WORLD REGIONAL GEOGRAPHY

Harper & Row Series in Geography
Donald W. Meinig, advisor

WORLD REGIONAL GEOGRAPHY
A QUESTION

PAUL WARD ENGLISH

University of Texas at Austin

OF PLACE

with the assistance of
JAMES ANDREW MILLER
University of Texas at Austin

HARPER'S COLLEGE PRESS

A department of Harper & Row, Publishers
New York · Hagerstown · San Francisco · London

PHOTO CREDITS

Title page. Aerial view, mandarin groves and rice paddies, Japan; Georg Gerster, Rapho/Photo Researchers. Power plant, West Germany; Paolo Koch, Rapho/Photo Researchers. Crowd, India; H. W. Silvester, Rapho/Photo Researchers.

Part opening pages. Pages xvi–1, cave painting, Altamira; photo, Spanish National Tourist Office, New York. Pages 58–59, camel market, Ajmer, India; photo Roland and Sabrina Michaud, Rapho/Photo Researchers. Pages 324–325, Sun City, Arizona; photo Georg Gerster, Rapho/Photo Researchers.

Section opening pages. *China:* Shih-t'ao (Tao-chi), *Reminiscences of the Ch'in Huai River.* Ink and color on paper, one leaf of an eight-leaf album; H 10^1/$_{16}$ in., W 7^{15}/$_{16}$ in. Ch'ing Dynasty. The Cleveland Museum of Art, John L. Severance Fund. *India:* Illustration to the Belaval Ragini, one of a series of 36 poems (*Ragmalas*) describing the 36 musical modes. Opaque watercolors and gold on paper; H 38 cm, W 29 cm. Mewar, second half of the 17th century. The Brooklyn Museum, A. Augustus Healy and Frank L. Babbott Funds. *Middle East and North Africa:* The court of a ruler, inside front cover, manuscript of the Diwan of Mir 'Ali Shir Nawa'i. Persian, dated 1499–1500. The Metropolitan Museum of Art, Gift of Alexander Smith Cochran, 1913. *Tropical Africa:* Wooden mask, Itumba region (border of Gabon and Congo Republic); H 14 in. Collection, The Museum of Modern Art, New York. *Latin America:* Stone relief of the goddess Chicomecoatl, H 38 cm. Aztec, Mexico, 15th century. The Brooklyn Museum, A. Augustus Healy Fund. *Western Europe:* Claude Monet, *Old St. Lazare Station, Paris.* Oil on canvas; H 23½ in., W 31½ in. 1877. The Art Institute of Chicago, Mr. and Mrs. Martin A. Ryerson Collection. *Russia:* Woodcut from an early book on Russia. Vienna, 1549. By permission of the Houghton Library, Harvard University. *Japan:* Ichiryusai Hiroshige, Sudden Shower at Ohashi, from *One Hundred Views of Famous Places in Edo.* Oban nishiki-e; H 33.8 cm, W 22.1 cm. Dated 1857. The Smithsonian Institution, Freer Gallery of Art, Washington, D.C. *North America:* David Walkowitz, *Metropolis No. 2.* Watercolor; H 29¾ in., W 21¾ in. 1923. Photo, Geoffrey Clements. Hirshhorn Museum and Sculpture Garden, Smithsonian Institution, Washington, D.C.

Chapter opening pages. Rise: The Pierpont Morgan Library. China: United Nations. India: United Nations. Middle East: United Nations. Tropical Africa: United Nations. Latin America: United Nations. Western Europe: German Information Center, New York. Russia: Wide World. Japan: Japan External Trade Organization, New York. North America: American Iron and Steel Institute.

Editor
Raleigh S. Wilson

Design
Gayle Jaeger

Editorial
Jeannine Ciliotta

Production
Abouchar & Jaeger, Inc.

Cover
Colos

Maps and art
Eric G. Hieber, EH Technical Services

Photo research
Myra Schachne

Color essays
Jeannine Ciliotta and Gayle Jaeger

Composition
Monotype Composition Company

Printing and binding
Kingsport Press

Library of Congress Catalog Card Number: 76–28555

ISBN: 0–06–167401–X

Library of Congress Cataloging in Publication Data

English, Paul Ward
    World regional geography.
    (Harper & Row series in geography)
    Includes bibliographies and index.
    1. Geography—Text-books—1945–   I. Miller, James Andrew, joint author. II. Title.
G128.E53   910   76–28555
ISBN 0–06–167401–X

To the three people
who shared this experience most fully:
Patricia Ann, Paul II, and Peter

CONTENTS

THE RISE TO ECOLOGICAL DOMINANCE

1

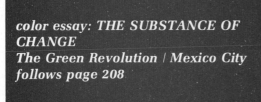

THE TECHNOLOGICAL WORLD

324

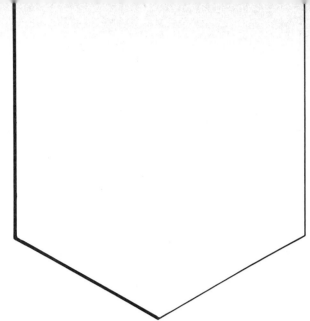

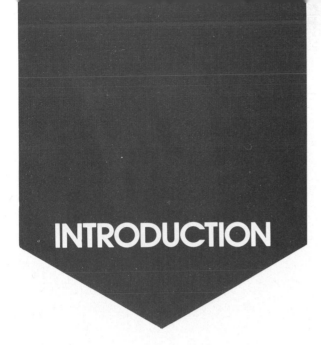

INTRODUCTION

One hundred years ago, the world's foremost research scientist, Thomas H. Huxley, visited the United States during its Centennial to deliver an address at newly founded John Hopkins University in Baltimore. He spoke of the future of America, warning his audience that size and wealth alone would not be sufficient to sustain this nation, and that the use to which America's vast resources were put would determine the country's course. In a democratic society, he argued, national goals must be set by the people, and the one condition of success—the sole safeguard against chaos—lay in the "moral worth and intellectual clearness of the individual citizen." The specialized clarity of the expert alone was not enough. A broader, more integrated understanding of the direction, momentum, and purpose of human affairs must reach to each world citizen.

A century later, Huxley's message rings clear. Americans are struggling with a complex set of interrelated issues of vital concern to each individual both within the nation and throughout the world. Everywhere, policies and decisions on population growth, utilization of resources and energy, equity and equality, pollution, progress, the preservation of human dignity and the quality of life are compelling personal and national issues. These set the direction, momentum, and purpose of life today. This book speaks to these issues as they have evolved throughout the world, and demonstrates the vitality of geography as an eclectic discipline suited to this present, rooted in the past, and anchored by the course humanity has set.

Geography has relentlessly refused to limit its realm of inquiry to a single body of facts or set of concepts. Seeking a more holistic universe than its neighboring disciplines in the physical and social sciences, geography's role lies in understanding the dialog between people and their environments, interpreting spatial patterns, and testifying to the regionality of human existence. In this book, nine world regions set the framework within which the sources of geographic knowledge—landscape, ecosystem, environment, diffusion, spatial structure, distance, and scale—are utilized to perceive the texture created by land and people. These areas do not form an exclusive set of world regions. There are many more. In a longer volume, Southeast Asia and Eastern Europe would merit separate analysis; Australia, the Pacific, and southern Africa would demand detailed attention; and the unique cultural complexes of Canada, the Caribbean, and the Indian Ocean could be treated more fully. But China, India, the Middle East and North Africa, Tropical Africa, Latin America, Western Europe, Russia, Japan, and North America do comprehend concrete and cohesive geographical and social experiences that have been fused in the consciousness of a people and expressed in the perception, symbolization, and organization of space. They illuminate the issues of today, and have elaborated the forces of change that give form and substance to the rise of human dominion over the earth.

Overriding issues link these world regions. The relatively recent human rise to dominance over the earth is first recorded in the environmental transformation, which created regional civilizations of farmers and urbanites. Then, over the last five hundred years, Europe unleashed upon the world a new kind of knowledge and technology—the scientific transformation—which penetrates all aspects of land and life today. First in Europe, then in the United States, Russia, Japan, and now throughout the world, technological innovations contribute to greater control over sources of power, higher levels of productivity, increasing stability of human settlement, less vulnerability to environmental hazard, and a technological destruction of distance. In the four regions of the technological world, a full elaboration of the modern experience has produced unprecedented levels of material well-being and yet unlearned mastery of environmental control. In the five regions of the developing world, this still new knowledge has only partly revolutionized traditional cultural matrices. In China, India, the Middle East and North Africa, Tropical Africa, and Latin America, the varied intensity and differing modes of scientific penetration have produced incomplete interpretations of the technological design. This differential modernization, where the chasm between rich and poor has widened to explosive proportions as the Malthusian scissors of population growth and resource production sharpen, generates great tension, but also serves to heighten distinctions between well-being and the purposeful direction of the present emerging from the past.

These contemporary forces have given us a new set of problems that will dominate discussion during the rest of this century. Distribution of population, food, and resources is at the heart of modern political and social dialogs between nations and among peoples. American grain shipments to Russia, hunger crises in South Asia, and oil embargos are harbingers of the patterns, problems, and solutions to come. Even a nation as vast and rich in resources as the United States is no longer self-sufficient. An Egyptian politician noted with undisguised satisfaction that the Arab oil boycott was the first world economic decision ever taken outside the West. Comprehension of the diversity of the world's people and regions—of the differing confines of physical space, modes of social organization, and forces of tradition—is particularly crucial today. For this reason, each region chosen develops basic geographical processes; the foundations of traditional society, regional landscapes, the resource base, and the introduction to and reinterpretation of the scientific transformation are examined in detail. Inserts, photographs, and photo essays have been selected to support and highlight these central themes with a view to understanding the essential humanity of change, process, and form throughout the world.

This volume cannot provide sets of solutions to the problems generated by the diversity of the human condition. While it is apparent that full integration of technology has released a substantial minority of the human population from lethal onslaughts of famine and disease, it is still not certain that this system of organization, with its extraordinarily high demand for and consumption of resources, can be sustained—much less lived out by the full complement of the human population. It seems that progress leads to paradox, and solutions bring new problems: medicine generates better health but crushing population problems; technological creativity releases societies from the bondage of physical labor while producing fatal weaponry; conquest of distance frees experience to a wider world, but builds clusters of megacities of unprecedented size; even as the world's economy and societies become more deeply intertwined, ancient racial, ethnic, and religious differences stubbornly persist and are placed in relief. The resultant complexity defies complete analysis of the global human condition, but demands the full attention of the coming generation. The resolution of these paradoxes lies inevitably with them, at a time when, as the French writer André Malraux notes, we are lost between civilizations, and no god is adding the finishing touches to world leaders. Perhaps neither followers nor leaders will emerge. Perhaps we will all learn and speak.

ACKNOWLEDG-MENTS

I would like to express my deep appreciation to several groups of people who contributed substantially to the creation of this book. First, to my colleagues at the University of Texas and elsewhere who contributed their thoughts and criticisms, among them James A. Bill, Ronald Briggs, Christopher Shane Davies, Robin Doughty, Hafez Farmayan, Robert Fernea, Charles Greer, Robert K. Holz, George Hoffman, Carl Leiden, Robert Mayfield, Donald Meinig, James Neely, and Walt W. Rostow; and to the many reviewers of the preliminary manuscript—Terry Jordan, Ross N. Pearson, Ronald F. Lockmann, John Hiltner, Phillip Bacon, Thomas P. Field, John C. Lewis, Merel J. Cox, Harry E. Colestock III, James Clarkson, Susan K. Williams, and Edmund Heger. Second, to my staff and assistants, who facilitated its development and production, especially Beverly Bowman, Barbara Burnham, Marilyn Duncan, Rebecca Gonzales, Patti Haardt, Curtis Jordan, Pamela Pape, Carla Richardson, Elizabeth Ross, Annette Baker Rushing, William Smallwood, William TeBrake, and Pamela Westfall. Third, to the editors and designers at Harper & Row, whose dedication and creativity were crucial, namely, Jeannine Ciliotta, Eric Hieber, Gayle Jaeger, Rhona Johnson, Walter Meagher, and Raleigh Wilson. Special thanks is due James A. Miller, who contributed directly to the writing and refining of much of the text.

P.W.E.

WORLD REGIONAL GEOGRAPHY

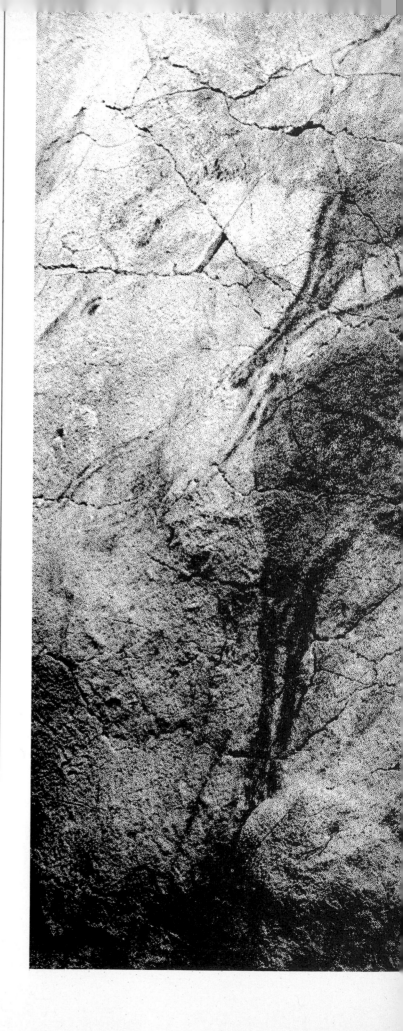

THE RISE TO ECOLOGICAL DOMINANCE

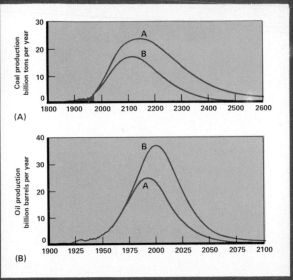

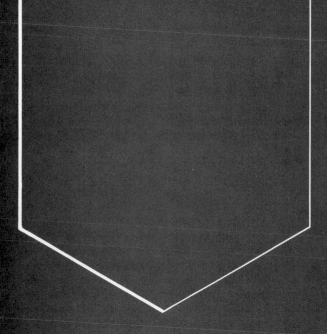

The growth of human understanding and control over *environments*° came about during two periods of explosive change that strongly affected the formation of our modern world. During the first period, the environmental transformation, people gained a revolutionary understanding of their relationships with nature. Between the seventh and third millennia BC, agriculture was invented, animals were domesticated, and cities were built in the *civilizational hearths*° of the Middle East and the Mediterranean Basin, Central Asia, North China, Southeast Asia, and somewhat later in the New World. Village life was organized, and villages became integrated within the service areas, or *hinterlands,*° of urban centers. Civilizations were supported by the new food supplies now within human reach. Hunters and gatherers were pushed—as agriculture diffused from the original hearths—into increasingly less attractive environments. Early farmers and urbanites forged new *sedentary*° patterns of life that every populous society from the early civilizations of Mesopotamia and the Nile to the medieval monarchies of Mogul India, Europe, and Russia came to share.

During the second period, the scientific transformation, a new scale and power of technological understanding emerged in a single *culture hearth:*° Europe. People harnessed inanimate sources of energy, and human potential expanded to global dimensions. Human understanding of nature increased beyond the imagination of those living just

Figure 1. A Matter of Perspective. The consumption of fossil fuels provides a measure of the rapid expansion of the scientific transformation. Graphs (a) and (b) show the production of coal and oil from the beginning of their intensive industrial use to the present, with projections to various times in the future at which, given current consumption, they will be exhausted as major energy sources. The shaded area in (a) shows the amount of coal mined and burned in the century beginning 1870; projections of future production are indicated by the A and B curves. *Adapted from:* M. King Hubbert, "The Energy Resources of the Earth," *Scientific American* (September 1971), p. 69. Copyright © 1971 by Scientific American, Inc. All rights reserved.

a few hundred years earlier. In the initial phase, the *agrarian*° basis of social life in medieval Europe changed, and new sources of biological energy supported emerging cities, industries, and elites. Commerce became a world venture; resource utilization, a global affair. The tentacles of an emerging international economy penetrated into even the most remote areas. As this system evolved and diffused, the world split into two: the nations of the technological world, the primary producers of industrial technology and the principal consumers of energy and resources; and the nations of the developing world, whose societies, subdued or subverted by this second transformation, now seek parity in an unequal world. These two worlds form the basis on which we can sensibly discern the different patterns and processes that so dramatically influence the geography of the twentieth century.

DISTRIBUTION OF WORLD POPULATION

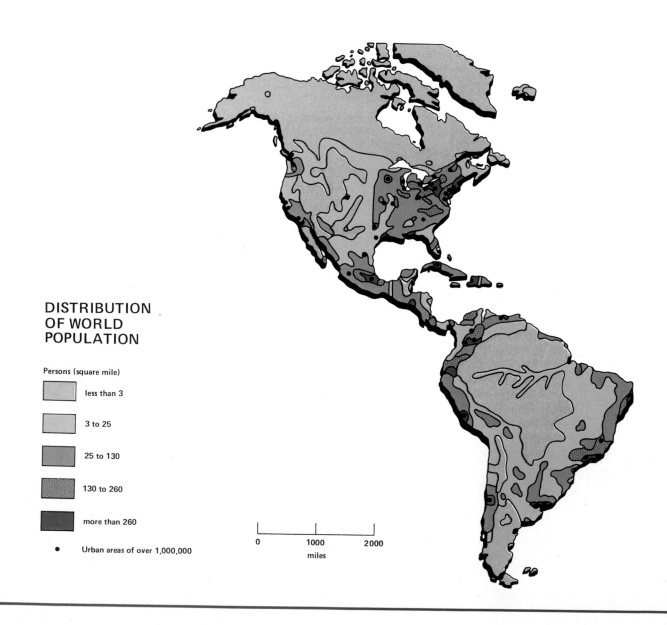

Persons (square mile)

	less than 3
	3 to 25
	25 to 130
	130 to 260
	more than 260
•	Urban areas of over 1,000,000

0   1000   2000

miles

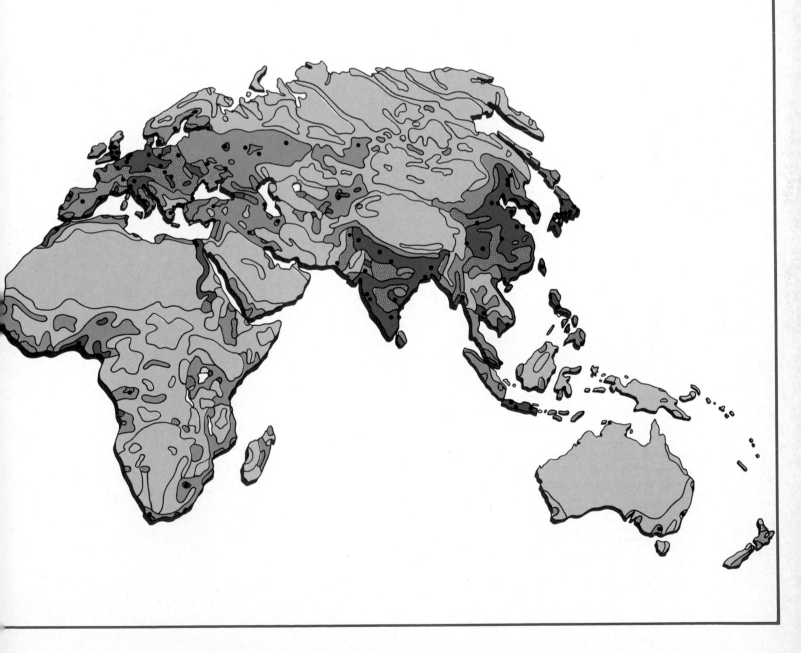

THE ENVIRONMENTAL TRANSFORMATION
1

The environmental transformation proceeded in two phases. First, food collectors discovered planting and domesticated animals. In the Middle East and along the shores of the Mediterranean, cereal cultivation, goat and sheep herding, the planting of tree crops, and the use of the plow formed the basis of village life. In North China, intensive hoe cultivation became the dominant economy, while in Southeast Asia, the planting of root crops and cuttings and the keeping of domesticated pigs and chickens formed the economic base. In the New World, squash, maize, and beans were the primary crops. In each area, agriculture was shortly followed by the founding of urban-based civilizations, the second phase of the environmental transformation. Although the archeological evidence is too slender to document fully the relative antiquity of these civilizations, important urban centers controlling sizable hinterlands existed in the river valleys of the Middle East in the fourth millennium BC, in the Aegean by the third, in West Africa and East Asia in the second, and in the New World 2000 years later. The dynamics of the environmental transformation must have differed substantially from one region to another, and the interconnections between the civilizational hearths are not fully understood, but it is generally suspected that the first farmers and the first urbanites lived in the Middle East. For this reason, and because evidence of the origins of agriculture and urbanism is more substantial for this region, the unfolding of the environmental transformation in the hills and valleys of the Middle East forms the central theme of this discussion.

THE DISCOVERY OF FOOD PRODUCTION
[FIGURE 2]

During the first phase of the environmental transformation, human beings made two deceptively simple discoveries: they learned how to plant and how to tame animals. These innovations opened the way to a humanized world by providing a reliable food supply. Before then, people had been few and settlements bare: landscapes evolved under the dictates of nature, barely touched by the efforts of hunters and gatherers to wrest a living from their environments. First in the Middle East, and later in North China, Southeast Asia, West Africa, central Mexico, and the northern Andes, agricultural societies sprang into being, altering the face of these favored cradle areas and then gradually extending their sway outward into more marginal environments. Forests were leveled, hillsides terraced, and dry lands irrigated. In transforming nature, these peoples transformed themselves and created the economic base for those stable, settled communities now found throughout the developing world.

The Middle Eastern Cradle Area
[FIGURE 3]

The earliest experiment in food production apparently took place on the hilly flanks of the Fertile Crescent in the Middle East. This region, called "fertile" because of its higher rainfall relative to surrounding deserts, sweeps northward in an arc from the coastal highlands of the eastern Mediterranean, encircling the Tigris-Euphrates Valley and then arching southward along the western slopes of the Zagros Mountains to the Persian Gulf. In these foothills, a variety of physical environments is found at different elevations. In general, grassy lowlands give way to hills covered by oak and pistachio forests at middle altitudes, with wooded mountain valleys and a scattering of alpine meadows above. In some places, grass-covered hills, upland **steppes,** and even **desert** conditions prevail, but the area generally receives enough precipitation to support cultivation without irrigation.

The optimum resource zone appears to have been the oak and pistachio forests at elevations of 1000 to 3000 feet, where the plants and animals later domesticated (wild wheat and barley, wild goats, sheep, and pigs) were native. In this setting, many plants and animals were available: wild grains, nuts, peas, lentils, land snails, freshwater crabs, boar, goats, gazelles, and sheep, among others. Thus, this region offered food collectors enough resources to provide settlements with stability and continuity during the long period of experimentation that must have preceded the achievement of full food production.

Preagricultural peoples were widely distributed in the Fertile Crescent. Larger and more stable populations were located in environments with more edible resources; smaller migratory bands probably occupied less favored areas. Once established in local environments, these patterns of living apparently remained relatively constant, with population densities well below a level that would lead to resource exhaustion. At Tell Mureybit on the Euphrates River in northern Syria, for example, hunters and gatherers were productive enough to live continuously in a settled village of some 200 houses, whose archeological record contains seventeen successive levels of cultural debris. Lacking agriculture, the people of Tell Mureybit hunted wild asses, cattle, and gazelles, and collected wild wheat, barley, and an assortment of seeds and nuts that were roasted in small pebble-filled fire pits. At higher elevations in the Zagros foothills, permanent or seasonal base camps occupied by a few families were the more common settlement units. Some of these sites (Zawi Chemi Shanidar, for example) were open-air encampments, demonstrating that men had begun to abandon caves well before the discovery of agriculture and the domestication of animals. Other groups maintained camps on the grass-covered plains of lowland Mesopotamia in the winter and in the mountain valleys of the Zagros in the summer, a seasonal shift designed to utilize *ecological*• zones during their seasons of greatest productivity. In addition to these settled groups, nomadic bands, who left little archeological evidence behind because of their migratory way of life, undoubtedly foraged throughout the region, living

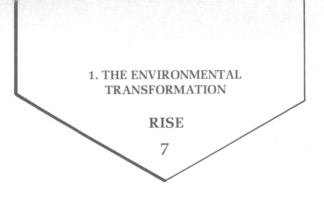

Figure 2. The Growth of Human Populations. The growth of human population is seen in different perspective when plotted arithmetically and logarithmically. Part (a) is plotted arithmetically and emphasizes the cumulative nature of population increase, the relatively recent impact of the scientific transformation, and the unprecedented nature of the population problem now confronting the world. Part (b), plotted logarithmically over a longer time period, emphasizes the impact of the environmental and scientific transformations as turning points in human capacities. *Adapted from:* (a) "How Many People Have Ever Lived on Earth," *Population Bulletin*, Vol. 18, No. 1 (February 1962), p. 5, Fig. 1. Courtesy of The Population Reference Bureau, Inc., Washington, D.C. 20036. (b) Edward S. Deevey, "The Human Population," *Scientific American* (September 1960), p. 52. Copyright © 1960 by Scientific American, Inc., All rights reserved.

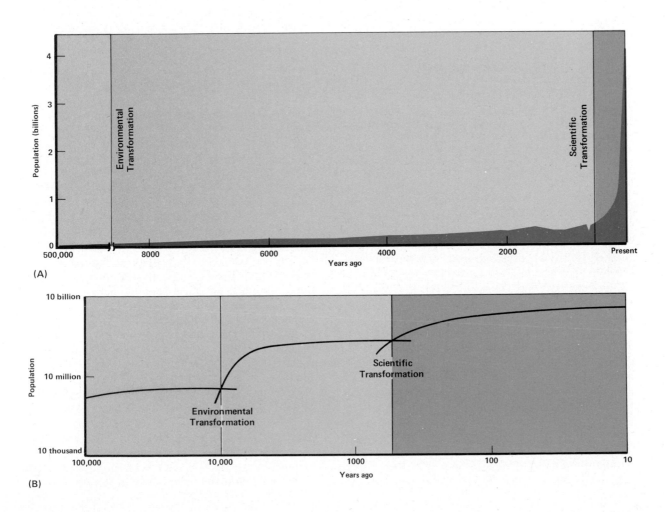

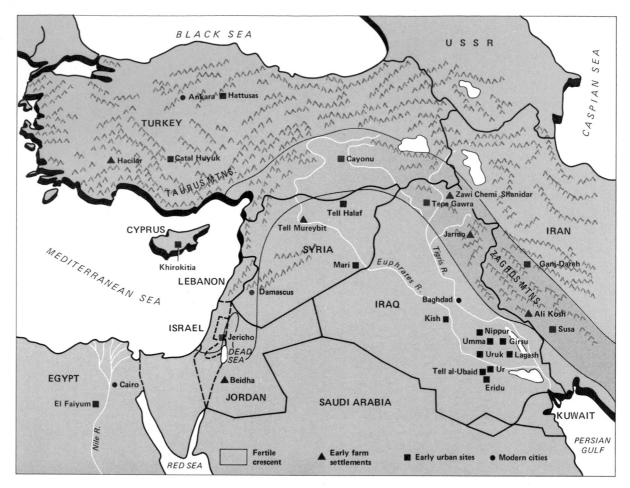

Figure 3. The Middle Eastern Hearth Area. The Fertile Crescent, a concave arc of productive, well-watered land extending from the highlands of the eastern Mediterranean through the foothills of the Taurus and Zagros mountains, formed the cradle area in which agriculture began in the Middle East nearly 10,000 years ago.

in caves and rock shelters in less favored environments.

About 20,000 BC, these people began to change their way of living, establishing new patterns of sustenance that characterized most subsequent cultures in the Fertile Crescent down to achievement of full food production at about 6000 BC. This change amounted to a considerable broadening of their diets to include greater and greater amounts of freely available food. Perception of food expanded to include a larger number and variety of wild resources—a shift away from dependence on large game to a more diversified pattern of collecting. Although hunting sites for those who relied on large game for 90 percent of their food supply still existed, most people in this region exploited an increasingly wider subsistence base.

This shift to a broader collecting pattern, in which everything from water turtles to land snails was

eaten, made a great deal of nutritional sense. Land snails, for example, although poorer in protein than meat, are richer in calcium. Among vegetable resources, acorns and pistachios have a very high caloric value, much higher than that of wild game. Mussels are a valuable source of vitamin A. Moreover, most of these additional food resources were small in size and could be stored. By 9000 to 7000 BC, underground storage pits, some plastered, were constructed at many sites, including Zawi Chemi Shanidar and Tell Mureybit. Somewhat later, pots and baskets appeared. This "container revolution," as the urban historian Lewis Mumford calls it, was only one of a series of changes in human behavior and technology that accompanied broad-spectrum collecting and contributed to the later development of agriculture and animal domestication. These two advances, in turn, made possible larger and more concentrated populations.

The new pattern of foraging probably involved women and children in the food economy to a much greater degree than was previously the case. Labor became divided between the sexes. Man, the organizer and director of the social unit, appears as the hunter in the archeological record; women and children led a complementary existence as gatherers of wild grains, nuts, and small invertebrates in large numbers and varieties. Their contribution to the total diet became more substantial, and their knowledge became important: it was they who identified the most useful plants, animals, and insects out of the thousands of species available.

Given this expanded perception of food resources, the overall productivity of local environments in the Middle East probably played a greater role in the regional distribution of population. As foragers gained insight into plant development, local environmental conditions, and seasonal changes, they became more concentrated in the oak and pistachio forests of the uplands which, for several reasons, formed an optimum collecting environment. First, the widest assortment of nuts, fruits, wild grasses, and small game was found in the uplands of the Fertile Crescent. Dense forest growth was inhibited by the low to moderate rainfall so that a rich spring groundcover of edible grasses and *legumes*•—such as peas, beans, and clover—flourished. Second, the soils of these forests could be worked with a digging stick, an implement later used for planting but in this period used to pry stones, prod plants, and uncover roots. Because of summer drought, annual plants harvested in the summer and early fall predominated over perennials. In addition, some of the large animals of this area—sheep, goats, gazelles, and wild asses—tended toward herd behavior, a feature understandably attractive to hunters.

One can assume, then, that hunters and gatherers peopled this rich environment in large numbers, but curiously enough, it may be that the actual beginnings of agriculture occurred not in the most favored parts of the oak and pistachio forest, the so-called nuclear zone, but in poorer valleys and *wadis*• or *arroyos*• on its margins, a paradoxical conjecture and speculation that needs some explanation. There are at least two obvious reasons why people alter their subsistence base: First, environmental stress caused, for example, by a change in climate could alter the ecology of a region sufficiently to require changes in settlement location and subsistence economy; second, an increase in population exerting *demographic*• pressure on the existing resource base could change patterns of resource utilization or cause migration. In the foothills of the Fertile Crescent, the most favored environmental niches may have acted as regional centers where growing populations in permanent settlements spawned "colonies" in less favored areas nearby. Demographic pressure of this type may have contributed to the discovery of grain cultivation.

In the nuclear zone itself, there was little stimulus toward planting because pure stands of wild grasses are found throughout the region. Today, on thousands of acres in these foothills, particularly in southern Turkey, wild wheat can be harvested from natural stands nearly as dense as those in cultivated wheat fields. An American agricultural expert recently established this point beyond doubt by harvesting enough wild wheat in one hour with the flint-bladed sickle used in early times to produce more than 2 pounds of clean grain. Interestingly enough, the wild grain proved to be twice as rich in protein as modern domesticated grain. This experiment suggests that an experienced family of food collectors could reap a ton of grain, more than a year's supply, in the three-week harvesting season— and without working very hard. Given these conditions, planting would clearly be unnecessary in the richer zones. In marginal regions, agriculture might have been a logical extension of collecting practices, an effort by migrants from the nuclear zone to recreate the dense stands of grasses that occur naturally in the heart of the optimum environment. It may be, then, that agriculture, with all its implications for the future growth of civilization, was in its earliest phases a supplemental alternative to hunting and gathering and only after long periods of experimentation became the dominant economy in the foothills of the Fertile Crescent.

If this is true—and the evidence is far from complete—the origins of agriculture and herding are not rooted in a dramatic environmental change or in the economic foresight of a prehistoric genius. Rather, these inventions occurred as a simple extension of the food-gathering practices of preagricultural hunters and gatherers spurred by a rather limited population explosion. People may have accidentally, unintentionally developed the capacity to control plants and animals.

The Domestication Process

By 7000 BC three domesticated grains—einkorn wheat, emmer wheat, and two-row barley—are found in village farming sites over a wide arc spanning the western flanks of the Zagros Mountains, southern Anatolia, and northern Palestine. At approximately this same time, the bones of domesticated sheep and goats (and later cattle and pigs) appear in these sites. In most places, cultivated plants and animals are found together. This was so at Jarmo, a prehistoric village of mud-walled houses located in the oak woodlands of northern Iraq, which was occupied by about 150 people for a period of 250 to 300 years between 7000 and 6750 BC. But at some sites (Zawi Chemi Shanidar, for example) domesticated animals preceded cultivated plants by almost 2000 years. All

Carvings and paintings used to decorate temples and tombs enable us to reconstruct the social and economic life of the Nile Valley, one of the first hearths of civilization. This beautiful fragment of raised limestone relief, which is dated to about 2420 BC, shows servants and herdsman leading the longhorn cattle prized by the ancient Egyptians. *Photo:* The Brooklyn Museum, Charles Edwin Wilbour Fund.

available evidence, however, points to the importance of the foothills of the Middle East as a primary hearth of both plant and animal domestication. The question is: How did domestication occur? How did men come to cultivate plants and herd animals to create the economic base for a new human environment?

One of the principal differences between wild cereals and cultivated varieties lies in the biology of seed dispersal, a process that must be accomplished one way or another if the plants are to survive and spread. Wild wheat and barley have very fragile, brittle, seed-holding spikes whose individual spikelets spread open at maturity. These characteristics ensure a wide dispersal of seed over surrounding territory because any movement of the plant caused by passing animals, by winds, or by collectors shakes seeds off the plants onto the ground. Furthermore, the arrow-shaped structure of the individual spikelets facilitates anchoring the seed in the soil, a fea-

ture of some importance in a climate with a summer drought. In cultivated grains, these structural adaptations disappear. The mature heads of cultivated wheat and barley cling tenaciously to the stalk until actually dislodged by threshing, and the elongated arrow shape of the spikelet has disappeared. In a natural setting, cultivated wheat and barley clearly would have had a low survival capacity. Where found in any numbers, these grains are instead associated with a new seed-dispersal mechanism—people. Botanists have been able to reconstruct and trace the spread of grain cultivation by noting changes of this type on imprints of einkorn wheat, emmer wheat, and two-row barley found in excavated village sites such as Jarmo in Iraq, Ali Kosh in Iran, and Catal Huyuk and Hacilar in Turkey. More important, they have also been able to gain insight into the patterns of human behavior that created these cultivated grains.

In wild wheat and barley fields, most plants have fragile, brittle heads, and only a minority of these cereal grains holds the ripened grain firmly on the stalk. When preagricultural collectors entered these fields with some regularity, however, plant populations began to change. Gradually, hard-holding wheat and barley plants gained preeminence as collectors ensured the dispersal of previously ill-adapted varieties by slapping them off the stalk and by collecting, carrying, and presumably dropping these seeds throughout the humanized area. Unconsciously, people ensured the spread of hard-holding varieties of einkorn wheat, emmer wheat, and two-row barley, and when they migrated to new environments they brought these plants with them. Through a natural extension of seed-collecting practices, the kind of grain needed for farming—grain picked from the plant rather than picked up off the ground—was unconsciously favored.

The domestication of animals in the foothills of the Middle East was also an unplanned, gradual process, probably pursued as a natural extension of the behavior of hunters and gatherers. The earliest animal domesticated in the Middle East was the sheep, which in those days looked much like a modern deer. Shortly thereafter, goats and probably pigs were domesticated in this region. Only after several thousand years did cattle become a part of human equipment.

The earliest physical evidence of animal domestication comes from Zawi Chemi Shanidar, where between 9000 and 8000 BC, a group of hunters and gatherers moved from caves to an open-air site where they lived in oval and circular stone houses. Simultaneously, sheep bones in the ruins began to outnumber those of goats by sixteen to one, suggesting the development of sheep herding and the beginnings of animal domestication. Somewhere between 8000 and 7000 BC, similar changes in goat populations begin to appear in other archeological sites. Goat horns shrink in size and change in shape; woolly sheep begin to emerge as a significant strain. These domesticated sheep and goats spread rapidly throughout the Zagros region, possibly dispersed by migrant herders. By 7500 BC, domesticated sheep and goats accounted for 30 percent of the meat eaten by the people of Ali Kosh in southern Iran. At Catal Huyuk, the bones of domesticated sheep and goats are found in the lowest archeological levels, and at Jarmo in 6750 BC both animals are fully domesticated.

Animal domestication must have posed certain problems to hunters and gatherers and even to early agriculturalists. First, herds of the smaller, more vulnerable domesticated sheep and goats had to be protected from wild predators, a task that was probably more easily accomplished by sedentary, or permanently settled, groups than by nomadic peoples continuously on the move. Second, herds had to be fed throughout the year and particularly during the summer drought when natural pastures in the lowlands dried up. Agriculturalists probably fed animals chaff and grain from their fields; ***transhumant*** nomads in the Zagros could take herds to alpine pastures in the mountains during the dry season. Finally, although herds were a source of food, adult females could not be slaughtered during the winter before spring lambing; thus, people involved in animal domestication, whether agriculturalists or collectors, had to have a reliable enough subsistence base so that they were not tempted to consume too much of their herding capital.

Yet to expend the considerable energy necessary for domestication, these people must have had a motive. Wild sheep and goats produce neither milk nor wool; both these products appear only late in the domestication process. Meat and hides already were acquired by hunters, so it is necessary to look beyond basic food and clothing needs to other aspects of the culture of these people to identify possible motives.

One of the most obvious reasons why animal domestication as we know it occurred in the foothills of the Middle East is that all the basic domesticates—wild sheep, goats, pigs, cattle, and even dogs—are native to this region. For thousands of years, hunters sought these animals for food and became familiar with their habits. In the case of scavenging animals such as the pig and dog, people probably developed a mutually beneficial, or symbiotic, relationship: the scavengers cleaned camp scraps and waste from the vicinity of the campsite or village, but occasionally paid for their hunger by becoming an evening meal. Larger, horned animals also played important symbolic and religious roles in the lives of these people. At Tepe Sarab south of Jarmo, for example, some of the earliest clay figurines depict lions, boar, and sheep. At Catal Huyuk, wall paintings of a huge bull surrounded by men reflect an elaborate art and religion centered on the cult of the bull, one of the most ancient and persistent Mediterranean religious symbols.

Thus, motives other than the food quest may have played an important role in the domestication of animals in the Middle East. Young animals that ultimately formed the nucleus of a herd may have been originally kept for religious purposes, for sacrifice at festivals, for example, or for the container value of their horns. Young animals brought into a village by a hunter may have survived as pets. Or young animals may have been kept as hunting decoys. By any or all of these means, once the nucleus of a herd of young sheep or goats was established, villagers would probably automatically select out of the herd the most aggressive, unmanageable individuals. As in the domestication of plants, these people must have begun an accidental, unplanned manipulation of animals that ultimately led to specialized stock breeding.

Village Farming in the Middle East

By 6000 BC, after 3000 years of experimentation and invention, the basic elements of the Middle Eastern food-producing complex—wheat and barley cultivation, domesticated sheep and goats (supplemented locally by pigs and cattle), and permanent village settlement—had spread throughout the uplands of the Middle East and into adjacent drier regions. Village farming combined with hunting and gathering had emerged as an attractive and reliable subsistence strategy. Under this new economic system, population densities probably increased ten to twenty times, and people appear to have concentrated at those sites most suitable for farming. In southwestern Iran, where an estimated one-third of the total area provided opportunities for a well-developed hunting and gathering economy, only one-tenth was suitable for farming. Such environmental limits resulted in fewer but larger human settlements in the uplands of the Middle East and marked the beginnings of a *population implosion* as people became increasingly concentrated in environmentally favored zones.

The discovery of agriculture and herding provided people with a more reliable and secure food base. But it would be a mistake to view the process as simply economic—life in these new sedentary agricultural villages must have differed substantially from that of hunters and gatherers. Life was increasingly tied to the seasonal activities of farming, which are based on understanding and controlling the annual cycle of nature. Sowing in the fall, harvest in early summer, lambing in spring, and moving herds to upland pastures in the summer were regular and repetitive events celebrated as festivals in early fertility religions. They formed the temporal basis of village life, a regular patterning of activity far more disciplined than that of hunters and gatherers.

This regularity of daily activity coincided with an expanding technology. We still refer to tedious situations as "boring" and to repetitive hard work as "the grind." These phrases hark back to this early period when patterned behavior became a hallmark of daily village life. The main methods of making tools out of limestone, sandstone, granite, or marble were by boring, grinding, and polishing. In earlier times, flint, amenable to chipping, had been virtually the only material used for fashioning tools and weapons. New techniques now extended the range of materials that could be used and thereby the technological capacities of society. In Catal Huyuk, for example, expert craftsmen were capable of delicate work in substances as hard as obsidian. They drilled holes in stone beads too small for a modern needle to pass and worked marble and alabaster into human forms. This accomplishment is impressive because grinding or boring even soft sandstone or limestone is extremely laborious and can only be accomplished by patient work.

Finally, the mixed farming system, which retained the older economies of hunting and gathering on a more sophisticated level, both expanded and limited human horizons. Geographically, patterns of movement became more restricted: the village, then as now, was a rooted community. Yet patterns of trade and commerce over large distances suggest that these communities were far from isolated and that a flow of goods and ideas existed in the Fertile Crescent from Palestine to the Persian Gulf. Recurring motifs in pottery decoration and religious symbolism attest to the fact that more than obsidian was being passed from one community to the next. Although personal knowledge of distant places and different environments must have been more limited in settled villages, the consequent deepening of local environmental experience probably contributed in no small way to the discovery that plant and animal resources could be controlled.

THE EMERGENCE OF URBAN LIFE

The rise of cities, the second phase of the environmental transformation, closely followed food production in each of the major hearths of civilization—in Mesopotamia, Egypt, the Indus Valley, North China, central Mexico, and the northern Andes. In each of these regions, only 4000 years separate the beginnings of agriculture from the emergence of larger and more complex urban settlements.

These cities intensified four major processes of change that had begun with the discovery of agriculture and the domestication of animals. First, population increased and became concentrated in more restricted and clearly defined ecological zones, thereby generating higher densities and more intensive human contact. Politically organized, class-stratified societies with full-time craft specialists could not have developed without such a population implosion. Second, space and resources were organized into larger units. These early cities had the capacity to levy taxes on rural hinterlands and maintain long-distance trade. Third, human manipulation of the environment became more explicit. New *cultural landscapes* were created, marked by irrigation channels, bounded fields, contour plowing, and *terraced* hillsides. Fourth, technological competence expanded with the discovery of the plow, the potter's wheel, the loom, control of metals, and the development of writing.

Before these cities could emerge, however, two preconditions had to be fulfilled. First, a reliable *food surplus* was needed to support the nonfarming populations of cities. The surrounding environment had to be sufficiently fertile for the production of rural agricultural surpluses to feed urban elites, craft specialists, merchants, and priests. Without such a surplus, no city, then or now, could long survive. Second, a *social organization* was needed to manage the collection, storage, and redistribution of food surpluses. Whether for religious, political, or economic reasons, rural farmers, fishermen, and herders had to be persuaded to exchange their annual surpluses for urban goods and services on a regular basis. The importance of these early cities, then, lies in the ordering and control of human energy. A "new" source of power (the agricultural product) was channeled and organized into "labor machines" capable of building walls, temples, and pyramids.

The following paragraphs describe first, the rise of urbanism in one center of civilization, Mesopotamia; second, the environmental base that produced a food surplus; and third, the political, social, and economic institutions that emerged to regulate human lives and expand group capacities. The narrative starts shortly after the discovery of food production, with fully agricultural people living in small villages of 250 to 500 people in the foothills of the Fertile Crescent, and culminates in the growth of large urban centers in the Tigris-Euphrates Valley 4000 years later. Although the rise of cities in Mesopotamia, the land between the Tigris and Euphrates rivers, is only one regional example of the emergence of urban society, all available evidence suggests that Mesopotamian cities predate others found in Egypt, the Indus Valley, North China, and the New World.

At about 4000 BC, early agriculturalists in the foothills of the Fertile Crescent moved down into the Tigris-Euphrates Valley, bringing with them wheat and barley; domesticated sheep, goats, and cattle; and a tradition of settled village life. Their movement is testimony to the success of agriculture in the foothills: the population literally ate and sowed its way down into the valley. The environment of the river valley, however, presented new problems and opportunities. The dryness of the lowlands made irrigation essential for cultivation. Wheat and barley fields interspersed with date palm groves (a new source of food) were planted on the marshy banks of stream channels and were watered by simple diversion channels. The summer sun, which scorched vegetation off the plains, made it difficult to support the cattle and donkeys needed for plowing. Since building stones were not available on the **alluvial plain,**˙ most structures were built of reeds or sun-dried brick, and these houses were periodically threatened by floods charged by the spring melting of snow on surrounding mountains. Adapting to this new environment must have been difficult, and the early Mesopotamian religious texts that survive describe a society living in fear of starvation.

Despite these environmental problems, the plains of Mesopotamia proved sufficiently rich to produce a reliable food surplus. The single most important factor in this development was probably the shift from **dry farming**˙ to **irrigation**˙ agriculture, which,

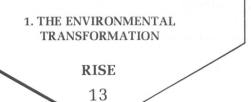
though precarious, is five to six times more productive than dry farming. The higher yields on irrigated land probably fed a growing population. And because irrigation agriculture was confined to the vicinity of river channels, settlements had to be located alongside them. Residential stability was thus reinforced, and a large, stable population evolved in the lowlands of Mesopotamia. What was lacking was a social structure capable of organizing this food surplus and channeling human energy into directed activities.

This direction and coordination were apparently provided by a specialized class of priests, who acted as economic administrators and spiritual leaders in early Sumeria, the first of a number of civilizations located on the Mesopotamian plains. Not surprisingly, religion at the time was intimately associated with ecological conditions in the valley. Early on, priests apparently became involved in the problem of feeding domesticated animals during the summer when drought parched local grazing lands. Agricultural land associated with temples was specifically set aside to grow fodder: the priests organized its winter storage and summer distribution to herdsmen. Not incidentally, this gave the priests partial control over wool, a major item of trade. Temples and priests became central to the organization of the agricultural economy. Ultimately, priests controlled and administered irrigation and mediated water disputes.

The growing involvement of priests in the management and supervision of the Sumerian economy led to the emergence of temples as the dominant institution in the cities of Mesopotamia. Walled temple complexes covered many acres of land and included a warren of storerooms, warehouses, and cult chambers occupied by priests, scribes, craftsmen, laborers, and their dependents. The main temple, typically located on a high terrace, evolved into a massive tower, the ziggurat. One such complex at the city of Uruk was so large that an estimated 1500 men working a ten-hour day for five years were required to complete it. This ability to organize labor reflects a forceful control of land and resources. Some land was directly owned by the temples and rented to farmers. In other cases, seed and plow animals were centrally maintained and special plowing officials organized the preparation of agricultural land. One text alone records a detailed accounting for some 9660 donkeys.

The Sumerian City-State

These processes of environmental exploitation and social differentiation culminated in the emergence of the first Mesopotamian urban civilization, Sumeria. The basis of this civilization, the **city-state,**[•] was organized and run by priests and kings, was occupied by a diversified population of merchants, craftsmen, and slaves, and was characterized by monumental structures, territorial control, and international trade. By 2500 BC, ten to twelve major Sumerian urban centers served a population of between 0.5 million and 1 million people and controlled a region of 10,000 square miles on the alluvial plains of Mesopotamia. Regional capitals such as Kish, Nippur, and Ur enclosed as much as 250 acres of land within their fortifications. The largest Sumerian city, Uruk, with a population of approximately 50,000, covered an area of 1100 acres encircled by a double wall approximately 6 miles long and reinforced by nearly 1000 semicircular towers. Each Sumerian city coordinated a hierarchy of settlements. The relatively small polity of Lagash, for example, consolidated an area of 620 square miles including twenty-five towns and forty or more villages. In addition, each city carried on long-distance trade, exchanging local textiles and grain for raw materials like copper from points as distant as Cyprus, Anatolia, and Oman.

By 2500 BC, every large city in Sumeria was a walled fortress whose battlements protected its people from occasional raids by nomadic groups and more frequent attacks by rulers of neighboring city-states. Fear of starvation had been replaced by fear of war; the Sumerians no longer prayed for subsistence but for safety. Hereditary kingship apparently emerged in response to incessant intercity warfare, and palaces grew to rival temples in size, wealth, and complexity. At the core of each Sumerian city were massive temples, palaces, and other public buildings; wide, straight, unpaved streets connected this core with the outer gates. The large houses of wealthy residents, which featured spacious courtyards and sewage removal, were located on major arteries and often covered as much as 2000 square feet of floor space. Off the major streets, the houses of the poorer classes were densely packed, less than 500 square feet in area, and sometimes even lacked the enclosed courtyard typical of Mesopotamian domestic architecture. Commercial activity was concentrated at the port or quay on the river banks and at the city gates. Large open areas in the city were still used for cultivation.

This differentiation in urban land use reflects the growing class stratification of society in the Sumerian city-state. At the top of Sumerian society were the king, palace administrators, priests, and temple officials. These leaders administered huge estates to supply the army, the palace, and the temple, and grew wealthy, as they do in modern

One of the distinctive features of the ancient Mesopotamian city was the ziggurat, a terraced tower of baked brick on top of which stood the temple of the patron god of the city. Although in ruins, the remains of the great ziggurat at Ur (c. 2125–2025 BC) give a clear idea of its original form and scale. *Photo:* **Hirmer Photoarchiv.**

societies, in the performance of their duties. Temple lands, which could not be bought or sold, amounted to 10 to 20 percent of the irrigated lands of the city. The palace estates accounted for another quarter of the agricultural land of the city, and this percentage probably gradually increased to meet the demands of constant warfare. Despite the great control exercised by the palace and the temple over human and agricultural resources in Sumeria, however, it appears that small agricultural producers cultivating their own lands formed two-thirds of the population and farmed 40 to 50 percent of the land.

Most people in Sumeria were still primary producers—herders, fishermen, and farmers—and it is unlikely that more than 20 percent of the total society was freed from subsistence labor at any one time. Slaves, at the bottom of society, were bought or sold at will and were owned by artisans, farmers, and minor administrators. Slave labor was used to build temples, canals, and fortifications, to row galleys, construct roads, and mine ores. Our most penetrating glimpse into the composition of Sumerian society stems from the Bau archives, the records of a temple in Lagash. From these we learn that among its community of 1200 people were 25 scribes, 20 or 25 craftsmen (including carpenters and smiths, leather workers, potters, stone cutters, and mat or basket weavers), 90 herdsmen, 80 soldier-laborers, 100 fishermen, 125 sailors, and 250 to 300 slaves. The majority of slaves were women, who probably worked at weaving, an important temple industry.

The Sumerian city-state, then, was a highly organized preindustrial economy and society, not unlike those in parts of the modern developing world. The elites of these early urban settlements collected food surpluses from **peasants**[•] and herdsmen and redistributed these foodstuffs to urbanites. A pattern of urban wealth and rural poverty, a leisured minority and a laboring majority, characterized each city-state.

THE DECLINE OF SUMERIA:
AN EARLY ECOLOGICAL
CRISIS

1. THE ENVIRONMENTAL
TRANSFORMATION

RISE

15

After a thousand years of growth, the center of civilization in the Tigris-Euphrates Valley shifted northward from Sumeria to Akkad in central Iraq, near modern Baghdad. Several reasons have been offered for this movement of the center of political power in Mesopotamia: the heavy military burdens placed on Sumeria's economy and society; progress in the art of metallurgy that gave an advantage to the mountain peoples of Armenia and Persia, whose territory included major ore deposits; and even a change in climate that led to the drying up of southern Mesopotamia. Recent evidence, however, suggests the changes in soil salinity and sedimentation generated by a thousand years of irrigated agriculture—in short, human abuse of the resource base—may have been the major contributing factor in the decline of Sumeria.

Salinization, the accumulation and concentration of salts in the soil, is a major problem wherever irrigation is practiced in arid or semiarid climates. If salts carried by irrigation water are allowed to accumulate on the field, the ability of plants to absorb water is substantially reduced, soil texture is damaged, fertility and yields decline, and then land is abandoned. Two approaches are used to limit the degree of salt accumulation in the soil. The first is to use water with a low salt content to lessen the rate of deposit in the root zone; the second is to flush accumulated salts from the root zone down into the groundwater by large-scale applications of water.

In Sumeria, salt accumulation was to some degree controlled by avoiding overirrigation and by cultivating land in alternate years. But these practices were not always successful in averting salinization, and the problem, which afflicted Sumeria for seven hundred years between 2400 and 1700 BC, was a causal factor in the decline of that early civilization.

For 150 years during this period, two neighboring cities, Girsu and Umma, located near tributaries of the Tigris and Euphrates rivers, had been in conflict over rights to fertile lands near their mutual frontier. When Girsu gained ascendancy, the people of Umma, located upstream in the watershed, blocked and diverted the canals that fed water to the disputed territory and thus were able to prevent cultivation. To resolve the issue, a king of Girsu, Entemenak, had a canal constructed westward directly from the Tigris River to supply water to the frontier zone. This canal gradually became an important source of irrigation water both for the border area

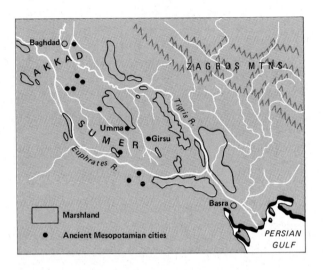

and for a larger region west of Girsu that formerly had been irrigated by water from the Euphrates only. The combined waters of the Euphrates and the Tigris Canal led to increased seepage, flooding, and overirrigation, and a rise in the water table with its accumulated salts.

Similar decisions spurred by conflict and underlying population pressure on the resource base must have been common in Sumeria. At Girsu, patches of saline ground appeared almost immediately after the construction of the Tigris Canal and surveys during the next 300 years prove that land previously described as salt-free had become saline. More generally in southern Mesopotamia, shifts from wheat cultivation to more salt-tolerant barley suggest that salinization was a chronic problem. About 3500 BC, wheat and barley were cultivated equally in this region, but a thousand years later wheat was grown on only one-sixth of the land. By 2100 BC, wheat amounted to 2 percent of the crop at Girsu; four hundred years later, wheat was no longer cultivated in southern Mesopotamia. Concurrently, the fertility of the land declined so that crop yields in 1700 BC were only one-third the size of those recorded for earlier periods. The implications of this erosion of the subsistence base for urban populations supporting massive temple complexes, palaces, and professional armies must have been staggering. The alluvial plains of Mesopotamia, once sufficiently fertile to provide a reliable food surplus, had been severely damaged by salinization.

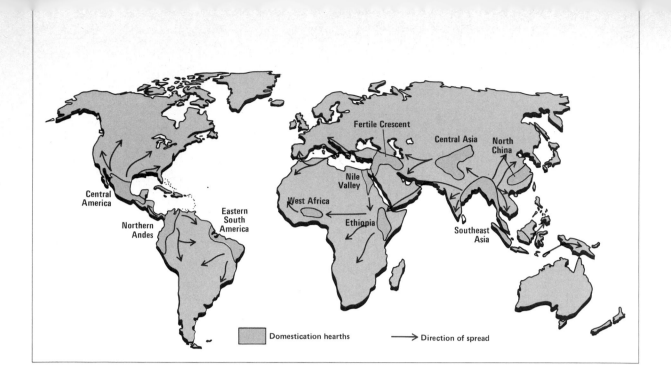

Figure 4. Origins of Domesticated Plants and Animals. *After:* Peter Haggett, *Geography: A Modern Synthesis.* New York: Harper & Row, 1972, p. 302, Fig. 13–3.

Religion was the central institution in Sumeria; its forms of expression pervaded all aspects of urban life. It provided a moral framework for social organization and centralized the managerial and bureaucratic skills basic to the existence of the system. For the majority of Sumerian citizens, this centralization of power gave rise to a division of labor that limited their horizons while providing subsistence security. But for the professional elite, the scribes, control of specialized knowledge carried with it mobility, security, and influence. These patterns intensified in Sumeria with the rise of militaristic groups, hereditary kingship, and continuous conflict. Professional armies (the first specialists in homicide) were supported by raising taxes. Fortifications were built by slaves recruited from among the disfavored.

In short, a civilization emerged in Sumeria similar to those that later arose in Egypt, the Mediterranean Basin, China, the Indus Valley, Europe, and the New World. Writing, an esthetic literary tradition, organized religion, huge public structures, and large-scale irrigation networks blended with militarism, exploitation and taxation of the weak, slavery, forced labor, bureaucracy, kingship, and environmental destruction.

THE DIFFUSION OF THE ENVIRONMENTAL TRANSFORMATION

The environmental transformation with its agriculture, domesticated animals, sedentary villages, and town life diffused outward from the various centers of discovery in the Old and New Worlds to new environments. The spread was slow and uneven. Centuries, not years, were needed for people, plants, and animals to adapt to different terrain and climates, and for the social organization required for urbanization to develop in different regions. Persistently, however, the world defined by this new relationship of people to their environment expanded at the expense of less complex social and economic systems. By AD 1500, immediately prior to European expansion, the world population of 500 million people was 100 times larger than before the development of food production. Sophisticated urban civilizations existed in the Middle East, the Mediterranean *littoral,*• China, India, Southeast Asia, Europe, Mexico, and Peru. Although the routes of diffusion and patterns of interaction among these centers still remain subjects of lively academic debate, the human world had been fundamentally reordered.

The Diffusion of Agriculture
[FIGURE 4, TABLE 1]

By the sixth millennium BC, the village farming way of life diffused out of the uplands of the Middle East. As we know from the evidence in Sumeria, the initial movement was vertical—down onto the alluvial lowlands of the Tigris and Euphrates and later the Nile. By 4000 BC, the food-producing revolution was fully established throughout the Middle East, and there were farming settlements in desert *oases,*• mountain valleys, and on the margins of stagnant marshes.

The essential elements of the food-producing complex spread westward from Anatolia into Europe,

TABLE 1. Probable Origin of Domesticated Plants and Animals

Note: ? indicates possible origin; occurrence of animals or plants in more than one hearth indicates likelihood of *independent invention*—unconnected domestication in different environments.

Sources: Marvin W. Mikesell, *Patterns and Imprints of Mankind,* from The International Atlas. Chicago: Rand McNally, 1969, p. xxx. © 1969 Rand McNally, & Co., R.L. 75–S–24. Encyclopaedia Brittanica, *Macropaedia,* Vol. 5, "Domestication, Plant and Animal." New York, 1974, pp. 936–942.

Hearth	Plants	Animals
OLD WORLD		
Southeast Asia	bamboo, yam, taro, eggplant, banana, sugarcane, citrus, mango, black pepper, tea	dog, cat? duck, goose, chicken, pig? cattle? water buffalo
North China	rice, sorghum, millet, soybean, radish, cabbage, mulberry, apricot, persimmon, peach, plum, tea	dog, chicken? pig? horse, silkworm
Central Asia	hemp, flax, walnut, almond, lentil, pea, turnip, onion, carrot, apple, cherry, pear, melon	dog, chicken, sheep, cattle, horse? yak, bactrian camel, reindeer, bee
Fertile Crescent	wheat, barley, rye, oats, almond, date, fig, olive, pea, onion, turnip, cabbage, rutabaga, grapes	dog, pigeon, sheep, goat, cattle? pig? dromedary camel, bee
Ethiopia	coffee	
Nile Valley	sorghum, millet, cotton, sesame, cucumber, pea, lentil, melon	dog, cat, donkey
West Africa	rice, kola, watermelon	
NEW WORLD		
Central America	corn, cotton, sunflower, cocoa, potato, tomato, red pepper, beans, pumpkin, squash, avocado, tobacco	dog, turkey
Northern Andes	potato, beans, pumpkin, squash, strawberry	guinea pig, llama, alpaca, vicuña, guanaco
Eastern South America	peanut, cocoa, sunflower, manioc (cassava), sweet potato, beans, squash, pineapple	dog, duck

moving slowly along river valleys—the Dnieper, the Danube, and the Rhône—and around the Mediterranean coast. Thousands of years were required for the ***diffusion*** of agriculture across Europe to the far corners of Scandinavia. Taken as an average, agriculture spread at a rate of one-half mile a year, but the exact routes and rates of dispersal are not fully known. The process may have been associated with migrations outward in search of new land. One of the earliest known European sites lies in Macedonia, where about 6000 BC, people subsisted on cultivated wheat, barley, and lentils and kept domesticated sheep, goats, cattle, and pigs. When cultivation and animal husbandry spread away from the Mediterranean, however, certain adjustments to different climates, soils, and vegetation were necessary.

The first non-Mediterranean area settled was the fertile Danube Valley. Here in the early fifth millennium BC, Danubians lived in long, rectangular, gabled houses in villages of 200 to 600 people, and practiced a form of ***shifting agriculture*** based on wheat, barley, lentils, beans, and peas. They also kept domesticated cattle and pigs, but sheep and goats were of minor importance, reflecting the poor adaptation of these animals to the environment of central Europe. The settlements of these people were restricted to areas of ***loess*** soil, suggesting that the fertile areas in the lowland river basins of western and central Europe were most attractive to early agriculturalists. Only later was cultivation extended into the more difficult to farm forest areas of Europe.

This later expansion of cultivators into the forests of central and northern Europe did not occur until approximately 3000 BC, when early agriculturalists began to clear the land by fire, to plant cereals in the ashes, and to herd animals in meadows created in newly cleared woodlands. Over wide areas of Europe, the face of the land was altered. Oak and elm forests, destroyed by encroaching farmers, were replaced, after temporary cultivation, by secondary growths of alder and birch trees. As these farmers moved into progressively cooler climates, wheat and barley were gradually replaced by hardier cereal grasses such as oats and rye. These agricultural clearings are found along the coasts of Denmark and southern Sweden, and southern England and Ireland, where large expanses of treeless ***heath,*** hitherto believed to have been too dry or infertile to support trees, were actually created by these early frontiersmen.

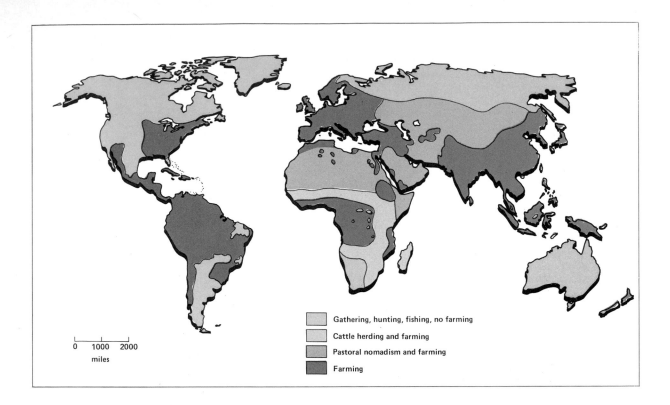

Gathering, hunting, fishing, no farming

Cattle herding and farming

Pastoral nomadism and farming

Farming

0   1000   2000
miles

Figure 5. World Patterns of Land Use, AD 1500. By 1500, the environmental transformation had diffused widely throughout the Old World and the New, and agriculture formed the basis of urban civilizations in East and South Asia, the Middle East, West Africa, Europe, and the New World. These patterns, evolved over several thousands of years, were radically reorganized when the scientific transformation gave Europeans a superior technology that enabled them to dominate the world.

At this same time, agriculture and herding also diffused westward along the North African littoral and up the Nile Valley as far south as Khartoum. The Mediterranean environment in this region was similar to that of the Fertile Crescent, so that little adjustment in subsistence strategy was needed. The climate of the Sahara, however, did require ecological adaptation, though this vast region was apparently wetter at about 5000 BC than it is now. Some cereal agriculture was practiced in a limited way in the oases of the Ahaggar Mountains, but the dominant economy that flourished in the Sahara in the fourth millennium BC was cattle herding. It is generally assumed that traders in the Nile Valley transmitted the knowledge of agriculture (but not the plants) into sub-Saharan Africa. Some writers, however, suggest that an independent center of plant domestication existed around 5000 BC in West Africa at the headwaters of the Niger River, but the archeological evidence is too scanty to sustain or disprove the argument.

The diffusion of Middle Eastern food production eastward into Asia was every bit as slow as its west-ward spread into Europe. By 5000 BC, wheat and barley were cultivated on the dry margins of the nuclear zone as far east as Baluchistan, eastern Iran, Afghanistan, and Pakistan. But beyond the Indus Valley, the evidence of food production is both more limited and much later in time. At 2000 BC, for example, at Navdatoli on the Narmada River in central India, farmers cultivated wheat, barley, peas, lentils, and rice, and kept domesticated cattle, pigs, and either sheep or goats. In North China, a farming pattern emerged in the Yellow River Valley, which fused Southeast Asian agriculture with the grain cultivation of the Middle East. In Southeast Asia, an independent pattern of farming was based on vegetative reproduction of plants through cuttings. Tuber plants played an important role, as did the pig and the chicken. The relationships between agriculture in this area and that in the Middle East are unclear, largely because the hot, wet climate of Southeast Asia has destroyed virtually all archeological evidence.

In the New World, an independent but parallel shift from food collection to food production took place in at least two locations, central Mexico and the northern Andes. Whereas in the Middle East people domesticated many animals and few plants, in the New World just the reverse happened. White and sweet potatoes were domesticated here, as well as two kinds of chili, amaranths, sunflowers, the peanut, four kinds of beans, pumpkins, a variety of squashes, and most important, corn. By contrast, the only large animals to be domesticated were the llama, the alpaca, and the vicuña of the Peruvian highlands.

The Spread of Urban Centers
[FIGURE 5]

In patterns similar to those of Mesopotamia, people soon concentrated in urban centers in the river valleys of Egypt, India, North China, and Southeast Asia after the emergence of Sumerian cities. In each case, the growth of cities closely followed the introduction of agriculture, suggesting that urbanism may have been a spontaneous response to dense sedentary populations and large food surpluses rather than the result of diffusion. In any case, by the third millennium BC cities existed in Sumeria, the Nile Valley, the Indus Valley, and shortly thereafter in the Mediterranean Basin. Most of these early cities were control centers for the organization of densely settled agricultural hinterlands. But very quickly they became exchange centers in an expanding network of interregional trade. By the second millennium BC, city life existed in the valley of the Yellow River in North China, in the river valleys of Southeast Asia, and along the Niger River in West Africa. Some 2000 years later, the Aztec and Inca civilizations in the New World were urban-based. By the time of the Roman Empire, world population had grown to around 300 million people. Fully 80 percent of this population was concentrated in three highly organized urban systems: an estimated 40 percent on the Indian subcontinent, another quarter in Han China, and the remainder in the Middle Eastern–Mediterranean core area. Beyond these fertile hearths of culture, vast regions remained thinly populated.

In the European culture hearth, for which the most evidence has been collected, nearly a millennium was required for urban institutions to spread from the Mediterranean to the western reaches of the continent. Under the Romans, this urban hierarchy spread north and west into Spain, France, and finally Britain. Population subsequently increased, particularly in the newly settled areas of western and east-central Europe. Although many of these centers collapsed with the fragmentation of the Roman Empire and the subsequent disorder and disruption of regional trade networks, some European cities reappeared in the medieval period as important centers of civilization. Similarly in India, China, and the New World centers, urban hierarchies spread out from the early centers to encompass larger regions and more diverse populations.

By AD 1500, on the eve of the scientific transformation, these overlapping diffusions of agriculture and urbanism had altered the economy of vast areas in the Old World and the New. Throughout Europe, the Middle East and North Africa, Central Asia, China, and India, cereal cultivation was the

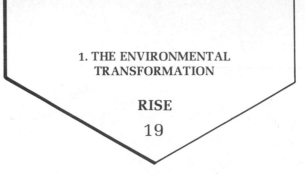

mainstay of human life. Expanding populations supported the emergence of urban societies comparable to those of Europe in Southeast Asia and Africa, where tuber cultivation was the basis of agriculture. Specialized nomadic herding economies existed in the deserts and steppes of the Middle East and North Africa and in the cold northern reaches of Scandinavia and Siberia. Agriculture had not spread to Australia, and scattered groups still practiced hunting and gathering in parts of southern and central Africa and along the Arctic fringe. By and large, however, sedentary agriculture had effectively replaced earlier economies as the predominant basis of human existence.

Similarly in the New World, cultivation of maize, beans, and squash was practiced throughout Central America and in humid eastern North America as far north as the Great Lakes, the Saint Lawrence River Valley, and Nova Scotia. In South America, only the dry temperate south, the uplands of northeastern Brazil, and scattered sections of the Amazon Basin did not have an agricultural economy. Complex urban civilizations existed in Mexico, parts of Central America, the northern fringe of South America, and the Andes highlands. Comparable in architectural sophistication, political organization, social stratification, and economy to the ancient civilizations of the Old World, these societies quickly collapsed before the superior military technology of expanding Europe.

Overleaf:
At the end of the fifteenth century, sowing was still done by the broadcast method, which gave equal amounts of seed to fields and birds. This miniature from the *Breviarium Grimani*, one of the many exquisitely illustrated books of prayer made for the medieval nobility, focuses on the all-important agricultural season as well as on another aspect of the life of the period, the town. *Photo:* The Bettman Archive.

THE SCIENTIFIC TRANSFORMATION

2

The environmental transformation created a world in which regional civilizations controlled different spheres of the globe, with no single society having the power to impose its will on the others. In China, India, the Middle East, the Mediterranean, and the New World, cities and empires held sway; trade networks were established; and advances in administration, religious thought, and architecture were accomplished. With the beginning of the scientific transformation, however, the European center of civilization became the first society with the capacity for global influence. First, during the medieval period (AD 500–1500), an expansion of settlement and population in northern and western Europe was stimulated by a series of social, economic, and technological changes in agriculture. New areas were brought into cultivation; the forests of Europe were felled. Larger agricultural surpluses supported larger and more intense human concentrations. In the phase that followed, generally called the Industrial Revolution, scientific knowledge was applied to technology, and inanimate sources of energy were brought under direct control. In the eighteenth and nineteenth centuries, England emerged as the first industrial urban nation. Largely as a result of this intellectual and technological growth, Europeans began to dominate all other world cultures, whether or not the latter came under their direct suzerainty. A new pattern of human relations was created in which an inner sphere of technologically secure nations, the technological world, began to control an outer sphere of technologically insufficient nations, the developing world. For the first time in history, the basic division between peoples across the face of the earth was based on the possession of scientific knowledge and technology. It was no longer a case of relative equality; power and wealth now depended on the ability to manipulate the physical world.

THE MEDIEVAL AGRICULTURAL REVOLUTION
[FIGURE 6]

In the Middle Ages, changes in the organization and productivity of agriculture in northern and western Europe gave rise to a major expansion of population and cultivation. In a period of 500 years, forests were cut, towns were established, and population nearly trebled. This initial phase of the scientific transformation established the agricultural basis for a flowering of European society in the later Middle Ages, providing food surpluses for growing cities, expanding commerce, and developing industries. The dramatic changes of this early period are often ignored because medieval patterns of growth were temporarily obscured by plagues and incessant warfare in the fourteenth and fifteenth centuries. Nonetheless, the distinctive features of modern Europe, the hearth of the technological world, are lodged in the changing rural life of the medieval period, in that prosperity of the countryside which fostered the advance of urban Western civilization.

In the early Middle Ages, rural life was universal in western Europe. England and Germany had virtually no urban centers. Elsewhere, towns were few and far between, small settlements embedded in the surrounding countryside. Agricultural productivity was so low that a cultivated area of nearly 7500 acres plus pastureland was required to feed a town of 3000 people. As a result there were few large cities, and in them, the vast majority of people (at least three out of four heads of households) were still directly engaged in agriculture.

Villages were the basic unit of settlement housing a stable peasantry clustered together for security. The normal background of human existence centered on these fixed points, widely separated one from another by empty spaces. The land on which these villages stood had special legal status and fixed boundaries. These boundaries were marked by hedges; entry into the enclosed area was forbidden, giving peasants an asylum from the relentless demands of medieval lords. Inside these enclosures were makeshift **wattle and daub**• huts, so fragile that a peasant could destroy a neighbor's house simply by sawing the central beam—an offense for which he was, according to English records of the time, fined. Animal pens and stables, stores of food, and vegetable gardens (tofts) were also inside the

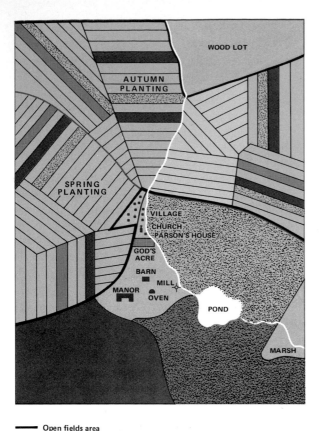

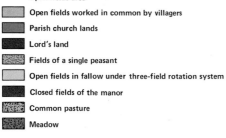

- ■ Open fields area
- ▦ Open fields worked in common by villagers
- ■ Parish church lands
- ■ Lord's land
- ▨ Fields of a single peasant
- ▨ Open fields in fallow under three-field rotation system
- ■ Closed fields of the manor
- ▨ Common pasture
- ▨ Meadow

Figure 6. The Typical Manse of a Medieval Lord. This generalized depiction of medieval land tenure and cropping shows the distinction between the closed fields of the large manse and the open lands of the village, held both in common and in private hands. With the three-field rotation system, the crops planted in the open fields, the dates of planting and harvesting, and the share of the harvest due the lord and the villagers were determined by the village commune, a corporate body directed by the lord or his steward. Villagers grazed a certain number of cattle on common land; some lords allowed timber and firewood to be taken from the woodlot. The enclosed fields of the lord's manse were not open to the villagers, although they labored there. The meadow in some cases belonged to the lord and in others was open to general use. A portion of the open fields was set aside for support of the church above and beyond "God's acre" (the parson's field).

enclosure. Strict legal definition of these refuge areas tended to discourage any dispersal of settlement by colonists and pioneers.

Villages also retained fixed locations for environmental reasons. The soil inside enclosures was more fertile than outside because of fertilization by household wastes and animal manure. On this interior land, peasants grew herbs, root crops, vines, and other vegetables that formed the *companaticum* (accompaniment) to bread, the staple of existence. These gardens were the only village land that was permanently cultivated. Outside the enclosures, grain fields of wheat, rye, and oats ringed with hedges were planted in the least exposed, most accessible, and most easily worked locations. In some cases, movable barriers surrounded these fields to discourage predators and keep out cattle. Severe penalties were levied on people who stole or moved these barriers.

Generally, the agricultural area was small, and over much of Europe the landscape was covered by natural pasture and forest. A good part of the peasant's food supply still derived from hunting, fishing, and trapping; the forests served as grazing areas for pigs; the meadows, for sheep, goats, and cattle. It was in these three zones—the enclosure, the cleared fields, and the wilderness—and through a combination of cultivation, animal husbandry, and gathering that the vast majority of people lived.

The family was the core of this rural medieval society, and villages (manses) were structured, lands distributed, and labor divided on a family basis. The term "manse" originally referred to the site of a single family hearth, but it was later extended to include the homestead, family lands both inside and outside the enclosure, and even communal rights to surrounding pastures. The manse of a lord, a monastery, or a religious order was simply a larger and more varied household that employed peasants and servants. And peasants in the vicinity of these larger estates often worked the land for the benefit of the aristocracy and the clergy, rarely owning their own.

In one unusual case, a couple named David and Dominique, who lived near the great abbey of Cluny in central France, was able to accumulate eleven parcels of land, which altogether amounted to about an acre. In the end, however, since the couple was childless, their land passed to the Church, contributing in a small way to the power and influence of the medieval clergy. As a result, the Church played an important role in the economic life of medieval Europe. In England, monasteries were widely distributed across the landscape, controlled large holdings of agricultural land, opened up new lands to cultivation in frontier regions like the English marshes, and were engaged in sheep raising in the uplands.

Most peasants, however, were too poor to accumulate land. The broader society of the period was dominated by small groups of lords and priests who controlled the activities of the vast mass of rural peasants. The wealthiest of these directly owned estates as large as 25,000 to 50,000 acres. The principal economic function of these large holdings was to support a few people in wealth and comfort, to maintain their style of life. An extensive retinue of followers traveled with each lord from property to property, consuming the profits of peasant labor on the spot and distributing alms and charity to paupers and monasteries en route.

Given this primitive system of production and consumption, western Europe was understandably lightly populated in the early Middle Ages. Human beings were far fewer than they have ever been since; settlement was sporadic, and vast tracts of land were probably deserted. The obstacles to communication between people were formidable. Roads were poor and unsafe; bridges were not maintained. A normal day's travel for a caravan of merchants amounted to only 19 to 25 miles, and this distance was often diminished by spells of bad weather or lack of forage for the animals. Trade was therefore restricted to a few routes, was low in volume, and was irregular in the extreme.

Most villages were located on light, easily worked, and well-drained soils. In England, this meant colonization of the uplands and avoidance of lowland regions of heavy clay soils covered with swamps, forests, and pastures. In Flanders, villages similarly avoided areas of heavy soils, creating a dispersed and spotty pattern of settlement. Agricultural expansion was prevented by the fragile wooden tools of the peasantry, which were not equal to the task of clearing wooded areas or turning heavy clay soils. As a result, although total populations were small, favored ecological zones tended to be overpopulated, and this population pressure could not easily be relieved by colonization. According to most manorial surveys, the manses of France, the Netherlands, western Germany, Switzerland, and northern Italy were overpopulated during the 200 years before the year 1000. The main preoccupation of the peasantry was to survive the perils of cultivating cereals with inferior tools in unfavorable climates, the ceaseless demands of landlords, periodic attacks by marauders, and the less frequent raids of invaders. Life was a hazardous, hand-to-mouth affair.

New Techniques

Several social, economic, and technological changes in medieval agriculture altered this fabric of country life in western Europe. These changes relieved the precariousness of peasant existence, reshaped the landscape of northern Europe, and created a vastly more productive agricultural system that indirectly contributed to the northward shift of civilization from the fringes of the Mediterranean to the plains

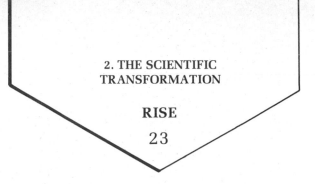

of northern Europe. The three most important elements in this second agricultural revolution were the heavy plow, which opened the wet clay soils of the north to cultivation; the use of horses for plowing and transport; and the development of a three-field system of **crop rotation,** which increased agricultural production to provide the biological basis for a population expansion.

The heavy plow, with a coulter or knife that cut the earth vertically, a plowshare that sliced it horizontally, a curved moldboard that turned the earth over in the furrows, and an adjustable frame by which the depth of the furrow could be regulated, came into use in northern Europe between the eighth and tenth centuries. Previously, the light scratch plow, well suited only to the climate and soils of the Mediterranean region, had been the principal agricultural implement in use throughout Europe. The development of the heavy plow, encouraged by a more widespread availability of iron when new mines in the Rhineland were opened, held three major advantages for agriculturalists north of the Alps. First, the heavy plow turned wet, thick soils so effectively that **cross plowing,** essential with the scratch plow, was no longer needed. This cut the labor of plowing in half, enabling peasants to cultivate more land in the same amount of time. Second, the new plow changed field structures from the square shapes produced by cross plowing to long, narrow fields with ridges and furrows. In wet years, crops grew on the ridges; in dry years they grew in the furrows, so that to some degree the climatic uncertainties of medieval agriculture were reduced by this new field system. Finally, the heavy plow enabled peasants to cultivate the heavy soils of the rich alluvial lowlands that were inherently more fertile than surrounding uplands and provided better crops. This combination of savings in labor, improvements in field drainage, and the opening of new lands to cultivation raised production and revolutionized agriculture in northern Europe.

The heavy plow also stimulated some important social and economic changes in the organization of peasant society. This plow needed eight oxen instead of the customary two to turn the soil effectively. Since few peasants owned eight oxen, a pooling of resources was required. This involved not only new patterns of social cooperation, but a reorganization of village lands into large open fields plowed in long strips. These strips were usually assigned to the group of peasants who owned the plow and oxen, and the land was worked communally, with disputes and management decisions placed in the hands of a village council. One benefit of this system of cultivation was that large communal fields, when *fallow,* could be used for grazing, a significant advantage particularly in later periods when *arable* land expanded at the expense of natural pastures.

Considerable regional variation existed in the rate of acceptance and utilization of the heavy plow in Europe. Its use was directly related to population density. In regions of low population densities, the average hamlet of ten families or less found it difficult to support the cost of the new plow. Regions in which the system of inheritance had already encouraged *strip farming* were more amenable. In any case, by the seventh century, agriculture and population expanded in south-central Germany and the Rhineland apparently coincident with the adoption of the heavy plow. At this same time, the plow was used in France north of the Loire and was later introduced into Britain by the Danes. By the end of the Middle Ages, the typical manorial economy involved the use of the heavy plow, strip farming of open fields, and communal husbandry.

A second major change in medieval agriculture was the growing use of horses for plowing and planting. The major advantages of horses over oxen lay in their greater speed and endurance. Although both animals had equivalent pulling power, horses plowed twice as rapidly and could work for one to two hours more each day than oxen. Not all medieval people accepted this evaluation, however. Walter of Henley, a noted thirteenth-century English agricultural writer, preferred oxen over horses because they ate less and could be sold for meat when old. Yet in eastern Germany, plowland was measured by the area that could be tilled either by one horse or two oxen. In any case, by the end of the eleventh century, horses were widely used for plowing on the plains of northern Europe, and a century later, they were common in England. Horses never penetrated Mediterranean Europe, probably because oats, their primary food, did not grow well there.

The shift from oxen to horses had important effects on communication and transport in medieval Europe. In the early Middle Ages, although every castle, monastery, or town was likely to be visited occasionally by wandering monks, peddlers, or a lord's retinue, connections between two inhabited settlements adjacent to one another were quite rare, and human isolation was much greater than in later periods. The widespread adoption of the horse altered this pattern. In the eleventh and twelfth centuries, hamlets in the vicinity of larger settlements were abandoned. Peasants shifted their residences to

larger centers and commuted to their fields on horseback. In parts of Germany, northern France, and England, substantial villages of 100 or more families with facilities such as a church, a tavern, and sometimes a school grew out of centrally located hamlets. This "urbanization" of the peasantry laid the foundation for the later shift in medieval society from rural to town life.

The three-field rotation system, the last and most important element of the agricultural revolution of the Middle Ages, was adopted in France north of the Loire, in Germany, in England, and in parts of the Netherlands during the thirteenth century. Under the traditional two-field system, half the village lands were planted to winter grain and half left fallow in alternate years in order to maintain soil fertility. With the advent of new soil-enriching legumes such as peas and beans, the land could be divided in thirds: on each third, winter wheat or rye was planted the first year; spring barley, oats, and legumes the second; and the third year the land lay fallow. This new system increased productivity. In the two-field system, half the land was unproductive (except as pasture), but with the three-field system only a third lay fallow. A greater number of people, therefore, could be fed from the same land area. Moreover, the larger spring planting of barley and oats was important for the feeding of horses, so that a change from the two- to three-field rotation often coincided with the shift from oxen to horses. In addition, triennial rotation distributed the labor of plowing, sowing, and harvesting more evenly over the agricultural year, and by diversifying crops, reduced the risk of famine.

The adoption of the heavy plow, the horse, and the three-field rotation system had a significant impact on life and landscape in medieval Europe. Past obstacles that had held population in check and limited cultivation were removed, and an intensive repopulation of the northern plains transformed the face of the land. New villages sprang up and old ones grew larger; towns began to dot the countryside. The Iberian plateau and the plains beyond the Elbe were colonized. Greater agricultural productivity and a better diet (protein-rich from peas, beans, and other legumes) provided the energy and capacity for new and demanding ventures. The great forests of the region were gradually destroyed, and when the empty spaces disappeared, closer patterns of human association were established. This medieval expansion of population and cultivation underlay the emergence of modern Europe.

Expansion of the Arable
[FIGURES 7, 8]

In the twelfth and thirteenth centuries, the population of western Europe grew sharply, nearly doubling—remarkable for a preindustrial society—from

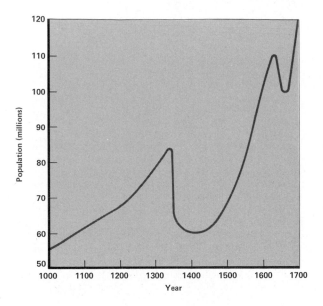

Figure 7. The Population of Europe in the Medieval Period. The population curve for medieval Europe shows the overall rise spurred by advances in agriculture between AD 1000 and 1350, and the devastating effects of bubonic plague in the fourteenth century.

an estimated 50 million in AD 950 to some 83 million in 1348, the year the Black Death swept over the continent. Everywhere, although birth rates were no higher, a larger number of people survived. As noted above, this population growth was based on improvements in agricultural techniques and basic changes in local food supply. For this reason, population grew at different rates in different places. In England, for example, the overall population rose from 1.1 million in 1086 to 3.7 million in 1346. But according to the *Domesday Book*, William the Conqueror's great survey of England's resources in 1086, the number of men in some hamlets in Lincolnshire in eastern England increased from six to twenty-four times, while Devon in the south remained a wilderness. In France, by far the largest country in Europe, the population tripled between 1086 and 1328 to reach a total of nearly 14 million. The number of households doubled in Provence in the southeast in the second half of the thirteenth century. The region near Paris, already relatively densely populated in the ninth century, likewise supported twice as many families five centuries later. Yet other regions were virtually uninhabited.

The reasons for local variations in the density of human occupance and the intensity of population growth are quite simple. First, the countryside of Europe during the medieval period was organized into small, closely knit regional units attached to growing market towns. In each of these units, agricultural conditions affected the spread of settlement and population. On this local scale, uncleared forests

stood next to long-settled communities, and broader, regional contrasts between, for example, the uncleared wilds south of the Thames River and the densely settled Wash were common. Second, the diffusion of agricultural innovations on which population growth was dependent proceeded unevenly. Marginal areas such as northern England, Scandinavia, and the plains of central Europe received them long after they were applied in the German-French **heartland.°** The rate of local acceptance was complicated by patterns of village organization, environmental conditions, and population density. Finally, changes in population varied simply because medieval peasants were considerably more mobile than is usually assumed, and the general pattern of movement was from old, settled, overpopulated regions into empty areas.

The larger number of people in Europe, then, was accommodated by an enlargement of the agrarian living space at the expense of forest, swamps, and pasture. In Holland, this meant the draining of **fens,°** the building of dikes, and the construction of **polders.°** In the forests of France and Germany, new land was cleared and new villages founded. In the mountains of southern Germany, Switzerland, and Austria, villages climbed the slopes of the Alps to elevations higher than those settled in modern times. A wave of colonization opened up the plains of eastern Europe. Generally this exploitation of virgin land, reshaping the landscape of medieval Europe, proceeded in three phases: first, enlargement of existing village territories from the eleventh century onward; second, the establishment of new villages at the end of the twelfth century; and third, a shift to **dispersed settlement°** and pastoral activities at the beginning of the fourteenth century.

The first phase of the assault on the European wilderness was accomplished in the eleventh century by peasant pioneers who, spurred by population pressure and possessing better tools and equipment, were no longer hemmed in by unconquerable waste and began to enlarge the cultivated lands in the vicinity of existing villages. Sometimes expansion was done furtively to escape the landlord's attention and, more especially, his rents. In this way, fields were brought into cultivation on the fringes of older settlements on sites previously cleared for temporary or shifting cultivation. Cultivated fields also sprang up in common pastures and were enclosed by

Victims of the Black Death in fourteenth-century Europe died in such numbers that the total population of the continent was reduced by half. These sufferers appear in an illustrated German bible of the sixteenth century. By then the great plague was long over, but regular outbreaks made it familiar to people all over the world into the twentieth century. *Photo:* **The Bettman Archive.**

hedges, to the chagrin of other villagers. This piecemeal nibbling of neighboring uncultivated land led to numerous lawsuits between village communities that strove to protect surrounding land where their horses and cattle grazed. At the very time when more animals were needed to plow virgin territory, there was less local room for livestock.

Deeper in the forests, peasants, hermits (who existed in large numbers in this period), charcoal burners, shepherds, iron makers, and wax collectors cut clearings in the woodland. In France, these new clearings (*assarts*) often bore the name of the peasant who first cut the trees, rooted out the stumps, and cleared the underbrush. Often, these pioneer efforts amounted to sizable migrations, as for example, at Brie in northeastern France, where some 20,000 to 30,000 people moved into forestland between 1100 and 1250, or in Germany, where the frontier advanced steadily eastward. Monks were not, as has

often been said, the chief agents of landscape change. The great abbeys of the Benedictines and Cistercians were almost always established on previously cleared land. However, many new religious orders settled the wilderness to rediscover, like members of modern communes, the dignity of manual labor. Peasants provided the necessary manpower; the masters with dominion over the waste consented to this extension of the arable. The forests of Europe, then, were first opened to settlement by isolated pioneers, but these sporadic individual efforts were soon replaced by more intense and coordinated group endeavors.

The second phase in the clearing of the European wilderness was characterized by the foundation of new villages (*villeneuves*) by groups of settlers organized and encouraged by prominent landlords. The unoccupied forests generally belonged to the highest nobility and the Church. Between 1150 and 1200, churchmen and nobles decided to support the exploitation and development of unused land. In some cases, the new villages were located on roads to ensure regular collection of tolls from passing merchants and pilgrims. In others, new villages were founded to generate additional sources of rents, dues, and **tithes**• to alleviate the financial distress

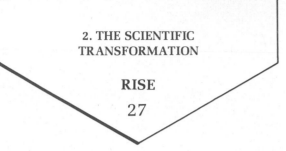

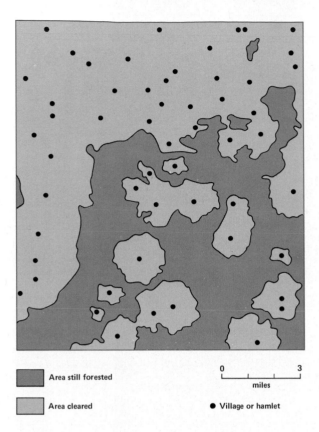

Figure 8. Stages of Forest Clearing in the Middle Ages. This map of a local area southeast of Munich, Germany, shows the various stages of forest clearing during the medieval period that left their mark on the European landscape. In the first stage, settlements (lower left) were isolated centers surrounded by forest; somewhat later, clearings were enlarged (center), until finally so much forest had been cleared that only patches of trees remained (upper right).

Area still forested

Area cleared

● Village or hamlet

0   3
miles

most lords experienced then. In the twelfth and thirteenth centuries, some 100 new towns were founded in Normandy, and still more were created in the Paris basin and in western Germany. The counts of Holland founded settlements on the polderlands. The inhabitants of these new **central places** were usually poorer peasants and younger sons. Overcrowded villages were beginning to act as nurseries for aggressive pioneers. Settlements in more remote locations attracted recruits with promises of new land, equipment, and houses. Elsewhere, groups of lay brothers attached to monasteries implemented the undertakings of their orders. In these planned colonial ventures, the plots of land assigned to each pioneer were laid out geometrically, creating the curious ribbon or herringbone villages that date from this period.

The third and final phase of settlement of the European wilderness was marked by an ebbing of the tide of new villages and a clearing of the intervening spaces by individual settlers living in isolated, dispersed single farmsteads. Often these colonists established predominantly pastoral farms specializing in animal husbandry and herding, activities that had been driven far from the centers of population by the expansion of the arable. Others were the houses of individual lords, complete with moats and battlements, constructed like miniature castles. Equally apparent were the dwellings of individual peasants who preferred solitude to the growing hubbub in the villages and towns of the period. In any case, the end of the thirteenth century witnessed the closing of the internal frontier, the settlement of the once impenetrable wilderness of western Europe, and the genesis of a landscape not unlike that of modern Europe.

The Changing Pace of Life

This growth of population and agricultural activity in medieval Europe dramatically altered not only patterns of settlement and environmental exploitation, but also systems of economic organization, commerce, and communication. The most immediate effect of these changes was to bring human groups into closer association, to intensify the human concentration. With the disappearance of the wilderness, travel was no longer so formidable, and new bridges and roads made distances easier to traverse. Across long distances, these roads connected the growing towns and nascent urban centers of western Europe. Here, a new urban middle class was developing, one less tied to agriculture and the rhythm of the seasons and increasingly indispensable to the changing economy of the region.

In the countryside, however, poverty still held sway. Hordes of starving people flocked to the monasteries and abbeys in times of plague and famine. At Cluny, this desperate migration averaged nearly 16,000 a year. Population had outpaced both the higher yields fostered by new techniques and the agricultural expansion, so that catastrophic famines repeatedly struck the countrysides of France, the Low Countries, and England in the thirteenth and early fourteenth centuries. After five centuries of change and upheaval, peasants were as poor as ever, though they lived in a new and different world.

And a major new element of this new world was the city. Cities had sprung up in every region of northern Europe in the twelfth and thirteenth centuries. Most of these towns were small, less than a

The small medieval walled town, its stone buildings crowded together within the security of the walls, its entirety easily encompassed by the eye, was far different from the great cities of the Roman Empire with their monumental buildings and huge open spaces. "A Tuscan Town," painted by Ambrogio Lorenzetti about 1340. Picture Gallery, Siena. *Photo:* Alinari–Art Reference Bureau.

half mile in radius. Their size was limited by water supply, by small local hinterlands, by primitive transport, and by municipal regulations. Usually, their jurisdiction covered no more than a peasant could walk (round trip) in one day, and this influenced their spacing. Some of these urban centers had existed since Roman times; others had become important as newer religious centers. Still others grew up around fortified points (*burgs*), protected by the strength of a lord's household. In any case, some 2500 new cities were established in Germany alone during this period, and though most were small, they attracted a swelling flood of peasants from the countryside. The largest cities of the period were Paris and Venice, with populations of 40,000. Although hardly large by modern standards, in them an urban mentality and social structure were incubated.

This growing urban population was made possible, at least in part, by improvements in transportation. All over Europe, bridges were thrown across rivers. Old roads were rebuilt and new ones constructed. The heavy bricks of the Roman *iter* (road) were replaced by light gravel surfaces that were easily changed or repaired. In England, these new roads cut wide swaths through the countryside after a statute in 1285 forbade trees within 200 feet of the highway to protect merchants from lurking highwaymen. On the Continent, roads twisted and turned tortuously to fit local conditions. One road in the Queyras (an alpine region of France), for which five bridges are sufficient today, had thirty bridges in the medieval period (seventeen of them were destroyed by flood in 1370). Nonetheless, the growth of land and water transport in this period contributed directly to the money economy and the increased commerce on which expanding urban populations relied.

In point of fact, the medieval urban middle class owed virtually everything to trade. In the Mediterranean, merchants of Venice and Genoa vied for control of coastal hinterlands; in the north, the Hanseatic League, an association of merchant groups that took political form, controlled commerce. Cloth dominated the medieval economy as completely as steel does now. In Flanders and Picardy, in Languedoc and Lombardy, city weavers produced cloth for local and foreign markets. The agricultural revolution in the hinterland had given rise to urban guilds of weavers, dyers, and cloth shearers who were of crucial commercial importance. This revival was stimulated by the flow of coinage and precious metals into western Europe. Previously trade had been exclusively for the purpose of supplying high-quality wine and fine cloth to a wealthy elite. By the fourteenth century, however, a countryman of Provence who was too poor to wed his daughter in cloth from Ypres or Champagne forced the husband-to-be to assume this responsibility. What had happened was a general widening and loosening of economic conditions, such that the peasantry was deeply affected by urban markets and by a growing awareness of broader horizons. Peasants now bought iron and cloth in the markets of neighboring towns. They sold grain and livestock to urbanites and became sophisticated in exchange. This flowering of culture and civilization in medieval Europe, despite the destruction of the plagues and wars that soon followed, formed the background of the Industrial Revolution of the eighteenth and nineteenth centuries. In a real sense, it was the womb in which the technological world was conceived.

THE INDUSTRIAL REVOLUTION

If the medieval period was marked by slow and gradual changes in life and livelihood in western Europe, the accumulated momentum of these changes gave rise to one of the most exciting and dynamic eras in human history. After centuries of looking backward toward the wisdom of Greece and Rome for inspiration, Europeans once more became adventurous—intellectually and geographically. In the middle of the fifteenth century, the scholars of Prince Henry the Navigator trained Portuguese pilots and mariners to man expeditions that charted the shores of Africa and brought gold and slaves back to Europe. In 1492, Christopher Columbus and eighty-seven other adventurers funded by the queen of Spain officially discovered the New World (having probably been preceded in their accomplishment by various Irish monks, Norsemen, and even Breton and Bristol fishermen). Encouraged by a vision of spoils to be won, Spain supported three more expeditions by Columbus to the New World—expeditions in search of gold, a maritime path to the East Indies, and new territories for the crown. Other explorers quickly followed, and a flood of new wealth, particularly gold and silver from the mines of Mexico and Peru, was injected into the European economy. These voyages culminated in Magellan's circling of

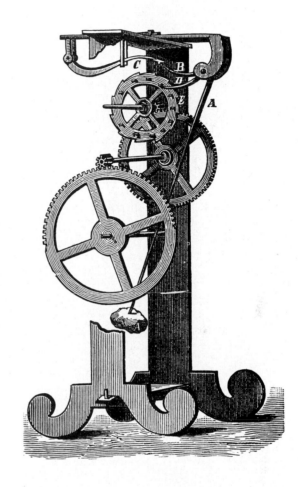

In the seventeenth century Galileo, one of the first modern scientists, verified the Copernican theory of the universe and discovered the principle of inertia. But he was equally interested in putting his discoveries to practical use: this plan for a pendulum clock was sketched by his son in 1641. The pinwheel at top, turned by the arms of the pendulum pivot, drove the clock. *Photo:* Culver Pictures.

the globe as the age of exploration unveiled a new and larger world to the Europeans. It ushered in a period when, for the first time in history, every part of the planet was accessible. Geographical exploration had captured the imagination of Europe.

Simultaneously, another new world—scientific and technological—was being explored by mathematicians and physicists like Copernicus, Kepler, Galileo, and Descartes. From their work, a world picture emerged that traditional concepts of space,

The diffusion of knowledge was one of the great changes brought by the scientific transformation. This etching shows the interior of a print shop in the early seventeenth century, when most of the work now done by sophisticated machinery was done by hand. At the rear of the shop type is being set; in the foreground, two men operate the press. *Photo:* The Bettman Archive.

time, motion, and matter could not explain. This new world was discovered by careful observation and experimentation, by what we now call the scientific method. The earth moved, and moved regularly. It formed a minor part of a broader universe, and was not even located at the center. Mechanical clocks controlled time, telescopes and compasses comprehended space. A thirst for new knowledge and discovery engulfed Europe, and soon this thirst filtered down to the artisan's workshop.

A host of technological inventions was discovered, leading outside observers to note the emergence of technological superiority in western Europe as early as the fifteenth century. No phase of life was unaffected. Progress was made in machine saws, textile and glass manufacture, the production of cast iron, mining, and printing. Incessant change marked the next two centuries, finally causing the irritable Sam-

uel Johnson to carp that even the gallows tree at Tyburn was not safe from "the fury of innovation," that now even hanging had to be done in a new way. It was in this climate of terrestrial and technological exploration that the Industrial Revolution occurred first in England.

The changes were sudden and violent, and for a time appeared to threaten the whole fabric of society. During the period, population grew at an unparalleled rate, and young people formed a significant portion of the total. The productive powers of machine technology unleashed a torrent of change— new sources of raw materials were exploited, industries emerged overnight, new patterns of trade and commerce developed, and production soared. This climate of progress and innovation fostered by the rapid pace of technological change undermined the traditional structure of economy and society.

The two great ideologies of the twentieth century, capitalism and Marxism, were spawned in the debate over the standard of living of industrial workers. These men and women had left their origins in the countryside and clustered together in the urban factories of the new industrial towns where the chimneys and smokestacks of "dark, satanic mills" erased church spires from the skylines. In cities like Manchester and Lille, merchants and entrepreneurs invested in the genius and gadgets of inventors and subsidized the development of new products in their factories. As laborers were harnessed to the tireless machines created by the inventions of Boulton, Watt, and Arkwright, men, women, and children came to be viewed and treated as things—as factors of production like land and capital.

In the countryside, change was no less violent. Village common lands were enclosed by fences and hedges and converted into sheepwalks to satisfy the rising demand for woolen cloth. Bitterly opposed by villagers, who saw themselves driven off their land by sheep and their houses and churches converted into stables, the movement by its end had "enclosed" some 10 million acres, nearly half the arable land in England. This enclosure movement was merely one facet of a trend toward more efficient, economic use of land. Vigorously encouraged by landlords like Lord "Turnip" Townshend and the eccentric Jethro Tull, "scientific" principles were brought to bear on agriculture and animal husbandry, not, however, without the payment of a price in human misery. Marshes and swamps were drained to create new agricultural land, and new field crops (most importantly the turnip) and rotation techniques were introduced. These innovations were diffused throughout England at countless cattle shows, wool fairs, and plowing matches. The resulting increase in agricultural productivity was striking; between 1710 and 1795 the average weight of a fattened ox brought to market had doubled from 370 to nearly 800 pounds.

This commercialization of agriculture was aided by the expansion of communications systems. New roads were built across England connecting emerging centers of industry; the twisting highways of medieval times were straightened and broadened. An era of canal construction made possible cheap bulk transportation of heavy commodities like coal, iron, stone, and timber, and integrated agricultural regions into a widening circle of exchange. In the north, the first rails were laid, and the era of mass transportation began. In short, the Industrial Revolution rationalized life on an economic basis, and although the new cities were the primary arenas of change, the impact was national in scope.

In this revolution that created a new society and a new landscape, four processes are of particular importance: first, the growth in population generated by a rise in birth rates and a decline in death rates; second, the pace of technological change, which harnessed inanimate energy and fostered rises in production to support the population expansion; third, the spatial reordering of society brought about by new patterns of resource utilization, communication, and growing urbanization; and fourth, the emergence of the industrial town as a new human environment. Virtually every problem shared

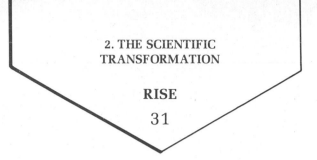

by the nations of the technological world—resource exhaustion, environmental decay, urban blight, ghettos, the declining quality of human life—was born in the Industrial Revolution that swept England between 1750 and 1850. Although it is not clear why this transformation first occurred here rather than elsewhere, it is certain that all subsequent industrial revolutions in Europe, the United States, Russia, and Japan strongly resembled the original.

A Surfeit of People

England and Wales embarked on the Industrial Revolution with a population of 6.5 million people. Fifty years later, in 1800, the total population of England and Wales had soared to 9 million, and by 1830 to 14 million. This spectacular doubling of population in less than a century, virtually unknown in preindustrial societies, was caused by the interplay of two forces—increasing birth rate and declining death rate.

The rising birth rate of the eighteenth century was principally caused by people marrying earlier and having more children. Previously, young men were tied to long guild apprenticeships, which had the effect of delaying weddings. The gradual replacement of skilled workers by machines manned by unskilled workers who married earlier led to a higher birth rate and larger families. Childbearing was also encouraged by the demand for child labor in the new factories. In the cotton mills, children were preferred as "apprentices" because they were more responsive to regimentation, had quicker hands, and could be paid at lower rates. In the mines, women and children were employed to drag coal from the mining faces of small, narrow cuts to the main passages and to drive the horses along these to the collection pit. The outrageous conditions of their employment are written in the "reforms" of the time: In 1819 children under nine were banned from the cotton mills; in 1842 children under ten could no longer work in the coal mines; in 1833 workers under eighteen (75 percent of the total labor force in the cotton factories) were limited to a 69-hour work week. And since as late as 1840 the average worker earned only 8 shillings a week and needed 14 for basic necessities, the stimulus to have children who could earn the deficit was substantial. In addition, family wages were supplemented by government subsidies on the basis of number of children after changes in the Poor Law in 1795. As Arthur Young, a spokesman for the new agricultural techniques, put it, "Come boys, get children—they are worth more now than they ever were."

At the same time the birth rate was increasing (reaching a peak of 37.7 per 1000 population in 1780), the death rate was declining because more children were surviving. In large part, this was due to improvements in medical techniques and the availability of hospitals in urban areas. Sanitary practices spread across England after the introduction of European clinical training for doctors around 1725. Between 1700 and 1818 some 100 hospitals and dispensaries were built in London. The impact of these hospitals can be judged by the fact that in one of them, infant mortality declined from 66 per 1000 population in the 1750s to only 10 per 1000 at the turn of the nineteenth century. Even so, infant mortality was still far higher than it is today and death in childhood was such a common human experience that the father of Edward Gibbon, the author of *The Decline and Fall of the Roman Empire*, named each of his sons "Edward" to preserve the name in case the eldest died.

This decline in infant mortality was part of a broader trend of lowering the death rate in England from a high of 35.8 per 1000 population in the 1730s to approximately 21.1 per 1000 early in the nineteenth century. A variety of factors was involved. Broad-scale famines were eliminated by increased agricultural productivity and the availability of meat year round. Improvements in medicine played a role —indeed, the elimination of smallpox in the last half of the eighteenth century is credited with lengthening the average life span of aristocratic women in England from thirty-six years at the beginning of the century to fifty-one years at the end. For common people, the availability of cheap cotton cloth and cheap soap, which killed the lice that carried typhus, was important. In later periods, the paving and draining of streets, the new slate roofs, the control of water supplies, and even the regulation of the quality of gin tended to lower the death rate.

As a result of these forces, by the beginning of the nineteenth century the population of England was increasing steadily at a rate of about 2 percent each year. This was largely due to the fact that (as in the developing world today) more people were surviving because of significantly better living conditions. The population therefore was principally composed of young people and was getting younger. The under-thirty generation made up 56 percent of the total in 1791 and 65 percent in 1821—a dramatic change. If industrial employment had not been available for these men and women in the cities of England at this time, Thomas Malthus's prediction of a disastrous famine would have become a reality. Industrial employment was available because of the rapid pace of technological change in eighteenth-century England.

A great growth in knowledge of the workings of the physical universe was one of the hallmarks of the scientific transformation. One such area of burgeoning knowledge was physics. This illustration, from his *Works*, published in 1744, shows Robert Boyle raising a column of water 33 feet by means of an air pump set up atop a London building.

TABLE 2. Major British, European, and American Inventions of the Eighteenth, Nineteenth, and Twentieth Centuries

Source: Marvin W. Mikesell, *Patterns and Imprints of Mankind,* from The International Atlas. Chicago: Rand McNally, 1969, p. xl. ©1969 Rand McNally & Co., R.L. 75–S–24.

Year	Invention	Country
1764	Spinning jenny	England
1765	Steam engine	England
1769	Self-propelled steam vehicle	France
1783	Puddling iron furnace	England
1785	Power loom	England
1786	Threshing machine	Scotland
1793	Cotton gin	United States
1802	Steamboat	United States
1811	Cylinder printing press	Germany
1824	Portland cement	England
1825	Steam locomotive	England
1831	Electric generator	England
1834	Reaper	United States
1839	Vulcanization of rubber	United States
1839	Photography (daguerreotype)	France
1844	Telegraphy	United States
1845	Rotary printing press	United States
1850	Corn picker	United States
1851	Refrigerating machine	United States
1855	Bessemer process of steel-making	England
1859	Gas engine	France
1859	Oil well drilling	United States
1861	Passenger elevator	United States
1866	Open-hearth steel furnace	United States
1867	Reinforced concrete	France
1869	Railway air brake	United States
1876	Telephone	United States
1876	Four-cycle gas engine	Germany
1879	Incandescent light	United States
1882	Steam turbine	France
1884	Photographic roll film	United States
1884	Linotype	United States
1884	Artificial silk (rayon)	France
1888	Pneumatic tire	Ireland
1892	Diesel engine	Germany
1892	Electric motor (alternating current)	United States
1892	Gasoline automobile	United States
1893	Motion pictures	United States
1895	Wireless telegraphy	Italy
1900	Caterpillar tractor	United States
1903	Airplane	United States
1906	Radio vacuum tube	United States
1907	Plastic (Bakelite)	United States
1911	Air conditioning	United States
1913	Radio receiver	United States
1913	Talking motion pictures	United States
1925	Television	Scotland-United States
1926	Liquid-propelled rocket	United States
1928	Helicopter	United States
1931	Cyclotron	United States
1935	Radiolocator (radar)	Scotland
1937	Nylon	United States
1937	Jet aircraft engine	England
1939	Helicopter	Germany-United States
1942	Atomic reactor	United States
1957	Extraterrestrial satellite	Soviet Union

The Pace of Technological Change
[TABLE 2]

A compelling interest in the application of science to technological problems characterized England in the late seventeenth and eighteenth centuries, and this interest was framed in a social and economic context that encouraged the growth of industrial manufacturing. The flow of money from two centuries of expanding commerce, slave trading, and piracy had injected new life into the economy. Merchants, who previously retired to the quiet life of country squires, now had capital to invest in new ventures at low rates of interest. Concurrently, the shift in economic development from the Mediterranean to the North Atlantic opened up new resource bases to the ships of British merchants. England was rapidly becoming one of the richest countries of Europe. At home, revolutionary changes in agriculture had, temporarily at least, banished the specter of famine from the English countryside. In addition, a broad stream of British scientific thought, based on the genius of Bacon, Boyle, and Newton, had spawned a generation of men keenly concerned with invention and technological application.

Given money, relative prosperity in the countryside, and a sustained interest in science, the critical inventions of Arkwright, Watt, and Boulton, along with a host of lesser innovations, harnessed new forms of energy and generated a surge in industrial production. These inventors were not academics; indeed, the combined freshman classes of 1750 at Cambridge and Oxford numbered only 317. Rather, they were the sons of artisans caught up in the popular enthusiasm for science and engineering that swept England during this period. Societies offered prizes for new inventions, and the most popular magazine of the day, *The Gentleman's Magazine,* was a cross between *Scientific American* and *Popular Mechanics.* Given this broad interest, the rate of invention rose rapidly after 1750. Of the 26,000 patents applied for in England in the entire eighteenth century, more were taken out between 1760 and 1785 than in the previous sixty years, and fully half of the total were granted in the fifteen years after 1785.

The effect of these technological changes struck first in the cotton textile industry. One of its major problems had been the inability of thread spinners to keep pace with the looms of the more technically

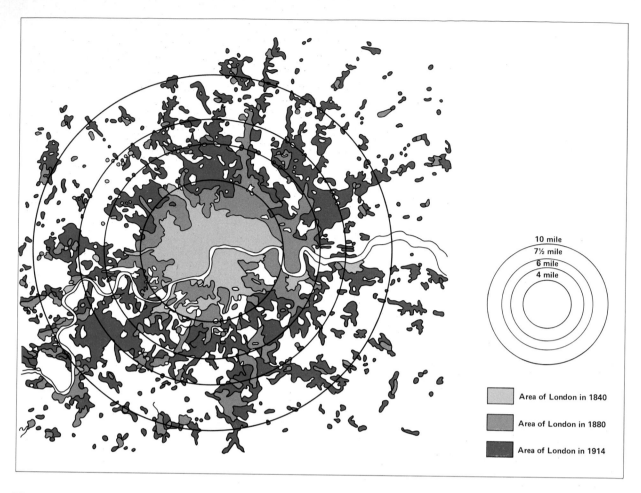

10 mile
7½ mile
6 mile
4 mile

Area of London in 1840

Area of London in 1880

Area of London in 1914

Figure 9. The Emergence of a Metropolis: London, 1840–1914. The explosive growth of London during the Industrial Revolution is dramatically portrayed by this diagram map. In 1840, the entire city was contained within a 4-mile radius. Forty years later, the built-up area had expanded to include places 6 miles from the city center, and by World War I, it extended over 10 miles along lines of transportation. *After:* S. E. Rasmussen, *London: The Unique City.* Cambridge, Mass.: MIT Press, 1967, pp. 134–139. Reproduced by permission of the MIT Press, Cambridge, Massachusetts. Copyright © 1967 by The MIT Press.

advanced weavers. In the 1760s a weaver-carpenter named James Hargreaves developed a hand-powered machine, the jenny, which women could use to spin as many as eighty threads simultaneously. Cheap, easy to construct, and small enough to fit in a spinner's cottage, more than 2000 jennies were distributed across the English landscape in the space of thirty years. Unfortunately, the thread from these machines was too soft to be used for the warp of the cloth, so that a good deal of thread still had to be spun by hand. In 1768, however, a barber from Manchester, Richard Arkwright, developed the water-powered spinning frame, which produced a strong, coarse cotton thread suitable for either warp or weft. This device could not be turned by hand and was too

large for cottage installation, so that mills and factories initially had to be situated on streams. But after 1790, when Watt's steam engine came into use, the growth of urban spinning factories was rapid. By the turn of the century, Manchester had fifty-two textile mills, all but two established after 1781. The factory town had been born.

Production soared. Raw cotton imports went from 5 million pounds in 1781 to 11 million in 1784; between 1800 and 1802 they rose from 43 million to 60 million pounds. England became the world's premier producer of cotton cloth, even though no cotton grew in England and the home market for it was limited by drafty buildings and cold winters. The cotton textiles made up 13 percent of Britain's total exports in 1800, and a phenomenal 40 percent six years later. A colonial commercial frontier was established overseas, in the American South, in the West Indies, and then later in Egypt and India.

The impact of technological change on the critical coal and iron mining industries was much slower and less dramatic. The extraction of these minerals remained essentially nonmechanized until late in the eighteenth century. Small independent contractors usually hired gangs of laborers to mine small quantities of coal and iron on order. The scale of iron making was so small that in 1750 a typical cutler or swordmaker probably used only 3 to 5 tons of iron a year. Even in the largest mines, the most significant technical advance in the first half of the eighteenth century was the introduction of ponies— a practice that freed men to do the mining and led to the hiring of women and children at cheap rates to control the horses. Illumination, ventilation, and flooding were major problems. In one operating coal mine in Warwickshire in central England, 500 horses had to work continuously hoisting water out of the mine bucket by bucket. Death in the mines was a common event.

Step by step, however, discoveries in metallurgy, machine tooling, and engineering led to the gradual replacement of wood by metal and to substantial increases in iron production. As early as 1709, Abraham Darby discovered a method of smelting iron with refined coal *(coke)*[•] instead of charcoal (made from wood). A half-century later, iron smelters were moved from the forests to the coalfields. John Wilkinson, himself the son of an old-fashioned ironmonger, invented a number of things—iron bellows (to replace leather), a rolling mill, a steam-powered lathe, and techniques for machining precise iron cylinders (replacing wooden ones). In 1784, Henry Cort discovered a coke-using technique for refining crude pig iron into the purer form of bar iron, and the forges joined the smelters in the coalfields. Production rose accordingly, though at a slower rate than in the textile industry. By 1800, coal production from the northern field around Newcastle had quadrupled; the rate of increase for the inland fields was probably higher. Nationwide total annual coal production was 11 million tons. The yearly production of iron, half of which had to be imported in 1750, grew to 227,000 tons by 1800, with half the total increase occurring in the last decade of the eighteenth century. The significance of these early increases lay less in their total volume than in the growing availability of cheap iron for the mechanization of other industries.

The rapid pace of technological change, based as it was on new knowledge, new forms of power, and new machinery, led to a substantial spatial reordering of society and economy in England. People migrated to urban factories, and the small farmer began to disappear from the English landscape. Industries relocated to take advantage of emerging resources. New patterns of commerce and communication favored the expansion of some cities, the decline of others. Regional specialization and the growth of manufacturing concentrations created the first industrial landscapes. England was the first nation to demonstrate these new patterns of spatial interaction. Other nations of the technological world, particularly those of northern Europe, soon followed the British example.

Changing Spatial Patterns
[FIGURE 9]

The industrialization of England prompted a spatial restructuring of society and economy on the basis of new criteria. Hand in hand with mechanization, several processes—virtually inevitable by-products of industrialization—were set in motion. Four were of critical importance: first, the rapid urbanization of the English population; second, the emergence of different patterns of resource utilization and industrial location; third, the expansion and growth of transportation networks; and fourth, the emergence of urban hierarchies and regional specialization.

When England became industrialized, it also became urbanized as the first generations of industrial workers abandoned the countryside and migrated to the mills of new industrial towns. At the beginning of the eighteenth century, over 60 percent of the English population lived in southern England in a band extending from Bristol in the west to London in the east. Less than a quarter of the total population lived in cities, and only London was of substantial size. But starting in 1750, the center of gravity began to shift toward the manufacturing centers developing on the coalfields of the northwest, so that by the turn of the century nearly half of England's population lived in the industrial north. The attraction, of course, was employment in the textile mills of Manchester and Liverpool and in the coalfields on both flanks of the Pennine Mountains. Between 1800 and 1900, the number of people living in urban areas increased from 27 to 64 percent. This tide from the countryside, what some have called "the transportation of the innocent," converted England from a country of farmers into a nation of city dwellers.

To accommodate this urban-directed flow, a spate of new cities developed. Between 1750 and 1850, the number of cities increased from 159 to 460. Most of these were small towns that expanded because of the influx from the countryside, the rising birth rate, and the growth of small-scale manufacturing. Their median size (if one excepts the ***primate city***[•] of London) was still quite small, between 3000 and 5000 residents. Only 24 of the 460 cities in 1850 were larger than 50,000 and only 4—London, Liverpool, Manchester, and Birmingham—could count more than 200,000 people.

Later in this period, principally after 1820, long-distance seaports and cities particularly favored by location and energy resources grew to metropolitan

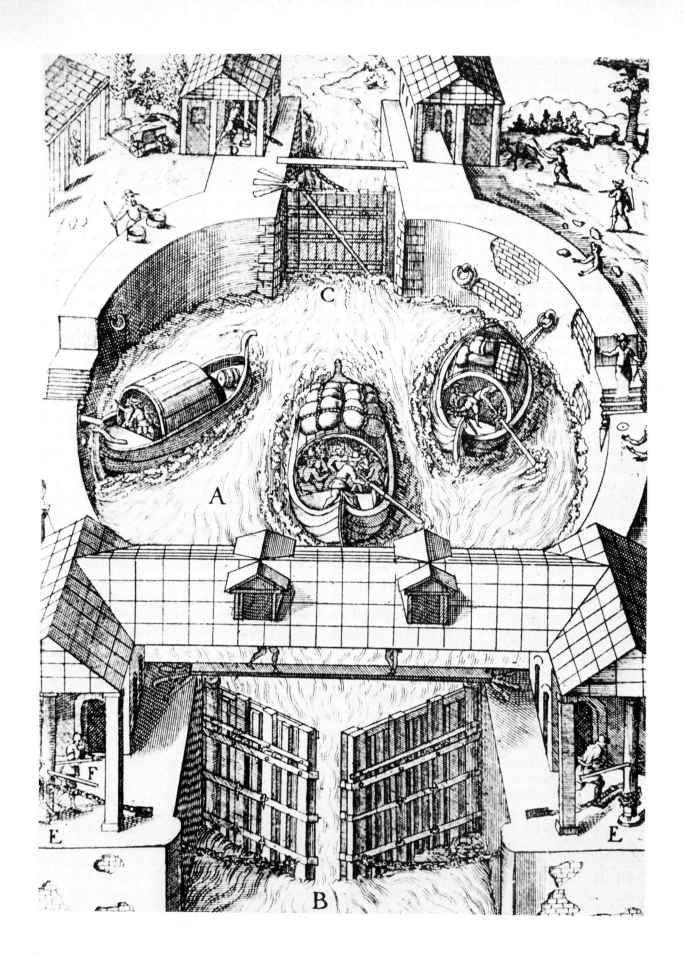

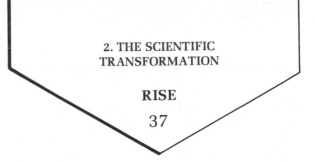

size. Manchester, the first industrial city, exemplified this later process. Called by Defoe a "mere village" in 1725, by 1775 it had a population of 25,000 and thirteen years later, 43,000. In 1830, the city of Manchester approached the 200,000 mark. Its explosive growth, like that of other great English cities, was the product of new patterns of resource utilization and industrial location created by the revolution in technology.

The most important new pattern of resource utilization was related to the substitution of coal for other energy sources. The impact of coal was most directly felt in the iron industry. Before this, it was the presence of trees rather than iron that determined the location of furnaces and forges, because it was cheaper to move the iron ore over long distances than to transport either wood or charcoal. Early iron making, then, was carried out in forests, and an estimated 10 acres of forest had to be cut down to produce 1 ton of iron. The technological innovations of Darby and Cort, however, freed iron making from the mechanical and spatial limitations of diminishing timber resources by substituting coke for charcoal. Because coke tended to crumble when being transported and once crumbled was useless for purifying iron, the iron furnaces and forges were forced to move to the coalfields. This concentration in turn led to the emergence of large, integrated industries that controlled the industrial processing of iron from the mine to the finished product. Iron production soon converged on the four major coalfields of Britain: the Midlands, the Northeast, Wales, and Scotland. Here the landscape was covered with pits and slagheaps, so thick in the "black country" around Birmingham that strangers were warned to be wary of roads undermined by shafts.

In the cotton textile industry, the relationship of the mill to cheap waterpower was originally paramount. The cotton mills of Lancashire, for example, were first located along streams on the western slopes of the Pennines. But with the shift from water to steam power, locational patterns changed. Manchester, for example, the commercial heart of this region, did not have a significant cotton spinning industry in 1775. Cotton mills were clustered in twelve industrial towns on the periphery of the city, their locations governed by the distribution of waterfalls whose energy was harnessed by waterwheels. When the steam engine replaced the waterwheel as the primary source of energy, location on the fringes of

The revolution in transport that was one of the outgrowths of the scientific transformation and then the Industrial Revolution was oriented toward moving goods (and later people) faster and cheaper. Canals—trouble-free inland waterways—were therefore constructed everywhere in Western Europe. This drawing is of a seventeenth-century design for hand-operated locks. *Photo:* **The Bettman Archive.**

the coalfield became not only desirable but virtually mandatory in order to reduce transportation costs. Cotton milling in cities only a few miles from the edge of the coalfield declined. Although waterwheels persisted for decades (accounting as late as 1840 for 13 percent of the total energy in the industry), the new urban cluster that emerged around Manchester was based on different locational principles.

Availability of resources, then, was critical to the development of industrial complexes in England. Since availability was frequently defined in terms of costs of transport, town leaders throughout England attempted to enhance the relative location of their cities with respect to resources and commerce by building roads and canals. And these canals were fundamental links in the early phases of the growth of regional transportation networks. The first long-distance canal, linking the cotton industry of Manchester with the growing port of Liverpool in 1767, cut the cost of coal in Manchester by half. Spurred by self-interest, merchants, industrialists, and entrepreneurs in other cities set up transportation trusts to build canal and highway networks. By 1775, every English city with a population of more than 20,000 was located on or near a navigable waterway. Within thirty years, all large cities in the Midlands were connected by canals, and in 1805, the Grand Junction Canal completed the network linking the metropolis of London to the industrial north. The age of canals (1775–1821) created the arteries that integrated the twin processes of urbanization and industrialization.

In the middle of the nineteenth century, this transportation network was reinforced by the construction of a network of railroads. Stephenson's steam locomotive was developed by 1813, but its use was delayed by the erroneous belief that a smooth wheel could not run on a smooth rail. After his Rocket won the competition in 1829 on the Manchester-Liverpool line, however, the potential of steam-powered rail transport of passengers and bulk commodities was realized. The journey between these cities was shortened from a day and a half by barge to two hours by rail. The cost of transport was once again halved, and in the first three months of operation 130,000 passengers made the intercity trip. By 1841, 1500 miles of track had been laid in England, and a decade later, 5132. In only twenty years, every major city in England was served by rail. These railroads

The Industrial Revolution changed not just modes of production and kinds and numbers of goods produced, but every aspect of life. People moved near the factories where they worked, creating new urban slums. Women left the home. This woodcut shows an early English pen factory employing only women. *Photo:* The Bettman Archive.

strengthened the emerging pattern of urban interdependence and industrial expansion; they contributed to regional specializations and the growth of urban hierarchies.

By the middle of the nineteenth century, the full impact of the Industrial Revolution on patterns of human settlement had been felt. Some 42 percent of England's population lived in an urban spine extending from London to Lancashire, and three urban hierarchies had emerged in the Midlands, northeastern England, and the Scottish lowlands to rival London. Reductions in transportation costs favored large industrial complexes that were already established, reinforcing the early predominance of cotton milling in Lancashire, woolen textiles in Yorkshire, and iron and steel manufacturing in the Midlands. Peasants migrating from the countryside in search of work and a more comfortable living were more attracted to these urban clusters than to other cities, and this spurred their already rapid growth. These clusters in turn extended their tentacles deeper into regional hinterlands to ensure the maintenance of a

regular and dependable food supply for the laborers in their mills. In the hinterlands, towns developed specialized functions congenial to local resources and tradition. The emergence of these urban hierarchies foreshadowed the later growth of megalopolises, first in England and later in other nations of the technological world, supercities that form the new human environment of twentieth-century technological societies.

Manchester—The First Industrial City

Manchester was perhaps the first industrial city to spring de novo from the economic and social revolution that swept England in the eighteenth and nineteenth centuries. In medieval times, Manchester was a small town, boasting a weekly market and an annual fair, and covering only 160 acres including Salford, its suburb across the Irwell River. By the second half of the eighteenth century, Manchester was a thriving commercial town, and in the nineteenth century it became an important industrial center and England's second largest city, after London. Following the development of the steam engine, Manchester became the cotton manufacturing center of the country, rising to dominance over a cluster of neighboring cities that once shared these laurels. Its population quadrupled in the first quarter of the nineteenth century and doubled every twenty years thereafter. Waves of migrants from the rural areas of Lancashire, Wales, and Ireland manned the weaving sheds, cotton mills, and foundries of the city. In the last quarter of the eighteenth century, 6500 new houses were built, and another 6000 in the first quarter of the nineteenth. Manchester, in short, experienced the explosive urban growth that appears to be an inevitable concomitant of industrialization. In the process, slums spread over large areas, and slum landlords fed off the poor. The wealthy fled to the suburbs; in the city, pollution, sanitation, and housing became major problems. Middle-class apathy diluted efforts toward reform. What is now called the "urban crisis" began in the city of Manchester, whose ecology in the nineteenth century carries a discouraging ring of familiarity today.

Poor rural migrants came to the factories of Manchester in search of economic security and moved into the densely crowded slums of the central city. By 1820, the density of population in central Manchester had risen to 70 people per acre (44,800 per square mile) as compared with less than 10 per acre in the suburbs. The greatest crowding was in the vicinity of the textile mills, located on the Irwell, Medlock, and Irk rivers. In these districts, land speculators constructed dense masses of cottages which they rented at exorbitant rates. The streets in these quarters were unpaved and unlit, the cellars frequently flooded; families of seven or eight lived in single rooms, and sanitation was so poor that on Parliament Street, a major avenue, one privy served 380 inhabitants. The streets of the **central business district**• were scavenged to remove waste, but in the poorer districts the main streets were cleaned only once a month. Lacking piped water, the urban poor had to rely on rain, polluted wells, and rivers. It was they who died of cholera.

The worst of these slums was the Irish ghetto, Little Ireland, where Catholic migrants clustered together in fear of the rabid Protestantism of the locals. Located on a swampy marsh, so low that the chimneys of three-story buildings barely reached road level, it was adjacent to the densest concentration of mills and was considered the most unhealthy part of the city. Here the Irish lived a marginal existence, many working as hand loom weavers for one-third the wage of factory workers.

Air pollution had already become a major problem. Even in the seventeenth century, the burning of coal cast a pall over the industrial cities of England that prompted the publication of John Evelyn's treatise on air pollution in London, *Fumifugium*. Occasionally the courts of Manchester fined factory owners for causing undue smoke, but only fifteen such cases were tried in Manchester between 1800 and 1815 (plus one for diverse stenches and vapors), and the fines were usually small. As a result, dense clouds of smoke covered the industrial sections of the city and the "nuisance committee" established to limit industrial smoke was predictably ineffective.

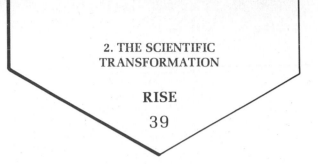

Conditions in the factories were little better. The mill worker labored twelve to sixteen hours a day, six days a week, with breaks of a half-hour for breakfast and an hour for lunch. Many were women and children who worked for a pittance to secure family survival in the face of uncertain wages. Some of the poor were taken off the street, sent to poorhouses, and forcibly employed in factories "to teach them industry." The absence of even rudimentary safety procedures produced legions of nine-fingered people. Objections to these working conditions took the form of petitions for a minimum wage, abortive strikes, riots in the streets, and the breaking of machines. From the viewpoint of the factory owners, however, any increase in wages contributed to laziness and drunkenness (which reduced profits), so that demonstrations were brutally put down. Industrial stability took precedence over social justice.

In spite of these grim conditions, the standard of living of the factory worker improved steadily throughout the course of the Industrial Revolution. Average per capita real income and per capita consumption of food and other consumer goods rose steadily. Bad as the industrial slums were, they were no worse than poverty in the countryside. The poor walked off the land and into factories as fast as the factories could take them, and they continue to do so. Thus, a new way of life and a new human environment emerged at Manchester—the city became the locus of technological society, the factory its social habitat.

THE DIFFUSION
OF THE SCIENTIFIC TRANSFORMATION

The diffusion of the scientific transformation from England and the European culture hearth to most parts of the world was not accomplished until the nineteenth century. During the previous three centuries, the growth of Europe was essentially internal: New towns and villages were founded, woodlands were cleared, and human settlement and communication intensified. Small colonies of religious dissidents settled along the coasts of North America, South America, and South Africa. But elsewhere only a handful of Europeans sought fortunes outside the European hearth: Spanish **conquistadors**• in Mexico and Peru, Dutch merchants in the East Indies, English and French traders in West and East

Africa, and the British East India Company in South Asia.

Except in Spanish America, where the leaders of the Aztec and Inca empires were quickly defeated by the military technology and political skill of the conquistadors, European colonization was confined to the coasts of the new continents, peripheral outposts on the flanks of sophisticated urban civilizations. Trading stations clung tenaciously to the oceanic rim of Asia and Africa; fortunes were made by acquiring and transporting luxury goods to the urban markets of Europe. The search for quick wealth became universal: gold and silver in Peru and Mexico; silk, spices, and tea in South and East Asia; sugar in the Caribbean and Brazil; and gold, ivory, and spices in West and East Africa. For the most part these traders survived by the grace of traditional native monarchs. They were confined by the Manchu emperors of China to port cities such as Canton; to Bombay, Madras, and Calcutta by the Moguls of India; and to the trading stations of West and East Africa by African kings jealous of their control of the trading routes in the interior. But in the nineteenth and twentieth centuries, this modest coastal presence expanded. A wave of some 52 million European migrants penetrated the continents, colonizing and settling the *midlatitudes*• in North America, southern South America, South Africa, and Australia, and establishing *plantations*• in the *tropical*• regions of Latin America, Africa, and South and East Asia.

European expansion by settler-colonizers was for the most part confined to temperate latitudes, where the agricultural experiences and preferences of the immigrants were more or less directly transferred to expanding frontiers in the New World, South America, Africa, and Australia. In North America, initial settlement along the eastern seaboard was forged by a variety of northern Europeans seeking greater freedom and economic opportunity. In Canada, French and English fur traders and fishermen established themselves on the rugged coast and penetrated the Saint Lawrence Valley. In New England and the Middle Colonies, dissident religious groups sought self-expression away from Europe, and in the South, gentlemen-adventurers searched for gold and spices but eventually settled for less. By 1800, two centuries after the founding of Jamestown, the European population of the United States was only 4.3 million. Gradually, however, commercial enterprises gave way to subsistence cultivation as a tide of European immigrants cramped in the industrial centers and densely settled agricultural regions of nineteenth-century Europe sought fortunes and land in the New World. Between 1840 and 1930, some 34 million immigrants, 80 percent of them from Europe, arrived on the east coast of the United States. Agricultural settlement expanded into the interior, dislodging and destroying native peoples. Europeans effectively occupied the continent.

In Australia, South Africa, and South America, European settler colonization took somewhat different forms. In Australia, settlement was not begun until late in the eighteenth century; in New Zealand, the nineteenth witnessed the first stages of European colonization. Perceived in Britain as an environment suitable only for criminals, the colonial population of these regions grew very slowly, numbering less than 200,000 persons as late as 1840. Expansion beyond the coastal frontiers of southeastern Australia and New Zealand did not occur until this century. And although recent European immigration has increased the population of the region to some 15 million, with a land area almost identical in size to that of the United States, these two countries remain thinly peopled. In South Africa, dense native African populations prevented the establishment of a predominately European population; conflicts between descendants of the Dutch and British immigrants and both European groups and native Africans soon became a dominant issue. In Argentina and Uruguay, the only nations in South America with European majorities, early Spanish influence and later German and Italian migrations established a significant European presence.

In time, each of these areas, populated by an emigrating European population of more than 50 million, aspired to independence from the mother country. But the ties of language and culture remained strong. The technological experience and skills brought to these regions by the immigrants gave the United States, Canada, Australia, New Zealand, the white minority of South Africa, and to a lesser extent leaders in Argentina and Uruguay, direct access to the fruits of the scientific transformation. In Europe new sources of energy were controlled. High levels of productivity were achieved by harnessing people to machines. The English industrialist Samuel Slater memorized the plans of the new textile technology and then himself emigrated to Rhode Island; others like him carried new knowledge and new techniques to regions of European settlement. The differential diffusion of the scientific transformation was thus culture-bound, and the presence of expanding European populations in the midlatitude colonies ultimately provided the capital, technology, social institutions, and labor needed to make them members of the inner sphere of the technological world.

In the tropical regions of Latin America, Africa, and South and East Asia, the impact of the scientific transformation was quite different. Although for the most part unattractive to European agricultural settlers, these areas produced raw materials highly valued in European markets. Collection of tropical agricultural products and minerals became the dominant economy. European overseers established plantations and mines; indigenous or imported laborers produced goods for export to Europe. In the Caribbean, tropical islands were planted to sugar as other parts of Latin America became known for the cultivation of coffee and rubber. In Africa, peanuts, cacao, rubber, and spices were produced in the west and east; diamonds, gold, and copper were mined in the south. In India, tea and opium plantations were founded; in Southeast Asia, rubber. The oil resources of the Middle East became the object of serious European commercial effort.

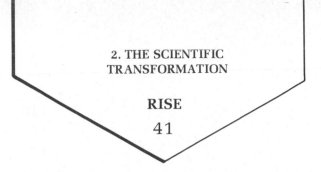

Everywhere Europeans formed a tiny minority that provided the capital and management skills. The maximum number of Europeans in India, for example, never exceeded 200,000—roughly 1 European for every 1500 Indians. Native peoples were used as cheap labor that served to enhance the profits of the Europeans. When labor demands in the New World outstripped local native populations, 10 million slaves from Africa were transported to Brazil, the Caribbean, and the American South. A similar coolie migration of contract laborers including 16.8 million Indians and several million Chinese was drawn to tropical plantations throughout the world. By the late nineteenth century, Europeans controlled every significant tropical area except China. The relentless hostility of the Chinese discouraged continental penetration, although the treaty ports of the coast drained the products of this region for export.

In all these regions, access to technology, capital, and science was retained by the European minority, who lived within but apart from the native cultures. The effect was to create economies subordinate to Europe and other expanding technological societies: entire nations became dependent on the production of a single crop. With the rise of nationalism, most of these colonial societies achieved political independence, but they did so in a world economically designed by Europeans. Blessed and cursed by the residue of colonialism, they share high birth rates and expanding populations, are dependent on exports to technological societies, and with rare exceptions remain less developed, poorer members of the outer sphere of the developing world.

Beyond these two worlds, the scientific transformation failed to penetrate vast stretches of the globe in much the same way as the environmental transformation diffused unequally and sporadically. In the heart of the tropics, the deserts of North Africa and the Middle East, the high mountains of South America and Asia, and the cold, high latitudes of North America and Eurasia, technological penetration remains minimal. Although individual mines, radar bases, oases, and plantations provide evidence of the tenacity of human purpose given good cause and sufficient resources, these regions remain stubborn reminders of the environmental limits of modern humanity.

THE TWO WORLDS

3

This differential development and diffusion of the scientific transformation divided the globe into two human domains—the rich and the poor, the haves and the have-nots, the underdeveloped and the developed, or as they are called here, the developing and technological worlds. Vast inequalities in the length and quality of life, standards of living, levels of education, rates of agricultural and industrial production, and command of political power now separate those societies that generated and have integrated the scientific transformation from those that, at differing rates, are striving to achieve modernization, development, and industrialization.

In the developing world a spectrum of nations with different traditions, economies, and environments is burdened by limited technology, burgeoning populations, poorly developed resource bases, inadequate capital, and neocolonial economies in the struggle to comprehend the scientific transformation. With few exceptions, the elites of these societies desire to modernize. Of their number, only Japan has thus far succeeded; except for the oil-rich nations of the Middle East and Communist China, few appear to have the human or physical resources needed to accomplish the task. In the technological world, by contrast, nations originally populated by Europeans continually expand their consumption of energy and resources, increase their standards of living, and maintain a balance of power in world affairs. In these direct offshoots of the European culture hearth, in Russia, and in Japan, urban industrial societies have achieved unprecedented levels of wealth and health.

Although the data on which this differentiation between the technological and developing worlds is based are incomplete and in many cases unreliable, and although the methods of measuring "levels of development" are relatively primitive and poorly understood, the overall impact of the scientific transformation on the nations of the world is abun-

dantly clear (Table 3). One-quarter of humanity is relatively well fed, healthy, and long-lived; three-quarters are not, and the most deprived 1 billion people on earth live in near total degradation and deprivation. The same proportions hold for literacy rates, energy consumption, income levels, and various other comparative measures of the quality of human existence. These differences occur not as isolated variables, but as a set of interlocking conditions that define the modern problems and prospects of essentially different human worlds. Although this global view obscures internal variations among different races, social groups, and regions within each country, the overarching similarities and differences among world nations provide a general framework for a comparative discussion of the geographical distribution and the increasing divergence of wealth and poverty in the modern world.

THE GEOGRAPHY OF DEVELOPMENT
[FIGURE 10, TABLE 3]

That poor people form a majority of the world's population is not surprising; this has always been the case. The rich get richer—the poor have children. In the twentieth century, however, a substantial minority of the world's nations is comparatively wealthy for the first time in history, and the resulting disparities between rich and poor generate tensions that are proving to be the central issue of our time. For the rich nations, those of the technological world, maintenance of political stability, the world economic system, technological superiority, and high standards of living is paramount. Endless international conferences and interventions in virtually every minor global disturbance form a scenario of dominance. On a more local level, specific national policies are forged to sustain supplies of food, fuel, and income that provide citizens levels of physical comfort attained only by royalty in the past. In the poorer nations, those of the developing world, national leaders strive to find a new place in the world economic system and to acquire the technology and skills needed to raise standards of living. The drama here is measured in changes in daily calorie consumption, lower infant mortality rates, miles of roadway constructed, and marginal gains in **gross national product**[*] beyond population growth. Local policies of birth control, land reform, agrarian change, and education bring teachers, doctors, and government representatives even to small settlements. The processes and problems of this struggle engage virtually everyone on a personal and private level; the scientific transformation has left only the most remote and isolated communities unaffected.

In each nation, policies and programs are uniquely designed to cope with differences in local culture and environment, national values and ideology. The Chinese, the Indians, the emerging nations of Africa,

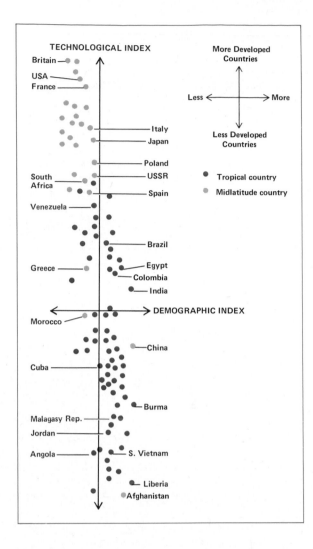

Figure 10. The Rich Nations and the Poor. In an effort to penetrate the complexity of the development process, one geographer, Brian Berry, measured variations in forty-three social and economic indices for ninety-five countries. From this mass of data, two indices were isolated: a technological index, which measured national product, energy production and consumption, transportation, and trade; and a demographic index, which measured births, deaths, population density, and rates of population growth. Plotted on a graph, the nations of the developing world are lower on the economic scale and higher on the demographic; they have colonial histories and tropical environments. By contrast, the nations of the technological world rank high on the economic and low on the demographic scale, are principally offshoots of the European culture hearth, and are located in middle latitudes. Although this graph pictures comparative levels of development in 1960, the general pattern is little changed today. *Adapted from:* Norton Ginsburg, *Atlas of Economic Development.* Chicago: University of Chicago Press, 1961, p. 113, Fig. 3. Copyright © 1961 by The University of Chicago Press.

and the countries of the Middle East and Latin America face development and modernization within the context of their own histories, economies, and societies. Similarly, the nations of Europe, Japan, the USSR, and the United States integrate science and technology differently within their own national systems. But at a more general level, the countries of the developing world possess one set of characteristics, and those of the technological world yet another.

Using forty-three economic and social indexes of development for ninety-five countries, one geographer, Brian Berry, has plotted the world distribution of rich nations and poor. The richer nations are those with extensive trade contracts, well-developed internal communications systems, dense transportation networks, high rates of energy production and consumption, and high gross national products. Their people are well supplied with medical facilities, have low rates of population growth, and are highly urbanized. The higher living standards in these nations of the technological world, all of which have midlatitude locations and environments of relative abundance, are the result of diversified commercial economies. The poorer countries of the developing world, by contrast, often have marginal environments, are weighed down by subsistence activities, and have high rates of population growth and low standards of living. Transport and trade networks are less developed; levels of energy production and consumption are relatively low. In population, economy, and spatial organization, these two worlds show significant and persistent differences.

Population Patterns
[FIGURES 11, 12]

Perhaps the most dramatic single effect of the scientific transformation on the modern world has been the postponement of death, the preservation of life. Tens of thousands of years were required before the human population reached 1 billion around 1800, only 125 years to attain 2 billion, 33 years to reach 3 billion in the late 1950s, and 17 years to reach 4 billion in 1975. The knowledge and techniques of environmental and medical technology combined with more productive economic systems have enabled more people to survive, and as births outstrip deaths, population grows.

TABLE 3. The Statistics of Development: Selected Social and Economic Indicators of Development, by Groups of Countries*

* Population and gross national product (GNP) per capita figures based on *World Bank Atlas, 1974*, Washington, D.C.: World Bank Group, 1974. Life expectancy, birth rate, death rate, and infant mortality data from Population Reference Bureau, "World Population Data Sheet," 1973, and Office of Population, U.S. Agency for International Development, *Population Program Assistance*, December 1972. Literacy rates from U.S. Agency for International Development, *Population Program Assistance*, December 1972. Energy consumption figures from United Nations, *Statistical Yearbook, 1972*.
† Not available.

Source: James W. Howe and the staff of the Overseas Development Council, *The U.S. and the Developing World: Agenda for Action, 1974.* New York: Praeger, 1974, pp. 144–153 (modified). © 1974 by Overseas Development Council.

Country	Population, mid-1971 (millions)	Per capita GNP, 1971 ($)	Life expectancy (yr)	Birth rate per 1000	Death rate per 1000	Infant mortality per 1000 live births	Literacy (%)	Per capita energy consumption, 1971 (kg)
POOREST DEVELOPING COUNTRIES								
Afghanistan	18.3	80	38	51	27	184	8	27
Bangladesh	83.4	70	46	43	16	125	22	n.a.†
Bhutan	0.9	80	n.a.	47	24	n.a.	n.a.	n.a.
Botswana	0.7	160	41	44	23	175	20	n.a.
Burma	29.6	80	48	46	17	139	60	68
Burundi	3.9	60	41	48	25	150	10	11
Central African Republic	1.6	150	40	46	25	190	5–10	60
Chad	4.0	80	40	48	25	160	5–10	27
Dahomey (Benin)	2.9	100	39	51	26	149	20	38
Ethiopia	26.8	80	39	46	25	162	5	32
Gambia	0.4	140	41	42	23	125	10	68
Guinea	4.2	90	40	47	25	216	5–10	108
Haiti	5.6	120	44	44	20	130	10	29
India	600.4	110	51	42	17	139	34	186
Kenya	11.7	160	48	48	18	115	20–25	171
Khmer Republic	7.7	130	52	45	16	127	41	24
Laos	3.2	120	50	42	17	123	15	91
Lesotho	1.1	100	45	39	21	181	n.a.	n.a.
Malagasy	7.2	140	38	46	25	102	39	n.a.
Malawi	4.8	90	40	49	25	120	22	49
Maldives	0.1	90	n.a.	46	23	n.a.	n.a.	n.a.
Mali	5.5	70	39	50	27	190	5	25
Mauritania	1.2	170	41	44	23	187	1–5	133
Nepal	12.0	90	42	45	23	162	9	9
Niger	4.2	100	43	52	23	200	5	22
Pakistan	68.3	130	50	51	18	142	16	96
Rwanda	3.9	60	43	52	23	133	10	10
Somalia	3.0	70	40	46	24	190	5	31
Sri Lanka	12.9	100	62	30	8	48	75	163
Sudan	17.4	120	50	49	18	121	10–15	119
Swaziland	0.4	190	41	52	24	168	36	n.a.
Tanzania	14.3	110	44	47	22	162	15–20	49
Togo	2.0	150	40	51	26	163	5–10	73
Uganda	9.3	130	49	43	18	160	20	72
Upper Volta	5.5	70	37	49	29	182	5–10	13
Western Samoa	0.2	140	63	41	8	56	86	112
Yemen	6.0	90	42	50	23	152	10	14
Yemen, South	1.5	120	42	50	21	152	10	n.a.
Zaire	19.3	90	43	43	23	115	15–20	77
OTHER DEVELOPING COUNTRIES								
Angola	5.6	370	34	50	30	192	10–15	157
Argentina	23.6	1,230	68	22	9	58	91	1,773
Bahamas	0.2	2,400	n.a.	28	6	37	91	5,600
Bahrain	0.2	640	46	50	19	138	29	7,186
Barbados	0.2	670	71	22	9	42	98	1,238
Bolivia	5.1	190	45	44	19	108	40	224
Brazil	95.4	460	61	38	10	94	67	500
Cameroon	5.8	200	41	43	23	137	10–15	97

Country	Population, mid-1971 (millions)	Per capita GNP, 1971 ($)	Life expectancy (yr)	Birth rate per 1000	Death rate per 1000	Infant mortality per 1000 live births	Literacy (%)	Per capita energy consumption, 1971 (kg)
Chile	10.0	760	61	26	9	88	84	1,516
China, People's Republic	787.2	160	50	30	13	50	25	561
Colombia	22.3	370	59	45	11	76	73	638
Congo, People's Republic	1.1	270	41	44	23	180	20	250
Costa Rica	1.8	590	66	34	7	67	84	446
Cuba	8.6	510	67	27	8	36	94	1,152
Cyprus	0.6	1,100	71	23	8	26	76	1,451
Dominican Republic	4.1	430	53	49	15	64	65	264
Egypt	34.1	220	53	37	16	118	26	282
El Salvador	3.7	320	55	42	10	53	49	223
Equatorial Guinea	0.3	210	41	35	22	140	20	183
Ghana	8.9	250	46	47	18	156	25	192
Guadeloupe	0.3	840	69	30	8	45	88	452
Guatemala	5.4	390	51	43	17	88	38	250
Guinea-Bissau	0.6	250	34	41	30	n.a.	3–5	103
Guyana	0.7	420	65	36	8	40	80	996
Honduras	2.6	300	49	49	17	115	45	234
Ivory Coast	5.2	330	41	46	23	159	20	265
Jamaica	1.9	720	69	35	7	39	82	1,338
Jordan	2.4	260	53	48	16	115	32	318
Korea, North	14.3	310	58	39	11	n.a.	n.a.	2,294
Korea, South	31.8	290	62	31	11	60	71	860
Lebanon	2.8	660	67	n.a.	n.a.	59	86	841
Liberia	1.6	210	43	50	23	137	9	368
Malaysia	11.2	400	66	38	11	75	43	421
Martinique	0.3	970	69	27	8	35	85	660
Mauritius	0.8	280	61	25	8	65	61	183
Mexico	52.5	700	63	43	10	69	76	1,270
Mongolia	1.3	380	58	42	11	n.a.	95	945
Morocco	15.4	260	51	50	16	149	14	205
Mozambique	7.8	280	41	43	23	140	7	178
Nicaragua	2.1	450	50	46	17	121	58	389
Oman	0.6	450	46	50	19	138	n.a.	62
Panama	1.5	820	64	37	9	41	79	2,121
Paraguay	2.5	280	59	45	11	n.a.	74	142
Peru	14.0	480	59	42	11	106	61	621
Philippines	37.9	240	59	45	12	67	72	298
Réunion	0.5	950	62	30	8	58	63	334
Rhodesia	5.5	320	51	48	14	122	25–30	618
Senegal	4.0	250	41	46	22	158	5–10	129
Sierra Leone	2.7	200	41	45	22	136	10	109
Singapore	2.1	1,200	68	23	5	21	75	851
Surinam	0.4	760	65	41	7	30	80	2,229
Syria	6.5	290	53	48	15	55	31	485
Taiwan	14.9	430	68	27	5	18	85	925
Thailand	37.3	210	61	43	10	68	68	296
Trinidad and Tobago	1.0	940	67	24	7	40	89	3,962
Tunisia	5.2	320	52	38	16	120	30	255
Turkey	36.2	340	54	40	15	119	46	516
Uruguay	2.9	750	69	23	9	43	91	958
Vietnam, North	21.6	100	50	33	21	n.a.	n.a.	n.a.
Vietnam, South	18.8	230	50	n.a.	n.a.	n.a.	65	n.a.
Zambia	4.3	380	44	50	21	159	15–20	458
OPEC COUNTRIES								
Abu Dhabi	0.2	3,150	46	50	19	138	20	802
Algeria	14.4	360	51	50	17	86	20	492
Ecuador	6.3	310	58	45	11	91	68	315
Gabon	0.5	700	40	33	25	229	12	1,028
Indonesia	119.2	80	48	47	19	125	43	123
Iran	29.8	450	50	45	17	139	23	895
Iraq	9.7	370	52	49	15	104	14	650
Kuwait	0.8	3,860	64	43	7	39	53	7,888
Libya	2.0	1,450	52	46	16	n.a.	27	571
Nigeria	56.5	140	37	50	25	157	25	59

TABLE 3 (Continued)

Country	Population, mid-1971 (millions)	Per capita GNP, 1971 ($)	Life expectancy (yr)	Birth rate per 1000	Death rate per 1000	Infant mortality per 1000 live births	Literacy (%)	Per capita energy consumption, 1971 (kg)
Qatar	0.1	2,370	46	50	19	138	10–15	2,025
Saudi Arabia	7.5	540	42	50	23	152	15	988
Venezuela	10.6	1060	64	41	8	49	76	2,518
DEVELOPED COUNTRIES								
Albania	2.2	480	66	35	8	87	72	631
Australia	12.7	2,870	71	21	9	17	98	5,395
Austria	7.5	2,200	71	14	13	25	98	3,231
Belgium	9.7	2,960	71	14	12	20	97	6,116
Bulgaria	8.5	820	71	15	10	26	90	4,029
Canada	21.6	4,140	72	16	7	18	85	9,326
Czechoslovakia	14.0	2,120	71	17	12	22	n.a.	6,615
Denmark	5.0	3.430	74	16	10	14	99	5,327
Finland	4.7	2,550	69	13	10	11	99	4,334
France	51.2	3,360	73	17	11	13	97	3,928
Germany, East	17.0	2,190	72	12	14	18	99	6,308
Germany, West	61.3	3,210	71	12	12	23	99	5,223
Greece	9.0	1,250	69	16	8	27	80	1,470
Hungary	10.3	1,200	70	15	11	33	98	3,291
Iceland	0.2	2,359	74	20	7	13	99	4,311
Ireland	3.0	1,510	70	22	11	20	98	3,285
Israel	3.0	2,190	72	28	7	23	84	2,710
Italy	54.1	1,860	71	17	10	28	95	2,682
Japan	104.7	2,130	72	19	7	13	98	3,267
Luxembourg	0.4	n.a.	n.a.	12	12	14	98	n.a.
Malta	0.3	694	71	17	9	24	83	981
Netherlands	13.2	2,620	74	16	9	11	98	5,069
New Zealand	2.8	2,470	71	22	9	17	98	2,934
Norway	3.9	3,130	74	17	10	13	99	5,189
Poland	32.7	1,350	70	17	8	29	95	4,374
Portugal	9.7	730	68	21	11	50	63	805
Romania	20.5	740	68	20	10	42	89	2,975
South Africa	22.7	810	49	41	17	138	35	2,895
Spain	34.0	1,100	70	19	8	28	86	1,614
Sweden	8.1	4,240	75	14	10	11	99	6,089
Switzerland	6.3	3,640	72	14	9	14	98	3,575
USSR	245.1	1,400	70	18	8	23	99	4,535
United Kingdom	55.9	2,430	71	15	12	18	99	5,507
United States	207.0	5,160	71	16	9	19	99	11,244
Yugoslavia	20.7	730	67	18	9	49	80	1,608

A sequential four-stage demographic transition accompanied economic development, occurring first in western Europe and particularly in Great Britain. In the first, or *high stationary,* phase, which lasted in England and Wales until about 1750, the high birth rate was canceled out by the high death rate, and natural increase was relatively limited. Fluctuations in the total population of 6 million to 7 million were largely a function of changes in the death rate as periodic famines and wars, balanced by times of peace and plenty, caused modest gains or losses. In the second phase, the *early expanding* phase, which extended from 1750 to 1875, the birth rate remained high but the death rate fell when improvements in health care, medical knowledge, sanitation, and standards of living began to take hold.

Life expectancy increased and the population of England and Wales quadrupled to 26 million. In the third, or *late expanding,* phase, between 1875 and 1925, the death rate remained low and the birth rate in the now urbanized, industrialized society of England and Wales began to fall. The rate of natural increase slowed substantially, although total population gained an additional 14 million. In the final, or *low stationary,* phase after 1925, both birth and death rates were low in England and Wales. Population growth was limited, but unlike the high stationary phase that preceded the scientific transformation, at this stage fluctuations in total population (which was now over 50 million) were caused by variations in the birth rate, not, as before, by variations in the death rate.

When this idealized four-phase model of population change is applied worldwide, a marked contrast between populations in the technological and developing worlds becomes apparent, although gradations along the entire continuum can be identified. In the technological world, some twenty nations in Europe and North America, the USSR, and Japan are in the low stationary phase. Rates of population growth are 1 percent a year or less and continue to decline. In a few nations, such as East Germany, *zero population growth*[•] has been achieved. In the developing world, remote and underdeveloped countries like Afghanistan, parts of Indonesia, and several countries of central Africa are still in the high stationary phase; more advanced developing nations like Cuba, Puerto Rico, Egypt, the Philippines, and China are in the late expanding phase. But substantial portions of Latin America, Africa, and tropical Asia fall into the early expanding phase, in which a high birth rate and a low death rate create substantial population growth, and the rate of natural increase is between 2 and 3 percent a year and even higher. Although these percentage differences seem relatively minor, growth at 1 percent doubles population every 87 years, at 2 percent every 35 years, and at 3 percent every 25 years.

As a result of this partial diffusion of the scientific transformation to the developing world, total world population is increasing at a rate of 75 million per year, and in the decade between 1960 and 1970 more than 80 percent of the 645 million people added to the population were born in those nations least able to cope. Whereas medical knowledge accumulated slowly over two centuries in western Europe, allowing time for social and economic adjustment to larger populations, in the developing world the instant spread of accumulated knowledge has caused much more rapid change. In Ceylon, for example, the death rate fell from 20 to 14 per 1000 population in a single year (1946–1947), after the introduction of DDT wiped out malarial mosquitos. The same thing happened in Mauritius, an Indian Ocean island, in the early 1950s. In Madagascar (the Malagasy Republic), control of venereal disease, which previously sterilized one-third of all women, led to a dramatic rise in the birth rate. As a result, changes in population profiles that took a century or more to accomplish in nineteenth-century England and Wales occur in less than a decade in some developing nations, creating unparalleled levels of social stress. New jobs, more food, and more houses are required for growing populations, and since the bulk of this growth occurs as a result of a lower infant mortality rate, children under fifteen now make up nearly half the population in many nations in the developing world, placing an enormous burden on nascent national education, medical, and social services.

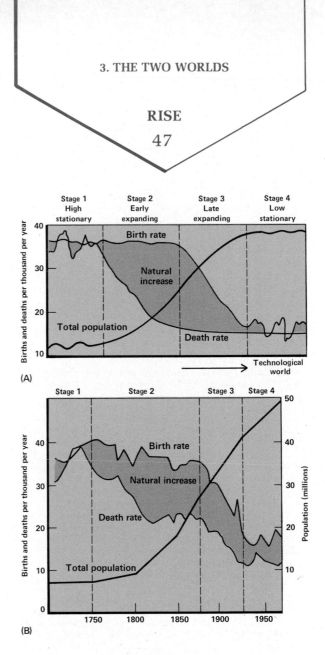

(A)

(B)

Figure 11. The Demographic Transition. These graphs portray the four-stage demographic transition, the change from low-survivor to high-survivor societies, in idealized form (a) and as it occurred in England and Wales (b). The first phase, which suggests limited control over the environment and high vulnerability to natural calamities, is characteristic of only the poorest nations of the developing world. Note that total population rises most dramatically in the early expanding stage but continues to grow at later stages because of the momentum of a larger base. Part (b) shows the effects of industrialization and urbanization on population in England and Wales from 1750 to the present. As the death rate begins to fall in stage 2, birth rates remain high, resulting in rapid population growth. In stage 3, birth rates plummet and death rates continue to decrease. Finally, relative stability occurs with both death and birth rates at low levels. *Adapted from:* (a) Peter Haggett, *Geography: A Modern Synthesis.* New York: Harper & Row, 1972, p. 174. (b) J. O. M. Broek and J. W. Webb, *A Geography of Mankind,* 2nd ed. New York: McGraw-Hill, 1973, p. 457.

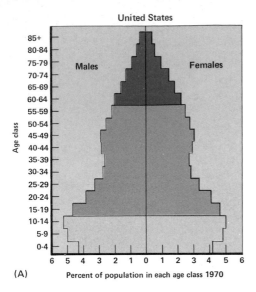

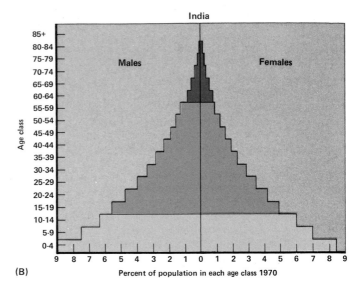

Figure 12. Population Profiles: The Developing and Technological Worlds. A nation's population can be visually projected onto a graph divided according to age and sex differences. The graph takes the form of a column, the shape of which can serve as a quick reference to the demographic characteristics of developing and technological societies. In general, a more pyramidal profile indicates rapidly rising birth rates and the sharp population increases of the developing world. More vertical profiles reflect populations approaching stability of age, sex, and number. Here, the United States serves as an example of the technological world. A tenth of the population is 65 years or older, reflecting improvements in health care and medical science. Two-thirds of the population is between age 15 and 64; anywhere from a quarter to one-third is younger than 15, demonstrating the lowered birth rates characteristic of urban-industrial societies. In India, as throughout the developing world, nearly half the population is 15 or younger. The working age population (15 to 64) is relatively smaller, and only a tiny minority lives beyond age 65. *Adapted from:* (b) "India: A Bleak Demographic Future," *Population Bulletin,* Vol. 26, No. 5 (November 1970), p. 3 (top). Courtesy of The Population Reference Bureau, Inc., Washington, D.C. 20036.

Economic Patterns
[FIGURE 13]

The different levels of living in the technological and developing worlds are produced by two markedly different economic systems. The scientific transformation enabled Europe to master new sources of energy in the form of coal, petroleum, and natural gas, which increased human productivity and spurred a reorganization of society and economy. In England, this knowledge became available at a time when wood, the traditional source of energy, was in increasingly short supply, large deposits of coal were available, and a class of maritime entrepreneurs had grown wealthy through a century of global commerce. This combination of ideas, resources, and capital led to an extraordinary increase in the amount of energy available to the society. Between 1860 and 1960, world production of inanimate energy increased by a factor of 33, nearly four times as fast as population growth. But while production of energy occurred in one part of the world, population growth occurred in another. Currently, the nations of the technological world, with approximately 30 percent of the world's population, consume 85 percent of all inanimate energy. Six nations—the United States, the USSR, China, Great Britain, West Germany, and Japan—account for two-thirds of the world's energy consumption, and any one of these countries individually consumes more energy than the eighty least developed nations combined.

In the technological world, these new energy budgets based on coal, petroleum, and natural gas (which in Civil War America accounted for only 10 percent of all energy as compared with 95 percent now) have had important effects on the nature of production and employment. New materials such as iron and steel form the basis of construction; steam and electricity concentrate energy in both space and time. New resources cause shifts in population to the source of production and the construction of transport networks with higher levels of connectivity and interdependence. Large factories of higher productivity and efficiency replace smaller, low-energy family enterprises. Per capita income rises with per capita energy consumption because of this higher productivity, and employment shifts from agriculture to manufacturing and service sectors. Industrialization defines a society as urban; seven of every ten Americans and more than half of all Europeans are urbanites. Less than one-quarter of the population in most technological societies is required for the production of food. Advances in agricultural technology have increased farm productivity. With mass production comes mass consumption and that dramatic increase in the material quality of human life which marks the wealthier nations of the world.

GRAND ILLUSION

CRYSTAL PALACE EXHIBITION 1851

In nineteenth-century England, for the first time in history, agricultural and industrial production consistently outstripped population growth. New energy sources and new technologies created the outlines of a distinctly new human geography. Manufacturing became oriented to national and international markets as a constellation of industrial towns linked by a network of canals and then railroads emerged on the landscape. Coal production tripled in 100 years. Population doubled. Iron, previously an expensive semiprecious metal, became a cheaply available necessity. In 1829, George Stephenson put his Rocket, the first steam locomotive, to the test, and proved the feasibility of steam power by hauling a 13-ton load at the unheard-of speed of 29 miles per hour. The costs of transport plummeted as its capabilities soared. In 1850, the rate of economic growth in Britain was unparalleled in the world.

Many more people than ever before became wealthy. But the very rapidity of change in Britain, although considerably slower than in modern developing nations, caused tension and class strife, strikes, and social inequities to tear at the fabric of British society. The flight from the land, the shift to mechanized factory employment, the new experience of city living, periodic financial recessions, and desperately inadequate environmental facilities in the smog-bound industrial towns were traumatic changes for all economic groups.

But the sure transition to industrial society was made. When the Great International Exhibition opened in London in 1851 in the huge glass building known as the Crystal Palace, all these tensions seemed to have disappeared. The Crystal Palace, opened by Queen Victoria on May 1, was the world's first prefabricated building. It had been erected in the amazingly quick time of seven months, and when it was completed it covered 19 acres in Hyde Park. It had 2300 cast iron girders, 3300 pillars, 30 miles of rain gutters, 202 miles of sashbars, and about 1 million square feet of glass. Joseph Paxton, its designer, who had begun as a gardener and whose 300-foot-long conservatory, built for the Duke of Devonshire, had been the model for the Crystal Palace, had so constructed the exhibition building that it could easily be taken down and erected elsewhere, as it later was. He had also included all kinds of "modern" conveniences: Canvas over the south elevation allowed a current of air between it and the glass roof. There were trellised boarding on the floor to avoid dust, mechanically controlled louvers for ventilation, retiring rooms and lavatories for visitors. Running on the gutter rails of the roof were little wagons

in which painters and glaziers could move about to do their work.

The 19,000 exhibits were divided into four categories: raw materials, machinery and mechanical inventions, manufactures, and sculpture and plastic art. They came from Britain and from foreign countries, and the skill and craftsmanship they displayed excited the wonder and awe of the 6 million people who saw them. But despite the artistry shown by foreign products, the exhibition was a clear demonstration of English achievements, for England at mid-century was the industrial workshop of the world.

The *Illustrated London News* reported the opening on May 1 in words that now seem naive but then were indicative of the optimism the Industrial Revolution had fostered:

[E]ven in a time when people are but little inclined to let their imagination run away with their judgment, . . . the fancy of the coldest and most calculating of the spectators was warmed into enthusiasm by the scene. It was not alone the sight of a youthful and beloved Queen, . . . lending the aid of a universal and well-won popularity to that solemn consecration of industry; . . . nor the concourse of strangers from every quarter of the globe . . .; nor the magnificent display of every conceivable article of usefulness or luxury invented by the ingenuity of men; nor the gay and brilliant appearance of the exterior of that Crystal Palace, glittering in the rays of a lovely May morning; . . . nor the reflection that forced itself upon all minds, how truly great and how full of good augury for all humanity such exhibitions might become hereafter; nor the pardonable exultation felt by Englishmen in the fact that in England alone at the present day such an exhibition was possible; it was . . . a combination of them all, . . . that made the scene within and without the Crystal Palace, the most affecting and cheering as well as the most remarkable event in the modern history of mankind.

(above) Testing the flooring. *Illustrated London News.*

(below) Exhibits being shipped at Paris. *Illustrated London News.*

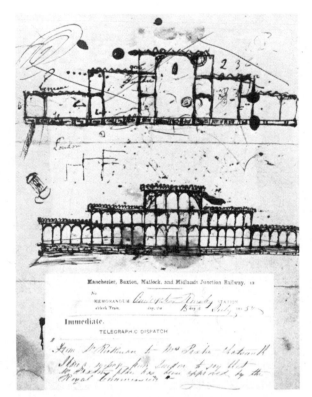

(above) Sketch of the Crystal Palace on blotting paper, with Paxton's note to his wife announcing approval of the design.

(above) Title page of a commemorative book. New York Public Library Picture Collection.

(below) Inside the Crystal Palace. New York Public Library Picture Collection.

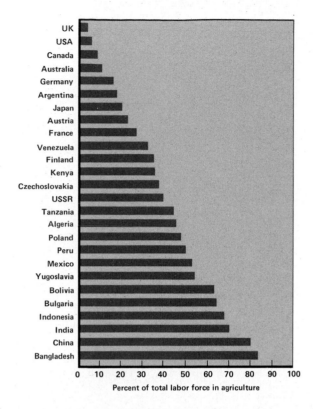

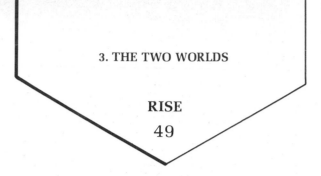

Figure 13. The Agricultural Sector in the Two Worlds. In the technological world, less than a third of the population is directly engaged in agriculture; in the developing world, it is as much as two-thirds. The problem for development specialists is that modernization requires capital, but if it is withdrawn from agriculture to build up industry, lower food production may result in widespread malnutrition or starvation. Which sector should be developed first, or whether both need to be developed simultaneously, is still being debated.

In the developing world, the shift from animate to inanimate forms of energy is under way, but men and animals are still the principal labor machines. As a result, productivity is low, per capita income is low, and the economic surplus is limited. People are distributed in villages, close to their fields, and 70 to 80 percent of the population is engaged in food production. Rising populations increase pressure on rural resources and encourage migration to industrializing urban centers; yet the necessary capital needed to create new jobs for these people is not available. Since many nations experienced modernization under colonial rule, dual economies with a modern, European-oriented, extractive sector and a traditional local agrarian sector cause growth without development. In Africa and Latin America, many countries rely heavily on the export of one or two raw materials to the industrial world. For most nations this means extreme vulnerability to fluctuations in international markets. Although energy production rises annually, population and consumer demands do as well. In India, for example, 70 percent

of commercial energy is used for domestic purposes that are not economically productive, whereas in the United States, 75 percent is used for industrial purposes.

For most countries in the developing world, the last twenty-five years have seen a political struggle to gain independence and an economic battle to transform the nature of their societies from an agrarian to an industrial base. The goal is to take advantage of those higher levels of productivity and wealth that accompany the shift from animate to inanimate energy; the problem is to accumulate the surplus capital needed to modernize agriculture, to construct roads and railroads, and to build factories and industry. Generally, high capital costs have frustrated development efforts, leaving many nations of the developing world trapped in cycles of poverty. Low levels of productivity, income, and savings generate an economy of stagnation, a mentality of underdevelopment.

Poverty breeds poverty. Whereas most developing countries can invest only 4 to 5 percent each year in industrial development, 12 to 15 percent is needed. Average incomes of less than $100 per year are common, of which well over half is spent for food. In these circumstances, investment in higher yields, irrigation projects, craft expansion, new businesses, or large-scale industry is difficult. The paralyzing lack of capital pervades the entire range of an underdeveloped economy. The whole industrial landscape of the technological economy is incomplete: too few factories, paved roads, power lines, machines.

Spatial Patterns
[FIGURES 14, 15, 16, 17]

These contrasts in the landscapes of developing and technological nations reflect differences in levels of technology and the social organization of space. In the technological world, a network of market centers or central places has evolved to facilitate the regular exchange of goods and services between buyers and sellers, producers and consumers. This systematic organization of space permits economic specialization, facilitates the growth of economic regions, and enhances maximal utilization of resources. The spatial basis of England's remarkable eighteenth-century economic growth can be found in the existence of a highly woven network of market towns—preindustrial central places. The emergence of trad-

CENTRAL PLACE DEFICIENCY IN THE DEVELOPING WORLD

A central place is any of the variety of dense human settlements (village, town, city) that offers goods and services for sale and acts as the receiver of goods produced in its surrounding area, or hinterland. The abundance or deficiency of central places is a universal yardstick of the relative density of market exchanges. The ratio of villages to towns or cities is an indication of the frequency, density, and patterns of market exchanges. In advanced technological societies, ratios tend to be low, with a median of sixteen villages for each town or city. In the Middle East, ratios are high except in industrial Israel, commercial Lebanon, and the tiny oil sheikdom of Kuwait. The median is 157, leaving Europe with roughly ten times as many central places per village as the Middle East. The data shown in the accompanying table are from 1961–1964 censuses.

Number of Villages for Each Central Place with Over 2500 Inhabitants, Europe and Middle East			
Country	Village	Central place	Ratio
Switzerland	1209	233	5
Luxembourg	67	9	7
France	5075	489	10
Denmark	1117	98	11
Sweden	2053	165	12
United Kingdom	4337	277	16
Netherlands	2378	147	16
Irish Republic	3077	122	25
Portugal	2810	74	37
Belgium	1931	49	39
Norway	4819	83	58
Finland	3445	59	58
Austria	4881	67	72
Israel	209	49	4
Lebanon	243	10	24
Kuwait	68	1	68
Muscat and Oman	1,682	16	105
Saudi Arabia	11,193	71	157
Turkey	44,175	219	201
Iraq	9,186	45	204
Syria	7,540	25	301
Yemen	9,532	15	635

Source: E. A. J. Johnson, *The Organization of Space in Developing Countries.* Cambridge, Mass.: Harvard University Press, 1970, Tables 5-1 and 5-2, pp. 174–175. © 1970 by The President and Fellows of Harvard College.

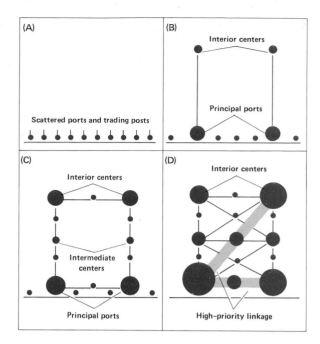

Figure 14. The Evolution of Transport Networks in the Developing World. This model, based on empirical research in Ghana, Nigeria, Brazil, East Africa, and Malaya, suggests a sequence of four stages in which transport facilities are extended inland like a diffusion wave. These are (a) scattered ports and trading posts, (b) penetration lines and port concentration, (c) early interconnections, and (d) emergence of high-priority linkages. It is not certain how widely this model can be applied beyond colonial seaboard areas, or indeed that all four stages can be clearly discerned in every developing country. *Adapted from:* E. J. Taaffe, R. L. Morrill, and P. R. Gould, "Transport Expansion in Underdevelopd Countries: A Comparative Analysis," *Geographical Review,* Vol. 53 (1963), p. 504. Copyrighted by the American Geographical Society and redrawn with permission.

ing towns in Belgium played a similar role in the transformation of what had been an undifferentiated agrarian landscape. In Meiji Japan, castle towns founded by earlier military rulers became focal points for markets and links between smaller villages and cities. This enhanced the rapid commercialization of Japanese society and space. Once railroads were able to overcome mountain barriers, this functional hierarchy of settlements formed the spatial basis of Japan's economic growth. The same economic rationalization of space occurred in the American Midwest despite the arbitrary linearity imposed on the landscape by the rectangular land survey and the railroads.

In the developing world, by contrast, landscapes reflect traditional human relationships imposed by landlords, religious leaders, and military elites. The underlying principles of spatial organization were designed to facilitate tax collection, the administration of justice, military control, and religious practice. Economic forces involved in the search for wealth played a proportionately smaller role in loca-

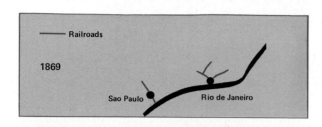

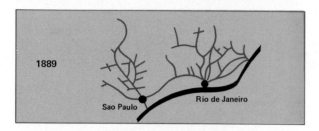

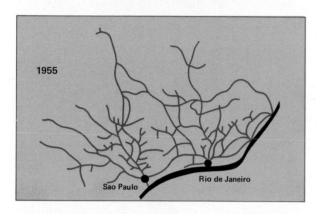

Figure 15. Growth of the Railroad Network in Southeastern Brazil. These diagrams show the growth of the rail system between São Paulo and Rio de Janeiro at three dates: 1869, 1889, and 1955. The extension and branching posited by the Taaffe network development model are clearly apparent. *Adapted from:* Peter Haggett, *Locational Analysis in Human Geography.* London: Edward Arnold, 1965, p. 81.

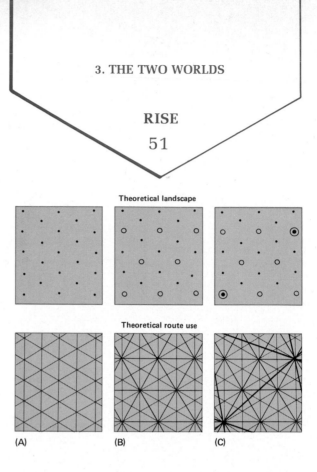

Figure 16. The Adjustment of Transport Networks in the Technological World. This model depicts network development by route substitution in advanced areas, here represented by the idealized landscape of the economist Lösch. In the initial stage (a), settlements are equally spaced and a network of intersecting routes links each settlement with the next. In the second stage (b), higher levels of economic development stimulate the growth of specialization and concentration of economic activity. A smaller number of higher-level centers emerges, with smaller places located on high-priority routes connecting the higher-level centers being bypassed. In the third stage (c), this process intensifies: a new and smaller set of major centers is connected by a new set of optimum routes, and a larger number of smaller centers is bypassed. *Adapted from:* Peter Haggett, *Locational Analysis in Human Geography.* London: Edward Arnold, 1965, p. 82.

tional decisions and the organization of settlements. Today, market centers are scattered, the integration of production and distribution is inadequately organized, and connections between villages, regional markets, and urban centers are poorly developed. All these landscape features reflect the disjunction between the past and the present.

Many of India's half-million villages, for example, have only minimal contact with higher level marketing centers, hindering the diffusion of modernization. In many former colonial nations in the tropics, railroads have only recently opened up landlocked areas to commercial development and economic exploitation. In China, by contrast, the imperial administrative network of *hsien* (county capitals) formed a functional marketing hierarchy that has facilitated economic development. But in most developing countries, two primary tasks are to shift

control of facilities and resources from traditional elites to national governments and to forge more efficient transport and settlement systems based on market forces.

The entire process of economic development in developing nations is closely related to the growth of communications networks. Based on research in Ghana, Nigeria, Brazil, East Africa, and Malaysia, Edward Taaffe and two other geographers developed a four-stage model that identifies certain regularities in the growth of transportation systems in the developing world. In the first stage, which in Africa lasted well into the nineteenth century, small ports and trading posts are scattered along the coast, inland connections are limited to immediate hinter-

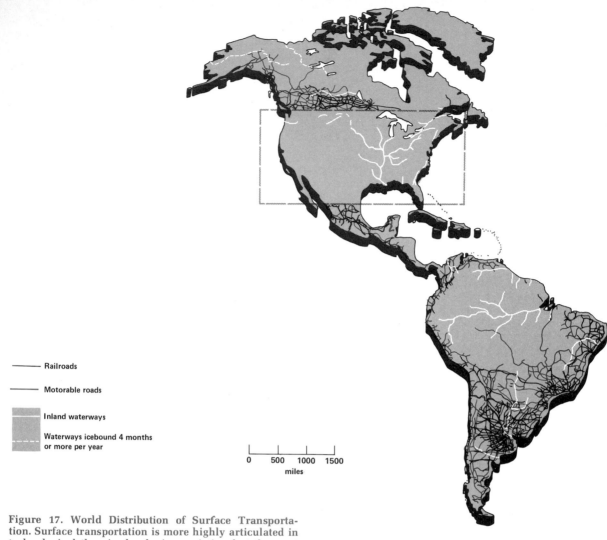

Railroads

Motorable roads

Inland waterways

Waterways icebound 4 months
or more per year

0   500   1000 1500
miles

Figure 17. World Distribution of Surface Transportation. Surface transportation is more highly articulated in technological than in developing societies, but the most striking contrast is between the densely inhabited and uninhabited world regions.

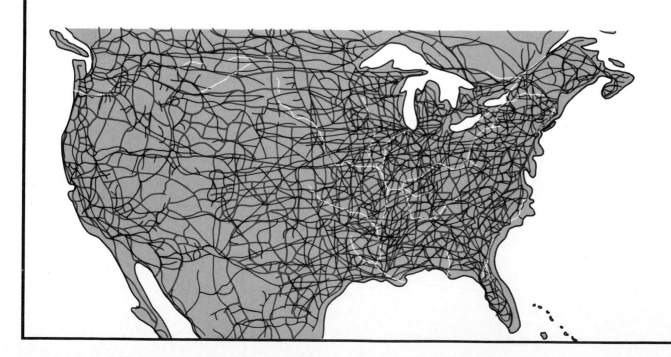

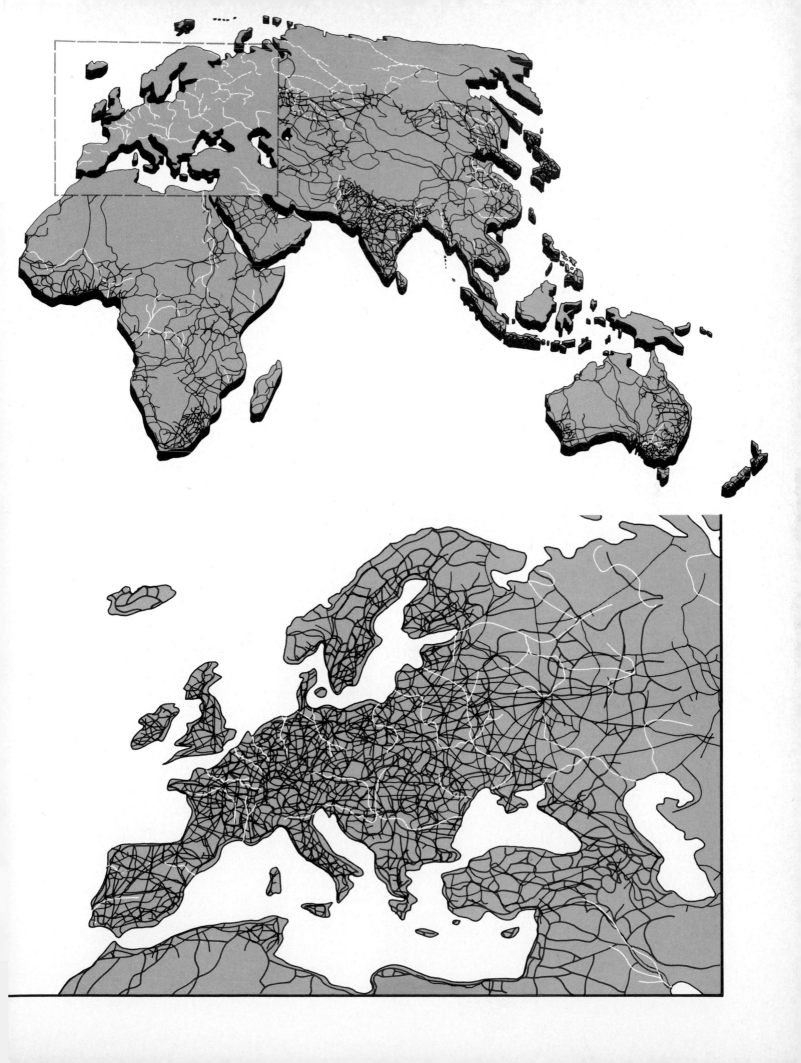

lands, and coastal linkages are weak. In the second phase, usually associated with colonialism, a few major lines of penetration connect selected coastal ports with specific areas in the interior where minerals or agricultural products are found. As the ports grow, local hinterlands expand and diagonal routes focus on these emerging centers. In the third stage, typical of many modern developing countries, both the seaport terminals and the interior centers continue to grow, and intermediate centers spring up along the routes of penetration. Connections between the coastal centers and between the inland centers forge linkages in the new network, and feeder routes penetrate deeper into the hinterlands.

In the final phase, high-priority linkages between the most important centers are formed, and the best paved roads, the most heavily used rail lines, and the most intense traffic occur along these "main street" routes. Lateral extensions and diagonal penetration of more remote areas cause certain centers to grow at the expense of others and foreshadow the emergence of a dense circulation system. For most countries in the developing world, the enormous costs of connecting resources by road or rail with industry and distribution points have prevented the full extension of an effective transportation network. All but a few highly developed regions within most developing countries still rely on primitive methods of transport, a spatial duality closely analogous to the dual economy of colonial states.

In the industrialized nations of the technological world, complex systems of roads, railroads, sea and air transport compete to carry passengers and freight. The central problem is not the construction of new transport networks: connections among resource areas, production centers, industrial districts, and markets have long since been established. Rather, the problem is to adjust existing systems to changes in industrial location, urban expansion, changing travel patterns (amounting in the United States to 4000 miles per person per year, of which 3600 are by car), and rising standards of living. In these technological societies, the functioning network adjusts by route substitution. Some centers attain greater importance than others, and old routes are modified to bypass smaller centers. Alternatively, new routes are created to accommodate increased traffic and reduce overuse, traffic congestion, and deterioration of transport facilities.

From a global viewpoint, these different patterns of spatial organization and communication in the developing and technological worlds stand out clearly. Adequate transportation is generally associated with higher levels of urbanization and industrialization. The most elaborate transportation networks, therefore, are found in the United States, southern Canada, western Europe, Japan, and the densely populated western part of the Soviet Union. Here, road and rail connections are nearly continuous, and virtually no region is inaccessible. Similar but less dense transportation networks are located in Argentina and eastern Brazil, in eastern Australia, in India (a colonial inheritance), and in parts of the Mediterranean Middle East. But vast reaches of the developing world remain unconnected: the arid cores of the Middle Eastern deserts, the tropical heartlands of South America and Africa, the interior of China, and the uninhabited eastern stretches of the Soviet Union and western Australia. In general, the distribution of surface transportation networks provides an index of the differential intensity of human occupance in the various world regions.

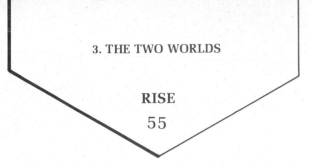

Building a highway in the American West. *Photo: Myron Wood/Photo Researchers. Villagers build a new road in India. Photo:* Chapelle/Monkmeyer.

THE RICH AND THE POOR

During the last twenty-five years, poverty and wealth have retained roughly the same world distribution. In spite of substantial infusions of foreign aid and intensive national programs of economic and social development, the rich nations have grown progressively richer, the poor relatively poorer. In the 1960s, per capita income in the developing world grew less than $50 per year as compared with 10 to 15 times that figure in the technological world. The income gap between the two worlds widened to 12:1, and this figure will probably increase to 18:1 or 20:1 in the near future. The sources of poverty vary. In India, Sri Lanka, and Bangladesh, population growth appears to be the critical variable. In North Africa and parts of the Middle East, aridity retards the development of resources. In central Africa, the legacy of colonialism weighs heavy. In South America, control of the physical environment is inadequate. In many nations, political leadership is corrupt and repressive. Whatever the reasons, poverty is now a persistent and pervasive feature of landscapes and lives in the developing world. And few experts think the condition will soon change.

One social scientist, Gunnar Myrdal, explains the stubborn resistance of depressed nations to developmental change in terms of a theory of *cumulative causation.* In this view, the "play of market forces" tends to increase rather than decrease the inequalities among nations. Developed regions attract greater development; less developed regions proportionately less. Two forces are at work: spread effects and backwash effects. Spread effects are centrifugal secondary impacts that diffuse from high-growth regions to less developed areas in terms of growing demand for raw materials and agricultural products.

Backwash effects refer to the magnetic centripetal attraction high-growth regions have for skilled and intellectually trained persons, new capital, and advanced technology. These differences in the levels of life between regions, lagging areas, or nations tend to intensify over time. The two forces, according to Myrdal, are usually not in equilibrium. Backwash effects frequently tend to dominate. Thus, once a nation gains an initial developmental advantage, a cumulative process sets in that progressively heightens this advantage by draining human and physical resources from hinterland regions. If the theory is true, the futures of many nations in the developing world may well be much like their pasts. These countries may remain outsiders to the world economy, contributing raw materials to more sophisticated and specialized nations, sharing only one-fifth of world trade, and experimenting with one new plan after another to accomplish the elusive goal of modernization.

Most observers believe this situation will grow worse. The highest rates of population growth, over 2.5 percent per year, are in Africa and Latin America. The greatest mass of population, nearly 60 percent of the world total, is located in the developing countries of Asia. Nearly a quarter of the world's population lives not in poverty, but in destitution. Scarcities of food and fuel are more intense today than at any time in this century. Only North America and Australia now produce an exportable grain surplus; world reserves are one-third less than fifteen years ago. Food is scarce because of rising population in the developing world and rising consumption in the technological world. The costs of energy are similarly rising, and rich and poor compete for oil. Several outcomes are possible: The wealthy may assist the less developed nations, although economic progress can hardly keep up with rising expectations; the poor may quietly grow poorer except in those nations where determined leadership, the discovery of new resources, or the successful integration of technology enables individual countries such as Venezuela, Iran, or Nigeria to move from one world to the other. Barring massive scientific breakthroughs in food and energy production, the nations of the technological world may be forced to curtail their standards of living in order to accommodate a rise in world standards. It is at this point that the experts on disaster—the prophets of war, famine, and environmental collapse—begin to speak.

BIBLIOGRAPHY

[1] THE ENVIRONMENTAL TRANSFORMATION
The Discovery of Food Production

Braidwood, Robert J. "The Agricultural Revolution," *Scientific American*, September 1960, pp. 130–148. Summary of the evidence from Jarmo.

Hole, Frank, Kent V. Flannery, and James A. Neely. *Prehistory and Human Ecology of the Deh Luran Plain.* Ann Arbor: Museum of Anthropology, 1969. A detailed field survey (including the data on Ali Kosh), valuable for its ecological viewpoint.

Isaac, Erich. *Geography of Domestication.* Englewood Cliffs, N.J.: Prentice-Hall, 1970. A survey of the evidence and major theories relating to the domestication of plants and animals.

Leonard, Jonathan N. *The First Farmers.* New York: Time-Life, 1973. A lavishly illustrated summary of the emergence of food production.

Mellaart, James. *Catal Huyuk.* New York: McGraw-Hill, 1967. An analysis of the excavations at Catal Huyuk. For a brief summary see: "A Neolithic City in Turkey," *Scientific American*, April 1964, pp. 94–104.

Sauer, Carl O. *Agricultural Origins and Dispersals.* New York: American Geographical Society, 1952. A brilliant speculative essay on the hearths of domestication of plants and animals.

Ucko, P. U., and G. W. Dimbleby (eds.). *The Domestication and Exploitation of Plants and Animals.* Chicago: Aldine, 1969. A symposium devoted to recent evidence bearing on plant and animal domestication. Note particularly the essays by Kent Flannery and David R. Harris.

The Emergence of Urban Life

Adams, Robert M. "The Origin of Cities," *Scientific American*, September 1960, pp. 153–168. A brief description of the rise of urbanization in Mesopotamia.

Adams, Robert M. *The Evolution of Urban Society.* Chicago: Aldine, 1966. A detailed comparative analysis of urban origins in Mesopotamia and pre-Hispanic Mexico.

Hamblin, D. T. *The First Cities.* New York: Time-Life, 1973. A beautifully illustrated survey of early urbanism.

Jacobsen, Thorkild, and Robert M. Adams. "Salt and Silt in Ancient Mesopotamian Agriculture," *Science*, Vol. 128 (1958), pp. 1251–1258. A description of the role of salinization and sedimentation in the decline of civilization of Mesopotamia.

Kramer, Samuel Noah. *The Sumerians.* Chicago: University of Chicago Press, 1963. A major volume devoted to the history, culture, and character of Sumerian civilization.

Lampl, Paul. *Cities and Planning in the Ancient Near East.* London: Studio Vista, 1968. A book studded with figures, plans, and photos of ancient Near Eastern cities, including those of Mesopotamia.

[2] THE SCIENTIFIC TRANSFORMATION
The Medieval Agricultural Revolution

Bloch, Marc. *Feudal Society.* Chicago: University of Chicago Press, 1961. A classic study of society and economy in medieval Europe.

Darby, H. C. (ed.). *A New Historical Geography of England.* London: Cambridge University Press, 1973. A series of essays on the changing geography of medieval England.

Duby, Georges. *Rural Economy and Country Life in Medieval Europe.* Columbia: University of South Carolina Press, 1968. An intensive discussion of changing conditions in rural Europe from the ninth to the fourteenth centuries.

Homans, George C. *English Villagers of the Thirteenth Century.* New York: Russell & Russell, 1960. A detailed case study of rural life in England in the thirteenth century.

Russell, J. C. "Late Ancient and Medieval Population," *Transactions of the American Philosophical Society*, Vol. 48 (1958), pp. 1–152. Comprehensive analysis of population change in Europe from Roman times through the medieval period.

White, Lynn T., Jr. *Medieval Technology and Social Change.* Oxford: Clarendon Press, 1962. A systematic description of the role of the plow, the horse, and the three-field rotation in the making of modern Europe.

The Industrial Revolution

Ashton, T. S. *The Industrial Revolution: 1760–1830.* London: Oxford University Press, 1948. Perhaps the best one-volume overview of the Industrial Revolution in England.

Habakkuk, H. J., and M. Postan (eds.). *The Cambridge History of Europe*, Vol. VI. London: Cambridge University Press, 1965. A basic reference on major aspects of the Industrial Revolution.

Lampard, Eric E. *Industrial Revolution: Interpretations and Perspectives.* Washington, D.C.: American Historical Association, 1957. An overview of critical issues and approaches to the Industrial Revolution.

Pred, Allen. *The External Relations of Cities During the Industrial Revolution.* Research Paper No. 76. Chicago: University of Chicago, Department of Geography, 1962. A study of changing spatial patterns generated by the Industrial Revolution using Göteberg, Sweden, as the example, but of general theoretical import.

Vigier, François. *Change and Apathy: Liverpool and Manchester During the Industrial Revolution.* Cambridge, Mass.: M.I.T. Press, 1970. A detailed analysis of the impact of industrialization on two of England's most important cities.

[3] THE TWO WORLDS

Berry, Brian J. L. "An Inductive Approach to the Regionalization of Economic Development." In Norton Ginsburg (ed.). *Essays on Geography and Economic Development.* Research Paper No. 62. Chicago: University of Chicago, Department of Geography, 1960, pp. 78–107. An early effort to develop a quantitative index of relative levels of development.

Cipolla, Carlo M. *The Economic History of World Population.* Middlesex: Penguin Books, 1970. A cogent treatise on the impact of the environmental and scientific transformation on population and economy.

Ginsburg, Norton. "From Colonialism to National Development: Geographical Perspectives on Patterns and Policies," *Annals, Association of American Geographers.* Vol. 63 (1973), pp. 1–21. A plea for

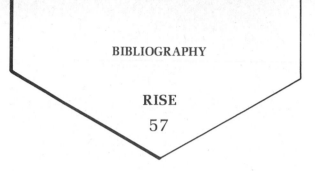
more geographical research into the dualistic nature of developing countries toward the goal of more effective developmental strategies.

Hoyle, B. S. (ed.). *Spatial Aspects of Development.* New York: Wiley, 1974. A high quality set of readings on the geography of development.

Johnson, E. A. J. *The Organization of Space in Developing Countries.* Cambridge, Mass.: Harvard University Press, 1970. A discussion of the role of spatial organization in the development process.

Myrdal, Gunnar. *Economic Theory and Underdeveloped Regions.* London: Methuen, 1957. The cumulative causation theory of the persistence of underdevelopment.

Overseas Development Council. *The United States and the Developing World.* New York: Praeger, 1974. Essays on emerging problems between technological and developing nations as well as recent data.

Rostow, W. W. *The Stages of Economic Growth.* London: Cambridge University Press, 1960. An evolutionary theory of development as discussed by an economic historian.

THE DEVELOPING WORLD

CHINA

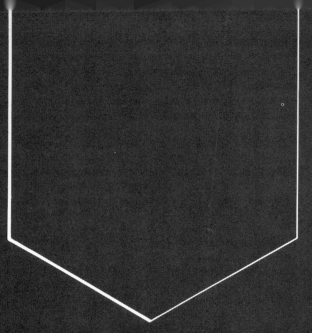

In 1967 the last of the Manchu emperors, Pu-yi, the Son of Heaven, died in Peking. Most of his life was spent in captivity, since he had been deposed as a child from the throne of the Middle Kingdom, the name by which the Chinese called their country. In his place, governing 800 million Chinese, one-fifth of humanity, was a peasant from Hunan, a remarkable revolutionary named Mao Tse-tung. This man, who miraculously survived the Nationalist purges and massacres that decimated Chinese Communist ranks in the 1920s and 1930s, had successfully led a revolution in which the peasantry overthrew the power of the landlord class.

The lives of these two men are intertwined, reflecting both this century of turbulence that has transformed the face of China and a past of stability and continuity that characterized Chinese civilization for 2500 years. Pu-yi was an infant in 1908 when his corrupt and infamous grandmother, the dowager Empress Tzu-hsi, died and he became the last emperor of China. Caught up in the ferment of twentieth-century China, he was a political pawn throughout his life. Forced to abdicate by Nationalist reformers in the 1911 revolution, he was restored to the throne for a few weeks in 1917 by a powerful warlord, then forced to abdicate again. The same process was repeated in 1934, when the Japanese temporarily declared him the puppet emperor of all the Manchus and sovereign over invaded Manchuria. Thus, Pu-yi was both the substance and the symbol of the death of the Chinese imperial system. Buttressed by a bureaucracy based on the precepts of Confucianism, the traditional belief system of China, it had endured for thousands of years and under many dynasties.

Mao, on the other hand, sprang from the stable base of Chinese society, the peasantry. Born in the village of Shao-shan in Hunan in 1893, he grew up in a rural society where 80 percent of the farmers were landless tenants working for landowners who

Photo: Wide World.

took 50 percent of each year's crops as rent and lent money at an interest rate of 30 percent. His early years were spent memorizing Confucian classics, the traditional educational path for escaping the fate of the masses and achieving a position of responsibility. Indeed, it was not until he was a grown man of twenty-seven that he was introduced to Communist writings. Mao's tumultuous path to ultimate control of the Chinese mainland in 1949 is one of the major events of the twentieth century. The lives of these two men, then, span the chasm separating the traditional society of Confucian China from the revolutionary life of the People's Republic.

This transformation of China from the world of the Manchus to the world of Mao is the central theme of this section. In "Traditional China," the ecological, political, and social foundations of Chinese civilization are analyzed. These were challenged after the decline of the Manchus, when a struggle to establish "A New Order" pitted the Communists, led by Mao Tse-tung, against the Nationalists of Chiang Kai-shek. The resolution of this struggle led to the establishment of "The New China," whose goals include a complete reorganization of agriculture, the building of a new industrial order, and the replacement of the Confucian tradition with a new society based on Communist principles.

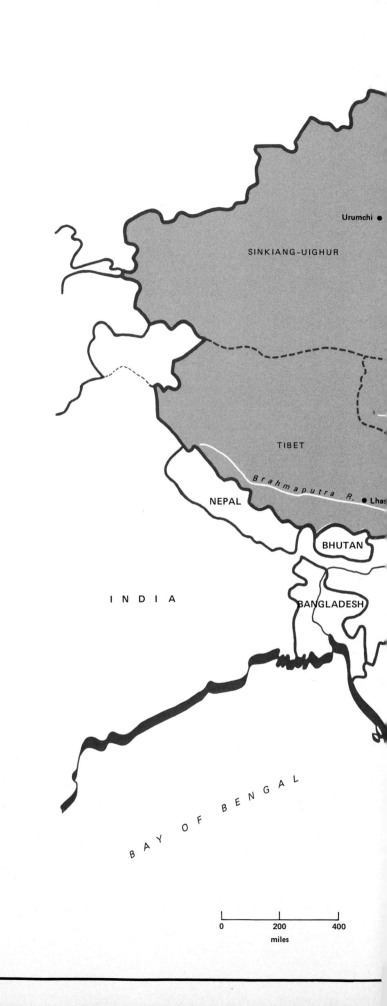

SINKIANG-UIGHUR

Urumchi ●

TIBET

Brahmaputra R. ● Lhas

NEPAL

BHUTAN

INDIA

BANGLADESH

B A Y   O F   B E N G A L

```
|————|————|————|
0    200    400
     miles
```

POLITICAL DIVISIONS

TRADITIONAL CHINA
1

Chinese civilization developed in the basin of the Yellow River (Huang Ho) in North China, a region of wind-driven **loess**• and alluvial soil, subhumid climate, and open vegetation. Because the fertile soils of this region were easily worked with a hoe or spade, local **ecology**• favored a style of agriculture different from that practiced in other centers of civilization. Irrigated **hoe cultivation**• of wheat and millet by means of intense human effort applied to small plots of land became the primary economy of the region. Drought was mitigated by simple **irrigation**• and drainage canal systems. The average peasant holding, 12 acres, was less than half that of a plow-using European contemporary in preindustrial times. Productivity per farmer was low, productivity per acre extremely high.

From a cultural viewpoint, the formative period of Chinese civilization began when a hunting people, the Chou, conquered the North China cradle area (in 1111 BC), settled as permanent farmers on the loess soil of Shensi, and established walled cities throughout the middle reaches of the Yellow River Valley. Their cities served as nuclei of relatively autonomous economic regions. From these bases, the Chou expanded their dominion eastward to the Shantung Peninsula and southward as far as the Yangtze River. Over the next 1000 years, a period of changing political structures, carpets of fields spread over the North China plain. **Terracing**• and irrigation systems were constructed. Key innovations and techniques—wet field rice, the ox-drawn plow, a formal style of writing, and a unifying single language—emerged in the region.

Finally, in 221 BC, the Chin (whence Chinese) ruler, Shih Huang-ti, consolidated all of North China into a single state and constructed a 1500-mile-long Great Wall to protect it from western nomads. It was Shih Huang-ti who laid the foundations on which his successors, the Han, would build a vast empire that would endure for two thousand years.

EXPANSION AND EMPIRE

During the four centuries of Han rule (207 BC–AD 220), the Empire of All Under Heaven extended its sway over what became modern China. In the west, the Chinese overran the Central Asian **oases**• at the foot of the Nan Shan Mountains and spread Chinese rule through the Tarim Basin as far west as the Jaxartes (Syr Darya) River.

In the north, Chinese armies maintained frontier control over Manchuria and much of Korea, reducing nomadic pressure on the core area of the Chinese state. The most important geographical expansion of the Han political and cultural system, however, lay to the south, which at that time was inhabited by a variety of non-Chinese Tai peoples native to Southeast Asia. Chinese peasants spread southward beyond the **alluvial plains**• of the Yangtze into the hill country of South China and onto the **tropical delta**• of the Hsi River. The Chinese conquered the Tai peoples of the south by assimilation, driving conservative, less responsive groups out of lowland **environments**• into the hills. Level land suitable for hoe cultivation was their goal. They concentrated on alluvial lowlands and loess plains to such a degree that even today nine-tenths of China's population is clustered on this one-sixth of the country.

The gradual drift of Chinese peasants into the tropics was apparently motivated by disaster in the north and the lure of new land in the south. According to some observers, nomadic pressures from the north and west on the Yangtze and Yellow river valleys produced a ripple effect that spread colonists farther and farther south. Floods and droughts also played an important role. Records exist of some forty-eight floods and seventeen droughts in North China during the Han period, each of which undoubtedly dislodged farmers from their land. The south, known and perceived as a land of plenty by peasants in North China, drew families in search of a better life—a fully justified view, since the south provides over 60 percent of the total food supply of modern China.

The southward advance of Chinese colonization spread a network of walled cities, called *hsien* or county capitals, throughout the valleys and **intermontane**• basins of modern South China. The rugged hills were left to Tai ethnic groups. The *hsien* functioned as administrative and economic centers for surrounding regions, and by the end of the Han period, this network of central places covered most of the territory of modern China. The Chinese Empire could then be aptly compared in size, population, and cultural complexity to its Western, Roman contemporary.

Over the centuries, the distinctive garden agriculture of the Han Chinese and their successors was sufficiently productive that China's population grew from 60 million in 1290 to 150 million in 1600, 179 million in 1750, and 430 million in 1850. Population

c. 1700–1100 BC
Shang dynasty: An early complex agricultural society centered on the Yellow River (Huang Ho).

c. 1100–256 BC
Chou dynasty: Consolidated and spread Chinese organization throughout the Yellow River core region of China.

221–206 BC
Chin dynasty: Short-lived, militaristic dynasty that united China.

202 BC–AD 220
Han dynasty: Confucian dynasty that ruled a Chinese empire equivalent to that of Rome in the West. Pax Sinica.

AD 590–618
Sui dynasty: A new dynasty that consolidated China and brought further peripheral peoples under Chinese cultural influence.

618–960, 960–1279
Tang and Sung dynasties: A glorious period of Chinese history, when China was clearly the most advanced nation in the world. Tang military prowess brought Central Asia, Southeast Asia, and Mongolia into the Chinese sphere.

1279–1368
Yuan dynasty: The Mongol dynasty that ruled China after the conquests of Genghis Khan.

1368–1644
Ming dynasty: Founded by a peasant rebel who defeated the Mongols, this dynasty reasserted Chinese culture.

1644–1911
Manchu (Ching) dynasty: A dynasty of foreign origins from Manchuria which faced the increasingly dominant power of the West.

pressure gradually pushed farmers into increasingly limited environments. In South China, a new rapid-maturing rice that cut the time from sowing to harvesting from 180 days to less than 90, making the growing of two rice crops in one year (**double cropping•**) possible, was introduced at the end of the first millennium. This new variety, called Champa rice, doubled the productivity of the land, required less water, and could be planted in hitherto marginal environments—on sloping land unsuitable for older rices and in regions of poorer soil and more rugged terrain. Dry-land crops like wheat, barley, and sorghum filtered southward from North China, further extending the environmental range of the Chinese agricultural economy. In the sixteenth century, the introduction of American crops—corn, sweet potatoes, and peanuts—pushed peasant cultivation deeper still into the dry hills and mountains of the south. The forests of central and southern China were cleared for cultivation. Similarly, in the north, dry-land crops were planted on easily worked hillsides. As many as 12 million acres of forestland were cleared for cultivation by colonists in search of land, leading to **erosion•** and abandonment in upland China, and silting and flooding in the lowlands.

THE POLITICAL SYSTEM IN TRADITIONAL CHINA

The twin problems of population and environmental pressure underlay the course of Chinese political history. Twenty-five times in 2000 years dynasties fell, leaving the administrations of new rulers to cope with environmental and social catastrophes caused by drought on the North China plain or floods in the tropical south. At the apex of society was the emperor, personally responsible for the well-being of the state. Beneath him were the scholar-officials of the imperial bureaucracy, who administered the state from the network of *hsien.* At the base of society, the Chinese peasants transformed the landscapes of China and lived out their lives in semi-autonomous, self-sufficient groups of villages called standard marketing communities by contemporary geographers.

The Emperor and the Bureaucracy

According to Chinese political theory, based on the teachings of Confucius (554–477 BC), a mandate was conferred on the emperor by Heaven, making him

CHINESE WALLED CITIES

As Chinese influence spread throughout East Asia, Chinese imperial authorities established walled cities to serve as county or provincial administrative centers. These were the hsien, the focus of imperial administrative power and authority, and the locus of central government policy. Since the hsien were built during the formative Chin and Han periods, their spread documents the diffusion of Chinese urban civilization.

Walled cities were almost always located on lowland waterways, in contrast to many cities of ancient Europe and the Middle East. The propen-

Adapted from: Tsung Ch'ing Hsien Chih, 1926.

sity to establish administrative, military, and commercial centers along rivers is largely the result of an agriculture system born in, developed in, and tied to riverine lowlands.

The drawing of a Chinese walled city included here shows land use patterns within the city, its location on flat ground, its symmetrical shape punctuated by four gates at the cardinal points, the seemingly random distribution of buildings and open spaces, and the clustering of homes, temples, and villas.

Houses were the main elements in these towns and it was on their location that the layout of streets depended. Entrances were placed facing south if possible for maximum sun in winter and breezes in summer. There is no separate, easily recognizable business district because dwelling and shop were usually in the same building. The shop fronted the street and the family lived in the back or above. The most elaborate buildings were the residence of the magistrate and the temple, the latter often surrounded by sacred forests that formed the open space within the city.

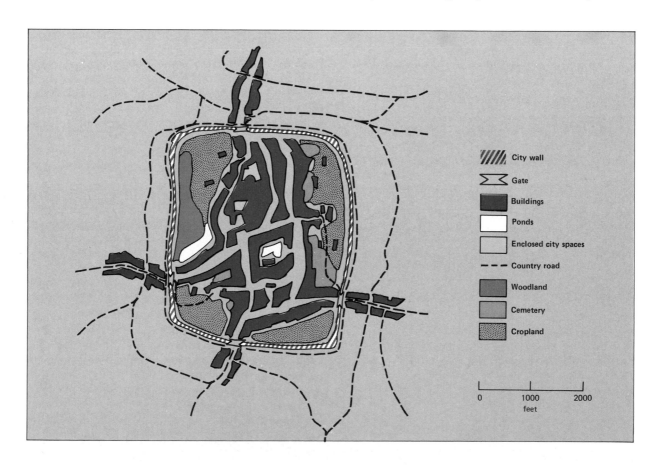

City wall
Gate
Buildings
Ponds
Enclosed city spaces
Country road
Woodland
Cemetery
Cropland

0   1000   2000
feet

universal monarch, the Son of Heaven. Inherently superior to all other rulers, his task was to conform to the will of Heaven through rituals and the practice of good government and moral conduct. Evidence of this harmony was found in human conditions in the realm. Drought, flood, famine, and disorder were signs that the emperor was failing to conform to Heaven's will. This personal responsibility, therefore, set limits on the emperor's power and justified his replacement by a new dynasty when it seemed that the mandate from Heaven was withdrawn.

Social conditions, then, were the responsibility of the ruling classes and depended upon their behavior, conduct, and example. A wise ruler treated his subjects as a father treats his children—instructing them in their obligations, caring for their needs, and demonstrating wisdom, virtue, and tact in the conduct of public affairs. The people in return demonstrated the same devotion and loyalty to the ruler that obedient and well-behaved children express to their fathers. Harmony existed when, as the proverb went, "Superior men diligently attended to the rules of propriety, and men in an inferior position did their best."

Although physical force might be necessary in overthrowing a corrupt imperial regime, authority was best exercised by "ritual and yielding," not by military power. For this reason, military training was deemphasized in mainstream Chinese dynasties. One did not, after all, waste good steel making nails; one should not, therefore, waste superior men creating soldiers. The ideal leaders in traditional China were not military leaders, but men of wisdom and learning: scholar-officials. This preference had a profound effect on the organization of traditional Chinese society.

The scholar-officials, or "mandarins," as the Portuguese called them, were representatives of the imperial government. They were bureaucrats who levied taxes, supervised public works, ran police forces, and administered law courts throughout China. Disdaining manual labor of any kind, they were men of learning, interested in music and literature, the fine arts, and fine conversation. Even the lowest ranks of this class commanded great influence, often being solely responsible for the public affairs of districts populated by as many as a quarter of a million people. They were the product of an elaborate recruitment scheme, the imperial examination system.

The Confucian principle that excellence was a matter of education and conduct rather than inheritance was applied to the task of establishing a reliable bureaucracy to govern the expanding territory and population of China. An exhausting series of ten local, provincial, and imperial examinations in each three-year period drew several hundreds of thousands of student-scholars from the lower reaches of

Tzu-hsi (1835–1908), the empress dowager and the epitome of imperial China, was the last of the Manchu dynasty truly to rule; her grandson Pu-yi ruled for just four years, until the revolution in 1911 gave birth to republican China. This photograph was taken shortly before Tzu-hsi's death by a Japanese photographer she invited to Peking for the purpose. Copies were sent to each of the foreign ministers at Peking and to the rulers they represented. *Photo:* New York Public Library Picture Collection.

society. Success quotas on some examinations limited the number who passed to less than 3 percent. But the rewards of the system were so great that all over China young men spent as many as twenty years honing to perfection their knowledge of Confucian teachings.

In the classic case, village communities (residents of marketing towns) pooled their resources to tutor the most promising local student. One writer has described the process as a "giant roulette game," for although scholar-officials were never allowed to directly administer their own localities, they invariably found indirect ways to divert wealth and

CENTRAL PLACE IN CHINA

The traditional Chinese landscape can be analyzed as a logical hierarchy of settlement—the basis of central place theory. While the real landscapes of China do not match the geometrical regularity of any idealized model, the spatial ordering of human activity becomes clearer by removing topographic, cultural, or political variations. The figure shows the discrepancies between the ideal landscape model posited in central place theory and the pattern actually found in China. In (a), 19 market towns are shown in two different counties. The only roads mapped are those that connect basic-level market towns to higher-level market towns. Part (b) is an abstraction of the real map, dividing the region into theoretical hinterlands associated with basic-level market towns and higher-level market towns. The brown lines connecting market towns form neat subdivisions of the landscape into higher-level marketing areas, each surrounding a higher-level market town. The hinterlands of the basic-level market towns are absorbed within the hinterlands of the higher-level market towns. Part (c) is a theoretical model in which all environmental and cultural differences have been filtered out. Seen in mathematical relief, all hinterlands and all central places revolve around the higher-level market towns of this district in a regular fashion. As a model of the complex human landscape, the simplified vision of reality suggests that there is a spatial order and logic underlying economic activity.

Adapted from: G. William Skinner, "Marketing and Social Structure in Rural China, Part I," *Journal of Asian Studies*, Vol. 24, No. 1 (November 1964), pp. 22–23, Figs. 2.1, 2.2, 2.3.

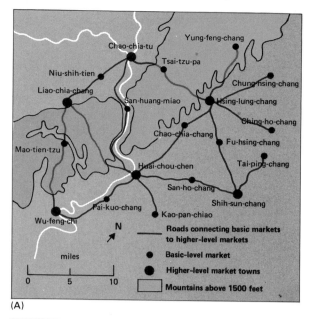

(A)

(B)

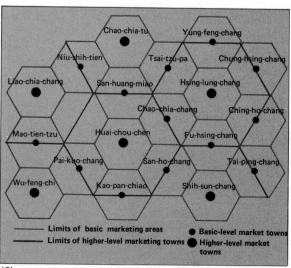

(C)

resources to their home districts. As a result, tremendous pressure was brought to bear on children to perfect their skills in reading and writing so they could compete in this scholastic marathon. They were taught the value of submissiveness to authority, respect for tradition, reverence for the past, love of traditional learning, decorum in social relationships, prudence, caution, and a preference for moderation. And this conservatism at the top of Chinese society was reinforced by an equivalent conservatism at the bottom in the semiautonomous marketing communities.

The Peasants and the Marketing Community

As is true of many traditional societies, the social and economic world of the Chinese peasant was rooted in a **market town**• lying within walking distance (2 to 4 miles) of the 900,000 farm villages of China. In densely settled eastern China, market towns served **hinterlands**• about 20 miles square in area. These, the simplest and most basic hinterlands in a hierarchy (ordered and graded series), are known as the basic **marketing areas**• of traditional China. Basic-level areas in lowland eastern China comprised fifteen to eighteen farm villages and a total population of some 7000 people. In less intensely settled mountain districts and in the deserts of Outer China, basic-level areas were larger and populations were smaller. Despite regional variations in settlement patterns, the basic-level market town and marketing area were the focus of peasant life throughout China. This economic structure of traditional China is an example of the regularity and rhythm in the human economy apparent in many preindustrial societies. Theoretical geographers who have studied this regularity and who have viewed the patterns of settlement in agriculture-based societies in terms of logic and deductive theory have thus been able to develop ideal models of complex human landscapes that reveal the almost geometrical precision of these patterns.

In nineteenth-century China, basic-level market towns were distributed across the landscape so evenly that virtually all peasants had access to the goods and services they offered. The basic-level town and its associated hinterland tended to stretch across China in a regular, almost mathematical pattern. The basic-level market town was thus the foundation in a hierarchy of **central places**• (towns and cities) that provided the countryside with urban services. They were centers for rural commerce carried on in a formal setting of bureaucrats and merchants. The range in the hierarchy of central places extended from the basic level of the market town and its marketing area up through progressively larger towns and cities and their collective marketing areas, each varying in size and importance according to environment and population. All over China, the agricultural products and crafts of the peasants were brought for sale

to market towns; manufactured and specialized goods filtered down through the hierarchy of central places and were exchanged for the peasants' products.

The basic-level market town, the "cell" in this pattern of economic exchange, was the Chinese hometown. It was a center of interaction between the worlds of the scholar, bureaucrat, and merchant, and the world of the peasant—the basic producer and mass consumer of goods in traditional China. Virtually every good or service needed by a peasant— soap, matches, oil, incense, a barber, a tailor, or a scribe—could be secured within the confines of this market town. The marketing area surrounding the town was the social terrain with which peasants were intimately familiar. By the time peasants reached age fifty, they had visited their market town more than 3000 times, dealt with merchants with whom they had become closely acquainted over the years, and recognized on sight an array of peasants from their own and nearby marketing areas. Since the population of these districts tended to remain stable over time, the social knowledge gained during these visits was cumulative. The contained life of the Chinese peasants extended from their nuclear village to the broader world of the basic-level market town.

In turn, each of these basic-level market towns was part of a network of larger settlements with an ever-increasing range of goods and services and larger populations. Higher-level market towns were important in traditional Chinese society because they were the major transfer points between the largest markets (the metropolises of China) and the local world of the peasant and the basic-level market town. Basic-level market towns formed patterned networks around the higher-level market towns. The hinterlands of the market towns were part of the area served by higher-level market towns. This relationship between populations and markets was repeated through each successive stage in the hierarchy of settlements, culminating in the largest central place of all, the imperial capital. At each higher level in the system, economic activities became more specialized, administrative functions broader, and occupations more diversified. In traditional China, then, the theoretical precision of the central place hierarchy model was closely approximated by the geographical distribution, the economic functions, and the administrative systems of the real world.

STATE AND LOCAL POWER IN THE DYNASTIC CYCLE

The Chinese dynastic cycle, a rise and fall of rulers, authority, and kingdoms, can be analyzed in terms of a sequence of five cyclical tendencies. Dissatisfaction and rebellion brought about a change of dynasty. The new dynasty pacified its constituency; the reconstruction of government then took place during a period of general prosperity and contentment known as the dynastic heyday. As the dynasty began to decline, control fell to increasingly local levels of organization. Unrest and rebellion followed, to be met by repression during a crisis period. Eventually a new dynasty emerged from the crisis period, beginning the cycle of pacification and reconstruction once again.

The relative openness or closedness of local systems was directly related to the cyclical nature of dynastic power. During dynastic heyday and early decline, local systems were open to cultural interchange of all types, but with decline and during a crisis, they began to close. Boundary-maintaining mechanisms grew stronger, aliens and expendables were forced out, feuds with nearby local areas flared up, and—perhaps most significant—local militarization began.

Adapted from: G. William Skinner, "The City in Chinese Society," unpublished manuscript prepared for the Conference on Urban Society in Traditional China, 1968.

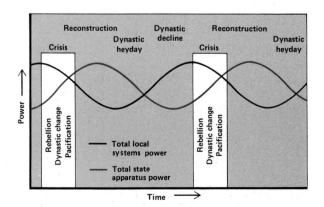

CYCLES OF CHANGE: PEASANTS VERSUS SCHOLARS

Except in isolated and remote regions, the Chinese peasant was a member of one of the economically organized units surrounding the 45,000 market towns that dotted the landscape. These cells were economic and socially autonomous units, including within them members of the leisured and literate **gentry**[*] class, merchants and shopkeepers, artisans, and, of course, farmers. Given this potential for economic self-sufficiency and social independence, the marketing community was able to respond to the opportunities and threats the cycles of Chinese history provoked by continuing population growth.

Chinese history can be seen in terms of cycles of dynastic change proceeding through five phases: social discontent, pacification, reconstruction, dynastic heyday, and dynastic decline. In each cycle, the marketing communities tended to fluctuate between periods of being closed and periods of being open to higher levels of central places. Whether they were closed or open depended upon the levels of social security or insecurity prevailing at the particular time within the broader external environment of the empire.

During the pacification phase, local systems tended to cooperate with the new rulers in eliminating brigands and bandits in the countryside and tracking down the last supporters of the previous dynasty. Once order had been restored, the emphasis shifted to reconstruction. Irrigation networks were rebuilt, roads cleared, canals dredged, and a uniform monetary system reestablished as the new empire attempted to restore the economic basis of Chinese society.

By the time dynastic heyday was achieved (for the Manchus this occurred in the middle of the eighteenth century), local systems participated rather fully in the broader society. Examinations were pursued on a regular three-year basis, and local candidates worked their way from the county (hsien) level, through the prefecture and provincial capital, to the imperial seat of power. Ambitious traders and merchants, artisans, and craftsmen followed the same path, moving up the economic ladder in search of broader and more lucrative opportunities. Since, as noted above, these men did not become estranged from their origins, but retained a deep sense of loyalty and allegiance to their home villages, benefits to the local system in the form of wealth, business opportunities, influence, and prestige were derived from the opening up of the local society to broader horizons. As a result, periods of dynastic heyday were marked by high rates of social and geographical mobility and intense interactions between the marketing community and higher levels in the economic hierarchy.

As the dynasty wore on, the pool of economic and

educational opportunities available from outside the local system began to dry up. In the nineteenth century, for example, only 40,000 government positions were available for the 1.1 million to 1.5 million people who were holders of degrees. As the efficiency of revenue collection began to decline, the state offered fewer rewards and the local system correspondingly more. Increased tension between local and national systems made the state use force (contrary to Confucius's teaching) to contain social unrest caused by increasing pressure on resources, local insecurity, and the threat of invasion.

In response to these changing conditions, local marketing communities tended to close their frontiers to the external world. Local myths, customs, and loyalties tended to intensify as the command of the imperial bureaucracy dissipated. A similar shrinkage of economic possibilities in the larger system tended to diminish the acquisitive spirit of merchants in favor of the security of local exchange.

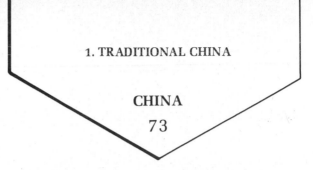

Finally, as the crisis period neared, peasant communities were essentially closed to outsiders, defensive crop-watching societies were formed, and local militia were recruited. In some cases, as in nineteenth-century Anhwei, earthen walls were thrown up around settlements to present a closed, hostile posture to the outside world. This national response to the chaos of dynastic change occurred with the destruction of the Manchu Empire and the rise of the People's Republic, as a struggle ensued to establish a new order in China.

CHINA

REGIONAL PATTERNS

PHYSICAL FEATURES MAP
POPULATION DENSITY MAP

Nearly the same size as the United States, some 3.7 million square miles in area, China's regional environments are equally complex. The western frontier of Chinese civilization, frequently called Outer China, includes the mountain core of the Asian continent, intermontane basins, high *plateaus,* and *deserts,* dominated by continental air masses and remote from oceanic sources of moisture. In general, Outer China is an inhospitable land, sparsely populated by a variety of non-Chinese ethnic groups concentrated in oases and mountain valleys, and remote from all but determined explorers. The core of the mountain fist is the 3-mile-high plateau of Tibet, to the north of which the two huge mountain-ringed basins of Sinkiang—the Tarim and the Dzungarian—are located. Still farther north, the cold, windswept plains of Inner Mongolia provide the only access to China from the west, which is precisely why the Great Wall was erected to keep out barbarian peoples.

Stretching eastward from Tibet, a series of mountain ranges—the Tsinling Shan and the Tapa Shan—reach like fingers into the lowlands of eastern or Agricultural China, forming and bounding the major Chinese river basins—the Yellow (Huang), the Yangtze, and the Hsi—which flow from the interior highlands to the sea. In eastern China, climate is determined by latitude, so that the north-south sequence of rainfall and temperature is much like that in the eastern United States, but comparable Chinese latitudes (Charleston, South Carolina, and Shanghai, for example) have an average annual temperature some 20 degrees cooler than in Atlantic America. This, the China that matters, is where 95 percent of the population lives, crowded into the three lowland core areas associated with the three major river systems. Densities reach 10,000 people per square mile on the North China Plain, in the Yangtze basins, and in the Hsi Delta near Canton,

as compared with 5 or 6 people per square mile in Outer China. In the north, where it is too cool for rice, the primary crops are wheat, millet, and sorghum. Rice is grown only south of a line paralleling and north of the Yangtze River. In the south, where rice is dominant, the climate is warm enough for double cropping, and in tropical areas, like Hainan Island, three successive crops a year can be grown. The topography of the south, in contrast to the flat, alluvial plains of the north, is dissected into once-forested rugged hills molded into terraced hillocks by the expansive agricultural economy of the Chinese. In view of the antiquity and permanence of Chinese civilization, one cannot speak of natural vegetation or soils in either region, as both have been so thoroughly altered by generations of peasants that "natural" phenomena are now cultural features.

In discussing the regions of China, then, a basic division can be made between Outer China and Agricultural China. The separating line stretches from northeastern India to northern Manchuria, closely following the 20-inch rainfall line. Within these two broad regions, Outer China can be subdivided on the basis of topography into Tibet, Sinkiang, and Inner Mongolia. Agricultural China consists of three lowland regions: the North China Plain, the Yangtze basins (including the Szechwan Basin), and the Hsi Delta and surrounding highlands.

OUTER CHINA

Outer China is a land relatively empty of people, fractured by a topography of high plateaus, towering mountains, and forbidding deserts. Taken together, the three major physiographical regions of Outer China—Tibet, Sinkiang, and Inner Mongolia—make up more than half the territory of China; but they produce less than 3 percent of China's food and contain only 4 percent of the total population. Vast areas, such as the high northern half of Tibet, the desert wastes of the Tarim and eastern Dzungarian basins, and the mountain deserts of Mongolia, are virtually uninhabited. The scattered inhabited areas of Outer China are principally occupied by nomadic herders and oasis cultivators, though extensive mineral finds point to industrial penetration in the future. Mao referred to this region, saying that of the three great assets of China—a large population, extensive territory, and abundant resources—the Han Chinese of China proper possessed the first, and the minority peoples of Outer China the remaining two.

Tibet

The Tibetan highlands, located for the most part at elevations of more than 10,000 feet, cover a vast frozen treeless area of 750,000 square miles occu-

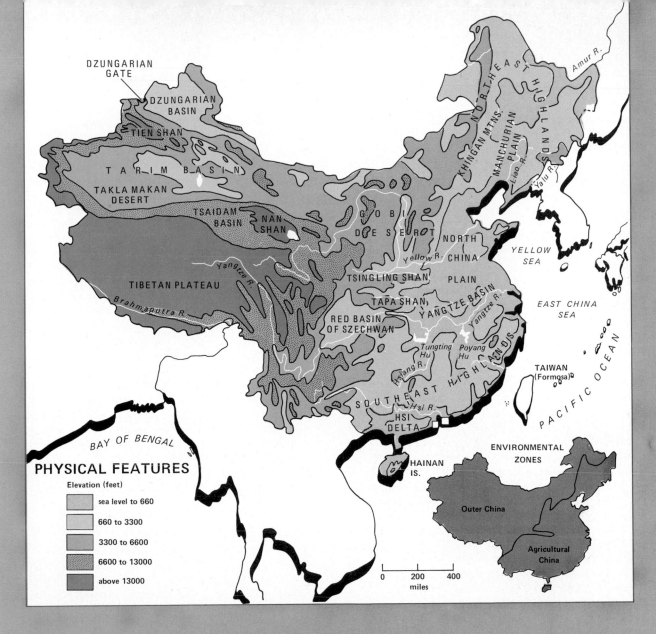

PHYSICAL FEATURES

DZUNGARIAN GATE
DZUNGARIAN BASIN
TIEN SHAN
TARIM BASIN
TAKLA MAKAN DESERT
TSAIDAM BASIN
NAN SHAN
TIBETAN PLATEAU
Yangtze R.
Brahmaputra R.
GOBI DESERT
Yellow R.
NORTH CHINA PLAIN
TSINGLING SHAN
TAPA SHAN
RED BASIN OF SZECHWAN
YANGTZE BASIN
Yangtze R.
Tungting Hu
Poyang Hu
Hsiang R.
SOUTHEAST HIGHLANDS
Hsi R.
HSI DELTA
BAY OF BENGAL
HAINAN IS.
KHINGAN MTNS.
NORTHEAST HIGHLANDS
MANCHURIAN PLAIN
Liao R.
Amur R.
Yalu R.
YELLOW SEA
EAST CHINA SEA
TAIWAN (Formosa)
PACIFIC OCEAN

Elevation (feet)

- sea level to 660
- 660 to 3300
- 3300 to 6600
- 6600 to 13000
- above 13000

0   200   400
miles

ENVIRONMENTAL ZONES

Outer China

Agricultural China

---

pied by some 5 million people, less than 3 million of whom are Tibetans. Until 1950, Tibetans were yak herders and marginal farmers organized by a landowning *theocracy*• dominated by monks and headed by the Dalai Lama. The Chinese invasion of 1950 began as an influx of Chinese settlement in regions adjacent to Tibet, particularly in the Hsining Basin of Tsinghai Province. In Tibet, the Chinese attempted to replace the Lamaist feudal system with agricultural cooperatives, but these were deeply resented by the Tibetans. In 1958 a revolt broke out among Khamba tribesmen and spread to the capital city of Lhasa. Chinese armies moved into the region in force and the Dalai Lama fled to India. Since then, the Chinese have consolidated their control over Tibet, driving the monks out of the monasteries, nationalizing their land, and starting a program of land reform. Although few Chinese have settled in Tibet proper, new roads have been constructed, fuel and energy sources have been developed, and sinification (absorption into Han control) pressures on Tibet have been intense.

Sinkiang

Sinkiang, located to the north of Tibet, is another sparsely settled expanse covering some 650,000 square miles, populated by about 10 million people. Two dry, mountain-ringed basins, the Tarim to the south and the Dzungarian to the north, are separated by the towering peaks of the Tien Shan range. The core of the Tarim Basin, the rainless dune-covered Takla Makan Desert, is settled only in a belt of oases stretching out on the *alluvial fans*• of the Tien Shan. Herding is the livelihood of only 2 percent of the population in Tarim, since land, apart from the oases, is too barren to support pasture. The colder Dzungarian Basin to the north receives somewhat more rainfall and is covered by a *steppe*• on which the 600,000 nomads of the region survive.

When the Communists assumed power in China in 1949, the population of Sinkiang was nearly totally composed of Turkish-speaking Muslim people similar in culture and language to their counterparts in nearby Soviet Central Asia. The largest of these groups, the Uigurs, numbered nearly 4 million and dominated the productive oases of the Tarim, along with the Kazakhs of northeastern Sinkiang, and the Kirghiz, who occupied the high mountain pastures of the southwest. Of a total population in 1953 of about 5 million, only 300,000 in Sinkiang were Chinese. Since that time, Sinkiang has doubled in population as a result of a concerted Chinese effort to develop the region for political as well as economic reasons.

The government policy of encouraging and enforcing migration from coastal to interior provinces of China has reinforced a centuries-long process of sinification by which the Han Chinese have established control over provinces on the western and northern peripheries. Historically, these peripheries were held by nomadic barbarian (non-Han) peoples, the focus of xenophobia and the object of a belligerent foreign policy. That Chinese fears were justified is illustrated by the fact that two of the major dynasties of the past were barbarian conquerors: the Yuan (Mongols) and the Ching (Manchus).

Traditionally, the Chinese assimilated the western conquerors, absorbing them into Chinese culture within a few generations. In the mid-twentieth century, this process has taken the form of officially sponsored migration and resettlement of Han Chinese into the western and northern provinces. Policymakers hope to produce a preponderantly Han population tied to inner China by educational and communications systems, the twentieth-century forces of *acculturation.*

Chinese immigrants, now about 30 percent of the population of Sinkiang, are predominantly urban people located in growing cities in the Dzungarian Basin and at a new oil field discovered at Karamai. New roads, constructed along historic caravan routes, connect the regional capital of Urumchi with Karamai and lower-level urban centers near the Soviet border. A railroad was built from Urumchi to Lan-chou in northwest China. The effect of these activities has been to establish a strong Chinese presence, an effective socioeconomic and political barrier, at the historic Dzungarian Gate. Traditional contact with non-Chinese peoples across the Soviet frontier has ended, and an explicit display of Chinese power in Sinkiang has been asserted.

Inner Mongolia

A similar pattern of dominance from the east has been imposed on Inner Mongolia, the third region of Outer China, although the origins of the Chinese presence here are more deeply rooted in the past than in either Tibet or Sinkiang. Physically, Inner Mongolia is composed of the rim of the Gobi Desert, which stretches in an arc from Sinkiang to the Amur River, extending eastward to the Great Wall of China. These northern desert and steppe plains give way to southern green hills more affected by the climate of eastern China. Good pastures are found nearest to the Great Wall; sand and gravel deserts dominate the west.

In this transitional zone, a contest for dominance has existed for centuries between Chinese cultivators and nomadic Mongols; the boundary between desert and sown land fluctuates with rainfall and political power. Today, 90 percent of the estimated 13 million people of Inner Mongolia are Chinese, concentrated along the irrigated upper stretches of the Yellow River where new dams and canals have made an expansion of grain agriculture possible. New industrial centers, notably the steel town of Pao-tou, have been developed, and the national road and rail network has been extended. The 900,000 Mongols left in the region are concentrated on the dry, windswept steppes of the north on the borders of Outer Mongolia. Active programs of *sedentarization* and acculturation seek to induce Mongols to settle as farmers in regions farther to the south. As in Tibet and Sinkiang, the Chinese are attempting to integrate these borderlands into the framework of the modern nation.

AGRICULTURAL CHINA

Agricultural China, covering less than half of China's territory, includes 95 percent of the total population. Three-quarters of these, an estimated 600 million to 650 million people, are clustered in three lowland core areas. These are the North China Plain of the Yellow River; the Middle, Lower, and Red basins of the Yangtze; and the Hsi River Delta of South China. In these areas, population densities average 500 to 1500 people per square mile, fantastically high figures for agricultural land, and rarely equaled in the world. Elsewhere in Asia, such figures are found in parts of the Indus and Ganges river valleys, along the Mekong and Red rivers in Southeast Asia, and on the island of Java. Since agriculture produces half the national income of Communist China and occupies 80 percent of the population, eastern China is the China of historical and political importance; it is the China that matters.

North China Plain

The North China Plain, which covers the provinces of Hopeh, Honan, and Shantung, includes only 5 percent of the Chinese earth, but has a population of 170 million people, 22 percent of the population, and 35 percent of the cultivated land of China. This region, the flat delta plain of the Yellow River

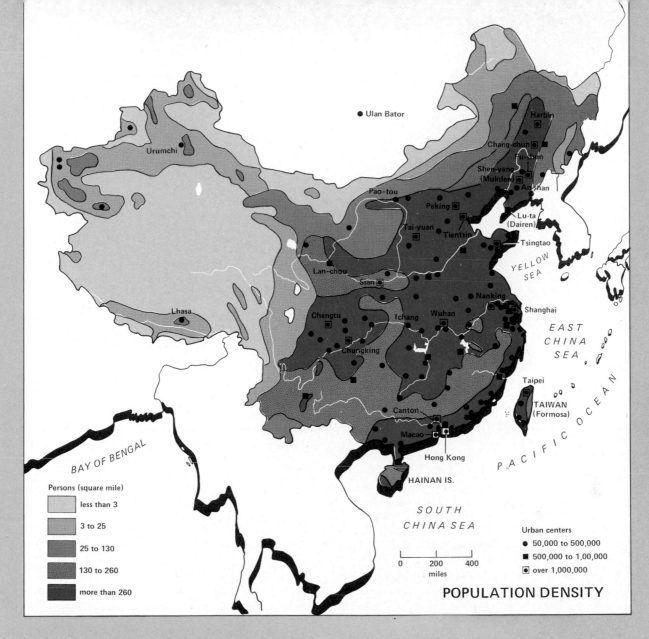

POPULATION DENSITY

Persons (square mile)

- less than 3
- 3 to 25
- 25 to 130
- 130 to 260
- more than 260

Urban centers

- ● 50,000 to 500,000
- ■ 500,000 to 1,00,000
- ◉ over 1,000,000

(Huang Ho), is covered with a dense carpet of agricultural fields. Too cold for rice, the fertile loess soils are planted to winter wheat, barley, millet, and a sorghum crop called kaoliang. Still farther north in Manchuria, cropping systems are similar, except that colder temperatures cause wheat to be replaced by soybeans. Unreliable rainfall, averaging 17 to 21 inches a year, makes agriculture hazardous, particularly on the western perimeter, where erosion of soil (later deposited as silt on the plain of the Yellow River) poses a constant threat of flooding. In spite of these environmental hazards, the North China Plain remains an important agricultural area and the center of political power in China. Peking, the national capital, has a municipal area of 6600 square miles; in 1970 its population was estimated to be 7,570,000. Together with its port city of Tientsin (3.3 million), Peking is the focus of a developing industrial region, based on the rich iron ores of Shantung and the coal deposits of Hopeh.

The Yangtze Basins

The Middle and Lower basins of the Yangtze, which group together the five provinces of Hupeh, Hunan, Kiangsi, Anhwei, and Kiangsu, cover about 9 percent of the Chinese territory and have a population of approximately 200 million, 26 percent of the total. In the Middle Yangtze Basin, agricultural densities reach 800 per square mile; the fertile, intensively cultivated lake basins at Tungting and Po-yang have been called the rice bowl of China. The urban focus of the Middle Basin is the tri-city hub at Wuhan, the site of one of the newest and largest steel complexes in the country. The Lower Yangtze Basin, the southern extension of the vast delta formed by the Yellow and the upper Yangtze rivers, stretches inland several hundred miles and 700 miles along the coast. The density of population here exceeds 1000 per square mile; over 50 percent of the region is cultivated, and agricultural productivity is immense. The Yangtze, unlike the Yellow

77

These terraced fields in the Tse-kiang Valley near Chungking show clearly the complexity of agriculture in the Szechwan Basin, where many crops can be grown in a small area at different elevations. The loudspeaker hung from a tree shows just as clearly that though the landscape may have changed little from ancient times, central government control effectively reaches everywhere. *Photo:* Marc Riboud/Magnum.

River, can be navigated by large vessels as far inland as Ichang, the positional center of China. The huge (10 million people) port city of Shanghai, near the mouth of this river artery, serves the entire Yangtze hinterland and is the largest city on the Asian continent.

It is on the Yangtze plain that the transition between northern and southern patterns of cultivation occurs. This transition, a significant agricultural and civilizational boundary in Asia, separates half of the Chinese cultivated area, but only one-third of total agricultural production lies north of the line. South of this boundary, irrigated rice fields spread out over the lowlands; tea and other tree crops are planted in the hills. Taken as a whole, the rice-tea agriculture of southern China produces 60 percent of China's food supply on less than half its cultivated area and contains a majority of the animal population of China—half the cattle and two-thirds of the pigs—the principal food animals.

This wheat-rice boundary also passes through the Szechwan Basin, the most remote and highest basin of the Yangtze. Located at the headwaters of the Yangtze 1000 miles in the interior, Szechwan Province has a population of some 95 million, two-thirds of whom live in the basin proper. Except for the Chengtu Plain, the landscape of the region is hilly, but the climate of Szechwan is milder than that of Shanghai. Because of rugged terrain, only 20 percent of the area is under cultivation, but owing to the local diversity of climate, cropping patterns in Szechwan are as complex as any in China. Terraced slopes are planted to rice in summer and wheat in winter. At higher elevations, sweet potatoes and corn are grown with tea and mulberry trees planted on hill slopes. Above Ichang, the gorge of the Yangtze separates Szechwan from lowland China, but its largest industrial city, Chungking (4.4 million), continues to grow, based on extensive local resources of coal, iron, petroleum, and natural gas.

The Hsi Delta

The third core area of Agricultural China is the Hsi River delta of South China. Separated from the Yangtze by the rugged hills of central China, this small plain—only 3000 square miles—has a population of 10 million. Pressure on the irrigated land is intense, and terracing and diking are common. Rice, the dominant crop, is supplemented by sugarcane, silk, and fruit. The southern location of the Hsi makes two rice crops per year common. The population of the plain and its great port city of Canton (3 million) is Chinese, but in the rugged interior hills some 9 million people speaking a variety of Tai languages have resisted acculturation. The largest of these groups, the Chuang, are lowland rice growers, number some 7 million people, and represent the largest minority in China. Other groups—the Miao-yao and the Tai—are subsistence cultivators in the more remote hills, although their traditional *slash-and-burn agriculture** has been discouraged by the Communist government.

A NEW ORDER
2

Between 1850 and 1864, imperial armies quelled revolts in virtually every Chinese province. Unable to deal with peasant unrest, unable to stop Western gunboats and warlord armies, the Manchu dynasty finally fell in 1912. During the ensuing fifty years, the first half of the twentieth century, two opposing groups attempted to reassert strong centralized control over the vast territory of China: the Nationalists under Chiang Kai-shek and the Communists under Mao Tse-tung. Despite the distractions of Western intervention, the Japanese invasion, and World War II, this struggle to establish a new dynasty has been the central issue in twentieth-century China. Mao Tse-tung, the peasant from Hunan, emerged victorious.

DYNASTIC DECLINE

At the beginning of the eighteenth century, the Chinese state was secure: the two forces that were to dislodge the Manchus—peasant anguish and Western intervention—were not yet apparent. In the countryside, population pressure was causing *fragmentation** of fields into tiny plots not large enough to sustain a family. Forced into debt, peasants lost their land to moneylenders, so that 30 percent of the farmers became landless tenants. These conditions were aggravated by the activities of corrupt tax collectors, men determined to squeeze an income from the peasantry in an imperial economy that derived 80 percent of its money from land taxes. But these processes were so gradual that the decline of the agricultural economy of China was not perceived until late in the century, when a general uprising, coinciding with the Revolutionary War in the United States, signaled the beginning of Manchu decline.

Nor had the Manchus perceived the growing economic and military power of the West. The physical isolation of China and a long-standing sense of cultural superiority had engendered in the Manchus, as

in their predecessors, a serene contempt for inferior peoples living beyond the borders of the Middle Kingdom. In 1715, European traders succeeded in establishing a commercial mission in Canton; but in 1793, when Lord Macartney sought, on behalf of Great Britain, better trading facilities, the eighty-three-year-old emperor of China sent him back to King George III with this advice: China had no need of Western manufactures and Britain should prepare to "swear perpetual obedience" to the emperor of China. A generation later, in 1816, a similar delegation led by Lord Amherst also failed.

Confucian China and the industrial West came into direct confrontation in the 1840s: the issue was the lucrative opium trade. Opium had been known in China for centuries and was prescribed as a curative for diarrhea and dysentery as early as the thirteenth century. In the eighteenth century, imperial edicts banned opium because of its growing use as an addictive drug. Yet, the number of opium addicts in China continued to grow, and European traders with access to the opium crops of British India were quick to fill this commercial vacuum. During the 1830s, some 30,000 chests of the drug were shipped annually from India to China in the holds of British, Dutch, and American ships. Stirred by the steady drain of silver from the Chinese treasury, the emperor finally appointed an administrator, Lin Tse-hsu, to eliminate opium smuggling in Canton.

This seemingly minor appointment precipitated the first direct confrontation between China and the West. An earlier incident at Canton in which a British sailor murdered a native had led the Chinese to demand that an Englishman—any Englishman—be surrendered to them for punishment. The ensuing misunderstanding based on two quite different visions of the law—an episode symbolic of virtually every encounter between the Chinese and Westerners in the nineteenth century—had already increased tension when Lin Tse-hsu arrived in Canton in 1839. He immediately ringed the foreign enclave on the Pearl River with troops, cut off all food supplies, and demanded that the Western traders surrender their opium. Some 20,000 chests of opium worth approximately $11 million were surrendered and publicly burned. Although the Chinese were acting within their sovereign rights, their actions so affronted British pride and threatened British trading interests that in 1840 Parliament declared war on China.

For three years during this First Opium War, the British inflicted one defeat after another on imperial Manchu forces. Manchu armies were completely overpowered by the gunboats and marine landings of the British, and the myth of Chinese invincibility abruptly vanished. In the Treaty of Nanking (1842), Chinese sovereignty was completely abrogated, a fact Chinese remember today with bitterness and humiliation. The island of Hong Kong, still a Crown Colony, was ceded to Britain in perpetuity; five other treaty ports—Canton, Amoy, Fu-chou, Ningpo, and Shanghai—were opened to Western trade. Lin Tse-hsu, the administrator who had enforced the imperial ban on opium in Canton, was exiled.

By the middle of the nineteenth century, China was open to the West, the opium trade was flourishing, and the Americans and French demanded and received most-favored-nation treatment, which granted them every right granted to any other foreign power. Chinese control of their land and economy was badly eroded. High-quality, low-priced textiles from mills in the industrial West destroyed markets for the more expensive handmade products of Chinese villagers. In the hinterland, the pressure of Chinese farmers on the land was reaching its environmental and technological limits. Forced to leave their fields, thousands of country folk became beggars in the treaty ports of Canton and Shanghai. Jobs in industry or commerce might have relieved the pressures of unemployment and destitution, but the dominant economic class, the landowning gentry, thwarted investment in new enterprise. In these deteriorating circumstances, bandits and anti-Manchu rebels sprang up across China.

The insurgent Hung Hsiu-chuan, a messianic Cantonese revolutionary who believed himself to be the younger brother of Christ, galvanized forces of discontent into a bloody civil war, the Taiping Rebellion. At least 20 million people, twice the number slaughtered in World War I, were killed during this protracted revolt. From 1850 to 1864, Taiping and Manchu forces criss-crossed the Yangtze plain, leaving in their wake epidemics, starvation, destroyed villages, abandoned fields, and many dead. Destruction was so severe that a century later, population in the five Yangtze provinces had still not recovered 1851 levels. This great peasant-based rebellion was finally crushed when Western mercenaries joined imperial forces to trap and destroy the Taiping rebels in Nanking.

This civil war held no lesson for the Manchus. When order was restored and their power made safe,

The Boxer Rebellion of 1900 was another sign of the turmoil in China in the nineteenth century. It failed, but the instability caused by a weak imperial government and growing Western penetration soon led to revolution. Here foreign troops enter Peking after the Boxers' defeat. *Photo:* New York Public Library Picture Collection.

they were unwilling or unable to initiate reforms. The overriding question was how to cope with materially superior Westerners; their answer was to return to an artificial and inward-looking revitalization of China's cultural traditions, particularly Confucianism. A few shipyards, arsenals, and coal mines were established, but basically China turned her back to the West and to industrialization.

Over the next fifty years, external intervention and internal disorder intensified throughout China. In 1856, the Second Opium War broke out and 30 gunboats and 3000 American, British, French, and Russian troops forced the Chinese to sign the Treaty of Tientsin, opening eleven ports and the interior of China to Western merchants and missionaries. In the sparsely populated northwest, Muslim rebellions flared on the periphery of the Middle Kingdom. Farther to the east, the 1877 drought on the North China Plain caused a famine that killed 9 million to 13 million people. In the northeast, China fought a reenergized Japan in 1894. The imperial Chinese forces were humiliatingly defeated; the Treaty of Shimonoseki forced China to recognize Korea's independence and cede the Liaotung Peninsula, the Pescadores, and Taiwan to imperial Japan.

Stung by these defeats, antagonized by missionary activities, and resentful of new European concessions for railroads and mineral rights, anti-Western and anti-Manchu secret societies emerged in the cities of China. The most important of these, the Boxers, whose members engaged in ritual shadow boxing to make themselves personally invulnerable, laid siege to the Foreign Legation in Peking for fifty-five days in 1900. A seven-nation expeditionary force defeated the Boxers, stripped the Manchu dynasty of effective power, and demanded heavy reparations. Finally, in 1911, an unplanned and accidental uprising overthrew the Manchus while its leader, Sun Yat-sen, curiously enough, was raising money in America. The stage was set for the emergence of a new China: the central question was whether the commercial, Western-oriented vision of Chiang Kai-shek or the ***agrarian,*** peasant-based society of Mao Tse-tung would prevail.

NATIONALISTS AND COMMUNISTS
China never became a political colony of Western powers as did India and most of Africa. European territorial control was confined to the treaty ports,

The house where Mao Tse-tung was born and grew up in Hunan, set amid terraced fields that show how endless and diligent is the labor required of the Chinese peasant, is shown here as it appears now. Mao's deep attachment to the countryside has been the basis for many of his policies. *Photo:* Marc Riboud/Magnum.

urban footholds on the fringes of the continent. Widespread disorder in the countryside and Chinese hostility to foreigners prevented Western traders and merchants from penetrating the heart of Chinese society in any permanent way. Few railroads were built into the interior; as a result, the industrial West was unable to control agricultural production or to restructure the economy.

Nevertheless, in Manchuria and in the port cities of China, Western industry and commerce did create a new class of merchants, bankers, and industrialists —called by the Portuguese the compradors—who facilitated the flow of raw materials (tobacco, tea, and fiber crops) from the interior to the ports; constructed and ran processing plants in cities like Canton, Shanghai, and Tientsin; and in general acted as middlemen between China and the West. A ***bourgeoisie**** began to emerge: by 1914, China had 1000 chambers of commerce with a membership of 200,000; nearly a million Chinese were employed in factory labor. Two leaders derived their support from this emerging middle class: Sun Yat-sen, the well-educated, Western-trained son of a Cantonese farmer, and his disciple and follower, Chiang Kai-shek, son of a middle-class Chekiang merchant.

The first ten years of the Republic of China did not mark the birth of a new dynasty, but rather the funeral of the old. Officials of the republic and the class they represented did not control the interior. Local rulers prevailed in the provinces as warlords or puppets; poverty was worsened by breakdowns in public order and by armed struggles between rival warlords and Communist factions. Finally, in 1922 Chiang Kai-shek, with financial aid from Russia, moved against the warlords and brought the Yangtze Valley and the northern capital, Peking, under Nationalist control. When Sun Yat-sen died of cancer in 1925, Chiang Kai-shek emerged as the most powerful figure in China. He purged the only viable competitors to his vision of a new China, the Communists, destroying thousands in pitched battles and leaving a tattered 10,000 survivors who still claimed affiliation with the Chinese Communist Party. Forty-five years ago, it seemed that the question of dynastic succession had been resolved and that a stable, unified China led by the comprador class and oriented to Western capitalism and mercantilism would begin the process of modernization.

In the villages of Hunan, however, one Communist —Mao Tse-tung—was inspecting Communist peasant associations in which 2 million villagers had enrolled and thereby escaped the anti-Communist purges of 1927. What he saw in Hunan convinced Mao, in his words, that "in a very short time, in China's central, southern and northern provinces, several hundred million peasants will rise like a tornado or tempest . . . and rush forward along the road to liberation." Himself the son of a poor peasant family who, by dint of enormous sacrifice, had managed to accumulate 3.5 acres of land, Mao had rarely eaten meat or eggs as a child, had grown up working in the fields, and was the only revolutionary—Com-

The Long March, a part of Communist China's historical and political heritage, is an epic tale of perseverance and human endurance. When Chiang Kai-shek without warning turned against the Chinese Communist party, which had been his ally against the warlords, he caught most members by surprise and tens of thousands were killed. Mao Tse-tung, the heretical Communist theorist who believed peasant rebellion was the key to a Communist revolution in China, was in the Chinese interior at the time and thus survived. During the next five years many came to follow his leadership as Communist peasant-oriented programs began to prove successful. By 1930 this group of self-sufficient, armed Communist revolutionaries had prompted Chiang to send armies four different times to wipe them out—each time unsuccessfully. His fifth effort in the fall of 1933, during which he fielded 400,000 troops, was more successful. The Communists, fearing encirclement, decided late in 1934 to break out of Hunan and Kiangsi and march north and west to Shensi Province. This move, which lasted until late December 1936, became known as the Long March.

Approximately 90,000 Communist troops set out with their families, local peasants who feared Nationalist reprisals, and all Communist leaders. Constantly harassed by units of the Nationalist army and fighting a series of pitched battles as they moved, these groups eventually marched 6000 miles to Yenan, where they established new headquarters. During the march, conditions were so bad that only 20,000 Communist troops and civilians—one of every five—survived.

Those who reached Yenan continued to foment revolution, although their activities were interrupted by the national cause of fighting Japanese invaders during World War II. After 1945 they defeated the Nationalist armies and eventually forced Chiang and fellow Nationalist leaders to flee the mainland. The leaders and molders of China—men like Mao Tse-tung and Chou En-lai— were revolutionaries in the 1920s, survived the Long March, and have effected a transformation of Chinese society since 1949.

munist or otherwise—who saw a new China built on the peasantry rather than on the urban working class. For the next decade, however, Chiang Kai-shek drove the Communists (or, as he called them, the bandits) deep into the recesses of rural China. In 1934, the survivors of the epic Long March had to cross eighteen mountain ranges and twenty-four rivers while fighting a running battle to escape Nationalist forces. By 1936, Mao and the Communists had retreated to the dry mountain interior of Yenan.

Communist Victory

The contest for dominion over China between the Communists in the interior and Nationalists on the coast was obscured for a time by the challenge of a new invader, the armies of Japan. Attracted by the important coal and iron resources of southern Manchuria, the Japanese invaded this region in 1931. While Chiang concentrated on the destruction of the Communists (and in a sense retained his focus on the main issue), Japan invaded China proper in 1937. Within a year, Japan conquered all of the lowland north, Nationalist armies lost 800,000 men, and Chiang Kai-shek retreated to Chungking in the mountain fastness of the Red Basin of Szechwan. The modest accomplishments of the Nationalists— 2000 miles of rail lines, 50,000 miles of road, and the growing industries of the port cities—fell into Japanese hands.

Immediately following the Japanese withdrawal from China at the end of World War II in 1945, the Communists and the Nationalists reengaged in the conflict that was to determine the future of modern China. Conditions then were as bad as they had been a century earlier. Death and starvation in the countryside seeped into the cities, and in Shanghai alone, 20,000 bodies were cleared from the streets each year. On the plains of eastern China, vast areas had been damaged by warring armies. Counting both soldiers and bandits, 5 million armed men had been living off the Chinese peasantry for two decades; the devastating taxation required to support these armies had resulted, to use the Chinese villagers' phrase, in "taking the fat off their fingers." The same peasantry, driven to desperation during the Taiping Rebellion a century earlier, was again ripe for revolt. It was this force the Chinese Communists hoped to harness. On the face of it, the Communists were at a disadvantage since they were outnumbered five to one in both manpower and materials. The National-

THE ECONOMY OF MISERY

. . . There were eleven of us children, eight brothers and three sisters. . . . Father was a tenant farmer. . . . Father died when I was eight, and then my eldest brother became head of the family. . . . [He] took the family and moved to the village of Hsiaotuwa, where he rented land. . . . We rented roughly twenty mu [less than 5 acres], for which we paid about 2000 jin [about 2000 pounds] of corn a year in rental. Besides this, there were various taxes: I cannot now remember them all in detail, but we paid tax every month, and once the rent and taxes had been paid, there wasn't much left, and in springtime we went hungry. . . .

What happened was that every year we had run out of corn and had had to borrow from the landlord, paying the loan back after harvest. The interest varied a bit from year to year, depending on what sort of harvest it had been. The lowest interest was when we borrowed 300 jin and repaid 390, the highest when we borrowed 300 and paid back 450. . . . We had to borrow money for clothes and tools. In the beginning, the interest on money was around three percent a month, but then it rose to five percent a month and finally it was up at ten percent a month. We could not always pay it, and our debts grew with interest being charged on the interest. . . .

It had been a hard time: 1928–9 was a period of famine. The 1928 harvest was bad and, in the spring of 1929, the slave dealers began coming to the villages of northern Shensi. They were out to buy children, and many were sold then. Children from northern Shensi were usually sold to Shansi and Hopeh. The boys went to childless families which wanted their name to continue, and the girls were sold as brides or to the towns. . . . Later that spring, people were dying of starvation.

The landowners were inhuman and cruel. They themselves had grain enough. They had big stores of grain. But they did not let those who had no land to pledge have any. They demanded security for a loan. They did not worry about people's distress. Yet, if Chang Ming-liang [the landlord] had sold his corn at normal prices, no one in our village would have starved to death. He had a big enough store. We thought he had, even then, during the famine, and later, in 1935, when we expropriated him during the revolution and examined his stores, we found a big hoard of grain dating back to before 1929. But he was a landowner.

ists had a monopoly of heavy equipment and transport and an unopposed air force. But in the countryside the Communists attracted firm popular support by opposing and where possible destroying gentry landowners and redistributing the land to peasant communes. This, and their appeal to an awakening national consciousness, caused Party rolls to swell to 1.2 million members by 1945. On this basis, they opposed the American-equipped 3-million-man army of the Nationalists.

In 1946, the illusion of Nationalist superiority dissipated as entire Nationalist regiments surrendered to the Communists. In 1948, Nationalist forces in Manchuria were surrounded and forced to surrender. In a battle of annihilation that had been raging for two months, central China changed hands on January 1, 1949, and a half-million Nationalist troops were killed or captured in the Huai River Valley. By the end of the year, Chiang Kai-shek fled from mainland China to Taiwan (Formosa), his military forces destroyed, and his last opportunity to lead the largest nation in the world gone. An unwanted refugee like Pu-yi before him, he left a China rent by civil war, corruption, starvation, disease, and inflation to lead a country from exile on Taiwan, an island 125 miles from the mainland protected by the guns of the "barbarian West." China had opted for the peasant from Hunan—the first and best example of a nation of the developing world pursuing modernization through a peasant revolution rather than an uprising of the middle class.

THE NEW CHINA

3

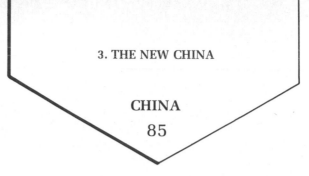

In 1949, the Communists set forth on a program to transform Chinese society, to reestablish the integrity of the Chinese state, and to provide some measure of security to the 550 million peasants of China. Mao's followers brought to this task a new social philosophy, the physical power to enforce it, and a disciplined (if small) Party of 5 million members. Communist goals were several: first, restructure the relationship between the Chinese people and the Chinese earth; second, build the industrial basis of a modern nation; and third, destroy the hold of the Confucian order on the Chinese mind. The object, in the end, would be to create a new society based on Communist principles as interpreted by Chinese leaders, specifically Mao Tse-tung.

The central problem, the paradox facing every aspiring nation of the developing world, was that farmers in the countryside had to provide the surplus needed for investment in the growth of industrialization and an advanced technology. In other words, the price of progress in China would have to fall where it had always fallen—on the backs of the peasants.

CHANGES ON THE GOOD EARTH

If economic development was to be achieved, the agricultural basis of Chinese society would have to be reorganized. An absolute increase in the production of rice and other foodstuffs was needed; more land would have to be brought into cultivation, more efficient techniques of cultivation employed, better protection afforded against the floods and droughts, and new transportation networks created to haul crops and processed foodstuffs to the urban centers where the power bases of an industrial China would emerge. In addition to increasing agricultural production, a more equitable distribution of the harvest among the peasants of China was necessary—the strong grip of the gentry class on rural production would have to be broken.

This goal of breaking the power of the gentry class was accomplished during the initial period of **land reform**• between 1949 and 1952; the Communists paid off a long-standing promise to the Chinese peasantry by redistributing agricultural land. Communist leaders classified landowners into four categories based on the amount of land they owned and whether they farmed it themselves. Large landlords (8 acres or more) and rich peasants (5 to 8 acres) who had collected taxes, lent money at high interest rates, and supported the Nationalists were brought to trial for "criminal activities" in thousands of Chinese villages. A million members of this class were killed by firing squads, lynch mobs, and in "reform through labor" camps. The Confucian gentry who had controlled the landscapes of rural China for 2500 years disappeared, and 120 million acres of land were redistributed among 350 million peasants.

Elimination of landlords and rich peasants led to problems: "land to the tiller" was not sufficient to change conditions in rural China. Redistribution of land left some peasants with agricultural land, others with draft animals, still more with tools but no land to farm. Partly to solve these problems and also to ensure political control over the countryside, the Communists started a program of **collectivization**• throughout village China. By 1954, 10 million mutual-aid teams were created in which groups of six to fifteen village households pooled their land, animals, and tools, sharing the harvest while retaining individual ownership of the means of production. As the paradoxes of individual ownership and collective gain became apparent, mutual-aid teams merged into larger agricultural producer cooperatives, in which individuals were paid on the basis of the amount of land and labor they contributed to the harvest. Finally, these cooperatives were reorganized into still larger collective farms, so that by 1957 some 740,000 of these units, averaging 168 households in size, accounted for 90 percent of China's rural population. All land was now commonly owned (even garden plots), all boundaries removed, and all workers paid on the basis of work-points and quota fulfillment.

The results of this social reorganization of Chinese agriculture were disappointing. Because of limited government investments in agriculture, afforestation projects, water conservation programs, and expansion of the **arable,**• the average annual increase in Chinese agricultural productivity was only 2.6 per-

In a landscape reminiscent of a scholar-poet's scroll painting of long ago, Chinese peasants work in a rice paddy. The season is late spring, when the densely packed seedlings must be transplanted and set out one by one in precise patterns in the flooded fields. Through all the hours of daylight, men, women, and children stand in mud, backs bent, patiently and deftly anchoring each plant in the soil. *Photo:* Marc Riboud/Magnum.

cent—barely enough to provide for the annual 2 percent growth in the Chinese population, certainly not enough to power any large-scale industrial expansion. Increasingly, the Chinese peasantry, without whom there could be no revolution, was proving an intractable problem. Given collectivized harvests, the peasants simply ate more; rigorous checks on consumption had to be instituted. Because the government was plunging all available resources into the growth of heavy industry, the economic relations between city and village became increasingly one-sided: harvests went to the city, little returned.

Further, many of the forestry projects and irrigation schemes were ill-conceived. In the province of Hupeh, for example, 82 percent of the newly constructed small reservoirs and ponds dried up in the drought of 1959. Similarly, half the 500,000 reservoirs in Kiangsu were useless. Deep wells sunk in marginal areas failed when variable climate made the wells vulnerable to both drought and flood. By 1957, the face of agricultural China had been transformed—spatially and socially—but this had not

solved the centuries-old problem of food shortage. The leaders of the new dynasty of the People's Republic were keenly aware of what starvation in the hinterland had meant to their predecessors.

A NEW INDUSTRIAL MAP
In the industrial sector, the results of a decade of Communist rule were much more encouraging. During the first five-year plan of the 1950s, China's industrial output (not counting handicrafts) rose by 240 percent, compared with a 25 percent expansion of agricultural production. The rapid expansion of industry was largely the result of direct imitation of development plans used earlier in the Soviet Union, in which 40 percent of the total budget was invested in primary industrial products like coal, steel, electric power, and oil; the agricultural sector received only 3 percent. Aided by Russian technicians and modest Soviet financial and technological investment, the Chinese Communists were intent on achieving the second of their goals, the construction of a modern industrial nation.

As in the West during the initial period of industrialization, coal, which represents 93 percent of energy sources in China, was important in the achievement of these aspirations. Within three years, the Communists had reached the Japanese war level of production for 1944 (60 million to 70 million tons) in the primary coal-producing region of Man-

This cartogram illustrates the pattern of land and animal ownership in a north Kiangsu community before the Communist assumption of power in 1949. It reflects the extremes of wealth and poverty in traditional agricultural society: Land was concentrated in the hands of a tiny number of landlords; water buffaloes belonged to rich and middle-class peasants; 90 percent of the population owned no land and, for all practical purposes, no water buffaloes. This concentration of the means of production in the hands of the rural gentry while the majority of peasants lived marginal, deprived lives provided fertile ground for Mao Tse-tung's peasant-based revolution.

	Families	Arable land	Buffaloes
Landlords			
Rich peasants			
Middle-class peasants			
Poor peasants and wage earners		= 10 Families = 10 Acres = 5 Buffaloes	

Adapted from: Keith M. Buchanan, *The Transformation of the Chinese Earth.* London: Bell, 1970, p. 119. By permission.

churia; by 1958, the government reported a total annual production of 270 million tons, third only behind the United States and the USSR. With high-quality coal reserves located at or near existing industrial sites, two-thirds of China's coal production is concentrated in the north and northeast, in the large strip mines at Fu-shun in southern Manchuria, in the *coke*• mines at Hao-kang, Shuang-ya-shan, and Chi-hsi in northern Manchuria, and in a broad arc sweeping across to the North China Plain from the Tang-shan fields near Peking to Cheng-chou in the south. Other coal-producing areas, from centrally located Hupeh Province and the Szechwan Basin westward to the Chinese borders of Inner Mongolia, enabled the Chinese to diversify and decentralize their industrial base—a politically desirable goal.

Recognizing that China's poverty was largely the product of an undiversified agricultural economy, Chinese leaders determined not only to intensify the growth of the coastal industrial complexes (three-quarters of China's industrial output), but also to introduce industry into the interior. The primary movement was toward heavy industry, especially machine building. The great steelworks at An-shan and Pen-chi in southern Manchuria remained the leading producers of steel, but centers of heavy industry were also developed in Tai-yuan based on the Shansi coal deposits, in Chungking to the south, in the tri-city hub of Wuhan, at Lan-chou to the northwest, and at Pao-tou north of the great bend of the Yellow River in Inner Mongolia. Shanghai retained its position of leadership in industrial production largely due to cheap electricity produced by inexpensive water-borne coal, but a new industrial map was emerging in China. Fully two-thirds of the major industrial projects launched during the first five-year plan (1953–1957) were located away from the coast.

As the first five-year plan progressed, it became clear that China had the resource base necessary for building a modern industrial state. Iron ore, although not available in either the quantity or quality of coal, was discovered and mined in Szechwan, Sinkiang, Inner Mongolia, and Hainan Island, supplementing production from the traditional mining centers of southern Manchuria. Important new discoveries of petroleum in Sinkiang, in Szechwan, and in the Tsaidam Basin led to the production of 3 million tons of oil from these western fields. More recently, a new field in northern Manchuria, Ta-ching, has become the major petroleum-producing region in China. Although not developed, the Yang-tze River has enormous waterpower potential—more than the total developed capacity in the United States—which could supplement and ultimately replace nonrenewable sources of energy.

To integrate these new factories and mines into the state economy, the network of roads and railroads in China was expanded. Between 1949 and 1958, 8000 miles of new track were added to the 16,200 miles the Communists inherited, and unknown numbers

This is the new China—factories operating at full capacity, workers' housing but a few steps away. This complex of new textile plants and apartments in the Peking area is one of many that have been constructed all over the country. In addition to a place to live, workers have access to all sorts of communal services, from day care centers for children of working mothers to food co-ops. *Photo:* Marc Riboud/Magnum.

of roads were constructed, repaired, and resurfaced. Over four-fifths of the new construction was in the less developed provinces of the west and northwest; the objectives of the new lines were both political and economic. Shanghai was connected to Canton, the Yangtze was bridged, and new lines were extended to the Straits of Taiwan and the borders of North Vietnam. The Communists were taking no chances on a Nationalist counterrevolution. In the west, the Lung-hai line was built from Peking to the steel plants of Pao-tou in Inner Mongolia and the oil fields of Urumchi in Sinkiang. A similar though less dramatic track was built northward through Ulan Bator, the capital of Outer Mongolia, to the Irkutsk Basin in Siberia, linking by rail the world's two largest Communist nations. As in agriculture and industry, the transportation network of Communist China was viewed through the prism of politics.

THE GREAT LEAP FORWARD
Despite the impressive industrial gains during the first decade of Communist rule, by 1957 a number of disturbing social and economic problems had appeared. In the cities, the growing estrangement of

intellectuals from the Party had led Mao to encourage free discussion and criticism ("Let a hundred flowers bloom"). But when open discussion became highly critical of the Communist party, or in other words the flowers became "poisonous weeds," numerous intellectuals were silenced and a return to "right thinking" was implemented. At the same time, the minority peoples of Outer China, particularly in Sinkiang, began to demand autonomy.

Of far greater significance, however, the glorious future that Party cadres had been promising agricultural cooperatives for several years was steadily retreating into the future. The policy of draining agriculture to support industry was reaping a harvest of peasant restlessness and resistance: rural food consumption continued to go up, productivity was declining. Agricultural surpluses were desperately needed by Communist planners to support continued industrial growth, to maintain the commercial activity funneled through Hong Kong, and to pay for the trade debts incurred by importing machinery in the early phases of industrialization.

Thus, when the level of China's food exports fell in 1957, it became clear that the gap between agricultural production and industrial aspirations would have to be resolved either by attracting financial and technical aid from the USSR or by changing internal economic strategy. When aid from the USSR was not forthcoming, the decision was made: China would not settle for a period of retrenchment and reconsolidation; the nation would advance by the disciplined labor of organized peasants and urbanites. In one Great Leap Forward China would overcome the central problem facing all developing nations: by sheer labor, regimented manpower would be converted into working capital.

The Great Leap Forward of 1958 demanded extraordinary feats of human labor from the Chinese people so that the industrial growth of China might continue unchecked. The Chinese peasantry would produce both bread and steel, a policy the Chinese called Walking on Two Legs. Millions of peasants labored by day tilling the fields and were forced to work in factories by night, the working day being extended to fourteen or sixteen hours. Cottage-style steel furnaces and forges were built in village China; within a matter of months approximately 600,000 of these backyard furnaces dotted the landscape. Production goals were revised upward almost monthly. Grain production, 185 million tons in 1957, was reported to have reached 375 million tons in 1958; steel production appeared to have more than doubled from 5.3 to 11 million tons. On paper, the Great Leap Forward had succeeded.

Simultaneously, one of the most revolutionary social changes of the century was taking place. The spatial basis of rural Chinese society and economy was completely reorganized: the 740,000 agricultural producers cooperatives were amalgamated into some 24,000 people's communes. The **communes** roughly equated with an ancient administrative subdivision, the county or *hsien*, and averaged 20,000 people on about 10,000 acres of land. People were housed in communal dormitories and mess halls; communal nurseries freed women for work in the fields, which continued, during this period, around the clock. In some villages, the walls of private dwellings were removed to create communal living quarters. Kitchen utensils, door hinges, and other bits of metal from these reconstructions fed village furnaces to increase the steel production of China. Of particular importance, in the communal dining halls food consumption was carefully supervised. A single ounce of grain per person per day in China, if saved, could amount to a surplus of 7 million tons of food a year.

Peking planners ordered great labor battalions to embark on large-scale irrigation and construction projects. The distance between crop rows was reduced on the theory that more rows of grain in a given space would produce more grain. Deep plowing was fostered by using winches to pull plows by cables across the rice fields. A campaign to kill sparrows and weaverbirds was launched because these birds ate newly sown seed; hundreds of men, women, and children danced and yelled to keep the birds in the air until they fell to the ground exhausted and were killed. In the final reckoning, a sparrow kill of 1 billion birds was claimed. On a larger scale, labor battalions constructed dams and irrigation projects, and new deep wells brought mar-

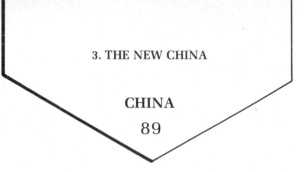

ginal land under irrigation. A nationwide drive for afforestation under the slogan "Make China Green" led to the planting of nearly 100 million acres to trees. As during the previous five years, the vast majority of capital investment—almost 65 percent—went into heavy industry; the peasants were increasing agricultural production with their bare hands, their traditional tools, and what had once been their leisure time.

The results of the Great Leap Forward in food grain and steel production are not known. The inflated announcement of 375 million tons of food grains in 1958 was eventually revised downward to 250 million tons, and some experts believe the actual harvest was 190 million tons, only 5 million tons greater than the 1957 harvest. In steel, the figure of 11 million tons was adjusted to 8 million tons, and it was admitted that 3 million tons produced in backyard furnaces was so poor in quality as to be useless. Whatever the truth, at the end of the effort, the work force of China was exhausted; illness and absenteeism were spreading.

Certain aspects of the experiment clearly failed: deep plowing where topsoil was thin turned up layers of infertile soil; faulty irrigation practices induced waterlogging of soils and increased salinity; the digging of deep wells in dry regions lowered water tables; and the massacre of the sparrows encouraged local insect population explosions. Above all, peasant resistance to the commune, which Mao had called "the most appropriate organizational form in China for accelerating socialist construction and the transition to Communism," was increasing.

At this critical juncture, environmental disaster hit China. Between 1959 and 1962, the three years following the Great Leap Forward, the specter of famine shadowed the Chinese landscape, and fear of hunger was the primary preoccupation of planner and peasant alike. Drought covered the North China Plain, and insect damage to crops was extremely high. In the tropical south, heavy floods and typhoons destroyed thousands of acres of cropland, and in 1960 a rare drought occurred in this normally humid region. The impact of these calamities on grain production was devastating. In 1959, the total grain crop was 20 million to 30 million tons below the previous year's harvest. The figures for 1960 were so low that no official announcements were made. Experts believe the total grain crop amounted to only 160 million tons, a harvest that could have

been considered exceptional in 1952, but that was totally inadequate eight years later with a Chinese population increase of some 50 million people, the equivalent of an entire Great Britain. To avert mass starvation, the Chinese were forced to buy large quantities of grain from Canada, Australia, and Burma.

The Great Leap Forward also led to changes in the communal organization of rural China, although the Communist commitment to the commune as the basic form of spatial and social organization remained firm. Centralization in the communes was reduced by making the production brigade, roughly equivalent in size to the old agricultural producer cooperative, the basic accounting unit of agricultural production. These brigades were subdivided into still smaller production teams, which corresponded reasonably well with the single Chinese village. The 550 million peasants of China were now allowed to maintain garden plots that covered 5 to 7 percent of the total cultivated area, and were even allowed to sell produce in free markets and to hold village fairs.

A NEW SOCIALIST PEOPLE

The social order of China was changing as drastically as the physical landscape. The Communist vision broke the long cyclical wave of Chinese history; the goals of communalization were to create a new social and moral order. Although this change is less measurable than are acres of cropland or tons of grain, it may be that the most fundamental change in the geography of China has been forged in the minds of its people.

Communist theory, which advocates self-determination for oppressed national minorities, has often come into conflict with the population mosaic of China and the traditional Chinese insistence on the superiority of the Han Chinese. Although the Han form the vast majority of the Chinese population, the 1953 national census counted 52 non-Han ethnic groups, including such diverse peoples as Tibetans, Mongols, Koreans, Thais, Vietnamese, Russians, and Muslim Turkic nomadic tribes: the Kazakh, Kirghiz, and Uzbek. Government policy has wavered between praise for the racial, cultural, and linguistic diversity of China and rigorous enforcement of the assimilation of minorities into common cultural patterns and national goals of the People's Republic.

Modernization of the country has required sending trained, politically reliable cadres of Han Chi-

In the new China, education is part of every moment of every day. In addition to classes and meetings, wall posters and billboards exhort each and every person to do his or her best to meet current national goals, whether they be production quotas or the extermination of disease. This billboard speaks for itself: Britain, once a power in China, is no longer in the race. *Photo:* Henri Cartier-Bresson/Magnum.

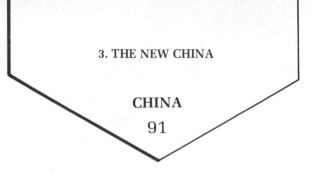

nese to direct programs of medical, educational, economic, and political integration. Conflict has developed because minority values are often at variance with those of the Han; when minority groups found themselves following and the Han leading; and when the traditional Han pride and scorn for other—"inferior"—peoples proved stronger than the ideology of brotherhood. The Cultural Revolution of the 1960s set out to eradicate the "four olds"—religious beliefs, traditional culture, customs, and habits—all of which are the basis of differences between minority peoples and the Han Chinese. Although cultural differences among different Chinese ethnic groups are still strong, it is unlikely that minorities will long remain distinct from the Han.

Education was the principal instrument available to create this new society; learning was considered one of the four collectivizations of Communist China, the other three being dining, living quarters, and labor. On the lowest level, adult education centers were established in the communes, in factories, and in the streets of the cities and villages of China. By 1958, 40 million people were attending basic classes, and another 31 million were studying part-time. The process was facilitated by the introduction of simplified Chinese characters and a phonetic romanized script. Primary school enrollments increased from 24 million in 1949 to 90 million a decade later; secondary schools increased proportionately, and some 810,000 students were enrolled in institutes of higher education. By 1960, over 90 percent of the school-age children of China were receiving education in one form or another. China, after a decade of Communist rule, had 50 percent more scientists than India.

The costs of this expansion of the Chinese educational system were borne by an application of the "Walking on Two Legs" policy. Students at universities and technical schools set up small factories; secondary and elementary school pupils built small dikes, cleared irrigation channels, and worked in the fields. Educational units became production units that were ideally self-supporting. This integration of study and practice in work was designed to avoid the ancient Confucian separation between mental and manual labor. The Chinese factory, like the Chinese commune, became in the words of Barry Richman (*Harvard Business Review,* January–February 1967) "a place where illiterate workers learn to read and write, and where employees can and do improve

One important goal of the Chinese Communist leadership is to prevent the formation of an intellectual elite whose lives, attitudes, and interests would be far removed from those of the mass of the people. Manual labor in the countryside has therefore been made mandatory for everyone. These student volunteers are helping to build a new community sewage system at Lan-chou in Kansu Province. *Photo:* Henri Cartier-Bresson/Magnum.

their work skills and develop new ones through education and training. . . . It is also a place from which workers go out in the fields and help the peasants with their harvesting." Emphasis was placed on technical and administrative training to fill the manpower needs of expanding industries. The curriculum, however, was political as well as technical, because the goal was not simply to produce engineers and chemists, but to create new socialist people.

Paralleling the drive for education, the Communists attempted to raise health levels in rural China through the elimination of the "five plagues and the four pests." As late as the 1930s, two-thirds of the people of South China were afflicted with malaria; a little-known disease called kala-azar, which affects the functions of the liver and spleen, was endemic to the North China Plain. In addition, typhus and plague, the diseases of poverty, were widespread throughout China. Some 10 million people had schistosomiasis, and from 50 million to 100 million suffered from hookworm, both parasite infestations. To cope with the five plagues—malaria, schistosomiasis, kala-azar, filariasis (another parasitic disease), and hookworm—Communist planners instituted campaigns of mass inoculation, improved sanitation, and established rural infirmaries. The four pests—flies, mosquitos, rats, and sparrows—

The new society of Communist China poses difficulties and value conflicts to the older generations of Chinese, particularly in relation to the new attitudes toward equality between the sexes and to marriage and family affairs. The following interviews in a Shensi village in the fall of 1962 discuss these problems. The speaker is Li Kuei-ying, a thirty-year-old woman active in implementing the policies of the new society in her village.

. . . [S]ome of the older people do not believe in marriage of free will. "How can a girl run off with the first chap she sees?" the older women ask. We have to talk to them and make propaganda for the new marriage. We have to remind them of how they felt when they were young and how they were made to suffer under the old system of marriage. It isn't so often it ever comes to a real conflict, but we did have a case in 1960.

That was when Tuan Fu-yin's eighteen-year-old daughter, Tuan Ai-chen, fell in love with a boy from Seven-Mile Village. But her parents refused to let her marry. They said that the boy was poor and that they wanted to marry her to somebody better off. One evening Tuan Ai-chen came to me and wept and complained. I went with her to her cave and talked with her parents. I said to them: "You have no right to prevent your daughter from marrying, you know that, don't you? Purchase marriage is not allowed in the new society. It is a crime to sell your daughter these days. Before, you could sell your daughter like a cow, but you can't do that any longer." I told them about the things that used to happen in the old days, about girls drowning themselves in wells, of girls hanging themselves and that sort of thing, about all the unhappiness purchase marriage caused. At first, Tuan Fu-yin tried to stand up to me. He said: "I had to pay dearly for my wife. Now I have been giving this girl food and clothes, I have brought her up and she just goes off. It isn't right. I just lose and lose all the time. I must get back something of all the money I have laid out on her. If she can't fall in love with a man who can pay back what she's cost, then it isn't right for her to marry."

I talked a long time with them that evening, and in the end I said: "You don't live badly in the new society. If you ever have difficulties, your daughter and son-in-law will help you. They are not rich, but they won't refuse to help you." Then they replied: "We must think about it." The next time I went there, only the girl's mother was at home. She had thought about it and she now told me her own story. . . . She said: "I was sold to Tuan Fu-yin when I was a little girl. I was sold in the same way you sell a goat. But my parents got a lot for me. Tuan's father had to take out a loan. That made them nasty to me. I was forced to work hard so as to make the loan worth while. They were all nagging at me. I can remember how much

I used to cry. Now that I think of that, I don't want my daughter to marry someone she can't like." Then she wept. Tuan Fu-yin didn't say anything more. But such cases are rare. It is the only one I remember. Tuan Fu-yin's sons had been allowed to marry in the new way, of course, because that meant that he did not need to pay anything for his daughters-in-law.

Source: Quoted from Jan Myrdal, *Report from a Chinese Village,* trans. Maurice Michael. New York: Pantheon; London: William Heinemann, Ltd., 1965, excerpts from pp. 224–225. Copyright © 1965 by William Heinemann, Ltd. Reprinted by permission of Pantheon Books, a division of Random House, Inc., and William Heinemann, Ltd.

---

were likewise the targets of extermination campaigns.

Most of these accomplishments were the product of an experiment in delivering health care to China's 550 million peasants—the "barefoot doctors." Upon completion of a year's training in the rudiments of both Western and traditional Chinese medicine, each barefoot doctor is sent out to an agricultural commune to labor with its members and provide health care as needed. Periodically, they return to a training center for refresher courses.

Both in education and in health, the Communist government tried to reduce the gap between conditions of life in the city and in the village, to prevent the emergence of an urban elite ruling in comfort over a starving peasantry. To a greater degree than most developing countries, China has succeeded. One effect of policies in education, health, and economic diversification has been to slow the rate of urbanization in China, an ancillary goal of the Cultural Revolution of 1967. In 1953 only 18.5 percent of China's population, or about 130 million people, were urban dwellers; only nine cities—Shanghai (6.2 million), Peking, Tientsin, Shen-yang (Mukden) (more than 2 million), Chungking, Canton, Wuhan, Harbin, and Nanking—had populations of more than a million. Although the number of million-person cities had risen to seventeen by 1960, the greatest increase in urban dwellers occurred in small towns of 50,000 or less. This broader problem of population growth may, in the end, pose an endless dilemma for the rulers and planners of China.

CHINA

THE INDUSTRIAL BASE

ENERGY AND MINERAL RESOURCES MAP

In 1953, Communist China launched an ambitious five-year plan of economic development. Fashioned after the Soviet example, the first plan was designed to create an industrial base for a new China. The emphasis was on capital rather than consumer goods, and on heavy industry rather than agriculture. Soviet industrial equipment and technical personnel provided the machines and know-how necessary to initiate the program; they were paid for by exports of Chinese agricultural goods, textiles, and minerals like tungsten, tin, antimony, and mercury. The impact of this selective investment in the industrial sector was dramatic: 1957 industrial output rose 240 percent over 1949 and handicraft production rose 83 percent; but agricultural production rose only 25 percent. These figures, however, were deceptive, because the underdeveloped nature of the Chinese industrial economy following the devastations of World War II made even relatively modest gains appear substantial.

Apparently dissatisfied with this rate of industrial growth, Chinese leaders started the Great Leap Forward in 1958. Heavy industry continued to be stressed, and a large number of rural industrial projects like backyard furnaces were begun. Reliance on Soviet technical assistance continued to be intense: over 70 percent of China's foreign trade was with the Soviet Union and Soviet-block nations, and 40 percent of her imports were heavy industrial equipment. But as the Great Leap Forward collapsed, the Russians withdrew their assistance from China, industrial growth was disrupted, and a statistical blackout was imposed on information regarding Chinese economic development.

In the economic crisis of 1960–1962 that followed, Chinese leaders abandoned the Soviet model of economic development with its emphasis on heavy industry in favor of a more moderate approach to economic growth called "Walking on Two Legs." This program reoriented industrial priorities toward the production of chemical fertilizers, farm machinery, and agricultural industries in an effort to increase food production by strengthening the rural sector. Imports of chemical fertilizer and agricultural goods supplemented industrial machinery, and China's foreign trade shifted to Japan and Western Europe. Although this balanced program of economic development was in turn disrupted by the Cultural Revolution of 1967–1968, it apparently remains the basis of Chinese economic planning in the 1970s. The extent to which this adjustment has influenced the growth of industry in China is not known.

Overall, the industrial development of Communist China during the last quarter-century has been impressive. Factories and mines still produce only one quarter of the *gross national product*• of the country, but reserves of most industrial raw materials appear large enough to support manufacturing complexes on a level comparable with those of the United States and the USSR. Although most sophisticated industrial equipment must still be imported, China's cadres of skilled managers, engineers, and scientists are growing, and few physical barriers to industrial growth appear to exist.

ENERGY SOURCES

Coal provides over 90 percent of the energy produced in China; it is used for cooking and home heating as well as for industry and transport. With proved coal resources of some 50 billion tons, China ranks third behind the United States and Russia and is gradually becoming a significant exporter of coal to South and Southeast Asia. Two-thirds of China's coal is located in the northeastern quadrant of the country, providing the energy base for the industrial complexes of North China and Manchuria. Recent exploration, however, has uncovered commercial *bituminous*• deposits throughout southern and western China, so that coal is important in determining the new spatial organization of Chinese industry. Coal has fueled the new iron and steel mills at Wuhan on the Yangtze and Pao-tou on the upper Yellow River, creating industrial employment in hitherto undeveloped areas of the Chinese interior.

Petroleum plays only a minor role in the Chinese energy economy at this time, but discoveries of major fields at Ta-ching in northern Manchuria and Sheng-li on the lower Yellow River have made China self-sufficient in petroleum products, eliminating her dependence on Soviet oil imports. Whereas older oil fields in Sinkiang and the Tsaidam Basin were located at great distances from centers of consumption, these new fields in densely populated North China now account for half of China's annual production of more than 10 million metric tons. Although refining capacity has in-

Oil and natural gas fields

Oil refineries

Hydroelectric plants

0   200   400 miles

■ Aluminum	△ Copper	□ Manganese
● Antimony	▲ Iron	⬡ Molybdenum
⬠ Coal	■ Lead and zinc	⬡ Tungsten

ENERGY, MINERALS, METALS

creased significantly in China, it has simply kept pace with crude oil production and appears to be the major factor limiting the expansion of petroleum production in the future.

Hydroelectric power is also a potential major source of energy in modern China, now producing one-fifth of the country's electric power. Enormous hydroelectric potential exists in China, particularly in the coal-poor south and southwest, and it is expected that hydroelectric resources, only 1 percent of which have been harnessed, will contribute more substantially to the economic growth of Communist China in the future.

MINERALS AND METALS

Communist China is well endowed with most minerals and metals, and the magnitude and quality of reserves compare favorably with those of the United States and the Soviet Union. Ferrous and ferroalloy minerals are sufficient to support a major iron and steel industry. Iron ore deposits are widespread, though all major mining areas now are located north of the Yangtze at An-shan in southern Manchuria, at Kalgan northwest of Peking, at Pai-yun-o-po near Pao-tou, and at Ta-yeh in Hupeh Province and Ma-an-shan near Nanking. Ferroalloys are also plentiful, although China is deficient in steel-hardening metals like chrome, nickel, and cobalt. China has the world's largest reserves of tungsten in the Nan Ling Mountains, and produces surpluses of molybdenum and manganese from mines in southern Manchuria. Other export minerals—antimony, mercury, tin, lead, and zinc—are produced in the rough mountain country of south-central China.

The regional distribution of mining activity in China still reflects the coastal development of mineral resources by foreign *concessionaires*• in the early years of the twentieth century. But since the vast terrain of western China is only now being explored geologically by the Communist Chinese and transport facilities to the interior are recent creations, sizable future discoveries of important energy and mineral resources can probably be anticipated.

PATTERNS OF INDUSTRIAL DEVELOPMENT

When the Communist Chinese assumed control of the mainland in 1949, an estimated 70 percent of China's industrial production, 85 percent of steel production, and 90 percent of machine tool industries were located in coastal provinces. To lessen this coastal concentration, economic planners attempted to create a new industrial map of China by initiating major new industrial projects in the interior regions. Fully two-thirds of industry started under the first five-year plan was located inland; this caused interior cities like Pao-tou, Tai-yuan, Wuhan, Hsi-an, and Chengtu to expand greatly in size and population. Despite this extraordinary effort to diversify the economy of the less developed regions of the country, the coast remains the most industrialized region in China because of the historical development of centers of manufacturing, the dense transportation network and raw material availability, and the heavy population concentration in lowland China.

Of the six economic coordination regions officially designated in China, the Northeast, the East, and the North—the coastal regions—rank highest in terms of industrial production. The Northeast, which comprises most of former Manchuria, has China's largest industrial concentration. Heavy industry is found in the south of this region, in cities like An-shan, Shen-yang (Mukden), Pen-chi, Fu-shun, and Lu-ta (Dairen). New heavy industrial concentrations have been built in the north at Kirin and Harbin. The Northeast is China's largest producer of iron and steel, electric power, petroleum, machinery, gold, and timber. East China, which includes the entire coastal zone from the mouth of the Yellow River southward to the northern boundary of Kwangtung, Canton's province, is the second leading industrial region of China. Although the smallest in area, East China includes one-third of the mainland population and is the leading producer of textiles and chemicals. The most important industrial center, China's largest city, is Shanghai. The third-ranking industrial region, North China, is located between the first two, and its industrial area is centered in a triangle extending between the cities of Peking, Tang-shan, and Tientsin. Though North China is the largest coal-producing region and an important producer of steel, most industry there is of recent origin.

The three remaining economic coordination regions in China—the Central South, the Southwest, and the Northwest—play a much less important role in the industrial economy. In the Central South, Canton is a center of light industry, particularly sugar processing, paper production, and silk textiles. The only centers of heavy industry located in this region are in the middle Yangtze Valley at Wuhan and Hsiang-tan and at Lo-yang in northern Honan. In the isolated and mountainous provinces of the Southwest, some industrial diversification has begun, but only mining, mainly of tin, copper, and lead, is of national importance. In the Northwest, the largest, least populated, and least industrialized region of China, the only major industrial centers, apart from petroleum production, are located in the east at Hsi-an and Lan-chou.

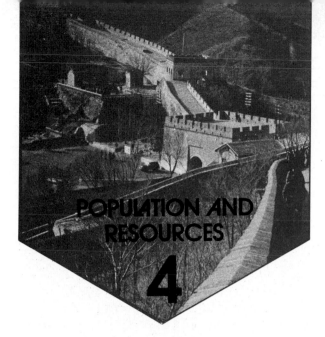

POPULATION AND RESOURCES

4

One-fifth to one-fourth of humanity, between 750 million and 900 million people, live in the People's Republic of China. Since no official population data have been announced in over a decade, estimates depend on projections applied to the 1953 census, which recorded a population of 583 million. Confusion on this issue exists even in China. In November 1971, the grain department believed that the population of China was 800 million; the ministry of commerce, 830 million, and the planning department, 750 million. Whatever the exact figure, the Chinese population has a seemingly boundless momentum; the agricultural base, however, is finite and stable.

FOOD PRODUCTION

Of the 11 percent of China which is under cultivation, only about 40 percent, mostly in the southeast, is double-cropped. This means that the sown area of China is roughly equal to that of the United States, but owing to the large Chinese population, only about 0.5 acre of cultivated land is available per person. In addition, the total population of China is increasing at a rate of 20 million people a year; in other words, it will increase at a rate equivalent to the entire American population every decade. By conservative estimates, China will have 1 billion people by 1980.

The primary response to the problem of numbers has been to increase the productivity of agriculture. In 1958, enormous amounts of energy were devoted to expanding the agricultural acreage in China by bringing millions of acres of marginal land under cultivation in Manchuria, Sinkiang, and the other subhumid fringes of Agricultural China. A year later this policy was abandoned in favor of intensified cultivation in the traditional croplands of eastern China. In many ways, the progress achieved since 1950 is remarkable. Mechanization, new varieties of seed, more efficient irrigation practices, and a disciplined, totalitarian reorganization of rural Chinese society have effected an increase in individual productivity sufficient to put China beyond the threshold of vulnerability to famine.

Chinese farms have yielded higher harvests due to applications of scientific knowledge, but the environmental and technological parameters of Chinese agriculture have remained remarkably stable. Population is distributed across the landscapes of the Middle Kingdom now as in the past; rising density levels have been repeatedly sustained. The stable agrarian living space today looms as the environmental confine that may thwart the goals of a planned Chinese state.

POPULATION POLICY

Producing a son in traditional Chinese society was not simply a device to ensure a comfortable old age, it was an act of moral responsibility, part of one's duty to honor and memorialize one's ancestors. Because the infant mortality rate in rural China was high, a peasant family strove to have at least three sons to ensure the survival of one. Given the laws of sexual probability, families of six or more children were the rule. The effects of this high birth rate were mitigated by malnutrition, disease, late marriage, and female infanticide, which was so widely practiced that as late as 1943 the Nationalist government of Chiang Kai-shek was prohibiting the drowning of girl infants. But large families remained a blessing in rural China, as in most agricultural societies. As a result, the birth rate was high; the best estimates suggest a rate of 40 to 45 births per 1000 population. In the 600 years for which estimates are available, the population of China grew ten times, the amount of cultivated land increased four times, and grain yields doubled. In spite of the clear implications of these reasonably well-known statistics, the Communist government of Mao Tse-tung was curiously ambivalent on the population issue.

When they assumed power in 1949, Communist propagandists asserted that China could support ten times her current population. Birth control was denounced, and people were considered to be "the most precious of all categories of capital." From the Marxist viewpoint, human misery was not produced by overcrowding, but by a social order defined by the nature of capitalism. But the results of the 1953 census changed planners' minds: 100 million extra Chinese turned up in the figures. Thereafter, abortion and contraception were viewed with greater leniency, and birth control was justified as desirable for the health and well-being of mothers and children. A firm distinction was maintained in official statements between "moderating the birth rate" and "restricting population growth." Not that it mattered a great deal, since even if the peasants rapidly abandoned their preference for large families, there were only enough contraceptive devices in China in 1958 to meet the needs of about 2 percent of the population. As a result, efforts to reduce the birth rate in the 1950s probably had no effect in rural China and only limited success in the cities.

The optimism of the Great Leap Forward of 1958 led to a reversal of government policy. The implausible argument that there was a labor shortage in China, that "a man's hands can produce more than his mouth can eat," was again disseminated. Disastrous food shortages and nationwide hunger over the next two years, however, led to a sustained program of birth control in the 1960s aimed at lowering the birth rate.

The approach was strangely indirect. Although marriage laws in Communist China allow a man to wed at twenty and a woman at eighteen, it was argued that early marriage was deleterious to work, study, and even health (through excessive sexual activity) and that the most appropriate age of marriage was twenty-three to twenty-seven for a woman and between twenty-five and twenty-nine for a man.

Premarital sex was considered totally reprehensible. These values took hold with the young, who make up a fertile two-thirds of the population of China.

To be effective, however, a variety of birth-control devices had to be introduced into the countryside. Abortion clinics were established; sterilization operations were made more readily available. More to the point, the thousands of peasants who were given rudimentary medical training, the barefoot doctors, were also made bearers of China's birth-control pills. Although it is difficult to determine which of these forces was most effective in lowering the birth rate in Communist China, by the end of the second decade of Communist rule the birth rate had dropped to about 32 per 1000 population.

During this same period, however, the death rate dropped from a 1949 rate of about 31 to 32 per 1000 to a current estimate of 17 per 1000. If these figures are close to reality, it means that the Chinese economy will have to absorb new citizens at a rate of 2.6 percent each year indefinitely—in other words, create employment and provide sustenance for 20 million or more new people each year. If China fails to accomplish this, the communes of the new society will communalize only hunger, and even harsher measures will be required to maintain order and social commitment in the world's largest society. It should be remembered, however, that of all nations of the developing world, China has succeeded in feeding her people while building industry with little foreign assistance; elsewhere, a quarter of the world borders on starvation.

BIBLIOGRAPHY

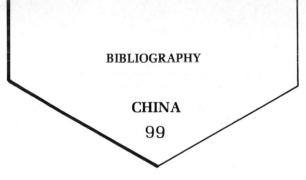

GENERAL

Clubb, O. E. *Twentieth Century China.* New York: Columbia University Press, 1964. For basic historical background.

Fessler, Loren. *China.* New York: Time-Life, 1963. Probably the best single brief introduction to China, except for the modern period.

Robottom, John. *Twentieth-Century China.* New York: Putnam, 1971. A well-written, well-illustrated introduction to China.

[1] TRADITIONAL CHINA

Chang, Sen-dou. "Some Aspects of the Urban Geography of the Chinese Hsien Capital," *Annals, Association of American Geographers,* Vol. 51 (1961), pp. 23–45. A study of the location and morphology of *hsien* capitals in China after the Han expansion.

Chang, Sen-dou. "The Historical Trend of Chinese Urbanization," *Annals, Association of American Geographers,* Vol. 53 (1963), pp. 109–143. A survey of urban growth in China based on local gazetteers.

Skinner, G. William. "Marketing and Social Structure in Rural China," *Journal of Asian Studies,* Vol. 24 (1964–65), pp. 3–43, 195–228, 363–399. An imaginative and detailed study of the spatial organization of rural China both before and after the Communist rise to power.

Skinner, G. William. "The City in Chinese Society." Unpublished manuscript prepared for the Conference on Urban Society in Traditional China, Wentworth, New Hampshire, August 31–September 6, 1968.

Weber, Max. *The Religion of China.* Glencoe, Ill.: Free Press, 1951. A classic analysis of society, economy, and religion in traditional China.

Wright, Arthur F. (ed.). *The Confucian Persuasion.* Stanford: Stanford University Press, 1960.

Wright, Arthur F., and David S. Nivson. *Confucianism in Action.* Stanford: Stanford University Press, 1959.

Wright, Arthur F., and Denis Twitchell. *Confucian Personalities.* Stanford: Stanford University Press, 1962. These three books by Wright and his colleagues constitute detailed studies of the role of Confucian thought in Chinese history and society.

[2] A NEW ORDER

Perkins, Dwight H. *Agricultural Development in China, 1368–1968.* Chicago: Aldine, 1969. The growth and development of the Chinese agricultural economy from Ming to modern times.

Whitney, Joseph B. R. *China: Area, Administration, and Nation Building.* Research Paper No. 123. Chicago: University of Chicago, Department of Geography, 1970. A detailed analytical study of the administrative geography of China, stressing the ways in which political power has been expressed in areal terms for two millennia.

[3] THE NEW CHINA

Buchanan, Keith. *The Transformation of the Chinese Earth.* London: Bell, 1970. An examination of the historical and modern parameters of China's economic geography.

Murphey, Rhoads. "Man and Nature in China," *Modern Asian Studies,* Vol. 1 (1967), pp. 313–333. An essay on the changing Chinese perception of environment before and after the Communist transformation.

Myrdal, Jan. *Report from a Chinese Village.* New York: Pantheon Books, 1965. A glimpse of village life in Communist China in the words of the villagers themselves.

[4] POPULATION AND RESOURCES

Ho, Ping-ti. *Studies in the Population of China, 1368–1953.* Cambridge, Mass.: Harvard University Press, 1959. A comprehensive survey of population trends in China from the Ming period to the Communist census.

Orleans, Leo A. *Every Fifth Child: The Population of China.* Stanford: Stanford University Press, 1972. The best and most up-to-date analysis of the population of China by a demographer.

Shabad, Theodore. *China's Changing Map: National and Regional Development, 1949–1971.* New York: Praeger, 1972. A detailed regional treatment of modern China, valuable as a reference.

In 1906, Mohandas K. Gandhi, a young Indian civil rights lawyer, took what he later called the most important vow of his life: a vow of chastity. Deeply rooted in Hindu tradition, this ascetic act marked the beginning of a lifetime of passive resistance to British rule. Gandhi's personal struggle against British colonialism inspired the birth of an independent India and made Gandhi, later called a *mahatma*, "great soul," the only saint to lead a traditional people to nationhood in the twentieth century. On August 15, 1947, after two centuries of rule in India, the British hauled down the Union Jack and went home. On that day, when the prime political goal of Gandhi's life became a reality, he was in Calcutta.

What had brought Gandhi to Calcutta was fierce communal rioting between Hindus and Muslims. Exactly a year before, 6000 people had died in riots in that city. With the approach of independence, the tide of violence between Hindus and Muslims had been rising. For a century, the British had contained separatist tendencies among Indian religious, cultural, and racial groups, achieving for the first time in history the ancient Indian ideal of a single nation stretching from the mountain banks of the Himalayas in the north to the sacred tip of Cape Comorin in the south. Now this unity was threatened. The Muslim minority in India, fearing Hindu revivalism, had demanded and formed a separate Muslim nation—Pakistan—from splinters of the northwestern and northeastern sections of the subcontinent. Gandhi alone had opposed this division, what he called this "vivisection of India," but he had failed. Now he came to Calcutta to call for peace between the two new nations about to be born.

There, Gandhi, the Hindu holy man and pacifist leader, met with two men to discuss ways of halting the bloodshed: H. S. Suhrawardy, the chief minister

Photo: Wide World.

of Bengal and a ruthless Muslim political boss, and Sir Frederick Burrows, the retiring British governor. In a dramatic plan of nonviolent action, Gandhi decided to take up residence with Suhrawardy in a Calcutta slum in an effort to change the hearts of the people in the very district where tensions were highest, and to stanch the flow of blood. The "miracle of Calcutta" flowered as the population stopped fighting and renounced bloodshed. Some 75,000 of their number marched to the crowded *shantytown* to observe a day of fasting and reconciliation with Gandhi and Suhrawardy. Five months later Gandhi was dead, assassinated at a Delhi prayer meeting, Suhrawardy had returned to a life of obscurity, and Burrows was writing his memoirs in England.

Though none of these men personally participated in the great issues facing independent India, they symbolize the three great cultural forces that until then had shaped life on the subcontinent: Hinduism, Islam, and British colonialism. The issues—basic food production, the planned industrialization of the subcontinent, internal political alignments, and above all, population policies—were left to the engineers, planners, and politicians of modern India, whose struggle to form a self-sustaining national state from disparate peoples is the central theme of this section.

This theme is pursued in four parts: "Traditional India" describes the enduring role of Hinduism, the caste system, and the village as preconditions to change; then the material on "The British in India" outlines India's metamorphosis into a society of burgeoning population, urbanized but not industrialized; "Development in an Asian Democracy" shows how the problems of population growth and the transformation of an agrarian society into an industrial society are attacked by state planners; and "The Statistics of Starvation" sets forth the current food crisis in India.

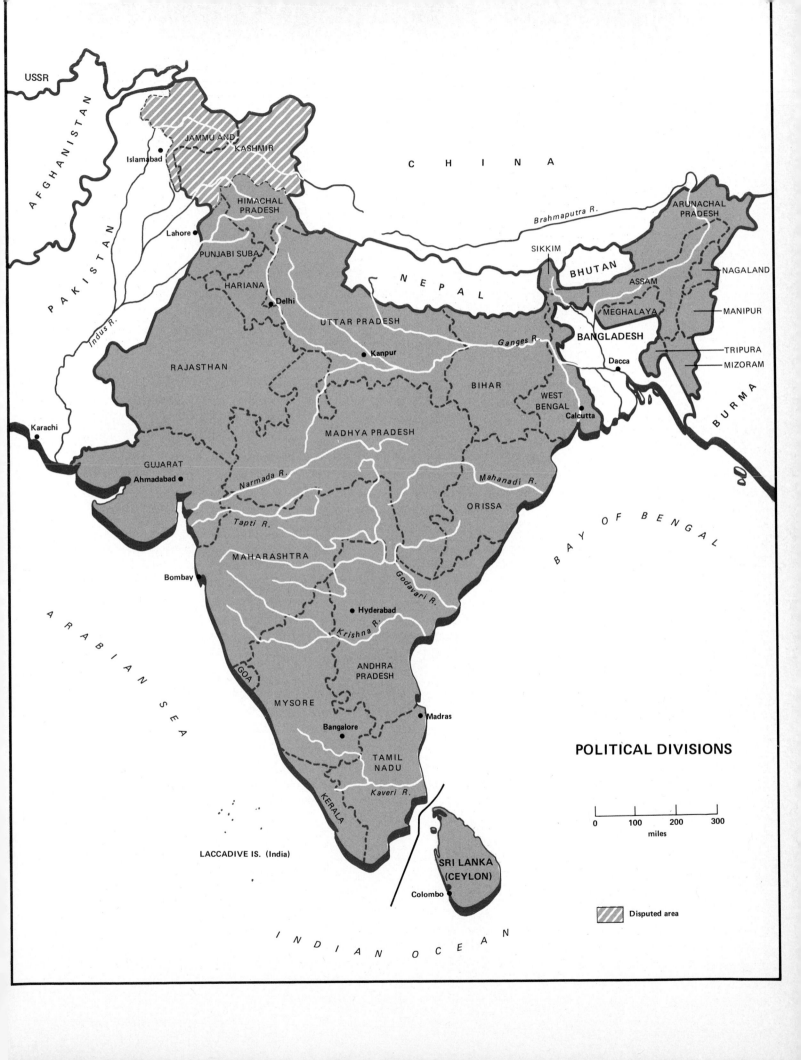

USSR

AFGHANISTAN

PAKISTAN

Islamabad

Lahore

Karachi

JAMMU AND KASHMIR

CHINA

HIMACHAL PRADESH

PUNJABI SUBA

HARIANA

Delhi

RAJASTHAN

UTTAR PRADESH

Kanpur

Indus R.

NEPAL

Brahmaputra R.

SIKKIM

BHUTAN

ARUNACHAL PRADESH

ASSAM

MEGHALAYA

BANGLADESH

Dacca

NAGALAND

MANIPUR

TRIPURA

MIZORAM

BURMA

GUJARAT

Ahmadabad

Narmada R.

MADHYA PRADESH

BIHAR

Ganges R.

WEST BENGAL

Calcutta

Tapti R.

ORISSA

Mahanadi R.

MAHARASHTRA

Bombay

Hyderabad

Godavari R.

BAY OF BENGAL

Krishna R.

ANDHRA PRADESH

ARABIAN SEA

GOA

MYSORE

Bangalore

Madras

TAMIL NADU

KERALA

Kaveri R.

POLITICAL DIVISIONS

0   100   200   300

miles

LACCADIVE IS. (India)

SRI LANKA (CEYLON)

Colombo

Disputed area

INDIAN OCEAN

TRADITIONAL INDIA
1

Before the Muslims converted a fifth of the people of the subcontinent to Islam, before the British built a colonial empire in India, before Gandhi and his colleagues began attacking the problems of creating an independent Indian nation, Indians were overwhelmingly Hindu by faith, caste members by birth, and villagers by circumstance. They still are. These three institutions—Hinduism, the caste system, and village life—have molded the culture, civilization, and human geography of the subcontinent for centuries. Four-fifths of the modern Indian population is Hindu; Muslims, Buddhists, Sikhs, Jains, and Christians—adherents of other devotional faiths—are notable religious minorities. Although Hinduism appears to have evolved in large part outside India, the religion took form when Aryan tribes invaded India between 1500 and 600 BC and set up rule among the native Dravidian peoples of the northwest. For generations, Indians have reared their children and lived out their destinies within Hinduism's defining characteristics. Today, the government of modern India is faced with orienting these traditional institutions toward national goals. But the persistent realities of the village as a spatial cell, caste as a social cell, and Hinduism as a localized, highly amorphous, individual faith have passively resisted and diverted the aspirations of national planners. As the three preconditions of the Indian cultural experience, they are fundamental to an understanding of economic development and culture change in modern India.

HINDUISM: THE PURSUIT OF SANCTITY

The glories of Greece were fading when, in the fourth century BC, the great devotional religion of Hinduism fully emerged in India. The outlines of this faith are difficult to define because Hinduism has no founder, no single code of belief, and no organizational structure. It is based on the concept of tolerating differences: different truths for one person and another, different lives through rebirth and reincarnation, different paths to salvation, and different duties or roles for each individual and group within society. Unlike Western faiths, Hinduism has a vast array of gods, popularly numbered at 330 million, any one of which may be appropriately worshiped in a given situation. Hinduism embraces a range of believers from rational, monotheistic Brahmans to pagan tribesmen barely touched by the modern world. As is true of any great religion, individuals of different classes, different temperaments, and different intellects can find a satisfying faith within the broad range of Hindu practice and belief. Yet three basic concepts are generally shared by all Hindus: dharma, or duty within society; reincarnation, the cycle of life, death, and rebirth; and karma, an accounting of good and evil behavior. Despite an apparent lack of structure, Hinduism forms the spiritual base of one of the most clearly defined social fabrics in the world.

In Hinduism, each individual is born with a personal duty, or *dharma*, within society consistent with caste and stage of life. Dharma sets forth a preordained role in life for the individual. In the *Bhagavad Gita* ("Song of the Blessed Lord"), written about the time of Christ, men are warned that it is better to fulfill this personal duty poorly than to pursue another well. The logic of the system rests on the fact that in India, the fundamental social position of the individual is set by one's group or caste. The caste system is a form of social organization in which groups are hierarchically positioned in society with their level preordained by myth, religion, or law. In traditional India, the rights, duties, and customs of caste groups were inviolable; the individual was socially immobile within this frame. Each caste has a duty (dharma) within society and when every group performs this duty, society functions in harmony. Hindus, then, have a personal destiny to follow which is conferred at birth by caste status. Since this destiny cannot be altered by education, by the accumulation of wealth, or by the attainment of power, social mobility and self-improvement have different meanings in the Hindu system than in the West.

The ideal Hindu society is separated into four broad, overarching caste groupings, each with its own dharma: Brahmans, who study, teach, and perform religious rituals and sacrifices; Kshatriyas, the warriors, political leaders, and kings; Vaisyas, farmers, tradesmen, and merchants; and Sudras, servants, so low in class that they are enjoined against reading sacred scripture on penalty of having molten lead poured in their ears. According to this idealized social plan, important religious distinctions separate the three upper classes from the lowborn Sudras. The upper classes were initiated into their castes through a sacred ceremony, a second birth that made them doubly holy (twice-born). Only after this second birth were they full members of Hindu society, leaving the once-born Sudras on the fringes of society. Beyond them, "in an external pen in outer darkness," were the quasi-human Untouchables. Until recently, this distinction pervaded Indian law: the twice-born had one law of marriage, adoption, and inheritance; the once-born, another. Identifying precisely which group was in one category and which in the other was the business of barristers such as young Gandhi.

Reincarnation, the cycle of life, death, and rebirth, is the second fundamental tenet shared by most Hindus. In this view, life is open-ended, with birth, growth, and death occurring repeatedly. The Western assertion that time moves in a straight, undeflected line from the past through the present and into the future plays no role in Hinduism. The body is conceived of as a suit of clothes, donned at the beginning of each life and discarded for another at death. Since the soul can occupy any life form from apes to insects, all creatures share sacred qualities in Hinduism. The tension inherent in the Western belief (ecologists excepted) that man and nature are separate finds no place in Hinduism. But only when a human body clothes the soul does the individual becomes responsible for the action he or she takes. People are capable of striving for release from this cycle of lives by the achievement of *nirvana*—an eternal spiritual understanding of life in which one is united with cosmic forces and thereby escapes the human processes of birth and death. As with everything else in Hinduism, different paths can be taken to achieve nirvana, reflecting the variety of travelers making the effort. Each path is called a *yoga*, or discipline, and four are widely recognized.

The Way of Knowledge is for those who approach the search for cosmic unity through reason and thought; the Way of Love, for emotional people, is pursued by prayers to one or another of the gods in the Hindu pantheon; the Way of Work is for socially active people like Gandhi; and the Way of Mystical Experience is for people who follow rigorous schedules of physical and mental self-discipline ranging from breathing through one nostril to slowing the heartbeat, all in pursuit of mastery over mind and body. In providing valid paths to nirvana for people of all temperaments, Hinduism retained the flexibility to unite diverse peoples into one general body of belief.

The third and final central tenet of Hinduism, the law of *karma*, can be thought of as a ledger in which an accounting, as impersonal and inexorable as the law of gravity, holds everyone responsible for his or her deeds and thoughts in all past existences: Good acts inevitably produce good results, such as birth into a wealthy Brahman family; evil acts produce the reverse, namely, rebirth as a lower creature

—an insect, an animal, or an Untouchable. Linked to the social order by the cycle of rebirth, karmic law justifies and explains with mathematical precision the relative position of each individual and group within the hierarchy of Indian society. Chance is eliminated, environment irrelevant; one's birth is no accident. Poverty, suffering, disease, and human degradation are not conditions to be eliminated by programs of social change. They are divinely ordained social states earned through past misbehavior and appropriate to each group and individual. Hindu belief is at the root of the caste system—the most rigid, diverse, and in some senses inhumane social order found in any nation of the developing world.

CASTE: IN SEARCH OF PURITY

The Portuguese explorers who arrived on the shores of India in the sixteenth century actually found the four broad orders of Hindu society (Brahman, Kshatriya, Vaisya, and Sudra) broken down into a host of smaller subgroupings called *castes* by the Portuguese and *jati* ("birth") by the Indians. Each of these castes formed an exclusive social group whose members ate together, often practiced the same occupation, intermarried, and shared the same dharma within society. Each group held a fixed position within the Indian social hierarchy; members of different groups lived apart from one another, touching lives only at the working level. By the nineteenth century, some 3000 of these groups existed in India; each village had a dozen or so castes, and each region anywhere from 100 to 200. Technically outside society, but actually grouped into their own castes, were the lowly Untouchables, who today make up nearly a seventh of the population of India.

At the root of this hierarchical social system was the fear that pollution through contact with spiritually unclean groups might lead, however accidentally, to defilement. Each caste held a ritual ranking in degrees of "cleanliness" within the Indian social pyramid; each was defined as either more or less pure than every other caste.

Brahman castes were usually accorded the highest rank, though frequently they were neither the wealthiest nor the most powerful group within the community. Orthodox Brahmans went to great lengths to preserve their high status: they took food

For the devout Hindu, to bathe in the Ganges at sunrise is a vital part of every pilgrimage to the holy city of Benares, a traditional act of worship as deeply satisfying as the Christian's going to Jerusalem or the Muslim to Mecca. *Photo:* United Nations/Jongen.

only from the hands of other Brahmans and were vegetarians; some groups would not eat beets (because the color was suggestive of blood) or eggs (considered nascent life); they avoided contact with lower castes, leading lives of near total isolation in groups as small as fifteen families. The extraordinary emphasis on food habits was based on the belief that the "soul stuff" of humans was the same as that of food they ate. As a result of this dietary fascination, many cooks are now Brahmans, and cafeteria and restaurant styles of eating require difficult adjustments for modern Indians.

At the other end of this graded scale of cleanliness were people considered so defiled as to be beyond the pale; people with "dirt under their skin," the Untouchables. In the nineteenth century, Untouchables were forbidden to use roads, as they would contaminate members of higher castes by their proximity; if the shadow of an Untouchable were to pass over food, no higher group, however hungry, would touch it. Yet even among the Untouchables the Hindu principle of hierarchy took root, and each caste within the Untouchables was scaled against the others. A leather worker, for example, would never degrade himself by eating with a sweeper; the highest caste of Untouchables, the washermen, would have nothing to do with either. Despite efforts to legislate new attitudes toward Untouchables and guarantee better places for them in Indian life by quota-hiring in government service (one-eighth of all jobs, one-seventh of the seats in national and state legislatures), each village retains a segregated Untouchable quarter outside the central precinct. Untouchables continue to perform the "contaminating" tasks of leather working, removal of the dead, and waste collection, for which they are generally despised and avoided.

Between these two extremes are hundreds of castes and subcastes, whose members know to the smallest gradation their places in this hierarchy. All economic, religious, and family life occurs within these closed social cells, and all decisions are considered as they relate or conform to the dictates of caste.

The Social Functions of Caste

Fear of spiritual pollution was a critical force in maintaining these relatively watertight social compartments in India, but it was not the only one. Although Indians accepted the dictates of Brahman superiority, acceptance was not wholehearted, and fees paid to Brahmans by farmers at harvest, by merchants when starting on a trip, and by craftsmen when beginning a project led to the North Indian proverb that there were three bloodsuckers in the world: "the flea, the bug, and the Brahman."

The caste system, while fixing a person's occupation, marriage, and place in society, also provided benefits to all but the lowest and most helpless groups on a day-to-day basis. Castes provided security for their members in the broad sense of a cultural group with shared customs and values and in the more narrow sense of assuming financial responsibility, whenever possible, for members struck by disaster or misfortune. In addition, each caste had its own internal system of justice regulated by a caste council that punished members for breaking caste rules and defended caste honor against outsiders. Finally, specialized caste occupations led to reciprocal exchanges of goods and services among castes in each community and region.

In each Indian village, there were hereditary castes of farmers, moneylenders, carpenters, potters, smiths, oil pressers, washermen, and landless Untouchable laborers. Each caste performed an exclusive function that others needed. Even if their task was viewed as unclean, they were, after all, fulfilling their dharma. They were contributing to the functioning of the total community, and in the final analysis, there were groups beneath them with fewer rights and privileges (surely a source of some satisfaction). In North India, the reciprocal exchange of services among landlords, dependent artisans, and field workers, the *jajmani* system, provided a share of the annual harvest to each contributing member of village society, however lowborn, and a place for each person within the social fabric. Stable, resistant to change, and until recently relatively isolated from outside influences, village India derived its social realities from Hinduism and caste.

The dominant climatic force affecting India is the monsoon. Suggesting violent, torrential downpours lasting weeks, a monsoon is defined as any air current, blowing steadily from one direction for weeks or months. India is affected by two monsoons: the wet summer monsoon, moving inland from the sea; and the dry winter monsoon, usually moving from the land to the sea. The summer monsoon pushes warm, moist ocean air over India from June through September, producing 85 percent of the country's annual rainfall. By contrast, the winter monsoon is a current of dry air moving south and east across the continent to the sea, producing little rain. Planting and sowing begin with the rains; the timing and amount of rain determine the harvest. With too little rain, the crops die before maturation; with too much, flooding may wipe out the entire year's crop and destroy whole villages as well.

Until recently, the monsoon was generally explained by the development of high- and low-pressure areas resulting from differential heating of land surfaces and the sea. The explanation of the summer monsoon went as follows: The interior of India becomes heated during the summer and a low-pressure area develops over the northwest. The land surface is then hotter than the Indian Ocean, where a high-pressure area has developed. The result is a pressure gradient in which air flows from the high-pressure area over the Indian Ocean toward the low-pressure area over northwest India. As the air moves across the sea, it picks up moisture, which later falls on India as rain.

The explanation of the winter, or dry, monsoon was based on the same principle. During the winter the interior of Central Asia becomes extremely cold, much colder than the ocean surfaces of southern Asia. A low-pressure area develops over the ocean, while a complementary high-pressure area develops over Central Asia. The resulting pressure gradient draws dry air from the Asian landmass to the ocean. The result is very little rainfall for India during the winter months.

Although differential heating patterns and pressure gradients are still considered part of the monsoon phenomenon, a newer theory proposes that the causal mechanism lies in the seasonal adjustment of heat between the northern and southern hemispheres and movements of the jet stream, a high-level river of air. During the summer months in the northern hemisphere, the southern branch of the

Photo: Lynn McLaren/Rapho-Photo Researchers.

westerly jet stream detours to the northern side of the Himalayas. Normally, it flows south of the Himalayas. Thus, the summer jet stream is north of the mountains and flows eastward, while the higher jet stream flows westward south of the mountains. These two currents of air set up a reverse circulation beneath them. The summer monsoon is the surface reaction to the circular pattern set up by the easterly jet above pulling air inland off the Indian Ocean. The winter pattern is the reverse. As temperatures drop in Central Asia, the westerly jet returns to its path south of the Himalayas and becomes the controlling mechanism of the Indian winter climate, causing cold, dry air to move from the Tibetan Plateau across India to the sea. That the jet stream reverses itself is now known; why this occurs is still under investigation.

This recent photograph is evidence of how little village life has changed in India. A young woman draws water from a well to fill the earthenware jugs at her feet. In order to meet her family's needs, she will perform this chore several times each day. *Photo:* United Nations/ Srinivasan.

THE TRADITIONAL INDIAN VILLAGE

Environmental and technological realities bind the lives of Indians in the traditional village as surely as Hinduism and the caste system. Of the various sources of poverty and misery that afflict villagers, none is more basic than the low productivity of the Indian farmer. Rice yield per acre in India (1438 pounds) is only one-third as high as that of Japan and one-half that of China; wheat yields average approximately 13 bushels per acre, compared with 27 in the United States and 40 in Japan. Extremely poor yields for the two largest food grain crops cultivated in India mean that over 80 percent of the population is engaged in a subsistence occupation of low productivity—and this in a country whose population is increasing at a faster rate than that of the United States or any other nation of the technological world.

Part of the problem is environmental. Large areas of India rely on the fickle rains of the monsoon for 80 to 90 percent of their rainfall. The Indian farmer copes with this by spreading seed thinly over the land and by cultivating only basic grains—agricultural practices that reduce yield and rule out profit. Most years the summer monsoon fails in one or another part of the subcontinent, forcing peasants to migrate, abandon their land and become tenant farmers, or simply fall deeper into debt. Even when rains are plentiful, most soils in India are so poor that their yields are minimal. The farmer with little

land and food cannot afford to set aside cultivated land in *fallow,* and the large-scale destruction of forests in the nineteenth century has increased erosion. Lack of wood forces peasants to burn cattle dung as fuel, thus eliminating from the field an important source of fertilizer that could be used to increase yields; fields are fertilized by what human and vegetable waste is left over—of considerable importance in light of the high ratio of people to land in rural India.

Fragmentation and Other Limitations
[FIGURE 1]

Population growth has intensified these problems; generation by generation, the fields of Indian villages have become more *fragmented,* forcing more people to live off the same amount of land. Currently 50 percent of India's farm families occupy less than 2.5 acres, and population growth, along with the Hindu and Muslim practices of subdividing land among the family sons, has produced a mosaic of tiny parcels of land. In one South Indian village that practices *strip farming,* it is possible to stand with one foot in one farmer's field, the other foot in a second farmer's field, and have a third narrow parcel run between the legs. In a Punjabi village with a cultivated area of 12,800 acres there are some 63,000 separate fields. The effect of fragmentation has been to create uneconomic holdings, generate thousands of lawsuits (nearly 2 million in 1939), leave *arable* land unused in field boundaries, and waste time in the daily journey to dozens of tiny parcels. Although 40 million acres of land in India have been consolidated into larger, more economic holdings, the unwillingness or inability of the Indian government to

THE ECOLOGY OF THE SACRED COW

The central fact of Hinduism is cow protection. Cow protection to me is one of the most wonderful phenomena in human evolution. It takes the human being beyond his species. The cow to me means the entire sub-human world. Man through the cow is enjoined to realize his identity with all that lives. . . . The motive that actuates cow protection is not "purely selfish," though selfish consideration undoubtedly enters into it. If it were purely selfish, the cow would be killed, as in other countries, after it had ceased to give full use. [Gandhi]

One of the most prevalent Western stereotypes of India pictures an overpopulated, starving country fanatically adhering to the Hindu taboo against slaughtering and eating its 175 million cattle and 50 million water buffaloes, thus forgoing a much-needed source of protein because of religion. If one looks at the role of the cow in India's ecology, however, one questions first, whether the food resources of the Indian population are lowered because of the competition for food between people and cattle, and second, whether the removal of the taboo would alter the present ecology of Indian food production. According to the research of anthropologist Marvin Harris, the relation between cattle and men in India is mutually beneficial, or symbiotic, not competitive, and people gain more than the cattle.

Cattle contribute to Indian food production by providing the traction necessary for plow agriculture. With 96 million bulls, including over 68 million working animals, two-thirds of India's rural households are still short of the minimum plowing team. When the monsoon arrives, draft animals cannot be shared because all farmers need them at precisely the same time; sowing must be done quickly during the first showers and harvesting begun when the grain matures.

Rural India must support a dense population of cows to ensure the birth of these vital draft animals. The problem is that farmers can provide little or no fodder for them. What fodder is available goes to working bulls, and cows must forage on unused hillsides or along roadsides. The resulting malnutrition of India's 80 million cows means that they breed irregularly and infrequently, but any bull they produce is a "free" asset to the farmer.

The second contribution of cattle, both cows and bulls, to the village economy is dung. Cattle scavenge for food, converting grain by-products and scrub vegetation into 800 million tons of dung

Photo: United Nations.

annually, the principal source of cooking fuel and manure in India. About 300 million tons (the equivalent of 35 million tons of coal or 68 million tons of wood) are used for fuel—a vital input.

The cow's third contribution is dairy products. Although buffaloes are India's primary milk producers, cows also contribute to the Indian diet. Admittedly they produce far less than their European or American bovine counterparts, but what they do provide is an important protein additive: approximately 8 billion pounds of whole milk annually. They also produce hides (roughly 16 million per year) to make leather products. Finally, when cattle die, most are eaten. The Hindu population may abstain from beef, but non-Hindu groups and Hindu Untouchables eat beef when it is available. Thus, the Indian use of the cow seems well adapted to agriculture, and it is questionable whether lifting the taboo against slaughtering and eating cattle would significantly alter the ecology of Indian agriculture.

Source: Quoted material from M. K. Gandhi, "How to Save the Cow." Ahmadabad: Navajivan, 1954, pp. 3, 5.

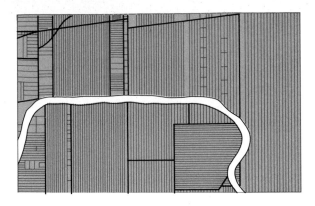

Figure 1. Fragmentation and Population Pressure, Punjab. Intense pressure on the land has been generated by population growth in the last century. Heavy lines show the boundaries of fields a hundred years ago, which averaged 10 acres in size; the lighter lines show subsequent fragmentation. *Adapted from:* Carl E. Taylor, "Population Trends in an Indian Village," *Scientific American*, Vol. 223 (July 1970), p. 109. Copyright © 1970 by Scientific American, Inc. All rights reserved.

reorganize ownership patterns in the villages makes fragmentation a basic fact of Indian agriculture.

As if cultivating infertile and unfertilized tiny patches were not enough, other factors contribute to the low productivity and low standard of living of the Indian farmer. The light scratch plow commonly used in India cuts the soil so shallowly that birds frequently eat large percentages of newly sown seed, and more seed is blown away. Even the scratch plow is beyond the reach of the poorest tenants, so that as much as a tenth of India's fields may be seeded unplowed, reducing yields to a minimum. After the crop is harvested, the peasant is frequently in debt at rates of interest as high as 300 percent to usurious traders and brokers who take advantage of the poor marketing facilities (some 250,000 settlements have populations of less than 500 people and are connected only by footpaths to the outside world) to relieve peasants of the small harvests their tiny fields produce. Landlords drain the Indian peasantry still further, leaving a standard of living so low that observers refer to the traditional Indian village as the one phenomenon that lasts where nothing else survives.

This persistence of form and substance characterized the three major institutions of traditional India —Hinduism, caste, and the village—until a company of British merchants forced India to adjust to the power and purpose of a modern technological society. Even now, Hinduism and the caste system remain strong in modern India, although secular attacks on traditional beliefs are common, and the government bans caste rankings from the census and other public accounts. Tensions are generated between the universal desire for a better life and the Hindu ethic in which this life is prescribed by caste and custom; between a faith that demands spiritual devotion and a reality in which monsoon rains and the availability of plow-pulling animals determine whether or not one eats. In the village, poverty and hunger remain the same for the modern villager as for his ancestors, and these problems plague the national planners of India as they did the Mogul and British princes.

INDIA

REGIONAL PATTERNS

PHYSICAL FEATURES MAP
POPULATION DENSITY MAP

The Indian subcontinent is a triangular *peninsula,*
1.5 million square miles in area, jutting 1000 miles
southward from the Himalayan mountain front into
the Indian Ocean. Within this *region,* virtually
every combination of climate and topography can
be found, but three major *environments* are clear:
the Himalayan Frontier, a 2500-mile arc of still
largely unexplored mountains and foothills extending from Kashmir in the west, through the Himalayan kingdoms of Nepal, Bhutan, and Sikkim, to
the forests of Assam in the east; the Gangetic Plains,
a 1500-mile-long ribbon of *alluvium* some 200
miles wide lying south of the Himalayas; and
Peninsular India, including the Deccan Plateau, a
tilted *tableland* south of the Gangetic Plain that
slopes irregularly from 2500 feet in the west to
about 1000 feet in the east.

THE HIMALAYAN FRONTIER

The concave arc of the Himalayas forms a forbidding, mountain-studded wall on the northern frontier of India some 150 miles thick, 2000 miles long,
and 4 miles high. In the west, these mountains
taper off into the desert ranges of Baluchistan and
Afghanistan; to the east, they grade into the jungle-
covered hills of Burma and Assam. The mountain
barrier, impressive as it is, was never impenetrable.
River-carved passes in the northwest, notably the
Bolan Pass, the Khyber Pass, and the Karakoram
Pass, served as gateways to the subcontinent, fun-
nels that channeled migrants and invaders down
through the hills of Punjab onto the Indo-Gangetic
Plains.

The only densely settled part of the Himalayan
Frontier lies in the northwest, in Kashmir, a former
princely state that has been in dispute between
India and Pakistan since 1947. The Indians now

control most of the fertile agricultural land, the
capital city, and 95 percent of the population in
this region.

The central portion of the Himalayan Frontier is
occupied by the states of Nepal, Bhutan, and Sikkim
—landlocked, mountainous countries that have
acted as refuge and buffer areas between the major
powers on either side of the Himalayas. Of the three,
Nepal, with an area of 54,000 square miles and a
population of 9.5 million, is the largest and most
independent. Sheltered behind a curtain of wet,
malarial jungles, Nepal was one of the few parts
of Asia never to come under Muslim domination
or the influence of Christian missions. In the fertile
Katmandu Valley southwest of the Everest *massif,*
the highest mountains in the world, there are population densities of more than 2000 people per square
mile.

Two smaller states, Bhutan (18,000 square miles)
and Sikkim (2800 square miles) have populations
of 8.5 million and 250,000, respectively (mostly
Buddhist yak herders and rice farmers). Bhutan is
for all intents and purposes a ward of India;
Sikkim is now incorporated into India.

The eastern reaches of the Himalayan Frontier include the hills and mountains of the Assam Himalaya, the Assam-Burma border ranges in the east,
and the valley of the Brahmaputra River in Assam.
This entire region, largely depopulated by incessant
Burmese invasions during the nineteenth century,
forms an economic as well as political frontier of
India. The entire area of the Assam Himalaya,
some 31,438 square miles, is occupied by less than
350,000 tribal people. The difficult terrain, extremely wet climate, and heavy forests of the region
have deterred colonization, leaving this area one of
the least developed and most remote in India. The
Assam-Burma border ranges, with 80 to 100 inches
of rainfall each year, are equally underdeveloped.
The various tribes of the region practice *shifting
cultivation.* By contrast, the 400-mile-long, 60-mile-
wide Assam Valley in which the Brahmaputra River
flows is a densely settled, peasant-tilled rice- and
jute-producing region. In the surrounding hills the
British introduced tea *plantations* in the nineteenth
century, and these now cover some 400,000 acres
and produce half the annual Indian crop.

THE GANGETIC PLAINS

The plains of the Ganges River form the spiritual,
economic, and political *heartland* of India. India's
densest rail network and road system connect a
string of major urban centers located between the
capital city of Delhi and the coastal port of Calcutta.
From the dry plains of Punjab in the west to humid
Bengal in the east, the Ganges Plain, 200 miles wide,
is densely settled, heavily populated, continuously

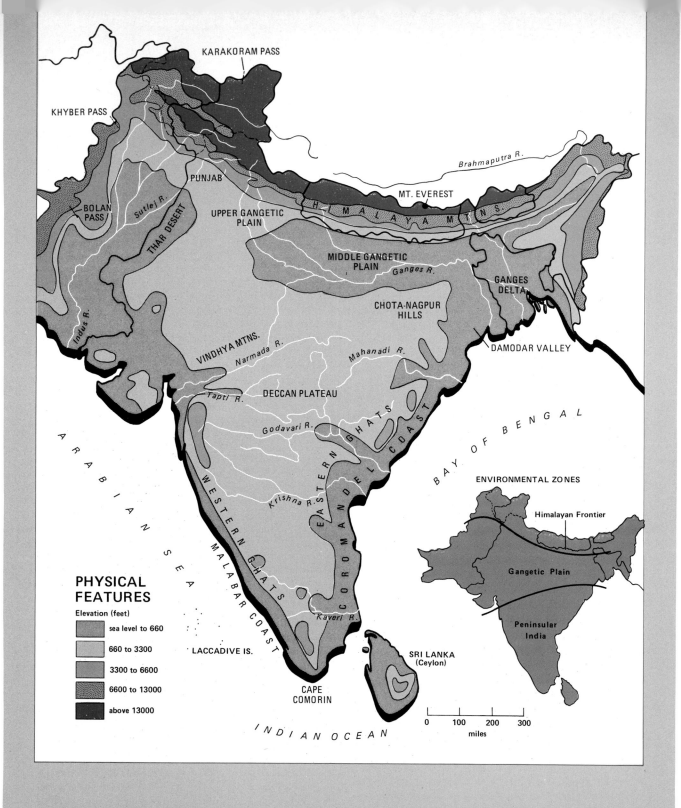

PHYSICAL FEATURES

Elevation (feet)

	sea level to 660
	660 to 3300
	3300 to 6600
	6600 to 13000
	above 13000

ENVIRONMENTAL ZONES

Himalayan Frontier

Gangetic Plain

Peninsular India

0   100   200   300
miles

cultivated, and highly productive. One can divide this vast plain into four subregions, which differ principally in terms of those agricultural changes induced by changing rainfall patterns: Punjab, west of the Ganges proper; the Upper Ganges plain; the Middle Ganges plain; and the delta.

The Indian Punjab forms an important physiographical divide separating the two great river systems of the subcontinent, the Indus Valley of Pakistan and the Ganges of India and Bangladesh. Located at the foot of the Himalayas, the dry plains of the Indian Punjab slope southward from the *piedmont* onto the flat alluvial plain. On the piedmont, where wells provide irrigation water, the destruction of forests has caused major *erosion,* and cultivation of commercial crops like wheat, cotton, and sugarcane is pursued high on the *alluvial fans.* On the plain itself, cultivation of wheat, barley, and other grains has expanded with the building of the Nangal and Bhakra dams, which will ultimately irrigate some 6.5 million acres of land. The hydro-electric power from these dams on the Sutlej River will undoubtedly lead to new industrial development in the major towns of the region. On the plains south of the river, rainfall is only 10 inches per year, and settlements are located at the few points where water is available.

The upper Gangetic plain extends over some 65,000 square miles eastward from the dry Delhi-Agra region. In this area the terrain is flat, and rainfall gradually increases to the east, although there is no marked boundary separating the wheat fields of the Upper Ganges from the rice land of the Middle Ganges. Irrigation is widely practiced as a hedge against the uncertainty of the summer monsoon. Wheat is the primary food crop, and sugarcane has replaced cotton as the principal commercial crop. Population densities are high, ranging from 650 to 1200 people per square mile. Pressure on resources is intense, farming methods rudimentary, levels of poverty and debt high, and the density of cattle as high as anywhere in India.

Although the region is overwhelmingly rural, there are a number of important urban centers in the upper Gangetic plain. On its western margin, the capital city of Delhi is the third largest city in India (1971 population, 3.6 million) and the largest inland city on the subcontinent. Farther east on the Ganges Plain, the traditional Hindu centers of Varanasi (Benares) and Allahabad, the Mogul city of Agra, and the post-Mogul settlements at Kanpur and Lucknow are of administrative and commercial importance.

The middle Gangetic plain is an area comparable in size (62,000 square miles) and terrain to the upper Gangetic plain to the west; only the climate is different. Rainfall, 90 percent of it associated with the monsoon, rises from 40 inches per year on the western border of this region to 70 inches per year in Bengal. Rice is grown on half of the estimated 20 million cultivated acres, followed by wheat, barley, sugarcane, and, in the east, jute. The transition is gradual: as one moves east, down the Ganges, irrigation becomes less pronounced, wheat fields increasingly rare, and *double-cropped* rice fields cover the landscape. Population density is extremely high, averaging 1500 people per square mile north of the river, 700 to 1000 south of the river, and 600 to 700 on the *floodplain* proper. Food production has not kept pace with population growth, creating an annual deficit in grain production of some 3 million tons. As a result, it is a region of bitter poverty, hunger, and malnutrition—the least industrialized, least urbanized densely populated region in India.

The easternmost stretch of the Gangetic Plain is the *delta,* a hot, wet plain formed by the confluence of the Ganges and the Brahmaputra rivers. Rainfall is heavy—50 inches in West Bengal (India) and 100 inches in Bangladesh—because the summer monsoon hits this coast earlier, starting in March or April. Although monsoon rains cause frequent large-scale flooding, these rains are essential to the cultivation of rice and jute. Almost 60 percent of the land is cultivated; of that total, over 80 percent is planted to rice, much of which is double-cropped, and 10 percent is planted to jute. As in other parts of India, land is highly fragmented, generating the familiar Gangetic pattern of poverty and hunger caused by overpopulation.

The new nation of Bangladesh, located on the eastern boundaries of the Ganges *watershed,* was established in 1972. It may well prove the least viable, most overpopulated country in the world. Here, some 75 million people live in an area of 54,500 square miles (smaller than Oklahoma).

PENINSULAR INDIA

The Deccan Plateau, a massive area of forests, fields, *scrubland,* and mountains, is separated from the Gangetic Plain by the low, forested Vindhya Mountains on the west and by rough, dissected Chota Nagpur Plateau on the east. These low ranges form a cultural divide between the Dravidians, who have occupied the Deccan since prehistoric times, and the Indo-European peoples who settled farther north on the Gangetic Plain. On either side of the Deccan Plateau two mountain ranges, the Western and Eastern Ghats, rim the peninsula, separating the grassy scrub of the interior from the lush, tropical coast. These coasts are heavily populated.

The northern frontier of the Deccan Plateau, roughly the triangle located between the Gulf of Cambay, Delhi, and the Bay of Bengal, is a complex region of *scarped plateaus,* river valleys, and *peneplains.* In the drier west, Rajasthan, the majority of people are cultivators who revert to herding when the monsoon fails. Where irrigation is possible, jowar (an Indian sorghum) and bajra (a local millet) are grown. In the Vindhya range to the east, rainfall increases to 20 or 25 inches per year. Cultivation is more permanent, with millet still the predominant crop. On the eastern side of the Deccan frontier in Chota Nagpur, development of the Damodar coalfields, the mica mines of Bihar, and bauxite and gypsum have brought a moderate level of prosperity, but generally these are among the poorest regions of India.

On the Deccan Plateau proper, a subhumid climate prevails, with rainfall reaching 40 inches per year in the northeast and 20 to 30 inches per year in the drier south and west. Only the mountain rims of

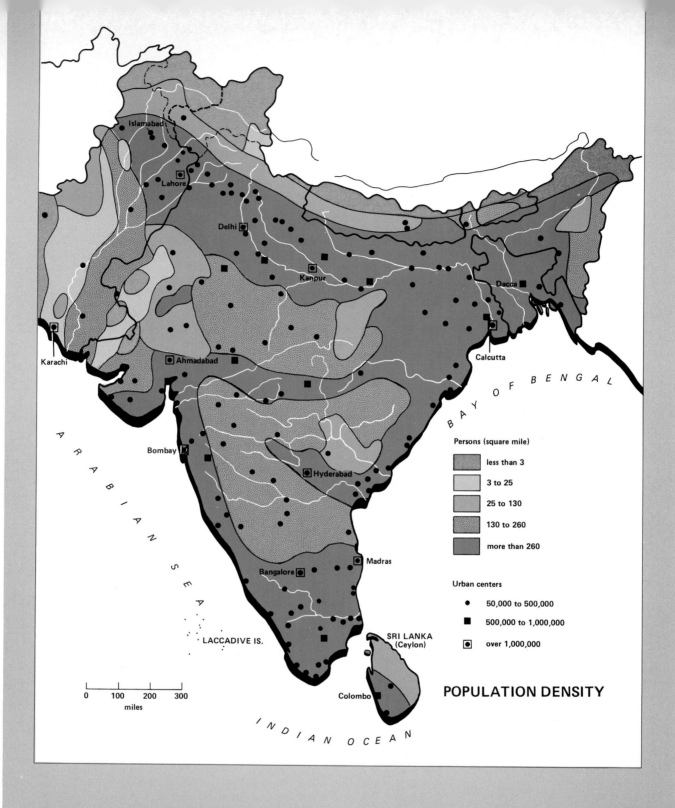

Persons (square mile)

- less than 3
- 3 to 25
- 25 to 130
- 130 to 260
- more than 260

Urban centers

- • 50,000 to 500,000
- ■ 500,000 to 1,000,000
- ◉ over 1,000,000

POPULATION DENSITY

the plateau, the Western Ghats and Eastern Ghats ("steps"), receive higher amounts of rainfall. As a result, the plateau is relatively sparsely populated, a blistering, parched land in which agriculture is dependent on the monsoon.

The heartland of the Deccan Plateau is formed by the Maharashtra Plateau, a flat, heavily eroded, deforested area with rich *volcanic soils.* In spite of low rainfall, it is relatively prosperous due to concentration on commercial crops, especially cotton. The chief grain is wheat, followed by jowar. Mechanized farming has recently been introduced on expanses of fertile volcanic soil, making this one of the better developed regions of India. Until the nineteenth century, the wet, forested *highlands*• of the peninsula's tip were the domain of tribal hunters and gatherers, but now they are covered with tea and coffee plantations.

The coastal *littorals*• of India—the Malabar Coast on the west and the Coromandel Coast on the east—are well-watered, tropical environments whose fertile soils make them the most productive agricultural regions in India. These coastal plains are carpeted with rice fields; in the nearby hills, rubber, tea, pepper, and coconuts grow. Farther northward, the climate becomes less equatorial, although rice remains the dominant crop. In the west, the coast broadens into the plains of Gujarat (the hinterland of Bombay), a major cotton-producing region. In the east, the coast narrows in Orissa and ultimately opens onto the delta of the Ganges and Brahmaputra rivers in Bengal and Bangladesh.

THE BRITISH IN INDIA

2

British rule introduced Western values, techniques of public administration, education, manufacturing, and armament to India. This introduction challenged, and continues to transform, Indian society. Beliefs are doubted; traditions questioned. The village has been undermined as the basic unit of social and economic organization. More people have become urbanites, but limited industrialization in a country of finite resources leaves most Indians living at very low levels of subsistence. Britain also created the spatial base for the establishment of a modern nation in India, drawing the diverse peoples and cultures of the subcontinent into a larger frame of reference. It began modestly.

December 31, 1600, was an auspicious day for England: Queen Elizabeth I chartered an association of 125 businessmen and merchants as the British East India Company, granting it exclusive privilege to ply the spice trade east of the Cape of Good Hope for fifteen years. India, then under Islamic Mogul rule, was an economically self-sufficient country, exporting both raw materials and finished goods to the world. By contrast, Britain was an underdeveloped one. The royal treasury of Elizabeth was only one-eightieth the size of that of her contemporary, the Mogul emperor Akbar (1542–1605), and British woolens were of poorer quality and coarser weave than Indian textiles. Gold or silver, pirated from Spanish galleons, was the only payment Indians would accept in exchange for silk, spices, and *indigo.* This led to a trading relationship so one-sided that the first British ambassador to India complained that Europe was bleeding "to enrich Asia."

For the first fifty years, profits were meager. The British clung to India in a trading outpost at Surat (later shifted to Bombay), a tiny enclave with a few buildings from which the British bought and sold cotton and indigo, and stockpiled cargoes for the return trip from the coast of India to the docks of London. Such were the humble beginnings of British suzerainty in India. By 1639 a similar naval factory was established at Madras, and in 1651 the British built a fort on the Hooghly River, later to grow as Calcutta, to tap the rich sources of silk and saltpeter (for gunpowder) available in Bengal. From these three commercial footholds on the western, southern, and eastern coasts of India, the British gained control of the Indian subcontinent.

THE MOGUL RULE IN INDIA (1526–1858)

When the British arrived in India, the subcontinent was ruled by a Muslim dynasty that had established its center of power in the Ganges River Basin after penetrating the Himalayas from the northwest and entering India. By the time the Portuguese discovered the maritime route to the East by rounding the Cape of Good Hope in Africa (1497–1498), Muslim rule in India was reaching outward under Babur (1494–1530). Ultimately, the Muslim rulers extended their hold over much of India, fusing elements of both Hindu and Muslim culture to create one of the most brilliant and dynamic empires in world history, the Mogul Empire (1524–1858). When the first three vessels of the British East India Company set sail from London in 1601, the Moguls were attaining their peak of power and cultural efflorescence. In the Indian court, Mogul rulers fostered a new and distinctive Indo-Islamic style of painting, music, and architecture; in the countryside, they conducted the first extensive land-use surveys in Indian history and established systems of taxation and land ownership on which the society and economy of India are still partially based.

Village India under the Moguls

The fundamental setting of life in Mogul India was the village, where four of every five Indians lived. In these subsistence settlements, people were bound by ties of religion, caste, **extended families,** and reciprocal obligations to other villagers. Disputes in villages were settled by councils of elders and caste organizations. There were no jails or imprisonment; the rich were fined, the poor mutilated. Any sizable village had its own priests, bankers, moneylenders, and shopkeepers. To some degree, caste groupings were regionally based, but incoherent communications tended to reinforce the self-sufficient, localized nature of village society.

From 1600 to 1900, there was little change in the technology and techniques of farming in village India. Cultivated land in northern India was generally planted to cereals and millet, with rice and sugar grown on the well-watered plains of Bengal. On the Deccan Plateau, cotton and jowar were planted. Throughout the peninsula, peasant life depended on the weather, and a good crop depended

The splendor of the Mogul rulers was but little diminished by the nineteenth century, though their political power had long since been taken over by the British. This drawing shows a raja riding in procession on his state elephant. *Photo:* **Culver Pictures.**

on the annual monsoon; agriculture was, in other words, a gamble on the rains. Yields were low, and peasants frequently hedged their bets by planting several crops in the same field. In the eighteenth century, new crops—tobacco, opium, and Gujarat indigo—became more widespread; but limited transportation networks hindered the development of large-scale commercial cropping. In Madras, for example, the cost of hauling grain doubled the value of the crop every 24 miles. River tolls were equally high, and roads were so poor that it took three months to go by cart from Delhi to Bengal. In these circumstances, overland transport was restricted to high-value goods and the two staples every village needed from the outside world, salt and iron. Yet conditions in village India then were probably not much different from those in preindustrial Europe.

The wealth that supported the Mogul court and army was derived from a well-conceived system of land taxation (***tax farming***•) which, at its best, was very good indeed. Instead of paying officials, military leaders, and others who performed public services directly from the royal treasury, Mogul emperors usually assigned the royal share of taxation for a given area, whether a single village or an entire province, to individuals as rewards. Land revenue, which ordinarily amounted to one-third the value of the crop, was assessed on the village as a whole and paid in kind, and was collected by local Hindu

authorities called *zamindars*. In this way, the Indian countryside was broken up into local ***despotisms***• with varying degrees of loyalty to the imperial throne.

The zamindar system worked effectively in India because the country was underpopulated and had large areas of uncultivated fertile land. In 1600 India had a population of about 100 million, probably larger than that of Europe at the time. The critical resource was not land but labor, and zamindars were loath to tax villagers too harshly, fearing they would flee to empty lands outside Mogul jurisdiction. The duty of peasants to cultivate their land was stressed by the authorities—so much so that, in one recorded case, a local governor physically split a village headman in two for refusing to sow his crop. The availability of free land to which the peasant might flee acted as a partial check on oppressive taxation.

Collapse of the Mogul Order (1658–1757)

The spatial jurisdiction of Mogul power expanded in the last half of the seventeenth century, and the population of India increased to 150 million. However, this period of the zenith of Mogul rule also saw the beginnings of dynastic decline. In 1658, Aurangzeb, the fifth son of Shah Jahan (the builder of the Taj Mahal), imprisoned his father, slaughtered his eldest brother, and dedicated the rest of his unfortunately long life to the militant conversion of Hindus to orthodox Islam. For fifty years, Aurangzeb fought a series of military campaigns to crush and convert both the Hindu Marathas of the Deccan Plateau and the Shiite Muslim kingdoms of the Coromandel Coast. The resources and treasury of the empire were poured into this ceaseless warfare. Aurangzeb was ultimately forced to move his capital from Delhi to the Deccan Plateau, where the court moved across the landscape like a plague of locusts. For twenty-five years, villagers were taxed unmercifully, milked by the government and marauding bands, and visited by famines and plagues spawned by the breakdown of the Mogul system of law and justice. When he finally died in 1707, Aurangzeb left behind the most spacious empire ever created on the subcontinent, but one so drained by the ulcers of war that fifty years later British merchants—coastal spectators during the Deccan wars—assumed direct territorial control over large portions of disintegrated Mogul India.

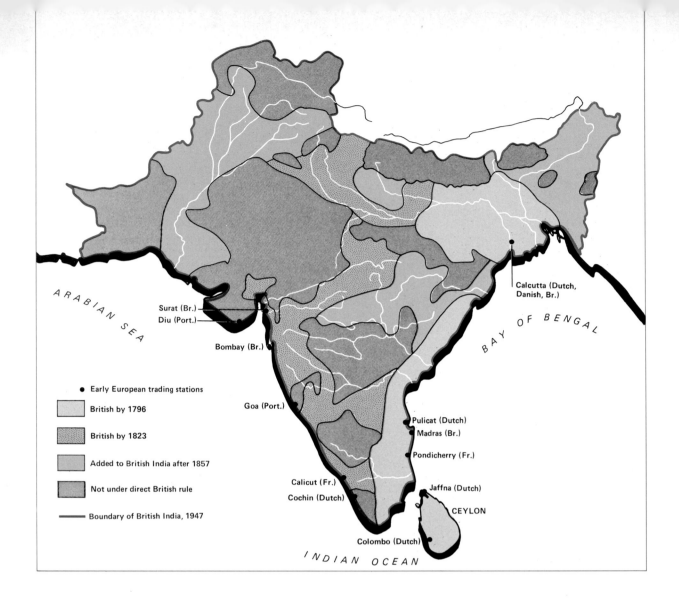

ARABIAN SEA

BAY OF BENGAL

Surat (Br.)
Diu (Port.)
Bombay (Br.)

Calcutta (Dutch, Danish, Br.)

Goa (Port.)

Pulicat (Dutch)
Madras (Br.)
Pondicherry (Fr.)

Calicut (Fr.)
Cochin (Dutch)

Jaffna (Dutch)

CEYLON

Colombo (Dutch)

INDIAN OCEAN

- Early European trading stations
British by 1796
British by 1823
Added to British India after 1857
Not under direct British rule
—— Boundary of British India, 1947

Figure 2. Growth of British Influence in India. British control of India came gradually; extension of colonial, commercial, and military zones of influence was effected in stages over a period of 150 years.

THE RULE OF THE BRITISH EAST INDIA COMPANY (1757–1858)
[FIGURE 2]

As Mogul rule deteriorated, the British East India Company, lodged in its coastal bases, began to assume increasing authority over local order and the organization of agricultural production. Everywhere, Marathas, Rajputs, Afghans, Moguls, and Sikhs were engaged in self-destructive warfare. Under these circumstances, an ambitious British officer, Robert Clive, a brooding bully whom Sir Frederick Burrows would have thoroughly detested, disobeyed orders and with 3000 troops put to flight the Mogul army in a mango grove at Plassey in 1757. In one stroke, the rich province of Bengal fell into East India Company hands, and Britain was irrevocably, if accidentally, committed to rule in India.

Bengal became a British possession in 1772; the kingdom of Mysore fell in 1799. Most of Madras was incorporated by 1803, and the western Marathas were defeated in 1818. Each conquest brought treasure in trade wrested from native merchants, who paid princely tributes to the company, and from artisans and weavers forced to work for the British. Conditions were so harsh that one writer claimed that the British in India had "outdone the Spaniards in Peru." Even so, the English brought their rule of law to the countryside, where the population had by now dwindled to 100 million. The benefits of peace may have outweighed the burdens of corruption. In any case, the political map of India in 1858 had taken the form it would keep until independence in 1947. Three-fifths of India was ruled by the company, and the remainder was indirectly controlled through 562 princely states scattered across the landscape in such a fashion that a traveler would cross thirty-six different frontiers in the 700-mile trip from Bombay to Delhi.

The British soon made changes in the system of

Ancient Period
3000–2500 BC
Civilization emerged in the Indus River valley, with large cities and sophisticated art.
1200
The Aryans from Central Asia invaded India through the northwest passes into the Punjab, spread across North India, and penetrated the Ganges River valley.
500
The Achaemenid (Persian) dynasty and later the army of Alexander the Great conquered the northwest and reoriented India to the West. Buddhism and Jainism rose in the north.

Medieval Hindu Period
300
Chandragupta conquered and united North India. The high point of the Mauryan age was the reign of Asoka (c. 273–232 BC), who ruled an empire approximate in area to modern India and sent Buddhist missionaries to Southeast Asia, China, and eventually Japan.
AD 400
The Gupta dynasty reunited India to launch India's classical age, whose art, literature, and science remain the Indian ideal today.
711
In 711 the Arabs conquered the northwest. For the next 250 years, rulers and dynasties tried unsuccessfully to weld another North Indian empire. After 977 the Muslim king of Ghazni in Afghanistan made annual raids into India.

Medieval Muslim India
1190
In 1192 the king of Ghazni opened India to Muslim rule, quelled Hindu rebellions, and united southern India.
1398
In 1398–1399 Timur Lenk (known in the West as Tamerlane) invaded North India and destroyed the capital, Delhi. Until the nineteenth century, North India was ruled by various local Muslim dynasties. The south remained Hindu.
1526
The most famous of the Muslim dynasties was the Mogul dynasty founded by Babur in 1526.

Modern India
1500
The Portuguese gained footholds in India, followed by the Dutch, French, and British in the seventeenth century. By the early nineteenth century, Britain controlled the affairs of whole regions, like Bengal, through the East India Company, until the Sepoy Rebellion of 1858–1859, when rule over India passed to the British crown.
1850s
The first railroads were constructed in India, precursors of the most extensive rail network in Asia.
1880s
The Indian independence movement began with formation of the Indian National Congress.
1947
British control of India was relinquished to the National Congress, with West Pakistan and Bangladesh (formerly East Pakistan) seceding from union with India.
1972
Bangladesh became an independent nation.

---

land taxation. Under the Permanent Settlement of 1793, the zamindars of North India were issued deeds to land on which they had previously collected taxes. In return for the payment of a fixed rate of taxes, the zamindars assumed the full rights of landlords, charging peasants exorbitant rentals if they so chose, throwing villagers off the land if they refused or were unable to pay. Peasants took out loans at interest rates of 35 to 50 percent to pay the cash rentals, and were foreclosed when they failed to pay. Property often ended up in the hands of urban moneylenders, accelerating a trend toward parasitic landlordism. By the middle of the next century, about 40 percent of the land in zamindar areas had changed hands in this fashion. In South India a type of directly assessed taxation prevailed, but as in the north, moneylenders became landlords so that the peasants fared as poorly as their northern counterparts.

But if the condition of the peasantry did not improve, moves toward the commercialization of agriculture in India did begin. The requirement of cash

The Sepoy Mutiny of the mid-nineteenth century had its origins in the kind of religious sensibility that still causes riots and communal tension in India today. In this case Indian troops, shown here attacking supply wagons, mutinied and killed their British officers because the cartridges issued them for their rifles were rumored to be greased with animal fat. The Muslims believed it was pork; the Hindus, beef. *Photo:* New York Public Library Picture Collection.

payment of taxes induced peasants and landowners to grow commercial crops, and the area cultivated in cotton, indigo, opium, and jute—all products for export—increased significantly. In parts of Madras, cotton acreage doubled between 1830 and 1850, and in Bombay, the area planted to cotton increased by 1.5 million acres in the decade 1840–1850. The cultivation of opium, principally in Bengal, was stimulated by the rising demand of the China trade. Increased demand for indigo spurred a similar expansion of production, and by the 1830s a million acres in Bengal produced this blue dyestuff for processing in 400 local factories. A similar pattern occurred in jute production, and tea and coffee, two products in great demand in Europe, were introduced to India. In sum, India became an agricultural **hinterland**• of Great Britain, an entire subcontinent assigned the task of producing raw materials to feed the mouths, machines, mills, and trade of industrial England.

The impact of the European Industrial Revolution was keenly felt in the urban centers of India, which lost population between 1800 and 1850. By the 1830s, cheap manufactured cotton cloth from the textile mills of Manchester and Birmingham was flooding the Indian market. Native spinners and weavers, unable to compete with these inexpensive machine-woven goods, were driven out of business. The impact was greatest in urban textile centers such as Dacca, whose population dropped from 150,000 to 30,000. By midcentury, 45 percent of all Indian imports were textiles, and a once flourishing handicraft industry, from which manufacturing might have emerged, was destroyed in India.

As if taxes and textiles were not sufficiently shocking to the Indian body politic, British reformers began to suppress certain Hindu practices. The English reformers, affronted by the collective injustice of the caste system, replaced caste courts by civil courts that were deeply resented by upper-caste Hindus. In 1829, the practice of *suttee*, in which widows were encouraged (often with ropes or drugs) to immolate themselves on the burial pyres of their dead husbands, was outlawed. Similarly, the practices of child sacrifice, ritual murder, hook hanging (a particularly painful path to nirvana), and female infanticide were made illegal. Finally in 1856, permission was granted Hindu widows to remarry, a major violation of traditional belief. Although these particular social reforms were not the only sources of Indian unrest at midcentury, it was an issue of this type that triggered the rebellion that was to lead to a transfer of power from the British East India Company to the British Parliament.

INDIA AS A BRITISH COLONY (1858–1947)

On May 9, 1857, thousands of Indian soldiers (sepoys) were forced to stand at attention in the sun while sixty of their fellows were enchained and imprisoned for refusing to bite the greased cartridges for the new Enfield rifles—cartridges rumored to be greased with either pig or beef lard and therefore unclean to both Hindus and Muslims. The next day, Indian troops north of Delhi rose in revolt, and for a year, full-scale war raged across the Indo-Gangetic Plain between native Indian troops and the English. Major battles were fought at Delhi, Kanpur, and Lucknow. When it was over, the better-equipped, more mobile British were firmly entrenched. But confidence in company rule had evaporated, and it was recognized by London that India was far too important an enterprise to be left in the hands of merchants. India became a British colony; said the prime minister, Benjamin Disraeli, to Queen Victoria, "I gift you India, the brightest jewel in your Crown."

Rural India under British Rule

The Sepoy Mutiny and subsequent British rule had a profound and debilitating effect on rural Indians—80 percent of the total population. Never again would the British rely primarily on Indian troops to defend their interests in the subcontinent. Some 60,000 British troops and 120,000 sepoys were garrisoned on Indian soil, and the enormous expense of this military machine absorbed from one-third to one-half of the total revenues of the subcontinent each year. For similar security reasons, the British spread a web of railroads across India. A decade after the rebellion, 5000 miles of railroad had been opened to traffic, and by 1939 India had the largest rail system in Asia, some 41,134 miles of track. The primary source of money to pay for these railroads was, as always, the land. New and heavier taxes pushed an already oppressed peasantry deeper into debt. In 1911, the total debts of villagers amounted to more than $500 million; thirty years later, this debt had grown six times larger. Three forces were at the root of this problem: the taxation policies of the British, the continuing commercialization of agriculture, and the growth of India's population.

Under the British, zamindars and moneylenders, who had in the past taken the peasant's crop, now took his land as well. Armies of landless peasants, migrating with the harvest, became a new feature on the Indian landscape. Land became a commercial commodity, and its price rose steadily during the last half of the nineteenth century. In the Punjab, land that had been worth 10 rupees an acre in 1866 cost 238 rupees an acre by the 1920s. During the same period, land increased in price from 7 to 260

times the value of its annual production. In the process, the traditional structure of the village was destroyed and the cultivators lost their land.

By the 1920s, the rate of indebtedness in India was 25 times higher than property taxes, and the men who had come to own the land, the moneylenders, made up one-fourth of the total tax-paying population. In this circumstance, few technical innovations were introduced into the wheat and rice fields of India, and the yields on crops remained substantially below those in nations like Japan and China. What emerged was a society with a tiny, enormously wealthy *elite,* which effectively drained the produce from the poor. In Madras, for example, 849 zamindars owned 27.5 million acres of cultivated land on which 4.5 million peasants, living poorly and briefly, were driven by debt into miserable circumstances. Landless cultivators increased from 13 percent in 1891 to 38 percent in 1931. Even after independence, when the zamindar system was abolished, one-fifth of the villagers in India owned no land, and one-half of the cultivators owned less than an acre.

Paradoxically, agricultural acreage increased during this period, reflecting the continuing commercialization of agriculture in India and an expansion of irrigation. In Madras, cultivated land increased by 25 percent in the last half of the nineteenth century, while the amount of land in cotton in Bombay increased 30 percent between 1860 and 1875. In the Punjab, irrigation extended the arable into what had been dry wasteland. Overall, in the twenty years prior to World War I, the amount of cultivated land in British India increased from 197 million to 219 million acres, and the amount of irrigated land doubled.

In part this happened because of the revolution in transportation. By 1880, there were 20,000 miles of surfaced roads in India, a figure that tripled by 1939. These roads fed into the rail system, carrying commercial crops from the agricultural hinterlands of interior India to the coastal ports of Bombay, Madras, and Calcutta. As a result, the production of commercial crops like cotton, jute, coffee, tea, and indigo (until synthetic dyes were invented) increased.

Underlying the impoverishment of the peasantry and the commercialization of agriculture was a third force, population growth, which first became noticeable in rural India at the beginning of the twentieth century. The rate of growth was slow between 1870

The British in India: Travelers stopping for coffee, 1859.
Lithograph. *Photo:* The Bettman Archive.

and 1920 because of famines, but even so, population increased 20 percent, from 255 to 305 million.

The immediate cause of famine was the failure of the monsoon rains, but the commercialization of agriculture, which took land out of food production, aggravated the situation. The level of misery was indescribable: In 1866–1867, one of every four people in Orissa State died of starvation; by moderate calculations, 15 million people died in the famines of 1877–1878, 1889, 1892, 1897, and 1902. Local famines caused by regional scarcity in prerailroad days were replaced by national famines generated by overall food shortages, high prices, and unemployment. In addition, during the second decade of the twentieth century, influenza epidemics raised the mortality rate, again retarding population growth. In 1918 through 1919 alone, influenza killed an estimated 12 million to 13 million Indians. But in the decades that followed, rudimentary Western medicine and sanitation practices took hold, and India's population began to grow at an annual rate of 1.2 percent. The proud boast of English writers that "British brains, British enterprise, and British capital" had transformed the face of India was true, but the face was one of misery.

Urban India and British Industry
Incredibly, at the end of the nineteenth century, India was no more urbanized than a century earlier; an estimated 10 percent of the population lived in cities in 1800, and only 9 percent in 1870. The reasons for this decline were clear: British policies inhibited the development of Indian industry to Britain's own advantage. The technological revolution in the West was reducing India to the status of a farm of limited capacity. In textiles, Britain protected domestic industry at home with tariffs while opening India to duty-free British cloth. For a while, Parliament even prohibited the export of machinery to India to retard industrial growth. These actions forced artisans out of the cities and drove them back into agriculture, so that whereas 61 percent of India's population was engaged in agriculture in 1891, by 1921 the figure was 73 percent. In the villages, population growth led to subdivision and fragmentation of the land, which had the effect of parceling out employment among larger numbers of people without increasing production. To be sure, limited urbanization and industrialization did occur. Commercial and factory growth in the large seaports of Bombay, Madras, and Calcutta converted these cities into metropolitan centers. The older religious and administrative cities of the interior grew or declined depending on their relation to the railroad network. The overall growth of manufacturing was, however, too slow to absorb an expanding population, and by the outbreak of World War II, less than 2 million people in India were employed in factories. And of those who were employed in the modern industrial sector of the economy, one-third worked in British-owned textile mills.

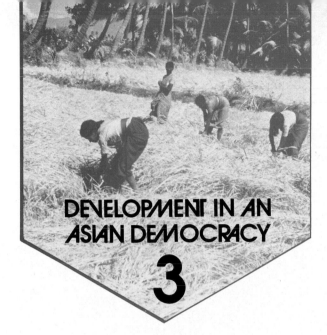

DEVELOPMENT IN AN ASIAN DEMOCRACY
3

Given this legacy of colonial rule, the national leaders of independent India faced three major problems that transcended both the joy of *svaraj* (self-government) and the pain of partition. First, divisive religious and linguistic loyalties created tensions between national unity and regional cultures that threatened to split the nation. Second, population growth, low productivity, and colonial agricultural policies had created an agrarian crisis of massive proportions in village India. Third, urbanization without industrialization had created slums across urban India, and the slow rate of industrialization meant too few jobs for too many people. If a strong, independent, democratic nation was to be forged on the Indian subcontinent, all three of these problems would have to be resolved.

NATIONAL UNITY AND REGIONAL CULTURES
[FIGURE 3]

The "Quit India" campaign finally succeeded; in 1947, the British did quit. Gandhi and his fellow Indians had achieved their primary political goal: self-government. *Svaraj* celebrations were muted, however, by the intensity of the communal riots between Hindus and Muslims in northern India and by the mass migrations and economic dislocations caused by division of the subcontinent. The Muslim-dominated regions of the northwest and northeast became the new state of Pakistan; the remainder, India. But the new borders left millions of Hindus and Muslims on the wrong side of their respective boundaries. Some 17 million people migrated—Hindus to India, Muslims to Pakistan. Nearly a million people died of torture, murder, and starvation. The legacy of bitterness between India and Pakistan spurred two wars, in 1948 and in 1965, over the disputed territory of Kashmir in the northwest; another war ended in the formation of Bangladesh from East Pakistan in 1972.

Economic disruptions caused by partition were many. West Pakistan, a principal food-producing region of the subcontinent, was separated from the iron and coal resources of India. The cotton fields of Sind and the jute plantations of Bengal belonged to Pakistan, yet the cotton mills and the jute factories were in India. Everything was divided: criminals, mental patients, government supplies, and railroad cars. Shared and divided as well were the underlying cultural and economic problems of the subcontinent: a rapidly expanding population, a slowly expanding and poorly exploited resource base, widespread and endemic poverty, and problems of local and regional separatism and isolation.

Hinduism was the only common cultural denominator on the subcontinent, providing, as the poet Rabindranath Tagore notes, "a unity of the spirit" that transcended local distinctions. Within this unity, a variety of races, religions, languages, and regional economies found their places, so that at independence, India embraced within her borders a greater array of cultures than ever existed on the entire continent of Europe. Though the nation was still splintered into 562 princely states, some of them large enough to have their own postal systems and currencies, these were quickly absorbed. Fourteen major languages and 845 separate dialects were spoken on the subcontinent. The largest language group (Hindi, Hindustani, and Urdu) accounted for 40 percent of the population but was confined to the Aryan north and therefore completely alien to the Dravidian-speaking south. In addition, the principal intermediaries between the Europeans and Indians, some of the most skilled and educated people in the country, lost credibility after independence. These Anglo-Indians, people of mixed European and Indian blood that fit no caste or other social category devised by Hinduism, played a limited role in the formation of the new nation. Thus the normal bases for communication and nationhood were weak. India had no means for incorporating all these differences: it was no melting pot. Welding a single nation out of these diverse peoples became the central goal of the new leaders of Indian society.

These people correctly perceived the centrifugal effects of provincial, linguistic, and religious loyalties as one of the most dangerous legacies of the Indian past. What they feared was a ***balkanization*** of the nation into a series of small religious and linguis-

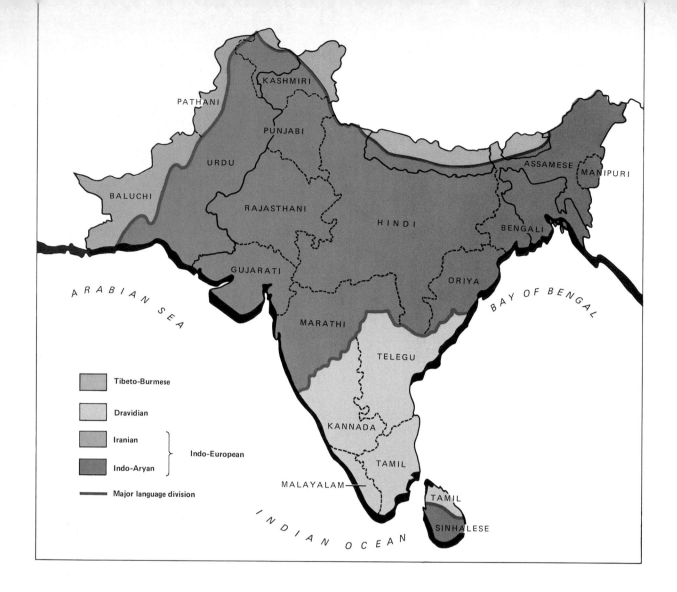

Figure 3. Main Language Groups of India.

tic states whose ties to Delhi would wither, whose religious problems and interregional rivalries would destroy the hope of a strong and unified twentieth-century India.

Under the direction of the urbane Jawaharlal Nehru, the new leaders of India turned to these problems. Their task was to transform the world's second most populous nation after China (there were 359 million Indians in 1950 and 574 million in 1973) into a modern industrial state, to achieve Gandhi's poetic ambition of "wiping every tear from every eye." These men brought to their task an honest and efficient civil service trained in the British tradition and a unified Congress party blooded by twenty-five years of passive resistance to British rule. Almost immediately, the new government dethroned the independent rulers of the 500 or so princely states of India, absorbing their area into the new republic and ensuring national territorial integrity. In 1949, a constitution was drawn up, guaranteeing that "all power and authority" would spring "from the people"; in 1950, the first election for state and federal offices was held. The Congress party won a popular plurality and a majority of seats in the lower house of Parliament. Its leader, Nehru, became India's first prime minister. Almost overnight, India became the world's largest democracy, with 173 million voters.

Language Groups and Political Fragmentation

After political partitioning had defused the principal source of religious disunity from the nation (although there were still 61 million Muslims in India in 1971), the problem of regional languages remained a threat to national cohesion. During their long struggle against British rule, nationalists had been forced to use English as their means of communication, their lingua franca. Regional subcommittees of the Congress party were organized according to linguistic divisions in Indian society. From the beginning, Indian nationalists were committed to redrawing state and provincial boundaries on the basis of regional languages.

Language, a mirror of history, reflects past battles and conquests, migrations and assimilation. Modern Indian languages express the historical experience of the subcontinent. India was wholly inhabited by Dravidian-speaking peoples until about 1500 BC when horse-riding Aryan nomads from Central Asia, speaking a variety of early Indo-European languages, moved through the northern passes of the Himalayas onto the plains of India. The Aryans introduced Hindi and related languages to the subcontinent. Over the next 1000 years, the invaders pushed the shorter, dark-skinned Dravidians southward into the Deccan hills and down the coasts of peninsular India. Here they remain: 24 percent of the Indian population, heavily concentrated in South India, speaking Dravidian languages. Four Dravidian languages are included among the fourteen recognized in the Indian constitution, and each is the principal language of a state: Telegu (Andhra Pradesh State), Tamil (Tamilnadu State), Kannada (Mysore State), and Malayalam (Kerala State) (see table).

Later in Indian history, Muslim Persians and Turks invaded northern India between the eighth and twelfth centuries. These conquerors developed a mixed language, Urdu, in order to speak with their Hindu neighbors, the Hindu women in their harems, and Hindu soldiers under their command. Originally an Indo-European language, Urdu borrowed words from Arabic, Persian, and Turkish, and was written in Arabic-Persian script. Today Urdu is still the language of educated Muslims throughout India and is one of the official languages of Pakistan. It has, however, always remained the language of the conqueror, while the subject peoples of northern India continued to speak the Indo-European languages of their homelands, principally Hindi. Despite centuries of Muslim rule, today, after partition, only 11 percent (61 million) of Indians are Muslim, whereas 83 percent (453 million) are Hindu.

At independence in 1947, it was assumed that English would gradually be replaced by Hindi, the language with the largest number of speakers in the country. But English has remained the language of Western culture, education, science, medicine, technology, and is the language of government when either party does not speak Hindi. English is spoken by only a small percentage of India's population, but this group governs and guides the country.

Major Languages of India, 1961 Census		
Source: Philip Mason (ed.), *India and Ceylon: Unity and Diversity, A Symposium*. Oxford, Eng.: Oxford University Press, 1967, p. 54. © 1967 Institute of Race Relations. Reprinted by permission of the Oxford University Press, Oxford.		
Language	Population (millions)*	Percentage of total population (439 million)
Hindi	133.4	30.4
Urdu	23.3	5.3
Punjabi	10.9	2.5
	167.6	38.2
Bihari†	16.8	3.8
Rajasthani†	14.9	3.4
	31.7	7.2
Telegu	37.7	8.6
Bengali	33.9	7.7
Marathi	33.3	7.6
Tamil	30.6	7.0
Gujarati	20.3	4.6
Kannada	17.4	4.0
Malayalam	17.0	3.9
Oriya	15.7	3.6
Assamese	6.8	1.5
Kashmiri	1.9	0.4
Sanskrit	0.002	0.00045

* These sixteen languages are used by 414 million speakers out of the total 439 million. More recent figures are not available.
† Not recognized by the Indian constitution, but included here because of their similarity to Hindi and their importance.

India, however, needed a national language of her own—continued use of English would widen the gap between the country's political elite and the masses of isolated population. Gandhi, himself a native speaker of Gujarati, sponsored the North Indian language of Hindustani (halfway between Hindi and Urdu), because with its closely related languages of Hindi, Urdu, Punjabi, Bihari, and Rajasthani, it was spoken by a plurality of the Indian population (in 1961 about 45 percent). The selection was not very popular with the Dravidian-speaking peoples of the

PLURALISM AND DIVERSITY IN CALCUTTA

The social and linguistic diversity of Calcutta is typical of other large Indian cities. Calcutta was founded late in the seventeenth century as a seaport and trading post of the British East India Company. As British power grew, Hindus from Bengal, mainly merchant castes (bankers, spice dealers, and gold traders), as well as upper-caste Brahmans, moved from smaller ports upstream on the Ganges to this growing commercial center. This group of upper-class Hindus formed the non-European elite of Calcutta and lived in the old "native quarter" north of the central square (maidan),

Adapted from: Nirmal K. Bose, "Calcutta: A Premature Metropolis," *Scientific American,* Vol. 213 (September 1965), p. 94 (right), p. 95 (left), p. 96. Copyright © 1965 by Scientific American, Inc. All rights reserved.

where specific castes like the Subarnabanik bankers and Kansari brassworkers still reside today. In time, they were joined by lower-caste Hindus who trickled into the city from hinterland villages for a variety of economic reasons. As the irrigation systems of Bengal began to break down in the late nineteenth century and malaria became epidemic in the region, a flood of migrants sought refuge in the city. Calcutta became, in Kipling's words, "the city of dreadful night": an overcrowded, diseased urban society. At the time of partition, in 1947, another tide of some 700,000 Bengali refugees from East Pakistan fled to Calcutta; this was repeated during the war in Bangladesh (the former East Pakistan) in 1970 and 1971. Now Bengali Hindus make up more than half the population of the city and are found in every quarter, pushed by circumstance from their village homes.

Although Bengalis dominate the upper and middle classes of Calcutta, other communities have also been attracted to the city. Members of the Rajasthani commercial castes and traders from Gujarat, including the famous Parsi or Zoroastrian community, have moved to Calcutta. Sikhs and Punjabis in the south of the city are important in urban transport. South Indians from Mysore,

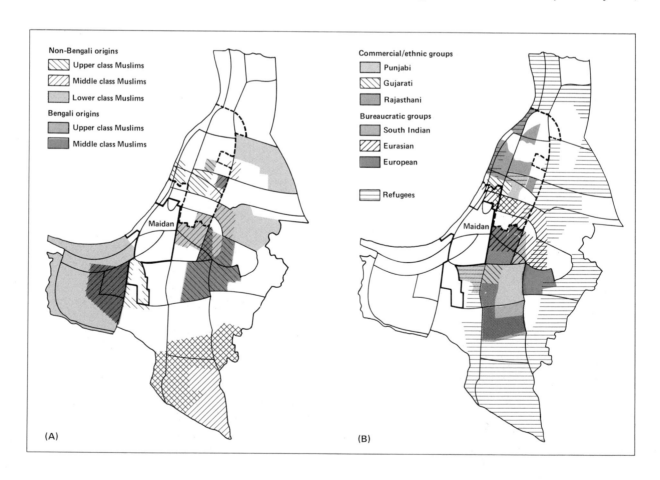

Kerala, and Madras have come to Calcutta for white-collar jobs in government offices. In addition, two large Muslim quarters are located in the southern and southwestern parts of the city.

Although Calcutta's fundamental cultural matrix is Bengali, and this group leads the city and at the same time constitutes three-quarters of the unemployed, the highly differentiated linguistic and religious texture of Calcutta demonstrates that cities in India cannot be likened to the melting pots of the New World. Calcutta schools teach Bengali, Hindi, Gujarati, and Oriya; pressures for linguistic homogenization are weak. The national government has tried to replace these divisive religious and linguistic loyalties with a sense of national consciousness, deploring the "fissiparous tendencies," as the Indian journalists call them, that split the nation. In fact, most observers concede that religious, linguistic, and caste consciousness has strengthened rather than weakened since independence, providing yet one more thorny problem for a nation with far too many.

south. But at independence, of all the languages and dialects scattered across the face of India, Hindi was designated as the "official language of the Union." English, spoken by about 1 percent of the population and 6 percent of all literate Indians, would "continue to be used" until 1965 for "official purposes." In addition to Hindi, the constitution recognized thirteen other "languages of India" —Urdu, Punjabi, Telegu, Bengali, Marathi, Tamil, Gujarati, Kannada, Malayalam, Oriya, Assamese, Kashmiri, and Sanskrit. The entire language problem was deferred until 1955 when a special commission would study the question.

But the issue was too highly charged with emotion to await the deliberations of a future commission, and between 1953 and 1960 the central government of India was forced to redraw its internal frontiers to give spatial and administrative expression to the demands of other regional language groups.

In 1952, the Telegu-speaking population of Madras, resentful of the dominance of Tamil-speaking bureaucrats in the province, demanded the establishment of a separate language-based state to be called Andhra Pradesh. In Delhi, Nehru argued against acceding to "foolish and tribal attitudes" that would strengthen provincialism, but when one of the Telegu leaders, Potti Sriramalu, died during a hunger strike, the central government acquiesced to local demands, and the new Telegu state was created in 1953. Three years later, the language commission recommended a spatial reorganization of India into fourteen states and six territories, recognizing "linguistic homogeneity as an important

factor conducive to administrative convenience and efficiency." But two of the most sensitive linguistic regions in India, Bombay and the Punjab, were not reorganized by the commission, and the demands of tribal groups were ignored.

The problem in Bombay State lay not in separate hinterlands of Marathi and Gujarati speakers, but in the city of Bombay itself, where the majority of the population spoke Marathi but the wealthy elite spoke Gujarati. As soon as the report of the language commission was issued, widespread rioting broke out in Marathi-speaking districts and the population of the region became polarized over the language issue. Again resisting further subdivision in India, Nehru appealed for a sense of national consciousness in Bombay, asking, "Who lives if India dies, and who dies if India lives?" Finally in 1960, Bombay State was subdivided into two new linguistic states, Gujarat and Maharashtra, with the city of Bombay included as a part of the latter. Gujarat received compensation for the loss of the major metropolitan area.

The next demand for regional autonomy in India came not from linguistic groups, but from tribal communities, which number some 30 million people in India and are mostly concentrated in remote hill and forest areas on the Deccan Plateau and in the foothills of the Himalayas. In the Chota Nagpur hills of southern Bihar, some 6 million Munda-speaking tribesmen, led by an Oxford-educated economist, demanded the establishment of an independent state to be called Jharkhand. Congress party leaders granted the tribes a series of important concessions, and temporarily at least averted the formation of a tribal state. But in the north, in Nagaland, the demand for a separate state in the hills along the Assam-Burma border posed a far more serious question. Administration was far more tenuous in this region, amounting only to an unenforced ban on headhunting and intertribal feuds. By 1956, the rebellion of Naga tribesmen against Indian rule had become so serious that a division of Indian troops had to be sent into the region. In 1963, the state of Nagaland was created under the jurisdiction of the state of Assam, but tribes aspiring to independent status continued to engage in guerrilla warfare against the Indian state despite the investment of large sums in the region in an effort to shift their allegiances from tribe to nation.

In the Punjab, a complex religious and linguistic problem involved one of the most militant communities in India, the Sikhs. This religious group, which originated in the Punjab in the sixteenth century, initially blended both Muslim and Hindu doctrines. Persecuted by the Moguls in the seventeenth century, the Sikhs became a fiercely independent, violently anti-Muslim people, and assumed their special characteristics—the beard, the turban, the dagger, and the universal name of Singh (lion). By 1960 they were requesting a separate Sikh state, a new Punjab (Punjabi Suba) based on linguistic grounds, which really amounted to a difference in script between the Devanagari writing of the Hindus and the Gurmukhi script in which the Sikh sacred texts, the Granth Sahib, were written. Once again, adherence to revived traditional beliefs and a strict pattern of personal asceticism arose to take the form of political action. After considerable agitation and fasting by Sikh leaders, the central government divided the Punjab into two states in 1966. Punjab, now 55 percent Sikh, was carved out of the western Sikh-dominated districts, and Hindu Haryana out of the east.

Consequences of Linguistic Fragmentation

The formation of linguistic states in India, despite persistent government opposition, has provided the geographical foundation for a fragmentation of the Indian union into subnational groupings not unlike the pattern that existed prior to British rule. The strength of these centrifugal forces is difficult to ascertain. Before secessionist movements became illegal, important Tamil-speaking leaders in Madras openly advocated the formation of a separate Dravidian nation in the south. As a result of these pressures, English was retained as an associate language in India, deferring the implementation of mandatory Hindi, considered an inferior language in the south. In the school system, instruction is in the regional language, although Hindi is required at the secondary level, and English is retained as an option in the public examination system for government positions. This three-language formula is an awkward attempt to resolve regional tensions that have persisted despite efforts to centralize the subcontinent in the past. From a cultural viewpoint, it may be that the Indian capacity for sustaining incompatibles will in the end be decisive. But the most significant economic factor in this conflict between state and federal power will be the allocation of government development funds, particularly in the agricultural sector, where a crisis of massive proportions has developed since independence.

THE AGRARIAN CRISIS

Few countries had such idealistic leadership at birth as India. Nehru and the Congress party were democratic socialists, whose goal of an "equitable distribution of the national wealth" aimed at the establishment of a socialist society. But the departure of the British created numerous vacancies in important positions with lavish privileges. The Delhi palace, which Gandhi wanted to convert into a hospital, became the president's residence, and throughout India the elite sought pomp, ceremonies, personal estates, and large cars. Lacking pressure from the masses, the politicians were soon separated from the people by a gulf of comfort and they postponed major reforms in the social and economic system of the country.

Publicly they condemned caste, communalism, lingualism, and provincialism—forces that fragmented national life; privately they sought the votes of caste lobbies and language groupings. Nowhere did the discrepancy between oratory and reality appear more striking than in the half million villages of India, where a peasant population of some 361 million existed on the fringes of starvation, earning a per capita income of less than $60 per year. Food imported from foreign sources was required to avoid famine. Clearly India's most compelling problems lay in the agricultural sector.

To cope with rural poverty and foodstuff insufficiency, the Nehru government proposed to follow two policies: first, the distribution of zamindar land to the peasants, and second, the growth of peasant productivity through assistance offered under a community development program. The abolition of landlordism would raise agricultural productivity by giving the cultivator actual title to the land and by reducing high rents and peasant indebtedness. But the passage of laws to accomplish this was left to the state assemblies, where landlord interests were strongly represented. Figures published in 1961 claimed that zamindar holdings had diminished to 8.5 percent of the cultivated area of India, but these statistics were illusory. In the mid-1950s, about half the total agricultural acreage in India was still held by less than one-eighth of the agrarian population. Unlike China, India did not restructure land ownership in the hinterland; the pattern of land ownership inherited from the British remained intact. The first prong of the Nehru policy failed, and this failure to alter the social structure of agriculture had a crippling effect on the community development program.

Under this program, which was begun to "improve all aspects of village life," the village was naively viewed in the new India as a vital repository of traditional Indian values, and so was selected as the spatial basis of a new rural Indian society. Adversely affected by the century of British rule, these villages were no longer meaningful social units, but nonetheless new schools, medical centers, and marketing facilities sprang up across the subcontinent. The idea was that peasants would respond to their "felt

Indian planners, following the ideological lead of Gandhi, used the village as the basic unit to introduce new methods and technology to agricultural producers. This approach is not viable in India. In The Organization of Space in Developing Countries, E. A. J. Johnson uses the example of the Kanpur region of Uttar Pradesh in northern India to illustrate the impossibility of using the village as the spatial and functional economic unit of Indian development.

Johnson sees the Indian dilemma as one in which the village farmer must experience repeated contact with a "package of practices": new technological and agricultural advances, supplies necessary to use these advances, equitable marketing facilities, a transportation network, and impartial credit. India's rural population has only limited access to this "package" and to the world outside their villages. The Kanpur region illustrates the problem.

Kanpur, with a population of over 1 million, is the major city of Uttar Pradesh. It is the urban center for a 17,000-square-mile region inhabited by 10 million people. Hierarchically, the Kanpur region has 11,239 villages, 24 urban centers officially recognized as towns, and 28 smaller urban centers plus the city of Kanpur. In the idealized terms of regional planning, each officially recognized town must serve 468 villages, an impossibility even with excellent transportation and communications networks. Only five or six of the smaller urban centers can serve as market centers for the town's surrounding hinterland. The arithmetic of this regional system shows its ineffectiveness: less than 60 central places must serve 10 million people living in 11,239 villages over 17,000 square miles. In fact, little meaningful contact exists between these villages and their market towns (central places), because over a third of the villages have no roads of any sort, and another third have unsurfaced roads unusable during the summer monsoon season. A second problem is the distance of villages from their market centers: 42 percent are more than 5 miles away, 18 percent more than 10 miles. All this means, in reality, that most villagers enter into the market economy on an irregular basis.

What Johnson terms the "crux of the spatial problem" focuses on the villages with no roads at all: over 36 percent of all Kanpur settlements, more than 3 million people in 4100 villages. This population, as large as that of Norway, is poorly integrated into the marketing economy of its region. The people must transport their produce or purchases on pack animals or their own backs to and from the market. Nearly half these villages without roads lie more than 5 miles from a market center, while almost a fifth are more than 10 miles away.

On this basis, it is clear that the marketing center, not the village, must be the basic economic unit in Indian regional planning. What is needed are roads, an organized system of market centers, and a set of practices to encourage investment and development on the local level.

Source: E. A. J. Johnson, The Organization of Space in Developing Countries. Cambridge, Mass.: Harvard University Press, 1970.

needs" when technological improvements were demonstrated, but the program ignored the caste system, property rights, and village unemployment, three important realities in village India. Tractors, new types of seed, new crops, commercial fertilizer, cooperative markets, and a host of long-tried elements of **land reform**● found their way into villages in every region of India; but the basic reform, a change in land ownership patterns, was ignored. As a result, the market surplus of India's villages continued to be drained off by the landlord elite, the spread of a market economy into rural areas was retarded, and agricultural productivity did not substantially increase.

This failure, however, was not immediately apparent to the economic planners. Huge irrigation projects constructed in the Damodar Valley west of Calcutta and on the Mahanadi River brought 3.4 million acres of land into cultivation. By the good luck of two beneficial monsoons in 1953 and 1954, the first five-year plan (1951–1955) succeeded in raising agricultural production by 22 percent. India's goal of self-sufficiency in food grains appeared to be within reach.

As a result, the second five-year plan (1956–1961) confidently apportioned a larger share of the total budget, nearly a fifth, to the development of mining

A human pile driver, Calcutta. *Photo:* Patrick Miller/Design Photographers International.

Nowhere are India's urban problems more pressing than in its largest city, Calcutta, where 7 million people are crowded into 400 square miles. Located on the wet, flat delta of the Ganges and Brahmaputra rivers, Calcutta is India's largest seaport and most productive manufacturing center, with a cosmopolitan population drawn from the diverse regions, religions, and language groupings of the subcontinent. The central business district along the Hooghly River is so crowded that an estimated half-million pedestrians and 30,000 vehicles cross the Howrah Bridge each day. Residential apartment complexes and slums surround the central city, and higher-class suburbs lie to the south. Three-quarters of the population live in overcrowded tenement districts; 57 percent live in unbaked brick houses. More than half the families in the city have only a single room to live in, with an average of 30 square feet of living space for each family member. In the slums, each water tap serves twenty-five to thirty people, each latrine about twenty; garbage is never collected. The figures are reminiscent of nineteenth-century London in the early stages of industrialization. The problem in Calcutta today is that industrialization is not proceeding rapidly enough to employ, house, and feed the population.

By 1960, no major progress in Calcutta's physical development appeared sufficient to cope with these conditions. Today in Calcutta, and specifically in the bustee *quarters, cholera is endemic. In addition, Calcutta has between 35,000 and 40,000 lepers in eight colonies around the city, the largest single concentration in the world. Epidemics are frequent, disease is commonplace. At least 400,000 men in Calcutta were jobless in 1961—a formidable array of beggers, day laborers, and pieceworkers—all urban hunters and gatherers. The social costs of hesitant planning in the face of these conditions have been high.*

tea of Assam, and most recently the industrial production of the Chota Nagpur district centered on Jamshedpur. Bombay, the second leading manufacturing city in India, tapped the cotton production of the Deccan Plateau, the hydroelectric reserves of the Western Ghats, and capitalized on its western location (closer to Europe) to become a major center of East-West commerce and banking. Delhi and Madras have maintained their roles as administrative and service centers. Each city grew by unplanned accretion, creating massive contemporary problems of housing, transportation, and sanitation. In some states, newly planned capital towns like Faridabad near New Delhi, Ulhasnagar near Bombay, Kandla in Gujarat, and the new steel towns of Durgapur and Rourkela incorporate advanced urban planning ideas; but in the largest cities, urban growth has been uncontrolled and may be out of control.

Approximately four-fifths of India's urban growth between 1951 and 1961 occurred by natural increase; only one of five city residents was a migrant from the agricultural hinterland. But these migrants moved to established urban centers, and at least partly for this reason, large cities grew more rapidly than smaller towns in India. Cities with more than a million people—which in 1961 included Greater Calcutta, Greater Bombay, Greater Delhi, Madras, Hyderabad, Ahmadabad, and Bangalore—increased by 26 percent between 1951 and 1961, cities between 500,000 and 1 million by 66 percent, and cities between 100,000 and 500,000 by 29 percent—all percentages higher than average. The attraction of these agglomerations continued during the 1960s so that by 1971 Calcutta alone had a population of 7 million, Bombay 5.9 million, Delhi 3.6 million, Madras 2.5 million, and two other cities, Kanpur and Poona, had been added to the list of Indian cities with populations over 1 million.

Rapid growth has generated slums, serious crowding, and almost unmanageable problems of public health and transport. The density of population in Calcutta averages 36,000 per square mile, Madras 28,000, Bombay 24,000, and Delhi 22,000; but in some sections, densities approach 500,000 per square mile. By contrast, New York has an average density of 24,000 per square mile, Chicago 16,000. Within these cities, dwellings are being added at a rate of 200,000 per year, but population increase demands a construction rate ideally eight times higher.

Urban centers also have grown without a commensurate shift in the occupational structure, making even menial jobs difficult to find. As a result, immigrants from rural India pile up on the outskirts of these cities in shantytowns, called *bustees*, lacking rudimentary water, medical, or sewage facilities.

In Calcutta, roughly one-quarter of the population lives in *bustees;* thousands more, even less fortunate, live and sleep in railroad stations, temple grounds, and on sidewalks. A count made in 1961 tallied 30,000 people sleeping in the streets; eight years later a newspaper counted 70,000 in a partial survey of a city that sprawls over 400 square miles. An estimated eight out of ten urbanites live in poverty, four out of ten in destitution, and the mortality rate in urban India in the 1950s remained higher than in rural areas. Underlying these conditions was, of course, India's growing population problem.

INDIA

THE INDUSTRIAL BASE
ENERGY AND MINERAL RESOURCES MAP

During the colonial period, the economy of the Indian subcontinent was oriented toward domestic consumption, and external trade was tied by colonial rule to the markets of the British Empire. Principal exports were agricultural commodities typical of those on which colonial trade relied—cotton, jute, tea, and spices—as well as a few minerals, such as mica used in the electrical industry and manganese for steel making. Imports were limited to small amounts of machine and manufactured goods, which left India with a favorable balance of trade, but low productivity in industry and low rates of internal industrial growth. This colonial economic pattern effectively ended with independence. Nehru and his successors have attempted to create a diversified modern industrial nation on the subcontinent; India is no longer content merely to produce raw materials for the industrial West.

To accelerate industrial growth, sophisticated machinery and scarce raw materials for manufacturing were imported to expand India's industrial capacity. Petroleum and lubricants, necessary to sustain industrial growth, and fertilizers, purchased to increase commercial agricultural production, became import items on the Indian balance sheet. In absolute terms, this policy had the desired effect: By 1970 the Indian industrial product had expanded four times since independence; finished steel production rose even more. In the context of India's economy, however, this rate of growth was too slow to shift a significant percentage of the population from agriculture to industry and too limited to provide the numbers and kinds of jobs needed by a rapidly expanding and unskilled population.

Cotton, tea, jute, tobacco, iron, coal, manganese, and mica continued as principal exports, but with policies of expanded industrial imports, Indian commodities are not of sufficient value to maintain a favorable balance of trade. Periodically, agricultural deficits force India to import foreign grains to avert famine; the currently rising cost of petroleum products threatens to absorb so much of India's foreign credits that imports of machinery and fertilizer may have to be curtailed, thereby slowing down industrial growth. Although modern India possesses an integrated national transportation system and the energy and mineral resources necessary to build a powerful industrial state, low agricultural productivity and high population growth have retarded the process. After twenty-five years of economic planning, 70 percent of the Indian population still relies directly on agriculture: economically, India has been treading water.

ENERGY SOURCES

India has the potential energy sources to sustain rapid industrial growth, but with the exception of coal, these resources have remained largely undeveloped. Coal is the principal source of industrial energy in India. Reserves of *bituminous*• and lower grade coals are substantial but high-grade *coking coals*• needed for steel making are quite limited. Annual coal production now amounts to over 70 million tons, making India the eighth leading producer in the world. Roughly one-quarter of this output is used up by the railroads, a fifth by heavy industry, and the remainder is used for light industry, power production, and domestic consumption. Some coal is exported.

Though coal reserves are scattered throughout the peninsula, mining is concentrated in the Chota Nagpur hills of northeastern India, where the Damodar fields yield 60 percent of the national output. This concentration of production creates a bottleneck in distribution, inhibiting industrial growth in regions remote from the producing fields. Two other factors have also presented problems: over 80 percent of the fields are owned or leased by small producers in the private sector, and most miners are tribesmen from the forested hills of Chota Nagpur. Labor strife has been acute.

Alternative sources of energy have great potential in India. Petroleum production in Assam, the Punjab, and Gujarat amounts to only one-eighth of India's needs, thus making oil imports a major drain on the Indian economy. The geological structure of the Indo-Gangetic Plain, the delta of the Ganges and Brahmaputra rivers, and the ocean floor off the northwest coast of India, however, appears to hold promise for future production, and considerable exploration for oil is now under way. Similarly, the hydroelectric potential of India is sizable, although this potential has been partially developed only along the Western and Eastern

139

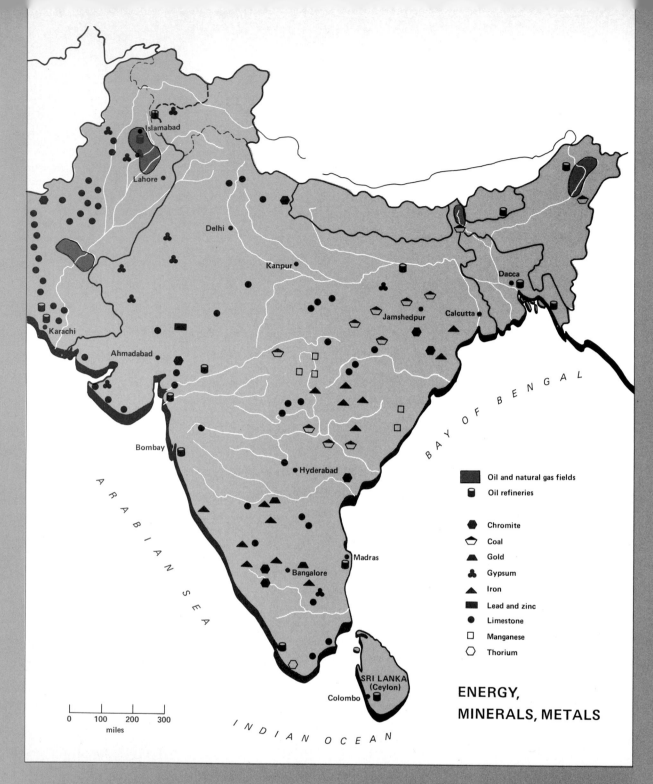

**ENERGY,
MINERALS, METALS**

Legend:

- Oil and natural gas fields
- Oil refineries
- Chromite
- Coal
- Gold
- Gypsum
- Iron
- Lead and zinc
- Limestone
- Manganese
- Thorium

Ghats and in the Damodar Valley. The greatest limitations on hydroelectric expansion are the high costs of multipurpose dam construction and the pronounced seasonal flow of India's rivers, which flood in the summer monsoon season and dry up in the winter.

Finally, in the long run, India has an abundance of resources that can be transformed into the raw materials of atomic energy. The world's largest deposits of thorium exist in the beach sands of the Malabar Coast and in *placer deposits* in Bihar; zirconium, used as a *refractory* in atomic reactors, is also found in the black sands, and uranium deposits exist in Rajasthan. India has exploded a nuclear device, and several atomic stations have been constructed near Bombay, in Rajasthan, and outside Madras. Other sources of energy, though perhaps less prestigious, remain less expensive.

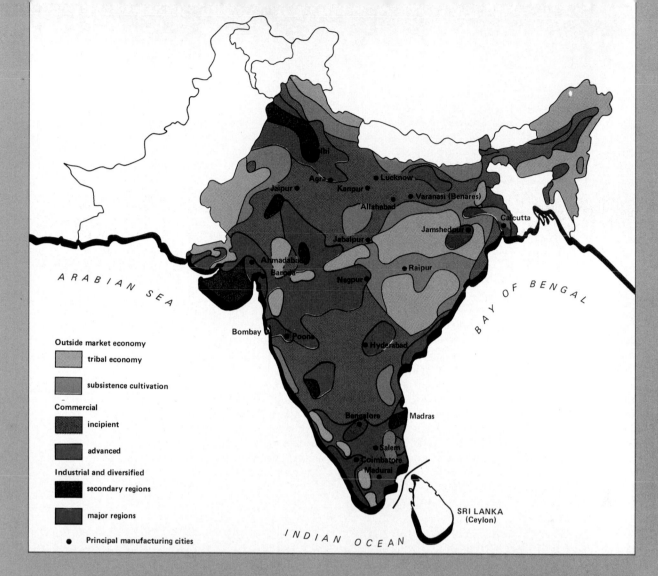

Figure 4. Levels of Economic Development. Levels of economic development in India vary from regions of tribal gatherers to heavily industrialized metropolitan centers. *After:* Joseph E. Schwartzberg, "Three Approaches to the Mapping of Economic Development in India," *Annals of the Association of American Geographers,* Vol. 52 (December 1962), p. 460, Fig. 5. Reproduced by permission.

MINERALS AND METALS

Except for insufficient coal of coking quality, India has the resources to support a major expansion of heavy industry; the largest reserves of high-grade iron ore in the world and substantial reserves of important *alloy minerals*[•] are found on the subcontinent. The major iron-producing area is in Bihar, where a range of iron some 40 miles in length is estimated to hold some 3 billion tons of exploitable ore. New iron fields in this region and in Mysore are being developed for export purposes, and considerable expansion of the annual production of 12 million tons per year is anticipated. Similarly, India is a world producer of manganese, and the fields in Orissa, Madhya Pradesh, and Mysore produce over a million tons a year, 80 percent of which is exported. Chromite is also mined

for export, as are gold, industrial diamonds, bauxite (for aluminum), and mica.

India is less well endowed with *nonferrous metals*[•]: over 90 percent of the copper, lead, zinc, and asbestos India needs must be imported. Tungsten, cobalt, and nickel are absent. Of those minerals used in fertilizer production, gypsum and limestone are plentiful, but phosphates must be imported from North Africa for use on fields planted in the new wheats and rices.

LEVELS OF ECONOMIC DEVELOPMENT
[FIGURE 4]

Although the efforts of Indian planners to modernize and diversify the Indian economy have not entirely succeeded, successive five-year plans have created a new map of levels of economic development in India. Five types of economic regions, based on levels of industrialization, degree of commercialization in the rural economy, and extent of urbanization can be identified: first, there are regions of industrial and economic diversification, heavily industrialized and highly urbanized, in which over half the population is engaged in nonagricultural pursuits; second, regions of advanced commercialization with relatively high rates of urbanization and a major emphasis on commercial agricultural production; third, regions of incipient commercialization characterized by modest rates of urban development and a limited amount of commercial agriculture; fourth, regions of subsistence cultivation in which virtually no land is devoted to commercial crops, agricultural manufacturing is limited, and urbanization is minimal; and fifth, regions of tribal economy which for all intents and purposes do not yet enter into the national sphere.

Industrial and Economic Diversification
Five major regions have emerged in India: Calcutta and Jamshedpur in the northeast, Bombay and Ahmadabad-Baroda in the northwest, Bangalore-Madurai-Coimbatore in the south. In 1967, these five regions with the addition of Uttar Pradesh produced three-quarters of India's industrial goods and accounted for seven of every ten industrial workers and two-thirds of all factories in India. Each of these regions is located on the coast or on a major river system, facilitating the transport of raw materials and manufactured goods. Peripheral to the five major *industrial nodes*• and such administrative and manufacturing centers as Delhi, Madras, Hyderabad, and Kanpur are city regions with high levels of economic diversification in which over half the population is engaged in agricultural processing and small-scale cottage industry. These regions are central intersections in India's extensive railroad system, which carries over half of all passenger traffic and three-quarters of all freight in the country. They are also the principal centers of innovation and modernization on the subcontinent, the focus of development schemes from which new concepts, new materials, and new techniques diffuse to village India.

Advanced Commercialization
These regions have a relatively high degree of urbanization and a strong emphasis on commercial agriculture, and are generally areas where the commercial cultivation of a single major crop has produced a higher level of economic development. In northern India, these regions include the tea plantations of Assam, the jute fields of Bengal, areas of sugar production on the Indo-Gangetic Plain, the green revolution wheat zones of Punjab, and the cotton-producing regions of Gujarat and Maharashtra. In southern India, production of commercial crops in regions of advanced *mercantilism*• is more diversified. Cotton, oilseeds, coffee, and new varieties of rice are grown in different parts of Tamilnadu (Madras), Mysore, and Andhra Pradesh. In all these regions, agricultural processing plants and small-scale manufacturing are widespread.

Incipient Commercialization
These regions form a transition zone between those areas in which commercial agriculture has become a major economic activity and areas of subsistence cultivation in which remote locations, unfavorable environmental conditions, and rural poverty have retarded the introduction of higher value crops. Two such broad regions are found, one stretching just south of the Indo-Gangetic Plain and separated from the second zone, located at the center of the peninsula, by the rich cotton-producing areas of the Deccan Plateau.

Subsistence Cultivation and Tribal Economy
The remaining regions are the very poorest areas of India. Subsistence cultivation is found on the dry frontiers of West Pakistan, in nontribal districts along the Himalayan Frontier, and in the river valleys which penetrate the tribal hills of the Chota Nagpur Plateau of east-central India. The regions of tribal economy are all located in the most extreme and remote environments of India: the forested hills of Assam, the Himalayan piedmont, the Thar Desert, and the rugged, inaccessible hills of the Western Ghats and Chota Nagpur. Except in the industrialized section of Chota Nagpur, the people of these regions are food collectors or *slash-and-burn agriculturalists.*•

THE STATISTICS OF STARVATION

4

Death control was introduced into India, but birth control was not; consequently, more babies live and more are born. In the fifty years since 1921, sustained population growth has doubled the number of people in India; 251 million became 546 million, and more. As noted earlier, before 1920, the high death rate was caused by malaria, plague, influenza, and famine; thereafter, these large-scale disasters were held in check. Until the 1950s, India's population grew at the relatively modest rate of 1.0 to 1.25 percent each year; but improved public health services have allowed the rate of growth to double to 2.5 percent. Each month India's population increases by more than 1 million, and each year by 13 million.

ECONOMIC STAGNATION
[TABLE 3]

While India's population has been doubling, the wealth of the nation has not. The work force and the economy are nearly the same now as they were at the beginning of the twentieth century. In 1901, 65 percent of India's men were farmers; fifty years later, 64 percent were farmers. No shift into manufacturing or service activities had accompanied the growth in population; thus in 1961 twice as many farm families were earning their living on a resource base that had not been substantially enlarged. During this period, factory and household manufacturing workers remained a steady 10 to 12 percent of the labor force.

As a result of this economic stagnation, the income of Indian families increased by less than 0.5 percent each year between the turn of the century and World War II. Crop output increased by 13 percent, but population by 38 percent, so that the average Indian farm family was eating less each year—20 percent less at independence than fifty years earlier. Between the mid-1950s and mid-1960s, food production increased by 27 percent, but balanced against

TABLE 3. Standards of Living in India and the United States

Source: John R. McLane, *India: A Culture Area in Perspective.* Boston: Allyn & Bacon, 1970, p. 47. Copyright © 1970 by Allyn & Bacon, Inc. Reprinted by permission of the publisher.

Indicators of living standards	United States	India
Doctors per 100,000 inhabitants	149	16
Dentists per 100,000 inhabitants	56	0.9
Percentage of the population over ten years of age which is literate	97	25
Students in higher education per 10,000 inhabitants	260	23
Radios per 1000 inhabitants	1000	7
Motor vehicles per 1000 inhabitants	454	13
Millions of tons of steel produced in 1966	121.6	6.6
Percentage of population living in urban or suburban communities	70	18

population growth, this amounted to a mere 2 percent increase in per capita food production. Currently, India averts widespread famine by massive imports of grain, but if population and food production continue to increase at comparable rates, India, which imported 7.5 million tons of food in 1965, will need three times that amount in 1980 just to keep abreast of the numbers of people.

These statistics measure India's slow retreat into deeper levels of poverty. Modern Indians have an average per capita income of less than $100 per year ($79 in 1966); 5 million people are totally unemployed in India, and millions more are underemployed. These people "economize" by not eating; the result is widespread malnutrition and undernutrition. In the *tropics,* "hunger" is defined as the consumption of food yielding less than 2100 calories of energy per person per day. The Indian average is 2110 calories per day; one-third of rural India subsists below the hunger line. Moreover, most of these calories come from low-protein rice and wheat, and consumption of high-protein foods, and particularly of fats and minerals, is very low. As a result, leading experts estimate that between 35 and 40 percent of India's children may suffer brain damage induced by protein deficiencies. But these statistics of starvation give only a hint of the depth of human misery in modern India.

मुले थोडी तरच संसारात गो

Famine and poverty will be part of Indian life until the sheer number of people is brought under control. Government efforts like this one, a pilot project undertaken with ILO aid, have so far had only minor effect. Here a project worker discusses the program with a village leader and his large family in front of a billboard that says "A Small Family Is a Happy Family" in the local language. *Photo:* United Nations/ILO.

POPULATION POLICY

Gandhi believed if only "all labored for their bread and no more," the resources of India would provide "enough food and leisure for all." But the majority of Indian leaders recognize that population growth must be checked if significant economic development is to occur on the subcontinent. By the mid-1950s, the population issue had been recognized as an urgent problem, so urgent that, according to an official, "even with utmost effort . . . to bring down birth rates, population pressure is likely to be acute." When the 1961 census indicated that population had grown by 21.5 percent in the preceding decade as compared with 13.3 percent between 1941 and 1951, the cautious approach of Indian planners to birth control was abandoned. India joined Japan as the second sizable nation in the world to inaugurate a serious effort to reduce the number of births.

During the first five-year plan, 147 birth-control clinics were established, mainly in urban areas; during the second plan, 1650. By 1963, there were 8443 such clinics, two-thirds of them located in rural areas. But in the Indian context of a half-million villages, these efforts amounted to little more than

pilot projects, and their results were not encouraging. In Manchai (a town near Poona), of 1255 women contacted, 388 generally approved of the idea of birth control but only 175 agreed to pursue a program of birth prevention. Similarly in Madras, of some 39,000 mothers given instruction in family planning, 92 percent expressed an interest in limiting their families, yet only 4 percent did anything about it. On this basis the government decided that a mass education campaign was needed. Throughout India, posters with inverted red triangles flanked by a family of four carried the message "Two children are respectable, three a menace." Billboards instructed the illiterate that "a small family is a happy family"; films and radios carried the same message. Since then, over 5 million men have undergone voluntary sterilization at sites as varied as railroad stations and community development offices. Some 2 million women have birth-control devices; 1 million take oral contraceptives.

These figures pale, however, in the face of the total population of India—an estimated 608 million in 1975—and a growth rate of 1 million a month. No **demographer** projects a population of less than 1 billion for India by the year 2000. Although the rate of growth in the 1960s, 24.6 percent, was less than anticipated, the lower level was the result of a slight rise in the death rate rather than any significant slackening in the birth rate. Even at this lower rate, population growth requires an additional 1.5 million tons of food grain each year, 2.5 million new houses, and 4 million new jobs. Despite such examples of progress as the green revolution and Jamshedpur, population growth has absorbed the benefits of virtually all economic progress since independence, leaving the people of India mired in poverty and plagued by a continuing food crisis.

INDIA'S FUTURE

No problem concerns Indian leaders more than their inability to raise standards of living; it is not accidental that the slogan of the majority Congress party in the last election was *garibi hatao* ("abolish poverty"). To some degree, the heirs of Gandhi and Suhrawardy have relied on slogans rather than performance, but it must be remembered that India's greatest accomplishment since independence has been to remain united and independent. The establishment of democratic institutions with free elections and freedom of speech in a major nation of the developing world is a considerable task. Some have argued that this commitment to gradual change, to evolution rather than revolution, has condemned

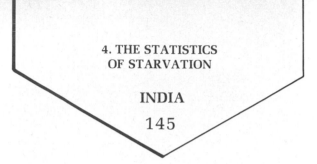

India to an uncertain future. In truth, India's rural poverty, cultural diversity, and growing population would pose critical problems to any government, however disciplined, whatever its ideology. Prime Minister Indira Gandhi's sudden lurch toward totalitarian rule in 1975 only emphasizes the difficult tasks facing Indian leaders. One thing is certain: India's future will be determined by the resolution of the twin issues of rural poverty and population growth. If these are not addressed with sufficient speed and force, the creation of the world's largest democracy will have been a Pyrrhic victory.

BIBLIOGRAPHY

GENERAL

McLane, John R. *India: A Culture Area in Perspective.* Boston: Allyn & Bacon, 1970. A small, well-written, and insightful introduction to the origin of the modern problems of India.

Moore, Clark D., and David Eldredge. *India Yesterday and Today.* New York: Praeger, 1970. A well-organized collection of original sources on social and economic life.

Myrdal, Gunnar. *Asian Drama: An Inquiry into the Poverty of Nations,* Vols. 1–3. New York: Twentieth Century Fund, 1968. The most detailed analysis of the sources of poverty in the developing world covering South and Southeast Asia.

Spate, O. H. K., and A. T. A. Learmouth. *India and Pakistan,* Vols. 1, 2. London: Methuen, 1967. The finest and most reliable geography of the region.

Spear, Percival. *India: A Modern History.* Ann Arbor: University of Michigan Press, 1961. A clear and objective history of India from Mogul to modern times.

Wolpert, Stanley. *India.* Englewood Cliffs, N.J.: Prentice-Hall, 1965. A well-written, concise introduction.

[1] TRADITIONAL INDIA

Basham, A. L. *The Wonder That Was India.* New York: Grove Press, 1967. A survey of Hinduism and Indian civilization in pre-Mogul times.

Hutton, J. H. *Caste in India: Its Nature, Functions, and Origins.* New York: Oxford University Press, 1963. The classic book on the Indian caste system.

Moon, Penderel. *Gandhi and Modern India.* New York: Norton, 1969. A biography of the father of modern India, a twentieth-century politician and a Hindu saint.

Simoons, Frederick J. "The Sacred Cow and the Constitution of India," *Ecology of Food and Nutrition,* Vol. 2 (1973), pp. 281–295.

Schulberg, Lucille. *Historic India.* New York: Time-Life, 1968. A beautifully illustrated, brief introduction to Indian history and values.

Schwartzberg, Joseph E. "The Distribution of Selected Castes in the North Indian Plain," *Geographical Review,* Vol. 55 (1965), pp. 477–495. An analysis of caste groupings on part of the Indo-Gangetic Plain.

Sopher, David E. "Pilgrim Circulation in Gujarat," *Geographical Review,* Vol. 58 (1968), pp. 392–425. A study of the role of religion in communication in western India.

Zinkin, Taya. *Caste Today.* London: Oxford University Press, 1962. Updates the superb historical description in Hutton.

[2] THE BRITISH IN INDIA

Moore, Barrington, Jr. *Social Origins of Dictatorship and Democracy.* Boston: Beacon Press, 1966. A brilliant comparative essay on the paths China, India, and Japan have followed in search of modernization.

Murphey, Rhoads. "The City in the Swamps: Aspects of the Early Growth of Calcutta," *Geographical Review,* Vol. 54 (1964), pp. 241–256. A detailed study of the origin of one of the three major ports established by the British.

[3] DEVELOPMENT IN AN ASIAN DEMOCRACY

Bose, N. K. "Calcutta: A Premature Metropolis," *Scientific American,* Vol. 213 (1965), pp. 91–102. The consequences of urbanization without industrialization in India's largest city.

Brush, John E. "The Distribution of Religious Communities in India," *Annals, Association of American Geographers,* Vol. 39 (1949), pp. 81–98. The impact of partition on the distribution of religious communities on the subcontinent.

Brush, John E. "Some Dimensions of Urban Population Pressure in India." In Wilbur Zelinsky et al. (eds.), *Geography and a Crowding World,* pp. 279–304. New York: Oxford University Press, 1970. An excellent study of urban population problems.

Chakravati, A. K. "Green Revolution in India," *Annals, Association of American Geographers,* Vol. 63 (1973), pp. 319–330. Regional variation of the impact of hybrid seeds on Indian agriculture.

Dube, S. C. *India's Changing Villages.* Ithaca: Cornell University Press, 1958. A description of the fruits of economic development programs in northern villages.

Frankel, Francine R. "India's New Strategy of Agricultural Development," *Journal of Asian Studies,* Vol. 28 (1969), pp. 693–710. Details of the new agricultural strategy.

Hardgrave, Robert L., Jr. *India: Government and Politics in a Developing Nation.* New York: Harcourt, Brace & World, 1970. A well-executed statement on the functioning of Indian democracy since independence.

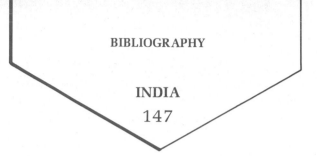

Jakobson, Leo, and Ved Prakash. "Urbanization and Regional Planning in India," *Urban Affairs Quarterly,* Vol. 11 (1967), pp. 36–65.

Johnson, E. A. J. *The Organization of Space in Developing Countries.* Cambridge, Mass.: Harvard University Press, 1970.

Karan, P. P. "Changes in Indian Industrial Location," *Annals, Association of American Geographers,* Vol. 54 (1964), pp. 336–352. A descriptive study of locational patterns of industrial growth between 1951 and 1961.

Ladejinsky, Wolf. "Ironies of India's Green Revolution," *Foreign Affairs,* Vol. 48 (1970), pp. 758–768. A balanced analysis of the problems and prospects of the green revolution in India.

Lewis, John P. *Quiet Crisis in India.* Washington, D.C.: Brookings Institution, 1962. An insightful analysis of the economic problems of modern India.

Neale, Walter C. *India: The Search for Unity, Democracy, and Progress.* New York: Van Nostrand, 1965. A brief survey of the problems of national economic development.

Rudolph, L., and S. Rudolph. *The Modernity of Tradition: Political Development in India.* Chicago: University of Chicago Press, 1967. A remarkable study of the flexibility of tradition in coping with modernization in India.

Schwartzberg, Joseph E. "Three Approaches to the Mapping of Economic Development in India," *Annals, Association of American Geographers,* Vol. 52 (1962), pp. 455–468.

Sopher, David E. "India's Languages and Religions," *Focus,* Vol. 6 (1956), pp. 1–6. A well-mapped, brief description of cultural diversity.

Wharton, Clifton R., Jr. "The Green Revolution: Cornucopia or Pandora's Box?" *Foreign Affairs,* Vol. 47 (1969), pp. 464–476. An overview of the impact of the green revolution in the developing countries of Asia.

[4] THE STATISTICS OF STARVATION

Nath, V. "Population, Natural Resources and Economic Development in India." In Wilbur Zelinsky et al. (eds.). *Geography and a Crowding World,* pp. 392–423. New York: Oxford University Press, 1970. A historical view of the economic setting of population growth in India.

Sen-Gupta, P. "Population and Resource Development in India." In Wilbur Zelinsky et al. (eds.). *Geography and a Crowding World,* pp. 424–441. New York: Oxford University Press, 1970. A regional analysis of the pressure of population on resources in India.

THE MIDDLE EAST AND NORTH AFRICA

In April 1974, the United Nations General Assembly convened to discuss the increasingly complex and volatile relationship between raw materials and economic development. United Nations Secretary General Kurt Waldheim outlined six parts of a global emergency facing both rich and poor nations: poverty among two-thirds of the world's people; population growth, which adds over a million people to the globe each week; food resources, currently at their lowest reserves in decades; energy, which quadrupled in price during 1973–1974; military requirements, on which $14 billion would be spent during the meeting; and world inflation. Henry Kissinger, speaking for the United States, pledged a "major effort" on the part of the industrial world to assist developing nations. He warned, however, against threats of pressure—this in response to the Arab oil embargo, which during the winter of 1973–1974 had reduced oil shipments to the industrial world pending a resolution of the deadlock between Arab and Israeli forces after the October War.

The keynote speaker and convener of the session, President Houari Boumediene of Algeria, argued eloquently for a radical change in the economic relationships between the industrial and developing worlds. Developing nations, he insisted, must become "masters in their own houses," by nationalizing foreign-owned property and creating producer-nation *cartels*° for raw materials (ranging from minerals to agricultural commodities such as coffee and tea), just as the thirteen-member Organization of Petroleum Exporting Countries *(OPEC)*° had done with petroleum. Furthermore, he emphasized, the developing nations should practice austerity and sacrifice at home in order to win victories over poverty, insecurity, and economic bondage. As an emerging spokesman for the nonaligned, nonindustrial world, Boumediene reflected the aims of his own life, of Algeria's revolutionary struggle against French colonialism, and more generally of the forces of change that are transforming Middle Eastern society.

Boumediene was born a half-century ago in a village near Annaba, a coastal city in eastern Algeria. One of seven children, he was from a family too poor to give him a French education—then the most promising path to success in Algeria—so he attended a traditional mosque school, memorizing the Koran and the principles of Islam. Reflecting one of the cultural goals of decolonizing North Africa, his speech to the United Nations was delivered in fluent classical Arabic. In the early 1950s, at the time of Nasser's revolution in Egypt, Boumediene was a student at Al-Azhar University in Cairo, a citadel of Islamic learning. Already deeply involved in the Algerian nationalist movement, he was planning armed resistance against the French. By 1962, he was a principal strategist of the Algerian National Liberation Front, and the French had been brought to a military standstill and political defeat as Algeria achieved independence after a century and a half of French colonial rule.

In the early 1800s Algeria was the westernmost province of the decaying Ottoman Empire. The French, on the pretext of an insult delivered to the French consul by the *dey* of Algiers, invaded the city, exiled Turkish officials, and established a European military presence in North Africa. For the next quarter-century, French armies extended their control over the Algerian countryside in the face of continuing resistance and began a policy of European colonization and land seizure. By 1900, the Algerians had been reduced to economic and cultural servitude. Some 3 million people had been killed, Berber tribal confederations in the mountains had been "pacified," and a European economy was established on the most fertile agricultural land in the country. Boumediene, himself deeply committed to Islamic tradition, grew up in a nation whose Muslim population had no voice and little economic power. Periodic rebellions were quashed by superior French military power. A million French colonists owned the farms, factories, and commercial enterprises of Algeria, which were centered in the large port cities of Algiers, Constantine, and Oran. When French rule ended in the early 1960s, the French, Jewish, and Spanish communities fled, leaving Algeria with few doctors, administrators, teachers, or skilled workers. Factories and farms were abandoned; 70 percent of the population was unemployed. The industrial landscape of Algeria lay devastated by the desperate eleventh-hour French terrorist efforts to combat the strategies of the independence movement. Over 1 million died in the rebellion; an additional 2.5 million out of a total population of 10 million were refugees or in camps.

Boumediene's determined opposition to poverty, insecurity, and economic bondage was a product of this environment. Assuming control of Algeria by military coup in 1965, Colonel Boumediene launched a program of radical economic and social change to improve the living conditions of the Algerian people. Lands abandoned by European colonists were nationalized and made state farms; large Algerian-owned estates were broken up into agricultural cooperatives. Small landowners, however, were left undisturbed. Thousands of acres of vineyards were plowed under and, converted to cereal cultivation and dairying to reduce Algeria's dependence on the export of wine. On the industrial front, Boumediene nationalized French oil holdings in Algeria in 1970 and, using the rising revenues generated by OPEC's renegotiations with oil corporations, invested in diversified industrial complexes. Moreover, throughout this period, over a quarter of the national budget was consistently invested in education, leading some observers to describe the New Algeria as a nation of urchins on the way to the classroom. Internationally, having broken diplomatic relations with the United States after the 1967 Arab-Israeli war, Boumediene remained a militant supporter of the Palestinian cause and provided a haven for a wide variety of Third World revolutionary groups, including American militants of the Black Panther movement.

These credentials—austere commitment to internal change within the framework of Islamic culture and determined opposition to colonialism—have made Boumediene a spokesman for the developing world and a symbol of the forces of change that have swept the Middle East. These forces are the central themes of this section. "Islamic Matrix, Cultural Mosaic" describes the traditional culture of Islam which Boumediene believes is "the most powerful religion in its struggle for the liberty of man" and the variety of minority faiths and peoples who coexisted for centuries in the Middle East and North Africa. Living briefly and poorly in three separate but related worlds—city, village, and tribe—Middle Easterners formed a coherent and stable civilization, delineated here in the section called "The Traditional Middle East." Confronted by the West and penetrated by commercial and colonial forces of economic and social change, the traditional Middle Eastern society and settlement system dissolved and was reorganized by "Imperialism, Nationalism, and Independence." Utilizing the powerful lever of their control of oil resources, the nations of the modern Middle East press the world powers for a satisfactory resolution of the struggle between the Arabs and the Israelis, a conflict between "Two Peoples, One Land."

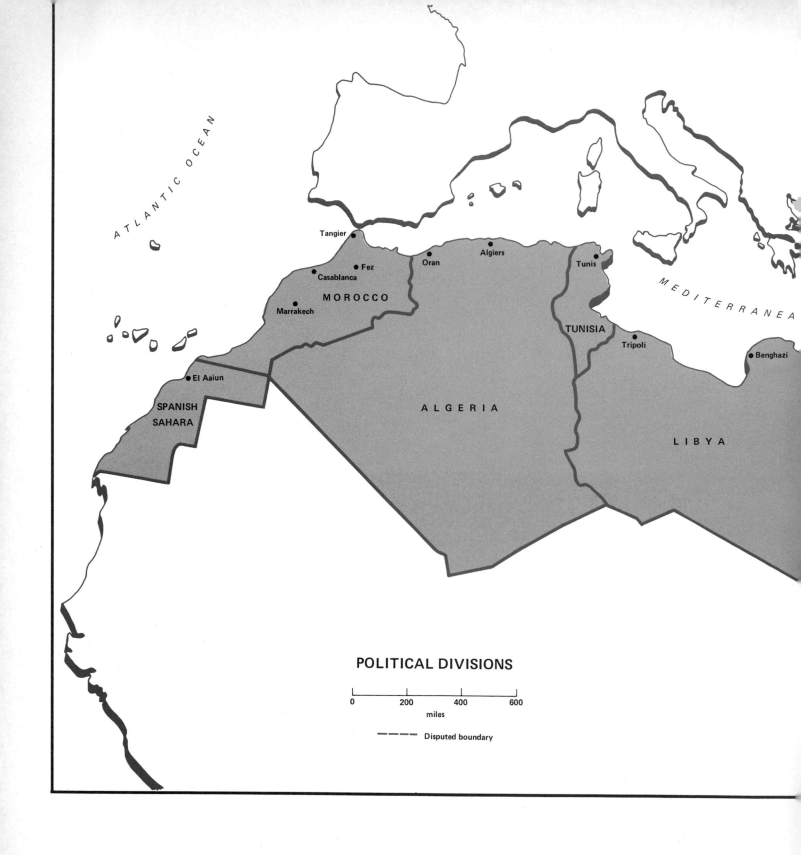

ATLANTIC OCEAN

MEDITERRANEA

Tangier

Fez
Casablanca

MOROCCO

Marrakech

Oran

Algiers

Tunis

TUNISIA

Tripoli

Benghazi

El Aaiun

SPANISH
SAHARA

ALGERIA

LIBYA

POLITICAL DIVISIONS

0	200	400	600

miles

– – – – – Disputed boundary

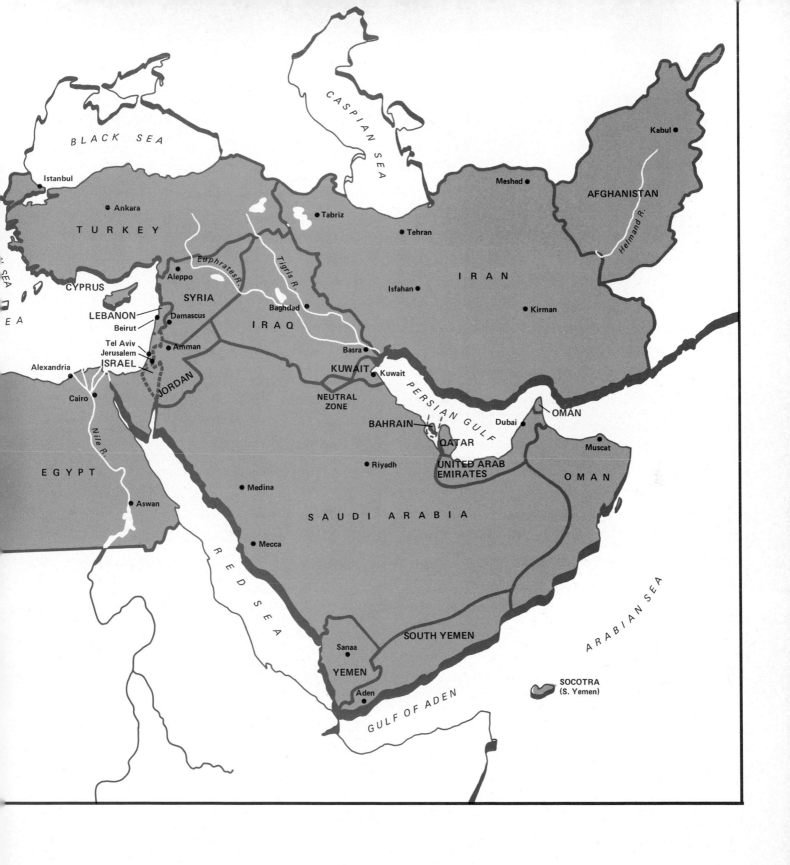

ISLAMIC MATRIX, CULTURAL MOSAIC 1

Some 1300 years ago, Arab armies propelled by a strong, monotheistic faith swept out of the Arabian *peninsula* and conquered Egypt, Syria, Iraq, and Iran in the name of their prophet. By AD 750, a century later, Muhammad's followers had incorporated a huge area, from *Iberia* to India, into a world empire, larger and more formidable than anything known in the Mediterranean Basin since Rome. Invading Arabs, a small military elite, established control of the *hinterlands* while living in the urban centers they conquered. Peoples of a variety of religions—Christians, Jews, and Zoroastrians—then occupied the region. But the Arabs managed over time to do what Persian, Greek, and Roman conquerors before them had not: they converted an overwhelming majority of the people of the Middle East and North Africa to a new religion, Islam. Muslims have been unquestionably dominant throughout the region from their initial expansion until today. Over 90 percent of the people of the Middle East are Muslim, although substantial Christian populations are found in Cyprus and the *Levant* (the countries of the eastern Mediterranean), colonies of Jews are dispersed throughout the region, and Judaism is the state religion of modern Israel. In general, Islamic beliefs and institutions form the focus and structure of Middle Eastern life.

Islam did not, however, absorb all peoples within its bounds, nor did it long remain monolithic. Within the Islamic world, a variety of ethnic, religious, and linguistic minorities retained distinctive customs and life styles for centuries. Isolated and protected in mountains stretching from Turkey to Iran, Kurds, Armenians, and a number of Turkish-speaking tribes lived until recently in virtual autonomy. In the Atlas Mountains of North Africa, Berber language and ways still survive. In traditional times, a bewildering variety of Christian and Jewish enclaves within every major city of the region lived side by side in religious and cultural isolation, clinging to their individual heritages, following their own laws and customs, and resisting assimila-

tion. Islam itself, while still a unifying force, has been fragmented over issues varying in time and place. In Iran and Yemen, Shia Muslims, followers of Muhammad's son-in-law Ali, became a majority of the faithful. In local areas, heretical Muslim sects such as the Druze of Lebanon, the Kharijites of Oman and North Africa, and the Alawi of northwestern Syria have maintained a geographical and cultural separateness. This mosaic of peoples, a distinctive feature of the region, is the social background of the new nation-states of the Middle East, complicating and confusing their search for identity and unity in the modern world.

THE ISLAMIC MATRIX

Late in the sixth century (c. AD 570) Muhammad the Prophet was born to a middle-class family in the town of Mecca, a small thriving caravan city near the Red Sea coast. After his parents' death, he was raised as a shepherd boy. At age twenty-five, he married a widow, entered the caravan trade, and raised a family of four daughters, all his sons dying in infancy. Until age forty, Muhammad apparently led the tranquil life of a Meccan trader who concerned himself with the transshipment of precious metals, leather, and spices from East Asia to the Mediterranean ports of Syria. But in 610 he retired to the desert wilderness and experienced a series of spiritual revelations. Muhammad returned to Mecca, announced that he had been chosen to be the messenger of God, and began to teach a monotheistic faith that today is practiced by one out of every seven human beings.

The Origins of Islam

Muhammad preached his relevations to the traders, shopkeepers, and artisans of Mecca, not to the nomadic tribesmen of the hinterland. The city, an *oasis* 48 miles inland from sea, is located in one of the dry, rock-filled *wadis* that crease the western slopes of the *Hijaz.* Sixth-century Mecca's raison d'être was trade: the city was a vital link in the overland trade chain between the Mediterranean and the Orient. Mecca's leading citizens were cosmopolitan businessmen who directed the caravan trade, sometimes organizing ventures of 2500 or more camels with goods worth as much as $3 million. Additional revenue came to Mecca from pilgrims visiting the nearby sacred sanctuary of the Kaaba, a temple where feuds could be resolved and no blood could be shed. Meccan society worshiped idols representing many gods; a Jewish community was also present. Not surprisingly, Muhammad's insistence on the oneness of God and his rejection of idols generated instant opposition from members of the Meccan business establishment, who anticipated a loss of income and influence if the sanctuary were closed.

Muhammad's first converts were drawn from younger, middle-class elements of Meccan society, who found that monotheism as revealed by God to

Muhammad offered answers to the social injustices of the times. Commerce had widened the extremes of wealth and poverty in Mecca, crystallizing class barriers and replacing bloodlines by the power of money. Muhammad's simple message of one god, justice, and social concern first appealed to the economically disaffected of indeterminate social standing. For seven years, agents of the Meccan establishment persecuted the early Muslims. Garbage was thrown on their doorsteps, they were beaten and insulted, and economic pressures were brought to bear upon them. Finally in 622, the Muslims fled northward from Mecca to the oasis city of Medina. This emigration (hegira) marked the emergence of Muhammad as a recognized social and political leader and the beginning of the Islamic calendar.

During the next ten years until his death in 632, Muhammad unified the tribes of western Arabia under the Muslim banner. Spreading northward from the Arabian peninsula, Arab armies broke through the southern outposts of Byzantine civilization and the western frontiers of the Persian Empire to conquer Egypt, Syria, Iraq, and Iran. The speed and success of conquest were extraordinary, and Islam's expansion remains one of the great religious movements of history. In a quarter of a century, Muslim armies established a new civilization with its own government, laws, institutions, language, and faith over all the Middle East except North Africa and Turkey. After a century of still wider conquests, Islam held sway from Morocco to the Indus River and had reached the borders of France; Muslim armies were camped at the gates of Constantinople (now Istanbul).

The expansion of Islam from its desert origins in Arabia has never been satisfactorily explained. **Demographers** estimate that the economy of Arabia during the period of conquest could not have supported more than 100,000 adult males, a much smaller population base than the Byzantine and the Persian empires the Arabs challenged. A new cultural synthesis had emerged that completely overshadowed contemporary Europe. How this came about may never be fully understood, but one fact stands clear. The golden age of Islam was made possible by a single fundamental force: the belief of a majority of the people of the Middle East in the divine inspiration of Muhammad's message and their common practice of a code of behavior and ritual based on his teachings.

The Five Pillars

Islam today provides the world's 530 million Muslims with a straightforward prescription for daily living. The model to be followed by each person is the word of God, as found in the Koran, and the life of the Prophet Muhammad, as described in oral tradition. Together, these testaments define the courses of action open to people in their daily lives and provide answers to the meaning of human existence. The task of interpretation and application of religious doctrine

is left to a group of respected and learned men, the ulama. By and large, however, Islam has no formal religious hierarchy similar to that of Christianity.

Complications, confusion, and schisms in Islam arose from the fact that no biography of Muhammad was written until well after his death. Nonetheless, for a majority of Muslims, the way of the righteous appears clear-cut, almost technical. Five basic acts upon which people must build their lives are universally stressed. These five pillars of Islam are bearing witness to God and to his messenger, Muhammad; practicing daily prayer at designated times and places; giving alms to the poor and the weak; fasting during the month of Ramadan; and making a pilgrimage to Mecca, the spiritual center of Islam, once in a lifetime. These patterns of behavior lend unity to the *dar al Islam* (the House of Islam) and bind Muslims of the Middle East and the world to common spiritual experiences. Without these five pillars, it is doubtful that a faith with an ill-defined hierarchy and minimal formal structure could have persisted and continued to expand over thirteen centuries.

The first pillar of Islam is the verbal expression of faith, as stated in the formula, "There is no god but God, and Muhammad is His Prophet." By making this statement, an individual becomes a believer and a member of the community of Islam. The simplicity of the act makes it relatively easy to gather converts. At least partly for this reason, Islam is currently the most successful religion in attracting new converts in Asia and Central Africa.

In times past, the distinction between being a Muslim and being another monotheist (Christian or Jew) or a pagan defined a person's legal rights, taxes, and residence in Middle Eastern society. This sense of religious identity remains strong in the Middle East. A person is known first as a Muslim, Christian, or Jew, and only secondarily as wealthy or poor, of good family or bad, of light or dark complexion. The unity of Islam, therefore, transcends national boundaries, and religious acts evoke much the same ritual and meaning in villages as in modern metropolises such as Cairo or Casablanca. In more isolated parts of the Middle East, this sense of religious identity is so strongly felt that if a motorist accidentally strikes a pedestrian, the first fact ascertained about the driver is his religion.

The second pillar of Islam, prayer, is required of all Muslims five times a day: at dawn, at noon, in the midafternoon, after sunset, and in the evening. The

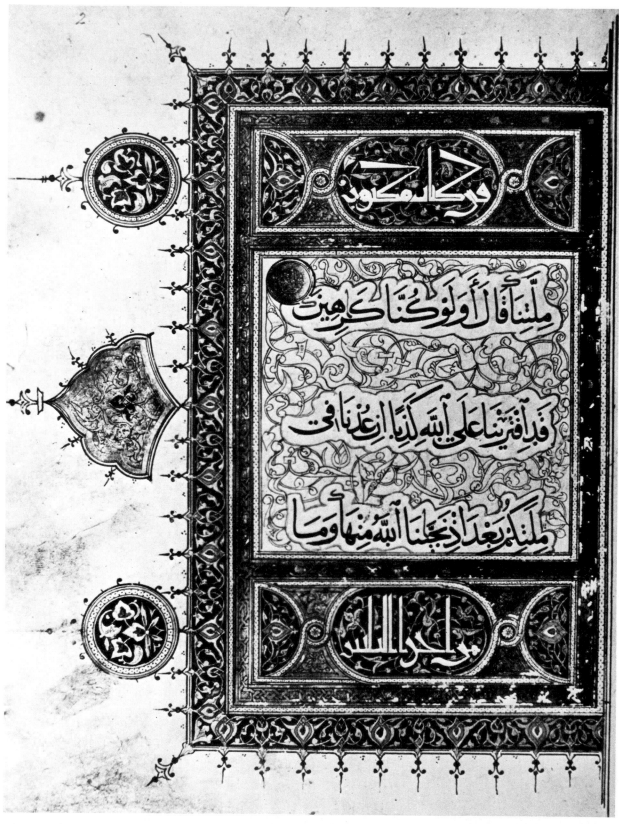

This page from a thirteenth-century Koran, like the illuminated manuscripts of the medieval West, is as illustrative of Islamic culture as it is of religious precepts. Its intricate blend of calligraphy and ornament delight the eye. *Photo:* The Bettman Archive.

334 BC

Alexander the Great launched a campaign of expansion and conquered Persia and Egypt, closing the period of the Achaemenid kings of Persia and establishing a far-flung empire. Four different states emerged under Alexander's successors.

146 BC

Romans seized Carthage; the Maghrib remained Roman for nearly 600 years. Latin rule in the Middle East extended from the first century BC until after the fall of Rome to barbarians.

AD 306–337

Rome accepted Christianity under Constantine.

330–1453

The Byzantine Empire (New Rome) was founded in the eastern half of the Roman Empire. After Rome fell to barbarians in 476, Western civilization survived in Byzantium, whose capital at Constantinople was the center of a Christian empire which at its height reunited elements of Rome from Algeria to Persia.

570

Birth of the Prophet Muhammad in Mecca.

622

The Prophet established his authority in Medina.

632

Death of the Prophet.

732

Invading Muslim armies reached their farthest advance and first defeat at Tours in France. By 750, Muslim rule was assured from the Pyrénées to the foothills of the Himalayas.

1095

Pope Urban II called for a Christian crusade to regain control of Jerusalem and the Holy Land. Jerusalem was held by the Christians from 1099 to 1187, when it was retaken by Muslim armies. In five successive military campaigns, the Christians failed to recapture Jerusalem, but right of Christian access was restored. Mixed spiritual and economic aims confused the meaning of the Crusades, which had varied political backgrounds.

1299–1326

Under the reign of Osman, the Ottoman Empire was formed out of a number of Muslim principalities in Anatolia. Byzantium, in retreat since the foundation of Islam, disappeared entirely with the Ottoman seizure of Constantinople in 1453. Thirty-six Ottoman sultans followed Osman in succession until the revolution of Ataturk in 1922.

form and content of the prayer vary little from one country to the next, and in the towns and cities of the Middle East, where the call to prayer is heard over loudspeakers, the rhythm of daily life is fixed in a framework of prayer hours. At the appointed times, the call to prayer is chanted to people below from the tall towers of the mosques. Small mosques and shrines dot the residential quarters of each town to facilitate daily prayer. In reality, few people—urban or rural—can pray at every specified time, and many countrywomen never learn how to pray at all, for lack of education. As in many traditional societies, the education of women is not stressed; women's important duties of child rearing, household tasks, and—in rural areas—tending animals are not seen as benefiting from education. Nonetheless, the mosque is the dominating feature in the city and a necessity in villages as well; every family owns a prayer rug or prayer stone to aid in the proper discharge of this religious responsibility.

Although private prayer is common, congregational prayer inside a mosque is preferred. The most important prayer meeting occurs on the day of assembly, Friday, when the entire community gathers at noon to pray. Inside the mosque, the faithful arrange themselves in rows, men forward, women to the rear, and are led in prayers by an imam, a man of learned authority in religious matters. Whether properly observed in the cities or only partially observed in the country, this ritualized communal prayer is a binding tie among Muslims and provides a disciplined rhythm to daily life.

The third pillar of Islam, almsgiving, obliges Muslims to give part of their wealth to the poor of the community as a sign of piety, a means to salvation, and an expression of the common concern of one human being for another. In Islam, the wealthy have a special social responsibility to care for the broader community; private property is validated by private benevolence. In early Islam, alms taxes were levied, with the rate of taxation varying according to the kind of property. Unirrigated field crops and fruits, especially grapes and dates, were taxed at a rate of 10 percent; irrigated crops at 5 percent. The rate on camels, oxen, sheep, and goats depended on whether they had grazed freely for the year or been used for work. The donkey, the beast of burden most commonly used by the poor of the region, was exempt from taxes. The tax on gold, silver, precious metals, and merchandise was a flat 2.5 percent.

THE PILGRIMAGE TO MECCA

The hajj, the potential duty and glorious desire of every Muslim, is an act of devotion that must be carried out between the eighth and the thirteenth days of the last month of the Muslim lunar calendar. Each year, tens of thousands of pilgrims arrive at the port city of Jidda by boat, plane, or bus beginning late in the eleventh month of the year. Six days after pilgrims begin the hajj at Mecca, they are back in Jidda, ready to depart for their homelands. The holy city of Mecca—45 miles distant from Jidda—is protected from entry by all persons of other religions by a geographical frontier called in Arabic the haram, a sanctuary protected not only from nonbelievers but from environmental molestation by the Muslims who may enter it. It lies outside Mecca from between 3 and 18 miles from the Kaaba—the symbolic starting point for each pilgrim, who re-creates in daily succession pious acts of the Prophet and is a symbol of human faith, weakness, and strength.

I. On the first day of the pilgrimage, the assembled travel to Mina, a village 5 miles east of Mecca. That night is spent in devotion at Mina, following the acts of the Prophet, in preparation for a day at the Plain of Arafat, 7 miles farther.

II. At dawn of the second day, the pilgrims arise to journey to Arafat, where the day is spent in prayer. Here, at the base of the hill called the Mount of Mercy, the Prophet delivered his last sermon during his own pilgrimage.

III. At sunset on the second day, the faithful return to Muzdalifa, a station on the route of pilgrimage. Pilgrims sleep under the stars and gather stones which are used later to throw at pillars symbolizing Satan—the unchanging evils of life in this world.

IV. On the third day of pilgrimage, the tenth of the month, the travelers return to Mina, using the pebbles collected along the road to throw at the pillars representing evil. At Mina, sacrifice to God is made by slaughtering a sheep offered to the less fortunate. The ritual is followed throughout the Muslim world on the same day—thanksgiving, unity, sacrifice, and need.

V. Usually, on the tenth or eleventh day of the month—the third or fourth day of pilgrimage, after the acts of devotion at Mina—the pilgrims return, shorn and obedient, to the holiest sanctuary of Islam, the Great Mosque in Mecca. The last day of formal pilgrimage is spent at the holy sites of the Great Mosque—the black stone of the Kaaba, the march between Mount Safa and Mount Marwa, and the well of Zamzam. Each act re-creates a mystery and the history of Islam.

Often a side trip to Medina, 277 miles to the north, follows the acts of pilgrimage at Mecca. In each act, the pilgrim follows a multitude of fellow worshipers, each believing in the same inspiration and the worthiness of the same acts. They return to their native countries imbued with a spirit of fellowship and congregational devotion.

Source: "The Hajj: A Special Issue," *Aramco World Magazine*, Vol. 25, No. 6 (1974).

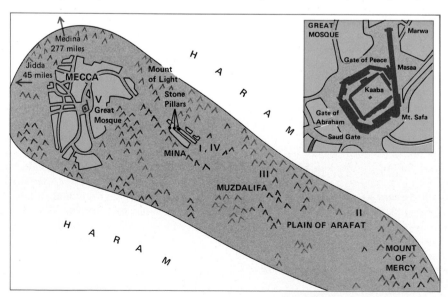

These alms were distributed to slaves, widows, orphans, new converts, debtors, and travelers. With gradual consolidation of the Arab conquests, alms taxes came to be rarely enforced. However, the principle remains, and still today alleviates the life of the poor and the sick in countries where hospitals, orphanages, and asylums are few, and extremes of wealth and poverty are common. In smaller towns, wealthy men personally distribute alms to the poor, particularly during the month of fasting, Ramadan. Recently, almsgiving was curiously modernized at Mit Ghamr, a town of 50,000 in Lower Egypt. Local leaders set up a bank account for the poor, and in one case purchased a horse for a carriage driver who had lost his means of livelihood in a traffic accident. Thus, although alms have rarely been collected in the precise amounts prescribed in Islamic law, almsgiving endures as a strong Muslim value to provide economic balance within the community.

By contrast, fasting during the month of Ramadan, the fourth pillar of Islam, is in all likelihood the most rigidly practiced obligation of Islam. Observation of the fast lasts twenty-nine consecutive days and requires abstinence from all food, drink, and sexual relations during daylight hours. Because the Muslim calendar (360 days) follows the phases of the moon, months rotate through the seasons, dropping back five days each year. When the month of Ramadan occurs in the summer and the daylight hours stretch out to sixteen or seventeen hours, a heavy burden is placed on the people of this region. But according to the Prophet, fasting is one-half endurance, and endurance one-half of faith. Only the aged, the sick, pregnant and nursing women, and travelers are exempt from the strict observance of the fast. When and if the exempting condition is relieved, the month of fasting must be immediately made up. This extended exercise in ascetic discipline binds Muslims in a community of abstinence that creates a solidarity among the Middle Eastern majority.

The regularity of daily life takes on a different form during the month of Ramadan. In some countries, public breaking of the fast is illegal, and restaurants are closed during the day. Feasts are held in the evenings and men gather in teahouses or cafés to hear storytellers recite legends of early Muslim victories. As the month progresses, anxiety and weariness rise and work declines. In Tunisia, the government has tried (and failed) to have the task of national development accepted as a basis for exemption from the fast. Gradually, as the stress of abstinence mounts, tempers flare and disagreements become common. One enterprising political scientist even finds a significant correlation between Middle Eastern political instability and the Ramadan fast. Despite these difficulties, the common people continue to view Ramadan as a symbol of the vitality of Islam and, conversely, of resistance to modernization and change.

The fifth and final pillar of Islam, the pilgrimage to Mecca, is the religious duty of every adult Muslim at least once a lifetime. The pilgrimage acts as a mechanism for uniting the community of Islam across national boundaries. The mentally ill, slaves, unescorted women, and the poor are exempt from this obligation, so that throughout the Middle East and Asia only about one in fifty Muslim males actually makes the pilgrimage. Each year, thousands of the faithful from Marrakech to Mindanao converge on Mecca. Until modern times, the majority of pilgrims came to Mecca by camel caravan, but pilgrims have preferred the safety and speed of sea and air travel in this century. In 1973, about one-third of the 645,000 foreign pilgrims came by air, another third by sea, and the remainder overland.

The fortunes of Meccan merchants vary greatly over the year, since for one brief month, the population of the city triples. The streets are lined with shops selling miniature illuminated Korans, whose price is determined by the binding, since the holy pages inside are always included free. Other stalls sell amber prayer beads, aromatic woods, incense, and an assortment of holy wares to the pilgrims. The majority of Mecca's shopkeepers are non-Arabs, the descendants of earlier pilgrims from Iran, Pakistan, Turkey, and other countries. Most are people who settled in the city to study religion, to make their fortunes, or simply to be closer to the beating heart of Islam. These shopkeepers reflect the one great integrative function of the Meccan pilgrimage —the sharing of a common social and religious experience by an international community of the faithful. Over the years, this common ground has provided holy men and political propagandists alike an opportunity to spread their doctrines over much of Asia and Africa.

THE CULTURAL MOSAIC

A mosaic of religious, linguistic, and ethnic minorities forms important cultural differences within the Muslim world. Religious diversity in this region is the legacy of three great world religions born in what is indeed the Holy Land: Judaism, Christianity, and Islam. Linguistic and ethnic minorities took root in the Middle East during the thousands of years of invasion and reinvasion when this region was the crossroads of the known world, a magnet for people from far beyond its borders.

Muslim culture spread far from its origins in Arabia. The mosque at Cordoba in Spain was begun by the Muslims in 786, then became a church after the Catholic reconquest in 1236. Its design is a blend of North African and Spanish influences that became the distinctive Moorish style. *Photo:* George Holton/Photo Researchers.

In a different setting, these minorities might well have disappeared by assimilation or extermination, but several factors militated against this happening in the Islamic Middle East. First, Islam has always recognized the spiritual sovereignty of the "peoples of the Book"—those who believe in a single God, the Day of Judgment, and the Prophets—as communities that should be tolerated and protected within Islam. Thus Jewish and Christian communities were able to retain and practice their own laws and customs, sustaining periodic persecution but surviving into the modern period. Spiritual martyrdom, as known in Europe, found no place in the traditional social relationships of the Middle East; recognition and acceptance followed the tolerance of Christian and Jewish beliefs.

Second, Islamic rulers were rarely able to control the vast desert and mountain regions of the Middle East effectively. Generally, the extent of central government influence was limited to the coasts and fertile lowlands of the region, leaving large areas where heretical sects and tribes could find sacred refuge and live in a geographical isolation that pre-

served language and tradition. Partly for this reason, the Islamic state ultimately came to view these various societies as separate communities who, if they paid their taxes and did not pose a threat to the government, were left to pursue their own beliefs and customs. In the nineteenth century, for example, the Ottoman Empire included a variety of religious communities (millets) whose leaders regulated the personal affairs of group members, reporting, when required, to the imperial government in Istanbul. Laws dealing with marriage, divorce, and property were determined by religious allegiance; common law as well was based on religion, not nationhood.

Clearly incompatible with modern nationalism, deeply ingrained allegiances to religious and tribal traditions—the plural tradition of the Middle Eastern mosaic—have proved an obstacle to the national unity sought by modern Middle Eastern leaders. Although all Middle Eastern countries have a tradition of pluralistic harmony, new boundaries, new aspirations, and new identities have forced a massive change in the cultural makeup and orientation of nations from Morocco to Iran.

Religious Diversity
Some 80 percent of all Muslims in the world belong to the orthodox or Sunni branch of Islam, the pre-

dominant faith of North Africa, Arabia save the Yemen, and Jordan, Syria, northern Iraq, Turkey, and Afghanistan. In a sense, Muhammad's prophecy that if Christianity had seventy-two varieties, Islam would have seventy-three came to pass. After Muhammad's death at age sixty-two, a struggle developed between the followers of his son-in-law Ali and several powerful Meccan families for a successor to the Prophet. Those Muslims who sided with the Meccans became known as the Sunnis, accepting the first four elected caliphs as rightful heirs to Muhammad. The caliph, the Prophet's successor, was the authoritative head of the Muslim community. Today, Sunni Muslims follow one of four schools of law, each of which is variously acceptable in different parts of the Muslim world. They base their religious beliefs and practices on the Koran and the Hadith, a compendium of sayings of the Prophet written after his death. The strictest and most orthodox of Sunni groups are the Wahabis, an eighteenth-century revivalist movement that grew to conquer Saudi Arabia early in this century.

In contrast, Shiism, the other major denomination of Islam, is based on the belief that the caliphate should have fallen to Ali, Muhammad's son-in-law, and his descendants. When Ali was assassinated in 661 and his two sons Hassan and Husayn were, respectively, poisoned and beheaded, a bitter schism erupted in Islam that engendered the formation of many of the seventy-odd Muslim sects found in the region. Shia Muslims accept the Koran and the Hadith as the fundamental sources of faith, but assign exceptional importance to Ali. They do not accept the legitimacy of the first three caliphs and differ among themselves about the proper line of succession thereafter. The largest Shia school, the Imami, which accepts twelve successors, is the state religion of Iran and a major sect in southern Iraq. The Ismaili, once powerful but now dispersed in Pakistan, Iran, and Syria, recognize seven successors, whereas the Zaidi of Yemen accept only five. Extremist sects that originated in one or another of these Shia schools include the Alawi of northern Syria, who believe that Muhammad was simply a forerunner of Ali; the Druze of the Lebanese and Syrian highlands, who relate that the last appearance of God was in the person of a Fatimid caliph who disappeared in 1020; and the Kharijites of Oman and North Africa, who felt that any Muslim was qualified to succeed Muhammad, broke off from the mainstream of Islam, and retreated to the desert.

Finally, mystical Sufi orders in which individuals strive for enlightenment through ascetic discipline are common to both Sunni and Shia Islam. In the past, Sufism has provided the basis of powerful political movements. Although these religious distinctions and associations often strike non-Muslims as remote and abstract, Muslims have built their lives and communities around them for centuries,

generally with considerably less bloodshed than similar Catholic-Protestant schisms in Europe.

Similar religious differences of separate communities with different languages, customs, and life styles mark the 4 million Christians of the Middle East. When Christianity became the official state religion of the Roman Empire in 313, four religious provinces were established with centers at Rome, Constantinople, Antioch, and Alexandria. Each ultimately gave rise to a separate Christian church. In a dispute over the nature of Christ, Egyptian Copts and Syrian Jacobites took the monophysite position that Christ's godhood and manhood could not be separated, "even for a twinkling of the eye"; they were subsequently declared heretics by the Church at Rome. The Copts, an important group in Egypt numbering over 1 million, claim direct racial descent from the ancient Egyptians from whom their original language was derived. Some 180,000 Syrian Jacobites still speak Syriac and Aramaic (believed to be the language of Christ) and are concentrated in Syria and northern Iraq. The Armenian Orthodox or Gregorian Church, which broke with Rome over the monophysite issue, has 600,000 members scattered throughout the Middle East, with primary concentrations in Iran, Turkey, and Syria. Other Christian sects include the Greek Orthodox, whose 600,000 members honor the Patriarch of Constantinople, denying the primacy of Rome and emphasizing the role of the Holy Ghost, and the Nestorian or Assyrian Church, a close-knit community of 25,000 in northern Iraq, whose patriarch now lives in political exile in Chicago.

Subsequently, an additional group of Christian sects, the Uniate churches, was created when subgroups of the Eastern schismatic religions reestablished their connections with Rome, renounced their heretical doctrines, accepted the supremacy of the pope, but retained their rites and customs. Only one group, the Maronites, completely reunited with Rome. Now forming a large minority of 425,000 in Lebanon, they speak Arabic, have retained a Syriac liturgy, and trace their history back to pre-Arab Phoenicians. Economic differences between these Lebanese Christians and the Muslim majority lie at the heart of Lebanon's recent civil war. Other Uniate churches include the Greek Catholic of Syria and Lebanon, the Armenian Catholic, the Coptic Catholic, the Syrian Catholic, and the Chaldean Catholic (an offshoot of the Nestorian or Assyrian Church).

Despite considerable internal distinctions, Middle Eastern Jewry is considerably less fragmented than either Christianity or Islam. A clear majority of Israel's 2.6 million Jews are Orthodox Rabbinites who accept the Talmud as interpreted by Orthodox rabbis or teachers. Old World Orthodox Jews, however, are subdivided into Ashkenazi or European Jews, who speak Yiddish, a language related to medieval German, and Sephardic or Oriental Jews, who speak Ladino, a dialect of Hebrew derived from fifteenth-century Spanish. Each of these broad groups has its own rabbinical courts, customs, and liturgy. European Jews in Israel range from recent American immigrants, to the extreme orthodox who do not accept Israel because it is a man-made creation, to Hasidic Jews whose dress is that of eighteenth-century Poland. Among Oriental Jews, each Middle Eastern community that migrated to Israel—a total of 600,000 people from Yemen, Kurdistan, Iraq, and North Africa—brought its own traditions, beliefs, and language. Beyond the orthodox, two small sects, the Karaites, who number 12,000 and accept the Bible but not the Talmud, and 500 Samaritans, whose interpretation of Judaism springs from the eighth century BC, now reside in Israel. Outside Israel, 200,000 Jews continue to live in Turkey, Morocco, and Iran—those parts of the Middle East least directly affected by the Arab-Israeli conflict.

In addition to the three major monotheistic faiths, adherents of a number of smaller faiths are found in the Middle East. In Iran, 30,000 to 40,000 Zoroastrians, who still practice the faith of the ancient Persian empires, have fire temples in the cities of Tehran, Yazd, and Kirman. An undetermined number of Bahai, followers of a nineteenth-century Persian reformer, live in Israel, Lebanon, and Iran. In northern Iraq, two religious groups of Kurdish origin are found: the Yazidi or devil worshipers, numbering about 70,000, concentrated in the province of Mosul; and the Shabak, a community of 10,000 to 14,000 who share shrines with the Yazidi and mix elements of both Sunni and Shia Islam. In southern Iraq, a group of 7000 Mandeans, whose ceremonial language is related to Aramaic, practice a fertility cult that combines aspects of Christianity and Manichaeism.

Ethnic and Linguistic Diversity

The distribution of language and ethnic groups in the Middle East is less complicated than religious patterns. A major language divide follows the southern and western slopes of the Taurus and Zagros mountains of the northern highlands. South of this boundary, Arabic, which spread throughout the region during the early Islamic conquests, is the predominant language of Syria, Jordan, Lebanon, Iraq, Arabia, Egypt, and North Africa. Hebrew, of course, is the national language of Israel. Although dialects vary considerably within the Arabic-speaking realm,

It was the medieval Arabs who recovered much of the philosophy, science, and medical knowledge of the ancient world, expanded upon it, and transmitted it anew to a Europe that was just recovering from centuries of chaos. This thirteenth-century manuscript page is from a treatise on astrology. *Photo:* The Bettman Archive.

the educated classes of these nations share a common knowledge of the classical form of the language, the language of the Koran. North of the highland boundary, Turkish has predominated in Anatolia since the thirteenth-century invasion by the Osmanli Turks, while Persian, an Indo-European tongue, is spoken on the Iranian plateau. Except for tiny minorities of Armenians, Aramaic-speaking Syrian Jacobites, enclaves of Greeks in Anatolia, and small Jewish and European communities in the larger cities, these three major languages predominate in the fertile, densely settled lowlands of the Middle East.

In the highlands, however, significant language minorities have persisted despite the long dominance of Arabs, Turks, and Persians in their respective realms. In North Africa, the original Berber language of the region is spoken throughout the highlands of Morocco, Algeria, and Tunisia. Berber consciousness has never been expressed in political terms, however, because tensions between the Arab majority of the lowlands and the highland Berbers are superseded by a common religious undertaking. But in the highlands of the **_Fertile Crescent,_**[•] some 2 million Kurdish-speaking people in Turkey, Iraq, and Iran have demanded self-determination and a separate political state for forty years. The problem is most acute in Iraq, where 800,000 Kurds, one-tenth of the country's population, have fought an unresolved conflict in northern Iraq for the last decade. In Iran, the Kurdish movement has been encouraged largely because its demands have been forwarded to Baghdad, not Tehran; a similar abortive claim to independence among the Turkish-speaking people of the northwestern province of Azerbaijan, however, was summarily extinguished. Other sizable Turkish-speaking nomadic tribal groups in Iran are scattered throughout the Zagros Mountains. Turkoman tribes inhabit the dry plains of the northeast along the Russian border. All these groups, semi-autonomous in the past, have been disarmed and forced to curtail their migrations by the strong central government at Tehran.

One final Middle Eastern cultural conflict, that between Greeks and Turks on the island of Cyprus, is deeply rooted in the centuries-long confrontation of these two cultures. Occupied by Greece in the eighth century BC and an early Christian stronghold, the island is viewed by modern Greeks and Greek Cypriots as part of their national homeland, despite its location only 40 miles from the Turkish coast. Turks began settling the Cypriot countryside late in the sixteenth century, setting a pattern of population distribution that lasted until now. Until 1974, nearly 80 percent of the island's 645,000 people were Greeks, and the Turkish minority was scattered in the less productive highlands. Greek demands for union with Greece provoked the Turkish invasion of the northern third of the island in 1974 and a sub-

sequent restructuring of the population along a de facto cultural divide. Ancient antagonisms between Greeks and Turks today override possible economic or commercial cooperation. Thus, because of Turkish military superiority, the probable outcome of recent conflicts will be the goal enunciated by Turkish Cypriots, that of ethnic partition.

The survival and persistence of these numerous ethnic, linguistic, and religious groups within the framework of Islamic civilization provided the cultural basis for the forces of divergence, dissidence, and conflicting loyalties to emerge when the Ottoman state began to crumble in the nineteenth century. Rooted in three distinctive human environments—city, village, and tribe—the allegiance and horizons of most Middle Easterners were framed within limited cultural and **_ecological_**[•] enclaves. The environmental basis of traditional life in the Middle East, an ecological trilogy, like the cultural mosaic, persisted for centuries. Ultimately both systems—cultural mosaic and ecological trilogy—disintegrated under the forces of nationalism, population growth, and developmental change that swept the region in the present century. They remain the sources, however, of the life experience of most Middle Easterners, the distinctive traditions that modern leaders must both alter and preserve.

THE MIDDLE EAST AND NORTH AFRICA

REGIONAL PATTERNS

PHYSICAL FEATURES MAP
POPULATION DENSITY MAP

The Middle East and North Africa form a vast swath of *deserts,*• *steppes,*• and mountain *plateaus*• located at the juncture of the three continents of Europe, Africa, and Asia. Nearly twice the size of the United States, this *region*• stretches 6000 miles eastward from the dry Atlantic shores of Mauritania to the high mountain core of Afghanistan. It includes twenty-three separate political states, most of which were created by colonial *cartographers*• in the nineteenth and twentieth centuries. By world standards, the population of the Middle East is small: less than 200 million people. But over half of the Middle East is too dry or rugged to sustain human life, and only 5 to 10 percent of the entire region is cultivated. As a result, a stark contrast exists between core areas of dense human settlement where water is plentiful, and the empty wastes of surrounding deserts and mountains.

Four regions can be identified in this huge area: the Northern Highlands, a 3000-mile-long zone of plateaus and mountains in Turkey, Iran, and Afghanistan, stretching from the Mediterranean Sea to Central Asia; the Arabian Peninsula, a million-square-mile desert quadrilateral jutting southward into the Indian Ocean and flanked on either side by the Persian (or Arabian) Gulf and the Red Sea; the Central Middle East, the rich valleys of the Nile in Egypt and of the Tigris and Euphrates in Iraq and the intervening Fertile Crescent countries of Israel, Jordan, Lebanon, and Syria; and North Africa, a band of watered mountains and plains set between the Sahara Desert and the Mediterranean Sea. Known by the Arabs as *al Maghrib al Aqsa*• (Land of the Setting Sun), it includes the nations of Tunisia, Algeria, Morocco, and Libya.

THE NORTHERN HIGHLANDS

The Taurus and Zagros mountains of southern Turkey and western Iran form a physical and cultural divide between Arabic-speaking peoples to the south and the plateau-dwelling Central Asian peoples of Turkey, Iran, and Afghanistan. Fully one-third of the people of the Middle East and North Africa live in the Northern Highlands, on the Anatolian and Iranian plateaus and the flanks of the Hindu Kush range of Afghanistan. Here, as throughout the Middle East, from 60 to 80 percent of the population are agriculturalists concentrated in areas of fertile land and sufficient rainfall. In Turkey and Iran, population growth has intensified the pressure on these fertile areas, even though extensive agricultural development programs have increased production, and cultivation has been extended into the dry margins of the plateau cores. Afghanistan remains one of the least developed, poorest nations in the world.

Turkey is a large, rectangular peninsula plateau bounded on three sides by water—the Black Sea on the north, the Aegean Sea to the west, and the Mediterranean Sea on the south. Except in the south, the Turkish coast is rainy, densely settled, and intensively cultivated. About 40 percent of the population is clustered onto the narrow, wet Black Sea coast, on the lowlands around the Sea of Marmara in both European and Asiatic Turkey, along the shores of the Aegean, and on the fertile Adana Plain in the southeast. By contrast, the center of Turkey—the dry, flat Anatolian Plateau—is sparsely settled. Cut off by the Pontic Mountains to the north and the Taurus to the south, the dead heart of the plateau is too dry to sustain dense agricultural settlement; in the east, the rugged terrain of the Armenian highlands limits agricultural development.

Turkey's current population of 36 million has doubled over the last forty years and continues to grow at a rate of 3 percent each year, but the country is still an *agrarian*• society where 70 percent of the population is on the land. Cultivation has penetrated less favorable environments on the dry plateau and has intensified along the more humid coasts. Overall, cultivated land has increased two and one-half times in the last twenty-five years, wheat harvests have doubled, and cultivation of cotton, tea, and citrus fruit has greatly expanded. However, rural Turks in search of economic security are increasingly migrating to cities such as Istanbul (2.2 million), Ankara (1.2 million), and smaller provincial capitals. Their success will depend on continued industrial and agricultural growth.

Although the environmental base of Iranian society is similar to Turkey's, the topography is more dramatic, and contrasts between the desert and the sown are more sharply drawn. High mountains ring the dry Iranian Plateau on all sides except the east. In the west and south, the folded ranges of the Zagros Mountains curve southeastward for a distance of 1400 miles from the northwest Turkish frontier to the deserts of Sistan in the southeast.

In the north, the steep volcano-studded Elburz range sharply divides the wet Caspian Sea coast from the dry Iranian interior. The encircled plateau covers over half the area of Iran, with large uninhabited stretches of salt waste in the Dashti Kavir to the north and of sand desert in the Dashti Lut to the south. As in Turkey, more than half the people of Iran are agricultural villagers. Because population has tripled from 10 million to 30 million in this century, settlement has imploded in regions favorable to agriculture.

Along the Caspian *littoral*,• which receives up to 60 inches of rainfall per year, the intensive cultivation of rice, tea, tobacco, and citrus fruits supports a dense rural population. Similarly, in Azerbaijan in the northwest and in the fertile valleys of the northern Zagros, rainfall is sufficient to support grain cultivation without irrigation. The higher pastures of this region support an estimated 3 million *transhumant*• nomads of Turkish origin. But in the rest of Iran, rainfall is inadequate and irrigation essential. Oasis settlement based on wells, springs, or underground horizontal water channels called *qanats* is common. In Khuzistan, on the Mesopotamian plain, new dams on the Dez and Karun rivers are aimed at creating a major industrial-agricultural complex. But the high growth rates of the small cities of the densely rural north and the mushrooming city of Tehran (3.4 million) as well as the growth of Isfahan, Meshed, and Tabriz (each with 0.5 million people) suggest that Iranian agriculture will not be able to support the country's future population growth. The basis of the Iranian economy will be the diversified industry now developing from the country's oil wealth.

In the small remote country of Afghanistan, the easternmost nation of the Northern Highlands, the processes of population growth, agricultural expansion, and urbanization have barely begun. The country's center is occupied by the ranges of the Hindu Kush, a rugged, snowbound highland that is one of the least penetrable regions in the world. Deserts to the east and south are cut by two major rivers, the Hari Rud and the Helmand, both originating in the central mountains of Afghanistan and disappearing into the deserts of eastern Iran. In the north, the Amu Darya (Oxus) flows into the Russian steppe. Settlements are found in scattered *alluvial*• pockets on the perimeter of the Hindu Kush, wherever there is level land and reliable water supplies. Over 70 percent of Afghanistan's estimated 18 million people live in scattered villages as cultivators of wheat and barley and herders of small flocks of sheep and goats. An additional 15 percent are nomadic tribesmen, whose political power is still felt in this traditional society. In central and eastern Afghanistan, Pathans are dominant; in the north, the Turkish-speaking Uzbeks and Persian-speaking Tadzhiks predominate. This cultural diversity reflects a tradition of isolation in a countryside that remains largely unconnected with the modern world. At least two-thirds of Afghanistan's rural produce never enters a market economy; urbanization is slight (Kabul has less than 400,000 people), and modern agricultural expansion has just begun with irrigation projects in the Hari Rud and Helmand valleys. Despite this, population growth has forced the country, formerly self-sufficient in foodstuffs, to begin imports of basic grains.

THE ARABIAN PENINSULA

The Arabian Peninsula is a huge desert platform bounded on three sides by water and on the fourth by the deserts of Jordan and Iraq. In the west, the rugged slopes of the Hijaz and the highlands of Yemen form the topographical spine of this platform. The remainder tilts eastward to the flat coasts of the Persian Gulf, rising only in the extreme southeast to the heights of the Jabal al Akhdar (Green Mountains) of Oman. Although the peninsula is the largest in the world and nearly four times the size of the state of Texas, it supports a population of less than 18 million people. The majority of these people live in two nations: Saudi Arabia (8.2 million), which governs nine-tenths of this region, and Yemen (6.0 million), whose highlands trap sufficient moisture to support cultivation without irrigation. Smaller states on the eastern and southern perimeters of the peninsula include Kuwait, Qatar, the United Arab Emirates, Oman, and South Yemen. All except the last have less than 1 million people.

The principal historical determinant of human settlement in Arabia has been the availability of water. Overall, the region receives less than 3 inches of rainfall each year, with a bit more in the north. Only the highlands of Yemen and Oman at the southern corners of the peninsula receive more than 10 inches. Daily temperatures commonly rise above 100 degrees Fahrenheit. Fully one-third of the central plateau is covered by a sea of shifting sand dunes, and much of the rest lies under boulder-strewn rock pavement. In the southern desert, the forbidding Rub al Khali (Empty Quarter), wind-worked dunes 500 to 1000 feet high, cover an area of 250,000 square miles to form a bleak, rainless no-man's land between Saudi Arabia and the states of the southern coast. Arching northward from the Rub al Khali, a 15-mile-wide river of sand, the Ad Dahna, connects the southern sands with the desert of Nafud 800 miles to the north. Given this harsh environment, the Arabian landscape has no permanent lakes or streams. Vegetation is sparse. Settlement is confined to oases, and only 1 percent of the region is under cultivation. Vast stretches of the peninsula are completely uninhabited, devoid of human presence except for the occasional passage of Bedouin camel herders.

165

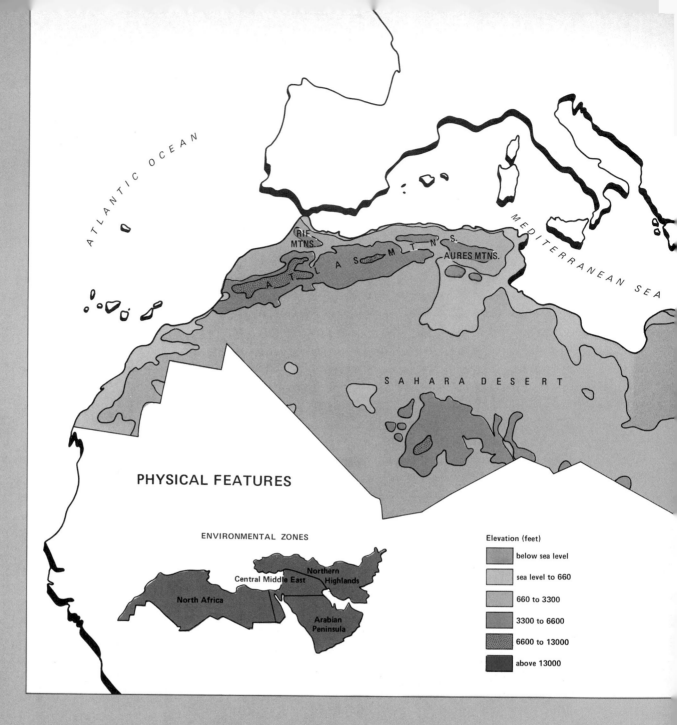

ATLANTIC OCEAN

MEDITERRANEAN SEA

RIF MTNS.

ATLAS MTNS.

AURES MTNS.

SAHARA DESERT

PHYSICAL FEATURES

ENVIRONMENTAL ZONES

North Africa

Central Middle East

Northern Highlands

Arabian Peninsula

Elevation (feet)

	below sea level
	sea level to 660
	660 to 3300
	3300 to 6600
	6600 to 13000
	above 13000

Within this difficult physical setting, two-thirds of the people of the Arabian Peninsula are rural agriculturalists, seminomads, and nomads. Their lives focus on oasis settlements where wells and springs provide water for the cultivation of dates—the staple food of Arabia—and the maintenance of herds of camels, sheep, and goats. The distribution of these oases is determined by a network of dry river valleys (wadis) carved into the surface of the plateau in earlier and wetter geological periods. These wadis provide the most favored locations for commercial and agricultural settlement and the most convenient routes for caravan traffic. In the western highlands, where population density is above average, the largest urban centers are Mecca, Medina, and Taif. In central Arabia, underground water percolates down from these uplands and surfaces through artesian (gravity-flow) wells, creating a string of agricultural oases both north and south of the Saudi Arabian capital of Riyadh. Farther east, on the shores of the Persian Gulf, this same water emerges as freshwater springs in Kuwait, eastern Saudi Arabia, and the United Arab Emirates. Similarly in South Yemen, springs in the Wadi Hadhramaut, a gash several hundred miles long parallel to the coast of the Gulf of Aden, provide the basis

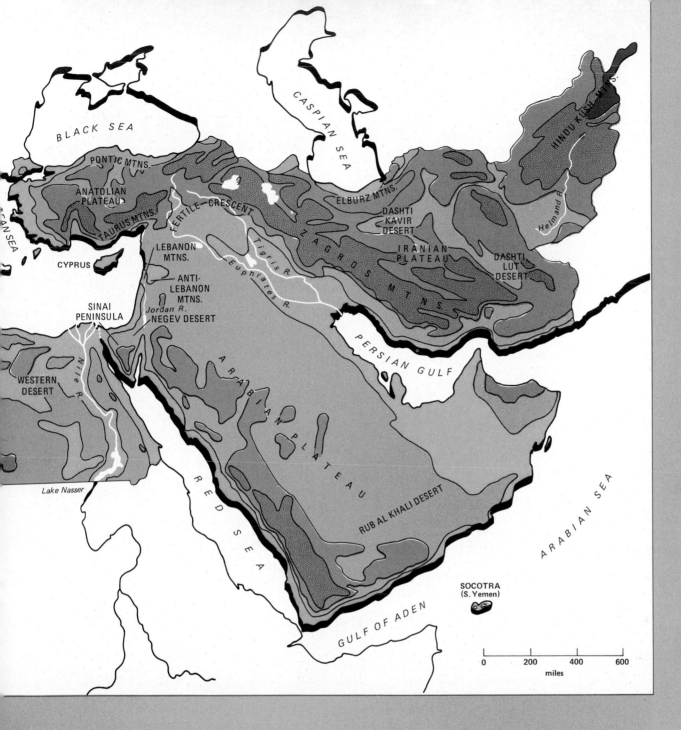

BLACK SEA
PONTIC MTNS.
ANATOLIAN PLATEAU
TAURUS MTNS.
FERTILE CRESCENT
CYPRUS
LEBANON MTNS.
ANTI-LEBANON MTNS.
Jordan R.
SINAI PENINSULA
NEGEV DESERT
WESTERN DESERT
Nile R.
Lake Nasser
CASPIAN SEA
ELBURZ MTNS.
DASHTI KAVIR DESERT
IRANIAN PLATEAU
ZAGROS MTNS.
DASHTI LUT DESERT
HINDU KUSH MTNS.
Helmand R.
Tigris R.
Euphrates R.
PERSIAN GULF
ARABIAN PLATEAU
RED SEA
RUB AL KHALI DESERT
GULF OF ADEN
SOCOTRA (S. Yemen)
ARABIAN SEA

0   200   400   600
miles

for oasis settlement. Only in Yemen and Oman is this dry-land oasis pattern broken. In Yemen, the highland rainfall allows terraced cultivation of coffee, cotton, and the profitable narcotic shrub *qat*. In Oman, grains, dates, pomegranates, and limes are cultivated, and cattle breeding is an important economic activity.

The prevailing harshness of the Arabian environment, however, has always required that any sizable settlement on the peninsula exist partially on resources brought in from outside—on revenues from the pilgrimage traffic, the coastal *dhow* trade in the gulf, or commerce in the Indian Ocean. Today,

oil resources in Saudi Arabia, Kuwait, the island state of Bahrain, the United Arab Emirates, and to a lesser extent, Qatar and Oman are providing the capital for rapid economic growth, leaving the southern states of Yemen and South Yemen in isolated poverty. In the gulf, cities like Dhahran, Dhammam, Ras Tannurah, Kuwait City, Manamah (the capital city of Bahrain), and emirate centers like Abu Dhabi, Dubai, and Sharjah are creations of the oil industry. Less directly but equally dramatically, the traditional centers of Riyadh (225,000), Mecca (185,000), and Jidda (194,000) are growing rapidly as farmers and Bedouins seek salaried

167

employment in expanding urban industries. This process of urbanization reflects an overall rate of human growth that has quadrupled the population of Saudi Arabia from 2 million to more than 8 million in the last forty years. With nearly limitless capital, the governments of the oil-producing states of the Arabian Peninsula are now drilling thousands of new water wells, establishing desalinization plants along the coast, and investing heavily in agricultural expansion and forestation—all to the purpose of establishing a viable post-oil economic base. Whether the marginal environment of the peninsula can long sustain the significantly larger populations that current growth rates promise is a matter of conjecture.

THE CENTRAL MIDDLE EAST
[FIGURE 1]

The central Middle East is flanked to the west and east by two great river valleys, the Nile of Egypt and the Tigris-Euphrates system in Iraq. Between these riverine states, the small nations of Israel, Lebanon, and Syria line the shores of the eastern Mediterranean; Jordan is landlocked. The total population of this region exceeds 60 million, reflecting the higher rainfall in the north delivered by winter storms coursing eastward through the Mediterranean Basin and the dependable fertility of the river valleys in the drier south. The environments of these nations are as complex as their histories. Four millennia of human civilization have left an essentially denuded landscape—barren hills, steppes overgrazed by sheep and goats, and rivers choked by the *erosional silt* of human activity. Faced with rapidly expanding populations, each state has developed strategies to cope with increasing pressure on environmental resources.

In Egypt, population pressure on agricultural resources is more serious than anywhere else in the Middle East. An estimated 96 percent of Egypt's 35 million people are crowded into the Nile Valley, a narrow trough 2 to 10 miles wide that cuts northward across the dry plateau of northeastern Africa to the Mediterranean Sea. East of the Nile Valley, the heavily dissected Eastern Highlands border the coast of the Red Sea, continuing past the Gulf of Suez into the Sinai Peninsula. Barren and dry, these highlands are occupied by nomadic herders, a few monasteries, and for the last twenty years, the armed forces of the United Nations, Egypt, and Israel. West of the Nile, the dune-covered rainless Western Desert stretches 300 miles to the Libyan border. Irrigated agriculture is practiced in a series of oasis depressions, optimistically called the New Valley, the largest of which are Kharga, Dakhla, Farafra, and Bahariya. The remainder of the Western Desert is occupied by a thin scattering of nomadic herders.

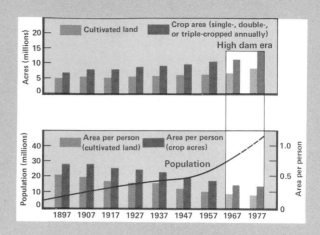

Figure 1. Cultivated Land, Crop Area, and Population in Egypt, 1897–1977. The amount of cultivated land and crop area per person has steadily diminished in Egypt, despite increases in crop yields and major efforts to expand the cultivated area. Population growth has outstripped resource development. *Adapted from:* U.S. Department of Agriculture data.

The sources of the Nile River lie 2000 miles south of the Mediterranean in the wet plains of the Sudan and the equatorial highlands of East Africa. The Nile's largest *tributary,* the White Nile, originates in Lake Albert and Lake Victoria and flows sluggishly through a vast swamp, the Sudd, in southern Sudan, before entering Egypt. The other major tributaries, the Blue Nile and the Atbara River, flow out of the Ethiopian highlands, draining the heavy summer rains of this region northward toward the desert. This summer rainfall pours into the Nile system, causing the river to flood regularly from August to December, and raises its level some 21 feet. For centuries, this flood formed the basis of Egyptian agriculture. Specially prepared earth basins were constructed along the banks of the Nile to trap and hold the floodwaters, providing Egyptian farmers with enough water to irrigate one and, in some areas, two crops of wheat and barley each year. Silt deposited by the swollen waters refertilized Egyptian fields and ensured continuing soil fertility and high yields.

In the twentieth century, British and Egyptian engineers constructed a series of *barrages* and dams on the Nile to hold and store the floodwater year round. Their goal was to change traditional *basin irrigation* into *perennial irrigation,* enabling the Egyptian peasant to plant three or four crops each year on land previously left *fallow* when the level of the Nile was low. Corn and cotton replaced wheat and barley as the primary crops, and rice and vegetables were grown for export. By 1960, the area under cultivation had increased from 4 million to 6 million acres, and crop yields of wheat and corn were up by one-third. This transformation of Nile agriculture was largely completed in 1970 with the construction of the Aswan High Dam, a massive earthen barrier more than 2 miles across, 0.5 mile wide at the base, and 120 feet high. Behind it, Lake Nasser, the dammed Nile River, stretches 300 miles southward to the Sudanese border. The dam will add about one-third to the cultivated area of Egypt. Unfortunately, that will not be enough. In addition, the environmental consequences of the High Dam may be severely negative in the long run, creating future problems that will compound the stress of population size.

As agricultural engineers labored successfully to increase the scope and productivity of Egyptian agriculture, the nation's population tripled from an estimated 10 million at the turn of the century to its current 35 million. During this same period, urban population expanded eight times, and Cairo (5.3 million) and Alexandria (2.1 million) emerged as the two largest cities on the African continent. The bulk of this population increase, however, was absorbed in the countryside; as a result, pressure on agricultural resources intensified. Peasants from Upper Egypt migrated from the less productive remnant areas of basin irrigation to richer agricultural areas downstream. In the *delta*° of Lower Egypt, rural densities in some areas increased to more than 6000 people per square mile. Overall, the average size of agricultural holdings in Egypt diminished from 5.7 acres in 1900 to 2 acres today, and the amount of crop area per person was halved. Contained within the narrow ribbon of fertile land in the valley and delta of the Nile, Egypt continues to grow at a rate of 800,000 people each year. Intense overcrowding and mounting population pressure can be relieved only by substantial emigration from Egypt or by military, political, or economic merger with other Arab states.

In contrast to Egypt, the central problem in the other great river valley of the Middle East, the Tigris-Euphrates of Iraq, is not overpopulation but environmental management. Both these rivers rise in the mountains of eastern Turkey and course southward for more than 1000 miles before merging in the marshes of the Shatt al Arab. North of Baghdad, both rivers run swiftly in clearly defined channels. To the south, they meander across the flat alluvial plains of Mesopotamia. East of the valley, the Zagros Mountains rise as a steep rock wall separating Iraq from Iran. To the west, a rocky desert plain occupied by nomadic herders stretches to the borders of Saudi Arabia, Jordan, and Syria. Only in the northeast, in the Kurdish hills, does rainfall sustain nonirrigated cultivation. Elsewhere in Iraq, human existence depends on the waters of the Tigris and Euphrates rivers. But unlike Egypt, where every available acre of farmland is intensively utilized, Iraq's agricultural resources are wasted. Only one-sixth of the potentially *arable*° land is under cultivation, and Iraq clearly has the

resources to support a substantially larger population than its current 10 million.

The Tigris and Euphrates rivers have always proved less manageable than the Nile. Fed by melting snows in Turkish highlands, spring floods 8 to 10 feet above normal pour down the river channels to Baghdad and then spread out over the vast plains of Mesopotamia, where the land is so flat that elevations change only 4 to 5 feet over distances of 50 miles. Since some 70 percent of the Iraqis are villagers in the south, these floods are a direct threat to the agricultural economy of the country. New *dikes*° and dams on the rivers have brought widespread flooding under control, but drainage and irrigation are difficult, and the accumulation of salts in the soil (salinization) is a constant problem over large areas (see Rise, p. 15). Progressive control of the environment, however, has encouraged nomads to settle as wheat and barley farmers in relatively good years in Mesopotamia and to revert to herding in bad agricultural years. Although cultivation is extensive, large areas still lie fallow, and yields are low. In the swampy marshes of the Shatt al Arab, which produce three-quarters of the world's dates, the environment is less hazardous, and dense populations of peasants produce an agricultural surplus. But growing population (now triple that of 1935) and urban advantages have caused a flight of villagers from rural areas to the cities, in particular to the dominant center, Baghdad (1.8 million). In spite of available agricultural land and relative underpopulation, many of the same processes that influence Egypt are affecting Iraq, although the available resources and oil revenues of the latter make future progress much more likely.

In the Fertile Crescent countries of Syria, Lebanon, Jordan, and Israel, which lie along the eastern coast of the Mediterranean between the river valleys of Egypt and Iraq, environmental patterns are extremely complex. The coastal plain, narrow in the north but widening southward, is backed by dissected, rugged highlands that reach elevations of more than 10,000 feet in Lebanon. Throughout their length, these uplands have been denuded of forests, notably the famous cedars of Lebanon, by centuries of overgrazing and cutting for economic gain. Winter rainfall is plentiful in the north but less in the south. In Syria, the highlands capture this ample rainfall in streams that support life in the oasis cities of Aleppo, Homs, Hama, and Damascus. In Lebanon and northern Israel, runoff from the highlands sustains important commercial and agricultural areas along the coast. Farther south, the highlands flatten out into the rainless wastes of the Negev Desert. Inland, a narrow belt of shallow, flat-bottomed *intermontane*° valleys separates these western highlands from the dry upland plateaus and mountains of the east. Between Israel and Jor-

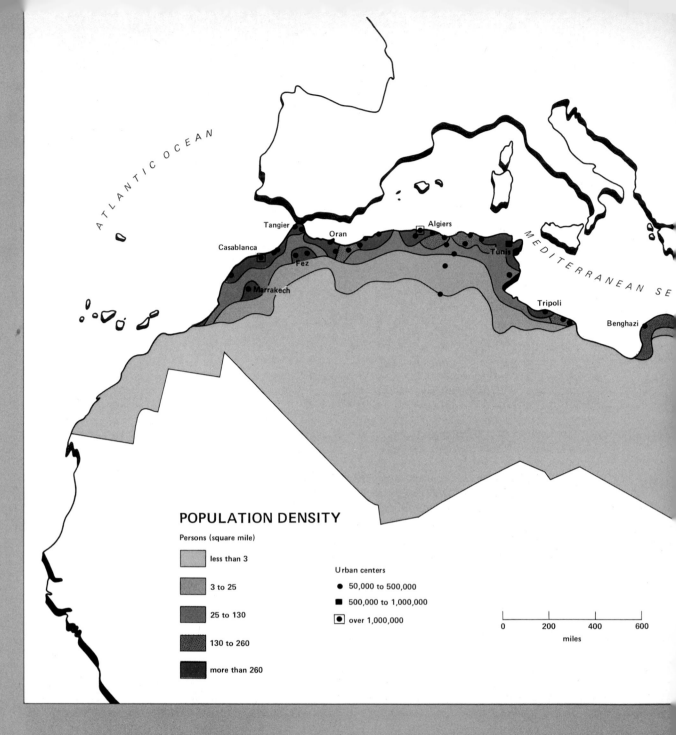

POPULATION DENSITY

Persons (square mile)

- less than 3
- 3 to 25
- 25 to 130
- 130 to 260
- more than 260

Urban centers

- ● 50,000 to 500,000
- ■ 500,000 to 1,000,000
- ◉ over 1,000,000

0   200   400   600

miles

dan south of the Sea of Galilee, the Jordan River flows along one of these valleys 150 miles southward to the Dead Sea, 1300 feet below sea level. Farther north, a similar trough in Lebanon, the Beqaa Valley, is drained by the Litani and Orontes rivers. East of these lowlands, rugged highlands grade inland to the grass-covered steppes of Syria in the north and the dry stone pavement of the Jordanian desert in the south.

In this varied terrain, the distribution of population is extremely uneven. In Israel (3.2 million), some 80 percent of the population is clustered on the northern coastal plain stretching from Haifa to Tel Aviv. In the south, the Negev, which makes up 70 percent of the area of the country, is virtually empty, although political considerations and ideological commitments have led to the establishment of some communal agricultural settlements (kibbutzim) in this desert. Similarly in Lebanon (2.6 million), population is dense along the coast and thinner in the interior highlands, with a secondary concentration in the Beqaa Valley between the Lebanon and Anti-Lebanon mountains. In both these countries, olives, grapes, citrus fruit, and other Mediterranean crops are grown commercially along the coast. Neither state, however, is primarily

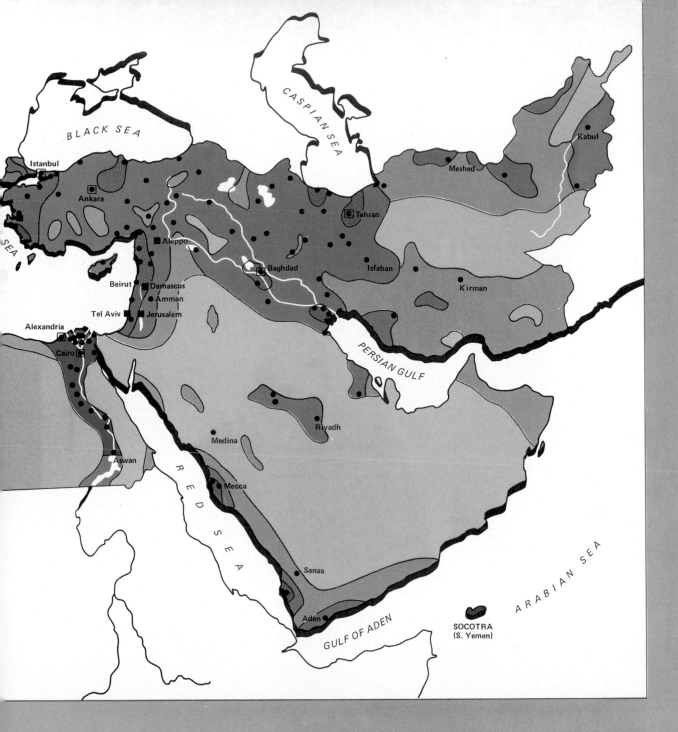

Map labels: BLACK SEA, CASPIAN SEA, Istanbul, Ankara, Aleppo, Beirut, Damascus, Amman, Tel Aviv, Jerusalem, Alexandria, Cairo, Aswan, Baghdad, Tehran, Isfahan, Kirman, Meshed, Kabul, RED SEA, Medina, Mecca, Riyadh, Sanaa, Aden, GULF OF ADEN, PERSIAN GULF, ARABIAN SEA, SOCOTRA (S. Yemen)

agricultural. Unlike most Middle Eastern countries, Israel and Lebanon are urban nations with sophisticated, literate populations and diversified economies. One-third of all Lebanese live in either Beirut or Tripoli; in Israel, a like percentage resides in Tel Aviv, Jerusalem, and Haifa.

In Syria and Jordan, the primary economic activity is village farming, and terrain and rainfall are decisive factors in the distribution of population. Some 90 percent of Syria's 6.6 million people live in the more humid western part of the country. On the narrow coastal plain and in the rugged limestone foothills of the Jabal Ansariah, wheat, olives, and

the famous latakia tobacco are cultivated by members of a Muslim sect, the Alawi. On the eastern slopes of the mountains, wheat fields interspersed with olive groves cover a vast plain stretching from Homs to Aleppo. In the far south around Damascus, olives, fruit, and wheat are primary products. In the interior, east of this strip of fertile stream-watered land, steppes and deserts cover two-thirds of Syria's territory. Oases and irrigation projects are found on the upper reaches of the Euphrates, but only in the far northeast, the Jezira, is rainfall sufficient to support nonirrigated grain agriculture. In Jordan (2.5 million population), five-sixths of the land is a

171

A new road and terraces to retard erosion and raise agricultural productivity are part of attempts to develop the poor, overpopulated mountainous area of the Western Rif in Morocco. *Photo:* United Nations.

desert plateau suitable only for a nomadic existence; the remaining sixth, the west bank of the Jordan River, has been occupied by Israel since 1967. In the highlands on either side of the Jordan River, subsistence wheat cultivation is supplemented by small vineyards and citrus orchards. This economy has been severely disrupted by warfare, and approximately half of Jordan's population is now composed of refugees from Israeli territory.

NORTH AFRICA

North Africa is the largest subregion of the modern Middle East, covering an area larger than the United States, but settled by only 50 million people grouped together on the southern shore of the Mediterranean Sea between water and sand. Much as Egypt is truly the gift of the Nile, cultural North Africa is the result of a physiographic event, the Atlas Mountains, which separate the Sahara Desert from the Mediterranean Sea and Europe beyond. Most of the territory of the modern nations of the Maghrib—Morocco, Algeria, Tunisia, and Libya—consists of Saharan wastelands that stretch 3000 miles across Africa from the Atlantic Ocean to the Red Sea. One-seventh of this area is sand dunes; the remainder is rock-strewn plains and plateaus.

Aridity in the Sahara is not interrupted even by the jutting peaks of the Ahaggar and Tibesti *massifs*• at 6000 feet, which receive as much as 5 inches of rainfall per year. Here, as well as in other scattered Saharan oasis environments, an estimated 3 million people wrest a living from what is earth's most difficult cultural environment outside the polar regions. Only in the north, along the mountain-backed coast of the Mediterranean, is rainfall sufficient to sustain substantial concentrations of people. The Atlas Mountains form a diagonal barrier isolating the nomads of the deserts and steppes of the south and east from *sedentary*• agriculturalists in the Mediterranean north.

The Spanish Sahara is the only North African country that is totally desert. Before the recent discovery of extensive phosphate deposits in the north and the possibility of rich iron ore lodes, this territory was of little interest to anyone but the 50,000 *pastoralists*• and 200,000 Spanish troops occupying the area. Both Morocco and Mauritania have claimed sovereignty over the region; Spain left the Sahara in 1976, and the territory has been divided between its two larger neighbors.

In Morocco, the Atlas Mountains form a succession of four mountain ranges dominating the landscape. In the north, the Rif, which is not geologically associated with the Atlas, is a concave arc of mountains rising steeply along the Mediterranean, reaching elevations of 7000 feet and orienting Morocco toward the Atlantic. In the center of Morocco, the limestone plateaus and volcanic craters of the Middle Atlas reach elevations of 10,000 feet; contact with Algeria is channeled through the Taza corridor, and this mountain barrier has isolated the Moroccan Sahara until modern times. Farther south, the snow-capped peaks of the High Atlas attain elevations of 13,400 feet and separate the watered north from life in the Sahara. Finally, the Anti-Atlas, the lowest and southernmost of the Moroccan ranges, forms a topographic barrier to the western Sahara. Historically, the Atlas have provided a refuge for the original Berber-speaking inhabitants of Morocco, whose descendants today make up half the nation's population. Throughout mountain Morocco, Berber populations maintain an agrarian tradition of transhumance of goats and sheep wedded to cultivation of barley centered around compact mountain fortresses. Density of settlement in the mountains depends on rainfall, which in general diminishes from west to east, and on altitude, which prohibits year-round settlement because of cold winter temperatures in areas much over 6000 feet.

Most of Morocco's 15.7 million people are Arabic-speaking farmers who till the fertile lowland plains and plateaus stretching from the Atlantic to the foothills of the Atlas. Two types of agricultural economy are intertwined and often juxtaposed in Morocco, as well as in Algeria and Tunisia. French colonists settled in areas suited to large-scale mechanized agriculture, and promoted the export-oriented cultivation of grapes, olives, wheat, citrus and other fruits, and vegetables. This new tradition, often based on crops alien to the domestic market, has been an important problem in these decolonizing countries. In Morocco, colonial agriculture prevailed along the Atlantic coast from Safi to Tangier, on the Gharb Plain, the Meknes-Fez area, and in the irrigated plains of Marrakech and the Sous River valley. In contrast, subsistence grain cultivation predominated on traditional North African farms, interspersed with domestic production of the great variety of fruits and vegetable crops native to the southern Mediterranean lands. All agricultural regions, however, have felt the impact of Morocco's rising population, which has more than tripled in this century. In the countryside, extensive government efforts to increase the cultivated area have not stemmed the flow of migrants from villages to the rapidly growing cities of Casablanca (1.5 million), Rabat, Meknes, and Fez.

Farther east along the Atlas complex, the primary environmental contrast in Algeria is once again the distinction between the fertile, well-watered, and densely settled coast and mountain ranges of the north, and the dry reaches of the Sahara Desert in the interior. The Algerian coast is backed by the Tell Atlas, a string of massifs 3000 to 7000 feet in eleva-

tion, which have formed an important historical refuge for Berber-speaking tribes. In the interior, a parallel mountain range, the Saharan Atlas, reaches comparable elevations in a progressively drier climate. Between these two ranges in western Algeria, the high plateaus of the Shatts, a series of flat interior basins, form an important grazing area. In eastern Algeria, the two ranges of the Atlas merge to form the rugged Aurès Mountains. South of these ranges, Algeria extends 900 miles into the heart of the Sahara.

Settlement and economy in these environmental zones closely parallel those of Morocco. The humid coast and mountain ranges of the north are densely settled; the desert interior is virtually empty. On the best agricultural land along the Mediterranean, some 1 million French settlers established vineyards, olive groves, and citrus orchards in the nineteenth century. Europeans controlled the exterior agricultural economy of Algeria until independence was achieved in 1962, after which most chose to return to France. The majority of Algeria's 14.6 million people cultivate small fields of wheat and barley, tend flocks of sheep and goats, and earn small subsistence incomes in environments marginal to former French interests. As in Morocco, population growth—currently estimated at more than 3 percent each year—has stimulated programs of land reform, land redistribution, and land reclamation, rationalizing production according to modern methods while diverting the flow of rural migrants to coastal cities. Algiers, however, already has a population of 1.2 million, and other northern cities—Annaba, Skikda, and Constantine—are also growing rapidly.

In Tunisia and Libya, topography is less dramatic than in Morocco and Algeria, but the same environmental sequence from northern coast to southern desert prevails. Two-thirds of Tunisia's 5.2 million people live in the humid northeast and in the eastern extension of the Aurès Mountains. The central highlands and interior steppes, marginally important in the past, have become sites of innovative development projects. Tunisia remains an example of self-motivated, serious, and successful state planning. In Libya, population (now estimated at 2 million) is concentrated on the coast and in the hilly back country of Tripolitania and Cyrenaica. In east and west Libya, commercial cultivation of Mediterranean crops prevails on the coast; to the south, except in the oases and oil towns, the desert beyond is vacant. Population throughout the eastern Maghrib is growing rapidly, and the large cities of Tunis (800,000), Tripoli, and Benghazi are attracting rural migrants in large numbers. Programs of agricultural expansion, funded in Libya by substantial oil revenues and in Tunisia by international assistance, are being undertaken.

THE TRADITIONAL MIDDLE EAST

2

The secular order of the Middle East was, until very recently, embedded in a cellular system of settlement composed of three different types of communities: the city, the village, and the tribe. Each of these components formed a distinctive human environment that was qualitatively different from the others. Their characteristics evolved over centuries of ecological experimentation and adaptation from the culture and institutions of Islam and from the social and economic realities that bound Middle Eastern horizons.

THE CELLULAR PATTERN:
CITY, VILLAGE, AND TRIBE

Middle Eastern cities shared a number of common features. The mosque, socially dominant and the symbol of the urban landscape, was directed by a religious intelligentsia. Commerce was pursued in nearby bazaars, whose structure and administration reflected the interplay of religious life with secular institutions. Residential quarters spread outward from the central bazaars. With one religion expressing shared cultural needs and practices from the Atlantic Ocean to India, and with common environmental problems and similar technologies, Middle Eastern cities were strikingly uniform in appearance and organization over vast distances. Villages, more closely tied to local conditions, were more diverse. Settlements in the Nile Delta, Anatolia, the Maghrib, and central Iran reflected the need to minimize the uncertainties of agriculture and stock breeding in different kinds of marginal environments—*riverine,** oasis, desert, and highland. Some patterns common to traditional Middle Eastern village economy and society can be identified: cooperative fieldwork, absentee land ownership, localized kinship systems, a simple technology, and the seasonal rhythm of the agricultural cycle. Similarly, traditional tribal nomads could be compared in terms of the migratory cycle, ecological adjustment to marginal resources, herd composition, and the role of agriculture in their own work. Nomadic life varied in intensity of movement ranging from the "pure" nomadism of the camel-herding Bedouins of the full desert, through transhumance (herding that moves seasonally over a fixed upland), to *seminomadism.**

The interactions among cities, villages, and tribes within areas, nations, and the whole of the Middle East delineated the regional variations of this part of the world. Networks of roads and camel caravan routes linked cities to one another, but the relations between individual cities and their hinterlands were complex and varied. In Anatolia, a hierarchy of agricultural settlements raised and traded the food surplus of the entire plateau to meet the needs of Istanbul and other Ottoman urban centers. In Iran, villages were often owned by an urban elite, which drained away the village products so that privileged urbanites might sustain a graceful way of life. In southern Mesopotamia, in Saudi Arabia, and on the Saharan fringe of North Africa, villagers paid tribute or were owned as slaves by nomadic tribes. In these areas where environment became difficult and distinctions between peasant and nomad, between the desert and the sown, were blurred by the need for people to master many tasks in the face of environmental uncertainty, urban dominance was usually at its weakest.

By the nineteenth century, this cellular system of settlement, although still intact, was in serious decline. Centuries of warfare with external invaders—Crusaders, Mongols, and Tatars—had exhausted the Middle East. The breakdown of order in the Ottoman state and the decline of long-distance trade reduced environmental control and human intensity to levels far below those experienced earlier. Syria's population of 2 million was only a third that supported during the Roman period, and large areas of once-cultivated land had been abandoned because of nomadic incursions; the case was much the same in Iraq. Egypt had a population of about 4 million; under the Romans, the Lower Nile had supported 8 million. In the countryside, *tax farmers** bled the peasantry, perhaps 80 percent of the total population, of their energy and their harvests. In the cities the death rate was so high that immigrants from village and tribe formed a significant percentage of the population. The economy of the Middle East was stagnant; its artistic life was sterile. Political power was in the hands of corrupt and ineffective rulers.

In the traditional Middle East, comfort, security, and sustenance were best found among one's own people. Interactions among the semiautonomous social worlds of the city, village, and tribe were few and formal because communications systems were poor and the countryside was insecure. Under such conditions, physical isolation was reinforced by an ingrained suspicion of strangers born of centuries of corruption and oppression. Although necessary exchanges of products and produce provided points of contact between diverse communities, loyalty to small groups and acceptance of existing conditions prevailed in the traditional Middle East.

THE TRADITIONAL MIDDLE EASTERN CITY

Muslim cities were the cornerstones of Islamic culture and civilization even though, as in other preindustrial societies, urbanites did not form a majority of the population. The preeminence of cities was especially strong in this region because Muslim political, religious, and economic leaders were almost always urban-based; the concept of a rural **gentry**• did not exist. Social and economic institutions were urban creations exported to the countryside. The peasant majority of the Middle East, organized into city regions—urban hinterlands—was the source of food supply and the recipient of political and social demands made by dominating urban centers.

In the early Islamic period, Arab geographers defined their cities in rather specific terms: any settlement with a mosque and a permanent marketplace or bazaar—two critical institutions of cultural and commercial leadership. Many of the cities settled by the Arabs had been established by Greek and Roman conquerors. But under the Muslims, cities in the Middle East came to share a new set of distinctive internal spatial patterns, characteristic forms of social and economic organization, and an urban milieu congenial to the practice and contemplation of Islam.

Until recently, the spatial patterning of Muslim cities differed markedly from that of industrial centers in the West. Several characteristics that consistently appeared in Middle Eastern cities were an emphasis on enclosure and security, both in urban structure and in domestic architecture; the allocation of central space to a mosque-bazaar complex; and the organization of residential space into semiautonomous quarters, usually with some degree of ethnic, occupational, or religious unity.

Every important Middle Eastern city (except Mecca, a sanctuary ringed by mountains) was surrounded by high walls and fortifications. Given the stormy history of this region, the time and energy spent building and repairing city walls were always wise investments. A circular or rectangular wall 40 to 50 feet high was penetrated only by monumental gates located at the ends of major avenues, which ran from a central mosque-bazaar complex to the walls. In many cities, a citadel with still stronger fortifications was built inside the city to protect the seat of local government from both internal and external uprisings. This emphasis on enclosure and security also influenced the structure of the residential quarters and houses. The internal patterns of the quarters were irregular: streets and lanes formed a maze of dark, twisting passageways, alleys, and culs-de-sac. Most streets were less than 12 feet wide and framed by the high outer walls of household compounds. Massive house doors were the only break in the façade of the street. Housetops were often studded with spikes or fragments of glass. There were no street signs and no numbers; the clamor of city traffic did not penetrate residential areas. Privacy, protection, and security were paramount in their construction.

Central space in these walled cities was allocated to the most prestigious institutions, the mosques and bazaars. The central mosque was often the most beautiful and impressive building in the city and the pivot of social and religious life. Some, like the Al-Azhar mosque in Cairo, Hagia Sophia in Istanbul, and the Masjidi Shah in Isfahan, were also major centers of education and administration. As cities evolved, new mosques became the focal point of new bazaars and the larger cities came to have several centers. Each mosque was a hub of activity for the ulama, who applied Islamic law to family life, regulated markets and even water supply, and managed the city's religious, educational, and legal institutions. The pervasive influence of Islamic values on the structure of Middle Eastern cities probably derives from the paramount importance of these men in urban administration.

The second central institution in these cities, the bazaar, was a welter of crowded lanes, covered stalls, and associated caravansaries far noisier and more aromatic than Western central business districts. The bazaar was the locus of virtually all wholesale and retail trade within the city. In the bazaar, central location was highly valued. Thus, a concentric hierarchy of trades and crafts often existed, with the shops of prestigious craftsmen such as booksellers, carpet merchants, jewelers, and silversmiths located at the center of the bazaar, and lesser crafts progressively nearer the margins.

Most of the space of the city was subdivided into residential quarters that were social and geographical entities bound by ties of religion, blood, occupation, and common origin. During the Ottoman period, the millet or community system recognized the legal existence of these separate and distinct social communities. In Antioch, for example, forty-five quarters existed with Jews. Armenians, Greeks, Europeans, and

This view of Bagdhad a generation ago shows the traditional Middle Eastern city pattern. The Khadimain Mosque, with its minarets and courtyards, dominates the city and sits at its center; around it, residences and shops linked by narrow alleys cluster in a random pattern marked by the lack of open space. *Photo:* The Bettman Archive.

Muslim sects each identified with specific sectors of the city. Every quarter formed an independent community walled off from the others, a city within a city, with its own mosque or church, its own customs, law, and milieu. At the turn of the nineteenth century, Cairo had a similar cellular residential pattern, although it did not encompass as varied a population. In smaller cities, walled quarters were usually absent. Nonetheless, differentiation on the bases of race, religion, and common origin was fundamental to Muslim urban social organization, and small, cohesive urban groupings were important features of the social ecology of traditional Middle Eastern cities.

In the nineteenth century, Middle Eastern cities were small, although a surprisingly high percentage of the region's total population, perhaps as much as a quarter, were town dwellers. Cairo, Baghdad, and Istanbul were the only cities in the region with populations larger than 250,000. Cities as famous as Aleppo and Damascus were slightly larger than 100,000; Jerusalem and the future capital of Iran, Tehran, had populations of only 10,000.

Both natural and social factors limited the size of each individual city. Although Istanbul, Damascus, Baghdad, and Isfahan were known in the West as international trading centers, less than one-tenth of their population was employed in commerce. Most city dwellers were engaged in producing, collecting, and processing raw materials from the hinterlands—wool for carpets and shawls; grain and vegetables to feed the urban population; and nuts, dried fruits, hides, and spices for export. Because regional transportation networks were poor, the size of the rural hinterland from which cities could draw agricultural surpluses was limited and so, therefore, was each urban center. Many Middle Eastern cities devoted much of the space within their walls to food production, and many city dwellers worked in fields surrounding the city. At the beginning of the nineteenth century, over half of Cairo's adult males were farmers or farm laborers.

Even when large territories were organized by the Ottoman or the Persian empires, highly centralized states, natural factors inside preindustrial Muslim cities limited their capacity to expand. When urban populations grew by migration from the countryside, problems of water distribution, poor sewage disposal, and inadequate food supplies caused a high urban death rate. Fires and earthquakes also took their toll. In Istanbul, for example, 160 fires were recorded in seven years, and the last of these, the great fire of 1865, reduced four-fifths of the city to ruins. Fez was substantially damaged by the great Lisbon earthquake of 1755. These physical and cultural conditions inhibited the growth of individual urban centers until the beginning of the twentieth century.

Qanats are gently sloping tunnels dug in loose, alluvial sediments. In excavating them the diggers must have fresh air and tunnel spoil must be removed, so the tunnels are connected to the surface with a series of vertical shafts through which fresh air enters and excavated dirt leaves. After the tunnel and shafts are constructed, ground water percolates into the tunnel and flows along its path to emerge at the surface. Unlike other traditional irrigation devices such as the counterpoised sweep (shaduf), the waterwheel (dulab), and the noria (na'ura), when the qanat is completed, no power source other than gravity is needed to maintain flow.

The size of a qanat may vary considerably. In the mountains short tunnels less than a kilometer in length are common [but some qanat tunnels are as long as 30 miles].... The deepest known qanat in Iran is located at Birjand; its tunnel begins at a depth of nine hundred feet. Usually qanats are constructed individually, but occasionally they are built in pairs, with twin tunnels constructed side by side connected by passages. This type of construction facilitates maintenance of the channels. Water can be diverted back and forth between the two channels as the workmen clean first one and then the other tunnel....

The ideal topography for qanat construction is a piedmont alluvial plain, where gently sloping tunnels can intersect a sloping water table. This setting exists in many arid regions of the Old World; in most, qanats are or have been used to bring irrigation water to the surface. In Iran, where alluvial plains are common, qanats are widely used.... It is estimated that nearly fifteen million acres of cultivated land, one-third to one-half of the irrigated area of Iran, is watered by 37,500 qanats, of which an estimated 21,000 are in fully operating order and 16,500 are used but need repair. Their aggregate length has been placed at more than 100,000 miles, their total discharge at 20,000 cubic meters per second....

East of Iran, qanats are used in Afghanistan, Central Asia, and Chinese Turkestan (Sinkiang). Here they are called by the Persian term (kariz) rather than the Arabic (qanat). In Afghanistan they are the major source of irrigation water in the south and southeast.... In China qanats were used in the second century B.C. and are still found in the Turfan Basin.

To the west, qanats can be found in Mesopotamia, the Levant, and Saudi Arabia. From there they were spread by the Arabs across North Africa and into Cyprus and Spain.... In the Levant qanats are found only in the drier parts of Syria and Jordan, where they are incorrectly believed to be of Roman origin.... In Arabia they are used in Oman, on the Hadhramaut coast, and in Yemen....

Qanats (foggaras) are found in North Africa on the northern and southern slopes of the Atlas Mountains and are particularly concentrated near the city of Mar-

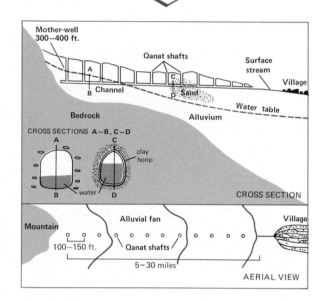

Adapted from: Paul Ward English, *City and Village in Iran.* Madison: University of Wisconsin Press, 1966, p. 31. Copyright © 1966 by the Regents of the University of Wisconsin.

rakech. ... They are used in Egypt only at the Kharga oasis, where the fifth-century B.C. Persian monarch, Darius, had infiltration channels dug in the soft sandstone to supplement surface water supplies. The Arabs introduced the concept of qanat technology into Spain, and from there it was carried to South America.

Source: Quoted from Paul Ward English, *City and Village in Iran.* Madison: University of Wisconsin Press, 1966, pp. 135–136. Copyright © 1966 by the Regents of the University of Wisconsin.

The village of Lalla Mimouna in Morocco has some 4000 inhabitants, most of them weavers of traditional clothing and small merchants. The women here do laundry the old way, but development projects sponsored by the government, with UN assistance, have brought shops, a dispensary, a community house, and a modern school. *Photo:* United Nations.

THE MIDDLE EASTERN VILLAGE

Villages were the economic foundation of traditional Middle Eastern society; 70 to 80 percent of the people in this region lived in rural agrarian communities. Occupied with cultivating wheat, barley, the date palm, and a host of lesser crops, villagers formed a majority in every major Middle Eastern region except Arabia and the Sahara, where nomads held sway. In general, villages were located wherever a reliable supply of water for cultivation either was available or could be made available through wells, horizontal tunnels (qanats), waterwheels, or other lifting devices. Particularly dense rural populations were found on the coasts of the Mediterranean, Black, and Caspian seas, in the uplands of the Fertile Crescent where winter rains provided water, and in the river valleys of the region. After millennia of human experimentation, only the highest mountain regions and the cores of the great deserts of the Middle East—the Egyptian Sahara, the Empty Quarter of Saudi Arabia, the Syrian desert, and the barren *kavir* and *lut* regions of the Iranian plateau —had no settled rural population.

Most Middle Eastern villages were small, compact clusters of dwellings with few facilities besides a mosque, a shrine, a few shops, and possibly a bath. The houses, dome-roofed cubes constructed of mud bricks or tamped earth, were nearly indistinguishable from the surrounding landscape. Houses were walled and faced inward to courtyards, creating even in small villages an external network of alleys that gave an illusion of urbanity.

Housing patterns varied with differing building materials, environmental constraints, and architectural traditions. In the marshes of southern Iraq, elaborate reed houses formed floating villages; along the western coast of Saudi Arabia, houses took a beehive form (also found near Aleppo, where they were built of stone). In the Saharan oases and in southern Saudi Arabia, palm fronds were a principal building material. In Libya, sandstone was used, and along rivers, adobe. In the highlands of Anatolia and Iran, wood and stone villages were interspersed with **troglodyte** settlements, where villagers solved the problems of construction and heating by living underground. In most cases settlements **agglomerated**; **dispersed** settlement was virtually nonexistent in the Middle East.

Watercourses are frequently social gradients in Middle Eastern villages. In Sehkunj (southern Iran), three distinct periods of growth illustrate this point. In 1800, Sehkunj was a small walled village clustered on an alluvial terrace where water emerged from the mountains. Prosperous households, the village mosque, and public baths were located in this cluster; poorer sharecroppers and fuel collectors lived downslope. Late in the nineteenth century, a local saint was buried in the cemetery below the town, and a shrine constructed over his grave attracted new settlers. Recently, the construction of a new qanat has encouraged the establishment of an entirely new residential quarter below the shrine. Significantly, the qanat enters the town at the shrine and not at the old center, and wealthy households have moved downstream to take advantage of the more plentiful water. Sehkunj is now divided in three sections: the old walled center, now in partial ruins, is occupied by the poor; a mixed residential quarter has developed above the shrine; and the new quarter below the shrine is becoming the social core of the village.

Source: **Paul Ward English,** *City and Village in Iran.* **Madison: University of Wisconsin Press, 1966, p. 55. Copyright © 1966 by the Regents of the University of Wisconsin.**

The specific sites of these clustered settlements were carefully adapted to local environments and the daily patterns of village life. Where water was plentiful and cultivation continuous, houses, mosques, and shops were frequently surrounded by orchards in which olives, dates, and other commercial crops were cultivated within walled enclosures. Grain fields radiated outward beyond the enclosed area; cultivation was limited primarily by the energy and determination of village families.

In some parts of the Middle East, where water came from a stream, a canal, an aqueduct, or a qanat, the village was strung out along the watercourse. The houses and walled gardens were located upstream, with grain fields fanning out downslope. In these villages, the location of each household compound determined the quality and quantity of its water supply. The homes of prosperous landlords, the village sheikh (acknowledged spokesman), and other distinguished villagers lay in the upper sections, where water was clean and plentiful; the poorer households of peasants, **sharecroppers,** and day laborers were located downstream, where water was polluted and diminished by use. In the Middle East, the administration of water was a critical social task, and conflict resolution a vital human theme.

Village life, then, was intimately tied to relatively isolated local environments. Most villagers were farmers whose lands provided the staple grain of their diet, whose few sheep and goats provided protein and wool products for clothing, and whose entire lives were regulated by the rhythm of the agricultural cycle. Plowing and planting for grain took place in the fall; the harvest, in late spring or early summer. In the winter, the villagers scoured surrounding wastelands for wood or worked as day laborers to accumulate small amounts of cash to purchase amenities such as mirrors, tea sets, or mats. Villagers were basically self-sufficient; their most important dealings were in kind. The local barber, potter, and carpenter were paid in grain at harvest time, with the amount largely dependent on the success of the harvest. The villagers' few cash ventures took place in the nearest town or city, which they visited infrequently.

Land Ownership and Tenure

The primary relationship between cities and villages in the Middle East was one of economic exchange,

A FAMINE WINTER IN AN ANATOLIAN VILLAGE

Mahmut Makal, son of a Turkish peasant, became the schoolteacher in a central Anatolian village at the age of seventeen. This excerpt from his controversial book, A Village in Anatolia, *describes the famine winter of 1947–1948 as experienced by the peasants of his village and their children, his students.*

How is the winter to be borne, unless one has a habitable house, clothing to protect one against the cold, something with which to fill one's stomach, and just a little fuel? With us, there's just nothing. Clothes are made once in five or ten years, and what is made is of the coarsest kind. . . . Some of the old men will adapt an ancient Army tunic, dye it, and pull it on; and under the jacket a pair of trousers, at least ten years old, and a smock, or simply a vest and pants alone. . . . Few wear shoes, and you rarely find anyone wearing socks. In any case there's nothing much to do on a winter's day, except to walk from the house along to the village common-room, and then from there back again. . . . As for the women, they wear even less, but for some reason they stand the cold better. It is they who work hard in winter. Such work as looking after the animals, watering them, and carrying water to the house, falls to them; whereas the men, having nothing to do, shiver through the winter. Many of them have nothing on their legs but a pair of the thinnest patched trousers.

People tell the villager who dries dung that "burning dry dung is a crazy thing to do," and that it is better to "spread it on the fields." . . . We count ourselves lucky when we find any dung to dry; we treat it with all the respect in the world. And what do you suppose the villager is to burn, if he doesn't burn dried dung? Has he ever set eyes on a bit of wood or coal? . . . Very often the dung, and the straw, and the other things will give out in the middle of winter. Then the village is in a pretty bad way. That is what happened this year. What a winter it was! . . . Everyone was waiting for the weather to clear; spring was on the way, and just as we were telling ourselves "It's over at last," it suddenly got worse, and we had a wind that blew incessantly, howling like a blizzard and as bitter as gall. . . .

I had fifty to sixty pupils still able to attend school. . . . When February came, and attacked us with all its venom, our knees gave way. Among all those pupils only one or two had a little dung fuel left in their homes. These were the children of the Agas, the more substantial villagers, who had more than two oxen. If I asked them to bring one piece of fuel every day, would their fathers and mothers agree, I wondered? And would they not soon run out of it themselves? . . .

On days when the children could stand the cold and come to school, we would give anything to go out when the interval came. Outside, with our lips and faces so frozen that we couldn't speak, we got some air, moved about a little, and got warmer. Like lizards crawling out of the ground, half dead, half alive, we reached the month of April. . . .

We grown-ups emerged from the winter with very little harm done; but the children! Ah, how the wretched children suffered! From the new-born to those a year old, not one survived. Pitiless children's diseases, profiting by the cold, swept the little creatures away. . . .

Our village has one hundred and thirty houses. . . . In [February] alone we inscribed the names of thirty-four children, not one of whom had lived to be one year old. . . .

Source: Quoted from Mahmut Makal, *A Village in Anatolia.* London: Valentine, Mitchell, 1954, pp. 7–12.

---

as the cities were dependent upon food surpluses produced at the village level. In the nineteenth century, most cultivated land in the Middle East was owned by absentee landlords, and land tenure agreements between urban landlords and village sharecroppers formed the basis of this exchange. While the terms of these contracts varied, generally the harvest was divided into five portions. Each portion was allocated to the party that supplied one of the five elements of production—land, water, plow animals, seed for planting, and labor. Peasants always received one-fifth of the harvest for their labor, and more if they provided either animals or seed. The success of the agricultural year often hinged on the more detailed provisions of land tenure contracts—the supply of fertilizer (if any), whether the stubble in a harvested field could be grazed by the villagers' animals, and whether the straw belonged to the peasant or the landlord. In a good year, peasants were able to provide their families with sufficient food and a bit besides. But in lean years, when drought or epidemic struck, peasants fell into debt. At this point, the landlord was expected to protect and guard the villagers from the threats of government tax collectors, marauders, and moneylenders.

Although absentee ownership of village land was the general pattern in the Middle East, wide variations in city-village relationships were produced by differences in location, economics, and terrain. In southern Iran, for example, sharecropping was part of a system of urban dominance designed to drain economic surpluses from surrounding villages, leaving the mass of the rural population quite literally without resources. Similar contracts in herding and weaving reinforced urban control of rural resources, so that village economic life was shaped by decisions made in the cities. In the Jordan highlands and

The dromedary, the single-humped camel, is the basis of nomadic life in the Sahara and the Arabian peninsula. Because of its adaptive characteristics, the camel serves as the principal food resource of the nomad, as a means of freight and personal transport, and as a source of leather and wool. Camel milk is the nomad's staple food; a milk camel produces 6 to 10 pints of milk daily for eleven to fifteen months. In contrast, sheep, goats, and cattle give milk only during the five months the wet season lasts. Although camels are slaughtered only for sacrifice or ceremony, camel meat is a derivative food equated locally with the meat of seven sheep. As beasts of burden, camels carry the entire camp, tents and furnishings, throughout the migration period. They produce additional income by being hired out as caravan animals in regional trade. With adequate herds to support them, the Bedouins of Arabia and the Tuareg, Teda, and Chaamba of North Africa were able to organize themselves in population units as large as several hundred tents in spite of the severe limitations of their environments.

The adaptations of this animal to the desert environment are well known. The camel needs water and pasture every three or four days in summer but can survive a month without water in the cool season because its hump is a fat-storage area and its stomach can carry up to 50 gallons of water. After a long period without water, a camel can drink 20 gallons of highly saline water in a single draught and, in a matter of minutes, increase its body weight 25 percent and recover from the effects of dehydration. Thick pads on its feet make it possible for the camel to cross both the sand dunes and the rock-strewn deserts. The swift racing dromedary of the Tuareg can cover 150 to 180 miles in a day; the slower and more common baggage camel usually averages only 15 to 20 miles a day.

other parts of the Levant, communal villages were found. Here, each male head of household owned the right to cultivate a share of the village lands, and these parcels were redistributed periodically within the village. In southern Iraq, large tribal confederations with both nomadic and sedentary sections owned land communally and maintained extensive irrigation systems. A more autonomous and independent pattern of ownership probably existed in villages distant from urban centers.

The lot of the peasant in the Middle East was one of hardship, toil, and poverty under all these tenure relationships. Moneylenders, landlords, nomadic tribes, and urban governments exacted their tolls from the only important source of revenue available —village produce. To be sure, the low population density of the Middle East in the nineteenth century meant that sufficient land was available, but peasants were rarely able to cultivate enough land to better their conditions. However, armed with family strength and a simple technology, they endured famine and plague, insecurity and drought. Comfort was found in the fact that most villagers were equally poor; security rested upon one's family and village. Thus, although sources of deep unrest and resentment existed in the Middle Eastern village, none surfaced as long as traditional society maintained its total integrity.

THE ECONOMY OF MIDDLE EASTERN NOMADS

Until this century, access to the limited communications and trade networks that existed across the dry reaches separating major population centers in the Middle East was controlled by some 5 million nomadic tribal peoples. The domain of the nomad included habitable portions of the Sahara and the watered Maghrib, the Arabian Peninsula, the Levant, and mountain and plateau regions of Turkey, Iran, and Afghanistan. The largest tribal federations—the Tuareg, Teda, and Chaamba of North Africa; the Bedouins of the Arabian, Syrian, and Egyptian deserts; the Kurds, Qashqai, Bakhtiari, and Baluch of the mountains and plateaus of Anatolia and Iran— were powerful groups in their own right.

Nomadic pastoralism as practiced in the Middle East can be organized into three idealized types: *horizontal nomadism,* the periodic movement of herds over large distances in search of pasture; *vertical nomadism* (transhumance), the seasonal shift-

An Afghan nomad camp in the Hindu Kush. This remote, inaccessible but incredibly beautiful landscape has yet to be touched by the forces of modernization. *Photo: United Nations/Siceloff.*

ing of herds of sheep and goats between lowland and highland environments; and *seminomadism*, a combination of herding and cultivation found on the margins of settled agricultural communities. In general, nomadic economies were adaptations to marginal resources beyond the perimeter of control of the central government.

Camel nomadism was practiced in the Sahara Desert, on the agricultural margins of North Africa, and in the twin desert cores of the Arabian Peninsula, the Rub al Khali in the south and the Nafud in the north. These regions have an extremely thin and scattered vegetation, a situation that stems partly from climatic reasons and partly from overgrazing. Fewer plant species are found in the Sahara than in any region except the polar zone, and most Saharan plants are succulents or thorny bushes low in nutritive value. Rainfall is so rare in some areas that houses in desert oases can be built of salt without danger of dissolving. By necessity, pastoral migrations took the form of movement in search of pasture for the camel herds.

Camel nomads tended to stay out of the desert as much as possible and set up camps on the steppe margins or in oases during the summer. In the Sahara, nomadic tribesmen lived in Cyrenaica, in oases in southern Algeria and southern Morocco, and in the **Sahelian°** zone of the southern Sahara. They ranged out from these bases into the desert in search of pasture, on long seasonal migrations covering as

much as 1000 miles and lasting as long as nine months. On the northern margins of the Sahara, migrations took advantage of the scanty winter precipitation maximum; in Arabia, annual grazing began in the autumn and lasted through early spring.

Despite the reliance of camel nomads upon their herds, every sizable tribe had access to agricultural products. These tribes rarely worked the land themselves; rather, they controlled the harvest in desert oases and steppe settlements. In the Sahara, only the peasants of the Souf and Mzab oases were able to free themselves completely from obligations to the camel-herding tribes. Commonly, nomads owned a quarter to a third of the date groves in the desert oases. In the central Sahara, the palm groves were tended by a slave caste of Africans, the Haratin, who for all practical purposes were owned by Tuareg and Teda tribesmen. In areas where tribes did not directly own cultivated land, they extracted tribute ("the brotherhood tax") from the villagers for protection of the oases. Camel nomads returned to the oases during the date harvest to collect their share. Similarly, in Arabia where the Bedouins controlled or owned the entire environmental infrastructure—desert pasturages, wells, the smaller oases, and even some large ones—oasis cultivators were the slaves, clients, or tenants of nomads. Until the introduction of Western technology in the Middle East, the desert **ecosystem°** was largely controlled by camel nomads.

In mountain and plateau areas of Turkey, Iran, Afghanistan, and the Maghrib, vertical nomadism (transhumance) was practiced on seasonal pastures not suitable for year-round grazing or permanent cultivation. The nomad system extended over summer pastures in the uplands and winter pastures in

These Tuareg nomads of North Africa have stopped to water their animals. Troughs made of hollowed tree trunks are filled by drawing water from the well in skin bags. The nomad way of life is under increasing strain as governments strive to modernize their countries. *Photo: United Nations.*

the lowlands. If sheep and goat herds had been kept in either zone year round, approximately 70 to 80 percent of the animals would have died; the logic of this system was to exploit each environment during its period of maximum productivity. For some transhumant tribes, migration to different elevations covered distances of 10 miles or less, and the migratory period was very brief; for others, the nomadic trek covered 100 to 1000 miles and the tribe was in virtual perpetual motion. Frequently a succession of tribes utilized the same pastures in different seasons. In the Zagros foothills of Kurdistan, for example, Kurdish sheepherders grazed their flocks in the lowlands during the winter. When they migrated to higher elevations, Arab camel herders moved in from the desert onto the vacated pastures, which were adequate for camels, although too barren for sheep. In the mountains of southwestern Iran, a

similar sequence of tribal occupance occurred, as various strains of sheep developed great resistance to changes in temperature and adapted to thin pasturage.

In Iran, transhumant tribes living in the Zagros and Elburz mountains owned a large proportion of the country's livestock. Patterns of nomadic herding often led to overgrazing and destruction of plant resources. The principal hedge against disaster was for each tribal family to maintain as many animals as possible; a transhumant family required a flock of forty sheep or goats. The primary threat was not drought, but cold spells during lambing time or at a crucial point in the migration, for frost could kill as much as 50 percent of a herd overnight. Maintenance of large herds therefore made sense in the short run; in the long run, it destroyed grazing resources. Despite these hazards, most transhumant nomads perceived village and city life as a poorer, less satisfactory type of existence.

The third type of nomadism found in the Middle East, seminomadism, encompassed a wide variety of agricultural and herding combinations designed to fit local environmental conditions. Patterns varied from year to year depending on rainfall, social and political conditions, and, in some cases, market factors. Along the Euphrates, short-distance sheep and goat nomadism was practiced to take advantage of nearby upland pastures. Occasionally a tribe tended herds belonging to a complex of villages, keeping the flocks one-half day's distance away so that milk would be daily available to the peasants. In North Africa, nomadic tribes frequently cultivated the steppe margins. Even among the mountain nomads of Iran and Afghanistan, some villages were peopled by sedentarized nomads who farmed when necessary and reverted to nomadism when conditions allowed.

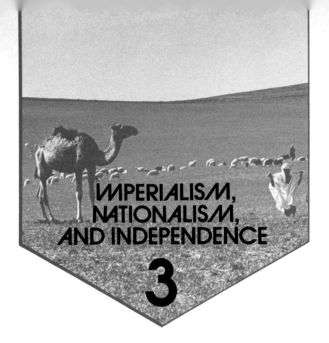

IMPERIALISM, NATIONALISM, AND INDEPENDENCE

3

The transformation of traditional society and the integration of the Middle East into larger systems of trade and communications were fostered by the acquisitive European search for new markets and raw materials during the nineteenth century. Other civilizations, notably India, China, and Japan, were feeling the same currents emanating from Europe at the same time. New boundaries appeared on the map of the Middle East as European powers vied for spheres of influence. Markets were opened to a flood of Western goods, and traditional handicraft industries were disrupted. This process moved the Middle East from subsistence to market economies. The self-contained religious, ethnic, village, and tribal societies of the region were dislocated; their isolation was broken and violated by ideologies, social and economic forces, and communications systems stemming from Europe. Western medicine and hygiene eliminated plagues and improved sanitation; the reduced death rate resulted in doubling and sometimes tripling population growth rates. Population growth, destruction of local service industries, and the entry of the region into the world economy presented a familiar picture of incipient, colonial-dominated industrialization.

The Middle East was slow to react to these Western intrusions until nationalistic aspirations, focused in the visions of new leaders such as Muhammad Ali of Egypt, Ataturk of Turkey, and Reza Shah of Iran, came to transform the traditional social mosaic of the region. Domestic social progress was stifled by European aims, which were limited to economic reorganizations that benefited the European economy. The assertion of independence from colonial rule by Middle Eastern nations reflected irrevocable changes in the social organization of the region. Communal ties were progressively replaced by contractual agreements, allegiance to tribe or sect by national ideologies. The settlement cells that formed the basis for social and economic interactions in the traditional Middle East were integrated into the new **nation-states**• of the region.

EUROPEAN IMPERIALISM IN THE MIDDLE EAST

Until the nineteenth century, an impenetrable cultural frontier between West and East lay athwart the Mediterranean Sea, separating Christian Europe from the Islamic Middle East and North Africa. Closer to Europe in distance than any other non-Western peoples, nineteenth-century Middle Easterners lived in isolation from the European scientific and technological discoveries that ultimately came to bear on their lives. Virtually no Muslims visited Renaissance Europe. European merchants in the Middle East generally acted in concert with local minorities—Lebanese Christians, Armenians, and Jews—the entrepreneurs of the region. Muslim universities were in decay, and the works of the great medieval Muslim scientists and philosophers such as Avicenna, al-Ghazzali, and ibn-Khaldun were no longer taught. High illiteracy rates were universal; hygienic conditions in Egyptian villages were probably among the worst in the world.

The feudal rulers of the Middle East remained aloof from the human condition. The Ottoman Empire was still territorially intact, but some petty dynasties had achieved quasi-independent status, and Bedouin incursions were increasing. When one of the Ottoman sultans attempted to introduce Western military techniques and weapons into his armed forces, however, the elite troops of the empire—the Janissaries—threatened revolt rather than adopt these "Christian devices." Plagued with ineffective rulers and without a Muslim commercial class, the Ottoman Middle East was poorly prepared to face the impact of an expanding, industrializing Europe when the first waves of the Industrial Revolution washed over this region in the latter half of the nineteenth century.

Weak central government in the Ottoman Empire was accompanied by the progressive breakdown of law and order. Tax revenues, primarily **tithes**• and livestock taxes levied on the peasantry, declined. In an effort to modernize their armies and civil service, the Ottoman sultans began to contract loans from European powers, but belated efforts at reform yielded little increase in military power. One by one the Balkan provinces of the empire (with the tacit or open support of European powers) attained independence. In North Africa, Barbary pirates virtually ruled the cities of Algiers, Tunis, and Tripoli. Throughout the Levant, adventurers carved out ephemeral kingdoms. In Anatolia itself, leaders of powerful local families called "valley lords" administered the law and refused submission (payment of taxes) to the Sublime Porte, the seat of Ottoman administration in Istanbul. Successive sultans signed commercial treaties with European powers in the search for additional revenue. In the 1840s, the British were granted trading rights anywhere in the empire, equal to those of Turkish nationals. Within a few years, Britain began to import substantial quantities of grain, carpets, wool, opium, and a variety of agricultural products from Anatolia in return for textiles and manufactured goods. Under constant pressure from other European powers, Ottoman sultans granted a series of **concessions**• to foreigners (capitulations) in return for lavish loans to support their palaces. Under the capitulations, Europeans were exempt from local taxes, could not be arrested by Turkish officials, had the right to be tried in their home countries for offenses committed in Ottoman territory, and were granted low export tariffs.

With these incentives, European banks were established in Mediterranean port cities, and European investors bartered for interior railroad concessions, mineral rights, public utilities, and agricultural land throughout the Middle East. Foreign loans to the sultans were secured by customs duties, tobacco and salt taxes, and other revenues due the Ottoman state from a burdened peasantry. Additional revenue was generated when sultans sold land in Palestine to early Zionists, a financial measure that had enormous repercussions on the future of the entire region. As the debt grew, so did European control of the Ottoman economy. Finally, in 1875, the once-powerful Ottoman state was declared bankrupt and turned over to international receivership. The Middle East had become an economic colony of Western Europe.

Commercial Penetration

The initial effects of European commercial activity in the Middle East were felt in the Mediterranean port cities—Istanbul, Izmir, Beirut, Alexandria—and spread progressively inland along existing trade routes. The introduction of machine-made European textiles had a devastating effect on traditional handicraft industries that had been fundamental to Middle Eastern commerce. Thousands of cotton spinners were driven out of business as cotton cloth, which had been an important Turkish export product in earlier periods, was imported in volume from the expanding mills of Europe. Indigenous textile products such as damask, muslin, and gauze disappeared from marketplaces. Local efforts to modernize production were foiled by high European import duties on textiles and by local Turkish tariffs, which were 5 percent on foreign imports and 12 percent on Turkish exports. Large numbers of spinners and weavers were subsequently driven out of urban occupations and forced into the countryside in search of work, a factor that undoubtedly retarded the emergence of an industrial class in the Middle East. As late as World War I, Turkey had less than 20,000 people engaged in manufacturing, and over half of these were employed in textile production and food processing.

As European economic penetration intensified, most of the important sectors of the Middle Eastern economy passed into the hands of foreigners or members of minority groups. Except in Egypt, all railroads and ports were foreign-owned and foreign-operated. In the large cities, public utilities such as water, electricity, and public transport were owned by foreign firms. And in North Africa—Morocco, Algeria, Libya, and Tunisia—every urban occupation including finance, commerce, real estate, and manufacturing came under European control. The local merchants used as intermediaries by the Europeans in these activities were usually non-Muslims: Greeks, Armenians, and other Christian minorities in Turkey and the Levant; Jews in Iraq and parts of North Africa. These groups appealed to the Europeans for special treatment as coreligionists, and by World War I the number of millets (separate communities) recognized by the Ottoman Empire had increased from three to seventeen.

Virtually every group found a sponsor in at least one European power. Frequently members of the minorities acquired passports and citizenship from European embassies in order to have the advantages of trading as a foreigner in the Middle East. Rather quickly, control of trade, which had been spurned by the Ottoman elite as an inferior occupation, fell into the hands of minority groups, with Muslims playing a distinctly minor role. In Egypt in 1914, foreigners and Jewish, Lebanese, Syrian Christian, and Armenian minorities made up only 3 percent of the population but owned 15 to 20 percent of the wealth. As the identification of these groups with Europeans increased, minorities became increasingly suspect by the Muslim majority—a significant break with the tolerance of the past.

In the countryside, the Western impact was no less dramatic. Progress was equated with increases in the production of raw materials. In Anatolia, mineral resources such as coal, lead, emery, borax, and chrome were mined for export. But in the Arab countries of the Middle East, the only available exploitable resource was agricultural land. Expansion of cultivation in Syria, Anatolia, and parts of Iraq was accomplished by restoring law and order, thereby enabling peasants to return to areas earlier abandoned. In southern Iraq and in Egypt, irrigation projects were constructed to enlarge the arable area. In North Africa, substantial portions of the cultivated land in the wetter Mediterranean zone were settled

For centuries, the court of the Ottoman emperor at Constantinople (the modern Istanbul) was the center of government for a vast area. Though by the nineteenth century Ottoman power was nearly gone, the empire itself was not formally dissolved until after World War I. Here the sultan moves in procession through the streets of the city. *Photo:* The Bettman Archive.

by European colonists, as France and later Italy extended their "zones of security." Two-fifths of the agricultural land in Algeria, one-fifth in Tunisia, one-fifteenth in French Morocco, and one-eighteenth in Libya were purchased, expropriated, or secured by deception from native farmers and tribesmen, inciting a pattern of out-migration to less fertile agricultural areas or to coastal cities.

The major agricultural change Europeans effected in the Middle East was the replacement of subsistence crops by commercial crops grown for export. Cotton became the principal crop of Egypt and parts of Anatolia; tobacco was introduced into Syria and Turkey. The export of dates from Iraq and coffee from Yemen became the basis of their economies. Generally the impact was greatest in the most accessible regions—coastal districts and areas penetrated by the spreading net of railroads. Even in these areas, however, little progress was made in the methods or technology of cultivation; improvements in the productivity or prosperity of the Middle Eastern peasantry were few. Development was accompanied by

economic and social backwardness. Change was horizontal, affecting and then reinforcing patterns of activity that were of benefit to foreign-dominated trade. Only later with the rise of nationalism was this structural change accompanied by social and intellectual change.

The Development of Egypt

Nowhere was this asymmetrical pattern of growth more pronounced than in Egypt. After the death of the brilliant and energetic ruler Muhammad Ali in 1849, the country came under the control of a series of unworthy successors. Egypt fell into debt, was declared bankrupt in 1880, and for all intents and purposes became a British colony. After 1860, Egyptian resources were developed rapidly in line with foreign interests; agricultural acreage was expanded and cotton was introduced as an export crop. Soil, climate, and water supply were ideal for the cultivation of cotton, and when the Civil War in the United States eliminated the American South as a major exporting area, cotton cultivation expanded to meet world demand. By 1865, Egyptian cotton production had quadrupled, and at the turn of the century cotton and cottonseed accounted for 90 percent of Egypt's exports.

But the industrialization of cotton in Egypt did not occur. The thirty-odd mills established by Muhammad Ali, with a production capacity of 1 million

ECONOMIC IMPERIALISM:
THE BRITISH IN THE
MIDDLE EAST

3. IMPERIALISM, NATIONALISM

THE MIDDLE EAST
187

David Urquhart, a nineteenth-century British observer, vividly described the economic ambitions and moral righteousness that motivated British imperialism in the Middle East. He conceived of the conversion of the region into a productive farm providing raw materials and a willing market for the products of the more industrious British. The decline in handicrafts, the relocation of "sixty millions of men" from textile production into agriculture, and the reorganization of the local economy were viewed as benefiting the people. Local preferences were of no account.

It is established, that our cottons and muslins, calicoes, chintzes, etc., are, if not better, infinitely cheaper than those of the East. Taste is gradually directing itself to our manufactures, and money less expended than formerly on furs, jewels, Persian and Damascus blades, amber mouthpieces and shawls. We may calculate . . . on supplying the necessaries as well as the luxuries of the whole of the eastern population, whose attention will thus be exclusively directed to agriculture, and the furnishing of raw produce; when we can take from them their produce in return for our wares, or find them the means of exchanging it. These changed circumstances are beginning to produce their effects. . . .

The manufacture of cotton is the principal in-door occupation of the greater portion of the East—of above sixty millions of men, with whom our future commerce will probably be carried on through . . . the Levant. . . . Throughout these vast and varied regions, these [men] have lain dormant . . . because hitherto the first object of necessity was not furnished to them cheap enough to induce them to forgo its manufacture, and turn their attention to cultivation. How important, then, is it to establish the fact, that our cottons are at a sufficiently low price to induce them to forego [it]!

Sources: Charles Issawi (ed.), The Economic History of the Middle East, 1800–1914. Chicago: University of Chicago Press, 1966, pp. 42–43. Quoted material from David Urquhart, Turkey. London, 1833, pp. 141–144.

yards of cloth, were liquidated. And the British made certain the textile industry did not revive. As Lord Cromer, the British consul general of Egypt, noted, "It would be detrimental to both English and Egyptian interests to afford any encouragement to the growth of a protected cotton industry in Egypt." When a small textile industry did attempt to develop, tariffs equivalent to foreign imports quickly drove it out of business. Thus, as late as World War I, the total number of Egyptians engaged in manufacturing enterprises amounted to only 30,000 or 35,000.

On the basis of a number of economic indexes, Egypt appeared to be a relatively well-developed society. With a population of 12 million in 1913, Egypt had a per capita income higher than that of Japan and more than twice that of India. In terms of foreign trade, only a small number of industrialized countries surpassed Egypt in value of foreign trade because such a large proportion of domestic agricultural production entered world markets. And with more than 2500 miles of railway associated with the navigable Nile, Egypt was as well provided with transport facilities as most countries in the world. In contrast, the level of social development was quite low. The illiteracy rate of 93 percent was higher than that in many less commercialized societies. During thirty-five years of British rule, school populations remained low, and less than 1 percent of the government budget was spent on education. Fewer than 300 Egyptians were sent abroad for training, and only one of every four studied engineering, medicine, agriculture, or any other field directly related to social and economic development.

The effects of this lopsided pattern of growth became apparent in the twentieth century. Order and good administration had increased agricultural production, but reliance on a single commercial crop led to severe economic fluctuations dependent upon world cotton prices. Internal transport networks, geared as they were to international marketing, had no multiplier effects in terms of Egypt's development. Most businesses and public services were, after all, in the hands of foreigners or minority groups. A native Egyptian middle class was virtually nonexistent. Finally, the growth of population spurred by advances in productivity and health exceeded agricultural expansion, and landless peasants piled up in the emerging cities of Egypt.

The colonial patterns of change—commercialization of the economy, low levels of social development, foreign control of important sectors of the economy, and orientation toward the production of raw materials for export—affected most areas in the Middle East. In the Persian Gulf, the primary interest was petroleum; in the Levant, agricultural production. In North Africa, nearly 2 million European settlers reorganized the agricultural economy of the Maghrib by introducing citrus orchards, vineyards, and commercial grain cultivation. Only the more remote parts of the region—the interior of Arabia, the Sahara, Afghanistan, and parts of Iran—were not substantially altered. In the more densely populated areas, however, European investment and initiative remained a compelling social and economic force until the rise of nationalism brought political independence and Middle Easterners reasserted control over their own destiny.

NATIONALISM AND INDEPENDENCE: THE TRANSFORMATION OF MIDDLE EASTERN SOCIETY

On the eve of World War I, Ottoman Turkey, the Sick Man of Europe, still retained territorial control over its Arab provinces in the Levant, Mesopotamia, and western Arabia. Great Power rivalries had preserved a delicate balance of distrust that enabled successive sultans to maintain physical and economic rule. But in 1914 the sultan, spurred by nationalists, rashly declared a "holy war" on the Allies and joined forces with Christian Germany. The European allied powers agreed by secret treaty to partition the Ottoman Empire. The Russians were to assume control of the Bosporus and the Dardanelles, the straits between the Black and Mediterranean seas, and Greece was to regain parts of western Anatolia. The Italians were to protect their substantial investment in the Adana region and the Zonguldak coal basin in northwestern Turkey, the British would remain in Palestine and Mesopotamia, and the French would receive Syria. In a ricochet from the shot at Sarajevo, the Turkish state faced political extinction.

Turkey and Iran. These plans were abandoned as Turkish nationalists, under the leadership of the army officer Mustafa Kemal (later called Ataturk), drove occupying French, British, and Greek armies from Anatolia and focused the national spirit of the Turkish people upon the establishment of an independent republic in the *heartland** of the Ottoman domain. The caliphate was abolished and religious courts were replaced by a Western code of civil law. The special privileges of the minorities were withdrawn, and a secular state was created. Efforts were made to develop the economic resources of Anatolia and to begin industrialization without foreign assistance and interference. Turkey, the first independent

In the Middle East, modern nation-states are a recent phenomenon. Kemal Ataturk (left) was the architect of Turkey, heart of the old Ottoman Empire. The ancient kingdom of Persia became Iran under Reza Shah (right), father of the present ruler. The two are shown during a meeting in 1934. *Photo:* Wide World.

Middle Eastern state, sought parity in the world through intensive Westernization.

Similarly, Iran was on the verge of becoming a dependency of the British Empire after Britain and Russia had competed for internal railroad, bank, tobacco, and loan concessions under the ineffectual Qajar rulers. But in 1921, Reza Khan, an officer in the Iranian cossacks, led a coup d'état in Tehran and took over the reins of the Iranian state. Like Ataturk, Reza Khan was an ardent nationalist. After subduing rebellious tribal groups in the Zagros, he embarked on an extensive program of modernization. Religious officials were stripped of authority and religious property was confiscated. Legal codes based on the French model were introduced and concession agreements with foreigners were abrogated. Over the next twenty years, the road system was extended from 2000 to 17,000 miles and the Trans-Iranian railroad, 865 miles long with 224 tunnels, was built to connect the gulf in the south with the fertile provinces in the north. Light industry was introduced, and some progress was made in agriculture, although the power of absentee landlords inhibited any fundamental land reform. As in Turkey, the pattern of developmental change was Western, although Iran maintained the traditional monarchical form of government with the designation of Reza Khan as shah in 1925.

The Arab lands. In the Arab Middle East and North Africa, no single charismatic leader emerged to unite national aspirations. Divided for centuries into separately administered provinces of the Ottoman Empire, islands of dense populations were separated from each other by deserts and mountains, by distances and cultural distinctions. Independence was achieved in different ways against each specific colonial regime. In Cairo, Damascus, Baghdad, Beirut, and the port cities of North Africa, secret national patriotic societies established by Western-educated intellectuals focused their energies in opposition to European colonialism in their countries. In the countryside, Arab governors, tribal leaders, and semiautonomous rulers fought to establish independent positions. But rivalries, geographical isolation, and the disruptive tactics of colonial authorities frustrated any concerted action among Arab leaders. Vague British promises of Arab independence in exchange for their support against the Turks in World War I were quickly converted into partition of the Arab domain under Western rule. Only in the Arabian Peninsula was independence attained: In the desert interior, the conservative Wahabis led by ibn-Saud conquered the Hijaz and unified most of the peninsula in 1933. Yemen remained independent as a result of its inaccessibility.

In Egypt, a traditional monarchy was established and granted nominal independence in 1924. But British influence remained strong in the Nile Valley throughout the interwar period, thwarting the aims of the nationalist Wafd party. British commercial and military interests remained paramount until the corrupt regime of King Farouk was finally dislodged by an army revolt in 1952 led by Gamal Abdel Nasser. In Iraq, a similar pattern developed. The British mandate was relinquished in 1932, but it was not until twenty-six years later that the pro-Western Hashimite dynasty was overthrown, again by a military revolt, and a program of developmental change begun. In the British mandate of Palestine, Jewish immigration and colonization led to a complicated international conflict between Jews and Arabs. A Hashimite monarchy was established in part of Palestine west of the Jordan River, which became the new state of Transjordan (modern Jordan). The British withdrew from the rest of Palestine in 1948, turning over to the United Nations the bitter territorial conflict between Israel and her Arab neighbors.

In Syria, the French were more determined than the British to retain their mandate. Severe fighting between Syrians and the French, including an unexecuted French plan to eliminate Syrian nationalism by demolishing Damascus, preceded final French withdrawal after World War II and the creation of two new republics—Syria and Lebanon. In North Africa, the struggle for independence was complicated by the presence of 2 million French nationals who were determined to remain in control in situ. Libya gained independence in 1952; Morocco

and Tunisia in 1956. The most severe conflict occurred in Algeria, where eight years of bloody guerrilla warfare were required to dislodge the French. With the removal of France and Britain (and earlier, Italy) from the Middle East, only a few isolated colonial territories remain. In Morocco, the Mediterranean ports of Melilla and Ceuta, long in Spanish hands, seem likely to remain so. South of Morocco, the Spanish Sahara faced division between Morocco and Mauritania.

Common problems. If the achievement of political independence was the predominant goal of the national leaders of the Middle East and North Africa during the first half of the twentieth century, the central issues facing Middle Easterners today are the development of national resources, the achievement of economic stability, and the quest for higher standards of living. These are increasingly viewed as necessities if Middle Easterners are to determine their own futures.

These goals, shared by virtually every government in the region, are being pursued within new social and spatial frameworks. The traditional social mosaic of religious, ethnic, and linguistic groups has broken down. Jewish communities have fled from the Muslim societies of the Middle East and North Africa to Israel; the Greeks and Armenians were driven by the Turks from Anatolia. Christian minorities in Egypt and the Levant are now highly Westernized. Tribal groups, except for the Kurds in Iraq and some Bedouin groups in Jordan and Arabia, have lost the independence of their environmental refuges. Traditional community allegiances are now submerged in state societies where loyalty to nation fires the imagination of individuals. Spatially, these states form a bewildering patchwork of political units on the Middle Eastern landscape. Of the twenty-two countries in the region, Turkey (35.6 million), Egypt (30 million), and Iran (29.7 million) are large, populous nations with organized resource bases. Only two other countries, however—Morocco (16 million) and Algeria (14.6 million)—have populations of more than 10 million. Seven of the new countries of the region—South Yemen, Cyprus, Oman, Kuwait, Bahrain, the United Arab Emirates, and Qatar—are microstates with a total population of less than 2 million.

Despite this tremendous diversity in scale, geographical resources, and populations, the countries of the Middle East and North Africa, whether led by

ARAB UNITY: NASSER'S PHILOSOPHY OF REVOLUTION

Arab unity is a powerful philosophical and emotional force in the Middle East, although economic and political realities have aborted attempts at unification such as the union of Syria and Egypt into the United Arab Republic and similarly proposed unions between Egypt and Libya and between Tunisia and Libya. Most Arab nationalists assert that artificial, arbitrary divisions of the Arab world were produced by British and French colonialism, although in fact the boundaries of the colonies accord well with the administrative divisions of the Ottoman state and the early Islamic empires. Nationalism and modernization have taken place within these separate nation-states, but the goal of a unified nation of all Arabs remains an ideal most articulately expressed by Gamal Abdel Nasser.

The age of isolation is gone.

And gone are the days in which barbed wire served as demarcation lines, separating and isolating countries from one another. No country can escape looking beyond its boundaries to find the source of the currents which influence it, how it can live with others. . . .

And no state can escape trying to determine its status within its living space and trying to see what it can do in that space, and what is its field of activities and its positive role in this troubled world. . . .

Can we fail to see that there is an Arab circle surrounding us—that this circle is a part of us, and we are a part of it, our history being inextricably part of its history? . . .

Can we possibly ignore the fact that there is an African continent which Fate decreed us to be a part of, and that it is also decreed that a terrible struggle exists for its future—a struggle whose results will be either for us or against us, with or without our will? . . .

There can be no doubt that the Arab circle is the most important, and the one with which we are most closely linked. For its peoples are intertwined with us by history. We have suffered together, we have gone through the same crises, and when we fell beneath the hooves of the invaders' steeds, they were with us under the same hooves.

Sources: George Lenczowski (ed.), The Political Awakening in the Middle East. Englewood Cliffs, N.J.: Prentice-Hall, 1970, pp. 121–123. Quoted material from Gamal Abdel Nasser, Egypt's Liberation. Washington, D.C.: Public Affairs Press, 1955, pp. 83–90, 109–110, 111–112.

democratic or socialist regimes, military elites, or traditional monarchs, face common problems in their pursuit of economic development and social modernization. Population growth, colonial economies, and technological change have transformed the Middle East.

POPULATION GROWTH AND URBANIZATION

The integration of the Middle East into large-scale modern economies led to the growth and redistribution of urban centers in the region. Historically, Middle Eastern cities were international trading centers, connecting points on continental trade routes crisscrossing the Old World. These cities were important **break-in-bulk points**• and staging areas for the international trade flowing between Europe and the Orient, and to a lesser extent between sub-Saharan Africa and the coasts of the Mediterranean. The largest cities were located in the interior. Many—Damascus, Aleppo, Yazd, and Kirman—were **entrepôts**• on the desert margins; others, such as Cairo and Baghdad, primarily fulfilled religious and administrative functions. Smaller cities were strung out like beads along the caravan routes between major centers and prospered or perished depending on local conditions of security, trade, food supplies, and water.

In the nineteenth century, as Western merchants and capital began to penetrate the region and integrate it into wider, Western-oriented trade networks, the distribution of urban centers altered, and seaports such as Istanbul, Beirut, Tripoli, Alexandria, Tangier, and Casablanca swelled in population and commercial importance. The great cities of the interior began to lose their demographic superiority. Industry changed the course of economic realities and Middle Eastern social geography.

Urban Growth
[FIGURE 2]

Urban growth in the Middle East has been so dramatic in this century that eight cities now have populations of more than 1 million and eighty are larger than 100,000. In North Africa, Casablanca (1.5 million) and Algiers (1.2 million) have grown from coastal backwaters to modern world metropolises. Cairo (5.3 million) is the largest city in Africa; its urban area has expanded from 5 to 75 square miles, making the old city a small district in the new. With Alexandria (2.1 million), these two cities house one-fifth of the Egyptian population. Tehran, the capital of Iran, has grown from 100,000 in 1940 to more than 3 million today; Baghdad has somewhat less than 2 million. In Turkey, the port city of Istanbul retains cultural supremacy with a population of 2.2 million, but the interior capital of Ankara has a population of more than 1 million.

In most Middle Eastern countries, a third or more

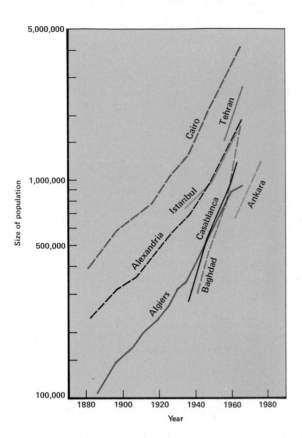

Figure 2. Growth of the Million Cities. Urban growth in the Middle East and North Africa has now generated eight cities with populations of more than a million, and eighty cities with populations larger than 100,000. *Adapted from:* J. I. Clarke and W. B. Fisher, *Populations of the Middle East and North Africa.* London: Hodder and Stoughton, 1972, p. 30, Fig. 1.2.

of the population lives in urban centers, a much higher percentage than in other regions of the developing world. As the **_primate cities_**[*] continue to grow at a rate of 6 to 10 percent a year, economic and political decisions are increasingly concentrated and played out on a national scale. Although growth rates vary in tempo and magnitude from city to city, two factors underlie this urban implosion; the doubling of population regionwide caused primarily by the declining death rate, and the immigration of peasants and tribesmen from the countryside to the expanding cities. Roughly two-thirds of the current urban population growth is a result of natural increase among urban residents. Better medical and health facilities have made the mortality rate lowest in the cities; rising aspirations and still limited educational levels have combined to maintain relatively high birth rates of 35 to 50 per thousand. The status of women in the Middle East, although improving slowly, is still hampered by early marriage patterns and the virtues attached to abundant procreation. Only in countries where the non-Muslim population is high—Israel, Cyprus, and Lebanon—is the birth rate relatively low. As a

result, overall population growth in the region is close to 3 percent per year, adding 1 million new citizens each year to countries like Turkey, Iran, and Egypt. The remaining third of the population growth in Middle East cities is generated by expanding rural populations who flow out of the countryside away from the villages and nomadic camps of another era into the new urban social and economic centers.

Structural Change

New cities are different physically and socially. Broad avenues suitable for motor transport cut wide swaths between the old quarters and more modern parts of the cities. Commercial activity has left the bazaar, and modern buildings have sprung up on the new streets. Skyscrapers house government offices, banks, hotels, and department stores; slum **_shantytowns_**[*] filled with poor new arrivals frequently occupy the interstices of incoherent urban centers. Urban sprawl has accompanied the enormous growth of population. Motorized suburbs have spread populations far beyond the confines of ancient city walls, and the cemeteries and shrines that once served as collars on urban expansion have been leveled. The exodus of the urban elite to suburbs where houses are less crowded and street patterns less tortuous has increasingly relegated the old sections of the cities to the lower classes.

These cities reflect the social premises the leaders of Middle Eastern societies have advocated for their peoples. Traditional emphasis on family ties, religious affiliation, and occupational groupings is weakening. Ethnic division of labor, the hallmark of the old social mosaic, will not be significant in the near future. Perhaps the most striking evidence of the impact of social change on urban structure has been the abandonment of religious segregation as a principle of town planning. In the small town of Kirman in southern Iran, for example, the Zoroastrian quarter dissolved in the growing modern atmosphere of religious tolerance. In the larger cities of the Middle East, a residential mix of different races and religions, previously unthinkable, is now quite common. A detailed social area analysis describes the movement of Cairo toward the general configuration of a modern, Western metropolitan society based on economic class. A new urban milieu is rapidly evolving in the Middle East.

The most important new social component in the

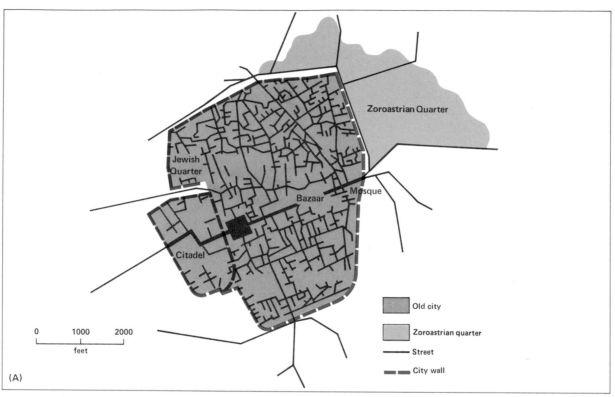

(A)

Zoroastrian Quarter

Jewish
Quarter

Bazaar   Mosque

Citadel

	Old city
	Zoroastrian quarter
——	Street
– – –	City wall

0   1000   2000

feet

(B)

Zoroastrian Quarter

Jewish
Quarter

Mosque

Bazaar

Citadel

	Old city
	New city
——	Street
– – –	Ruined city wall

0   1000   2000

feet

Adapted from: Paul Ward English, "Nationalism, Secularism, and the Zoroastrians of Kirman: The Impact of Modern Forces on an Ancient Middle Eastern Minority," in Fred E. Dohrs and Lawrence M. Sommers, eds., *Cultural Geography: Selected Readings.* New York: Crowell, 1967, Figs. 2, 3, 4.

THE ZOROASTRIANS OF KIRMAN

In the nineteenth century, Iranian urban life was medieval in character and feudal in organization. Religion was the organizing principle of the state, and life was difficult for minority groups such as Christians, Jews, and Zoroastrians. In Kirman, a small walled city of 40,000 people in southern Iran, the Zoroastrian community lived apart from, but embedded in, a Muslim society. As part (a) of the figure shows, the Zoroastrians were forced to reside in their own quarter outside the city walls, a precarious location. As nonbelievers, they had no legal rights in Muslim courts, and their community was constantly drained by conversion to Islam. Buildings were restricted to one story, because Muslims allowed no rivals to the beauty and majesty of their mosques. Zoroastrians were forced to wear mustard-colored robes, could not wear eyeglasses or stockings, and could not ride any animal that would raise them above the eye level of a Muslim. Despite these restrictions, the Zoroastrian community continued to practice a faith as old as the Achaemenid kings and to regulate its own internal affairs.

In the twentieth century, under the leadership of Reza Shah, new viewpoints were injected into Iran's feudal society. A constitution was established, and a secular state declared. The religious elite was stripped of its power over law and education as Iran strove to enter the modern world. In Kirman, as part (b) of the figure shows, the effects of these changes were rapidly felt. With increased security, the walls of the old city were destroyed and residential settlement spread into suburbs as population increased by a third to 60,000. For the Zoroastrians, the decline of clerical power meant release from the old restrictions. And the new nationalism that stressed the glories of Iran before the Arab conquest left them a favored group—the only people who had preserved the religion of ancient Iran. In this new atmosphere of tolerance, Zoroastrians migrated from rural villages to Kirman, and from Kirman to the capital city of Tehran to seek their fortunes. The coherence of Kirman's Zoroastrian community—preserved in a ghetto bordered by intolerance—began to give way to the subtle forces of assimilation into broader Iranian society. By the 1960s the Zoroastrian quarter, as the (c) diagram shows, was integrated (nearly a third of its houses occupied by Muslims), and the principle of religious segregation no longer held in this provincial city.

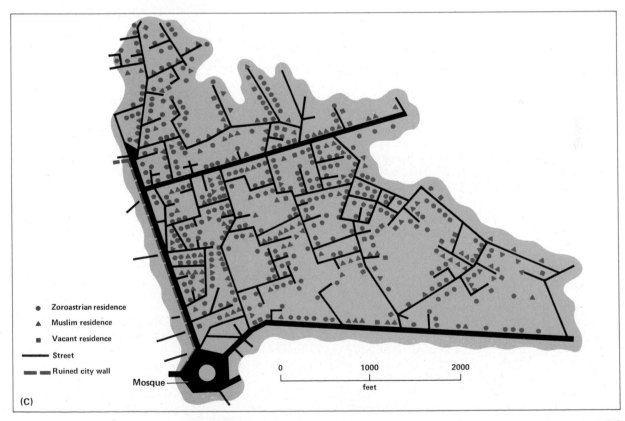

- ● Zoroastrian residence
- ▲ Muslim residence
- ■ Vacant residence
- ▬ Street
- ▭ Ruined city wall

Mosque

0   1000   2000

feet

(C)

How different in style and structure the new cities of the Middle East are from the traditional pattern is strikingly clear in Riyadh, the mushrooming capital of Saudi Arabia. The model here is twentieth-century modern, and is another sign of the social change sweeping the Muslim world. *Photo:* J. Allan Cash/Rapho-Photo Researchers.

urban Middle East is the emerging middle class. City dwellers, still numerically small, account for 10 percent of the populations of Turkey, Iran, Egypt, Lebanon, and the Maghrib; in Saudi Arabia, Yemen, Afghanistan, and other traditional societies the middle class is far less important. Yet the aspirations of this handful of men and women have had a dramatic impact on life and landscape in the Middle East and North Africa. Armed with the knowledge and skills of modern education, the middle class has broken the traditional confines of **guilds,** **extended families,** and religious associations to play important roles in the development and transmission of ideas, in the formulations of plans to modernize society, and in implementing programs of reform. This group staffs the petroleum industry and other state and private corporations engaged in discovering and utilizing the natural resources of their countries. They work in government bureaus and agencies devoted to land reform, land distribution, and campaigns against illiteracy and medical and sanitary ignorance—all considered inappropriate activities under traditional Islamic rulers.

CHANGE IN THE COUNTRYSIDE

In the rural Middle East, population growth and the transition from subsistence to commercial farming intensified pressures on agricultural resources already severely limited by the natural difficulties of arid climate and rugged terrain. In addition, a substantial portion of the cultivated land was traditionally held by absentee landlords, tax farmers, and tribal sheiks who took cunning advantage of

Western law codes emphasizing private property during the colonial period. And vast tracts of pasturage were under the autonomous control of tribal nomads. The early twentieth century found the mass of tribesmen and peasants poverty-stricken and chronically in debt to an unconcerned elite resistant to change. Given these conditions, national programs of economic and social development in the countries of the Middle East and North Africa have taken similar directions, despite important cultural and ecological variations. Among their common objectives were the settling of the nomads, the institution of **land reform** and land distribution, and the expansion of the cultivated area.

The Settling of the Nomads

The introduction of modern transport and military technology gave national leaders in most Middle Eastern countries the capacity to control their own territories. Nomadic tribes, which had for centuries contested government rule in marginal environments, were quickly brought to heel. National boundaries cut across the historical grazing areas of their forefathers and were patrolled by well-equipped government troops. Tribal raids to redress the balance were met with machine guns, tanks, and airplanes.

In North Africa, this process was accomplished during the French and Italian "pacification" periods. Army posts were constructed throughout the Sahara; tribal pastures were occupied, a fact bitterly resented by the nomads. The tribes fought with a determined resistance and lost; chronicled warfare in the Sahara ended. In the new security imposed by Western forces, peasant cultivation was extended onto the Maghrib steppe formerly grazed by tribesmen. In the oases of Algeria, Tunisia, and Morocco, the Haratin slave caste was freed from tribal control. Peasant and nomad paid taxes—a great disgrace—to the central governments. The nomads suffered a double loss in revenue as their protection services for camel caravans lost out to trans-Sahara motorized traffic. Constricted in space, reduced in prestige, economically pressed, and led by government-appointed chieftains, the Teda, Tuareg, and Moorish tribes of the Sahara began to settle down in villages on the steppes, at wells in the deserts, and in the rapidly growing cities on the Mediterranean coast.

In the mountains and plateaus of Iran and Turkey, the transhumant tribes of the Zagros and Caucasus were also stripped of their economic and political independence. Reza Shah led army campaigns against tribesmen in northwestern and northeastern Iran, but the powerful Lur, Qashqai, and Bakhtiari confederacies continued to deal as independent states with foreign countries until after World War II. Then, a series of brutal raids by well-equipped government forces disarmed and disbanded the tribes by breaking their patterns of migration, destroying their flocks, and settling them on marginal land in northeastern Iran. In Anatolia, the process of tribal pacification was less violent and less complete, and many groups in eastern Turkey have retained their traditional pastures while accepting the supremacy of the central government. In Israel, Syria, Jordan, and parts of Egypt, nomadic groups have been trapped in the ongoing warfare between Arabs and Israelis. Only in Iraq, where the Kurds successfully defied the central government in Baghdad well into the 1970s, has tribal autonomy been maintained, but the recent withdrawal of Iranian support may soon end Kurdish resistance.

In Saudi Arabia, where Bedouin nomads make up as much as half the population, a similar process of sedentarization is being pursued, but for quite different reasons. Here, the government, which itself has nomadic origins, drilled wells in the desert to create a series of watering points for the nomads. The goals of this expensive program were administrative on the part of the reigning Saudi dynasty, whose own immediate history is one of consolidating tribal alliances on a national level, and religious on the part of the powerful sect of conservative Islamic reformers, the Wahabis. Their aim was not simply to settle the Bedouins for purposes of security and control, but to enable the nomads to lead truly religious lives in fixed locations where mosques could be built. These new oasis settlements, called al-Hijra after the flight of Muhammad to Medina, now number more than 200 in the Najd region of central Arabia. Plans exist for settling an additional 10,000 nomads in the vicinity of Riyadh, a project requiring the planting of some 600,000 tamarisk trees to fix the soil and prevent encroachment by sand dunes.

The effect of these varied government policies on the traditional economic and social life of nomads has been disastrous. Nomadism and tribalism are in serious decline, leaving a void in resource utilization in those regions unsuitable for cultivation but productive under a grazing economy. Despite the cost in unproduced meat, milk, and wool products, the governments of the Middle East have been determined to destroy the independence and mobility of the tribes, preferring peace and order to protein. As a result, less than 7 percent of the people of the Middle East and North Africa continue to live a predominantly nomadic way of life: 2 million to 3 million in the Sahara, an estimated 1 million to 2 million in Arabia and Turkey, less than 1 million in Iran, and 300,000 to 400,000 in Syria and in Iraq.

Land Reform

The widespread poverty and low standards of living of most peasants in the villages of the Middle East and North Africa derive from three sources. First, in many countries, absentee landowners held a monopoly over both the cultivated land and the capital to develop it. Huge individually owned estates were

parceled out to families of sharecroppers who tilled the land in traditional fashion, paid high rents, and had little security of tenure. Second, during the course of colonial rule, few new agricultural techniques were introduced on the peasant level. Except in Egypt, parts of Lebanon, the Zionist settlements in Palestine, and European farms in North Africa, per capita productivity and income remained extremely low. Finally, because of low rainfall and rugged terrain, the agricultural base of the Middle East and North Africa was and is extremely limited. Only five countries—Turkey, Syria, Israel, Lebanon, and Cyprus—cultivate more than a fifth of their total land surface; an equal number of countries cultivate less than 1 percent. The cumulative effect of these factors meant that hopes for progress in the villages of the Middle East focused on three areas: elimination of the landlords, introduction of modern agricultural techniques, and expansion of the arable.

Land redistribution was effected in one country after another by a series of social and political revolutions. When Nasser came to power in Egypt in 1952, 72 percent of all farmers owned less than 0.5 acre of land, although 2 acres was considered minimum subsistence level; an additional 1.5 million peasant families were totally landless. The bulk of Egypt's highly productive commercial agriculture was in the hands of less than 300 urban landlords, who together owned a tenth of the country's rural resources. The revolution eliminated the landlords, confiscated the royal properties of King Farouk, and limited individual holdings to 200 acres and subsequently to 50. In the next fifteen years, a fifth of Egypt's agricultural land was redistributed to tenant cultivators.

In Syria, a land distribution law was passed in 1958 as the government attempted to break up large holdings and provide land for peasants. In Iraq, the overthrow of the monarchy in 1958 led to the expropriation of large estates, limits on the size of private holdings, and redistribution of the land to tenant farmers, although implementation, particularly in the tribal south, has been slow. In Algeria, an estimated 2.5 million acres vacated by French colonists in 1962 was expropriated by the government; more recently, large Algerian-owned farms have been converted into collectives. In Iran, where an estimated 70 percent of the fertile land was owned by a small number of large landlords, the shah's White Revolution (signifying bloodless change) has limited land ownership to one village per landlord. Despite these reforms, great disparity still exists between the wealth of landlords and the poverty of peasants in the Middle East and North Africa.

The introduction of modern agricultural techniques into the region has gradually accelerated in the last decade. A web of new roads, communications media, and government hierarchies is spreading out from the cities, introducing new crops and field methods, marketing cooperatives, agricultural credit, and educational programs to the rural hinterlands. In one remarkable Syrian case, urban merchants invested in mechanized agriculture in the rain-fed north; grain production increased by 60 percent, and cotton yields increased by a factor of eight. Similarly, in Egypt agricultural techniques are now sophisticated enough to produce wheat, corn, and cotton at higher yields per acre than in the United States and Europe. In Israel, great pride is taken in the transformation of desert wastes into gardens, fields, orchards, and new forests—in "making the desert bloom."

But overall, the productivity of Middle Eastern peasants is estimated to be only one-eighth to one-quarter that of their European counterparts. This stems from a variety of environmental and social factors. Many soils in the region have low organic content because of dry climate, high soil temperatures, and the historical deforestation of much of the region. Irrigated fields, the most productive agricultural systems of the Middle East, are subject to salinization. In addition, illiteracy is common, diet often marginal, poor health endemic, and debt chronic in many areas. Although the programs for universal primary education, national health services, and agricultural reform that now exist in all but the most remote countries of the region may ultimately transform both the peasantry and land use patterns in the Middle East, today's growing populations and attendant food shortages must be met by an increase in productivity.

Expansion of the arable is not an unlimited option in dry lands. In Turkey, the cultivated area has tripled from 27 million to 65 million acres in twenty-five years. Significantly, wheat harvest totals in the same period only doubled, reflecting the extension of agriculture into increasingly marginal environments. In Morocco, Algeria, Syria, and Iran similar extensions of cultivation have been effected by the construction of dams, the drilling of new wells, and the cultivation of semiarid steppes. Regionwide, however, agricultural production has failed to keep pace with population growth, and the Middle East is now a net importer of food. After a quarter-century of development and planning, average rural income in the Middle East and North Africa remains well below $250 per year except in Kuwait, Lebanon, Israel, and Cyprus.

Expansion of the Arable

Nowhere have the frustrations of the failure to raise standards of living been more acute than in the large riverine systems of Egypt and Iraq, both of which transformed the environmental basis of their agriculture in an effort to increase production. In Iraq, the historical decimation of forests and the subsequent **erosion,**• silting of the rivers, and flooding over a long period of time badly damaged the environmental basis of irrigated agriculture. The primary effort, therefore, has been to control annual variations in the flow of the Tigris-Euphrates river system through the construction of a series of dams to reduce flooding (Baghdad was ravaged by flood in 1968) and to open up new areas for cultivation. Four major irrigation works were built: the Samarra Barrage on the Tigris, the Ramadi Barrage on the Euphrates, the Dukan Dam on the Little Zab River, and the Darbandikhan Dam on the Diyala River. These projects and those currently planned were expected to double the agricultural area of Iraq, provide adequate protection against floods, and supply electricity for industrial development.

But these massive irrigation projects, combined with the programs of land reform and land distribution fostered by the revolutionary leaders who came to power in 1958, failed to raise significantly the standard of living in rural Iraq, partly owing to population growth, but mainly owing to environmental problems on the alluvial plains of Mesopotamia. In this region, flat terrain and impermeable soils cause water to stand rather than run off. As these pools of water evaporate, salts are deposited on the land, accumulate, and eventually render the soil infertile. Iraqi farmers coped with these environmental limitations by cultivating the land only every other year. Small groups settled on the land, constructed canals, and irrigated soil. When salt levels began to rise and harvests fell, these groups moved on to new areas, leaving the land to lie fallow and eventually recover. This traditional pattern of agriculture was able to support the smaller population of Iraq in the past, but with nearly 10 million people today and an annual growth rate of 2.5 percent, the new agricultural projects are designed to develop a more productive form of intensive agriculture.

The earliest of these schemes, at Dujaila near Al Kut on the Tigris River, saw 1000 plots of land, 60 acres each, distributed to landless peasants who cultivated the soil under government supervision. In the early stages, the Dujaila project and others like it succeeded in increasing both agricultural production and the peasants' standard of living, but salt levels began to rise early in the second year of cultivation, and the land became progressively less fertile. Elsewhere, the new dams that expanded the agricultural area of Iraq also increased the total amount of water and salts brought to the land. This inten-

All over the Middle East and North Africa, modern irrigation techniques are being used to bring desert areas under cultivation and thus expand agriculture. Concrete conduits have been used to cut down on evaporation in this new system in Jordan, which is part of a Bedouin settlement program. *Photo:* United Nations/Rice.

sified the process of salinization, leading to progressive abandonment of large areas at an estimated rate of 1 percent each year. Thus Iraq, self-sufficient in foodstuffs prior to revolution and land reform in 1958, now must import grains and vegetables.

In Egypt, as in Iraq, the Aswan High Dam converted Egypt's agriculture from the traditional one-crop system of floodplain irrigation into two- and three-crop perennial irrigation. The agricultural area was increased by one-third, and crop production rose even more. But these gains were completely absorbed by Egypt's galloping population growth. In addition, it now appears that serious environmental problems associated with the transformation of the Nile have emerged. The rate of evaporation over Lake Nasser behind the dam was seriously underestimated, and the dam holds less water than the two smallers dams and natural flow it replaced. Engineers are studying the feasibility of spreading acetyl alcohol over the surface of Lake Nasser to reduce evaporation, or alternatively of cutting a canal through the Sudd swamps above the lake to increase flow. Water is also seeping in beneath the dam, undermining its structure; some specialists estimate that the life span of the system may be as short as twenty years. The trapping of sediment behind the dam has also had serious effects farther downstream: the coastline of the delta is eroding for lack of natural siltation, fishing in the Mediterranean has been seriously damaged as the nutrient content of Nile River water pouring into it has decreased, and increased use of pesticides is polluting a wide part of the eastern Mediterranean.

For the Egyptian farmer, the Aswan High Dam has been a mixed blessing. Although new land was made available to a growing population, the high cost of commercial fertilizers to replace the fertile silt that previously was deposited by the Nile has reduced the average farm income from $75 to $60 per year. Lower cost delta soil has been trucked to inland areas at a cost of $240 per acre, but supplies are now running out. Levels of salinity are rising in the water table, and the installation of tile drains to flush the soil would cost nearly as much as the construction of the dam itself. In addition, with water now standing year round in the lake and in irrigation canals, the incidence of waterborne disease is more common than ever. Malaria and schistosomiasis (parasitic diseases transmitted, respectively, by mosquitoes and snails that breed in quiet water) have reached epidemic proportions. Faced with a doubling of population to 60 million in thirty years or less, Egypt's leaders have little choice but to try to improve and understand this new ecosystem and to resolve the new ecological problems it has created.

THE ECONOMICS OF DEVELOPMENT
Despite the relatively modest progress most new nation-states of the Middle East have made in the improvement of life in their societies, recent changes

in the economics of oil have transformed parts of this region into some of the richest in the world. Unlike other developing countries that must limit industrialization and agricultural growth because of economic strangulation, the oil-producing nations of the Middle East have abundant cash reserves and foreign credits with which to finance vast programs of economic and social development. In the five largest producing countries—Iran, Saudi Arabia, Kuwait, Libya, and Iraq—over 60 percent of the total revenues of each government and 70 percent of their foreign exchange earnings accrue directly from oil. Similar figures apply to the lesser producers, and in a derived fashion to the transit countries of Jordan, Syria, and Lebanon through which oil is piped to Mediterranean ports. These revenues have risen rapidly since the oil-producing nations joined together in the Organization of Petroleum Exporting Countries (OPEC) in 1960 and renegotiated oil concessions and contracts with European and American oil companies. As a result, the rate of economic growth in the Middle East is now approximately 5 to 6 percent per year, double that of any other region in the developing world.

Nowhere have the potential effects of this rapid rate of economic growth been more apparent than in Kuwait and the other principalities on the east coast of the Arabian peninsula, where oil is financing the transformation of the area from one of the poorest and most backward in the Middle East to a major industrial zone. Before the discovery of oil, Kuwait was a small, flat desert sheikhdom whose population of 50,000 was occupied as nomadic herdsmen, date growers, pearl divers, fishermen, and sailors. The major local industry was the construction of sailing vessels (dhows) out of timber imported from East Africa. Kuwait now has a growing population of 700,000 people, possesses the highest per capita income in the world, and is the seventh ranking world producer of petroleum. Technically speaking, Kuwait is also one of the most highly urbanized nations, as virtually every Kuwaiti is the resident of an urban belt that stretches from Kuwait City to Ahmadi. Advanced social welfare schemes provide free education, housing subsidies, telephones, and health care. Proportionately, the nation has the same number of doctors and hospital beds as the United States. Oil and associated **petrochemical**• industries account for 90 percent of this rapidly developing country's income.

Although larger and more complex nations like Iraq and Iran will require much longer to achieve high levels of social development, and Libya and the smaller principalities on the Persian Gulf have barely begun to modernize, the inflow of billions of dollars into this region each year is bound to quicken the transformation of Middle Eastern society. A certain risk, however, is involved. The world's most advanced industrial nations are now intimately entwined economically and strategically with distant, small, and relatively underdeveloped Middle Eastern nations. The industry, employment, and social welfare of Western Europe, Japan, and to a lesser extent the United States, depend on the uncertainties of Middle Eastern politics and local control of the vital flow of crude oil and natural gas. Further complicating this new economic reality is one of the most explosive and difficult political struggles of this century, the continuing conflict between the Arabs and the Israelis.

THE MIDDLE EAST AND NORTH AFRICA

THE INDUSTRIAL BASE

ENERGY AND MINERAL RESOURCES MAP

Until recently, industrial growth in the Middle East and North Africa was quite limited, and manufacturing probably employed less than 15 percent of the population. Colonial rule had discouraged the emergence of a middle class and the development of local industry. Foreign capital was invested in the production and export of agricultural products, raw materials, and minerals. Egypt became a cotton farm for the British textile mills in Manchester; North Africa produced grain, citrus crops, and grapes for European markets; and Ottoman Turkey was a European condominium, with a variety of colonial powers holding specific concession rights to the land and mineral resources of the empire. On the shores of the Persian Gulf, a massive petroleum complex—foreign-owned and foreign-managed—has barely touched the lives of neighboring peasants and Bedouin nomads during most of its history of operation.

Since independence, the nations of the Middle East have tried to stimulate industrialization and undo their colonial inheritance, but growing population, increasing urbanization, and intensifying pressure on farmland have forced these governments to invest heavily in social welfare programs and land reform. Few states have had the human or capital resources to subsidize the establishment of major industrial complexes. In addition, mineral resources in the Middle East (except for oil) are widely scattered, of variable quality, and distant from labor pools concentrated in cities. The paucity of coal in the region has meant that most other ores could not be processed or concentrated locally and have been carried in raw form to distant ports or foreign countries for refining. But the quadrupling of oil prices in the early 1970s and increased local control of the oil industry have suddenly provided producing nations such as Iran, Iraq, Saudi Arabia, Libya, and Kuwait with the capital necessary for the development of broader, more diversified industrial

economies. Although light industries, particularly textiles and food processing, still predominate in the large cities of the region, the political and economic aspirations of these states to achieve economic independence in the post-petroleum era have led to a more intensive search for industrial raw materials and new mineral discoveries that will change the industrial map of the Middle East and North Africa.

ENERGY SOURCES

The Middle East and North Africa make up the largest oil-producing and oil-exporting region in the world, and petroleum is by far the most significant resource of the region. In the early 1970s, the Middle East and North Africa produced over 40 percent of the world's crude oil; new discoveries continue to be made. The costs of producing oil in this region are quite low. In the Persian Gulf, the production costs of a barrel of oil range from 6 cents in Kuwait to 35 cents offshore Dubai, compared with the $3 per barrel cost in the American Southwest. The primary reason for this cost differential is that Middle Eastern wells are close to the surface and free-flowing, and an average well produces 4500 barrels of oil per day as compared with 15 in the United States. As a result, the Middle East, until recently, was the world's major supplier of cheap crude oil. The people of the Middle East utilize only a small proportion of the region's vast production. Even with higher prices, the Middle East and North Africa, with over 70 percent of the world's proved petroleum reserves, will undoubtedly remain the world's primary exporter of oil.

In the technological world, imported oil is an economic fact of life. Japan, for example, depends on oil for 75 percent of its energy needs. Western Europe depended on oil for 30 percent of its energy needs in 1960; by 1970, this figure had risen to 53 percent. The United States, which imported 20 percent of its oil in the 1960s, will import 50 percent in the 1970s. With consumption increasing in all these nations at a rate not unlike that of Japan (20 percent a year), intense competition for Middle Eastern oil foreshadows an emerging world energy crisis in which the political and economic decisions of Middle Easterners will play a crucial role.

The Middle East oil industry began early in the twentieth century as the need for oil to power the expanding machine technology of the Industrial Revolution led to European penetration and exploration of this region. In 1901, W. K. D'Arcy, a British adventurer who had made a fortune in Australian gold, negotiated a concession covering all of Iran, and in 1908 oil was discovered on the western slopes of the Zagros. Shortly thereafter, the Turkish Petroleum Company was established with the combined interests of Deutsche Bank, Royal Dutch, and

199

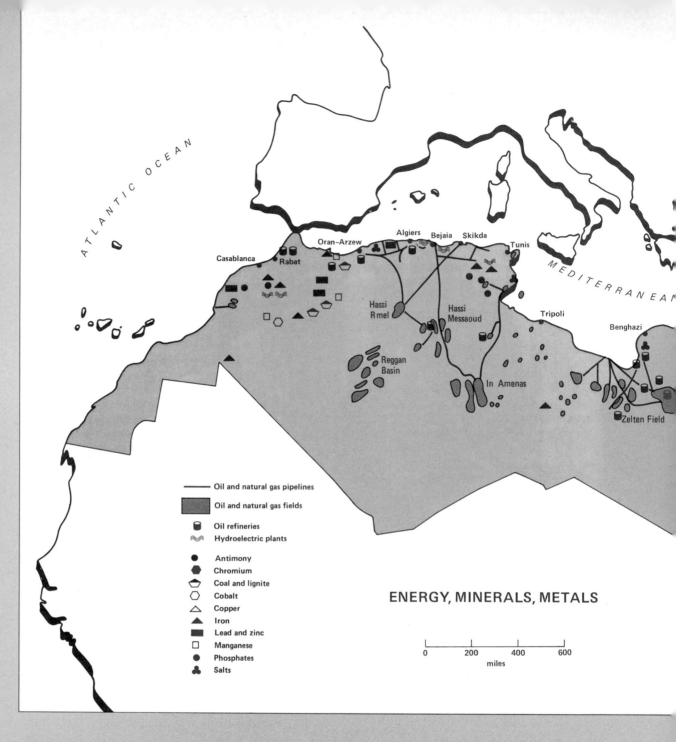

ATLANTIC OCEAN

MEDITERRANEAN

Casablanca
Rabat
Oran–Arzew
Algiers
Bejaia
Skikda
Tunis
Tripoli
Benghazi

Hassi
R'mel

Hassi
Messaoud

Reggan
Basin

In Amenas

Zelten Field

—— Oil and natural gas pipelines

▮ Oil and natural gas fields

⬢ Oil refineries

〰 Hydroelectric plants

● Antimony

⬡ Chromium

⬠ Coal and lignite

◯ Cobalt

△ Copper

▲ Iron

▬ Lead and zinc

◻ Manganese

● Phosphates

♣ Salts

ENERGY, MINERALS, METALS

0   200   400   600

miles

Anglo-Persian Oil; at the same time, the Armenian entrepreneur Calouste Gulbenkian gained concessionary rights in Iraq. In the 1920s, Aramco appeared in Bahrain; it later expanded its interests over much of Saudi Arabia. Currently, a variety of national companies and international corporations, operating now in partnerships in which Middle Eastern governments have controlling interests, are engaged in producing the symbiotic flow of oil to the consuming markets of North America, Western Europe, and Japan and cash and credits to the producing states of the Middle East.

The most important oil-producing field in the Middle East is located in a vast *sedimentary basin* known geologically as the Persian Gulf geosyncline. Lining the gulf shores, the largest oil-producing countries are Iran, Saudi Arabia, Kuwait, and Iraq; lesser but important producing areas lie in Abu Dhabi, the Kuwait–Saudi Arabia Neutral Zone, Qatar, Oman, Bahrain, and Dubai. The largest oil fields in Iran, the Khuzistan fields, lie on the western flanks of the Zagros Mountains just north of the Persian Gulf. Here, oil trapped in a subsurface limestone reservoir is brought to the surface and piped to the huge port and refinery complex at Abadan and to a ten-berth, deep-water tanker terminal at

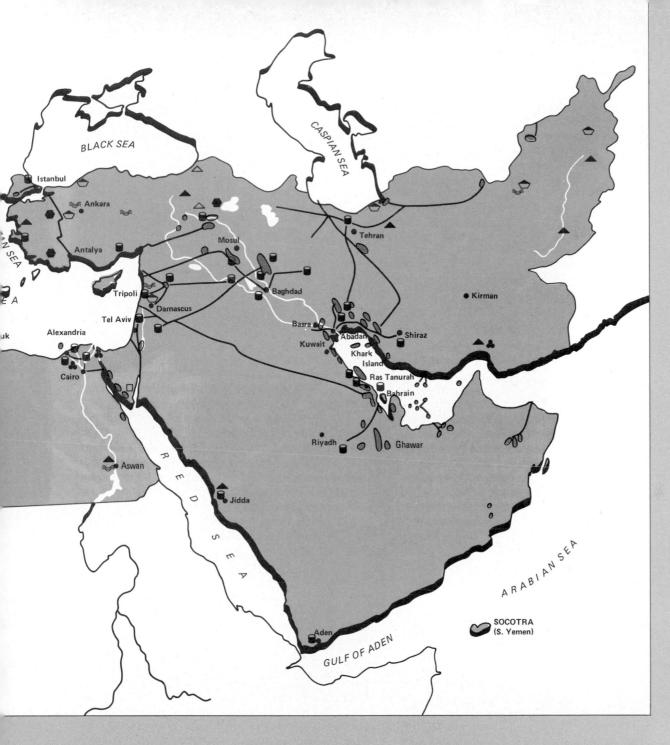

Khark Island. Since 1957, Iranian oil has been produced by the National Iranian Oil Company (NIOC) in partnership with a variety of foreign firms. In 1973, Iran, the second largest producer of oil in the Middle East, assumed direct control of all concessionary rights and operations. In Iraq, the largest oil field is located in the north and is directly connected by pipeline to Mediterranean ports in Lebanon and Syria. Other important fields are located still farther to the north near Mosul, and in the deep south near the port city of Basra. Iraqi oil was worked by the Iraq Petroleum Company (IPC), a consortium of British, Dutch, French, and American interests (along with Gulbenkian's 5 percent), until the company was nationalized in 1972.

The oil industries of the other Persian Gulf states were not developed until after 1945. The postwar expansion of oil production in Kuwait transformed that country into the largest Middle Eastern producer of crude oil, a position only recently relinquished to Saudi Arabia and Iran. During the 1960s, some 2 million barrels of crude oil flowed each day from eight Kuwaiti fields. Produced at exceptionally low cost, since the oil is near the surface and under water pressure, Kuwaiti oil is transported less than 15 miles from the oil fields to refining and port

Crude oil from this well deep in the Libyan desert flows 250 miles by pipeline to the Mediterranean, and then to the rest of the world. *Photo:* Monkmeyer.

facilities. The Kuwait Oil Company (KOC), the largest of three companies operating in the country, is a combine of British Petroleum and Gulf, now 60 percent controlled by the Kuwaiti government.

In Saudi Arabia, Aramco, the principal and the largest oil company in the world, has been bought outright by the Saudi government. Here, Ghawar, an enormous oil pool 150 miles long and up to 22 miles wide with reserves equivalent to those of the entire United States, was discovered in the late 1940s. This field, and others farther to the north and offshore, pipe oil to two refining terminals at Ras Tannurah and Bahrain and nearly 2000 miles westward to the Mediterranean. These fields have propelled Saudi Arabia into first position in Middle Eastern oil production. Similar patterns in the production and export of Persian Gulf oil on smaller scales are found in the Kuwait–Saudi Arabia Neutral Zone, Bahrain, Qatar, Dubai, Abu Dhabi, Oman, and the other sheikdoms of the Persian Gulf.

Similar, though less spectacular, discoveries of oil on the North African *shield*° have converted this region into a major exporter of crude oil and natural gas. In Libya, a dozen major fields clustered in Cyrenaica now have approximately 1000 producing wells. The largest of these fields, Zelten, was not discovered until 1959; an equally large field at Idris is currently under development. All Libyan fields have the advantage of being located relatively close to the Mediterranean, and pipeline terminals now exist at five locations on the Libyan coast. Farther to the west, in Algeria, the third largest natural gas field in the world was discovered at Hassi Rmel some 200 miles south of Algiers near Ghardaia. Already supplying industrial producers in Britain, Algerian natural gas will soon be shipped in liquefied form from Arzew on the Mediterranean to the east coast of the United States by arrangements made between El Paso Natural Gas Company and the Algerian national oil company, which is called SONATRACH.

In addition, a series of major oil strikes have been made in the interior of southern Algeria, and four pipelines now connect these fields with the Mediterranean. In Tunisia, offshore oil near Kerkennah Island is now in production. Morocco has had less success in discovering oil, but exploration has expanded owing to the finds in the contiguous Algerian Sahara. Similarly, in Egypt, which has recently begun to export oil from offshore finds in the Gulf of Suez and older wells at El Alamein, the scope of oil operations has improved since the return of the Sinai oil fields held by Israel after the 1967 war to Egyptian control.

The petroleum industry of the Middle East and North Africa, in all its phases—from exploration and discovery to pipelining and distribution—is perhaps the most complex and strategic of all world industries. The international tensions that bear on every aspect of the industry lend to it an air of immediacy and of global strategy. Middle Eastern domestic priorities, Arab politics, multinational capitalism, and global energy needs all play a part in rendering the Middle Eastern oil industry perhaps the most critical in a world of growing aspirations and limited resources.

The Middle East remains weak in other energy sources. The largest deposits of coal in the region are found in Turkey at Zonguldak on the Black Sea coast, where irregular fractured seams of *bituminous coal** of good quality are mined. Production amounts to less than 8 million tons a year, and mining costs are so high that the venture must be subsidized by the national government. Similarly, in Iran, coal is found in the Elburz Mountains northeast of Tehran, in eastern Mazandaran, and at Bafq, north of the desert city of Kirman. These coal deposits are of variable quality; their seams are discontinuous, and total production is, in global terms, negligible. Algeria and Morocco also have minor coal deposits. The development of hydroelectric power, although also quite limited in the Middle East, is beginning to play an important role in a number of countries for internal industrial and agricultural expansion.

The production of hydroelectric power was a primary object in the construction of the Aswan Dam, and this facility will increase Egypt's electric power capacity by twelve times. In western Turkey a series of much smaller power projects on rivers draining northward to the Black Sea will soon be supplemented by a much larger facility at Keban on the upper Euphrates. In Lebanon, some electric power for domestic use is generated on the Yarmuk River. In addition, the numerous short rivers streaming down the slopes of the Atlas Mountains of the Maghrib have been tapped by the construction of several dams. In Algeria and in Morocco, in particular, hydroelectric power, what is called the *politique des grandes barrages*, is seen as allowing rapid industrialization in the near future.

MINERALS AND METALS

Many small deposits of a wide variety of minerals and metals are found throughout the Middle East and North Africa, but only in exceptional cases are these resources significant in world markets. Although iron ore is found in appreciable quantities in a variety of places—east-central Turkey, on the fringes of the central desert in Iran, at Aswan in Egypt, in Syria north of Aleppo, and in parts of North Africa—heavy industry is virtually absent in the region. A steel mill has been constructed with Soviet assistance at Isfahan in Iran, and electric power from the Aswan Dam is being used to process local iron ores for use in the Helwan steel complex south of Cairo. Both these projects, however, will fail to satisfy local demand. Given the scattered and remote nature of coal and iron resources and the high costs of their exploitation in the Middle East and North Africa, it seems likely that this region will continue to rely on imports of heavy machinery and steel for some time to come.

With respect to other minerals, Turkey is the world's second leading producer of chromium, from deposits in the southeast; Morocco is a significant producer of cobalt and manganese; an important copper find has been made at Sar Cheshmeh in southern Iran; manganese is found in the Sinai; and Cyprus produces asbestos and copper. In addition, recent exploration has uncovered important deposits of copper, nickel, silver, and gold in western Saudi Arabia along the Red Sea. With the exception of oil, however, the most important mineral resource in the region is phosphate, a fundamental source of chemical fertilizers and hence basic to food production in industrial nations. Morocco is the second largest producer of phosphates (after the United States) and the world's leading exporter. Vast deposits in neighboring Spanish Sahara have become a focus of international tension. Increased demand for phosphates and a tripling of their price in 1974 have contributed substantially to the phosphate-exporting economies of Morocco, Tunisia, Jordan, and Israel.

TWO PEOPLES, ONE LAND

4

In the late nineteenth century the brutal persecution of large Jewish communities in Russia and Eastern Europe led to the formation of Zionism, a worldwide Jewish philosophical movement devoted to securing a political refuge for the Jews. Nearly 2000 years of Christian intolerance had convinced Zionists that lasting safety for Jews could be guaranteed only by the establishment of an independent Jewish state. They explored alternative sites in Africa and Latin America, but none held the powerful religious and emotional appeal of Palestine.

It was in Palestine that the last sovereign Jewish community existed until the Roman legions entered the region in the second century BC, ultimately ravaging Jerusalem in AD 70, destroying the temple of Herod, and dislodging the Jews from their Holy Land. Thereafter, during the long diaspora, Jews lived as alien minorities in no country they could call their own; they were frequently unwanted and often confined to urban ghettos and barred from full economic and social franchisement. Orthodox Jews believed that the land of Palestine, sanctioned in their scriptures, had been promised to them by God. Others felt that in Palestine, Jews would experience a cultural rebirth and a spiritual redemption by which they would reestablish self-identity. Small groups of Zionists had already migrated to Palestine from Eastern Europe during the nineteenth century. For these reasons, the First Zionist Congress, held at Basel in 1897, defined its primary goal as the creation of "a home in Palestine secured by public law" for the Jewish people. Twenty years later, as the Ottoman Empire was physically disintegrating during World War I, the opportunity arose. Influential Zionists secured a commitment from the British government in the Balfour Declaration to support the "establishment in Palestine of a national home for the Jewish people." Subsequently, in 1920, Palestine became a British mandate under the League of Nations, and Zionists were convinced they had succeeded in bringing "the land without a people to the people without a land."

PALESTINE UNDER BRITISH MANDATE
[FIGURE 3]

Had Palestine in fact been a "land without a people," the British would have had little difficulty in fulfilling their pledge to the Zionists. But 750,000 people lived in Palestine in 1920. The majority of the Arabs, who composed 87 percent of the native Palestinian population, were Muslim farmers living in the thousand or so villages that dotted the fertile coastal plain and lowland valleys of Palestine. Some 98 percent of the land in this region had been in Arab hands for fifty generations. (The Ottoman government had forbidden foreign ownership of land, so only a small percentage was in the hands of outsiders.) But land tenure patterns had changed in the twentieth century, when the growing value of commercial crops encouraged urban landlords and merchants in Beirut, Damascus, and Jerusalem to invest in agriculture. Communal tenure systems had given way to large private holdings, increasing the insecurity of Arab peasants throughout the region.

This had little effect, however, on the Jewish minority of 83,000, who formed 11 percent of the population of Palestine in the early 1920s. Three-quarters of the Jews were urban residents who lived in Jerusalem and in Tel Aviv, the new Jewish suburb of Jaffa. Although Zionist ideals stressed a Jewish return to the land, most Jewish immigrants, urban in outlook and training, tended to settle in the cities. Zionist agricultural colonies had been established at Safad and Tiberias in the north, but Jews owned and occupied only a tiny percentage of the land. It was clear from the start that until both demography and land ownership were radically changed, Palestine could not be a home for the Jews.

For the Zionists, physical possession of the land was a political imperative: more Jews had to come to Palestine, more of Palestine had to belong to Jews. Seven villages were bought in the Jezreel Valley, and large tracts of fertile land were occupied in the Vale of Esdraelon. Zionist objectives were to build up population concentrations in core areas and to estab-

Figure 3. **Population and Land Ownership in Palestine, 1944. On the eve of civil war, Jewish land ownership was concentrated in the Vale of Esdraelon and Galilee in the north, on the Plain of Sharon south of Haifa, and in Tel Aviv–Jaffa. In the hilly interior and the southern deserts, land ownership was overwhelmingly Arab (a). Jews comprised a substantial portion of the population only in the urban centers of Jerusalem, Tel Aviv–Jaffa, and Haifa. Elsewhere, Arabs predominated (b).** *After:* **(a) John Ruedy, "Dynamics of Land Alienation," in Ibrahim Abu-Lughod, ed.,** *The Transformation of Palestine.* **Evanston, Ill.: Northwestern University Press, 1971, p. 121; (b) Janet Abu-Lughod, "The Demographic Transformation of Palestine," in** *ibid.,* **p. 158.**

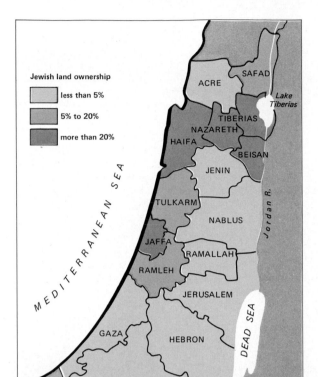

Jewish land ownership
- less than 5%
- 5% to 20%
- more than 20%

MEDITERRANEAN SEA

ACRE
SAFAD
Lake Tiberias
TIBERIAS
NAZARETH
HAIFA
BEISAN
JENIN
TULKARM
NABLUS
Jordan R.
JAFFA
RAMALLAH
RAMLEH
JERUSALEM
GAZA
HEBRON
DEAD SEA
BEERSHEBA

(A)

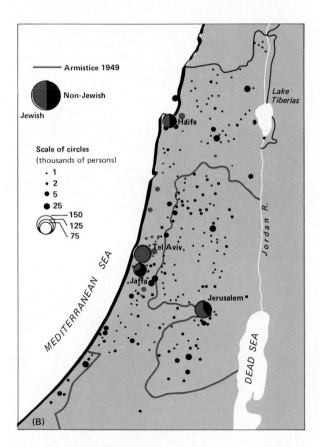

Armistice 1949

Non-Jewish
Jewish

Scale of circles
(thousands of persons)
- 1
- 2
- 5
- 25
- 150
- 125
- 75

MEDITERRANEAN SEA

Lake Tiberias

Haifa

Tel Aviv
Jaffa
Jerusalem

Jordan R.

DEAD SEA

(B)

lish a Jewish presence elsewhere. Some cultivated land was reclaimed in the Kabbara swamp, in the Huleh marshes, and in the dunes that border the Mediterranean south of Tel Aviv. But a majority of the land, upward of 90 percent, was purchased from absentee landlords who evicted the Muslim tenant farmers who worked the land. With an estimated 29 percent of Palestine's farmers then landless in Palestine, Jewish land acquisitions sparked a political response. Arab riots ensued, and Britain's mandate adminstration was caught between the opposing impulses of the Arabs and the Zionists.

British policy vacillated between restricting Jewish immigration and land sales in deference to Arab pressure and relaxing regulations because of pressure from the Zionist lobby in London. By 1931, the Jewish population of Palestine had doubled to 174,000 through immigration. But a falling death rate and a high birth rate among the Arabs swelled the population of Palestine to over 1 million, so that Jews remained a minority of 16 percent. Still overwhelmingly urban despite Zionist programs of land settlement, 68 percent of the Jews in Palestine lived in either Jerusalem or Tel Aviv-Jaffa, where they constituted 49 and 48 percent, respectively, of the total population. In large areas of the countryside, in the Negev and the hilly wilderness of central Palestine, Jewish settlement remained negligible.

Tensions between the Arab and Jewish communities began to mount, foreshadowing the hostilities that dominate the eastern Mediterranean today. In 1929, a trivial incident—the stabbing of a Jewish boy who had kicked a football into an Arab's garden—triggered bloody urban riots in Jerusalem. By 1933, Arab demonstrations against the British administration were frequent, and outbreaks of violence between Arabs and Jews flared throughout Palestine. Underlying these clashes were the competing national aspirations of two peoples for one land. By 1936, a tide of Jewish immigration from Nazi Germany increased the Jewish population to 385,000, 28 percent of the Palestinian population. Jewish land purchases doubled and redoubled; taxes on land transactions quadrupled in three years; and the price of land soared well beyond the means of most Arab farmers. The increase in Jewish immigration, widespread fear of the establishment of a Jewish national home, the growing militancy of Arab nationalists, and a declining local economy sparked a six-month general strike. This soon deteriorated

into a guerrilla rebellion that lasted until the beginning of World War II.

During the war years, Jewish immigration continued despite British efforts to limit the flow. A high Arab birth rate and a falling death rate offset Jewish immigration gains. By 1947, the British decided to wash their hands of the situation they had so deviously created by promising Palestinian homelands to the Jews in the Balfour Declaration and to the Arabs in the McMahon correspondence. They turned the issue over to the United Nations, which devised a scheme for partitioning Palestine into two countries: a Jewish state, composed of 56 percent of Palestine including the Mediterranean lowlands from Haifa to south of Tel Aviv, the fertile north, and the Negev; and an Arab state, 43 percent of Palestine, including Acre and Nazareth in the north, the central hill lands and the Jordan Valley, Gaza, and part of Beersheba. Jerusalem was to remain under permanent United Nations administration.

The Jews agreed to partition, the Arabs did not; both communities prepared to fight. On the eve of civil war, the 590,000 Jews in Palestine, still heavily concentrated in the urban districts of Jerusalem, Tel Aviv-Jaffa, and Haifa, made up 31 percent of the population and owned 450,000 acres of land or roughly 7 percent of the entire area. Arabs formed 69 percent of the population of 1.9 million and owned 93 percent of the land. Zionist plans and programs had only partially succeeded in altering demography and land ownership in Palestine.

THE EMERGENCE OF ISRAEL

On May 14, 1948, the British withdrew from Palestine, the state of Israel was created, and war between the Arabs and the Jews began. In fourteen months the Arab armies of Egypt, Syria, and Jordan were decisively defeated, and Israel achieved what decades of immigration had not accomplished. Palestine was transformed into a Jewish homeland. Under the armistice of 1949, Israel occupied nearly four-fifths of the territory of the former mandate and virtually all its good agricultural land. Roughly 750,000 Arabs fled or were driven from Israeli-controlled areas and became refugees in the Gaza Strip or in Jordan, Syria, and Lebanon. Over 80 percent of the land administered by Israel, including 1.1 million acres of agricultural land, still technically belonged to these refugees. But through a variety of devices this land was soon confiscated. Meanwhile, Jewish survivors of concentration camps, Jews from Eastern Europe, those released from British detention camps, and Jews from the Arab countries of North Africa and the Middle East flocked to Israel. Some 250,000 arrived in 1949 alone, and the Jewish population of Israel

Two peoples, one land: The Damascus Gate in the old section of Jerusalem. *Photo:* **Sam Falk/Monkmeyer.**

increased a staggering 108 percent in only four years. According to the Israeli census of November 1948, the non-Jewish population of Israel had shrunk to 156,000, and Jews, firmly in control of the land, now composed more than 80 percent of the population.

In the next quarter century, the ingathering of Jews from various world regions proceeded under the Law of Return, which provided that "every Jew shall be entitled to come to Israel as an immigrant." By 1962, 2 million Jews lived in Israel; a decade later, 2.7 million. Israel, which at independence contained 7 percent of the world's Jewish population, now held nearly a fifth. The sources and rates of immigration varied with changing world conditions. In the first six years, 576,000 immigrants arrived from Europe and the Arab states of the Middle East and North Africa. The ancient Jewish communities of Iraq and Yemen (145,000 of them) were airlifted to Israel. In 1956 and 1957, the Hungarian uprising and a Polish government decision to release 40,000 Jews brought a new influx of Eastern European immigrants. Subsequently, in the 1960s, rising nationalism in the Maghrib brought an additional 200,000 North African Jews. Then Russia relaxed emigration restrictions and tens of thousands of Soviet Jews arrived. By the early 1970s, over half of Israel's population had been born abroad, and second-generation Israelis composed only 17 percent of the population.

These diverse cultural origins of the Jewish population posed massive problems of integration and assimilation to the Israeli state. At independence, Israel was totally dominated by European leaders, institutions, and ideals. Today approximately half of the population derives from African or Asian origin. These Oriental Jews with their lower levels of education, limited control of Hebrew, and nontechnical skills have had difficulty adjusting to the tempo and organization of the planned, Western, and industrial society of Israel. An additional 500,000 non-Jews, most of them Arabs, still live in Israel.

Israel attempted to absorb the tide of new immigrants by expanding agricultural settlement into the less densely populated parts of the country. The motivations were several: first, the Zionist commitment to cultural redemption by a return to the soil appealed to a strong minority; second, the heavy concentration of Jews in Haifa, Tel Aviv, and Jerusalem posed security problems; third, self-sufficiency in food seemed a desirable goal given the continuing hostility of the Arab world; finally, the considerable

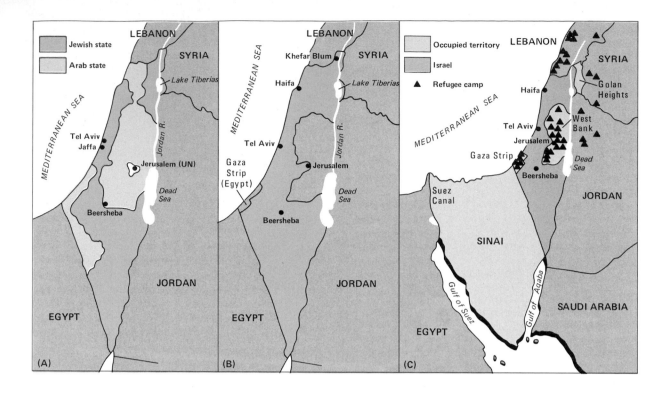

Figure 4. The Expansion of Israel. In the wars of 1948 and 1967, Israel displaced over a million Palestinians and expanded in area. The competing national claims of these two peoples for the same land is the heart of the Arab-Israeli conflict. (a) Palestine according to the UN partition plan, 1947; (b) Israel, 1949–1967; (c) Israel and occupied territory since June 10, 1967.

lands abandoned by Arab refugees provided an attractive economic resource.

A master plan based on Christaller's **central place** theory was designed to achieve an optimum distribution of the Israeli population and to create a close-knit hierarchy of settlement. At the lowest level were primary villages: the kibbutz, a unique Israeli collective farm, and the moshav, a cooperative composed of independent small farmers. Although these settlers were never a significant percentage of the population, the tough survival philosophy forged in these pioneer settlements, now numbering 600 and including more than 200,000 people, has a strong influence on Israeli national policy. At higher levels in the hierarchy, rural service centers, small towns, and urban centers are linked in a network composed of twenty-four planning regions including the three large cities of Jerusalem, Tel Aviv, and Haifa.

By 1970, the number of rural settlements in Israel had doubled and virtually all agricultural land in the country was occupied. Thousands of acres had been reclaimed from deserts and marshes, and 480,000 acres of land—nearly half the total in cultivation—were under irrigation. The traditional extensive **dry-farming** methods of former Arab farmers were replaced by modern intensive scientific horticulture. Cultivation of citrus crops became an important agricultural sector and oranges the largest export product of Israel. Dairying, cattle raising, market gardening, and cereal cultivation also expanded.

This transformation of agriculture in Israel, a land long subject to human abuse, attracted international acclaim. Making the desert bloom became both a spiritual goal and a political slogan in Israel. Thousands of evergreens were planted on the barren limestone uplands of Galilee, Samaria, and Judea from which an estimated 3 feet of topsoil had been scoured by centuries of erosion. The malarial swamps of the Jezreel Valley were converted to agriculture. In the south, Beersheba, once occupied by nomads and dry farmers, became an important center of irrigated farming. Experiments in **drip irrigation, hydroponics,** and the use of brackish underground water extended human settlement deep into the Negev wastes. Despite these well-publicized efforts, however, Israel remained an urban nation, and the concentration of population in the urban centers of the well-watered north has gradually been accepted by Israeli planners. Severely limited by insufficient water, 85 percent of which is already used for agricultural purposes, farming occupies only 8 percent of the labor force and accounts for 6 percent of the national product. By contrast, fully a quarter of Israel's national income derives from manufacturing, the highest such figure for any Middle Eastern country.

THE SUBSTANCE OF CHANGE

The differential development and diffusion of the scientific transformation divided the globe into two human domains—the rich and the poor, the haves and the have-nots, the underdeveloped and the developed, or, as they are called in this book, the developing and technological worlds. Vast inequalities in the length and quality of life, standards of living, levels of education, rates of agricultural and industrial production, and command of political power now separate those societies that generated and have integrated the scientific transformation from those that, at differing rates, are striving to achieve modernization, development, and industrialization. In the developing world, a spectrum of nations with different traditions, economies, and environments is burdened by limited technology, burgeoning populations, poorly developed resource bases, inadequate capital, and neocolonial economies in the struggle to master the scientific transformation.

During the last twenty-five years, despite substantial infusions of foreign aid and intensive national programs of economic and social development, the rich nations have grown progressively richer, the poor relatively poorer. In the 1960s, per capita income in the developing world grew less than $50 per year, compared with 10 to 15 times that figure in the technological world. The sources of poverty vary: In India, Sri Lanka, and Bangladesh, population growth appears to be the critical variable. In North Africa and parts of the Middle East, aridity retards the development of resources. In central Africa, the legacy of colonialism weighs heavily. In Latin America, population growth is explosive, control of the physical environment inadequate. Whatever the reasons, poverty is now a persistent and pervasive feature of landscapes and lives in the developing world, and few experts think the condition will soon change.

These nations may remain outsiders to the world economy, contributing raw materials to more sophisticated and specialized nations, sharing only one-fifth of world trade, and experimenting with one new plan after another to reach the elusive goal of modernization. The highest rates of population growth, over 2.5 percent per year, are in Africa and Latin America. The greatest mass of population, nearly 60 percent of the world total, is located in the developing countries of Asia. Scarcities of food and fuel are more intense today than at any time in this century. Only North America and Australia now produce an exportable grain surplus; world reserves are one-third less than fifteen years ago. Food is scarce because of rising population in the developing world and rising consumption in the technological world. The costs of energy are rising, and rich and poor compete for the oil that is needed to run a modern industrial economy and to maintain modern urban centers.

In the developing world, urbanization and the shift from animate to inanimate forms of energy are under way, but men and animals are still the principal labor machines. As a result, productivity is low, per capita income is low, and the economic surplus is limited. Although there have been advances in agriculture like the green revolution, rising population increases pressure on rural resources and encourages migration to industrializing urban centers. Yet the necessary capital to house, educate, and employ these people is not available. Since many nations experienced modernization under colonial rule, dual economies with a modern, European-oriented, extractive sector and a traditional local agrarian sector cause growth without development. Food and energy production rise annually, but population and consumer demands rise faster.

For most countries in the developing world, the past quarter century has encompassed a political struggle to gain independence and an economic battle to transform their societies from an agrarian to an industrial base. The goal is to take advantage of those higher levels of productivity and wealth that accompany the shift from animate to inanimate energy; the difficulty is to accumulate the surplus capital needed to modernize agriculture, to construct roads and railroads, to build factories, to set up and staff educational systems, to build and run modern urban infrastructures. The problems of Mexico City and of the green revolution in India are but two examples of this struggle, the substance of change in the developing world.

THE GREEN REVOLUTION

As late as 1957, Krishna Menon, one of Nehru's most trusted advisors, claimed that Indians were born with "two hands capable of work and only one mouth to feed." He was not alone in underestimating the seriousness of the food-population race in the subcontinent; the long-run consequences of the world-wide surge in numbers was not yet high priority on the international agenda. Yet by 1961, India's population had increased to 439 million people, unemployment was widespread, and the fruits of development that would have meant a 42 percent increase in personal income for the 361 million people of 1951 were reduced to 16 percent. This multiplication, combined with low grain production, left the villages with too little food, too many mouths to feed, and rising food prices.

When in 1966 30 million urban Indians were obliged to ration food strictly and 200 million in the countryside had to endure partial rationing, the government adopted a new strategy. The goal was "self-sufficiency in food grains by 1971," raising total food production from a base of 90 million tons in 1965 to 125 million tons in 1971. New seeds and agricultural techniques were to be introduced in areas where irrigation could be practiced, and price incentives would be offered to encourage participation. The new seeds and techniques would come from the results of an agricultural program in Mexico set up by the Rockefeller Foundation in partnership with the Mexican government, which had produced new strains of dwarf wheat, maize, and rice with extraordinarily high yields—a "green revolution." These cereals, however, required modern scientific farming and reliable water supplies, conditions uncharacteristic of most of India, where traditional subsistence techniques and dependence on the monsoon persisted.

The core area of India's green revolution was therefore the Punjab, the country's traditional breadbasket, where 80 percent of the land was devoted to "miracle" wheats. Punjabi farmers were more prosperous and progressive, and irrigation had always been used. The results were startling. In the rice-producing areas, however, there were significant increases in yield only in certain districts. The new varieties were susceptible to pests and diseases, and most South Indian farmers could not afford chemical fertilizers and pesticides. Unlike the Punjabi farmers, they did not have sufficiently reliable irrigation facilities. And the new varieties of rice did not look, cook, or taste like those to which people were accustomed.

The breakthrough in food production made possible by the green revolution did avert widespread famine in India, but it is far from a full-fledged agrarian revolution. Only a tiny minority of India's 60 million peasant families have benefited from the introduction of the new crops, and since over three-quarters of the agricultural land is dry-farmed rather than irrigated, this may remain true for the foreseeable future. The green revolution created islands of prosperity in a barren landscape, and now these islands are threatened by the rising price of fertilizers and pesticides caused by the energy crisis.

In the rest of India, two-thirds of the rural population still has no land or less than 5 acres and lives in abject poverty on annual equivalent incomes of about $20. The situation is even more difficult for the 103 million landless tenants, and there is no growing pool of jobs in industry to take the surplus from the rural areas. For in the decade since the new high-yielding dwarf wheat and rice seeds were introduced into the villages of the subcontinent, India's population has increased by more than 100 million people. Even if the green revolution achieves maximum success in raising the productivity of Indian agriculture, it may simply postpone for one decade a Malthusian disaster in India. The problem is not only enough food: it is also enough jobs for those who now flood the cities looking for the work that cannot be found in the countryside. And in India, as in most nations of the developing world, urbanization has gone forward without industrialization.

(opposite) Crossbreeding rice. Andhra Pradesh University, Hyderabad. Marc & Evelyne Bernheim, Woodfin Camp.
(left) Agricultural extension officer demonstrates a spraying machine in a rice field, South India. Marc & Evelyne Bernheim, Woodfin Camp.
(right) A traditional good-luck statue guards a miracle rice field, South India. Marc & Evelyne Bernheim, Woodfin Camp.
(bottom) Experimenting with dwarf banana plants, Coimbatore Research Institute, South India. Marc & Evelyne Bernheim, Woodfin Camp.
(overleaf) Miracle rice fields at Andhra Pradesh University, Hyderabad. Marc & Evelyne Bernheim, Woodfin Camp.

(left) Harvesting wheat grown with water wheel irrigation, North India. Marc & Evelyne Bernheim, Woodfin Camp.

(top) Threshing in the traditional way. Marc & Evelyne Bernheim, Woodfin Camp.

(bottom) Family harvesting wheat, with a transistor radio. Marc & Evelyne Bernheim, Woodfin Camp.

(overleaf) A farmer and his wife winnow the new wheat crop, North India. Marc & Evelyne Bernheim, Woodfin Camp.

MEXICO CITY

In the Plaza of the Three Cultures in Mexico City stand the ruins of an Aztec temple and ball court and the old Spanish Church of Santiago; facing it are the red, yellow, and orange buildings of Nonoalco, a new government housing project. Its inhabitants are themselves people of "three cultures," for Indian ways still persist, as does the Catholicism that is Spain's lasting legacy, amid the modern structures and life styles of this Latin American primate city.

In the Valley of Mexico before the Spanish conquest, the capital city of the Aztecs, Tenochtitlán, stood in the middle of a lake and was surrounded by settlements along the shores. Tenochtitlán itself was a vast and rich city of stone surrounding a central plaza, with thriving markets in which could be found in abundance the gold and feather work of excellent craftsmen. It was this magnificence that Cortès and a handful of Spaniards destroyed in 1521. On its ruins they built Mexico City, which became the capital of New Spain, as the conquerors called Mexico, and then that of independent Mexico.

The new city was a fortress, not a monument; the new places of worship were cathedrals, and colonial viceroys and prelates lived in palaces built in the ornate Spanish style. Once the conquest was over, the pattern typical of all Spanish Latin America appeared in Mexico: Urban centers in which lived a few Europeans who ruled the mass of the people were built at strategic places; and the population clustered in these areas or in the few environmentally favored parts of the region. Between settlements were vast empty areas.

This distribution of population has not changed from colonial times: those areas already densely settled continue to receive a constant stream of migrants. In 1970, 25 percent of all Latin Americans were crowded onto 3 percent of the land area, while half the region was occupied by only 5 percent of the population. The largest cities are located in these islands of settlement, and they have been growing three to four times as fast as the population at large, which itself is growing faster than that of any other world region.

One cause of this growth has been the lowering of the death rate by advances in medicine, sanitation, and personal hygiene; another has been the wealth of the modern cities, particularly that of the primate cities, which has created images of a better life that draw rural migrants who are then encouraged to have children. These primate cities, a feature of Latin American urbanization, have created great concentrations of people in single political and economic centers. Mexico City, for example, is a conurbation of more than 7 million. The two next largest urban centers, Guadalajara and Monterrey, are just over 1 million each. And these cities, once staging areas for outward movement into the countryside in colonial times, have become magnets for those seeking advance and adventure. By 1960, Mexico's Federal District (which includes Mexico City) contained 15 percent of the country's population.

But industrialization has not kept pace with urbanization in Latin America. Numbers and jobs do not match. Manufacturing employed less than one-fifth of the urban workforce in 1970, roughly the same proportion as in 1925. The poverty and unemployment of the countryside have been transferred to the cities. Colonies of makeshift shacks without sewage systems, water, or electricity have appeared on vacant city land and in suburbs, and these shanty-towns house perhaps a quarter of the populations of urban centers like Mexico City. The flight of this miserably poor and depressed class of people to the city has overwhelmed the capacity of urban planners to provide adequate housing, education, and health services.

Aware of the problems of overconcentration and of the exaggerated prominence of primate cities in their economies and societies, modern Latin American governments are moving to develop the periphery and integrate frontier regions into the national economy. Mexico is opening up new agricultural land in the Yucatán and the northeast, and the construction of new factories in Mexico City (which already has the preponderance of modern industry) has been forbidden. Within the city, squatters have been moved from caves and tenements to planned communities like Nonoalco, which houses 90,000 people. There are schools and supermarkets, a splendid subway system, a downtown marked by stunningly imaginative architecture. Yet the gap between rich and poor persists, as do traditional ways. Scribes still do business in the plazas; Indians still approach the shrine of the Virgin of Guadalupe on their knees; the white minority still forms the professional class. And population continues to grow, lowering the chances for the orderly management of change. The Plaza of the Three Cultures is neither anachronism nor symbol; it is the reality of modern Mexico.

(left) Mexico City from the top of the Hotel de Mexico. Albert Moldvay, Woodfin Camp.

(top) Interior of the house of the jeweler Porfirio Fenton. Albert Moldvay, Woodfin Camp.

(center) Cave dwellers within the city limits. Albert Moldvay, Woodfin Camp.

(bottom) Interior of a one-room slum apartment. Marc & Evelyne Bernheim, Woodfin Camp.

(top) Nonoalco housing complex. Marc & Evelyne Bernheim, Woodfin Camp.

(left) A supermarket. Marc & Evelyne Bernheim, Woodfin Camp.

(right) Sunday in Chapultepec Park. Marc & Evelyne Bernheim, Woodfin Camp.

(bottom) Housewives line up for the garbage collector. Marc & Evelyne Bernheim, Woodfin Camp.

(opposite) The shrine of the Virgin of Guadalupe. Marc & Evelyne Bernheim, Woodfin Camp.

(top) Fruit and vegetable stand near Nonoalco. Marc & Evelyne Bernheim, Woodfin Camp.

(left) Woman scribe and client, Plaza de Santo Domingo. Marc & Evelyne Bernheim, Woodfin Camp.

(right) Snack stand. Marc & Evelyne Bernheim, Woodfin Camp.

(opposite) Courtyard of a house in the slum area of Vecindad. Marc & Evelyne Bernheim, Woodfin Camp.

(overleaf) Cityscape, Paseo de la Reforma. Thomas Hopker, Woodfin Camp.

THE PALESTINIANS, THE ARABS, AND THE JEWS

[FIGURE 4]

If Westerners applauded Israel's success in establishing a modern industrial and agricultural economy in an ancient and ravaged land, this view was not shared by the displaced Palestinians or their Arab supporters. In the Western view, Israel was a special case, the Jews a special and deserving people. Many felt guilty about the treatment Jews had received in Christian Europe; there was indeed a debt to be paid. After 2000 years of dispersal, the Jews had returned to their biblical home and revived a wasting and holy land to productive use. Initial support for Israel was based on a world conscience aroused by the tragedy of the concentration camps of World War II. This sentiment soon gave way, however, to admiration for the courage and determination of the Israelis in creating a permanent home against formidable odds. Ultimately, after twenty-five years, Israel remains a political reality, and the pragmatic leaders of Western states who themselves have reconciled differences with defeated enemies are puzzled by the continued intransigence of the Arabs and the bitter hostility of the Palestinians.

For the Arabs, Israel was a colonial nation created by Europeans during a time when Westerners were able to impose their culture on others and dispose of territory as they chose. Israelis were imperialists who, like the Crusaders before them, had occupied the homeland of the Arabs and had succeeded, at least temporarily, in dislodging the legitimate population of Palestine. Throughout the developing world, nations which in one fashion or another secured independence by driving out European colonialists are coming to compare Israel to the remaining white-ruled states of southern Africa. By the Palestinians, stateless, rejected, living as burdens in other Arab countries or as wards of the United Nations, Israelis are viewed as a foreign population occupying the land where they, the Palestinians, lived for 1400 years. For the Palestinians and the Israelis alike, the continuing conflict ultimately rests on their deep and unrelenting common attachment to the same land.

For twenty-five years, this impasse has persisted and gradually escalated into the current Arab-Israeli conflict. After the 1948 war, the Arab nations—humiliated in defeat—refused to absorb the 760,000 homeless Palestinian refugees because to do so would be to acknowledge the permanence of Israel. A few tens of thousands were permitted repatriation to Israel, but most Palestinians ended up in temporary United Nations refugee camps where they have lived for the last generation. Intermittently, Palestinian frustrations were vented by border raids into Israel. These were met by massive Israeli retaliation. In 1956, threatened by Nasser's nationalization of the Suez Canal, Israel joined France and Britain in an

invasion intended to return the canal to European control. Israeli armies swept across the Sinai and into Gaza, but under heavy pressure from the United States, all three nations were forced to abandon this adventure and return the invaded territories to Egypt. Over the next decade, Arab guerrilla raids increased, as did political confrontations between the Arabs and the Jews. Finally in 1967, when Nasser imposed a blockade on Israeli shipping through the Straits of Tiran at the southern tip of the Sinai Peninsula, Israel launched a preemptive strike on Egypt, Syria, and Jordan that resulted in a catastrophic defeat for Arab forces and the transformation of the political map of the eastern Mediterranean.

In six days of fighting during the June 1967 war, Israel occupied the Sinai Peninsula, the Gaza Strip, the Golan Heights in Syria, and the entire west bank of the Jordan River. An estimated 380,000 Arabs fled eastward across the Jordan, and Gaza's population diminished by 50,000. In 1971, 1.5 million Palestinians were registered as refugees with the United Nations, half of them in Jordan, a third in Gaza, and a quarter on the West Bank. In the occupied territories, 1 million Arabs were under Israeli administration and the area of the Jewish state had quadrupled in size. The Arabs protested to the United Nations; the United Nations passed resolutions. The Israelis, having secured safe borders, refused to withdraw and initiated an extensive building program in the occupied territories.

Forty-eight settlements were constructed in the vicinity of Jerusalem, including eleven on the west bank of the Jordan River. New roads, water reservoirs, and nineteen villages were built on the Golan Heights. In the Sinai, captured Egyptian oil wells were brought into production, and military settlements were founded in Gaza to increase security. Palestinian guerrilla activity took the form of terrorist attacks on isolated settlements, as the fedayeen, organized into the Palestine Liberation Organization (PLO), attempted to focus world attention on the issue. In October 1973, Syrian and Egyptian armies attacked Israel in the Sinai and Golan Heights. After bitter fighting, a cease-fire was signed with Israel still in control of the occupied territories. But the Arabs had fought creditably for the first time.

The October War and the oil embargo that followed revealed the growing political and military power of the Arab states. To cope with these new realities, the world's industrial nations embarked on efforts to reconcile the conflict between the Arabs, the Palestinians, and the Jews. At immediate issue were the seemingly unresolvable territorial disputes among five nations. The Arabs demanded return of all territories occupied in the 1967 war. Strong international support for their position was apparent when Yasir Arafat, the leader of the PLO, was allowed to speak for the Palestinian cause to the United Nations General Assembly.

For the Israelis, the creation of a Palestinian state on the West Bank poses a direct threat to national security; for the Palestinians, it is a minimal demand. The sparsely populated wastes of the Sinai Desert and the Golan Heights appear to be negotiable, but the city of Jerusalem remains a difficult emotional and symbolic issue. The Israelis annexed the Old City in 1967 and returned the Wailing Wall, Judaism's most sacred place of worship, to Jewish control for the first time in 2000 years. Also a religious center of Islam, the Arabs view Jerusalem as non-negotiable. Complicating this territorial search for peace in the Middle East are thirty-five years of bitterness generated in the struggle between the Palestinians and the Israelis for national identity on the same land.

Out of this quandary of international politics, religion, and culture, several irrefutable points arise. The first is that the historical and continuing attraction of Israel to the world Jewish community serves to underscore the spiritual viability of a physical state of Israel. Second, the protracted opposition of the Arabs to the creation of Israel in Palestine illuminates their view of Zionism as a foreign-inspired philosophy that has no place in the indigenous matrix of Middle Eastern society. Yet Israel, the creation of Zionism and British and United Nations indecisiveness in the Middle East, is a physical reality. And this reality, tenuous as it may be, creates and focuses the problems of the Middle East.

BIBLIOGRAPHY

GENERAL

Berger, Morroe. *The Arab World Today.* Garden City, N.Y.: Doubleday, 1962. A concise, informative paperback introduction to the modern Middle East.

Bill, James A., and Carl Leiden. *The Middle East: Politics and Power.* Boston: Allyn & Bacon, 1974. A fine volume on the nature of political systems in the modern Middle East.

Fisher, Sydney Nettleton. *The Middle East: A History.* New York: Knopf, 1968. An extremely well-written history of the Arabs from the rise of Islam to the modern period.

Fisher, W. B. *The Middle East: A Physical, Social and Regional Geography.* London: Methuen, 1971. The best detailed regional geography text available on the Middle East.

Taylor, Alice (ed.). *Focus on the Middle East.* New York: Praeger, 1971. Brief essays on the modern geography of the Middle East with excellent maps.

Van Nieuwenhuijze, C. A. O. *Sociology of the Middle East.* Leiden: Brill, 1971. A detailed theoretical analysis of the nature of Middle Eastern society.

[1] ISLAMIC MATRIX, CULTURAL MOSAIC

Gellner, Ernest, and Charles Micaud (eds.). *Arabs and Berbers: From Tribe to Nation in North Africa.* London: Duckworth, 1973. A superb collection of essays on the impact of change on Arabs and Berbers in North Africa.

Gibb, H. A. R. *Mohammedanism.* London: Oxford University Press, 1949. A brief introduction to Islam.

Hourani, Albert. *Minorities in the Arab World.* New York: Oxford University Press, 1947. Religious, linguistic, and political minorities of the central Middle East.

Planhol, Xavier de. *The World of Islam.* Ithaca: Cornell University Press, 1959. A speculative essay on the impact of Islam on the geography of the Middle East.

Shiloh, Ailon (ed.). *Peoples and Cultures of the Middle East.* New York: Random House, 1969. A study of contemporary peoples and cultures in the Middle East.

[2] THE TRADITIONAL MIDDLE EAST

Briggs, Lloyd Cabot. *Tribes of the Sahara.* Cambridge, Mass.: Harvard University Press, 1960. A fine volume on the tribal peoples of the Sahara.

Coon, Carleton S. *Caravan: The Story of the Middle East.* New York: Holt, Rinehart & Winston, 1958. An engaging description of the peoples and landscapes of the traditional Middle East.

Gibb, H. A. R., and Harold Bowen. *Islamic Society and the West,* Vols. 1 and 2. London: Oxford University Press, 1950, 1957. Traditional Muslim life in the eighteenth century and the early intrusion of the West.

Lawrence, T. E. *The Seven Pillars of Wisdom.* New York: Doubleday, 1935. The life of Lawrence of Arabia with the Bedouins.

Patai, Raphael. *Golden River to Golden Road.* Philadelphia: University of Pennsylvania Press, 1967. An anthropologist's view of traditional Middle Eastern culture and society.

[3] IMPERIALISM, NATIONALISM, AND INDEPENDENCE

Antoun, Richard, and Iliya Harik (eds.). *Rural Politics and Social Change in the Middle East.* Bloomington: Indiana University Press, 1972. Modern forces of change in the Middle Eastern village.

Brown, L. Carl (ed.). *From Madina to Metropolis.* Princeton: Darwin Press, 1973. A beautifully illustrated volume of articles dealing with the transformation of the traditional Middle Eastern city in modern times.

Clarke, J. I., and W. B. Fisher (eds.). *Populations of the Middle East and North Africa.* New York: Africana, 1972. A country survey of modern population growth and urbanization in the Middle East.

Clawson, Marion, Hans H. Landsberg, and Lyle T. Alexander. *The Agricultural Potential of the Middle East.* New York: American Elsevier, 1971. A survey of the environmental resources in the Middle East concluding that agricultural output can be tripled.

English, Paul Ward. *City and Village in Iran.* Madison: University of Wisconsin Press, 1966. A detailed study of city-village relationships in southern Iran outlining the Middle Eastern pattern of urban dominance of rural hinterlands.

Issawi, Charles (ed.). *The Economic History of the Middle East: 1800–1914.* Chicago: University of Chicago Press, 1966. A selection of original sources documenting the transition from medieval to modern economy and society in the Middle East.

Polk, William R., and Richard L. Chambers (eds.). *Beginnings of Modernization in the Middle East.* Chicago: University of Chicago Press, 1968. Excellent articles on the early impact of the West on traditional Middle Eastern society.

UNESCO. *The Problems of the Arid Zone.* Paris: UNESCO, 1962. The impact of modernization on Middle Eastern nomads.

Warriner, Doreen. *Land Reform and Development in the Middle East.* New York: Oxford University Press, 1962. A classic study of the introduction of land reform into Egypt, Syria, and Iraq.

[4] TWO PEOPLES, ONE LAND

Abu-Lughod, Ibrahim (ed.). *The Transformation of Palestine: Essays on the Origin and Development of the Arab-Israeli Conflict.* Evanston, Ill.: Northwestern University Press, 1971. An excellent collection of original articles supporting the Arab case in the conflict over Palestine.

Halpern, Ben. *The Idea of the Jewish State.* Cambridge, Mass.: Harvard University Press, 1961. The goals, ideals, and aspirations of Israel.

Lowdermilk, Walter C. "The Reclamation of a Man-Made Desert," *Scientific American,* Vol. 202 (1960), pp. 55–63. Israel's efforts to introduce modern agriculture into a badly eroded dry land environment.

Orni, E., and E. Efrat. *Geography of Israel.* Jerusalem: Israel Programs for Scientific Translations, 1964. A physical and historical geography of Israel.

Turki, Fawaz. *The Disinherited.* New York: Monthly Review Press, 1972. The exile of the Palestinians.

TROPICAL AFRICA

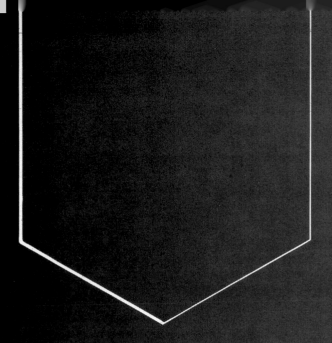

The conference to partition Africa convened in Berlin on November 13, 1884, and lasted three months. Fourteen nations, including every major European power, the Ottoman Empire, and the United States, debated the future of this continent, 2.2 million square miles larger than North America and three times the size of the United States. The specific political issue at hand was deepening Anglo-French rivalry in the Congo and West Africa; at stake, however, were the conflicting commercial and imperial ambitions of five major European powers—France, Germany, Great Britain, Portugal, and Belgium, or rather its king, Leopold.

Chancellor Otto von Bismarck of Germany, the most powerful political figure in Europe, called the meeting. He wished to further German interests in four widely scattered parts of Africa: Togoland, Cameroon, East Africa, and Southwest Africa. Jules Ferry of France arrived, intent on solidifying French claims in the Senegal Valley. Granville, the representative of Gladstone's government in Britain, spoke for free trade, since Britain's advanced industrial position gave the English a dominant hand in African commerce. Portugal already held the mouth of the Congo (and still dabbled in slavery). Five years of exploration by the American adventurer Henry Stanley had given 900,000 square miles of land in the Congo Basin to Leopold II, the king of the Belgians. The meeting was a charade, a colonial game, a paper partitioning of a little known part of the world. In 1884, over 90 percent of the continent was still under native rule, but no African was at the conference. Within twenty years, however, the game became a reality, and all but a tiny fraction of Africa was under European rule. The factors involved in this "scramble for Africa," as some historians call it, ranged from trivial personality conflicts between European politicians to the relentless European search for raw materials and markets in the developing world.

In the case at hand, friction between the British and the Germans had intensified after the Franco-Prussian War of 1870. Bismarck, the German chancellor, had no use for Gladstone, prime minister of Great Britain; Gladstone was, according to him, a man "fit only to chop down trees and make up speeches." But this might not have mattered, in Africa at least, had it not been for Granville's incompetence. In February 1883, Bismarck requested British support for a German commercial settlement in Africa at Angra Pequena on the barren coast of South-West Africa. Receiving no reply from the British, Bismarck repeated his request in December 1883. Granville dawdled for another six months while making vague allusions to British claims in the district. After an embarrassing exchange of messages between the two governments (which revealed that at least one British minister didn't know where Pequena was) Bismarck, piqued at the British, declared the territory under German sovereignty.

The scramble for Africa then began in earnest. Leopold sought treaties of annexation along the Lower Congo; French agents combed the Nigerian coast for territorial treaties. Britain sent consul E. H. Hewett on a treaty-making mission along the coast of West Africa, but the French and Germans had already secured "title" to the region: Hewett's efforts secured him his nickname, "Too-late Hewett."

It is not surprising, given this atmosphere of tension, competition, and conflict, that the resolutions of the Berlin Conference of 1884–1885 were never implemented. Conference resolutions I, II, and IV guaranteed freedom of trade and navigation on the Niger and the Congo rivers and the internationalization of the Congo Basin. In fact, the Congo became the private domain of Leopold II, and the British levied high tariffs on trade on the Niger. Resolutions VI and IX guaranteed the "preservation of the native tribes," the improvement of their "moral and material well-being," and forbade "trading in slaves" in the African interior. But within a very few years the Congo and the Niger became sites of extraordinary colonial brutality.

The Berlin Conference proved in the end to be a turning point in African affairs, a pivot that altered the spatial and economic environments of modern African societies. The catalyst in this process was embedded in resolution XXXV, which required "establishment of authority" and "effective occupation" as validation of European claims to African territories. This resolution intensified the scramble for Africa and sent adventurers, explorers, and government representatives speeding into uncharted regions in search of local rulers who could be bribed, coerced, or convinced to sign treaties. The British secured the island of Mussa off the coast of Libya for ten bags of rice. Mineral rights in the

Matabele territories in Central Africa cost a German industrial cartel $300 per month, 100 breech-loading rifles, and an armed steamer on the Zambezi River. On the Benue River in Nigeria, the French won a treaty from the emir of Muru by supplying him with troops to defeat his neighboring enemies. Out of such haphazard arrangements forged in haste, a continent of colonies emerged whose borders split tribal groups and dissected economic hinterlands, but whose territorial boundaries survived to form the spatial frame of independent Africa.

The European rationale for this imperial intrusion, the dual mandate, also emerged from the Berlin Conference. In this view, the new European rulers of Africa had two duties: first, to stop the slave trade and introduce the material and moral benefits of European civilization; and second, to make the trade and resources of Africa available to the rest of the world. Europeans, who for four centuries had been content to grope along the coastal fringes of the Dark Continent, delineated the spatial and social outlines of modern Africa in a brief half-century of conquest.

The transformation of Africa into a series of independent nation-states is the central theme of this section. In "The Dark Continent," four centuries of slavers, missionaries, and explorers introduce Africa to an avid European public. Based on images generated in this period and the driving need of industrializing countries for raw materials and markets, the scramble for Africa resulted in African subjugation and European settlement: "Colonialism." Although this period lasted only a half-century, the social, economic, and spatial parameters of the new nation-states of Africa were already set when "The Winds of Change" replaced colonies with independent states. In the south, however, Europeans remain in power, making the central issue in that part of the continent "A Question of Color."

215

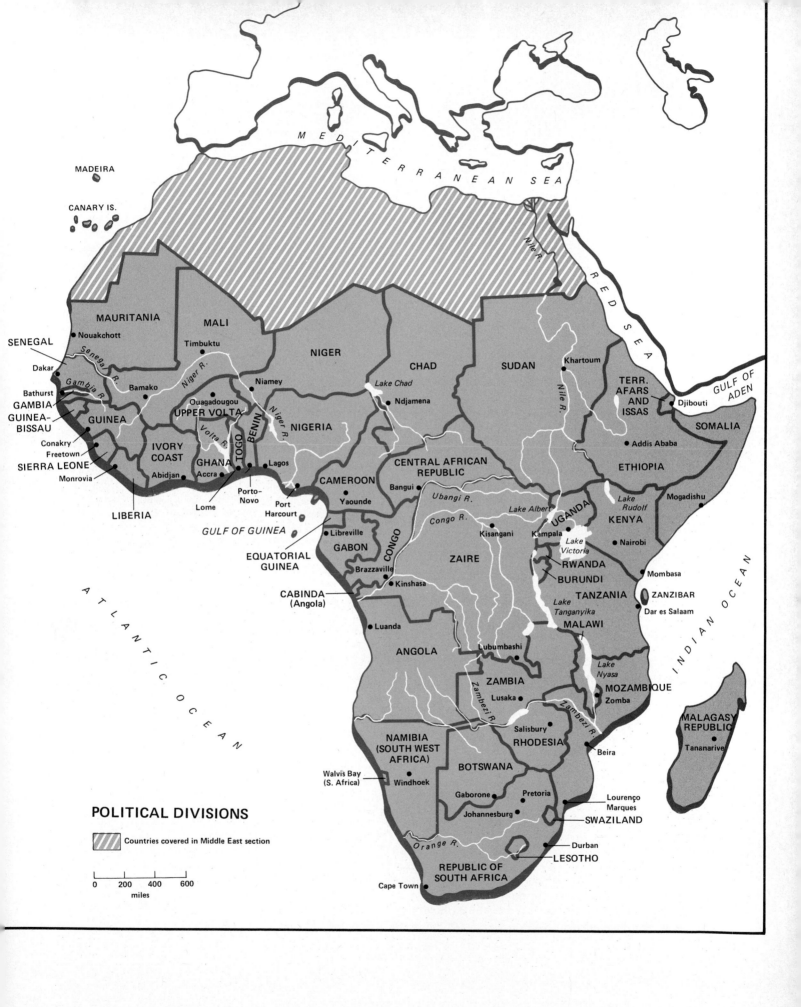

MEDITERRANEAN SEA

MADEIRA

CANARY IS.

SENEGAL
Dakar
Bathurst
GAMBIA
GUINEA-
BISSAU
Conakry
Freetown
SIERRA LEONE
Monrovia
LIBERIA

MAURITANIA
Nouakchott
Senegal R.
Gambia R.
GUINEA
IVORY
COAST
Abidjan

MALI
Timbuktu
Bamako
Niger R.
Ouagadougou
UPPER VOLTA
GHANA
Accra
Lome
Porto-
Novo
Port
Harcourt

Niamey
Volta R.
TOGO
BENIN
Niger R.
NIGERIA
Lagos

NIGER

CHAD
Lake Chad
Ndjamena

CAMEROON
Yaounde

EQUATORIAL
GUINEA

GULF OF GUINEA

Libreville
GABON
CONGO
Brazzaville
Kinshasa

CABINDA
(Angola)

Luanda

ATLANTIC OCEAN

CENTRAL AFRICAN
REPUBLIC
Bangui
Ubangi R.
Congo R.
Kisangani

ZAIRE

Lake Albert
UGANDA
Kampala
Lake
Victoria
RWANDA
BURUNDI
Lake
Tanganyika

SUDAN
Khartoum
Nile R.

Nile R.

TERR.
AFARS
AND
ISSAS
Djibouti
SOMALIA
Addis Ababa
ETHIOPIA

Lake
Rudolf
KENYA
Nairobi
Mombasa

TANZANIA
Dar es Salaam
ZANZIBAR

RED SEA

GULF OF
ADEN

Mogadishu

INDIAN OCEAN

ANGOLA

Lubumbashi

ZAMBIA
Lusaka
Zambezi R.

MALAWI
Lake
Nyasa

MOZAMBIQUE
Zomba

Zambezi R.
Salisbury
RHODESIA
Beira

NAMIBIA
(SOUTH WEST
AFRICA)

Walvis Bay
(S. Africa)
Windhoek

BOTSWANA

Gaborone
Johannesburg

Orange R.

Cape Town

Pretoria
Lourenço
Marques
SWAZILAND

Durban
LESOTHO

REPUBLIC OF
SOUTH AFRICA

MALAGASY
REPUBLIC
Tananarive

POLITICAL DIVISIONS

Countries covered in Middle East section

0   200   400   600
miles

THE DARK CONTINENT
1

Despite the proximity of Africa to Europe, the Dark Continent remained obscure to the European mind well into the nineteenth century. A combination of **environmental** and economic circumstances produced Europe's ignorance of Africa. In the north, the Islamic world, stretching from Morocco to the Asian interior, had served for centuries as a barrier between the peoples of Europe and of **tropical** Africa. Although the products of Africa—principally gold, ivory, and slaves—were highly prized in the Mediterranean, the routes of commerce across the Sahara Desert were controlled by the Muslims of North Africa and the Sudan. For Africans in the tropics, the stimulus for the Saharan trade was salt, a commodity not found in West Africa but plentiful in the Sahara. The exchange was effected by Barbary traders, who carried salt southward from desert mines to Timbuktu and traded it in that city's bazaars for gold, kola nuts, ostrich feathers, ivory, ebony, and slaves. All these products were of high value in the marketplaces of the Mediterranean, but barred by Muslims from direct contact with these African natives, the Europeans remained distant and envious consumers of Africa's exotic wealth, so uninformed that they incorrectly believed a great semimythical Christian kingdom, the land of Prester John, lay south of the Islamic Sahara.

EARLY EUROPEAN CONTACTS

It was not until the fifteenth century that direct European contact with tropical Africa by sea became technically possible. Once possible, the struggle for African commodities, and eventually territory, was on. A visionary member of the Portuguese royal family, Prince Henry the Navigator, became convinced that well-constructed ships could sail down the West African coast and then eastward to the Indies. Previously no European vessel had dared voyage beyond Cape Bojador, 200 miles south of Morocco, because trade winds blowing steadily to the south and west for most of the year pushed venturesome ships into the oblivion of the South Atlantic. No way was known to get back north. After considerable experimentation by the scholars and mariners assembled by Prince Henry, they developed the **caravel,** a vessel equipped with triangular lateen sails that could carry the Portuguese beyond the African bulge and tack into the winds to bring them back again. In 1446, the Senegal River was reached; the Gold Coast was visited by 1475. Contact with the Kingdom of the Kongo (the modern Congo region) was established in 1483, and five years later Bartholomeu Diaz rounded the Cape of Good Hope. But Portuguese mariners discovered few natural ports or harbors on the west coast of Africa, and most trade was carried out by ships anchored offshore at the mouths of rivers.

During the next four centuries, from the time of these early Portuguese contacts to the late nineteenth century, European traders conducted business on the coastal fringes of the Dark Continent, while the interior of Africa remained a mystery. The early traders—Portuguese, Dutch, British, and French—constructed forts and trading posts at key points along the west coast of Africa from Mauritania to southern Angola. Inland from these "factories," as they have been called, a web of trading partnerships introduced European trade goods to ever-enlarging **hinterlands** from Senegal to Angola, encompassing the market structure of two-thirds of the African population. Over time, New World crops (corn and manioc), cloth goods, metals, and firearms diffused throughout a wide area of sub-Saharan Africa. In the interior, leaders of highly organized agricultural peoples vied for control of economic hinterlands and the trade routes along which gold and slaves flowed to the coast. Cooperation between native African kingdoms and European traders required a European coastal presence only. But even if economic motives had attracted Europeans to the African interior, physical deterrents to such penetration were formidable.

The interior of most of Africa is a plateau flanked by coastal lowlands; less than 10 percent of the continent lies at elevations below 500 feet, a smaller coastal fringe than on any other continent. Only a limited amount of Africa can be explored by river canoes, the simplest means of transport, because great waterfalls and **cataracts** occur along sharp breaks in elevation not far inland. Bypassing these river barriers by portage and pack animals was difficult because of the dangers posed to men and animals by the disease-carrying tsetse fly, endemic to the tropical forests of the African lowland. Thus, any trading expedition entering the African interior not only risked hostile tribes jealous of their trading rights, but also had to be large enough to carry all goods by hand.

In the early seventeenth century, long before the great scramble for territory, the Dutch had joined the Portuguese in a struggle for maritime control along the West African coast. These Dutch ambassadors are welcomed by King Alvaro II of Kongo. *Photo:* New York Public Library Picture Collection.

Beyond physical obstacles, perhaps the single most important factor that discouraged European entry into the African interior was disease, specifically malaria, dengue fever, and yellow fever. Africa developed a well-deserved reputation as the "white man's grave" because of the extraordinarily high death rate among Europeans. A song of the time warned sailors to beware the Bight of Benin because "for every one that comes out, forty go in." Some 40 to 60 percent of newcomers from Europe died during their first year of residence in Africa. For all these reasons, Europeans stayed out and stayed ignorant. *Cartographers** labeled the interior of Africa as "uninhabited," meaning that only Africans lived there. African societies, African people formed an unknown mass, objects of trade until slavery was abolished and invisible thereafter.

THE ATLANTIC SLAVE TRADE
In 1517, Bartolomé de Las Casas, a Spanish priest from Haiti known as the Apostle of the Indies, returned to Spain to plead with the king for the lives of the Carib Indians, a once-proud Caribbean people who had risen in revolt and been crushed by the Spaniards twenty-two years earlier. In the mines and plantations of New Spain, the Carib had been decimated by disease and forced labor and were rapidly dying off. As an act of mercy, Las Casas convinced Charles V of Spain to import black slaves into America, at a rate of twelve per colonist, to replace the Carib in the fields and mines of the New World. In response, the Spanish king granted an import license, the infamous *asiento* (assent), to a favorite courtier entitling him to import 4000 slaves into the West Indies. In the next year, 1518, a cargo of slaves was shipped from the Guinea coast to Haiti and the Atlantic slave trade began.

Actually, the taking of slaves from Africa had been going on sporadically since the first Portuguese vessel rounded Cape Blanc off the north coast of Mauritania in 1441 and returned with twelve blacks as a gift for Prince Henry the Navigator. Three years later, in 1444, a fleet of six Portuguese vessels raided the Moroccan coast and brought back a profitable cargo of 235 men, women, and children, who were sold in European cities for use in domestic service, in the fields, and on ships. By the turn of the century an estimated 3500 slaves were imported annually from the West African coast to the slave markets of Portugal and Spain. In the 1550s, the traffic became so heavy that an official census of Lisbon listed slaves as 10 percent of the total population.

Even the practice of importing black slaves for the economic development of new territories had precedent. In the Canary and Cape Verde islands, and on São Tomé and Principe in the Gulf of Guinea, slaves were imported from the African mainland to tend vineyards, sugar fields, and orchards on Spanish and Portuguese plantations. But it was the Atlantic trade that opened up an almost infinite market for human cargoes from Africa, a 400-year episode in human brutality which denied any standard except profit and loss and numbed the hearts of all who participated—trader, sailor, and slave alike.

African Slaves in the New World
[FIGURE 1]
Las Casas proved correct: black slaves from Africa were better able to survive the pressure of work under Spanish overseers in the New World than American Indians, who lacked immunity to common Old World diseases and died in a series of devastating imported epidemics of measles, smallpox, typhus, and yellow fever. Available statistics suggest that the death rate among blacks was only one-third that among American natives. As a result, African slaves became an economic solution to the labor shortage in the Americas, and gangs of blacks working under military discipline provided the muscle needed for large-scale production of tobacco, sugar, rice, and later cotton. By 1515, twenty-five years after Columbus's historic voyage to the New World, the first cargo of slave-grown sugar was shipped from the West Indies to Spain.

The need for manpower to expand New World production intensified, and so did the demand for African slaves. Between 1600 and 1650, Spanish and Portuguese colonies in the Americas imported an estimated 7300 slaves each year. The first ship

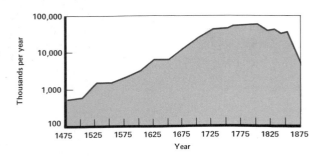

Figure 1. Slave Imports to the New World, 1475–1875. Some ten million African slaves were imported to the New World during the four centuries of the Atlantic slave trade. The traffic reached its peak in the eighteenth century but did not decline appreciably until the middle of the nineteenth. *Adapted from:* Philip D. Curtin, *The Atlantic Slave Trade: A Census.* Madison: University of Wisconsin Press, 1969, p. 266, Fig. 26. Figure by UN Cartographic Lab. Copyright © 1969 by the Regents of the University of Wisconsin.

arrived in British North America a year before the *Mayflower*. Thereafter, competitive French and British economic interests in the New World doubled the rate of importation to 14,700 per year between 1650 and 1675, 28,000 per year from 1675 to 1700, and 45,000 per year by 1720. By the third quarter of the eighteenth century, 65,500 slaves a year were being drained from the African continent for enforced labor in the Americas. After 1810, the slave trade began to decline and after 1840, dropped sharply. By 1870, slaving was illegal in the Western world and except for a minor amount of smuggling, ceased to exist. All told, nearly 10 million Africans worked as slaves in the Americas; it was the largest enforced migration in history. Probably three times as many were actually abducted into slavery but died before reaching America—on the brutal journey from the African interior to the coast, in the slave pens of the coastal factories, below deck on the notorious six- to ten-week middle passage across the Atlantic, or in rebellion against their captors.

From 1650 on, Africans outnumbered Europeans in the New World. Approximately half the African slaves brought to the New World were sent to the Caribbean and another third were imported to Brazil. Less than one in twenty, a recorded 399,000, arrived in the United States. For reasons that are not clearly understood, slaves in the United States achieved a low death rate and a relatively high birth rate very early, so that by the middle of the eighteenth century, the already existing slave population in North America was increasing rapidly apart from new imports. In the Caribbean and Brazil, however, a high death rate and high labor demands on these regions' expanding sugar and coffee plantations continuously required new cargoes of slaves. Disease rates were higher in the tropics, and planters, pre-

THE MIDDLE PASSAGE

Two schools of thought existed among the slaving captains of the Guinea coast: some preferred "loose packing," others "tight packing." The latter, who came to ascendancy after 1750, argued that by packing slaves as tightly as possible into the cargo holds of their schooners, the net receipts of each voyage were higher despite the higher mortality rate among the slaves. A survey conducted by a Captain Parrey of the Royal Navy showed that each captain "made the most of the room available" even to drawing miniature black figures on ships' plans to illustrate the most effective method of packing in the human cargo.

On the Brookes, which Captain Parrey considered to be typical, every man was allowed a space six feet long by sixteen inches wide (and usually about two feet, seven inches high); every woman, a space five feet, ten inches long by sixteen inches wide; every boy, five feet by fourteen inches; every girl, four feet, six inches by twelve inches. The Brookes was a vessel of 320 tons. By the law of 1788 it was permitted to carry 454 slaves, and the chart, which later became famous, showed how and where 451 of them could be stowed away. Captain Parrey failed to see how the captain could find room for three more. Nevertheless, Parliament was told by reliable witnesses, including Dr. Thomas Trotter, formerly surgeon of the Brookes, that before the new law was passed she had carried 600 slaves on one voyage and 609 on another.

A typical day during the six-to-ten-week passage across the Atlantic was as follows:

If the weather was clear, [the slaves] were brought on deck at eight o'clock in the morning. The men were attached by their leg irons to the great chain that ran along the bulwarks on both sides of the ship; the women and half-grown boys were allowed to wander at will. About nine o'clock the slaves were served their first meal of the day. . . .

After the morning meal came a joyless ceremony called "dancing the slaves." . . . Dancing was prescribed as a therapeutic measure, a specific against suicidal melancholy, and also against scurvy—although in the latter case it was a useless torture for men with swollen limbs. While sailors paraded the deck, each with a cat-o'-nine-tails in his right hand, the men slaves "jumped in their irons" until their ankles were bleeding flesh. . . . Music was provided by a slave thumping on a broken drum or an upturned kettle. . . .

While some of the sailors were dancing the slaves, others were sent below to scrape and swab out the sleeping rooms. It was a sickening task. . . .

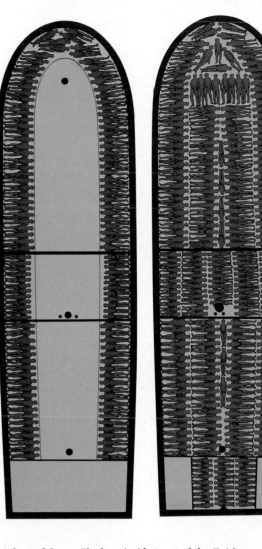

Adapted from: Clarkson's *Abstract of the Evidence,* 1791.

At three or four in the afternoon the slaves were fed their second meal, often a repetition of the first. . . . That second meal was the end of their day. As soon as it was finished they were sent below. . . .

In squalls or rainy weather, the slaves were never brought on deck. They were served their two meals in the hold, where the air became too thick and poisonous to breath. . . . Not surprisingly, the slaves often went mad. . . . Men who went insane might be flogged to death, to make sure that they were not malingering. . . .

Source: Quoted from Daniel P. Mannix and Malcolm Cowley, *Black Cargoes: A History of the Atlantic Slave Trade, 1518–1865.* New York: Viking Press, London: A D Peters & Co., Ltd., 1962, pp. 107, 113–116. Copyright © 1962 by Daniel Mannix. All rights reserved. Reprinted by permission of the Viking Press, Inc., and A D Peters & Co., Ltd.

ferring men for heavy field work, imported two men for every woman. The number of new births was therefore halved, children were not numerous, and with an infant mortality rate of 40 to 50 percent, the slave population could not be maintained without additional imports. It was also a matter of economics: buying new slaves was cheaper than improving the health and family lives of existing slaves. At the beginning of the eighteenth century, a slave cost the same as sixteen muskets or 600 pounds of raw sugar on the London market. In addition, newly arrived slaves were more easily manipulated than indigenous veterans; even minor infractions committed by slaves were punished by castration or the removal of half a foot. Since the black slave population far outnumbered white planters, maintenance of control through terror was considered an essential policy.

The Middle Passage
[TABLE 1]

For traders, the mass transport of human cargoes from West Africa to the Americas was simply one leg of a triangular trade among Europe, Africa, and the New World. European manufactured goods were sold in Africa for slaves; slaves were brought to the Americas (the middle passage in this network) and sold for sugar, tobacco, and rum. These products of the New World were then sold in the United States or Europe, and the expedition set sail again. Profits were made by investors in Lisbon and Spain, by their counterparts in France and England, and by New World planters. In addition, the entrepreneurs directly involved—the slaving captains, traders on the African coast, and African kings in the interior— made high profits. In 1827 Captain Theodore Canot, a slaver on the Guinea coast of Africa, loaded 220 slaves on the Cuban schooner *La Fortunata* for consignment to Havana. The balance sheet of this slaving voyage shows that only three slaves died in the middle passage and that the survivors, purchased in Africa for $55 apiece, were sold in Havana for $357 each, netting the vessel's Cuban owners a tidy profit at 104 percent. It is not surprising that so lucrative an enterprise brought its practitioners no social censure.

But the risks of slaving were high, too. Slaving parties in the African interior, attacked by competing tribes on the long routes to the coast, frequently

TABLE 1. The Economics of Slavery: Balance Sheet of a Slaving Voyage by *La Fortunata*

Source: Daniel P. Mannix and Malcolm Cowley, *Black Cargoes: A History of the Atlantic Slave Trade, 1518–1865*. New York: Viking Press, 1962, p. 199.

EXPENSES OUT	
Buying and fitting out a 90-ton schooner	$6200
Provisions for crew and slaves	1115
Cargo (to be exchanged for slaves)	10,900
Advance on wages	1340
Hush money	200
	19,755
Commission on this at 5%	987
Total expenses out	$20,742
EXPENSES BACK	
Head money on slaves (for officers of schooner)	$3492
Wages, officers and crew	2938
Total expenses back	$6430
EXPENSES IN HAVANA	
Bribes to government officers (at $8 per slave)	$1736
Factor's commission	5565
Consignees' commission	3873
Slave dresses (217 at $2 each)	434
Extra expenses of all kinds	1200
Total expenses in Havana	$12,808
Total of all expenses	$39,980
RETURNS	
Vessel sold at auction	$3950
Proceeds of 217 slaves	77,469
Total returns	$81,419
Net profit on voyage	$41,439

ended up as cargo themselves. European traders on the coast died of malaria and drunkenness—poorly paid, illiterate men unable to build lives in their native countries. On the ships themselves, seamen died in the middle passage of scurvy and tropical diseases at rates higher than their captive slaves. On nine voyages for which full records were kept, 11 percent of the sailors but only 6.5 percent of the slaves died. Toward the end of the 1700s, more than one-fifth of the seamen on slave ships out of Bristol and Liverpool died in passage; fully one-half never returned to Britain.

Slaves were money: Nets were slung around the vessels to make suicide more difficult; minimum water and medical treatment were afforded. It is reckoned that about one of every eight slaves died on ship before reaching port—in the holds beneath decks, thrown overboard for suspected smallpox, whipped to death for attempting to escape, or victims of the "fixed melancholy," refusing to eat or to live. It was a despicable and degrading business, a commerce that altered the human geography of both the Americas and Africa.

THE SLAVE TRADE IN AFRICA

Europeans did not start the slave trade. It had existed in Africa for centuries before the Portuguese ever sailed southward along the West African coast. African groups had sold slaves to each other and exported slaves to the Mediterranean world and to Asia at least 1000 years before the birth of Christ. Nor did European slaving expeditions comb the African interior in search of manpower for the plantation economy of the Americas. Topography, disease, and African trading policies restricted Europeans to the coastal margins of the continent. Only one or two of every hundred slaves shipped to the New World were actually captured by Europeans; the rest were caught, transported, and sold into slavery by fellow Africans.

Nor were the Africans who profited from the growth of the Atlantic slave trade in any sense "primitive" peoples. All of West Africa, from the coast to the grasslands of the interior, was populated by thriving agricultural societies ruled by kings in centrally organized states. The West African kingdoms were part of a trading region that linked West Africa with the Sudan, the Sahara, and North Africa beyond. It was to these states that European ships came filled with trade goods to exchange for slaves; and African kings entered into partnership with slave traders, lured by the products of industrializing Europe. This introduction of the commercial and industrial revolutions to Africa is comparable to what happened in other parts of the developing world, although the legalized, international trade in people that evolved was particularly vicious. In Africa as elsewhere, Europeans opened up new commercial horizons, reorganized internal political and commercial networks, and introduced an abundance of new goods, techniques, and ideas.

The Atlantic Trade System

The arrival of European traders in West Africa meant that the old Islamic trans-Saharan trade links were bypassed. The Sahara diminished in importance as north-south trade declined; West and Central African products could be directly transported to European markets by Europeans. Previously, the centers of economic activity in West Africa lay in the interior, where powerful groups like the Kanem-Bornu of Lake Chad and the Songhai and the Hausa states of the Niger controlled crossroads locations where the products and people of tropical Africa converged for transshipment northward to market centers in the ***Maghrib.**** States near the west coast were peripheral to this Sudan trading network by reason of distance. With the emergence of Atlantic commerce, however, the coastal regions became centers of a new, important commercial system. This directional shift in the economy of West Africa never completely destroyed the vitality of the interior trading network, but the flow of goods to the Atlantic coast increased and that northward across the Sahara diminished.

The Atlantic trade system centered on eight major *entrepôt*• regions where natural transportation routes provided relatively easy access to interior hinterlands. Two of these trade regions were located on the northern Atlantic coast: at the mouth of the Senegal River, goods flowed to the coast from the interior of what are modern Mauritania and eastern Mali; several hundred miles to the south a similar trade center existed in the islands off the mouth of the Gambia River. For the next 1000 miles eastward along the African coast beyond Sierra Leone, trade was intermittent and trading stations were few until the Gold Coast (modern Ghana), where twenty-seven different European outposts were established along 220 miles of coastline. Some of these stations were elaborate fortresses such as Elmina, to which the Portuguese brought 600 artisans and workers in 1481 to construct a massive stone fort designed to protect the flow of gold from its source among the Ashanti in the interior. Other trading posts were simple houses and storage buildings flanked by heavily fenced pens holding slaves awaiting shipment.

Although trade was heavy along the entire coast of the Gulf of Guinea, four major trading centers can be discerned. The Gold Coast was a natural outlet for goods from the Volta River Basin in the interior, the eastern sections of the Ivory Coast, and western Togo. The bulk of the early slave trade filtered from eastern Togo, Benin, and western Nigeria to the port cities of the Slave Coast: Ouidah, Ardrah, and Lagos. The next major trade center was located at the *delta*• of the Niger, the so-called Oil Rivers, which tapped the wealth of the upper reaches of the Niger and Benue rivers. Finally, along the Bight of Biafra east of the Niger delta, the easternmost trade center of West Africa was located at the mouth of the Calabar River.

European-oriented trade was limited along the next 700 miles of the African coast as it veers southward along the shores of southern Cameroon, Rio Muni, and Gabon. Farther south, two coastal trade complexes located at the mouth of the Congo and stretching southward to Luanda in Angola carried on a rich trade with the organized states of central Africa. South of Luanda, the coast merges into the dry Namib Desert, a poor, thinly populated region that held little interest for European traders.

The products of Europe flowed through these eight major trading regions into the most densely populated sections of Africa. Manufactured cloth, metal goods, knives, brass kettles, copper and iron bars, rum, brandy, tobacco, and firearms and gunpowder passed through the hands of one African king to another from hundreds of colonial trading stations. The most significant innovations, however, were New World crops: corn entered the Congo in the sixteenth century and by 1900 covered the cultivated

lands of the *savanna*• grasslands and some converted forests in the Congo Basin; manioc entered Angola after 1600 and by 1853 was cultivated in Rhodesia.

Over a long period of time, African societies became dependent on these imports and foreign-derived foods. In parts of the Gold Coast, for example, native metal working declined because of the steady source of inexpensive European axes, hoes, and knives; the same was true of cloth weaving. More socially disruptive, however, were the African rulers who came to rely on the wealth of merchandise passing through their kingdoms—the luxury goods that attracted loyal retainers and the firearms that enabled Africans to participate in the European trade as vendors of slaves rather than as human merchandise.

As the demand for slaves in the Americas focused European interest in African trade on this sole export, the social, political, and economic life of West Africa became dependent on a steady outflow of human cargo. The area between Senegal and southern Angola produced roughly 80 to 85 percent of all the slaves exported to the New World, but fluctuations in trading conditions, prices, and changing local politics were so complex that it is difficult to reconstruct an accurate economic geography of the area. In Benin, for example, the slave trade was a tightly controlled royal monopoly upon which the state was almost completely dependent. In the Senegal Valley, the Futa Toro tribe were never slavers or enslaved, but they profited by taxing shipments of slaves passing through their territory. In the Niger delta, a series of city-states like Bonny, divided into trading houses based on family ties, operated armed war canoes with as many as a hundred oarsmen whose object was to penetrate the interior to collect slaves for export. In Nigeria one subgroup of the Ibo people, the Aro, converted a traditional system of religious belief into a sacrifice of men offered in export through complex trading networks to European interests on the coast. The Aro system was so effective that the Bight of Biafra, as the Nigerian coast is known, was the origin of only 2 percent of all slaves exported in the 1720s, whereas the area provided 42 percent a century later.

The vast majority of slaves, however, were captured in intertribal wars. In the view of some observers, native warfare increased dramatically with the introduction of firearms, which may have pre-

Two of the legendary figures of the period of European exploration of Africa—Livingstone and Stanley—are shown here in a drawing made by a *Harper's Weekly* artist for the August 31, 1872, issue from sketches supplied by Stanley. It was the missionary Livingstone rather than entrepreneurs or soldiers who crossed Africa from the west coast at Luanda to the mouth of the Zambesi on the east. *Photo:* New York Public Library Picture Collection.

cipitated a gun-slave cycle, where native people were provided with arms, arms were used to enslave enemy tribes for a profit, and the profit bought more guns and increased dominance. This certainly occurred in Benin, which derived its wealth and power almost exclusively from the slave trade; elsewhere the evidence is ambiguous.

The Impact of Slaving on Africa

The long-term impact of the slave trade on Africa is equally difficult to discern. Only two areas, Angola on the west coast and Mozambique on the east, show any evidence that this massive export of human beings caused extensive depopulation. In West Africa, which produced the largest number of slaves between 1700 and 1850, the slave trade may simply have drawn off a population increase that could not have been locally supported given the existing economy and technology of the region. Paradoxically, then, although 30 million of the healthiest people of Africa were withdrawn from their societies over four centuries, there is little evidence that this had any extended impact on the **demography** of the continent.

The effects of the slave trade on African politics and economics are more direct but equally contradictory. Some states and peoples were literally elim-

inated by the slave trade, but others like the Ashanti and the Yoruba rose to prominence, at least in part through the wealth generated in the Atlantic trade. Poorly organized societies like the Ibo suffered the greatest losses; highly structured societies like Benin, the least. One effect cannot be denied. As the tentacles of the slave trade reached deep into the continent, distrust, fear, and warfare were generated among the peoples of Africa. Already culturally fragmented into 264 Sudanic languages, 182 Bantu languages, and 47 Nilo-Saharan languages, Africans were further alienated from one another by the terror associated with the trade in lives.

The most enduring effects of the slave trade on Africa and its people may have been psychological, strongly influencing the concepts Africans hold of each other, the separate history of black Americans, black people elsewhere, and the European perception of Africans. White prejudices, supported by a weak body of pseudoscientific literature, were generated by a basic ignorance of the societies and environments of Africa. Tales abounded of tribes of 6-inch men in the Congo Basin, of savagery, cannibalism, and human degradation. But more actively, these deeply rooted notions of African inferiority were produced by the Atlantic slave trade, which selectively supported the vision of Africans as "the most ignorant and unpolished people in the world" through relations based solely on the price of a human being. When the slave trade finally became both distasteful and unprofitable in nineteenth-century Europe and America, it was a curious distortion of these biases that laid the foundation for European conquest. Explorers seeking the unknown and the unusual penetrated the interior in search of the fable; missionaries came to enlighten the "savages" by spreading the precepts of Christianity and the benefits of Western civilization.

EXPLORERS AND MISSIONARIES

The classical period of the exploration of Africa by Europeans opened with the journey of the explorer Robert Bruce to the highlands of Ethiopia in 1769 and ended 104 years later with the death of the missionary David Livingstone near Lake Bangweulu in East Africa. When Bruce left Massaua on the Red Sea coast to climb the **escarpment**· into the kingdom of Abyssinia (Ethiopia), the African interior was virtually unknown to Europeans. Bruce was first an explorer and second a geographer, a huge Scotsman drawn to Africa by curiosity. His goal was to discover the source of the Nile, and though he failed in this purpose, his writings fired the imagination of Europe, which in the late eighteenth century had embarked upon a new age of adventure and exploration. His example initiated a series of explorations by men who, like Bruce, were obsessed with the drama and glory of conquering the Dark Continent and played a significant part in opening up Africa to the Western world.

The "Discovery" of West Africa

In 1788, a dining club called the Association for Promoting the Discovery of the Interior Parts of Africa was formed by twelve wealthy English gentlemen who, intrigued by the unknown, joined together to solve the riddle of the Niger River—to identify its source, the direction of its flow, and whether it ended in an interior lake or was the same river known on the coast. The club's first four expeditions were disasters, but the fifth, led by Mungo Park, succeeded in establishing that the Niger flowed eastward. More explorers were lost before cartographers could delineate with confidence the major features of the West African interior. Hugh Clapperton, a Scottish seaman, crossed the Sahara and discovered Lake Chad. Alexander Laing reached the fabled city of Timbuktu in 1825; the Frenchman René Caillie arrived there two years later. The acclaim for these heroic journeys even penetrated the corridors of Cambridge University, where a young scholar named Alfred Tennyson won the chancellor's Gold Medal in 1829 for his verse on Timbuktu, the trading capital of Saharan Africa.

As questions concerning the topography of the lands of the Niger were answered, impetus for continued exploration of the African interior came from a new motivation: the evangelical movement in Europe to abolish slavery in Africa. This humanitarian goal was accomplished in England in 1772. In a historic decision, Lord Chief Justice Mansfield freed a fugitive slave named James Somerset on the basis that "as soon as any slave sets foot on English ground he becomes free." But slavery was still prac-

ticed in the American colonies and in Africa. As moral sentiment to suppress slavery grew in Europe, penetration of the African interior was deemed essential to eliminate the slave trade at its source.

Slavery was abolished in all British colonies in 1833; later that year an elaborate expedition fitted out with two steamships sailed up the Niger River for the purpose of eliminating slavery. Aboard was a variety of merchants and traders who supported the new effort to open up Africa to the West; they sought trade in palm oil, ivory, and wild rubber to fill the economic void created by the decline of slavery. The expedition ended in disaster (thirty-eight of forty-seven Europeans died of disease), as did a similar expedition eight years later. But by the 1850s, the discovery of the antimalarial properties of quinine greatly enhanced the life span of European explorers in Africa. Thereafter, a number of expeditions established British consulates and private commercial stations on the lower Niger and French missions in Senegal and the upper Niger. Western Africa was by now relatively well known to Europe, and trading depots were proliferating along the three great rivers of the region—the Senegal, Gambia, and Niger—thus setting the stage for the conflicts of interest that would emerge at the Berlin Conference.

Exploration of East Africa

Somewhat the same complex of events and motives opened up East Africa to nineteenth-century Europe. Richard Burton, an erratic and learned man, published his account of a dangerous expedition across Somaliland to the unknown city of Harar. Shortly thereafter, accompanied by J. H. Speke, he traveled inland from the island of Zanzibar to Lake Tanganyika, igniting the celebrated controversy between these two radically different men about the source of the Nile. Speke returned to Africa to prove, along with Baker and Stanley, that Lake Victoria was the ultimate source of the Nile, riveting the attention of contemporary Europe on a part of Africa which until then had been remote from European interests.

But an even more serious motive than geographical curiosity brought the greatest of the African explorers, David Livingstone, to East Africa; he believed in the redemption and conversion of Africa to Christianity. After eight years of missionary activity in what is now Botswana, Livingstone moved on, crossing the Kalahari Desert in 1849 in search of the rich agricultural lands of the interior of east-central

ON THE PROBLEMS OF BEING AN AFRICAN EXPLORER

Tropical Africa was a terrain for walking and river navigation. Mungo Park was the first to test what this involved. Park's preparations included a servant, a horse, provisions for two days, a change of linen, an umbrella and a "small assortment of beads, amber and tobacco" as trade goods for barter. His instruments consisted of a pocket sextant, a compass and a thermometer. His armament was two fowling pieces and two pairs of pistols. One of his qualifications for the assignment was that he spoke Mandingo. His plan was to purchase food and shelter with his trade goods as he advanced. He quickly found that the price of his laissez passer from successive chiefs was very high, and that virtually everything a white man had was plunder to the impoverished natives. At Jong half his stores were taken, at Koonitang half of what remained was taken by the chiefs of the territories through which he went; finally he himself became the prisoner of the "moors" or Fulani who robbed him of his horse and compass. Here was the first lesson of African travel over any distance: how did one retain enough of one's stores to get any distance, for the exactions laid on travellers were so heavy from the outset that one soon became a pauper. Park was reduced to selling the buttons off his rags to buy food.

The white traveller proved to be not only a walking store of wealth to be stripped, but a store of technical knowledge to be exploited. Park was only the first explorer in Africa to be ordered to mend the broken guns and other imported European gadgets for his hosts who lacked the skills to do so. Park also learned to live off little but his curiousity value for four years. He brought back the information that the Niger flowed eastwards.

Source: **Quoted from Roy Lewis and Yvonne Foy, *The British in Africa*. London: Weidenfeld & Nicolson, 1971, pp. 32–34.**

Africa to open up new fields of missionary activity. For the next fifteen years, Livingstone tramped across Africa from Luanda on the west coast to the mouth of the Zambezi River on the east. He was the only explorer to reject what he called "the stupid prejudice against color" and the first missionary to bring the sufferings of the African people to the attention of Europeans.

What Livingstone embodied were the three great motives and rationales for the European conquest of Africa: curiosity, Christianity, and commerce. As a result, his influence on the course of African history was immense. His explorations attracted interest to possibilities of economic ventures in the fertile reaches of the Zambezi River. The population of the Zambezi at that time was being ravaged by slave raids organized by Arab and Indian traders from the island of Zanzibar and the adjacent African coast. As Livingstone put it, "Africa is bleeding out her life's blood at every pore."

This eastern slave trade, although smaller in volume (total exports, 2 million Africans) than the defunct Atlantic trade, was similarly organized. Native leaders bought cloth, metal goods, and guns from slavers in return for captives, who were marched in chains to Arab sailing vessels on the coast. The abolitionists, who had eliminated the west coast traffic in human beings, were inspired by Livingstone to demand a cessation of slavery in the east. An expedition similar to those on the Niger was sent into the Zambezi interior to open up East Africa to Christianity and commerce. By 1873, Britain had forced the sultan of Zanzibar to prohibit the export of slaves, and the civilizing and evangelizing followers of Livingstone and their commercial counterparts were entering the highlands of East Africa.

On the eve of the Berlin Conference, then, although the political partitioning of Africa had barely begun, its economic and moral foundations had been laid. In the west, the British and French were establishing themselves along the Atlantic coast between Senegal and the Niger delta. Liberia and Sierra Leone had been founded as homes for freed slaves by American and British philanthropists. Farther south, the American Stanley was exploring the basin of the Congo River after finding Livingstone, and had interested Leopold II in "this grand highway of commerce to west-central Africa." In South Africa, discussed in detail below, British and Boer colonists had broken over the question of slavery, and the Great Trek of the Calvinist Dutch into the interior brought them into direct conflict with the powerful Zulu nation. Meanwhile, Cecil Rhodes was advocating a contiguous British colony extending from the Cape of Good Hope to Cairo. Although European interests on the east coast were minor, the Portuguese retained their established stations in Mozambique, and the British watched Zanzibar.

Thus, information on the geography, peoples, and economic conditions in Africa flowed into Europe through the journals of an increasing number of explorers and through the accounts of missionaries. Yet only three countries maintained a serious presence in Africa—Britain, France, and Portugal—and the swift partitioning of Africa, although seemingly inevitable in hindsight, must have come as a total surprise to most Africans. After four centuries of European contact, all Africa except Liberia and the mountain kingdom of Ethiopia fell under direct European political control within three decades.

CLONIALISM
2

taking. Imperialists, missionaries, and humanists agreed. There was, as native African writers have noted, a curious affinity between the vaunted humanitarianism of the abolitionists (slaves were obsolete in the new industrial age) and the imperialists' insistence on the replacement of the slave trade with commerce in raw materials.

After the Berlin Conference of 1884, the imposition of colonial rule on the peoples of Africa was swiftly and ruthlessly accomplished. Contrary to common belief, the process was far from peaceful. During the first thirty years, European nations crushed resistance and rebellion in virtually every region of Africa as their well-equipped, technologically superior armies gave them a clear military advantage.

The motives for this rapid and determined invasion of the African interior were both political and economic. The Berlin Conference had defined the rules for the partitioning of Africa: new annexations in Africa were to be recognized as valid by other European powers only when accompanied by *effective occupation*. Politically, then, the scramble for Africa was not so much a conscious race for the acquisition of new territory as sound nineteenth-century defensive politics: Each European nation "had" to establish a presence in Africa wherever possible so that it would not be excluded from the development of trade and resources by some other colonial power. The justification offered was that the Europeans were, in the long run, opening up Africa for the benefit of its peoples, but African opposition was viciously eliminated, and European interests were dominant.

From an economic viewpoint, the transformation of Europe from a **mercantile*** to an industrial economy in the nineteenth century demanded new markets and raw materials for the rising output of British and European factories. By the end of the nineteenth century, however, the last major area in the world available for European territorial acquisition was Africa. Although the economic potential of most of Africa was poorly known at this time, the fear of missed economic opportunities weighed heavily on the minds of European decision makers. This was a reason for their focus upon the highways of imperialism in Africa—the rivers Niger, Nile, and Congo—all viewed as dazzling economic prizes available for the

THE PROCESS OF COLONIALIZATION
[FIGURES 2, 3]

Common European political and economic goals governed the colonialization of Africa, although differing levels of native opposition varied the scope and intensity of the process from one region to another. The methods employed to achieve European aims were adapted to fit regional environmental and economic conditions and reflected each nation's approach to colonial rule, the differing sizes of the colonial presence, and the differing political philosophies of the colonizing powers.

The first thirty years of European action in Africa after 1884 were given over to "pacification" and partition of society and territory. The progress of commerce and settlement demanded security, so that as elsewhere in the developing world, European interest in order prevailed over European concern for justice. Boundaries forged in bitter commercial competition were arbitrarily drawn on new and increasingly detailed European maps. These boundaries reduced clashes between rival European powers seeking similar spheres of influence, but native societies and economies were disrupted by the new political barriers.

With the establishment of European law and order, each region of the African continent was successively opened to trade and new sources of raw materials were identified and introduced. African manpower was organized to produce and transport goods for export to Europe. Throughout the continent, laborers left their traditional livelihoods and entered cash economies oriented to European needs. The development of transportation systems, plantations, and mines was financed by taxes and duties on Africans. Africa was not only to be conquered, it was to be conquered cheaply.

Although the colonial era spanned only seventy years, complex and fundamental changes were set in motion that catapulted Africa into the world econ-

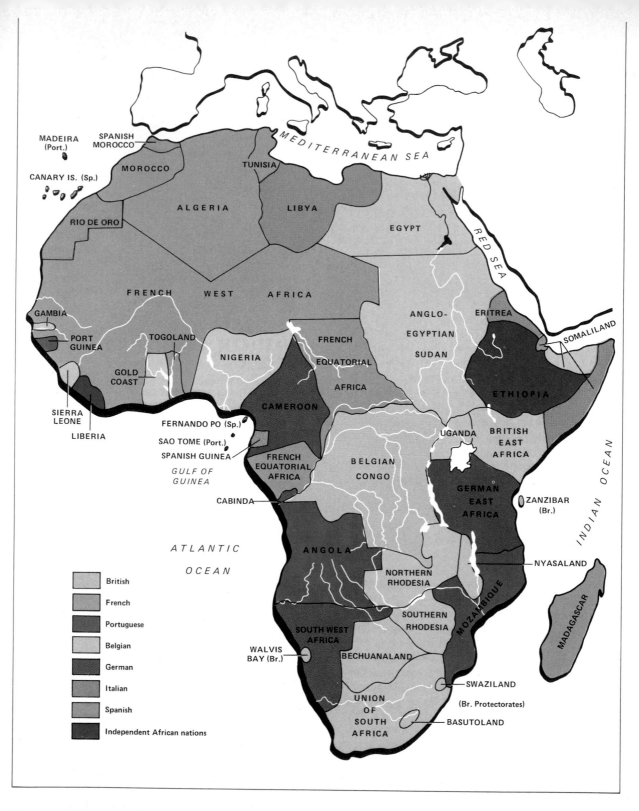

Figure 2. The Scramble for Africa. Between the Berlin Conference of 1884 and the outbreak of World War I, European colonial rule was established throughout the African continent except in the mountain kingdom of Ethiopia and in Liberia, the homeland for freed slaves on the Guinea coast. *After:* Raymond F. Betts, ed., *The Scramble for Africa.* Lexington, Mass.: D. C. Heath, 1972, pp. xiii, xiv. Reproduced by permission of the publisher, D. C. Heath and Company.

omy and laid the foundations of its modern human geography. Territory was subdivided by Europeans into what would become the modern nation-states of Africa. Whether traditional political hierarchies were destroyed or subordinated, or whether colonial rule took direct or indirect form, the effect was essentially the same. Even the poorest peasant farmers and herdsmen ultimately understood that power lay with the colonial administrators; they hoped that their children would attend schools and universities in Europe to benefit from the new system.

Similarly, the economic dimensions of Africa were transformed in the colonial period. Transportation systems developed to facilitate the maintenance of order and the exploitation of Africa's resources. Africans planted new crops introduced by Europeans and labored in the mines, railroads, and ports of a continent in the midst of economic transformation. The process of change was not confined to a small urbanized elite like the "trouser blacks" of British Africa who adopted European dress, tastes, and attitudes. It reached out into the countryside of Africa in the form of new economies, continuous taxation, forced labor, and Western patterns of administrative organization. Viewed from Europe, Africans were unproductive and undisciplined, their continent lay undeveloped; European guidance would now open up new horizons for an unorganized people. For Africans, colonialism was an invasion of European political and economic interests that shattered their society and culture. The course of colonialism, despite improvement in modernized economic sectors, ultimately proved humiliating for Africans and Europeans alike. Variations in African subjugation and European settlement determined modern conditions in each region of Africa.

WEST AFRICA: COLONIAL ADMINISTRATORS, PEASANT PRODUCERS

The European presence and level of influence were modest in West Africa in the middle of the nineteenth century. The French colony of Senegal consisted of the port of Saint-Louis, a nearby island, and a few upriver trading posts with a total population of 18,000, of which only 300 were Europeans. The British colony of Sierra Leone occupied 400 square miles, and its population of 40,000 was principally composed of liberated slaves from Britain and the Caribbean; there were fewer than 100 Europeans in residence. Similarly, Liberia, founded as a homeland for freed American slaves, had a population of only 3000 reverse immigrants dispersed in settlements along 300 miles of coast. British and French trading posts existed on the Ivory Coast, on the Gold Coast, and in the Oil Rivers area in the Niger delta, and were principally involved in transshipping gum, palm oil, and rubber gathered by Africans in the interior. All told, there could not have been more than 1000 Europeans in West Africa in 1850; yet from these unimposing outposts colonial empires were launched that partitioned one-third of Africa's sub-Saharan population into seventeen different nations.

The Scramble for Territory

French expansion in West Africa in the late 1800s, a major reason for convening the Berlin Conference,

began with a strengthening of coastal garrisons in Senegal and at the port cities of Conakry (French Guinea), Abidjan (Ivory Coast), and Porto-Novo (Benin). Pushing eastward from their primary node of settlement in Senegal, French armies conquered the grasslands of the Sudan from the coast to Lake Chad and after several years of fighting destroyed the Muslim empire of Hajj Umar centered on the headwaters of the Niger. Moving southward into the Upper Volta River region, the French encountered stiff resistance from the Muslim leader of the Mande peoples, a man named Samori. After fifteen years of guerrilla activity, the Mande were finally defeated and Samori was exiled in 1898. The purpose of this latitudinal advance was to cut off British expansion into the African interior from the Guinea coast. Liberia, Sierra Leone, Gambia, and the Portuguese stations were now encircled by French boundaries. The declaration of colonies in French Guinea and the Ivory Coast in 1893, and in Benin (after bloody fighting) in 1900, prevented any east-west British expansion along the coast.

Because of this, all the British could do in West Africa was to extend their four existing footholds on the Gold Coast, the lower Niger, and to a lesser extent Gambia and Sierra Leone as far inland as possible. In the Gold Coast, the Fante states of the coast were rather easily occupied by the British, but the powerful Ashanti of the interior were not. Two British expeditionary forces were sent to quell Ashanti resistance in 1896 and 1900; after a bloody nine-month war, the Ashanti territories were annexed as a crown colony stretching inland 400 miles and encompassing more than 2 million people. When boundaries were drawn between French and British territories and the German colony at Togoland (created out of only 40 miles of coastland), the Ewe tribes were split between the Gold Coast and Togoland, and the Twi-speaking states between the French-ruled Ivory Coast and British domains.

In Nigeria, British occupation was launched from three different directions: the island colony of Lagos, the British consulate in the Niger delta, and trading posts in the interior. On the coast, the Lagos settlement expanded to become a protectorate including most of the territory of the Yoruba. Similarly, the Niger delta consultate expanded its authority inland, but effective control was not achieved until African chiefs with established trading monopolies in the region were subdued and replaced in the 1890s. The

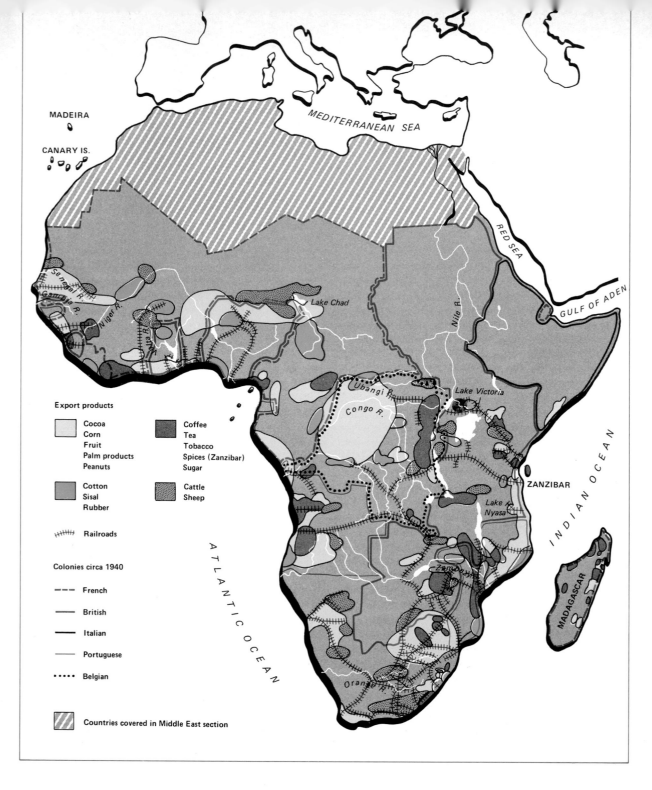

MADEIRA

CANARY IS.

MEDITERRANEAN SEA

RED SEA

GULF OF ADEN

Senegal R.

Gambia R.

Niger R.

Bila R.

Lake Chad

Nile R.

Ubangi R.

Congo R.

Lake Victoria

ZANZIBAR

Lake Nyasa

INDIAN OCEAN

ATLANTIC OCEAN

Zamb...

MADAGASCAR

Orange R.

Export products

▢	Cocoa Corn Fruit Palm products Peanuts
▨	Coffee Tea Tobacco Spices (Zanzibar) Sugar
▨	Cotton Sisal Rubber
▨	Cattle Sheep

⊬⊬⊬⊬ Railroads

Colonies circa 1940

– – – French

———— British

▬▬▬ Italian

——— Portuguese

•••• Belgian

▨ Countries covered in Middle East section

Figure 3. Colonial Economic Development. *After:* Roland Oliver and Anthony Atmore, *Africa Since 1800*, 2nd ed. Cambridge, Eng.: Cambridge University Press, 1972, pp. 144–51, 190–93.

process of colonial unification ended when Benin was occupied and its king deported in 1897.

In the Nigerian interior, in the land of the Hausa, the treaties of George Goldie's trading company with the Fulani emirate formed the basis for British claims over this region. Goldie's claims were backed up by his private army, the West African Frontier Force. Warfare was averted by British confirmation of the Fulani emirs, and a policy was set of ruling "indirectly" through existing African political structures. Finally, in 1914 the three separate districts—the Lagos Protectorate, the Oil Rivers Protectorate, and northern Nigeria—were amalgamated into the colony of Nigeria, Britain's largest possession in West Africa both in area and population.

The French in West Africa

By the turn of the century, the French had carved out an empire in West Africa nine times the size of metropolitan France, and were faced with problems of administration and development on a scale not previously undertaken by the French government. A consistent policy, based on the French experience in Senegal, was applied to the newer colonies of the Sudan (modern Mali), Mauritania, Upper Volta, Niger, Guinea, Ivory Coast, and Benin, all of which were amalgamated into French West Africa shortly after 1900. In these seven territories, centrally administered by a governor-general in Dakar, military forces were replaced by a hierarchy of civilian administrators that reached down to the village level, the only locale in which Africans had any voice in government affairs. In theory, every West African subject could become a citizen of France through the French policy of *identité* or cultural assimilation; in practice, only Africans born in the older urban centers in Senegal actually achieved French citizenship, since education in French, military service, and ten years of French employment were requirements. By 1937, of the 15 million people under French rule in West Africa, only 2500 from the seven newer colonies had met these conditions and become French citizens.

Economic policy in French West Africa was strongly influenced by the successful French experience in peanut cultivation on the grassy plains of the Senegal Valley. Since the great majority of territory under French control was covered by savanna grasslands and only the coastal colonies of Guinea and the Ivory Coast were located in the ***rain forests,*** the principal goal was to convert the African population of this vast area into commercial cultivators of crops for export to France. Except on the coast, however, the population of the region was thinly scattered and trade patterns were poorly developed. To cope with transport difficulties, railroads were constructed connecting Kayes inland on the upper Senegal River with Bamako on the Niger to bypass the turbulent headwaters of both rivers, from the old port of Saint-Louis to the deep-water harbor at Dakar, and finally in 1924 from Dakar to the inland city of Kayes. Head taxes were levied on the population to finance these developments; taxes had to be paid in cash, thereby forcing Africans into the cultivation of commercial crops.

Despite these developments, inland cultivation of peanuts and cotton never proved profitable, and French attention rapidly concentrated on coastal environments where cocoa, timber, coffee, and bananas from the Ivory Coast, palm products from Benin, and bananas from Guinea became important export commodities. Railroads were built inland from the port cities of Conakry, Abidjan, and Porto-Novo, generating narrow corridors of considerable wealth. But the vast majority of French West

Africa's 17 million people were scattered over 4.8 million square miles of countryside, most of which remained isolated and undeveloped during the colonial period. These differences in regional development stimulated large-scale labor migrations to islands of development on the coast in times of economic stress.

The British in West Africa

By contrast, the four British colonies in West Africa were smaller in area, more densely populated, and possessed of important mineral as well as agricultural resources. After the Ashanti were defeated, the Gold Coast rapidly became the richest territory in West Africa. Initially wild rubber was a major export, but after railroads were constructed from the coast to the Akan gold fields, gold, manganese, and bauxite became important export products, although these were later overshadowed by the large-scale commercial development of cocoa plantations. The development of Nigeria was slower because most of the colony's 24 million people lived in the northern provinces in the interior. Eventually, however, two railroads from the coastal ports of Lagos and Port Harcourt opened up peanut cultivation in the interior to supplement Nigeria's export of palm oil and cocoa from coastal districts. In Sierra Leone, a similar pattern evolved. A railroad from Freetown into the interior facilitated the cultivation of palm trees and kola nuts, although the colony remained relatively poor until the discovery of iron deposits and diamonds in the interior in the 1930s. Lastly, the tiny colony of Gambia, although an important source of peanuts, remained the poorest of Britain's West African colonies.

Unlike the French, the British never developed a consistent method of administering their possessions in West Africa, preferring instead to follow a policy of empiricism that allowed local conditions to dictate the techniques of government. As in the French territories, revenues generated by peasant producers on the coast were used to finance the development of the interior, although the greater productivity of the British colonies enabled them to rely on export duties instead of head taxes. In the Gold Coast, this money financed the construction of railroads, which were profitable and secured military control over the still-powerful Ashanti in the interior. Ultimately, the coastal districts and the Niger River delta were governed by direct British

The Europeans who came to West Africa in the nineteenth century and established colonies found cities there much like the one shown in this sketch, which was made in Ghana (then the Gold Coast Colony). *Photo:* New York Public Library Picture Collection.

rule, while the interior was administered indirectly through pacified Ashanti leaders and Fulani emirs. In Nigeria, the Gold Coast, Sierra Leone, and Gambia, the great increase in trade that followed the extension of British rule and railroads in West Africa created a sizable mercantile class of well-educated Africans who spoke for developments in medical services, education, and social services to a far greater degree than in French West Africa.

Liberia

In Liberia, the only noncolonial territory in West Africa, none of this happened—neither the establishment of European rule nor economic development. Unable to generate revenue or to control the interior effectively, the immigrant government of American-Africans in Monrovia clung to the coast, lacking the wealth, the trade, and the cultural power to run the country. Finally in 1925, the Firestone Rubber Company leased 1 million acres of Liberian forests and developed rubber as the one-crop economy of this state.

CENTRAL AFRICA: THE CONCESSIONAIRES

In the Congo River basin of Central Africa, the course of colonial development was influenced by different environmental and economic conditions than in West Africa. The tropical rain forests of the region were thinly populated by unsophisticated, isolated multiethnic groups of hunters, fishermen, and subsistence farmers. The commercial trading kingdoms of West Africa had no corollaries in Central Africa. Denser populations on the northern and eastern rims of the Congo Basin did maintain limited trading connections between the rain forest and the Sudan to the north and Zanzibar to the east, but the potential for large-scale exchange of European trade goods was quite limited. Central Africa, then, had neither precolonial economies nor trading systems upon which the various European colonies—Leopold's Congo Free State, the French colonies of Equatorial Africa (modern Chad, Central African Republic, Congo, and Gabon), and to a lesser extent the British colonies of Nyasaland (Malawi) and the Rhodesias (Rhodesia and Zambia)—could graft a system of colonial development and exploitation.

Central Africa had few peasant producers to convert to commercial farming, no substantial trading networks to tax for revenues, and no dense, settled populations from which head taxes could be collected. The formidable task of developing the Congo into an area of modern commercial production had to be financed by risk capital, money invested by private European entrepreneurs seeking large long-term gains. Mineral and agricultural rights (concessions) were granted over large sectors of the interior of Central Africa to any private company that guaranteed to finance the construction of highways, railroads, and navigational routes to stimulate commercial production. Central Africa thus became the realm of the concession company.

Leopold's Congo Free State

The process began when Leopold II of Belgium employed Henry Stanley to explore the Congo River system. Through a series of political maneuvers at the Berlin Conference, the king managed to achieve international recognition of his personal domain, the Congo Free State (modern Zaire). In 1886, a concession company was granted rights to 3000 square miles of territory in return for constructing a railroad from Matadi on the coast near the lower Congo rapids to Leopoldville (Kinshasa) in the interior. This amounted to nearly 9 square miles of land given for each mile of track laid. Similar contracts were signed for the construction of rail lines from the upper Congo River to Lake Tanganyika and from the upper limits of navigation on the Kasai River to the heart of mineral-rich Katanga.

Early in this process policies were introduced to facilitate and accelerate the growth of commercial exploitation. All lands not under cultivation, named "waste land," were declared government property and available for contract to a concession company. Since most farmers in the Congo Basin undertook *shifting cultivation,* moving from one area to another every several years as crop yields declined, the effect on the native African agricultural economy was disastrous. Forced labor and payment of taxes were considered the obligation of all natives, and a pervasive armed police force ensured that these obligations were fulfilled. Rebellious chiefs were punished and fined; entire villages were sometimes burned. Failure to pay taxes led to a public trial, after which the offender's hand or ear was cut off. In a reign of terror that lasted nine years, from 1889 to 1908, roughly half the population of the Congo was killed by arms, forced labor, starvation, and malnutrition. This estimate, arrived at by an official commission of the Belgian government, is undoubtedly conservative. Leopold burned all his records when he was forced to cede the Congo to the Belgian government in 1908, saying, "They can have my Congo, but they've no right to know what I've done there."

The first products brought out of the Congo were ivory and rubber, but as the tracts ceded to the concession companies were developed, cotton plantations, palm groves, sisal farms, and mines were established. Stimulated by the invention of the pneu-

matic tire in Europe, a rubber boom led colonial officials and company administrators to force Africans to leave their patches of cultivated land to tap rubber trees in the forests. As the demand for wild rubber declined with the establishment of rubber plantations in Southeast Asia, similarly brutal tactics were employed to provide labor for other commercial enterprises. The resulting destruction of the food economy of the Congo was the principal reason for the severe reduction of the population in the basin. Although the Belgian government ameliorated the worst of Leopold's excesses after assuming control, it never questioned the ethics of forcing Africans to work for European profit. Following a policy of paternalism, the Belgians confined education to the primary level and provided Africans with only the minimum of services necessary to meet the Belgians' main objective: economic development.

French Equatorial Africa

In the French territories in Central Africa, a similar pattern of economic development through concession companies was pursued, though the execution was less vicious than in Leopold's Congo. These companies were granted commercial monopolies over large territories in the four colonies of Gabon, Middle Congo (modern Congo), Ubangi-Shari (modern Central African Republic), and Chad, which were amalgamated into French Equatorial Africa in 1910 to lower the costs of colonial administration. Native laborers were forced to work on palm plantations in Gabon, to harvest wild rubber in the forests of the Middle Congo, and to tend coffee and cotton plantations in Ubangi-Shari. But the presence of a central administration in Brazzaville tempered the methods, if not the zeal, of the concessionaires for profit, although the effects of reorganizing African labor from subsistence to commercial production were much the same.

SOUTH AFRICA:
THE BOERS AND THE BRITISH

In South Africa, the imposition of colonial rule followed a quite different course than in West Africa with its commercial peasant farmers, or Central Africa with its company employees. The Europeans who came to South Africa ultimately sought lands for settlement, although they originally came as traders. In 1652, the Dutch had established a trading

NEGRITUDE AND COLONIALISM

The colonialization of Africa has caused some Africans to reject Western values such as objectivity, progress, and productivity. In the view of Aimé Césaire, Africans who "never invented anything, explored anything, conquered anything" have unique and precious attributes—emotion, sensibility, and comprehension—that taken together make up négritude, the quality of being African. This is the basis of Césaire's passionate condemnation of colonialism as a force of alien destruction.

It is my turn to formulate an equation: colonization equals thingafication.

I hear a storm of protest. They speak to me of progress and "accomplishments," sickness conquered, higher standards of living.

I speak of societies emptied of themselves, of trampled cultures, undermined institutions, confiscated lands, of assassinated religions, annihilated artistic masterpieces, of extraordinary possibilities suppressed.

They throw up to me facts, statistics, the number of kilometers of roads, canals, and railways.

I speak of thousands of men sacrificed in the Congo ocean. I speak of those who at the time I am writing are in the process of digging out the port of Abidjan by hand. I speak of millions of men torn away from their gods, their land, their customs, their way of life, their livelihood, their dance, and their wisdom.

I speak of millions of men in whom fear, trembling, feelings of inferiority, despair, toadyism were knowingly inculcated and who were brought to their knees.

They have kept me fully informed about the tonnage of cotton or cocoa exported, the acres of olives or vines planted.

I speak of destroyed food crops, the beginnings of undernourishment, of agricultural development directed only toward the benefit of the metropole, of the seizure of produce and primary goods.

They boast about suppressed abuses.

I also speak of abuses, but in order to say that on top of the old very real abuses they have superimposed others that are very detestable. They speak to me of local tyrants who have been "straightened out," but I declare that in general they keep themselves in office very well with the new ones, and that a network of good services and complicity between the old and new tyrants has been established to the detriment of the people.

They speak to me of civilization; I speak of proletariatization and mystification.

For my part, I would systematically vindicate these para-European civilizations.

Every day that passes, every denial of justice, every police bludgeon, every workers' demonstration put down in blood, every scandal hushed up, every punitive ex-pedition, every car of the secret service, every policeman and every soldier impresses us with the value of our old societies.

They were communitarian societies; never all for only a few.

They were not only ante-capitalist societies, as they say, but also anti-capitalist.

They were democratic societies, always.

They were cooperative societies, fraternal societies.

I would systematically vindicate those societies destroyed by imperialism.

They were fact—they had no pretense of being idea. They were, in spite of their faults, neither contemptuous nor contemptible. They were content with being. Neither the word failure, nor the word avatar made any sense to them. They kept hope intact.

Source: Quoted from Aimé Césaire, "On the Nature of Colonialism." In I. L. Markovitz (ed.), *African Politics and Society.* New York: Free Press, 1970, pp. 41–42. Reprinted with permission of Macmillan Publishing Company, Inc. Copyright © 1970 by The Free Press, a division of The Macmillan Company.

---

station at Cape Town in the shadow of Table Mountain on the southwestern tip of the continent. The prime function of this colony was to provide cattle, wheat, and fresh water to ships making the long haul from the ports of Europe to the Dutch East Indies. During the next century the European presence on the cape grew relatively slowly. A trickle of German Protestants and French Huguenots joined the Dutch in South Africa and spread out from Cape Town to establish large farms on which **indentured**• Malay, West African, and local slave labor worked in wheat fields and vineyards. As the frontier of settlement moved inland, the Dutch exterminated pastoral Hottentot and Bushmen groups in their path. It was not until 1770 when the Dutch were migrating toward the fertile lands of the eastern cape that they encountered well-organized resistance from the Bantu-speaking Xhosa people east of the Great Fish River, a native people who were agriculturalists as well as pastoralists.

By this time, after a century in residence, the Dutch, called Boers (farmers), had developed a distinctive rural culture whose language, Afrikaans, was simpler than standard Dutch and in whose rigid religious beliefs of orthodox Calvinism they found justification for the master-slave relationship they promoted. Nonetheless, major conflict between the Boers of the coast and the Bantu of the interior might have been averted had not Britain, in the wake of the Napoleonic wars in Europe, seized Cape Town in 1806 to protect its growing naval interests in the Indian Ocean.

By 1820, some 5000 British immigrants had settled in their new Cape Colony as town dwellers. Friction arose between British colonial authorities and the pastoral Boers. Each Boer considered it his birthright to possess 6000 acres when married; the Boers thus insisted on an aggressive policy of territorial expansion that generated continuous strife on the northern and eastern frontiers separating the Boers from the Bantu. The British were appalled by Boer cruelty to native Africans—the Boers treated blacks like cattle. In 1828, the British extended legal protection to remnant Bushmen groups in the Cape Colony, and in 1834 London forbade the Boers to keep slaves. These acts deeply offended the Boers, who resented Africans being, as they put it, "placed on equal footing with Christians, contrary to the laws of God and the natural distinction of races and religion."

In 1836, when the British restored a large tract of land in the eastern cape to Bantu control because it was too expensive to administer, the Boers began to leave. One by one, in ox-drawn wagons, they trekked northward across the Orange River to escape the confines of British rule. This Great Trek of the Boers into the interior immediately brought them into conflict with the Xhosa, Sotho, and other peoples who occupied the rich pastures of the high *veld.*[*] At the same time, the rapid military expansion of the Zulu of Natal had expelled Bantu groups from their lands. They also streamed onto the plateau through passes in the Drakensberg Mountains, moving westward toward the Cape Colony to escape the feared fighting regiments of the Zulu. On the high veld, the trek Boers and scattered Bantu groups vied for control of the fertile lands of the interior of South Africa.

Boer Republics, British Colonies

At midcentury, the issue was resolved in favor of the better-armed Boers. The Bantu peoples of the high veld were subjugated and two Boer republics, the Orange Free State and the Transvaal, were established north of the Orange River beyond the reach of British influence. In the east, in Natal, Boer raiders defeated the Zulu and annexed their territory. The British, however, took Natal back, fearing Boer access to ocean ports and potential commercial and naval competition.

By now, the combined European population of the British Cape and Natal colonies and the interior Boer republics amounted to about 300,000. In these territories and in many independent kingdoms and chiefdoms, the largest of which were Zululand and Basutoland, the African population numbered between 1 million and 2 million. As European rule spread and land was alienated from the Africans, desperate measures were taken by African tribes. After repeated defeats by whites moving eastward from the Cape Colony, the Xhosa, for example, followed the prophecy of a young girl that the Europeans would be driven into the sea if all native cattle and grain supplies were destroyed on a certain day. The day came, 100,000 cattle were slaughtered, grain was burned, yet the Europeans pushed on. In a pat-

tern that recurred, Africans left their land in the wake of the resulting famine and migrated to the cape in search of work and food.

The pattern of African migration to white-dominated urban centers intensified as the British and Boers settled on the best farmland, leaving poorer, less fertile environments for native peoples. Urban jobs were created by the discovery of diamonds at Hopetown south of Kimberley in 1867 and of gold at Witwatersrand near Johannesburg in 1884. Nonetheless, sporadic warfare continued as it had for three centuries between Europeans and the Xhosa of the eastern frontier, the Bapedi of Transvaal, and the Zulu of Natal. Gradually, however, centers of African strength like Basutoland, Swaziland, and Zululand were disarmed and forced to submit.

The great mineral finds of South Africa intensified problems between the British and the Boers as thousands of foreign miners, entrepreneurs, and adventurers, mostly British, immigrated into the heartland of the Boer republic of Transvaal. Led by Cecil Rhodes, the British sought an alliance with the Boers in order to develop the wealth of South Africa and to extend British rule northward into East Africa. The Boers, already outnumbered, feared their distinctive way of life would be destroyed by British intrusions. The resulting tensions ultimately triggered the fierce Anglo-Boer War at the turn of the century which, after 4000 Boers and 5700 British had lost their lives, ended in British victory. The Union of South Africa was formed in 1910, composed of the British Cape and Natal colonies and the Boer Orange Free State and Transvaal.

The Union of South Africa

During the next half-century, this union of British and Boer interests transformed South Africa from an agricultural to an industrial economy. Economic change occurred faster and on a larger scale here than anywhere else in Africa; the Witwatersrand developed into a major industrial and mining complex centered on Johannesburg, the largest city in tropical Africa. A web of railroads flung across the country connected the inland industrial districts with the ports of Cape Town, Port Elizabeth, East London, and Durban. The Africans were pushed into reserves, frequently located in the least desirable areas of South Africa. The Transkei Territories in Natal were set aside as "native reserves," and protectorates were established in Basutoland (modern Lesotho),

At the turn of the century, the Boer War pitted two groups of Europeans, the descendants of the Dutch who had settled Cape Town in the seventeenth century and the British who had come in the nineteenth, in a contest for control of the mineral resources of South Africa. The British army, shown here advancing on Johannesburg in 1901 complete with balloon corps, finally won, but not until 10,000 lives had been lost. *Photo:* The Bettman Archive.

Bechuanaland (modern Botswana), and Swaziland, foreshadowing the policy of **apartheid**• (apartness), later rigidly enforced.

Africans participated in the economic development of South Africa only as cheap labor in the mines and factories of the industrial centers and on the cotton, rice, and sugar plantations of Natal. Asian laborers who formerly worked these plantations emigrated to the towns to become shopkeepers. Although Africans made up three-quarters of the population, their reserves formed but 13 percent of the land area; although South Africa's economy depended on gold mined by Africans, the native population earned one-eighth the income of whites in similar jobs and lived in slums in restricted areas

near the larger cities. Thus when the tide of nationalism swept Africa after World War II, South Africa differed substantially from other areas of the continent: Here the largest European population on the continent had built a modern economy on the backs of a subjugated majority, and unlike colonial regimes elsewhere in Africa, they remained determined to stay in Africa and in power.

EUROPEAN SETTLERS IN EAST AND SOUTH-CENTRAL AFRICA

In the highlands of East Africa from Kenya southward to the Cape of Good Hope and in related coastal areas, lands sparsely populated by Africans and climatically attractive to European settlement were available. Policies of settler immigration were encouraged by the British, the Germans, and the Portuguese. In the British territories of Kenya, Uganda, the Rhodesias (modern Rhodesia and Zambia), and Nyasaland (Malawi), policies varied with local conditions. In the German colonies of South-West Africa (modern Namibia) and Tanganyika

(Tanzania) and in the Portuguese colonies of Mozambique and Angola, the impress of colonial rule was rigid and inflexible despite very large differences in climate, terrain, local society, and economy.

The British in East Africa

Although British policies in East Africa varied from colony to colony, the development of a cash economy to support the costs of administration and to generate trade provided a common thread of English motivation. In Kenya, settler plantations were encouraged by local governors, and 17,000 square miles of good land in the sparsely settled highlands were reserved for Europeans, although no official government policy of immigration was declared. In Nyasaland, dense African populations on the best farmland limited European settlement. In Uganda, the powerful Buganda people who had assisted the British in conquering the area received in return large grants of land. Aided by a railroad pushed through from Mombasa on the coast to Kisumu on Lake Victoria, the Buganda became a landholding aristocracy and converted large areas into highly profitable commercial cotton production.

In the Rhodesias, Cecil Rhodes's South African Company promoted European settlement to further his dream of a cape-to-Cairo axis. Large grants of land were set aside for settlers from South Africa and the British Isles; other immigrants were attracted by jobs in the copper mines of Katanga. Both the Shona, the original inhabitants of the Rhodesian plateau, and the Matabele, the conquerors of the western half of the region, lost large tracts of land to incoming whites. In a major revolt which broke out in 1893 and lasted several years, these two traditional enemies collaborated and forced Britain to bring in troops to retain control of the region. Eventually, the remaining natives were herded into reserves after the death toll in Rhodesia reached 10,000. But compared with events in the German colonies, British rule in East Africa was relatively peaceful. By 1914, there were more than 10,000 British settlers in southern Rhodesia, 3000 each in northern Rhodesia and Kenya, and much smaller numbers in Nyasaland and Uganda.

The Germans in South and East Africa

In contrast to Britain, Germany was committed to colonization as well as colonialization; German settlers were exhorted to emigrate to overseas African colonies, particularly Tanganyika and South-West Africa. In both colonies, the intent was to impose German discipline and techniques of production on the native labor force, to create a new German homeland in Africa for the large and growing peasant population of the mother country, and to produce revenue and raw materials as efficiently as possible. German administrators backed by military garrisons and conscript troops ruthlessly sup-

pressed opposition to colonial rule, levied heavy taxes on native peoples, and forced African subsistence farmers into commercial agriculture. In both Tanganyika and South-West Africa, the German impact on native peoples was disastrous.

German colonists began to arrive at Walvis Bay and Lüderitz in South-West Africa in the late 1880s, and a railroad was constructed to the interior capital of Windhoek. German policy called for the concentration of the African population into environments in this dry region that could support the cultivation of commercial crops. But most natives in South-West Africa were Bantu-speaking Herero people, a seminomadic group of cultivators and herders who lived in small settlements well adapted to the arid climate. Enforced settlement, therefore, met with Herero resistance. In 1904 war broke out, and a German military force exacted reprisals for Herero incursions on German settlements. Herero territory was declared part of the German colony; according to this decree, Africans no longer owned any land on which to graze animals, hence they were forbidden to own any cattle (a feat of circular logic). By 1906 two-thirds of the Herero population, 60,000 to 75,000 people, had been killed, and the remaining 25,000 to 30,000 had fled to neighboring Bechuanaland or entered employment on German farms and ranches.

When the Germans lost their African territories in the aftermath of World War I, South African farmers moved into South-West Africa to buy up cheap vacated farms and treated the Africans as harshly as the Germans had. In 1935, the 32,000 European settlers in South-West Africa owned one-third of the land; the remainder was mostly desert. The Africans were settled in reserves and labored in European enterprises to secure cash needed to pay European taxes.

In Tanganyika, African resistance began almost immediately upon the German establishment of colonial rule after buying the coastline from the sultan of Zanzibar in 1884. By 1888, the coastal Swahili people had forced the Germans to evacuate their garrisons at Lindi, Kilwa, and Mikindani, and had launched an attack on the important German settlement at Dar es Salaam. Better armed and in control of the coast, the Germans were able to suppress this resistance in two years. But in the interior, much larger groups—the Hehe and Gogo peoples of central Tanganyika, the Chagga people of Mount Kilimanjaro, and the Yao and Ngoni tribes of southern Tanganyika—fiercely resisted the implantation of garrisons. The Germans responded with a scorched-earth policy, burning villages, destroying fields, and brutally torturing leaders of African resistance.

After pacification, the continuing harshness of German colonial rule provoked one of the largest African uprisings on the continent, the Maji-Maji Rebellion, in which native religious leaders over wide areas of Tanganyika convinced their followers that German bullets would turn to water (*maji*) and that freedom from colonial rule would thus be achieved. In four bloody and chaotic years, between 75,000 (the German estimate) and 125,000 Africans died in battle or of starvation. The settlement system of Tanganyika was virtually destroyed and the country laid waste. After the British acquired a League of Nations **mandate**• over this territory following World War I, conditions improved. But the mark of the German colonial rule on the population of Tanganyika was so strong that development in this territory was retarded for two generations.

The Portuguese in South-Central Africa
In the colonies of Angola and Mozambique, the Portuguese practiced one of the least coherent, most radical colonial policies on the African continent. Professing a desire to assimilate the Africans into Portuguese culture and society, a policy of **miscegenation**• was encouraged with the ultimate aim of producing a population of **mulattos**• or at the very least of black Portuguese who would form an elite group loyal to the mother country. The practice, of course, was quite different from the theory. Some 3 million blacks were shipped as slaves to Brazil from Angola, seriously depopulating this dry, relatively thinly inhabited region. Until the twentieth century, fewer than 1000 Portuguese clinging to the port capital of Luanda organized this trade and settled on coffee plantations in the adjacent hinterland, forcing the Africans, as elsewhere, to labor in commercial agriculture. In Mozambique, palm and cocoa plantations were hacked out of the coastal jungles. When local sources of labor failed, Indians, many of them Christians from Goa, were imported from South Asia to work on the estates of the Portuguese colonists. Despite the theoretical altruism of the Portuguese policy of assimilation, fewer than 1 percent of the African population achieved citizenship status as an *assimilado,* and the lowest levels of literacy and health care in Africa existed in the two Portuguese "provinces" of Angola and Mozambique.

TROPICAL AFRICA

REGIONAL PATTERNS

PHYSICAL FEATURES MAP
POPULATION DENSITY MAP

Tropical Africa is a massive, compact block of land extending 3200 miles southward from the Sahara Desert to the Cape of Good Hope. Approximately three times the size of the United States and 4600 miles at its widest, this *region* lies astride the equator so that climates from South Africa to the northern tier of the *Sahel* (the sub-Saharan zone) are either tropical or *subtropical*. Despite this relative uniformity of climate over distance, tropical Africa is thinly peopled; its average density of thirty people per square mile is lower than that of any other continent save Australia. The reasons for this are environmental. Africa has a greater proportion of valueless land than most other world regions: The lowlands of western and central Africa are infested by tsetse flies and have poor, heavily leached, *lateritic* soils; rainfall in the highlands of eastern and southern Africa, in the Kalahari Desert, and on the plains of the Sahel is either too little or too unreliable. Thus, in Africa, whose population is increasing faster than that of any world region except Latin America, the pressure of people on the resource base—despite relatively low densities—is a serious problem.

As one might expect, population pressure varies in cause and intensity from one environment to another in tropical Africa, although natural regions are less clearly defined here than on other continents, where major divides like the Alps, the Andes, and the Himalayas compartmentalize and isolate human activity. In Africa, extensive transition zones are more common than compartments: north-south transitions from the hot, wet, equatorial forests of central and western Africa northward through the grasslands of the Sahel to the Sahara and southward to the *steppes* of the Kalahari; east-west transitions from the lowlands of western and central Africa to the highlands of eastern and southern Africa. On the basis of these two variables, rainfall and elevation, the following regions

can be identified. Lowland Africa, west of a line drawn from western Ethiopia to northern Angola, lies at elevations of less than 3000 feet and includes two subregions: the tropical rain forests and savannas of central and west Africa and the grassland steppes of the Sahel which stretch from the plains of Senegal through Mali, Upper Volta, Niger, Chad, and southern Sudan to the highlands of Ethiopia. Highland Africa, east of this line and above 3000 feet, includes the African Horn, composed of the Ethiopian *massif* and the deserts of Somalia; East Africa, the European-settled uplands of Kenya, Uganda, and Tanzania; and southern Africa, the eastern highlands of Zambia, Rhodesia, and South Africa and the dry Kalahari Desert and steppes of Namibia (formerly South-West Africa), Botswana, and western South Africa.

LOWLAND AFRICA: CENTRAL AND WEST

Tropical rain forest covers much of the Congo Basin of Central Africa, a vast, shallow saucer ringed by low hills, and the lowland coasts of the Gulf of Guinea. Bisected by the equator, all parts of this region are constantly wet. Rainfall of more than 60 inches a year and no dry season supports the most imposing and luxuriant plant association known: a three-tiered canopy of evergreen trees at 50, 100, and 150 feet arches over the land, blocking out sunshine from the surface. Along river channels, where sunshine can penetrate to the ground, a dense *gallery forest* stretches unbroken along the banks, an impenetrable tangle of mangrove shrubs, palms, and lianas (vines). An estimated two-thirds of the Congo forest remains intact, the rest having been cleared by lumbermen and shifting cultivators. Along the Guinea coast, forest lines the shore from Sierra Leone eastward to Benin and western Nigeria, where a wide tongue of savanna cultivated in palm trees breaks its continuity. On the outer fringes of the rain forest, in the hills of Cameroon, Congo, Gabon, and the Central African Republic that ring the Congo Basin and in the middle zone of West Africa, the evergreen vegetation gives way to *deciduous* woodlands and savannas.

Despite the luxuriant vegetation in rain forest areas, this *ecosystem* is sensitive to change, delicately balanced, and vulnerable to human activity. The myth of the encroaching jungle suggests rapid growth, but in truth tropical forests grow twenty to one hundred times slower than forests in the mid-latitudes. Areas cleared for cultivation or lumbering take generations to recover; the complexity of the plant association with as many as one hundred different species found in 1 square mile precludes replanting. Further, these forests are underlain by thin, acid lateritic soils leached of plant nutrients by heavy rainfall and susceptible to erosion when forest cover is removed.

239

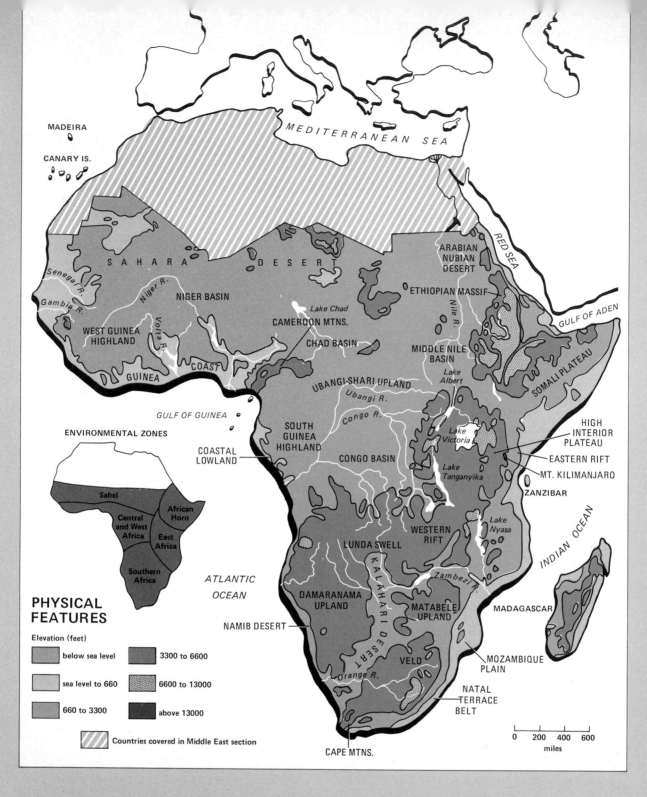

MADEIRA

CANARY IS.

MEDITERRANEAN SEA

S A H A R A   D E S E R T

ARABIAN
NUBIAN
DESERT

RED SEA

Senegal R.

Niger R.

Gambia R.

NIGER BASIN

Volta R.

WEST GUINEA
HIGHLAND

Lake Chad

CAMEROON MTNS.

CHAD BASIN

ETHIOPIAN MASSIF

Nile R.

GULF OF ADEN

GUINEA   COAST

UBANGI-SHARI UPLAND

MIDDLE NILE
BASIN

SOMALI PLATEAU

GULF OF GUINEA

Ubangi R.

Congo R.

Lake
Albert

COASTAL
LOWLAND

SOUTH
GUINEA
HIGHLAND

Lake
Victoria

HIGH
INTERIOR
PLATEAU

EASTERN RIFT

ENVIRONMENTAL ZONES

CONGO BASIN

Lake
Tanganyika

MT. KILIMANJARO

ZANZIBAR

Sahel

African
Horn

Lake
Nyasa

INDIAN OCEAN

Central
and West
Africa

East
Africa

WESTERN
RIFT

Southern
Africa

ATLANTIC
OCEAN

LUNDA SWELL

KALAHARI

Zambezi R.

DAMARANAMA
UPLAND

MATABELE
UPLAND

MADAGASCAR

PHYSICAL
FEATURES

NAMIB DESERT

DESERT

MOZAMBIQUE
PLAIN

VELD

Elevation (feet)

Orange R.

NATAL
TERRACE
BELT

below sea level	3300 to 6600
sea level to 660	6600 to 13000
660 to 3300	above 13000

Countries covered in Middle East section

0   200   400   600
miles

CAPE MTNS.

A disturbed ecosystem has already become a problem in the densely populated coastal belt of West Africa, where a year-round growing season, the *alluvial soils*° of river deltas, and trading opportunities have encouraged intensive commercial cultivation of cocoa, palm products, and rubber as well as the usual subsistence crops. In Ghana, Togo, and Benin over half the population lives on the coast; similar clusters of population are found near major

ports in the Ivory Coast, Liberia, and Guinea. In Yorubaland in western Nigeria, the higher quality soils of the forest-savanna border support agricultural densities of 400 to 500 people per square mile.

In selected parts of West Africa, these nodes of population have set in motion forces of environmental deterioration. In Sierra Leone, for example, rising population has pressured *slash-and-burn*° farmers into shortening the fallow period in the rain forest from a traditional seven to ten years to only three; soil destruction, infertility, and *erosion*• have ensued. A similar process of erosion is afflicting densely settled parts of Iboland in eastern Nigeria and the uplands of Cameroon, where growing numbers of agriculturalists have produced gully erosion, *fragmentation*• of holdings, declining soil fertility, and frequent land disputes. In the vast rain forests of Zaire, Congo, Gabon, and the Central African Republic, however, population pressure is not yet a dominating problem, as poor soils, dense vegetation, and swarming tsetse flies have kept population densities low for as long as anyone knows. In this area, roughly the size of Europe, the total population is only 25 million.

On the northern fringes of the rain forests of the Guinea coast and the Congo Basin, the forest grades into savanna grasslands and open woodlands. In West Africa, this middle belt, as it is called, is thinly populated compared with the dense populations of the coast and the commercial farming areas on the savanna-steppe boundary of northern Nigeria. Here, tsetse flies are more common than on the coast, soils are poorer in quality than those of the interior, and rainfall is too low to support tree crops. None of these reasons, however, sufficiently explains the relative underdevelopment of this region.

Farther inland, in the northern belt of West Africa, although the dry season lengthens, it is not underpopulation but overpopulation that is the problem. In the densely settled nodes of the old emirates (Muslim kingdoms) around such cities as Kano, Katsina, and Zaria, the high natural fertility of the grassland soils has been maintained by heavy applications of fertilizer. But in outlying areas where overgrazing has reduced herds, continued cultivation without fertilization destroys the natural basis of the agricultural economy, leading in places to land abandonment and migration to urban centers. Recently this migration has turned into a human flood as the interior of West Africa, a transition zone between the tropical environments of the equatorial zone and the desert to the north, has been afflicted by a southward movement of Saharan climatic influences, a seven-year invasion that has spread drought across sub-Saharan Africa.

LOWLAND AFRICA: THE SAHEL
[FIGURE 4]

On the northern margins of the western and central African savanna, annual rainfall diminishes to 20 inches or less and the long grasses of the humid south are replaced by the short-grass steppes of the Sahel. Here the six French-speaking nations of Senegal, Mauritania, Mali, Upper Volta, Niger, and Chad face an environmental crisis of major human proportions. With the exceptions of the peanut-

Seen from the air, a village of the Sahel stands parched and isolated in a vast inhospitable area of dust and sand. *Photo:* Sue Habachy.

growing valley of the Senegal River and the cotton farms of the Upper Niger, this 4000-mile-long region is thinly populated, with most cultivation restricted to the humid south, and cattle and camel herding in the dry, tsetse-free north.

In the early 1960s, it is believed that the population of the northern regions of the Sahel among herding peoples such as the Tibu of Chad, the Fulani of Niger, the Tuareg of Mauritania, and the Baggara of the Sudan, probably doubled when vaccination programs and the drilling of deep wells improved the chances for man and animal to survive. In the south, population growth was reflected in soil exhaustion, forcing a spatial shift in the peanut zone of Senegal and bringing large-scale erosion to the Mossi country of Upper Volta. Population pressures were already felt when drought invaded this region in 1966, as the Sahara Desert migrated southward, in some places by as much as 100 miles.

The impact of this drought has been disastrous: in a wide band from the Atlantic Ocean to the Red Sea as many as one-third of the 51 million people of the Sahel (Ethiopia included) face resettlement or starvation. The major rivers of the region, the Senegal and the Niger, now record their lowest water levels in a century; Lake Chad has evaporated to one-third its former size, leaving shoreline fishing villages 18 miles from the new waterline. A cycle of drought, famine, and death has been initiated. Induced partly by worldwide climatic readjustment (similar droughts are occurring at this latitude in Latin America and India), the impact has been intensified by preexisting overpopulation.

In Mauritania, for example, three-quarters of the cattle are dead and epidemics of cholera and diphtheria have broken out. In Mali, Upper Volta, and Chad, an estimated one-half of the cattle have died; in Niger there are no cattle, and most camels have died as well. Herdsmen have fled to more densely settled, better watered regions to the south and west. In Senegal, *shantytowns*• have sprung up on the outskirts of Dakar to house emigrants from Mauritania; along the Niger River, refugees from Mali and Niger occupy resettlement camps set up by international assistance.

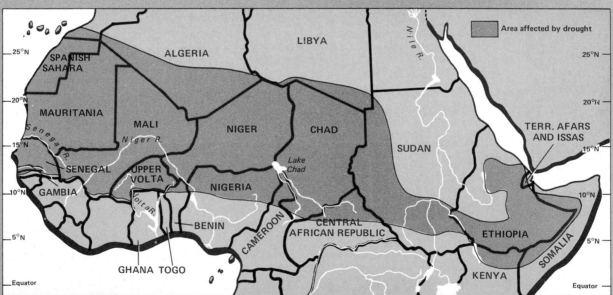

Figure 4. The Southward March of the Sahara. Changes in climate threaten the existence of the 51 million people who live in the six nations of the Sahel, the southern Sudan, and Ethiopia. As the photograph shows, animals died by the thousands all over the Sahel as water supplies vanished and people fled to other areas to survive. *Photo:* Jerry Frank/Design Photographers International.

The drought has had a ripple effect southward through the vegetation zones of West Africa: Ni-geria's peanut harvest has been cut by two-thirds; coffee and cocoa crops in the forests of the Ivory Coast, Ghana, Togo, and Benin have dropped off sharply. If this drought is caused by a basic shift in weather patterns, the six nations of the Sahel may well deteriorate into chaos. Even if rainfall increases, the reestablishment of vegetation, herds, and former livelihoods may prove impossibly difficult.

HIGHLAND AFRICA:
THE AFRICAN HORN AND ETHIOPIA

The African Horn, the northernmost region of Highland Africa, is composed of the two nations of Ethiopia and Somalia, which are believed to have populations of 25 million and 3 million, respectively, although neither country has taken a census. Rugged escarpments separate the Ethiopian massif from the plains of the Sahel; the dry plains of northern Kenya isolate the region from East Africa. The highland itself is partitioned by the Great Rift Valley which runs southward through the middle of Ethiopia, separating the densely settled western highlands from the dry hills of the eastern upland.

The entire region is broken into a jumble of hills, mountains, scarps, canyons, and valleys; a dissected complex mass that maintained a variety of peoples in cultural isolation. Over 90 percent of Ethiopians are agriculturalists, generally clustered on the 10 percent of the country neither too dry nor too rugged to be cultivated—the western highlands between Addis Ababa and Lake Tana. By contrast, the lowlands of Ethiopia and Somalia are hot and dry, covered with bush scrub, and suitable mainly for grazing. Three-quarters of the people here eke out livings as cattle and camel herders, still today collecting and selling frankincense gum to supplement a bleak existence.

Although overgrazing by cattle and camels has depleted the none-too-rich resources of the dry lowlands of Somalia and northern Ethiopia, and cereal cultivation on the eastern plateau has induced some soil erosion, the well-watered western highlands of Ethiopia have long been viewed as underpopulated. Some enthusiastic development specialists have even speculated that this highland would become the breadbasket of the Middle East.

Since 1966, however, when the southward migration of Saharan influences did not stop at the western escarpments of the highlands, Ethiopia has been in the grip of drought, much the same as the nations of the Sahel. In the dry provinces of the north, famine and cholera took between 50,000 and 100,000 lives in 1973. In the barren deserts of Harar Province, the Danakil tribesmen are in danger of extinction. Over 4 million people are now affected, and since between one-third and one-half of the Ethiopians live more than 20 miles from any transportation link, there is little likelihood of effective food distribution. Whereas in the Sahel overpopulation existed before the drought, in Ethiopia the drought has begun a change in environment significant enough to damage badly the once productive potential of the land.

HIGHLAND AFRICA: THE EAST

The highland countries of East Africa, Kenya Uganda, Tanzania, Rwanda, and Burundi form the roof of the continent, a high plateau studded with volcanoes (the highest of which is Mount Kilimanjaro at 19,340 feet), and bordered on the west by a branch of the Rift Valley. A second branch of the Rift, 30 to 80 miles wide, cuts through the center of the plateau; Lake Victoria lies between the two branches in a shallow depression that is the core area of a densely populated, productive agricultural zone of East Africa. In the northern and southern highlands, the plateau slopes gently to a broad coastal plain fringing the Indian Ocean; in the central section, the coastal zone is quite narrow.

Vegetation varies with elevation and precipitation. In the north, the steppes of Kenya grade imperceptibly into the dry lands of Somalia and southern Ethiopia; an arbitrary political boundary drawn between the two regions divides and isolates related groups of Somali cattle herders. But the vast majority of the plateau is covered by open parkland, rich, tree-dotted grasslands that form the premier big game hunting region of Africa. Forests make up only one-seventieth of the region and are primarily found on the slopes of the higher volcanoes. Coastward, the upland savanna gives way to mangrove swamps in the deltas of rivers that course down the eastern slope of the plateau.

The distribution of reliable rainfall in East Africa has strongly influenced population patterns, as to a lesser extent have soil fertility and the distribution of the tsetse fly. About 30 inches of rainfall are required for settled intensive cultivation in this region, and nearly all densely populated parts of East Africa, whether on the coast, the highland plateau, or the elevated peaks, are in areas where this amount of rainfall is attained four out of every five years. Thus in Kenya, where only one-sixth of the land receives this much rainfall on a regular basis, nine-tenths of the population is clustered in well-watered zones on the shores of Lake Victoria extending eastward into the former White Highlands, the land taken over by the colonists. Except for nodes of population around coastal ports like Mombasa, the rest of Kenya is thinly settled: three-quarters of the country has less than ten people per square mile.

In Tanzania, similar stretches of low rainfall and low population are found on the Masai Plain, the Serengeti Plain, the central plateau, and large areas of the low eastern plateau. Since over 60 percent of the region is infested with tsetse flies, this factor, as well as unreliable rainfall, may explain the distribution of people. Tanzanian population clusters occur around Lake Victoria, on the eastern shores of Lake Malawi, along the coast, and at sites favored by fertile soil or above-average rainfall. Population is also dense in the fertile, well-watered crescent of southern and eastern Uganda and in the highlands of Rwanda and Burundi, which have the highest population densities of any countries in Africa.

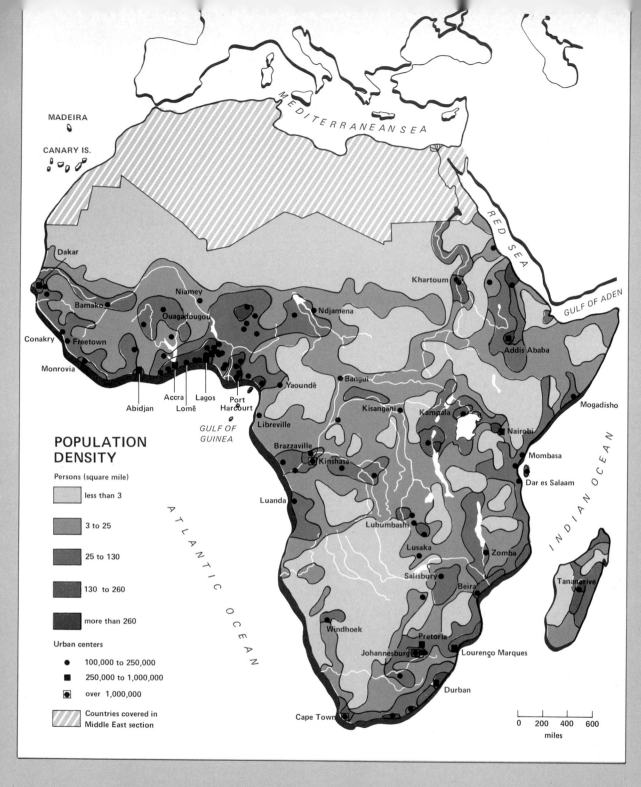

POPULATION DENSITY

Persons (square mile)

less than 3

3 to 25

25 to 130

130 to 260

more than 260

Urban centers

● 100,000 to 250,000

■ 250,000 to 1,000,000

◉ over 1,000,000

Countries covered in Middle East section

MADEIRA

CANARY IS.

MEDITERRANEAN SEA

RED SEA

GULF OF ADEN

Dakar

Niamey

Khartoum

Bamako

Ouagadougou

Ndjamena

Conakry

Freetown

Addis Ababa

Monrovia

Yaoundé

Bangui

Mogadisho

Abidjan

Accra

Lagos

Port Harcourt

Lomé

Kisangani

Kampala

Nairobi

Libreville

Brazzaville

Mombasa

Kinshasa

Dar es Salaam

Luanda

GULF OF GUINEA

Lubumbashi

Lusaka

Zomba

Salisbury

Beira

Tananarive

ATLANTIC OCEAN

INDIAN OCEAN

Windhoek

Pretoria

Johannesburg

Lourenço Marques

Durban

Cape Town

0   200   400   600

miles

Europeans were attracted to the temperate, tsetse-free regions of highland East Africa and strongly influenced the development of the agricultural economy of this region. Commercial and subsistence crops were planted on the rich *volcanic soils** in the highlands; plantations of tea, coffee, and pyrethrum (a chrysanthemum used in the manufacture of insecticide) were established in areas of reliable rainfall; cattle ranches were developed in the drier zones. In Kenya, and to a lesser extent in Tanzania,

this had the effect of pushing Africans into more marginal environments. This, combined with population growth, has generated pressure on the resource base of selected parts of East Africa.

In the Masai country, for example, a minimum of six cattle per person is required to maintain the tribal way of life. Since 10 acres of the dry plains are required to support one animal, areas where densities rise above ten people per square mile are likely to be overgrazed. Similarly in parts of Kikuyuland, one-third of the adult males are landless and half the agricultural holdings are smaller than 3 acres, the size generally assumed to be needed for subsistence cultivation. Even the fertile lands of the Lake Victoria basin are experiencing population pressure, where densities reach two to three times the assumed critical point in areas of cotton cultivation. Here, as elsewhere, pressure on the land is marked by a decline in food supply, a lower quality of diet, deforestation and attendant erosion, soil exhaustion, fragmentation of holdings, migration to islands of development, and social conflict.

HIGHLAND AFRICA: THE SOUTH

South of the highlands of East Africa and the lowland Congo Basin to the west, a vast *peneplain*• defines an arc stretching from the Muchinga Mountains of eastern Zambia through Rhodesia and Botswana to the Atlantic coast of Angola and the dry Kalahari Basin of Botswana, South Africa, and Namibia. This upland plain is generally covered by thin, deciduous woodland, with heavier vegetation on its northern tropical margins; on the south, it grades into grassland steppes. Favorable for neither agriculture nor pastoralism except for higher elevations in Rhodesia and Angola, economic development in this part of Africa has relied on mining, creating isolated centers of population with poorly developed hinterlands.

To the southeast, the Rift Valley plunges between Malawi and Mozambique, reappearing in the form of the rugged Drakensberg Mountains of the eastern cape. The escarpments of the Drakensberg range separate the high veld plateau of the interior from the densely populated, subtropical coast of Natal. Although environmental factors have played an important role in this southern half of tropical Africa, racial policies discussed elsewhere have also conditioned human occupance of the land to a degree found nowhere else.

Except for the urban, industrial centers of the Copperbelt, the factors that influence the distribution of population in Zambia are dry-season water supplies (half the year has less than 1 inch of rain), the presence or absence of tsetse flies, and fishing opportunities along the important rivers of the region. Except for the Barotse Plain, the Luvale country on the upper Zambezi, and various fishing grounds in the swamps of Lake Bangweulu, the country as a whole is either sparsely populated or virtually empty. This is also true of western Rhodesia, Botswana, and the lowland regions of South Africa and Namibia where the dry desert and steppe country of the Kalahari and the coastal *fog desert*• of Namibia have discouraged dense populations except in favored local environments.

In Malawi, the better watered lands of eastern Rhodesia, the uplands of Mozambique, and the high veld of South Africa, rainfall appears to have been an important determinant of the type of rural economy. Most European settlement in these temperate uplands is mixed farming, although *plantations*• are also well developed. In Rhodesia and South Africa particularly, the native African population has been precluded from settling the better watered, more fertile lands, forcing these cultural majorities into unfavorable environments either in the Zambezi and Limpopo lowlands or on the dry margins of the good earth.

Along the coasts of Mozambique and South Africa, population densities increase southward, reflecting the more temperate, less tropical climate of the region as well as the intensity of European development. In Mozambique, subsistence cultivation is the rule except in the hinterlands of the port cities of Lourenço Marques and Beira where sugarcane and cotton are cultivated. In South Africa, the well-watered coast of Natal is densely populated and sugarcane, cotton, citrus fruits, and bananas are grown.

Two factors have caused population pressure on the resource base of southern Africa: the Kalahari Desert, which spreads inland from the southwestern quadrant of the continent to western parts of Zambia and Rhodesia, and the racial policies of European colonists who have usurped African land. In Rhodesia, both factors come into play as the African reserves, overstocked and overpopulated, constitute only one-fifth of the land area of the country but support two-fifths of the population. In independent Zambia, population pressure is less severe, although population growth in favored areas described above foreshadows future problems.

By contrast, the entire country of Botswana, the domain of the Hottentots and the Bushmen, suffers from severe overgrazing and overpopulation, and appears destined to remain a perennial recipient of relief supplies from private and international agencies. In South Africa, population pressure is artificial, a matter of race, not resources. In general, population increases eastward with rainfall, but the enforced settlement of Africans on restricted reserves has generated serious problems.

THE WINDS OF CHANGE

3

Independence spread across tropical Africa almost as swiftly as colonialism entered a half-century earlier. Political turbulence grew in the years following World War II, but in 1955 only two nations, Liberia and Ethiopia, were independent. A decade later, however, thirty-one new nation-states existed in Africa, seventeen created in 1960 alone. The process began in West Africa, where the Gold Coast, under the charismatic leadership of Kwame Nkrumah, became an independent state renamed Ghana in March 1957. In Guinea, the militant nationalist Sekou Touré campaigned for "liberty in poverty," and the abrupt French withdrawal in 1958 ensured both. By 1960, virtually all the European colonies of West and Central Africa had declared their independence, and East Africa soon followed suit. In the south, the Portuguese reluctantly withdrew from Angola and Mozambique in 1975. Only in Rhodesia, South Africa, and Namibia have white settlers remained in control.

THE COLONIAL MATRIX

The colonial powers left and the government of tropical Africa returned to native political leaders. But a legacy of fifty years of European political and economic dominance was the matrix within which newly independent African states were forced to seek their destinies. The colonial boundaries of the new nations set the spatial perimeters within which each country struggled for independence and now seeks social and economic prosperity. The dual European-African economic system created by colonial administrators engendered growth without development, wealth without well-being, leaving Africa the most underdeveloped of continents. More than in any others, the twin factors of European-designed boundaries and European-oriented economies have conditioned patterns of political and economic development.

States in Search of Nations
[FIGURE 5]

In the late nineteenth century, competing European powers divided Africa into colonial compartments inside which precolonial African states and ethnic groups were amalgamated. The frontiers between these colonies were drawn arbitrarily with little regard for the African environment and even less for the African population. As a result, when independence came to Africa, 44 percent of all boundaries were **parallels** or **meridians,** another 30 percent were straight lines or arcs of circles, and the remaining 26 percent were drawn along rivers, mountain ranges, watersheds, or valleys. Thirteen states—Mali, Upper Volta, Niger, Chad, the Central African Republic, Uganda, Rwanda, Burundi, Malawi, Zambia, Botswana, Lesotho, and Swaziland—were entirely landlocked, having no access to the sea. Others—Gambia, Sierra Leone, Togo, Benin, Equatorial Guinea, Guinea-Bissau, and Cabinda—were absurdly small. An estimated 187 ethnic territories were divided by national political boundaries, although the difficulty of defining ethnic groups or "tribes" with any precision makes this figure somewhat unreliable. In any case, like people were separated and unlike people were joined by a colonial spatial system superimposed on the African continent.

Political leaders in the new nation-states of Africa, therefore, inherited truly new countries of great ethnic and cultural diversity. The problem they faced was a complete reversal of the European national experience, where nations of people aspired to becoming independent states. Here independent states aspired to national unity. In Zaire, when the Belgians precipitously withdrew in 1960, three major secessionist movements in Katanga, South Kasai, and Kisangani (Stanleyville) threatened to fracture the former colony into several smaller states. After five years of confused fighting and United Nations intervention, the secessionist movements, rooted in cultural diversity, were suppressed and central political control by the majority Kongo group was reimposed. In nearby Burundi, civil war between the Tutsi (about 15 percent of the population) and the majority Hutu people culminated in 1972 with the massacre of virtually all literate Hutu leaders and the maintenance of Tutsi rule.

The same tendency toward fragmentation led to war in Nigeria, where at one time or another minority groups in the northern, eastern, and western provinces threatened secession from the federation. The most populous country in Africa, Nigeria has more than 250 ethnic groups, ten of which make up 80 percent of the population. In 1966, minority groups throughout Nigeria tried to strip decisive power from the three largest ethnic groups, the Hausa, Yoruba, and Ibo; the coup was a failure. A year later, one of these peoples, the Ibo of eastern

Nigeria, seceded from the federation and declared the independence of the state of Biafra. Bloody fighting between federal Nigeria and secessionist Biafra ended with a starvation blockade of the Ibos in 1970 and the reestablishment of federal control. Although most new nations in Africa have not experienced such violent attempts at boundary revision, the local and regional interests of ethnic and linguistic groups continue to threaten the security and stability of new states throughout the continent.

Despite the problems these precolonial loyalties have posed for the new states of Africa, no major colonial boundary has been changed since independence, mainly because these frontiers circumscribe not only larger, more heterogeneous populations but also the circulation channels within which people, goods, and knowledge move. By 1914, colonial entrepreneurs had constructed 50,000 miles of railroad track on the continent to bring the mineral and agricultural resources of the African interior into the orbit of the world economy. Most of these communication lines connect interior trading cities with coastal ports and acted as channels for the **diffusion**• of colonial influence. As the system matured, feeder lines were added to open up inaccessible regions; still later, a road network intensified interconnections between channels of penetration and centers of economic activity.

But all this took place inside the boundaries of each colony; few roads or railroads crossed colonial frontiers (except to gain access to the sea), so that most colonies had closer connections with Europe

than with their immediate African neighbors. This circumstance has confined the processes of change and modernization into what the geographer Edward Soja calls communication "bubbles." They exist to such a degree that when the president of the Central African Republic wished to visit Uganda, a little over 1000 miles away, his most direct route was through the Paris airport. African leaders have verbally supported the concept of pan-Africanism and the notion of an amalgamation of former colonies into larger political units, but these circulation systems tend to isolate potential partners and defeat unification. Each country pursues its plans for social and economic development within compartments defined by the frontiers of colonial Africa, and these plans, like the spatial domain in which they are effected, are influenced by the colonial legacy.

As the monarch of Dahomey (modern Benin) and his court look on, prisoners of war, dressed in white robes and red caps, are displayed before being thrown into a 12-foot pit and beheaded. Lithograph, mid-nineteenth century. *Photo:* **New York Public Library Picture Collection.**

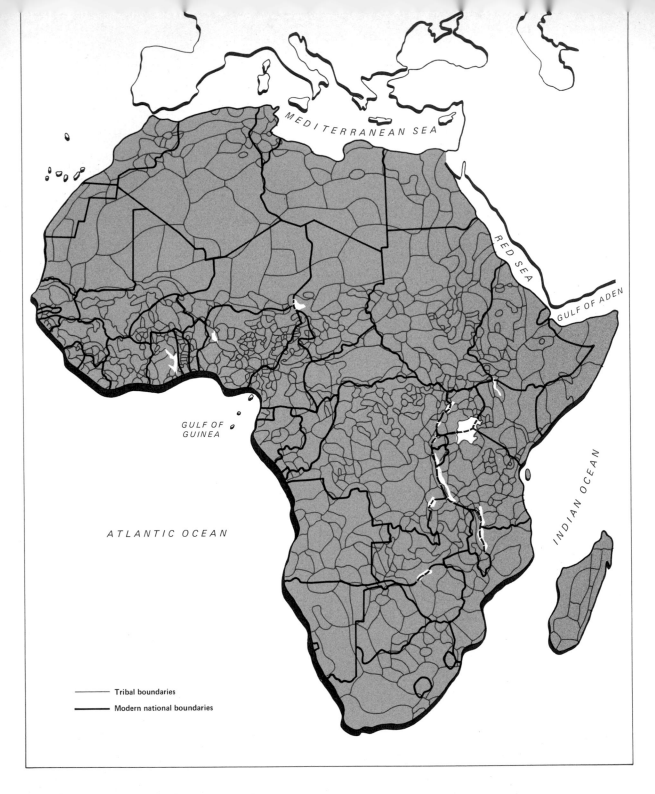

MEDITERRANEAN SEA

RED SEA

GULF OF ADEN

GULF OF GUINEA

INDIAN OCEAN

ATLANTIC OCEAN

——— Tribal boundaries
——— Modern national boundaries

Figure 5. The Colonial Reorganization of African Space. The colonial boundaries of the new nation-states of Africa make the population of each ethnically diverse and difficult to weld into a unified group because of the way in which tribal boundaries were ignored by European colonizers.

Growth Without Development

Perhaps the greatest paradox of this colonial legacy, at least from an economic viewpoint, is that no one, except a few entrepreneurs like George Goldie, profited. After a half-century of development and investment, the standard of living of the average African peasant had not improved; in many places it had declined. In a majority of countries, less than one-tenth of the adult population was literate, few lived in towns, and only a small percentage worked for wages. Most lived as pastoralists and subsistence peasants, aware of but not connected to the currents of economic change that were sweeping Africa. Nor did the European powers substantially benefit from the possession of a continent; their colonies were, for European governments, liabilities rather than assets. They produced a few scarce minerals and some luxury tropical foods, but Africa proved an insignificantly small market for industrial goods and, in the end, played a minor role (about 5 percent) in the pattern of world trade. Colonialism impoverished the Africans without enriching the conquerors. Even Portugal, which at the end of World War II derived one-quarter of its budget from Mozambique, Angola, and other minor African colonial possessions, until withdrawal in 1975 spent 40 percent of its national wealth maintaining its presence on the continent. Colonialism, then, was an all-round failure, mainly because the colonial economy initiated growth that demanded investments beyond the scale of colonial interests.

This growth without development was most intense in resource-rich regions like South Africa, Rhodesia, and Zaire; in poorer countries like Niger, Gabon, Chad, and Mali there was neither growth nor development. Growth meant more miles of railroad track, larger cities, better roads, a shift to commercial agriculture, intense pressure on the resource base, and a deceptive rise in per capita income. In fact, the native population in wealthy regions remained impoverished, living poorly in the native reserves of South Africa, the mining compounds of Witwatersrand and Katanga, and the shantytowns of cities in West and Central Africa. Two exceptions to this pattern were Ghana and Uganda, where small farmers engaged in the commercial growing of cotton, coffee, and cocoa, and were able measurably to improve their standards of living.

Generally, the shift to commercial agriculture, in which plants were grown for export rather than local consumption, did not increase the social well-being of Africans. The expansion of peanut, cotton, palm oil, cocoa, and coffee cultivation engaged Africans as wage earners through the inducement of forced taxation. Colonial powers invested heavily in commercial plantations and ignored the subsistence agriculture of the African majority. Transport networks were geared to the export market. What African leaders inherited at independence, therefore, was a dual economy: a relatively small, modern commercial sector devoted to the production and international sale of selected minerals and agricultural products coexisting with a much larger subsistence agricultural economy whose methods of cultivation, crops, land tenure systems, and patterns of social organization were virtually ignored by the colonial powers.

The effect of this process was to create islands of economic growth in Africa, whose expanding cities, mines, and commercial farms attracted migrant wage laborers from undeveloped hinterlands. Because most of these areas depended on a single crop or mineral, the economies inherited by independent

Africa were generally unstable and precarious with uncertain labor markets. The rising or falling price of any specific commodity on the world market could expand or contract the economy of a given region in a matter of days. In addition, industrial nations soon developed synthetic substitutes for crops like rubber, cotton, and sisal. In short, the colonial economic matrix, like the spatial matrix, has been a stricture on independent Africa. It has created economic dilemmas that appear virtually insoluble for most of its countries.

The Dual Economy
[TABLES 2, 3]

Poverty is Africa's central problem, and this is not likely to change in the foreseeable future. The poverty level income of $3000 for an American family is fifteen to thirty times larger than the annual income of an *average* African family. The total **gross national product (GNP)** of the African continent, approximately $40 billion, is one-twentieth that of the United States and is equal to the amount added to the American GNP each year. Even compared with large areas of Latin America and Asia, Africa stands out as an underdeveloped area, although overpopulation and food shortages have generally been less intense. The speeches of African leaders usually stress "closing the gap" with industrial economies and achieving "economic independence" to match their international sovereignty. But during the 1960s, Africa's rate of economic growth was less than that of any major world region.

These data, although useful for comparative purposes, tend to mask the great regional variation in scale and level of development that exists among the forty nations of tropical Africa, most of which are small as well as poor. Currently only six of these countries have populations of more than 10 million—Nigeria, Ethiopia, South Africa, Zaire, Tanzania, and Kenya. An additional nine nations have between 5 million and 10 million people; the remaining twenty-five countries, less. South Africa stands out with a per capita GNP of over $700 as the only developed economy in tropical Africa; two others have per capita GNPs of more than $600, eleven between $200 and $500, and the remaining twenty-six less than $200. Even these relatively low income levels are not secure, since so many African countries rely on one or two products for wealth. Seven nations gain two-thirds or more of their export income from

TABLE 2. African Raw Materials Economies

Source: Adapted from Ian Livingstone, "Agriculture in African Economic Development," in *Africa: South of the Sahara, 1975.* London: Europa, 1975, p. 34, Table 1.

Country	Major export			Percentage of total exports
ONE MAJOR EXPORT				
Zambia	Copper metal			95.5
Mauritania	Iron ore			79.6
Nigeria	Crude petroleum			74.4
Liberia	Iron ore			72.2
Zaire	Copper metal			67.1
Chad	Raw cotton			65.5
Ghana	Cocoa			64.3
TWO MAJOR EXPORTS				
Gambia	Peanuts	Peanut oil		88.2
Uganda	Coffee	Cotton		79.8
Sudan	Cotton	Oilseeds		77.6
Somalia	Animals	Bananas		76.0
Sierra Leone	Diamonds	Iron ore		74.8
Rwanda	Coffee	Tin ores		69.5
Gabon	Petroleum	Wood		67.7
Ethiopia	Coffee	Oilseeds		67.0
Malawi	Tobacco	Tea		65.8
THREE MAJOR EXPORTS				
Central African Republic	Diamonds	Coffee	Cotton	82.4
Ivory Coast	Coffee	Cocoa	Wood	78.8
Upper Volta	Animals	Oilseeds	Cotton	77.2
Togo	Phosphates	Cocoa	Coffee	73.3
Congo People's Republic	Wood	Fertilizers	Veneer sheets	69.1
Mali	Animals	Cotton	Oilseeds	67.6
Niger	Peanuts	Metal ores	Cattle	66.7
Cameroon	Cocoa	Coffee	Wood	64.1
Angola	Coffee	Petroleum	Diamonds	63.5
MOST IMPORTANT EXPORTS				
Benin	Cocoa, cotton, palm kernel oil, oilseeds, palm oil			
Kenya	Coffee, tea, petroleum products, chemicals			
Madagascar	Coffee, cloves, vanilla, meat			
Mozambique	Fruit and vegetables, cotton, sugar, petroleum products			
Rhodesia	Tobacco, food, asbestos, machinery			
Senegal	Peanut oil, natural phosphates, fish, oilseed cake			
South Africa	Gold, diamonds, machinery, fruit and vegetables			
Tanzania	Cotton, coffee, diamonds, spices			

a single product. Zambia's only export, for example, is copper; Mauritania's, iron; Chad's, cotton; and Gambia's, peanuts. Two-thirds of the nations of tropical Africa export three or less products, and nearly half of Africa's agricultural exports are made up by only two crops—cotton and cocoa. The producing areas for these raw materials are nucleuses of urbanization and industry, zones of dense population, and focuses for migration from vast and thinly populated subsistence hinterlands.

ISLANDS OF DEVELOPMENT

Sixty years of European exploitation of agricultural and mineral resources created islands of economic activity in Africa linked directly to the world economy. These islands include the largest cities in tropical Africa, every important industrial complex, the most productive zones of commercial agriculture and mineral production—in other words, the European sector of Africa's dual economy. Three types of economic locations are noteworthy. The first is the coastal zones of commercial and urban development: the coastal belt bordering the Gulf of Guinea in West Africa from the peanut fields of Senegal in the west to the oil fields of Nigeria and the cocoa plantations of Cameroon in the east; the port centers of South Africa (Cape Town, Port Elizabeth, East London, and Durban); and the entrepôts of East Africa (Dar es Salaam and Mombasa). The second type is the areas of commercial agricultural development in the interior, including the peanut farms of Nigeria and the coffee and cotton plantations of the Lake Victoria highlands in East Africa. The third type consists of the major zones of mineral production: the Witwatersrand in South Africa, the highlands of

Country	Population (thousands)	GNP per capita (US $)	Population growth rate (%)
Nigeria	55,070	120	2.9
Ethiopia	24,625	80	2.2
South Africa*	22,160	760	3.0
Zaire	18,800	90	2.8
Tanzania†	13,270	100	2.5
Kenya	11,250	150	3.1
Uganda	9,814	130	2.7
Ghana	8,640	310	2.6
Mozambique	7,729	240	1.9
Malagasy Republic	7,310	130	2.6
Cameroon	5,836	180	2.1
Angola	5,501	300	1.3
Upper Volta	5,384	60	2.1
Rhodesia	5,310	280	3.3
Mali	5,018	70	2.1
Ivory Coast	4,941	310	3.0
Malawi	4,440	80	2.6
Zambia	4,136	400	2.5
Niger	4,020	90	2.9
Guinea	3,980	120	2.6
Senegal	3,870	230	2.1
Rwanda	3,596	60	3.0
Chad	3,640	80	1.8
Burundi	3,544	60	2.0
Somalia	2,828	70	2.4
Benin	2,708	90	2.9
Sierra Leone	2,555	190	1.4
Togo	1,956	140	2.9
Central African Republic	1,552	140	2.6
Liberia	1,520	240	3.0
Mauritania	1,170	140	1.9
Lesotho	923	90	2.0
Congo	899	300	1.5
Botswana	611	110	2.0
Guinea-Bissau	560	250	0.7
Gabon	489	630	1.0
Swaziland	423	180	2.9
Gambia	360	120	2.0
Equatorial Guinea	291	210	1.8
French Territory of Afars and Issas	95	670	1.6

TABLE 3. Population and Poverty in Independent Africa, 1970

Source: International Bank for Reconstruction and Development, World Bank Atlas, 7th ed. Washington, D.C.: IBRD, 1972.

*Including Namibia.
†Mainland Tanzania.

Rhodesia, the Copperbelt of Zambia, and the Katanga region of Zaire. Each of these economic regions, as well as the important urban centers of Kinshasa, Brazzaville, Luanda, and Lobito, have been destinations for hundreds of thousands of labor migrants.

Coastal Economic Development

By far the largest and most diverse region of coastal commercial development is located in West Africa in the twelve nations that extend from the western bulge of the African continent in Senegal along the Gulf of Guinea to Cameroon in the Bight of Biafra. With a total population of nearly 100 million, this section is the most densely populated, highly urbanized, and economically diverse region in Africa. Only white-dominated South Africa is more highly developed.

The economy of this coastal region gained momentum in the postslaving period at the end of the nineteenth century when the cultivation of palm oil in West Africa and the Industrial Revolution in Europe brought these two economies into close contact. Trade in palm oil, whose cultivation was confined by climate to the wetter portions of the coast, particularly in the Niger (formerly Oil Rivers) Delta, was gradually supplemented by other commercial crops. In the dry plains of the Senegal Valley, peanut cultivation was introduced and spread throughout the savanna interior of West Africa. In Guinea and the Ivory Coast, coffee and bananas became important products, as did cocoa in Cameroon and Ghana, and rubber in Liberia. Only in Togoland, under German rule, was a major effort to generate a diversified economy made during this developmental period.

These patterns of resource utilization have conditioned the continuing economic growth of the nations of West Africa since independence. The export trade in commercial agricultural products and selected minerals such as diamonds from Sierra Leone, aluminum from Guinea and Ghana, iron ore from Liberia, manganese from Ghana, and phosphates from Togo remain the significant generators of wealth in this region. Peanuts, for example, make up four-fifths of Gambia's exports; iron ore, 70 percent of Liberia's; diamonds and iron ore, 75 percent of Sierra Leone's; cocoa and aluminum, 70 percent of Ghana's. Since all railroads go to the sea, less than 1 percent of Nigeria's trade is with other West African nations; the figures for Ghana and Sierra Leone are under 4 percent. Although some new crops have been introduced since independence—ginger in Sierra Leone, and tapioca in Togo—and a major oil find has been developed in eastern Nigeria, the pattern of West Africa's economy remains basically what it was under colonial rule.

The major urban centers of West Africa are coastal ports, terminuses of interior railroads that tap rich and densely populated environments. Most colonial economies were dependent upon a single major port city—Dakar in Senegal, Bathurst in Gambia, Bissau in Guinea-Bissau, Conakry in Guinea, Freetown in

Much of Niger, on the southern edge of the Sahara, is unpopulated, and even in populated areas the climate is such that agriculture is severely limited. The most important problem is water; with it, a cattle industry could be developed. Here tribesmen fill skin water bags at a well newly drilled by a UN crew operating in the area as part of cattle ranching project aimed at helping nomadic peoples settle in villages. *Photo:* United Nations.

This worker carries a replacement for a band-saw blade at a sawmill in Nigeria that is part of what may one day be a modern lumber industry based on scientific management of rain forests and reforestation programs. A Forestry Service has been established, along with a course program at the university level to train the managers of the future in forestry policy, law, management, and technology. *Photo:* United Nations.

Sierra Leone, Monrovia in Liberia, Abidjan in the Ivory Coast, Accra in Ghana, Lomé in Togo, Porto-Novo in Benin, and Douala in Cameroon. Only Nigeria, of the twelve coastal states of West Africa, is large enough to sustain two major port cities, Lagos and Port Harcourt. Most of these cities include half of the urban population of each country, but it should be noted that with the exception of tiny nations like Senegal and Gambia, the urban populations of West Africa make up less than one-tenth of the total population. Except for Dakar (population 693,000), Lagos (665,246), and Accra (633,900), the West African city is small by Western standards. Nevertheless, these cities and the areas of intense commercial cultivation around them are today focuses of fast-paced, often incoherent economic development.

The patterns of labor migration to these cities and their surrounding areas are complex, but in at least two ways they reflect general characteristics of tropical Africa. Men, usually not accompanied by wives and children, move long distances to work for a few months or years in the mines, factories, and fields of the economically advanced areas. Since many of the agricultural and mineral developments in Africa are remote from population centers (although this is less true of coastal West Africa), the lure of cash wages draws tribesmen from villages to urban recruiting

agencies that seek workers to fill the labor needs of company and government enterprises. Both the employer and the employed are reluctant to form continuing relationships. Few rural Africans have been attracted to cities on a permanent basis, one reason why Africa is the least urbanized continent; for their part, employers do not want to provide housing and other facilities needed by a permanent labor force. For these reasons, hundreds of thousands of Africans live out their lives in two worlds, driven from the countryside by lack of opportunity and land, attracted to but uncomfortable in the cities, mines, and factories of developing Africa.

In Senegal and Gambia, some 75,000 *navétanes* (nomadic farmers) migrate seasonally to Dakar and nearby peanut farms from Mali, Guinea, and subsistence areas in Senegal. Cultivating the landlord's fields, these workers receive the right to farm a plot for themselves, a variation of traditional sharecropping arrangements. In Liberia, four-fifths of the labor force that tends the 12 million rubber trees on the Firestone plantations are migrants; the same is true in the diamond fields of Sierra Leone. In developed regions of these countries, men outnumber women two to one, reflecting the pattern of male migration mentioned above.

In the Ivory Coast and Ghana, two important migrant destination areas in West Africa, the cocoa and coffee farms, mining areas in southwestern Ghana, and coastal urban centers draw so many workers from the dry interior of the Saharan fringe that in the 1960s less than half the labor force of the Ivory Coast were natives of the country. Similar movements, though on a smaller scale, occur in the coastal regions of Togo, Benin, and western Nigeria. All told, 1 million people are migrant laborers in West Africa, over half of whom migrate to the Ivory Coast and Ghana. These migrations intensify rather than alleviate regional disparities between the islands of development and subsistence hinterlands.

The industry and commerce of coastal ports in South Africa such as Durban and Cape Town and to a lesser extent Port Elizabeth and East London are more highly developed than in the cities of West Africa, reflecting the fact that South Africa is easily the richest, most powerful, and most advanced country in tropical Africa. In Cape Town, despite apartheid, only 40 percent of the population is now white, the remainder being Bantu migrant laborers attracted by factory employment in this city which, with its suburbs, has a population of 1.25 million. Cape Town may well be the most diversified city on the African continent: it processes the agricultural products of the southwestern part of the cape, and is the second leading port of South Africa and a major center of textile manufacturing, light industry, and fishing. Durban, a metropolitan center of 1 million people, plays a like role in the eastern area of the cape and in addition is the leading port in South Africa because of its rail connections with the Witwatersrand mines. In addition, Durban has sugar refineries, textile factories, oil refineries, and other industries sufficient to rival Cape Town in commercial output. As in Cape Town, Bantu laborers, many of them migrants living in conditions of poverty and humiliation, provide the muscle for industrial growth.

The East African entrepôts, Dar es Salaam and Mombasa, form a third area of coastal commercial activity in Africa. Dar es Salaam, the capital of Tanzania and the starting point of a railroad to the interior of East Africa, now has a population of more than 250,000. As the leading port in the country, it handles the export of commercial crops like cotton, coffee, sisal, cloves, and cashew nuts. The largest industrial city on the East African coast, it attracts migrant laborers from the interior to work in the oil refineries, meat-processing plants, and textile factories as well as seasonal agricultural laborers during the clove-harvesting season. Mombasa, the major port of Kenya, plays a similar role in that country. Linked by rail to the coffee- and cotton-growing regions of Lake Victoria, it is developing into an important industrial center approximately the same size as Dar es Salaam. Recent mining discoveries north of the city have attracted migrants to the coast, above and beyond those working on landlord-owned

coconut, mango, and citrus orchards in the immediate hinterland.

Interior Agriculture

The two major regions of highly developed commercial agriculture in the African interior are located in the highlands of East Africa near Lake Victoria and the Nigerian interior. The East African highlands of Kenya and Uganda are densely populated, well-watered lands that have been zones of historical conflict. Europeans penetrated to Lake Victoria in Kenya and constructed a railroad into the interior at a time when the Masai and the Kikuyu, the two largest ethnic groups in the region, had been weakened by smallpox and cattle epidemics. Attracted by the fertile environment and temperate climate of the highlands, European settlers established farms on apparently vacant land. Some 12,000 square miles of this well-watered high country on either side of the Rift Valley, reserved for European farmers in the 1930s, came to be called the White Highlands. About half this area is developed in mixed farming, and the remainder is given over to ranches and coffee, tea, and sisal plantations. At independence, the 12,000 Europeans in these Kenya highlands employed about 150,000 African farm laborers, the majority of them descendants of the displaced Kikuyu. Nairobi, located astride the rail connection between this rich farming region and the coast, developed into a metropolis of 500,000 people. After the Mau-Mau uprisings of the 1950s, many Europeans left Kenya and most of the mixed farming areas were transferred to African hands, but the plantations and ranches remain European and still employ thousands of local and migrant workers in this very densely populated, productive agricultural region.

In neighboring Uganda, a fertile crescent of highly developed commercial agriculture like that in Kenya is located on the well-watered northern shores of Lake Victoria. The developmental history of this region, however, differs from that of Kenya and indeed is unique in tropical Africa. When the British assumed control over Uganda in the 1890s, they signed an agreement with the most powerful kingdom in the region, Buganda, located north of the lake, confirming the power of tribal leaders and awarding them official estates. The full significance of this concession to African land ownership did not become apparent until the main commercial crops of the region, cotton and coffee, were introduced some-

This complex of terraces, roads, and pits has changed the landscape of Mount Nimba in Liberia, but the iron ore it produces will contribute to the spread of economic development in Africa. The mine, opened and developed by Europeans, utilizes the most modern labor-saving machinery. *Photo:* Marc & Evelyne Bernheim/Woodfin Camp & Associates.

what later. When the British were attracted to these farms in the 1930s, 80 percent of the agricultural production of Buganda was in native hands, an African success story paralleled only by Ghanian cocoa cultivation.

The original land grants to 4000 people have been subdivided by inheritance and sale so that there are now 130,000 African landowners in Buganda. The expansion of coffee and sugar cultivation, the development of copper mines near Tororo, and the growth of light industry in nearby Kampala have made this one of the most advanced regions in East Africa, attracting large-scale labor migrations from Kenya, Rwanda, and Burundi. Despite the recent expulsion of the Asian commercial community and the administrative restructuring of the Buganda kingdom, this densely populated agricultural region remains the core of the Uganda economy.

The second major region of commercial agriculture in the African interior is located in northern Nigeria, the largest and most populous region in the sub-Saharan savanna. The land here is cultivated by **sedentary**˙ Hausa tribes. Sorghum, millet, and beans are grown for subsistence; cotton and peanuts are raised for cash. In the vicinity of the Muslim city of Kano (population 300,000), population densities approach 500 per square mile, and an estimated 2 million people live within 30 miles of the city. Although the Muslim north has traditionally been the most conservative region of Nigeria, deeply re-

sistant to modern change, the cultivation of commercial crops was readily adopted throughout the savanna in the colonial period for obvious environmental reasons. Until recently, the region attracted thousands of migrant laborers from throughout Nigeria who arrived to harvest the cotton and peanut fields of the north. The drought of the early 1970s, however, has reversed the flow of migrants; today, Nigerians from the north, the agricultural Hausa, and the pastoral Fulani are migrating southward to the coast, reducing the pressure on resources in their interior homelands.

Mineral Exploitation

The third major type of modern economic activity that created European islands of development in Africa was the discovery and exploitation of the rich mining belt which sweeps northward from the Witwatersrand district of South Africa through Rhodesia to the Copperbelt of Zambia and Katanga Province in Zaire. Development began in 1867, when the children of a Dutch farmer near Hopetown on the banks of the Orange River were found playing with a 22-carat diamond; within three years, 50,000 miners were combing the South African interior for diamonds and other precious metals, and the Kimberley mines were established. Twenty years later gold was found on the Witwatersrand some 300 miles to the northeast, and a year later Johannesburg, destined to become the largest city of tropical Africa, was founded nearby. The wealth from the Kimberley diamond mines provided capital for the development of the gold mines of the Witwatersrand; the wealth from gold has played a vital role in the sustained growth of the South African economy.

A complex combination of geological events created a rich mineral-bearing region in the Witwatersrand. In an area of a few thousand square miles, base metals, coal, precious minerals, and underground water are found next to one another. This resource base now supports a 50-mile-long, 20-mile-wide industrial and commercial complex centered on Johannesburg with a population of about 3 million. Gold is still the most important single mineral resource in the region, accounting for one-half of South Africa's mineral output and employing 500,000 workers, but the production of uranium, platinum, nickel, coal, iron ore, and manganese has increased substantially. Because extracting 1 ounce of gold from the mines requires crushing 3 to 4 tons of rock, other economic minerals, particularly uranium, are processed from the vast *tailing hills*• found in the mining regions.

The major problem in the Witwatersrand remains securing enough labor to work in the mines, steel mills, and factories of the urban belt. At the turn of the century, some 50,000 indentured Chinese were imported for this purpose, but they were later repatriated. Since then, labor has been recruited from native Bantu populations in neighboring countries—Mozambique, Botswana, Lesotho, and Swaziland. Only single males are allowed into South Africa, and they cannot remain in the country after their labor contract is fulfilled. In small Lesotho, whose men have been specialists in sinking shafts in the gold fields for three generations, three-fifths of the adult male labor force is absent from the country at any one time. In South Africa, this labor policy has discouraged the emergence of a resident black work force that might demand what it is not now receiving: fair treatment.

In Rhodesia, similar but less extensive mining opportunities were an incentive for European settlement of the region. Gold had been mined in Rhodesia by native Africans for nearly 1000 years, from the founding of the great ancient religious center of Zimbabwe to the beginnings of European penetration. After the Matabele, a fierce Zulu tribe, were defeated by British troops in 1893, settlers and miners made their way northward from South Africa into Rhodesia in search of another Witwatersrand. They found one, though on a much more limited scale, in a belt extending from the capital city of Salisbury southward 300 miles to Bulawayo. Initially, gold was the most important mineral produced, although in export terms asbestos, coal, pig iron, and chrome are now more significant. The recent discovery and development of nickel ores at Bindura, north of Salisbury, may be of sufficient importance to double the value of mineral exports from Rhodesia.

As in South Africa, laborers in these mines and the 100,000 factory workers in associated industries are native Bantu, so that Africans outnumber Europeans in the two largest industrial centers, Salisbury and Bulawayo. Rhodesia is a less important magnet for

migrant laborers, however, than the Witwatersrand; fewer than 60,000 men work in the mines. But the same pattern of bachelor migration, the same repatriation regulations exist for laborers from Mozambique and Zambia, and the same wage rates are found: Africans who labor in the mines and factories of Rhodesia earn one-tenth as much as Europeans employed there.

The two remaining mineral and mining regions of tropical Africa, the Copperbelt of Zambia and Katanga Province of Zaire, abut on a border originally drawn to separate the competing colonial claims of Cecil Rhodes for British South Africa and King Leopold II for his Congo. In Zambia, the huge ore resources of the Copperbelt were developed in the 1930s to meet growing world demand in the electrical and automotive industries. Currently this region covers a zone 80 by 20 miles whose seven towns make up nine-tenths of Zambia's urban population and an equivalent share of its industrial and mining activity. The copper from this region is produced in sufficient quantity to rank Zambia as the third leading producer of this metal; more important, it provides half the government's revenue and is Zambia's only important export. Unlike the situation in South Africa and Rhodesia, a series of worker strikes and labor laws have bettered the living conditions and wage scales of the 40,000 miners and 20,000 factory employees who work here. As a result, most migrant laborers have brought their families to the Copperbelt, creating a relatively stable working population, a situation barred by policy in the white-dominated states.

In Zaire's Katanga Province, mining activities were developed by concession companies under the Belgians. As in neighboring Zambia, copper became the most important mineral export from the region, but in addition Katanga produces major amounts of tin and zinc, two-thirds of the world's cobalt (a steel alloy), and almost all the world's radium. The labor force in the mining and smelting centers of Lubumbashi (Elisabethville) and Likasi (Jadotville) is relatively stable, although the need for workers in the mines still attracts migrants from throughout Central Africa. The position of Katanga as an island of European development in Zaire was an underlying force in the attempt by this province to secede at independence; its vital contribution to the economy of the nation makes it of great value to the central government.

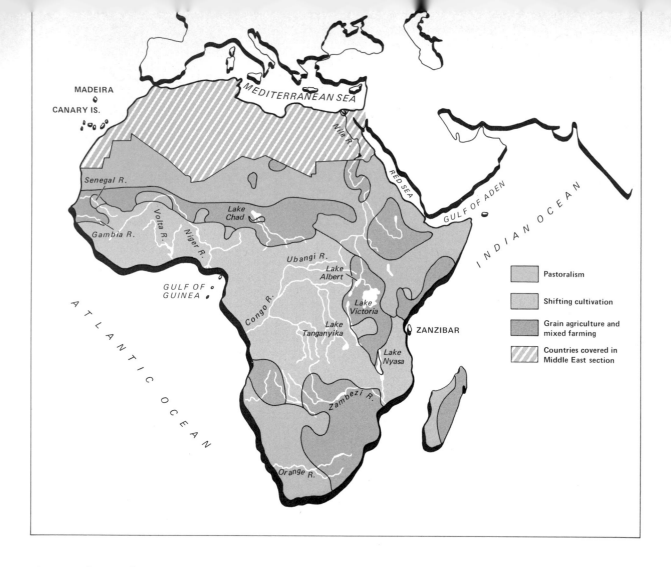

Figure 6. African Subsistence Economies.

Legend:
- Pastoralism
- Shifting cultivation
- Grain agriculture and mixed farming
- Countries covered in Middle East section

AFRICAN SUBSISTENCE ECONOMIES
[FIGURE 6]

Away from the port cities, the commercial farming areas, and the mining centers of these islands of modern commercial development, the vast majority of Africans continue to depend on their fields and herds for survival. Only one out of ten modern Africans is an urbanite and an even smaller percentage work in the European labor markets established during the colonial period. Thousands of families never entered the economic orbit of the European sector, were never touched by expanding transportation networks, market economies, and the spreading waves of commercialization. For them, society and economy continue to be pursued in small, semiisolated ethnic groups, closely tied to local environments, separated from other groups by language and belief, poor in terms of cash equivalents but until recently rarely threatened by famine. A majority of Africans today, perhaps as much as 60 percent of the population occupying the 4 million square miles of tropical Africa, live as subsistence cultivators and herdsmen in this traditional sector of the African dual economy.

The small scale of these traditional economies differs sharply from the social context of industrialized Western societies. In part, the incredible cultural diversity of Africa, where 750 to 1000 mutually unintelligible languages separate ethnic groups from one another, limited the degree to which larger scale settlements and marketing systems could emerge. But these local economies also reflect critical environmental limitations in tropical Africa. In the wetter tropical areas of West and Central Africa soils are of poor quality, with less than one-tenth the organic content of cultivated soils in the United States and Western Europe. Over much of East Africa, rainfall is low and erratic, and the level of environmental risk is frequently directly proportional to the density of population. Diseases of animals, tsetse flies and ticks, and human diseases like malaria and bilharziasis, further militate against the emergence of dense agricultural populations except in highly favored environments. The rudimentary technology of African agriculture also restricts the area of cultivation to the limits of physical endurance. Faced with these conditions, small-scale economies are the rule in Africa, though they are neither simple nor crude.

The three major traditional African economies—shifting cultivation in the wet, tropical core of Central Africa and parts of the Guinea coast; grain agriculture and mixed farming in the more temperate belt running eastward from the interior of West Africa and southward through the highlands of East Africa to the South African veld; and pastoralism in the dry sub-Saharan fringe, parts of East Africa, and the margins of the Kalahari—are sophisticated African social adjustments to the diverse environments of the continent. African cultivators have adapted their methods and patterns of cropping to the limitations of the environment: they *fallow*[•] to increase soil fertility, move when a minimum threshold of agricultural productivity threatens the well-being of the group, and employ patterns of land use which if unsuccessful in preserving and/or enhancing the environment at least minimize soil deterioration. Similarly, *pastoralists*[•] use complicated and flexible patterns of animal husbandry, adapting migrations to annual and seasonal grazing resources to maintain the size and quality of their flocks. This is not to suggest that preindustrial African societies achieved complete harmony with their environments: epidemics decimated populations, plant and animal diseases destroyed the physical bases of life, and entire cultures fled to new regions to escape slavers, wars, and political subjugation. But the economies of traditional Africa did achieve at least some degree of equilibrium with complex environments, so that the chronic hunger and starvation found throughout history in Asia rarely visited the African continent.

All these systems, however, were predicated on precolonial economic conditions and precolonial concepts of space, property, and resources that are now threatened by changes stemming from the modern sector of the economy. In most African groups, concepts of private property and individual ownership of land and resources do not exist. Instead, regions and their raw materials are conceived of as cultural domains that any member of the tribe, clan, or *extended family*[•] has the right to utilize. In this system, each member of the group has access to land, grazing areas are communal, and no one lacks the basic elements needed to pursue a livelihood. Unlike most of the developing world, where a small landowning elite controls production and a mass of commoners labors for shares, in Africa space and resources are viewed in communal, egalitarian terms as are the crises of human existence.

But the colonial intrusion disturbed this equilibrium between the Africans and the land. The introduction of medicine and health care spurred population growth at a rate of increase of 2.5 percent per year, exceeded only in Latin America. Traditional economies, well adapted to small populations

and extensive resource areas, feel the impact of rising population in terms of the fragmentation of cultivated land into small, unproductive holdings and the overgrazing of communal pastures. In Central Africa, the colonial sale of "unoccupied" land to concession companies took away those areas to which shifting cultivators could move when soil fertility declined. In East Africa, national boundaries block pastoral migrations. In the hinterlands of Zambia, Rhodesia, and parts of South Africa, the flight of the men from villages to factories has made the pursuit of subsistence agriculture impracticable. And in the settler areas of South and East Africa, Europeans took land for themselves by force of arms. The amount allocated to each group, to the "civilized" Europeans and the "primitive" Africans, was based on a dual standard of "need." In South Africa the Europeans needed nine-tenths of the land, in Rhodesia and Swaziland a disproportionate half, and in Angola and Mozambique an equivalent share. All these forces have created new pressures on the traditional agricultural and pastoral economies, pressures most experts, African and others, believe are forcing their integration into the commercialized national economies of independent Africa.

Shifting Cultivation

Shifting cultivation—or as it is sometimes called, slash-and-burn agriculture—is widely practiced in the tropical forests of Central Africa and the Guinea coast and in the savanna reaches of the West African interior and highland East Africa. In both these regions, land is cultivated in hillside patches as long as it retains sufficient productivity to support the group, usually four or five years. Then the group moves to a new location and establishes new fields, leaving the former fields to lie fallow long enough to regain their fertility. The key variable in the system is the character of the soil. On the rich volcanic soils of Mount Kilimanjaro and in Buganda, near continuous cultivation of bananas and plantains is achieved. On weak, highly leached soils in the rain forest it takes from twenty to twenty-five years for the soil to recover sufficiently to be recultivated. Given the nature of the system, a vast amount of land is required to support densities of population that in most regions rarely exceed 15 people per square mile. For this reason and because it was considered destructive of vegetation, most Western experts until recently considered shifting cultivation to be a most

At a desert well some 10 miles from Khartoum, nomads use donkeys to pull out the water-filled gourds and cans. The cans are the only things that make this scene different from that of thousands of years ago; though drought in the area has exacerbated the difficulty of survival, life has as yet changed little for the people of the Sahel, despite efforts to introduce modern irrigation and well systems that could alter the landscape. *Photo:* Marc & Evelyne Bernheim/ Woodfin Camp & Associates.

primitive form of agriculture. In fact, this system is a sophisticated form of economic improvisation designed to cope with changing soil and weather conditions, levels of health, and other circumstances beyond the control of either the individual African or the cultural group.

In forested regions, the settlements of shifting cultivators usually amount to a dozen or so huts surrounded by vegetable gardens, plantains, and valuable palm or fruit trees. Paths radiate out from the village to patches of land, cleared by burning in the forests, where maize, yams, cassava, and manioc are planted. The clearings, usually located on slopes, are opened to sunlight by chopping down smaller trees and girdling and burning the larger ones. Most families can clear, weed, and cultivate only 2 to 3 acres a year. Plants are scattered in the most favored micro-

environments: bananas on the most fertile soil, pumpkins and sweet potatoes in areas with high ash content, yams in moist depressions, and grains where nothing else will grow. In the first year fertility is high, but as the forest begins to close in, as soils stripped of vegetation erode, as the crops drain nutrients from the poor, **leached soils,** the productivity of each patch declines. As long as an adequate food supply is produced, the plants are cleverly selected so that they mature at different times of year, and the settlement remains fixed. When fertility declines and the distance between patches and the village becomes overlong, the group moves to a new location, abandoning the fields to the natural processes of forest growth. The system works where population density is light. But when population grows, as it has in the uplands of Sierra Leone and the Ibo country of southeastern Nigeria, the abandoned patches do not have time to recover fertility before being recultivated, and a downward ecological spiral of soil erosion and declining agricultural productivity occurs.

In the savanna, shifting cultivation varies considerably with local environment and tribal traditions. On the northern plateau of Zambia and in southern Zaire, ash burning is practiced: trees are cut over a large area, stacked on the fields, and burned. The ash residue fertilizes the soil as potash, and heat from the fires breaks the soil down, making cultivation easier. Sorghum, millet, cassava, and other crops can be grown for at least two years before soil exhaustion forces abandonment. But in other areas of the savanna, more advanced systems of cultivation have evolved. Among the Hausa of northern Nigeria, for example, the application of animal fertilizers to burned areas prolongs soil fertility and postpones the necessity of relocation. Similarly, other groups located near towns and large villages utilize manure to make their agricultural locations more permanent.

The standard of living of these groups is usually quite low, because the major advantage of an agricultural way of life, the growth of settled communities, is negated by the periodic necessity to shift locations. Seasonal droughts, pests, and epidemic diseases afflict many, and as in most marginal environments, the risk is high and so is the death rate. Food intake, however, is generally sufficient to prevent malnutrition, but protein deficiency is acute. Kwashiorkor, a disease that causes anemia, learning disabilities, and distended bellies in children, is widespread. Because the economy is noncommercial, people eat only what they grow—carbohydrates, not proteins. To some degree, farming is supplemented by hunting, fishing, and collecting, depending on local environmental opportunities, but few animals are kept because most of Central Africa is infested by the disease-carrying tsetse fly. The distribution of protein deficiencies and tsetse fly areas from which cattle are barred accord well in Africa, suggesting the importance of this insect in determining the human economy. Only in South Africa are cattle raising and protein deficiencies found in the same region: the whites have the cattle; the blacks have the protein deficiencies.

Grain Cultivation and Mixed Farming
[FIGURE 7]

A belt of grain cultivation and mixed farming encircles the equatorial core of tropical Africa, occupying the subhumid transition zone between the constantly hot, wet environment of the rain forest and the deserts to the north and south. Grain is a staple food in the savanna belt from Senegal on the Atlantic Ocean to the Ethiopian highlands, as it is in a north-south strip from the highlands of East Africa to the high veld of South Africa. Among Africans, mixed farming is rare, and where found usually represents collaboration between two ethnic groups, a pastoral group on the dry steppe margins of the savanna and an agricultural group in the more humid fringe. In the temperate highlands of East and South Africa, however, mixed farming is extensively practiced by white planters who transferred this agricultural economy from Europe to Africa.

Rice is cultivated in villages in Senegal, Sierra Leone, Liberia, and the Ivory Coast, but rain lessens eastward in the West African interior, and sorghum, millet, and corn become the principal crops. Conditions of cultivation vary with elevation, rainfall, local soil conditions, and the technological skill of the cultivators. In more remote sections of this grain belt, the digging stick is still the principal agricultural implement, although commonly a short-handled hoe is used to till the soil. In northern Nigeria, villagers employ the pastoral Fulani to herd their flocks; similar exchanges occur between the cattle herders of East Africa and nearby settled farming communities. Africans rarely, however, engage in mixed farming in the European sense of combined animal and crop raising. Among the exceptions are the people of Ukara Island in Lake Victoria, whose intensive mixed farming economy supports a population of 600 people per square mile, and the Kabré hill dwellers of northern Togo, who crop irrigated fields fertilized by cattle kept in corrals.

In areas of colonial settlement—the White Highlands of Kenya, the plantations of Mozambique, the ranches of Angola, and in the mixed farming belt of South Africa—combined crop and cattle raising is quite common. Western technology, knowledge of fertilization and crop rotation practices, and seizure of the most suitable agricultural environments from the Africans enabled the colonialists and their descendants to establish permanent farms on the African continent.

These regions of permanent settlement and sedentary life have already felt the impress of modernization and have begun to make the transition from subsistence to market agriculture. In northern Nigeria, Ghana, and Uganda, full commercial agriculture exists; in the less well located regions of West Africa, a system of *periodic markets* provides the basis for agricultural exchange. In East Africa, the growth and evolution of circulation networks and settlement hierarchies are integrating rural Africans into national systems. The transformation of African agriculture is the single most important economic change now taking place on the continent: as it progresses, regional inequities generated by the colonial dual economy may be eased.

The geographer Peter Gould studied this process in Tanzania to identify the underlying factors in the diffusion of modernization across Africa. In the 1920s, the *modernization surface* in Tanzania as

A Kereyu tribesman in Ethiopia herds the distinctive long-horned African cattle along a highway toward a new grazing ground. Though Ethiopia is one of the oldest known countries of the world, its modernization is still many years away. *Photo:* United Nations.

Figure 7. Tanzania: The Spatial Impress of Modernization. In Tanzania in the 1920s, urban centers—most prominently Dar es Salaam—were the only nodes of development and modernization. Part (a) shows the distribution of modernization then in terms of contoured areas in a lighter tint spreading out from the urban centers; part (b) shows that by the 1960s modernization was more widespread, but the pattern was a spatial replica of that of the 1920s. *After:* Peter R. Gould, "Tanzania, 1920–1963: The Spatial Impress of the Modernization Process," *World Politics,* Vol. 22, No. 1 (1970), pp. 152, Fig. 2; 167, Fig. 6. Copyright © 1970 by Princeton University Press.

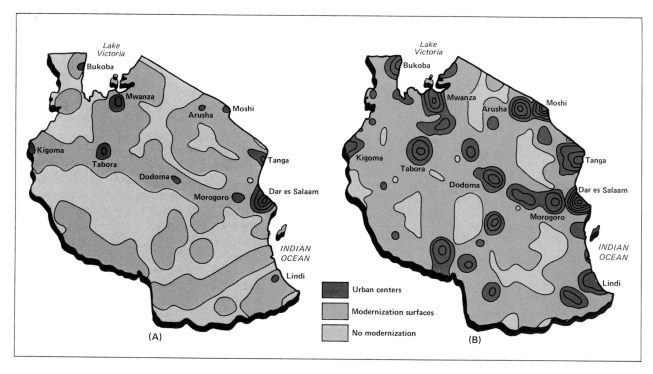

defined by an infrastructure of roads, railroads, hospitals, and government administrative offices appeared in a few islands of development focused on Dar es Salaam and the lower-order cities of Mwanza, Tabora, and Tanga floating, as Gould puts it, "in a millpond of traditionalism." By the 1960s, despite a host of additional measurable variables such as telephones, hospitals, postal stations, and electrical consumption, the spatial pattern of modernization resembled what it had been forty years earlier. Modernization was more intense and widespread, but the major urban centers of Tanzania remained the crucial areas of change. This intimate relationship between the spread of modernization, the emergence

of a **central place** hierarchy, and the dynamics of urbanization reinforces the view that "the town is the door through which Africa is entering the modern world."

Pastoralism

The majority of African pastoralists are cattle keepers who live in environmental transitional zones between desert and forest on the dry-land margins of the grain belt from Senegal to Lake Victoria, through highland East Africa to South Africa, and between the forests of the Congo Basin and the Kalahari Desert. Camel herders are found on the Saharan fringe and in the eastern part of the African Horn;

goats are widespread on the continent and are herded in large numbers on the Serengeti Plain of Tanzania and in other areas of East Africa. The greatest concentrations of cattle are found on the dry plateaus east of Lake Victoria, along the coast of Natal in South Africa, and in the Senegal and Niger river valleys. But vast areas with low precipitation, particularly in East Africa, are inhabited by a sparse scattering of pastoralists. In Kenya, for example, three-quarters of the country has a population density below 10 people per square mile; these are the lands occupied by the cattle-keeping Masai, Jie, and Turkana tribes. Similarly in Tanzania, the Serengeti Plain, Masai Plain, and the dry central plateau are occupied by pastoralists. The distribution of these people is directly related to climatic conditions, to the nature and quality of grazing resources, and to the absence of tsetse flies.

African cattle keepers live much as pastoralists do in other world regions; grazing land for the herds, the critical need, is met by moving animals from one pasture to another throughout the year. Although most pastoralists occupy dry lands not suited for agriculture, complex patterns of cooperation, conflict, tension, and trade mark the boundaries between settled farmers and nomadic herders. Migration routes and patterns of social organization vary widely. Among the Baggara, who herd cattle between the White Nile and Lake Chad, a strategy of constant moves—as many as 60 per year—is typical. In the highlands of the eastern cape, Lesotho and Swazi herders migrate only with the changing of the seasons.

The Turkana, who live west of Lake Rudolf, herd more than 1 million animals between dry lowland plains with as little as 2 inches of rainfall per year and massive granite hills that seasonally receive 20 inches. Split up into tiny groups to maximize use of thin pasturelands, the Turkana lack political cohesion as compared with their relatives the Jie, a tribe living in better watered country in northeastern Uganda. In Nigeria, groups of the nomadic Fulani cattle herders have settled as town dwellers and farmers in the wetter south, so that exchanges of animal and crop products between groups in two distinct environments are handled within the larger tribe. Each system is keyed to local ecology, but in many areas, environmental circumstances have already been altered by the impact of the forces of modernization.

The overall impact of modernization on pastoral groups in Africa has been, directly and indirectly, to encourage sedentarization. In the early years of this century, the great rinderpest epidemics that decimated cattle herds in West and East Africa forced the Fulani, Kikuyu, and Masai to settle temporarily. When Europeans entered East Africa, these newly vacant lands were occupied by white colonists who prevented the expansion of the tribes into former pastures when their herds recovered. Although Europeans controlled the epidemics and cleared environments of tsetse flies, the most favorable areas were taken from cattle herders, reducing their realm and therefore increasing environmental risk. Paradoxically, however, the introduction of pest control in Africa led to a dangerous expansion of the herds in the new nation-states. Most pastoralists continue to view their herds as bank balances—the larger, the better—and higher survival rates among cattle have led to overgrazing and deterioration of pastures.

Indirectly, the growth of population has also played a role in the reduction of pastoralism by pushing agriculture farther into the dry margins of cultivation, denying the herders their most reliable pastures. In addition, the new nation-states of Africa are more eager to count and control their populations than their predecessors, the colonial administrators. Taxes on cattle are high, reducing the herders' margin of profit; raiding, a dignified and honored method of increasing herds in the past, is not tolerated. The future of pastoralism in Africa, therefore, is dim, as mixed farming and cattle ranches increasingly supply the protein needs of settled populations. Pastoralists are being pushed deeper into unattractive environments. This process has been going on for some time; the first white settlers at Cape Town, for example, stole cattle from the Hottentots, drove the tribesmen into the interior of South Africa, and introduced a new and different question into the environment and society of tropical Africa: a question of color.

TROPICAL AFRICA

THE INDUSTRIAL BASE
ENERGY AND MINERAL RESOURCES MAP

Before independence, tropical Africa, except for South Africa, was essentially a continent of subsistence agriculture and an export producer of unprocessed mining products (diamonds, gold, copper, cobalt, manganese, uranium, platinum) and of tropical agricultural products (typically coffee, cocoa, peanuts, and palm oil). Only in the last twenty years has serious attention been paid to building industrial complexes in the region.

Most nations have continued to export raw materials to generate capital, fully realizing that production in the agricultural sector is increasing at a rate of only 2.5 percent each year, slightly less than population growth. Although market prospects are currently favorable for most African commodities, especially petroleum, copper, manganese, cobalt, and uranium, more diversified industrialization is seen as a prerequisite to lightening the burden of poverty that characterizes most of the continent today. In 1970, only 1.5 million Africans south of the Sahara were employed in mining and manufacturing. If the independent states of tropical Africa remain agriculturally based, as is true of 80 percent of the population today (and many of the smaller countries have little choice), Africa will undoubtedly remain the poorest and most underdeveloped part of the developing world for the foreseeable future.

ENERGY SOURCES
Tropical Africa is rich in potential hydroelectric power, has modest petroleum reserves, and except for the states of South Africa and Rhodesia, has virtually no coal resources. Consumption of primary energy, generally regarded as a reliable index of industrial development, is extremely low. Most African countries still rely on the muscles of men and animals and consume 400 to 500 times less energy per capita than does South Africa. Although the total energy capacity of the continent suggests that development can occur rapidly, the massive initial costs of energy projects, chronic shortages of technological personnel, small local markets in most countries, and the requirement of regional cooperation among African countries have thus far retarded exploitation and development of known energy sources.

Tropical Africa possesses 28 percent of the estimated world electric power potential, a gift of rivers running to the sea from the interior plateaus. But the region has developed only 1 percent of its potential capacity; most of this is only recently harnessed or in the developmental stage. In Ghana, the Volta River project will provide energy for an aluminum smelting complex, for the city of Accra, and for export to nearby Togo and Benin; in Uganda, the Owens Falls Dam is located on the Nile at Lake Victoria. The Kainji Dam on the Niger River is capable of fulfilling Nigeria's electrical needs for some years to come; the Kariba Dam on the Zambezi River supplies electricity to the mines and factories of the Copperbelt of Zambia and central Rhodesia; the Inga Dam, upstream from Kinshasa on the Congo River, is in the first stages of construction. According to some estimates, the Congo rapids alone have a greater hydroelectric potential than all the proved waterpower resources of the North American continent.

Petroleum resources, more limited and more localized, are significant factors in the economy of only three countries: Nigeria, Gabon, and Angola. Only Nigeria is a world producer (ninth), and its high-quality, sulfur-free petroleum has special value on world markets. Production of crude oil from wells along the eastern coast reached 1 million barrels a day in the early 1970s. Petroleum is now Nigeria's most valuable export product, generating 75 percent of total revenues, and a refinery has been built at Port Harcourt.

Although production is more limited in nearby Gabon, petroleum and natural gas have had a similar economic impact. A refinery at Port Gentil provides for internal consumption and some regional export. In Angola, the discovery of petroleum near Luanda and later strikes offshore at Cabinda now produce 150,000 barrels of oil a day. Although Africa produces less than 2 percent of the world's coal, and that in only two countries, coal is significant as the only local source of power for the Rhodesian economy.

MINERALS AND METALS
At first glance, the array of minerals and metals found in tropical Africa is impressive. This region produces more than half of the world's cobalt

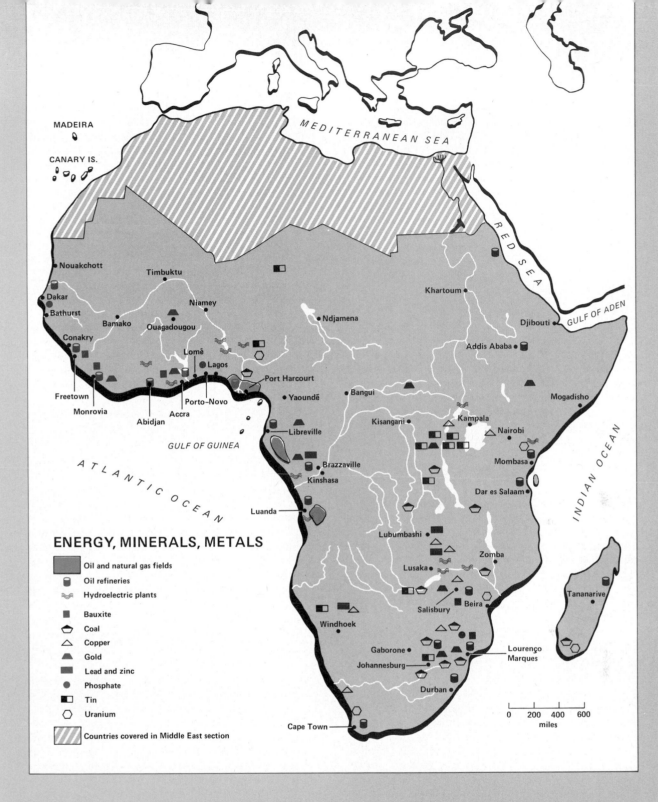

ENERGY, MINERALS, METALS

▨	Oil and natural gas fields
⬢	Oil refineries
≈	Hydroelectric plants
■	Bauxite
⬠	Coal
△	Copper
▲	Gold
▬	Lead and zinc
●	Phosphate
◨	Tin
⬡	Uranium
▨▨	Countries covered in Middle East section

Map labels:

MADEIRA

CANARY IS.

MEDITERRANEAN SEA

RED SEA

GULF OF ADEN

Nouakchott · Timbuktu · Khartoum

Dakar · Bathurst · Niamey · Ndjamena · Djibouti

Bamako · Ouagadougou · Addis Ababa

Conakry · Lomé · Mogadisho

Freetown · Lagos · Porto-Novo · Accra · Abidjan · Monrovia · Port Harcourt · Yaoundé · Bangui · Kisangani · Kampala · Nairobi

GULF OF GUINEA · Libreville · Mombasa

ATLANTIC OCEAN · Brazzaville · Kinshasa · Dar es Salaam

INDIAN OCEAN

Luanda · Lubumbashi · Zomba

Lusaka · Tananarive

Salisbury · Beira

Windhoek

Gaborone · Lourenço Marques

Johannesburg

Durban

Cape Town

0 200 400 600 miles

(Zaire), diamonds (Zaire, South Africa), and gold (South Africa); one-quarter of its manganese (South Africa), platinum (South Africa), copper (Zambia, Zaire), and chromium (South Africa). Africa also produces significant quantities of asbestos (South Africa), iron (Liberia), tin (Nigeria, Zaire), and uranium (South Africa, Gabon). The usual conclusion to this listing is that Africa is well endowed with mineral resources, particularly at the four major mining complexes in the Witwatersrand of South Africa, the Copperbelt of Zambia, in Central Rhodesia and in the Katanga Province of Zaire. Although this may be true, the derivative assumption that the mineral resources of tropical Africa provide the basis for a major world industrial complex will not stand scrutiny except in South Africa.

263

The minerals and metals of this region are scattered from Ghana to Mozambique, often in remote locations, generating considerable regional disparities. Since independence, the integration of the mining centers into more diversified industrial urban regions has proved a slow and diffficult process. For the foreseeable future tropical Africa is likely to remain an exporter of raw metals and minerals to the industrial world because few countries appear to have the human or physical resources to sustain broadly based industry, and patterns of regional integration and cooperation have been slow to develop.

ECONOMIC PATTERNS

Except for South Africa, whose industrial economy is mature, only two nations in tropical Africa—Nigeria and Zaire—have sufficient size and scale to become important industrial nations.

Nigeria, the most populous country in Africa (55 million), has the human and natural resources to make possible economic development on a national scale. During the 1960s, the first Nigerian development plan, a rather conservative document, emphasized expansion of the infrastructure of the country and further cultivation of traditional agricultural export products like cocoa, palm oil, and peanuts. The Kainji Dam was begun, roads were built to reorganize the colonial railroads into a national transportation network, ports were improved, and a petroleum refinery was constructed at Port Harcourt. Agriculture remains the most important sector of the national economy from a statistical viewpoint: 70 percent of the population is engaged directly or indirectly in agriculture; half the nation's income and 40 percent of its exports come from this sector.

But the rapid expansion of petroleum production on the eastern coast, increasing five times in the late 1960s, is the most important factor in the Nigerian economy today. Although the total budget of Nigeria is only one-third that of New York City, the flow of capital generated by demand for sulfur-free Nigerian oil is providing the financial resources necessary to develop industry. Furthermore, Nigeria has more native educated technical people than any other African state, a legacy of British colonial rule. If the country remains unified and secessionist movements like Biafra's do not again

attempt to fragment the territory and resources of the nation, Nigeria will remain one of the few states in tropical Africa with the potential rapidly to raise the standards of living of its people.

The same long-term potential exists in Zaire, although progress since independence has been less rapid. A large nation of only 18.8 million people spread over an area one-fourth the size of Europe, Zaire controls the mineral resources, arable land, and waterpower potential to sustain a balanced, productive economy. As elsewhere in tropical Africa, the colonial economy stressed the production of agricultural and mineral raw materials for export. In Zaire, these are numerous and diverse. A producer of copper, tin, silver, uranium, cobalt, and tungsten, with unexploited deposits of bauxite and iron, Zaire has the minerals and metals to sustain the development of both heavy and light industry when the potential power of the Congo River is harnessed. Similarly, the huge territory of the country encompasses both tropical and subtropical climates and a richer variety of agricultural resources than most African nations.

The abrupt departure of the Belgians and the attendant political upheaval that followed, however, disrupted anticipated patterns of economic development. Wars of secession, insecurity and corruption throughout the countryside, declining health services, rapid urbanization, and a rate of population growth estimated at 4.2 percent (the highest in the world) have all retarded the growth of an industrial economy. And the delayed impact of the Belgian discouragement of advanced education for native people has had an impact upon current development.

The remaining nations of tropical Africa are small, poorly located, or dependent on the export of one or two raw materials. Some, like Angola and Gabon, whose petroleum products are in high demand, may succeed in raising standards of living and reducing the poverty of their people. For others —the numerous drought-ridden nations of the Sahel, the small landlocked enclaves of Lesotho and Swaziland, and resource-poor regions like Botswana—prospects are bleak. Barring the emergence of regional patterns of economic cooperation and the input of intensive technological and financial assistance, the extreme levels of poverty that have been characteristic of tropical Africa until now will prevail.

A QUESTION OF COLOR

4

It began on April 6, 1652, when three ships of the Dutch East India Company anchored in Table Bay in Cape Town. On landing, the Dutch were met by a party of about fifty pastoral Hottentots. Within six weeks, the Dutch captain, Jan van Riebeeck, faced with finding the labor needed to establish a colony, hatched a plan to capture the Hottentots, seize their cattle, and sell the able-bodied men into slavery.

It was not that the Hottentots were nonwhite, but rather that they were non-Christian, "pagans beyond redemption," according to Dutch Calvinism. Thus they could be enslaved. Discrimination in these early days was based on religion rather than race, a fact that explains the considerable intermarriage in the early years between European whites and converted, Christian Africans which created a mixed race, the Cape Coloureds, who live in the vicinity of Cape Town today. But prejudice on a racial basis has a long history in South Africa. In 1660, a wild almond hedge was planted on a hill above Cape Town beyond which no Hottentot was supposed to venture. The color bar had been established.

For the Dutch, the "welfare of the settlement" demanded that blacks be subjugated, dispossessed of their lands and herds, and forced to labor in the colonists' fields. When sufficient slaves could not be found locally, others from Java, Madagascar, and India were imported, so that until the nineteenth century, slaves outnumbered their white masters by a substantial margin. The Dutch and other colonialists who followed were, after all, simply saving the "natives" from "leading an indolent life." As European control spread across the African continent, the colonial stereotype of Africans as an inferior, lazy, ignorant people, devoid of the finer human qualities and lacking in history and culture, became both the rationale and the justification for the establishment of stratified color-based societies. As this system evolved, the maintenance of master-servant relations between white and black also became fundamental to the political and economic structure of the European regime.

When the winds of change swept Africa after World War II, European governments reassessed the costs of maintaining white rule in their African possessions in the face of the rising tide of African nationalism; one after another, however reluctantly, the colonial powers found the price in money and lives too dear. The British, French, Belgians, and Germans abandoned their colonial empires. In the colonies of Angola, Mozambique, and Portuguese Guinea, which provided revenue amounting to 25 percent of the total budget of the home country, the Portuguese stayed until a change in government in Lisbon forced a reassessment of the Portuguese role in Africa in the 1970s. In areas of dense white settlement in South Africa, Namibia, and Rhodesia, however, white minorities were determined to stay, and stay they have.

In Angola and Mozambique, large numbers of Portuguese settlers—300,000 in Angola and 100,000 in Mozambique—were enticed to Africa to run the diamond mines and agricultural estates on which substantial numbers of native Africans labored. As racial tensions rose and nationalist movements in the large African populations of 5.5 million in Angola and 7.7 million in Mozambique began to resist colonial rule, Portuguese troops were brought in to crush native rebellions. A bloody campaign of guerrilla resistance was waged in both Angola and Mozambique, with Portuguese rulers determined to build and maintain the fiction of a Greater Portugal in Africa until the 1974 coup d'état in Lisbon. Similarly in Rhodesia, a white minority of 250,000 asserted their right to remain the rulers of 5 million black Rhodesians and declared their unilateral independence from Great Britain in 1965. Despite economic sanctions and world censure, the European minority has retained control in the face of increasing racial violence and guerrilla attacks. Nowhere has the exercise of white racism been more efficient or pronounced than in South Africa (and by extension Namibia). The early dominance of van Riebeeck's Dutchmen has been translated into an official government policy of racial segregation, apartheid, a territorial and social solution to the problems of multiracial living more extreme than any racial policy yet devised, except of course that of German National Socialism.

A street in Johannesburg. *Photo:* Jerry Frank/Design Photographers International.

APARTHEID: A GEOGRAPHICAL SOLUTION TO RACIAL PREJUDICE
[FIGURE 8]

In 1948, the Boer or Afrikaans national party in South Africa was elected to power on a platform of apartheid, or separate development, which promised to segregate the Bantu-speaking African majority from the European minority. The object was to transform a multiracial society colored black at the bottom, Asian and Cape Coloured above, and white at the top into a union of color-coded, semi-independent territories. In these territories, or homelands, each group could presumably develop its own society and traditions. Cultural and racial pollution would be averted, and white dominance over the greater part of South Africa would be maintained. Some 260 fragmented areas in South Africa were set aside as Bantu reserves, from which eight native African Bantustans (Bantu states) would emerge. Similar plans of residential segregation were developed for the Cape Coloured and the Asians, with specific locations set apart from the white population for each group. By the late 1950s, the planning stage was finished, all nonwhites were denied the right to vote, and a spate of apartheid legislation was passed, giving spatial and racial segregation the force of law.

Society and economy in South Africa have for some time been guided by the determination of the white minority to retain control of the country. The conscious development of apartheid as a government policy stemmed from white fears that in any inte-

JOHN MVALO, MIGRANT LABORER: A MAN OF TWO WORLDS

John was conceived during one of his father's visits home from the mines, and he was born in 1906 at Chatha. . . . When he was six years old his mother took him with her to the trading store where for the first time he saw a white man. When he was a little older he began to help herding the cattle and playing with the other boys. His parents were pagan and he never went to school. . . . From the older boys he heard much about life in town and in 1922 when he was 16 years old his father, who was at home at the time, said he could go to work in East London. He travelled there with a friend from Chatha, who had worked in East London before. They both lived with his mother's sister who had a shack in the West Bank location. He was there for two years during which time he had six different jobs. . . . He then got into some trouble with the police and returned home to Chatha. His father, who was at home, said it was time for him to become a man. So he attended the initiation school and was circumcised in July 1924. After this was over he went to work on the mines from September 1924 to July 1925 and then came home for six months. He made five further trips to work on the mines with visits home between each. When in 1931 he returned home from his sixth visit to the mines he had some money saved, and his father helped him with cattle so he was able to marry.

He stayed at Chatha for two years seeing the birth of his eldest child, but money was needed for the support of his family, . . . so he went off to work again. This time he went to Cape Town and worked in the Royal Dairy as a milk delivery boy. . . . He stayed there three years before returning home, but he sent money back to his wife regularly. He made several further visits to Cape Town, where he often worked for the same dairy; but he once had a job as a domestic servant, and once as a cleaner at the post office. His next job was at the ISCOR steel works in Pretoria. This was in 1942, and the war led to good wages. Then he had a job at the Drill Hall, in Johannesburg in 1945.

He came home in 1947. He was now over forty years old. His wife had borne him four sons (one of whom had died in infancy), and two daughters. Although he was still pagan, he insisted that his children went to school because he wished them to learn to read and write. He had now eight head of cattle and ten sheep. His eldest son was 15 years old and would soon be able to go out to work, so he thought he would stay at home. In 1948, however, there was a serious drought in the Ciskei, six of his cattle died and the mealie crop failed completely. He set off to work again—this time to Port Elizabeth, where he found employment in the Eastern Province Herald office moving rolls of paper. He worked there for four years with two short visits home, but in 1953 he returned home to settle there permanently. He was then 47 years old, and the eldest son of 21 years was doing his second stint on the gold mines.

Of his working life from the age of 16 to 47 (31 years) 36 percent of his time was spent at home and 64 percent in employment away. He had had 34 different jobs, and the average length of a job had been 47 weeks.

Source: Quoted from D. Hobart Houghton, "Men of Two Worlds: Some Aspects of Migratory Labor in South Africa," *South African Journal of Economics,* Vol. 28 (1960), pp. 179–180.

4. A QUESTION OF COLOR

TROPICAL AFRICA

267

grated society, the Europeans would be demographically swamped by the overwhelming Bantu majority. In 1970, South Africa's total population of 22.1 million was composed of 15.5 million (70 percent) Bantu-speaking Africans, 3.8 million (17 percent) whites of Afrikaans or English descent, 2.2 million (10 percent) Cape Coloured, and 664,000 (3 percent) Asians of Indian extraction.

The African majority are almost all Bantu speakers from two major groups, the Nguni and the Sotho. Originally herders and farmers who lived in small villages, these people were either crowded on homeland reserves by the 1970s, living as squatters on white-owned Afrikaner farms, or huddled in the working-class districts of the four major industrial regions of South Africa in the vicinity of Johannesburg, Durban, Port Elizabeth, and Cape Town.

Two-thirds of the 3.8 million whites in South Africa are native speakers of Afrikaans, and one-third are English speakers. Thus the descendants of the Boers definitely outnumber the British, particularly in the old Boer republics of the Orange Free State and the Transvaal. The Boers have guided the economic development of South Africa, dominating every aspect of life in the country, ruling the mining and industrial establishments and the plantations, and holding positions of power in society. Originally rural dwellers, two-thirds of the whites now live in urban centers while retaining control directly and indirectly of the most fertile, productive parts of the South African countryside.

The 2.2 million people known as Cape Coloured in South Africa are products of three centuries of mixed breeding between Europeans, Africans, and Asians. Nearly 90 percent live in the city of Cape Town, and except for a small English-speaking group in Natal, the majority speak Afrikaans. Originally holding an advantageous position over the Bantu-speaking Africans because of their close affiliations with the Europeans, racial discrimination has condemned them to menial tasks as farm laborers, servants, and factory workers with the highest mortality rate of any group in the country. The smallest racial group, the Asians, are Indians who were imported to the sugar plantations of Natal in the 1860s as indentured laborers. Now traders and market gar-

deners in Natal, their standard of living approaches that of the Europeans.

Faced with these demographic realities and the success of African nationalist movements in Central and West Africa, the Afrikaaners decided on apartheid as the only policy that would keep them in South Africa and in power. On May 5, 1964, the first **Bantustan** was established in the Transkei; in theory more than 250 other Bantu reserves would be consolidated into seven "historicological" tribal centers in Tswanaland, Vendaland, Pediland, Swaziland, Zululand, Xhosaland, and Sotholand. In fact, Bantu reserves are scattered throughout northern and eastern South Africa primarily on infertile, isolated, desolate land. All cities, industries, railroads, and most of the fertile agricultural lands were retained in the white homeland. Only 13 percent of South Africa is devoted to the Bantustans, on land so destitute of resources that by Afrikaaner reckoning it would take an average 111 acres for a farm family to earn an income of $168 per year. Outside these reserves, Bantus are not permitted to own land or occupy property, cannot vote, are forbidden to join any group or association, and are restricted to some 150 "black spots" located in the vicinity of the larger cities and industrial areas. In one stroke, the policy of apartheid twisted a well-established pattern of economic growth based on African labor and European management and distorted the entire functioning of South Africa as a geographical complex.

ECONOMIC INTEGRATION, SPATIAL SEGREGATION

The political and social engineering of South Africa's population into this program of separate (and unequal) development denies the necessities of an integrated national economy. From the middle of the nineteenth century on, native Africans migrated to the emerging industrial and mining centers of South Africa, to Johannesburg, Cape Town, Durban, Pretoria, and Port Elizabeth. Currently over half the population of the Witwatersrand industrial complex near Johannesburg is composed of native Africans, and though the total Bantu population is still predominantly rural, no major city in South Africa has a white majority. After a century of life and work in these urban centers, few Bantu were allowed to acquire either the skills or the education necessary in the management of a modern economy. But their

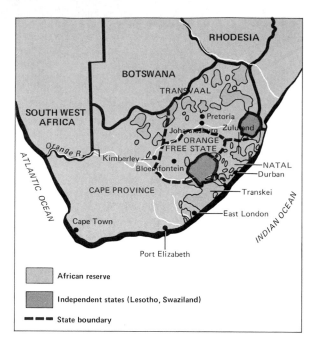

Figure 8. African Reserves in South Africa. The African reserves are the spatial bases for the Bantustans created by the policy of apartheid.

contribution to industrial production is vital to the economy of South Africa. When separate Bantu homelands were established in the hinterland of the industrial centers, these urban Bantu were stranded in white homelands without rights, faced with the alternative of returning to the rural bush where there were no cities and no jobs.

This problem is compounded by a flow of migrant laborers from Bantu reserves to white areas, an exodus which at any one time probably amounts to 40 percent of the able-bodied work force. On the Bantu reserves, every male is forced to pay both a poll tax and a hut tax in cash, and every young man in search of a bride must one way or another accumulate the cash or kind to pay her parents. As a result, the majority of Bantus leave the reserves to become permanent residents in white homelands, returning to the Bantu reserves only for occasional visits. Over 60 percent of the Bantu now live outside their homeland, roughly half working as laborers on the farms, the other half in urban industry. This migration leaves the reserves an economy without manpower; the migrants are transients in two worlds —one without jobs, the other without rights.

Whatever the theoretical attractions of separate cultural development, of apartness, for Bantus, the remarkable cynicism of the South African government in implementing apartheid has disenfranchised the African majority from the land and resources of the nation, reducing them to poverty, humiliation, and pain. On the Bantu reserves, the economic crisis is so intense that an official government commission reported that fully half of the population would have to be removed for the remainder to achieve minimum agricultural subsistence. Given the Afrikaner penchant for shaded figures, these statistics may be understated. Although plans exist for programs of agricultural stabilization and industrial transformation in the Bantu reserves, these goals would have to be accomplished in regions devoid of resources, lacking in transportation facilities, without cities, among people who have never participated in urban, industrial life.

The policy of apartheid, therefore, can only be viewed as a decisive political effort by a white minority to retain supremacy over an impoverished African majority. In the short run at least, it has been successful: the British (except in Rhodesia), Portuguese, French, Belgians, and Germans have all been forced out of Africa; but the Afrikaners remain. Yet the price is heavy, both economically and politically. Each year violence and suppression increase in South Africa, Namibia, and Rhodesia. Incidents on the frontier between the states of white-dominated South Africa and those of black-controlled Central Africa are becoming more frequent. The outcome of these clashes will ultimately decide whether tropical Africa will become a black continent.

BIBLIOGRAPHY

GENERAL

Bernard, Frank E., and Bob J. Walter. *Africa: A Thematic Geography.* Washington, D.C.: United States Department of Health, Education, and Welfare, 1971. A human geography of Africa based on four themes: perception, diffusion, population, and modernization.

Bohannon, Paul, and Philip Curtin. *Africa and Africans.* Garden City, N.Y.: Natural History Press, 1971. Probably the best-written one-volume introduction to Africa; coauthored by an anthropologist and a historian.

Church, R. J. Harrison et al. *Africa and the Islands,* 3rd ed. New York: Wiley, 1971. A basic regional geography of the entire continent.

Grove, A. T. *Africa: South of the Sahara.* London: Oxford University Press, 1970. A well-illustrated, well-written regional geography of sub-Saharan Africa.

Kimble, George H. T. *Tropical Africa,* Vols. 1, 2. New York: Twentieth Century Fund, 1960. Highly detailed geographical analysis of modern Africa.

Paden, John N., and Edward W. Soja. *The African Experience,* Vol. I. Evanston, Ill.: Northwestern University Press, 1970. An interdisciplinary prospectus on the state of African studies.

Prothero, R. Mansell. *A Geography of Africa.* New York: Praeger, 1969. A series of excellent regional essays by prominent geographers of Africa.

[1] THE DARK CONTINENT

Curtin, Philip. *The Atlantic Slave Trade: A Census.* Madison: University of Wisconsin Press, 1969. A heavily documented statistical analysis of the slave trade. Conclusions summarized in "The Atlantic Slave Trade, 1600–1800." In J. F. Ade Ajayi and Michael Crowder (eds.). *History of West Africa,* Vol. I, pp. 240–268. New York: Columbia University Press, 1972.

Davidson, Basil (ed.). *The African Past.* New York: Grosset & Dunlap, 1964. A collection of original sources documenting the growth and development of the continent.

Mannix, Daniel P., and Malcolm Cowley. *Black Cargoes: A History of the Atlantic Slave Trade, 1518–1865.* New York: Viking Press, 1962. A detailed descriptive piece covering the Atlantic slave trade from inception to abolition.

Murphey, E. Jefferson. *History of African Civilization.* New York: Crowell, 1972. A comprehensive, well-written history of the continent with emphasis on the post-European period.

Vansina, J. "Long Distance Trade Routes in Central Africa," *Journal of African History,* Vol. 3 (1962), pp. 375–390. A detailed analysis of trading networks related to the slave trade in the Congo Basin.

[2] COLONIALISM

Betts, Raymond F. (ed.). *The Scramble for Africa.* Lexington, Mass.: Heath, 1972. A collection of articles on the significance and consequences of the Berlin Conference of 1884.

Johnson, Hildegard Binder. "The Location of Christian Missions in Africa," *Geographical Review,* Vol. 57 (1967), pp. 168–202. A spatial study of the role of missionaries in shaping African societies.

Lewis, Roy, and Yvonne Foy. *The British in Africa.* London: Weidenfeld & Nicolson, 1971. Detailed description of various lives and life styles assumed by British men and women in Africa.

Oliver, Roland, and Anthony Atmore. *Africa Since 1800.* London: Cambridge University Press, 1972. A well-written and insightful one-volume history of Africa during the nineteenth and twentieth centuries.

Perham, Margery, and J. Simmons. *African Discovery.* Evanston, Ill.: Northwestern University Press, 1963. One of the many volumes on the course of African exploration.

Rotberg, Robert I. (ed.). *Africa and Its Explorers.* Cambridge, Mass: Harvard University Press, 1970. Accounts of the travels of the greatest European explorers of Africa.

[3] THE WINDS OF CHANGE

Ewing, A. F. *Industry in Africa.* London: Oxford University Press, 1968. A discussion of the problems and prospects for industrialization in Africa.

Gould, Peter R. "Tanzania, 1920–63: The Spatial Impress of the Modernization Process," *World Politics*, Vol. 22 (1970), pp. 149–170. A detailed analysis of the spread of modernization processes through the central place structure of an African state.

Hance, William. *Population, Migration, and Urbanization in Africa.* New York: Columbia University Press, 1970. A detailed analysis of demographic conditions in contemporary Africa.

Hanna, William J., and Judith L. Hanna. *Urban Dynamics in Black Africa.* Washington, D.C.: Center for Research in Social Systems, American University, 1969. Detailed study of the characteristics of emerging urban centers in modern Africa.

Kamarck, Andrew M. *The Economics of African Development.* New York: Praeger, 1971. A systematic study of the economic problems of African countries in their efforts to diversify and develop.

Prothero, R. Mansell. *Migrants and Malaria in Africa.* Pittsburgh: University of Pittsburgh Press, 1965. The relationship between migration patterns and the distribution of malaria in tropical Africa.

de Wilde, John C. *Experiences with Agricultural Development in Tropical Africa,* Vol. I. Baltimore: Johns Hopkins University Press, 1967. A lucid synthesis of traditional African agricultural systems.

Yudelman, Montague. *Africans on the Land.* Cambridge, Mass.: Harvard University Press, 1964. A study of the dual economy, European and African, that characterizes agriculture in Africa with data specifically drawn from Rhodesia.

[4] A QUESTION OF COLOR

Cole, Monica M. *South Africa.* London: Methuen, 1961. An enormously detailed treatment of the systematic and regional geography of South Africa.

Fair, T. J. D. "Southern Africa: Bonds and Barriers in a Multi-Racial Region." In R. Mansell Prothero (ed.). *A Geography of Africa.* New York: Praeger, 1969. Apartheid and other racial policies in the white-dominated southern part of the continent.

Green, L. P., and T. J. D. Fair. *Development in Africa.* Johannesburg: Witwatersrand University Press, 1962. The changing economic structure of southern Africa.

Pollock, N. C., and Swanzie Agnew. *An Historical Geography of South Africa.* London: Longmans, 1963. The evolution of patterns of resource utilization in South Africa from the seventeenth to the twentieth centuries.

Sabbagh, M. Ernest. "Some Geographical Characteristics of a Plural Society: Apartheid in South Africa," *Geographical Review,* Vol. 58 (1968), pp. 1–28. A sensitive delineation of the impact of pluralism on the functioning of South Africa as a geographical complex.

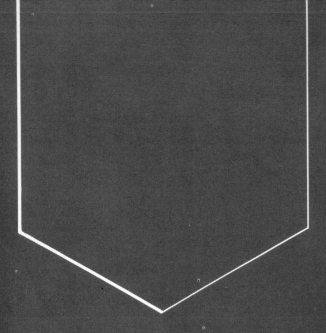

Like many individuals long celebrated in memory for great events, Christopher Columbus led a life that merited anything but the accolades awarded him after death. Columbus devoted most of his adult years to a single-minded quest for weath and fame. He yearned to become a "knight with golden spurs," a man to be reckoned with—no small ambition for a son of a Genoese wool weaver. In the summer of 1476, when he was twenty-five, a Flemish merchant ship on which he had enlisted as a seaman was attacked and sunk by a French naval force off the coast of Portugal, and the penniless sailor was forced to swim to shore. For the next eight years, Columbus lived in Lisbon, the most lively and exciting center of navigation in Europe, earning his way as a mapmaker and bookseller. A sophisticated *cosmographer,* Columbus negotiated a marriage with the daughter of the governor of Madeira, who was from one of Portugal's oldest families. This match gave him access to the court of King John and an opening to pursue his schemes and ambitions.

No one knows precisely when Columbus struck upon the notion of sailing across the Atlantic in search of the fabled Indies; but in 1484, he presented a proposal to the Portuguese king demanding the money and titles due the leader of a westward expedition to what was called Cipango (probably Japan). A royal commission appointed to study his petition determined that the island did not exist. The next year he was again refused; his wife died, and a disappointed Columbus left Portugal for Spain with his five-year-old son, Diego.

At the court of Ferdinand and Isabella, Columbus reformulated his plea, again demanding one-tenth of all tribute, the title Admiral of the Ocean Sea, Viceroy and Governor, and a variety of other privileges and honors as well as funds to support a transoceanic expedition. A commission of Spanish savants studied the question to their satisfaction and concluded correctly that Columbus's estimate of 5000 nautical miles as the distance between Europe and Asia was short by more than half, and incorrectly that the caravels of the day were not capable of such an extended voyage. For the next six years, Columbus followed the Spanish court from one city to another as the Catholic monarchs drove the last Moorish kings from Spain. His threadbare living was gained through family loans and a small royal due. The final report of the royal commission simply confirmed the earlier judgment that Columbus's concept of the globe was mistaken, and Columbus—now gray-haired and forty but stubbornly holding out for titles and percentages—decided to leave for France. In January 1492, a royal messenger from the Spanish court overtook him 10 miles outside Granada: Isabella was prepared to sponsor a voyage.

Just ten months later, the island of San Salvador in the Bahamas was sighted on October 12, 1492, by Rodrigo de Triana, the lookout aboard the *Pinta.* The uneventful trans-Atlantic voyage ended when Columbus went ashore in one of the *Santa María*'s boats, laid claim to his titles and to a continent he believed to be China, and achieved immortality. Within months, Columbus was back in Spain, a public hero, making preparations for a second voyage to the Indies. The seventeen ships he assembled at Cádiz formed the first of many great fleets to sail between Spain and the New World. Some 1500 settlers, with horses, domestic animals, seed, building stores, and weapons, set sail with Columbus on his second voyage as the Spanish colonization of the New World began. They arrived off the coast of Hispaniola in the Caribbean on November 27, 1493.

For Columbus, his second expedition to the New World marked the beginning of a series of unremitting personal disasters that ended only upon his death in 1506. The town of Isabella was successfully established on the northern coast of Hispaniola, with a church, a military storehouse, and a viceroy's residence ringing a central plaza. But Columbus, uninterested in administrative problems and himself ill, sent an expedition into the interior in search of gold. He had, after all, promised his monarch all of China, then known as Cathay. But his ships returned to Spain with only a small quantity of gold and a cargo of Indian slaves. Columbus persistently requested more supplies and livestock, promising to pay for them with additional cargoes of Indians.

Conditions in the colony meanwhile had deteriorated as settlers fell sick from poor diet, malaria, and syphilis. So many men were ill that Columbus drafted gentlemen and priests as laborers; the doctor of the expedition demanded overtime pay. Mutiny and insurrection threatened, and in 1496, the town of Isabella was abandoned for a more favorable site at Santo Domingo. Undaunted, Columbus, now suffering from arthritis, malaria, and a severe

POLITICAL DIVISIONS

MEXICO
Monterrey
Guadalajara
Mexico City

GULF OF MEXICO

BELIZE (Br.)
Belize

GUATEMALA
Guatemala

HONDURAS
Tegucigalpa

EL SALVADOR
San Salvador

NICARAGUA
Managua

COSTA RICA
San Jose

PANAMA
Panama

CANAL ZONE
(USA)

CARIBBEAN SEA

ATLANTIC OCEAN

PACIFIC OCEAN

GALAPAGOS IS.
(Ecuador)

ECUADOR
Quito

COLOMBIA
Bogota

Cauca R.
Magdalena R.

Caracas
Orinoco R.
VENEZUELA

Georgetown
GUYANA
SURINAM (Neth.)
Paramaribo
FRENCH GUIANA
Cayenne

PERU
Lima

Amazon R.

BRAZIL

Sao Francisco R.
Recife

Salvador
(Bahia)

La Paz

BOLIVIA

PARAGUAY

Paraguay R.

Parana R.

Brasilia

Belo Horizonte

Rio de
Janeiro

Sao Paulo

Asuncion

Parana R.

CHILE

ARGENTINA

Uruguay R.

URUGUAY
Montevideo

Santiago

Concepcion
Bio-Bio R.

Valdivia

Buenos Aires

La Plata R.

0   200   400   600
miles

FALKLAND IS. (Br.)

DISCOVERY, CONQUEST, COLONIZATION

1

By the end of the fifteenth century, Spain and Portugal emerged among the strongest and most aggressive European nations, ready to undertake adventures in the New World. For over 700 years, a strong military caste of mounted noblemen (the Spanish caballeros) had fought the Muslim Moors and progressively reconquered the Iberian Peninsula for Catholicism. In the spring of 1492, the last Moorish sultan evacuated the fortress of Alhambra in Granada and retired to Morocco. Spain, a nation of 10 million people, was spiritually and territorially united under the Castilian rule of Ferdinand and Isabella.

Attention in Spain now shifted from warfare with the Moors to trade. The fabled wealth of the East Indies excited interest throughout Europe in voyages aimed at exploration, discovery, and conquest. In neighboring Portugal, Prince Henry the Navigator assembled a stable of **cartographers** and cosmographers to guide Portuguese ships as they groped southward along the African coast. The shipyards of Venice were set busy building larger and swifter craft with cargo holds and space for provisions for longer voyages. Men like Christopher Columbus listened to Renaissance thinkers who claimed that the earth was round and that the East could be reached by sailing west. In this atmosphere Queen Isabella of Spain dispatched a messenger to bring Columbus to her court and pledged him $30,000 to finance the first organized European venture to bring the Old World into contact with the New. Later that same year, 1492, the Niña, the Pinta, and the Santa María sailed west. In October, Columbus landed on the tiny island of San Salvador in the Bahamas, and the Caribbean was claimed for Spain.

THE CARIBBEAN EXPERIMENT

Columbus returned from the New World to Spain with a small amount of gold, some Caribbean parrots, a few spices, six Bahamian Indians, and the electrifying news that land lay only thirty-three days' sail west of Europe. Within a year, a large fleet was outfitted with equipment, seed, and livestock, and some 1500 settlers were recruited to colonize the large island Columbus called Hispaniola. Spain transplanted an Iberian society in miniature to the New World. The threefold purpose of the Spaniards was to find the wealth of the Indies, to convert native peoples to Catholicism, and to establish permanent settlements in order to discourage Portuguese interests and so serve as a base for further Spanish exploration.

In November 1493, the seventeen ships charged with these responsibilities arrived on Hispaniola and established the town of Isabella on its northern coast. Within a few years, 12,000 Spanish colonists moved to the West Indies, and thirteen chartered towns were established. The interests of the Spaniards were quickly realized: Gold was mined in the interior and cotton and sugar fields were planted in the lowlands. All the larger islands in the Antilles were explored. Despite this rapid start, these islands remained the central interest of the Spanish for only thirty years. But in these first thirty years, the Spanish forged the elements of colonial policy that were to endure for over three centuries of direct rule.

Since no European nation had discovered a continent before, Spain had no precedent to follow. The guiding principle in establishing policies and solving problems was to create colonies that would become a credit to both Spain and the Catholic Church. In this early period, extensive power was given to colonial governors, the first of whom was Columbus. These men collected taxes, dispensed law (an *audiencia* or court soon curtailed individual power), and distributed land grants. Consistent with the Spanish desire to establish permanent bases for further exploration, early governors directed the first colonists into agriculture. Columbus introduced horses, sheep, donkeys, cattle, and chickens as well as a variety of agricultural crops—wheat, barley, melons, and cucumbers—to the New World. Later governors introduced grapes, olives, citrus fruits, figs, bananas, and sugarcane. The agricultural economy of the Mediterranean world was gradually reproduced in the Caribbean; because little gold was ever discovered on the islands, the new colonists settled into agriculture and cattle raising.

Most Spanish colonists detested manual labor, and institutions were soon created to force native Indians (and later Africans) to labor in the fields, tend the livestock, and mine the gold. The first of these labor systems was the *repartimiento,* the allotment of Indian labor to Spanish colonists on a temporary basis for specific projects: building a church, clearing a field, or planting an orchard. By 1514, 700 repartimientos had been granted on Hispaniola and 20,000 Indians—peaceful Arawaks and hostile Caribs—labored to sustain the island's new economy. Slavers

A sixteenth-century woodcut of Columbus studying the globe. Not too long before, people believed the earth was flat and that if one sailed too far, one simply fell off the edge. The ship at anchor in the background may be one of the three that made the first voyage to the New World. *Photo:* The Bettman Archive.

combed the Antilles to obtain this labor supply. When word of native deaths from abuse, overwork, and epidemic reached Spain, a second institution, the *encomienda,* was established for the purpose of protecting the Indians. Under the encomienda, Indians were grouped into ecclesiastical hamlets under the control of a Spanish protector who converted and fed them in return for their labor. Unfortunately, the effect of the encomienda was to give the Spanish permanent control of Indians and their land, subordinating their entire lives to the ambitions of Spanish colonists. Needless to say, these institutions failed to protect the Indians; by the 1530s, the native Caribbean labor force was virtually exhausted—slain in abortive rebellions, shipped to Castile as slaves, decimated by epidemics of measles and smallpox, or worked to death in the ***placer mines*** on the rivers of the larger islands.

The economic health of Spain's Caribbean colonies rapidly declined. With native laborers in short supply, farms were abandoned and mines closed down. Although small quantities of gold were discovered on Hispaniola, Puerto Rico, and Cuba, it seemed that El Dorado, the mythical golden city of fabulous

wealth, lay ever elsewhere. The original colonists, who had never had any intention of settling as farmers, joined adventurers dedicated to the quest for fabulous wealth. Two important adventurers, Cortés and Pizarro, headed north to Mexico and south to Peru. The total depopulation of the Caribbean was averted only by meting out dire penalties to colonists who tried to leave. Those caught leaving Hispaniola, for example, were punished by having a leg cut off. Despite these deterrents, old colonists slipped away and new colonists bypassed Spain's island foothold in the New World and immigrated to the mainland. The economy of the islands lapsed into subsistence agriculture and cattle grazing, and Spain's Caribbean colonies retained importance only as defensive and strategic strongholds. Attention shifted instead to the conquest of the mainland as rumors of populous and wealthy Indian civilizations in central Mexico lured Cortés to the land of the Aztec and the Maya.

THE CONQUEST OF MEXICO

The Aztec Federation that Cortés attacked in the sixteenth century was the latest of several native American civilizations to occupy the fertile central ***plateau*** of Mexico. Migrants into the region in the 1300s, the Aztec were the inheritors of the cultures and economies of their predecessors. They had conquered and built an empire extending from the Pánuco River in the north to the border of Guatemala in the south. The Aztec diet reflected the importance of more than ninety separate plants that had been domesticated in Mesoamerica (Middle America). The most important of these—corn, squash, and beans—formed the basis of the Aztec economy. In the Valley of Mexico, a basin 30 by 40 miles wide, an agricultural population of between 1 million and 2 million supported the capital city of the Aztecs, Tenochtitlán. Utilizing the ingenious chinampa system of cultivation (in which artificial gardens were built on reed beds and extended into freshwater lakes to create floating gardens), the Aztec capital was a densely populated region in pre-Columbian Middle America. Elsewhere, intensive cultivation, terraced farming, and irrigation were used in the fields of small, dispersed villages to produce three to four crops in succession during the year. On the eve of the Spanish conquest, this economy supported a population of 12 million to 15 million

guzmā. mıchvacā.

The conquest of Mexico in a contemporary illustration. This colored drawing shows Cortés in battle against the Aztec, whose bows and arrows and magic birds are of no avail against the sword-wielding Spaniards on horseback. *Photo:* The Bettman Archive.

people in central Mexico, an additional 1 million in the highlands of Chiapas and Guatemala, and 500,000 in the Yucatán.

This population was by no means homogeneous, culturally or politically. At the time of the Spanish conquest, eighty different languages belonging to fifteen language families were spoken throughout Middle America. The best known of these groups, the Maya, had developed a civilization of artistic and agricultural sophistication in the tropical *rain forests*[•] and surrounding dry *highlands*[•] of the Yucatán *peninsula.*[•] The Maya were led by a class of priests, and their religion centered upon the careful observance of time and astronomical phenomena. Their economy, based on the cultivation of corn,

was sufficient to support a substantial population in the wet Yucatán lowlands until the Maya abandoned their ceremonial centers around AD 900 and moved to the drier northern part of the peninsula and to the highlands of the interior.

By 1500, much of this region was still controlled by decadent remnants of the Maya, but the powerful Aztec Federation with whom the Maya traded was pressing southward. Both the Aztec and their western neighbors on the central plateau, the Tarascan, were powerful tribute states; the alien towns they conquered paid annual gifts of grain, gold, textiles, cocoa, and human sacrifice to Aztec nobles in Tenochtitlán, the Aztec capital. The Aztec made no effort to integrate the varied people of the empire into their society. Political unrest was therefore considerable, and the military garrisons that dotted the Aztec domain maintained order and ensured the payment of tribute. It was among these disaffected tribes, particularly the Tlascalan, that the Spanish found support in their bid for power, making it possible for Hernán Cortés, the gentleman from Estremadura, to conquer a nation of millions with a handful of men.

Cortés sailed from the port of Santiago, Cuba, in 1518 with 11 ships, 508 soldiers, 109 seamen, 16 horses, and just a few cannon. After landing on the Mexican coast and establishing the city of Veracruz, with the support of dissident tribal groups, Cortés mounted the eastern *escarpment*• of the central plateau of Mexico, marched on Tenochtitlán, and on November 8, 1519, met the emperor of the Aztec Federation, Montezuma. Less than two years later, after complicated maneuvering, the Spanish, aided by the smallpox they brought with them, killed Indians by the thousands and burned the Aztec capital to the ground. The most important center of high civilization in Middle America was destroyed.

In the next decade, the men of Cortés, as they were called, extended Spanish control throughout the Aztec realm. Indian laborers were parceled out in encomiendas granted to all the Spanish officers; Cortés himself received a grant of 25,000 square miles, twenty-two villages and 23,000 Indians. Catholic priests arrived to preach Christianity to the natives and to establish missions on the settlement frontier. Areas of dense population such as the central plateau basins and the valley of Oaxaca were particularly attractive to the Spanish, who retained the Aztec system of tribute and slavery and collected the gold, cotton cloth, and cocoa that had formerly been paid to the Aztec. Higher populations meant more tribute so that populated areas of New Spain (Mexico) were anchored by new Spanish cities of substantial size: Mexico City was founded on the ashes of Tenochtitlán in the Valley of Mexico, Antequera (Oaxaca de Juárez) was built in the valley of Oaxaca, and Colima developed in the rich mining area on the Pacific slope of the western *cordillera*• that had formerly provided the Tarascan state with gold, silver, and copper. Smaller towns were established at strategic locations to maintain order.

There was little resistance to this extension of Spanish rule across the central plateau for two reasons: First, the maintenance of the Aztec tribute system affected most natives as a simple change of rulers; and second, virulent epidemics of smallpox, measles, and typhus slaughtered the Aztec and Tarascan populations. During the first century of Spanish rule, the Indian population of Middle America declined 75 to 80 percent, from an estimated 12 million to 15 million at the time of conquest to 2.5 million in 1600. As early as 1540, encomienderos complained of low populations and diminished tribute from villages where Old World crops such as wheat and sugarcane were established, and from the highland pastures and lowland *savannas*• where livestock had been introduced.

The primary interest of the Spanish, however, remained gold. The highlands of southern Mexico

and the escarpments of the central plateau were quickly brought under their dominion in order to control Aztec and Tarascan sources of mineral wealth. As settlement progressed outward from the Aztec core area, the Spaniards met stiff resistance from warlike Indians in the highlands of Chiapas and Guatemala, and from remnant Maya groups who resisted Spanish incursions until the 1540s. Similarly, in the northern frontiers of the Aztec realm, the Spanish encountered the hostile, nomadic Chichimec Indians, who allied with local farmers and fought standing battles against the Iberian invaders. After one such battle north of Guadalajara, the rich Zacatecas silver mines were accidentally discovered in 1546, leading to a rush of Spanish colonists to northern Mexico. In the silver belt, mining camps and missions became centers of Spanish influence, but the more remote unproductive highlands of northeastern Mexico and the deserts of Baja California were not fully brought under control until nearly two centuries later.

THE CONQUEST OF PERU

Francisco Pizarro's conquest of Peru in the 1530s closely paralleled the earlier conquest of the Aztec Federation in Mexico. Like Cortés, Pizarro left Estremadura in southern Spain to seek fortune in the New World. After a series of expeditions in Central America, he launched the conquest of the Inca Empire in 1531. With 3 vessels, 180 men, and 27 horses, Pizarro set sail southward from Panama along the Pacific coast of South America to find a wealthy civilization reputed to exist in the mountains beyond the coast. A year later, after a brutal forty-five-day climb from Tumbes on the dry coast into the high Andes, Pizarro confronted the Inca ruler, Atahualpa, at Cajamarca, and made him hostage to ensure the good behavior of the Inca army. A ransom of 20 tons of gold and silver, fifteen times the value of that seized by Cortés in Mexico, was collected from the empire for the release of the Inca ruler. In August 1533, Atahualpa was garroted, a favor granted by the Spanish, who agreed not to burn him if he converted to Christianity before his death. Almost immediately, the Spanish marched southward on the Inca capital of Cuzco, destroyed its temples, and took control of the Inca Empire. Within two years, this small band of Spaniards conquered the largest and best organized state in South Amer-

The great Inca city of Machu Picchu in Peru is now in ruins and active only as a tourist site, but even the remnants show how splendid it once was, and how awesome state religious ceremonies must have been in such a setting. *Photo:* United Nations/Rothstein.

ica. Although Indian rebellions continued sporadically for the next forty years, Spanish dominance, once established, was never seriously challenged.

At the time of conquest, the Inca controlled an empire of 380,000 square miles, 1500 miles long and 300 miles wide, extending along the Andes from the southern border of Colombia through Ecuador and Peru to the fertile central valley of Chile. This territory, equivalent in size to the Atlantic states of the United States, had a population of between 4 million and 16 million, most of whom had been conquered by the Quechua-speaking Inca and had been socially and economically integrated into the Inca state. The center of the empire, Cuzco, a town of 100,000 people, was located in an ***intermontane**** basin high in the Peruvian Andes at an elevation of more than 11,000 feet. From Cuzco, 5000 miles of roads extended outward in a network equivalent in size and quality to that of the Romans and spanned the most difficult terrain in the New World. The authority of the Inca ruler, relayed along these roads by runners, was implemented by a highly centralized bureaucracy. The smallest, most distant

corners of the state were kept well in control and in touch with Cuzco. The empire was divided into four regions, within which households were arranged in standardized social groups ranging in size from 10,000 to 40,000 families. A systematic distribution of people with respect to resources was constantly maintained by resettlement of families into new colonies.

The economic basis of the Inca state was the cultivation of potatoes, corn, manioc, peppers, tomatoes, beans, and squash in irrigated valleys along the coast, in basins on the high plateau, and on terraced hillsides in the Andes. ***Guano**** was imported as a fertilizer from offshore islands to increase productivity; fertile soil was carried from the lowlands to the highlands to enrich ***arable**** land. A well-planned system of canals, aqueducts, and reservoirs attested to the skill of Inca engineers; communal pastures were grazed by restricted herds of llamas and alpacas.

In theory, all land belonged to the state, but in practice, one-third of the harvest was allocated to the producing community, one-third to the Inca priestly class, and one-third to the ruler and his family, who held a monopoly on precious metals and stones. Private property did not exist, and work on communal land was allocated according to family size within each agricultural community. Surplus food was placed in public storehouses for distribution in

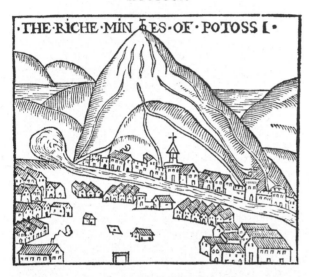

THE
DISCOVERIE AND CONQVEST
of the Prouinces of *PERV*, and
the *Nauigation in the South*
Sea, along that Coaft.
And alfo of the ritche Mines
of *POTOSI.*

·THE·RICHE·MINES·OF·POTOSSI·

¶ *Imprinted at London* by Richard Ihones. *Febru.6.1581.*

The title page of an early account of the conquest of Peru and the discovery of the mineral riches of South America, in this case the silver mines of Potosí in Bolivia, published in London in 1581. *Photo:* The Bettman Archive.

drought years; the cycles of poverty and hunger that characterize large parts of this region today did not exist under the Inca. In short, Inca rulers established a benevolent dictatorship (or more properly theocracy) in the very difficult environment of the Andes. Personal freedom, from choice of residence to choice of wife, was severely restricted, but lifetime social security was assured.

The high level of Inca organization and submission worked to the advantage of the Spanish conquistadors. Once the Inca ruler Atahualpa was disposed of and the capital city of Cuzco taken, the entire Inca domain and its thousands of acres of fertile land worked by hundreds of thousands of Indians fell under the purview of Pizarro's small group of invaders. The coastal city of Lima was founded in 1535 to connect the Spanish conquest of Peru with the European world. The road system of the Incas was abandoned. As in Mexico, the Indians were parceled out to the conquerors in encomiendas; Francisco Pizarro organized one estate northeast of Lima with 100,000 Indians; his brother Gonzalo founded the mining center of Charcas (modern La Paz) in Bolivia as his encomienda. Complex irrigation networks gradually fell into disrepair, and traditional Inca techniques of maintaining high rural agricultural productivity were neglected. When thousands of Indians were taken from lowland oases for work in silver mines at high altitudes, both food supply and population began to fall. The impact of smallpox and measles on the Andean population was much the same as in Mexico: within fifty years, the number of people in the Inca realm was reduced by a third. At the same time, Spanish settlers flowed into Peru to manage farmlands, organize work in the mines, work as shopkeepers and artisans in new Spanish cities, and as always to pursue still further the search for El Dorado.

Quito, the northern capital of the Incas, was taken and looted very early in the colonial period, and a dissident group of Pizarro's soldiers launched an expedition southward into Chile. But as the Spanish pushed outward from the well-ordered domain of the Inca, they encountered poor, hostile, uncivilized Indians who strongly resisted attempts at conquest and conversion. The fierce Araucanian Indians south of the River Maule proved a continuous problem, although the city of Santiago was founded in 1540, Valparaíso in 1544, and the southern towns of Concepción and Valdivia six years later. Other expeditions from Spain's colonies in Peru and Chile crossed the Andes into Argentina, ultimately reaching the Plata *estuary.*• In the north, expeditions pushed over the Bolivian and Colombian Andes, but the dense jungles and savage Indians east of the mountains discouraged most Spanish, except for a few pioneering missionaries. As a result of this Spanish disinterest, the Portuguese were able to press territorial claims granted by the pope under the Treaty of Tordesillas in 1494, settle the Brazilian coast, and penetrate deep into the interior of the Amazon Basin.

THE PORTUGUESE IN BRAZIL

In 1494, two years after Columbus's first voyage, Pope Alexander VI grandly divided the unexplored world into two spheres of influence to avoid competition between Spain and Portugal. The pope's line, as it was called, was drawn 370 leagues west of the Cape Verde Islands along the fiftieth *meridian,*• which cuts through the shoulder of modern Brazil from the mouth of the Amazon to south of São Paulo.

All lands west of this line were granted to Spain; those east of it were ceded to Portugal. On this basis, the Portuguese mariner, Cabral, claimed sovereignty for Portugal when he landed at Bahia on the northeastern coast in 1500. But this discovery stirred little interest in Portugal.

Brazil was occupied in pre-European times by a thin scattering of Tupi-Guaraní Indians who lived as hunters, fishermen, and *shifting cultivators*[•] along the coast and produced no gems, spices, or gold. The only product of value was a red dyewood, which early European ships brought back to Portugal along with parrots and monkeys. Unlike the Spanish, the Portuguese were not interested in colonization or conversion. A nation of less than 1 million people, Portugal lacked both the population and the religious fervor to engage in large-scale schemes of conquest in the New World. For thirty years, the Brazil colony was viewed as a wretched business, unworthy of note, until Portuguese voyages around the Cape of Good Hope to the East Indies became so risky that Portugal was paying "a drop of blood for every grain of pepper," as a common saying of the day put it. At the same time, French and Spanish expeditions to the Brazilian coast forced the Portuguese either to press forward with settlement on the South American coast or to abandon claim to the New World.

Portugal established firm possession of Brazil by dividing the entire coast from the Amazon to south of São Paulo into fifteen *capitanias*, large tracts of land extending inland, each granted to a wealthy Portuguese family. These families held the right to found towns, levy taxes, and hold economic monopolies in their territories; in return, they were expected to bring in settlers, organize the countryside, and return a fifth of all profits to the Portuguese king. Colonies were established at São Vicente near Santos, at Olinda near Recife, and at Bahia (Salvador). Results were uneven—several of the noble families never came to South America, some went broke financing new settlements; few made large profits. By 1550, however, Brazil could count sixteen towns. Portuguese colonists were exporting dyewood, sugar, cotton, and tobacco, and were cultivating European grains and raising cattle. Competition and conflict between the separate capitanias were eliminated in 1549, when all of Brazil was brought under the control of a governor-general appointed by Portugal.

The initial Portuguese impact on native society in Brazil was less devastating than that of Spain in the New World. Eventually the capitania families, themselves large landowners in Portugal as well, began to sense the potential profits in establishing sugar *plantations*[•] worked by local laborers and imported African slaves. The first plantation was established in 1532 at São Vicente in the south, but the favorable location of northern capitanias, closer to Euro-pean markets, soon led to expansion of sugar cultivation in the northeast. In 1576 Bahia had forty-seven sugar mills, and Santos, Recife, and Olinda were wealthy towns. Native Indians died by the thousands on the sugar plantations, and slaving parties in the Brazilian *hinterland*[•] were unable to meet the demand for new laborers. As a result, the Portuguese began to import slaves from Africa for the sugar plantations of Brazil as they had done earlier on farms on the island of Madeira off Africa. By 1600, an estimated 25,000 Portuguese colonists had settled along the coast of Brazil, the northeast had emerged as the world's chief source of sugar, and 14,000 African slaves and 18,000 Christianized Indians labored in the fields of the Portuguese New World.

THE NEW WORLD IN 1600

Twenty years before the Pilgrims landed in New England, the greater part of Central and South America and every densely populated native society had been colonized by the Spanish or Portuguese. Where tiny bands of conquistadors had destroyed and pillaged native empires eighty years earlier, small groups of colonists—perhaps as few as 150,000 in the entire New World—were building cities and establishing plantations and mines. The destinies of those native Americans not already destroyed by warfare, labor, or disease were totally controlled by the Iberian settlers. In the Caribbean, important fortresses at Santo Domingo, Havana, Portobelo, and Cartagena protected the gateway to the Spanish New World against French and British incursions. On the larger islands, commercial sugar plantations and a trickle of African slaves foreshadowed the economic and social future of the area. On the mainland, all of Mexico and Central America except the northern *deserts,*[•] remote lowland *jungles,*[•] and isolated highlands was firmly ruled from Mexico City, the seat of the viceroyalty of New Spain. In the later 1500s, Mexico City was the largest urban center in the Western Hemisphere, with a Spanish population of 20,000. Delegate courts (*audiencias*) were located at Guadalajara in the mining north and at Guatemala City to the south.

In South America, an arc of Spanish settlement had been established stretching from the *isthmus*[•] at Panama—itself an unhealthy, malarial town of 8000 —along the Andes to Bogotá, Quito, Lima, La Paz, and Santiago; eastward over the Andes to the frontier outposts of Mendoza, Asunción, and Buenos Aires. In the Andes, Indians labored in gold and silver mines to maintain a steady flow of precious metals to the coffers of the Spanish king; on the frontiers of the *pampas,*[•] natives effectively resisted the spread of tiny colonies of Spanish agriculturalists and livestock herders. The internal frontier of this arc of settlement, a border 7000 miles long, stretched the length of South America, separating unconquered

In the seventeenth century, Mexico City, flooded with riches from the silver mines to the north, was a turbulent city of perhaps 40,000. These excerpts from the diary of Don Gregorio Martín de Guijo reflect the headlines of the time: the droughts, famines, epidemics, pirates, church affairs, and colonial decisions of New Spain.

April 26, 1648. A frigate sailing from Campeche, with a cargo valued at 100,000 pesos, is driven ashore by pirates and looted.

December 9, 1648. The Manila galleon has been sighted off the south coast, the first one to arrive in two years. Great rejoicing and ringing of bells.

July 8, 1649. Juan de Alcocer, administrator of the sale of papal bulls, has a corn removed. Gangrene sets in, his leg is cut off, and he dies eleven days later.

July 29, 1649. A free mulatto is hanged for stealing a lamp from the Augustinian convent.

December 26, 1650. Don Guillén de Lombardo has escaped from the prison of the Inquisition. No ships have arrived from China, and the resultant scarcity of cinnamon has raised its price to a peso a pound. [Cinnamon was and is considered indispensable in the manufacture of chocolate.]

September 23, 1651. The flota from Spain arrives at Vera Cruz. It had put in for water at the island of Virgita, where the landing party was attacked by Indians and thirty men were killed, among them two Jesuits and a Dominican. One vessel sank in Vera Cruz harbor.

April 17, 1652. The Indians of Parral are reported to be in rebellion. They have eaten a Jesuit.

June 17, 1653. Miraculous intervention of the Virgin to relieve a drought. Her image is paraded through the streets for two weeks, at the end of which a violent storm interrupts the procession.

May 18, 1654. The French and Dutch pirates of the island of Tortuga quarrel over division of their spoils. The Audiencia of Santo Domingo sends two vessels; the pirates are surprised, and a million pesos in treasure are recovered. The pirates are brought to Santo Domingo and, it is a safe guess, are hanged.

August 15, 1655. A fifty-gun ship from Spain arrives at Santo Domingo and forces the enemy to lift the siege. The enemy loses 3,000 men. Great rejoicing in Mexico City, with bell-ringing and thanksgiving services at the cathedral.

September 8, 1655. The English take Jamaica. Prayers are ordered in all the churches.

June 6, 1656. The flagship of the treasure fleet sinks off Havana, with a loss of 5,000,000 pesos and 400 passengers.

June 14, 1661. One of the worst droughts ever recorded causes heavy losses of cattle. The image of Nuestra Señora de la Asunción is paraded through the city, fol-

lowed by an immense crowd. A few drops of rain fall. The procession is repeated on the eighteenth, with the Sacred Host added as a further inducement, whereupon it rains for twenty-eight days without stopping.

February 7 and March 28, 1663. The office of treasurer of the mint is sold to Juan Vázquez de Medina for 300,000 pesos. He is jailed for failure to deliver 200,000 pesos of the price.

June 22, 1663. Violent outbreak of smallpox. Dreadful heat by day and frost by night, which kills the crops. Religious processions bring a little rain. They are repeated, and it rains steadily until July 8, when the epidemic ceases.

September 9, 1664. A Negro girl is accused of assaulting her mistress with a machete. While she is being led to the gallows, her owners withdraw their complaint and she takes refuge in a church. The viceroy sends a halberdier to fetch her out. Two Mercedarian friars and a secular priest protest this violation of sanctuary. A mob of Negroes, Indians, and mulattoes rescue the girl and bring her to the cathedral. She is given in custody to the convent of La Concepción. She is not otherwise punished.

Source: Excerpts quoted from Lesley Byrd Simpson, *Many Mexicos.* Berkeley: University of California Press, 1966, pp. 143–147. Copyright © 1966 by the Regents of the University of California. Reprinted by permission of the University of California Press.

Indian lands from zones of Spanish dominance. On the Brazilian coast, the Portuguese moved inland from centers at Recife, Bahia, Rio de Janeiro, and São Paulo. Although the interior of South America—the eastern slopes of the Andes, the Amazon Basin, the *llanos* of Venezuela, and pampas of Argentina—remained free of European domination for some time, the future path of Latin America was apparent in 1600; the spatial and social dimensions of the continent were fixed.

COLONIAL DEVELOPMENT AND CULTURE CHANGE

Spain successfully transplanted Iberian patterns of administration, settlement, economy, and culture to the New World over the course of the next two centuries. The New World institutions of rule, modeled on those of Castile, were modified perforce by local conditions in America. The basic relationship between the colonies and Spain was based on the premise that the Spanish Empire was the private property of the Spanish king. The duties of the colonists were to claim land for the Spanish flag, fill the coffers of the Spanish monarch, and convert native peoples into useful Catholic subjects of Spain. A centralized system of political and economic administration was imposed on the colonies by the Council of the Indies, a board composed of a handful of nobles, lawyers, and members of Spain's richest families. Their decrees filtered down through the viceroyalties and audiencias of New Spain in Mexico and Peru. A network of 250 colonial towns, 14 of which later became capitals of independent nations, anchored Spanish colonial rule. Rigid control of colonial trade and immigration was maintained by the House of Trade. Missionaries pushed the frontier of Spanish settlement deep into the continent, often at their own peril. Spain governed this empire in the New World for three centuries, repelling the territorial incursions of other European nations jealous of riches pouring into Spain. Parallel to the vast Spanish dominion in Central and South America was the Portuguese colonial empire established in Brazil.

The Colonial Economy

Despite the consuming Spanish quest for gold and precious metals, the basis of the emerging New World economy was agriculture. In most years, the value of agricultural exports to Spain exceeded that of the mines. As a result the accountants of the Council of the Indies soon paid close attention to patterns of land tenure and land use in the colonial possessions of the king. Wherever possible Spanish commercial agriculture was introduced alongside the subsistence economy of the Indians; wheat, barley, olives, and grapes were planted on vast tracts of land. On the Caribbean islands and in the tropical colonies of the mainland, Indians and African slaves worked sugar, tobacco, cocoa, and *indigo*• plantations. Olive trees were planted in the irrigated oases of coastal Peru, and Lima exported olive oil to the rest of the New World. Vineyards sprang up in central Mexico, the central valley of Chile, and the Argentine *piedmont.*• In recognition of the potential of this wealth, great tracts of land, called *haciendas* in New Spain and *latifundios* in South America, were bestowed upon favorites of the king. As in contemporary Europe, land was owned by the wealthy few, and the masses—in this case Indians, Africans, and a growing mestizo (mixed European and Indian) population—labored in servitude.

On the northern and southern margins of the Spanish Empire, a livestock industry unparalleled in the Old World arose. Herds of wild horses and cattle, descended from Iberian stock, flourished on rich grasslands. A new culture of rancher-cowboys populated these regions—the *vaqueros* of the Rio Grande del Norte (Texas), the *gauchos* of Argentina and Uru-

guay, and the *llaneros* of the Orinoco lowlands of Venezuela. Sheep were introduced to provide wool for a textile industry. Textile factories hired large numbers of skilled Indian weavers from one end of the continent to the other to produce cheap cotton and woolen cloth. Labor conditions in some of these mills were so notorious that reform-minded provincial officials imported African slaves and Chinese weavers to relieve the burden on Indian workers. The mules and horses of Peru, Colombia, and Venezuela died by the thousands in the mines and on the steep trails connecting highland work sites to the coastal ports. Despite the policies of the Council of the Indies, which limited the amount of land distributed to cattlemen to a maximum of 3 leagues apiece, the stock-raisers guild was so powerful that the Council of the Indies was ignored. Great cattle ranches were established in northern Mexico, the Plata lowlands, and the plains of the Orinoco.

Supplementing this agricultural economy was the mineral wealth that had attracted the Spanish to the New World in the first place. The king of Spain held subsoil mineral rights on all occupied lands, and a fifth of all metals went to the royal treasury. In Mexico, Colombia, Peru, and Bolivia, gold and silver miners worked feverishly to meet the escalating demands of Spain for raw gold and silver ore. Alexander von Humboldt, a famous geographer, estimated in 1803 that the New World exported more precious minerals to Spain in three centuries than all the world had previously produced. To do this, of course, required a virtually unlimited supply of labor.

In the Andes, where precious ores tended to be located close to the surface, forced-labor gangs of Indians dug small pits in the ground and carried baskets of ore up ladders to the surface. In the early colonial years, some 80,000 Indians were employed at the San Luis Potosí mines in Bolivia alone. Thousands died of mistreatment, underground flooding, and overwork; the replacement of exhausted workers was a major colonial problem. By contrast, the rich silver mines of northern Mexico were, by the end of the eighteenth century, generally worked by free Indian labor. Here, mining was a more sophisticated venture involving connecting shafts, underground drainage, ventilation, and deep tunnels. Because of the special skills required in these mines, untutored labor gangs recruited from the fields were inefficient and costly. In the end it was cheaper to hire free laborers trained in the complexities of ore collection and processing. The labor contracts offered to skilled workers of northern Mexico engendered considerable discontent among laborers recruited under the repartimiento earning only one-eighth as much.

Labor problems remained an issue throughout the colonial period. The Spanish steadfastly refused to perform manual labor, so the entire economic structure of the Spanish New World depended on the labor of native populations and Africans. Starvation, slavery, and death in the Caribbean led the Spanish to institute what in those days were considered reforms. Even after the encomienda system was abolished in law, landlords continued to hold the Indians in debt bondage much as **serfs**[*] were bound to feudal lords during European medieval times. More brutal were the forced labor drafts for public works, the repartimiento of Mexico, and the mita of South America. These were ultimately abolished and replaced by wage labor.

Complicating the labor system of the Spanish domain was the paradox of saving the souls of the Indians while placing harsh demands upon their bodies. Out of this emerged a confusing conflict between church and secular authorities concerning the treatment of Indians. Although immense cathedrals were built with forced labor, some enlightened church leaders criticized and ultimately eliminated the worst abuses of the mining haciendas and the lowland plantations. Other missionaries attempted to establish utopian religious communities between the zone of Spanish colonization and unconquered Indian lands, teaching their charges a new faith and a new way of life. Curiously, this clerical concern for Indians almost never extended to Africans imported by the Portuguese, Dutch, and Yankee slavers. Never as important in Spanish America as in Brazil, black slaves populated the Caribbean and the lowland coasts of the mainland—costly imported human merchandise.

A Monopoly of Trade
[FIGURE 1]

From Spain's viewpoint, the overseas empire existed to supply raw materials to the mother country in return for a supply of manufactured goods. Europe became an international trading society; the gold, silver, and agricultural products from tropical colonies provided the backing for wealth and power. The New World proved a storehouse of treasure: Between 1570 and 1820, the mints of New Spain coined the equivalent of $2 billion in pieces of eight and an additional $2 billion in silver was exported as ingots; Peru contributed another $1 billion—all this in an age which, as one writer notes, still counted its wealth in pennies. The impact of this flow of metals on Spain was disastrous. Inflation drove prices beyond the reach of both peasants and artisans; depression followed, and the economy of Spain's cities was virtually destroyed. No one connected the flow of silver and gold to the economic plight of Iberia; for several centuries both Portugal and Spain mistakenly exerted every effort to maintain strangleholds on the trade of the New World.

The House of Trade in Madrid maintained a sizable bureaucracy to supervise trade and immigration

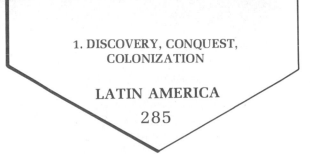
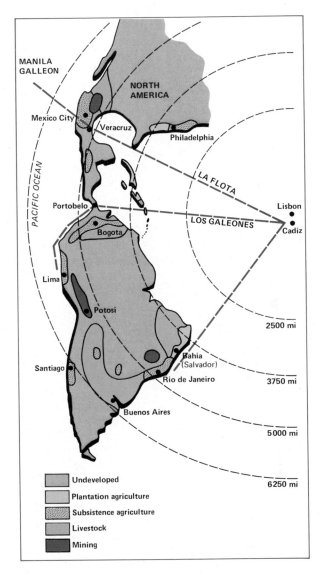

Figure 1. The Colonial Economy and Distance to Europe. Throughout the colonial period, export economies were developed on the Atlantic coast closest to Europe and in the specialized mining centers of Mexico, Brazil, and the Andes. Regional economies grew up in the temperate regions of Brazil, Chile, Mexico, and North America. Areas more than 5000 miles from Europe in the interior remained undeveloped. *After:* John P. Cole, *Latin America: An Economic and Social Geography.* London: Butterworths, 1973, p. 76, Map A.

with the New World. Its objectives were to maintain a total monopoly on all exchange, particularly that in gold and silver, and to prevent other European nations from engaging in trade with the Spanish colonial empire. Two fleets of all ships licensed to trade with the New World assembled each year at Seville or Cádiz, the two designated ports of departure, and made the difficult voyage to New Spain along a route patrolled by pirates and corsairs. The spring fleet (*la flota*) sailed to Veracruz and returned to Spain with hides and sugar from the Caribbean and silver from Mexico. The autumn fleet (*los galeones*) landed at Portobelo on the Isthmus of Panama to collect Peruvian silver, emeralds from Colombia, and pearls, spices, and cocoa from Venezuela. Goods from Spanish possessions in Asia were transported by a single ship, the Manila galleon, which brought silks, porcelain, and ivory from the Orient to Acapulco on the west coast of Mexico.

This total regulation of trade between the colonies and Spain created considerable hardship in the New World. The Veracruz *flota*, if it survived scurvy, hurricanes, and pirates, brought manufactured goods that were transshipped to the upland town of Jalapa, where a great fair was held. Wholesale merchants and middlemen from all over Mexico, Central America, and the Caribbean brought raw materials for sale and bought European manufactures to sell in provincial towns and large settlements throughout the region. The routes to the fair, nothing but mule tracks, were threatened by bandits, groups of runaway slaves, and hostile Indians attracted by the mule trains carrying silver bars, precious stones, and valuable agricultural products. At the fair, the value added and taxes on manufactured goods were enormous.

As the depression in Spain deepened, the quality of the textiles, hardware, implements, military supplies, and luxury goods from Europe deteriorated. A similar fair for *los galeones* was held at Portobelo for merchants who survived long and dangerous journeys from all over South America. In theory, no manufactured goods reached the Spanish New World except through these constricted and heavily regulated channels. Buenos Aires, for example, was forbidden to trade with Europe except through Portobelo and Lima, a journey of thousands of miles. Trade between colonies was limited by distance, terrain, and the orientation of each area to similar patterns of raw material production for export. In this situation, illegal smuggling replaced legalized piracy; the colonists solved their problem by quietly defying Spain.

The Spatial Distribution of Economic Activity

By 1600, direct European control of virtually every aspect of life in the New World had resulted in a spatial distribution of economic activity that remained essentially the same until the nineteenth century. The interests and aims of Portugal and Spain were crucial factors; distance from Western Europe also played an important role. In tropical areas closest to Europe, 3500 to 4000 miles away, sugar, cocoa, indigo, and tobacco plantations were established in coastal Brazil, the Guianas, and the islands of the Caribbean. The substantial risk and high costs of land transport restricted the cultivation of these bulk commodities to the Atlantic coast. Even moving them across the Isthmus of Panama was so difficult that tropical exports were not grown in any quantity in the Pacific lowlands.

South of this belt of tropical plantations an economy of subsistence cultivation supported populations in the more temperate Brazilian highlands and La Plata territory. Europe's lack of interest in trade with these regions meant less control and less regulation and encouraged local enterprise. Similar regional economies evolved near the mining centers of Mexico and Peru to support the adventurers, immigrants, and laborers drawn to the silver and gold centers of Latin America. In the temperate grasslands more than 5000 miles from Europe, a livestock economy was established on the pampas, the llanos of Venezuela, and in northern Mexico. In the Amazon region, southern South America, and the southwestern interior of North America—areas remote from colonial centers of power and located in inaccessible environments—vast stretches remained the domain of hostile Indians, runaway slaves, missionaries, pioneers, and occasional traders.

INDEPENDENCE IN LATIN AMERICA

The distances separating Spain from the New World possessions made it difficult for the mother country to maintain a tight rein on colonial society. In the course of three centuries, a new and complex society evolved in Latin America with a Spanish-born European elite (*gachupins*), a colonial-born European commercial and landowning class (creoles), and mestizos and **mulattos,** native Indians, and Africans. In the early nineteenth century, an estimated 23 million people lived in Spanish America, nearly half of whom were Indians, a third mestizos, a fifth pure whites, and 5 percent blacks. Increasingly, these colonial societies felt confined by Spanish control of their destinies. Trade restrictions imposed by the crown were circumvented by large-scale smuggling with Spain's European adversaries. Local officials ignored unpalatable instructions from Spain. Spain came to distrust anyone born in the colonies as a result, and appointed only affiliates of the court to positions of power and influence in the New World. The most incompetent gachupin was preferred to a well-qualified creole, so that in two centuries, only four of Mexico's viceroys and 14 of 602 governors and captains-general were born in America. Bitterly resentful of official discrimination, creoles, who formed a wealthy, well-educated social nucleus, brought independence to Latin America in the nineteenth century.

It is remarkable that Spain held so tight a rein on the New World for so long. Obedience and submission were traditions reinforced by the powerful hierarchy of the Catholic Church. Revolts were brutally suppressed by administrators backed by garrisons of colonial troops. Any concerted rebellion was hindered by the long distances and poor communications between the colonies. Thus, despite inept leadership and continual warfare both in Europe and on the northern margins of Spanish America, the Spanish presence in the New World was intact (save minor losses to Britain, France, and Holland in the Caribbean) as the eighteenth century began. It was then that a series of enlightened Bourbon kings instituted a series of reforms in colonial government, economy, and trade to forestall the growing friction between Spain and Spanish America. The tax system was consolidated to increase efficiency and reduce corruption and graft; visitations by agents of the crown ensured their implementation. Recognizing the need for a decentralization of political power in the colonies, new viceroyalties were established at Bogotá and Buenos Aires and new captaincy-generals in Cuba, Guatemala, Venezuela, and Chile. Some creoles were even allowed entrance into the colonial administration.

Additional measures were taken in the late 1700s to strengthen the economy of the colonies. Trade restrictions were relaxed, and laws against smuggling were strictly enforced. The unwieldy convoy system was abandoned. Individual ships were allowed to trade in the Caribbean. The monopoly of the Cádiz merchants over trans-Atlantic trade was broken; all Spanish ports could now trade with the colonies. The greater volume of commerce between Spain and the New World drove smugglers out of business, and a class of creole merchants grew wealthy during this period. Buenos Aires maintained bimonthly trading contacts with Spain. The

number of hides exported in 1790 was ten times that in 1770. In Chile, freer trade strengthened the agricultural economy, and a growing urban population of 150,000 creoles and mestizos inhabited fifteen large colonial towns. Similarly, Cartagena, Havana, Veracruz, and Acapulco profited from the growth in trade among the colonies and with Spain.

But these concessions to colonial interests were too few and came too late. By the beginning of the nineteenth century, many citizens of Spanish America were ready to view their colonial homelands as separate from Spain. The revolt of the North Americans against British rule provided an example; the doctrines of free trade and equality of classes preached in the French Enlightenment appealed to the wealthy, embittered sons of creole merchants and landowners as they questioned the authority of the Spanish crown.

In 1804, creoles led an estimated 25,000 regulars and 127,000 militiamen who had fought in frontier warfare in South America and the northern reaches of Mexico. The stage was set for rebellion. Local revolts in Venezuela, Colombia, Argentina, Mexico, Central America, and Peru ended ultimately in independent republics. The five nations of Venezuela, Colombia, Ecuador, Peru, and Bolivia were created by the extraordinary leadership of a young Venezuelan aristocrat, Simón Bolívar. Argentine creoles led by Manuel Belgrano overthrew the viceroyalty of Buenos Aires. Independence came peacefully to Brazil when the Portuguese dynasty fled the armies of Napoleon and retired to the New World. In only a decade, 1815–1825, the Portuguese and Spanish empires in the New World disintegrated, and eighteen independent nations emerged in the quarter-century of chaos that followed.

LATIN AMERICA

REGIONAL PATTERNS

PHYSICAL FEATURES MAP
POPULATION DENSITY MAP

Latin America is a landmass consisting of the two triangles of South America and southern North America that join at the narrow Isthmus of Panama. The *region* extends nearly 6000 miles from north to south and forms a land area of 7.9 million square miles, more than twice the size of the United States. The northern triangle, composed of Middle America and the Caribbean islands, is 1 million square miles in area and forms the southern extension of North America. The southern and much larger triangle, South America, is set so much farther east than its northern counterpart that the shortest distance between South America and Africa is only half that separating North America and Europe.

The equator slices across this region from the mouth of the Amazon to the Ecuadorian Andes, so that most of Latin America lies within the tropics. Like Africa, the other tropical continent, the overall density of population in Latin America is quite low —less than 40 people per square mile. Clusters of dense population are found only along the east coast of South America, in highland pockets in the Andes Mountains and Middle America, and on the large islands of the Caribbean. These stand in juxtaposition to the empty stretches of the Amazon lowlands and the Andean cordillera. This uneven distribution of modern Latin American peoples is the result of two forces: first, the nature of Spanish and Portuguese colonial settlement in the New World, which tailored the development of this huge area to the needs of a European peninsula only one-fortieth as large; and second, strong regional environmental variations. One-quarter of the land is mountainous, another quarter is covered with tropical swamps, and an additional tenth of Latin America is barren desert.

This interplay of settlement history and physical environment forms the basis on which Latin America can be subdivided. The northern triangle of Middle America and the Caribbean includes two sub-regions: the Mainland, a tropical and subtropical highland occupied by mixed European-Indian (mestizo) people, traditionally organized by the economy of the hacienda; and the Rimland, a tropical lowland environment occupied by mixed Indian and black peoples organized in a plantation economy. The much larger, more diverse southern triangle of South America includes three major subregions: the towering Andean Cordillera, arching southward along the western coast of the entire continent and occupied by mixed Indian peoples; the Midlatitude South, the southern midlatitude extension of that landmass occupied mostly by Europeans; and Brazil, the densely populated coast and tropical interior of Portuguese-speaking eastern South America.

MIDDLE AMERICA AND THE CARIBBEAN

Middle America and the Caribbean together have a population of 110 million, one-third of the total population of Latin America on only one-eighth of its land area. Two generalized human habitats are recognized: the Mainland and the Rimland.

Mainland Middle America

Mainland Middle America is a band of tropical and subtropical plateaus and mountains that sweep cross-compass, northwest to southeast, through eight countries linking the North American landmass with its southern counterpart. In the north, steep escarpments 7000 to 13,000 feet in elevation flank either side of the central plateau of Mexico. A mile above sea level, and even higher in its southern portions, this plateau is 500 miles wide at its broadest and tapers southward where the eastern and western cordilleras converge to form the mountain spine of Central America.

The central plateau of Mexico. With an area of 761,000 square miles and a population of 50 million, Mexico is the largest and most significant country in mainland Middle America. The economic and social core of the country is located in the southern part of the central plateau. Here, at elevations of 6000 to 7000 feet, adequate rainfall, a temperate climate, and rich *volcanic soils* favored the early growth of a dense nexus of agricultural settlement. Consequently, half of Mexico's people, primarily mestizo, are concentrated in this section of the central plateau.

As in earlier periods, intensive cultivation of corn, beans, squash, and wheat supports rural population densities of 200 to 300 people per square mile, some of the highest in Latin America. In especially favored locations, such as the central valley of Mexico, rural settlements blanket all but the steepest slopes with densities of 500 to 1000 people per square mile, figures rarely attained outside the rice-growing regions of Asia.

PHYSICAL FEATURES

Elevation (feet)

sea level to 660
660 to 3300
3300 to 6600
6600 to 13000
above 13000

GALAPAGOS IS.
(Ecuador)

ENVIRONMENTAL ZONES

Rimland

Mainland

Portuguese Brazil

Andean Cordillera

Midlatitude South

ATLANTIC OCEAN

GULF OF MEXICO

BAJA CALIFORNIA

CENTRAL PLATEAU

CENTRAL VALLEY

YUCATAN

Rio Grande

CENTRAL AMERICAN RANGES

PACIFIC OCEAN

GREATER ANTILLES

LEEWARD IS.

LESSER ANTILLES

WINDWARD IS.

CARIBBEAN SEA

Cauca R.

Magdalena R.

LLANOS

Orinoco R.

AMAZON

BASIN

Amazon R.

MONTANA

SERTAO

Sao Francisco R.

ALTIPLANO

Lake Titicaca

ATACAMA DESERT

CENTRAL VALLEY OF CHILE

GRAN CHACO

Paraguay R.

Parana R.

Parana R.

Uruguay R.

PARAIBA VALLEY

Bio-Bio R.

PAMPAS

ATLANTIC OCEAN

PATAGONIAN PLATEAU

FALKLAND IS. (Br.)

TIERRA DEL FUEGO

0   200   400   600
miles

ATLANTIC OCEAN

GULF OF MEXICO

Monterrey

Guadalajara

Mexico City

Havana

CARIBBEAN SEA

Guatemala

Managua

San Jose

Caracas

GALAPAGOS IS. (Ecuador)

Medellin

Cali

Bogota

Quito

Guayaquil

PACIFIC OCEAN

0   200   400   600
miles

Fortaleza

Recife

Lima

La Paz

Brasilia

Salvador (Bahia)

Persons (square mile)

less than 3

3 to 25

25 to 130

130 to 260

more than 260

Belo Horizonte

Rio de Janeiro

Sao Paulo

Asuncion

Cordoba

Santiago

Rosario

Porto Alegre

Montevideo

Urban centers

● 50,000 to 500,000

■ 500,000 to 1,000,000

⊡ over 1,000,000

Buenos Aires

ATLANTIC OCEAN

POPULATION DENSITY

FALKLAND IS. (Br.)

In northern Mexico, rainfall decreases to less than 20 inches per year. The densely settled fields of the central plateau give way to scattered oasis-like villages, ranches, and mining centers; population densities fall to less than 20 people per square mile. In the states of San Luis Potosí and Zacatecas, discoveries of silver, lead, zinc, copper, and gold were the basis of Spanish settlement. The nomadic hunting tribes who previously occupied the area, mainly Chichimecs, were driven into the drier north. Here, Indian influence and speech are much less pronounced than in the rest of Mexico.

In southern Mexico, as in the north, landscape and culture change as one moves away from the central plateau. Rainfall increases, cloaking the broken upland ranges of the escarpments with a mantle of evergreen* forest that grades into the tropical rain forests of the Mexican south. Regional population densities are low—the entire south has a total population of only 8 million. In Morelos state, sugarcane and rice fields supplement the staple subsistence crops of Middle America. Farther south, in Oaxaca, wheat, coffee, oranges, and tobacco are cultivated in the tierra templada (temperate land, or cooler piedmont uplands). In the Chiapas highlands, the agricultural economy is distinctly tropical and the major commercial crops are cocoa and bananas. This pattern is repeated in the wetter part of the Yucatán, the lowland Caribbean appendage of southern Mexico which is now an important producer of sugar, oranges, copra,* and bananas. Throughout southern Mexico, the people are Indians, 50 to 80 percent of whom still speak indigenous languages.

The mountains of Central America. The densely forested mountain core of Central America is formed by two volcanic ranges: One cuts east-west across Guatemala, Honduras, and Nicaragua with active volcanic peaks rising 11,000 to 13,000 feet above sea level; a second, less imposing range trends northwest to southeast through Costa Rica and Panama. Both ranges are wet and densely settled. Roughly 80 percent of the 17 million people of the region live in highlands above 2000 feet. Most are of Indian, European, or mestizo descent, in contrast with the people of the *tierra caliente* (hot and humid lowlands) of the Caribbean coasts of Panama, Costa Rica, Nicaragua, Honduras, and Belize.

In Guatemala, roughly 60 percent of the population of 5.2 million are pure-blooded Indians—subsistence hoe cultivators who grow maize, squash, beans, and a variety of commercial crops on the mountain slopes and in the basins west of Guatemala City. By contrast, the rich commercial coffee, cotton, and sugar haciendas of the Pacific piedmont and coastal plain, which produce 95 percent of Guatemala's exports, are run by a mestizo (or, as they are called, *ladino*) aristocracy. In neighboring Honduras, population densities in the uplands are quite low, and the inhabitants of this region—overwhelmingly mestizo—operate small, archaic gold and silver mines, raise cattle in the oak and pine forests of the highlands, and cultivate hillside plots.

By contrast, El Salvador is the most densely populated country in Central America. With 27 percent of its land in cultivation—the highest percentage in Latin America—average densities approach 400 people per square mile. The best lands in the *tierra templada* are owned by a European elite, reputedly numbering only fourteen families, who grow commercial coffee and cotton. But most of the population are subsistence farmers whose diet is as meager as anywhere in Latin America. In Nicaragua, the Honduran pattern is repeated, with coffee haciendas in the *tierra templada,* cotton and banana plantations in the lowlands, low overall population densities, and a preponderance of mestizo subsistence cultivators.

Costa Rica, however, is a nation of small farmers (83 percent of whom claim European descent), stable government, a high literacy rate, and a high standard of living. Over half of the 1.7 million Costa Ricans are clustered in the central highlands cultivating coffee, sugarcane, and a variety of food products on small holdings. In Panama, the more general Central American pattern reappears: a predominantly mestizo population, low densities of population, and subsistence cultivation. Only the Canal Zone, the American-leased transit area between Colón and Panama City, breaks this pattern.

The Caribbean Rimland

The Caribbean Rimland is a tropical lowland environment where the vast majority of the population lives at elevations below 1000 feet. Less isolated than the Mainland, the Caribbean was a focus of competition among colonial powers. The Spanish ultimately maintained predominant influence over three of the four major islands of the Greater Antilles: Cuba, the Dominican Republic, and Puerto Rico. Northern European colonists held sway in Jamaica (British), Haiti (French), and the Lesser Antilles (British, French, and Dutch). Colonialists developed profitable sugar plantations in the islands and along the Caribbean coast of Central America. For three centuries slaves were imported from Africa to labor in the fields, and eventually blacks became the dominant population virtually everywhere.

The Greater Antilles. The Greater Antilles, composed of the four large islands of Cuba, Jamaica, Hispaniola, and Puerto Rico, includes nine-tenths of the land area of the West Indies and an even larger percentage of the Caribbean population. The largest island, Cuba, is 800 miles long and has a population of 8.5 million. The majority of its 44,000

291

The natural beauty of the Caribbean islands is their chief resource; there is little else to sustain a modern economy. *Photo:* Addie Passen/Design Photographers International.

square miles is flat or gently rolling terrain with three small mountainous areas rising to elevations of 3000 to 6000 feet above sea level. The climate of Cuba is subtropical and rainy, a natural endowment that has made the island the world's largest source of sugar.

On Hispaniola, the second largest island in the Caribbean, some 9 million people inhabit a land area far more mountainous and one-fourth smaller than Cuba. Four major mountain systems dominate Hispaniola, with people clustered along the coasts and in lowland ribbons located between parallel ranges. Climate and vegetation vary with altitude and exposure, creating a complex of microenvironments now occupied by the Hispanic and European peoples of the Dominican Republic and the black African population of Haiti.

Jamaica, the third largest island in the Greater Antilles, is one-tenth the size of Cuba and has a population of slightly less than 2 million. Most of the island is a heavily dissected limestone plateau, a marginal land occupied by peasant cultivators. Under three centuries of British rule, the windward coasts and lowlands were carved into sugar plantations. Puerto Rico, the smallest and most easterly of the Greater Antilles, is, like Jamaica, spanned by a dissected plateau with a mountain core. Its wet, coastal lowlands are cultivated in sugar.

Despite this diversity of environmental conditions and colonial experiences, the four islands of the Greater Antilles with their lowland plantations and African populations share common problems: burgeoning populations and dependence on the export of tropical plantation products. In Cuba, Spanish occupation resulted in limited economic growth. In 1900, only 3 percent of the island was cultivated, and Cuba's population of 1.5 million was clustered on the coast with most of the interior still wilderness. After independence at the turn of the century came the eradication of yellow fever, an infusion of capital from the United States, and preferential tariffs on Cuban sugar in American markets, which led to the expansion of sugar and tobacco cultivation and tourism.

Some 3.5 million acres were planted to cane. Large estates covered over half the arable land in the country, and Cuba became completely dependent on a single crop. Sugar and molasses made up 80 percent of exports; 40 percent of food needs were imported. Fluctuations in sugar prices created periodic crises in the economy. The annual rhythm of sugar planting and harvesting threw a quarter of the island's people out of work for half the year. After Castro's revolution in 1959, the great estates were dissolved and sugar land was expropriated by the government. Despite growing agricultural and industrial diversification, the fourfold increase in Cuba's population since 1900 is beginning to pressure this, the best-endowed environment in the Caribbean.

A surprisingly similar developmental pattern occurred in Puerto Rico, despite contemporary contrasts in political orientation. Like Cuba, Puerto Rico remained peripheral to Spanish colonial designs. Sugar and slaves were introduced to both islands in the sixteenth century. In the nineteenth and twentieth centuries, sugar cultivation in Puerto Rico expanded along the coastal plains and the interior valleys, tobacco estates were established in the humid east, and coffee was introduced into the western highlands. By World War II, large estates controlled 85 percent of the cultivated land, and the usual problems of a one-crop economy had emerged. After the war, *land reform*• programs were instituted, diversified manufacturing introduced, and the lucrative tourist industry expanded.

But this economic growth was partially offset by a population increase which, despite emigration, has tripled the population in seventy-five years to its current 2.7 million people. Given the eroded mountain core and thin *alluvial soils*• of Puerto Rico, population densities on arable land have soared to 1700 per square mile. Over 40 percent of the population is found today in the capital of San Juan (452,000 people) and smaller cities like Mayagüez and Ponce. Although Puerto Rico's standard of living is one of the highest in Latin America, contemporary problems revolve around the fact that the limited land base cannot support its population.

On Hispaniola, contrasting patterns of population and resource utilization evolved in Haiti and the Dominican Republic. Under French rule in the eighteenth century, Haiti became the richest plantation colony in the Caribbean. But at the end of the century the slaves revolted, threw out the French, and destroyed the sugar mills and estates. Desperately poor Haitian cultivators are now squeezed onto the western third of Hispaniola, a country with 80 percent of its terrain in mountains. With a total population of 4.8 million and average densities of more than 300 people per square mile, Haiti has the lowest standard of living in Latin America. In the Dominican Republic, a somewhat smaller population (4.3 million) occupies a territory twice as large as Haiti. Scarcity of land is not a problem; large sugar and coffee plantations dominate the landscape, and the predominantly mulatto population has a substantially higher standard of living.

In Jamaica, the familiar pattern of sugar estates and banana plantations was established by British colonists on the humid coastal lowlands, with peasant farmers in the limestone uplands. A population of over 2 million and a meager resource base (only 15 percent of the island can be cultivated) have caused land hunger. Unlike the other Caribbean islands, however, Jamaica is endowed with a major mineral resource, bauxite, from which aluminum is made. Producer of 20 percent of the world's supply and with huge reserves, Jamaica uses the revenues from mining as the financial base for an important expansion of the island's economy.

The Lesser Antilles. Similar patterns of tropical agricultural development mark the economies of the Lesser Antilles, a 700-mile-long concave band of islands that sweeps across the Caribbean from Puerto Rico in the north to the coast of Venezuela. These islands are the peaks of a double line of submarine volcanoes: an outer ring of low islands, old volcanoes, and limestone banks (the Leeward islands), and an inner ring of higher volcanic peaks (the Windward islands), which link near the coast of South America with Trinidad, Barbados, and the Netherlands Antilles—islands with a quite different geological history.

The largest of the low-lying (Leeward) islands are Guadeloupe (French) and Antigua (British). The mainstay of their economy is sugar grown on large estates with the usual problems of poverty and unemployment endemic to the Caribbean plantation system. On the higher (Windward) islands, agriculture is quite varied, despite their similar terrain and tropical environmental conditions (forested mountain spines of between 3000 and 4000 feet, rich volcanic soils, little level land, and abundant rainfall). Saint Vincent (British) produces arrowroot, a starchy tuber; Dominica (British), limes; Grenada (British), cocoa and nutmeg; Martinique (French) and Saint Kitts (British), sugar; Saint Lucia (British), bananas; and Montserrat and Nevis (both British), cotton. On some islands, such as Grenada, small holdings dominate; on Martinique and Saint Lucia, however, so much land is devoted to commercial estates that food must be imported. More than 1 million people live on these islands, over half on the two French islands of Guadeloupe and Martinique.

Approaching the South American coast, the Lesser Antilles joins with a string of continental islands, the most important of which are the former British territories of Trinidad and Barbados and the two largest islands of the Netherlands Antilles, Aruba and Curaçao. Barbados most closely emulates the Caribbean economic pattern: 95 percent of all exports are sugar, molasses, and rum; population densities reach levels of 1400 per square mile. In Trinidad, settled much later, a mixture of black Africans (43 percent of the population), Hindu Indians (37 percent), and Chinese and Portuguese were imported to work on sugar plantations in the nineteenth century.

Although sugar and rum are still the major agricultural exports, petroleum has been discovered on the southern third of the island, and Trinidad now produces and refines more than 100 million barrels annually, providing an economic balance rare in the Caribbean. In Aruba and Curaçao, petroleum refining is about the only economic activity. Near-desert conditions limit agricultural development, and water is so scarce that distillation of seawater is required to maintain the population.

293

SOUTH AMERICA

South America, which includes two-thirds of Latin America's 330 million people, is seven times larger than Middle America. On the basis of variations in environment, settlement history, and contemporary culture, three subregions can be distinguished: the Andean cordillera, the Midlatitude South, and Brazil.

The Andean Cordillera
[FIGURE 2]

The Andean cordillera rises from the waters of the Caribbean in eastern Venezuela and extends southward over 4000 miles in a sinuous curve that forms the backbone of the continent. Much of the Andean highlands is 10,000 feet above sea level, with individual ice-covered peaks in Ecuador, Peru, Bolivia, and Chile soaring to 22,000 feet, a full 4 miles above sea level. In the Andean cordillera as in the mountains of Central America, the same pattern of environmental diversity is repeated. Three environments of human settlement and economy can be distinguished, the *tierra caliente, tierra templada,* and *tierra fria*—lowlands, piedmont, and highlands.

In this middle section, the Andean system broadens to a width of 400 miles in Bolivia. In Chile to the south, it narrows to a width of only 20 miles. Throughout most of their course, however, the Andes form a 200-mile-wide band of parallel mountain ranges, walls of ice and stone, cut by fertile intermontane valleys and pocked with mountain-rimmed basins and plateaus that are the primary centers of settlement for the Indian population. The eastern slopes of the Andes are heavily watered, deeply dissected, and covered by tropical forests that extend into the Amazon Basin. Virtually inaccessible, this *transmontane*• region includes half of the national territory of Colombia, Ecuador, Bolivia, and Peru, but is inhabited by only a thin scattering of tribal hunters and gatherers and a few hardy missionaries and pioneer settlers.

Tropical rain forests also cover the western slope of the Colombian and Ecuadorian Andes, where moisture-laden winds from the Pacific drop more than 100 inches of rainfall each year. South of the Gulf of Guayaquil, however, a stretch of desert trends along the coast of Ecuador, reaching its greatest intensity in the dune-covered Atacama Desert of northern Chile and cutting diagonally across the Andes to the south as it reaches into Patagonia. This coastal *fog desert*• is produced by a cold north-bound ocean current, the Humboldt, which lowers the temperature of on-shore subtropical air masses, reducing their moisture content and limiting rainfall. Settlement here is limited to coastal oases dotted along streams originating in the Andes. Farther south, the Chilean Andes reach into the midlatitudes, producing a *Mediterranean climate*•

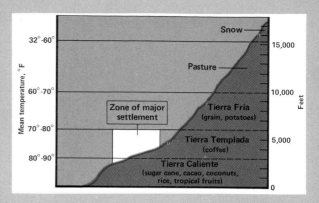

Figure 2. The Altitudinal Zones of the Andean Cordillera. Throughout the Andean cordillera, altitude is a principal factor in human settlement and economy. Temperature decreases and rainfall increases with elevation. Typically, *tierra caliente,* hot and humid lowlands, are dominated by a tropical plantation economy; *tierra templada,* warm piedmonts, are characterized by dense populations and mixed commercial and subsistence cultivation; and *tierra fria,* cool uplands, by subsistence cultivation and mining. The elevations and temperatures shown here are from the central highlands of Venezuela. *After:* Gilbert J. Butland, *Latin America: A Regional Geography.* London: Longman Group Ltd., 1972, p. 195, Fig. 41.

in the fertile central valley and cold, wet, fogbound forests southward toward Tierra del Fuego.

The northern Andes and the Guianas. In the northern Andes, the Andean cordillera splits into several parallel ranges that slice through Ecuador, Colombia, and Venezuela to create three distinct environmental zones: the tropical coastline thinly populated by a mixed mestizo and African population; interior valleys and plateaus occupied by mestizo and Indian peoples; and a transmontane eastern rain forest drained by the Orinoco and Amazon rivers. These nations were the object of Simón Bolívar's early dream of a north Andean nation to be called La Gran Colombia. Though they share common cultural and environmental characteristics, Ecuador, Colombia, and Venezuela have had different patterns of development, as have the Guianas, a coastal area that attracted neither Spanish nor Portuguese settlement.

The bulk of Venezuela's population of 10 million is located in the country's richest agricultural zone, the interior central highlands, where plantations of cocoa, sugarcane, cotton, and coffee support a large portion of the mestizo and European population. Although agriculture remains the principal economic activity, Venezuela's mineral wealth makes it the richest country in Latin America. The 6500 oil wells of the Bolívar coastal field in the Maracaibo Basin yield 10 percent of the world's petroleum and 90 percent of Venezuela's export earnings.

Oil capital has made it possible for Venezuela to launch an ambitious program of industrial diversification in the llanos (grasslands) of the Orinoco Basin to the east. In the llanos, previously dominated by a cattle economy, vast deposits of iron at El Pao and Cerro Bolívar are being developed, new oil fields are being brought into production, and a multipurpose dam is being constructed on the Guárico River. Although less than 5 percent of Venezuela's labor force is engaged in industry and its population is growing at the extraordinary rate of 3.6 percent per year, Venezuela is endowed with a resource base capable of supporting a modern economy. In eastern Venezuela, the Guiana Plateau grades into the three countries of Guyana, Surinam, and French Guiana, where sugar, rice, coffee, and bauxite production are the bases of more static economies.

In Colombia, the largest nation in the northern Andes, the mountains divide into three separate cordilleras that finger northward toward Panama and Venezuela and are separated by the valleys of the Cauca and Magdalena rivers. Most of Colombia's 22 million people are scattered in fourteen separate population clusters dotting the valleys and basins between the highlands. Gold initially attracted the Spaniards to the area, but later cotton, sugarcane, cocoa, cattle, and coffee became important economic products.

Two major regions of the country have never attracted significant populations: the forested slopes of the Pacific coast, where settlement is quite limited except for Buenaventura; and the grasslands east of the Andes, the *llanos orientales,* which constitute 60 percent of the area of Colombia. On the Caribbean coast, a stock-raising area, population is concentrated around a series of port cities, notably Barranquilla and Cartagena, which are exterior outlets for agricultural products grown in the highlands.

In contrast to Colombia, Ecuador is clearly divided into three separate environmental and cultural regions. The narrow Ecuadorian coast is populated by a small population of Indians, mestizos, and blacks who produce virtually all the agricultural and mineral wealth of the country. Cocoa, once the principal economic product of the coast, has given way to a large-scale expansion of rice and banana cultivation. All three products are exported through Guayaquil, Ecuador's largest city and most important port.

In the Andean highlands, where most of Ecuador's 6 million people live, the population is predominantly Indian; population pressure in the highlands is intense; subsistence cultivation of corn, barley, wheat, and potatoes has been a persistent agricultural pattern. Over the mountains, the vast tropical forests of four Ecuadorian provinces in the Amazon headwaters are the homelands of the warlike Jivaro Indian tribes, whose previously undisturbed existence is now being disrupted by the

discovery of oil in this, one of the most remote regions in Latin America.

The central Andes. The mountain spine of South America broadens to a width of 400 miles and commonly reaches elevations above 20,000 feet in Peru and Bolivia. In Peru, two cordilleras flank a broad, flat *tableland* 10,000 to 14,000 feet high studded by jagged mountain blocks; in Bolivia, the tableland becomes a plateau basin of interior drainage, the *altiplano.* These uplands were the core of Inca civilization in Peru and Bolivia; subsistence cultivation on valley floors, windswept plateaus, and the mountain slopes of the Andes sustained a relatively dense and prosperous New World civilization. Both the dry, dune-covered coastal zone of Peru and the Amazonian forests were thinly settled.

The Spanish did not, however, establish their capital in the heavily populated uplands of Peru as they had in Mexico, Colombia, and Ecuador. Instead they founded Lima as a commercial port to link the wealth of the Andes to Europe. Colonial land tenure patterns and commercial mines were introduced to the mountains. The social and economic gulf that developed between the dominant mixed European population of the coast and the isolated Indian population of the highlands has been a characteristic of central Andean society ever since.

Most modern Peruvian economic development has taken place along the 1500 miles of desert coast, a bleak dune- and cliff-studded strip 20 to 80 miles wide. European-owned sugar and cotton plantations are located in the fertile valleys of streams that cascade down from the Andean highlands. Roughly one-third of Peru's population, along with the richest agricultural land and most of the country's manufacturing, fishing, and petroleum production, is found along the coast. Until recently, a relatively small European elite owned 90 percent of the cultivated land and the factories in which mestizo and black populations labored. Although land reform is now underway, the coast continues to be the economic heartland of Peru, and efforts at industrial diversification and agricultural expansion inevitably focus on the capital city of Lima.

By contrast, the Andean highlands (where most of Peru's 14 million people live) and the Amazon forests beyond are virtually undeveloped—even unknown. Quechua-speaking Indians, the descendants of the Inca, cultivate terraced fields of wheat, barley, and potatoes in the deep intermontane valleys and high plateaus, and tend herds of sheep, llamas, and alpacas in mountain pastures. Only three areas of dense settlement are found: around Lake Titicaca, where the moderating influence of the lake makes corn cultivation possible at high elevations; near Cuzco, the capital of the Inca Empire; and the min-

The road between Mendoza and Santiago, Chile, winds over the majestic but forbidding terrain of the Andes. If the mineral resources thought to be in this part of the Andes can be located and extracted, the road will become a major highway and Mendoza, whose economy is still predominantly agricultural, will become an important mining and industrial center. *Photo:* United Nations.

ing complex of Cerro de Pasco, inland from Lima. Desperately poor and short of land (only 2 percent of Peru is under cultivation), the people of this region—and particularly the Indians—live outside the mainstream of Peruvian life.

In Bolivia, this social dichotomy is compounded by an extremely difficult natural environment. Trapped between the Atacama coastal desert and Amazon rain forests, most of Bolivia's 5 million people live in small communities on the altiplano, the roof of the Andes, in the gorges of streams flowing eastward to the Amazon, and in narrow intermontane valleys. Over one-third of Bolivia is 1 mile or more high, and much of the rest is either rain forest or semiarid *steppe.* The people, two-thirds of whom speak indigenous languages, are divided by race, language, and local economy; national integration is an elusive goal. The most significant concentration of population is found in the basin of Lake Titicaca.

Elsewhere, settlement is limited by climate and terrain, and primary settlement nodes are almost all determined by the location of Bolivia's mining economy (tin and other metals), which provides 80 percent of the country's exports. Although petroleum production and some commercial agriculture have sprung up on the eastern slopes of the Andes and a program of land reform has broken the traditional grip of the elite on farmland, the limited natural resources of Bolivia and its landlocked and

varied environment make it one of the poorest nations on the continent.

The southern Andes. The Andean cordilleras converge in their southern half to form a mountain spine sweeping 2500 miles southward to outline the long, narrow Pacific republic of Chile. Despite the steep rise of the Andes from a narrow coastal plain, climate, rather than terrain, has been the primary determinant of human settlement in Chile. In northern Chile, the Atacama Desert extends 600 miles along the coast, watered only by mists generated by warm air blown landward across the cold Humboldt current. Agriculture and herding are significant activities only in the southernmost part of the coastal deserts. Rich nitrate deposits located in an upland trough some 500 miles long and copper ores mined at Chuquicamata, El Salvador, and Potrerillos are the vital contributions of the Chilean north to the national economy. The upland mines are connected by rail to Pacific ports such as Arica, Antofagasta, and Iquique, which serve as supply bases and outlets.

Elsewhere, the barren landscapes of the north are virtually uninhabited. The southern extreme of Chile, from the Bió-bió River to the tip of Tierra del Fuego, is also thinly populated. The cool, damp environment of forests and *fjords* in the Chilean south was a refuge for Araucanian Indians driven from their homelands by the Spanish. Until the last century, the Chilean south was physically and culturally outside the society and economy of the nation. Today forestry on the Pacific coast, sheep raising on the plains east of the Andes, and petroleum discoveries in Tierra del Fuego have integrated this region into the national economy.

The heartland of Chile lies between the northern deserts and the southern forests in the central valley, where some 65 percent of the nation's 11 million people live. Marked by Mediterranean climate (warm annual temperature averages and cool season rainfall maxima), the rich alluvial soils of the basin make this the most favored agricultural region of Chile. Until 1965, land in the central valley was held in large haciendas, or *fundos*, which raised wheat and beef cattle. Although small irrigated orchards of citrus fruits, vineyards, and market gardens dot the valley, extensive ranchland dominates the agricultural pattern. The rapidly growing Chilean population, unable to expand in a countryside of fenced ranchland, has been forced to migrate to industrial centers such as Santiago and Valparaíso. By the early 1970s, two-thirds of the Chilean population was urban. After considerable political turmoil the great estates have been confiscated, but national development plans aimed at the redistribution of agricultural land and the introduction of more productive modern forms of agriculture stand in question. As one of the richest agricultural areas on the continent, the central valley holds the key to the Chilean future.

The Midlatitude South

The three temperate countries of Argentina, Uruguay, and Paraguay are part of a midlatitude prairie that stretches from the piedmont of the Andes to the South Atlantic. Drained by the Paraná-Paraguay-Uruguay river system, this region focuses on the estuary of the Río de la Plata, the region's outlet to the world. In the colonial period, these grasslands remained the domain of Indian hunting tribes, and the region was a backwater of the Spanish Empire. Colonial towns were founded on the Andean piedmont, but the eastern grasslands were penetrated only by bands of missionaries who were frequently martyrs to their Christian ideals. Thus separated from the rest of Spanish America, the Midlatitude South was peopled relatively later by immigrants from Europe during the nineteenth and twentieth centuries.

Argentina. In Argentina, a distinctive Latin hybrid has been created by recent European immigration, earlier colonialization, and the belated economic development of the fertile grasslands of the *pampas* in the age of industrialization. The process was reminiscent of the American conquest of the Great Plains. As late as 100 years ago, this region of temperate climate and rich *loess* soil supported a population of only 1.5 million; Buenos Aires, now the second largest city in the Southern Hemisphere, was a small town. Since the 1880s, 7 million Europeans, nearly half of them Italians and one-third Spanish, have immigrated to Argentina. Indians were driven from the pampas, and cattle ranches were founded to feed the expanding populations of industrial Europe. European grasses, windmills, barbed-wire fencing, and six-shooters played their roles in the settlement of this South American prairie. The range was parceled off and wheat cultivation began, heralding the same struggle between rancher and farmer that occurred slightly earlier in the North American Central Plains. A dense network of railroads followed—the best on the continent—to connect the pampas with the bustling port of Buenos Aires.

The pampas are now the undisputed social and economic core of Argentina. Two-thirds of Argentina's population, some 15 million people, live on this grassland, which produces 80 percent of the nation's exports. Buenos Aires, with a population of 5.5 million, is a *primate city*—no other Argentine urban center approaches its size and power. The rural economy of the grasslands is directly influenced by decreasing rainfall starting in the west and worsening to the south, and by distance to market. A hierarchy of economic intensity circles outward from Buenos Aires: market gardens are found nearest the city; intensive farming of wheat, fruit, corn, and flax farther out; and a purely cattle-ranching economy on the periphery. Yet less than a fifth of Argentina's labor force is agricultural despite the preponderant importance of farming in the national economy. Buenos Aires has grown by a factor of fifty in this century, and two-thirds of Argentina's population is urban.

The three backward regions of Argentina—the *scrub forests* of the Chaco in the north, the rugged Andean piedmont to the west, and the bleak wastes of Patagonia to the south—have gradually been welded into the national economy. Until recently, the hot, wet, forested plains of the Chaco were marginal to anyone's interests save Jesuit missionaries and their Indian converts from Paraguay and Brazil. Largely due to modern-day immigration from Europe, the Chaco is now a pioneer region where lumbering and cattle raising are supplemented by cotton, sugar, and tobacco. Still largely populated by Indians, this frontier region has 12 percent of the nation's population today.

A similar process of economic integration is occurring in the dry plateaus and mountain valleys of the Argentine Andes, an area previously linked to the colonial economies of Peru and Bolivia and the principal supplier of mules to the mining camps of the Andes. The province of Tucumán is today the largest sugar-producing area in Argentina, and the irrigated oases of San Juan and Mendoza are important fruit- and grape-growing regions. Although livestock and wheat retain primary importance, urban centers such as Córdoba, Argentina's third largest city, have grown. Improved transportation links with the pampas encourage the rapid expansion of commercial agriculture here and a growth in population now amounting to 20 percent of all Argentines.

On the barren tablelands of Patagonia, which stretch from the pampas 1000 miles south to the tip of the continent, population growth was historically limited by political enmity between Chile and Argentina and by environmental constraints. Less than 3 percent of the Argentine population lives in Patagonia. They are concentrated in deep valleys that provide sufficient shelter from cold winter winds to support sheep ranches. Some 40 percent of Argentina's oil supply is produced at Comodoro Rivadavia; iron resources have been discovered farther south, and Patagonia's role in the Argentine economy has increased in the last decade.

Uruguay and Paraguay. The two smaller nations of the Plata lowlands, Uruguay and Paraguay, are studies in contrasts—in environment, population, and social and economic development. Uruguay, a nation of mild climate, low rolling terrain, and rich grasslands, became an independent state as a buffer zone between the two large and powerful nations of Brazil and Argentina. Although originally settled by the Portuguese, Uruguay's first European settlers of importance were Spanish gauchos hunting wild cattle for their hides. They later subdivided the pastures of the country and settled as large cattle ranchers. With the introduction of sheep and the immigration of 500,000 people from Spain and Italy, Uruguay's population of 3 million is racially European and its economy is deeply anchored in animal husbandry. Sheep and cattle outnumber people by ten to one; wool, hides, and meat products compose 70 percent of the country's exports; and 70 percent of the territory of the country is pastureland.

Yet in Uruguay, the expectable social pattern of a wealthy landowning elite and a poverty-stricken farm working class did not evolve. The haciendas were complemented by large numbers of medium-sized and small farms on which wheat, flax, wine, and vegetable production has doubled in recent years. Enlightened government policies have provided social welfare to the poor; the Uruguayan population, half of which is in the primate city of Montevideo, has the highest literacy rate, the lowest rate of population growth, the best diet, and the highest standard of living of any South American country.

In Paraguay, the evolution of society and economy followed a quite different course. Settled as a base from which the Spanish could penetrate the continent in search of gold, the eastern third of Paraguay with its rich soils, luxuriant grasslands, and gentle terrain became a productive agricultural region under the guidance of Jesuit missionaries, while the western two-thirds, scrub forest of the Chaco, remained a wilderness. The expulsion of the Jesuits in the eighteenth century and a series of disastrous wars and revolutions in the nineteenth and twentieth centuries devastated Paraguay, literally erasing the economy of the country. After the worst of these, the five-year War of the Triple Alliance against Brazil, Argentina, and Uruguay in the 1860s, the mestizo and Guaraní Indian population of Paraguay was halved from 525,000 to 221,000. Only 28,000 adult males were still alive, and Paraguay lost 55,000 square miles of territory. The country has never recovered from this catastrophe.

Currently, the only productive agricultural zone in Paraguay lies in the immediate hinterland of Asunción, where 50 percent of the country's 2.5 million live on only 5 percent of the land. Cotton, tobacco, cattle ranching, and market gardening are important here, but throughout the remainder of Paraguay *slash-and-burn cultivation*° of corn, manioc, and beans, and extensive cattle ranches are the rule. In the Chaco, the *quebracho* forests along the rivers provide tannin and lumber, but except on the 2100-square-mile colony recently granted by the government to Mennonites, modern agriculture and herding are nonexistent. This backward economy supports a Paraguayan population increasing at a rate of 3.4 percent a year, already one of the poorest and most illiterate in Latin America.

Brazil
[FIGURE 3]

Discovered inadvertently in 1500 by Pedro Cabral, a Portuguese, and Vicente Pinzón, a Spaniard, Brazil is the largest nation in Latin America, comparable in size to the United States. Largely through Spanish indifference to the tropical forests which form the core of South America, Brazil became a Portuguese empire in the New World.

Throughout most of Brazil's history, its population has been concentrated along the eastern coasts. Today, however, Brazil (which covers half the area of the continent) has a population of more than 100 million, increasing at a rate of roughly 2 million each year. Of demographic necessity, the penetration of the interior is progressing. Stretching 2300 miles north-south and an equivalent distance into the interior, Brazil is unequaled in Latin America in the diversity of its environments and natural resources.

Coastal Brazil. Northeastern Brazil is the *cultural hearth*° of Portuguese America. It was here that European colonists first established permanent settlements, developed institutions and social patterns which influenced the entire country, and introduced sugar plantations and African slave labor to the New World. The warm, rainy coasts of the northeast are well suited to sugar cultivation, and even today, despite unchanged cultivation techniques, this area produces one-third of Brazil's agricultural product. In some places, the fertile red soils of these lowlands have been producing cane crops and cocoa for up to 400 years. On the drier coasts and the fringes of the interior uplands, cotton cultivation has been introduced.

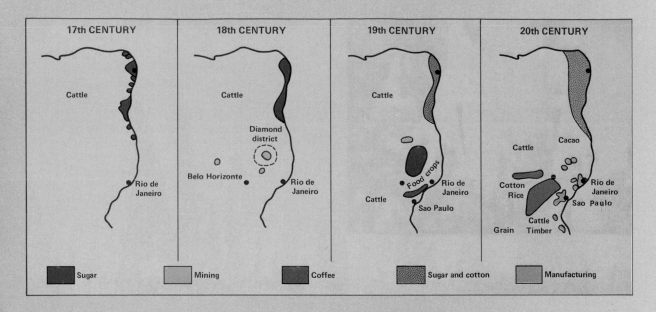

Figure 3. The Economic History of Brazil. The boom-bust economy of Brazil, "harvesting the fruit without planting the trees," has retarded the development of Latin America's largest nation. In the seventeenth century, a sugar boom led to the settlement of the northeast; in the eighteenth century, a gold and diamond mining boom in Minas Gerais evolved into the growth of Belo Horizonte to the east; in the nineteenth century, coffee cultivation developed in the Paraiba Valley. In this century, the growth of an urban industrial complex centered on São Paulo and Rio de Janeiro has been the focus of Brazilian life. *After:* John P. Cole, *Latin America: An Economic and Social Geography.* London: Butterworths, 1973, p. 76, Fig. 4.4 (d).

The bulk of the northeast's population of 400 million lives near the coast; the major cities of the region are Recife and Salvador, which have a combined population of 2 million. In contrast, the interior upland of the northeast, the dry *sertão*, is a poor, barren, thinly peopled land covered by dryland grasses and thorn scrub forest. Used primarily for open-range cattle, the sertão is subject to periodic droughts, the latest of which occurred during 1969–1971. These two regions, the coast and the sertão, are sharply differentiated, but despite their contrasting densities of population, both parts of the northeast are overpopulated. Droughts intensified by deforestation and overgrazing have propelled large-scale migrations of peasants and herdsmen out of the sertão. The government has even closed roads to attempt to stem the tide of this emigration. On the coast, the persistence of rigid social barriers, absentee patterns of cultivation, and exhaustion of the soil have encouraged migration away from the northeast to the more dynamic regions of contemporary Brazil.

Eastern Brazil covers only one-tenth the land area of the country but has nearly one-half the population. The two largest cities—São Paulo (6 million) and Rio de Janeiro (4.5 million)—form the most ma-

ture and diversified industrial region in Latin America. They developed late, however. The well-watered forested plateaus behind the coastal escarpment held little appeal for colonial Portugal. Roving bands of pastoral adventurers criss-crossed the area in the search for gold and precious stones. When gold and diamonds were discovered in the river gravels of Minas Gerais state in the eighteenth century, thousands rushed to this new El Dorado. The plateau was opened to settlement and Rio de Janeiro was founded as an outlet for the mineral wealth of the interior.

By the nineteenth century the gravels had panned out, but subsistence agriculturalists cleared land in southern Minas Gerais and pastoralists herded cattle in the savannas to the north. On patches of fertile red soil coffee estates (*fazendas*) were established in the nineteenth century, and the hinterland of São Paulo and the Paraíba Valley inland from Rio de Janeiro became important, serving European and North American markets. A stream of 2 million European immigrants, principally Italians, Portuguese, Spanish, and later Japanese, flowed into this region after 1880 to labor on coffee estates in the interior and on sugar, rice, and cotton farms along the coast and in river valleys.

In the twentieth century waterpower on the Tietê River has been harnessed, and an integrated steel complex constructed at Volta Redonda based on the rich iron, manganese, and tungsten ores of the Serra do Espinhaço. São Paulo now produces 40 percent and Rio de Janeiro 20 percent of all Brazilian manufacturing. Despite extensive penetration of the upland interior, the coast remains the nexus of Brazilian population. One of every four people in this region lives in either São Paulo or Rio de Janeiro, the two metropolises, or in the densely settled Paraíba Valley.

The Amazon Basin, one-third of the area of Brazil, plays little part in the economy, although it does supply some rubber, here shown harvested by hand. *Photo:* United Nations.

The Brazilian south, which encompasses one-sixth of the nation's population, experienced colonization in waves that successively penetrated the interior, transforming the landscape of the dissected upland plateau. But the sequence of occupance and the traditions of the settlers in the south were quite different from those in the zones to the north. The first European settlers were pastoral adventurers who filtered southward from São Paulo and ultimately settled on the rolling temperate grasslands of Rio Grande do Sul State and established a cattle- and sheep-raising economy not unlike that of neighboring Uruguay. At this same time, during the seventeenth and eighteenth centuries, small numbers of Brazilian colonists spread southward along the Atlantic coast seeking gold. They established fortified outposts at São Francisco do Sul, Florianópolis, and Pôrto Alegre—footholds on the southern perimeter of the Portuguese Empire in America. In the nineteenth and twentieth centuries, these coastal centers were bases for a second major wave of colonization by foreign immigrants from Germany, Italy, and eastern Europe.

The first to penetrate the interior were Germans, who established a mixed-farming economy of corn, rye, and potato cultivation and pig raising in the river valleys of Rio Grande do Sul. Italian immigrants later bypassed the German settlements, clearing forests and planting vineyards deeper in the interior. The third major wave of colonization into the south is the current sweep of the agricultural frontier southward from São Paulo into northern and western Paraná State, where occasional frosts prevent the establishment of a coffee-based economy and encourage agricultural diversification. On the basis of this sound agricultural economy, the Brazilian south is growing rapidly in economic importance; Paraná doubled its population to 8 mil-

lion during the 1960s; Santa Catarina and Rio Grande do Sul added 2 million during the decade.

The Brazilian interior. The vast interior of Brazil, the central states of Goiás, Mato Grosso, and Amazonas, covers an area two-thirds the size of the United States, but it is occupied by less than 10 million people. Hailed as one of the world's last frontiers the interior is the territorial basis for Brazilian plans to double the country's population to 200 million people by 1990. But the region's tropical environment has stubbornly resisted all but the most determined efforts at permanent settlement. It remains one of the least known and most misunderstood regions of Latin America.

The early history of the plateaus of the central states was one of small gold rushes and quickly abandoned mining towns. Savannas supported extensive cattle raising and subsistence agriculture, but only in southeastern Goiás and in the Paraguay basin of Mato Grosso are there soils of sufficient fertility to support intensive cultivation of coffee, corn, and sugar. The new capital city of Brasília, a symbol of the Brazilian desire to conquer the interior, was founded in the late 1950s in the central states. In the first decade, population increased by 80 percent, and since then the central states have gained an additional 50 percent as settlers from São Paulo and Minas Gerais moved westward. But the continued expansion of the pioneer frontier in the central states will depend on the productive exploitation of the acid soils of savanna scrub forests, which thus far have impeded the development of a strong agricultural economy.

Settlement in the northlands of the Amazon is more limited than in the central states. Over half the population of the vast Pará state live near the mouth of the Amazon or farther inland on patches of arable land along the rivers that support the larger centers of Manaus, Santarém, and the port city of Belém. Although the 3900-mile-long Amazon River is navigable as far inland as Iquitos in Peru, the hot, humid climate and infertile soils of the tropical rain forests that cover this flask-shaped basin keep it almost unoccupied. In the interior, Indians collect rubber and Brazil nuts and practice slash-and-burn agriculture; on the dry savanna margins of the rain forest, cattle are raised.

A brief rubber boom at the turn of the century was defeated by the inaccessibility of the area, plant diseases, and labor shortages. The Ford and Goodyear plantations are today in ruins. The government's determination that the empty heart of Brazil should no longer remain empty has led to the construction of roads that link the major population centers of the Amazon. But many of these roads have already fallen into disrepair, and unless oil is discovered in the farther reaches of the Amazon or significant advances are made in tropical agriculture, the Amazon north will remain a wilderness.

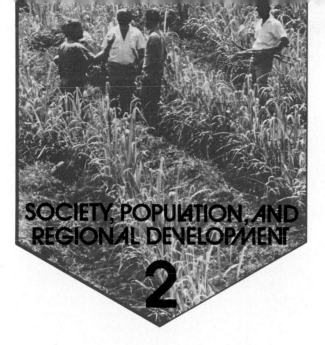

SOCIETY, POPULATION, AND REGIONAL DEVELOPMENT

2

South American revolutions did not bring the independent prosperity, economic development, and social improvement that the complementary revolution in the United States had effected. In many ways, they should have. When English colonists to the north revolted against King George, the nations of Latin America had more people (nearly 25 million), larger cities, and better universities than North America. The culture, laws, languages, and religions of her people derived from a common European culture hearth, although by the nineteenth century, Iberia itself was in serious decline. After three centuries of European exploitation, the agriculture and mineral production of Latin America far exceeded that of the United States. Indeed, the export value of sugar from Haiti alone was greater than the value of the total export product of British North America during the entire eighteenth century. In both North and South America, vast reaches of valuable land awaited conquest in the interior.

Yet today, after 150 years of independence, Latin America remains relatively undeveloped. The combined domestic product of all of Latin America is equal to only one-tenth that of North America; Latin standards of living are many times lower than those found north of the Mexico–United States border. For a variety of reasons, the Industrial Revolution, which truly transformed life in Europe and European-settled North America, Australia, and New Zealand, took root in a very different form in Latin America. Latin leaders, who were and remain cultured in the same Christian tradition, have not organized the region's extensive area and resources as effectively as the North American population. Only the large nations of Latin America—Brazil, Mexico, and Argentina—have gross domestic products comparable to those of the tiny Western European nations of the **Benelux.**

Latin America thus remains on the periphery of the industrial world, a primary producer of raw ma-

terials, with higher standards of living and literacy than those found in most of Africa and Asia, but far behind the nations of the technological world in all indexes of social and economic development. Despite European origins and inspirations, a primary cause of the delayed Latin American pattern of growth has been the persistence of the value system and institutional structure inherited from sixteenth-century Spain and Portugal.

THE SOCIAL MATRIX

The revolutions in the Spanish New World succeeded in liberating the colonies from Spain; the gachupins lost control and returned to Europe. Simón Bolívar, a brilliant orator and revolutionary leader, called for the first Pan-American Congress in 1826. He dreamed of a federation of South and Central America whose proposed capital at the Isthmus of Panama would become the center of a dynamic new civilization. But only four nations sent delegates; Bolívar himself was entangled in Lima and unable to attend.

By 1850, the Spanish New World had crumbled into eighteen independent states. By 1900 there were twenty; today there are twenty-four. Central America broke away from the Mexican Empire and within twenty years was subdivided into five quarrelsome states—today's Guatemala, Honduras, El Salvador, Nicaragua, and Costa Rica. Bolívar's north Andean nation, La Gran Colombia, was torn in 1830 into Colombia, Ecuador, and New Granada (now Venezuela). Later that same year, the defeated liberator, penniless and dying of tuberculosis, retreated to a plantation near Cartagena and his death. With the sole exception of Portuguese Brazil, local factions were triumphant; political (and thus economic) fragmentation prevailed. Regional differences, vast distances, and formidable physical barriers separated the centers of population as before, but the presumptuous personal ambitions of the military leaders of Latin America aborted all efforts at political unification. Perhaps the most striking difference between independent North and South America was this absence of the emergence of a single powerful state from the Latin revolutionary struggle.

In most of the new nations, the long wars of revolution devastated agricultural land and disrupted local economies. Plantations lay in ruins; mines were flooded and abandoned. Insurgent bands led by

The Catholic Church proved far stronger in Latin America than the armies and officials of the Spanish king: Elaborate churches like this one in Bogotá are still as active today as they were when they served Spanish colonial administrators centuries ago. *Photo:* Corporacion Nacional de Turismo, Colombia.

local chieftains came to exploit the vacuum of authority by roaming the countryside to vie for power, wealth, and prestige. New methods of government were discussed by creole aristocrats in the drawing rooms of Mexico City, Lima, Bogotá, and Buenos Aires. Monarchies were rejected out of hand. The seven postrevolutionary kings of Brazil, Mexico, and Haiti met bitter ends: three were banished, two were executed, one was assassinated, and one committed suicide. Except in public speeches, democracy was not a serious consideration; the creoles dreaded the consequences of political power in the hands of the Indian and mestizo masses. Lacking experience or training in public administration, one state after another evolved into a highly centralized republican form of government led by victorious generals, the so-called men on horseback.

The pattern arose and was repeated again and again. Local chieftains (*caudillos*) developed personal followings and launched revolutions against incumbent strong men much like themselves. Personalities were more important than programs; the cult of the individual prevailed. Hailed as protec-

tors, saviors, redeemers, and liberators, new leaders squandered their resources to prevent emergence of other caudillos. Some were cultured aristocrats. Others were savage imperators such as the one Charles Darwin met on his voyage up the Paraná River whose hobby was hunting Indians; he managed to kill forty-eight during Darwin's brief visit. The military dictators of the twentieth century are the cultural descendants of these nineteenth-century caudillos, men who filled the vacuum at the termination of Spanish rule.

Largely because of this kind of leadership, independence did not introduce social changes into the highly stratified colonial society of Latin America. Creoles retained the upper hand, replacing the exiled gachupins; mestizos moved up to fill the creoles' shoes. Black people gained legal freedom but little else; Indians, who existed mostly outside the political process, gained nothing. Latin American economies were ordered by an *oligarchy** of landowners, mine operators, priests, merchants, intellectuals, and military officers whose interest in the welfare of the population was minimal.

A Dual Economy
[FIGURE 4, TABLE 1]

The revolutions did, however, free Latin America from the commercial restrictions of Spain. Trade with Britain, France, Belgium, and later Germany,

Italy, and the United States increased substantially. In the throes of the Industrial Revolution, Europeans exported manufactured goods and invested capital wherever possible. In Latin America, the European demand for foodstuffs was balanced by local need for the manufactured goods of the age; trade expanded rapidly. In a single year, Britain's Latin American investments increased by one-third, and during the latter half of the 1800s, Britain became the banker and financial trustee of Latin America. Railroads were thrown across the pampas of Argentina and up into the Andean cordillera; European capital paid. The commercial wool industry of Uruguay and Argentina was established; later, oil exploration was begun in Venezuela, and in the 1920s, the nitrate and copper deposits of Chile were brought into production by American investment. American associates of President Porfirio Díaz drilled oil wells along the Mexican coast in the early twentieth century; the banana empire of the United Fruit Company was created in the Caribbean at the same time. Since almost all government revenues in the nations of Latin America derived from trade tariffs, successive governments attempted to form lasting trade alliances between foreign capitalists and the creole ruling class.

In the more advanced parts of Latin America, a dual economy was implanted which was in some respects similar to those of the same period in colonial Africa, the Middle East, and India. The most productive agricultural lands were given over to the growing of export crops oriented to European interests. Brazil became world famous for rubber and coffee; Argentina grew wheat and beef. The sugar production of the Caribbean declined when sugar beet cultivation in Europe expanded, but other plantation crops (cotton, cocoa, and bananas) came to replace it.

Improvements in transportation expanded the potential area of single-crop agriculture: Railroads opened hinterlands away from the coasts; larger and faster refrigerator cargo ships made it possible to ship bulky and perishable goods from Latin America to the ports of Europe within weeks instead of months. The mineral exports of a few countries—tin from Bolivia, copper and nitrates from Chile, bauxite and gold from the Guianas, and oil from Venezuela—were selectively exploited by modern mining ven-

---

TABLE 1. Principal Exports of Latin America as Percentages of Total Value of Exports, c. 1960

Source: John P. Cole, *Latin America: An Economic and Social Geography.* London: Butterworths, 1973, p. 427.

Country	Product	%	Product	%	Product	%
Brazil	Coffee	56	Cocoa	8	Vegetable fibers	6
Mexico	Cotton	21	Coffee	9	Sugar	7
Argentina	Meats	31	Cereals	29	Wool	26
Colombia	Coffee	72	Crude oil	17	Bananas	3
Peru	Copper	22	Cotton	17	Fish	12
Chile	Copper	70	Iron ore	6	Nitrates	5
Venezuela	Oil	91	Iron ore	7	Coffee	1
Cuba	Sugar	76	Tobacco	10		
Ecuador	Bananas	62	Coffee	15	Cocoa	14
Guatemala	Coffee	66	Bananas	17		
El Salvador	Coffee	69	Cotton	14		
Honduras	Bananas	46	Coffee	19	Wood	10
Nicaragua	Coffee	34	Cotton	26	Gold	12
Costa Rica	Coffee	49	Bananas	28	Cocoa	7
Panama	Bananas	73	Coffee	4	Cocoa	3
Haiti	Coffee	56	Sisal	12	Sugar	11
Dominican Republic	Sugar	50	Coffee	13	Cocoa	8
Puerto Rico	Textiles	25	Sugar	21	Machinery	11
Jamaica	Bauxite	49	Sugar	24	Bananas	9
Trinidad	Oil	84	Sugar	8	Chemicals	2
Netherlands Antilles	Oil products	98	Chemicals	1		
Guianas	Bauxite	44	Sugar	30	Rice	10
Bolivia	Tin	65	Lead	7	Silver	7
Paraguay	Meats	26	Quebracho	11		
Uruguay	Wool	35	Meat	24	Hides	6
Latin America	Oil	28	Coffee	17	Sugar	8

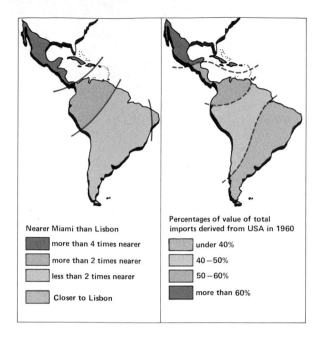

Nearer Miami than Lisbon

■ more than 4 times nearer

▒ more than 2 times nearer

▒ less than 2 times nearer

□ Closer to Lisbon

Percentages of value of total imports derived from USA in 1960

▒ under 40%

▒ 40–50%

▒ 50–60%

■ more than 60%

Figure 4. Location and Trade in Twentieth-Century Latin America. As the United States became an industrial power, locational advantages led to a substantial increase in hemispheric trade. Now most of Latin America imports half or more of all manufactures, machinery, and food from the United States. *After:* John P. Cole, *Latin America: An Economic and Social Geography.* London: Butterworths, 1973, p. 4, Figs. 1.2(d), 1.3(b).

A plantation worker in Ecuador packs a newly cut stem of bananas for shipment to market. The fibrous trunk of the tree is peeled away and used to protect the fruit. Increasing its exports of this and other agricultural products such as coffee and cacao is part of this Latin American country's efforts to develop a viable and diversified economy that will enable it to move into the world of the twentieth century. *Photo:* United Nations.

tures subsidized by foreign companies and governments. National economies and transportation networks became geared solely to the maintenance of this flow of goods. Broad-scale economic development remained at a minimum in areas outside the realm of commercialized agriculture. As a result, large regions floundered into unfocused economic backwardness. The eighteenth-century economy of large landholdings, debt slavery, and subsistence cultivation remained intact well into the present century. **Peons**• produced what food they could on the margins of large estates and hauled their produce by mule and ox-cart over bad roads to be cheated in the market towns. Rural poverty remained intense.

Nowhere were the damaging effects of this symbiotic relationship between the ruling classes of Latin America and the bankers of Europe and the United States more apparent than in Argentina. At the turn of the century, British capital was invested in the construction of railroads, port facilities, packing plants, and public utilities—the vital elements that opened up the pampas to production of meats and grains for the British market. In the Argentine pampas and in the temperate zones of Brazil and Chile, a stream of migrants—mostly poor German, Swiss, and Italian farmers—followed the direction of European overseas capital. By World War I, Argen-

tine politics and economics were intimately linked to the British standard of living, and Argentina was indisputably the most developed country in Latin America. Elsewhere, Britain became the owner of 118 railroad lines, 45 port facility companies, and 112 public utilities, as well as electric power plants and waterworks throughout Latin America.

In a typical exchange, British ships carried wheat, meat, corn, and linseed to European markets; on the return voyage, British coal was exported to satisfy the energy needs of Argentina. This classic example of complementary agricultural-industrial interdependence had the effect of significantly reducing local Argentine interest in the development of a balanced manufacturing and industrial economy in their country. Here and elsewhere in Latin America, the Industrial Revolution had the effect of only partially modernizing local economies and then only for the benefit of landlords and politicians. The change was not sufficiently powerful to create autonomous systems capable of generating their own internal economic growth.

During the twentieth century, North American investments gradually replaced European capital in Latin America, and the same encouragement of one-crop export economies prevailed. Almost half of all American investment abroad in the 1930s was in

Latin America. Before World War II, Bolivia was the most heavily subsidized nation per person. A confusing array of Latin American military dictators drew heavily on American banks and arms; security took precedence over national development. Since riots, rebellion, and rural unrest disturbed production on the plantations, haciendas, and mines, movements for social change were uniformly perceived as threats to export economies and were ruthlessly suppressed. In Mexico, the revolution of Emiliano Zapata (1910–1915) was an exception. The large Mexican haciendas were confiscated, land was redistributed to the peasants, the oil industry was nationalized, and Indians were granted some measure of social dignity. The Cuban revolution of the late 1950s brought the same objectives of economic balance and social equality to bear, but the pernicious dependence of the island upon sugar exports still exists.

The growing role of the United States in Latin American economic affairs was prompted by the emergence of America as a world industrial power after World War I and by simple locational factors. The Caribbean is four times closer to the United States than to Europe; northern South America is twice as close. Only beyond the eastern shoulder of Brazil is Latin America nearer to Europe than to North America. As a result, nearly two-thirds of Mexico's imports come from the United States; half the imports of the Caribbean nations and most countries of South America come from the United States. Only Argentina and Brazil import less than 40 percent of their manufactured and food needs from North America. Thus, the balance between Latin America production of tropical agricultural products and raw materials for the needs of industrial North America has been the primary focus of exchange.

Heavy dependence upon the export of particular crops or minerals, therefore, remains an economic pattern throughout Latin America, despite government prodding to diversify. For example, oil accounts for 90 percent of the export revenues of Venezuela and a quarter of the value of Latin American exports as a whole. Tin plays a similar role in the Bolivian economy, as does copper in Chile and bauxite in Surinam and Jamaica. More than half of the exports of Brazil, Colombia, Guatemala, and El Salvador are directed to North American markets. Fluctuations in the prices of these commodities on world markets periodically shatter the welfare of these societies. Sugar is still the mainstay of Cuba and the Dominican Republic; bananas are pivotal in the Honduran and Panamanian economies, as they were in Ecuador prior to the recent development of oil production.

Overall, agricultural products generate four-fifths of all exports of fifteen nations of Latin America. Mexico looms as the only large nation with a

balanced export pattern. Brazil has attempted to diversify its production of food crops, cotton, and sugar; Colombia has moved to boost production of sugar and cotton; the Central American countries are interested in balancing bananas with cotton; in Venezuela and Chile, the iron industry is being promoted. But in general the reliance on a single product remains as strong today in Latin America as in the past. Paradoxically, by using the best lands to cultivate agricultural exports, Latin America in the 1970s must import one-tenth of its food needs.

Latifundismo
[FIGURE 5]

The Spanish and the Portuguese passion for land acquisition led them to institute a regime of feudal-like estates in Latin America. This landholding system, *latifundismo,* relied on the availability of cheap land, open markets for abundant produce, a submissive labor force, and an armed elite capable of controlling unrest. These conditions prevailed in the New World. A century after conquest, 100,000 square miles in Mexico alone were bestowed as land grants on the aristocracy of New Spain. From these roots were born the haciendas of mainland Middle America, the *estancias* of Argentina and the early La Plata states, the *fundos* of Chile and Peru, the coffee *fazendas* of Brazil, and the sugar plantations of the Caribbean. Rural society in Latin America became divided into two classes. A wealthy, landed elite of leisure and power, owners of the great estates, the latifundios, and the mass of the peasantry whose tiny plots, minifundios, were unable to sustain a family and thus forced the peasant to work as a sharecropper. Currently, half the agricultural land of Latin America is held in estates of 37,000 acres or more; two-thirds of the peasantry (13 million rural families in 1960) are landless laborers or small holders.

In Argentina, the pampas have been subdivided into huge estancias on which beef and dairy cattle, sheep, and horses are raised. Until recently, the 100 wealthiest cattle baron families owned more than 10 million acres; the 2000 largest farms represented one-fifth of the total area of Argentina. In earlier periods, nearly 1 million Italian and Spanish farm workers made annual migrations to Argentina during the European winter to harvest wheat and corn and then returned to Europe during the South American off-season. Millions more, a European-born

This village on the road to Otalvo, north of Quito, Ecuador, is one of 10,000 small rural settlements in Latin America still characterized by poverty, disease, and illiteracy. *Photo:* United Nations/Guthrie.

tenant peasantry, stayed on to work the great ranches, where overseers maintained a staff of servants and supervised the villages of tenant farmers, **sharecroppers,*** and day laborers. These peasants and ranch hands earned the equivalent of $40 a month in the 1960s cultivating the wheat fields and tending the herds belonging to absentee landowners.

Although market pressures and the inheritance system have broken up some estancias, 60 percent of Argentina's arable land remains in holdings larger than 5000 acres. In Uruguay, sheep ranches are operated in similar fashion; 3800 of these occupy some 60 percent of the national territory. The Uruguayan government has made an effort to increase small agricultural holdings, but only an insignificant amount of land has been transferred to such ownership. Large estates are also dominant in Paraguay, and although half the country's labor force is engaged in agriculture, only 3 percent own their own land. The resultant population pressure makes land squatting a common Paraguayan pattern.

In Peru, until the current government program of land redistribution took effect, 400 families owned half of the agricultural land in the fertile central valley; one estate was as large as the state of Israel in its pre-1967 form. In the 1960s, half of Chile's farm families—185,000—were landless, and three-quarters of the rest owned only 5 percent of the land. The same pattern was repeated on the coffee hacien-das of highland Colombia, where 2 percent of the landowners controlled 43 percent of the agricultural land in units of 250 acres or more. The ownership of Brazil's agricultural land was equally imbalanced, although on the largest estates, the coffee fazendas of São Paulo, the living conditions of the share-croppers of European descent are better than in most of Latin America. These farmers live in fazenda colonies, tend up to 1000 coffee trees each, cultivate private garden plots, and tend livestock nearby. This model of agriculture with its emphasis on the cultivation of a single crop for export is repeated on the commercialized modern sugar and banana plantations of the Caribbean. Despite a long history of slavery and the vagaries of price fluctuations, these plantations and the state-owned farms remain the only modern, efficient agricultural systems in Latin America.

Rural poverty. These restrictive forms of land ownership are a fundamental source of rural poverty, agricultural stagnation, and social inequality in Latin America. Typically, landowners, cultured and urbane people, maintain their haciendas for status and income. There is little impetus for investment in more intensive land utilization or modernization of cropping and marketing methods. At the bottom of the agricultural and social pyramid, the minifundio is so small, so inefficiently run that it produces barely enough food to sustain a peasant family. Such families' diets are inadequate, and their incomes are commonly below $100 per year. Hidden and outright unemployment is high in rural areas; dissatisfied tenants can easily be replaced.

BANANA PLANTATIONS
IN CENTRAL AMERICA

2. SOCIETY AND
REGIONAL DEVELOPMENT

LATIN AMERICA
307

At the end of the nineteenth century, commercial banana plantations were established on the Caribbean coast of Central America. Efficient standardized production was achieved by the United Fruit Company and its competitors on large tracts of unoccupied alluvial soils in the hot, rainy lowlands of the Caribbean tierra caliente—*ideal conditions for banana cultivation. Administrative centers were established on the coast, and large numbers of black laborers from the West Indies, chiefly Jamaica, were imported to work in the banana groves of Honduras, Nicaragua, Costa Rica, and Panama.*

By 1930, 48 million banana stalks (the average stalk has 170 bananas) were being exported to the United States each year, more than half from the Honduras coast. But then plague and leaf blight entered the area; thousands of acres of banana land were abandoned and workers discharged. The banana industry shifted to the Pacific coast, but the diseases followed and this new area of cultivation was also abandoned. Banana cultivation has recovered in some places on the east coast, but the focus of activity is today more selectively intense as greater efficiency demands greater concentration of the crop. Although many economists cite the banana plantation as the most efficient form of plantation agriculture in Latin America, the plantations—particularly in the banana republics of Honduras and Panama—have not substantially benefited the people of these countries. Dependence on a single crop has removed fertile land from diversified food production, created a mobile force of discontented migrant laborers uncertain of their jobs, and led to severe local economic fluctuations instead of integrated regional development.

A Guatemalan peasant returns from market with his new piglets on a leash. *Photo:* United Nations WHO/Almasy.

In some areas, out of desperation peasants have squatted illegally on open cropland. In Peru, some 200,000 Andean peasants occupied private estates in the 1950s until repressed by the military. Similar peasant moves occurred in Mexico and Venezuela during the same period. More frequently, the dispossessed move to the cities or become migrant laborers traveling from one rural scene to another. In Guatemala, 200,000 people—nearly one-third of the rural labor force—descend from the highlands for the coastal coffee harvest each year. Experienced observers estimate that one of every two minifundio peasants regularly migrates in search of seasonal employment. Family farms similar to those of the United States and Europe are found only in southern Brazil, parts of Argentina, Colombia, south-central Chile, and Costa Rica.

With over half of all Latin Americans engaged in agriculture, rural poverty is the most compelling problem facing national governments. Agricultural productivity per worker declined by 3 percent in the 1950s. In the 1970s, arable land is increasing at a rate of only 1 percent per year. Thus, population pressure on agricultural land has become more intense, and the average size of the minifundio has steadily decreased. Governments have responded to these conditions by initiating land reform programs, but even these small gains, which are being made as a matter of political expedience, meet with continuing resistance from an entrenched elite.

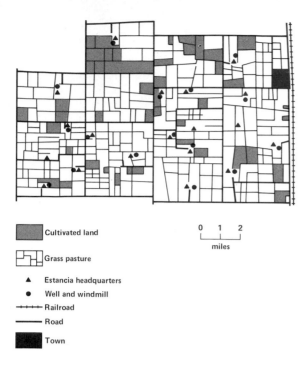

Cultivated land

Grass pasture

▲ Estancia headquarters

● Well and windmill

┼┼┼┼ Railroad

───── Road

■ Town

0 1 2
miles

Figure 5. The Argentine Estancia. The pampas of Argentina are subdivided into cattle ranches called *estancias,* **great blocks of land 5000 acres or larger. Headquarters is usually a palatial mansion, flanked by a well and windmills, set in rolling pastures on which beef and dairy cattle are grown. The** *estancias* **are slowly breaking up into small farms with more land in cultivation and less in pasture. Market demands for food in the Buenos Aires metropolitan area are increasing, but since land is held for prestige, not profit, the change has been gradual. Planners still complain of the "green blight" of pastureland around Buenos Aires that makes it necessary to import food from distant areas—while in North America and Europe, efforts are being made to create greenbelts around urban centers.** *After:* **Pier Luigi Beretta,** *Bollettino di Societa Geografica Italiana,* **Series IX, Vol. VII (1966), p. 549. By permission of the Societa Geografica Italiana, Rome.**

Agrarian revolt. Three social upheavals in Latin America resulting in the destruction of the landlord class have struck fear of revolution into this elite. The early revolt of the illiterate tenant farmer Emiliano Zapata in Mexico left the states of Morelos and Guerrero in ashes; according to a song of the day, "only four cornfields were left." The great estates were broken up and peasant cooperatives were established. "Land and liberty," the objectives of the peasants, were achieved; but productivity on the cooperatives remains low even today. In Cuba, Castro's agrarian reforms of 1959 banned large landholdings and sharecropping. Huge American-owned sugar estates were confiscated and redistributed to Cuban farmers in lots of 67 acres each. Later these were recombined, and cane cutters now work on large government farms organized under a state monopoly—a huge national sugar factory in the

fields. Sweeping social reforms in 1952 in Bolivia were similarly dependent on the transformation of the traditional social order. More than 2 million new small landholders were given parcels of land secured by the nationalization of the great estates, but environmental problems and limited financial resources have rendered Bolivian agriculture as socially inadequate as before.

Elsewhere, agrarian reform has been more tentative. An estimated 1000 to 1500 families in each country received land from expropriated private estates through land reform programs during the 1960s. In Venezuela significantly larger numbers of people—10,000 to 12,000 families a year—were given land, a benefit of capital from oil exports disbursed to the Venezuelan peasantry. With population growing at increasing rates and land reform and industrial production providing limited relief, rural poverty and social inequity are evidence of a continuing failure of leadership in Latin America.

POPULATION GROWTH AND URBANIZATION

The population of Latin America, currently estimated at 330 million and increasing by 8 million a year, is growing faster than that of any other continent. In some countries of mainland Middle America and tropical South America, the population growth rate is two to three times that of modern

Figure 6. Population Growth, 1920–1970. The population of Latin America, doubling every twenty-three years, is growing faster than any other world region. Part (a) uses 1920 as a base to show rate of increase by year; (b) shows that most nations of Latin America have tripled their populations over the last fifty years. *Adapted from:* **Gilbert J. Butland,** *Latin America: A Regional Geography.* **London: Longman Group, Ltd., 1972, pp. 22, 23.**

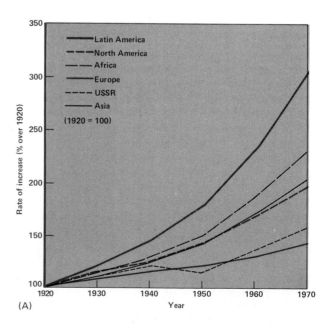

China. Although the balance between population and resources is more favorable in Latin America than in either India or China, the population has doubled since 1950, and this jeopardizes recent efforts to raise standards of living and improve the quality of life. People have fled to the cities, and there the poverty of Latin America has become more apparent.

Some countries are approaching the extent of their natural resources; others lack the finances and organization needed to provide education, jobs, and social services to larger segments of society. Some of the more developed countries, notably Argentina and Uruguay, have minimal population growth problems. Brazil, the giant of the region, has embarked upon a dubious plan to double its population to 200 million by the end of the century in an effort to conquer with numbers the emptiness of the Amazon. It is clear, however, that population growth acts as a brake on economic development in Latin America, and planners are scrambling to provide a reasonable life for an urban population that will double in size in less than twenty-five years if the current growth rate continues.

Population Growth
[FIGURE 6]

Between 1930 and 1960, an unprecedented rapid decline in the death rate in Latin America served to extend the average life span from thirty-five years to fifty-five years. Previously, the high birth rate was offset by a high death rate, and the rate of population

growth was limited to 1.1 to 1.3 percent per year. Before the 1940s one of every three children died before age five; at birth, a Latin American had only a 50 percent chance of living to age thirty-five. But by the 1960s, the crude death rate fell to 10 to 15 per 1000, and the birth rate remained high. The three major killers—malaria, yellow fever, and typhoid— were brought under control. The *Organization of American States** subsidized hospitals, medical training, water supply, and sewage systems throughout Latin America. Communicable and infectious diseases, which had traditionally decimated the population, were replaced by the chronic diseases of old age. As a result, by the mid-1970s, Latin America's population of 330 million was five times larger than the 63 million Latin Americans in 1900.

The population explosion in Latin America does not stem simply from the medical effort to lower the death rate by advances in medicine, sanitation, and personal hygiene. The wealth in such cities as Rio de Janeiro creates strong images of a better life in the minds of migrants, encouraging them to have children. In addition, from Mexico to Buenos Aires,

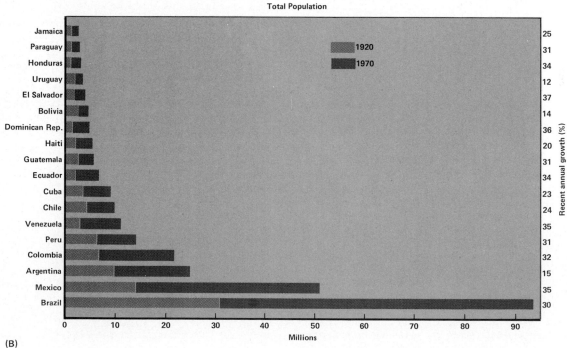

(B)

Latin America is a Catholic society. And the Church, while under social pressure to change its views, adamantly opposes artificial methods of contraception. As a result, no Latin American nation is able to sponsor official public birth-control programs. Interestingly enough, the phrases "birth-control program" and "Roman Catholic Church" are not indexed in contemporary volumes on Latin America's population.

The distribution of population growth in Latin America has been concentrated in areas already densely settled. Pioneer settlement is hindered by environmental difficulties, the grip of latifundismo, and the heavy concentration of economic and social development programs in and around existing urban centers. As a result, in 1970, a quarter of all Latin Americans were crowded onto 3 percent of the land area, while half of the region—nearly 4 million square miles—was occupied by only 5 percent of the population. The regions of highest density today are the islands of the Caribbean and central Mexico, the Andean agricultural highlands from Venezuela through Colombia and Ecuador to Peru, and a Brazilian coastal band 100 miles deep from the shoulder to the Plata estuary. Small clusters of settlement are found in the central valley of Chile, the Bolivian highlands, and parts of Central America. Elsewhere, people are few: the vast rain forests of the Amazon, the scrub forests of the Chaco, and the bleak wastes of Patagonia have less than ten people per square mile. For all intents and purposes, South America has remained an empty continent surrounded by islands of people.

Urbanization

The largest cities in Latin America are located at the cores of these islands of settlement. They have been growing three to four times as fast as the population at large. In 1950, one-fourth of all Latin Americans lived in cities larger than 20,000 people. A decade later, this figure had risen to one-third. Between 1960 and 1970, the urban population of Latin America increased from 68 million to 125 million, resulting in a considerably more urbanized population than in either Asia or Africa. Currently, sixteen cities in Latin America, nine of them national capitals, have populations of more than 1 million. The conurbations of Mexico City and Buenos Aires have populations of more than 7 million each. São Paulo and Rio de Janeiro, the two largest cities in Brazil, have respective populations of 6 million and 4.5 million. Bogotá, Lima, and Santiago have 2 million or more; Guadalajara, Monterrey, Caracas, Medellín, Havana, Recife, Belo Horizonte, Pôrto Alegre, and Montevideo are greater than 1 million in size.

A *favela* clings to a hillside in Rio de Janeiro. *Photo:* **Gerard Oppenheimer/Design Photographers International.**

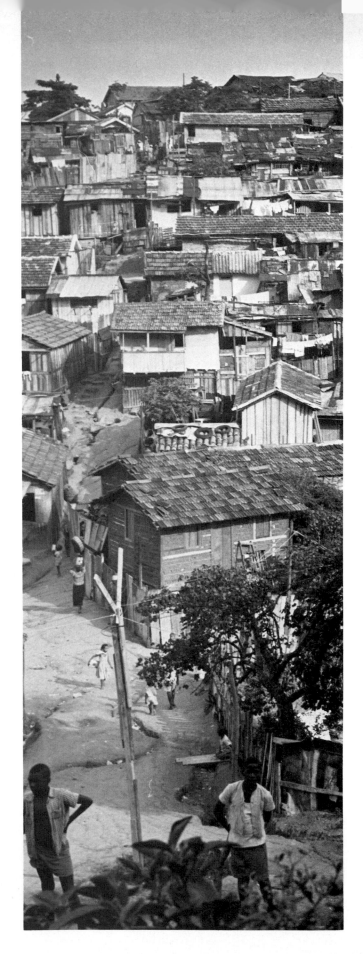

The following are excerpts from the diary of Carolina María de Jesus, Child of the Dark. When her journal was first published in her native São Paulo, it caused a literary and a social furor, forcing Brazilians to reexamine their relationship to the neglected poor who live on the margins of a better life in the favelas. These few days in her life point out the pain-filled existence of the urban poor in Brazil's islands of development.

May 3. I went to the market at Carlos de Campos Street looking for any old thing. I got a lot of greens. But it didn't help much, for I've got no cooking fat. The children are upset because there's nothing to eat.

May 10. I went to the police station and talked to the lieutenant. . . . The lieutenant was interested in my boys' education. He said the favelas have an unhealthy atmosphere where the people have more chance to go wrong than to become useful to state and country. I thought: if he knows this why doesn't he make a report and send it to the politicians? . . . Now he tells me this, I a poor garbage collector. I can't even solve my own problems.

Brazil needs to be led by a person who has known hunger. Hunger is also a teacher.

Who has gone hungry learns to think of the future and of the children.

May 11. Yesterday I got half a pig's head at the slaughterhouse. We ate the meat and saved the bones. Today I put the bones on to boil and into the broth I put some potatoes. My children are always hungry. When they are starving they aren't so fussy about what they eat.

May 15. . . . The neighbors in the brick houses near by have signed a petition to get rid of the favelados. But they won't get their way. The neighbors in the brick houses say:

"The Politicians protect the favelados."

Who protects us are the public and the Order of St. Vincent Church. The politicians only show up here during election campaigns. Senhor Candido Sampaio, when he was city councilman in 1953, spent his Sundays here in the favela. He was so nice. He drank our coffee, drinking right out of our cups. He made us laugh with his jokes. He played with our children. He left a good impression here and when he was candidate for state deputy, he won. But the Chamber of Deputies didn't do one thing for the favelados. He doesn't visit us any more.

I classify São Paulo this way: The Governor's Palace is the living room. The mayor's office is the dining room and the city is the garden. And the favela is the back yard where they throw the garbage.

May 21. Who must be a leader is he who has the ability. He who has pity and friendship for the people. Those who govern our country are those who have money, who don't know what hunger is, or pain or poverty. If the majority revolt, what can the minority do? I am on the side of the poor, who are an arm. An undernourished arm. We must free the country of the profiteering politicians.

Yesterday I ate that macaroni from the garbage with fear of death, because in 1953 I sold scrap over there in Zinho. There was a pretty little black boy. He also went to sell scrap in Zinho. He was young and said that those who should look for paper were the old. One day I was collecting scrap when I stopped at Bom Jardim Avenue. Someone had thrown meat into the garbage, and he was picking out the pieces. He told me:

"Take some, Carolina. It's still fit to eat."

He gave me some, and so as not to hurt his feelings, I accepted. I tried to convince him not to eat that meat, or the hard bread gnawed by the rats. He told me no, because it was two days since he had eaten. He made a fire and roasted the meat. His hunger was so great that he couldn't wait for the meat to cook. He heated it and ate. So as not to remember that scene, I left thinking: I'm going to pretend I wasn't there. This can't be real in a rich country like mine. I was disgusted with that Social Service that had been created to readjust the maladjusted, but took no notice of we marginal people. I sold the scrap at Zinho and returned to São Paulo's back yard, the favela.

The next day I found that little black boy dead. His toes were spread apart. The space must have been eight inches between them. He had blown up as if made out of rubber. His toes looked like a fan. He had no documents. He was buried like any other "Joe." Nobody tried to find out his name. The marginal people don't have names.

Once every four years the politicians change without solving the problem of hunger that has its headquarters in the favela and its branch offices in the workers' homes.

May 23. . . . I've come to the conclusion that for those who aren't going to Heaven, it doesn't help to look up. It's the same with us who don't like the favela, but are obliged to live in one. . . . It doesn't help to look up.

Source: David St. Clair (trans.), *Child of the Dark: The Diary of Carolina María de Jesus* (*Beyond All Pity* in the British Commonwealth). New York: Dutton; London: Souvenir Press, 1962, pp. 37–50. English translation copyright © 1962 by E. P. Dutton & Co. and Souvenir Press, Ltd. Reprinted by permission of E. P. Dutton & Co. and Souvenir Press, Ltd.

Figure 7. Unequal Regional Development. *After:* John P. Cole, *Latin America: An Economic and Social Geography.* London: Butterworths, 1973, p. 424, Fig. 19.5(a).

Outline of coast from *Oxford Atlas,* Oxford University Press.

This extraordinarily rapid urban growth in such a short period marks a reversal of the role of cities in Latin America. During the colonial period, cities were founded as staging areas for the assault on the wilderness. Adventurous colonists moved out from urban centers to exploit the agricultural and mineral potential of the natural surroundings. Individual cities often foundered as local misjudgments of the environment frustrated the expectations of settlers. But the stable core of colonial Latin America was based on several hundred Spanish towns with central plazas, cathedrals, and grid-patterned street plans. From the towns, the outward movement into the countryside was staged.

With the coming of independence, the new capital cities of Latin America became cauldrons of national politics and irresistible magnets for budding caudillos and their followers. Some cities became important commercial centers when Spanish trade restrictions disappeared. Townspeople, newly freed slaves, unemployed workers, political refugees, and peasants began to congregate in cities. In 1900, at a time when urban growth was just beginning to gain momentum in Latin America, nearly one-third the population of Lima, some 30,000 people, were described as "urban drifters." By the 1940s, rural immigrants accounted for half the population increase of Mexico's cities and 70 percent in the six largest cities of Brazil. Twenty years ago, two-thirds of the growth of Caracas and Cali (Colombia) was the result of the flow of peasants to the city. Now, however, natural increase has taken over as the primary source of current urban growth.

Unfortunately, industrialization has not kept pace with urbanization in Latin America. Numbers and jobs do not match. Manufacturing employed less than a fifth of the urban work force in 1970, roughly the same proportion as in 1925. In the midst of increased numbers and stagnating urban economies, the poverty and unemployment of the countryside have been transferred to the cities. During the 1930s, colonies of makeshift shacks without sewage systems, water supply, or electricity began to appear on vacant city land and urban peripheries. In Rio de Janeiro, shanties were thrown up at a rate of 1000 a year in the 1930s and 2700 a year in the 1940s. Currently, nearly 1 million people, one-fifth of the population of Rio de Janeiro, live in the 232 slum communities (*favelas*[•]) that blanket the hillside margins of the city. In Lima, a quarter of the population resides in squatter settlements inside the city and on its margins. A similar percentage is found in the slums of Buenos Aires and Mexico City. Overall, as many as 7 million to 8 million people may live in the slum fringes of Latin America's largest cities. They are a miserably poor and depressed class whose flight to the city in search of an alternative to poverty has overwhelmed the

capacity of urban planners to provide them with adequate housing, education, and health services.

PRIMACY AND REGIONAL DEVELOPMENT
[FIGURE 7, TABLE 2]

The irreversible flow of immigrants from rural areas into the largest cities of this region has reinforced and intensified the already concentrated population distribution of Latin America. If life in the slums of the city is harsh, it is probably no worse than conditions in decaying regional towns and villages with their entrenched social structures, conservative landowners, dominating caudillos, declining agriculture, and impoverished peasantry. Primate cities are poles of economic and social growth, centers of influence, and theaters of change. During the last century, the growth rates of the capital cities of the twenty largest nations of Latin America have outpaced the national population growth rate. A third of all Argentines and Uruguayans live in either Buenos Aires or Montevideo. Lima, Santiago, Havana, Caracas, Asunción, Panama City, and San José account for one-fifth of the various national populations. In seven other countries 10 percent or more of the population lives in one major urban center. Dominating in numbers and influence, urban primacy is a more obvious and recurrent theme in Latin America than in any other world region.

Although the political and economic dominance of contemporary Latin America's primate cities was established in the colonial times, the cities were often not population magnets until the modern period. Caracas, for example, was designated as the capital of a new captaincy-general in 1777, and bureaucratic offices, courts, military barracks, seminaries, and a university were constructed to form an administrative urban core. Cultural and political leadership, however, did not make Caracas a center of commerce. The city did not keep pace with the national population growth rate during the nineteenth century. But under the impact of the petroleum industry, Caracas has become a diversified commercial and industrial center so attractive to rural immigrants that it now houses 17 percent of Venezuela's population. Santiago is another example of an early center of Spanish rule whose long role as political and cultural capital was not accompanied by growth indicative of primacy. Now

TABLE 2. Population Growth and Primacy of
Buenos Aires

Source: Richard M. Morse, "Trends and Issues in Latin
American Urban Research, 1965–1970," *Latin
American Research Review,* Vol. 6 (1971), p. 42. Data
from Franciso de Aparicio and Horacio A. Difrieri,
La Argentina: suma de geografia, Vol. VII, pp. 94,
201, 202; Vol. IX, p. 138. Buenos Aires, Argentina,
1958–1963.

Year	Population of Argentina (a)	Population of Buenos Aires (b)	(b) as % of (a)
1825	578,000	55,416 (1822)	9.59
1837	675,000	62,228 (1836)	9.22
1855	1,271,000	90,076	7.09
1869	1,913,029	239,059	12.50
1895	4,046,761	781,611	19.31
1914	8,044,294	2,034,799	25.29
1947	16,058,765	4,723,918	29.42
1960	20,735,200	6,751,769	32.56
1970	23,360,000	8,352,900	35.76

Note: Material for 1970 added to original data.

housing a quarter of Chile's total population, Santiago has based its expansion over the last thirty years upon treatment of raw materials to processed and manufactured goods for the Chilean market. In a quite different case, Buenos Aires experienced a loss of population to the interior immediately after independence, but capitalized on locational advantages, a rich hinterland, and large-scale foreign immigration and investment to become a Latin American primate metropolis containing one-third the population of Argentina.

The exaggerated importance of primate cities in the development of modern Latin American economies and societies has led to a growing disparity between the core regions of urban development and the rural periphery. Lima, for example, with one-fifth of Peru's population, handles virtually all the country's financial affairs, supports half its commerce, employs two-thirds of its industrial workers, and produces between 80 and 90 percent of its manufactured goods every year. Over 60 percent of the new factories constructed in Mexico between 1940 and 1970 were built in Mexico City. With a total population of more than 7 million, the federal district of Mexico is the commercial, financial, and industrial core of the country. Similar urban concentrations surrounded by intensive agriculture characterize the heartlands of Venezuela, the Carib-

bean, eastern and southern Brazil, the central valley of Chile, and highland Colombia. These islands of dense human settlement are the geographical focuses of opportunity that have attracted the rural poor from the stagnating countryside.

Modern Latin American governments, concerned with patterns of unequal regional growth within their countries, are now moving to develop the periphery and integrate frontier regions into national economies and societies. In a dramatic move to counter its pattern of restricted development, Brazil decided in 1956 to shift its capital city to a semi-arid forested plateau 600 miles deep in the undeveloped wilderness of the interior. Within a decade, the new city of Brasília had a population of 300,000; it has since grown to nearly 750,000. A plan to divert migration from São Paulo and Rio de Janeiro via a network of roads into the Amazon interior is under scrutiny. In the Andean countries of Colombia, Bolivia, and Peru, roads have pushed eastward over the Andes into the Amazon forests in search of petroleum. In Venezuela, the Orinoco lowlands are projected as a secondary center of population. Mexico is opening up new agricultural lands in the Yucatán and the northeast, and has forbidden the construction of new factories in Mexico City. Settlers in Argentina are moving south and west of the pampas. Only the densely populated islands of the Caribbean have no frontiers to be conquered.

It is difficult, however, to predict whether this "new colonization" will successfully transform the distribution of human activity in Latin America that was established during the colonial period. In many countries, areas of new intensive economic development are close to national borders, reflecting the political desire of each country to protect its territory from intruding neighbors. Migrants continue to prefer the established core areas to life on the periphery. Furthermore, the redistribution of economic activity is taking place within more than twenty self-contained states whose integration with one another is so poorly developed that only 10 percent of South America's foreign trade takes place within the continent. If, as predicted, the population of Latin America doubles in the next twenty-five years and the proportion of urbanites rises from 40 to 60 percent, it seems likely that the existing urban cores will become even more dominant in the economies of most countries. At that time, the 250 million city dwellers of Latin America concentrated in these clusters of settlement will pose problems of a magnitude barely suggested by present conditions.

LATIN AMERICA

THE INDUSTRIAL BASE
ENERGY AND MINERAL RESOURCES MAP

Latin American countries are today engaged in efforts to diversify their economies, reduce their dependence on the export of raw materials, and achieve higher standards of living, but the dual economies of the colonial period have lingered until very recent times. Until World War II, large-scale Latin American industry was almost completely financed by foreigners. European and North American capital paid for the development of the externally oriented oil industries of Mexico and Venezuela, the copper mines of Chile, tin in Bolivia, bauxite in Jamaica and the Guianas, and the plantation agriculture of the Caribbean. Internal infrastructures—railroads, roads, and ports—were constructed for the export of raw materials to the industrialized West. With the exception of the textile industry, local manufacturing was limited.

In the postwar period, major urban centers such as Mexico City and Monterrey in Mexico, Medellín in Colombia, Lima, Santiago, Buenos Aires, São Paulo, and Rio de Janeiro became centers of diversified light industry. But this late start, together with rapid population growth, political instability, inadequate leadership, and environmental difficulties, have sapped progress toward economic growth and diversification. In the 1960s mining and manufacturing employed just 10 percent of the work force of Latin America; only Southeast Asia and Africa recorded lower figures. Consumption of steel was roughly equivalent to the level of pig iron consumption attained in the United States in the 1870s, and consumption of energy, considered a reliable index of economic development, is well below that of the industrial countries even in the larger, more advanced Latin American nations like Venezuela, Argentina, Mexico, and Brazil. The least developed Latin American countries—Paraguay, Bolivia, Peru, Nicaragua, Honduras, and Haiti—are among the poorest of all the nations in the developing world.

ENERGY SOURCES

Latin America produces about one-fifth of the world's petroleum, holds an untapped potential of large-scale hydroelectric power, and except in Colombia, has virtually no coal. Despite eternally optimistic estimates of future development, the economies of Latin America are likely to remain in their complex state of underdevelopment for some time. Large areas in the interior of South America are only now being explored for petroleum and other sources of natural wealth. Mobilization of the resources necessary for the construction of expensive hydroelectric power sites is beyond the reach of many of the smaller countries. Limited local energy markets require patterns of regional interdependence and cooperation that have been slow to develop. In general, the largest nations—Mexico, Colombia, Venezuela, Brazil, and Argentina—are likely to play a dominant role in the development of new sources of energy. The smaller, resource-poor countries of the Caribbean, Central America, and South America are likely to become energy dependencies.

The Caribbean is the focus of Latin America's developed petroleum resources. Of the five countries with an appreciable surplus of petroleum and natural gas—Venezuela, Mexico, Colombia, Trinidad, and Ecuador—four are located in this subregion. Venezuela is by far the most important, producing roughly two-thirds of Latin America's petroleum and exporting 3.4 million barrels a day, about half of which goes to the United States. Refining this petroleum sustains the economy of the islands of Aruba and Curaçao in the Netherlands Antilles. The primary Venezuelan oil field is located in the Maracaibo lowlands, where 6500 wells tap the richest petroleum deposit in Latin America. Venezuelan production accounts for 10 percent of the world total, and additional discoveries have been made in the Orinoco lowlands. New discoveries in Mexico, the world's largest petroleum producer in the 1930s, should return that country to a prominent position in the world energy economy. The declining coastal deposits near Tampico and Veracruz are still locally important, but newly discovered fields offshore and in the southern states of Chiapas and Tabasco will fill domestic needs and allow modest exports. The additional development of oil reserves in the northern states of Baja California, Chihuahua, and Coahuila may make Mexico equivalent in importance to Venezuela in the export of oil.

Elsewhere in Latin America, more modest petroleum production and reserves are crucial to the development of local economies. In Ecuador, a member of *OPEC,** oil deposits in the Aguarico Basin, a *tributary** of the Amazon, have been linked by a pipeline across the Andes to reach the coastal port of Esmeraldas. Oil is providing much-needed

315

ENERGY, MINERALS, METALS

Oil and natural gas fields

≋ Hydroelectric plants

Silver

■ Bauxite

⬠ Coal

△ Copper

▲ Iron

▬ Lead and zinc

□ Manganese

⬡ Nitrate

◖ Tin

capital for internal development and can be credited with reducing Ecuador's historical dependence on bananas. Similarly, the discovery of the Soladado oil field in Trinidad, an eastern exten-

sion of the Venezuelan deposit, has strengthened the economy of this island nation. The same is true in Colombia, whose oil field at Barrancabermeja produces only 5 percent of the Venezuelan total but is well located in the valley of the Magdalena River and vital to the Colombian economy. The oil fields of eastern Bolivia may provide some momentum to South America's poorest economy.

But if these countries have prospered through their control of developed energy resources, most Latin American nations have suffered. All of Central America and most countries in the Caribbean rely on high-priced oil imports to sustain industrialization. The Brazilian oil field at Recôncavo in the northeast supplies only a fraction of the country's needs. In Brazil and in Peru, potential reserves on the eastern slopes of the Andes are undeveloped. Peru, therefore, is dependent on the coastal Talara field for 80 percent of its petroleum production. The interior oil fields at Salta, Mendoza, Plaza Huincul, and the Patagonian field at Comodoro Rivadavia barely supply Argentina's national oil requirements. Chile's only source of petroleum is in Tierra del Fuego; Paraguay and Uruguay have no proved petroleum deposits.

The principal alternative energy source for most nations is hydroelectric power. Latin America has extensive and generally well distributed hydroelectric power potential, but less than one-tenth is developed, so that production throughout the entire region is only one-fifth that of the United States—roughly equivalent to that of Norway. In Brazil, the expensive construction of a power plant at the Paulo Afonso falls of the São Francisco River is designed to provide electricity and industrial power to the depressed economy of the northeast. In southeastern Brazil, waterpower is the principal energy source for the rapidly expanding industrial regions of São Paulo and Rio de Janeiro. In an extraordinary feat of engineering, the Tietê River was reversed to generate power for São Paulo.

The Itaipu project, a joint Brazil-Paraguay venture on the Paraná River, will be one of the largest hydroelectric complexes in the world when it is completed. Additional hydroelectric projects are under expansion in the south, in Minas Gerais, and in the interior near Brasília. Hydroelectricity is fairly well developed in central Chile, near Lima in Peru, in central Uruguay, eastern Venezuela, the Cauca River valley in Colombia, and in central and northern Mexico. The tremendous cost of these installations has limited construction and expansion, but projected energy needs in Latin America will probably have to be met from this source.

Coal plays an important role in the economies of Colombia and Chile only. The mines are small and the fields limited, so that only local markets are supplied from these domestic sources and exports are not feasible. Throughout the rest of Latin America, coal imported from the United States is less expensive than development of local deposits. In Colombia, the coal field at Paz del Río has probably the largest reserves in Latin America, with an output of 3 million tons per year; it supports an integrated iron and steel complex. The Arauco–Bió-bió coal fields in south-central Chile contribute to the industrial growth of Concepción. The only other large coal deposit in Latin America is located in Coahuila in northern Mexico. Overall, coal accounts for less than 5 percent of the energy produced in Latin America, and the limited availability of this critical resource has, in the opinion of many observers, been an important factor retarding the expansion of industry in Latin America.

MINERALS AND METALS

Despite the strong association of certain Latin American countries with mineral production and their historical dependence on mining exports, this region accounts for less than one-tenth of the non-Communist world's production of minerals. Oil and natural gas account for three-quarters of all mineral revenue. In selected minerals and metals, however, various parts of Latin America are major world sources. Almost one-half of world bauxite production comes from Jamaica and the Guianas; Mexico and Peru are significant producers of lead and zinc. Chile is an important source of nitrates and the world's fourth leading producer of copper; Brazil is a leading manganese producer. Bolivia accounts for better than one-tenth of the world's tin, and Mexico and Peru continue to produce one-third of the world's silver. Most of these mines were developed by foreign capital, and only a limited but growing amount of raw material processing is done in Latin America. As a result, mining employs an insignificant portion of the population, but produces an important, if uncertain, source of foreign credits.

Perhaps more important to the development of Latin America is the gradual growth of iron mining and local steel industries in the larger nations of the region. In 1935, the iron and steel output of Latin America was less than 1 percent that of the United States. Since then, production has doubled every five years, although by world standards it is still quite limited. Nine-tenths of all iron ore in Latin America comes from four regions: the Itabira mines of Minas Gerais in Brazil, which have this region's largest reserves; the Cerro Bolívar mines of eastern Venezuela; and smaller iron deposits in central Chile and southern Peru. The lack of *coking coal,** an obstacle to the growth of a significant steel industry, has been solved in various ways: by the use of charcoal derived from eucalyptus trees in Minas Gerais, hydroelectric power in eastern Venezuela, and imported coke in a number of coastal locations. Only at Paz del Río in Colombia and Monclova in northern Mexico are iron and coal both found in the same vicinity, so that future development of heavy industry in Latin America will depend on alternative sources of energy (primarily hydroelectric power) and exploration for new sources of ore.

A MIXING OF RACES

3

A half-century after the Europeans conquered Mexico and Peru, a new race began to appear in the Latin New World, combining the culture and blood of Europe, Africa, and America. The mingling of Europeans with American Indians resulted in a mixed-blood mestizo element in the population. With few European women available, the Church permitted and even encouraged marriages between these two races. Europeans also mixed with African slaves brought to Brazil and the Caribbean, creating a mulatto population. But marriages were quite rare between these two groups: the common union was between a European plantation owner and his female slave concubines. Zambos were crosses between Africans and American Indians, and these red-black half-breeds came to be scorned and distrusted by Europeans, Africans, and Indians alike. In 1800, the Latin American population of 20 million was estimated to consist of 4 million Europeans, 8 million Indians, 2 million Africans, 5 million mestizos, and 1 million or so mulattos and zambos. These six groups represent only the simplest racial combinations; contemporary Spanish records recognized as many as eighty racial mixtures with variations extending to nineteen degrees of relationship.

With the passage of time, people of mixed blood came to outnumber those of pure racial lineage in Latin America, but this melting pot produced social layers of blood and color rather than a lessening of racial perceptions. Whites retained the highest positions of social and economic power, forming a superior caste closed to people of color. The result was denigration at all levels and loss of selfhood among persons of color. Black mothers in the West Indies would tell their misbehaving children to "stop acting like niggers." Mestizos in Mexico referred to themselves as "white" when as little as one-sixteenth of their blood was European. Culture was dominated by European manners and modes, and whites set the tone for the aspirations of the other races in Latin America. Pure-blooded American Indians and Africans remained near the bottom of the social scale, and both groups became food producers and laborers in Latin America. While differing greatly in language and customs, they shared extreme poverty, low standards of living, poor diets, and short lives. Between the European whites at the top and the Indians and Africans at the bottom was a bewildering variety of mixed-blood mulattos and mestizos. Mestizos were viewed as people of reason as compared with pure Indians, and they formed the middle class of officials, tradesmen, and artisans which became the binding core of Latin American society. In Brazil, where they were called *caboclos* (the copper-colored people), these mixed bloods were considered to have higher physical and moral endurance than mulattos.

RACE AND ASSIMILATION
[FIGURE 8]

Although deep underlying racial prejudices and a recognized ladder of color leading from darkest to lightest persist in parts of Latin America, the rigid color bar dividing whites and nonwhites characteristic of North America, Africa, and other regions settled or colonized by Europeans does not exist here. The mixing of races and the absence of a color bar are not the results of a more tolerant racial ethic by Spanish and Portuguese colonists compared with northern Europeans, however, nor was racial mixing in Latin America the creation of more enlightened colonial policies. Gilberto Freyre, a Brazilian historian, notes that the mulatto population of the sugar regions of Brazil sprang not from racial tolerance but from sadism directed at African slaves by a decadent planter aristocracy and from the purely economic benefits to be gained by siring mulatto slaves. In Spanish Latin America, racial intermingling went hand and hand with the wholesale and deliberate destruction of indigenous cultures, decimation of native political leaders, and the elimination of existing religions and conversion to Christianity. In neither Brazil nor New Iberia was racial tolerance an important factor in the mixing of races. Instead, the intense Europeanization of the peoples of Latin America and the twining of blood from three races were created by distinctive patterns of conquest in the New World.

The Spanish and Portuguese came to the New World as conquerors and still rule as the dominant elite in Latin America. Social relationships between Europeans and their Indian and African subordinates were complicated by two factors that encouraged a mixing of races and the Europeanization of the population. First, plantation and large estate agriculture required large numbers of submissive laborers who, in Latin America, were organized into a stable system of peonage and slavery. The

This Indian woman, wearing a bowler copied from the headgear of the Spanish conquerors, works at a modern cotton mill in La Paz, one of the few such factories in Bolivia. *Photo:* United Nations.

paternalistic, semifeudal social structures of the hacienda, the fazenda, and the plantation were vehicles of **acculturation**[*] that encouraged Indians and Africans to abandon their native cultures in favor of Christianity and Westernization. Second, the scarcity of white women in the New World forced the Europeans to abandon questions of racial purity; a bond of fraternization was created between master and slave, hacendero and serf, that rapidly produced a population of varied race. The superiority of the white and the inferiority of others was never questioned in these affairs, but the expanding number of intervening combinations became quickly confusing. Racial mixing and assimilation were extraordinarily rapid—within two generations, substantial portions of land were divided between the hispanicized mestizo sons, legitimate and illegitimate, of the Spanish ruling class. The role of latifundismo in promoting racial mixing is highlighted by the few places where it is noticeably absent. In the central Costa Rican highlands, an enclave of unmixed Spanish blood has existed since the sixteenth century, the result of settlement on a farm-family basis where European women were available.

Currently, mestizos form the single largest Latin American racial component. Over one-third of the population—perhaps 130 million people—are mestizo. They predominate in Mexico, highland Central America, Colombia and Venezuela, the settled coastal zones of western South America, and the accessible interior of eastern Brazil. Pure Indians—approximately 45 million in number—

remain strong elements of the population principally in the more remote regions of western Mexico and the Yucatán, Central America, the Andean highlands of Ecuador, Peru, Bolivia, and Chile, and the Amazon interior, where the last remnants of hunting and gathering groups are now being rounded up and placed on reservations.

Where the Iberians encountered sparsely populated areas, local inhabitants were rapidly eliminated by warfare, disease, or starvation. In Argentina, Uruguay, and southern Brazil, Indians were brushed aside by waves of European colonists in the nineteenth and twentieth centuries, creating a large area of essentially white population in Latin America. But in other regions, notably northeastern Brazil and the Caribbean rimland, African slaves were imported to replace local Indian populations killed in smallpox epidemics. Here, plantation slavery and the lack of white women produced much the same result as in the areas of dense agricultural settlement. Mulattos, quadroons, octaroons, and the other more complex racial mixtures became locally important segments of the population.

Whether under Portuguese, British, Dutch, or French rule, the ruthlessly efficient conditions of plantation slavery destroyed African cultures and replaced them with the language and mores of the respective planter culture. Currently, Africans number some 40 million in Latin America and are concentrated in the old sugar plantation regions of northeastern Brazil, the West Indies (notably Haiti), and the coastlands of the Gulf of Mexico. An equivalent number of mulattos of varying degrees of racial mixture are found in the same area. The red-black zambos, most of them descendants of runaway slaves, occur in much smaller numbers, since blacks were principally imported into regions lacking an adequate supply of Indian labor—in the Brazilian interior, the Guiana highlands, and the Colombia lowlands.

SOCIAL RACES

The extensive mixing of races in Latin America, although born of oppression and not of racial tolerance, has made this region a laboratory of race relations where prejudice and discrimination are comparatively subdued. In most Latin American nations only one or two of the possible racial combinations are prominent in the population, and only

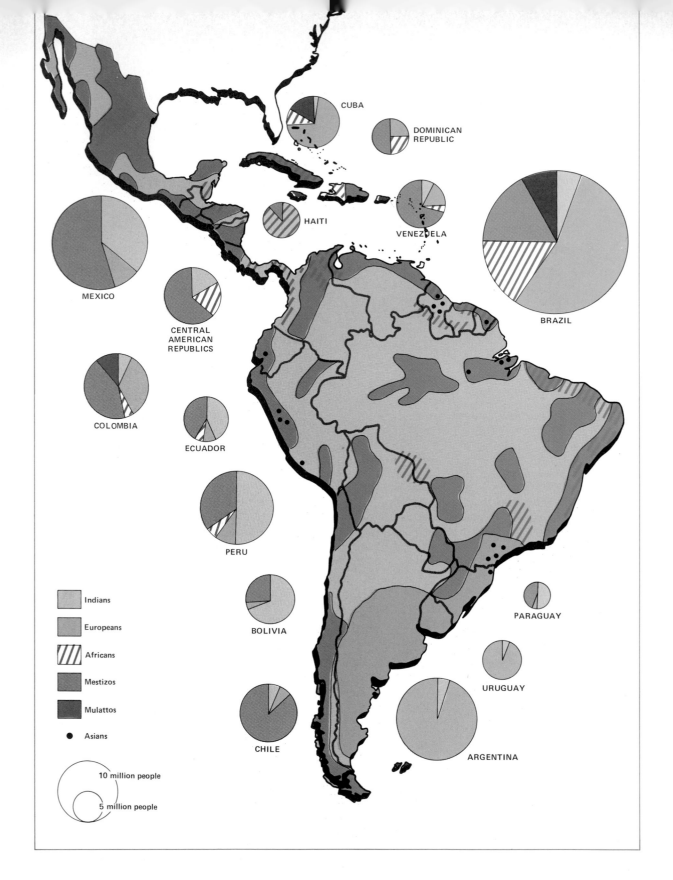

Figure 8. Distribution of Races in Latin America. *After:*
Harry Robinson, *Latin America: A Geographical Survey,* rev. ed. London: Macdonald & Evans, Ltd., p. 44, Fig. 21.

Brazil has significant numbers of all six basic mixtures. In Mexico, a new *indianismo* movement is building pride among a downtrodden and alienated Indian population. In the West Indies, differences of color inhibit social development and individual identity. Yet if it is true that the social pyramid throughout Latin America is consistently lighter in skin color at the top than at the bottom, it is equally true that despite differences in rights and advantages, there is no race problem comparable to those of the United States and South Africa. The three races of Latin America live in peace.

One can think of Latin American society as composed of a series of "social races," whereby individuals classify each other in the hierarchy of power and prestige according to characteristics of which skin color is only one. Social values attached to race vary from region to region. In Vila Recôncavo, the traditional sugar center of northeastern Brazil, the slave heritage of the population and the persistence of patriarchal social patterns have preserved a separation of race and class to a degree unusual in contemporary Brazilian society. In the sertão of the interior, by contrast, the more independent and democratic social forms of the cattle raising frontier are dominant, while the slums of São Paulo and Rio de Janeiro contain the dispossessed of all races. In the Chiapas highlands of southern Mexico, the primary distinctions are between poor rural Indians and more commercialized mestizos or ladinos. In Central America, race relations are complicated by the contrasting economic systems of the highland Indian and European populations and the lowland

plantations worked by Africans. In the West Indies, where black and colored people make up a majority of the population, color and class prejudice are still visible, but primary allegiances are to island societies and racial problems vary with locale. Chinese, for example, form a substantial proportion of Trinidadians, and in the Guianas the race issue is complicated by the presence of a substantial East Indian population.

The multiracial history of Latin America has made simple correlations between race and education, wealth, culture, and character less consistent and more complex than in any other world region. Although no Latin American is unaware of, inexperienced in, or unaffected by interracial contacts, the question of color is more subtle and muted, less aggressive and abrasive, than elsewhere. This is an important and distinctive characteristic of this region. A clear understanding that modern tolerance derives not from past goodwill but from specific sets of historical social and economic realities may prompt less moralizing and more corrective action in those societies where racial discrimination distorts the values and habits of their people.

BIBLIOGRAPHY

GENERAL

Bailey, Helen Miller, and Abraham P. Nasatir. *Latin America: The Development of Its Civilization.* Englewood Cliffs, N.J.: Prentice-Hall, 1973. An extremely well written basic history of Latin America.

Butland, Gilbert J. *Latin America: A Regional Geography,* 3rd ed. New York: Wiley, 1972. A detailed regional geography in the British tradition.

Cole, John P. *Latin America: An Economic and Social Geography.* Totowa, N.J.: Rowman & Littlefield; London, Butterworths, 1973. A modern regional geography notable for its inventive maps.

James, Preston E. *Latin America,* 4th ed. New York: Odyssey Press, 1969. The most complete, detailed regional geography of Latin America.

West, Robert C., and John P. Augelli. *Middle America: Its Lands and Peoples.* Englewood Cliffs, N.J.: Prentice-Hall, 1966. A superb cultural and historical geography of Middle America by two prominent geographers.

[1] DISCOVERY, CONQUEST, AND COLONIZATION

Bradford, Ernie. *Christopher Columbus.* New York: Viking Press, 1973. A beautifully illustrated modern biography of the explorer from Genoa and his four voyages to the New World.

Foster, George M. *Culture and Conquest: America's Spanish Heritage.* Chicago: Quadrangle Books, 1960. The acculturation of native Indians under Spanish rule.

Portilla, Miguel León (ed.). *The Broken Spears: The Aztec Account of the Conquest of Mexico.* Boston: Beacon Press, 1962. A fascinating account of the coming of the Spanish and the destruction of Tenochtitlán from the Aztec point of view.

Prescott, William H. *History of the Conquest of Peru.* New York: Dutton, 1963. A definitive account of the Spanish conquest of the Inca Empire.

Rippy, J. Fred. *Latin America: A Modern History.* Ann Arbor: University of Michigan Press, 1958. A descriptive history of Latin America with emphasis on the nineteenth and twentieth centuries.

Rowe, John. "Inca Culture at the Time of the Spanish Conquest." In Julian Steward (ed.). *Handbook of South American Indians.* Bulletin No. 143, Vol. 2, pp. 183–330. Washington, D.C.: Smithsonian Institution, Bureau of American Ethnology, 1947. A thorough description of the Inca state and society in the early sixteenth century.

Sauer, Carl O. *The Early Spanish Main.* Berkeley: University of California Press, 1966. Impact of Spanish discovery and conquest on the Caribbean and adjacent shores, its peoples and landscapes.

Simpson, Lesley Byrd. *Many Mexicos.* Berkeley: University of California Press, 1966. A delightful history and geography of Mexico.

[2] SOCIETY, POPULATION, AND REGIONAL DEVELOPMENT

Chaplin, David (ed.). *Population Policies and Growth in Latin America.* Lexington, Mass.: Heath, 1971. Essays on population growth and planning in the context of economic and social change in Latin America.

Farley, Rawle. *The Economics of Latin America: Development Problems in Perspective.* New York: Harper & Row, 1972. A dry, comprehensive study of the economics of Latin America in developmental terms.

Feder, Ernest. *The Rape of the Peasantry: Latin America's Landholding System.* Garden City, N.Y.: Doubleday, 1971. A trenchant account of the impact of *latifundismo* on the rural poor.

Furtado, Celso. *Economic Development of Latin America: A Survey from Colonial Times to the Cuban Revolution.* London: Cambridge University Press, 1970. Historical treatise emphasizing institutional obstacles to economic development in Latin America.

Miller, John, and Ralph A. Gakenheimer. *Latin American Urban Policies and the Social Sciences.* Beverly Hills: Sage, 1971. Excellent series of articles on urbanization and regional development in Latin America.

Morse, Richard M. "Trends and Issues in Latin American Urban Research, 1965–1970." *Latin American Research Review,* Vol. 6 (1971), No. 1, pp. 3–52; No. 2, pp. 19–75. An excellent review of major issues in urban research in Latin America with an extensive bibliography.

Nelson, Michael. *The Development of Tropical Lands: Policy Issues in Latin America.* Baltimore: Johns Hopkins University Press, 1973. The environmental complexity of tropical land use systems with development case studies.

Sanchez-Albornoz, Nicolas. *The Population of Latin America: A History*. W. A. R. Richardson (trans.). Berkeley: University of California Press, 1974. The most competent study of Latin American demographic history and its contemporary patterns.

[3] A MIXING OF RACES

Freyre, Gilberto. *The Masters and the Slaves*. New York: Knopf, 1956. The classic study of the evolution of racial relations in Brazilian history.
Lowenthal, David. *West Indian Societies*. New York: Oxford University Press, 1972. A beautifully written volume by a prominent geographer on the Caribbean as a laboratory for the study of race relations.

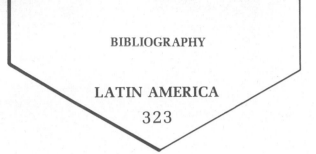
Wagley, Charles (ed.). *Race and Class in Rural Brazil*. New York: UNESCO, 1963. A series of penetrating articles on the interrelationship between race and class and its significance in five rural Brazilian communities.

THE
TECHNOLOGICAL
WORLD

WESTERN EUROPE

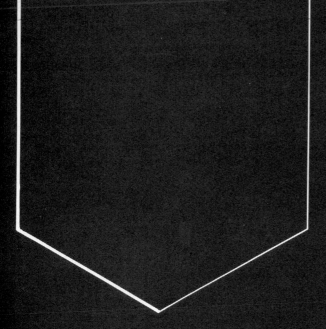

The Wealth of Nations was published on March 9, 1776, in two volumes over 1000 pages long at a price of better than $60. The author, Adam Smith, a professor of moral philosophy, had devoted twelve years to his manuscript, writing and rewriting in an effort to clarify his views on the nature of economic behavior and why nations grow and prosper. The book sold well; the first edition was exhausted in six months despite its length and complexity. The scope of the discussion reflected Smith's fertile mind and keen powers of observation, as well as the mastery of science, philosophy, art, and literature he had already demonstrated in an earlier work, *Theory of Moral Sentiments* (1759). From a detailed description of the making of pins at the beginning to a recommendation that Britain abandon her colonies at the end, *The Wealth of Nations* pieced together the themes of the age into the first complete and coherent theory of the economic system known as capitalism. It laid the intellectual foundations of the system that launched Western Europe and later the United States on the longest period of sustained wealth and prosperity in human history.

Self-interest, Smith argued, was the strongest of human drives, and it was not opposed to the common good because the desires of millions of people to gain personal wealth would, in a free marketplace, bring prosperity to all. The butcher, the brewer, and the baker do not provide us with food out of benevolence, he noted—they do it for money. Similarly, no nation trades with another except for gain, and indeed trade does not exist, under normal circumstances, unless both parties benefit from the exchange. Only this fundamental force, selfish as it is, moves people to produce the goods society wants and needs, and only in a free market based upon supply and demand will the collision of these motivations produce prosperity. If, for example, the price of meat rises steadily and butchers reap high profits, an "invisible hand" will draw other shop-

A contemporary portrait of Adam Smith. *Photo:* Culver Pictures.

keepers into the trade in their own search for profits. The ensuing competition will drive the least efficient butchers from the field when consumers, themselves motivated by personal gain, seek out the least expensive and best meat from the more efficient producers.

The result is a self-regulating market in which goods and services flow freely and everyone benefits. When competition is restrained by government tariffs or subsidies, this remarkable balance of forces is disrupted; the results are higher costs, greater inefficiency, and less prosperity. If Scotland, for example, prohibits the importation of wine, excellent grapes will be grown in Scottish greenhouses, but the wine they yield will cost approximately thirty times more than French claret and burgundy. Sales will be lower and prices higher. And should butchers convince city councils to tax meat brought in from other towns or to limit competition among the fraternity of butchers, the inevitable result will be higher meat prices. Even education, Smith's own "unprosperous" profession, yields to the law of self-interest. When professors at Oxford were paid subsidies, Smith claimed, courses were no longer taught for the benefit of students. Pay professors according to the number of students they can attract, he caustically noted, and teaching will improve quickly enough.

His treatise, radical at the time, put an end to the remnants of medieval society and struck hard at the trade walls that had been erected around the nation-states of Europe. By 1790, a German writer called Adam Smith "the mightiest monarch in Europe, next to Napoleon"—unexpected praise for a modest philosopher and apostle of free trade who ironically was living out the last year of his life as Scotland's commissioner of customs. In the nineteenth century, politicians took up Smith's economic ideas, and free trade and an international economy reigned. Entrepreneurs accumulated and reinvested capital in unfettered business environments, and production multiplied enormously as markets expanded. Populations grew when capitalism produced the goods and food to keep them alive. All were caught up in the accelerating tempo of social and technological change. The philosopher had prophesied correctly: self-interest could bring prosperity, and the face of Western Europe, reshaped by capitalism, took on the modern dimensions that form the themes of this section. In "The Ascent of Europe," the spread of industrialization across Western Europe creates an urban and technological society of such productive potential that Europeans come to dominate the world until the capitalistic competition that bred prosperity takes the form of national wars and depression. In "The Quest for Unity," a diminished Europe, its capitalism now monitored by government planning, again seeks affluence and a new world role through economic integration on a larger geographical basis.

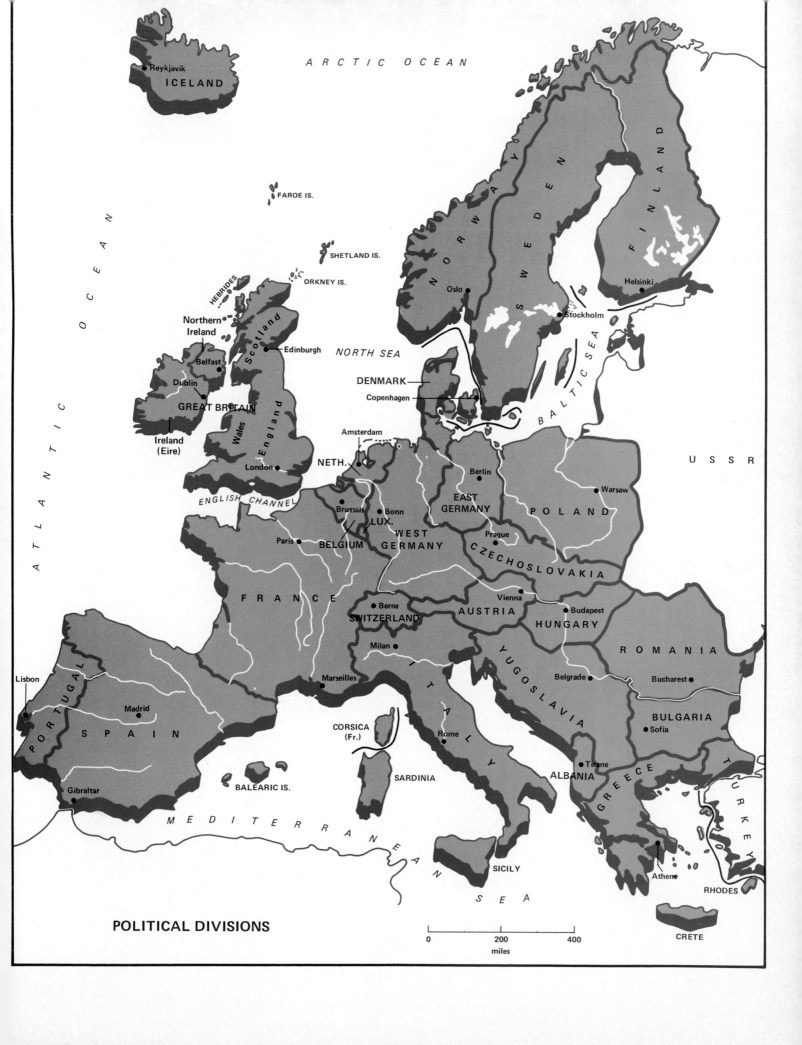

POLITICAL DIVISIONS

ARCTIC OCEAN

ICELAND
Reykjavik

FAROE IS.

SHETLAND IS.

ORKNEY IS.

HEBRIDES

NORWAY

SWEDEN

FINLAND

Oslo

Stockholm

Helsinki

Northern
Ireland

Scotland

Edinburgh

NORTH SEA

BALTIC SEA

Belfast

Dublin

GREAT BRITAIN

Ireland
(Eire)

Wales

England

London

DENMARK

Copenhagen

USSR

ATLANTIC OCEAN

ENGLISH CHANNEL

Amsterdam

NETH.

Berlin

Warsaw

Brussels

Bonn

EAST
GERMANY

POLAND

LUX.

BELGIUM

Paris

WEST
GERMANY

Prague

CZECHOSLOVAKIA

FRANCE

Berne

Vienna

Budapest

SWITZERLAND

AUSTRIA

HUNGARY

Milan

ITALY

YUGOSLAVIA

ROMANIA

Belgrade

Bucharest

Lisbon

Marseilles

PORTUGAL

Madrid

SPAIN

CORSICA
(Fr.)

Rome

BULGARIA

Sofia

Tirane

ALBANIA

GREECE

TURKEY

Gibraltar

BALEARIC IS.

SARDINIA

MEDITERRANEAN

SEA

SICILY

Athens

RHODES

CRETE

0   200   400
miles

THE ASCENT OF EUROPE
1

The economies of Europe developed a productive capacity of unprecedented strength and wealth in the nineteenth century. New technologies were harnessed in agriculture and industry, population grew, society urbanized, and a new and complex way of life emerged. This Industrial Revolution occurred first in Britain and then spread to the European continent. By the latter half of the century, Europe held a virtual monopoly on machine technology, and its newfound military strength dominated the globe. The technological conquest of distance brought natural resources for industry under European control, and by colonization and colonialization, this small continent came to govern vast stretches of the globe. But in 1914 nationalism within Europe led to World War I and by that time, the bases of capitalism in Europe—free trade, free enterprise, and private property—had spawned new and competing centers of industrial power in Russia, Japan, and the United States. The international economy of the West collapsed in the Depression of the 1930s, and Europe, drifting toward yet another continental conflict, lost its position as the central force in the world economy. This chapter looks at the beginnings of industrialization in Britain (see also Rise, "The Scientific Transformation"), its diffusion across the European continent, the growth of the international industrial economy as the basis of European power, and finally the decline of Europe as the leader of the technological world.

THE BEGINNINGS OF INDUSTRIALIZATION
[FIGURE 1]

While revolutions in America (1776) and France (1789) were creating new models of political and social life in the eighteenth century, a development of even greater significance was occurring in Britain. For the first time in history, agricultural and industrial production was consistently outstripping popu-

lation growth. New energy sources and new technologies were creating the outlines of a distinctly new human geography. Manufacturing was becoming oriented to national rather than local markets.

A constellation of industrial towns linked by a network of canals, and then railroads, emerged on the British landscape. Coal production tripled in 100 years. Population doubled. Iron, previously an expensive, semiprecious metal, became a necessity cheaply available to many. In 1800, iron production was 250,000 tons; fifty years later, output was ten times that. In 1829, George Stephenson put his Rocket, the first steam locomotive, to the test, and proved the feasibility of steam power by hauling a 13-ton load at the unheard-of speed of 29 miles per hour. This new method of transport worked against self-sufficient local economies by liberating more specialized and efficient economic activities from the dictates of distance (see also Figure 16, Rise). The costs of transport plummeted as its capabilities soared. Coal could be moved cheaply; factories could be located in more diverse settings. In 1850, British cotton textile production was equal to that of continental Europe, and the rate of economic growth in Britain was unparalleled in the world.

These growth rates in economic productivity in Britain during the period 1750–1850 enlarged the privileged economic class. Many more people than ever before became wealthy. But the very rapidity of change in Britain, although considerably slower than in modern developing nations, obscured steady gains in income, health, education, and food made by the average person. The flight from the land, the shift to mechanized factory employment, the new experience of city living, periodic financial recessions, and desperately inadequate environmental facilities in the smogbound industrial towns—in short, industrialization and urbanization in rapid sequence—were traumatic changes for all economic groups. For the poor, untutored in methods of capitalizing on economic and social opportunities, these changes were frequently catastrophic. Not only were trades, ancient skills, and small communities jeopardized, but traditional values and regional ways of life were disappearing. Tension and class strife, strikes, and social inequity tore at the fabric of British society, but the sure transition to industrial society was made. When the Great Exhibition of London opened in 1851, a cavernous Crystal Palace, symbol of technique and artifice, was built of 300,000 panes of glass and 5000 iron girders to demonstrate the achievements of British industry. Only there could a "palace" be made of crystal. Britain had become the primary supplier of textile goods, machinery, and railroad materials to continental Europe; England was the industrial workshop of the world.

Why the Industrial Revolution occurred in Britain, rather than elsewhere in Europe, is still a matter of

A traffic jam in a London street in 1872. Woodcut. *Photo: The Bettman Archive.*

Figure 1. A Question of Distance. The reduction in travel time between London and other British cities between 1750 and 1850 emphasizes the degree to which railroads improved communications and fostered the development of a national economy. Transport costs were reduced, travel became possible the year round, and the isolation of rural life diminished. This telescoping of time and distance foreshadowed the coming age of mass transit. *After:* E. J. Hobsbawn, *Industry and Empire.* London: Penguin, 1969, Fig. 16. Copyright © E. J. Hobsbawn, 1968, 1969. Used by permission of Penguin Books, Ltd.

conjecture, although several factors played important roles. First, the union of England and Scotland (1707) gave Britain a large internal market for manufactured goods; this larger population could absorb increased production. In addition, the population of England and Wales doubled between 1750 and 1832, in effect doubling the size of the domestic market. In 1830, London was already an immense city of 2 million people; the populations of Manchester and Glasgow had doubled in the preceding eighty years. Population growth in this case acted as a powerful incentive to more efficient production on a larger scale. Second, within its boundaries, Britain was a free-trade area. Domestic exchange barriers, common in eighteenth-century France, Italy, and the German states, did not hinder the growth of England's national economy. By 1800, various regions were already highly specialized in industrial output: cotton textiles were the basis of life in Lancashire, as were woolens in the West Riding district, finished steel and cutlery in Sheffield, and heavy metal goods in Birmingham and the Midlands *black country.* Regional specializations that translated into efficiency in manufacturing had never before been so geographically dispersed. Third, Britain played a key role in the triangular trade among West Africa, the Caribbean, and Europe; British domestic exports had increased two and one-half times during the eighteenth century. This international traffic laid the

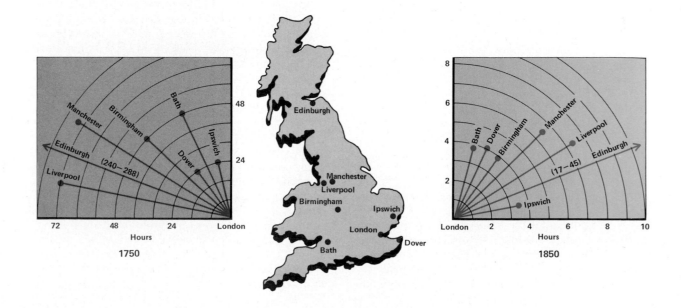

THE TWO APPRENTICES
(HOGARTH)

1776.

A Hogarth engraving shows an English factory in the late eighteenth century. *Photo:* Culver Pictures.

foundations for colonial expansion and filled British coffers with the wealth that was used to finance industrial expansion at home. Finally, technological progress was a powerful stimulus to the growth of manufacturing in Britain. Ingenious scientists and inventors collaborated with entrepreneurs and investors to seek new methods of production in both agriculture and industry. These factors, detailed in "The Rise to Ecological Dominance," thrust Britain into the lead, a pioneer on the new frontiers of the technological world.

By contrast, continental Europe at the time of the French Revolution was still a realm of country estates, peasant holdings, and domestic workshops little changed by the sweeping reorganization of land and life across the Channel. Even by the middle of the nineteenth century, Britain, with a population only half that of France, was still producing two-thirds of the coal and more than half of the iron and cotton cloth of the world. Early efforts to emulate the British example generally failed; a series of obstacles to industrialization slowed the spread of the Industrial Revolution on the Continent.

The first of these obstacles was the scale and complexity of the European landmass. The sheer size of Europe, broken by physiographic barriers, made transportation difficult and expensive. In contrast to Britain, roads were terrible in Europe in the late 1700s, and only the Low Countries were well endowed with navigable waterways. Even on the best roads and rivers travel was interrupted by numerous local toll stations that made long-distance exchange of all but the dearest commodities prohibitive. A second reason for the advance of Britain over the Continent was that the resource base of continental

A SLAVER'S EPITAPH

An important part of Great Britain's wealth in the triangular trade came from slavery—The Middle Passage from Africa to the New World (see also Tropical Africa). One wealthy trader had this epitaph carved on his tombstone when he died in the mid-1700s:

A merchant whose honesty, competence, and insight into mercantile things earned himself and his country riches and esteem; an administrative officer who upheld the cause of righteousness with prudence and impartiality; a good Christian, God-fearing and exemplary in the exercise of all his duties; a friend of virtue; a father to the needy, an enemy only to vice and indolence.

The merchant referred to here, Mr. Foster Cuncliffe of Liverpool, was a prominent slave trader. A Swedish observer wrote:

He had four ships constantly trafficking in slaves, each one containing 1,120 slaves. "A father to the needy" is no empty phrase. . . . Cuncliffe was a father to 4,480 needy people per cargo trip.

Source: Göran Palm, *As Others See Us* (trans. Verne Moberg). Indianapolis: Bobbs-Merrill, 1968, pp. 40–41.

Europe was less favorable to industrialization. The textile industry in France, Germany, and the Low Countries was stifled by the necessity of importing cotton from sources where British agents held monopolies; most of their wool, too, came from foreign sources. By contrast, cotton from India, the American South, and Egypt was at Britain's maritime doorstep, and Scotland was the "sheep belt" of the world. In addition, though coal and iron resources on the Continent were accessible, they were usually widely separated from one another. France, for example, lacked deposits of ***coking coal,*** and in Germany, the resources of the Ruhr remained undiscovered. Furthermore, the widespread availability of timber in Europe prolonged traditional charcoal methods of iron production. Finally, the poor of continental Europe were poorer than the poor of Britain, limiting the market for inexpensive manufactured goods. At the beginning of the nineteenth century, the British traveler Arthur Young noted that in the Dordogne (southwest France) "all the country girls and women are without shoes or stockings, and the ploughmen . . . have neither *sabots* [wooden shoes] nor feet to their stockings." With considerable business sharpness, he concluded that this was a poverty "that strikes at the root of national prosperity." For all these reasons, economic activity remained a social enterprise on the Continent, and **guilds** retained control over the scale and techniques of production. To be sure, there were some beginning centers of specialized economic activity: Flanders, Normandy, and Saxony in woolen textiles; Switzerland and southern Germany in cotton cloth; and the upper Marne Valley, the Siegerland east of the Rhine, and Upper Silesia (in modern Poland) in iron production. But by and large, the markets and manufacturing output of continental Europe remained preindustrial, focused on small, self-sufficient markets served by local craftsmen and artisans, until after the Napoleonic wars in the early nineteenth century.

THE SPREAD OF INDUSTRIALIZATION TO THE CONTINENT

Had Britain been able to maintain a monopoly on industrial technology, the Industrial Revolution could be treated as a specific event, a conjoining of special conditions that created a local productive anomaly. And for years, Britain tried to do just that by placing embargoes on the export of machinery and the emigration of artisans. But industrial technology and awareness of its importance diffused to the Continent and to North America, little hindered by British restraints. The jealously guarded secrets of British manufacturers were smuggled to Europe by Dutch drainage experts, German mining engineers, French civil engineers, and Britons who took the opportunity to profit from their valuable knowledge.

For the governments of Europe, the British challenge was unavoidable. Economic growth was accurately seen as the key to increased wealth. A favorable balance of trade was the basis for the substantial increases in taxes that maintained political power, and governments saw that full employment was important in preserving long-term domestic order. But the geographical and social limitations on industrialization in Europe remained strong long after the technology of industry was widespread. A knowledge of mechanics and machines was one thing; the implementation of an industrial revolution was quite another.

Slow Diffusion: 1800–1850
During the first half of the nineteenth century, the **diffusion** of technology from Britain to the Continent was sporadic. Unlike the situation in Britain, where specific industries clustered in favored locations to take advantage of availability of labor or

natural resources, a large number of varied small and less efficient industrial centers persisted in Europe. The growth of large-scale industrial nuclei comparable to Yorkshire or the Midlands was retarded by poor transportation networks, limited markets, and a pervasive resistance to industrial life.

The French textile industry is a case in point. In France, the principal Continental producer of cotton cloth, the textile industry was scattered across the country, with primary centers in Normandy, Lille, and Alsace. Alsace was the most progressive and technically sophisticated of these areas, but Normandy, the largest producer, was technologically backward because locational advantages tended to slow the rate of acceptance of technological change and to reinforce the use of traditional processes. This manufacturing environment was temporarily secure despite its rejection of the new geography of technology. Cotton textiles were manufactured in virtually every province of France with a wide range of efficiency, quality of product, and technology. In a typical example, when the sophisticated Dollfus textile mills of Mulhouse in Alsace attempted to sell obsolete machines for scrap iron, the machines instead were bought by cotton mills in the Vosges and used for years. These inefficient and outdated methods preserved the small shop in France, so that at midcentury, the 3 million French industrial workers labored in 1.5 million establishments—an astounding two workers per enterprise. European textile factories remained small, family-run concerns with fewer than five workers. Although there were concentrations of cotton mills in Ghent, the Rhine Valley, Saxony, Silesia, and Bavaria, the industry remained widely dispersed. The industrial technology developed in Britain was seen on the Continent as destroying the old system of production with no assurance that it would create a new one.

The changeover to new techniques and new fuels was equally slow in heavy industry. In 1850, three-quarters of the iron of France was still produced in small charcoal-burning forges located near sources of iron, timber, and water. Conversion to modern iron production was retarded by the low quality of local coal and iron ore and by British competition. Similarly, in the German states, iron smelters continued to be widely dispersed and to follow craft techniques. At midcentury London's coal consumption exceeded the total production of Prussia, and a German representative at the Great

By the mid-nineteenth century, the Industrial Revolution and the factory system had spread to the Continent. This engraving shows a French manufacturer of safes. *Photo: Culver Pictures.*

Exposition in 1851, unaware of the extent of the coal resources of the Ruhr, doubted that Germany could ever match Britain's production of coal and iron. Several forges in the Ruhr and the Saarland were, in fact, as modern as any in Britain—the great capitalist entrepreneur Krupp was able to surprise the world by casting a 2-ton block of steel for the 1851 exposition—but these operations were the exception rather than the rule. In Italy, where transport duties were so high that goods moved 37 miles from Mantua to Padua were taxed six separate times, iron and coal resources were poor, and heavy industry remained limited. South of the Pyrénées and in Scandinavia, there was virtually no heavy industry.

Only Belgium, of all the states on the Continent, kept pace with Britain; its modern landscape of factories, mines, and row housing—a continental analogy to the British Midlands—reflects early industrialization. The seeming abundance of the Belgian coal and iron fields near the Sambre and Meuse rivers and the scarcity of charcoal made conversion to modern methods more attractive there than elsewhere. By midcentury Belgium was the largest coal producer on the Continent and was exporting significant quantities of iron to Germany. In 1835, Belgium inaugurated the first national railroad network in continental Europe, and the length of its rails, hard-surfaced roads, and navigable waterways per unit area soon exceeded those of Britain. Only in

Belgium were the foundations of a sizable industrial complex comparable to the ***primary manufacturing districts*** of England laid in Europe; elsewhere, industry was pursued in traditional cities and towns newly swollen by a tide of migration from small farms and large estates.

In 1850, then, the countries of the Continent lagged a full generation behind Britain in industrialization. At a time when half the population of England and Wales was urban, less than a quarter of the people of France and the German states lived in towns. Even in Belgium, the most highly industrialized nation in continental Europe, over half the labor force was still agricultural. Elsewhere, the proportion of farmers was higher still, and in Iberia, Greece, and Italy south of Florence, essentially nothing had changed. The concentration of industrial workers in urban factories had barely begun, and nothing like the slums of Manchester could be found. Contemporary writers in France and Germany congratulated themselves on avoiding the penalties of unbridled growth, citing the horrors of child labor in British textile mills, women in the coal mines of Newcastle, the pall of smoke that hung over the black country, and the slums of industrial Birmingham and Leeds as appalling human environments which they had the good sense to avoid. But the persistence of the old social order on the Continent also meant a persistence of rural poverty, less visible in dispersed villages than in great cities, but nonetheless real. With populations growing throughout Europe and few industries to absorb their labor, a reckoning was bound to come. In the 1840s, depression and famine produced misery and death from Flanders to Silesia. Strikes, riots, and popular uprisings alerted political leaders: the price of retarded industrialization was as high as the price of progress.

Closing the Gap: The Conquest of Distance
[FIGURE 2]

In the second half of the century, the pace of economic life on the Continent quickened and the gap between Britain and the rest of Europe closed rapidly. Perhaps the single most important factor promoting this transformation was the building of railroads, a web of steel that stretched across Western Europe to include even the slowly developing countries of Iberia and Italy.

Between 1850 and 1870, the rail network of Europe tripled in length. Some 50,000 miles of new line were laid, and strategic trunk lines connected state capitals, industrial centers, and ports. In the German

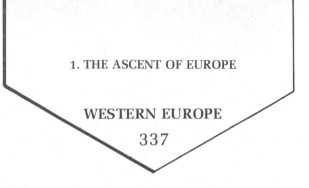

states that banded together in 1834 to form a customs union, the Zollverein, railroads were built more quickly than elsewhere; Cologne emerged as the most important **railhead**• west of the Elbe River; Berlin assumed new significance in the east. The coal of the Ruhr shuttled across Germany, and the growth of the ports of the North Sea was greatly accelerated by Germany's search for export markets abroad. In France, railroad lines radiated out from Paris like spokes of a wheel. In the south, railroad engineers pierced the Alps with the Mont Cenis and Saint Gotthard tunnels to bring Mediterranean Italy within hours of Central Europe. A line traversed the Pyrénées to connect France and Spain. Everywhere the effect of these railroads was similar: the commercial and natural barriers to trade on the Continent were broken, and many inefficient industries previously protected by distance and topography were eliminated. Heavy raw materials moved from one end of Europe to the other on strands of steel, and the population discovered a new mobility.

Figure 2. Railroads and Industrial Growth in Europe. This figure demonstrates the close correlation between the growth of railroads and the expansion of heavy industry in the United Kingdom, Germany, and France. Railroads broke down the barriers of distance: transport of heavy industrial goods became feasible. Note the extremely rapid rise in German productivity, the gradual slowing of the British industrial revolution, and the relatively modest growth of heavy industry in France. *Adapted from:* William L. Langer, ed., *Western Civilization,* Vol. II. New York: Harper & Row, 1968, pp. 433, 441. Used by permission of the publisher.

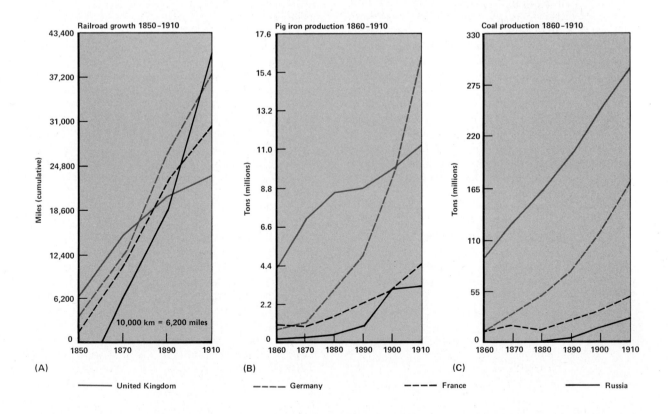

This conquest of distance stimulated an extraordinary breakthrough in industrial activity; the appetite of European economies for raw materials grew apace. An industrial economy was recognized as a political necessity—a matter of national prestige—and the basis of a modern military. Nowhere was this more appreciated than in Germany, determined under Chancellor Bismarck to secure that nation's "rightful place in the sun"; nowhere did industrialization proceed more rapidly. By 1870, German iron and coal production exceeded that of France, and the Ruhr emerged as the greatest center of industrial activity in Western Europe. After German unification and the defeat of France in the Franco-Prussian War in 1871, Germany's steel production doubled in each decade until the end of the century. By the 1890s, German steel production surpassed that of Great Britain and was second only to that of the United States. This phenomenal rise to industrial leadership was fostered by programs of government-sponsored industrialization not unlike those of Japan.

In France and Holland, by contrast, the pace of industrial growth was slow, almost stately, leading some observers to claim that the French to this day have never experienced an industrial revolution. In northeastern France, in the Nord (Lille) and Pas de Calais, a zone of heavy industry developed based on the Lorraine iron ores and coal from the Saar. But the devastating losses of the Franco-Prussian War and the conservative, measured French approach to industrial growth caused France to fall farther behind Britain, Belgium, and Germany in industrial output as the twentieth century approached. Elsewhere, industrial centers developed in the Po Valley of northern Italy and in northeastern Spain around Barcelona. In Sweden, new railroad lines stimulated the export of iron ore and timber. In Denmark, the technological revolution found its place in agriculture, and the dairy and poultry industries were reorganized and mechanized. In short, by the turn of the century, Europe held primacy in the world economic order and the economic map of Europe took the form it has maintained to the present. As early as 1870, Britain, Germany, and France produced 60 percent of the world's total manufactures. Although the overall Continental proportion fell to 40 percent by the beginning of World War I largely because of increasing competition from North America, Europe began the twentieth century as the cockpit of the world, the core area in a new world economy and society.

A Second Industrial Revolution
[FIGURE 3]

A large part of Europe's preeminence sprang from a new generation of scientific and technological advances in the second half of the nineteenth century. The age of coal and iron was replaced by a new age

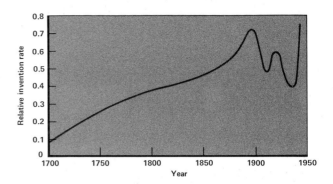

Figure 3. Inventions and Economic Progress, 1700–1950. This graph shows a "relative invention rate" by weighting the importance of mechanical inventions developed during different periods of world history. The 1890s reflect the European discoveries in electricity, steel production, and organic chemistry that spurred a second cycle of industrial growth. Although this graph is speculative, it is supported by patent statistics. *Adapted from:* S. Lilley, *Men, Machines and History.* London: Cobbett Press, 1948, p. 193, Fig. 52. Used by permission of Lawrence & Wishart, Ltd.

of steel and electricity, which spurred a second cycle of industrial growth, a second industrial revolution. The Bessemer converter made it possible for forges to remove the precise amounts of carbon from iron necessary to convert varying grades of ore into steel, a material of surpassing strength, hardness, and flexibility. The Bessemer process and open hearth methods of steel production cut the cost of steel by a factor of ten, and the discovery of a simple method of removing phosphorus from iron ore opened up new phosphorus-rich iron mines to large-scale production. In the cities, coal was harnessed for electrical power, illumination, and telecommunications. Shortly thereafter, the petroleum industry blossomed and internal combustion engines were developed for automobiles. Machines for both commerce and the home—sewing machines, scissors, manufactured shoes, watches, and typewriters—became commonplace.

Equally profound changes were occurring in the countryside. Scientific advances in organic chemistry produced chemical fertilizers far less expensive than the guano (bird dung) imported from Chile; these fertilizers rejuvenated the ancient agricultural soils of Europe, doubling and sometimes tripling local harvests. Synthetic dyes, chemical drugs, synthetic cloth (rayon), and dynamite were additional products of this new science. One proud British industrialist, somewhat carried away, called this period the "golden age of the Leblanc soap industry" in celebration of the sudden widespread availability of cheap soap with its attendant implications for health, sanitation, and social grace. The dark, chlorine-laden fumes that poured from his factory towers over the surrounding Lancashire countryside were happily ignored, an environmental blindness

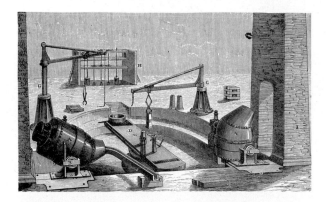

The second Industrial Revolution was marked by a new spate of inventions that made possible much greater volumes of production utilizing far more sophisticated methods. One such invention was the Bessemer process for making steel, the equipment for which is shown in this contemporary drawing. *Photo:* Culver Pictures.

shared by every early industrial society. His triumph was brief, however; German scientists soon discovered electrolytic methods of preparing alkali, chlorine, and sulfuric acid that put the huge Leblanc plant out of business.

Leblanc was simply one of many entrepreneurs, followers of Adam Smith, who engaged in stiff competition for raw materials and markets in the four industrialized nations of Western Europe—Great Britain, Germany, France, and Belgium. As leadership shifted from Britain to Germany largely because of the keen German appreciation of the application of scientific principles to industrial production, free trade began to give way to tariffs, ***protectionism,*** isolation, and a pattern of international competition. German, French, Belgian, and American manufactures began to dislodge British products both at home and overseas. Impassioned speeches in the British Parliament railed against the importation of Bavarian lead pencils, brushes made by German convicts—even playing cards and buggy whips. But in the ever closer marriage of science and technology, the Germans were outpacing the British.

In part, this shift was a normal maturation, or as the British called it, "climacteric," a change of life in the growth of the British economy. But it also reflected Britain's spirit of pride in its practical inventors (the barber Richard Arkwright, the mechanic James Watt, and the clergyman Edmund Cartwright) and a certain scorn for the book learning of technical education. Compulsory elementary education was not introduced in Britain until the 1870s, and even then, a London inspector of schools justified elementary schools as a means of preventing the city from being overrun by "hordes of young savages." Technical education was badly neglected in Britain. By contrast, universal education in Germany was a long-standing idea. In 1820 Prussia enrolled all children under fourteen years of age in school,

and by the 1890s, Prussia had twice as many university students per capita as Great Britain. With the growth of science, the German government sponsored well-staffed technical schools and universities with the most modern laboratories. Teutonic faith was lodged in technicians, not tinkerers.

Other factors important in the rise of Germany to its position of industrial preeminence were complacent British merchants who took markets for granted, conservative English industrialists who were slow in developing new products, and the higher cost of changeover than of initial industrialization. As Britain's industrial monopoly gave way to Continental competition, the contradictions between the interdependence of the world economy and the politics of nationalism in Europe became apparent.

THE INTERNATIONAL ECONOMY

What the railroads did to economic organization within Europe, the steamship did to communication among the continents. Economic interdependence among technological countries and between them and the rest of the world increased sharply. The value of international trade expanded from an estimated $4 billion in 1850 to nearly $40 billion in 1913. The progressive reduction of international shipping rates had important effects both in Europe and abroad. The price of a bushel of American wheat in Western Europe fell by three-quarters, making it uneconomic for European farmers to compete with cheap grain from the grasslands of the New World, southern Russia, and the Antipodes (Australia and New Zealand). Argentine beef and Australian mutton found new markets in Europe, as did European manufactures abroad. Millions of European emigrants sought new homes in the United States, Canada, Latin America, Australia, and New Zealand. Less developed regions began to specialize and become known for particular products—Egyptian cotton, Indian tea, Malayan rubber, Cuban sugar, Chilean nitrates, Brazilian coffee, Bolivian tin, and the minerals of the Congo Basin. European capital financed these commercial developments; by 1914, Britain, the banker of the world, had one-quarter of its national wealth invested abroad. For the most part, Europeans controlled both ends of these trade lines. Although the historical Third World countries experienced sudden prosperity as new markets for

The *Viceroy*, shown here at anchor in Galway Bay, inaugurated steamship communication between England and New York in 1850. *Photo:* Culver Pictures.

their raw materials opened up in Europe, they also became vulnerable to a world economy so sensitive to fluctuations that in 1873 a bank panic in Vienna led to worldwide economic disturbances; in the United States, 200,000 railroad workers were suddenly unemployed as the financing of their business collapsed.

Imperialism

With the world reaching toward a spatially interlocked economy for the first time in history, greater political cooperation might have been anticipated during the second half of the century. Instead, the industrialized nations of Europe launched a competitive scramble for colonial possessions that in one generation brought most of the earth under their jurisdiction. Africa is a prime example of the progression of European colonialism. In 1875, less than a tenth of tropical Africa was under European control; a decade later 5 million square miles and 60 million Africans were under European rule. On the eve of World War I, only the kingdom of Ethiopia and Liberia remained independent. In the process, the French acquired an African domain twenty times the size of France; elsewhere, they consolidated their hold on Indochina. Britain maintained India under colonial status and realized the dream of Cecil Rhodes in Africa, a Cape to Cairo territorial axis. Germany acquired territory in southwestern Africa and the Gulf of Guinea; Belgium took the Congo; Italy settled for Libya and parts of Somalia; and the Dutch held Indonesia. French North Africa expanded to include Tunisia and Morocco as well as Algeria, taken earlier. Russia moved into Central

Asia and eastward toward Manchuria, while Japan took Korea and Taiwan. The United States "liberated" Cuba, Puerto Rico, and the Philippines from Spain and forced Europeans to stay out of the New World in a reconstruction of the Monroe Doctrine. When the spasm was over, a geography book of the time noted that "nearly all the waste spaces had already been staked out." Britain had gained 4.5 million square miles of territory; France, 3.5 million; Germany, 1 million; Belgium, 900,000; Russia, 500,000; and Italy, 185,000. In addition, nearly all laid claim to China, whose gigantic territory was carved into "spheres of influence." Never had so few governed so many: Europe controlled 20 million square miles of foreign territory and the destiny of 500 million people.

The motivations behind this sudden geographical expansion into Asia and Africa were complex and contradictory. On the economic side, industrialists and merchants were attracted by markets for industrial goods, control over sources of foodstuffs and industrial raw materials, and outlets for surplus capital and population. Trade, it was said, would follow the flag. One English politician spoke of a "great British commercial republic" with its factories in England, its farms overseas, and a constant flow of people and goods between them. Even opponents of imperialism thought colonies would be profitable. In fact, both groups were wrong.

At its maximum, only one-eighth of Britain's trade was with its colonies, a far smaller exchange than with the self-governing dominions of Canada and Australia. For other European powers, colonial trade was even less significant: France traded with its overseas territories for only 11 percent of its exports; Japan, 4 percent; and Germany and Italy, less than 1 percent. Although locked in fierce commercial competition, the industrial powers did more

"Imperialism" is not a new epithet: as this 1882 political cartoon shows, the race for colonies in the late nineteenth century was not always regarded as a good. *Photo:* Culver Pictures.

business with each other than with their underdeveloped colonies. In terms of foreign investment, both France and Britain directed more capital into Russia and the United States than into their own colonies. Commercially and culturally, Saint Petersburg was virtually a French dependency. But migration to overseas colonies in the fifty years after 1885 amounted to fewer Europeans than would sometimes emigrate to the United States in a single year. The new territories were too poor to absorb industrial goods, too expensive to administer, and most often environmentally unattractive to Europeans.

Instead, the conquest of new lands and new markets was an issue of national prestige, a guarantee of the well-being of future generations carried out in an atmosphere not unlike the race to the moon between Russia and the United States a half century later. Statesmen believed that the day of small countries was over, that spheres of influence, a balance of power, and empires were essential to preserve or attain great power status. For the British it was a choice between Little England and Imperial Britain; for the Germans, a place in the sun; for the French, *la mission civilisatrice*; and for the Italians, a new Roman Empire. If one nation failed to seize territory, it was certain that another would, moving the conqueror one rung higher on the ladder of imperial competition. Further complicating the issue was the confident belief that Europe had a spiritual duty to spread modern culture and civilization to the more backward peoples of the world. Rudyard Kipling's "white man's burden" summed up this patronizing moral goal. Well-intentioned humanitarians followed the explorer Livingstone into the farthest

reaches of Africa and Asia, frequently giving their lives for their faith. Often they served to protect natives from the disregard shown them by the colonial regimes everywhere. This curious combination of economic imperialism, nationalist passion, and evangelical spirit was summarized by Lord Curzon, the English statesman and viceroy of India, who wrote: "In Empire, we have found not merely the key to glory and wealth, but the call to duty and the means of service to mankind."

The Dispersal of the Europeans
[FIGURE 4]

In the new international economy of 1850–1914, Europeans began to move about as freely as goods and capital—from one European nation to another, from the countryside to the city, and overseas. Passports and visas were not required; steamship companies offered cheap fares to migrants who served as the human ballast that enabled the Cunard Line, among others, to show a profit. The mass movement of the European population began in the 1840s when potato blight destroyed the agricultural economy of Ireland. From then on, each political or economic crisis sent forth fresh waves of migrants. Between 1850 and 1900, an average of 400,000 a year left European ports for overseas; after 1900, this figure rose to over 1 million a year. All told, from 1870 to 1914, 34 million Europeans left the Continent; 27 million came to the United States, and the rest went to Canada, Argentina, Brazil, Australia, and South Africa. The Irish continued to form an important part of the exodus from the British Isles. Germany was a principal source of migrants until 1890. After 1890, the less industrial periphery of Europe—Central Europe and the Mediterranean states—formed the principal platform for emigration. Never in European or for that matter world history had so many people migrated by choice. In effect, migrants were maximizing their economic opportunities with their feet.

This vast migration that Europeanized North America, South America, and Australia and implanted compact colonies in parts of Africa and Asia was produced by the interplay of two forces—population growth and industrialization. The **demographic transition**[•] (see Rise) spread southward from northwestern Europe to the Mediterranean during the nineteenth century. The death rate fell while the birth rate remained high, and population pressure

The *Ballengeich* leaves Southampton in August 1852 for Australia, carrying about 250 men, women, and children who had joined a "family emigration" plan. The departure, one of the first from that port (emigration was growing so that London and Liverpool could no longer handle the traffic), was reported in the *Illustrated London News*, which also published this engraving. *Photo:* Culver Pictures.

intensified. Twenty years later, as this new generation sought jobs, waves of migrants from these regions found employment overseas. Some 60 percent came to the United States, but in terms of intensity of migration, an even higher proportion of the populations of Brazil, Argentina, Australia, and New Zealand were affected. As industrialization took hold in Britain and then spread to the rest of Western Europe, emigration rates fell as growing factory towns absorbed the bulk of the population increase.

It was not, however, simply a movement of peasants from overcrowded Europe to the frontiers of the Great Plains, the ***pampas,*** and the ***outback.*** Artisans and craftsmen migrated as well: early in the twentieth century, the movement of unemployed urban Polish, Italian, and Ukranian families to the factories of Pittsburgh and Chicago was substantial. Nor did all migrants find their new homes congenial. A full 9 million returned to Europe from the United States. The new mobility created a class of working-class globe-trotters: English housepainters worked in Philadelphia in the spring, Scotland in the summer, and England in the fall; the Italian *golondrinas* (swallows), who left Genoa and Naples in November, harvested wheat and corn in Argentina until April and returned home for the Italian harvest in May. The repatriation rate for the United States may have been as high as 30 percent, and except for the Irish and the Jews, who had little to return to, this inter-

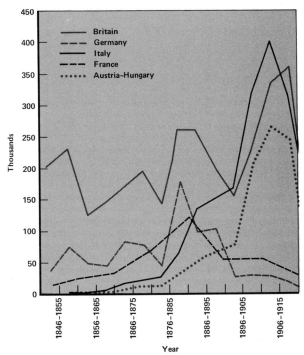

Figure 4. European Emigration, 1846–1915. In the second half of the nineteenth century, a mass exodus of some 55 million Europeans changed the complexion of the North and South American and Australian populations. The colonies established in Africa and Asia became the objects of political and racial friction in the twentieth century. Great Britain, with its limited resource base, was the principal source of emigrants. German migration was greatest in the 1890s; Italians and Austro-Hungarians peaked a decade later. French migration was quite limited throughout the period. *Adapted from:* William L. Langer, ed., *Western Civilization,* Vol. II. New York: Harper & Row, 1968, p. 446. Redrawn by permission of the publisher.

continental shuttling was common among most migrant groups. Overseas employment undoubtedly reduced social tensions and population pressure in Europe, although at no time did international migration draw off more than 40 percent of the natural population growth in any single country. The sheer scale of this movement, however, reflected the human dislocations unleashed by the new social and economic forces at work in Europe.

THE PROUD TOWER: SOCIETY IN CHANGE

The inhabitants of the Proud Tower, as the contemporary writer Barbara Tuchman calls Europe before World War I, had absorbed and turned to their advantage the most accelerated rate of change in history. For most Europeans, the superiority of their values and the diffusion of their civilization across the globe were facts—articles of faith—that demonstrated a unique European capacity to adapt to technology, seize new opportunities, and create a society of prosperity and peace. In retrospect, they were merely the first to cross the watershed between traditional and modern societies; their capacities in transportation and communication, production and consumption, energy and commerce had expanded enormously. If large-scale emigration was a symptom of underlying tensions, it was also an example of European ingenuity and confidence. If there were new pressures of wealth and need, of crowded cities and class antagonisms, of national pride and international tensions, the inhabitants of Europe, the Proud Tower, would withstand them and accommodate change. Underlying these pressures to expand, which along with industralization propelled the European continent to world domination, were three forces: population growth, urbanization, and the rise of new classes.

Population Growth

Between 1800 and 1900, the European population doubled from 150 million to 312 million, an increase larger than any previous total population on the Continent. The birth rate remained steady or rose in most countries, while the death rate was halved by advances in medicine and reliable food supplies. This created an unprecedented rate of natural increase, which even in relatively underdeveloped countries like Hungary and Italy amounted to 300,000 people per year in 1900. Although emigration drained off a significant portion of this surplus, population densities across Europe were rising, thickening the human texture, and generating competition for land and for personal advancement. The advanced industrial countries proved capable of maintaining levels of population that would have proved lethal in any agrarian society pitted against the environmental constraints of Europe. Belgium, for example, had an overall population density of 600 people per square mile and in some districts

1000, figures never before achieved on the European continent. As a result, by the turn of the century, one of every four human beings was European as compared with one in five in 1800.

Increased agricultural and industrial production, stemming from technological progress, supported this larger population, although the distribution of the increase varied considerably from one part of the Continent to another. Britain (42 million) and Germany (50 million) were the most populous nations in 1900, with their growth rate holding steady at better than 1 percent per year. England relied on cheap grain from the North American prairies, the pampas of Argentina, and the **chernozem**• belt of the Ukraine to feed an increasingly urban, industrial population. As the saying went, an Englishman could "produce more food making shoes than growing wheat." The British and the Belgians became the Europeans most highly dependent on international trade. By contrast, German peasants were emancipated from **serfdom**• in the 1850s and were protected as independent farmers from foreign competition by government tariffs on food imports. Thus, Germany remained essentially self-sufficient in foodstuffs, although at a high price. With the application of scientific principles and new technologies to agriculture, German farmers ultimately achieved grain yields three times those of Russia and twice those of the United States. Along with the Dutch and Swiss, whose populations doubled in the nineteenth century, and the Danes, who tripled in number, the Germans became the richest and most productive farmers in Europe. In Spain and Italy, in the underdeveloped southern periphery of Europe, population growth was not matched by comparable levels of industrial or agricultural progress despite enclaves of modernity in Catalonia and the Po Valley. Land remained in the hands of the state, absentee landlords, and the Church; overpopulation led to rural poverty, **fragmentation**• of land, declining rural standards of living, and other problems common in developing nations today.

Perhaps most unusual, however, was the fact that France did not experience the surging population growth prevalent everywhere else in Europe. In 1800, France was the richest and most populous country in Europe; a German peasant adage, pungent with jealousy of the abundant agricultural resources of France, described heaven as being "happy as a peasant in France." But between 1800 and 1850, the

WHERE I WAS BORN: HOLLAND BEFORE INDUSTRIALIZATION

In this selection from his autobiography, Days of Our Years, *Pierre Van Paassen recounts his memories of childhood around the turn of the twentieth century. It was a period when not much had changed for Dutch villagers from what their ancestors knew, but indications of the century to come were at hand.*

The population of the community of Gorcum [in Holland] in which I was born had been stationary between twelve and thirteen thousand for fully three centuries, ever since the foundation of the Dutch Republic. Hemmed in by a ring of old-fashioned bastions, palisaded redoubts, and deep moats, the town was incapable of expansion. For the building of a doghouse or a cowshed outside the gates, permission from the war department was necessary, and since that body invariably refused to sanction the erection of anything "that might offer a visible target to enemy guns," the burghers had long ago given up trying. We lived ina house that was built in 1644. The building next door was a hundred years older. It bore a sculptured inscription on the facade which read: PRAISE THE LORD. HONOR HIM. FOR THE DAY OF RECKONING IS BEARING DOWN UPON YOU! *Cannonballs were embedded in its walls, and of one of these projectiles the story was told, that before coming to lodge between two windows, it had taken off the head of my maternal great-great-grandfather as he stood quietly smoking his pipe in the cool of the evening. The argument as to whether it was a Prussian or a French ball that had decapitated the old gentleman was occasionally revived in our family.*

Although farm machinery had begun to make its appearance, we noticed on our roaming in the rural regions of Holland and Flanders that the peasants still cut their grain with a scythe. Children of orthodox parents in the outlying hamlets, where no "School with the Bible" existed, walked four or five miles to town and back in their wooden shoes every day. We sliced our long beans by hand in the late summer, and made apple cider in November; the wheat was ground to flour between flat stones turned by a windmill. But a change was in the air. I well remember the first automobile puffing up to the ferry, and the shower of stones with which the peasants pelted the occupants of the monster that frightened their horses. The sight of a motorcar was said to turn the milk in the cows' udders. For years, one of my schoolmates bore the humiliating nickname of "the liar" because, having been taken for an automobile ride in a southerly direction, he had returned a few hours later, declaring that he had been as far as where the signposts by the roadside were in the French language.

[My] Uncle Kees was one of those men who looked upon industrialization with mingled feelings of pride in human achievement and fear for the future. He was not optimistic about the miracles of technique and the invention of more and more ingenious machinery for the production and distribution of goods. Unless the whole human race could benefit from this change, he saw in technical advance a limitation placed on human progress rather than a spur. "Some day," he would say, "the common people will pay dearly for these newfangled contraptions." He was not wrong in that prediction. For industry, as time went on, engaged armies of workers whom the countryside furnished, and then threw them into unemployment and poverty for ever longer periods of depression. Not till after the war did the blighting effect of the industrialization process become quite apparent to all—crowded cities and depopulated villages.

Source: Excerpts from Pierre Van Paassen, *Days of Our Years,* New York: Dial Press, 1946, pp. 9–10, 14–15. Reprinted courtesy of Mrs. Van Paassen.

French population grew slowly, from an estimated 27 million to 36.5 million, and in the second half of the century inched up to only 41 million. By contrast, Germany grew by 32 million people in the nineteenth century; Austria-Hungary, by 23 million; Britain, by 26 million; and Italy, by 16 million. France, with a net gain of only 14 million, had become a medium-sized state despite major advances in industry, agriculture, and health.

What happened was that the French birth rate fell almost as rapidly as the death rate, a departure from the expected demographic transition that population specialists have been attempting to explain ever since. Some have suggested that inheritance laws, which required a division of property among all children in the family, caused French peasants to limit their number of children. Others have pointed out that abortion and birth control, outlawed as early as 1556 by Henri II, were more prevalent in France, despite its Roman Catholic faith, than elsewhere in Europe. Indeed, abortionists were among the first prisoners released from the Bastille at the time of the French Revolution. Finally, some modern demographers suggest that France had a low birth rate because it was a more advanced country than others in Europe, that high levels of education and aspiration, growing cities, and an expanding middle class tended to limit population growth. Whatever the reason, by the turn of the century more than half the districts of France had achieved zero population growth, and abandoned villages were becoming a common feature of the landscape. Probably no factor played a greater role in the social geography of France in the twentieth century than the pattern of low birth and death rates established previously.

Urbanization

Most of Europe's immense increase in population was absorbed by old medieval and even Roman cities that outgrew their fortified walls and spilled onto the countryside. Industrial resources such as iron ore, coal, and waterpower were more location-bound than the population. It was cheaper to move people than raw materials; new centers sprang up alongside the mines and mills. At the beginning of the nineteenth century, 60 percent of the English and Welsh populations were rural, compared with 75 percent in France, the Low Countries, Germany, and Italy, and upward of 90 percent in the less industrialized northern and eastern periphery of Europe. But in 1914, 80 percent of the British population, 60 percent of all Germans, 45 percent of the French, and a third of the populations of less industrialized countries such as Denmark and Poland were urban. In the Ruhr Valley, the English Midlands, and the French northeast, factory towns had devoured the intervening countryside and formed smoke-palled **conurbations.** Traditional administrative and political centers such as London, Paris, Brussels, Vienna, and Madrid also expanded, casting a magnetic attraction for urban life over country people now able to migrate to cities because increasing industrial productivity supported ever larger urban populations. London in 1900 was a sprawling city of 6.6 million people—a full 15 percent of the population of the nation. Paris had a population of 3.7 million; Berlin, 2.7 million; and Vienna, 1.7 million. The industrial centers of Manchester, Liverpool, Birmingham, Hamburg, and Barcelona grew to more than 500,000 people, as did the political capitals and port cities of Glasgow, Marseilles, Brussels, Amsterdam, Copenhagen, Budapest, Rome, and Milan. In a continent that had had barely twenty cities with populations of 100,000 in 1800, a massive shift in the human center of gravity had occurred, creating a new social environment to herald the beginning of a new century.

The rapid growth of urban centers in the nineteenth century completely transformed the nature and setting of life in Europe. In 1800, except for England and to a certain extent the Netherlands, European cities were centers of court and religion populated by the nobility and bureaucrats, politicians, soldiers, priests, artisans, and craftsmen. Madrid was such a city, as were Paris, Vienna, and Rome; all reflected long-standing patterns of cultural and social homogeneity buttressed by time and tradition. The influx of millhands and factory workers from the countryside into the cities destroyed this traditional urban culture and society as surely as sprawling acres of tenements and workers' cottages altered the size and physical appearance of the cities. The tensions and budding antagonisms accompanying this human invasion were played out in squalid districts of cities ill-equipped to deal with large increases in population. In Manchester, Lille, and Essen, slums grew up around the factories, railroads, and mills, spreading uncontrollably outward from the medieval urban core. Living conditions were ghastly, though probably no worse than in the preindustrial villages of the European past so romanticized by later generations.

Throughout urban Europe, buildings were so poorly constructed that entire blocks sometimes collapsed. Miserable quarters, the worst of which were Saint Giles in London, Little Ireland in Manchester (see Rise, "The Scientific Transformation"), and Voightland in Berlin, were hastily constructed to meet the needs of the expanding work force, and these areas rapidly declined into slums. Minority groups suffered the worst degradation—the Poles in the Ruhr, the Irish in Liverpool and Manchester. Water supplies were inadequate, and facilities for sewage and garbage virtually nonexistent. Crowding was so intense in the Ruhr city of Essen that nearly a fifth of all households were lodged in attics at the turn of the century. Europe, as Benjamin Disraeli, the British prime minister, put it, was fast splitting into two nations—the rich and the poor—and both were thrown together in the city. Urban critic Lewis Mumford, who has dubbed such cities "Coketowns," asserts that "never before in recorded history had such vast masses of people lived in such a savagely deteriorated environment."

The New Classes
[FIGURE 5]

In these cities, two new social orders—the middle and the working classes—put their stamp on the nineteenth century. The upper middle class, composed of industrial entrepreneurs, bankers, businessmen, and professionals, set the tone of urban life, replacing the rolls of an older order—the aristocracy, the Church, and the gentry—who gradually receded from the realities of the industrial age.

The ethics, manners, and tastes of these people were remarkably uniform from one nation to another. Neatness, thrift, preservation of order, and avoidance of sensual pleasure were the primary virtues. In Protestant countries, wealth was viewed as heaven's reward and poverty as the product of laziness and irresponsibility. Any man of ordinary talents, it was believed, could achieve high social standing through hard work, careful discipline, and self-improvement. The family was the core of middle-class society; education and manners were matters of crucial importance, and sexual restraint a mark of character. At a time when one in eight Aus-

After the Industrial Revolution, the new symbol of human pride became the industrial exposition, which absorbed the talents and energies that centuries before had gone into the building of cathedrals. At the Paris Exposition of 1900, the new Eiffel Tower proclaimed the accomplishments of technology. *Photo:* Culver Pictures.

trian and one in four French children were born out of wedlock, the middle class was quick to condemn as immoral the behavior of a significant proportion of society and impose its code of morality on European society as a whole.

However, it was the upper middle class that pressed for social reforms and was responsible for abolishing serfdom in Europe; removing discriminatory religious and ethnic laws; and sponsoring public education, the emancipation of women, and the organization of labor unions, reforms that probably spared Europe—given the antagonisms of the time—widespread and bloody revolution. Artistically eclectic and obsessed by morality, the upper middle class molded public aspirations and social ideas in Victorian England and on the Continent. Beneath it, a lower middle class of shopkeepers, bureaucrats, and domestics copied its manners, eager to climb the social ladder. By the turn of the century, domestic servants formed a staggering one-seventh of the total labor force in Britain—2.7 million workers, as compared with 1.6 million in agriculture. Living downstairs, they hoped their children would live upstairs.

For that other new class, the working class, high aspirations were unrealistic. Having abandoned the rhythm of the farm in search of a better existence in the city, factory workers, miners, and mechanics were plagued by the most basic forms of social insecurity—unemployment, illness, and death at an early age. Harnessed to machines and engaged in monotonous work, they became, as socialists Marx and Engels called them, "degraded hands" who bitterly resented the luxury and security afforded the upper and middle classes. The industrial death rate was high: in the Sheffield cutlery industry, thirty-two was the average age of death for scissors grinders; wool-shear grinders lived to be thirty-three, and tableknife grinders, thirty-five. Fatal accidents in the coal mines of the Ruhr rose from an annual rate of 26 in 1850 to 537 in 1900. In France, workers were compelled to carry identity cards, so police and employers could trace their movements, usually to collect debts. Each trade was known for its own health risk: for potters, it was lead poisoning; for miners, tuberculosis and black lung disease; for spinners, bronchial illnesses; and for match makers, phosphorus poisoning. Mass production had made more creature comforts available to more people, but, rather than providing material goods, this progress filtered down to the poor in the form of basic municipal improvements: paved streets, sewers, lighting, water supply systems, plumbing, hospitals, police and fire protection—those services that made urban life less dangerous for all social classes.

The only other significant rise in the standard of living of the working poor came near the end of the century when cheap food from overseas led to better diet. Even so, a study of York, England, at the time showed that 27 percent of the town's population was suffering from "primary poverty," that is, insufficient income to support an acceptable level of nutrition. At the time of the Boer War, one of every three British recruits was rejected as unfit for military service because of physical disability. The festering tensions that resulted from the economic gap be-

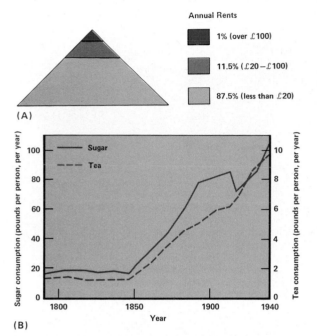

Annual Rents

■ 1% (over £100)

■ 11.5% (£20 – £100)

□ 87.5% (less than £20)

(A)

(B)

Figure 5. The New Society. At the end of the nineteenth century, British society was composed of the rich (2%), the middle class (11%), and the working class (87%)—or, as Matthew Arnold trenchantly called them, the Barbarians, the Philistines, and the Populace. These divisions were so widely recognized that seating on railroads mirrored the social divisions of the nation—first, second, and third class. The structure of rents in Britain in 1862 (part a) suggests the scope of class differences. By the late nineteenth century, the diets of the working class (part b) had begun to show significant improvement, an important change because over 50% of working-class salaries was spent on food. Meat, beer, tea, and sugar consumption rose. Yet in 1913, studies on British schoolchildren showed that the offspring of the working class were an average of 5 inches shorter than the children of the privileged upper class. *After:* E. J. Hobsbawn, *Industry and Empire*. London: Penguin, 1969, Figs. 44b, 46. Copyright © E. J. Hobsbawn, 1968, 1969. Used by permission of Penguin Books, Ltd.

tween working-class poverty and middle-class ease generated labor movements that forced European governments to better the conditions of factory employment and job security and to provide the economic basis for a life of reasonable comfort.

Denouement

For most Europeans, the dawn of the twentieth century boded well, and many considered it a golden age, the Belle Epoque. Paris had become the playground of world society, of American millionaires, European aristocrats, and captains of industry. Few Europeans seriously thought that rising nationalism, imperial competition, and social unrest would spawn a conflict of unprecedented destructiveness, World War I.

When war came, it was sparked by a trivial incident. In June of 1914, Serbian terrorists assassinated the Austrian Archduke Francis Ferdinand in the ob-

scure town of Sarajevo in modern Yugoslavia. The assassination itself was not an unusual occurrence, for during these years anarchists had killed prominent statesmen with frightful regularity. In 1894, a printer named Vaillant threw a bomb into the French Chamber of Deputies (parliament); shortly thereafter, President Carnot of France was stabbed to death by a baker's apprentice; Empress Elizabeth of Austria was slain by a vagrant Italian workman; and in the United States in 1901, an unemployed Polish-American named Leon Czolgosz shot and killed President McKinley in a receiving line at the Pan-American Exposition in Buffalo, New York. But in the case of Francis Ferdinand, Austria gave Serbia an ultimatum and demanded and received support from Germany. Serbia asked for help from Russia, which in turn invoked its treaty of alliance with France. Britain, worried about possible German dominance on the Continent, joined in. Through action and reaction, an intricate series of European treaties and countertreaties forged a chain of reciprocal responsibilities that ensnared virtually everyone in a continentwide conflict.

The Proud Tower, free from large-scale war since Napoleonic times, entered the fray happily, welcoming a release for the pent-up energies produced by the Industrial Revolution. In one year, however, the illusions and enthusiasms of 1914 were shattered. It was the first war in which modern technology was applied to the art of killing, and the loss of human lives and property was enormous. Machine guns, artillery, and poison gas—basic equipment for trench warfare—created a four-year stalemate on the battlefield. A generation of European men was destroyed by inept generals who launched one frontal assault after another on entrenched positions in an effort to bleed their opponents white. In the Somme offensive, the British, after losing 60 percent of their officers and 40 percent of their ranks on the first day, penetrated German lines a distance of 7 miles at a cost to both sides of 1 million men: one body for each 4 yards of contested ground. The psychological consequences of this mechanical slaughter were devastating: in 1915, a Belgian poet dedicated his work "with emotion to the man I used to be." Overall, 10 million people died and the cost ran to hundreds of billions of dollars. When it was over, France had lost 1.5 million men, half the prewar male population of military age. Germany, ringed by the British naval blockade, faced starvation, and the British

The "war to end all wars" stopped at 11 AM on November 11, 1918, and in the streets of Paris soldiers from the Allied countries in this first world war were heroes to a people who had lost a generation of young men in four years of unbelievable slaughter. But the "normality" that everyone sought lasted barely a generation; the same scene would be repeated less than thirty years later. *Photo:* Culver Pictures.

themselves were deeply in debt. The Europe that had dominated the world was shattered.

THE DECLINE OF EUROPE

Europeans longed for a return to normality, to pre-1914 life. For most, this meant an end to killing, renewed prosperity, the revival of trade, reconstruction of the devastated landscape, and continued dominance over the world. But World War I had accelerated a shift in the world balance of economic and social power and created a new set of international conditions that made this impossible. Industrial leadership had shifted to the United States. After the Revolution of 1917, Russia withdrew from the international economy. Nationalism had spread from Europe to the colonies, and new competitors such as Japan vied for markets and produced merchandise previously monopolized by Europeans. The free-trade system that had brought such prosperity to Europe began to weaken and, during the Depression of the 1930s, collapsed. This, in turn, led to the rise of economic nationalism and a breakdown of the world economy. Europe, fragmented by the Treaty of Versailles that ended World War I, played an increasingly secondary role in world affairs. The internal weakening of the middle class and the rise of autocratic regimes highlighted a drift toward yet another destructive war in Europe twenty-five years later.

The Breakdown of the International Economy

Europe emerged from World War I a debtor continent. Huge loans contracted with the United States to sustain the costs of the conflict had to be repaid. The Treaty of Versailles held Germany responsible for $33 billion in reparations, to be used for the reconstruction of the European Allies—"loser pays" had long been a principle of European warfare. Dismembered by the war, Germany could not pay without loans for reconstruction; the United States would not accept imports in payment of European loans for fear of competition with domestic American manufacturers. A new cycle of international commerce ensued: Britain and France paid their debts to the United States; private American lenders extended credit to Germany, which in turn used the proceeds to pay reparations to the European victors. America replaced Europe as the banker of the world.

European trade declined substantially. German trade in 1920 was one-quarter the prewar level, and Sweden's trade balance was cut by half. French and British exports were reduced to one-quarter and one-half former levels. Although a temporary wartime loss of markets had been expected, it soon became clear that the nature of overseas markets had permanently changed. The United States was now a prominent industrial exporter, and Japan had taken over markets in the Pacific. India, Argentina, Australia, and a number of other less developed countries created local industries in the absence of dominating European exports. Cloth and textile machinery, coal, and steel, which had formed the bulk of Europe's offerings to the world, were being produced in new centers of production outside the European sphere of control.

In Great Britain the three leading industries—coal mining, iron and steel production, and textile

When Italy suddenly seized Turkey's last province in North Africa and the Balkan War devastated the southeastern corner of Europe, my liberal teachers at the Gymnasium, which was not a denominational institution, casually dismissed these outbreaks of violence in the continent's most backward areas as the last spasm of a dying medievalism. Western Europe, they argued with facile optimism, had grown too enlightened to have recourse to such barbaric practices. The Dark Ages lay behind. Democracy was breaking through in the most remote corners. Even Russia now had a parliament, and Bulgaria had just accorded its citizens equal franchise. Day was breaking at last, and the heavens would soon be all aglow. Man was about to reach the summit in his long and weary climb toward the human ideal. It was merely a question of time before the nations of the world would be walking hand in hand on the road of progress and prosperity. That was the optimistic interpretation given us of contemporary history. . . . Only the rector of the college . . . who was a social democrat, said to me one day as we walked home from school together that Europe and the world, instead of moving toward a greater era of well-being and happiness, were on the threshold of a period of violent readjustments. He thought that the period of upheaval that we faced might well last a century or more.

Source: **Quoted from Pierre Van Paassen, *Days of Our Years*. New York: Dial Press, 1946, p. 40. Reprinted courtesy of Mrs. Van Paassen.**

---

manufacture—all experienced great difficulties. German reparations in the form of coal from the Ruhr deprived Britain of European markets for her product, and the relative inefficiency of British coal mining made production costs high. Similarly, British steel mills were, compared with those of Germany and the United States, obsolete. Britain, once the world's leader in iron and steel manufacture, was now open to invasion by cheaper steel from new centers of production. Finally, Britain's cotton textile industry contracted and declined by half in the early 1920s. Japan and India had emerged as major textile exporters, with their newer and more efficient machinery and far lower labor costs. It was still necessary for Britain to import large quantities of raw materials to sustain its industrial economy, but the island nation began to experience a high rate of domestic unemployment and an unfavorable balance of trade.

Germany, carved up by the Treaty of Versailles, had lost one-third of its coal resources, three-quarters of its iron mines, and one-tenth of its population. France took Alsace-Lorraine, Denmark received northern Schleswig, and Belgium the three small communes of Eupen, Malmédy, and Moresnet. The Saar region and its coalfields was placed under French control for fifteen years. In the east, the Posen region was granted to the new state of Poland as were the industrial centers of Upper Silesia; West Prussia became a Polish corridor to the sea separating German East Prussia from Germany proper. Combined with high reparations payments, these territorial losses saddled the German economy with unmanageable inflation. France, by contrast, was relatively better off, having gained important resources in Alsace-Lorraine and maintained its balanced, less industrialized economy.

In Eastern Europe, a number of new nation-states were created from the defunct Austro-Hungarian and Ottoman empires in line with Woodrow Wilson's principle of self-determination of peoples. Serbia united with several Austrian provinces to become Yugoslavia; the Czechs and Slovaks merged in the state of Czechoslovakia. Poland regained an independence lost in the eighteenth century, its new national territory composed of former parts of Germany and Austria. Hungary became an independent country but lost Transylvania to Romania. Austria, which had been the second largest state in Europe with 50 million people in 1914, lost the Tirol and Trieste to Italy in the south, and emerged as an insignificant power of 8 million people, smaller than Bulgaria. This confusing wholesale creation of new sovereignties left Eastern Europe fragmented into small and economically illogical nations.

Economic Nationalism, Social Change

In these circumstances of divided states, cycles of debt, and a changing world economic order, the nations of Europe struggled to build their separate economies while bound in one way or another to the powerful financial structure of the United States. When the New York stock market crashed on Black Thursday in 1929, the impact on Europe was direct and immediate. In a single year, prices and production fell precipitously all over the world; in Europe, unemployment increased by half. In Austria and Germany, banks closed. A general economic depression settled over Europe.

Thrown back on its own resources, each country withdrew to the extent possible from the international economy. A collection of closed-off, largely antagonistic national units resulted. The first victims were the depressed agricultural countries of Eastern Europe, which threw wave after wave of products on the world market while causing prices to fall still further and completely dislocating their domestic economies. Month by month, the volume of world trade fell; by 1932, it was one-third that of 1929. Every nation erected barriers—tariffs, quotas, and embargoes—to imports while seeking agreements with other nations that would maximize exports. Production everywhere became oriented to domestic markets, and for Europe as a whole this meant a drastic contraction of jobs and wealth. In the world labor force, 30 million people—a fifth of the total— were jobless.

The breakdown of free trade was soon followed by the decline of two other basic European institutions —liberal democracy and the power of the middle class. Rampant inflation beggared middle-class investors, wage earners, and pensioners in Germany; taxation accomplished the same in France. In Britain, inheritance and income taxes made the accumulation of wealth and its transfer to children so difficult that a primary motive for capitalistic enterprise was muted. Adam Smith would have dis-approved. For peasants, the decline in agricultural prices spelled poverty, and labor unions plagued by falling production struck for equity in a collapsing world economy. Faith in liberal democracy, badly damaged by the devastation of World War I, was strained by these new social tensions. Breadlines and bankruptcies became common. Extremists of the political left and right gained credibility as the old bases of European economic strength crumbled. The smaller democracies that had remained neutral in the war—Switzerland, the Netherlands, and the Scandinavian countries—found themselves involved in the disintegration. Even before the Depression, Hungary, Spain, Portugal, and Yugoslavia had opted for more dictatorial regimes, and in Italy fascism took root under Mussolini. Germany, humiliated by treaty and economically deprived, was taken over by Hitler's National Socialist Party. Like its future ally, Japan, Nazi Germany strove to create an empire independent of the world economy. Europe plunged into World War II. This second struggle among Europe's fragmented nation-states completed the destruction of the Continent as a world political and economic power. After this war, no illusions remained about a return to the normality of pre-1914; it was clear that the center of gravity had shifted. In a world dominated by Russia and the United States, Europeans were forced to seek a new role.

WESTERN EUROPE

REGIONAL PATTERNS

PHYSICAL FEATURES MAP
POPULATION DENSITY MAP

Western Europe is a landscape of industrial nations set in mid to north latitude *environments.* The climates of the Atlantic coasts of Portugal and Norway are as different as those of Los Angeles and Juneau, Alaska. But in Europe, north-south bands of climate and vegetation—so prominent in the Soviet Union and North America—are distorted and compartmentalized by two factors: the maritime influences of the Atlantic Ocean and the Mediterranean Sea, and the discontinuous mountain terrain.

The maritime influences of the Atlantic and its north European arms, the North and Baltic seas, as well as the Mediterranean, moderate the effects of Western Europe's northerly position. In southwestern Ireland, for example, at the same latitude as Calgary, Alberta, temperatures below 20 degrees Fahrenheit have never been recorded. At the same latitude as Sept Isles, Quebec, palm trees can be grown on the British coast. Rome and Athens in southern Europe are at the same latitudes as Philadelphia and Washington, D.C., but cannot be considered "southern" except as compared with the northerly position of the rest of Western Europe. Indeed, European centers of population are clustered further north than in any other world *region*: maritime influences have contributed substantially to making it an attractive human environment.

From the time Benjamin Franklin observed the northeastward drift of Atlantic waters, it was believed that northwestern Europe basked in warm water from the Gulf of Mexico, directed north and eastward across the North Atlantic. However, *meteorologists* and *geohydrologists* have now determined that the current of warm Atlantic water influencing Europe, the North Atlantic Drift, surges out of the central Atlantic and is deflected northeastward toward Europe. The warming action of the Mediterranean, a closed continental sea, plays a similar moderating role in southern Europe. The Strait of Gibraltar, 9 miles wide, is relatively shallow—water depths are only 700 feet, compared with 3000 feet within the Mediterranean. The deep Mediterranean, therefore, acts as a heat reservoir, its waters warming rapidly in spring and early summer, and cooling very slowly during the autumn.

Separating and outlining the limits of Atlantic and Mediterranean influence in Europe are chains of mountains that have served historically as boundaries of human activity. The highest of these—the Pyrénées between Spain and France, and the Alps of France, Italy, Switzerland, Germany, and Austria—form a barrier between the Atlantic north and the Mediterranean south. Both ranges are highly dissected by *glaciation.* The Alps stretch 650 miles and at some points are 155 miles wide—a block of difficult terrain nearly 80,000 square miles in area. Wide alpine valleys, distinguished by U-shaped contours and often dotted with lakes, tend to make the Alps relatively accessible and penetrable despite their height and extent. In contrast, the narrow, V-shaped valleys of the Pyrénées make it one of the most effective barriers to human contact in Western Europe. Between the mountains and the Atlantic, the broad expanse of France, West Germany, and the Benelux countries forms a transition zone between the maritime north, the mountains, and the Mediterranean south.

Partly on these environmental bases, Western Europe can be divided into five broad subregions—the British Isles, Scandinavia, Continental Europe, Mountain Europe, and the Mediterranean—to provide a framework for viewing large-scale similarities. But the 335 million people of Western Europe live in a small, intensively exploited realm; so much so that if world agricultural productivity were to reach Dutch averages, a global population of 25 billion could be sustained. And each nation of Western Europe has its own language, mass media, universities, and ideals; each is in global terms a self-contained and powerfully communicative culture. As a result, Europeans speak to their landscapes in small terms. France, for example, is conceived of as a succession of distinctive countrysides (*pays*), each representing a culture and a region in its own right. Like their European neighbors, the French refer to their landscapes in discrete terms that reflect a long history of human occupance: a nationscape of individually defined regions. This microscopic scale of geographical perception masks the broad complementarity of the subregions of Western Europe.

THE BRITISH ISLES

Set apart from the European mainland by the North Sea and the English Channel, the British Isles, with a population of 58 million, nearly a fifth that of Western Europe, are composed of two main islands: Ireland in the west and Great Britain in the east, along with some 5500 others. England, Scotland, and Wales are geographically united on Great Britain, but each has its own language, culture, and outlook. The United Kingdom includes these three cultures as well as Northern Ireland. The Irish Republic (Eire), independent of the United Kingdom since 1922, shares common origins with its island neighbors but has experienced a separate evolution marked by both its isolation from and its proximity to the British.

Much of the physical geography of the British Isles is characteristic of northwest Europe in general: glaciated landscapes, poor soils, and a continually moist climate. Although gaining in winter harshness to the north, this region is distinguished by its mild winters and cool summers. Seen from the air, the agricultural lands of Britain and Ireland resemble those of Belgium, Germany, and northern France—a mosaic of neat farmsteads, well-kept pastures, meadows, and cropfields outlined by hedgerows. Although British farms are highly productive, only 7 percent of the area of the United Kingdom is devoted to the production of foodstuffs consumed directly by its population. Britain must buy one-fourth the beef available on the world market and more dairy products than any other country to sustain its population.

About 3 percent of the British population is employed in agriculture. A fuller measure of life in Britain, and for that matter in much of northwestern Europe, is visible from the night sky: chains of urban lights illuminate the industrial basis of modern Europe. Over 60 percent of Britons live in cities with more than 50,000 inhabitants, and fully 77 percent are townspeople. With the exception of London, most large British cities are located on or near coalfields, but topography has also shaped patterns of occupance. Highland Britain, generally a treeless land, deforested by grazing sheep and goats, shares the geology of Norway and Sweden. Although now sparsely settled, the environmental barrenness of much of Britain's highlands points out that every part of the country has been exploited at some time in history.

The United Kingdom:
Scotland, England, Wales, Northern Ireland
The *highlands** of Scotland are divided by the Scottish Lowlands, which extend coast to coast from the River Clyde to the Firth of Forth. Four-fifths of the Scottish population is clustered in the lowlands; the Glasgow metropolitan area (1.7 million), the industrial capital of Scotland, and Edinburgh (453,000), the political and cultural capital, are complementary lowland centers. Outside this lowland belt, Scotland has extensive open lands, relatively thinly populated by virtue of rugged terrain and the harshness of North Atlantic weather. Much of the Scottish northwest resembles the Norwegian

ENVIRONMENTAL ZONES

coast with *fjords** and small, self-contained fishing and farming communities, far removed in spirit from the lowland industrial complex based on specialized trades—tobacco, whisky, heavy metals, shipbuilding, and *petrochemicals.** To the south, a T-shaped block of highlands breaks the ribbon of urbanization. The southern uplands of Scotland are much lower than the northern highlands, only around 2000 feet in elevation, but they have served as an effective barrier between the Scots and the English.

The Pennine Mountains course southward 135 miles from Scotland to the English Midlands, their length broken by an important series of west-east gaps connecting the farmlands and pastures of Yorkshire in the east with the urban complex of Merseyside in Lancashire in the west. Here, a belt of cities developed during the Industrial Revolution on the basis of coal and iron mines in the Pennines, available waterpower, and agricultural resources. In the east, in Yorkshire and West Riding, wool gave rise to the textile industry; Leeds-Bradford (1.7 million) and Sheffield (516,000) are its largest urban centers. West, across the Pennines, in the metropolises of Liverpool (1.3 million) and Manchester (2.4 million), commerce turned from woolens to cotton textiles and other colonial products brought to the ports on the River Mersey. Known together as the cities of the Merseyside, Liverpool and Manchester form a *megalopolis** which, with the centers of Yorkshire to the east,

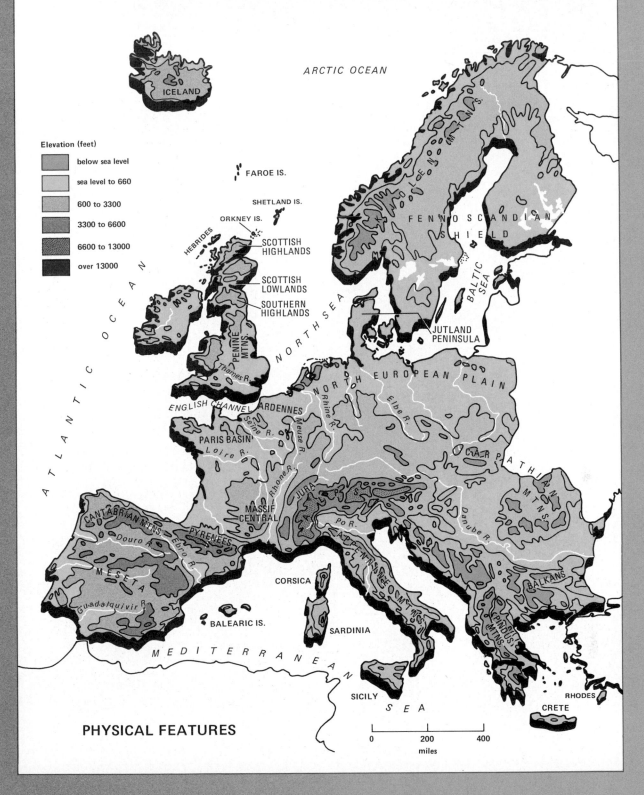

ARCTIC OCEAN

ICELAND

FAROE IS.

SHETLAND IS.

ORKNEY IS.

HEBRIDES

SCOTTISH HIGHLANDS

SCOTTISH LOWLANDS

SOUTHERN HIGHLANDS

FENNO SCANDIAN SHIELD

BALTIC SEA

JUTLAND PENINSULA

NORTH SEA

NORTH EUROPEAN PLAIN

ATLANTIC OCEAN

PENNINE MTNS.

Thames R.

ENGLISH CHANNEL

ARDENNES

PARIS BASIN

Seine R.

Loire R.

Meuse R.

Rhine R.

Elbe R.

CARPATHIAN MTNS.

Rhone R.

JURA

MASSIF CENTRAL

Po R.

Danube R.

CANTABRIAN MTNS.

Douro R.

PYRENEES

Ebro R.

MESETA

Guadalquivir R.

APENNINES MTNS.

CORSICA

BALKANS

PINDUS MTNS.

BALEARIC IS.

SARDINIA

RHODES

SICILY

CRETE

MEDITERRANEAN SEA

PHYSICAL FEATURES

0   200   400
miles

may become a single urban mass strewn from the west coast to the Yorkshire countryside.

In northeast England, the Pennines are flanked by the cities of the Tyneside and the River Tees on the North Sea. The Industrial Revolution was born here in the rich coalfields of Northumberland and Durham. Newcastle, a transshipment point for coal since the 1300s, was its center. The Tyneside mines have been depleted over the centuries; today some seams have been mined so thoroughly that they reach 3000 feet below the earth and some mines have tunneled under the North Sea. Still, the coalfields of northeast England rank second among British fields.

As the narrow ridge of the Pennines flattens out to the south, the Midlands form a southern indus-

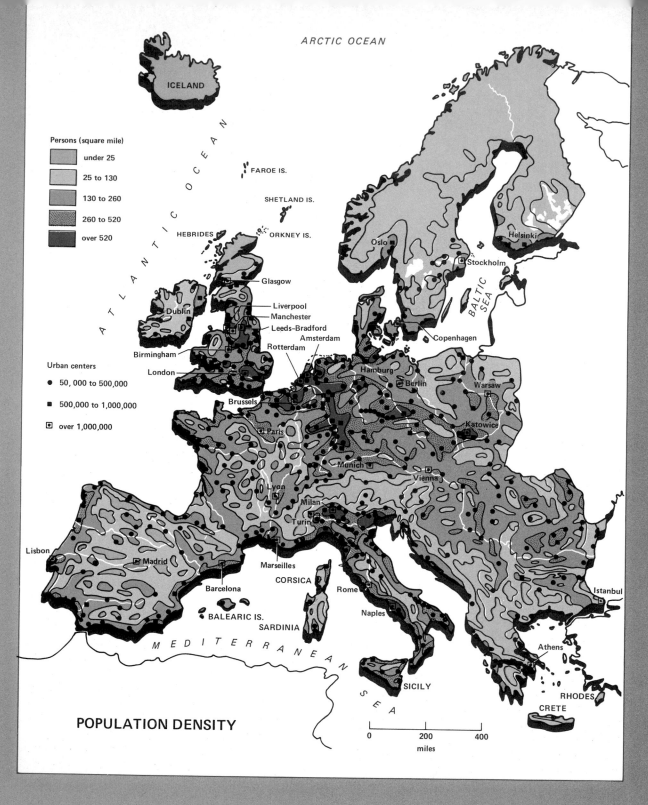

ARCTIC OCEAN

Persons (square mile)

under 25

25 to 130

130 to 260

260 to 520

over 520

Urban centers

● 50,000 to 500,000

■ 500,000 to 1,000,000

⊡ over 1,000,000

POPULATION DENSITY

ICELAND

FAROE IS.

SHETLAND IS.

ORKNEY IS.

HEBRIDES

Glasgow

Liverpool
Manchester
Leeds-Bradford
Amsterdam
Rotterdam

Dublin

Birmingham

London

Brussels

Paris

Lyon

Milan

Turin

Lisbon

Madrid

Barcelona

BALEARIC IS.

Marseilles

CORSICA

SARDINIA

Rome

Naples

Oslo

Stockholm

Helsinki

Copenhagen

Hamburg

Berlin

Warsaw

Katowice

Munich

Vienna

BALTIC SEA

Istanbul

Athens

RHODES

CRETE

SICILY

MEDITERRANEAN SEA

ATLANTIC OCEAN

0   200   400
miles

trial ring around the highlands. The West Midlands, centered upon Birmingham (2.4 million), is the heart of the black country of England—an area so long and so densely industrialized that a local species of green-camouflaged butterfly has evolved into a gray-colored insect over the last 150 years. Smaller in population than the West Midlands (2.5 million), the East Midlands continues the patterns

of urbanization between Northampton and Nottingham. The coalfields of Nottingham produce about half the total British output, making this the nation's most important mining district. The southern extension of the Pennine chain is ringed by a U-shaped band of cities from Leeds to Sheffield to Birmingham and from there north to the Merseyside in the west. In terms of modern communications, Leeds is only three hours by car from Birmingham, and Birmingham little more than an hour's drive from Liverpool. This intensity of industrial activity and concentration of population is matched in Europe only by the German Ruhr.

Southwest of this industrial belt, the rugged mountains of Wales have isolated that country and its people and preserved their Celtic identity. But Wales, conquered by the English in the thirteenth century, has not escaped industrialization and urbanization. South Wales has a major coalfield now in decline (see "The Quest for Unity") that formed the basis for an important industrial region whose major port, Cardiff, developed much like Newcastle in the English northeast as an export center for the *hinterland.*

With the exception of Cornwall and Devon in the far southwest, most of southern England is lowland country dominated by London, only recently replaced by Tokyo and New York as the largest city in the world. Much of the English southeast plain is productive agricultural land devoted to the cultivation of grains, cattle, and intensively worked vegetable farms and orchards, but London's influence in this part of the British Isles is near total. Some 40 miles from the mouth of the Thames on the North Sea, 12.8 million Londoners, one-fifth of the British population, live in a city open to the world by trade, the primary focus of British society. The city spreads out over a considerable portion of the southeast countryside. Its size, remarkable among British cities even before the Industrial Revolution, has been attributed to its proximity to the Continent and its populous and productive hinterland. London houses the headquarters of almost all British firms and is the seat of a government that until recently directed the largest of all European colonial empires. Not surprisingly, more air traffic passes through London than through any other European city. The area covered by urban London has grown many times in the last 100 years (see Rise, Figure 10), devouring precious farmland in a country whose finite land resources make unrestricted urban growth unrealistic. Government policies of reserved open lands (forests and farmlands) near London protect a continuous *greenbelt* from being entirely engulfed by urbanization. *New towns,* entirely planned before construction, have been built beyond the greenbelt as successful experiments in urban geography.

The United Kingdom also includes the territory of Northern Ireland centered around Belfast and Londonderry. These 5460 square miles of hilly landscape are a political remnant of the English domination of Ireland. Northern Ireland's population of 1,525,000 is divided on religious grounds that have their origins in the English control of all of Ireland from the time of Cromwell (1642) to the establishment of the Irish Republic in 1922. Protestants—descendants of English and Scottish country gentlemen, tradesmen, and industrialists—are a minority in Ulster (Northern Ireland). Serious civil strife has continued since 1969 between these people and the more numerous Catholics (indigenous Irishmen), who form a relatively depressed majority.

Republic of Ireland

Ireland (Eire) shares a heritage of Celtic civilization and language that once flourished in Scotland, Wales, Cornwall, and Brittany. Although the intensity of Celtic culture has diminished greatly under French and English influence elsewhere, Ireland retains its separate language and literature.

Most of Ireland is a level plain under 500 feet elevation studded by glacial *moraines,* barren rock outcrops, and deeply etched valleys whose lower extremities are drowned in the Atlantic. The coast, except in the east, is rimmed by low mountains that shelter centers of population in coastal indentations. Dublin (670,000) is the primary seaport and manufacturing center of the republic; Cork, the second largest city, has only 132,000 people. Over half of Ireland's 2.9 million people remain tied to agriculture, and in the west they form a poverty-stricken group whose economy has been singled out by the European Economic Community (Common Market) for regional development. Emigration from Ireland continues—the island as a whole now has just over half the population of 8.2 million recorded in 1841 before the great potato famine struck the land. Even with this small population, however, Ireland faces grave questions of regional underdevelopment and lacks industrial raw materials, capital, and markets; furthermore, rainy weather and poor soils render expansion of the agricultural base extremely difficult.

SCANDINAVIA

Scandinavia, the northernmost subregion of Western Europe, is composed of the continental nations of Norway, Sweden, Denmark, and Finland and the island of Iceland. With a combined population of slightly more than 21 million people living on one-third of the total area of Western Europe, Scandinavia is very thinly populated, a consequence of the harsh climate, glacial landscapes, and acidic soils that generally prevail. In Norway, Sweden, and Finland people are concentrated in the warmer south; only Denmark has an overall population density of more than ten people per square mile. Fishing, forestry, and agriculture play important roles in the economies of these countries. Despite small populations and limited natural resource bases, Scandinavia has high standards of wealth and pioneering programs of social services that provide living environments as unique as its landscapes.

355

The landscape of Norway is characterized by fjords, narrow valleys where the mountains meet the sea. *Photo: Brownlie/Rapho-Photo Researchers.*

Iceland

Iceland, an island nation proud of its separate heritage as an outpost of Norse trans-Atlantic exploration, was colonized during what may have been a warmer period in climatic history from about AD 874 to 900, when Norwegians fled political disturbances at home. The Danes took the island in 1381 and used it as an outfitting center for further exploration and fishing—a satellite state within the orbit of Greenland and Newfoundland. Today a center of fisheries and communications in an otherwise inhospitable sea, Iceland is distinguished by Arctic mountains reaching over 5000 feet, glaciers, *crevasses,* caverns, *geysers,* fierce winds, and volcanoes. Settlement is restricted to the southwestern part of the island, where proximity to the North Atlantic Drift has enabled a population of 82,000 to survive in Reykjavik, the capital, and the remainder of the 204,000 Icelanders in the area around it.

Norway

Norway, which occupies the western half of the 1200-mile-long Scandinavian *peninsula,* is dominated by the rugged landscapes of the Fennoscandian *shield,* an outcropping of the ancient continental crust. Stretching far to the north, Norway has severe Arctic climates and *tundra* vegetation; were it not for the moderating influence of the North Atlantic, it would be a Siberian wasteland. Punctuating the Atlantic coast are fjords, Norway's most distinctive landscape feature. Fjords are U-shaped valleys that reach outward from the heartland of the Kjölen Mountains, the highland spine of the Fennoscandian shield. Scooped out by glaciation, the fjords have partially filled with seawater in the postglacial period. Although quite deep and well protected from the Atlantic, the typical fjord provides limited space for human settlement. Despite this problem, a succession of fjords stretching from the Finnmark or northernmost Norway through the Nordland (above 65 degrees north latitude) southward to the milder southwest has served as a multicored nucleus of Norwegian economic activity tied by necessity to the resources of the sea. The only cities that have substantial populations and relatively large hinterlands—Bergen (116,000), Trondheim (128,000), and Stavanger (82,000)—are located in the most protected fjords in the south. The other towns along the western Norwegian coast are quite small and serve specific extractive industries.

The Finnmark is occupied by Lapps, native *pastoral* reindeer herders numbering some 30,000 in Norway, northern Sweden, and Finland, who are now threatened by industrial civilization. The town of Narvik (13,000) has been developed to serve as an ice-free port for high-grade Swedish iron ores shipped overland by rail. Northern Norway, like much of Sweden and Finland, is a modern frontier where the fishing, waterpower, timber, and mineral resources of the area are being harnessed.

In the past, the traditional heartland of Norwegian culture oscillated between the amenable fjord environments of Trondheim (where the fjord stretches inland for over 100 miles) and Bergen; today, the Norwegian population and economy center on Oslo (579,000) in the east. In contrast to the Atlantic coast, eastern Norway is a land of wide, wooded valleys with lower rainfall and warmer summers, dotted by a variety of urban centers with diverse industrial bases. It now accounts for more than half the national population (3.9 million) and is growing much more rapidly than the Atlantic regions. But in European terms, Norway is an empty land, with most of the population clustered in small parcels of the nation's 125,000 square miles of territory. The harshness of the environment and limited economic opportunities have prompted more than half the population to emigrate overseas in the last century.

Sweden

East of the Kjölen range and protected from the immediate effects of the North Atlantic is Sweden, a low-lying landscape of glacial features. The fast-flowing rivers of the north (the Norrland) are succeeded in the central part of Sweden and the southern half of Finland by lakes and streams partitioned by numerous eskers, morainic deposits of assorted rocks and soil left behind by retreating glaciers. In southern Sweden, the climate is warmer as the martime influences of the North Sea penetrate farther inland than elsewhere in Scandinavia.

Scania, the southernmost Swedish province, is separated from Denmark by the strait of the Öresund, only a few miles wide. A population of 1 million makes this the most densely populated district of Sweden, Norway, or Finland. Small farms, few over 50 acres, are intensively cultivated; dairy cattle and poultry are complemented by wheat, sugar beets, and fodder crops. Malmö (445,000) is the principal port and center of population in Scania, its economy based on the supply, refinement, and export of agricultural products.

Central Sweden is the heartland of Swedish population (8.1 million) and commerce. Dominated by the Stockholm metropolitan region (1,345,000), it is an area of large-scale agriculture and diversified urban centers. Three great lakes—the Mälaren, Vättern, and Vänern—are practically inland seas, covering 3500 square miles, linked by rivers and canals. Göteborg on the west and Stockholm on the east frame a region noted for abundant natural resources of high-grade iron, manganese, copper, zinc, and lead ores in the east, and timber and grain in the west. Although industrial pursuits dominate the area today (67 percent of Sweden is urban), the traditional agricultural organization of central Sweden, the *bergslag*, provides the basis of the social solidarity and democratic institutions for which the country is famous. The *bergslag* was a royal corporation founded during the Middle Ages that provided Swedish workers with a degree of autonomy over the production of foodstuffs and manufactures in their district. The *bergslag* was conceived as a self-sufficient economic unit, a programmed counterpart of the French *pays*. As Sweden pushed the frontier of settlement north and west of the lakes in the eighteenth and nineteenth centuries, the *bergslag* became the basis of communal economic organization. Today, the area just north of the central lakes is commonly referred to as the Bergslagen, a legacy of the chartered development of the frontier.

Like the Norwegian north, northern Sweden has very low population densities. The Norrland, 100,000 square miles in extent, is an immense forest of pine, spruce, and birch. Settlement has progressed inland since the 1600s from ports on the Gulf of Bothnia in search of timber; today, the streams of the Norrland provide cheap hydroelectric power for a developing chemical industry in the cities of Sundsvall and Umeå. In the far north, the Norbotten is a rugged sub-Arctic land of tundra, the summer pastures of the Lapps. Since the turn of the century, several rich deposits of high-grade iron ore have been developed in the pioneering regions of Kiruna and Gällivare. Luleå, the capital of the Norbotten on the Gulf of Bothnia, is the principal Swedish transshipment point for bulky ores and lumber from the deep north.

Finland

Finland stands apart from Norway and Sweden, its population of different origin and its easterly position farther removed from temperate Atlantic influences. The 4.6 million Finns are a Central Asiatic people who came to the lake-dotted lowlands of this westernmost extension of the Russian landmass in the eighth century. Finland's climate is more continental than elsewhere in Scandinavia. As a whole, winters are colder and drier; summers are hotter. Although the average July temperature at Helsinki, the capital, is a relatively mild 62 degrees, higher than in Oslo, Stockholm, or Copenhagen, frosts are possible in June and September and harbors on the Gulf of Finland are jammed with ice for a good part of the winter.

Finnish settlement patterns mirror those of the other Scandinavian nations. Yet the topography of the country imposes special problems. The coast, facing the Gulf of Finland on the south and the Gulf of Bothnia on the west, is a low-lying plain much more intensely settled than the interior lake country. Uusimaa Province, along the southern coast, has a population density of over 300 per square mile, which includes the city of Helsinki (804,000); the lake provinces have densities of just 40 per square mile. The economy of the country, based on timber, agricultural products (oats, potatoes, dairy goods, and meat), furs and hides, and some new industries, is typically Scandinavian. But the development of Finland has been hampered by a terrain shredded by glaciation and a history of political subservience. Finland was Swedish territory until 1809, and then belonged to Russia until 1917. After siding against the Soviet Union (but not with Nazi Germany) in World War II, Finland was forced to cede 18,000 square miles to Russia in 1944. Since that time, the country has remained apart from Western European efforts at economic and political cooperation and maintained an absolute neutrality.

Denmark

Denmark, with a population of 4.9 million, is much less rugged and more evenly settled than any of the nations to its north. No point in Denmark's 16,629 square miles rises above 550 feet; with the exception of isolated undrained marshes, the landscapes of the Jutland Peninsula and the islands of Fyn and Sjaelland forms an unbroken carpet of rich agricultural land laced by a network of villages and market towns. Agriculture is a highly specialized, export-oriented industrial enterprise in Denmark. About 76 percent of Jutland and an even higher proportion of Fyn and Sjaelland are cultivated, and average yields on poultry and dairy products are among the highest in the world. Yet Denmark must import large quantities of grains, fruits, and vegetables. And despite its image as an agricultural nation, Denmark is organized around a small number of important cities. Copenhagen, the capital, is a metropolis of 1.4 million people, fully one-fourth of the Danish population. It is the premier port of the Baltic and the site of almost all Danish industry. The cities of Odense on Fyn and Åarhus and Åalborg on Jutland are secondary urban centers.

CONTINENTAL EUROPE

The core of Western Europe—France, West Germany, Belgium, the Netherlands, and Luxembourg —has a combined population of 135 million people (40 percent of the total) and is located in a transitional environment between maritime Britain, the Scandinavian north, the mountains of Central Europe, and the Mediterranean south. Each face of this region reflects a different influence; its 335,000 square miles of territory accommodate great diversity. The population core of Continental Europe is concentrated in a band of industry that streams inland and south from the Benelux countries and northern France along the Rhine. On the glacial plains north of this industrial zone, and in the French Mediterranean south, agriculture predominates. The economic core of Western Europe and the Common Market, these five countries have been the pivot of modern European history.

France

Compared with other nations in Western Europe, France has a favored environment. For the most part unglaciated, France borders both the Atlantic and the Mediterranean as well as the North Sea. It has a varied topography, with the Alps (15,771 feet at Mont Blanc) forming a formidable barrier to the east and the Pyrénées, an 11,000-foot mountainous crest, separating it from Spain. Strong regional differences characterize France, which, with 212,973 square miles, is the largest of all West European nations and four-fifths the size of Texas. Like Italy, Sweden, and West Germany, France has strong latitudinal differences, and the natural and human environments of the south (the Midi) are profoundly different from those of the north. But the origins of the human regions of France—the distinctive *pays*—belong to the past, not the present. France today, with a population of 50.8 million people, is a highly centralized state, dependent upon the resources and services of Paris for the structure and function of its culture, economy, and administration.

Paris stands at the confluence of several important river systems—the Oise, Marne, Seine, Yonne, Loire, and Eure—which converge in north-

Six important river systems converge at Paris in north-central France, the geographical heartland of the country. This view shows the Seine. *Photo:* Maurice Chardonnieres/Rapho-Photo Researchers.

central France on the Paris Basin. This basin commands the geographical heartland of France. To the northeast, along the North Sea, the Paris Basin leads to marshlands settled by the Dutch and Flemings; to the east, Germany is rimmed by the upland topography of the Ardennes and the Vosges with only the Lorraine lowland between them, an open gate to the east. Brittany to the west, a vestigial Celtic *culture hearth* long incorporated into France, projects 100 miles into the Atlantic. The English are across the 20-mile-wide channel that the French call La Manche (the sleeve). The rich French countryside that extends south from Paris, including Anjou, Poitou, Touraine, the Beauce, Champagne, and Bourgogne, has been the undisputed homeland of the French nation since the Middle Ages.

In northern France, a tapestry of cities weaves outward from Paris. Orléans, Rouen, Amiens, Reims, and Troyes form a first ring some 70 to 80 miles away. Rouen (370,000), the largest, is dwarfed by the capital's metropolitan population of 8.2 million—a sixth of the total French population. A second web of cities farther outward includes the industrial districts of Lille, Metz, Nancy, and Strasbourg in the north and east. Lyons to the south communicates with both the Nord and the Midi, and is located in the enclosed Rhône Valley surrounded by the highlands of the Auvergne and the Massif Central on the west and the jagged Alps to the east. Northern France ends in this valley, and the Midi stretches southward to embrace the cities and countryside of the Mediterranean lowlands of the Rhône.

To the west of Lyons, Clermont-Ferrand is an isolated industrial center at the foot of the Massif Central. This second band of cities is larger and more distinguished than those closer to the capital.

To the west and southwest of Paris, the intensity or urbanization is much less; a line arcing 100 miles outside Paris would include Caen, Le Mans, and Tours, but these cities, like Cherbourg, Rennes, Angers, Poitiers, and Limoges still farther from Paris in the west and southwest, are only of local importance. This part of northern France remains predominantly agricultural, its cities integrated into the specialized products of their surrounding *pays*. Consequently, only two coastal ports of entry, Nantes and Bordeaux, have national importance.

South of Lyons, the Rhône Valley gradually widens from Orange in the north to Montpellier in the west and Marseilles in the east. The Mediterranean coast of France—the ancient Provence—spreads out, a densely settled region identifiable by its Mediterranean climate and agriculture. The whole of Mediterranean France has a history of distinctive languages and political affiliations, more independent of Parisian influence than regions farther north. A ribbon of coastal cities at the foot of the Alps stretches east from Toulon to Nice toward Italy; Narbonne and Perpignan arch southward on the lowland plain toward Spain. Toulouse controls the southwest land passage, the Pass of Lauragais, that connects Atlantic France to the Mediterranean. The primary urban center of the Mediterranean is Marseilles, the only French city of international importance outside Paris. A conurbation of 964,000 people, Marseilles is a major seaport and manufacturing center.

Unlike its industrial neighbors to the north and the United Kingdom, France remains an important agricultural nation, the largest food producer in Western Europe. Some 46 million acres of diversified cropland employ 14 percent of the French labor force, and some 2 million workers are imported from North Africa, Senegal, and the poorer Mediterranean lands to labor in both French agriculture and industry. With large expanses of good farmland in diverse environments and important industrial resources, France is a favored nation in Western Europe.

West Germany

Neither as large nor as favorably endowed as France, West Germany with a population of 61 million includes two distinct environments: the northern plains and the more mountainous south. The North European Plain, broadening to the east, is rolling countryside mostly below 300 feet elevation. As in Denmark and coastal Sweden and Finland, the plain has been glaciated; moraines, *bogs*,* and lakes occur frequently. The plain covers the northern third of West Germany from the Ruhr

conurbation in the west to Hannover in the east, widening east of the Elbe River to include most of East Germany, Poland, and Russia beyond. Toward both the North and the Baltic seas, glacial depressions have warped the land into low-lying fields and marshes. West of the Weser River, the landscape dips toward the North Sea and is composed of peat bogs, marshes, and heavy, damp soils. It resembles Holland, but much of the land lies unreclaimed, providing havens for wildlife. The most fertile sections of the North European Plain are located in East Germany and Poland, historically germanized. Today isolated, the metropolis of Berlin (2.1 million) was once the urban core of the eastern plain. Yet West Germany's north does have an expanding economy, as the traditional port cities of Hamburg (the largest German city after Berlin, 1.8 million), Bremen, Kiel, and Lübeck have developed diversified industries within the European Economic Community and have been the primary resettlement zone for 10 million refugees from East Germany.

South of the North European Plain, West Germany rises in a series of low mountain ranges that culminate in the Alps at the Swiss border. Densely settled lowlands alternate with highlands generally under 2500 feet throughout southern Germany. The uplands hold important reserves of timber; the lowlands are a checkerboard of prosperous small farms that vie for space with urban centers. The first lowland north of the Alps holds Munich (1.3 million), the third largest city, whose rapid growth during the last century has eclipsed all other south German towns. Augsburg, originally a Roman colony and an important medieval trading link with the Mediterranean, has lost many of its commercial functions to Munich. Stuttgart on the Neckar, a *tributary** of the Rhine, is linked to the intense urbanization that follows the Rhine northward to the sea. Nürnberg is set off to the north of Munich, and like many West German cities, it has lost its traditionally larger hinterland to the closed, Soviet-oriented economic system of East Germany.

The cities of the Rhine are dense urban clusters. In the Middle Rhine, the port cities of Karlsruhe, Heidelberg, Mannheim, Darmstadt, Frankfurt, Wiesbaden, and Mainz form a ribbon of industrial towns whose contemporary importance is rooted in their early industrialization. Together, they contain over 2 million people, not counting the inhabitants of secondary towns and associated rural areas. To the west of the Rhine, tucked away in territory historically disputed between Germany and France, is the Saar. It is a center of heavy industry set in an area known for the excellence of its agricultural products (wines and fruit).

Farther downstream, the Rhine broadens to accommodate ocean-going vessels and is a main artery of European maritime traffic. Few landscapes

The Rhine is a center of intense industrialization and urbanization for almost its entire length. This picture was taken in the Ruhr. *Photo:* Paolo Koch/Rapho-Photo Researchers.

in the world can rival that of the lower Rhine for intensity of urbanization and industrialization. From Bad Godesberg in the south to Dortmund and Münster in the northeast and Aachen in the southwest, the Rhineland is an immense alluvial fan of cities. The area, usually called the Ruhr, is the largest megalopolis of continental Europe. Over sixty cities of note lie in this industrial belt: the largest are Cologne (866,000), Essen (705,000), Düsseldorf (681,000), Dortmund (647,000), and Duisburg (458,000). Within a perimeter of 100 miles, 9 million people are engaged in the treatment of ores, the production of metals, and the manufacture of a wide variety of finished products.

West Germany, then, has a highly industrialized economy and a strongly urbanized society: 70 percent of the population are city dwellers. Yet on the plain in the north and in the mountains of the south, the country retains much of its wilderness past. Its open lands, whether restricted to agriculture and protected from urbanization or insulated from society as natural reserves, contrast strongly with the intense human landscapes of its neighbors toward the sea—Denmark, Holland, and Belgium.

The Benelux Countries
[FIGURE 6]

In the Benelux countries, the level North European Plain sweeps westward and south along the North Sea, unbroken to the hills of Artois and the Plain of Picardy in northeastern France. The Netherlands is totally included within this arc, and only the Condruse Plateau and the Ardennes uplands in the Belgian interior and the independent Duchy of Luxembourg (999 square miles) are not part of the North European Plain. With a total population of 23 million people, 7 percent of the Western European total, and only a tiny fraction of the continental landmass, this area is more intensively utilized than any other in Europe.

The Netherlands sits astride two great rivers: the Maas, which originates far to the south in French Lorraine, and the Rhine, which enters the country as one river and quickly divides into numerous *distributaries.* In this *delta* land of swamps and marshes, the Dutch have created a human landscape out of drained *estuaries* and shallow sea bottom. *Polders,* land protected from the sea by seawalls, *dikes,* and dams, cover a significant proportion of the modern Dutch landscape. Reclamation began in the early Renaissance and has continued to the present, aided by increasing technology and growing capital expenditures. Between 1960 and 1970, 323,000 acres—nearly 50 square miles—were added to the Dutch national territory. Where the Rhine and the Maas enter the sea, Holland is slowly sinking, and continuous effort is required to maintain the status quo.

Modern reclaimed areas, carefully organized into productive farmland, give Holland a scientifically designed landscape, one developed for maximum utilization. Polders are intensely cultivated; land is restored to fertility by letting hay and grasses grow as groundcovers to create topsoil. Although dairy foods, poultry, and flower bulbs are produced for export, Holland must import most of its food. In the eastern Netherlands south of Groningen, poor

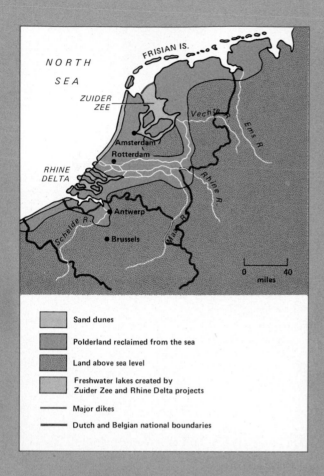

Figure 6. The Dutch Against the Sea. Much of The Netherlands and substantial parts of Belgium would be shallow sea bottom were it not for persistent hydraulic engineering and tedious land reclamation efforts. The Rhine Delta project area and the drained Zuider Zee are the largest of a considerable number of modified landscapes in the Low Countries.

sandy and peat-laden soils never covered by the North Sea but severely degraded by glaciation have been partially rejuvenated by extracting the peat and adding heavier soils and massive doses of fertilizers.

Overall, however, the Netherlands, with a population of 13 million, is an urban nation. Only 7 percent of its people are employed in agriculture, and the country relies on its trading location at the mouth of the Rhine and on skilled labor for industrial products. In this respect, Holland mirrors Denmark's agricultural patterns (though more restricted) and Switzerland's industry (though less limited in scope). Amsterdam is the premier metropolis of the country, with an urban zone whose influence extends over the entire nation. A service center for the far-flung Dutch colonial empire, Amsterdam's port still moves many tropical commodities—tin, sugar, rubber, tea, coffee, spices, copra,* and tobacco. An extensive industrial *infra-*

*structure** and skilled trades such as diamond cutting support a metropolitan population of just over 1 million.

In the south of Holland on the Maas, Rotterdam, another city of 1 million people, is the busiest port in Europe. Much of Rotterdam's postwar growth has been rooted in the oil and natural gas industry, and its new deep harbor—Europoort—handles much of the Middle Eastern oil flowing into the European continent. Besides Amsterdam and Rotterdam, the Dutch landscape is dotted by other urban centers—Hilversum, Haarlem, Utrecht, Leiden, The Hague—all linked by the nation's 3478 miles of canals. The Netherlands is a small country (14,192 square miles) with high standards of living. However, the Dutch pay the price of density: emigration has been and remains high; water pollution and the lack of open space are serious problems.

South of the Netherlands, Belgium forms a transition between centers of German and Dutch culture to the north and the influence of the French to the south. Belgium unites two diverse populations: the Flemings, who speak Flemish (a variety of Dutch) and the Walloons, who speak French with a distinctive accent. Flemings are more numerous—55 percent of Belgium's 9.7 million people—but the Walloons, with 33 percent of the population, dominate the cultural and political life of the country. Only one in five Belgians is bilingual, and tensions occasionally surface as Flemings perceive themselves in a situation of cultural, economic, and political discrimination.

The landscape of Belgium reflects the general patterns found around the continental North Sea coast—coastal lowlands, and an interior plain, succeeded by highlands. Most of the Belgian population was, until modern times, concentrated on the transitional zones between these three distinct landscapes. Bruges, now a small town (52,000), was the medieval port of entry to Flanders, inland from the coastal lowlands, and to the Brabant Plateau, the heartland of Belgium today. Liège, 100 miles east of Bruges across the plain and at the foot of the Ardennes, has developed into an integrated industrial region of 444,000 people in the Meuse Valley. But Brussels and Antwerp dominate Belgium today. Brussels, the national capital set in the middle of the rolling plain of the Brabant, is the headquarters of both the European Economic Community and the *North Atlantic Treaty Organization (NATO).** Primarily a city of *tertiary** economic activities, it is connected by canal to the Schelde River, granting its population of 1.1 million access to ocean-going vessels and prompting growth in the industrial sector. Antwerp, the port rival of Rotterdam, is the second city of Belgium, with a metropolitan population of 673,000. Its harbor facilities are impressively modern, and it attracts cargo by rail and canal from northern France, Germany, and Switzerland.

The smallest of the Benelux countries, Luxembourg, with a population of only 339,000, remarkably has survived as an independent nation. Located on hilly land in the Ardennes and surrounded by Belgium, West Germany, and France, Luxembourg is a significant world producer of steel made from iron ore deposits in the area adjoining French Lorraine. The Luxembourgeois retain a separate language related to both French and German. A remnant of a much larger medieval state, Luxembourg has been politically independent since 1867, although tied to Belgium by economic union since 1922 and to NATO by military alliance since 1948.

MOUNTAIN EUROPE

Switzerland and Austria are landlocked nations framed by high mountains and similar environments, but quite different in their historical experiences. Austria is a vestige of the Austro-Hungarian Empire of the southern Germans, culturally conceived within a greater Germany that no longer exists; Switzerland is half as large, has a denser population (16,000 square miles and 6.2 million people compared with Austria's 32,000 square miles and 7.4 million people), and is the geographical center of Western Europe, straddling three streams of cultural influence—Italian, French, and German. Together, the two upland states constitute 4 percent of the land area and population of Western Europe.

Switzerland

Switzerland is a remarkable multinational state whose national cohesion has been formed in a geographical zone where different linguistic and cultural groups meet. The Swiss population is well educated: primary education has been free and compulsory since 1874. Yet unlike most other West Europeans, the Swiss do not speak a common language; 72 percent of the Swiss speak German; 21 percent, French; 6 percent, Italian; and 1 percent, an ancient dialect of Latin, Romansh. All four languages hold equal status in national affairs. Nor is there uniformity of religion in Switzerland: 40 percent are Catholic and 60 percent are Protestants. It is thus an exception to the general West European pattern of cultural uniformity derived from competitive nationalism. The origins of confederation in Switzerland were based on cultural cooperation, a rare quality.

The territory of the Swiss confederation is confined on the west by the heights of the Alpine Jura and on the south and east by the Italian and Austrian Alps, which cover over half the area of Switzerland. Stretched between these two mountain ranges lie the Swiss "lowlands," a fertile highland plain holding nearly three-quarters of the na-

tional population on one-third the national space. This alpine corridor has been the focus of Swiss life since its rolling, forested topography was cleared and drained in the Middle Ages. Within it, a series of compartmentalized subregions, each dominated by a single culture and set of cities, is found. Population density in the lowlands is very high—800 per square mile—approaching the Dutch average. Agricultural production of dairy products, poultry, and grains is intense.

In the southwest, the city of Geneva is the center of French language in Switzerland and a meeting point for world organizations and conferences. Across several lowland valleys and the centers of Fribourg, Neuchâtel, and Biel in the upper Aare River valley, Zurich in the northeast is the largest city (675,000). Nearly a sixth of the Swiss population lives in Zurich and its suburbs. The city's financial markets and banks make it as important in international commerce as New York, London, or Paris. Basel to the northwest, located on a strategic bend in the Rhine, is an important manufacturing center with a metropolitan population of 373,000. Dependent on the rest of the world for most of its fuel and raw materials, Switzerland has been able to base its industry on a highly skilled urban labor force; 92 percent of the Swiss population is employed in nonagricultural pursuits. Exporting precision mechanical and electronic gear and a variety of finished goods from locomotives to rifles and binoculars, the Swiss have developed far beyond the limits of their natural resources.

Austria

Framed by the upper Danube River valley in the north and the eastern prolongation of the Alps in the south, contemporary Austria is a fraction of its former size. After World War I, when the new independent states of Yugoslavia, Hungary, and Czechoslovakia were created from the old Austro-Hungarian Empire, Vienna, the imperial capital, emerged bereft of its eastern hinterland. Modern Austria is a nation attempting to reformulate its national existence by harnessing the resources of two different environments, the upper Alps and the Danube Valley.

The Alps arc horizontally west-east across southern Austria. Unlike the Swiss Alps, the Austrian mountains are not broken by wide agricultural valleys, although the Brenner Pass opens the Austrian Alps (the Tyrol) to north-south traffic. But the environments of the Austrian Alps do contribute specific resources to the national economy; sheep and cattle grazing predominate in the upland zones of human occupance, with patches of fertile lowland soils worked much like gardens. Forest covers 38 percent of the country, and lumber and wood products contribute heavily to the Austrian economy. The fast-flowing alpine rivers sweep down into the Danube to provide hydroelectric power for modern industries—particularly iron and steel, paper, textiles, and electrical machinery. In addition, highland Austria is potentially a large producer of *geothermal electricity*• harnessed from geysers and contains large reserves of magnesite (used as a hardener in steel), graphite, and timber.

Lowland Austria is a narrow section of the upper Danube Valley. In the northwest, Linz developed on the valley floor as a railroad hub and textile center in the first wave of industrialization that swept Central Europe in the mid-1800s. Downstream, Vienna long controlled the entire length of the Danube, which flows southeast toward Budapest and Belgrade and eventually empties into the Black Sea. Vienna grew rapidly from the time of the Empress Maria Theresa (1740–1780) until World War I and became a graceful city combining Western and Eastern influences with a population of 2 million. After World War I Vienna's eminence declined, as Austria, a country reduced in population from 50 million to 7 million, was annexed by Nazi Germany in 1938. After World War II, Austria was occupied by the Allied Powers—Britain, France, the United States, and the Soviet Union—until 1955, and Vienna was administered much like Berlin. After reaching a population low in 1951, Vienna grew back to 1,603,000 by 1971, an adjustment to the reduced size of the nation.

THE MEDITERRANEAN

The four nations of Mediterranean Europe—Portugal, Spain, Italy, and Greece—have a combined population of 106 million, nearly a third that of Western Europe, and a comparable share of its land area. Yet population pressure in this region is intense, in part because long abuse of the environment has resulted in widespread deforestation and soil *erosion,*• in part because of relatively underdeveloped economies. The Mediterranean environment, with its dry summers and wet winters, is quite sensitive to human pressure, and successive layers of civilization—Phoenician, Minoan, Greek, Roman, Byzantine, Arab, and modern—have severely stripped the resources of the region. Only now industrializing, the countries of Mediterranean Europe are still dependent on agriculture and with growing populations are a source of emigrant laborers to the industrial centers farther north.

Iberia: Spain and Portugal

The two Iberian nations of Spain and Portugal form a separate European reality. Cut off from France by the Pyrénées and from the nations of Atlantic Europe by distance, Iberia is nearly surrounded by the Mediterranean and the Atlantic. The Iberian heartland is a high, dry landscape outlined by coastal mountain ranges. Like Greece, Iberia has been strongly affected by non-European cultures; it was an integral part of Muslim civilization for over three centuries.

Spain, the second largest European nation in area, has a population of only 34 million and a population density that is among the lowest in Europe—some twenty-five people per square mile. The central plateau, the Meseta, dominates the country in size, aridity, and rural poverty. The Mediterranean coastline, rimmed by nearly continuous high mountains, is punctuated by a series of lowland indentations where rivers from the Meseta and the coastal mountains sustain dense agricultural and urban populations. The northern coast has an Atlantic climate and is separated from other centers of economic activity by a range of west-east highlands, the Cantabrian Mountains. Stretching from France to Africa, Spain is a nation of contrasting landscapes and sharply defined human habitats.

The north is a relatively fertile land rimmed by a succession of mountain ranges that intensify maritime influences on the coast and distinguish it from the drier and colder interior. Galicia, in the northwest, is Spain's most humid region, with annual rainfall of over 65 inches. This highland region resembles western France: farmlands are planted to northern crops such as apples, rye, wheat, and potatoes. The coastline is deeply etched by bays that extend far inland and provide shelter for the three most important urban centers—Vigo, La Coruña, and El Ferrol—port cities with a growing industrial base. Farther east along the Atlantic coast, high-grade iron ore deposits near Bilbao and the country's primary coalfield at Oviedo have given rise to a zone of heavy industry at the foot of the Cantabrian Mountains, which grade eastward into the Pyrénées. In Spain, the Pyrénées have been called a "dead end" because their valleys are narrow, steep penetrations which do not reach across the crests into France.

Central Spain, the bulk of the Iberian peninsula, is occupied by the Meseta, a series of high plains bordered on the north by the Cantabrian Mountains and the Ebro River and on the south by the Guadalquivir River and the high Sierra Nevada. The Meseta is a harsh landscape: almost uniformly above 1500 feet elevation, it is arid, lacks adequate sources of water, and is largely deforested by the grazing of sheep and goats. The northern Meseta, or Old Castile, is more sheltered from drought and heat than New Castile, the southern Meseta, which is in large part a near-desert (La Mancha), although fertile and well watered by mountain streams along its periphery. Madrid, the capital of the nation and a cultural focus for the entire Spanish-speaking world, is located at the foot of the Guadarrama range separating the two mesetas. The old riches of Spanish colonization concentrated here attract a modern population of 3.1 million.

The Mediterranean coast is bordered by a succession of fertile lowlands where intensive cultivation of citrus, olives, nuts, and other fruit trees is often interspersed with vegetable crops grown for local markets. This garden cultivation of the restricted, fertile coastal valleys (*huertas*) is found throughout Andalusia (southern Spain) and the Spanish Mediterranean. The *huertas* have long attracted dense populations, and numerous cities dot the coast. In the northeast, along the Costa Brava, Barcelona (1.7 million) is the primary port and industrial complex and the capital of Catalonia, one of the ancient provinces of Spain. It is the most developed part of the country: hydroelectric power has been harnessed to provide energy for cotton mills and chemical factories; the Ebro and its tributaries have been tapped for irrigation. Farther south along the Mediterranean coast, a number of regional capitals are important centers of farming and industry. Valencia, the largest of these, is famous for its high-grade citrus crops and has a diversified industrial base of textile mills, iron and copper foundries, and food-processing facilities. Alicante, Cartagena, and Almería are similar but smaller coastal towns. Málaga, on the Costa del Sol, is the largest city of southern Spain and an important center of tourism. The rural core of Andalusia, however, is the rich valley of the Guadalquivir River—the largest expanse of agricultural land in Spain. Cádiz, Seville, Córdoba, and Jerez organize this lowland environment, which stretches some 160 miles to the Atlantic.

Although Portugal, with a population of 9 million, is the most Atlantic-oriented of all the continental nations of Western Europe, its climate and vegetation are decidedly Mediterranean. It is a continuation of Spain in climate and topography; yet its cultural landscape is clearly different. It is an intensely manicured countryside of Mediterranean agriculture.

There are three subregions. Rainfall decreases and temperatures increase southward; vegetation is more lush and relief is greater to the north. Northern Portugal is centered on the Douro River valley, a region of winter snows and oak and pine forests. The Douro and its hinterland are famous for cork (Portugal produces over half the world total) and wine (rosés, made from red grapes which do well on the *humus*-laden soils of the terraced slopes). Oporto, the second city of Portugal, is the core of this intensely inhabited region, which has 1400 people per square mile, one of the highest densities in Europe.

The farmlands of the Mediterranean coast of Spain are intensely cultivated, as this aerial view of the citrus orchards and vineyards of Alicante, a regional center of industry and farming, show. *Photo:* Georg Gerster/Rapho-Photo Researchers.

Southward, the Tagus River valley extends over 100 miles inland, carving out the largest expanse of farmland in the country. Rice, fruit orchards, and forests of cork oak trees alternate with extensive irrigated fields. Lisbon, the nation's capital, is a good example of a *primate city*; its population of 1.6 million is twice that of Oporto and seven times that of the next largest city. Lisbon functions as the center of virtually every facet of Portuguese life. South of the city, the country is considerably drier; agriculture is dependent on irrigation, and sheep grazing is important. The Algarve Mountains frame the southern coast and enclose a region undergoing extensive development as a center of tourism.

Portugal, however, remains an agriculture-based country. Some 71 percent of the population is rural; an important number of Portuguese are fishermen, and catches of flounder and cod from Newfoundland and sardines from the Moroccan coast are important national assets. Industrialization has only just begun to change the face of Portugal. A limited number of textile mills and chemical plants has been developed to capitalize on the nation's resources of waterpower; West German, British, French, and Italian firms have set up local assembly plants for electronic equipment and automobiles. But traditional patterns hold sway: a limited urban network, few urban job opportunities in industry, and a record of out-migration to northwestern Europe. Portugal, like Greece, also faces political problems as the loss of the African colonies of Angola and Mozambique throw the country back on its own resources and the aspirations of its population outpace the rate of economic growth.

Italy

Italy, in 1870, was one of the last countries in Europe to unite under one government. Yet even today, its population of 54.5 million remains two nations, north and south: one in race, language, religion, and political structure, it is economically divided.

The Italian north, highly industrialized and focused on the rich agricultural plains of the Po River, stands in strong contrast to the south. The steep slopes of the Alps and the northern face of the Apennines provide ample sources of water for the Po. The central Po Valley is a reclaimed marshland, and its *watershed* is characterized by early fall flooding when summer *meltwater* from the Alps combines with fall rains in the Apennines. An intensive, highly mechanized agriculture of rice, corn, hemp, olives, and fruit on only 15 percent of the land area makes Italy a primary West European food producer—an exporter of grain, wine, and olives. The Po Valley is dotted with large agricultural towns—Pavia, Cremona, Mantua, Ferrara, and Padua—none of which holds more than 300,000 people. Along both the Alpine and Apennine foothills, the Po lowland is ringed by important centers of commerce. In the western Po Valley, Turin (1.2 million) is the capital of the Piedmont, a province with strong historical attachments to France. Milan, more central in position, rules the plain and is the headquarters of many Italian companies and the financial capital of Italy. The second largest city in Italy after Rome, its metropolitan population approaches 2 million.

Farther eastward, Bergamo, Brescia, and Verona, all with populations of less than 300,000, are nestled in the foothills of the Alps. In the south, where the Po meets the Apennines, another string of industrial towns—Parma, Modena, and the rapidly growing Bologna—flank the southern Po. The urban outlet of the Po plain is Venice, 30 miles north of the delta at the head of the Adriatic Sea. Long a center of east-west trade and of fine arts, Venice is today a city beset by environmental difficulties.

Venice's regional population of 368,000 is spread across a unique urban landscape of land and water, its historical center located on 118 tiny islands grouped together to form a 3- by 1.5-mile pontoon of architectural majesty set in a shallow *lagoon.* Some 116,000 people live in this Renaissance creation. Nearly two-thirds of the population, 202,000, live in "industrial Venice," a city that has grown up on the mainland, Marghera. This section of Venice has had a disastrous effect on the Renaissance city, polluting air and water and diverting water. Today, the old city of Venice is sinking below sea level; floodwaters rushing into the lagoon swamped the city in 1966. International efforts—organized by the United Nations Educational, Social, and Cultural Organization (UNESCO)—have attempted to save the Renaissance buildings, and their efforts have to some degree succeeded, although frustrated by regional development plans that call for even more industry.

In many ways, Venice mirrors the problems of modern Italy: population pressure in the countryside has forced the Italians to sponsor industrial expansion at all costs; jobs are scarce and emigration remains substantial. Much of Italy is characterized by out-migration to northern centers of economic activity. During the 1960s, 250,000 Italians sought work each year in Continental Europe; some 30,000 Italians left the country permanently each year. Within Italy, each segment of the labor force—postal workers, Fiat employees in Turin, hotel personnel on the coast—is highly organized and sensitive to anything less than booming industrial expansion. As a result, civil strife makes Italy far less tranquil than either France or West Germany.

East of the port city of Genoa (842,000), the Apennine Mountains trend southeastward across the peninsula. Though not generally over 5000 feet in elevation, they are a considerable barrier to

A canal in the old city of Venice, whose survival is endangered by the industrialization that brings jobs. *Photo:* Eisner/Rapho-Photo Researchers.

movement. Cut by short streams and narrow valleys on the Adriatic Sea coast and longer, more mature rivers on the west, the Apennines are the source of most of Italy's major rivers, each associated with a separate economy and major city. In the north, Florence is distinguished by its artistic past and present. Its position on the Arno River is ecologically precarious, and the ancient core of the city was severely damaged by floodwaters in 1966. Rome, on the Tiber River at the geographical center of Italy, is a congested national capital with a metropolitan population of 2.7 million. The center of empire in classical times, it has since unification drawn people to its expanding industry, and now boasts a population ten times larger than that of 1870.

Naples is the regional capital of southern Italy, a sprawling industrial port city of 1.3 million, an island of industrialization and job opportunities in the backward Mezzogiorno. The problems of the Mezzogiorno—feudal landowning practices; an environment of rugged, broken mountains and low rainfall; a large peasant population subsisting on a finite resource base—are all reflected in the urban texture of Naples. Although one of only four European cities with a population over a million in 1800, Naples never became a modern metropolis: it has been instead the point of departure for millions of Italian emigrants seeking opportunities abroad.

The misery of the rural Mezzogiorno intensifies south of Naples, and the island of Sicily across the Strait of Messina is equally underdeveloped. A region of almost primeval beauty, Sicily is dependent on Mediterranean agricultural products that meet stiff competition in world markets: citrus, olives, and wine. Italy's other island, Sardinia, lies 170 miles west of Rome and 250 miles northwest of the Sicilian capital of Palermo. It is less densely populated than most of Italy and still isolated from the mainstreams of modern civilization.

Greece

Greece, about the size of Florida and with a population of 8.8 million, has figured large in its contributions to Western civilization. It is a mountainous country consisting of a main peninsula; the Peloponnesus (the southernmost extension of the Balkans), connected to the mainland by the Isthmus of Corinth and separated from it by the Corinth canal; the large Mediterranean island of Crete to the southeast; and 165 smaller inhabited isles along the coast of the Ionian Sea and in the Aegean Sea that together compose a fifth of the Greek land area.

Northern Greece is a broken landscape dominated by the Pindus Mountains. Its three important coastal lowlands contain substantial populations and are the most productive farmlands in Greece. In the far north, Macedonia and Thrace have traditionally been centers of emigration, although these areas are agriculturally important. Wheat, barley, and corn are the chief crops; tobacco is also important. The north is now undergoing delayed and rapid industrialization, as are a variety of other centers throughout Greece, the most important of which is the city of Salonika, a free port also open to Yugoslav exports. Farther south, Thessaly is a well-watered plain hemmed in by the high ranges of the forested Pindus and Olympus mountains.

Some 140 miles to the south, the landscape of Attica is quite different: dry, hot summers and a limestone topography characterize this eastern Mediterranean environment. Athens (2.5 million), the primate city of Greece, is located here. Athens is seven times larger than Salonika, Greece's second city. The administrative, industrial, educational, and political life of the nation is concentrated in Athens to a degree unequaled elsewhere in Europe; more than a fourth of the modern Greek population is located within 30 miles of the ancient Acropolis.

The Peloponnesus is a rugged rural landscape with over half its area above an elevation of 1500 feet; mountains higher than 6000 feet are not uncommon. Beyond Patras, a regional food processing center, urban centers and industrialization are noticeably absent: it remains, for the most part, a countryside of olive trees, vineyards, and pasture.

The Greek islands stretch out over an area several times larger than their land surface. Communications are difficult with all but the largest—Crete, Rhodes, Chios, Lesbos, Corfu; the Greek loss of Ionia (western Turkey) in the early 1920s worked to the disadvantage of many islands because trans-Aegean navigation was curtailed.

The problems of Greece—isolation from the main currents of industrial Europe until very recent times; an environment subjected to drought, heat, erosion, deforestation, and earthquake; rural overpopulation and a history of emigration—are masked by the beauty of the landscape, worked through time by successive layers of civilization. Greece is a transition nation, and to the south and east, Muslim civilization and the drier Mediterranean lands follow a separate path.

THE QUEST FOR UNITY

2

Compared with the United States and Russia, Western Europe at the end of World War II faced a bleak future. The war-damaged landscapes and impoverished economies of the Continent were physical symptoms; the heart of the problem was Europe's political disunity. Proud national traditions, linguistic and ethnic differences, varying levels of development, and harsh economic competition separated the eighteen West European states from one another. Indeed, these differences had been at the root of two twentieth-century wars that threatened to destroy the heartland of Western civilization. Overall, the region had a substantial and talented population (285 million in 1950) and an adequate resource base. But Europe's industrial and agricultural economies were geared to eighteen small, protective national markets. Even today, thirteen countries have fewer than 10 million citizens each, and only four—West Germany, Britain, Italy, and France—have populations larger than 50 million. Productivity inside these national compartments has mostly been geared to the size of the national population; the large investments and huge enterprises common in the economies of the United States and the Soviet Union were beyond the reach of any single nation. Trapped between Communist Russia to the east and the United States to the west, divided Europe seemed destined to fall steadily behind both superpowers as the twentieth century progressed.

But Europe found a solution to these problems through economic integration, the merger of individual national economies into larger units. The nine-member European Economic Community (the Common Market or EEC) pooled labor, market, and transport to remove trade barriers among its six member nations in stages, starting in 1958. In the east, the Communist satellite countries of Eastern Europe formed a parallel organization, the Council for Mutual Economic Assistance (COMECON). Thus Europe embarked upon a quarter century of sus-

tained economic growth and prosperity. Industrial productivity, particularly in the highly technical fields of electronics and durable consumer goods, increased substantially in Western Europe; and automobiles transformed and integrated resources, production, and population as surely as the railroads had a century earlier. The contrast between the dynamic industrial cores and the less developed areas of Western Europe became more intense, although partially ameliorated by migration from the job-poor countries of the Mediterranean to the labor-hungry industry centers of the north. Overconcentration brought the usual problems of urban slums, pollution, and crowding, but indicative (rather than imperative) government planning, a mixture iof socialism and capitalism, worked to provide basic services and continued economic growth while preserving the central ideals of liberal democracy. Through cooperation rather than competition, Europeans enjoy standards of living second only to those of North America. In this sense, Europe provides a model for economic progress for the states of Latin America, Africa, Southeast Asia, and the Middle East, which have found difficulty in fostering industrial growth and competing in the world economy.

ECONOMIC INTEGRATION

The basic idea was as old as the notion of free trade. Adam Smith had enunciated it two centuries earlier as a principle of economic growth: "The division of labor is limited by the extent of the market." A large market makes possible economies of scale, greater specialization among industries and regions, and more economical locations for human activity. Intent upon avoiding the stagnation that characterized the period between the two world wars, European leaders recognized the need for the modernization, technological improvement, and competitiveness that could be achieved in larger geographical contexts. Six nations—West Germany, France, Italy, the Netherlands, Belgium, and Luxembourg—formed the Common Market to accomplish these goals. The much looser European Free Trade Association (EFTA), composed of the "outer seven"—Great Britain, Ireland, Norway, Sweden, Iceland, Switzerland, and Austria (later joined by Portugal)—stood on the perimeter. In 1973, Great Britain, Ireland, and Denmark joined the Common Market, reducing the effectiveness of EFTA. Through these organizations, Europe has again become a dynamic economic center, accounting for 40 percent of world trade, of which two-thirds takes place within Europe itself.

At the end of World War II, Western Europe's economic problems were similar to those following World War I. For nearly a century, this region had depended on international trade to sell industrial products worldwide, which in turn paid for foreign imports of raw materials and food. Many foreign investments had been lost or liquidated; the historical trade relationship with the agricultural countries of Eastern Europe had been blocked by the iron curtain; rising populations in the developing world were consuming food previously exported to Europe; and industrialization had progressed in a number of countries that had not participated in the war. The initial costs of reconstruction were sustained by the United States under the Marshall Plan. Loans, grants, and investments totaling $14 billion were channeled into Western Europe between 1947 and 1952. Within five years after the war, transportation systems and industries were rebuilt, and although housing was in short supply and agriculture recovered more slowly than industry, most European countries had achieved or surpassed prewar levels of production.

During the war, the governments of Europe had organized production, employment, and resource allocation to meet the military crisis. Postwar demands for full employment and welfare programs reinforced this tendency toward government planning, and many European countries developed economies characterized by publicly funded corporations. The Marshall Plan encouraged national planning to avoid the inefficient allocation of resources during reconstruction. In Britain, coal mines, communications, electric utilities, insurance, and the Bank of England were nationalized. Heavy taxation reduced income differences, and a national health program was initiated. In France, economic planning was also accepted, and the same institutions—insurance, communications, banking, and coal mines—were brought under government control. Planning was more cautious in West Germany, however, because close government control raised memories of the Third Reich. But in Scandinavia, extensive programs of social welfare were implemented. In Eastern Europe, command economies using central planning of the Soviet type were imposed on the satellite countries. The new economic order, based on national planning, expanded into international regional planning. By 1949, Paul Hoffman, the administrator of the Marshall Plan, was encouraging "the formation of a single large market within which quantitative restrictions on the movements of goods . . . and, eventually all tariffs, are permanently swept away." Hoffman was anticipating nothing less than the integration of the entire Western European economy.

A most important step in this direction occurred in 1951, when France, West Germany, Belgium, the Netherlands, Luxembourg, and Italy agreed to place their coal and steel industries under a single authority, the European Coal and Steel Community (ECSC). The principal motive for this union was to end the historical rivalry between France and Germany: the French feared an independent West German industrial complex in the Ruhr; the West Germans preferred a European union to internationalization or

occupation of the Ruhr. Yet the European Coal and Steel Community was not an unqualified success. With mines getting deeper, labor costs rising, and petroleum products competing for the energy market, the coal industry stagnated. Ultimately the union was forced to set up a social fund to aid unemployed, displaced miners. In steel, by contrast, expanding domestic and world markets led to rapid development and modernization, and even Italy, lacking sizable coal and iron resources, expanded production significantly. More important from a political viewpoint, the European Coal and Steel Community established patterns of cooperation among the member states that led to the formation of the European Common Market.

The six members of the European Coal and Steel Community reorganized into a more effective economic union in 1958. The goals of the European Economic Community were wider, envisioning social and political integration as well as economic cooperation. First, internal barriers to trade were progressively abolished over a period of ten years. Goods flowed freely from country to country, and when the process was complete in 1968, mutual trade had tripled in volume. Second, a common tariff on external trade was imposed on goods flowing into the Common Market, discriminating against those European nations, especially Britain, that had failed to join, as well as against non-European competitors such as the United States and Japan. Despite these barriers, the increasing prosperity of the Common Market countries attracted a great volume of imports, and trade with nonmember nations doubled in the first decade of its existence. In 1968, free international movement of labor was allowed in the Common Market, providing manpower from depressed agricultural regions of southern Europe for the industrial areas of northwestern Europe. Finally, in 1973, Britain and Ireland withdrew from EFTA and, along with Denmark, joined the Common Market. The dream of an economically unified Europe with a population equal in scale to the United States or the Soviet Union was realized. Closely joined in the pursuit of affluence and economic growth, the member nations did not, however, relinquish political sovereignty. The hopes of the founders of the Common Market for a political union in the form of a United States of Europe, a "second America in the West" as Jean Monnet called it, have not been realized.

THE PURSUIT OF AFFLUENCE

A keen awareness of the economic, political, and social limitations of their small national size propelled Europeans toward economic integration. A century earlier, Japan had been rudely awakened to a more advanced technology; now Europeans—the founders of the Industrial Revolution—were bracketed between two superpowers, the United States and Russia, whose military and industrial potential completely overshadowed their own. The old leaders, Winston Churchill and Charles de Gaulle, still spoke compellingly about the British Empire and the glory of France, but two wars and a depression had shattered those old dreams. Modern politicians discussed tariffs and wages, employment and price supports, topics less grand than the old ones, but more realistic to a European populace painfully adjusting to its own diminished world role. Most leaders recognized that Europe had fallen sharply behind the United States and Russia in technology, power, and productivity; if this recognition was galling, it was also an impetus for change.

The people of Western Europe, weary of war, demanded social and economic reform and a just measure of stability and prosperity from their respective governments. Complacent assumptions about the superiority of European culture and society lingered on in some circles, but the old order had been discredited. An emerging class of technocrats—industrialists, politicians, and labor leaders—spurred by the example of America and Russia as the samurai of Japan had earlier been goaded by exposure to Europeans, undertook a quiet revolution that transformed the industrial and agricultural landscapes of Europe. Except in Eastern Europe where satellite regimes were imposed by Moscow, Communist influence was confined to social reforms within democratic frameworks. Leaders influenced by the remarkably high standard of living in the United States and the comparative deprivation of their own people introduced new techniques and technologies into Europe and launched the Continent on its pursuit of affluence.

Technological renewal and economic integration were the two keys that unlocked this new era of prosperity. National incomes doubled between 1950 and 1960 and again between 1960 and 1970 in most countries. The greatest gains were recorded in Spain and Greece, where the late arrival of the full effects of the Industrial Revolution caused sudden social shifts and fostered rapid economic growth. But in all countries, regional differences between the wealth of the industrial cores and metropolitan centers and the poverty of rural areas intensified, as did problems of crowding and pollution generated by migration to cities and the more affluent life led in them.

Although many people did not fully participate in this economic miracle, European life and livelihood changed dramatically. A consumer society took root in the 1950s and 1960s when families purchased

The supermarket, symbol of American-style affluence, has spread throughout Western Europe in the postwar period as European life styles have changed with new prosperity. This is the Kaufpark supermarket near Frankfurt in West Germany. *Photo:* **Christa Armstrong/Rapho-Photo Researchers.**

automobiles, television sets, refrigerators, and other household appliances just as Americans had first done in the 1920s. Industries that supplied consumer goods expanded rapidly compared with the declining iron and coal industries, which formed pockets of poverty and social tension in many countries. Skyscrapers changed the look of cities; supermarkets began to replace groceries; and chain stores took the place of small shops. Many condemned these developments as a new paganism which was destroying an older, and presumably more ennobling, way of life. In a provocative volume, *The American Challenge,* Jean-Jacques Servan-Schreiber warned that Europe was in decline and that a managerial invasion from across the Atlantic was drowning Western civilization in a sea of mass-produced goods. De Gaulle attacked "dollar colonization." Europeans, however, voted with their pocketbooks for material progress and reshaped the social and industrial configuration of their continent.

INDUSTRIAL RESURGENCE

The industrial resurgence of Europe was based on new techniques, better organization, and greater effi-

In France, a patelin *is a hicktown, two blinks and a dip, a one-horse town. In 1965, the patelin of Plodémet, the town seat of an isolated region in Brittany, was subjected to intensive investigation by teams of professional social scientists interested in recording contemporary social change in a small town. Plodémet (population 1200) preserves traditional Breton language, customs, and foods. Yet its modern economy of small-scale farming and summer tourism depends on national food markets and outsiders' appreciation of its picturesque landscape, isolation, and rural way of life. Like most of the European countryside, Plodémet is set apart from the mainstream of modern life and takes pride in local traditions, but also shares an avid desire for modernization.*

The affair of the Maison Kérizit [in Plodémet] was revealing in this respect. An early eighteenth-century three-story house, standing by itself opposite the crossing of the [main] road, it was the oldest secular building in the town. The municipality had bought it in a dilapidated state with the intention of demolishing it to make way for a parking lot. Jean-Claude Le Bail, who is an architect as well as municipal councilor, failed to persuade his colleagues to preserve the building. He appealed to the Ministry of Culture, and the day before the demolition was to begin a telegram to the mayor placed the house under the protection of the State, pending further decision.

From then on, passions were inflamed against the house that had been preserved by a "plot"; only a small minority led by Jenny Le Bail and Mme. Luc, a retired schoolmistress, wanted to save it. Mme. Luc launched an "appeal to the authorities to restore the Maison Kérizit to its former splendor," and proposed that it be converted into either a [regional] museum, a youth center, or even a town hall. Eventually, the obstinate municipal council succeeded in having the old house demolished in March 1966.

The few supporters of preservation were . . . isolated individuals, like the educated farmer Cloédic ("It's got something about it"), a union activist ("The façade is beautiful"), the proprietress of the . . . crêperie ("It's very beautiful, we ought to save it"). Among the old peasants, we noted respect for the size of the building, rather than aesthetic admiration. Among the tradespeople, there was marked dislike. "It's a horror. It ought to be pulled down," said Marie of the Café des Droits de l'Homme.

"Certainly, the Maison Kérizit has to be pulled down, mainly because it's ugly. I can't understand how people can like such things," declared Hervé, the pork butcher.

The . . . teen-agers of the town all found it "old, ugly, and ready to be pulled down." The teacher Le Bellec said, "In my opinion, it's not a beautiful building." In the course of the debate in the municipal council a majority judged it to be ugly. "I've no artistic education," one councilor said, "but ordinary people know what's beautiful. . . ."

The anti-Kérizit group published an article in the newspaper Ouest-France (December 1, 1965), complete with photograph, claiming that "this decrepit building stands in the way of traffic development" and "detracts from the beauty of the church and the war memorial." The final outcome was, above all, an aesthetic condemnation of the old-fashioned.

Source: Edgar Morin, *The Red and the White: Report from a French Village* (trans. A. M. Sheridan Smith). New York: Random House, London: Penguin Press, 1970, pp. 213–214. Copyright © 1970 by Random House, Inc.; copyright © 1971 by The Penguin Press. Reprinted by permission of Random House, Inc., and Penguin Books, Ltd.

---

ciency in resource utilization. No new finds of coal or iron, of chemicals or minerals, spurred this growth (the North Sea oil finds are only now coming into production). Nor was there a significant shift in the spatial location of industry, which remained densely clustered in the "golden triangle," the economic heartland of Europe stretching from London to Milan to the Ruhr, and containing the industrial agglomerations of the English southeast, the Paris Basin, the Low Countries, the Ruhr, and the Po Valley. Rather, modernization and innovation in three major industries—steel, chemicals, and automobiles—increased Europe's industrial strength.

The Common Market produces over 120 million tons of steel each year, making its nine members an important market and a formidable competitor for the United States and Japan. In France and West Germany, government and Common Market loans were invested in automating and computerizing steel production, and the Italians developed one of the most modern steel complexes in the world at Taranto in the south. High-grade iron ore is now largely imported from Sweden, Mauritania, Venezuela, and Canada; ports on the North Sea were adapted to take bulk ore carriers, as were Holland's Europoort and Port Talbot in South Wales. The size

The Volkswagen factory at Wolfsburg, West Germany, where finished cars roll off the assembly line at the rate of one every two minutes. By the early 1970s, Common Market countries were producing nearly 9 million cars. *Photo:* Fritz Henle/Rapho-Photo Researchers.

of steel plants increased substantially, and although productivity is still lower than in the United States and Japan, it has improved steadily. A partial shift to coastal locations has occurred in France, the Netherlands, and Belgium, but by and large the steel industry remains tied to traditional locations on the coalfields of Europe.

The chemical and automobile industries particularly benefited from changing patterns of European consumption and the enlarged market created by economic integration. The chemical industry developed at twice the rate of other large-volume industries, accounting for a third of the world's output. Production of plastics and synthetic fibers doubled in West Germany, France, Britain, and Italy between 1960 and 1970. American investment by companies such as Du Pont, Union Carbide, and Monsanto was attracted to the expanding European market; technological and managerial innovations from across the Atlantic were imported intact. By the early 1970s, the Common Market countries were producing nearly 9 million automobiles, and the European auto market was approaching that of the United States in size. Upward of 60 million cars streamed across Western Europe, one for every four people in indus-

trial countries such as Sweden, France, Belgium, and West Germany, and one for every ten or more in Ireland, Portugal, Spain, and Greece. The largest manufacturers—Fiat, Volkswagen, Renault/Peugeot, British Leyland, and the American Big Three (General Motors, Ford, and Chrysler)—expanded to fill domestic demand and entered world markets. Assembly plants for European automobiles are scattered throughout the Third World and even in Canada and Russia. In France, the car industry now absorbs a quarter of national steel production, and the Fiat plant at Turin is the social and economic backbone of the industrial complex in the Italian north. Heavily infiltrated by American investment, which controls one-half of British, one-third of West German, and 15 percent of French production, the automobile industry has become critical to the European economy.

Despite these impressive industrial gains, European leaders were deeply concerned when a technological gap between Europe and the United States was revealed in the late 1960s. The United States, it was discovered, was spending six times as much on industrial research and development as the Common Market and three times as much as Western Europe as a whole. For Europeans, dependent on technological advancement for their high standards of living, it was a shock. In advanced technological fields such as computers, nuclear energy, and space, Europe is not competitive with either Russia or the United States. Discoveries in data processing, telecommunications, meteorology, and oceanography—all regarded as fields of the future—are being rapidly developed without European competition. In computers, for example, the market in Europe is increasing at a rate of 20 percent a year, but American corporations, notably International Business Machines, are the principal suppliers. Boeing aircraft outsell European equivalents even in the tariff-protected Common Market. In nuclear energy, the Euratom project stumbled on national differences; dependence on the United States for military and space hardware leaves Western Europe a bystander in fields that will shape the social, economic, and industrial structure of Europe in the future. British prime minister Harold Wilson called for action, lest Europeans become "industrial hewers of wood and drawers of water." Few agreed with the economist Lord Keynes, who, when asked if this technological gap meant that Britain would become the forty-ninth state, glumly replied, "no such luck."

Part of the problem was that large European industrial companies such as Phillips in Holland, Fiat in Italy, and Imperial Chemical Industries in Britain had outgrown their small domestic markets, but genuinely European corporations comparable in scale to the industrial giants of Russia and the United States had not emerged. Strong national affiliations and loyalties slowed such mergers. For example, the joining of the Fiat and Citroën automobile corporations was first opposed by de Gaulle and then approved in limited form in 1968. Education was a second factor in creating the gap. Considerably fewer children finish secondary school in the Common Market countries than in either Japan or the United States. Moreover, social status plays an important role in university attendance, with the upper class, perhaps 4 to 5 percent of the total population, contributing one-third to one-half of the university population. The impact on industrial management is direct: whereas 80 percent of Japan's industrial managers had university educations in the early 1970s and half the members of Russia's elite were scientists, only 30 percent of Britain's industrial leaders were similarly qualified. In France, women account for only 2 percent of all engineering graduates; in Britain, 0.1 percent. In Russia, the figure is 35 percent. Further, as many as 50,000 to 60,000 scientists, doctors, and engineers migrate across the Atlantic each year to seek their fortunes in more dynamic industries, universities, and laboratories in North America. Since Europe, no longer a primary producer of industrial staples, must live by its wits and must export technology and services to the world, these losses of human resources (the brain drain) are of crucial importance to its future.

A second set of problems in Europe's industrial progress is generated by increasing dependence on imports of energy. With 9 percent of the world's population, Western Europe consumes 20 percent of

the world's total energy output and refines 30 percent of the world's oil. For every four units of energy produced, six must be imported—and energy consumption is increasing by nearly 10 percent a year. As in other parts of the technological world, petroleum has replaced coal as the principal source of industrial energy and accounts for two-thirds of Europe's consumption. Dependence on foreign oil, three-quarters of it from the six Middle Eastern countries of Libya, Kuwait, Saudi Arabia, Iraq, Iran, and Algeria, places Europe in a delicate position, particularly since the price of oil has been sharply increased and threats of boycott became, for a time, reality. Hydroelectric power is important in Switzerland, Italy, France, and parts of Scandinavia; sixty nuclear power plants were in operation in Western Europe in 1970. But for most nations, dependence on imported energy has precipitated a financial crisis of major proportions that may only be relieved if and when North Sea oil deposits are brought into full production in the early 1980s.

Compounding this adverse energy balance has been a steady decline in Western Europe's coal mining industry, which provides 30 percent of total energy needs and dropped in absolute production from 463 million tons in 1960 to 349 million tons in 1970. The rapid and unplanned exploitation of major coalfields in the nineteenth century produced an uncoordinated network of mines, factories, and towns. Many of these mines have now closed, mining employment has dropped, and some of the oldest industrial regions have become depressed areas. In the Ruhr, which contains a tenth of the West German population and produces nearly three-quarters of its coal, iron, and steel and a substantial part of its chemicals, employment in the coal industry dropped by 200,000 in the 1960s and local iron mines closed when reliance on high-quality ores from imported sources increased. Similarly, in South Wales, the number of coal miners dropped from 85,000 to 36,000 during the 1960s. Unemployment has been alleviated by the introduction of new industries, retraining of the younger miners, and a variety of welfare programs, but as in America's Appalachia, these efforts have met with limited success. In a landscape dotted with obsolete factories, old-fashioned mines, and poor housing, and plagued by widespread air and water pollution, textile manufacture and mining have become depressed industries, their workers social casualties.

THE DECLINE OF INDUSTRIAL SOUTH WALES

those who cannot leave face a future as bleak as the landscape. Modern technological change has largely bypassed the obsolete factories and deep mines of South Wales. The land, long laid waste by industrial activity, is dotted with slag heaps; the rivers are polluted by tin-plate, sheet-tin, and galvanizing works and steel mills.

South Wales, with a population of 1.8 million in 1970, is a coal-based industrial region now in decline. Mines have closed, unemployment is high, and government efforts to create planned communities and build new steel factories have met with limited success. Young people leave the region for opportunities in London and other metropolises;

After: John Bartholomew & Son, Ltd., *The Bartholomew-Scribner Atlas of Europe.* New York: Charles Scribner's Sons; London: Frederick Warne & Co., 1974, p. 45. Copyright © 1974 by John Bartholomew & Son, Ltd., and Frederick Warne & Co., Ltd. Used by permission of Charles Scribner's Sons, New York; and John Bartholomew & Son, Ltd., and Frederick Warne & Co., Ltd., publishers of *The Atlas of Europe.*

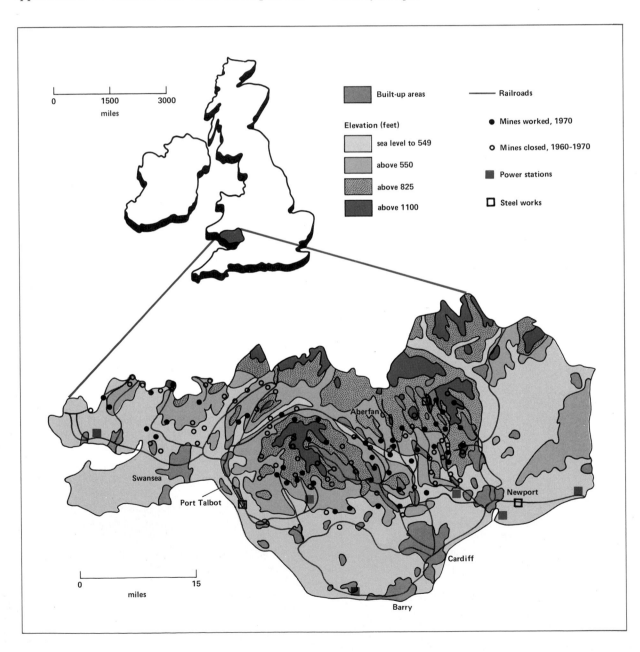

MODERN AGRICULTURE
[TABLE 1]

Europe's farmers were also drastically affected by the industrial resurgence of the Continent. Rapid population growth in the nineteenth century was accompanied by agricultural expansion as the remnants of feudalism slipped away. The European *arable*• expanded in most regions; machines came to the farm as more extensive markets encouraged modernization. The nationalism of the Belle Epoque and then war led to a drive for agricultural self-sufficiency in most countries. Indeed, Germany's collapse in World War I demonstrated the harsh fate that awaited nations which lacked an organized food base. Even politically neutral countries such as Sweden and Switzerland designed agricultural policies to produce as much food as possible from their own resources. Only Britain, confident of her control of the sea lanes of the world, revoked agricultural subsidies (as Adam Smith suggested) in favor of less expensive imported food from former colonies such as Canada, Australia, and New Zealand.

The principal effect of this siege mentality on European agriculture was to encourage farmers to remain on the land. After World War II, significant areas of Western Europe, poorly endowed by nature, were still being farmed by small holders producing the highest priced food in the world. Two-thirds of the farms in the future Common Market countries were smaller than 25 acres. Only 3 percent were larger than 125 acres and these were concentrated on the fertile expanses of the Beauce Plain south of Paris, the Rhône Delta, and the Po Valley. Even the industrious farmers of Denmark and Holland were hard-pressed to compete in world markets because the small national hinterlands they served prior to economic integration did not encourage efficient production. Only Britain, whose policies had already driven small farmers off the land and into the cities, had a sound agricultural economy.

As a result, when the Common Market formed, European agriculture faced major problems. With too many farmers, and particularly too many inefficient farmers, the income gap between industrial workers and agriculturalists widened significantly. Rural poverty became a dangerous political issue in France, West Germany, and Italy. When farmers began to use chemical fertilizers, improved seeds, and new techniques of production in an effort to better their incomes, the resulting overproduction at prices far above world market levels became a critical issue. Further, the less efficient farmers in more isolated parts of the Continent, in regions untapped by rail lines, became vulnerable to competition from outside areas because of the introduction of truck transport.

As late as 1960, a third of all workers in France, Austria, Ireland, and Norway and a fifth in West Germany, Denmark, Switzerland, and Sweden were still farmers. Around the Mediterranean, farmers formed half the work force in Spain, Portugal, and Greece, and 40 percent of the workers in Italy. Although 400,000 farmers had left the land every year since 1950, there were still 12 million agriculturalists in the original six Common Market countries in 1970. The sheer scale of the farm problem made agriculture a sensitive political issue, perhaps the most difficult the Common Market faced in effecting economic integration. The Common Market decided to guarantee farmers high prices for their products, to protect them from outside competition by import tariffs, and to expand food exports through government supports guaranteeing farmers prices equal to those on world markets.

The Common Agricultural Policy of the EEC immediately led to gross overproduction. High prices created massive surpluses of wheat, butter, and sugar. France and Denmark were producing wheat for export, as were Sweden and Finland, but the costs of production rendered the price of the European crop substantially higher than the world market would allow. By 1970, an enormous 400,000 tons of surplus butter had accumulated, a "butterberg" that one wag noted was equal to the weight of the total population of Austria. With subsidized prices, farmers produced more, and urbanites paid three times the world price for butter while surpluses were dumped in foreign countries at great losses. Large surpluses of sugar beets in Belgium, Luxembourg, France, and Denmark produced a similar market situation in sugar. Drastic structural reforms were clearly needed. With the entrance of Britain into the Common Market in 1973, it has been proposed that 5 million European farmers be encouraged to leave the land and that the agricultural acreage of Western Europe be cut by a tenth.

The European farmers that the Common Agricultural Policy now envisions retiring, retraining, and moving off the land have already been strongly influenced by the transportation revolution that occurred when Europe truly entered the automobile age in the 1950s. The network of *central places*• in Western Europe was established in the age of foot and water traffic. The railroad grid, superimposed on existing settlements in the nineteenth century, did not substantially alter this locational matrix. Great as the indirect effects of railroads were on European agriculture, they did not reach down to reorganize the structure of farming in large stretches of rural

The poverty of isolated rural areas in Europe stands in sharp contrast to the affluence elsewhere. These Spanish farmers still bring in the harvest the traditional way. *Photo:* Oppersdorff/Rapho-Photo Researchers.

France, Germany, and Holland. But the automobile penetrated these regions, exposing the upland farmers who account for much of the cultural variety and economic poverty in Europe to new competitive forces. As the spatial dimensions of markets shift and expand, hill towns in central Italy, southern France, and parts of Austria are dwindling in size, wiping out settlements whose occupants have farmed the land and tended herds for generations.

Cars and trucks have also rationalized agricultural marketing, driving small, uneconomic farms deeper into debt. Refrigerated trucks can easily bring fresh meat to most rural regions, and small local slaughterhouses and meat markets are being driven out of business. For centuries, local municipalities operated their own meat markets, drawing on local supplies and taxing townspeople for their meat. Only in Scandinavia and the Netherlands was agricultural marketing unchaotic before World War II. In the mid-1960s there were nearly 6000 commercial slaughterhouses in the Common Market countries, compared with 15 in the American Midwest. With the advent of new, highly mechanized livestock facilities drawing on wider hinterlands, many of these old slaughterhouses have closed, and even the famous central food market of Paris, Les Halles, has moved to suburban Rungis to take advantage of highway connections. Both food processing (flour and sugar beets) and commodity marketing (eggs, fruits,

and vegetables) are being restructured across the Continent. While these new facilities and marketing procedures are bringing efficiency and lower food costs, the highly diversified European landscapes geographers have described with such enthusiasm are gradually disappearing, and large zones of rural underdevelopment and poverty today stand in juxtaposition to prosperous, but crowded, industrial cores.

Between 1960 and 1970, the number of farms in Western Europe fell by more than 100,000 each year. This was an unprecedented flight from the land, even greater than the rural exodus that marked the early phase of the Industrial Revolution. Large acreages throughout Europe were abandoned or lost to urbanization during 1960–1970: 3.4 million acres in France, 2 million in Sweden, 1.7 million in West Germany, and 1.5 million in Britain. In Portugal, Spain, Greece, southern Italy, and Ireland, high rates of rural unemployment and low incomes launched a stream of migrants into the major industrial zones in northern Italy, France, West Germany, and Britain. In 1973, West Germany employed over 2 million foreign workers; most were from Turkey, Yugoslavia, Italy, and Greece. France drew slightly fewer from Mediterranean Europe and North Africa. The Irish continued to flow into industrial Britain, and one of three jobs in Switzerland was held by a foreigner. This transnational migration from rural areas has reorganized the social fabric of Europe, disrupting the "ordered whole," as the French anthropologist Levi-Strauss calls it, that existed in the region until the middle of this century.

Urban poverty is also characteristic of the backward pockets of Western Europe. This Naples street scene is typical. *Photo:* Carl Frank/Rapho-Photo Researchers.

TABLE 1. Regional Differences, 1971

Source: Overseas Development Council, *The U.S. and the Developing World: Agenda for Action, 1974.* New York: Praeger, 1974, pp. 148–153.

Country	Per capita income ($)	Life expectancy (years)	Infant mortality per 1000 births	Percentage literate
W. Germany	$3210	71	23	99%
Netherlands	2620	74	11	98
Greece	1250	69	27	80
Portugal	730	68	50	63
Turkey	340	54	119	46
Morocco	260	51	149	14

The disintegration of traditional rural communities in parts of Western Europe has precipitated a serious problem of regional underdevelopment in central and southern France, the Alps, southern Italy, northern Britain, and Scandinavia. Part of the problem is environmental: the northern climates are suited only to raising animals, and overproduction of dairy products in these restricted environments is driving marginal farmers off the land; in France, the rocky and barren lands of the Massif Central, the Pyrénées, and the Alps are not profitable in terms of modern agriculture; in many parts of the Mediterranean, eroded soils, cultivated since antiquity, are exhausted. The economies of these regions are deteriorating rapidly, although in most countries, regional planners have attempted to stem the tide by encouraging decentralization of industrial growth. Factories have been implanted in Brittany and in central and southwestern France in an effort to create nuclei that will spur local economic revivals. Italy envisions a ten-year allocation of public investment to the poorest, most backward parts of the country: the Mezzogiorno, Sicily, and Sardinia. In Britain, incentives are given new industrial ventures to locate outside the London conurbation to create a more balanced regional growth. But the costs of combating rural poverty are frequently complicated by cultural differences, and inflation, mounting social demands, and high energy costs make it questionable whether this balance can be achieved.

ENVIRONMENTAL POLLUTION
[FIGURE 7]

The continued growth of urban industrial centers at the expense of the rural fringes in Western Europe has led to dense concentrations of people and industry. Over the last century, the amount of land available per person has been halved, so that today 335 million Europeans live in an area one-third the size of the United States. Twenty-eight European metropolitan areas have populations of 1 million or more; all are capital cities, ports, or industrial centers. Urbanites form better than 60 percent of the populations of Britain, West Germany, France, the Netherlands, Belgium, Luxembourg, Sweden, and Iceland. In Denmark, Norway, Ireland, and Portugal most of the people still live on the land, but their number dwindles yearly. With nearly 220 million people living in cities, an average density of nearly 300 people per square mile, and an industrial economy, Europe, not surprisingly, has serious environmental pollution. Pollution controls, expensive additions to any industry, have met with substantial corporate resistance. And, perhaps most important, much of Europe's industrial plant was created before pollution was perceived as an evil.

Air Pollution
With local exceptions, automobile exhaust has affected the structure and the feel of every city in Europe, and increased use of high-sulfur petroleum from the Middle East for industry and domestic heating has also raised air pollution levels. Today, Euro-

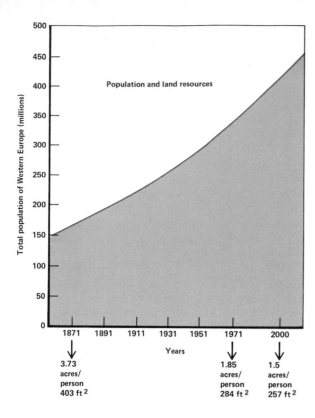

Population and land resources

Total population of Western Europe (millions)

500, 450, 400, 350, 300, 250, 200, 150, 100, 50, 0

Years: 1871, 1891, 1911, 1931, 1951, 1971, 2000

↓ 3.73 acres/ person 403 ft² (1871)

↓ 1.85 acres/ person 284 ft² (1971)

↓ 1.5 acres/ person 257 ft² (2000)

Figure 7. Competition for Land. The land-use patterns of contemporary Western Europe stem from the concentrations of city dwellers that followed the course of nineteenth-century industrialization. In Britain, the Netherlands, Belgium, and Germany, population densities now range between 700 and 1000 people per square mile—about one acre of land per person. In contrast, Ohio, for example, had 243 people per square mile in 1973. *After: John Bartholomew & Sons, Ltd., The Bartholomew-Scribner Atlas of Europe. New York: Charles Scribner's Sons; London: Frederick Warne & Co., 1974, p. 70. Copyright © 1974 by John Bartholomew & Son, Ltd., and Frederick Warne & Co., Ltd. Used by permission of Charles Scribner's Sons, New York; and John Bartholomew & Son, Ltd., and Frederick Warne & Co., Ltd., publishers of The Atlas of Europe.*

pean governments are enacting harsh clean air legislation.

After a smog over London in December 1952 was declared medically responsible for some 3000 to 4000 deaths, public demands for the improvement of air began. During the next decade, a series of clean air acts was put into effect in Britain to control smoke and levels of particulate emissions. By 1970, smoke levels had fallen by more than half and sulfur dioxide concentrations by a third. Winter sunshine levels showed remarkable improvement. West Germany has recently enacted a stringent antipollution bill to accomplish this same purpose, adopting the Japanese formula of forcing polluters to pay. In addition, France, Belgium, the Netherlands, and Italy have passed or are considering various pollution-control measures, from limitations on emissions from gas and diesel engines to control of industrial wastes.

The international dimensions of pollution problems in Europe are clearly demonstrated by recent Scandinavian claims that industrial air pollution in northwestern Europe, particularly Britain, has increased the level of acid in the rain and snow that fall in Norway and Sweden. Holt-Jensen, a Swedish geographer, has been able to trace the source of high sulfate and acid levels in Scandinavian precipitation to the heavily industrialized areas south and west of the North Sea, and since 1971 he has successfully predicted the incidence of acid rains. Temperature inversions and stagnant air over the Midlands or the Ruhr create masses of pollutant-saturated air which the general westerly circulation of the atmosphere then carries north and east. Rain from this airmass falls on Scandinavia, and gray snow (from soot and ash) and rain with a high level of sulfuric acid are deposited on the peninsula. The already high acidity of the soils of Scandinavia (mostly **podzols**•) and the sensitivity of vegetative growth to the acid solution falling on it give cause for immediate concern. Significant changes in the acid levels of rivers have led to fish kills in some cases.

Sorting out the causes and costs of air pollution among the small, crowded nations of Western Europe demands complex scientific as well as political strategies. The nine-member Common Market is attempting to forge a common environmental policy, but its successful implementation will require an unprecedented degree of cooperation.

Water Pollution
[FIGURE 8]

Water pollution is more intense, or at least more apparent, in Western Europe than air pollution. Most large cities are located on rivers that provide water for domestic and industrial purposes. As the European population has grown and become more concentrated, urban and industrial pollution has severely damaged the rivers. In France, the distribution of polluted rivers coincides almost directly with population density; the waters of the Seine, Rhône, Loire, and Garonne, as well as the canals of the industrial north, are chronically polluted. In the Netherlands, river water can be neither drunk nor used on gardens without filtration. In Britain, clean water acts have revived the Thames, but an estimated 2000 miles of polluted inland waterways remain. Even the alpine lakes of Switzerland, West Germany, Italy, and France are contaminated by airborne pollutants deposited on glaciers and by domestic sewage. The fish populations of Lake Geneva and Lake Constance have diminished rapidly. Measurements at Lake Maggiore in the Italian Alps indicate an input of 2400 tons of nitrates and 600 tons of phosphates each year. At Lake Lugano, hydrogen sulfide in the

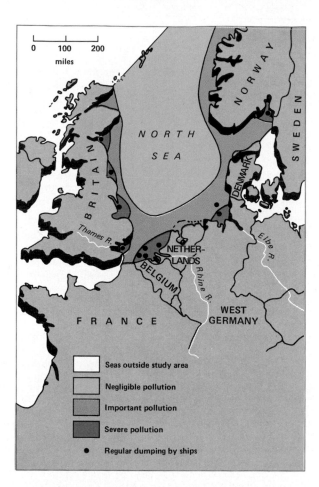

Figure 8. Pollution of the North Sea. Streams from nine north European countries flow into the North Sea. Along its southern shores—near Britain, Belgium, The Netherlands, Germany, and southern Sweden—water pollution is severe. Heavy industrial concentrations, high population densities, and offshore marine traffic all contribute to the environmental decline of this important water body. *After:* Günter Weichart, "The North Sea," *Environment,* Vol. 16 (1974), p. 32, Fig. 1. Copyright © 1974 by Scientists' Institute for Public Information.

water has led to temporary bans on swimming. To the south, the beaches of the Riviera must be regularly sprayed to limit the spread of communicable diseases such as cholera and to dissolve the tar dropped by tankers carrying Middle Eastern oil.

Some forty international conferences have been held in Europe over the last 100 years to discuss water pollution, many of them concerned with the Rhine River. Despite this attention, pollution in the Rhine has risen with population density and industrial growth, reaching critically toxic levels. As the Rhine flows northward, it passes through five different countries and a near-continuous band of dense urbanization and heavy industry. Waste water and sewage from Basel's 373,000 inhabitants and dyestuffs from large chemical factories begin the process, so that by the time the river reaches Strasbourg,

swimming is forbidden. Along the French border, potash mines around Mulhouse dump 7.5 million tons of salt a year into the Rhine, a full 40 percent of the total, and a primary reason water must be desalinized before agricultural use in the Netherlands. In West Germany, chemical industries at Ludwigshafen contribute their poisons to the Rhine, and the Neckar River, which joins the Rhine after serving as the sewage disposal system for Stuttgart and Tübingen, adds more pollutants. At Koblenz, the seat of the international pollution commission, nuclear plants constructed on the banks of the river raise water temperatures and encourage bacterial action, thereby reducing the water's oxygen level. Farther north, industrial wastes from the Lorraine iron mines, the Saar coalfields, and more potash mines pour into the river. Thereafter, the Rhine enters the industrial Ruhr, and when it crosses the Dutch border at Emmerich, it is carrying a staggering total of 24 million tons of solid waste a year, 66,750 tons a day. Industries depend on the Rhine, some 17,000 vessels a year ply its waterways, and nearly 20 million people rely directly or indirectly on it for domestic water.

The process continues. The Rhine and other rivers from nine north European nations ultimately dump their waste materials into the North Sea, one of the most heavily polluted water bodies in the world. Salts from potash mines, phosphates in urban sewage, heavy metal wastes from steel mills, and agricultural pesticides flow into the North Sea in unmodified form. Some 15,000 tons of phosphorus and 60,000 tons of fixed nitrogen reach the North Sea from the east coast of Britain each year; an additional 40,000 tons of phosphorus and 500,000 tons of fixed nitrogen come from the Rhine, Elbe, Weser, and Ems rivers. The Rhine alone contributes 80,000 tons of iron, 20,000 tons of zinc, 6000 tons of manganese, and more than 1000 tons of chromium, nickel, copper, lead, and arsenic. Additional pollutants are introduced by shipping, the development of offshore oil, and direct dumping of colliery wastes, London sludge, titanium dioxide, and various organic chemicals and radioactive substances. Since the North Sea is cleansed by water from the Atlantic circulating around Scotland in the north and west, pollution concentrates in the south of the North Sea, the area most heavily used and most densely ringed by population.

Pollution is symptomatic of a deterioration in the quality of the European environment that has paralleled this region's remarkable surge to affluence in the postwar period. Urban congestion, traffic, inadequate housing, and excessive noise are now characteristic of most European metropolises; yet, expanding urban economies continue to attract increasing numbers of people. Although planners have partially disrupted this flow through devices such as London's greenbelt, concentration intensifies.

A NEW WORLD ROLE

In the summer of 1975, the leaders of thirty-five nations converged on Helsinki to acknowledge the postwar frontiers of Europe. Except for Albania, all Europe was represented; the United States and Canada rounded out the group. The document produced, a masterpiece of evasive language, confirms Soviet dominance in Eastern Europe and the existing division of the Continent into two separate social and economic worlds. The largest gathering of European heads of state since the Congress of Vienna in 1815, the conference was nonetheless curiously obsolete. Europe is no longer the headquarters of the world, and disputes over its national boundaries, which earlier in this century precipitated wars, seem minor in a world governed by larger, more powerful societies and caught up in the problems of development in the Third World. For Europeans themselves, the central question was not how to strengthen their respective frontiers, but how to weaken the confining political and economic bonds national borders placed on material progress. In the modern age, it seems that only countries continental in scope, like Russia and the United States, can successfully develop within their own national frontiers. And it is questionable how long even these superpowers can maintain their relative self-sufficiency.

To meet this challenge, proponents of European political and economic integration envision a united Europe comparable in size and resources to the United States and Russia. Under a single political leadership, they argue, Western Europe can regain a prominent place in world affairs, a place it lost almost overnight when empires dissolved and 500 million colonial people became citizens of independent nations. Gone are the days when twenty-one civil servants and twelve policemen could secure British rule over 17.5 million people in Bengal, as they did in 1907. Even when Europeans tried desperately to maintain their colonial possessions—as, for example, the Portuguese did in Angola and Mozambique —the price in blood and treasure proved too high. Decolonization signified the demographic and economic dwarfing of Europe. This enforced withdrawal from world governance has had a profound psychological effect on Europeans and was a principal force behind the establishment of the Common Market. While still maintaining strong relationships with former colonies, Europeans have turned inward on themselves in search of a new geographical solution to their diminished economic and political position in the twentieth century.

The Common Market, Europe's most compelling example of cooperation, remains, despite the visions of its founding fathers, an elaborate customs union forged for mutual economic benefit. Yet it is successful beyond measure. Whether the next logical step, political union, will become a reality depends on the strength of cultural and national allegiances compared with opposing economic pressures for international merger. If a united Europe should arise— and countries such as Germany and Italy were themselves born of such ideals in earlier times—Western Europe would provide a model for integration in such geographically incoherent areas of the developing world as Central America, South America, and Africa, whose national resource bases are too limited to fulfill the aspirations of their people.

WESTERN EUROPE

THE INDUSTRIAL BASE

ENERGY AND MINERAL RESOURCES MAP

Virtually any map of Western Europe—depicting transportation networks, population distribution, urban centers, or land use—reflects the crucial role of industrial resources and production in the complexion of the region. European statistics document the high productivity of this society; methods of increasing industrial productivity, the source of Europe's affluence, preoccupy political leaders, labor unions, and the populace at large. The industrial base of Western Europe, therefore, is central to its human geography, and this has been true for some time.

PREINDUSTRIAL PATTERNS

A number of important centers of specialized manufacturing predated the Industrial Revolution in Europe. Capitalizing on the skills of craft workers in trade guilds, on locally available mineral or agricultural resources (wool, leather, iron ore, lead), or on favorable locations in the links of land and water trade routes, these centers developed a tradition of manufacturing, and their products were widely known. But before the technological revolution swept over Britain in the eighteenth century and spread to the Continent in the nineteenth, these cities were small and, like their relatively self-sufficient hinterlands, oriented to the fulfillment of local needs first and special manufactures second.

The largest of these early industrial centers were located on the Continent, especially in Mediterranean Europe. A variety of towns such as Toledo, famous for its high-quality steel swords and knives, and Córdoba, known for its supple and artfully designed leatherwork, were dispersed over Europe. But two large regional groupings of cities, specializing in what was then large-scale production of manufactured goods, grew up in northern Italy and Flanders. Northern Italian cities gained wide importance as producers of fine silk textiles, glass,

weapons, and seaworthy ships. The rise of the Italian city-states to medieval eminence resulted from the dominance in Mediterranean trade achieved by the merchants of Venice, Genoa, Milan, and Florence. Although northern Italy declined after the fifteenth century, when the discovery of new trade routes increased the importance of cities open to the Atlantic, this region long retained the reputation of being the most developed part of Europe. To the north, the cities of the Belgian coastal plain, Flanders, experienced a similar economic growth in the 1200s and became the textile center of northern Europe. Bruges, Ghent, and Ypres drew on local supplies of flax and wool and some imports from Spain and Britain to achieve preeminence in the production of woolens and linen. Early stirrings of an industrial revolution can thus be traced to seventeenth-century Europe, to these local centers of specialized manufacture that transformed the specialties of their hinterlands into finished products. It is important to note, however, that all these manufacturing centers drew upon readily available, high-quality raw materials and maintained their importance through excellence in production and political dominance. Thus, the iron ore of Toledo, although limited in quantity, was the best known in preindustrial Europe; the silver of the Apennines was worked by Florentine silversmiths of the highest degree of mastery; the same was true for the glassblowers of Venice and the gunsmiths of Liège.

THE INDUSTRIAL REVOLUTION

The Industrial Revolution began with a transition to new energy sources: first waterpower and, somewhat later, coal. Wherever in Europe these new environmental resources could be found, industrial technology eventually followed. The changeover began with waterpower mechanically harnessed by the application of principles of gears and levers first understood by Leonardo da Vinci (1452–1519). The textile industry was transformed by this new technology, and shortly afterward, the steam engine, which could burn wood but was more efficiently run by coal, enlarged industrial possibilities to other manufactures, particularly metals.

The first regional combination of these elements—wool, water, coal, and iron ore—occurred in Yorkshire, which like other European primary manufacturing districts, developed around these basic resources (see Rise, "The Scientific Transformation"). Yorkshire reorganized the spatial structure of its economy from the production and weaving of woolens on cottage farms to the factory production of woolen cloth in riverside mills in Leeds and Bradford at the foot of the Pennines. In the center of this emerging industrial district, at Doncaster, coal mining became the focus of an energy-extraction industry; 15 miles to the southwest, at Sheffield, iron ore deposits had been mined for centuries. With new technologies of steel production, coal brought from Doncaster could be burned to remove the impurities from iron on a scale not previously possible. Other early centers of industry in Britain as well as on the Continent replicated this pattern.

Centers of industry arose according to the availability of sources of energy—coal or waterpower—and the supplies of raw materials awaiting transformation. Cloth and metals were the first manufactures to become "industries." Thus, the textile industry of Lancashire moved to riverfront mills where waterpower could transform into cloth the cotton imported from abroad to the Liverpool docks. Similarly, the metal industry of Sheffield shifted from craftsmen's stalls to machine factories. At the same time, population migrated to expanding mines, furthering the growth of Doncaster as a center of energy extraction specializing not in a finished product but a raw material—coal. Lancashire and Yorkshire are two early examples of primary manufacturing districts in Britain similar to the later developed Ruhr and Saar in Germany, the valleys of the Sambre and Meuse rivers in Belgium, the Pas de Calais and Lorraine in France, the Po Valley in Italy, the Bergslagen in Sweden, and Bilbao and Barcelona in Spain.

Improvements in technology ensured and reinforced the importance of the primary elements of industrialization. The technology of transport—canals, the railroad, and long-distance ocean shipping—made it possible to import large quantities of raw materials and export finished products anywhere in the world. Through progress in production techniques, manufactures previously done only by craftsmen were possible in factories. Colonial ports of trade tapping a world network of raw materials became centers of industry: Liverpool, London, and Amsterdam illustrate this point. The railroad grid of Europe allowed industry to develop wherever the energy sources and raw materials of the Industrial Revolution met.

In Belgium, for example, an axis of industrialization grew up between the port of Antwerp, the seat of government at Brussels, the valleys of the Sambre and the Meuse, and the French border district of the Pas de Calais. As in Yorkshire, the elements of the industrial age came into focus in a small triangle, 90 miles at its widest. Colonial products could be unloaded at Antwerp and shipped to any part of Belgium by rail or canal. Extractive energy—coal from the limited mines near Mons or Liège or from the rich mines of the Saar—was nearby. Iron ore was available from a variety of domestic and foreign sources. Textile, iron, and steel production multiplied rapidly; later, the same factors of industrial location—market, labor supply, raw materials, transportation, energy sources—were at work as cities in Belgium retained textiles, iron, and steel as

the backbone of their economy but expanded to more varied industrial production: finished consumer goods, chemicals, electronics. But Belgium is no longer a closed industrial system. Local deposits of coal and iron ore are exhausted, and Belgium must import iron ore from Sweden, Canada, and Russia, and coal from French or West German sources. And today, Belgium follows the general European trend toward industrial conversion from coal to oil and natural gas.

The problems of Belgian industry, then, are problems of old age. Favored in the early stages of the Industrial Revolution, no other world region contains so many industrial zones based on the local availability of coal, iron ore, and waterpower. The Peninne conurbations, the British Midlands and South Wales, the Ruhr, the Sambre-Meuse, the Pas de Calais, and the Lorraine all evolved on the basis of proximity of resources. Today local mineral deposits are fully exploited, and many have been worked out. Europe's industrial output must diversify, while coping with obsolete factories, inadequate housing, unemployment, and pollution of air, soil, and water—an inheritance from the Industrial Revolution.

ENERGY SOURCES

Dramatic increases in industrial output and standards of living have increased Western Europe's demand for energy. Petroleum, the fuel of the age, must be imported to meet this demand. But the search for alternative sources of energy is perhaps more intense in Western Europe than in any other world region. With 9.2 percent of the world's population, the eighteen nations of Western Europe consume 20 percent of the global energy output.

Coal

[FIGURE 9]

The backbone of European industry has historically been coal, but in 1970 only a declining 30 percent of

Figure 9. Changing Energy Sources in Great Britain. *Adapted from:* Michael Chisholm, ed., *Resources for Britain's Future.* Newton Abbot, Devon: David and Charles, 1970, p. 78, Fig. 1.

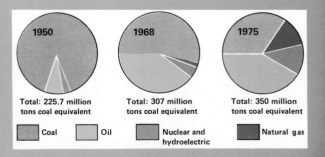

Total: 225.7 million tons coal equivalent

Total: 307 million tons coal equivalent

Total: 350 million tons coal equivalent

☐ Coal   ☐ Oil   ☐ Nuclear and hydroelectric   ☐ Natural gas

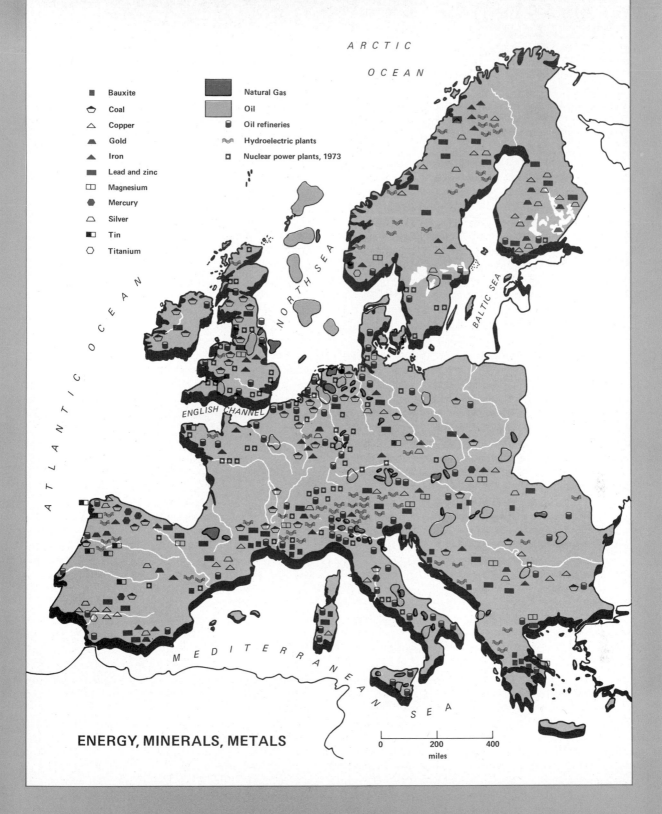

Legend

- ■ Bauxite
- ⬠ Coal
- △ Copper
- ▲ Gold
- ▲ Iron
- ▬ Lead and zinc
- ▭ Magnesium
- ⬢ Mercury
- △ Silver
- ▣ Tin
- ⬡ Titanium

- Natural Gas
- Oil
- 🛢 Oil refineries
- 〰 Hydroelectric plants
- ▢ Nuclear power plants, 1973

ARCTIC OCEAN

ATLANTIC OCEAN

NORTH SEA

BALTIC SEA

ENGLISH CHANNEL

MEDITERRANEAN SEA

ENERGY, MINERALS, METALS

0   200   400

miles

Europe's energy needs were met by coal. Indeed, 1970 coal production was only 75 percent that of 1960, and the coal mining labor force has declined even more sharply. Although several European nations remain significant world producers (the United Kingdom, West Germany, and Austria hold fourth, sixth, and ninth positions, respectively, in world output of coal), Western Europe is a net importer of coal. Exporters of coal within Western Europe include Sweden, France, Norway, and Spain —France being the only country that finds it practical to both export and import coal. Higher world prices for oil may enhance the position of coal in the European economy.

383

Oil and Natural Gas

Western Europe now imports 53 percent of its energy needs in the form of petroleum. It has increased its dependence on petroleum, as have the countries of the developing world and the other technological nations—Japan, the Soviet Union, the United States. Oil refineries are the new coalfields of Europe, and old port cities such as Rotterdam, Amsterdam, Hamburg, Le Havre, and Marseilles have been rejuvenated as refining centers, nodes in a 4400-mile-long pipeline network connecting tanker terminals to inland refineries. No West European country yet produces much petroleum, although minor operating fields are located near Karlsruhe and on the North German Plain (in association with natural gas) in West Germany, in the Paris Basin and near Bordeaux in France, and near Vienna in Austria. All West European nations (except Iceland) produce some natural gas, but only the Netherlands (one of the world's largest fields is near Groningen), the United Kingdom, West Germany, Italy, and France are significant producers. Faced with large trade deficits from the costs of imported Middle Eastern oil and natural gas, northwestern Europe is counting on the development of a major new oil and natural gas field in the shallow bottom of the North Sea. Under United Nations auspices, five nations bordering the North Sea—the United Kingdom, the Netherlands, West Germany, Denmark, and Norway—have settled and mapped concession areas, and some gas and oil fields off north-central England are already in operation. If the full potential energy reserves of the North Sea are realized in the early 1980s, some favored European nations may become energy exporters of global importance.

Alternatives

Coal, oil, and natural gas make up 91 percent of the total energy budget of Europe. But hydroelectricity is well developed and provides 80 percent of the electrical power in Switzerland, 40 percent in France, 35 percent in Italy, and substantial amounts in Austria, Norway, and Sweden. In Scandinavia, the development of hydroelectric reserves following World War II has been instrumental in opening up new mining districts and supporting industrialization in the Arctic north. But the growth of energy demand, nearly 10 percent each year in the 1960s. has been so strong that even Switzerland must now use petroleum to generate electricity. In 1975, most of the best sites for hydroelectric dams were already in use.

In Austria and Italy, possibilities exist for harnessing subterranean hot water to produce geothermal electric power; the French have successfully experimented in the production of electricity from strong tides on the Breton coast. Both geothermal and tidal electricity, however, will remain isolated and at best regionally important energy sources.

More important, Western Europe is turning to nuclear energy as an alternative to both coal and petroleum. With the exceptions of Austria, Luxembourg, Ireland, Portugal, and Iceland, all Western European nations either have or are planning to generate nuclear power. By the mid-1970s, nearly fifty nuclear power plants were in operation; some sixty others were under construction or planned. Britain is already generating 10 percent of its national needs from atomic energy.

MINERALS AND METALS

In Western Europe, heavy demand, thorough domestic exploration and exploitation of local resources, and high production proportional to proved reserves have required large imports of minerals and metals. Iron ore, an essential reserve behind any modern industrialized economy, is found in abundance in Sweden and France, which rank fifth and seventh, respectively, in world production. Even so, the demands of the West European iron and steel industry are such that 64 percent of iron ore must come from outside sources, primarily Canada and the Soviet Union. West Germany alone purchases nearly 20 percent of the iron ore available in world markets.

Western Europe is also an important consumer of nonferrous minerals and metals—aluminum, bauxite, copper, lead, zinc, and tin. West Germany, Sweden, and Norway import 31 percent of the copper sold on the world market; Belgium, Luxembourg, France, and West Germany import 62 percent of exported lead ores; Britain consumes 44 percent of the world market's supply of tin. Sweden is a major producer of lead and zinc; Greece has significant deposits of bauxite; Finland ranks high in zinc output. Some West European countries have deposits of other minerals: West Germany has large deposits of silver; Norway is an exporter of magnesium; Spain is the largest producer of mercury; Finland is a primary source of cobalt and vanadium. But on the whole, the balance of exports versus imports of metal ores requires vast foreign expenditures. Western Europe is likely to become even more import-oriented in the future, requiring the production of large quantities of finished goods to pay for raw materials.

BIBLIOGRAPHY

GENERAL

East, W. Gordon. *An Historical Geography of Europe.* London: Methuen, 1962. A historical geography of settlement and economy prior to the Industrial Revolution.

Gottmann, Jean. *A Geography of Europe.* New York: Holt, Rinehart, & Winston, 1969. Perhaps one of the best volumes of this type ever written; a perceptive regional geography.

Hoffmann, George (ed.). *A Geography of Europe.* New York: Ronald Press, 1975. A well-organized and accurate regional geography of Europe.

Jordan, Terry G. *The European Culture Area: A Systematic Geography.* New York: Harper & Row, 1973. A concise and up-to-date systematic geography.

Langer, William L. (ed.). *Western Civilization: The Struggle for Empire to Europe in the Modern World.* New York: Harper & Row, 1968. A well-written survey of the ascent and decline of modern Europe.

Nystrom, J. Warren, and Peter Malof. *The Common Market: European Community in Action.* Princeton: Van Nostrand Searchlight Series No. 5, 1962. A geographical analysis of economic integration and its political implications.

[1] THE ASCENT OF EUROPE

Dickinson, Robert E. *The West European City.* London: Routledge & Kegan Paul, 1963. A detailed geographical study of form and function.

Habakkuk, H. J., and M. Postan (eds.). *The Cambridge Economic History of Europe,* Vol. VI. London: Cambridge University Press, 1965. The authoritative treatise on the Industrial Revolution.

Hohenberg, Paul. *A Primer on the Economic History of Europe.* New York: Random House, 1968. A lucid introduction to the social and economic forces that swept Europe into the industrial age.

Moller, Herbert (ed.). *Population Movements in Modern European History.* New York: Macmillan, 1964. An excellent collection of articles on the complexities of population in nineteenth- and twentieth-century Europe.

Rostow, Walt W. *How It All Began: Origins of the Modern Economy.* New York: McGraw-Hill, 1975. A skillful interpretation of the events and consequences of the Industrial Revolution.

Tames, Richard. *Economy and Society in Nineteenth-Century Britain.* London: Allen and Unwin, 1972. The impact of the Industrial Revolution on Britain.

Tuchman, Barbara W. *The Proud Tower.* New York: Macmillan, 1966. A brilliant description of culture and society in Europe before World War I.

[2] THE QUEST FOR UNITY

Barzanti, Sergio. *The Underdeveloped Areas Within the Common Market.* Princeton: Princeton University Press, 1965. An outline of underdevelopment in southern Italy and central France and, by analogy, in other pockets of poverty in modern Europe.

Beck, Robert H., et al. *The Changing Structure of Europe: Economic, Social, and Political Trends.* Minneapolis: University of Minnesota Press, 1970. An interdisciplinary survey of the postwar transformation of European land and life.

Browne, Geoffrey S. (ed.). *Atlas of Europe: A Profile of Western Europe.* New York: Scribner, 1974. More than simply an atlas; a penetrating statistical description of changing conditions in Europe.

Council of Europe. *Freshwater Pollution Control in Europe.* Hamburg, 1966; *European Conference on Air Pollution.* Strasbourg, 1964. Two of a number of Common Market reports on environmental conditions in Europe, marked by political rhetoric, but basic documents none the less.

Graubard, Stephen R. (ed.). *A New Europe?* Boston: Houghton Mifflin, 1964. Essays on the possible political future of modern Europe.

de La Mahotière, Stuart. *Towards One Europe.* Middlesex, England: Penguin Books, 1970. An analysis of the European Common Market.

Ney, John. *The European Surrender: A Descriptive Study of the American Social and Economic Crisis.* Boston: Little, Brown, 1970. A well-written argument that all Europe is Americanized.

Thomas, David. *London's Green Belt.* London: Faber, 1970. One of a number of geographical studies delineating problems of the urban environment and planning efforts to correct them.

RUSSIA

И. В. СТАЛИН.

Stalin as a young revolutionary in his native Georgia. *Photo:* Wide World.

On February 5, 1945, according to *Time*, Joseph Stalin was "the most important person in the world." The week's news had been climactic: Russian armies, having broken German resistance, were rolling across the plains of Poland into eastern Germany. Industrial Silesia had been captured; East Prussia was cut off from the Reich; the German eastern front lay in ruins. The armies of Romania, Bulgaria, Hungary, and Finland had been knocked out of the war; Czechoslovakia had fallen to national partisans, and the Germans had withdrawn from Greece. In two years, the Soviet Union had recovered from a crushing 1300-mile Nazi thrust into the Russian interior, had blunted the German advance, and was systematically destroying the invading German armies.

The final defeat of the Third Reich was nearing, and Allied political leaders were deeply concerned about the future shape of Europe. The Russian front sliced 800 miles through Central Europe and would soon become what Churchill termed an Iron Curtain. In the occupied territories of Eastern Europe behind the front, satellite Communist regimes were being organized into a multinational buffer zone along the entire length of Russia's western border. Future control of Germany, the economic and strategic heart of Europe, was in question. It was clear, however, that Stalin's Soviet Union was emerging from the throes of war as the strongest force in European politics.

Absolute ruler of the 200 million people of the Soviet Union, Stalin had come to power both slowly and unexpectedly. He was born in 1879 in a small town near Tiflis in the Georgian Caucasus, where his father was a shoemaker known for his drunkenness; their home, a frame hovel, reflected the family's low status. The boy was so frequently and unmercifully beaten by his father that damage to his elbow at age seven left Stalin's left arm several inches shorter than his right. This withered arm, combined with his pocked face (the result of a severe case of smallpox), his small adult stature (5 feet 4 inches), and his nine toes (two on the left foot grew as one), made him the butt of considerable childhood cruelty—facts some psychohistorians have proposed as an explanation of his determination, iron will, brutality, and inhumanity in later years. While his future Western counterparts, Roosevelt and Churchill, were maturing on the playing fields of Groton and Harrow, Stalin, expelled from the theological seminary at Tiflis, was organizing revolutionary cells in Georgia and conducting raids on the Imperial Bank to finance revolution. When that revolution finally came in 1917, Stalin was released from an Arctic prison camp and returned to Moscow to join Lenin in the task of creating a new society.

In the early years of the Bolshevik Revolution, Stalin—the "gray blur," the "bureaucrat's bureaucrat," or in Trotsky's words "the outstanding mediocrity of our party"—was dismissed as a nonentity by his colleagues. But this patient and silent man who spoke Russian with a thick Georgian accent gradually packed party offices with his supporters, outlasted more intellectual rivals, and in 1928 assumed total control of the Communist party and the Soviet Union. Stalin believed that he alone was capable of leading Russia and that his means, however ruthless, were justified in pursuing this goal. Although dedicated to communism, he was first and foremost a Russian nationalist, more a spiritual descendant of Ivan the Terrible and Peter the Great than a socialist colleague of Lenin. The men he brought to power shared this cast of mind.

In Stalin's view, Russia's backwardness was at the root of the country's isolation from the West and its military inadequacy. His driving purpose was to make the Soviet Union the independent equal of the nations of the industrialized West. He saw Britain, France, Germany, and America as both models and enemies to be surpassed. An invincible army, modern heavy industry, and productive agriculture became Stalin's three goals as he began the transformation of the peasant nation of the tsars into a world power. He imposed his inexorable will upon this vast nation; Russia was to be forced into the modern world regardless of human price. Asked when he would stop killing people after a million Communist party members had already been liquidated in the purges of the 1930s, he replied, "When it is no longer necessary." And if people deplored his methods and suffered extraordinary hardships because of them, the overwhelming majority of Russians shared his vision and understood his spirit.

Today, more than twenty years after his death, Stalin stands as the principal architect of the Soviet state, his mark deeply etched upon the human geography and personality of the Soviet Union. Stalin's life spanned the crucial epoch of Russian history during which a social and economic revolution was implanted and a modern nation constructed. In "The Modernization of Russia" Stalin and his contemporaries consolidate the Bolshevik Revolution and design the framework of a new Soviet society. Through a succession of state-controlled five-year plans started in 1928, the vast natural resources of the Soviet Union are harnessed, new industrial centers created, and industrial technologies imported to further the advance of a tightly controlled program of industrialization. Peasants are forcibly collectivized as Communist control is imposed on all aspects of life. Russia reassumes the atmosphere of a social prison; 10 million citizens are jailed or flee into exile. The Soviets, however, discipline and organize the population to a degree that makes possible the defeat of the formidable military machine of Nazi Germany. In "The Soviet State" the modernization of Russia broadens and new problems of state economic planning, socialized agriculture, urbanization, and dissent appear. Stalin's successors must grapple with the complexities of a diverse and literate population while simultaneously attempting to perfect a classless society in the most complex multinational state in the world. Stalin's vision of transforming a primitive, illiterate nation into a highly advanced country was accomplished in little more than a generation. Today, Soviet leaders must produce the rewards promised during that period of struggle and sacrifice.

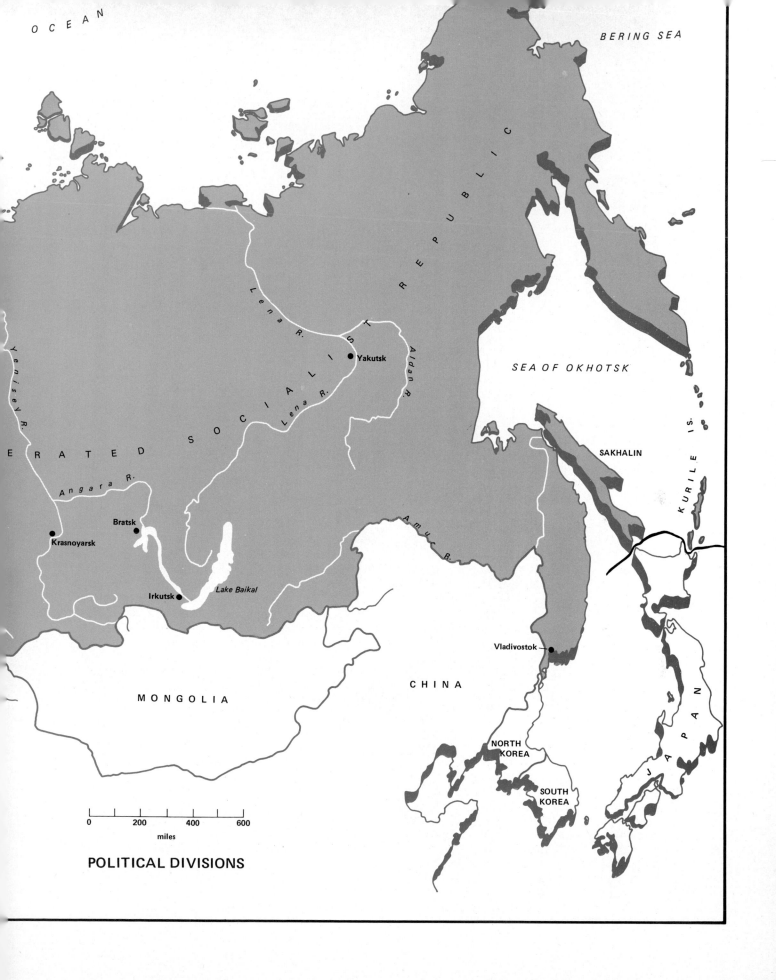

OCEAN

BERING SEA

SEA OF OKHOTSK

Yenisey R.

Lena R.

Lena R.

Aldan R.

● Yakutsk

E R A T E D   S O C I A L I S T   R E P U B L I C

Angara R.

KURILE IS.

Bratsk ●

SAKHALIN

● Krasnoyarsk

Amur R.

Irkutsk ● *Lake Baikal*

Vladivostok ━●

MONGOLIA

CHINA

JAPAN

NORTH
KOREA

SOUTH
KOREA

0   200   400   600

miles

POLITICAL DIVISIONS

THE MODERNIZATION OF RUSSIA

1

At the beginning of the twentieth century, Russia was a gigantic *agrarian*• land stretching from the eastern frontiers of Europe thousands of miles across Asia to the Pacific. It was neither European nor Asian. Ruled for three centuries by the *autocratic*• Romanov tsars, Russia lagged far behind the industrializing West in economic and political strength and gradually declined from first- to second-class military status. Like many modernizing countries today, Russia had a low per capita income—the lowest in Europe—and a dual society composed of a majority of faceless peasants isolated from the small, modernizing urban class that held economic monopoly over the country. The central problem was the transformation of this agricultural society into an industrial power, but the huge investment required to construct an industrial society was greater than Russia could pay. Through a combination of foreign aid and peasant repression, the last of the tsars, Nicholas II, tried to sponsor industrial growth and to some extent succeeded, but economic progress was aborted by the entry of Russian armies into World War I and the social upheavals which resulted from that defeat. In 1917, a small group of *Bolshevik*• revolutionaries picked up the reins, determined to create a new socialist society out of the confusion of civil war, peasant rebellion, and revolution.

A decade later, one of these men, Joseph Stalin, assumed total power within the Bolshevik party and Russia, and he effected this social revolution. In 1928, he launched a forcible drive to modernize Communist Russia. No aspect of society was left untouched; the cultural geography of one-sixth of the world was transformed. Collectivized peasant farms and state industries arose in the Soviet Union. Russia became an industrial giant at a fearful cost in human life. By the end of the 1930s, Russia had developed—through state planning—the outlines of a modern industrial economy, an example of rapid, programmed industrialization that is not lost on developing so-

cieties today. Because of the relentless discipline imposed by the will of this dictator, the Soviet Union survived devastation during World War II to emerge as one of the two most powerful nations in the entire world.

THE LEGACY OF THE TSARS

In the spring of 1917, few suspected that Russia was on the brink of a revolution, a social hurricane that would topple the 300-year rule of the Romanovs and set Russia on a course of cultural experimentation. The three crucial figures in this revolution were all in exile. A disheartened V. I. Lenin, in Zurich, was convinced that the decisive battles of the revolutionary struggle would not occur in his lifetime. Leon Trotsky, having escaped from Siberia, was living on the Lower East Side in New York. J. V. Dzugashvili (Stalin), who a decade earlier had masterminded a daring bank robbery in Tiflis to finance the Bolshevik cause, was brooding in the snowbound town of Achinsk, thousands of miles from the capital on the Trans-Siberian Railroad. True, demonstrations occurred daily in Petrograd (before 1914, Saint Petersburg; after 1924, Leningrad), but food shortages, bread riots, strikes, and peasant uprisings were common features of the social landscape of tsarist Russia. No one in power considered them unusually important or dangerous. On March 6, the British ambassador cabled London from Petrograd: "Some disorders occurred today, but nothing serious." He was wrong. The Russian Revolution had begun; the rule of the tsars was over.

Personal dictatorial rule by the tsar had held the vast empire of the Russians together for centuries. Nicholas II, the last tsar, was convinced that only through autocracy could Russia survive as a nation and progress. His empire stretched through eleven *time zones*• from the Baltic Sea to the Pacific Ocean, an 8.5-million-square-mile reservoir of illiterate peasants and untapped resources. Most of this land was barren of human exploitation, an endless expanse of *tundra,*• forest, *steppe,*• and *desert.*• Only at the turn of the century had Russia's population of 130 million begun to spread eastward from its traditional European *heartland*• in western Russia, across the Ural Mountains and into Siberia and Central Asia. Of the total population of Russia at that time, 55 million spoke Russian as their native tongue and were thus ethnic Russians; an additional 36 million Belorussians, Ukrainians, and Poles spoke related Slavic languages. The remainder of the population formed a non-Slavic linguistic and cultural mosaic: Jews (5 million); Tatars (4 million); Baltic peoples (4 million); Caucasians (3.5 million); Germans (2 million); and Central Asian Uzbeks, Kazakhs, and Turkmenians (7 million). Some 200 nationalities speaking 146 languages belonging to dozens of religious groups occupied Russian soil.

The overwhelming majority of these people were simple peasants whose lives were mired in persistent poverty and drained of hope by taxes, landlords, droughts, early frosts, and famine. Relatively few lived in cities or worked in factories, despite the fact that Russia had experienced a modest **economic takeoff** during the last thirty years of the nineteenth century. To rule and control this vast and varied land was a monumental task. When Western Europeans criticized Nicholas II for his repressive measures, his finance minister Count Sergei Witte responded that the marvel of Russia was not that it had an imperfect government, but that there was any Russian government at all—however autocratic.

The World of the Peasants:
Traditional Russia

Russia had always known great extremes of wealth and poverty. The social and economic gulf separating the ruling nobility and landowning class from the world of the peasantry was an age-old obstacle to reform and progress. In the eyes of the West, Russia was a nation lost in its own vastness—a land of wretched roads and vermin-ridden villages located on the fringes of Asia. From the European viewpoint, this was true; a journey from London to Moscow in 1900 was an expedition into the unknown. At the beginning of the twentieth century, the tsar's urban

subjects included 300,000 convicts, 17,000 students, 2 million bureaucrats, merchants, and soldiers, and 2.4 million industrial workers. In the countryside, 110 million peasants scraped meager livings from the soil, and their numerical superiority and economic inferiority constituted Russia's greatest problem.

Earlier, Tsar Alexander II made a serious effort to solve this problem by emancipating the **serfs** and releasing them from their condition as the baptized property of the landowning nobility and the crown. In 1861, some 20 million peasants were given land, principally on the Russian frontier where enormous labor was required to incorporate new lands into the nation's **arable.** In the rich black-soil areas of the Ukraine, however, the nobility retained 45 percent of the best agricultural land. Although most peasants

An old woodcut showing the Kremlin, for centuries the symbol of imperial Russia. *Photo:* Culver Pictures.

One of the causes of revolution in Russia was the misery in which the great mass of the people lived. Serfdom, for example, was not abolished until the middle of the nine-teenth century. *Photo:* Culver Pictures.

received less land than they had previously tilled for their owners, these changes built an unshakable peasant conviction that the tsar wanted them to have the land; it was the landlords who did not. Although these early reforms produced a small class of fairly wealthy and prosperous farmers, the rural majority remained yoked to taxes and redemption payments. Their ethic, brutally simple, was for each to look out for himself; as they put it: "Another's tears are water." Emancipation from serfdom had not im-proved their lot.

At the turn of the twentieth century, therefore, Russia was still a nation of peasants. Four of every five Russians were villagers and three out of four were farmers. The low productivity of Russian agri-culture defined the peasants' existence. A typical peasant ate 3 pounds of bread a day (5 pounds dur-ing harvest season), with cabbages, beets, and cu-cumbers the other major elements of their diet. In most areas, land was still worked with wooden plows unchanged from medieval times; grain was harvested by sickle and threshed by hand. One-third of the farms had but one horse; another third had no horse at all—the soil was turned by men and women yoked to primitive agricultural implements. Some 90 percent of Russia's agricultural land was

planted to grain, but yields were one-third those in Western Europe. And annual variations in yields—reflecting climatic differences between good and bad years—were three times greater in Russia than in Western Europe.

As the new century unfolded, the situation grew worse. Russia's population of 60 million in 1850 had doubled to 130 million by 1900; in 1913 it reached 160 million. Most of this increase was absorbed within village structures, which had become increas-ingly communal in organization following the eman-cipation of the serfs. In the communal village, the *mir*, the newly rich peasants who had prospered when serfdom was abolished, collected taxes and communal dues, allocated justice, and periodically redistributed fields to the poorer peasants. But farm-land became increasingly fragmented because the population increase was barely matched by greater yields and Russia's farmland was forced to accom-modate more people. The "surplus" rural popula-tion, as the government knew them, was considered to number between one-third and two-fifths of all rural dwellers. As a result, by 1900 some 4 million villagers had fled to urban areas; in some cities, the population doubled within a generation. An addi-tional 2.5 million migrants sought jobs along the railroad lines in the Siberian wilderness. Because movement required permission from the village **commune**⁎ and an official internal passport, most Russian peasants remained bound to their home villages. In this spectacle of growing rural destitution, the Russian government provided no relief. Its policy was to export grain to Western Europe in order to pay for imported urban and industrial goods. In the face of growing hunger in the countryside, a tsarist minister declared, "We shall undereat but we will export." The peasant underate.

This situation exploded in 1905 when riots broke out in numerous Russian cities. Ostensibly generated by the disastrous war with Japan, these riots reflected the social imbalance that accompanied the first phases of modernization in Russia. Peasants, kept home during the grip of winter, took up the banner when spring arrived; crying "the land is God's," they burned farm buildings, occupied estates, and raided towns throughout Russia. In retaliation, thousands were exiled to Siberia; the rest were summarily shot. The tsar's authority was not to be questioned, so in Saint Petersburg, troops slaughtered 2000 peaceful demonstrators on Bloody Sunday, January 22, 1905. The facile reforms that followed these uprisings were too late to save Nicholas and the Romanovs.

Modernizing Russia: The Dual Society
[FIGURE 1]

Despite the backward and isolated nature of the peasantry on the eve of the Revolution of 1917, Russia was simply not the dim, feudal world so often described by revolutionaries and Western travelers. Broad-scale social changes were at work. Starting in the 1890s, Russian industry had expanded by more than 8 percent a year, a rate unmatched in the early industrialized West. After a lull between 1900 and 1907, industry continued to expand by 6 to 7 percent each year. The principal factor that stimulated economic takeoff was the state-sponsored expansion of the railroad system, which opened up new regions for colonization and new resources for exploitation. By 1917, Russia had 47,000 miles of track, including the longest single line in the world, the 5700-mile-long Trans-Siberian Railroad. Although most new railroads were built for military reasons, towns sprang up along the track, mines were established along the right-of-way, and previously isolated regions provided new internal markets for Russian manufactures. New machinery was imported, and so many factories and mines were financed by French, Belgian, and German capital that by 1900, half the total investment in Russian industry came from foreign sources. ***Iron smelting*** expanded at a rate three times faster than in Germany and eleven times faster than in England during the thirty years preceding World War I. A new heavy industrial complex in the Donets Basin in the Ukraine overtook the original industrial base built by Peter the Great in the Urals in the early 1700s. Moscow became an important textile center, and tsarist Russia for a brief period produced more petroleum than the rest of the world combined.

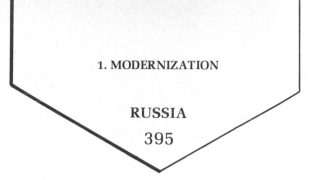

Russia, like Japan and Germany, was catching up after a late industrial start.

By 1914, Russia was a budding industrial power. But conditions in the factories and mines were scandalous, far worse than in Western Europe or North America. The work day averaged over twelve hours and was, more often than not, sixteen to eighteen hours. It was forbidden to employ night workers more than ten continuous hours, lest they fall asleep at the machines. Women and children made up nearly half the labor force, and low wages were ensured by the endless flow of impoverished peasants —potential factory workers—who coursed across the Russian landscape and into the cities in search of work. Average pay in the Moscow region was $7.35 per month in 1914; peasants in the vicinity, however, netted only about $20 per year from their land, so willing workers were always available. In Siberia, where exiles and felons formed the bulk of the work force, the repression and torture so meticulously described a half century later in Soviet writer Aleksander Solzhenitsyn's *The Gulag Archipelago* took root. Armed cossacks, the tsarist paramilitary, guarded the factories and mines. Between 1912 and 1914, over 2000 strikes were recorded each year involving nearly 1 million workers, a fifth of the total industrial labor force. For these people, the Marxist appeal to revolt, "You have nothing to lose but your chains," made good sense.

Industry had begun to restructure the face of Russia. Cities grew so fast that by 1917 nearly one of every five Russians lived in an urban center. In 1910, Saint Petersburg had a population of 2 million, and Moscow's population was 1.5 million. The number of cities with populations greater than 50,000 increased from thirteen to forty-four in the last half of the nineteenth century. An influx of villagers swelled into cities poorly equipped to house, employ, and provide any newcomers with municipal services. Discontent was widespread but unfocused.

Large as these urban and industrial statistics were in sheer numbers, Russia remained a nation of peasants and lagged far behind the West in per capita wealth. A dual society not unlike those of some modern developing nations separated city from village, modern technology from traditional ways. After the serious disturbances of October 1905, the government attempted to find ways of assuaging the peasants' hunger for land. Growing rural populations and declining availability of land were driving farmers to

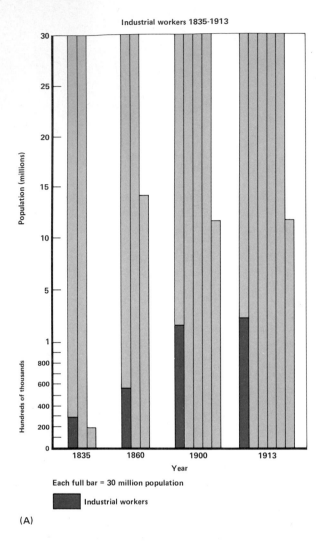

Industrial workers 1835-1913

Population (millions)

Hundreds of thousands

Year

Each full bar = 30 million population

■ Industrial workers

(A)

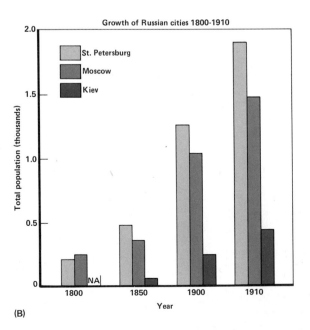

Growth of Russian cities 1800-1910

St. Petersburg

Moscow

Kiev

Total population (thousands)

NA

Year

(B)

desperation. The contest between landlord and peasant for land, a thread of blood running through centuries of Russian history, threatened the very roots of Romanov rule. Peasant deputies in the newly formed parliament, the Duma, clamored for the distribution of land from the great estates; landlords, having ridden out the revolutionary squall of 1905, would have none of it. In 1906, the minister of the interior, a politician named Peter Stolypin, offered a compromise plan: peasants were allowed to divide their communal *mir* land (that not in landlord estates) into independent holdings. His policy was to "wager not on the needy and drunken but on the sturdy and strong." It anticipated a Darwinian elimination of the weaker members of the peasantry among whom drunkenness, a major problem, was a national pastime. According to a peasant saying, three days were required for a proper binge: one to drink, a second to be drunk, and a third to sober up. Because of the heavy taxes on liquor, the government could not afford to limit the flow of spirits.

The government was hoping to develop a class of private landowning peasants who would form a sober, conservative bulwark against revolt and anarchy without reducing the privileges of the landowning nobility. To some degree this happened. In the decade before the 1917 Revolution, one-third of the 9 million peasant households in European Russia shifted to private tenure. This was less true in the north forests than in the Ukrainian steppes, for in the north a long winter and short growing season compressed the agricultural year into four to five months and communal cooperation was virtually required. In Asiatic Russia (mainly Siberia, the Altaic region, Central Asia, and the Caucasus), land-hungry peasants were settled on virgin territory.

But these reforms were largely ineffective in diverting the dramatic course of history. By 1917, modernizing Russia was moving toward social change of a most basic kind under the autocratic rule of a small class of medieval-like nobility. In the cities, industrialization had created a dissatisfied working class of substantial size. Demonstrators carried placards with basic demands: "Bread," "Down with the Autocracy." In the countryside, peasants—drained of their crops to pay for imported machinery and by taxes to pay the costs of World War I—were in ferment. Trapped in the midst of an incomplete indus-

Figure 1. The Modernization of Russia. This graph shows the growth of Russia's urban population in relation to the growing number of industrial workers in the nineteenth century. Although industrial workers remained a minor percentage of the total population, the burgeoning of Petrograd, Moscow, and Kiev reflects the urbanizing effects of even partial industrialization. *Adapted from: David Floyd, Russia in Revolt, 1905: The First Crack in Tsarist Power.* New York: McGraw-Hill; London: Macdonald and Jane's, 1969, p. 33. Copyright © 1969 by David Floyd; used by permission of the McGraw-Hill Book Company and Macdonald and Jane's Publishers.

trial revolution, the rule of Nicholas II crumbled under the impact of two different revolutions emanating from the two social worlds of Russia: urban **proletariat**• and rural **peasantry**.• In Petrograd, grumbling urbanites revolted, and the soldiers refused to fire on them: a war-weary Tsar Nicholas was forced to abdicate the throne. Shortly thereafter, in region after region of the Russian countryside, peasants rose up and rampaged, cast out the landlords, burned forests and manor houses, and seized the land. In this vacuum of chaos, the three who made a revolution—Lenin, Stalin, and Trotsky—returned to Petrograd from exile in the summer of 1917.

THE BEGINNINGS OF COMMUNIST RULE

Stalin, traveling out of Siberia, arrived first in Petrograd on the Trans-Siberian Railroad. Trotsky, then lecturing in Canada, set sail from Montreal. Lenin was transported from Switzerland across Germany to Russia in a special "sealed" railroad car courtesy of the enemy German government. After six months of confused political maneuvering, this Bolshevik faction overthrew the provisional coalition government in an armed coup d'état and seized control of Russia with a program for action designed by Karl Marx. According to Marx (1818–1883), the roots of contemporary problems were economic in origin, the result of the exploitation of one economic class by another. By luck and skill one class, capitalists, had gained control over the means of production and distribution. According to Marxist theory, this economic power was used to enslave and impoverish workers. In Marx's view, the entire social system was primarily designed to reinforce the power of the capitalist class and to protect its property. Shatter that system, impose a revolution to overturn the basis of society, and a better, more rational world—a world of social equality—would arise. The first step in this experiment would be the abolition of individual property rights. Class differences based on ownership would no longer exist. While it puzzled Lenin, Stalin, and Trotsky that the long-awaited Communist revolution had taken root in their own backyard rather than in one of the older industrialized countries of Western Europe, they nonetheless were determined to construct a new socialist order and to forge a classless society in Russia under the absolute control of the Bolshevik party.

Civil War: Bolshevism (1917–1921)

Between 1917 and 1921, the Bolshevik Revolution struggled with a number of issues crucial to all Russians: a humiliating peace treaty with Germany, a nationwide civil war, peasant revolt, and famine. Russia withdrew from World War I under the terms of the Treaty of Brest-Litovsk and was forced to give up vast areas along its western frontier—territory painstakingly acquired by the tsars during the previ-

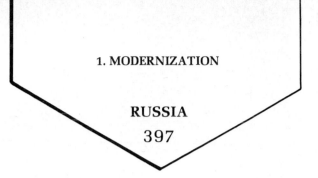
ous three centuries. Poland, the Baltic states (Estonia, Latvia, and Lithuania), the Ukraine, and part of Belorussia were lost. Finland gained its independence and Bessarabia was later transferred to Romania. The Bolshevik promise of peace with Europe was kept, but Russia was economically and geographically torn apart. Some 62 million people and 1.27 million square miles of territory, including one-third of the country's most fertile lands, one-third of its factories, and three-quarters of its coal and iron mines no longer belonged to the Russian state. Lenin hoped that the treaty, disastrous as it was, would provide breathing space for the Bolsheviks to consolidate their control over Russia, a formidable task for a party numbering less than 300,000 in a nation of tens of millions. Instead, civil war broke out between two factions: the Communists (Reds) and the opponents of the revolution (Whites).

White forces controlled the Baltic provinces, Siberia, the Caucasus, and the Crimea—virtually all non-Russian Russia. They received half-hearted support from British and American troops who had occupied the northern port cities of Murmansk and Archangel during World War I to prevent war materials from falling into the hands of the Germans. The Communists held Moscow, Petrograd, and the Great Russian heartland. The bulk of both armies consisted of apathetic peasants forcibly pressed into service.

In three years of savage warfare, famine and disease (typhus) took the lives of an estimated 9 million people. By 1920, a third of the population in the cities and towns of northern and central Russia had fled to the countryside in search of food, reflecting the tenuous nature of urbanization at that time. Industrial manpower declined by half; grain production by a third. Anarchy prevailed in many regions; the so-called green revolutionaries, peasants concerned less with ideology than with land, took the Russian landscape by force. Special detachments of Communist troops fanned out from the cities in search of the food peasants cunningly hid. Villagers stood their ground and were slaughtered. The entire country was in the throes of a war for bread, and the people generally had little use for either the Communists or their opponents. A peasant folksong of the time aptly described the politics of the rural majority: "Oh you little apple, oh so bright; bash the Whites from the left and the Reds from the right." But by 1921, the Reds, although widely disliked, had defeated the still more hated Whites. Russia lay in

The main street of Petrograd in May 1917, as the discontent and disorder World War I had brought to a peak erupted into revolution. In 1905, then known as St. Petersburg, the city had been the site of the slaughter of Bloody Sunday, the beginning of the first open revolt. *Photo: Wide World.*

ruins, its industry, transport system, and food production shattered by six consecutive years of war since the opening of World War I in 1914.

The New Economic Policy: NEP (1921–1928)

Immediately after the 1917 Revolution, the market economy, so important in Europe's modernization, was abandoned by Lenin, who nationalized every important sector of the Russian economy in line with orthodox Marxist thinking. Upper-class urbanites—those with property—were shorn of their assets, and by 1921, most heavy industry was owned by the state. In the countryside, lands belonging to the crown, the Orthodox Church, and the **gentry*** were nationalized. Although 125 million acres of land were transferred from the state to peasant control, the flight of 8 million city dwellers to the villages during the chaos of civil war absorbed whatever benefits this transfer could bring. An additional 125 million acres of agricultural land were subsequently confiscated from the previously unaffected richer peasants, the *kulaks* or "fists," but it is not clear how much kulak land was redistributed to poorer peasants or how much was simply subdivided among the kulaks themselves. In these early years, Lenin blindly persisted in viewing peasants in Marxist terms as "the class that represents barbarism within civilization." But lacking an effective arm of control over territory,

Lenin in effect legalized peasant control of the land. Social upheaval in four years had been sweeping: in both city and village the Communists had leveled the population into a primitive state of social equality. But this social transformation of Soviet Russia had had such awesome economic consequences that by 1921 the very survival of Russia as a nation was at stake.

In the civil war, Communist forces had been denied the grain of the Ukraine, the cotton of Turkestan, and the coal and iron of the Donets Basin because White forces controlled 60 percent of Russia's railroads. Even more basic problems were the dictatorial policies of the Bolsheviks, the necessity to requisition farm products at bayonet point, and the inefficiency of the newly created Soviet bureaucracy. As the decline in industrial and agricultural production became more acute, the need for a new economic policy became clear. By 1921, the bread ration in Moscow and Petrograd, already at starvation level, had to be cut by one-third. A fuel crisis shut down the largest factories in these cities. In the province of Tambov in the middle Volga region, all the peasants were in open revolt. Sailors in the naval garrison at Kronstadt in the Gulf of Finland, themselves sons of peasants, rebelled and demanded an end to Bolshevik tyranny. The Communist Revolution, only four years old, was trapped, as Trotsky described it, in a pair of open scissors: the prices of manufactured urban goods rose as money declined in value, while the prices paid for farm products plunged. The widening gap between these lines on a graph—the two blades of the economic scissors—meant that peasants ate more of their produce and provided less

A Communist poster of 1919 urging workers and peasants to use their power against the forces that oppressed and exploited them—church, czar, and capitalist. The struggle for power that eventually resulted in victory for the Bolsheviks consumed several years; begun in 1917, the revolution was not over until 1921. By that time Russia lay in ruins, its industry, transport system, and food production shattered by six consecutive years of war since the beginning of World War I in 1914.

ЦАРЬ, ПОП И БОГАЧ
НА ПЛЕЧАХ У ТРУДОВОГО НАРОДА.

BORIS ALEKSEIVICH: REVOLUTIONARY

"I was born in Odessa—the most cosmopolitan, sophisticated city in Russia. It was the most important port in czarist times, just as it is now—a magnificent city—brawling, bawdy and cultured, all at the same time. It seemed to me when I was a child that you could hear ten different languages being spoken at once as you walked down the street. . . . I came from a family that had belonged to the upper-middle-class intelligentsia for several generations. My father owned various kinds of real estate and was a provincial school superintendent—exactly the sort of job Lenin's father had in Kazan. My mother was a concert violinist . . . and a music teacher. We spoke Russian in our home, although everyone in the family was bilingual in French. . . . My father thought the Romanovs would never survive because they had been too stupid to give up some of their powers, unlike the more intelligent English monarchs. . . .

"I was thirteen years old (in 1917) and from that time on politics became my whole world. Two of my older brothers, who had immediately joined the Bolshevik Party, decided I could be useful because of my gift for languages. We were in Sevastopol . . . at the time of the revolution; my father had been promoted in 1916, and we had left Odessa so he could take over his new job. . . . The years between 1918 and 1920 were a time of constant civil war and foreign intervention. It seemed that we had one government on one side of the street and one on the other, with a third on the rooftops. The English occupied Sevastopol, the French were in Odessa and the coastline was blockaded. . . . In 1920 the French took off and the rule of the Soviets was established in Odessa. I immediately joined a Komsomol [Communist party youth group] training course. I was sixteen then. From that point on, the revolution became my life. My parents had their doubts and emigrated to France with my sister. They said they might return when things settled down, but they feared there would be no place for the old intelligentsia in the new Soviet state. I said very sarcastic things to them about getting out with their money after all the talking they had done about revolutionary politics. I laughed at their fears; I was utterly convinced of the rightness of our course. . . . My father, who knew more about the rest of the world than I did, tried to talk to me about the modifications being made in industrial capitalism in England and America. I didn't listen. We believed that world revolution was inevitable, that the old order was dying everywhere. . . .

"So. I was a Komsomol organizer for fifteen years. I traveled to all of the Soviet republics, setting up loyal Komsomol organizations. I was particularly careful to look out for unorthodox political tendencies in the republics that had hoped for independence from Russia at the time of the revolution. Those were my instructions, and I carried them out. Of course, weeding out the unorthodox didn't mean sending them to camp, not at that point. I believed in persuasion; I talked myself hoarse with people who didn't agree with me. . . .

"I was arrested . . . in early 1935. The official grounds were that I had been a friend of someone in Leningrad who was accused of being a conspirator in the Kirov murder and a secret Trotskyite. I had known the man only slightly, when I was based in Leningrad for two years. I was in Kiev when they (the secret police) came to take me away. Why was I really arrested? Who knows—there were never any reasons for arrests in those days. . . . The only blessing is that my parents and sister never returned to Russia, unlike some other emigrés who were fooled by the good face Stalin put on for the rest of the world. But I don't blame the rest of the world for being fooled; we ourselves didn't realize what was happening until it was too late."

Source: Quoted from Susan Jacoby, *Moscow Conversations.* New York: Coward, McCann & Geoghegan, 1972, pp. 56–62. By permission of Coward, McCann & Geoghegan, Inc. Copyright © 1972 by Susan Jacoby.

---

to the cities. Unless the gap between the two blades were closed, to pursue Trotsky's analogy, the Communist Revolution was in danger of being beheaded.

In the face of these realities, Lenin retreated from socialism toward private enterprise. He yielded to the demands of the peasantry and launched the New Economic Policy (NEP), a profound change in direction. The objective was to encourage private entrepreneurs and foreign investment in order to get Russia's crippled economy moving. But during the first year of the NEP, 1921, drought in the Volga River basin caused famine to stalk the Russian landscape. An estimated 22 million people faced starvation; American aid directed by Herbert Hoover fed 10 million Russians. Some 5 million died, but the new policy soon took hold. The previously vilified kulaks, the wealthier and more energetic peasants, were encouraged to increase production and to trade freely in urban markets. This freer policy spread to industry; by 1923, nine of every ten factories were run by private enterprise, and production was stabilizing. For the first time since before World War I, Russia experienced a return to normality, and an economic revival ensued. By 1927, Russian industrial production had returned to prewar levels. The Russian census of 1926 reported a population of 147 million, only slightly larger than in 1917; with normal growth rates, it would have been 175 million. Statistically speaking, 28 million people had vanished or not been born. Individual farming was carried out on 25 million small holdings, and peasants made up 73 percent of the population. Restrictions on hiring

In 1925, the Bolshevik party authorized a study of 32,730 peasant households in Penza Province in the middle Volga region to ascertain the causes of rural poverty. This unique data base provides insight into the roots of rural discontent. In the districts under study, believed to be representative of European Russia at that time, between one-quarter and one-half of all peasant households were defined as poor. The primary cause of poverty was the dearth of able-bodied men in the villages, brought about by war, drought, famine, and migration. The old, the unfit and the mad, the disaffected and widows were left on the land. In this survey, a disaster was defined as crop failure, famine, fire, or death of a horse. The unfit were those with persistent bad luck and failure; layabouts were those who spent their summers sleeping in idleness, gossiped, and spent their money foolishly.

Causes of Rural Poverty, Penza, 1924–1925

Source: N. Rosnitskii, *Litso derevni* (1926), pp. 27–28. Adapted from Teodor Shanin, *The Awkward Class.* Oxford, Eng.: Clarendon Press, 1972, p. 172, Table 9.11. Courtesy of Oxford University Press.

Causes	Percentage of all rural poor
Shortage of family labor	14–38
Long illness or invalidism	10
Military service of main worker	10
Natural disaster	20
Fragmentation of land	10–26
Not being fit people for farming	5–8
Being layabouts	5
Being poor over generations for unknown reasons	6–12
All	100

labor, leasing land, and investing capital—all practices abhorrent to orthodox Marxists—were relaxed. Lenin's death in 1924 disturbed little, and in the next four years the gradual ascendancy of Joseph Stalin to control of the Communist party went largely unnoticed by the Russian people. Dismissed by most of his colleagues as a mediocrity, Stalin would wield absolute power over Russia for the next quarter century and would become the architect of a new Russian empire after World War II.

COLLECTIVIZATION AND INDUSTRIALIZATION

Alone among prominent Bolsheviks, Joseph Stalin was a Soviet nationalist and not an internationalist, having never lived in the West or learned any Western language. His belief that Russia should go it alone, that "socialism in one country," not a world revolution, should be the Bolshevik objective, stood in marked contrast to the pronouncements of Lenin, whom he outlived by nearly three decades, and Leon Trotsky, whom he had assassinated in Mexico in 1940. To Stalin, Russia was a country ringed by powerful enemies who had eternally taken advantage of the country's internal backwardness, underdevelopment, and expanse. He profiled this attitude in a 1931 speech: "The history of Russia was that she was ceaselessly beaten for her backwardness. She was beaten by the Mongol Khans, she was beaten by the Turkish Beys, she was beaten by the Swedish feudal lords, she was beaten by the Polish-Lithuanian Pans, she was beaten by the Anglo-French capitalists, she was beaten by the Japanese barons, she was beaten by all for her backwardness. . . . We are fifty or a hundred years behind the advanced countries. We must make this lag good in ten years. Either we do it or they crush us."

Few in power disputed this view, and its appeal to the Russian people was considerable. But for most Bolsheviks, change was seen as a matter of timing and tactics, with moderates counseling against drastic shifts in policy from the NEP for fear chaos and peasant revolt would plunge the country into another civil war and destroy the regime. But once in firm control of the party, Stalin became convinced that headlong collectivization of agriculture and rapid industrialization were essential to Russia's survival. In 1928, grain shipments to the cities had fallen far behind urban requirements and, indeed, were 2 million tons short of fulfilling the basic needs of Russia's 30 million city dwellers. Once again, the Russian peasants were holding the cities to ransom. Urban famine posed a real threat to Bolshevik power, and the small, inefficient private farms were not producing enough food to provide an urban surplus. Somehow the peasants must be forced to feed the cities and to provide capital in the form of grain to pay for investment in heavy industry. Stalin was determined to impose his will on Russia whatever the cost; his five-year plans would transform Russian agriculture and industry.

Collectivization
[FIGURE 2]

In 1929, a new policy of collectivizing the 100 million peasants of Russia was inaugurated. Within a year more than half the farmland in Russia and half the peasantry had been organized into *kolkhozes,* a transitional type of collective farm in which several villages pooled their labor and land under government supervision and were paid proportionate shares of the harvest. A small number of state farms, or *sovkhozes,* on which peasants were paid cash wages, were also established. Kulak land was confiscated by the state to become part of these commonly owned state collectives. Since distinctions between kulaks, middle class, and poor peasants were vague, anyone who failed to join a collective farm voluntarily was treated as a kulak. The peasants responded with predictable fury, their traditional craving for private land again thwarted by government edict. Faced with confiscation, peasants killed animals and burned crops rather than give them up to the collectives. In 1929, 18 million of the 34 million horses in Russia were killed. Half the cattle and two-thirds of all sheep and goats were slaughtered in the next four years. Nonetheless, two-thirds of the peasants were collectivized in 1934; by 1937, 93 percent were under collective status. Villages became battlefields where troops were sent to collect food, subdue riots, and protect the collectives; the countryside was once again on the verge of civil war. When famine broke out in the Ukraine and along the Volga in 1932, Stalin continued to sell grain on world markets to purchase machinery while 5 million peasants starved. The kulaks, who had remained outside the socialist sphere and had threatened the revolution, were liquidated as a class. Millions of these people were stripped of their property, deported to Siberia and the Arctic, or shot in their fields. Some years later in a moment of candor, Stalin estimated the losses at 10 million and confided to Winston Churchill that compared with collectivizing the Russian peasants, defeating the Nazis was relatively easy. Collectivization was, he felt, an absolute necessity if the land were to be worked with tractors.

Despite the enormous human cost, by the end of the Second Five-Year Plan in 1938, the government had solved the problem of feeding the urban population and subsidizing the growth of heavy industry by reorganizing agriculture. The 24 million to 25 million individual peasant holdings had been amalgamated into 250,000 kolkhozes under Communist control and organization. By the middle 1930s, agricultural production had recovered to its pre-World War I level, and some 5800 machine tractor stations were spread throughout the agricultural core of Russia. Nearly two-thirds of the arable land was tractor-plowed and 90 percent of the grain mechanically threshed. Even if peasants were not reconciled to the new collective system, resistance was muted by the

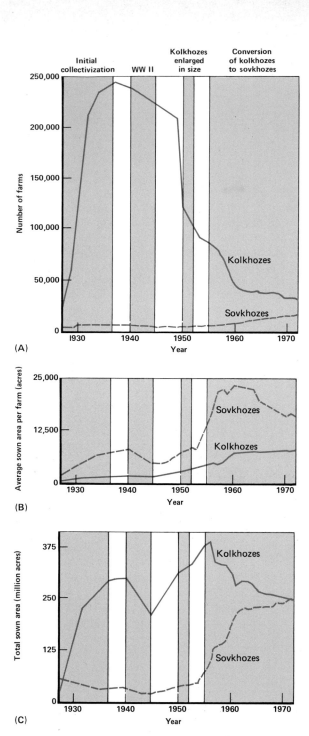

Figure 2. The Collectivization of Agriculture. These three graphs illustrate the rapid collectivization of agriculture during the 1930s. Two kinds of collective farm, the *kolkhoz* and the *sovkhoz,* evolved out of the 24 to 25 million individual peasant holdings of tsarist Russia. Kolkhozes have been consolidated into larger units and a number converted to sovkhozes. From a geographical viewpoint, Stalin's collectivization of the peasantry marked the real socialization of Russia, a transformation of man and land that distinguishes the Soviet Union from all other industrial nations.

The open hearth furnace of the Magnitogorsk steel combine in the Urals, which in the period of intense industrialization between 1929 and 1940 was the primary iron and steel center of Russia. It grew during that time from a collection of huts to an industrial city of 146,000 people. *Photo:* Wide World.

threat of withdrawal of machine services. Peasants continued, however, to evade collectivization as much as possible and concentrated their energies on their private garden plots: their one cow, one pig, and four sheep. They actually managed to divert, foot by foot, some 5 million acres from collective to private use. Severe penalties for such obstructionism were meted out, grain pilferers faced death, and bureaucrats on the collective farms carefully monitored all agricultural activities. By the end of the 1930s, Russian grain production was 50 percent higher than in 1928; population had risen to 170 million—23 million more than in 1926; consumption of food in the emerging industrial centers was rising, although levels were still far below standards of Western Europe; and the rural masses of Russia had been integrated into a socialist state, their opposition broken by the determination of Joseph Stalin.

Industrialization

Collectivization exacted a brutal price from the Russian people and disrupted society, but in Stalin's

view, it was a sacrifice required for the young Soviet socialist nation to overtake and surpass the West in industrial and military power. Ironically, when Stalin instructed his economists to devise a plan for accelerated industrial growth, they turned up a tsarist economic blueprint drafted prior to World War I and revised it. In the course of the 1930s, the foundations of a new industrial society were laid. All industrial plants were brought under state control and assigned production quotas. In 1937, steel and pig iron production was between 16 million and 17 million tons each, two and a half times the levels of five years earlier. And by 1940, Russia was producing 165 million tons of coal and 30 million tons of petroleum as new fields were developed between the Volga and the Urals. The vast mineral resources of the country, until then barely tapped, were brought into production: aluminum, copper, zinc, tin, nickel, and magnesium were needed in the new blast furnaces and rolling mills constructed during this crash program of industrialization. New railroad lines laced the countryside to link industrial centers; the Trans-Siberian Railroad and the network connecting Leningrad, Moscow, the Donets Basin, and the Volga were double-tracked. Canals were built connecting Moscow with the Volga, and the distance from the northern port of Archangel to Leningrad was cut by a factor of four by a new canal.

Some 20 million people migrated from the villages to the cities of Russia over the period 1926–1939; at the same time, the number of cities with populations of 200,000 or more increased from twelve to thirty-nine. The two largest cities—Moscow (4 million) and Leningrad (3.2 million)—doubled in size. In these Communist metropolises, the proletariat was exhorted to increase production quotas; a day's absence from work meant dismissal. A Ukrainian coal miner, Alexei Stakhanov, improved the output of his mining team and achieved fame and heroic status in the Soviet Union. The Stakhanovite movement was formed to encourage greater efforts on the part of all for Mother Russia. For the most part these pleas fell on a dispirited population, sullen with hardship and deprivation. For the one out of three Russians who lived in a city, rapid urbanization had brought housing shortages and inadequate services. In Russia, 9 square yards of living space per person was regarded as the minimum, but in 1939 available living space was less than half that figure. The skeleton of a modern industrial state was being forged in Russia, but the resultant human dislocations caused by urbanization and industrialization—social tensions that had been absorbed in Britain during a century—were forced upon Russians in a decade.

The geographical distribution of Russia's new industry was influenced by political and economic factors. In conformity with Marxist philosophy, a more even allocation of industrial activity throughout the country was considered desirable so that backward regions would not be exploited by powerful concentrations of economic activity in previously established centers. An attempt was made to locate industries as close as possible to sources of fuel and raw materials and to reduce dependence on interregional transport. And because of Stalin's obsessive fear of military conquest from the West, which in World War II proved justified, a major effort was made to reduce the concentration of industry in European Russia, the area most vulnerable to attack.

A second coal and steel concentration, the Urals-Kuznetsk combine, was constructed in the east. Magnitogorsk, the primary center in the Urals, grew in eight years from a collection of huts to an iron-processing city of 146,000. Iron was shipped from Magnitogorsk to the Kuznetsk coal mining district in Siberia, and to the emerging city of Karaganda on the steppes of Kazakhstan. Coal was moved westward, iron eastward, and steel mills were established at both ends, an integrated industrial combine spanning more than 1200 miles. In addition, petroleum fields were developed in the Volga region to relieve Russia's heavy dependence on oil from the Caucasus. Population growth in Central Asia and Siberia was triple that of European Russia as a new east-west industrial axis formed along the Trans-Siberian Railroad. Although the process of industrial growth was incomplete at the outbreak of World War II when German armies swarmed over the traditional industrial complexes of European Russia and the Ukraine—which still produced two-thirds of Russia's coal, iron, and steel—the new industrial pattern in Asiatic Russia contributed substantially to Russia's survival in the war and formed the basis of Russia's later rise to world power.

RUSSIA

REGIONAL PATTERNS

PHYSICAL FEATURES MAP
POPULATION DENSITY MAP

Today as in the tsarist past, Russia is the largest nation in the world and embraces within its 38,000-mile borders the eastern half of Europe and the entire northern half of the Asian landmass. Two and one-half times the size of the United States and one-sixth of the world's land area, Russia is the general term used to refer to the Soviet Union or Union of Soviet Socialist Republics (USSR), a nation of landscapes and peoples unevenly distributed within the broadest of all national frameworks. Specifically, "Russia" refers to the homeland of the Russian people—one ethnic group among nearly 100 in the Soviet Union. However, in common and historical usage, "Russia" refers to the entire landmass encompassed by the Soviet Union.

Most of this sprawling country lies at latitudes north of the Canadian-United States border, and the largest population centers of Russian society—Moscow and Leningrad—are located at latitudes comparable to those of southern Alaska. Monotonous stretches of treeless Arctic waste (tundra) and snowbound *evergreen* forests (taiga) cover the northern half of the country. In the south, outliers of the Himalaya *massif* thrust northward into the deserts of Soviet Central Asia. These harsh environmental conditions at least partly explain why Russia has an average population density of just over twenty-five people per square mile, half the world average. Between these extremes of latitude and climate, a triangular wedge of fertile, well-populated land defines the core of the modern Russian state, the Fertile Triangle. The Fertile Triangle, broad in the relatively mild, well-watered European west, tapers eastward along an axis of Soviet industry and agriculture into south-central Siberia. Within these generalized environments, virtually every set of climatic variation short of the tropical can be found; sheer immensity ensures a national landscape of abundant variety and distinctions. Furthermore, the cultural landscape is peopled by perhaps the most complex national population in the world.

In the tsarist period, Russia was frequently characterized as a "prison of peoples" not simply because of the absolute autocracy of the Russian state, but also as a description of the great cultural diversity of the nation. Over the course of several centuries, Russians have progressively expanded from their traditional homeland in the forest between the Oka River and the *headwaters* of the Volga to conquer Baltic and related Slavic peoples on their western borders, the Muslims of Soviet Central Asia to the south, and numerous Asiatic peoples located in lands that extend 6000 miles between European Russia and the Pacific Ocean. The modern Russian state, 242 million people in 1970, includes more than 100 different racial, ethnic, linguistic, and national groups within its territory. Environmental diversity is thus complemented by cultural variation. Not surprisingly, patterns of human occupance are extremely complex, and local variations in levels of social and economic development are uneven.

Within this complexity of vast distances, cultural differences, and environmental difficulties, Russia's problems, today as in the past, resolve to questions of the size of the landmass, the degree of environmental harshness, the isolation of much of that land, and effective settlement in vast areas marked by a relative lack of human dominance. Thus, the human *regions* of Russia are defined by their environmental accessibility, effective settlement, and economic integration within the country as a whole.

Three generalized regions basic to Russian life can be identified: the Fertile Triangle, the Russian North, and the Southern Periphery. The western boundary of the Fertile Triangle lies at Russia's European frontiers and its apex extends eastward to Lake Baikal. It contains two-thirds of the Russian population, three-quarters of all Soviet agriculture and industry, and a majority of the country's sources of energy, minerals, and metals. This region includes the long-settled European core of the Soviet Union—the Moscow region, the Baltic, and the Ukraine—as well as a more recently developed Asian frontier stretching from the Volga River through the Ural Mountains to beyond the Kuznetsk Basin in south-central Siberia. The Russian North encompasses more than half the land area of the country, a 1000- to 2000-mile-wide band of tundra and forest that stretches across the entire breadth of Russia. Thinly populated until recently, the North contributes only marginally to the Soviet economy through mining and lumbering. Climate in the Arctic and Siberia poses special problems to settlement. Siberia, almost totally within the Russian North, is the traditional name given to the geographical area extending from the Ural Mountains to the Pacific Ocean across the Soviet Union. The

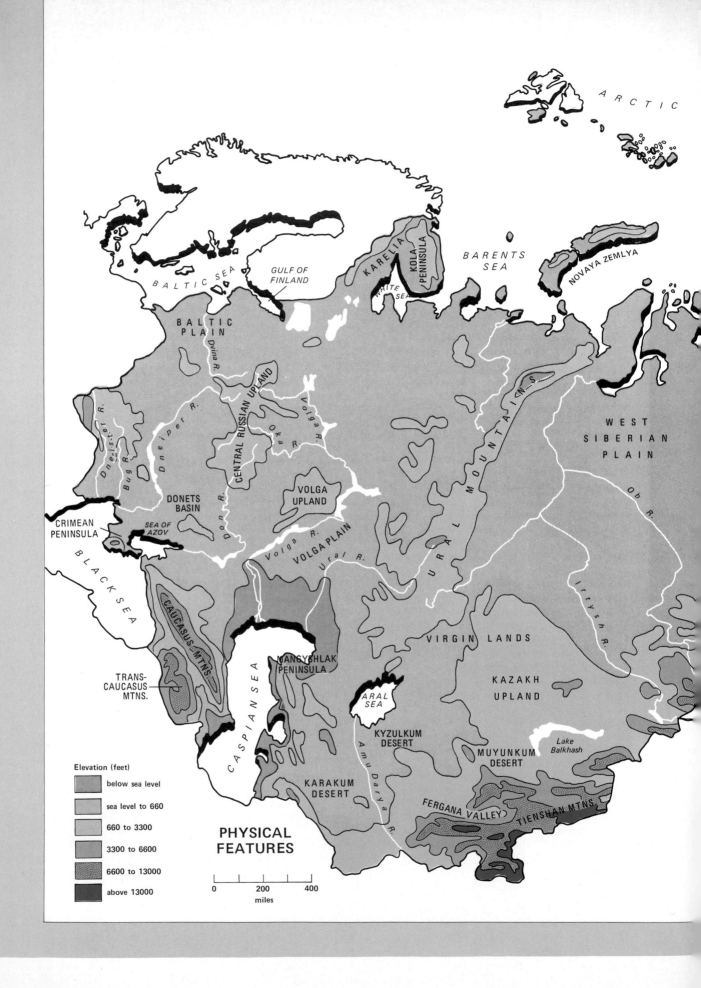

ARCTIC

BARENTS
SEA

KARELIA

KOLA
PENINSULA

WHITE
SEA

NOVAYA ZEMLYA

BALTIC SEA

GULF OF
FINLAND

BALTIC
PLAIN

Dvina R.

Dneister R.

Bug R.

Dnieper R.

CENTRAL RUSSIAN UPLAND

Oka R.

Don R.

Volga R.

WEST
SIBERIAN
PLAIN

U R A L   M O U N T A I N S

Ob R.

VOLGA
UPLAND

DONETS
BASIN

CRIMEAN
PENINSULA

SEA OF
AZOV

Volga R.

VOLGA PLAIN

Ural R.

Irtysh R.

BLACK SEA

CAUCASUS MTNS.

TRANS-
CAUCASUS
MTNS.

CASPIAN SEA

MANGYSHLAK
PENINSULA

ARAL
SEA

VIRGIN LANDS

KAZAKH
UPLAND

Lake
Balkhash

KYZULKUM
DESERT

MUYUNKUM
DESERT

Amu Darya R.

KARAKUM
DESERT

FERGANA VALLEY

TIENSHAN MTNS.

Elevation (feet)

below sea level

sea level to 660

660 to 3300

3300 to 6600

6600 to 13000

above 13000

PHYSICAL
FEATURES

0   200   400
miles

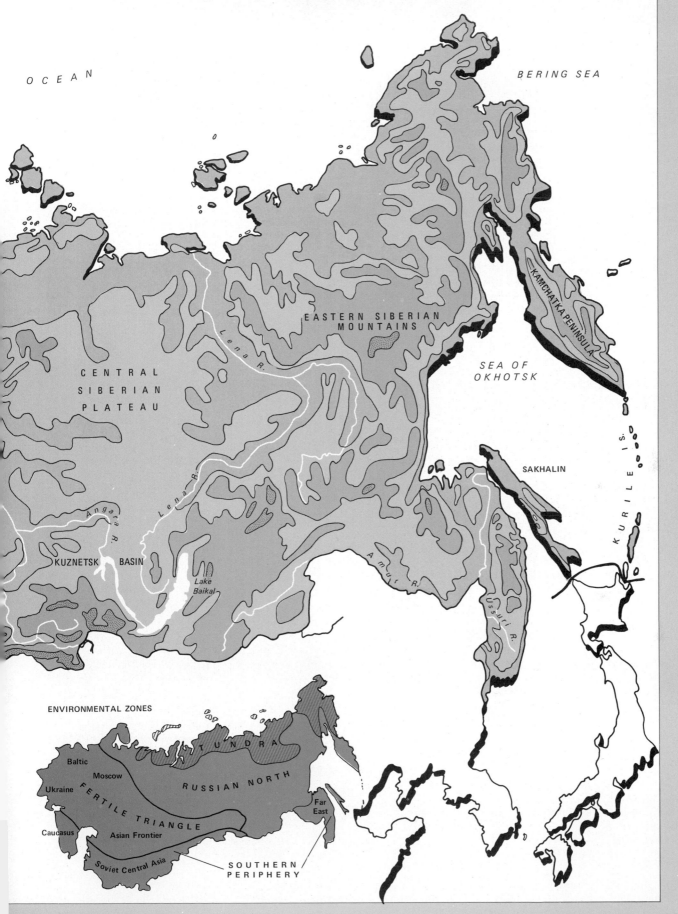

OCEAN

BERING SEA

EASTERN SIBERIAN
MOUNTAINS

CENTRAL
SIBERIAN
PLATEAU

Lena R.

Lena R.

Angara R.

KUZNETSK   BASIN

*Lake
Baikal*

Amur R.

Ussuri R.

KAMCHATKA PENINSULA

SEA OF
OKHOTSK

SAKHALIN

KURILE IS.

ENVIRONMENTAL ZONES

Baltic

Moscow

Ukraine

Caucasus

Asian Frontier

Soviet Central Asia

T U N D R A

RUSSIAN NORTH

FERTILE TRIANGLE

Far
East

SOUTHERN
PERIPHERY

Southern Periphery extends through the Caucasus, Soviet Central Asia, and the Far East to include a discontinuous band of mountains, steppes, and deserts along the southern borders of the Soviet Union. Like the northlands, this region is thinly populated, contributes little to the national economy, and was occupied solely by non-Russian peoples until modern times. In many ways a region defined only by location, the Southern Periphery contains a strategic band of cultural spillovers from the countries that abut Russia in the south—Turkey, Iran, Afghanistan, Mongolia, and China.

THE FERTILE TRIANGLE

The agricultural and industrial heart of Russia, the Fertile Triangle is a region of social and environmental complexity that anywhere else on earth would be a country by itself. It lies wedged between Arctic Siberia to the northeast and the deserts and mountains ringing the Soviet Union's south-central perimeter. The historic centers of Russian civilization—Moscow, Kiev, and Leningrad—anchor its northern quarter. These early established administrative and trading cities were supported by *hinterlands** of peasants cultivating the brown forest soils of the rolling plains of European Russia and benefited from the longer growing season and milder winter that prevail in this area. To the south, forests yield to the grasslands of the Ukraine, whose thick, fertile black soils (chernozems) support the highest rural population densities in Russia; the heavy industrial complex of the Donets Basin follows farther east. The Ukraine and the long-established cities of northeastern Russia form the European core of the Fertile Triangle. East of the European core, Soviet settlers have been drawn by opportunities progressively farther east—to the vast oil fields of the Volga plains, the mineral resources of the Ural Mountains, the grasslands of northern Kazakhstan, and the raw materials of the Kuznetsk Basin—in a migration in some ways similar to that of the American pioneers to the West. Overall, the Fertile Triangle supports 190 million of Russia's 240 million people, creating far higher densities of population than in the rest of the Soviet Union. It contains most of Russia's good agricultural land and all five of the major industrial concentrations—the light industries of Moscow and Leningrad and the heavy industries of Donets, the Urals, and Kuznetsk. By any measure, this is the heartland of Russia. Its six identifiable subregions—Moscow, the Baltic, and the Ukraine in the European core; the Volga, the Urals, and the Kuznetsk Basin on the Asian frontier—although considerably different from one another culturally and environmentally, stand apart from the Russian periphery by reason of their high levels of social and economic development. Although for ideological and strategic reasons Soviet planners have tried to divert development away from this core area and into Siberia, Central Asia, and the Far East, the Fertile Triangle has been and will remain the fulcrum of the Russian state.

The European Core

The European core of the Fertile Triangle can be subdivided into three areas—Moscow in the north, the Baltic in the northwest, and the Ukraine in the south. The Moscow subregion, the original homeland of the Russian people, is a gently rolling, forested plain located in the transitional climatic zone on the southern taiga margins. Moscow benefited from its position at the hub of the extensive river system of the East European Plain—the Volga, the Don, the Dnieper, and the Dvina—to become a trading and artisan center; later, Moscow served as the springboard for Russian migration south into the Ukraine and east into Siberia. This locational advantage helped compensate for the meager resources of its hinterland—acidic, poorly drained forest soils that produced low grain yields; cold, damp winters with six months of snow; no energy resources except wood and *peat;** and few significant mineral deposits. In the nineteenth century, however, Moscow's historical position as the social and political capital of the Russian people was reinforced by the growth of the railroad network, which made Moscow the *railhead** of the nation, and by canals which linked the city with the Baltic, Caspian, and Black seas. Food, raw materials, and energy resources flowed along these routes into the administrative capital, promoting the emergence of the Moscow region as an industrial center that today supports 35 million people. With a current population of nearly 7 million, the city of Moscow is ringed by satellite industrial cities and suburbs, an economic landscape of textile mills and metal and machine plants on the Russian plain, whose combined product is the largest in the nation.

The Baltic region west of Moscow and north of the Ukraine is a *glacial** landscape of *bogs,** lakes, and forest. It is located so far north that the sun in midwinter barely rises above the horizon and in midsummer barely sets.

Its importance in the national economy stems from Russia's historical drive toward the Baltic Sea to gain access to Europe. This drive culminated in the establishment of Saint Petersburg (Leningrad) in the early eighteenth century on the poorly drained *delta** of the Neva River, the point on the Baltic shore closest to Moscow. Like Moscow, Saint Petersburg—Tsar Peter the Great's "window on the West"—was founded in an infertile region whose poorly drained, glaciated soils, northern location, and paucity of energy and mineral resources had long retarded development. Centuries of conflict among Germans, Poles, Swedes, and Russians for political dominance in the Baltic necessitated the establishment of strong rail and water connections between Leningrad and the farmlands and resources of the Ukraine, Moscow, and the Urals. Although much of the countryside around the city has remained a poor farming area, resources imported from elsewhere in the Soviet Union have made the region an important industrial center. Coal, iron ore, and other materials shipped by rail and barge and oil and gas moved by pipeline have spurred the city to achieve importance as a port and center of manufacturing.

Leningrad, with a population of nearly 4 million today, is a major center of engineering, electronic, chemical, and metal-working industries, although it is clearly located outside the mainstream of contemporary Russian economic growth. Despite the firm Russian development and occupation of the area, its precarious location on the Baltic *march-land** has left a residue of complex cultures in this region unusual in the Slav-dominated Fertile Triangle. Only a third of the nearly 25 million people in this region are Great Russians, another third are Belorussians with their own distinctive language, and the remainder are Lithuanians, Latvians, and Estonians who were unwillingly incorporated into the Soviet Union at the end of World War II.

The third subregion in the European core of the Fertile Triangle is the Ukraine, offering the best-endowed and most productive farmland in Russia. Forested in the north and covered by grasslands in the south, almost the entire region is underlain by *humus**-laden chernozem soils. Its relatively southerly location defines a far more moderate climate than either the Moscow or Leningrad regions, allowing a longer growing season. These environmental factors make the Ukraine the breadbasket of Russia, a land of rolling *plateaus** and *escarpments** etched by parallel northwest to southeast rivers—the Bug, the Dniester, the Dnieper, the Donets, and the Don.

Until the nineteenth century, the Ukraine was a Cossack frontier, a backward area in contrast to the more densely populated woodlands to the north. Extensive wheat- and sheep-raising estates were established in pioneer fashion by noblemen; with the discovery of the iron deposits of Krivoy Rog and the coal of the Donets Basin, the Ukraine was transformed into the agricultural and industrial heartland of the Russian state. Currently, nearly 60 million people live in this region spread across the old agricultural districts of the north and west (centered on Kiev) and concentrated in a belt of industry located between the Donets Basin and the Dnieper bend. The entire region is populated by Slavic-language speakers, two-thirds of whom are classified as Ukrainians.

The Asian Frontier

East of the European core of the Fertile Triangle, a wedge of fertile agricultural land narrows eastward from the Volga plains to the low ranges of the Urals, past the *watershed** of the Ob River, and into south-central Siberia. The longitudinal rivers and mountains of this expansive region are crosscut by latitudinal climatic zones that converge eastward to narrow this strip of moderate climate and cultivable land which runs between northern forests and southern mountains and deserts. A limited industrial complex was established in the Urals during the reign of Peter the Great in the eighteenth century; some settlers filtered into this region with the construction of the Trans-Siberian Railroad. But for the most part this remained a backward area, an Asian frontier beyond the Volga, which for many years formed the boundary between the civilized regions of European Russia and the Asian unknown. In the last thirty years, this region has been opened to new settlement and exploitation; the discovery of vast energy resources and raw materials in the region has formed the basis for a new industrial axis of some 70 million people. The Volga, longest river in Europe, traditionally marked the outer rim of Russia but today connects the resources of the east and the dense populations of the west.

Russians conquered the Volga plains and founded the cities of Kuybyshev, Saratov, and Volgograd in the middle of the sixteenth century. Except along the Volga, a north-south highway of trade connecting the Caspian Sea with the Baltic Sea, the region remained a plains landscape of peasant grain cultivators coping with periodic drought and famine caused by uncertain rainfall. Although endowed with navigable streams and timber resources, the Volga River region was not industrialized until the Soviet period. After World War II, the discovery of immense oil reserves on the Volga plains transformed the economy and society of the region. New settlers and industries were brought to the Volga Basin, vast hydroelectric projects were begun, and engineering and *petrochemical** plants were established in the older towns. The population has increased to nearly 30 million, and the influx of Russians from the west has submerged the non-Slavic minorities who dominated the area until modern times—the Tatars, the Bashkir, and the Chuvash. Now the fastest-growing industrial region in Russia and producing four-fifths of the country's petroleum, the Volga capitalizes on its intermediate location between Moscow and the Urals.

The Ural Mountains and the flat plains of western Siberia attracted some 7 million Russian migrants from the European core at the turn of this century. On the wetter northern margins of the grassland steppes, grain farms were established as peasants gambled on adequate rainfall when new railroads provided access to European markets for their wheat and butter. In the Urals, the antiquated charcoal-based iron industry originally constructed by Peter the Great offered employment to a growing

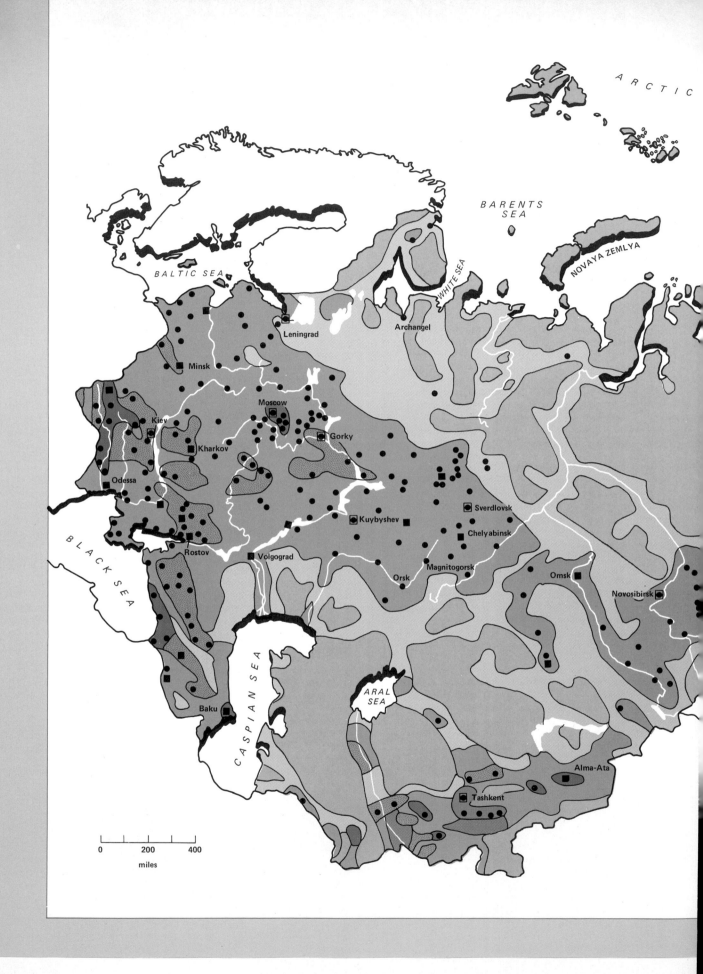

ARCTIC

BARENTS
SEA

NOVAYA ZEMLYA

BALTIC SEA

WHITE SEA

Leningrad

Archangel

Minsk

Moscow

Kiev

Gorky

Kharkov

Odessa

Sverdlovsk

Kuybyshev

Chelyabinsk

Rostov

Volgograd

Orsk

Magnitogorsk

BLACK SEA

Omsk

Novosibirsk

CASPIAN SEA

ARAL
SEA

Baku

Alma-Ata

Tashkent

0   200   400

miles

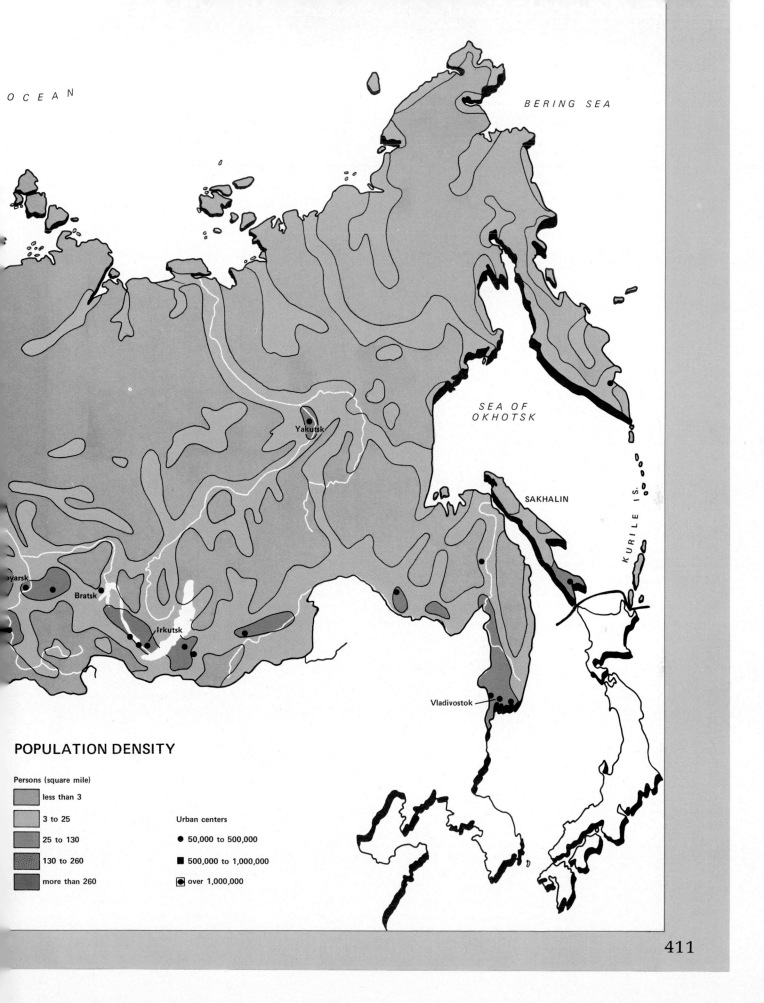

OCEAN

BERING SEA

SEA OF
OKHOTSK

Yakutsk

SAKHALIN

KURILE IS.

oyarsk

Bratsk

Irkutsk

Vladivostok

POPULATION DENSITY

Persons (square mile)

less than 3

3 to 25

25 to 130

130 to 260

more than 260

Urban centers

● 50,000 to 500,000

■ 500,000 to 1,000,000

◉ over 1,000,000

Rural Siberia in the late 1960s. For centuries a backward area, the boundary between European and Asian Russia, in the last thirty years south-central Siberia has been opened to settlement and exploitation. *Photo:* Wide World.

working class. But regional development on the Asian Frontier lagged until the 1930s, when the decision was taken to modernize industry in the Urals through the establishment of the Urals-Kuznetsk combine. Coal is shuttled 1200 miles westward to the Urals from the Kuznetsk Basin in Siberia; iron ore is sent east to Kuznetsk, and steel complexes exist at both ends of the line. Greatly accelerated during World War II, industry in the Urals was facilitated by the discovery of a rich storehouse of metals and minerals, the most important of which are high-quality iron ore, copper, and a variety of *ferroalloys.*

Sverdlovsk emerged as the principal center of a northern cluster of industrial cities, and to the south, Chelyabinsk, Magnitogorsk, and Orsk are growing more rapidly than any other cities in the Soviet Union. The energy problem has been solved by sending coal from Karaganda (in Kazakhstan) and Kuznetsk; oil is shipped eastward from the Volga Basin to the Urals, thereby making the Urals an indispensable industrial base on the Asian frontier. In addition, some 90 million acres of land in the southern steppes of this region on the borders of Kazakhstan were plowed under the virgin lands program of the 1950s. Migration to these marginal

farmlands has pushed the population of the Urals and associated lowlands to nearly 20 million, but as in the American prairies, the threat of erosion, drought, and the possibility of *dust bowl* conditions make the permanence of today's agricultural experiments uncertain.

The Kuznetsk Basin and associated industrial areas near Lake Baikal form the tapering eastern end of the Fertile Triangle. Like the Urals to the west, the Kuznetsk Basin has experienced rapid industrial growth in the modern period. The terrain is rugged; cold northern climates and southern deserts converge at the Kuznetsk to pinch off good arable land. Only in the black-soil country of the Altai steppe at the headwaters of the Ob is adequate rainfall available; this region attracted early agricultural immigrants with the construction of the Trans-Siberian line. Modern development, however, has centered upon industry, as the Kuznetsk coal basin and the hydroelectric power resources of the Angara, Yenisei, and Irtysh rivers form Russia's most powerful source of industrial energy. Despite environmental liabilities and great distance from Russia's principal centers of population, coal- and steel-based cities, the largest of which are Novosibirsk and Novokuznetsk, have mushroomed in the Kuznetsk Basin. The construction of huge hydroelectric stations at Bratsk on the Angara River and Krasnoyarsk on the Yenisei has fostered parallel urban and industrial explosions. On this basis, a third metallurgical base for the Soviet Union with a current population of 20 million is developing in the Kuznetsk, the distant frontier tip of the Fertile Triangle.

THE RUSSIAN NORTH
[FIGURE 3]

The Russian North, a 4-million-square-mile area larger than Canada or the United States, contains only 5 million people and is the least populated, least known, and least exploited region in the Soviet Union. Along the rim of the Arctic, tundra environments prevail over a tenth of the country. Here winters are long and bitter, and despite continuous daylight in summer, average monthly temperatures remain below 50 degrees Fahrenheit. The only trees that can grow are stunted birches. Vegetation is composed of mosses, lichens, and ferns thinly rooted on the bare rock surfaces and in the frozen bogs of this glaciated region. Inhabitants consist of reindeer herders, miners of the scarce and valuable minerals in the area, and the personnel of military bases and prison camps.

South of the tundra, land essentially deprived of trees by cold, an enormous evergreen forest, the taiga, stretches 4000 miles across the country in a belt 1000 to 2000 miles wide. Most taiga is unpopulated and unused. Although temperatures are warmer than in the Arctic, the soils of this forest are some of the poorest in the world. These soils, *podzols*,° lack humus and have been *leached*° of nutritive value and clay, so that cultivation requires heavy soil reconstruction. Standing bogs cover much of the region. In many areas, the subsoil is permanently frozen, a condition called permafrost, and the alternate winter freezing and summer thawing of the topsoil provide an unstable foundation for rail lines, roads, and buildings. Across the northern half of Russia's vast territory, therefore, human occupance is tentative and economic development limited and selective.

Yet certain regional differences in levels of utilization can be identified in the Russian North. In the European section, where four-fifths of the population of the Russian North resides, the moderating influence of Atlantic air masses ameliorate the winter cold, limit permafrost conditions, and push vegetation boundaries farther north. Murmansk, an ice-free port, is connected by rail to Moscow. Fish and forest products are shipped south to the populated core of European Russia, and the Kola Peninsula has emerged as an important iron mining center as well as the primary source of apatite, a phosphate ore used for fertilizer. East of Karelia, however, a low, marshy glacial plain mostly devoted to fishing and hunting extends to the northern Urals. East of the Urals, the West Siberian Plain and the Central Siberian Plateau stretch monotonously to the rugged mountains of the Far East beyond the

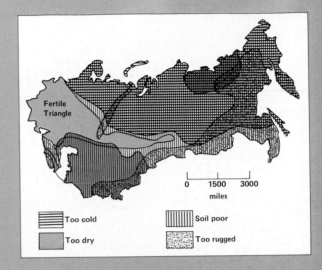

Figure 3. Environmental Limitations. Throughout most of Russia, environments are unfavorable for agricultural settlement: In the north the climate is cold and soils are poor; in the south it is too dry; and in the east it is too cold and rugged. Only the Fertile Triangle has a significant area of comparatively good land. *Adapted from:* John P. Cole and F. C. German, *A Geography of the U.S.S.R.* London: Butterworths, 1970, p. 116, Fig. 9.2.

Lena River. Except for Norilsk, a nickel and copper mining and treatment center near the *estuary*° of the Yenisei, and some gold mining centers in eastern Siberia, the region is virtually unoccupied. Although two-thirds of Russia's coal reserves and a comparable proportion of its hydroelectric power potential are located in the frozen Siberian north, these resources are not likely to be developed except under very unusual circumstances. The various reindeer-herding tribes who now number a million probably will retain control of the northern environment, with Russians concentrated in isolated urban mining and lumbering centers.

THE SOUTHERN PERIPHERY
The Southern Periphery is composed of the Caucasus, Soviet Central Asia, and the Far East. Like the Russian North, it lies outside the primary axis of social and economic development. The Caucasus, located between the Black and Caspian seas, is a mountain refuge where non-Russians make up 80 percent of the nearly 20 million people in the region. Of the thirty different ethnic groups in the Caucasus, Muslim Azerbaijanis and Christian Georgians and Armenians are the most numerous, although the 3 million Russians clustered in the cities of the region, principally Baku, wield disproportionate influence over the economy and politics of the area. The broken terrain of the Caucasus has generated considerable cultural complexity—a mixed economy of grazing in mountain pastures, corn growing in Transcaucasia, and the cultivation

413

The mountains of the Caucasus between the Black and Caspian seas shelter a large non-Russian population, mainly Muslim Azerbaijanis and Christian Georgians and Armenians. *Photo:* Wide World.

of tea, citrus, and vegetable crops on the Black Sea coast and the lowlands bordering the Caspian Sea. The national significance of this region, based on the oil production of Baku, has declined substantially with the opening of the Volga oil fields, leaving the Caucasus outside the migratory stream of Russian industrial development in the Fertile Triangle to the north.

Soviet Central Asia is also peripheral to the modern Soviet economy. Separated from the Fertile Triangle by the deserts of Middle Asia (the Kara Kum, Kyzyl Kum, and Muyun Kum), this region is the least industrialized and most rural in Russia. Conquered by Russians in the 1880s, the nomadic tribes of Central Asia were gradually *sedentarized.*• Central Asia is the ancient homeland of Muslim Uzbek, Tadzhik, Kirghiz, and Turkmenian peoples, an extension of the Middle Eastern cultural complex into Soviet territory. Settlement is concentrated in ancient *oases*• such as Samarkand, Bukhara, and Khiva at the foot of the eastern mountains that rim the southern borders of Soviet Central Asia. In more recent Russian history, some cities have undergone considerable expansion, notably Tashkent, the center of the region's railroad network and a city of 1 million. Less than 10 percent of the 20 million people in Central Asia are Russians. Although commercial cotton cultivation in the irrigated Fergana Valley, the Tashkent oasis, and the lower Amu Darya River and the discovery of natural gas at Gazli west of Bukhara have transformed the economy of Soviet Central Asia, its people have resisted assimilation into Soviet society. It is one of the few remaining areas in the world conquered by colonizing Europeans in the nineteenth century that has failed to secure status as an independent nation.

By contrast, the Far East, the third region of the Southern Periphery, is almost completely occupied by Russians. Most of its 5 million Russian inhabitants, however, did not migrate to the Far East until the twentieth century, after the Trans-Siberian Railroad provided a lifeline to the Russian heartland. Overall, the Far East remains a landscape of densely forested mountains rich in game (particularly tiger and bear). The only Russian territory east of the Yenisei River whose soils are not underlain by permafrost are found in the basin of the Amur River, the dominant watershed of the Far East. Agricultural settlement is confined to patches of soil in the valleys, the largest at Khabarovsk at the confluence of the Amur and the Ussuri rivers, while fishing settlements are found on the Pacific coast, ice-free only during the summer months. Vladivostok to the south is one of Russia's few good harbors. In general, this region provides little to the Soviet economy except fish; were it not for its strategic location on the eastern rim of the Soviet domain, its population would probably decline. Chronically short of food and with few energy or industrial resources, the modest assets of the Far East remain distant and perhaps too difficult to secure to make any significant difference economically.

Overall, the regional patterns of the Soviet Union reflect the aspirations of the Russian people over a domain in small part theirs for centuries and in large part a far-flung country of difficult environments and different peoples only recently associated by tsarist imperialism and Soviet development.

THE SOVIET STATE
2

The victorious Soviet Union emerged from World War II as one of the world's two great industrial powers. Only the United States could challenge Russia in resources and production. The country had gained a new empire through warfare. Estonia, Latvia, Lithuania, and parts of eastern Poland, East Prussia, and Finnish Karelia had been incorporated into the Soviet state; in the southwest, Bukovina, Ruthenia, and Bessarabia became part of Russia. In Asiatic Russia, southern Sakhalin and the Kurile Islands fell under Soviet dominion, as did Tannu Tuva, a fertile valley on the Mongolian border larger than the state of New York but known only to stamp collectors. In addition, Soviet troops and influence held sway over 100 million people in the so-called satellite countries of Eastern Europe—Poland, Hungary, East Germany, Romania, Czechoslovakia, Bulgaria, and Albania—to form a broad buffer zone between Western Europe and the Russian homeland. Yugoslavia remained Communist but independent of Moscow's authority.

But for all its new international standing and despite immense territorial gains, the Soviet Union was on the brink of economic ruin and close to social collapse. Four years of savage warfare had wrought havoc across the Russian landscape. Some 20 million Russians died in the war; this staggering loss only became known when the 1959 Soviet census revealed a total Russian population of only 200 million. Nearly 70,000 villages and 1710 towns in European Russia had been leveled; an estimated 25 million people were homeless in 1945. Some 31,000 factories employing 4 million people had been destroyed; 40,000 miles of railroad track lay uprooted. Food, clothing, and housing were rationed; approximately one-quarter of all material goods in Russia had disappeared during the war. The immediate problem facing Russia was the revival of agricultural productivity and the reconstruction of industry in a land laid waste in the struggle for victory. Recon-struction was a persistent theme of Soviet life in the postwar era. As the Soviet economic order evolved and matured, defects became apparent in the strategies used to shape the Russian urban and agricultural environments. "The Soviet State" discusses these present-day Russian social dilemmas as questions posed by the multicultural society of the USSR.

REBUILDING
[FIGURE 4]

The Soviets considered three paths toward reconstruction: Russia could rely on its own resources and exhausted people to rebuild the nation; massive reparations could be demanded from the defeated enemy; long-term credits from the United States could finance redevelopment. The latter course was rejected out of hand by orthodox Marxists, who viewed assistance from the West as ideologically incompatible with the goals of a Soviet socialist state. The Allies prevented the payment of reparations by Germany, believing that the harsh peace treaty imposed at the end of World War I was an important factor in the rise of the Nazi party. Stalin, however, fearing invasion from the West, was already anticipating a resurgent Germany that could invade Russia yet a third time in three generations. In Soviet eyes, the domination of Eastern Europe was essential to Russian security. But to the West, the Russian dominance created an Iron Curtain separating the free world from the Communists. As mutual suspicions deepened, the United States decided to rebuild wartorn Western Europe under the Marshall Plan. The Soviets stripped Eastern Europe of much of its industrial *infrastructure,* moving entire factories by rail from Czechoslovakia and East Germany to Russia. Stalin perceived Russia as encircled by capitalists determined to destroy the revolution. Confrontations in Iran, Korea, and Greece intensified cold war hostilities; in the background, the power of nuclear weapons demonstrated at Hiroshima loomed large in the thinking of Russian leaders. For these reasons, Stalin determined that Russia would go it alone. As in 1928, the Russian people would have to forego material goods and leisure: if Russia did not match and exceed the military power of the West, the nation would again be beaten for its backwardness.

The economic targets projected for the First Postwar Five-Year Plan (1946–1950) seemed impossibly high, but they were part of Stalin's absolute determination that Soviet industrial production should overtake that of Western Europe and the United States. Some 3000 medium- and large-scale industrial plants were rebuilt; 2700 new factories were created. Special emphasis was given to revival of the traditional industrial centers of western and southwestern Russia, the Moscow region, and the Ukraine. This did not represent, however, a reversal of the goal to enlarge eastern industrializing centers;

rather, total production was to be increased everywhere. Huge dams were constructed on the Volga and Dnieper rivers; the electrical output of Kazakhstan was doubled. The network of concentration camps, the Gulag Archipelago (fundamental to Russia's wartime effort), was maintained intact with as many as 10 million inmates—a figure continuously depleted by premature death but constantly replenished by new prisoners.

In society at large, the wartime work week of forty-eight hours was retained; malingering, laziness, obstructionism were summarily punished. The Russian people were exhorted by a barrage of domestic propaganda campaigns to reconstruct the Russian landscape and safeguard the aims of the revolution. By 1952, overall Soviet industrial production was 2.5 times higher than in 1940. Stalin's long-term goals of an annual production of 500 million tons of coal, 60 million tons of steel, and 60 million tons of petroleum—dismissed as unrealistic, imaginative ramblings by competent Western observers—were met by 1960. The harsh demands of the Russian government succeeded particularly in heavy industry. However, two problems—slow agricultural recovery and low production of consumer goods—continued to plague Stalin's successors after his death in 1953.

Figure 4. Urbanization of Russia. These graphs illustrate the changing size and urbanizing nature of Russia's population. Although Russian demographic patterns have been drastically altered by war, revolution, and social reorganization, the figures demonstrate that Russia has experienced the general effects of industrialization. Birth and death rates have progressively declined, and the population is increasingly concentrated in cities. Russia today exhibits the relatively low rate of population growth of other nations of the technological world.

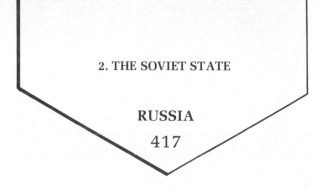
The Soviet Union exploded its first atomic bomb in 1949 and added hydrogen bombs to its military arsenal four years later. Russia successfully tested the first intercontinental ballistic missile (ICBM) in 1957, thereby enlarging the strike capability of nuclear weapons across continents and oceans. A few weeks later, the Soviet Union electrified the world by launching the first earth satellite, *Sputnik*; in 1961 Yuri Gagarin became the first man to enter space. The United States was forced to reevaluate its space and weapons program, educational goals, and military posture in the world in the light of Russian advances. The Soviet assertion that communism was the wave of the future came to dominate the global strategies of war and peace as the cold war heightened. Nowhere did the Soviet example attract more attention than in the newly independent nations of the developing world. By 1972, ten years after the decade of independence, Marxist-Leninist political parties had been established in sixty-two nations of the developing world.

To many, the Russian example provides a clear-cut method of attaining rapid industrialization and modernization and serves as an alternative form of social and economic organization to the capitalist system that most of the developing countries experienced as subject colonial peoples. The ideological

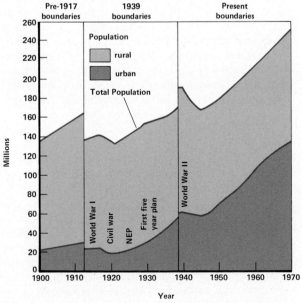

(A)

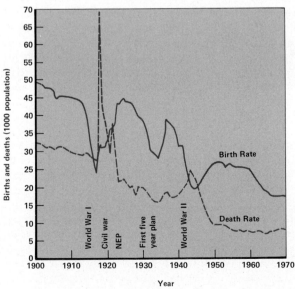

(B)

World War II brought destruction and chaos in Russia on a tremendous scale: 20 million people died and 25 million were left homeless; nearly 70,000 villages and 2,000 towns in European Russia were leveled. According to the caption of this German photograph received in Lisbon in 1943, the scene is of a destroyed Russian tank on a street in Stalingrad, a city that endured a terrible siege as well as near-total destruction. *Photo:* Wide World.

struggle for the hearts and minds of these nations, begun in the 1950s, has not ended. The economic achievements of the United States compared with Russia and of Western Europe compared with Eastern Europe became the substance of international debate and diplomacy in the post-World War II and postcolonial era. The substantial achievements of the Soviet Union, and particularly its quick transformation from a backward, agrarian society into a modern industrial state, are alluring. To many, Soviet communism offers a seductive and practical model for meeting the ***revolution of rising expectations*** in the developing world. Obscured from world view, however, have been the inefficiency and arbitrariness of the Soviet economic order, the brutal and dictatorial suppression of the Russian people, the staggering human cost of the developmental process, and the vast natural endowment of the Soviet earth—all factors that directly contribute to the rapid economic progress of the Soviet Union today.

THE SOVIET ECONOMIC ORDER

Lenin once defined communism as "Soviet power plus electrification." In modified form, these two principles—the power of the state over economic functions and the rigorous emphasis upon heavy industry and energy exploitation—have remained values central to the Soviet organization of Russian life. Unlike the nations of the industrial West, the Soviet Union has a command economy. All natural resources, sources of production, and financial institutions are owned by or are at the command of the state: water, land, minerals, property, transport, and communications. According to Marx, state ownership of property would open up limitless economic vistas. But for these economic horizons to be realized, a new and evolving form of economic organization had to arise out of Communist doctrine. The resulting difficulties in coping with ideological heritage and Russian isolation, environment, and organization unfold in the recent history of the USSR. The militaristic emphasis of the early Soviet period of industrialization has left Russia a nation with a highly arbitrary economic system. In the Soviet Union, state planners and bureaucrats—not simple market demand—determine social and economic priorities by projecting the kind, quantity, location, and price of all industrial and agricultural production as well as the wages and salaries of both

A steel plant in the Ukraine in 1939, symbol of the Soviet determination to construct a modern industrial base where none had existed before in the shortest possible time. *Photo:* Wide World.

managers and employees. Collective bargaining and strikes do not occur in this system. In Russia, every act dealing with resources and production is decided at the top and in the center.

State ownership and control of all important sectors of the economy can be credited with both the past successes and current problems of the Soviet Union. Stalin's headlong drive for rapid industrialization in the 1930s favored key economic sectors, namely, those needed to support a strong military. Unlike the situation in modernizing nations today, the goal of achieving a higher standard of living for the Russian people was secondary to the improvement of the military. Indeed, those who proposed a more balanced program of economic growth were condemned as ideological deviationists. Agriculture, housing, consumer needs, and social services waited until the nation became a first-class military power. Enormous engineering projects such as the Magnitogorsk steel complex, the Urals-Kuznetsk combine, and the great dam on the Dnieper were undertaken during this period to boost Soviet industrial statistics. The will and strength of the Russian people, bent on the construction of an industrial

base, reached a frenzy when Nazi Germany threatened national survival. The organizations entrusted with directing these tasks were the Supreme Economic Council and the State Planning Commission, Gosplan.

The basic aims of Stalin's politically motivated economic policies were fulfilled: Russia became one of the two most powerful nations in the world and the second leading industrial producer, despite World War II. Stalin, the architect of Soviet modernization, radically altered the distribution of population in Russia, the structure of life in urban and rural areas, the distribution of industry and economic growth—indeed the entire human geography of one-sixth of the earth. His successors inherited a nation transformed by his personal interpretation of socialism. The face of Russia today reflects this impact as the debate over economic policy continues: heavy industry versus light, industrialization in populated areas versus less developed regions, agricultural production against urban consumption, consumer goods as opposed to capital equipment, the relative importance of material versus moral incentives. Given the highly centralized nature of the Soviet economic order, all decisions on these issues directly affect the land and the direction of life in Russia.

Urbanization and Population Growth
[FIGURE 5]

Although centralized control governs most phases of Russian life, patterns of urbanization and population growth in the Soviet Union are generated by underlying forces similar to those at work in the non-Communist nations of the technological world. In the 1970s, the majority of Russia's 242 million people are concentrated in the more favorable environments of the Fertile Triangle, the long-settled agricultural region of European Russia, and the new eastern industrial complexes selected for development because of their wealth of specific industrial resources. About 56 percent of Russians, 136 million, are urban today, compared with only 15 percent in the 1930s. Strewn across the Soviet landscape are 221 cities with more than 100,000 people and 10 cities with more than 1 million, in addition to the metropolises of Moscow (7 million) and Leningrad (4 million). Rural population is steadily decreasing, particularly in the old agricultural lands of the European core. The industrial modernization of the So-

These apartments in Moscow are indistinguishable from thousands of others in Russia, where standardized housing marks the planned socialist city. *Photo:* Wide World.

Figure 5. Population Profiles of the USSR and the USA. In this population pyramid of the contemporary Soviet Union, age-sex distributions indicate the direct effects of wars (World War I, the Civil War, and World War II) upon the adult male population as a deficit and the indirect effects of the loss of that child-rearing population: a shortage in the youthful population between the ages of 20 to 24. Contrasted to the profile of the American population, the pattern of the Soviet Union's population is interrupted and sex-disadvantaged. *Adapted from:* Paul E. Lydolph, *Geography of the USSR.* New York: Wiley, 1970, p. 339, Fig. 13–2. Copyright © 1964, 1970, by John Wiley & Sons, Inc. Redrawn by permission of the publisher.

viet Union, therefore, is progressively converting Russia's sea of peasants into a nation of urbanites. Russia's current level of urbanization, more than 50 percent of society, was achieved in Britain around 1860 and in the United States in 1920.

The Soviet Union is also beginning to exhibit a population profile that is characteristic of the technological world. Russia is entering the final stage of the **demographic transition,**[•] as low birth and death rates create a modest rate of population growth. In the decade 1960–1970, Russian population grew by only 16 percent; by the end of the 1960s, the birth rate hovered around 18 per 1000 population and the death rate at about 8 per 1000. The low death rate, one-third that of thirty years ago, is a result of ad-

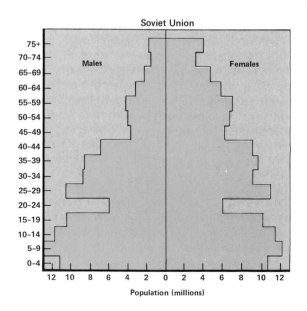

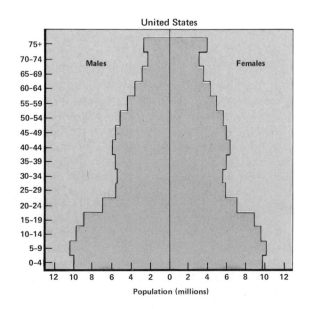

vances in medicine, sanitation, and the control of communicable diseases. It is lower today than that of the United States. Life expectancy in the Soviet Union is sixty-six years for men and seventy-four for women. The low birth rate, particularly in western Russia, is the result of the large number of adult men killed in World War II (there are nearly 10 percent more women than men in the Soviet Union) and the general demographic effects of rising standards of education and rates of urbanization. The Soviet Union is unique in the world in that the state sponsors a high fertility rate: the more children a woman has, the more generous the reward. Family allowances, birth payments, stipends to unwed mothers, and the distribution of medals (Order of the Mother Heroine) to women with ten or more children are public policy. But because Lenin, a pillar of moral organization, contended that either sex should have the right to decide whether a child should be born, abortion is free and contraception holds no social stigma. To the consternation of Soviet demographers, the birth and population growth rates among the non-Russian peoples of the Caucasus, Kazakhstan, and Soviet Central Asia are double those of Russians, meaning that Russians may soon become an ethnic and cultural minority within their own country.

The pattern of urbanization in Russia has been determined by the dynamics of ethnically non-Russian growth as well as by the planned industrial growth of the Soviet state. The five major industrial zones before World War II—Moscow, Leningrad, the Donets Basin, the Urals, and the Kuznetsk Basin— stood as islands of modernization in the countryside. During the 1920s and the 1930s, cities such as Magnitogorsk and Karaganda mushroomed in developing areas, and the urban population of Russia trebled in little more than a decade. Intervening spaces were bypassed in the rush to modernization; regions of extreme environmental difficulty such as the Russian North remained relatively underdeveloped despite the Communist ideological commitment to balanced regional growth. After World War II, in the 1950s, the industrial region between the Volga Plain and Lake Baikal continued its earlier advance as a **growth pole,** strengthened by the discovery of large oil fields and the belated Soviet energy shift from coal to petroleum. During the 1950s, cities in the Asian frontier grew faster than cities in southern California. In the 1960s, urbanization gained further momentum: 478 new towns and 158 cities were established. Since the urban networks and settlement hierarchy of the Russian heartland were relatively complete, the impact of urbanization was greatest in growth pole areas. The regions of important urban growth today are located in the Caucasus, Kazakhstan, and Soviet Central Asia, where new oil and gas discoveries attract willing Russian emigrants and the rate of population in-

crease among the local population is high. In the underdeveloped fringe of European Russia—the Baltic, Belorussia, Moldavia, and the southern Ukraine—cities are growing by immigration. During the 1960s, rural populations decreased everywhere except in the Southern Periphery. More than 16 million people left farming communities; two-thirds of these migrants were young people seeking educations, jobs, and urban amenities. As this human tide continues to flow, it generates problems of urban congestion and rural decay in Communist Russia similar to those of the capitalist industrial nations of the West.

The Planned Social Matrix
[FIGURE 6]

To a greater degree than in other technological societies, Russian planners have been able to channel and divert the flow of urban migrants from one destination to another through administrative devices. Their objective has been to implement and integrate urban with regional planning and to maintain a balance among city size and regional environmental resources, population size, and other conditions in surrounding hinterlands. Action has been taken to limit the growth of the larger cities—Moscow, Leningrad, and Kiev. Migrants are barred from these cities unless they have jobs assigned to them. Police permits are required for people to leave collective farms, and new industries have been implanted in smaller towns; industrial and residential penetration is carefully controlled in **greenbelts** that girdle the largest cities. Despite efforts to avoid the overcrowding, crime, and social unrest apparent in Western cities— and to fulfill Lenin's dictum that there should be a gradual abolition of the distinction between town and country—Russia is today a nation of cities and a society of urban problems. Two-thirds of Russia's forty-seven cities larger than 500,000 population lie within the Fertile Triangle. Despite official restrictions, Moscow figures as the premier Russian city with over 7 million people and 500,000 daily commuters from the suburban zone outside the 6-mile-deep forest belt. Leningrad and the industrial centers in the Ukraine, Volga, Urals, and Kuznetsk continue to grow steadily. But no Russian city has achieved the size and complexity of New York, London, or Tokyo, suggesting that restrictions on growth have been at least partially effective in deflecting the tide to smaller urban centers.

Figure 6. The Socialist City. A 700-square-mile greenbelt encircling Moscow is under direct municipal control. Principally used for recreation, it is also the residence of nearly a million people. The suburban zone, extending up to 45 miles from the city center, houses an additional 2.4 million people, many of whom are daily commuters to the central city. Encroachments along communication lines suggest that planning control has been less than total, although far more effective than in any large American city. Part (b) depicts the *microrayon* or communal apartment district, the universal planned community for residential construction in Russian cities. This blueprint, reproduced in hundreds of cities thousands of miles apart, consists of apartment buildings for 6000 residents grouped around community facilities and services. *Adapted from:* (a) V. A. Kamenskii et al., *Prigorodnyye zony Krupnkykh gorodov* (The Suburban Zones of the Largest Cities). Leningrad: Stroiizdat, 1963, p. 15. (b) N. Baranov et al., *Osnovy sovetskogo gradostroitel'stva*, Vol. II. Moscow: Stroitzdat, 1967, p. 102.

Russian cities are structured by Communist ideology to such a degree that contemporary urban geographers debate whether socialist cities merit treatment as a special type of human environment. The standardization of housing, consistent with Communist principles that a classless city should reflect a uniformity of form, dominates all Russian cities. Residential areas of low-cost, mass-designed three- and four-story apartment buildings are prevalent. The amount of interior space per family, determined by the state according to family size, averages about one-quarter that of American norms. Since all land is owned by the state, competition is eliminated and the internal patterning of urban space is less dynamic and more controlled than in Western cities. Integration of land use, rather than separation into distinct residential, retail, and industrial areas, is a guiding concept. The central city plays the role of a cultural and social node; it does not function as a rigidly defined **central business district.** A strong effort has been made to create self-sustaining social units which possess shops, services, and maximum sources of employment for local residents. Ideally, these self-contained communes include residences, service facilities, and a factory in which 2000 to 3000 Soviet citizens lead communal lives and share all tasks, following Marx's theories of social justice as a blueprint for socialist urbanism. In reality, a transitional form of the commune, the *mikrorayon,* is more common. The *mikrorayon* ("small stage") is a housing complex including residences, services, schools, and playgrounds, whose occupants work in industries located outside the neighborhood. Although these units do not totally fulfill the Marxist ideal, they create a distinctive urban structure in the Soviet Union—an administrative design of urban space less related to market forces and social distinctions than is true in Western cities.

The Planned Economy

By the time of Stalin's death in 1953, the Soviet Union had become a global superpower, one of two important nations far surpassing all others in environmental resources and industrial output. The Soviet gross national product rose at a rapid rate in the post-World War II period, but more slowly than that of Japan. It was second in size only to that of the United States. Stalin relied on critical investments in a few economic sectors—mining, manufacturing, and heavy industry—and required a harsh degree of discipline to marshall vast natural resources. The Soviet Union, while achieving breakthroughs in those sectors, was still beset by problems. The Supreme Economic Council had become a sprawling collection of departments; the Council of Economic Ministers had grown to seventy members, reflecting the increasing complexity of the Russian economy and an increasingly centralized and inflexible planning process. The result was high levels of inefficiency and very low labor productivity (one-third that of the United States). Further, the emphasis on achieving quantitative goals in terms of tons of steel, numbers of car loadings, and kilowatts of energy typically led to severe distortions in economic balance. One factory produced chandeliers so heavy no ceiling could hold them; another shipped tank cars filled with water across Russia to meet an allotted number of shipments only to find the railroad cars split open as the water froze in winter. Ministries competed for coal, iron, timber—hoarding resources so their individual quotas would be met. Local factories set production goals as low as possible to reduce the risk of failure. In the pyramid of central planning, consumer goods held low priority, as did agriculture; not until 1958 did the real wages of Soviet workers match the level of 1928. The Soviet planning system, unparalleled in size and completeness, slowed down as it became larger, less interconnected, and more rigid.

To cope with these problems, the leaders of the post-Stalin era have attempted to overhaul the nation's economic administration to provide a more flexible and responsive regional base for state economic planning. In 1957, the system of central ministries each with its own specialized industrial empire was abolished and replaced by 105 regional economic councils (*sovnarkhozy*) responsible for local allocations of resources and the rational use of transport within their regions. At the center, Gosplan, the State Planning Commission, was to serve as the supreme planning authority. The objective of this decentralization was to provide industrial plants and regional planners with the incentive to boost production and with the authority to rejuvenate and balance industrial growth on the regional level.

Although heavy industry and the development of nuclear weaponry retained priority, some concessions to consumer needs were made by the develop-

ment of industries based on new petrochemical installations, the reduction of the work week to forty-one hours, and improvement of wages, benefits, and pensions. In agriculture, the virgin lands scheme was initiated in Kazakhstan with optimistic predictions that food shortages in the Soviet Union would become a thing of the past. Khrushchev promised to overtake the United States in milk and meat production. A new national resources policy was implemented when the forced-labor camps of Siberia were abolished and economic rather than punitive forces came into play in the development of those areas. A major manpower shortage was created overnight in the east when prisoners returned to their homes in the west. New industrial projects in these underpopulated regions were now restricted to capital-intensive, energy-oriented industries whose labor needs could be accommodated from local sources with a minimum of migration. New labor-intensive industries were scheduled for the well-populated towns of European Russia. In a decade Stalin's spatial organization of economic planning was revised, the drive to the east was blunted, and consumers began to receive some attention. It appeared to many observers that the Soviet decision-making process under Khrushchev was becoming more responsive to economic forces and less dictatorial—some even predicted a convergence between the Soviet command economy and Western capitalism.

In 1964, Khrushchev was dismissed, condemned for his "wild and harebrained scheming" with the Soviet economy. Russia's new leaders were faced with the old problems of central versus regional planning, capital versus consumer investment, and priorities in the allocation of Soviet resources. Khrushchev's scheme of regional economic administration was abandoned and the ministerial system reinstated. The economy of the Soviet Union was once again reorganized; eighteen economic planning regions based on location, physical setting, industrial composition, and cultural homogeneity were created. Reduced to seven regions in 1973, these economic units are the spatial matrix of production, transport, and industrial development in Russia today. All crucial industrial commodities—coal, oil, iron, steel, chemicals—are under direct central ministerial control. To some degree the tendency to measure progress in quantitative terms has diminished; at the same time, the Soviet economy

Mechanized feeding pens at a state sheep farm complex in the Alma Ata region. Khrushchev's grandiose scheme to eliminate private enterprise and convert all food production into huge collective operations foundered, and Soviet policy is now aimed at collectivizing slowly and in units of manageable size. *Photo:* Wide World.

seems to be reaching maturation: industrial output increased in the early 1970s at a rate only slightly greater than that of the 1960s. However, there has been a marked shift toward the production of consumer goods. Private automobiles, formerly restricted in supply and use to the highest ranks of power, numbered 3.7 million in 1975. For the first time, investment in the agricultural sector is substantial. Although still suffering from bureaucratic inflexibility, Soviet planners are beginning to compromise rigid doctrine in the location and composition of industry and are providing monetary incentives to workers and management to achieve a more rational economy.

Strategies for Socialized Agriculture

After three decades of Communist control, Soviet agriculture was still plagued by lack of motivation to work, low productivity, and uncertain harvests on the farm. As a result, agricultural productivity was the most pressing problem facing Stalin's successors in the 1950s. The Communist party had been unable to win the confidence of the peasants; Lenin's dictum that the material and social conditions of rural areas be equalized with those of the cities was never successfully implemented. During World War II, peasants sequestered 14 million acres of public land for private use and lavished their efforts on these private plots at the expense of their collective farms. A fearful drought in the Ukraine in 1946 clearly demonstrated that collectivization alone had not solved the agricultural problem. Grain and livestock production, large-scale operations possible only on collective land, fell behind social demand. The livestock sector was revealed to be weaker than before the 1917 Revolution. The need for agricultural reform and more effective political control of the countryside demanded a reorganization of the collective farms. Between 1949 and 1952, the total number of collective farms was consolidated from 252,000 to 94,800. Sovkhozes increased at the expense of kolkhozes. It was hoped that this consolidation would make farming more manageable and efficient and that mechanization would be furthered. The peasants were even less attracted to these huge collectives than they had been to the smaller ones, but Khrushchev, the designer of this new policy, optimistically talked of the establishment of agrograds, agricultural cities where farming would benefit as had industry from an economy of scale. In his view, production would rise and the civilized amenities of the agrograd would mute peasant resentment.

The grain harvest was still far short of the needs of Russia's growing population in 1953, and upon Stalin's death and Khrushchev's rise to leadership of the Soviet state, spectacular new measures were announced to revitalize Soviet agriculture. Khrushchev's major proposal was to open up virgin lands in western Siberia, Kazakhstan, the Volga Plain, and the northern Caucasus to the cultivation of wheat and other grains. It was thought that the level, semiarid steppes of black soil (chernozem) east of the Volga could be easily brought into production. In a single year, 32 million acres were put to the plow. In 1960, over 115 million acres of new land—an agrarian space larger than that of West Germany, France, and Great Britain combined—were in cultivation. Some 150,000 workers and technicians, mostly young people motivated by patriotic appeal, were encouraged to migrate and settle on the sovkhozes of the new agricultural frontier. This gigantic undertaking was a gamble. Climate in Kazakhstan and western Siberia—a long and severe winter, a short growing season, and frequent summer droughts—renders large-scale grain farming a hazardous undertaking. Traditional Marxist thought, however, suggested that a socialist society, suitably organized, could triumph over nature and that spirit and determination would minimize environmental risks.

Furthermore, in a bizarre academic debate that became national policy, an uneducated Ukrainian, T. D. Lysenko, argued that the genetic structure of plants could be altered by environmental manipulation; by proper treatment ("vernalization") of seed, he argued, the growing season of winter wheat could be shortened to the point that seed could be planted in spring and yet produce an abundant and reliable harvest. Successfully eliminating his intellectual rivals, Lysenko convinced Khrushchev that "genetics, like chess, was a hobby" not a science, and that plants could be trained to adapt to the severe environments beyond the margins of the Fertile Triangle. Complementing this massive virgin lands cultivation of wheat was the conversion of the more reliable agricultural lands of the Ukraine to corn production. In the next five years, the area planted to corn in the Soviet Union expanded by a factor of seven, from 10 million acres to nearly 70 million. In one fell swoop, Khrushchev planned to solve the persistent food shortages of the Soviet people: the virgin lands would produce their bread; the Ukraine would serve as an immense factory for corn and beef production. Between 1953 and 1958, Russia's total agricultural production increased by 50 percent as crop and livestock production alone expanded by more than 40 percent. It appeared that Khrushchev's extraordinary gamble to push back the frontiers of Soviet agriculture had succeeded through concerted effort and daring. Cultivation had been liberated from the climatic boundaries of the narrow wedge of the Fertile Triangle.

Encouraged, Khrushchev disbanded one of Stalin's most important creations, the machine tractor stations, and sold off the equipment to collective farms. Khrushchev also denounced the private household plots as a distraction to farm workers motivated by petty bourgeois tendencies not in keeping with Marxist principles. In fact, private plots dramatically demonstrated the persistent peasant rejection of collectivization and highlighted the relatively low productivity of collective farms. In 1959, for example, the private sector occupied only 3 percent of the agricultural land but produced a quarter of all field crops, nearly half of all livestock products, 80 percent of Russia's eggs, 60 percent of the potatoes, and half the green vegetables consumed in the Soviet Union—impressive testimony to the private enterprise of Russian farmers. The production gains of the collective farms by contrast were the result of the expansion of the arable blessed by climatic respite on the new frontiers. They did not reflect peasant cooperation. Following 1959, crop production fell; in 1963, disastrous droughts hit Russia, forcing the importation of 11 million tons of wheat from the United States, Canada, Australia, and Argentina. The planned 70 percent increase in food production expected from the virgin lands amounted to only a 10 percent increase in national agricultural output. This was not sufficient to fulfill the needs of a growing population with rising consumer demands. Only one-fifth of the corn planted in the new acreage was able to mature in the short summer of southern Russia. In the political crisis that ensued, Khrushchev was ousted from power. Russian farmers, hating party bureaucrats much as their fathers had hated landlords, destroyed Khrushchev's dream of agricultural self-sufficiency as much as the vagaries of Russia's climate.

Khrushchev's successors have taken a more practical and less dictatorial approach to problems in Russia's agricultural sector. Environmental limitations are increasingly viewed in proper perspective; the Marxist assumption that human mastery of the environment is always possible has become subdued. The campaign against private plots has ceased, and restrictions on their use have been lifted. It has been belatedly recognized that only when communal agriculture provides the worker with the economic incentive to produce does the private plot diminish in importance and the productivity of the collective farms increase. The merger of collective

SOVKHOZES AND KOLKHOZES

Although the natural environment of the Soviet Union poses special difficulties to farming, there is no doubt that the land is capable of producing far more food than Russia's 240 million people need. In an age of global food shortages, the agricultural strategies of every nation are thrown into sharp relief. For many, chronic and increasing food shortages pose questions of immediate social survival. Russia, both in tsarist times and in the Communist present, is a nation whose agricultural sector has been consistently unable to meet all the food demands of its population.

At the time of the Bolshevik Revolution, the leaders of the new socialist state had few ideas about what role and what form the Russian farm would take under their new rule. The Communists inherited a poorly understood, poorly organized morass of small peasant holdings, sharecroppers, rural renters, and peasants bound as debtors and employees to the noble and landed gentry. It was on the estates of the rich, confiscated during the revolution, that the first conceptual move toward the collectivization of Russian agriculture took place. Although most peasants continued to operate their holdings independently during the first eleven years of the Soviet state, the administration organized the land of the gentry into state farms—the parents of the sovkhozes of today.

On these farms, large, contiguous blocks of land were farmed as a single unit, managed and worked by peasants acting in the name of the state. This first kind of collectivity, the sovkhoz, has been revised and expanded to the point where today the sovkhoz holds more ideological importance in Soviet aims than its parallel farm-organization form, the kolkhoz. The sovkhoz is a state enterprise, seen in the same light as a mine, fishing cooperative, dress factory, or any other form of business in the Soviet Union. Its workers are state employees, paid wages and receiving fringe benefits in a managerial setting similar to industry in an urban environment. The state has direct control over the location, land, management, sociological structure, tools, and orientation of the farm. Sovkhozes tend to be very large (42,000 acres), single-purposed (cereal grains or cotton in developing areas; vegetables or dairy products near large urban centers), and operated on a cost-accounting basis: they are expected to show a profit. As the collectivization drive began in the early 1930s, sovkhozes tripled in number; the virgin lands, some 115 million acres brought into pro-

Seventy miles south of Moscow, this sovkhoz is devoted to the production of vegetables, potatoes, and milk for the markets of the Soviet capital. The farm workforce is 925 persons, with a total sovkhoz population of about 3250. It is currently undergoing reorganization as the settlement pattern of prerevolutionary villages is restructured through consolidation—that is, some villages will be removed; others will become consolidated centers.

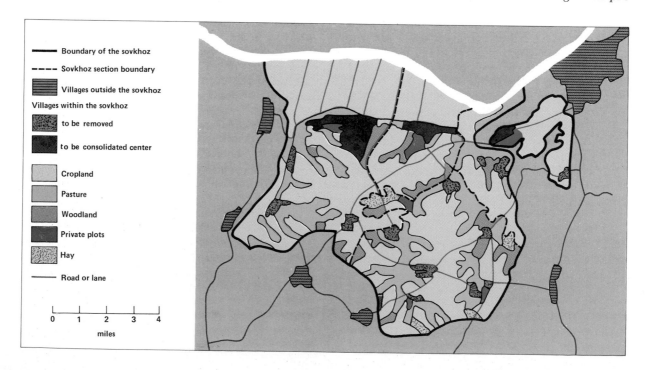

Boundary of the sovkhoz

Sovkhoz section boundary

Villages outside the sovkhoz

Villages within the sovkhoz

to be removed

to be consolidated center

Cropland

Pasture

Woodland

Private plots

Hay

Road or lane

0 1 2 3 4
miles

Toting up accounts of work completed in a 1930s collective. *Photo:* Wide World.

ductivity in the 1950s, were organized primarily around modern sovkhoz lines; sovkhozes again tripled in number in the early 1960s when Soviet agriculture was reorganized and kolkhozes were consolidated into sovkhozes.

The Soviet kolkhoz was a compromise to the problems faced by Russian authorities at the beginning of Communist rule. Already a nation of peasants, Russia was also a nation of small villages poorly connected to a hierarchy of markets, industry, and finance. Restructuring a countryside of complex and historical peoples and cultures as well as medieval agricultural practices was no small task, and the kolkhoz was the logical Soviet response to Russian rural society. The key element in the kolkhoz is the family, the kolkhoznik and his wife—she too is a full-time kolkhoz worker—their children, and other relatives. The kolkhoz family lives in a cottage—often a structure dating from before the revolution—set in a 1-acre private plot near their village neighbors. Surrounding them is the state-owned land upon which the villagers labor as partners in the production of foodstuffs for the state and society at large. Kolkhozniks and kolkhoznikas are expected to work full-time with their workers' brigade, a squad of fellow villagers who till the rent-free state-owned land as a cooperative enterprise. They own the tools and share as individuals the benefits of the crops they reap.

However, neither the kolkhozniks nor their sovkhoz counterparts manage the orientation, purchasing, merchandising, or safekeeping of their crop. Decision making on both the sovkhoz and the kolkhoz is the power of the agricultural management of the Communist party of the USSR. The sovkhoz farm director or the kolkhoz chairman determines what use is to be made of the earth, keeping in mind ideological considerations advanced in local party committees.

and state farms into progressively larger and more unwieldy units has been halted at 50,000 since the early 1960s. Currently, Russia's 550 million acres of cultivated land are organized equally into state farms (the sovkhoz) and the kolkhoz, where workers receive shares in the harvest. The ultimate objective remains to convert all units into state farms where all agriculturalists will be wage laborers similar to their industrial counterparts. In addition, the state now provides substantial funds for agricultural research into higher yields through better plant varieties (Lysenko fell from favor), greater use of fertilizer, better tillage practices, improved machinery, and better farm management. For the first time since Stalin's drive to industrialize began in 1928, the agriculture sector is receiving high priority.

By the early 1970s, relaxed Soviet economic measures resulted in a one-third increase in Russia's total crop production in ten years. Agriculture has made gains well above the 16 percent rise in population that occurred between 1960 and 1970. Now the world's leading producer of bread grains and potatoes, crops that do well in northern climatic conditions, Russia appears to have reached a turning point in agriculture, although problems persist, and imports from the West are still required. Yields remain considerably lower than those in other technologically advanced societies, and it requires 25 percent of Russia's population to produce the country's food supply, compared with 5 percent in the United States. The continuing migration of the young to urban centers has created regional labor shortages, particularly in the east. These shortages have been partially offset by an ambitious program of rural consolidation in which 16 percent of all rural settlements—110,000 in number—have been selected for intensive development, while it is planned that the remainder will be eliminated or remain at present size. Private plots still produce a third of Russia's food, reflecting the continuing reluctance of the Russian peasant to farm collectively. Although Russian agriculture is clearly improving, it remains tenaciously resistant to the collective patterns of organization set forth in classical ideology and the least productive sector of the national economy. The Soviet Union purchased $2 billion worth of grain from the United States in 1972—partly the result of difficult weather, perennial mismanagement, and the farmers' indomitable individualism—but also of increasing attention to consumer demands.

TOWARD A HOMOGENEOUS SOCIETY

Many observers have suggested that the Soviet Union, the United States, and other industrial nations are converging toward a similar form of society—the technocratic state. Despite differences in history, environment, social order, and national temperament, it has been argued that forces unleashed by industrialization and urbanization are sufficiently powerful to eliminate age-old distinctions of race, religion, and nationality. In this view, mass communication, international interdependence, compulsory education, urbanism, and geographical mobility have led to a secular, technology-oriented, mass-production consumption society within the technological world. In the United States, the policies of compulsory education and equal opportunity stemming from national ideals at first glance appear to support a melting pot hypothesis that spells an end to racial and ethnic distinctions in the American population. In the Soviet Union, Marxism presumes the gradual obliteration of social and national differences and the subsequent emergence of a national society without class distinctions. But in both countries, these expectations are slow to be realized. The persistence of ethnic, religious, and national feelings has been sufficiently intense to cast doubt on the homogenizing power of modernization and industrialization. In the Soviet Union, the old distinctions are potent despite fifty years of Communist rule.

Nationalities
[TABLE 1]

In a prophetic essay, *Will the Soviet Union Survive until 1984?* the dissident Russian writer and historian Andrei Amalrik portrays the leaders of the Russian state as mindless and subservient bureaucrats, immobilized by their own incompetence and dedicated to the existing state of affairs to support an ideology that is not Marxism but an arbitrarily crude form of Russian nationalism. Predicting a protracted guerrilla war between Russia and China along their common 4000-mile border in the 1980s, Amalrik foresees violent responses within the Soviet population to the ensuing wartime decline in standards of living and the financial bankruptcy of the state. In this scenario, these irritations foster uprisings among the non-Russian peoples of the Baltic, the Ukraine, the Caucasus, and Central Asia that tap preexisting national animosities in a Soviet multinational state where "certain nations enjoy privileged status." The Marxist Revolution, having delayed the breakup of the Russian Empire, succumbs to a revival of ancient national enmities. Though few envision such an eruption of nationalism in the Soviet Union, Amalrik was sentenced to two and one-half years of exile in Siberia, condemned as a "social parasite" for his comments.

In the 1970s, Russians constitute a bare majority of the 242 million people in the Soviet Union, 129 mil-

TABLE 1. National Composition of the Soviet Population, 1959 and 1970 (in millions)

Source: Pravda, April 17, 1971. A full table in translation is available in *Current Digest of the Soviet Press,* Vol. 23 (May 18, 1971), pp. 14–18. Percentage data have been computed. Omitted are data on sixty-nine nationalities numbering less than 1 million, plus a residual figure for very small national categories.

	1959		1970	
Nationality	Population	Percent of total	Population	Percent of total
All nationalities	208.8	100.0%	241.7	100.0%
Russian	114.1	54.6	129.0	53.4
Ukrainian	37.3	17.8	40.1	16.7
Uzbek	6.0	2.9	9.2	3.8
Belorussian	7.9	3.8	9.1	3.7
Tatar	5.0	2.4	5.9	2.4
Kazakh	3.6	1.7	5.3	2.2
Azerbaijani	2.9	1.4	4.4	1.8
Armenian	2.8	1.3	3.6	1.5
Georgian	2.7	1.3	3.2	1.3
Moldavian	2.2	1.1	2.7	1.1
Lithuanian	2.3	1.1	2.7	1.1
Jewish	2.3	1.1	2.2	0.9
Tadzhik	1.4	0.7	2.1	0.9
German	1.6	0.8	1.8	0.8
Chuvash	1.5	0.7	1.7	0.7
Turkmenian	1.0	0.5	1.5	0.6
Kirgiz	1.0	0.5	1.5	0.6
Latvian	1.4	0.7	1.4	0.6
Mordvinian	1.3	0.6	1.3	0.5
Bashkir	1.0	0.4	1.2	0.5
Polish	1.4	0.7	1.2	0.5
Estonian	1.0	0.4	1.0	0.4

lion or 53.4 percent of the total population. Ukrainians (40 million) are the largest minority culture, followed by Uzbeks and Belorussians with less than 10 million each. In the Southern Periphery, Tatars, Kazakhs, Azerbaijanis, Armenians, and Georgians form separate national groups of 3 million to 6 million people each. On the European frontiers of Russia the Estonians, Latvians, and Lithuanians of the Baltic region and the Germans, Poles, and Moldavians farther south are significant non-Russian cultural groups. Some sixty-nine different nationalities have populations of less than 1 million each. With a declining birth rate among Slavic nationalities and a high birth rate among the peoples of Armenia, the Caucasus, and Central Asia, the slight Russian majority in the Soviet population will predictably disappear in the near future.

In Lenin's view, the national allegiances incorporated into the Soviet Union would die a natural death under the social and economic equality found under communism. Viewing the Russian Empire of the tsars as an oppressor of all national groups, the early Communists established a federal system in which national groups were encouraged to assert

A beggar in the bazaar in Samarkand in 1969. The Muslim Uzbeks and the Belorussians are the second largest minority groups in the Soviet Union, where Russians constitute a bare majority of the population. Despite nearly two generations of Communist rule, religious and cultural distinctions persist. *Photo:* Wide World.

their rights in preparation for the ultimate disappearance of both national and class differences. But from a practical viewpoint, Russia's place in the world depended on its ability to retain control of the resources of the non-Russian areas of the Soviet Union—the soil of the Ukraine, the oil of Baku, Central Asian cotton, and Polish coal. As commissar of nationalities, Stalin, himself a Georgian, promoted a study of the 180 Soviet nationalities to determine which local traditions should be encouraged. But in the social turmoil of the 1930s and World War II,

Stalin blatantly appealed to Russian nationalism for the preservation of Mother Russia from the crisis facing the nation. Minorities in the Caucasus and the Crimea as well as 1.5 million ethnic Germans along the Volga were forced into Siberian exile. Since that period, the Soviet Union has stressed the benefits of the annexation of non-Russian territories to undermine the strength of national customs and traditions and encourage the fusion of minorities into a common Russian-dominated culture.

Population migration has proved the most effective method of spreading Russian language and culture in the Soviet Union. Russians are today a numerical majority in the large cities of the Ukraine (the Russian component in the population of the Ukraine has increased by a quarter in the last decade) and a growing number of Ukrainians identify Russian as their primary language. Heavy migration into the new economic regions of Kazakhstan has made this traditionally Asian region predominantly Russian today. Similarly, Russian migration into the Baltic has intensified—not, however, without some friction with local cultures. To some degree economic policy has been manipulated to implant Russian culture in specific cultural regions, as, for example, during the extensive industrialization of Lithuania during the 1950s. Since all police permits register an individual's nationality within the Soviet Union, the state bureaucracy has the capacity to use population movements to dilute ethnic distinctiveness. Official policy under Khrushchev and Brezhnev has been to encourage population movements in all directions to eliminate "national narrow-mindedness" and create a new "Soviet people." It is difficult, however, to estimate to what degree this ethnic objective has guided state decisions as compared with economic development, manpower needs, or other forces. But it is undeniable that official migration has effected a blending of peoples in the Soviet Union, although the process has been slow. In the 1960s, nearly 10 percent of all marriages were contracted between members of different nationalities, with a high rate of 15 percent in Latvia and the Ukraine, and a low rate in Central Asia and Armenia (3 percent). Not surprisingly, such cultural mixing is greatest in large cities and least in rural areas.

Language policy has been a second method for encouraging the Russification of the Soviet population. After the revolution, local languages were officially recognized in the Soviet Union to combat illiteracy

YOSIF AND MARINA: A JEWISH COUPLE LOOKS BACK

Yosif and Marina were born in Kiev, the capital of the Ukraine. Their escape from the fate of most Ukrainian Jews under the Nazi occupation profoundly influences their reactions to many seemingly unrelated aspects of life in the Soviet Union today. . . .

Yosif . . . has worked as a cook, a bookkeeper and a designer of holiday greeting cards. He was trained as an electrical engineer in his youth and is now the assistant manager of an electrical parts factory in Moscow. The other jobs were part of the . . . life he and Marina were forced to lead between the beginning of the war and Stalin's death in 1953. . . . After leaving Kiev (during World War II) Yosif and Marina thought he would be able to find an engineering job in Moscow. Instead they were required to spend most of the war in Siberia in a special settlement with other refugees from the western Ukraine, the Baltic republics and various Eastern European countries. Stalin did not trust refugees either from foreign countries or from the border regions of the Soviet Union; he was afraid they would engage in espionage and sabotage among the populace if they were allowed to live in areas near the military front. At the same time—through the . . . double-think of the period—Soviet citizens who remained on occupied territory were widely distrusted because they had not retreated east with the Soviet Army.

"We could have proven our patriotism more thoroughly by waiting until the Germans were marching into Kiev," Yosif said, "or better yet, by dying there. . . . It was true that some people from the border republics collaborated with the Germans, but how could anyone have thought a Jew would do that? We ran away to escape them." In 1944, when the Russian-German front had moved far west of Moscow and Allied troops had landed in Normandy, Yosif and Marina were allowed to leave Siberia and return to the capital. . . .

Yosif and Marina were not able to lead what might be considered a normal life until Stalin's death. The policies of the regime became more openly anti-Semitic after the war than they had been during the 1930's. Virtually all Jewish cultural institutions were closed, [and] leading Yiddish-language writers were secretly tried and executed. . . . "We kept on the move constantly, living in six towns between 1947 and 1954. . . . You know that Russians don't talk very much about the Stalin years," she said. "Well, Yosif is a Jew on top of being a Soviet citizen. He lived through two separate catastrophes, and he always bore the main burden of worry—first in persuading me to leave Kiev ahead of the Nazis, then in seeing that we had food in our mouths for eight years after the war. He always said we would live longer than Stalin. He never forgets how much better life is now than it was then. I don't forget either, but I still can't keep my mouth shut about things that are wrong now. . . ."

After Stalin died, Yosif and Marina returned to Moscow and a happier life. Their daughter Nadezhda was a year old. "She was an accident—we thought an unhappy one because we were still on the run from town to town," Marina said. . . .

Yosif has been working steadily since 1955 in the profession for which he was trained. He was promoted to a supervisory job in 1960 and has been an assistant manager of his electrical parts plant since 1966. Marina is a Ukranian-Russian translator specializing in scientific and technical material. . . . Although Yosif and Marina [are] quite satisfied with the way their own lives had turned out, they [are] not at all sure the Soviet system [offers] the kinds of opportunities they wanted for their children. "We have seen progress in our own lives," Marina said. "We have better housing, better clothes, better food than we did ten years ago, not to mention the period after the war. We also feel more free—we are no longer terrified of a knock on the door at night that would send us away to a camp. But that isn't enough for our children. You like to give your children something much better than you had, and I don't know if that's really possible here. Things were so bad twenty years ago, and they have improved so much, that I don't think the comparative improvement can be as great in the next twenty years. . . . Despite their problems, though, my children cannot imagine a different life. They are Soviet citizens; their life is here. They would not think of applying to go to Israel. Most of their friends are Russian; I think it's unlikely that they will marry Jews. If they did, it would be by sheer accident. . . .

"For every Jew who was proud," Marina said, "there must have been one who was scared and tried to declare himself as being of another nationality. You can do that sometimes if your last name isn't obviously Jewish and you speak only Russian. There's something else you have to remember too. The rate of intermarriage between Jews and Gentiles is now quite high; I know that from my own experience and that of my friends. A child of intermarriage can pick the nationality of either parent, and I don't know how many such

children would freely choose to be identified as Jews on their passports." . . .

Yosif and Marina are assimilated because their parents believed in assimilation as the ultimate solution to anti-Semitism. But as survivors of Hitler and Stalin, they no longer have complete faith in it. "Anyone who lived through what we did, and still thinks you can forget about being a Jew, is crazy," Marina said. "We would have liked our children to learn something about Jewish culture in a more organized way than we were able to provide at home. But that is impossible in the Soviet Union."

Source: Quoted from Susan Jacoby, *Moscow Conversations*. New York: Coward, McCann & Geoghegan, 1972, pp. 139, 141–145, 148–149, 151–152. By permission of Coward, McCann & Geoghegan, Inc. Copyright © 1972 by Susan Jacoby.

---

and as a means of introducing the Russian alphabet (local languages were taught in Russian transliteration) into areas such as Central Asia and the Far East. During the 1920s, instruction in sixty non-Russian languages was introduced into elementary education, although the language of higher education remained exclusively Russian. In 1958, an educational reform introduced Russian as a second language in all Soviet schools with the choice of language studied by each child left to the parents. But despite the economic and social advantages to be gained through knowledge of Russian, the common language, surprisingly few people have abandoned their native tongues. Between 1926 and 1970, the number of non-Russians who claimed Russian as their primary language doubled from 6.5 million to 13 million, but the number of those speaking non-Russian languages increased from 60 million to 100 million. While Ukrainians and Belorussians, fellow Slavs, have tended to adopt Russian, the Baltic, Caucasian, and Central Asian minorities have retained the use of local languages at levels of 95 percent or more. The official goal of making Russian a universal language in the Soviet Union has progressed slowly, and it remains to be seen whether modern communication networks will accelerate the process.

God and Communism

As with national identity, the goal of Soviet leaders has been to create a setting in which organized religion would disappear. Religion, in the Communist view, was a tool of the tsars. Religion was viewed as an institution that reconciled the oppressed to their condition in life. It was likened to a drug, the "opium of the people." During the

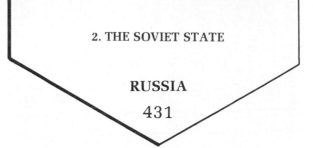

1920s, a temporary accommodation was worked out between Russia's churches and the fledgling Soviet state, but in the following decade, it became clear that the Communist party was committed to the creation of an atheistic society. The League of the Militant Godless, a group of militant antireligious agitators, was formed in 1929. Churches were closed; Sunday was abolished as the universal day of rest; clergymen were persecuted; and churches were stripped of all social functions. A remarkable personal diary of the thirty-three-year religious career of one Russian Orthodox bishop showed that between 1921 and 1944 he spent 33 months as an active prelate, 32 months at liberty but without position, 76 months in exile, and 254 months in prison and labor camps. During World War II, this pressure was relaxed when the Russian Orthodox Church was used by Stalin to encourage patriotism. But Stalin's successors have continued to apply administrative sanctions against religious activities in an effort to reduce religion as a separate and parallel socializing force to the lowest possible level. In the early 1960s an estimated 10,000 places of worship were closed, and all clergymen were forced to register with the state or risk becoming "unregistered servants of cults," a criminal status.

Nonetheless, religion remains a powerful force in the Soviet Union. The Russian Orthodox Church continues to function despite severe harassment. Although membership figures are unknown, Moscow churches are estimated to have an annual income of $6 million largely derived from the manufacture of candles. Increasing social unrest encouraged by the Russian Orthodox Church suggests that it is still a viable cultural force. By far the most active and aggressive religion in the Soviet Union today, however, is the Baptist Church, which cannot be identified with tsarist exploitation and has thereby escaped the worst effects of official antireligious actions. Membership is estimated at more than 500,000, five times what it was in 1917, an achievement remarkable in the face of government hostility. The Muslims of Central Asia have also enjoyed a favored position, largely because of the Soviet policy of encouraging closer relations with the Middle East. Religious groups identified with Ukrainian and Belorussian nationalism, by contrast, have been virtually eliminated. In the last census that made any reference to religion (1937), one-third of the Russian population identified them-

A Russian Orthodox priest conducts a service at the ancient monastery of Zagorsky near Moscow, which has been continuously active for six centuries. Despite repression and propaganda campaigns, the Orthodox Church remains a cultural force in the Soviet Union and religion still a part of the lives of many people. *Photo:* Wide World.

selves as believers in one or another faith. The Marxist expectation that religion would wither away without state support has not yet occurred, and the strong nihilism and search for purpose in modern Soviet society suggest that communism has failed to provide a new morality of sufficient power to uproot the ethic of the past.

Perhaps no religious group has proved more perplexing to the leaders of the Soviet Union than the Jews. Unlike other nationalities, Jews have traditionally proclaimed themselves a nation despite their lack of a national territory. The Soviet formula allowing some regional expression of national rights found no ground with Russia's Jews. An effort to create a Jewish homeland in the Amur River valley in the Far East in the 1920s failed for lack of interest. The growing identification of some Soviet Jews with Israel since World War II, their high level of urbanization and education, and their status as a religion as well as a nation pose further complexities. Furthermore, only a minority of Soviet Jews speak a separate language, Yiddish, as their mother tongue. Most are native Russian speakers, unlike Ukrainians or Tatars, for example. Before World War II, Jews appeared to be becoming secularized and Russified as the lifting of the anti-Semitic legal restrictions of the tsarist period offered them access to new opportunities. Many of the Bolshevik revolutionaries were Jews. But the Nazi extermination of Soviet Jews, responsible for reducing their number in Russia from an estimated 5 million in 1939 to 2.2 million in 1970, helped mold a resurgent Jewish identity. This Jewish sense of separate identity denies the Soviet arguments for an assimilated society; recent demands by Soviet Jews for the right to emigrate without restrictions have produced inter-

national repercussions. As in other aspects of Soviet society, a half century of Communist effort to eradicate religious and national heritage through closing synagogues, restricting services, and harassing religious leaders has not been effective in quelling the aspirations of individual motivation.

DISSENT AND DETENTE

The Bolshevik Revolution of 1917 threw down a gauntlet to the industrialized West. It projected an ideology that rejected all forms of capitalism and predicated the Russian national purpose upon the ultimate downfall of the societies of Europe and North America under a wave of similarly inspired Communist revolutions. Although the first three decades of Soviet rule were influenced by resource scarcities, social upheavals, purges, and wars, this framework of national identity guided the process of modernization and industrialization in the Soviet Union. In the rhetoric of the 1961 Communist party program, every citizen is expected to make the triumph of communism "the greatest purpose of their life and the banner of a nationwide struggle." Operating from within these principles, born into the bondage of a difficult history and harsh environment, Russia has interpreted the scientific revolution within its own cultural and mental framework and has restructured the geography of its land and people in terms unique to itself.

Despite Marxist predictions that communism and capitalism lead to radically different ways of life and personality, a convergence of Russian and Western societies is anticipated by many. Changes generated in the Soviet system by the economic and social effects of urbanization, industrialization, universal education, and social complexity may come to moderate the totalitarian political organization and ideological rigidity of the Communist party. One questionable prediction holds that an educated populace demands ever greater levels of participatory democracy. In Russia this would open up the bureaucracy to the influence of a multitude of individuals and pressure groups who presently have no voice there. Since the Russian public is highly literate today, the validity of this assumption is doubtful. Yet dissent exists. Another belief is that consumer demands multiply at a certain stage in the industrialization process, so that Russian consumer demands will temper the national demands for energy and sacrifice, leading to a more individualistic economy of choice and mobility akin to those in the West. Some, like Amalrik, see nationalism resurgent among Soviet peoples as it is in much of the developing world. Nationalism would at least force Marxist leaders to retreat from their efforts to create a "new Soviet man." In all these models, a central theme of liberalization prevails, forecasting a reduction of the administrative manipulation of indi-

THE QUALITY OF LIFE

For the nations of the technological world, the scientific transformation ushered in a period of what seemed to be endless expansion and advancement. Particularly since World War II, in Europe and North America, and also in Japan, supplies of food, fuel, and income have provided whole populations with a level of physical comfort attained only by royalty in the past. The people of these nations turned from a struggle to earn food and shelter to a pursuit of affluence and its concomitant, leisure, on a scale never before known. In Europe and Japan, national incomes doubled between 1950 and 1960 and again between 1960 and 1970 in most countries. And although many people did not fully participate in the postwar economic miracle, life and livelihood changed dramatically. A consumer society took root: families purchased automobiles, television sets, refrigerators, and other household appliances just as Americans had first done in the 1920s. Skyscrapers changed the look of cities; supermarkets replaced groceries; chain stores took the place of small shops.

The industrial resurgence of Europe was based on new techniques, better organization, and greater efficiency in resource utilization. There were no new discoveries or changes in location: rather, modernization and innovation in three major industries—steel, chemicals, and automobiles—increased industrial strength. In Japan, a great push to convert to heavy industry and industrial export products achieved the same result. But once economic growth had done its job—had changed the style of life and the physical surroundings in which it was lived—other effects began to appear.

One was the persistence of pockets of poverty and backwardness amid affluence, the fixing in place at the bottom of the socioeconomic scale of a class of rural and urban poor despite campaigns to educate, house, and train that have absorbed the energies of government planners and the dollars of taxpayers with very little result. In North America, and particularly in the United States, the affluence that led the surge to the suburbs and to other parts of the country from the old urban centers of the North and East left only the very rich and the very poor—the unskilled, the economically "hopeless"—in cities already declining and unable to maintain levels of service sufficient for the working and middle classes. "White flight" drained them of strength just as they were flooded with a largely nonwhite migration of rural poor looking for a better life, for a share of the affluence all around them. Crowded into crime- and drug-ridden slums and more dependent on government than the medieval serf, these people are rapidly becoming an underclass—a group that does not now have a functioning place in the society.

Another unforeseen effect of prosperity was serious environmental pollution, particularly in the densely populated and heavily industrialized but physically small areas of Europe and Japan. With local exceptions, automobile exhaust has affected the structure and the feel of every city in these regions. Today, European governments are enacting harsh clean air legislation. West Germany has recently enacted a stringent antipollution bill that adopts the Japanese formula of forcing polluters to pay. France, Belgium, the Netherlands, and Italy have passed or are considering various pollution control measures, from limitations on engine emissions to control of industrial wastes. The international dimensions of pollution in Europe are clearly demonstrated by recent Scandinavian claims that industrial air pollution in northwestern Europe, particularly Britain, has increased the level of acid in the rain and snow that fall in Norway and Sweden, and by the environmental disruption generated by great industrial complexes like the Ruhr that line the Rhine, which flows through five countries.

In Japan, where more economic activity takes place in less space than anywhere else in the world, the consequences of such human concentration in te. ms of noise, air, soil, and water pollution have been acute. By 1970, the gains in comfort and convenience achieved by a single-minded devotion to economic expansion at any cost began to be questioned as isolated "environmental incidents" in urban-industrial centers clustered and spread, and as feverish competition, congestion, inadequate services, and alienation began to replace the slower-paced and more spartan—but also far more harmonious and secure—patterns of traditional Japanese society. The Japanese refer to these problems as the agonies, the evils of overconcentration caused by rapid economic expansion. As the complaints about the "quality of life" grow in volume and intensity, there are those who look to the rice cycle, the traditional organizing principle of Japanese life, with its nurturance of the environment and of those who existed in it, as a symbol of what has been lost.

GHETTO LIFE IN NEW YORK

With a metropolitan area population of 16.2 million in three states, New York is the world's largest city. Urbanization spreads from two groves of ninety buildings over 500 feet high in Midtown and Lower Manhattan outward for more than 60 miles to Connecticut, the lower Hudson Valley, Long Island, and New Jersey. Forty-eight states, all with greater natural resource potential, have populations smaller than the New York metropolitan area. New York's black population is considerably larger than the entire population of Atlanta; New York's Puerto Rican population dwarfs that of San Juan.

New York has as well some of the worst—or most infamous—slums. Denounced by Jacob Riis in his classic study, *How the Other Half Lives*, in 1890, the tenement slum remains a persistent component of this city's urban landscape. Seventy years old, having served generations of immigrants, the same crumbling buildings today house new New Yorkers —black and Puerto Rican Americans who have exchanged rural for urban hovels and bitterly resent their impoverishment in a land of obvious plenty.

Since World War II, Americans have enjoyed higher standards of living than any previously experienced. Between 1950 and 1970, personal incomes quadrupled, and former luxuries became necessities. The search for a better, easier life led to the suburbs and to the southern and western parts of the country, with the result that older cities of the Northeast began to lose jobs and people. At the same time, those who had always come to the cities in search of better lives found themselves trapped in the decaying urban cores. The urban poor now form a lower class frozen by racial discrimination, poor education, or inadequate skills into continuing economic deprivation. Segregated in ghettos, they remain outsiders in a society that yields easy affluence to the well educated and the technically able.

The geographical shift of poverty to the cities occurred in the 1960s; 60 percent of the poor live in urban centers today, compared with 44 percent in 1960. Rural poverty is slowly diminishing as highways and development programs change life, but in the black and Hispanic ghettos of the large urban centers, there are few signs of improvement. And poverty remains closely identified with race; the urban poor are predominantly nonwhite.

An explosive demand for factory labor in World War II brought blacks out of the South in great numbers; between 1950 and 1970, some 3 million moved to the North and West. Whereas two of every three were southerners in 1950, only 53 percent of America's 23 million blacks still lived south of the Mason-Dixon line in 1970. This migration was more than a simple geographical shift; it was an economic move from field to factory, a social transition from small town to metropolis, a cultural leap from the segregated small-town South to the city streets of the North. Puerto Ricans undertook a similar migration from a rural, agricultural society to the city, and at about the same time. For both groups, the timing was wrong.

By the 1970s, the central cities were hardly areas of opportunity. The white middle class had moved to the suburbs in a steady exodus that began in 1950 and been replaced by the rural poor, racial minorities, and immigrants from countries new to the American experience, such as Korea, Haiti, and Trinidad. Economic growth in the core areas declined, and the demand for unskilled labor disappeared. Those who worked in the great office buildings were educated whites who lived in the suburbs. Efforts at residential integration were frustrated by discriminatory real estate practices, white flight, and newly formed resistance groups. Businesses found it more profitable and pleasanter to move to the suburbs—a spatial dislocation that left the unemployed poor geographically and socially removed from new job opportunities. New York, with revenues declining, is saddled with salary demands by city service workers; with high energy, rent, and land costs; with high taxes, obsolete buildings, and a disproportionate share of society's disadvantaged. This metropolitan center, once a dynamic core, is now an economic and social disaster zone.

Within that disaster zone, traditional slum areas such as Harlem and the Lower East Side in Manhattan and Brownsville in Brooklyn expanded; now there is Spanish Harlem as well, and the symbol of inner-city collapse, the South Bronx. Landlords abandon buildings, fires are constantly set, drugs abound, gangs rule what is left of the streets. The unemployment rate for males is estimated at 70 to 80 percent. Police, firefighters, and social agencies barely contain the disorder in the area and speak of it as one would of a war zone. Within it, a new generation of the hopeless grows up amid destruction and decay.

A burning tenement. Hugh Rogers, Monkmeyer.

(opposite) A ghetto street. Hugh Rogers, Monkmeyer.
(top) Neighborhood group painting a wall. Hugh Rogers, Monkmeyer.
(left) A main street in the ghetto. Hugh Rogers, Monkmeyer.
(right) Crime being reported to the police. Sam Falk, Monkmeyer.

(top) A Puerto Rican wedding. James Theologos, Monk-meyer.
(left) A Puerto Rican storefront church. Bill Anderson, Monkmeyer.
(right) Harlem street scene. Hilda Blut, Monkmeyer.
(opposite, top) Street in Spanish Harlem. Allyn Baum, Monkmeyer.
(opposite, bottom) Spanish Harlem grocery. Allyn Baum, Monkmeyer.

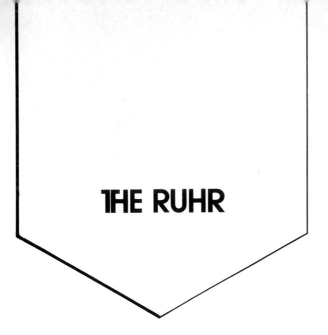

THE RUHR

In the second half of the nineteenth century, the pace of economic life on the Continent quickened and the gap between Britain and the rest of Europe closed rapidly. Perhaps the single most important factor promoting this transformation was the building of railroads, a web of steel that stretched across Western Europe to include even the slowly developing countries of Iberia and Italy. This conquest of distance stimulated an extraordinary breakthrough in industrial activity; the appetite of European economies for raw materials grew apace. An industrial economy was recognized as a political necessity—a matter of national prestige and the basis of a modern military. Nowhere was this more appreciated than in Germany; nowhere did industrialization proceed more rapidly.

By 1870, German iron and coal production exceeded that of France, and the Ruhr, a coal mining area in the Rhine Valley, emerged as the greatest center of industrial activity in Western Europe. The great Krupp works were here, at Essen, fabricating steel and from the steel ships, armaments, and industrial machinery. Germany's steel production doubled each decade until the end of the century. By the 1890s, it surpassed that of Great Britain and was second only to that of the United States.

Since industrial resources such as iron ore, coal, and waterpower were more location-bound than the population, it was cheaper to move people. New cities therefore sprang up alongside the mines and mills. By 1914, 60 percent of all Germans, 80 percent of the British, and 45 percent of the French were urban. In the Ruhr, factory towns devoured the intervening countryside and formed smoke-palled conurbations. In a continent that had had barely twenty cities with populations of 100,000 in 1800, a massive shift in the human center of gravity had occurred, creating a new social environment. The influx of millhands and workers from the countryside into the cities destroyed traditional urban culture and society as surely as the sprawling acres of tenements and workers' cottages altered the size and physical appearance of the cities. In Essen in the Ruhr, slums spread uncontrollably outward from the medieval core. Living conditions were ghastly. Water supplies were inadequate, and facilities for sewage and garbage virtually nonexistent. Crowding was so intense in Essen that nearly a fifth of all households were lodged in attics at the turn of the century.

The new urban working class, having abandoned the rhythm of the farm in search of a better existence in the city, was plagued by the most basic forms of social insecurity—unemployment, illness, and death at an early age. The industrial death rate was high: fatal accidents in the coal mines of the Ruhr rose from an annual rate of 26 in 1850 to 537 in 1900. Harnessed to machines and engaged in monotonous work, they became, as Marx and Engels called them, "degraded hands" who bitterly resented the luxury and security of the middle and upper classes.

The cities of the Ruhr, stretching all the way to the North Sea, are today still dense urban clusters. In the middle Rhine, the port cities of Karlsruhe, Heidelberg, Mannheim, Darmstadt, Frankfurt, Wiesbaden, and Mainz form a ribbon of industrial towns whose contemporary importance is rooted in their early industrialization. Together they contain over 2 million people, not counting the inhabitants of secondary towns and associated rural areas. Farther downstream, the Rhine broadens to accommodate ocean-going vessels and is a major artery for maritime traffic as well. Few landscapes in the world can rival that of the lower Rhine for intensity of urbanization and industrialization; it is an immense alluvial fan of cities. The Ruhr is, in fact, the largest megalopolis of continental Europe. Over sixty cities of note lie in this industrial belt: the largest are Cologne (866,000), Essen (705,000), Düsseldorf (681,000), Dortmund (647,000), and Duisburg (458,000). Within a perimeter of 100 miles, 9 million people are engaged in the treatment of ores, the production of metals, and the manufacture of a wide variety of finished products.

The continued growth of urban industrial centers like the Ruhr at the expense of the rural fringes of Western Europe has led to such dense concentration of people and industry that today 335 million Europeans live in an area one-third the size of the United States. With nearly 220 million people living in cities, an average density of nearly 300 people per square mile, and an industrial economy, Europe, not surprisingly, has serious environmental pollution. And nowhere is pollution more evident than along the Rhine and in the Ruhr.

Some forty international conferences have been held in Europe over the last hundred years to discuss water pollution, and many of them have been concerned with the Rhine. Despite this attention, pollu-

tion in the Rhine has risen with population density and industrial growth and has now reached critically toxic levels. The industries of five countries depend on the river, some 17,000 vessels a year ply its waterways, and nearly 20 million people rely directly or indirectly on it for domestic water. Yet by the time it reaches Strasbourg, swimming is forbidden because of the waste water, sewage, and industrial by-products dumped in by the Swiss. In West Germany, chemical industries at Lugwigshafen contribute their poisons, and the Neckar, which joins the Rhine after serving as the sewage disposal system for Stuttgart and Tübingen, adds more. At Koblenz, the seat of the international pollution commission, nuclear plants on its banks raise water temperatures and encourage bacterial action, thereby reducing the oxygen level. Farther north, industrial wastes from the Lorraine iron mines, the coal fields of the Saar, and potash mines pour into the river. Then the Rhine enters the Ruhr, and when it crosses the Dutch border at Emmerich, it is carrying a staggering total of 24 million tons of solid waste a year, 66,760 tons a day. The Rhine and the Ruhr alone contribute 80,000 tons of iron, 20,000 tons of zinc, 6,000 tons of manganese, and more than 1,000 tons of chromium, nickel, copper, lead, and arsenic to the immense load of pollutants dumped into the North Sea by nine north European nations. The severity of environmental deterioration in an area like the Ruhr has paralleled the remarkable surge to affluence of the postwar period: Its people now pay a heavy price for their television sets, supermarkets, and automobiles.

A castle on the Rhine. Thomas Hopker, Woodfin Camp. (*overleaf*) The steelworks at Reinhausen. Rene Burri, Magnum.

(opposite) Steel making, Krupp works, Essen. Erich Lessing, Magnum.
(left top) Worker inspecting parts. Erich Lessing, Magnum.
(left bottom) Tram and bus factory, Krupp works, Essen. Rene Burri, Magnum.
(right bottom) Worker with parts ready for shipment, Krupp works, Essen. Erich Lessing, Magnum.

(top) A view of the Ruhr at Essen. Erich Lessing, Magnum.
(left) The Krupp shipyards, Essen. Erich Lessing, Magnum.
(opposite) View along the Rhine. Thomas Hopker, Woodfin Camp.

THE JAPANESE RICE CYCLE

Rapid industrialization during the late nineteenth and early twentieth centuries and the "economic miracle" of the postwar period have made of Japan a world economic power, but they have also so polluted the four small islands of that country that today it is, in the opinion of one environmentalist, much like the canary in the cage that warned coal miners of the presence of deadly gases. People have been disabled and have died of poisoning from industrial wastes; air pollution in some areas is so severe that free medical care is given to those stricken with chronic respiratory diseases; and in 1973 the discovery of tainted fish in Tokyo's main market caused a national uproar as fishermen dumped catches they could not sell at corporate and government doors and housewives rationed their families' intake of a food that is part of almost every meal.

But the damage caused by industry and urbanization stands in stark contrast to another aspect of life and culture in Japan—the rice cycle. Rice farming, introduced into the islands around the third century BC, was traditionally so practiced by the Japanese as to form a perfect ecological cycle: Seeds were sown in spring in special seedbeds and the seedlings then set out by hand in flooded paddy fields fertilized with organic materials and tended by intense labor. When harvested, the plant was separated into four elements: rice, straw, bran, and hulls. Every element was fully used and eventually returned to the soil as organic waste.

The polished rice was (and is) eaten as food in various forms. *Gohan*, boiled rice, was the staple food for every meal. Glutinous rice pounded to a doughy consistency became *mochi*, rice cakes offered at Shinto shrines and made for holidays; when cut into thin pieces, dried, grilled and flavored with soy sauce, it became *senbei*, rice crackers eaten as a snack. Powdered rice mixed with water and shaped, steamed, and seasoned became confections, *dango*. Rice malt combined with steamed rice and fermented became *sakè*, rice wine; the sediment was used to make the pickled vegetables that also accompanied every meal.

Rice straw was used as livestock feed; as organic fertilizer; as cooking fuel; as the foundation for *tatami*, the floor matting of the traditional house; as ropes, containers, apparel (the traditional raingear, hat, and snow boots of the farmer), toys, and ceremonial religious objects. The ash from burned straw was used in braziers and in firing pottery. Bran, which contains oil, proteins, and vitamin B_1, was made into oil for cooking, pickling ingredients, and chicken and livestock feed. Wrapped in a little cloth pouch, it was also used for skin care. Hulls were used as fertilizer, as packaging for fragile objects, and in ash form to create a special pottery glaze.

The rice cycle regulated the rhythm and style of life as well. The communal effort that wet rice cultivation requires made the Japanese an intensely group-oriented people. At the heart of village life, the *ie*, an extended patriarchal family embracing both ancestors and the living, tied individuals in a web of close relationships. Personal concerns were subordinate to family and village welfare, for harmony was necessary to maintain complicated irrigation and drainage systems. The hallmark of the entire system was order and continuity—and a frugality permitting no waste.

Industrialization, commercialization of the countryside, population growth, and modern education have disrupted these traditions; changing life styles have relegated many of the products of the rice cycle to handicraft shops selling decorative objects for the urbanite to display in a city apartment. By the middle 1950s a massive migration of labor from the land swept into industrial Japan, driven by population pressure and attracted by the amenities, jobs, and individuality of urban life. Agriculturalists form a declining percentage of the labor force each year, and family fields now are left to women and children and grandparents. Traditionalists mourn the declining importance of the *ie*, the village life it defined, and the weakening of values that are falling victim to the urban industrial ferment of modern Japan. There is constant discussion, especially since the oil crisis, of whether economic progress alone is a sufficient national goal, of the value of an ever-rising GNP, of whether the values embedded in the rice cycle are not after all better adapted to a reasonable social and physical environment and to a sense of personal dignity and worth.

(opposite) Two women threshing rice. Herbert Lanks, Monkmeyer.
(overleaf) Transplanting rice in flooded fields. Japanese National Tourist Office, New York.

(opposite, top) Community meeting. Takeshi Takahara, Woodfin Camp.

(opposite, bottom) Harvesting rice. Takeshi Takahara, Woodfin Camp.

(top) Sacred straw rope, Izumo Shrine. John Nicholias, Woodfin Camp.

(left) Tatami maker, Asakusa, Tokyo. John Nicholias, Woodfin Camp.

(right) Sake offerings, Izumo Shrine. John Nicholias, Woodfin Camp.

(overleaf) Rice fields in midsummer. Dennis Stock, Magnum.

(last page) Farmhouses and rice fields in autumn. Japanese National Tourist Office, New York.

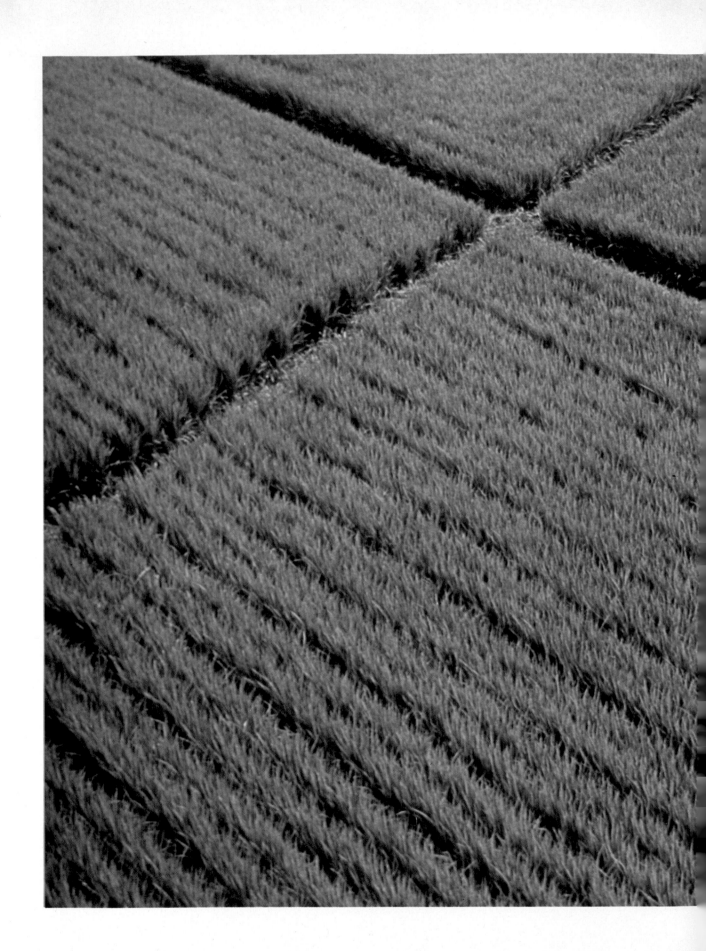

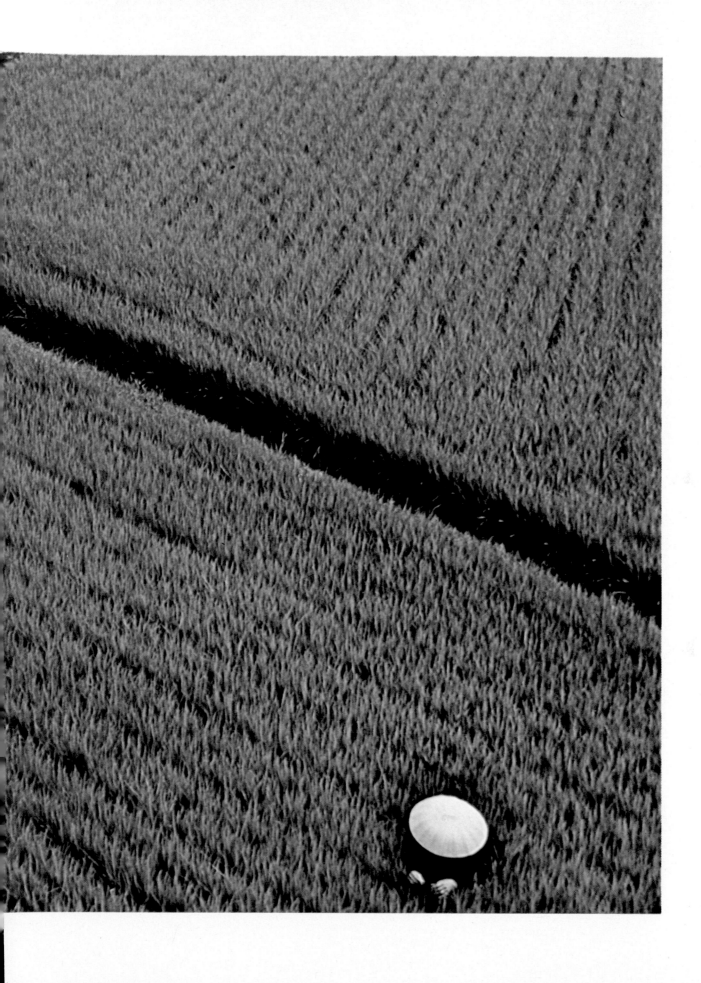

vidual lives in the name of the people. It appears that the people of the Soviet Union may yet discover their own power—collectively, democratically, and individually.

To a certain degree, the forces that gave special character to Russian modernization and distinguished it from the patterns set in the rest of the technological world have moderated. The extreme anti-Western, nationalistic sentiments of the Russian administration have been tempered by technology itself: literacy, intensive international communication, and the attainment of material comfort. Although the USSR is the most isolated of all technological societies, indeed more insulated from world currents than many Third World countries, Russia's defensiveness has been eased by control of a European buffer zone and its attainment of military power. Détente between Russia and the United States is, in some areas, a reality. Yet the most salient characteristic of Russia's modern evolution, the sole initiative of the state and the bureaucracy in all phases of cultural and economic life, remains inviolable. In a sense, modern Soviet leaders are trapped in the dilemma of the tsars: the creation of an efficient modern society requires the delegation of power and authority to a widely based population whose interests automatically threaten the authority of any small class of leaders. This internal contradiction was not anticipated by Marx. In his dictatorship of the people, the two primary social classes,

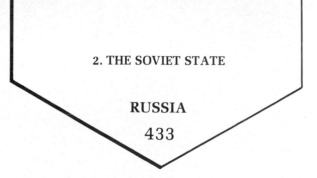

the workers and the peasants, would themselves hold the position of power. The privileged position of "mental workers," the intelligentsia, would simply dissolve as society in general became the repository of all power. But in fact the intelligentsia, the members of the Soviet bureaucracy, dominate the Communist party and wield the social and economic power to make all decisions that determine the human geography of the Soviet Union. The current problem is to raise the standard of living of the Soviet people and to provide the economy of abundance so frequently promised by Communist leaders while simultaneously resolving the internal tensions generated by a privileged bureaucratic class in a society whose ideology demands classlessness. Unlike other industrial societies, where countless individual decisions determine trends and policies, the concentration of power in the hands of so few makes judgments upon the future direction of Russia more a matter of understanding ideology than of understanding social and environmental forces.

RUSSIA

THE INDUSTRIAL BASE
ENERGY AND MINERAL RESOURCES MAP

Western, European Russia is a densely settled, fertile, and well-populated region that produces the bulk of the country's food and manufactured goods but possesses few of the raw materials of industry. To the east, Siberia stretches to the Pacific Ocean over a difficult and thinly peopled environment rich in the necessities of modern economy—energy resources, minerals, metals, and other raw industrial materials.

During the early Stalin years, Soviet planners embarked on a program of industrial development in the east near sources of raw materials. This move was prompted by two strategic necessities: the removal of the balance of Russian industry from its vulnerable position near Europe and the rationalization of the Russian economy in the context of internal development. The industrial and population centers gradually shifted eastward under the five-year plans of the 1930s, which pursued this locational policy and favored economic growth in the Urals, Central Asia, and Siberia. Thousands of Slavic peoples were transferred eastward. Some migrated in a patriotic response to the national planning goals, but most new Siberians came east as Stalinist purges staffed the emerging industries of Asiatic Russia with convicts, enemies of the state, and hapless innocents trapped in the web of Stalin's secret police. This heralded eastward movement did not, however, significantly shift the distribution of Russian industry before World War II. In 1940, two-thirds of Russia's energy was produced in European Russia along a north-south axis stretching between the coalfields of the Donets Basin and the oil fields of the Caucasus. The building of new industrial centers in the east, far from diminishing the industrial dominance of the west, had demanded the continued expansion of older centers of heavy industry in European Russia so that new areas could be constructed and equipped. But the German onslaught in 1940 succeeded in restructuring Russia's industrial distribution where planners had failed. Within months after the opening of the war, some 1360 major industrial enterprises in European Russia and the Ukraine were loaded onto flatcars, workers atop, and transported east to the Urals, Kazakhstan, and western Siberia.

At the end of World War II, European Russia's industrial base lay in ruins while the centers of mining and manufacturing in the Urals and Siberia were intact. However, the continuing disparity between the densely populated, resource-poor west and the thinly populated, resource-laden east remained a central problem for Soviet planners. They have come to realize that it is more efficient and less expensive to move the raw materials of Siberia westward to industrial centers than to move the population eastward into Siberia and create urban centers in the wilderness. Furthermore, the advent of missile warfare in the postwar era made strategic considerations obsolete. A new energy axis emerged in Russia eastward from the established industrial terminus of the Donets Basin to the Volga-Urals oil fields and to the coal and hydroelectric reserves of the Kuznetsk Basin and Baikal. Meanwhile, a web of pipelines and railroads was constructed to carry oil and coal to the rebuilt centers of heavy industry in the Ukraine and the central industrial region (Moscow and its nearby hinterland).

This spatial reorganization of mining and manufacturing was coupled with a tremendous postwar expansion of industrial production: by the early 1970s Russian annual coal production exceeded 600 million tons, more than that of the United States; oil production was above 2 billion barrels a year; annual steel production passed 100 million tons, equal to the combined output of Great Britain and the *European Common Market.* This explosive growth propelled Russia into its current position as the second leading industrial power in the world after the United States. With vast territories only partly explored and huge proved energy reserves and mineral and metal resources, Russia has the raw materials to support extensive future industrial expansion.

ENERGY SOURCES

The Soviet Union claims more than half the coal reserves on earth, a third of all natural gas, and more petroleum reserves than any other country. Although methods of estimating energy reserves vary, it is clear that Russia has an energy base comparable to and perhaps larger than that of the United States. Until 1950, coal was the source of two-thirds of the industrial energy of the Soviet Union. Widely distributed and more fully exploited than hydroelectric power or petroleum, coal was the basis of Russian industrialization until World War II. But one-sixth of the millions of tons of coal

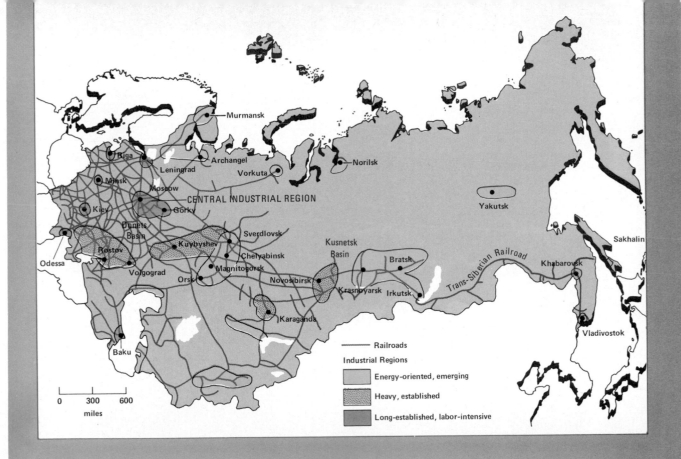

Figure 7. Centers of Industry. The traditional centers of heavy industry in European Russia have been supplemented by an east-west industrial axis based on raw materials that extends thousands of miles eastward from Moscow and the Donets Basin through the Urals and the Kuznetsk Basin to the shores of Lake Baikal in Asiatic Russia.

shipped by rail over huge distances to sustain the industrial growth of the country was burned up in transport. Today, four separate fields integrated to nearby industrial development yield 60 percent of total production and account for a large proportion of higher grade *anthracite*• and *bituminous coals*• as well as most of the country's *coking coal*.• The Donets Basin in the Ukraine produces 200 million tons per year and is the leading field. Although the coal seams of the Donets are thin and heavily worked, the high quality of the product and its nearness to Russia's centers of population and industry have maintained the primacy of this field. The Kuznetsk field in western Siberia, 2000 miles to the east, produces a fifth of Russia's coal. The Kuznetsk field is characterized by thick, easily worked seams, some as wide as 50 feet, capable of being *strip-mined*.• The fact that these mines produce twice as much coal per worker as those in the Donets compensates for the locational disadvantage of Kuznetsk. The Karaganda field, located between the Ural Mountains and the Kuznetsk Basin, and the Pechora fields in the Soviet Arctic also produce significant but smaller quantities of high-grade coal.

Other notable Russian coal-producing regions include *lignite*• mines in the Urals industrial region and the Moscow Basin, the newly developed mines of eastern Siberia in the Irkutsk Basin east of Lake Baikal, and the vast undeveloped Tungus and Lena coal basins of eastern Siberia, containing nearly half the coal reserves of the Soviet Union. Although coal currently accounts for only 40 percent of the total energy consumed in the Soviet Union, compared with 65 percent twenty-five years ago, it is still produced and used in greater quantities than in any other industrial nation. With three-quarters of domestic reserves—enough to maintain current consumption levels for 15,000 years—located in the remote and relatively undeveloped expanses of eastern Siberia and the Far East, coal will continue to play a significant role in Soviet economic planning and industrial development.

In the 1950s, the energy patterns of the Soviet economy were transformed by the development and exploitation of the Volga-Urals oil fields, a series of basins clustered near the great bend in the Volga River and extending northeast some 500 miles. Previously, Russia had relied on the vulnerable Baku and Grozny oil fields in the Caucasus for its relatively limited consumption of petroleum products. But the development of huge Volga-Urals deposits, which produce 80 percent of Russia's current annual production of 2 billion barrels, has led to a shift from the inefficient and expensive transport of coal by railroad to the more flexible trans-

435

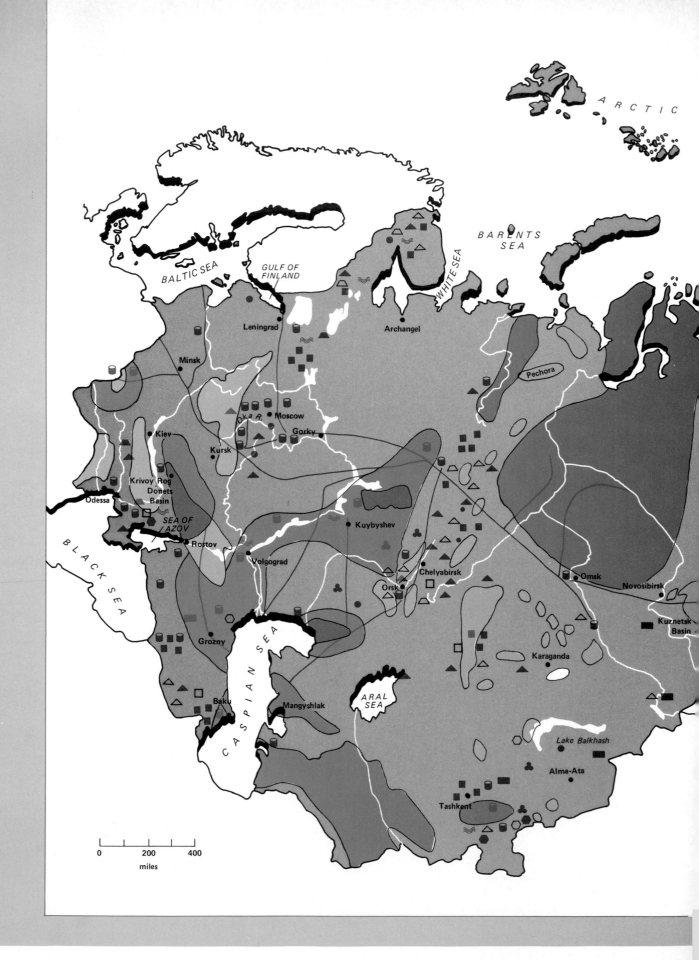

ARCTIC

BARENTS
SEA

BALTIC SEA

GULF OF
FINLAND

WHITE SEA

Pechora

Leningrad

Archangel

Minsk

Oka R.

Moscow

Kiev

Gorky

Kursk

Krivoy Rog
Donets
Basin

Odessa

SEA OF
AZOV

Kuybyshev

Rostov

Volgograd

Chelyabirsk

Omsk

Novosibirsk

Orsk

BLACK
SEA

Kuznetsk
Basin

Grozny

Karaganda

CASPIAN SEA

Baku

Mangyshlak

ARAL
SEA

Lake Balkhash

Alma-Ata

Tashkent

0   200   400

miles

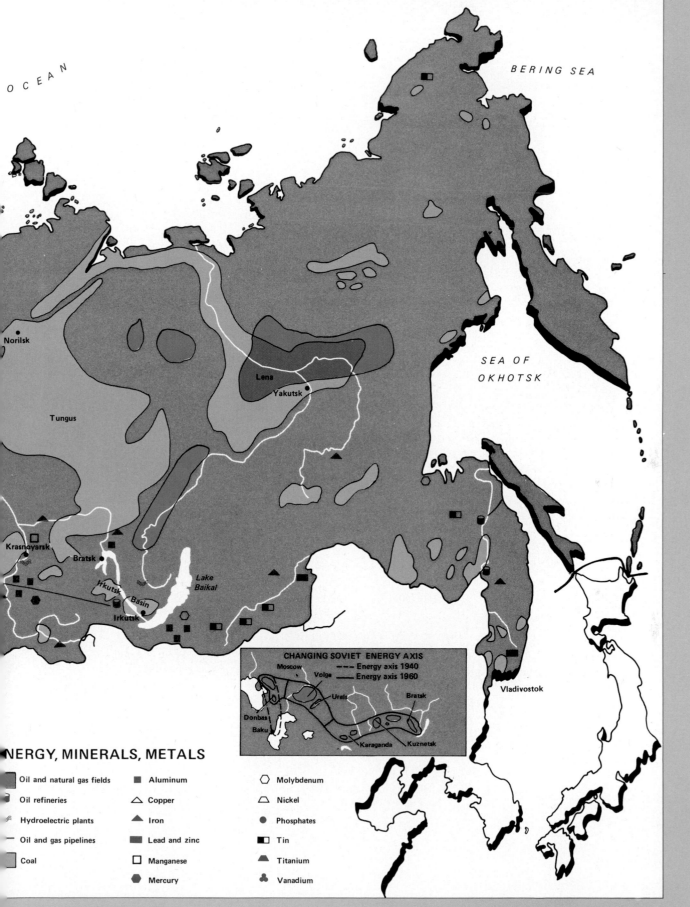

OCEAN

BERING SEA

SEA OF
OKHOTSK

Norilsk

Lena

Yakutsk

Tungus

Krasnoyarsk

Bratsk

Irkutsk Basin

Lake
Baikal

Irkutsk

Vladivostok

CHANGING SOVIET ENERGY AXIS

Moscow

Volga

Urals

Bratsk

Donbas

Baku

Karaganda

Kuznetsk

- - - - Energy axis 1940
———— Energy axis 1960

NERGY, MINERALS, METALS

◼ Oil and natural gas fields	◼ Aluminum	⬡ Molybdenum
◣ Oil refineries	△ Copper	△ Nickel
⋙ Hydroelectric plants	▲ Iron	● Phosphates
— Oil and gas pipelines	▬ Lead and zinc	◧ Tin
▨ Coal	☐ Manganese	▲ Titanium
	⬢ Mercury	♣ Vanadium

port of oil by pipe. Great pipeline systems have been laid eastward from the Volga to Novosibirsk in the Kuznetsk Basin and beyond to Irkutsk in eastern Siberia. Oil is piped west to the industrial centers of European Russia, an energy web connecting Moscow, Leningrad, Kiev, and the Donets concentrations. Additional oil fields have been developed on the Mangyshlak Peninsula on the eastern shore of the Caspian Sea and in the valley of the Ob River in western Siberia. The natural gas industry experienced a parallel rapid growth in the 1950s and 1960s as productive fields were developed in the Ukraine, the Volga region, and Soviet Central Asia. Carried by pipe directly to most sizable cities in European Russia and to the Urals as well, natural gas production increased tenfold during the 1960s, making Russia the second largest gas producer in the world. Together, petroleum and natural gas account for nearly 60 percent of the energy currently consumed in Russia and have become important export products.

Although hydroelectric power plays a relatively small role in the Soviet energy economy, Russia's waterpower potential is estimated to be 12 percent of the world's total, second only to that of the basin of the Congo River in Zaire. Huge waterpower projects have been constructed at Kuybyshev and Volgograd on the Volga River, at Bratsk on the Angara, and at Krasnoyarsk on the Yenisei. Overall, Russia's waterpower resources are less fully developed than in any other major industrial nation. The largest rivers are located in eastern Siberia, thousands of miles away from the centers of population, and are susceptible to strong seasonal variations in flow.

MINERALS AND METALS

The Soviet Union is equally richly endowed with mineral and metal resources; it is virtually self-sufficient in the most important industrial ores—iron, copper, aluminum, lead, and zinc. Russia has been the world's largest producer of iron ore for nearly fifteen years, and the current Russian annual production of some 200 million tons is nearly double that of the United States, today forced to rely on imported iron ore. Two-thirds of Russia's iron production comes from two locations: Krivoy Rog, near the bend in the Dnieper River in the Ukraine (these deposits supply the Donets industrial com-

plex and with associated fields near Kursk are substantial enough to cause a *magnetic anomaly**), and the Urals, where a series of deposits, most importantly at Magnitogorsk ("iron mountain"), form the resource basis for the Urals-Kuznetsk industrial combine. Secondary iron-producing districts are found at Kerch in the Crimea, at Tula and Lipetsk south of Moscow, at Olenogorsk near Murmansk on the Kola Peninsula, and in the Kuznetsk Basin itself. With existing technology, current levels of iron production can be maintained for a century, but as in the United States, higher quality ores are being depleted, so that over half the iron ore mined requires concentration. Necessary ferroalloys are also in plentiful supply: manganese deposits at Nikopol in the Ukraine and Chiatura in Georgia produce two-thirds the total world supply; nickel and chromium deposits found throughout the Urals produce, respectively, one-third and one-sixth of the world total; and titanium, molybdenum, and tungsten are scattered from the Urals eastward through the mountains of Central Asia, Siberia, and the Far East.

Russia is an equally important producer of non-ferrous metals, although data on mineral production and distribution are sketchy. Copper is mined at a number of sites: the Urals, in northern Kazakhstan where the largest proved reserves in the country are located, at Almalyk south of Tashkent in the foothills of the Tien Shan Mountains, and in Soviet Armenia. Lead and zinc, often found in association with other minerals in Central Asia, are mined principally at Leninogorsk in the Altai Mountains and at Chimkent in the Tien Shan. Zinc is also found in the Urals and west of the Kuznetsk Basin. In recent years, aluminum refining has expanded substantially at huge plants in Bratsk, Krasnoyarsk, and near Irkutsk, where large hydroelectric facilities provide power. The various bauxite ores that feed these mills come from the Ural Mountains, Kazakhstan, and Transcaucasia. In European Russia, ore from the Kola Peninsula supplies plants at Volkhov and Boksitogorsk east of Leningrad.

Russia's diverse mineral and metal economy is extremely strong, and only the United States has a comparable resource base. Currently, the Soviet Union is the world's first, second, or third leading producer of ten minerals and metals: iron, manganese, molybdenum, chrome, nickel, tungsten, copper, bauxite, asbestos, and gold.

BIBLIOGRAPHY

GENERAL

Cole, John P., and F. C. German. *A Geography of the U.S.S.R.* London: Butterworth, 1970. A detailed economic geography treating Russia as a coherent spatial system.

Gregory, James S. *Russian Land, Soviet People: A Geographical Approach to the U.S.S.R.* New York: Pegasus, 1968. By far the most detailed and intensive analysis of the geography of Russia in print.

Grey, Ian. *The First Fifty Years: Soviet Russia 1917–67.* New York: Coward-McCann, 1967. A well-written general history of Russia after the revolution.

Hooson, David. *The Soviet Union: People and Regions.* Belmont, Cal.: Wadsworth, 1966. A brief but comprehensive regional geography of Russia.

Jackson, W. A. Douglas. *Russo-Soviet Borderlands.* Princeton: Van Nostrand, Searchlight Series No. 2, 1962. An interpretive essay on the foundations of Chinese-Soviet relations by a prominent geographer.

Lydolph, Paul E. *Geography of the U.S.S.R.* New York: Wiley, 1970. An authoritative and detailed systematic and regional geography with excellent maps by the cartographer Randall Sale.

Parker, W. H. *The Soviet Union.* Chicago: Aldine, 1969. An integrated geographical study of the landscapes of Russia.

[1] THE MODERNIZATION OF RUSSIA

Billington, James H. *The Icon and the Axe.* New York: Knopf, 1966. The culture and civilization of Russia from the medieval period to the present.

Black, Cyril E. (ed.). *The Transformation of Russian Society.* Cambridge, Mass.: Harvard University Press, 1960. A comprehensive series of essays on the modernization of Russian society.

Floyd, David. *Russia in Revolt, 1905: The First Crack in Tsarist Power.* New York: American Heritage, 1969. A well-illustrated and incisive introduction to the decline of tsarist rule in Russia.

Pipes, Richard. *Russia under the Old Regime.* London: Weidenfeld and Nicolson, 1974. A thoughtful interpretation of prerevolutionary Russia.

Shanin, Teodor. *The Awkward Class: Political Sociology of Peasantry in a Developing Society, Russia 1910–1925.* Oxford: Clarendon Press, 1972. A well-argued essay on the Russian peasantry and their resistance to alienation from the land.

Troyat, Henri. *Daily Life in Russia under the Last Tsar.* New York: Macmillan, 1962. Vignettes of the life of commoners at the turn of the century.

von Mohrenschildt, Dmitri (ed.). *The Russian Revolution of 1917: Contemporary Accounts.* New York: Oxford University Press, 1971. Eyewitness accounts of the revolution that transformed Russia.

[2] THE SOVIET STATE

Harris, Chauncy D. "Urbanization and Population Growth in the Soviet Union, 1959–1970," *Geographical Review*, Vol. 61 (1971), pp. 102–124. A regional analysis of the demographic and urban revolution in the Soviet Union.

Laird, Roy D., and Betty A. Laird. *Soviet Communism and Agrarian Revolution.* Harmondsworth: Penguin Books, 1970. The impact of Communist doctrine and practice on food production in Russia.

Matthews, Mervyn. *Class and Society in Soviet Russia.* London: Allen Lane, 1972. An analysis of Soviet society in the light of recent statistical data.

Meissner, Boris (ed.). *Social Change in the Soviet Union.* Notre Dame, Ind.: University of Notre Dame Press, 1972. The development and evolution of the Soviet Union as a modernizing system.

Osborn, Robert J. *Soviet Social Policies: Welfare, Equality, and Community.* Homewood, Ill.: Dorsey, 1970. A discussion of welfare, equality, and community in Soviet Russia.

Osborn, Robert J. *The Evolution of Soviet Politics.* Homewood, Ill.: Dorsey, 1974. An analysis of the organizational dynamics of the modern Soviet state.

Salisbury, Harrison E. (ed.). *Anatomy of the Soviet Union.* Camden, N.J.: T. Nelson, 1967. A brilliant series of essays on Russia after a half century of Communist rule.

Shaffer, Henry G. *The Soviet Treatment of the Jews.* New York: Praeger, 1974. The changing Soviet policies toward the Russian Jewish community.

Treml, Vladimir G. (ed.). *The Development of the Soviet Economy.* New York: Praeger, 1968. Comprehensive essays on the Soviet economic order.

JAPAN

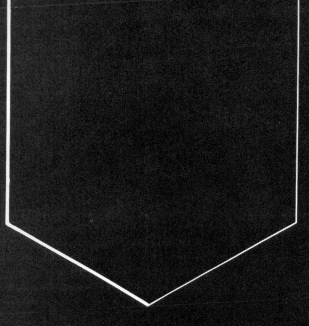

Yukio Mishima gestures as he addresses officers and enlisted men, November 25, 1970. *Photo:* Wide World.

On the morning of November 25, 1970, Japan's most celebrated novelist and three-time candidate for the Nobel Prize dropped the final pages of a manuscript into a mailbox and drove off with four young men to seize the Eastern Division headquarters of Japan's Self-Defense Force. At noon he addressed a jeering crowd of 800 men of the Thirty-Second Regiment from the roof of the headquarters building, imploring them to "rise and die" and to be "true men and *samurai*" (warriors). Yukio Mishima railed against complacent corruption in modern Japan and lives ordered by the pursuit of material gain. He evoked images of the idealistic young officers who assassinated reluctant generals and liberal politicians in the 1930s to lead Japan's quest for empire and spoke of the sacrifices made by the pilots of the "divine wind" (*kamikaze*) who crashed their planes into American ships during the last summer of World War II. Inside and unheard by the soldiers, Mishima removed his jacket, knelt, plunged a short sword into the left side of his abdomen, drew it across his stomach, and was then beheaded. Through the act of ritual suicide known in the West as *hara-kiri,* Yukio Mishima, a brilliant and erratic voice of modern Japan, admonished with his death the politicians and businessmen of Japan, Inc., and on a more personal level achieved in glorious death a peace he had never found in life.

Despite the legend that now surrounds Mishima, his family did not come from the samurai class but from peasant stock, people so low in the social hierarchy that they lacked a surname until early in the nineteenth century. By 1925 when Mishima was born, however, his family had moved into upper-middle-class status through wily land purchases, moneylending, and trade. His father, an unbending misanthrope who worked as deputy director of fisheries, educated his son at the prestigious Peer's School and Tokyo University. Mishima, frail and unsure of his manhood, wrote his first published work, *The Forest in Full Bloom,* in 1941. Composed in archaic style, this romance was an achievement comparable to a novel written by an American adolescent in the language and fluent idiom of the colonial period. It gained attention. His father, upset by Mishima's growing commitment to literature rather than a more practical field, opposed him and used to enter Yukio's room several times a week to collect and destroy manuscript. Mishima, deeply influenced by the nationalistic militarism of the war, persisted. At the end of the war, he wrote the work that made his reputation, *Confessions of a Mask,* a brilliantly conceived confessional account of his emotional development that exposed his erotic attraction to men and his fascination with the beauty and pathos of death. When the emperor surrendered to the Allied Powers on August 14, 1945, Mishima's deep identity with nation, traditional values, and destiny was jolted. He later looked on the surrender as a betrayal of the many who had chosen death above dishonor by the emperor and his advisers. Mishima's father, shallow and obtuse, reversed course and decided that his son could freely write because defeated, Japan must now enter an age of "culture."

At that point, if anyone had predicted his station at age forty-five, the year he ended his life, a reasonable guess would have projected Mishima as a somewhat frazzled, middle-aged intellectual vainly striving to maintain a middle-class academic existense. Not so. After nine months as a reluctant bureaucrat in the ministry of finance, Mishima resigned and devoted himself to writing. Discredited because of his nationalism in the "liberalism" of postwar occupied Japan, he was transformed into a new literary giant by the publication of *Confessions of a Mask* in 1949. Over the next two decades, Mishima produced a dazzling variety of novels, plays, and essays—a total of thirty-six volumes— culminating in a four-volume cycle, *The Sea of Fertility*. Although much of his work is published in the West, its significance is not well understood or its context well placed. His personal life was as varied as his literary production: he undertook a program of body building, developed a cult of physical prowess, starred in gangster and samurai films, recorded jazz songs, and created the Shield Society, a small private army designed to shield the emperor, the living repository of Japanese tradition, from any attack. His writings became more nationalistic as his understanding of the impact of the West on Japan grew. Paradoxically, Mishima was extremely anxious to be read outside Japan,

and his failure to win the Nobel Prize was a significant personal disappointment. He saw his nation as decadent, afflicted by an Oriental strain of a Western disease: the consuming desire to produce, export, gain, and progress. A return to the ideals of Old Japan, a revival of the warlike spirit of the samurai, was required; the unique identity and destiny of Japan must be rekindled, the commercialization of life must be rejected. Brilliantly aware of the needs of his own society and sensitive to others, Mishima fits no cultural category—he is a truly modern figure. He symbolizes the confusions, contradictions, and transformation of the Japanese environment and society during a century of turbulent change.

The century of change that transformed Japan from a nation of rice-growing peasant farmers into the fastest growing economic state in the technological world is the central focus of this section. In "The Modernization of Japan," the samurai warriors of traditional Japan lead their country from self-imposed isolation to a position of world political power by combining Japanese values with Western technology. Although their nation is defeated in a quest for empire, "The Industrial State" achieves far greater wealth in the postwar period than was imaginable in 1945. The martial spirit of the samurai is transferred to the pursuit of business and economic growth, and the social and environmental problems of industrial maturity become national issues.

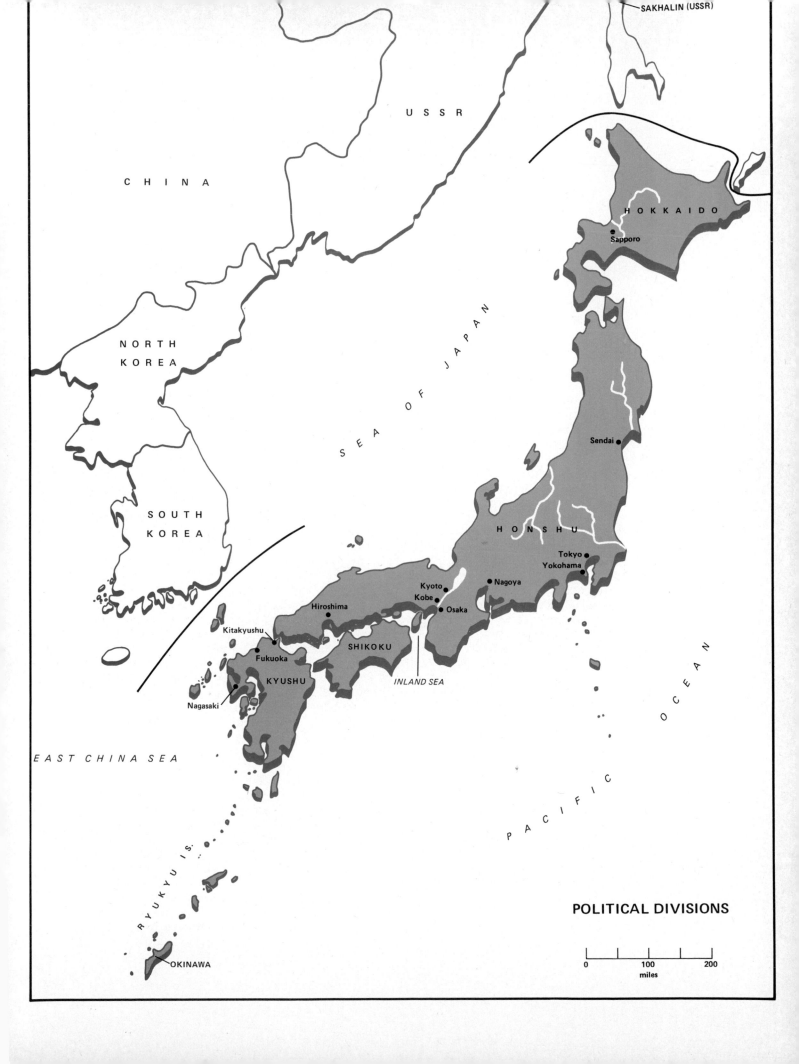

SAKHALIN (USSR)

U S S R

C H I N A

HOKKAIDO

Sapporo

NORTH
KOREA

S E A   O F   J A P A N

Sendai

SOUTH
KOREA

HONSHU

Tokyo
Yokohama

Kyoto
Kobe
Osaka

Nagoya

Hiroshima

Kitakyushu

SHIKOKU

Fukuoka

INLAND SEA

KYUSHU

P A C I F I C   O C E A N

Nagasaki

EAST CHINA SEA

RYUKYU IS.

OKINAWA

POLITICAL DIVISIONS

0   100   200
miles

THE MODERNIZATION OF JAPAN

1

In April 1868, the modernization of Japan was launched with the symbolic signing of a brief, five-sentence document by Mutsuhito, the adolescent emperor of Japan. Known by the name given to his reign, the Meiji emperor became the figurehead leader of a revitalized Japanese government consisting of a handful of young samurai. The document, known as the Charter Oath, embodied a set of principles by which these young men planned to eliminate *feudalism,* open the island nation to Western technology, and build a powerful Japanese state based on a combination of Eastern ethics and Western science. Their objective was accomplished in less than fifty years: an isolated and introverted agricultural society was transformed into the first non-Western industrial state. Unlike the situation in Russia and later China, peasant unrest and revolution were not spurs toward modernization; unlike the case in Western Europe and the United States, a discontented middle class did not demand liberal social and economic progress. Instead, modernization in Japan was motivated by a reinterpretation of traditional values—pride and a keen sense of national spirit—carried out by the upper classes. These were wedded with modern science and technology to accomplish an unparalleled leap to economic and political power as Japan took its place as the first cultural hybrid in the technological world.

THE TOKUGAWA INHERITANCE

The restoration of the emperor to direct rule in 1868 ended 250 years (1603–1867) of feudal military rule in his name under a succession of *shoguns* (generalissimos) of the Tokugawa clan. After an initial contact with the West, in the sixteenth century, Tokugawa Japan severed connections with the outside world and developed a static, inward-looking society. In the seventeenth century, a series of government edicts had imposed economic and cultural

isolation on Japan. No foreigners were allowed to enter Japanese ports save a limited number of Dutch and Chinese, who were permitted to trade on the man-made island of Deshima in Nagasaki Bay. Foreign merchants could not travel elsewhere in Japan except by special permission, and the quantity of trade was limited to two cargoes a year for the Dutch and thirty for the Chinese. Japanese ships could not leave the country; shipyards, in fact, were prohibited from building oceangoing vessels. Japanese living abroad were not allowed to return to Japan; those who did were executed. Western books were banned, and the half million or so Japanese Christians whom the Jesuit missionary St. Francis Xavier and his successors had earlier converted from Buddhism or the native Shinto religion were brutally persecuted and forced underground. Foreign religions were officially banned. Some Western, or "Dutch" (as it was called by the Japanese), learning continued to filter into Japan, but for more than a century the primary task of the Tokugawa government was the insulation of Japanese life from foreign influence—the removal of Japan from the world of nations.

Peace and Prosperity
[FIGURE 1]

These measures of self-imposed isolation were part of a broader impulse to retard economic change and preserve existing patterns of social organization. Government policies as laid down by the shogun, the true ruler of Japan, underlined the conservative, self-protective nature of Tokugawa rule. Society was rigidly divided into four classes: the *daimyo* or feudal barons; their retainers, the samurai warriors; the *peasants*; and merchants. The daimyo, numbering less than 3000, composed the elite from which the Tokugawa family sprang to power. The daimyo were a landed elite who held the agricultural plains of Japan in 200 to 250 separate feudal domains. They were subservient to the shogun, who directly or indirectly controlled a quarter of the labor and agricultural produce of the country. On a spiritual level, both the Tokugawa shoguns and the daimyo paid homage to the emperor, who became a shadowy, symbolic figure residing in Kyoto in relative obscurity and under careful Tokugawa supervision. Holders of great wealth and power, the daimyo were required to bear heavy expenses for their economic and political privileges under the Tokugawa. They were obligated to maintain elaborate residences at the seat of the *shogunate* in the city of Edo (modern Tokyo) and to live there in alternate years; their families were left behind as hostages when the daimyo returned biennially to their personal estates. Even so, the daimyo and particularly the "outside lords," who ruled remote areas of Japan, were largely autonomous within their own domains after they had satisfied the requirements of the shogunate for the proper tax revenues, maintaining social order, and seeing that social regulations were enforced. However, the daimyo were never allowed to communicate directly with the emperor or to repair or fortify their castle towns.

Socially below but economically bound to the daimyo were 2 million samurai, a class trained in the Confucian tradition of loyalty, obedience, and service. Samurai pride, loyalty to lord, and military preparedness were encouraged and applauded, despite the potential threat the samurai posed to the stability of Tokugawa rule. Any internal military actions were ruthlessly suppressed, and foreign adventures were precluded by the national policy of seclusion. Below the samurai were 28 million peasants, 80 percent of the population, on whom the economic burden of the country fell. Peasants bound to the soil and to their lord could not change residence or occupation, and their lives were ordered in minute detail. Only grains could be grown; millet (not rice) was the appropriate diet of peasants, and rigid obligations forced peasants to cultivate all the feudal **arable.** What spare time peasants had was devoted to the production of necessary handicrafts: ropes and sandals, woven textiles, and thread. Frugality was essential, and diversions such as smoking, tea drinking, or consuming sake (a rice-based alcoholic beverage) were prohibited. Taxes paid in rice commonly amounted to 40 to 50 percent of a peasant's yield and provided 80 percent of the revenues of the Tokugawa state. Failure to pay taxes meant dishonor and disgrace, and, more to the point, confiscation of the peasant's property, wife, and even children. In one case, a village **headman** pleaded in desperation for a reduction in taxes; the reduction was granted but the headman was executed for having the audacity to ask. The general policy of the ruling class toward peasants was aptly summarized by an elder Tokugawa official, who wrote: "Sesame seed and peasants are much alike, the more they are squeezed, the more one extracts." The fourth class, theoretically below but actually more wealthy than the peasants, were the artisans and merchants, townspeople who lived in the incipient urban centers of Tokugawa Japan. Although merchants were considered inferior because of the orthodox Confucian belief that money corrupts, the ruling daimyo and samurai classes eventually came to rely on them for cash to sustain new urban styles of life.

Tokugawa rule brought social stability, peace, and prosperity to Japan; embedded within this matrix, however, were the seeds of an urban and commercial revolution that ultimately undermined and broke the rigid social solidarity of feudal Japan. At the beginning of the seventeenth century, Japan had four large cities with a combined population of 400,000: Kyoto, Fushimi, Osaka, and Sakai. Grouped together at the eastern end of the Inland Sea, they were all within a radius of 25 miles of one another. This curious urban concentration in a nation of iso-

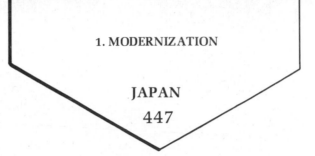
lated villages and subsistence farmers was complemented by occasional castle towns or ports of a much lower order. However, the establishment of the Tokugawa shogunate inspired an unprecedented increase in urbanization throughout the feudal **heartland.** Castle towns, the nuclei of feudal domains, became the loci of local military and administrative activities. And as the role of the feudal elite broadened and the daimyo consolidated their control over large areas of rural Japan, the role of castle towns became ever more important. New castle towns were built not in outlying mountain passes where the old defensive fortresses were found, but in the economic and strategic centers of the various domains. A network of urban centers based on the economic functions of the **fiefdom** and the administrative role of the elite was established throughout the fertile lowlands of the **archipelago.** As this network of cities, the physical embodiment of the growing power of the feudal elite, came under the control of the shogunate, the spatial base for a new centralized state was formed.

This shift of the feudal elite—lords and their retinues of samurai—from the countryside to emerging castle towns created a dichotomy of rural and urban functions between peasants remaining on the land and the newly urbanized feudal class in the towns. Because of their origins as garrison towns, fully 50 percent of the urban population were members of the samurai class. As Tokugawa rule became ever more involved in the organization of rural life and agricultural production, the castles of Japan came to house bureaucracies which served as the focal points of economic transactions. The commerce of the freer marketplaces of new castle towns was a first step in the transition of Japan to a market-oriented society. Feudal lords came to rely increasingly upon the merchants to bridge the gap between city and countryside and to provide links between their agricultural domains, the castle town, and the national market system. The merchant class, the *chonin*, was the vital and aggressive element in a growing economy that was very much of its own making. By the beginning of the eighteenth century, Tokugawa urbanism had fully matured and Japan contained some of the largest cities in the world at that time. Edo (Tokyo) had nearly 500,000 people; Osaka and Kyoto had populations of 300,000. Kanazawa and Nagoya had grown to about 100,000, and an estimated 10 percent of the Japanese population lived in cities

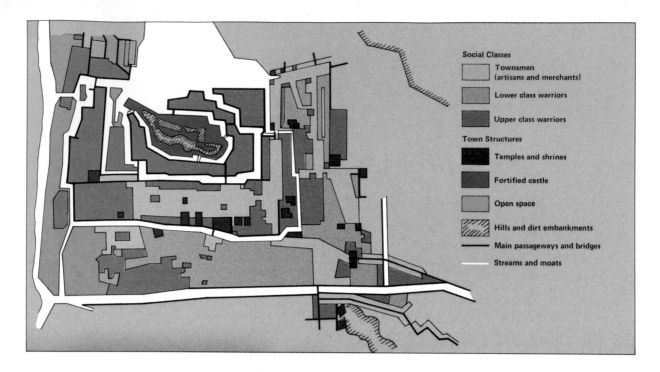

Social Classes
- [ ] Townsmen (artisans and merchants)
- [ ] Lower class warriors
- [ ] Upper class warriors

Town Structures
- [ ] Temples and shrines
- [ ] Fortified castle
- [ ] Open space
- [ ] Hills and dirt embankments
- Main passageways and bridges
- Streams and moats

Figure 1. The Rise of the Castle Town. Castle towns emerged as the consolidation of the daimyo's feudal domains resulted in the development of strategic centers for the political, military, religious, and economic affairs of the region. The social patterning of the town shows the castle of the daimyo at the center, surrounded by moats; wealthy samurai close to the castle; lower-class samurai on the edge of town; and the artisans and merchants in well-defined quarters. Fully half the population of the castle towns was drawn from the warrior class. *After:* Takeo Yazaki, *The Japanese City: A Sociological Analysis.* Tokyo: Japan Publications Trading Company, 1963, pp. 2, 4.

with populations larger than 10,000. Feeding the urban population and meeting its sophisticated needs had emerged as the major business of Japan.

The burden of sustaining the growing urban population predictably remained the task of the peasantry. Occupied with growing rice in wet lowlands and wheat, barley, millet, vegetables, and tea in the uplands, Japanese peasants were continuously exhorted to produce the food, fibers, timber, and fish demanded by the expanding towns. The Japanese arable doubled between 1600 and 1730 as farming extended outward from the plains of the warm southwest to the untouched shallow bays and *lagoons*• of the north. Cultivation of wet rice increased, commercial fertilizer came into use, double cropping (the cultivation of more than one crop in the same field in a given agricultural year) became more widespread, and yields increased. Waterwheels and treadmills were introduced, and the number of varieties of rice increased from 175 to more than 2000. Given this increase in agricultural production, the market economy of the castle towns spread to

outlying rural areas. Industry-oriented crops such as mulberry leaves for silkworms, cotton, sugarcane, indigo (for blue dyes), and tobacco were put into cultivation in suitable climates and soils. Handicraft industries grew in importance, and peasants, who began to receive cash payments for their produce, supplemented their incomes by spinning silk, brewing beer, making sandals, matting straw, and weaving cotton textiles. By the late Tokugawa period, regional preindustrial specializations were developing—*sericulture*• on the Pacific coast of northern Honshu, sugar refining near Edo, and hemp weaving along the Sea of Japan in west-central Honshu. Villages became product-oriented. Enterprising and resourceful peasants bought land and rented it out to a new generation of *tenant farmers.*• Peasant landlords controlled village life and worked to maintain the proper peasant deference to social status. Through this commercialization of the Japanese landscape, villages were welded into the national spatial and economic system.

Commercial and urban growth in Tokugawa Japan created tensions that ultimately cracked the foundations of feudalism. The daimyo and samurai classes could not generate the income needed to sustain their urban way of life within a nonindustrial agricultural economy. Forced into debt, the feudal lords lowered the lucrative rice grants traditionally paid to their now largely symbolic and idle samurai retainers. Deep resentment infected the proud and militant samurai, and when inflation further eroded their fixed incomes, large numbers of masterless samurai roved from city to city, frustrated and deprived of role, seeking jobs in the bureaucracy or in

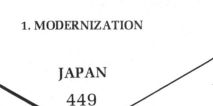

the military academies that flourished in the larger urban centers. The merchants, although benefiting enormously from the growth in commerce and trade, were deprived of foreign opportunities and were under continuous scrutiny by Tokugawa administrators who remained unyielding in their perception of commerce as a despised activity. This arrogance was muted by a healthy awareness of the financial power of the merchants, whose anger could strike terror to the heart of a debt-ridden nobleman. Peasant life remained unrewarding. Some 2809 peasant disturbances ranging from tax protests to rice riots were recorded during the Tokugawa period, marking the desperate response to systematic economic deprivation. Although some wealthier peasant landlords did benefit from the introduction of a money economy into rural Japan, money merely increased the costs of village life and heightened the level of silent misery for most. Thus the seeds of change and social discontent were deeply embedded in Tokugawa society long before Commodore Matthew C. Perry steamed into Edo harbor in 1853 and exploded Japan's self-imposed isolation.

The Intrusion of the West
All the internal problems confronting the Tokugawa in the middle of the nineteenth century—large num-

bers of unemployed, masterless samurai congregating in the cities, the growing power of the merchant class for whom there was no place in the feudal hierarchy, peasant unrest near the point of open rebellion, and restiveness among some of the outside lords—were intensified by the external threat posed by Perry's small naval squadron. Japan, which had so long ignored the outside world, could do so no longer; a growing awareness of the technical superiority of the West weakened confidence in shogunal rule. Enough European knowledge had filtered into Japan so that authorities respected the firepower potential of the American vessels. They were also aware of the disastrous collapse of the Chinese in the Opium Wars with Britain a decade earlier. Perry demanded better treatment of shipwrecked sailors, aid for American vessels seeking shelter and supplies, and an opening of trade with the West. Nationalists demanded that the shogun expel the "barbarians." Perry left to give them time to think it over.

Commodore Perry meeting the imperial commissioners at Yokohama. *Photo:* Culver Pictures.

THE UNITED STATES AND JAPAN, PART 1: PERRY

Two events involving the United States stand as introduction and postscript to Japan's entry into the modern world—the arrival of Commodore Perry's fleet and the unleashing of the atomic bomb. On March 31, 1854, Commodore Matthew Perry and ministers of Imperial Japan signed the Treaty of Amity and Friendship at Kanagawa, some 12 miles south of Edo (Tokyo), the Tokugawa capital. This paved the way for the opening of Japanese civilization to trade with the outside world. And the Japanese reinterpretation of modernization and industrialization began. Nearly a century later, 100 years during which Japan became the dominant military power in East Asia, war broke out between Japan and the United States. On August 6, 1945, the B-29 bomber Enola Gay dropped an atomic bomb on the city of Hiroshima, Japan's eleventh largest urban center. The 1-megaton bomb unleashed a force that killed over 100,000 of Hiroshima's population of 280,000; world peace was simultaneously sealed and threatened by a new terror. These two acts frame a crucial period in Japanese-American relations.

Matthew Perry, born in 1794 to an illustrious Rhode Island family, became a naval officer extraordinaire. His lifetime was one of service to his country—the resettlement of freed slaves in Liberia, naval reform, peacekeeping on the Barbary Coast, and battles in the 1848 war with Mexico. In 1853, Perry was asked to open negotiations with the emperor of Japan. The voyage to Japan was conceived as a full-scale diplomatic mission. Perry was granted freedom in negotiating with the Japanese, an unknown society, and was given instructions comparable to those handed to Columbus by Isabella. Expanding American interests in the Pacific necessitated the opening of the Japanese Empire, a government closed to outsiders behind a bamboo curtain. The marine engines of the day burned so much coal that steamships had little space left over for cargo and passengers, so a refueling stop was needed. The Pacific Mail Line planned regular service between San Francisco and the Chinese treaty ports by steamer, and Japan loomed as a strategic location. There were other concerns. American seamen lost at sea in Japanese waters often received hostile treatment when washed ashore in Japan. The potential for lucrative international trade further strengthened America's determination to "open" Japan.

Perry was the ideal choice to lead this mission. The commodore had a strong grasp of the Japanese character and was able to deal with the shogunate where other European nations had failed:

> He felt that it was well to teach the Japanese, in the mode most intelligible to them, by stately and dignified reserve, joined to perfect equity in all he asked or did, to respect the country from which he came, and to suspend for a time their accustomed arrogance and incivility toward strangers. The Japanese so well understood him that they learned the lesson at once.

The treaty was concluded amid an exhibition of presents made to the emperor by his "good friend, [U.S. President] Millard Fillmore." The gifts, a diplomatic survival kit of America in the 1850s, were intended to demonstrate Yankee ingenuity, technology, and craftsmanship.

> Commander Adams went ashore on 12 March [1854] to set up the miniature railway with the help of engineer officers, to run a telegraph wire from Yokohama to Kanagawa, and tune the instruments at each end. He also brought ashore a patent metal lifeboat, the Audubon elephant folios, a telescope, sundry agricultural implements, a case of books, several cases of firearms, a barrel of whiskey, several baskets of champagne, all for the Emperor. In addition there were about three dozen Yankee clocks, seeds of American plants, and a quantity of wines and liquors for the Commissioners' consumption. . . . The miniature railway in particular was a succès fou. It consisted of a locomotive, tender, and passenger car, with a circular track of 18-inch gauge, 350 feet in diameter . . . many Japanese insisted on having a ride; and it was quite a sight to see a samurai on the roof of the car, robes flapping in the wind, while the train huffed, puffed and whistled around the track. . . .

Perry's mission impressed the Japanese. Perry himself spoke to the potential for transformation inherent in his mission:

> In the practical and mechanical arts, the Japanese show great dexterity. . . . Their handicraftsmen are as expert as any in the world, and, with a freer development of the inventive power of the people, the Japanese would not remain long behind the most successful manufacturing nations. . . .

Perry's prediction proved true. After three generations of national effort, the Japanese were major competitors in the "race for mechanical success." In August 1945, the denouement of that effort appeared imminent as Allied forces prepared to invade the Japanese homeland.

Source: Quoted material from the official narrative of the Perry mission, reproduced in Samuel Eliot Morison, "Old Bruin": Commodore Matthew C. Perry, 1794–1858. Boston: Little, Brown and Atlantic Monthly Press, 1967, pp. 324, 371–372, 428.

He returned a year later with eight vessels. Rent with dissension and indecision, but terrified by this show of force, the shogunate reluctantly agreed to open two ports to American vessels—Hakodate on remote Hokkaido and Shimoda on the isolated Izu *Peninsula* south of Edo. Celebrations were held. The technological import of the American gifts presented to the shogun was not lost on the Japanese. Additional trade agreements were soon signed with England, Russia, France, and the Netherlands; Japan's long period of seclusion came to an end. Under this stimulus, commerce increased rapidly during the 1860s as Japanese raw silk, tea, and copperware were exchanged for imported cotton textiles, sugar, and ironware. Opposition to shogunal rule, which had begun to form before midcentury, now crystallized around a formidable core of young samurai whose motto was "revere the emperor and expel the barbarians." Never intending that the emperor should have real power, these warriors saw his traditional symbolic status as a powerful rallying point for opposition to the Tokugawa. As antiforeign sentiment grew, some Japanese leaders decided that the only way to cope with the West was to adopt its military technology. After a severe defeat at the hands of Western forces, the Choshu clan in extreme western Honshu began to form mixed battalions of samurai and commoner soldiers equipped with modern arms. In an important incident in 1862, a visiting English businessman, Charles Richardson, failed to dismount his horse when passing the daimyo of Satsuma (in southern Kyushu). Satsuma samurai immediately killed him, and the British shelled the daimyo capital of Kagoshima in response. The Japanese responded not with despair but with admiration for British naval power, and the barons hired British officers as naval advisers. In January 1868, the lords of Choshu and Satsuma pooled forces, marched on Edo, overthrew the shogunate, and proclaimed the restoration of the emperor. It was the leaders and samurai of these two rural domains who mainly ruled Japan under the symbolic guidance of the Meiji emperor, by whose reign name this period of Japanese history is known.

THE MEIJI RESTORATION

The year 1868 was a date as important in the development of Japan as 1066 in England or 1776 in the United States. In that year, the new imperial government launched a program of reform and reorganization that reacted directly to the Western intrusion. Although Japan's economy had crystallized along feudal lines and had been left technologically naive by the isolationism of the Tokugawa period, other facets of the Japanese society and environment were far more advanced than they are today in many parts of Asia, Africa, and Latin America. Fully half the men and 15 percent of the women of Japan were re-

ceiving formal education in the 1860s. More than a million commoners were enrolled in religious schools; many merchants and the majority of samurai were well-educated people. The rewards of the traditional education system were to be translated into a rapid understanding of new ideas and an adaptability to new technical methods. In addition, this literate population had absorbed the sophisticated urban culture of Edo, Osaka, and Kyoto. And although the Tokugawa refusal to deal with outsiders had isolated Japan from the technological inventiveness of the West, it had insulated Japan from the effects of the colonialism that enveloped Africa, Latin America, and other parts of Asia at the same time. With a centrally governed society, well-organized market centers linked by road to a hierarchy of urban centers, and a strong moral code of work, loyalty, and patriotism, the Japanese were well prepared to face the twentieth century.

Wealthy Nation, Strong Military

Modernization was a calculated, official policy of the young samurai leaders of Meiji Japan. Their aim was to upgrade Japan's position on the ladder of world power, to convert their small group of islands, scattered "like millet seeds in the wind" on the rim of the Pacific, into a respected military and commercial nation. Their motivations, then, were political, rather than economic. Wealth was viewed as the source of power; the samurai code of discipline, loyalty, sacrifice, and selfless labor was harnessed to provide the momentum to propel Japan into a position of world leadership. Traditional values, "the spirit of Old Japan," were preserved and reiterated in the culture of New Japan. Only those elements of Western science and technology that strengthened the nation were consciously acquired. Foreigners were accepted for their usefulness, and delegations were sent to the United States and Europe to select the best models for the new society (and new goods) the Japanese were determined to create.

To accomplish modernization, considerable reorganization of space and society was required. The capital of the new regime was established at Edo, which was then renamed Tokyo, or Eastern Capital— a symbolic break with the Tokugawa past. The 200 or so feudal daimyo domains were abolished and consolidated into the forty-six prefectures that remain the basic regional unit of government in modern Japan. Although in some new prefectures

The opening of the first railway in Japan in 1872. The procession is led by the emperor and his ministers and courtiers, followed by the representatives of the leading Western powers. *Photo:* Culver Pictures.

feudal lords were installed as governors and paid generous stipends, the hereditary daimyo monopoly on national territory was essentially broken. Tolls and other economic barriers between the old domains were eliminated, and ports were thrown open to foreign commerce. Within four years, the first Japanese railroad was running the 18 miles between Tokyo and Yokohama. Within a decade, this line was carrying 2 million passengers and considerable freight. By the turn of the century Japan, a country of short distances, had constructed more than 2000 miles of track; by 1914, 7000 track-miles were complete. As elsewhere, the railroad was an effective measure of the progress of modernization. A post office with telegraph and telephone service was inaugurated linking the islands of Japan by wire. In less than a decade, reflecting the growth of foreign and internal trade, the merchant marine doubled in size. By World War I, half of Japan's foreign trade was carried in Japanese vessels. Innovations in mechanized transport and communications, and less sophisticated improvements such as the construction of a network of dirt roads and the introduction of rickshaws (invented in 1870) and carts exerted a powerful influence on the development of the Japanese economy. The landscapes of rural Japan, already integrated into a network of castle town marketing centers, were welded into a unified national economy and central state structure.

The emergence of a unified national space was paralleled by reforms aimed at creating a national society. The restrictive class barriers of the feudal period were eliminated; all occupations figured in social competition. Universal conscription was introduced; a strong army and navy followed. This military role, previously reserved to samurai, brought rural and urban Japanese together and bridged the rigid class distinctions of earlier times. The long-guarded right of the samurai to carry both long and short swords and to cut down commoners at will was abolished, and their stipends were reduced by half. Compulsory education was introduced in 1872, only two years after a similar advance in Britain. Within fifteen years, two-thirds of all boys and one-third of all girls were in school; by 1900, 95 percent of the Japanese population was literate. The educational system stressed state supremacy; the welfare of the nation was the highest priority. Only then, as one leading educator emphasized, could Japan "become strong in the arts of peace and war and take a place in the forefront of the progress of the world."

The forefront of Meiji initiative was in industrialization, following the earlier Western model of modernization. The heavy industry needed to support an effective up-to-date military was especially favored. An iron foundry at Nagasaki formerly owned by the shogun was modernized, as were the shipbuilding yards of the Satsuma clan at Kagoshima. A variety of shipyards, machine works, and steel mills were built on northern Kyushu and in Osaka and Tokyo. Finished steel production reached 250,000 tons in 1914; 21 million tons of coal, mostly from the mines of northern Kyushu, were produced in that same year. Government-sponsored factories producing cotton and woolen textiles, silk, iron, paper, glass, and other manufactures were set up as models to introduce Western technology to the Japanese. As early as 1880, scarcely a decade after the Restoration, the government owned 3 shipyards, 10 mines, 75 miles of railroad, and a telegraph system. At the

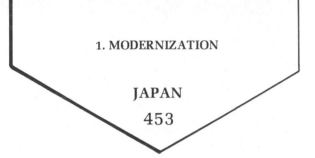
same time, the government both subsidized industries funded by private families and sold model government factories to private entrepreneurs, merchants, and industrialists. Virtually every modern Japanese industry was begun during the early Meiji years. The Industrial Revolution was being deliberately copied on the eastern rim of Asia.

New factories, administration of the feudal domains, Western technology and advisers, and building a modern military were expensive ventures indeed. Once again, the costs of modernization were borne by the backbone of Japanese society—the peasants. Early in the Meiji period, feudal restrictions on land use and sale were abolished, and peasants came into direct ownership of the land they worked. Taxes were assessed (at a rate of 3 percent) on land valuation instead of the traditional harvest portion. Although peasants initially resented the new regulations because they were more difficult to circumvent than the old, incentives for increased production and more intensive land use were built into the system.

Reform in agriculture was crucial to the Meiji government because 90 percent of state revenues in the 1870s came from that sector. New seeds were introduced; intensive use of fertilizer, irrigation, double cropping, and better weeding practices became common. Rice yields increased 80 percent between 1880 and 1920 as the arable expanded by a third. Competition from foreign imports forced a change in cropping patterns. Home-grown sugar and cotton (principally cultivated on the shores of the Inland Sea) were replaced by mulberry trees, tea, fruits, and vegetables. During this period, tea and silk were the primary export products of Japan. Indeed, in the 1890s, raw silk accounted for nearly half of all Japanese exports. Experts disagree about the rate of agricultural progress, but the agricultural product of Japan increased steadily, between 1 and 3 percent each year. Some claim that the recorded advances were caused by the colonization of Hokkaido and the correction of wasteful practices in the north, traditionally more resistant to change than the south; others claim that the fairs, lectures, demonstrations, and classes—so typical of rural Victorian England of the day—were responsible for a **diffusion*** of beneficial innovations. In either case, it was the peasants who sustained Japan's plunge into technology by providing the labor supply for industrialization while simultaneously feeding a growing urban and industrial population.

Social Change

The rapidity of modernization transformed the foundations of Japanese society. Peasant unrest became a serious problem as expectations outpaced structural changes in society. In 1873, thirty-seven different rural disturbances related to the family costs of military conscription, compulsory education, and high taxes were quelled. Major riots involving 300,000 people broke out in southern Honshu and in the mountains north of Tokyo. In the latter, authorities meticulously recorded the destruction of 4590 buildings and 181 telegraph poles. Steady taxation and falling food prices were causing considerable misery. By 1884, the debt of the agricultural population reached a total of 200 million yen—a significant figure when it is reckoned that the average annual rice harvest per peasant family was worth 53 yen. Some 100,000 farm families went bankrupt in 1885, and the number of tenant farmers rose sharply. Emigration throughout the Pacific and to North America was one release. The suicide rate rose, although a majority of the poor starved in silence rather than break the law. Of greater concern to the government, however, was the distress of the samurai, who had been stripped of privilege and income and were a dangerous and dissatisfied element in the urban population. Jobs were created in industry for displaced samurai, and government bonds were issued them for investment in new family enterprises. The more reactionary samurai, nineteenth-century counterparts of Yukio Mishima, rebelled and were crushed. The new rulers of Japan were convinced that men of their class uniquely possessed the necessary qualities of morality, determination, and character to lead Japan in the national quest for power, so that many samurai were integrated into the industrial leadership. For factory workers, life in Japan was much like that in nineteenth-century Europe. In the textile factories, women—half under the age of twenty—were used as cheap labor. Conditions in the mines were dreadful. Twelve-hour shifts kept industry producing day and night; low wages preserved capital for factory expansion. Strikes were prohibited. Cheap housing and crowded workers' quarters sprang up in the cities as industry reshaped the urban environment.

Despite these social tensions, the Japanese faced modernization with a sense of common national purpose. All classes recognized the importance of national power, and self-sacrifice to this ideal was seen as every citizen's duty. Unlike other developing areas, industrialization in Japan did not alienate rulers from the governed. Rather, the traditional sense of loyalty to one's family and the emperor were intensified, and the stern ethic of the samurai became the prevailing ideal for all society. Change was predictably slower in rural areas than in cities,

Japanese soldiers pose with a Russian captured during the siege of Port Arthur in the Russo-Japanese War in 1905. *Photo:* Culver Pictures.

but no important segment of the population questioned the goal of national power. To have done so would have been to cut themselves off from their cultural past and its rejuvenated values. Through sheer will and determination, traditional institutions were dropped while traditional values were maintained. In one generation, a medieval **agrarian**• state was transformed into an industrial nation—a feat most countries of the developing world have yet to duplicate.

With newfound power, in 1895, modern Japanese forces defeated China in war, were awarded Taiwan, and secured the independence of Korea, although Japan was compelled by the Great Powers to relinquish its claims and conquests in southern Manchuria. Then, in 1905, the Japanese destroyed the Russian fleet by night attack at Port Arthur, captured the city by land, and annihilated a relief fleet steaming through the Korean Straits. A shock wave reverberated through the industrial West after the defeat of European Russia on its Asian frontier by a non-Western nation. The Japanese took the seat they so coveted among the powerful nations of the world, despite an abundance of environmental obstacles and a dearth of geographical assets.

EXPANSION AND EMPIRE

When the Meiji emperor died in 1912, the revolution planned by the young samurai during the previous half-century was by any measure a success. Japan's population had increased from 30 million to 50 million, reflecting the rapid rise in birth rate typical of incipient industrialization. The industrial and commercial foundations of the Japanese economy had, through the hard work and thrift of the peasantry, reached a **take-off stage,**• and the standard of living of the country as a whole had risen. Recognized as a major military and political force in world affairs, Japan embarked upon a twenty-year period of territorial and economic expansion. Following World War I, Japan was awarded a League of Nations mandate over the Caroline, Mariana, and Marshall islands in the western Pacific and captured trade areas throughout East Asia that the old colonial powers were no longer able to supply. The industrial sector of the Japanese economy, however, developed much faster than the rural economy, and in the early depression years of the 1930s this dual system played a major role in the rise of militarism in Japan. With a growing population, Japan sought new sources of raw materials and new markets. An industrial economy was implanted in Manchuria following the Japanese invasion in 1931. Japanese forces entered China itself, a key region in the concept of the Japanese empire (known as the Greater East Asia Co-Prosperity Sphere), in 1937. In 1941, Southeast Asia was attacked and integrated into this empire, and the Japanese ruled from Mindanao in the Philippines to Manchuria. With an immense field of commercial and industrial expansion in the offing, spurred by American embargoes on oil and scrap iron and a British threat to cut them off from Southeast Asian oil, the militant Japanese attacked Pearl Harbor and overreached their military capabilities. The political ambitions that had accompanied the modernization of Japan had reached their greatest extent.

The Dual Economy

In the first quarter of the twentieth century, Japanese industry and commerce expanded rapidly while the agricultural sector grew at a much slower rate. Cotton textiles and silk manufacturing tripled in production, and half of Japan's 2.5 million industrial workers were employed in these industries. Steel production rose to 2 million tons a year, although half the needed iron ore was imported from China and Malaya. Domestic coal output reached more than 30 million tons and was supplemented by imports of high-quality **coking coal.**• A diversified industrial core stretching from Tokyo to northern Kyushu began to emerge. A variety of heavy industrial plants—metallurgy, machinery, cement, and shipbuilding—were constructed in a string of cities along this 600-mile axis. These large establishments were complemented by small domestic firms that continued to flourish. Japan's pattern of trade reflected its rapid industrial growth, and manufactured products formed an ever-increasing share of exports while raw materials became vital imports.

Change in agriculture was much more limited, and a gap developed between this traditional sector wrought, saw only boiling dust and dancing flame—a perfect mushroom cloud.

"My God, what have we done?"

Source: The New York Times, *Hiroshima Plus 20.* New York: Delacorte Press, 1965, pp. 41–42. Copyright © 1945, 1951, 1963, 1964, 1965 by The New York Times Company. Used with the permission of Delacorte Press.

On the ground in Hiroshima a new human distress was being played out:

There was no sound of planes. The morning was still; the place was cool and pleasant.

Then a tremendous flash of light cut across the sky. Mr. Tanimoto has a distinct recollection that it travelled from east to west, from the city toward the hills. It seemed a sheet of sun.... he ... reacted in terror—and ... had time to react (for [he was] 3,500 yards, or two miles, from the center of the explosion).... Mr. Tanimoto took four or five steps and threw himself between two big rocks in the garden.

Source: John Hersey, *Hiroshima.* New York: Knopf, 1958, pp. 8–9.

A survivor recounted on the day after the explosion:

"It was a horrible sight," said Dr. Tabuchi. "Hundreds of injured people who were trying to escape to the hills passed our house. Their faces and hands were burnt and swollen; and great sheets of skin had peeled away from their tissues to hang down like rags on a scarecrow. They moved like a line of ants. All through the night, they went past our house, but this morning they had stopped. I found them lying on both sides of the road so thick that it was impossible to pass without stepping on them....

"The sight of the soldiers, though, was more dreadful than dead people floating down the river. I came onto I don't know how many, burned from the hips up; and where the skin had peeled, their flesh was wet and mushy. They must have been wearing their military caps because the black hair on top of their heads was not burned. It made them look like they were wearing black lacquer bowls.

"And they had no faces! Their eyes, noses and mouths had been burned away, and it looked like their ears had melted off. It was hard to tell front from back."

Source: Michihiko Hachiya, *Hiroshima Diary.* Chapel Hill: University of North Carolina Press, 1955, pp. 14–15.

The surrender of Japan to terms set by the Americans on August 14 was followed by the American occupation of Japan during the first week of September 1945. Time *magazine reported:*

The invasion proceeded with machine-like precision. Transport planes floated down on the airstrips at four-

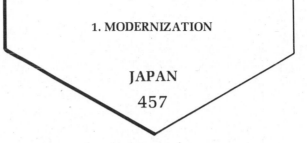

minute intervals. U.S. and British battleships, cruisers and destroyers marched in stately file through the treacherous Uraga Channel into Tokyo Bay. It was almost too smooth.

Source: Time magazine, Vol. 46, No. 11 (Sept. 10, 1945), p. 28.

Ninety-two years before, Perry's diplomatic squadron first made contact with Japanese officials at the town of Uraga, then a small fishing village. The commodore assured the Japanese that he had not come to invade their country; he said, "I have come here as a peacemaker." General MacArthur later inscribed these words on a monument in Japan dedicated to the opening of the nation by Perry. As negotiations between Perry and the Japanese proceeded, a small wooden building was constructed about a mile and a half south of Uraga for the exchange of diplomatic letters. The area is now a baseball field.

often assassination. The militarists, having succeeded economically, were determined to establish a self-sufficient empire by gaining political control over sources of raw materials. In 1937, Japan invaded China and provoked a full-scale war, mobilizing the national economy and society on an emergency basis. Having earlier walked out of the League of Nations (which had censured the aggression in Manchuria), the Japanese became increasingly isolated and resentful of what they perceived as international encirclement. When the United States banned exports of strategic materials such as scrap iron, steel, and oil to Japan, the decision for war was taken. Japan would secure economic self-sufficiency by conquest of Southeast Asia and the Pacific. In December 1941, the military party under Premier Tojo gave the signal to carry out a plan for a surprise attack on the American fleet at Pearl Harbor in Hawaii. The attack, intended to immobilize the United States in the Pacific and give Japan time to consolidate a hold on China and Southeast Asia, was a gamble that failed.

JAPAN

REGIONAL PATTERNS

PHYSICAL FEATURES MAP
POPULATION DENSITY MAP

The Japanese archipelago is formed of four main islands—Hokkaido, Honshu, Shikoku, and Kyushu—and 3400 lesser islands that arc 800 miles to the south and west along the eastern rim of Asia. These islands are the volcanic peaks of young mountain chains, a discontinuous, fragmented string of rugged highlands sunk in the Pacific Ocean. With an area smaller than that of California, they now support more than 100 million people. Because the Japanese have occupied this island home for centuries, differences in race, religion, and culture are relatively minor from one *region*• to another. The principal distinctions are environmental—mountain versus plain, the cold north versus the subtropical south. Forested highlands dominate the landscape and constitute nearly four-fifths of the area of the four main islands. Human activity is concentrated on small *alluvial plains*• located on the coast where streams plunge to the sea, and in a few *intermontane*• basins. In these areas, agriculture and industry compete for space. Because less than a quarter of the country is level enough for either activity, the human density per square mile of cultivated land in Japan is the highest in the entire world.

Climate is a second important factor in regional differences: if aligned along the eastern coast of the United States, the main Japanese islands would curve from the border of Maine and New Brunswick southward to north Florida. The subtropical south is the nucleus of Japanese civilization, a landscape of terraced rice fields and mulberry and tea plantations; the north, by contrast, has a short growing season and snowbound winters, and remains an area of frontier settlement even today. On these bases, the Japanese recognize three generalized regional divisions of their country: Hokkaido, the northernmost island of Japan; Tohoku, the northern third of the island of Honshu, a transition zone between the core and the frontier; and Central and Southwestern Japan, the subtropical heartland of Japanese industry, agriculture, and population.

HOKKAIDO

Hokkaido, the second largest island of the archipelago, differs from all other regions in Japan in its topography and climate, its isolation from the centers of Japanese civilization to the south, and its recent settlement. Hokkaido's subdued volcanic mountains and *plateaus*• contrast sharply with the dramatic peaks and plunging cliffs of Honshu. With a climate like northern New England's, much of the island is forested, and the cold, snowbound winters and acid soils allow only one crop a year. At the beginning of the Meiji period, when only 58,000 Japanese lived on Hokkaido, most of the island's inhabitants were fishermen clustered in small coastal villages on the southern Oshima peninsula. Most of Hokkaido was occupied by a thin scattering of Ainu hunters and fishermen, a caucasoid people of uncertain origin, who probably never numbered more than 30,000. Modern Japanese colonization was initiated in 1869, when military settlements were established to defend northern outposts from Russian incursions and to extract local fish, lumber, and mineral resources. Later colonists received subsidies to settle the region, so that Hokkaido had a population of 1 million in 1900 and 3 million by 1930. In 1970, 5.2 million Japanese lived on Hokkaido, which, with an area of 78,000 square miles, a fifth of Japan, is the least densely settled region of the island archipelago. Only the port of Sapporo, with a population of slightly more than 1 million, is a major city.

During the military and early colonial period of settlement, a grid-pattern system of land ownership modeled on the American township and range system was imposed upon the landscape of Hokkaido. Nineteenth-century settlers adopted agricultural patterns similar to those in northern Europe by cultivating potatoes, oats, and hay on 12.5-acre rectangles. When cold-resistant and early maturing strains were developed at the turn of the century, rice was introduced to Hokkaido. The original core of settlement, the relatively fertile, protected Ishikari Valley in western Hokkaido, has been complemented by later settlement on less fertile eastern uplands and more recently, on land reclaimed from the forested slopes and bamboo brushlands of the eastern coast. Although *rice paddies*• cover a fifth of the agricultural landscape of Hokkaido today, beans, potatoes, oats, and sugar beets are much more important than elsewhere in Japan. Animals, especially beef and dairy cattle, play a significant role in this area's agricultural economy. Until a century ago, the Japanese did not kill four-footed animals and had no tradition of animal husbandry or of mixed farming. Japanese agriculture in this

Irrigation projects and improved farming methods (better seed, chemical fertilizers) have all been used to increase Japan's food supply. This aerial view shows Makio Dam, part of a project in Aichi Prefecture that brought under perennial irrigation 42,000 acres of paddyland and 40,000 acres of upland areas. *Photo:* United Nations.

northern frontier region, therefore, reflects a practical cultural adaptation to environmental possibilities. The nonagricultural economy of Hokkaido is still primarily extractive: fish, lumber and coal, and oil from the Ishikari Valley. Incomes are high and settlement is not intense—land holdings are four times the national average size. Although Hokkaido drew a heavy stream of migrants in the 1950s, it has proved increasingly less attractive. Most Japanese prefer the amenities of the urban-industrial core in the south to Hokkaido's harsh northern landscapes.

TOHOKU

Tohoku, the northern third of the island of Honshu, forms a transition zone between Hokkaido to the north and the subtropical south. A hilly and mountainous area in which level land is scarce, the *relief** of Tohoku is dominated by three highland zones that slice north-south through the region. Population is clustered in the separate intermontane basins

between these volcanic and forested uplands. Although moderate by Hokkaido standards, winters in Tohoku are still cold and long. Except in protected inland basins, only one crop a year is grown, even along the east coast where the land is chilled, as fog from the clash of the warm, northward-moving Kuroshio ocean current and the cold, polar Kurile current drifts inland.

Although settled between the seventh and ninth centuries, Tohoku is still viewed by the Japanese as a backward frontier region. It is less urbanized and more rural than any comparable region in Japan, and low incomes have led to considerable outmigration. With 18 percent of Japan's area, Tohoku has a population of less than 10 million; average population densities, while higher than on Hokkaido, are only half those of Central and Southwestern Japan. Mountainous topography, the isolation of inland population centers from the coast, lack of raw materials, and absence of deepwater ports have all combined to retard industrial expansion. The region remains a bastion of rural settlement, with over half the labor force engaged in agriculture and other primary economic activities.

The broken relief of Tohoku is the primary factor influencing the distribution of rural population. The rugged eastern plateau, frequently called the Tibet of Japan because of its isolation, is a granite platform covered by poor volcanic ash and *bog** soils

459

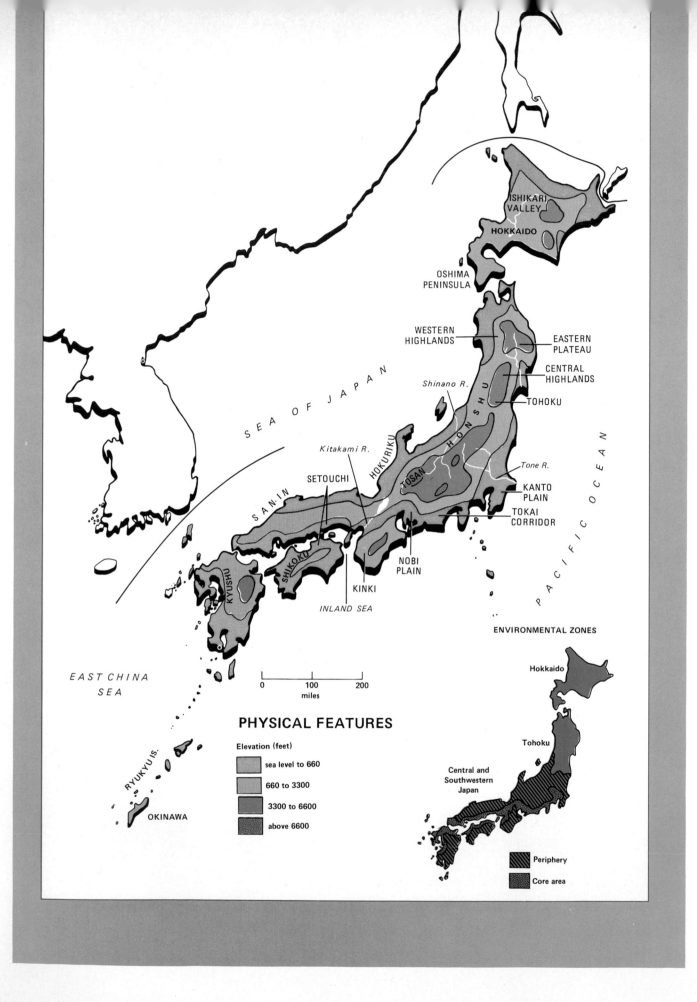

ISHIKARI
VALLEY

HOKKAIDO

OSHIMA
PENINSULA

WESTERN
HIGHLANDS

EASTERN
PLATEAU

CENTRAL
HIGHLANDS

Shinano R.

TOHOKU

Kitakami R.

SEA OF JAPAN

HOKURIKU

HONSHU

Tone R.

SETOUCHI

TOSAN

KANTO
PLAIN

SAN-IN

TOKAI
CORRIDOR

SHIKOKU

KINKI

NOBI
PLAIN

KYUSHU

INLAND SEA

PACIFIC OCEAN

EAST CHINA
SEA

ENVIRONMENTAL ZONES

Hokkaido

Tohoku

RYUKYU IS.

OKINAWA

Central and
Southwestern
Japan

| 0 | 100 | 200 |
miles

PHYSICAL FEATURES

Elevation (feet)

sea level to 660

660 to 3300

3300 to 6600

above 6600

Periphery

Core area

where farm yields are low and only the narrow valley floors are used for rice cultivation. The climate is too cold for winter rice, tea, or citrus cultivation, but mulberry trees and sweet potatoes, not found on Hokkaido, can be grown. In the longitudinal basins that separate the eastern plateau from the more rugged central highlands, however, settlement is dense, and unirrigated terraced fields climb protected slopes. Although farms are small and fragmented, rice occupies two-thirds of the cultivated area, and yields are high. Unlike other Japanese farm regions, in Tohoku supplemental industrial and craft activities play a minor role in the family economy, and the primary nonfarm occupations are charcoal burning and lumbering in the *coniferous** forests of the highlands. This same pattern of populated lowlands and sparsely occupied highlands extends through the western highlands to the west coast of Tohoku. There, the heavy fertile soils of the narrow coastal plain are irrigated by spring meltwater from the snow cover that cloaks the western highlands in winter. Conditions are ideal for rice cultivation, and this area, sometimes called the rice basket of Japan, produces a quarter of the country's grain.

CENTRAL AND SOUTHWESTERN JAPAN
South and west of Tohoku, the traditional heartland of Japanese civilization stretches from central Honshu westward to include the southern islands of Shikoku and Kyushu—a variegated landscape of small farms, tidy villages, terraced rice fields, tea gardens, orange groves, growing cities, and industrial mills. Over three-quarters of Japan's population and most of its economic activity are set within this topographically diverse region: forested highlands typically flank alluvial plains trapped between mountain and sea. Here, intensive agricultural and industrial complexes vie for level land to support Japan's growing population. From the volcanic peaks of Tosan (central Honshu), a mountain fist 2 miles high sometimes called the Japanese Alps, several ranges trend westward along the Inland Sea to form the tree-covered spines of southern Honshu, Shikoku, and Kyushu islands. The subtropical climate and ample rainfall of this area enable farmers to cultivate year round; terraced fields climb hilly slopes to much higher elevations than in the colder frontier regions of Tohoku and Hokkaido.

Regional distinctions are more difficult to define in central and southwestern Japan than in the north: each subregion is a mixture of hills and mountains that ring plains on which urban and industrial centers have developed. Typically, the cities of the plain are surrounded by paddyland, which is in turn flanked by terraced fields on more elevated agricultural land; highland coniferous and *decidu-* *ous** forests complete the regional framework. This pattern is illustrated in the primary core areas of the center and south: Tokyo, Nagoya, and Osaka. The entire area has been settled by the Japanese for centuries and shares a common tradition of land use and settlement. But the recent economic growth of Japan has sharpened regional differences; the mixing of two cultural traditions has provoked sharp contrasts between the industrial, urban landscapes of the Core Area and the less developed, more rural subregions of the northern and southern Periphery.

The Core Area
The Core Area of Japan is a latitudinal belt of disconnected lowland plains stretching 600 miles from the Kanto Plain in the east along the shores of the Inland Sea to northern Kyushu in the west. The Kanto Plain is Japan's largest patch of lowland, a 2500-square mile plain blanketed by the country's fastest growing industrial complex, the Tokyo-Yokohama *conurbation,** and a substantial agricultural expanse on which a tenth of this region's 24 million people cultivate rice, mulberry groves, and truck garden crops. Dairy farming is also important. The western side of the plain is far more intensively exploited than the east, which is isolated from Tokyo by the marshes of the lower Tone River. Surrounding uplands are little used because of a scarcity of irrigation water, and much land remains in its natural state of bamboo brush. East of Kanto, the narrow Tokai corridor connects a series of small, isolated *deltas** running along the Pacific coast to link Tokyo with Japan's second largest plain, the Nobi Plain of Nagoya, and with the center of ancient Japanese civilization, Kinki, at the head of the Inland Sea with its large urban centers of Osaka, Kobe, and Kyoto. Along the Tokai corridor, a mild subtropical climate and plentiful rainfall have made the area a center for the production of tea and mandarin oranges, whose groves cover south-facing slopes. On the Nobi Plain, the Chukyo industrial core is set around the city of Nagoya, which is surrounded by vast *poldered** rice fields with vegetables and other grains grown on nearby hillsides. Kinki includes the second largest industrial conurbation of the nation, several important second-order urban centers, and lowland rice fields and terraced gardens, ringed by largely deforested uplands.

This industrial-urban complex continues along Setouchi in the form of a number of smaller-order urban centers scattered on both the Honshu and Shikoku shores of the Inland Sea. The Inland Sea unites this region; communications between centers on southern Honshu and northern Shikoku have historically been easier by water than overland. The Core Area ends in northern Kyushu, where coal mines fostered early Meiji heavy industry. This area has now been eclipsed by the trade-oriented port complexes of Tokyo, Nagoya, and Osaka-Kobe

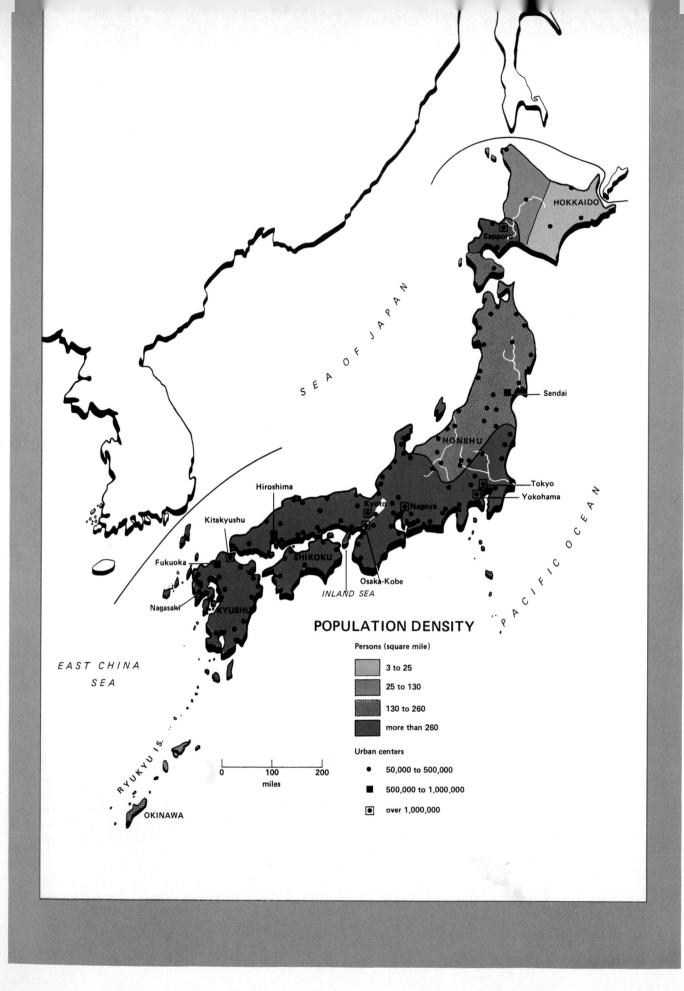

SEA OF JAPAN

HOKKAIDO

Sapporo

Sendai

HONSHU

Tokyo
Yokohama

Hiroshima

Kitakyushu

Kyoto
Nagoya

Fukuoka

SHIKOKU

Osaka-Kobe

Nagasaki

INLAND SEA

KYUSHU

PACIFIC OCEAN

EAST CHINA
SEA

POPULATION DENSITY

Persons (square mile)

3 to 25

25 to 130

130 to 260

more than 260

Urban centers

● 50,000 to 500,000

■ 500,000 to 1,000,000

⊡ over 1,000,000

RYUKYU IS.

0   100   200
miles

OKINAWA

farther east. Throughout the Core Area from Kanto to Kyushu population is extremely dense. Mills, houses, and cultivated land are tightly packed; human occupance is intense. Blighted by smog and air pollution, this area is the vital heart of Japanese life today.

The Periphery

The Periphery of central and southwestern Japan flanks the Core Area to its north and south and includes San-In, Hokuriku, and Tosan on the island of Honshu and the less industrialized southern halves of the islands of Shikoku and Kyushu. San-In, an area of low, forested ranges with poor soils on the uninflected coast facing the Sea of Japan on southwestern Honshu, is a thinly populated and rather undeveloped region. Called "the shady side," its raw winter climate, dearth of level land, and isolation from urban centers have retarded industrial and agricultural development. Farther northeast along the coast of the Sea of Japan, farming is somewhat more intensive in Hokuriku. Scattered lowlands are the focus of settlement, and a variety of fruit and vegetable crops are grown, as well as rice. Some important industry has developed on the narrow coast between Niigata and Fukui, where five *riverine* plains provide space in this largely mountainous region for extended settlement.

Inland from Hokuriku, the rugged mountain complex of Tosan, the roof of Japan, forms the topographic core of Honshu and separates the rich, well-settled plains of the Pacific coast from the cold, sparsely occupied regions of the Sea of Japan. Here, in several separated basins, light industry, diversified agriculture, and tourism have become important in traditional silk production centers. The two remaining areas of the Periphery, southern Kyushu and southern Shikoku, have been isolated from the mainstream of Japanese economic and industrial development. In southern Kyushu, *folded block mountains* and volcanoes limit communications with the Core Area; the region lacks level land or ports, and its forested highlands are occupied by subsistence farmers and *shifting cultivators.* Similarly, southern Shikoku is a backward, sparsely populated mountain region, although its warm climate makes double cropping possible wherever water is available and alluvial soils are found.

Altogether, Japan is a nation of great environmental diversity, set over 15 degrees of latitude and many degrees of development and isolation, of human density and relative wilderness. The same nation that was hard put to remove snow from the 1972 Winter Olympic trails also had difficulty in providing adequate space in crowded Tokyo to coordinate facilities for the 1964 Summer Olympics. Although the degree of attachment with which Americans have dealt with the Japanese over the last several generations has been high, the Japanese environment remains confused in the American perception. Forest temples and Datsun-choked freeways coexist in modern Japan; so do the traditional land of the peasant and the urban landscape of the factory worker. The twin notions of isolation—the serene harmony of the being in nature so aptly depicted in Japanese art and literature—and of the increasing density of industry, urban populations, and agricultural interstices provide a forum of *ecological* problems and choices set in an Oriental environment.

THE INDUSTRIAL STATE
2

At the end of World War II, Japan lay in ruins and its population was exhausted. Two-thirds of Tokyo and Osaka had been burned to the ground in air raids, and one of every four houses in Japan had been destroyed. Hiroshima and Nagasaki were atomic wastelands obliterated in the last days of the war. Industry, shipping, transportation networks, and power plants were devastated. Some 13 million of the labor force were without employment. The territorial empire had vanished, and the Japanese were once again limited to the four islands of the homeland—the same area they held at the time of Commodore Perry's visit a century before.

For the first time in history, the Japanese faced foreign occupation; the American victors were determined to demilitarize, democratize, and render Japan incapable of waging war in the future. Armed forces were banned; antimonopoly legislation was passed to break up the commercial and industrial empires of the *zaibatsu;* a **land reform** program virtually eliminated absentee landowners by restricting land ownership to 10 acres per family. Compulsory education was increased from six to nine years, and new textbooks—democratic in tone—were introduced into the schools. Midway through the seven-year American occupation of Japan, however, emphasis shifted from democratization and demilitarization to defense and rapid recovery. The Communist victories in China and the outbreak of the Korean War convinced the United States to view Japan as a potential ally rather than as a defeated enemy. In 1952, the occupation ended and control of Japan was returned to the Japanese.

RICH NATION, STRONG ENTERPRISE
In the thirty years following World War II, the Japanese experienced a phenomenal rate of economic growth and transformed what could be termed a premodern manufacturing society into an industrial state of the first order. Overall, the Japanese economy expanded faster than that of any other country, at a rate of 10 percent per year—double the average world rate during the 1950s and 1960s. An industrial complex equal in scale to the German Ruhr, the English Midlands, or the American Great Lakes Plain expanded between northern Kyushu and the Kanto Plain of Tokyo. Manufacturing shifted from labor-intensive industries such as textiles to heavy industrial goods and products of advanced technology. Japanese exports grew twice as fast as average world rates, to the point where its merchant marine now ranks among the largest in the world. These economic shifts intensified rural-urban migration as the labor force responded to opportunities in the rapidly expanding industries. At the same time, advances in agricultural modernization progressively released rural labor for urban job markets. Despite a net population increase of 30 million between 1945 and 1970, the standard of living of Japan's people rose substantially to approach the standards of Western Europe and the United States. In the process, Japan completed the program of modernization begun during the Meiji Restoration. Under the new motto, "rich nation, strong enterprise," growth was pursued with single-minded skill and determination to increase the nation's economic output.

Industrialization
[FIGURES 2, 3]

Japan's extraordinary postwar rate of economic growth was based on a rapid expansion of industry and manufacturing. Large-scale steel complexes planned to receive giant carriers of imported iron ore and coal were constructed at coastal locations. By the early 1970s, Japan was producing 100 million tons of finished steel and 70 million tons of **pig iron** a year, figures four times as large as the output of Great Britain and second only to the United States. Metal, chemical, and engineering industries today employ over half of the Japanese work force; Japanese production of heavy industrial machinery (especially ships and automobiles), as well as specialized scientific apparatus, cameras, binoculars, and electronic goods, is today a substantial percentage of the world's total. The textile and silk industries, traditionally prominent in the Japanese economy, declined considerably. Japan has surrendered these labor-intensive activities to newly developing countries in Asia such as Korea, Taiwan, China, and India. Japan's economy has assumed the structural characteristics of industry in other nations of the technological world.

But unlike most industrial nations, Japan has a rather limited natural resource base with which to sustain high levels of industrial production. Japan must live by trade. With virtually no oil, Japan imports 95 percent of its petroleum needs from the

Middle East—a full half of total energy requirements. Similarly, the steel industry imports most of its iron ore and coking coal; taken together, fuel and ores constitute a third of all imports. Cotton and food, mostly wheat and soybeans, are also imported in large quantities; the limited arable land of Japan cannot supply the food needs of its present population. Some 70 percent of Japan's current imports are raw materials, but paradoxically, with the exception of oil, most of these primary goods come from the United States, Western Europe, and Australia—other industrial nations. In turn, Japan sells automobiles, advanced electronic equipment, television sets, and other highly specialized goods to nations in both the technological and the developing worlds.

Partly because of the need to trade, but also for topographical and historical reasons, Japan's large-scale industry is densely concentrated along a narrow coastal band extending from Tokyo in the east 600 miles westward to northern Kyushu. More than three-quarters of Japan's industrial production and four-fifths of the total industrial labor force are located in this zone of Japan. Four cores of particu-

In Kawasaki, an industrial city between Tokyo and Yokohama, refineries, power stations, and chemical plants blot out the landscape and cause chronic respiratory diseases. *Photo:* **Paolo Koch/Rapho-Photo Researchers.**

larly dense industrial activity can be identified: Kanto on Tokyo Bay, Chukyo on Ise Bay, Keihanshin on Osaka Bay at the head of the Inland Sea, and the Kanmon complex in northern Kyushu. The first three of these industrial areas are located on bays rimmed by densely populated plains where large rivers enter sheltered harbors—excellent locations for concentrations of labor, water, and access to trade. The fourth center, northern Kyushu, developed as an early industrial region because of access to the nearby Chikuho coal mines. These four industrial cores produce 85 to 90 percent of Japan's iron and steel, two-thirds of all engineering and textile products, and one-half of all chemicals. With port facilities capable of handling fuel, ore, and raw fiber imports, and a readily available labor force, this level land adjacent to protected harbors is at a premium in a country that is 80 percent moun-

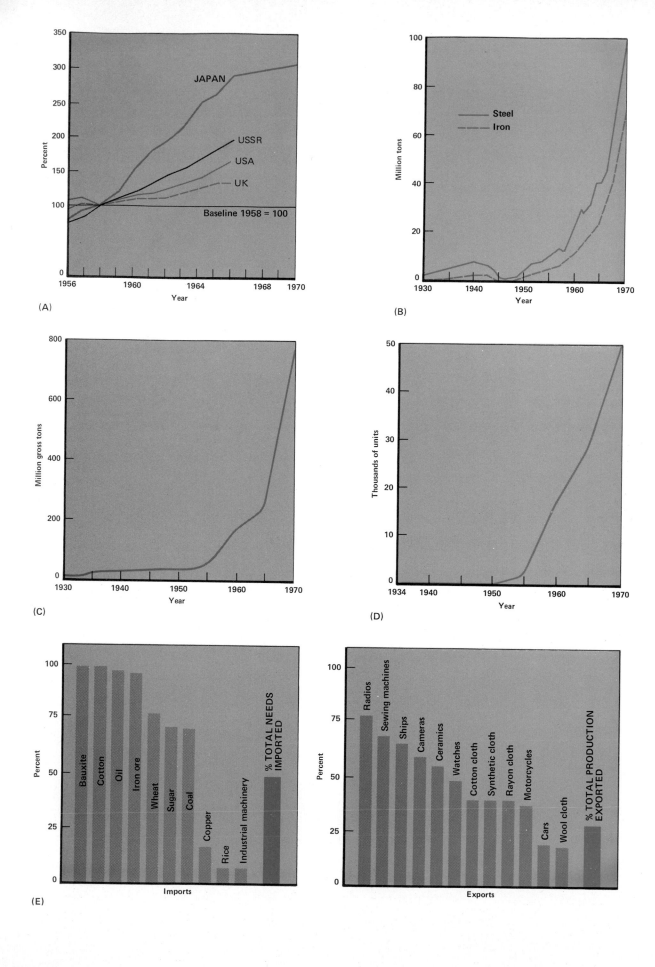

Swordmaker Takeshi Yamamura prepares a blade for tempering in his small shop, equipped only with traditional tools and a kerosene stove. *Photo:* Ted Grant/Design Photographers International.

tainous. The industrial core of Japan continues to grow in size and complexity despite high levels of congestion, land values so high that coastal reclamation is profitable, housing shortages, transport problems, and severe ecological pollution. There is growing awareness of the long-run consequences of such concentration, however, though it has as yet had little practical effect.

The Kanto core, consisting of the cities of Tokyo, Yokohama, Kawasaki, and Chiba, forms a conurbation of 24 million people responsible for 35 percent of Japan's industrial production in 1970. Chemicals, light industry, and iron and steel are most important, with textiles playing a much less vital role than in other industrial nodes. Factories and rice fields blanket the entire plain, a carpet of concrete and paddy, whose political and economic primacy in Japan continues to attract a stream of migrants from smaller urban centers and rural areas in general. The Keihanshin node on the Inland Sea, the oldest commercial and industrial center in Japan, includes

Figure 2. Indices of Japanese Economic Growth. Since World War II, Japan has emerged as a modern industrial state, a primary producer of iron and steel, automobiles, engineering goods, and electronic equipment. These five graphs display Japan's industrial growth (a) compared with that of the USA, UK, and USSR (1958 = 100%); (b) in iron and steel production; (c) in shipbuilding; (d) in the production of automobiles, radios, and television sets; and (e) as reflected in dependence on trade. *Adapted from:* (a), (b), (e) Prue Dempster, *Japan Advances.* London: Methuen, 1969, pp. 181, 213, 281. (c), (d) G. C. Allen, *A Short Economic History of Modern Japan.* London: Allen and Unwin; New York: Praeger, 1972, pp. 226, 227. © George Allen & Unwin, Ltd., 1972. Used by permission of Allen & Unwin, Ltd., and Praeger Publishers, Inc., New York.

the three major cities of Osaka, Kobe, and the ancient imperial capital of Kyoto; it produces one-fifth of Japan's manufactures. Heavy engineering and shipbuilding are the primary industries, but iron and steel, oil refining, chemicals, and textiles are also important. The Chukyo industrial core is centered on Nagoya; it constitutes somewhat less than a fifth of total industrial production, and is Japan's leading producer of cotton, wool, and synthetic textiles. Kanmon, in northern Kyushu, is based on local coal supplies rather than port facilities and is a declining center of heavy industry, less well adapted to the emerging pattern of Japanese commerce and industry—namely, the importation of raw materials, the processing of them into a variety of products, and the export of manufactured goods abroad.

While the national landscape and the structure of large-scale Japanese industry has assumed the general characteristics of other industrial nations in the technological world, the social organization of manufacturing remains distinctively Japanese. Old *zaibatsu* firms such as Mitsui and Mitsubishi, which manage two-thirds of Japan's trade, have reemerged to control a mass of financial and industrial activities. Newcomers such as Honda, Toyota, and Matsushita have joined the national fabric of **cartels**• (now called the *zaikai*) that play a crucial role in the Japanese national scene. Looser and more amorphous than the rigid family-dominated combines of the past, the modern *zaikai* conglomerates retain a traditional respect for loyalty, obedience, and mutual obligation which takes the form of industrial stability. Strikes are rare, job security is high (a worker is hired for life), and increased industrial productivity is a consuming value. But alongside these vast corporations, a significant share of Japan's industry consists of small family firms who employ few workers, use simple techniques, and pay low wages. More than four-fifths of the factories (a third of the total industrial labor force) in Japan employ fewer than thirty workers. These workshops specialize in the traditional craft industries—lacquerware, dolls, prints, fans, silk brocades, and basic domestic needs such as bread, cushions, and kimonos; they also figure strongly in the expanding specialized manufacture of cameras, television components, and radios. Although productivity and wages are lower than in large-scale industry, family tradition, skill, and willingness to work have enabled these firms to persist in Japan.

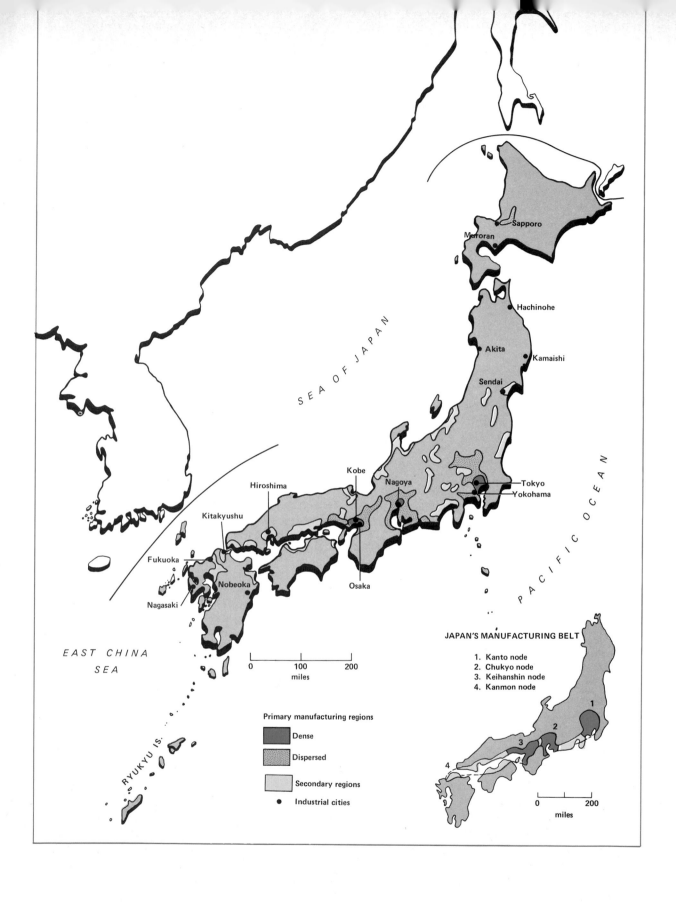

SEA OF JAPAN

Sapporo
Muroran

Hachinohe

Akita
Kamaishi

Sendai

Kobe
Hiroshima
Nagoya
Tokyo
Yokohama

Kitakyushu

Fukuoka
Nobeoka

Nagasaki
Osaka

PACIFIC OCEAN

EAST CHINA
SEA

RYUKYU IS.

0   100   200
miles

JAPAN'S MANUFACTURING BELT

1. Kanto node
2. Chukyo node
3. Keihanshin node
4. Kanmon node

Primary manufacturing regions

Dense

Dispersed

Secondary regions

● Industrial cities

0   200
miles

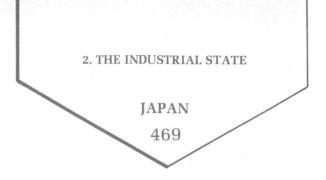

Urbanization

[FIGURE 4]

The very rapid growth of the Japanese industrial economy has reordered the distribution of population in Japan. Labor drawn from the farming communities of rural Japan has relocated in the sprawling cities of the flat, coastal plains of the core area. Long tied to their fields by the high labor requirements of rice cultivation, Japanese farmers resisted urbanization for some time. As a result, a third of the Japanese work force—some 13.6 million people—were still engaged in agriculture as late as 1960. This extraordinarily high figure for an industrial nation represented approximately the population on the land during the early Meiji period. But by 1970, this figure declined by nearly half, to 7.7 million people, 16 percent of the labor force. Population

Figure 3. The Industrialization of Japan. An industrial landscape along the Pacific coast with manufacturing nodes on the Kanto Plain, the Chukyo region near Nagoya, the Keihanshin region at the head of the Inland Sea, and the Kanmon area of northern Kyushu is the modern Japanese heartland. Together, these areas produce more than 80 percent of Japan's industrial goods and employ a similar percentage of the industrial labor force. *After:* Glenn T. Trewartha, *Japan: A Geography.* Madison and Milwaukee: University of Wisconsin Press, 1965, p. 269, Fig. 8.5. Copyright © 1965 by Glenn Thomas Trewartha.

Figure 4. Urbanization in Japan. The growth of Tokyo, Yokohama, Nagoya, Osaka, Kobe, and Kyoto—the Big Six—has resulted in the emergence of the Tokaido megalopolis, a densely settled and multinucleated conurbation extending along the Pacific coast of Japan. As part (a) shows, Tokyo, the primate city of Japan with 14 percent of the nation's population, has grown as the principal industrial center and political capital of the country. Beyond the six cities shown, only Kitakyushu, a group of five cities in northern Kyushu now tallied as a unit, and Sapporo in Hokkaido have populations of more than 1 million. Part (b) compares the overall rate of Japanese urbanization with that of India and England. In Japan, urbanization has been recent and rapid, reflecting the nature of Japanese industrialization. *Adapted from:* Prue Dempster, *Japan Advances.* London: Methuen, 1969, pp. 262, 264; Figs. 136, 138.

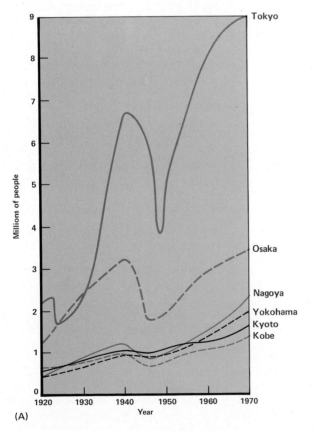

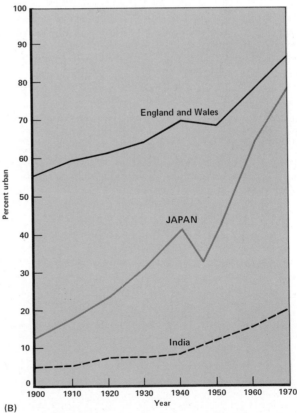

Blocks of concrete apartment buildings have been built all over Japan by government and industry to relieve the housing shortage. Though functional, they retain nothing of the traditional harmony with nature. *Photo:* United Nations.

pressure in the villages and hamlets and high urban wages have attracted Japanese youth to urban life. In 1970, 72 percent of all Japanese lived in cities larger than 50,000. Thus, after a century during which the Japanese population tripled from 30 million to over 100 million, all the added people were urbanites.

The factors that have influenced the growth and distribution of cities in Japan are, of course, related to the patterns of modern economic growth. But the role of topography in controlling urban location and development continues to operate today as it has throughout Japanese history. Japanese cities are primarily confined to the coastal plains, particularly in the core zone along the Pacific coast. A few are found in mountain basins. Size and location are directly related to availability of level land. Four-fifths of all cities are located on the one-quarter of Japan that is relatively flat, and no city larger than 100,000 is located in the mountains. The largest cities, the so-called Big Six, all with populations of 1 million or more, are located on the fertile alluvial plains that line the core zone of south-central Japan. Tokyo, on the Kanto Plain, had a 1970 population of 11.4 million. By some definitions, it is the largest city in the world. Extending to include Yokohama, the Kanto conurbation gathers an estimated 24 million people, nearly a quarter of the country's total population. Farther west, Nagoya, with more than 2 million, dominates the Nobi Plain; at the head of the Inland Sea, the three cities of Osaka (more than 3 million) and Kobe and Kyoto (more than 1 million each) have spread inland from the Settsu Plain into the traditional heartland area of Japanese civilization. With the exception of Kyoto, the cultural and religious center of Japan, all these large urban centers extend to the sea, are equipped with port facilities, and have densely settled agricultural **hinterlands.** These and most other large cities in Japan, including thirty-four of the forty-six prefectural capitals, are former castle towns, indicating the persistent attractions of fertile soil and mild climate in the core area of Japan to both the seventeenth-century daimyo and the modern corporation.

Japanese urban geographers today call the belt of urban and industrial activity between Tokyo and Kyoto the Tokaido Megalopolis, named after an earlier post road, the "avenue along the eastern sea." Along this route the palanquins of Tokugawa nobility, the rickshaws of Meiji, and more recently, modern rail and highway systems link the premier industrial center of Tokyo and the imperial city of Kyoto. This elongated urban belt includes the Kanto Plain (population 24 million), the Chukyo region (9 million), and the Keinshan complex (14.5 million). Some 47 million people, nearly half of the total population of Japan, are clustered in these three ancient agricultural regions that together make up less than 1 percent of the land area of Japan. This extraordinary concentration of people, industry, commerce, and agriculture has generated fierce com-

A Tokyo street, packed with shops and restaurants, people and vehicles, under a canopy of power lines and signs: what life is like with too many people and too little space. *Photo:* **Herb Levart/Rapho-Photo Researchers.**

petition for space; problems of congestion considerably more intense than those of the eastern seaboard of the United States have resulted. Linked by highway and monorail, this complex continues to grow despite government efforts at industrial dispersal and balanced regional development.

Rural Japan
[FIGURE 5]

The dramatic modernization of the urban and industrial landscapes of the core zone of modern Japan had no counterpart in rural areas of the island archipelago. Described by one writer as a country "where the stones show human fingerprints; where the pressure of men on the land has worn through to iron rock," the Japanese agricultural landscape remains a patchwork of intensively tended lowland rice fields and staggered upland terraces. Rice, the primary crop, is grown on nearly half the agricultural land; other crops such as wheat, barley, soybeans, and fruit are planted as winter crops and wherever rice is not practicable. Plots of land are tiny; seven of every ten Japanese farmers own less than 2.5 acres of land, an area one-twentieth the average British farm and roughly equivalent to two football fields. Yields, however, are among the highest in the world and continue to rise because Japanese farmers lavish time, energy, and fertilizer

on their small plots. With two-thirds of Japan in forested upland and only 20 percent in cultivation, this intensive agriculture has overcome the problem of size through sheer labor. However, population densities in the coastal plains and narrow upland valleys of agricultural Japan are greater than 4000 per square mile, triple those of the Netherlands. The total agricultural acreage of Japan remains steady at 14 million acres, with newly reclaimed land on the coast and in marginal environments counterbalanced by losses of agricultural land to urbanization. Overall, then, the distribution and complexion of agriculture—crops grown, high yields, and patterns of intensive cultivation—have changed little compared with the postwar flood of technology and capital that has washed over urban Japan.

The social structure of agriculture, however, underwent a fundamental reordering. Believing the poverty and misery of Japanese peasants a primary cause of militarism in Japan, the leaders of the American occupation forces implemented land reform programs aimed at the removal of the landlord class by confiscating agricultural land and redistributing it to tenants who worked the land for rent. A total of 4.8 million acres of land was purchased by the government; more than 27 million separate tracts—one-third Japan's agricultural land—were transferred to reformed titles. The number of tenants fell from 46 to 8 percent of the agricultural work force, and in a single stroke, rural Japan was converted into a nation of peasant proprietors. Considerable areas of paddyland were reorganized and reshaped into larger, more rectangular plots. Resented by peasant farmers who were deeply attached to the small bits of land they had acquired over the years by renting, buying, inheriting, and trading, consolidation of fields made rice farming more susceptible to mechanization by garden tractors and power tools. This, combined with better drainage and irrigation and land recouped from former field boundaries, increased yields as much as 15 percent in some areas. Gradually, mechanization, scientific use of fertilizers, better grade seeds, and rationalized agricultural practices spread; agricultural production in Japan increased by 45 percent between 1955 and 1970.

During this same period, farm incomes rose and closed the standard of living gap which traditionally existed between the urban industrial popula-

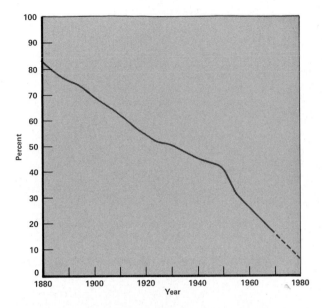

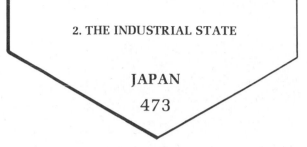

Figure 5. The Declining Role of Agriculture in Japan. The declining role of the farmer in the Japanese workforce reflects the concurrent urbanization and industrialization of Japanese society. The consequent disappearance of traditional rural society, seen by some leaders as a crucial reservoir of the true Japanese culture, is a topic of national debate. *Adapted from:* Prue Dempster, *Japan Advances.* London: Methuen, 1969, p. 73, Fig. 31.

tions and countryfolk. By 1971, almost every farmer had a television set, and three-quarters could afford refrigerators and washing machines. This was made possible by two factors. First, agricultural production was subsidized by the government, guaranteeing farmers a minimum rice price, and limiting foreign imports of agricultural products (especially rice, wheat, and sugar) which sell on the world market at two-thirds the Japanese price. Despite declines in the early 1970s, Japanese farmers produce a rice surplus, although political pressure is currently mounting in urban areas to reduce the rice price and to open Japan to food imports from Korea, Taiwan, and mainland China. The second factor which increased farm incomes was the commercial penetration of the countryside by industrial firms in search of cheap labor. By 1970, three-quarters of all Japanese farmers were working part time in small factories, fisheries, and craft activities, and 60 percent of their total incomes came from nonagricultural activities. Fields tended on weekends primarily by women signaled a special transformation of the close-knit family and village structure Japanese politicians consider so essential to the preservation of true Japanese culture and values.

The Japanese landscape is vertical and enclosed: terraced fields in precise patterns fill all the arable area, and farmhouse compounds are squeezed into unusable space; above rise the mountains. *Photo:* Georg Gerster/ Rapho-Photo Researchers.

At the heart of village life, the *ie*, an extended patriarchal family embracing ancestors and the living, tied individuals in a web of close family relationships. Personal concerns were subordinate to family welfare, and greatest authority was attached to the head of household. Female marriage patterns tended to benefit the *ie* by forming allegiances with other village families. The ideal family had three children: "one to sell (a daughter), one to follow (the first son), and one in reserve (a second son)." Families in each village were related not only by marriage but also by the cooperative labor required to maintain complicated rice irrigation and drainage systems. Village harmony was a duty and a necessity; the hallmark of the entire system was order and continuity. But the commercialization of the countryside, population growth, and modern education have disrupted these traditions. By the middle 1950s, a massive migration of labor from the land swept into industrial Japan, driven by population pressure on cultivated land and attracted by the amenities, jobs, and individuality of urban life. Agriculturalists form a declining percentage of the labor force each year. Japanese family fields are left to women and old people, who now constitute two-thirds of the farm population. Traditionalists mourn the declining importance of the *ie*, the village life it defined, and the weakening of those values of obedience, loyalty, and personal sacrifice that are falling victim to the urban industrial ferment of modern Japan.

ZONE OF EMPTINESS

In his novel, *Zone of Emptiness*, Hiroshi Noma portrays the Japanese army as an organization built on repression, whose men were morally impoverished by empty sacrifices made for glory, obsessive loyalty, and the quest for national prestige. He explains the arrogance and cruelty of the Japanese soldiers who occupied China and Southeast Asia as expressions of an emotional vacuum, a "zone of emptiness," generated by suppression of personal expression and individuality. After the war, the government, having lost both political and economic independence, made economic growth the top national priority. The disciplined Japanese began to pursue increases in gross national product as a matter of national honor, and the condition of the country was perceived and measured in terms of manufacturing tonnage and

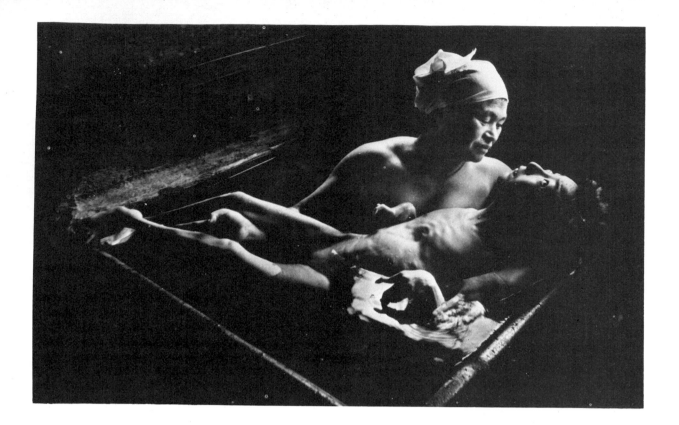

A woman bathes her daughter, a victim of Minamata disease. Her child was born deformed nearly twenty years ago because she ate mercury-contaminated fish caught in Minamata Bay. It has taken nearly that long for the determined victims to force the company responsible to make some compensation. *Photo:* Eugene Smith.

world trade figures. The goal of catching up with and surpassing the West remained the same, but was interpreted anew.

The Japanese succeeded beyond all expectations, achieved the world's second largest gross national product, and compiled in recent years a record of unmatched industrial development. The benefits of economic growth have penetrated all levels of Japanese society. Life expectancy is seventy years for men, seventy-five for women; standards of living have risen, and Japanese incomes are the fourteenth highest in the world. The literacy rate approaches 100 percent, and the material trappings of the technological world—television sets, automobiles, radios—have become ubiquitous. These gains in comfort and convenience have been achieved by the social devotion to economic expansion at any cost. For some, this policy has created a new zone of emptiness, a new personal vacuum, characterized by feverish competition, congestion, air and water pollution, inadequate services, and alienation—the sacrifices required to fulfill the single-minded Japanese drive for economic preeminence.

Pollution

In Japan, more economic activity takes place in less space than anywhere else in the world; the gross national product per area is higher than in any other country. The consequence of this human concentration in terms of noise, air, and water pollution has been acute, although generalized data are difficult to assemble. Complaints about pollution began to increase in the late 1960s, tripling from 20,000 to 60,000 per year between 1966 and 1970. In this same period, the number of prefectures defined as "free of environmental disruption" dropped from seventeen to six. Isolated environmental incidents in the urban-industrial centers began to cluster and spread, forcing the government to recognize pollution as a national problem. Recent measurements show that dust and soot levels in the atmosphere have diminished with the shift from coal to petroleum as the primary industrial energy source in Japan, but sulfur dioxide, carbon monoxide, and other petroleum-based residues rise steadily. Between 1968 and 1975, industrial production on the Kanto Plain doubled in value, and sulfur pollutants also doubled to more than 1 billion tons a year. Only one-tenth of these pollutants are treated. The problem is intensified by heavy reliance on Middle Eastern oil, which has a high sulfur content (2 to 3 percent), and by the growing use of personal automobiles, which number 2.3 million in Tokyo alone and 21 million in total. Smog domes now cloud the

1950
Chisso Corporation opens an acetaldehyde factory in the port city of Minamata. The factory produces CH₃CHO, a compound with a pungent, fruity odor used primarily in the silvering of mirrors and in organic synthesis, and begins to discharge industrial effluents into Minamata Bay, long famous as a fisheries center.

1953
Citizens of Minamata begin to suffer from an unknown disease that produces severe convulsions and leaves its victims crippled, deaf, blind, or insane.

1953–1963
Over a decade, 106 citizens of Minamata die from what becomes known as the Minamata disease.

1963
Scientists determine the cause of the disease: mercury poisoning. Methyl mercury is pinpointed as one of the industrial pollutants discharged into Minamata Bay by the Chisso Corporation since 1950. The government bans fishing in the bay; Chisso is ordered to stop contaminating the bay with methyl mercury and quickly abandons the use of mercury altogether in its production techniques.

Scientists relate the tale of mercury poisoning. Highly toxic methyl mercury travels through the food chain of the region. Small organisms in the bay collect mercury during their life processes; their toxicity is passed on through several orders of fish in the aquatic life of Minamata Bay. Toxicity passes to the human population via the larger fish which compose a substantial portion of the diet of the citizens of Minamata.

1970
Compensation to the victims of the Minamata disease begins under the "three-P policy" (polluters pay for pollution). In the following five years, Chisso Corporation pays $67.3 million to 793 victims. Suspected victims numbering 2700 may yet receive up to $60,000 per person.

1973
One of Chisso's plants is partially destroyed by explosion.

1974
Chisso Corporation sells $200 million worth of petrochemicals, yet loses $12 million overall. Chisso asks the government's national development bank for a $13 million loan to repair its damaged facilities and restore its slipping economic fortunes.

1975
Public outcry erupts as Chisso's development bank request becomes known. Japanese environmentalists castigate Chisso as a corporate murderer and denounce the use of public funds for corporations whose activities undermine social well-being. Prime Minister Miki states that "Chisso wants the loan to pay not for the consequences of pollution but to repair its damaged production system."

Chisso Corporation, devastated by compensation payments, faces a clouded future.

Japan, a finite environment with a dense population in large part dependent in its diet upon the products of the sea and bound to an industrial economy, faces an ever-tightening dilemma of ecological well-being and social responsibility.

---

atmospheres of every large city, and incidents of photochemical smog and lead poisoning have increased in the urban-industrial core along the Pacific coast.

Most dramatic, however, has been the water pollution in the Inland Sea and coastal bays, where high densities of shipping and peripheral industry are found. During the 1950s and 1960s, residents who ate fish caught in Minamata Bay were struck by a disease of the central nervous system caused by mercury poisoning originating from discharges from a local polyvinyl chloride factory. At Niigata, a similar case of mercury poisoning from industrial pollutants led to a judgment against a local industry on the west coast. These and other cases against mining and petroleum industrial complexes have provoked public outrage and decrees of compensation for victims of asthma from sulfuric acid mist and the *itai-itai* disease caused by cadmium discharges. Under heavy pressure, the government

The monorail line over Tokyo Bay, 1974. Once a place of great natural beauty, celebrated for centuries by poets and artists, the shoreline now offers this grim vista of ugliness to passengers riding the monorail from Haneda airport into downtown Tokyo. *Photo:* John Orr/United Nations.

adopted a policy of "polluters pay for pollution," which has already threatened at least one major corporation with bankruptcy. But given the extraordinarily high concentration of Japan's people and industry, the limited possibilities for industrial dispersion in the mountainous interior, and the high costs of environmental management, the Japanese will be forced to review critically rates of industrial growth in order to improve environmental quality—a reversal of the policy the nation has pursued for decades.

Quality of Life

The determination to maximize the rate of economic growth has left Japan deficient in public services despite its great prosperity. Japan lags far behind other technological nations in roads, water and sewage supply systems, city parks, number of rooms per person, and other measures of social development. The single exception is medicine. Japan has only one-eighth as many roads as Great Britain, and only one-third of them are paved. Traffic jams, called "traffic wars" by the Japanese, are legendary, particularly in Tokyo where only 11 percent of the land is given over to streets, compared with 25 percent in London and Paris and 35 percent in New York.

The rate of movement in the Tokaido Megalopolis is 5.6 miles per hour during rush hours and even less on major arteries. On commuter trains, government "pushers" are hired to cram people into trains, and these have been supplemented by "pullers," who detach those who cannot possibly fit to allow doors to close. Currently, all commuter lines in Tokyo run at at least 250 percent of capacity.

These measures of congestion, most intense in Tokyo but also typical of the Chukyo, Keihanshin, and Kanmon industrial core regions, are extremely high, due partly to the recentness of urbanization in Japan and partly to government disinterest in social investment. Housing shortages are acute, and spiraling land prices in urban centers, which in Tokyo amounted to a sixfold increase between 1960 and 1970, prohibit many from living in traditional single-family dwellings. Under the slogan One House for One Family, the government constructed 6.7 million new urban houses during the 1960s, but the housing shortage has not noticeably changed. Similar problems of inadequate water supply systems frequently forcing summer shortages, brownouts due to inadequate power sources, sewage systems which link only one house in ten to central systems, and park areas which in Tokyo amount to only one-half those of Paris and one-tenth of those in New York City, all point to a serious deterioration of the Japanese urban environment.

The Japanese refer to these problems as the agonies, the evils of overconcentration caused by rapid economic growth, the limitations of Japanese topography and resources, and the national policy of growth at any cost. With a declining birth rate and longer life expectancy, the proportion of Japanese over sixty-five has doubled in a society that spends less on social welfare than any other technological nation. The migration of the young to rented rooms and apartments in the larger cities has weakened family ties, leaving the old less able to rely on their traditional sources of support. Furthermore, the postwar generation has proved less willing to make sacrifices for national development and is critical of the government's lack of concern for the less fortunate; a growing number of strikes and student riots marks this dissent. In the modern industrial state of Japan, then, discussion progresses on the question of whether economic progress alone is a sufficient national goal. Whether the concept of "rich country, strong enterprise" can in the future provide a reasonable social environment and individual dignity or whether a new zone of emptiness will develop among the embittered old, the urban poor, and industrial laborers is open to debate and question.

JAPAN

THE INDUSTRIAL BASE
ENERGY AND MINERAL RESOURCES MAP

Japan does not possess the domestic sources of energy and minerals needed to sustain independent modern industrial growth. Like Great Britain, Japan must compete in world markets for the raw materials from which the products of Japan are made. Despite these limitations, the country's rate of energy consumption has been increasing at double the world rate—nearly 10 percent a year—and iron and steel production is growing four times as fast as in other leading industrial nations. It seems doubtful that this rate of economic growth can be sustained, or that other nations will be willing to satisfy, under reasonable terms, Japan's expanding appetite for raw materials. The quadrupling of oil prices in 1973 shocked the Japanese economy. Few nations in the world are as keenly aware of their economic future and as sensitive to commodity prices, domestic production, and exports as Japan. The rapid growth of Japanese industry and trade based on cheap raw materials, inexpensive labor, and available technology may be permanently slowed in the near future by Japan's poverty of resources.

ENERGY SOURCES
Until 1955, coal fulfilled half of the country's energy needs and was the primary source of power in Japan. Coal today accounts for only a quarter of Japanese energy consumption as rapid industrialization has outpaced declining domestic production. The primary coalfields of Japan are located in northern Kyushu and Hokkaido, and together these two fields produce 90 percent of the 45 million to 50 million tons annually mined in Japan. In the Kyushu field, severe faulting of thin, poor quality coal seams, underground springs, and trapped gas make mining difficult, dangerous, and expensive. Coal production per worker is one-tenth that of the

United States. The better quality coals of Hokkaido are less expensive and easier to mine, but the main fields at Ishikari are 35 miles from the coast and 600 miles from Tokyo. For these reasons and despite government subsidies, the coal industry is declining in both production and employment. Some 200,000 Japanese coal miners have lost their jobs in the last decade, and small and medium sized coal mines have closed because of the plummeting demand for coal as an energy resource and the conversion of industry to petroleum.

Petroleum now supplies two-thirds of Japan's total energy, but less than 1 percent of the oil needed is locally produced. Minor oil fields extend along the west coast of Japan from central Honshu northward to Hokkaido; production is controlled by a single company. Since the fields have been thoroughly explored, there is little likelihood of major new petroleum discoveries. Additional sources of energy in Japan include some 1500 hydroelectric plants scattered throughout the country, most of them of limited capacity; 400 thermal electric plants powered by coal or oil; and a small number of atomic power stations. The latter, fueled by uranium imported from the United States, are seen as a major future source of energy in Japan. It seems unlikely, however, that atomic power will significantly decrease Japan's long-term dependence on foreign imports for over 80 percent of the country's energy needs.

MINERALS AND METALS
Minerals and metals in Japan are equally limited. Japan produces only 3 percent of the iron ore used in its heavy industry, so that the iron and steel industry, the backbone of Japan's industrial growth, is heavily dependent on imports from Australia, India, Peru, and Chile. With respect to other mineral production, Japan is self-sufficient in copper, lead, zinc, and silver; the only mineral produced in surplus is sulfur. Small quantities of tin, gold, manganese, tungsten, chromium, and molybdenum are also produced. The mines are scattered throughout the archipelago; many are small, inefficient family operations that mine small quantities of several minerals. Costs of production are high and barely competitive with foreign sources. Nickel, cobalt, and bauxite are not found in Japan, and deficiencies in *ferroalloys*[*] and auxiliary minerals are a serious industrial problem. The absence of phosphates for fertilizer poses a comparable problem in agriculture. Currently, Japanese leaders are searching for mineral concessions and purchase agreements throughout the developing world. As with energy, however, Japan can expect to pay a high price for the raw materials needed to sustain future economic growth.

477

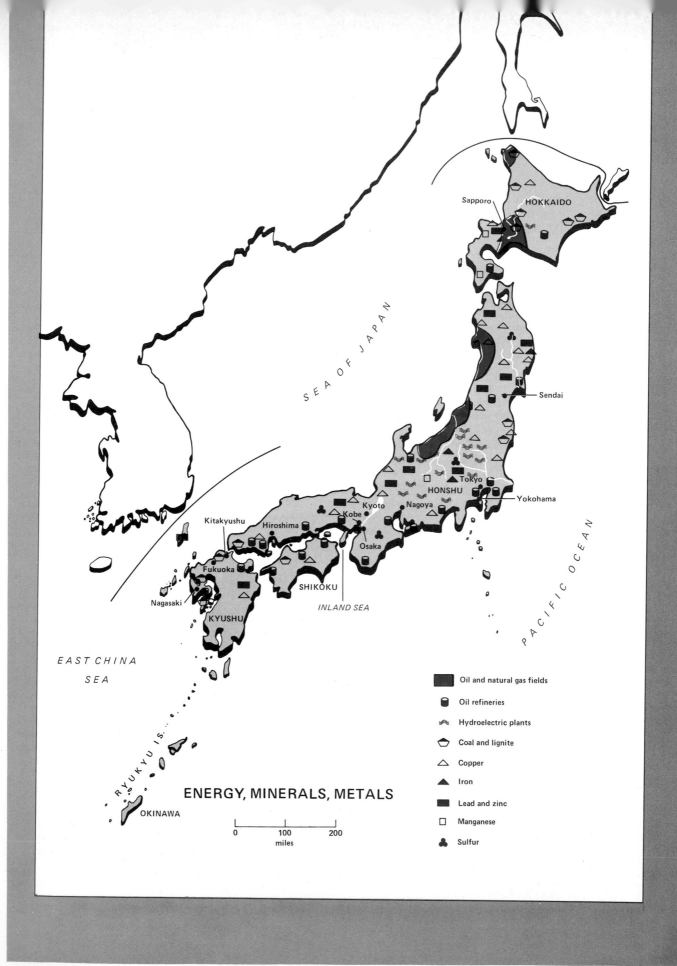

SEA OF JAPAN

PACIFIC OCEAN

EAST CHINA SEA

HOKKAIDO
Sapporo

Sendai

HONSHU
Tokyo
Yokohama
Nagoya
Kyoto
Kobe
Osaka

Kitakyushu
Hiroshima
SHIKOKU
Fukuoka
INLAND SEA
Nagasaki
KYUSHU

RYUKYU IS.

OKINAWA

ENERGY, MINERALS, METALS

0   100   200
miles

Oil and natural gas fields

Oil refineries

Hydroelectric plants

Coal and lignite

Copper

Iron

Lead and zinc

Manganese

Sulfur

BIBLIOGRAPHY

GENERAL

Association of Japanese Geographers. *Japanese Cities: A Geographical Approach.* Tokyo: Association of Japanese Geographers, 1970. A detailed series of articles on various aspects of urban Japan.

Dempster, Prue. *Japan Advances: A Geographical Study.* London: Methuen, 1969. A thematic volume devoted to the changing economic geography of Japan in the modern period.

Reischauer, Edwin O. *The United States and Japan.* New York: Viking Press Compass Books, 1965. A perceptive and thoughtful volume on Japan and its relations with the wider world.

Trewartha, Glenn T. *Japan: A Geography.* Madison: University of Wisconsin Press, 1965. An accurate, authoritative, and exhaustive systematic and regional geography of Japan.

[1] THE MODERNIZATION OF JAPAN

Allen, G. C. *A Short Economic History of Modern Japan.* London: Allen and Unwin, 1972. A detailed analysis of the economic development of modern Japan.

Barr, Pat. *The Coming of the Barbarians.* New York: Dutton, 1967. An insightful sketch of the opening of Japan to the West in the middle of the nineteenth century.

Beasley, William G. *The Meiji Restoration.* Stanford, Calif.: Stanford University Press, 1972. A definitive study of the political, social, and economic dynamics of this watershed period of Japanese history.

Beasley, William G. *The Modern History of Japan.* London: Weidenfeld and Nicolson, 1973. An excellent general history of Japan from the Restoration to the postwar period.

Borton, Hugh. *Japan's Modern Century, from Perry to 1970,* 2nd ed. New York: Ronald, 1970. Good general history of Japan from the end of its isolation in the nineteenth century.

Morton, William Scott. *Japan: Its History and Culture.* Newton Abbot, England: David and Charles, 1973. A brief, well-written history of Japan.

Ohkawa, Kazushi, and Henry Rosovsky. *Japanese Economic Growth.* London: Oxford University Press, 1973. The twentieth-century growth of the Japanese economy with special emphasis on the modern period.

Hall, John Whitney. "The Castle Town and Japan's Modern Urbanization." *Far Eastern Quarterly,* Vol. 15 (1955), pp. 37–56. A brilliant essay on the spatial basis of Tokugawa society.

[2] THE INDUSTRIAL STATE

Fukutake, Tadashi. *Japanese Rural Society.* London: Oxford University Press, 1967. A penetrating analysis of the subtle social changes in village life that have accompanied the industrialization of Japan.

Gibney, Frank. *Japan: The Fragile Superpower.* New York: Norton, 1975. A well-written volume which argues that despite a growing population, industrial pollution, and trade problems, the Japanese have been well able to cope with contemporary industrial life.

Hall, Robert B., Jr. *Japan: Industrial Power of Asia.* Princeton, N.J.: Van Nostrand Searchlight Books, 1973. A brief introduction to major facets of the geography of Japan.

Kahn, Herman. *The Emerging Japanese Superstate: Challenge and Response.* Englewood Cliffs, N.J.: Prentice-Hall, 1970. A superficial but widely quoted work which projects Japan as the most powerful economic and financial nation in the world by the year 2000.

Kawahito, Kiyoshi. *The Japanese Steel Industry.* New York: Praeger, 1972. A detailed study of the remarkable growth of the Japanese steel industry.

Tanaka, Kakuei. *Building a New Japan.* Tokyo: Simul Press, 1973. Primarily a propaganda piece by a former Japanese prime minister, but with interesting insights into the problems generated by rapid economic growth.

Vogel, Ezra. *Japan's New Middle Class.* Berkeley: University of California Press, 1964. The changing role of family and community in modern Japanese cities.

NORTH AMERICA

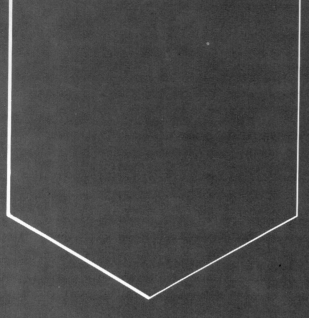

Alexis de Toqueville in 1844. Chasserian Collection. *Photo:* Bulloz.

On May 12, 1831, a well-born young Frenchman, Alexis de Tocqueville, landed at New York City after a 38-day voyage from the French port of Le Havre. Ostensibly on a mission from the French government to investigate the American prison system, his purpose was, in fact, much more ambitious. Tocqueville wanted to study "that vast American society which everyone [in Europe] talks of and nobody knows," to comprehend the basic mechanisms which powered the young democracy in the New World. With his companion, Gustave de Beaumont, Tocqueville planned to collect "the elements of a fine work"—a book that would win him public acclaim by introducing America's new social order to his countrymen. To accomplish this task, as Beaumont noted, they "must see America . . . its inhabitants, its cities, its institutions, its customs." In the next nine months they did just that. Traveling more than 4000 miles by steamboat and stage from Boston to Green Bay, from Quebec to New Orleans, they visited virtually every large North American city, steamed down the Ohio and Mississippi rivers from Pittsburgh to New Orleans, ventured upon the western frontier in the Michigan Territory, and saw each of the twenty-four states of the Union. Laden down with notebooks, the two men sailed for France the following February. Three years later, in 1835, when he was not quite thirty years old, the first two volumes of Tocqueville's masterful and penetrating study of American society and culture, *De la démocratie en Amérique*, were published.

The youngest son of a noble family, Tocqueville was born in a small chateau in Normandy in 1805. Amiable but aloof, he grew up an aristocrat in a middle-class age—a lover of dogs, an excellent marksman, a strong swimmer, a country gentleman and local magistrate who aspired to becoming a statesman of France. This dream was shattered, however, when the rising tide of democracy in Europe led to the Revolution of 1830 and the overthrow of the Bourbon king, with whom the Tocqueville family was closely identified. Fearing that France was drifting toward chaos (and perhaps partly to keep his quest for high political office alive), Tocqueville swore allegiance to the new king, Louis Philippe, whose supporters were middle-class merchants, bankers, and industrialists. This decision left young Tocqueville in midstream—an outcast in aristocratic circles, yet not trusted by the new powers because of his background. When his superiors demanded a second oath of allegiance, Tocqueville recognized that his hopes for real political influence under Louis Philippe were unrealistic. Not wishing to become too closely identified with the new dynasty, he determined to leave France. The central tension in his life had become the battle between the old monarchists and the new socialists, and Tocqueville was too liberal for the former and too traditional for the latter. He resolved to write a book about the New World, where the irresistible movement from aristocracy to democracy had been accomplished without destruction or anarchy.

It was this conception of a democratic revolution that enabled Tocqueville to clearly grasp the essentially middle-class nature of North American society and culture. Unlike France, he noted, North America had no entrenched aristocracy, no land-holding elite, and no centralized bureaucracy. As a result, he viewed the extremes of wealth and poverty within society of small moment—North Americans formed one great, homogeneous class-less society (except in the South). In his view, the settlers of this new land had from the first striven for social and political freedom, economic inde-pendence, and equality. Under optimal conditions, they had succeeded in imposing this landscape of the mind on half a continent, and had proved that democracy was a feasible social and political organization. This realization burst on Tocque-ville as a genuinely new idea. Drawn from a society where the clashes between rich and poor were strong, where the aristocracy had been broken but not replaced, Tocqueville came to see North America as a laboratory for the future, as a new world that exemplified not only what was inevita-ble, but what was possible; a real choice for his beloved France. His work received immediate acclaim in France and Tocqueville was elected to the French Academy in 1837. He continued to write on political questions until his death from tuber-culosis in 1859.

Tocqueville probed the anatomy of the American republic to determine how equality of condition affected the customs and mores of the people, to discover the mainsprings that had enabled democ-racy to become an actuality. He examined how political parties, public assembly, freedom of the press, landholding systems, education, and com-merce gave weight, size, and shape to North Ameri-can society. "A new science of politics is needed for a new world," he claimed, and he brought intellect and verve to his study. In the process he delineated a number of lasting tendencies in the growth of American civilization—a belief in individualism, an acceptance of change, the relentless pursuit of material wealth, and a strong faith in progress. These values were central to the creation of the first new nations from the implantation of European culture on the Atlantic coast to the rise of fully articulated, geographically united North American societies two centuries later. And although Tocque-ville strongly underestimated the impact urbaniza-tion and industrialization would have on modern North America, he was one of the first to appreciate that the United States, a struggling republic built on new and questionable principles, would have the momentum and stamina to become a world power.

ARCTIC OCEAN

ALEUTIAN IS.

KODIAK I.

Yukon R.

ALASKA

Anchorage • Fairbanks •

GREENLAND
(Denmark)

YUKON

NORTHWEST TERRITORIES

Mackenzie R.

*Great Bear
Lake*

*Great Slave
Lake*

PACIFIC OCEAN

VANCOUVER
I.

BRITISH COLUMBIA

Peace R.

Fraser R.

C   A   N   A   D   A

Columbia R.

Vancouver •

ALBERTA

SASKATCHEWAN

Saskatchewan R.

MANITOBA

Churchill R.

Nelson R.

HUDSON
BAY

NEWFOUNDLAND

Saguenay R.

Sacramento R.

Snake R.

*Great
Salt Lake*

UNITED

Missouri R.

Winnipeg •

ONTARIO

QUEBEC

GREAT LAKES

Montreal •
Ottawa •

Toronto •

St. Lawrence R.

Connecticut R.

Hudson R.

PRINCE
EDWARD I.

NOVA SCOTIA

NEW
BRUNSWICK

Colorado R.

STATES

Arkansas R.

Red R.

Mississippi R.

Ohio R.

Tennessee R.

ATLANTIC OCEAN

Rio Grande

MEXICO

GULF OF MEXICO

POLITICAL DIVISIONS

0   200   400   600
miles

HAWAIIAN IS.

Honolulu •

0   100   200
miles

CUBA

San Juan •

PUERTO
RICO

THE FIRST NEW NATIONS
1

Alexis de Tocqueville's insights into North American society brought to the attention of Europeans the degree to which the new society of the United States and Canada differed from that in the Old World. For him, Americans were "born free instead of becoming so," and they inhabited "one vast forest in the middle of which they carved some clearings." Struck by America's dynamic mobility, enormous resources, individualism, and faith in progress, Tocqueville underestimated the difficulties and hazards that faced the pioneers who gave these two democracies form.

In the colonial period, four culture hearths were precariously implanted on the east coast of North America by people of varied backgrounds with differing ambitions, linked only by their willingness to explore the unknown. After nearly two centuries, however, their descendants won their independence from Europe, swept westward across the continent, and dominated the resources of an extraordinarily rich swath of **midlatitude**• land. After a century of independence, the centennial celebration of freedom in the United States witnessed the emergence of two vibrant, expansive democratic societies—the world's first new nations.

COLONIAL BEGINNINGS
[FIGURE 1]

The Spanish and Portuguese colonial empires in America were 100 years old before the French and the British even began to colonize the New World. European explorers had groped along the Atlantic coast of North America and were familiar with its outlines, but conditions in northwestern Europe in the sixteenth century did not favor large-scale colonization. John Cabot's voyages to Newfoundland in the 1490s had unearthed no treasure. The Indians he encountered did not "possess anything worth five *sous*"—nothing exciting enough to spark the enthusiasm of the British crown or of England's financial community. The voyages of the Breton sailor Jacques Cartier to the Gulf of Saint Lawrence had similar results. His description of the barren rock shores of Labrador as the "land God gave to Cain" stifled what little interest existed in France for establishing a New World colony. French, British, and Dutch explorers were searching for a northwest passage to China, a highway of trade across the northwestern sea to bring Europe closer to the wealth of the Indies. Failing that, finding no gold, the explorers who established temporary settlements from Quebec to Florida on the Atlantic coast were unable to generate sufficient interest at home to sustain colonial adventures. The geography of North America was too forbidding, and the monarchs of Britain and France were preoccupied with wars, political intrigues, and religious strife at home.

But by the beginning of the seventeenth century, conditions in France and Britain had stabilized, and new European energies were released to colonize North America. In France, quarrelsome regional political factions and religions were brought to heel. The predecessors of Louis XIV imposed order on the country by pressuring the Protestant Huguenots out of France and reasserting the dominance of Catholicism. The previously independent French noblemen lived under virtual court arrest during this period. In England, after forty-five years of rule, Elizabeth I died in 1603; her successor, James I, finally united England and Scotland and was eager to launch foreign ventures.

The first spur to colonial development was the hope that American colonies would provide gold, spices, and naval stores (tar, pitch, turpentine, and rope)—commodities not available at home. Impassioned speeches in Parliament urged New World colonization to free Britain from dependence on foreign sources of raw materials, speeches similar to those favoring energy independence for the United States today. Second, both France and Britain wanted to challenge **Iberian**• dominance in the New World; North American colonies, it was argued, could be bases for French pirates and English privateers to plunder the **Spanish Main.**• Third, unemployment was then high in England, and a new class of urban drifters had arisen. Discharged soldiers and sailors, monks evicted from monasteries, students and beggars no longer supported by the Church, and peasants driven off their land by the conversion of common pastures into fenced estates —all congregated in the towns and cities of England. Known as the "roguish nation," this army of thieves and cutthroats posed a social threat to British law and order. Better for England to let them migrate. Finally, there were dissident religious minorities seeking liberty to exercise their beliefs, adventurous nobles who sought new conquests outside the ordered world of Western Europe, and families in

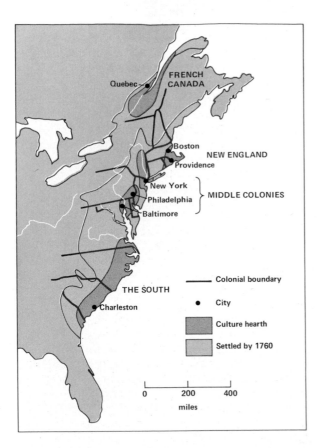

Figure 1. Colonial Culture Hearths. With their individual social origins, economic evolution, and political forms, each of the four North American culture hearths took on regional characteristics. The local environment exerted subtle but profound influences on European immigrants restricted to the coast by the densely forested ridges of the Appalachians (except in the case of the French) and isolated from Europe by 3000 miles of ocean. *After:* Preston James, *One World Divided.* New York: Blaisdell, 1964, p. 153, Fig. 44. Copyright © 1964 by Blaisdell. Used by permission of John Wiley and Sons, Inc.

search of land. In the seventeenth century, therefore, emigrants came to the New World: tens of thousands from England, a thin trickle from France, a thousand or two from Spain, and an even smaller number from Holland and Portugal. Varying purposes and methods of colonization and different adaptations to the environments of the New World produced a variety of ways of life. Out of these desires for gold, religious freedom, new prospects, land, and empire came a new geography of North America. Within a quarter century, four distinct colonial **culture hearths** emerged: French Canada, New England, the South, and the Middle Colonies.

French Canada

The first permanent French settlements in Canada were established at Annapolis Royal (1604) in

Acadia (now Nova Scotia) and at Quebec (1608) by the French explorer, Samuel de Champlain (1567?– 1635). Scouting inland to the west but pushed northward by hostile Iroquois Indians, Champlain and his successors staked out an elongated French empire along the glacial waterways draining the southern rim of the Canadian **Shield.** There they found a forested, severely **glaciated** land, pockmarked by lakes and streams, endowed with shallow and stony soils, and subject to long, cold winters. Although poor for agriculture, much of this region was ideal habitat for beaver, which subsist upon a diet of birch and poplar bark. This discovery precipitated a rush of trappers and fur traders into the Saint Lawrence Valley eager to make fortunes in the fur trade. Christianizing missionaries soon followed, and Louis XIII granted a fur monopoly to a crown company which exported as many as 25,000 beaver pelts a year from Canada to France. Every spring, fleets of Indian canoes came down the rivers to Montreal, Trois Rivières, or Quebec, and Indians bartered furs for pots and pans, guns, blankets, and liquor. Somewhat later, the French moved out to Indian settlements deep in the forests and dealt directly with the Indians on their own ground. Thinly scattered across a forest frontier penetrating 2000 miles into the North American interior, the traders and priests of New France probably numbered no more than 2000 by 1650, of whom a third were clustered in the town of Quebec.

With the English populations of New England and Virginia increasing rapidly and British plans for expeditions into Hudson Bay in progress, Louis XIV recognized that France must establish a more substantial presence in North America. In 1663, he made Canada a province of France governed directly by the crown. Enormous grants of land were given to feudal lords, *seigneurs,* who cleared the forests and served the French crown in time of war. These estates were subdivided and rented out to tenants, with the seigneur retaining timber rights, the right to draft tenant labor for road building, and certain other prerogatives. Men, livestock, and seed were sent out from France to tame the wilderness. Shiploads of women were provided from French orphanages, and a marriage market was established in Quebec. French bachelors in the New World were heavily taxed; the impetus to marriage was considerable. Only Catholics were allowed to emigrate to New France; the Huguenots were denied this right. As a result, society in New France took on a feudal cast and had a smaller middle class than did contemporary English settlements on the Atlantic coast.

The seigneurial system of landholding created a distinctive cultural landscape in French Canada. To avoid road building, colonists used rivers for transportation; but because taxes were levied on the basis of river frontage, owners attempted to arrange their farms so that as little land as possible bordered the water. Long strips of farms, often ten times longer than wide, came to line the Saint Lawrence and its *tributaries.*

Despite efforts by the crown to encourage colonization in New France, population remained low; settlement, difficult in the harsh climate, proceeded slowly. By 1750, when France and Britain stood poised for conflict in the New World, the 80,000 Frenchmen dispersed from the Saint Lawrence to the Great Lakes and down the Mississippi River to the Gulf of Mexico were flanked by more than 1 million British colonists tightly clustered on the Atlantic coastal plain. Although French penetration of the continent started earlier and brought France control of the two major *riverine* gateways to the American interior, the Saint Lawrence and the Mississippi, the French were too thinly scattered over too large an area to effectively hold their territory. Britain emerged as the primary political power in the New World, and English perceptions, political and social institutions, settlement forms, and systems of thought came to dominate the geography of North America.

New England
While the first French settlers were struggling at Champlain's outpost in Quebec, James I of England was entertaining proposals to subdivide the northern coast of Atlantic North America, from Philadelphia to Newfoundland, into royal *fiefdoms* to be developed by British aristocrats. But these plans never materialized. So it happened that in December 1620, a small group of religious dissenters, Pilgrims bound for Virginia in their ship the *Mayflower,* missed their destination and landed at what is now Plymouth on Cape Cod. Rather than risk a continued winter sea voyage farther south to Virginia, they decided to disembark. Only 41 of the 102 members of the Plymouth Colony actually belonged to the Pilgrim sect that had earlier fled from England to Holland to escape religious persecution. Discouraged by life as expatriates, they decided to establish a new settlement where they could live as "a distinct body by themselves"; they were joined by 61 British artisans, *indentured* servants, and soldiers. Half the members of the expedition died of starvation and disease in the unexpected cold of that first New England winter. But the Plymouth Colony survived, and within a decade grew to some 300 people.

At the same time, in Britain King Charles I had come under the influence of Archbishop Laud, a fiercely religious man determined to cleanse England of all heresy. As one religious sect after another fell under Laud's persecution, the so-called heretics fled Britain for New England. The largest of the groups, the Puritans, landed 900 settlers at Massachusetts Bay in 1629. By 1640, some 25,000 emigrants had journeyed from Britain to the Commonwealth of Massachusetts in search of religious freedom.

This freedom, however, rarely extended beyond members of each individual sect, and discord broke out among religious leaders. Splinter groups left Massachusetts and established new colonies in Rhode Island, Connecticut, New Hampshire, and Maine. Virtually every religious dispute produced a new settlement. Small, compact clusters of believers, New Englanders created a landscape of tightly organized religious townships, a topography of the mind superimposed on the wilderness of a new England. Having fled Europe for religious freedom, they never looked back. This distinguished the settlers of New England from those of the three other culture hearths on the Atlantic coast of North America.

The typical unit of settlement in New England was a small town—the only true village in the United States—inhabited by a single religious congregation and located in one of the many narrow valleys that trend southward between the sweeping Appalachian folds. Houses with yards were built close together; public buildings usually consisted of no more than a church, a meetinghouse, a courthouse, and an inn. The cemetery adjoining the church took up a substantial and central part of village land. In town meetings citizens of the community debated local issues as a strong tradition of political freedom and majority rule was firmly established. Higher education began with the establishment of Harvard College in 1636, only sixteen years after the landing of the Pilgrims at Plymouth. Rigorous codes of conduct were laid down: young men could not fish or wander in the woods on Sunday; cooking on the Sabbath was forbidden; smoking was banned. Offenders were subjected to public scorn and ridicule in the pillory or the stocks, on the ducking stool, or by branding on thumb, cheek, or forehead with an *A* for adultery, a *B* for burglary or blasphemy, and so on.

Common action arrived at by common consent was an important force enabling New Englanders to cope with their difficult environment. The coastal plain was narrow, the soils of the interior stony and sandy—a glacial landscape of forest and bare rock unsuited to agriculture. The Puritans were firm believers in the values of the Old Testament, and the direction of settlement in New England was seen in Biblical terms: "Make straight in the desert a highway for our God. Every valley shall be exalted, and every mountain and hill made low; the crooked straight, and the rough places plain." With great labor and unwavering belief, fields were cleared of trees and stones, and the farmlands owned and worked by a single family lay within walking distance of the village. In some places, abandoned clearings belonging to the departed Indians were available, making the task considerably easier. An estimated 85 percent of the early New Englanders became subsistence farmers. Indian crops such as corn, beans, and squash—all new plants to the Europeans—were cultivated, and European grains suited to the severe winter and cool summers of New England were also planted. Poultry and livestock were imported from Europe. Cod fishing proved a profitable supplement to agriculture, as did fur trading and the export of timber. A relatively self-sufficient society of free farmers, businessmen, fishermen, and artisans reshaped the landscape of New England and on the anvil of this new land hammered out the values of hard work, thrift, piety, and equality—an ethic that has played a continuous role in the growth of a distinctive American civilization.

The South

In 1605, two merchant companies petitioned James I for the right to colonize Virginia for commercial purposes, hoping to find mines of gold and silver like those in Peru and Mexico. Sir Walter Raleigh, a lordly rogue and a favorite of Queen Elizabeth I, had already made two unsuccessful attempts to establish a colony on Roanoke Island off the North Carolina coast. The members of the first Raleigh colony returned to England in a year, after an appalling loss of life; the second group of settlers totally disappeared, their fate remaining a mystery to this day. When Elizabeth I died, Raleigh's security vanished; he fell into debt and languished in jail, facing execution. His dreams of conquest and wealth, however, were seized by others.

In May 1607, a group of about 100 settlers sponsored by the London Company arrived in southeastern Virginia to found Jamestown, the first English settlement in North America. The members were taken from what were, in the words of one British historian, "ne'er do wells and misfits." The contract they signed, which required seven years of labor for the company before taking up private land, failed to attract respectable farmers and artisans. Furthermore, the company insisted that colonists devote themselves to such futile and exotic pursuits as hunting for gold, glassblowing, silkworm raising, wine making, and exploring for a passage to China. Ignorance of the geography of the New World took its toll. Poorly led, the Jamestown settlers established themselves in a malarial lowland because it seemed easily defensible against Indian attack. They

failed to get a first-year crop in the ground. Each year many colonists died from disease, starvation, and Indian raids. By 1622, only one of every three settlers (2000 of 6000) sent over by the London Company was still alive.

What saved Jamestown was tobacco, a New World crop introduced to Europe by Spanish explorers from the West Indies and then in great demand. Tobacco production in the American South increased from 2500 pounds in 1616 to 500,000 pounds in 1627 and to nearly 30 million pounds per year in the late seventeenth century. Tobacco provided southern settlers with funds to pay for imported manufactures from Europe, and a rich export trade between Virginia and England ensued. As colonies prospered, new grants of land were secured by English aristocrats and merchant companies: Lord Baltimore was given territory north of Virginia; merchant groups invested in the Carolinas to the south. Tobacco flourished in the warm, wet summers and rich soils of both the *tideland*• and the inland *piedmont.*• But the labor requirements of tobacco cultivation were high: its tiny seeds (10,000 to a teaspoon) were planted in special beds; the young plants were transplanted to fields, where careful weeding and trimming were required. Finally, the leaf had to be harvested, cured, and prepared for shipment. In England, colonization was run as a commercial contest. One sales pitch that lured settlers to Virginia went: "In Virginia land free and labour scarce; in England land scarce and labour plenty." And when supplies of indentured servants and laborers fell short, black slaves were imported from Africa to work in the tobacco fields, on rice *plantations*• bordering the tidal rivers and freshwater swamps of the southern coast, and in the upland piedmont where the indigo plant was grown to provide a blue dye needed by British woolen manufacturers.

The commercial production of tobacco, rice, and indigo had important effects on the development of southern society. Prices of these commodities fluctuated widely, driving small planters off the land. Moreover, tobacco is a crop that quickly exhausts the soil, and small farmers, lacking sufficient land to move their cultivation from one field to another, were frequently broken by the competition of wealthy planters with large holdings worked by slaves. As market instability grew and competition became stiffer, the gulf widened between the landed planters on the **tidewater**• and the small farmers of the Appalachian piedmont. And because the landed planters traded directly with British merchants from their own docks and warehouses on coastal inlets, no middle class of merchants emerged in Virginia. Neither did a middle class of industrialists develop: Since quality manufactures were readily available from England, the incentive for industrialization was weak—so weak that barrel making was the largest southern craft. Even Charleston, the only city of importance in the colonial South, a community of 12,000 in 1750, had no outstanding craftsmen or artisans and few businessmen to offset the pervasive influence of the landed **gentry**.•

Slavery further distorted the social pattern. Government was by the rich, the well-born, the propertied, and the able; schooling for most was rudimentary and haphazard, but the children of the wealthy were educated by European tutors. Despite the early founding of the College of William and Mary (1693), education in the South remained confined to the upper class. More a reflection of contemporary Europe than any other colonial culture hearth, the American South developed some of the prominent characteristics of many countries of the developing world, particularly Latin America: rigid class lines, dependence on agricultural exports, a dual economy, and a dual society imposed on the environment of the New World. But to the west, on the Appalachian frontier, society was more egalitarian, and subsistence farmers soon turned their backs on the colonial South and moved west.

The Middle Colonies

The Middle Colonies—Pennsylvania, New Jersey, New York, Delaware, and Maryland—formed a geographical and social transition zone between the New England society of compact villages set in an environment of rocky soils and severe winters and the tidewater plantations and piedmont farms of the warm, humid South. Commercial crops such as sugar, tobacco, rice, and indigo were not as productive here as in Virginia and the Carolinas, but such food grains as wheat and corn grew far better in the rich soils of the mid-Atlantic coastal plain than in glaciated New England. Europeans of diverse ancestries and faiths came to the Middle Colonies. Dutch colonists came to New Netherland, or New York, as it became known in 1664; Swedes came to Delaware; Quakers, Mennonites, and Moravians settled in William Penn's community in Pennsylvania; Huguenots and Jews were attracted by the religious tolerance of Lord Baltimore's colony of Maryland; and waves of English, Germans, Scots, and Irish were drawn to the rich, open lands of the mid-Atlantic region. Both northern and southern types of economies developed. Dutch landlords (patroons) established large estates along the Hudson River, and some small tobacco estates with slaves were successful in eastern Maryland. But most settlers in the Middle Colonies became freehold agriculturalists on single-family farms dispersed across the countryside—a departure from the European pattern of clustered village settlement. Education in the log-cabin schoolhouses extended basic reading, writing, and arithmetic to the public. Towns became **central places**• serving agricultural hinterlands; Philadelphia and New York, with 4000 people each in 1690, emerged as the largest urban centers. Differences in faiths and backgrounds bred tolerance; there was neither the religious and social coherence necessary for a close-knit town life modeled on New England nor the large-scale agricultural base for a southern-style plantation elite. More balanced and diverse in both economy and society, the Middle Colonies produced self-educated frontiersmen who pioneered the wilderness, religious liberty and democracy in the modern American sense, and the roots of commerce and trade that would expand dramatically as the colonial period ended in independence in 1776.

The Expansion of the Colonial Economy
[FIGURE 2]

In the seventeenth century, the American economy, like other aspects of colonial life, was relatively crude and underdeveloped. Cities such as Boston, New York, and Philadelphia were small but active seaports. Population was sparse and labor continually in short supply; 95 percent of the colonists were farmers involved in clearing forests and fields, combating hostile Indians, and bringing the land into productivity. In the eighteenth century, however, these tasks were largely accomplished east of the Appalachians, and populations in the culture hearths began to increase rapidly.

Between 1700 and 1750, the population of the Atlantic coast rose from 250,000 to 1.6 million. In 1750, New England had a population of 500,000; the South, around 700,000; the Middle Colonies, the fastest growing, had 400,000 people. Virginia, with 231,000 people, was the largest colony; Georgia, with less than 5000, the smallest. Eastern Massachusetts, Pennsylvania, and Connecticut were among the most densely settled regions; Rhode Island, New Hampshire, and Delaware were the least populous. Even though most Americans still lived on the coast, settlement was beginning to push west beyond the Appalachian Mountains, through the Cumberland Gap into Tennessee and Kentucky, up the Susquehanna River onto the Allegheny Plateau, and along the Hudson and Mohawk valleys into the Lower Great Lakes Plain. Since most of the increase in population in the colonies resulted from very high American birth rates, the coastal areas of New England, the Middle Colonies, and the South remained predominantly English in population and culture. But other nationalities, drawn by the reported attractions of the New World and set upon by hardship in Europe, began to emigrate, settle, and transform the ethnic map of North America.

Of all coastal regions, the tightly woven social fabric of New England was the most hostile to outsiders; incoming German, Scottish, and Irish immigrants were frequently deflected southward to other colonies. Maine, Vermont, and New Hampshire were still mostly wilderness in the generation before the American Revolution. In New York and New Jersey, the cultural imprint of European Lowlanders was strong, although the Dutch formed less than a tenth of the colony's population. German immigrants had bypassed Dutch landholdings in the Hudson River valley and occupied the northern frontier of settlement in the Mohawk River valley. The most distinctive regional concentration of German immigrants, however, was in Pennsylvania, where 100,000 people, a third the colony's rural population, were popularly called the Pennsylvania Dutch (from *deutsch*, meaning "German"). Moving inland, German settlers also occupied the rich farmlands of the Lehigh, Susquehanna, and Cumberland valleys and swung southward into the Shenandoah Valley, a 600-mile long band of German settlement in the shadow of the Appalachians. As other German colonists settled in South Carolina, the English began to fear they would be culturally engulfed, since more than 5000 Germans were arriving at American ports each year. Highland Scots settled central Georgia, but most immigrants from Britain in the mid-1700s were Scotch-Irish (from Northern Ireland) and Irish settlers. Flinty and aggressive solitary types poorly adjusted to indentured labor or village life, these new arrivals populated the back country of the Appalachian frontier and gained fame as hunters, trappers, and Indian fighters. After the War of 1812, they became the landed politicians of Tennessee and Kentucky. In the South, nearly 300,000 slaves formed the backbone of plantation agriculture; in South Carolina, blacks outnumbered whites three to one. On the eve of the American Revolution, only 60 percent of the colonial population was English; 14 percent was Scottish or Scotch-Irish, and 9 percent was German. As American author Thomas Paine observed in *Common Sense*, "Europe, and not England, is the parent country of America." He forgot Africa. In 1776, 2.7 million people inhabited coastal America—a fifth of them African, a smaller number Indian, and the remainder whites. They were people with diverse languages and backgrounds, thinly scattered over 200,000 square miles of organized territory.

With a growing population and an expanding agricultural economy, colonial America emerged as an important trading nation in the eighteenth century. Its ports had become active centers of a new trans-Atlantic commerce. By 1775, Philadelphia was the second largest city in the English-speaking world, with a population of 40,000. New York contained

over 20,000 people; Boston, 17,000; and Charleston, 16,000. Of the twenty largest cities in the colonies, nineteen were ports. Only Lancaster, Pennsylvania, in the midst of the prosperous countryside of the Middle Colonies, could support an urban population of 6000 without an export-oriented trade. Each city specialized to some degree, reflecting both the productivity of preindustrial *hinterlands* and the environmental diversity of the Atlantic seaboard.

In New England, where about a quarter of the population depended on nonagricultural pursuits such as fishing, lumbering, and commerce, farms produced little to export; the region imported a considerable part of its grain from the Middle Colonies. But the sea proved a profitable alternative for New Englanders. The fish catch from the waters off the coast of Newfoundland and the Grand Banks was far superior to that from the North Sea. In the 1770s, 10,000 men on 665 ships were bringing cod to New England ports, and 72,000 tons of fish were exported to southern Europe and the West Indies. On Nantucket, whaling became a major activity. Some 150 ships reaped 30,000 barrels of whale oil each year, sustaining over a dozen candle-making factories in nearby Rhode Island.

Related New England industries were based on forest products—shipbuilding, lumber, and naval stores. Shipyards dotted the coast from Maine to Philadelphia, and by the outbreak of the Revolutionary War, over a third of Britain's ships were American made. Tapping the interior forests along the entire coast, the colonies exported 42 million board feet of lumber, 15,000 tons of timber, and 20 million barrel staves to Europe, which was rapidly becoming deforested as industrialization progressed. Masts, then the most precious and costly part of any vessel because they came from trees over 2 feet in diameter, were exported for ships of the royal navy at the rate of 3000 tons in 1770. Agents of the king, exercising an ancient royal prerogative, placed the king's mark—a broad arrow—on large trees all along the Atlantic coast and forbade colonists to use them. Naval stores were additional exports, as was iron produced from a growing number of forges from Pennsylvania to Massachusetts. According to one estimate, America in the 1770s produced one-seventh of the world's iron.

The Middle Colonies produced a large exportable surplus of wheat and flour. Some 750,000 bushels of wheat, 20,000 tons of bread and flour, and lesser

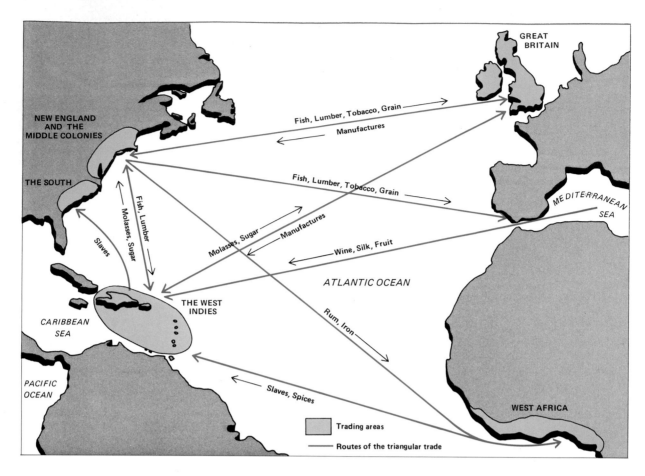

Figure 2. Colonial Trading Patterns. Colonial America based its prosperity on trade carried out across the North Atlantic. The most famous of the trade triangles involved the shipment of distilled rum and iron from ports in New England and the Middle Colonies to West Africa, where they were exchanged for African slaves, who in turn were brought to the Caribbean and the American South for sale. In the New World, slaves were exchanged for the molasses and sugar distilled into rum, so that the cycle was profitable in three locations and with three commodities. Ships operating out of Boston, New York, and Philadelphia participated in the slave trade; and Newport, Rhode Island, supported two dozen distilleries. *After:* Max Savelle, *A History of Colonial America,* 3rd ed. New York: Dryden Press, 1973, p. 526, map 18. Copyright © 1973 by The Dryden Press. Used by permission of Holt, Rinehart and Winston. John F. Kolars and John D. Nystuen, *Geography.* New York: McGraw-Hill, 1974, p. 215, Fig. 12–10. Copyright © 1974 by McGraw-Hill, Inc. Used by permission of McGraw-Hill Book Company.

amounts of flaxseed, corn, beef, and pork were exported from New York, Philadelphia, and Baltimore to Europe in 1770. Farther south, in Maryland and Virginia, tobacco was the principal export product; in the Carolinas and Georgia, rice and indigo sustained plantation society. Trade, particularly with England, tripled between 1750 and 1775, and although the value of colonial exports never kept up with the price of imported manufactures from Europe, the exports began to play a key role in some European economies. Although some statesmen in England believed that one sugar-producing island in the West Indies would be worth more than all New England, and others even suggested trading Canada for the French Caribbean island of Guadeloupe, it was clear by the time of the American Revolution that the New World had a rich and diverse resource base.

Commercial relationships between England and America were clearly defined: the colonies were to produce staple goods in return for manufactures from Europe. The board of trade, which regulated colonial commerce, actively discouraged "the making of any manufactures [in America] made in England, it being against the advantage of England." So the export of colonial hats was forbidden, as was the construction of rolling mills. Taxes were levied on imports, and all European goods sold to the colonies had to be reexported through Britain. Although these restrictions would certainly have hampered a more complex American economy, complementary needs in Britain and America kept conflict to a minimum, and relations were generally harmonious. Besides, English administrators in the New World were notoriously incompetent and in many

The capture of a fort, 1759, from an old woodcut. With their victory in the French and Indian War, the British emerged as the primary political power in the New World. *Photo:* New York Public Library Picture Collection.

cases corrupt, so that the growing merchant and business classes in the colonies could generally function as they wished.

This situation changed, however, after the successful defeat of the outnumbered French by British and colonial troops in the French and Indian War (1758–1763). Britain had gained half a continent, although the costs were sufficiently high to double Britain's national debt. From the British point of view, the prosperity of the colonies was the result of Britian's generosity—mild laws, substantial investments, and an expensive war to eliminate the French threat to the western frontier. It seemed only right that the colonies should pay part of this financial burden, and in 1763, the year the war ended, the British enacted a series of tax measures toward this purpose. The Americans viewed the war against the French as a means of enlarging British territory in North America (when European antagonisms were falsely extended to the New World ground), not as a simple matter of protection. Why, therefore, should Americans pay Britain's debt? As resistance to taxation spread, British leaders increasingly came to view the colonists as ungrateful subjects, a quarrelsome people who, left to their own devices, would engage in civil war from one end of the continent to the other. When the Stamp Act imposed taxes on every legal and business document and every piece of printed matter (including playing cards) in 1765, the colonists reacted violently and with surprising unanimity. Lawyers, merchants, newspaper editors, and tavern keepers in every colony were antagonized, and their combined protest swayed public opinion. In the end, little money was collected, and stamp collectors were chased across colonial boundaries and hounded until they re-

signed. The Stamp Act was ultimately repealed, but British sovereignty in the New World had been openly questioned.

Tensions between crown and colony intensified. In Virginia, Patrick Henry believed that Britain had no right to tax the colonies at all, and announced, "If this be treason, then make the most of it." In *Common Sense,* Thomas Paine challenged loyalists to "show a single advantage that this continent can reap by being connected with Great Britain." In Massachusetts, tons of tea were dumped in Boston Harbor, and battle was joined at Lexington and Concord. In England, George III opted for conflict rather than conciliation, stating, "We must either master them or totally leave them to themselves." The war lost, loyalists fled north to Canada and gave root to the proud independence Canadians maintain with respect to the United States today. Britain had underestimated the strength of the competitive, individualistic living that characterized its New World descendants and never understood the degree to which a wide ocean separated the two peoples. As the British geographer James Watson has noted: "Few places or times offered more freedom than North America, and few peoples carried freedom so far." This was as true after independence as before, when the new American nation turned its back on Europe and looked to its uncharted West.

FORGING A NATION

After independence, Americans turned to the West as an outlet for growth and development. No longer hemmed in by the Appalachians and no longer pinned to the sea as a coastal extension of European administration, settlers swept into the interior plains of North America. As a society, Americans had a bent toward migration and movement, always attracted by greener pastures, better soils, and greater opportunity. As one saying put it: "If hell lay to the west, Americans would cross heaven to reach it." The pace of westward expansion was rapid, and in three generations the migration was over. Individuals, families, and small groups, largely on their own initiative, built homes in the wilderness, harnessed the resources of a continent, forged the territorial outlines of modern America, and created a myth and an ideal of freedom, individualism, and self-sufficiency that remains deeply rooted in modern American culture.

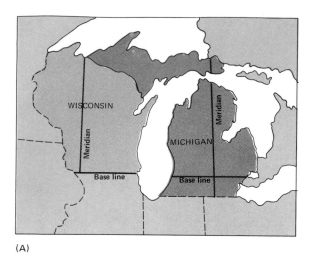

(A)

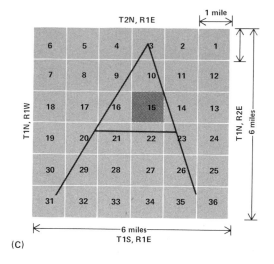

(C)

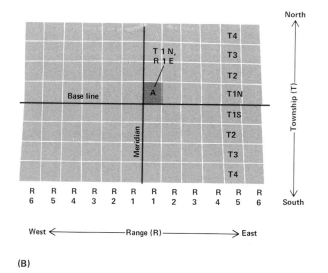

(B)

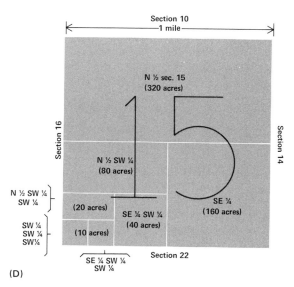

(D)

Figure 3. Township and Range. The organization of western lands into orderly civil divisions began with the survey of the Old Northwest—the territory lying north and west of the Ohio River—authorized by Congress in 1785. Part (a) shows Michigan and Wisconsin organized by two surveyor's reference lines: an east-west base line, or "geographer's line," corresponding to one degree of latitude; and meridians, lines of longitude running north-south. Part (b) enlarges the perspective to show the organization of the land into townships and ranges. The location of individual units is identified by townships, counted off in sets of four north and south of the base line, and by ranges counted in sets of six east or west of the meridian. A township is thus identified by its north-south and east-west location in relation to a base line and a meridian. Here, township A is labeled T1N, R1E—in the first set north of the base line (Township 1 North) and in the first set east of the meridian (Range 1 East). In part (c), each township, 6 miles square, is divided into 36 sections; in part (d), each section, 1 mile square, can be subdivided into many units. *Adapted from:* Arthur N. Strahler, *Introduction to Physical Geography*, 3rd ed. New York: Wiley, 1973, p. 447, Figs. AII.17, AII.18, AII.19, AII.20. Copyright © 1973 by John Wiley and Sons. Used by permission of John Wiley and Sons, Inc.

Pioneering became a common experience. Pioneers crossed plains described as so large they were bounded only by the Day of Judgment. They crossed the Rocky Mountains, which one congressman advocated as the western border of the United States because it stood like "a Chinese Wall," an impregnable barrier. Everywhere the frontier outpaced the lawmakers, and in the resulting chaos, vast herds of buffalo were exterminated, Indians were decimated or relegated to reservations, and forests were leveled. Open land, considered an American birthright, was added in great chunks—the Louisiana Territory, Texas, California, and New Mexico—any one of them as large as a substantial European nation. At the end of forty years, the American West had accumulated a population as large as the thirteen British colonies of the eastern seaboard had achieved in a century. The new nation, though yet barely formed, doubled and tripled in size until it stretched from ocean to ocean.

The Moving Frontier
[FIGURE 3]

At the close of the Revolution, few Americans knew what lay beyond the Allegheny Mountains, but trappers, small groups of pioneers, and land speculators (among them George Washington, who had surveyed land in western Pennsylvania) were aware of the rich potential of the western lands. Soon Scotch-Irish and German settlers began to penetrate the region, creating a landscape of small farms cut out of towering forests and small towns spaced along primitive roads and trails. A new geography began to take shape. Immigrants, escaping the New World feudalism of the plantation South and the religious rigidities of New England, spread into Ohio, Kentucky, and Tennessee to carve out individual farmsteads. The *diffusion*• was sporadic and irregular; settlers generally followed rivers in search of fertile land, bypassing more rugged terrain that was occupied much later. Indian resistance was fierce. Of the 256 men who in 1780 drew up the first state government of Tennessee, for example, just a dozen were alive in 1790 and only one had died of natural causes. But settlers continued to come, pouring through gaps in the Appalachian Mountains to plant corn patches in the forest, living in isolated log-cabin homesteads in a wilderness so unending and a forest so dense that people speculated at the time that a squirrel might travel for thousands of miles from tree to tree without ever touching the ground.

In this frontier environment, settlers developed a new sense of social and economic independence. Indeed, historian Frederick Jackson Turner saw the westward advance of the frontier as a movement away from the influence of Europe and toward a steady growth of American character. In his view, the frontier bred toughness, resourcefulness, individualism, and resilience—traits Turner felt were the hallmark of American civilization. He viewed the closing of the frontier in 1893 as holding dangerous implications for American society, though in fact more free land was *homesteaded*• after 1900 than before. In any case, frontier independence bred conflict between the settled areas of the East and the unfolding West. In the Carolinas, differences between the back-country settlers on the piedmont and the tidewater gentry of the coast nearly led to civil war. In Pennsylvania, President Washington's tax on frontier rye whisky led to the Whisky Rebellion in 1794—an uprising whose defeat required a force of 12,000 soldiers, a larger army than Washington had ever commanded during the Revolutionary War. Similar problems existed between coastal and upstate New York, Boston and western Massachusetts, the plantation South and the small farms of the piedmont. However much Turner admired the frontiersmen, many leaders of American society in growing urban centers such as Boston, New York, Baltimore, Philadelphia, and Charleston considered

them unruly, uneducated people, prone to violence and impatient of law, and were delighted to see them leave the well-ordered coastal societies.

As western lands increasingly proved too valuable to be left to random pioneer settlement, the area between the Appalachians and the Mississippi River was declared public land in 1802. A federal plan was initiated to regularize settlement. In the South, the warrant system was in use: individuals took out warrants, or rights, to new land and traveled into the interior settling wherever they wished. New England, however, followed a more organized system of land development with tier after tier of townships planned to regulate the western advance. The growing dispute between North and South over the way the West should be organized was mirrored in the settlement forms created by the streams of migration into the trans-Appalachian interior. Ultimately, the patterns of the North prevailed; all public lands were divided into townships 6 miles square, which in turn were subdivided into thirty-six sections of 640 acres each. Every second township was sold as a unit to groups of settlers in a variation of the community tradition of New England. The others were auctioned off by single sections, a compromise to the southern system of individual pioneers. In this way, a geometrical grid was imposed on the new lands east of the Mississippi; regardless of terrain, this pattern overlaid much of Ohio, Indiana, Kentucky, and Tennessee. After the Louisiana Purchase in 1803, public lands were extended to the Rocky Mountains. With the acquisition of Oregon and California, the artificial geometry of the *township and range*• system was impressed on the American landscape from the Appalachians to the Pacific coast.

By 1820, the population of the United States was 9.6 million, triple that of 1790; during those thirty years, the country had doubled in area to nearly 1.8 million square miles. Almost all population growth was due to natural increase—only 250,000 new immigrants arrived at Atlantic ports during that period. In 1790, some 100,000 white settlers were living beyond the Appalachians; by 1820, 2.2 million had been drawn by the lure of nearly free land. By 1840 the population of the United States had again nearly doubled to 17.1 million, and hordes of settlers continued to roll westward. Between 1830 and 1840, the population of Arkansas tripled, and Missouri attracted 200,000 new immigrants. In the 1840s,

DANIEL BOONE'S PARADISE: TWO MONTHS ALONE

A recurrent theme in the American personality is the concept of self-discovery in the wilderness—alone by oneself, in touch with the spirit of nature. The legend of Daniel Boone (1734–1820) obscures his occupation as a North Carolina farmer forever in search of "elbow room." This passage, adapted in 1793 from his earlier autobiography, depicts Boone as a man initially frightened and then calmed by his first experience alone in the wilderness:

On the first day of May, 1770, my brother returned home to the settlement by himself, for a new recruit of horses and ammunition, leaving me by myself, without bread, salt, or sugar, without company of my fellow creatures, or even a horse or dog. . . . A thousand dreadful apprehensions presented themselves to my view, and had undoubtedly disposed me to melancholy, if further indulged.

One day I undertook a tour through the country, and the diversity and beauties of nature I met with in this charming season, expelled every gloomy and vexatious thought. Just at the close of day the gentle gales retired, and left the place to the disposal of a profound calm. . . . I had gained the summit of a commanding ridge, and, looking round with astonishing delight, beheld the ample plains, the beauteous tracts below. On the other hand, I surveyed the famous river Ohio that rolled in silent dignity, marking the western boundary of Kentucky with inconceivable grandeur. At a vast distance I beheld the mountains lift their venerable brows, and penetrate the clouds. All things were still. I kindled a fire near a fountain of sweet water, and feasted on the loin of buck, which a few hours before I had killed. . . .

Thus I was surrounded with plenty in the midst of want. I was happy in the midst of dangers and inconveniences. In such a diversity it was impossible I should be disposed to melancholy. No populous city, with all the varieties of commerce and stately structures, could afford so much pleasure to my mind, as the beauties of nature I found here. . . .

Shortly after, we left this place . . . and proceeded to Cumberland river, reconnoitring that part of the country until March, 1771, and giving names to the different waters.

Soon after, I returned to my family (in North Carolina) with a determination to bring them as soon as possible to live in Kentucky, which I esteemed a second paradise, at the risk of my life and fortune.

Source: Daniel Boone, *The Adventures of Colonel Daniel Boone, Containing a Narrative of the Wars of Kentucky.*

Iowa's population quadrupled to 192,000; Wisconsin registered 300,000 settlers; 10,000 Americans had trekked to Mexican Texas; and a few had filtered westward as far as Spanish California and the Oregon country. An Irish journalist, John L. O'Sullivan, captured the mood of the new nation when he referred to America's "manifest destiny to overspread the continent." It was an idea of powerful geographical logic that subdued those who believed the Great Plains west of the Mississippi were uninhabitable desert and the Far West too remote to be effectively governed.

Stage by stage, westward expansion enveloped the continent; statehood was accorded to Texas in 1845, Iowa in 1846, and California in 1850. In 1853, the Gadsden Purchase of the Gila River country of southern Arizona and New Mexico rounded out the frontiers of the continental United States. In Canada, the union of the provinces of New Brunswick and Nova Scotia with Quebec and Ontario in 1867 marked the beginnings of nationhood and provided a method for assimilating the expanding western provinces. Whereas the Spanish New World became fragmented into a host of medium- to small-sized countries, the United States and Canada governed regions continental in scope, a principal geographical key to the markedly different evolutions of North and South America in the modern period.

A Revolution in Transport
[FIGURE 4]

The enormous land acquisitions and westward expansion of the United States and Canada posed difficult questions of communications and transport. The high demand for food and cotton fiber in urban America, Europe, and the Far East sustained continual westward expansion to open up new lands for agriculture. But in 1800, only farmers located near seaport cities or on navigable streams could market their grain, cotton, tobacco, or timber. Overland transport was so prohibitively expensive that the cost of moving goods 30 miles over roads in New England was roughly equal to prices paid for shipping goods 3000 miles across the Atlantic from Europe to America. In Philadelphia coal from Liverpool, England, sold for less than coal from Richmond, Virginia. The cost of transporting wheat from Buffalo to New York was three times the Buffalo market price; for corn, the price rose six times; for oats, twelve. Small wonder that pioneers became subsistence farmers, that Americans remained pinned to the Atlantic coast for nearly two centuries, and that Pennsylvania farmers rebelled when their one movable product, corn liquor, came under taxation. Even along the eastern seaboard, roads were inadequate. Indeed, during the Revolutionary War, news of the signing of the Declaration of Independence took twenty-nine days to reach Charleston from Philadelphia.

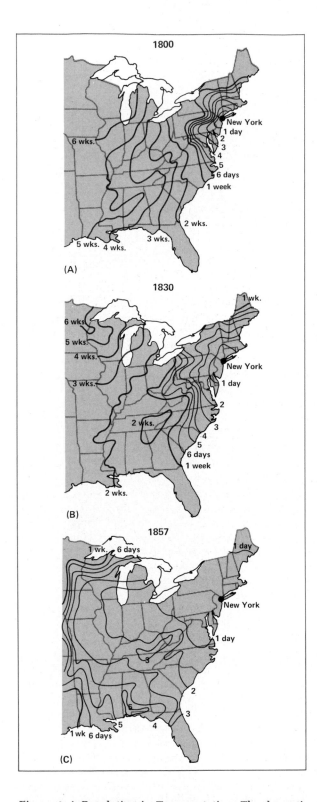

Figure 4. A Revolution in Transportation. The dramatic increase in geographical accessibility of the North American interior in the first half of the nineteenth century, stimulated by new forms of transport (turnpikes, canals, railroads), is illustrated by overland travel times in 1800, 1830, and 1857. *After:* Charles O. Paullin, *Atlas of the Historical Geography of the United States.* Carnegie Institution of Washington, D.C. and New York Geographical Society. Redrawn by permission.

Robert Fulton's steamboat, the *North River* or *Clermont,* 1807, from a sketch published in Woodcroft's *Origin and Progress of Steam Navigation,* 1850. *Photo:* New York Public Library Picture Collection.

In the first half of the nineteenth century, however, efforts were made to stimulate commerce by improving communication. Private stock companies as well as state and provincial governments built graded and paved turnpikes to link the cities of the coast with the developing interior. The most ambitious of these was the National Road, or as some called it, the Cumberland Road, a federal project that ran from Cumberland, Maryland, west to Vandalia, Illinois. The principal economic effect of the turnpikes was to reduce the cost of short hauls, but given the long distances involved, roads could not effectively connect the agricultural lands of the interior with eastern markets.

More important was the steamboat, developed and tested by Robert Fulton in 1807, which enabled goods to be transported thousands of miles—even upstream—along inland waterways. In 1820, 60 steamboats were plying the Mississippi and its tributaries; by 1860, there were more than 1000. Goods moved five times faster on steamboats than in wagons or on keelboats. Downstream moving costs were cut by a factor of four; upstream costs, by ten or even twenty. The effective range of the **market economy** was vastly extended by steamboats, opening the central part of the United States and to a lesser extent Canada to commercial agriculture and industry.

Canals were built to facilitate the movement of goods. The first, opened in 1825, was the Erie Canal, a 364 mile-long ditch linking Albany on the Hudson River with Buffalo on Lake Erie. Thomas Jefferson had labeled the project "a little short of madness," but soon grain and other foods were flowing eastward in exchange for manufactures from

The steamboat and the canal improved internal communications, but it was the railroad that enabled Americans to conquer the continental dimensions of the United States and bind its sections into an independent national economy. *Photo:* **New York Public Library Picture Collection.**

New York City. People could now travel from New York to Detroit for less than $10. A water road to the west had been opened. The volume of traffic was so heavy that tolls paid the entire cost of construction in only nine years. Pennsylvania built a competing canal system linking Philadelphia with Pittsburgh. In the Middle West, canals joined the Ohio and Mississippi river systems with the Great Lakes. Between 1816 and 1840, 3326 miles of canals were constructed in the United States.

The steam railroad, however, provided the most successful means of conquering the continental dimensions of the United States and binding the North, South, and West into an independent national economy. In the 1830s, a few minor railroad lines were built outward from Boston, Charleston, and Baltimore—coastal cities prevented by terrain from developing inland water connections. By 1840, the United States had 3300 miles of rail in operation, compared with Europe's 1800. Over the next two decades, the railroad network of the eastern part of the country grew at a geometrical rate: 8900 miles in 1850; more than 30,000 miles in 1860. All the major market cities of the North were linked by rail, and trunk lines spanned the Appalachians to connect the East and the West. Chicago became the rail hub of the center of the continent. Over 20 million acres of public land administered by both federal and state governments were given to private rail construction. According to American writer Henry David Thoreau, railroads became an "institution [that] regulates the whole country." Even he was caught up by the splendor and force of the steam locomotive, noting at Walden: "When I hear the iron horse make the hills echo . . . it seems as if the earth had got a race now worthy to inhabit it."

The magnitude of this effort transformed the structure of the American economy. Goods that took more than fifty days to travel from Cincinnati to New York in 1817 could be hauled by rail in six days in 1860. Granted access to world markets by these gleaming lines of iron, farmers in the fertile prairies of the upper Mississippi Valley and cotton planters in the interior South expanded production enormously. America became the world's single greatest source of food, as the railroad system brought American farmers next door to Europe. In the words of historian Allan Nevins, the growth of the railroads in America forced "the yeoman farmer of Yorkshire and the *junker* of Prussia to the wall. American bread was baked for the table of the Berlin workman, American cheese was eaten by the French artisan, and American bacon used for the breakfast of the British clerk." Back home, America became a nation of movers endlessly and anxiously catching trains whose schedules were, their boosters claimed, "as inexorable as fate."

THE RISE OF SECTIONAL ECONOMIES

At midcentury, the United States was growing and changing rapidly. A national economy had arisen, piecing together the regionality of American production. In a nation previously composed of relatively independent and isolated states, improvements in transport—turnpikes, canals, railroads—had bound the sections together and encouraged regional economic specializations that fostered spectacular increases in commercial agricultural production. Areas beyond and on the frontier of settlement were brought into this national orbit on the basis of what they could produce and contribute to the national economy.

Three reasonably distinct economic regions began to emerge: the Industrial North, the Agricultural South, and the variegated West. In the North, the Industrial Revolution traversed the Atlantic, and a landscape of mills and factories, growing populations, and expanding urban centers was re-created in America. In the South, cotton replaced tobacco as the principal agricultural commodity, and the slave population swelled to fill the labor demands of growing numbers of plantations; slavery and cotton became big business. The West was perhaps most keenly affected by evolving transport networks. In an area as far distant from large urban markets as the Rockies, commercial agriculture, mining, and livestock herding supplanted subsistence farming. Clashes between regional economic interests reinforced differences in culture and society. Human gulfs separated New England from the South, and both these culture hearths found composite re-creations of their strengths and weaknesses in the several culture regions of the frontier West. Ultimately, these regional tensions led to the Civil War, a bloody five-year struggle that was joined over the issue of slavery, and whose wounds remain tender even to the present.

The Industrial North

The spread of commercial agriculture in the West and the growing accessibility of both southern and western markets proved strong impetus to the development of industry in the northern United States. As early as 1850 the United States led the world in manufactures that required the use of precision tools—clocks, rifles, sewing machines, pianos, and locks, for example—and 65 percent of all industrial goods in the United States were produced in the northeastern states. The reasons for this rapid growth were several. First, Americans in the North were remarkably receptive to technological change; Yankee ingenuity was not an idle eastern boast. Craft arts were strong and highly refined. A French traveler, Michel Chevalier, described New Englanders in 1839 as "laborious ants; industrious, . . . sober, frugal." Other Europeans noticed the high level of education among working men in the North, their liking for invention, and their desire to improve on traditional procedures—a strong contrast to contemporary European laborers. Second, the opening of the western prairies made grain agriculture in New England progressively less profitable. According to local humor, soils in New England's glaciated valleys were so stony that the noses of sheep sharpened as they grazed between the rocks. Given this natural endowment, only specialized dairy and market garden agriculture catering to the needs of local urban centers could prosper in New England. Some farmers left the land and traveled west; others turned to factory work. Finally, because their cities had been **entrepôts**° of trans-Atlantic trade for more than a century, New Englanders had considerable expertise in commerce. This initial advantage accelerated when the natural resources of the West were harnessed and cotton

production expanded in the South. The cities of the eastern seaboard sprouted agricultural processing industries: flour mills, textile factories, leather works, and distilleries. Of the ten leading American industries in 1850, eight were based on agricultural resources. Most of the goods that found their way to domestic and world markets, although produced far inland, were processed in the cities of the Northeast.

As in Britain, the textile industry in America was the first to mechanize. Samuel Slater, formerly a textile worker in England, opened a mill in 1790 in Pawtucket, Rhode Island, from plans he reproduced from memory; the factory had seventy-two spindles and employed nine children, who worked for wages of 12 to 25 cents a day. Soon cotton and woolen mills sprang up throughout southern New England, particularly in cities such as Providence, Fall River, and Hartford on the **fall line.**° The first large-scale textile mills, however, were constructed at Waltham and Lowell, where proud young women from New England farms ("Lowell girls") were housed in dormitories and boardinghouses in the charge of women of the highest respectability, to provide a cheap, reliable labor force. In 1833, Lowell was described as "a pile of huge factories, each five, six, or seven stories high, capped with a little white belfry." These were some of the first factories in the world to combine all textile operations under one roof. They led one awed visitor to describe them as "a Yankee phenomenon . . . that took a bale of cotton in at one end and gave out yards of cloth at the other, after goodness knew what digestive process." Keenly aware of technological inventions in Europe, the cotton textile industry grew rapidly, and the factory system was applied to other industries such as shoe manufacturing in southern New England and woolen production in the Middle Atlantic states. Meanwhile, iron production was concentrating in Pennsylvania, endowed with rich resources of iron, coal, and wood. By 1860, Pennsylvania produced half of the **pig iron**° in the United States. As the use of steam power grew in industry, Pennsylvania coal fueled the further growth of New England factories. During the 1850s, American output of cotton textiles increased 77 percent; of woolens, 42 percent; of shoes, 70 percent; of carpets, 45 percent; of pig iron, 54 percent; and of railroad iron, 100 percent. In the same decade, New England

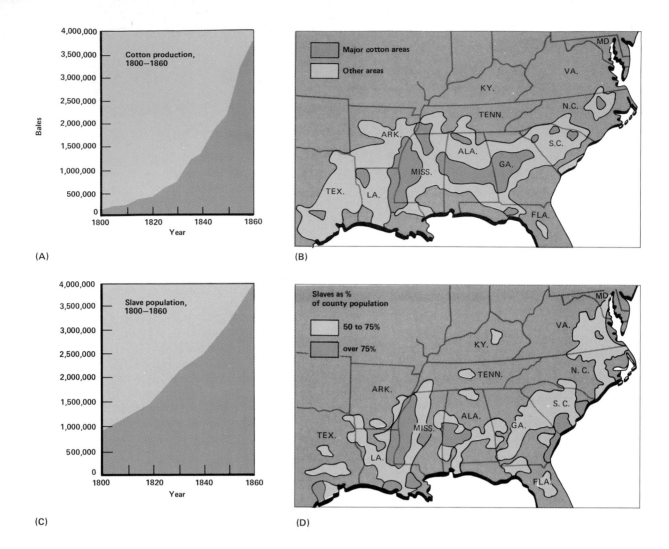

(A)

(B)

(C)

(D)

Figure 5. Cotton and Slaves, 1800–1860. By 1860, the distribution of slaves in the American South was closely correlated with major areas of cotton production. Exceptions to this rule were coastal Texas, where sugar was the principal plantation crop; the Mississippi Delta, where sugar and rice were grown; and the coastal fringe of South Carolina and Georgia, also major rice-producing areas. *After:* (a), (c) John A. Garraty, *The American Nation: A History of the United States to 1877.* New York: Harper & Row, 1971, p. 267. Redrawn by permission of the publisher. (b), (d) Richard Hofstadter, William Miller, and Daniel Aaron, *The United States: The History of a Republic,* Englewood Cliffs, N.J.: Prentice-Hall, 1967, p. 349.

manufactures grew 62 percent in value, compared with 7 percent in the Middle Atlantic region and 10 percent in the West. An industrial ***heartland***° was taking shape in the northeastern United States. The pull of industrialization was so intense that to Tocqueville's observant eye, "the pursuit of industrial callings" could be identified as the psychic drive that motivated the new American nation and the new breed of people who formed it.

The Agricultural South
[FIGURE 5]

In the South, large-scale agriculture, not industry, was the commercial mainspring of the region. Southern agriculturalists concentrated very early on the production of a few cash crops for export. The cultivation of tobacco, rice, sugar, and cotton fixed the plantation system and slavery with fateful certainty over large areas extending from Maryland to Georgia. But by the turn of the nineteenth century, this agricultural economy was in serious decline. More than half the population of Virginia, Maryland, and North Carolina depended directly or indirectly on tobacco cultivation, and acres of once rich and fertile land were being ruined by this soil-exhausting crop. Plantations were being abandoned daily. Owners retired with their slaves inland to the Appalachian piedmont and beyond to carve out new estates from virgin soil. Because of this westward drift, more tobacco was grown west than east of the Appalachians during the 1840s. Gullied, brush-strewn, and exhausted fields came to line the long-cultivated banks of the Atlantic coastal rivers and the tidewater.

As the plantation economy of the South languished, the price of slaves fell, and substantial numbers of black people were freed. Tobacco growing, which had sustained the early expansion of the southern economy, became, as Thomas Jefferson had said earlier, "a culture productive of infinite wretchedness." Elsewhere in the South, except for enclaves of wealth on the rice plantations of the Carolina lowlands and the sugar estates of the Mississippi Delta, abandoned farmsteads on ravaged lands marked the passage of farm families who never stayed long enough in one spot to learn to use their land well.

What revived this faltering southern agricultural economy was a simple machine. The cotton gin was invented by Eli Whitney, a young schoolteacher fresh from Yale, while on a visit to a plantation in Savannah, Georgia, in 1793; the problem of separating the thorny seeds of short-staple cotton from the precious lint was solved. Demand for raw cotton in the mills of New England and industrialized Europe was then high, and southern planters were eager to experiment with the crop. In the 1790s, long-staple "sea-island" cotton was grown on the warm, wet coastal lowlands and offshore islands of Georgia and South Carolina. Highly susceptible to frost, however, this long-staple cotton could be cultivated only on the tropical perimeter of the American South. Elsewhere, short-staple "upland" cotton was grown, but removing the seeds from short-staple cotton by hand was so laborious that it took an able-bodied man a full day to de-seed a single pound.

In ten days, Whitney—who had never before seen a cotton field—constructed a simple hand-driven machine that made it possible to clean fifty times as much cotton in a given period of time. Whitney later attributed his notion of plucking the cotton from its seeds to watching a cat claw at a chicken; it kept missing the bird but coming away with the feathers. Large mule- and water-driven gins spread widely among the plantations; the costs of constructing these "absurdly simple contrivances" were modest. Development of the cotton gin allowed cotton to be grown profitably wherever rainfall was more than 24 inches a year and the frost-free growing season longer than 200 days—in other words, throughout the entire South. Cotton cultivation spread inland throughout Georgia and the Carolinas, engulfed the rich black soils of central Alabama and northern Mississippi, and extended westward through Louisiana into Texas, where unreliable rainfall formed a natural limit. The forests of these regions, some of the densest in the nation, were systematically felled. Cotton production soared from 300 bales (each weighing about 450 pounds) in 1790 to 100,000 bales a decade later; 400,000 bales were produced each year in the 1820s. And nearly

4 million bales a year were produced on the eve of the Civil War.

By the 1850s, cotton was king; it was the most prosperous and dynamic element in the emerging export-oriented national economy of the United States. The *arable*• South had bloomed into a 1000-mile-wide landscape of cotton, 1 million square miles of raw wealth that produced three-quarters of the world's cotton and two-thirds of the export value of the United States. Vessels from Europe and New England landed at ports from Charleston to New Orleans to purchase bales of cotton for the mills of the industrial world, trading cheap cloth, diverse manufactured goods, and the luxury products of the age in exchange. This new wealth sustained the graceful mansions and showplace plantations of a rich planter class that ever since has remained a model and an ideal of a regional golden age. In fact, a good deal of the South's cotton was produced on ramshackle farms Mark Twain called "one-horse cotton plantations."

To the west, the steamboats that plied the Mississippi hauled cargoes of raw sugar northward to refineries at Saint Louis and Cincinnati, buying cheap corn, hogs, and vegetables for the South, whose cotton lands were too valuable to be planted in any other crop. In the Mississippi Valley and along the rivers flowing into the coastal plain of the Gulf of Mexico, cheap food from the Central Plains made it possible for planters to keep their best land in continuous cotton cultivation. In less accessible areas, such as mountainous Virginia, North Carolina, and parts of South Carolina, however, more land was devoted to wheat, corn, and livestock raising in order to feed local populations. The pressure on the South was relentless: no matter how much cotton was produced, prices remained high, profits substantial, and the demand of northern mills insatiable. Something like the earlier triangular trade of the Atlantic emerged, drawing the sectional economies of the United States closer together: southern cotton flowed northward; northern manufactures traveled south and west; and western food went north and south. Embedded in and basic to the structure of this triangular national economic exchange was the labor of legions of slaves in the South.

The expansion of cotton cultivation, a crop ideally suited to large-scale plantations worked by gangs of unskilled laborers, rapidly led to a revival of slavery. Immediately after the Revolutionary War, slavery had become a declining, stagnant institution. In 1808, a federal law forbade the import of slaves, and numerous states outlawed their interstate transport. Between 1790 and 1810, the number of freed slaves in the United States rose from 8 to 13 percent of the black population. The excess of slaves prompted colonization schemes to return blacks to Africa on land purchased in modern Sierra Leone and Liberia. But cotton changed all that. With one field hand needed for every 5 acres, the demand for cheap labor soared. As the world looked on in fascination, a quarter of the United States became the world's premier commercial cotton farm. In a nation ostensibly devoted to freedom and the belief that all men were created equal, the American South became a stronghold of slavery, an institution already deemed barbaric in other technological societies.

The number of slaves in the South increased from less than 1 million in 1800 to 4 million in 1860. Between 40,000 and 250,000 of these, the so-called Gullahs from Angola, were smuggled into South Carolina, but the quadrupling of the South's black population was principally a result of natural increase. Prices paid for slaves soared, tripling in the 1830s and reaching $1800 for a prime field hand in 1860 (a figure equivalent in modern dollars to the price of tractor). Slavery again became big business. Crop value per slave increased from $15 per acre in 1800 to $100 per acre in 1860. Trainloads of blacks were illegally shipped from the declining tobacco-growing regions of Virginia and the Carolinas to the emerging cotton and rice fields of Alabama, Mississippi, Louisiana, and Texas, altering the distribution of the black population in the Southeast. Virginia exported 300,000; South Carolina about 170,000. Gangs of slaves were marched hundreds of miles in chains overland from Virginia, Kentucky, and North Carolina into the Deep South. Freed blacks from as far north as New York and New Jersey were entrapped by slavers and transported to southern markets. Some planters went into the vicious business of raising slaves, like cattle, for sale on the auction blocks of Charleston, Savannah, Mobile, and New Orleans. Families were broken apart by private sale or auction. Poet John Greenleaf Whittier's refrain, "Gone, gone—sold and gone; To the rice-swamps dark and lone," captured the pathos of these forced separations. It was a cruel and brutal business, frowned on by the best people and managed by the most depraved, but patronized by all who needed labor.

Conditions of life for southern slaves in the pre-Civil War South varied from one plantation to the next and from region to region. Conflicting contemporary accounts abound. Some describe whippings (most southern towns had always maintained a public whipper), brandings, and sadistic sexual abuse. More accurate is the picture of a wretched, insecure life of poverty set forth in Harriet Beecher Stowe's *Uncle Tom's Cabin.* Tempering mistreatment, however, was the monetary value of the slave: maiming a slave lowered his price, imprisonment lost the owner his time, and short rations impaired his health. Other reports describe healthy, high-spirited, hard-working agricultural slaves much as Jefferson Davis, later president of the Confederate States, pictured them—"peaceful and contented laborers." A controversial modern view, *The Time on the Cross,* contends that slaves were not materially worse off than their white farmer counterparts in the North. But there were revolts: Denmark Vesey, a freed black man, enlisted slaves to capture the city of Charleston in 1822; he was betrayed and executed along with 36 of his followers. In 1831, the visionary Nat Turner led a slave insurrection in Virginia in which 57 whites and 100 blacks were killed before Turner was hanged and 40 to 100 of his followers executed. In 1845, 75 unarmed slaves from southeastern Maryland tried to fight their way through to Pennsylvania and freedom, but were rounded up and shot 20 miles north of Washington, D.C. Spurred by fear, southern states passed severe legal prohibitions against blacks, and except in New England, where there were few blacks anyway, black people could not vote, testify in court, intermarry with whites, obtain anything but the most servile jobs, get an education, or hold a meeting. In Canada, there were virtually no blacks. By 1860, with fully 40 percent of the South's population of 9 million enslaved, one disgusted Virginian proclaimed that "the land of Washington, Jefferson, and Madison had become the Guinea of the United States."

On the eve of the Civil War, the economy of the South was overwhelmingly agricultural; with slavery now a symbol of enterprise, southern society took on a different cast from society elsewhere in North America. New Orleans, with 170,000 people in 1860, was the sole southern city of substantial size; Charleston had a population of only 40,000; Mobile, 29,000; and Savannah, 22,000. Less than 8 percent of the South's white population lived in towns larger than 4000 people; the urban middle class was small in size and influence. The immediate profits from tobacco, rice, sugar, and cotton were higher than profits from industrial ventures, causing most southern capital to be invested in land and slaves. Those few people with industrial interests, such as Cyrus McCormick, moved north because manufacturing was viewed as sordid and dirty. Charleston even enacted city ordinances against machinery as a potential smoke nuisance. As a result, in 1860, less than 200,000 southerners worked in factories; the town of Lowell, Massachusetts, had more textile mills than did the entire South; only 10 percent of the nation's manufactures were produced south of the **Mason-Dixon line.**° Few immigrants, therefore, were attracted to the South;

in 1860, 19 percent of the nation's total population was foreign born, but immigrants made up less than 5 percent of the population of the South.

At least partly for these reasons, the aristocratic planter families who actually profited from the plantation system, although less than 1 percent of the South's population, set the cultural tone for the entire region. Fewer than 2000 of these masters owned as many as 100 slaves; two-thirds of the 385,000 slave owners had fewer than 10 slaves; and at least three-quarters of the white population did not deal at all in slave labor. Most southerners were relatively poor, near-subsistence farmers who cultivated corn, cereal grains, sweet potatoes, and sorghum cane on small holdings tucked between plantations in the tobacco and cotton country and concentrated in the inland South. In the mountains, these small farmers, the hillbillies, formed a proud and distinctive group. Even they maintained the mentality of class. Below them, the poor white trash, or crackers, as they were variously known, were a class of illiterate, uncouth victims of parasitic and diet-deficiency diseases who became the most vigorous and embittered defenders of slavery— their color their only source of pride and self-esteem. All aspired to the chivalrous society of the gentry and the romantic mystique of plantation life; all obeyed the emotional, authoritarian preaching of diverse Protestant sects and shared a coherent, unified—if guilt-ridden—regional culture. It was this southern white culture—its moral attitudes, literature, language, and sense of tragedy—that was so disastrously and valiantly defended in the Civil War. Pitting a population of 9 million against the North's 22 million, and with New York producing more manufactures than the whole South, southerners fought for four years with verve, courage, and brilliance in a war for southern independence. Short of men, supplies, and resources, the South battled to certain destruction; the Cotton Kingdom was destroyed and the plantation system culturally debased.

Several Wests
[FIGURES 6, 7]

While industry flourished in the North and cotton in the South, manifest destiny was being converted from a slogan to a reality in the American West, that vast expanse of land stretching from the Appalachian Mountains to the Pacific Ocean. The impulse to settle open land and a prevailing faith and optimism that the future offered greater opportunities for wealth and satisfaction than the present propelled people westward. They went by the thousands—farmers, miners, adventurers, entrepreneurs, religious groups, and ragged regiments of immigrants from Europe—with such speed and force that it seemed the headlong rush of Americans to the West might depopulate the older, established

regions of the East. One Harvard minister feared that "wretched hermits in overgrown graveyards" would be all that was left behind. East of the Mississippi, in what is today the Upper Midwest, the agricultural frontier marched steadily westward, and the wilderness and the rich soil resources of the continental heartland were exploited. At the Great Plains this steady advance faltered. Daunted by a treeless expanse of prairie, the Great American Desert, wagon trains of settlers set out for what the environmental understanding of the time held to be more fertile, forested land in the Far West, in Oregon and California. They were soon joined by thousands of fortune hunters lured westward by an explosive and erratic scramble for gold and silver in California and the Rocky Mountains. Finally, the "last West," the Great Plains, was occupied by cattlemen and farmers; remnants of the American Indian population were destroyed or interned, and the shape of the nation was complete.

Between 1800 and 1830, settlers poured into the tangled wildernesses between the mountains, into the Susquehanna Valley of Pennsylvania, the Mohawk and Genesee valleys of New York, and the rolling hill country of southern Ohio, Indiana, and Illinois beyond the mountains—a region known as the Old Northwest. Isolated clearings and wilderness farms soon gave way to more organized commercial agriculture, and the eastern broadleaf forest was hacked away by an avalanche of new settlers. On turnpikes, steamboat routes, canals, and railroads a stream of wheat, flour, corn, pork, and beef flowed eastward and southward from the fertile interior to seaboard cities, southern plantations, and European markets. Towns sprang up to process the agricultural surplus of this lush land and to serve the needs of a growing rural population. Cincinnati was "the Porkopolis of the West"; Saint Louis and Chicago grew rapidly. A booster magazine for the Genesee Valley boasted that "the starving millions of Europe were waiting upon the action of Rochester's mills," which, it insisted, "were among the most stupendous works of modern art." Railroad companies and land speculators sold millions of acres to eastern farmers and immigrants with stories of cornstalks as large as tree trunks and cucumber vines that grew fast enough to strangle an unwary farmer. The wheat left ungleaned in a farmer's field, advertisements stated, could feed an entire English parish; the apples left rotting in Ohio orchards would "sink the

Despite hostile Indians, cyclones, blizzards, disease, and exhaustion, in the 1840s more than 5000 American farmer-settlers made the 2000-mile trek to Oregon by wagon, traveling in trains like this one. *Photo:* Association of American Railroads.

British navy." Soon agricultural settlements of English, Welsh, German, and Norwegian pioneers dotted the Upper Midwest. With land to spare and labor rare, each state, such as Illinois, attracted new settlers with claims of having the "greatest tracts of fertile land on the surface of the globe." Other resources also developed—lead mining in Missouri and southern Wisconsin, copper mining in Michigan, and iron mining near Pittsburgh and later along the shores of Lake Superior.

As the agricultural frontier edged westward onto the prairie fringes of the unforested Great Plains (author Hamlin Garland's Middle Border country), farmers in northern Indiana and Illinois, central Wisconsin and Minnesota, Iowa, and eastern Kansas and Nebraska faced a new set of environmental problems. The thick, tough, root-matted grassland soils required a plow drawn by as many as fourteen oxen to cut and turn the turf. Professional land breakers with massive plows had to be hired at considerable expense; poorer folk used sledgehammers and axes. Timber for building and fuel was scarce, as were sources of good water. There were no acorns and nuts to feed the hogs, and having carved their way westward through 1000 miles of forest, many settlers viewed land without trees with considerable suspicion. Yet the richness of the Middle Border soils was such that even with the tools of the day (which limited to 40 acres the amount of land a farm family could cultivate) they produced substantial agricultural surpluses. Mastery of this environment, however, was accomplished not by manpower but by machines; between 1840 and 1860 the Middle Border began to emerge as the breadbasket of America.

In the 1850s, John Deere, an Illinois blacksmith, produced 13,000 steel plows a year at his factory in Moline. Light enough to sling over the shoulder, these instruments could cut clean, deep furrows into the prairie soils and could be drawn by a horse. At the same time, Cyrus McCormick began the manufacture of mechanical reapers in Chicago. At first ridiculed as a cross between "a flying machine and a wheelbarrow," the reaper cut the cost and labor of harvesting by a third. William H. Seward, who later stirred controversy by purchasing more than 500,000 square miles of Arctic waste in Alaska as secretary of state, credited reapers with pushing forward the farming frontier at a rate of 30 miles a year. By the time McCormick died in 1884, 500,000 reapers were in operation doing the work of 5 million hands. Binders, threshers, and other farm machines were rapidly developed and used; these inventions produced a golden torrent of grain. In the 1850s, American corn production rose 40 percent; wheat production climbed 75 percent. By the middle 1850s, Chicago, which had arisen from a marshy village of 200 squatters ten years before, could convincingly claim to be the primary grain market in the world; 8 million acres of new land were brought under cultivation in Illinois alone during the 1860s. Thus, even at the height of the Civil War, with large numbers of young men at war and a large army to support, the productivity of Midwestern agriculture was so great that the United States still exported 140 million tons of grain.

As the grain farmers of the Middle Border edged onto the eastern margins of the Great Plains, other Americans set their eyes on more distant horizons, lured by stories of rich land for free in Oregon and California. Trappers, fur traders, and mountain men had come to know parts of this region during a half century of penetration. But until the Lewis and Clark expedition opened up the Oregon Trail in 1804–1805, the Far West was too remote for most Ameri-

A common thread in immigration to America was the gradual movement of a family, member by member, seeking out possibilities for their collective enrichment in the New World. If one family member prospered, money was sent to the "old country" to bring others across the ocean. Andrew and Jane Morris, husband and wife, left the turbulent society of their native village in Lancashire in 1829. They were followed in three years by two sisters and two brothers and their families as well as their parents; only one brother of the entire Morris family remained in Lancashire, and he contemplated emigration for years. His younger brother wrote him from the republican hills of Ohio in 1842:

Aurelius, Ohio, 13 Aug. 1842

Dear Brother,

After reflecting, studeing and consulting about what could be the cause that we heard nothing for so long from the only branch of our family remaining in England, we received your truly welcom letter on the 18 day of April, dated Feby 26th. We are sorry to hear that times is so bad in England and that their are so many people out of imploy, but it is nothing but what we expected, knowing as we do the smallness of the island and emance population and that all the property belongs to the rich and they having the makeing of the laws can consequently do as they pleas with the working class. There is no prospect ether for the presant or riseing generation. Things is very different here although times is wors than ever they was known to be through bank failures and scarcity of money; yet there is an excelent prospect for both the presant and riseing generation and perticulary the latter as there are hundreds of miles of first-rate land in excelent climits for 1¼ dollars per acre. . . .

You ask if we have good roads. Our roads are good considering the newness of the country. You ask are we far from a town or vilidge. We are 20 miles from Marietta, a very nice town on the bank of Ohio River at the mouth of the Muskingam River. It is pleasantly situated and has 2 market days in a week. We can go with a wagon in half a day. The market hours are from daylight until 9 oclock Wedensday and Saterday. We frequently go in the night with butter &c. in the wagons, sell out in the morning and come home the same day. Their are three little vilidges nearer. You ask if the country is pleasant. . . . It is broken or rowling and a great deal of the land is prity steep. So we answer it is pleasant for a broken country. You ask if there any farms on sale part cultivated, to wich we answer Yes, plenty. You ask can we sell our produce and get money for it, to wich we answer Yes, there has not been a time since we came here that we could not get money for produce

though at presant, it is very low. You ask can we injoy society, to wich we answer Yes. Our neighbourhud is quite throng enough. You ask is there any railways near, as to wich we answer No. . . . You ask are we much trubled with reptiles or wild beasts or bugs or fleas or midges, to wich we answer No, there are no wild beasts except some wild turkeys and a few dear; bugs are not as bad as in England. Fleas we have none and midges are not near as bad here as there. We have some snakes but not many. You ask do we consider we have made a good choice. We should think so if we did not hear of so many other parts that is so much supearier, but if times gets better we shall very likely some of us go and look and if we like sell our property here and go. You ask do we live in rude log houses. We answer Yes. When people buys Congress land in the woods they build what they call temperary log cabins untill they get a farm cleared and fenced and cultivated so as to grow produce enough for there own use and some for market an where they find themselves able they can build a house to there own likeing. There is hewn log, brick and frame houses in our nabourhood which are all very comfortable. You ask how we spend our time. We have plenty of work and are likely to have untill we get enough of land cleared and our farms in good order and then we think we could do very well by working one half or two thirds of the year. . . . If you come here you can come from Philadelphia to Pittsburge by canal and railroad and from Pittsburge to Marietta by steamboat. . . . From yours affectionately,

ANDREW AND JANE MORRIS

Source: Charlotte Erickson, *Invisible Immigrants: The Adaptation of English and Scottish Immigrants in Nineteenth-Century America.* Coral Gables, Fla.: University of Miami Press, 1972, pp. 169–170. Reprinted courtesy of the publisher.

---

cans to worry about. As late as 1828, one congressman felt that the only reason anyone would go to Oregon was "to become a savage." And when a Boston trading brig, the *Owhyhee*, returned from the Northwest with a cargo of pickled Columbia River salmon in 1831, President Jackson's treasury department taxed the catch as "foreign-caught fish."

But in the 1840s, Oregon fever struck. Pioneers from Iowa, Missouri, Illinois, Kentucky, and New England, attracted by tales of the fish-filled Columbia River, virgin forests, and fertile valleys, began to surge across the Great Plains. The prairie schooner, or covered wagon, was hit upon as the best means of

A boomtown in the West in 1889: the city marshal's office, the sign painter's establishment, and the lunch room and grocery. *Photo:* **Western History Collections, University of Oklahoma Library.**

transport, and wagon trains gathered at Independence, Missouri, and Council Bluffs, Iowa, to follow the course of the muddy Platte River across the plains. The hardships were severe: hostile Indians, cyclones, blizzards, disease, drowning, and exhaustion. An estimated 34,000 died in the early pioneer years. Many people walked across the entire continent to save their animals. Too large a wagon train ran out of grazing area for its animals on the High Plains, but smaller groups were inviting targets for attack by bands of Cheyenne, Blackfoot, or Crow Indians. Stragglers with broken wagons, limited supplies, or weak animals disappeared; the Oregon Trail became lined with discarded equipment, hidden graves, and advice to followers written on the skulls of fallen oxen. The worst parts of the journey lay beyond the plains, on the alkali flats of the arid Wyoming Basin and the following 800 miles through the Rockies and down the Snake and Columbia rivers into the Oregon country. With some luck, a party that left Missouri in May arrived in Oregon by Christmas. In the early 1840s, despite the many dangers, better than 5000 American farmer-settlers had made the 2000-mile trek and taken up property and livelihood in the lower Willamette Valley. By 1848, competing British and American claims to territory in the Pacific Northwest were settled by a compromise agreement defining the Canadian-American border along the forty-ninth *parallel,*• a pact that left both countries outlets to the Pacific Ocean in Puget Sound.

Although most transcontinental migration veered northward to Oregon in the 1840s, a few thousand Americans and Mexicans filtered into California, attracted by its fertile land and moderate climate, and established themselves as traders and ranchers in what was then Mexican territory. Some pioneers cut southward through mountain passes in the Rockies, others plunged west from Santa Fe, and a few arrived on clipper ships from eastern ports. One of these, a Swiss pioneer named John Sutter, set up his own California colony on 49,000 acres along the Sacramento River which he received as a Mexican land grant in return for maintaining a fort —an administrative subcenter—for the Mexican governor. In his colony, named New Helvetia, Sutter hired Indians and brought in Hawaiians to tend cattle and grow wheat; he established there a distillery, a tannery, and a blanket factory; 50 miles away on the American River in the foothills of the Sierra Nevada, he built a sawmill. In January 1848, two years after the United States had wrested California from Mexico, a Scottish carpenter named James Marshall discovered gold nuggets in the mill-race of this sawmill.

Hamlin Garland's 1917 autobiography of his boyhood on the newly settled prairie is the story of a family lured ever westward by the attraction of more fertile land. The great-great-grandparents of modern Americans grew up in a restless society. In the late 1860s, Hamlin's father uprooted the family from its well-organized Wisconsin farm and took them to Iowa, first to Winnesheik and then to Mitchell county. As they made their third trek westward in less than two years, they left the familiar scenery of the hardwood forest and entered the prairie:

Late in August my father again loaded our household goods into wagons, and with our small herd of cattle following, set out toward the west, bound once again to overtake the actual line of the middle border. . . .

Each mile took us farther and farther into the unsettled prairie until in the afternoon of the second day, we came to a meadow so wide that its western rim touched the sky without revealing a sign of man's habitation other than the road in which we traveled.

The plain was covered with grass tall as ripe wheat and when my father stopped his team and came back to us and said, "Well, children, here we are on The Big Prairie," we looked about us with awe, so endless seemed this spread of wild oats and waving bluejoint.

Far away dim clumps of trees showed, but no chimney was in sight, and no living thing moved save our own cattle and the hawks lazily wheeling in the air. My heart filled with awe as well as wonder. The majesty of this primeval world exalted me. I felt for the first time the poetry of the unplowed spaces.

Work came early and lasted late on the new land:

The cabin on this rented farm was a mere shanty, a shell of pine boards, which needed reinforcing to make it habitable and one day my father said, "Well, Hamlin, I guess you'll have to run the plow team this fall. I must help neighbor Button wall up the house and I can't afford to hire another man."

This seemed a fine commission for a lad of ten, and I drove my horses into the field that first morning with a manly pride which added an inch to my stature. I took my initial "round" at a "land" which stretched from one side of the quarter section to the other, in confident mood. I was grown up!

The soil was the kind my father had been seeking, a smooth dark sandy loam, which made it possible for a lad to do the work of a man. Often the share would go the entire "round" without striking a root or a pebble as big as a walnut, the steel running steadily with a crisp craunching ripping sound which I rather liked to hear.

In truth work would have been quite tolerable had it not been so long drawn out. Ten hours of it even on a fine day made about twice too many for a boy. . . .

Day after day, through the month of October and deep into November, I followed that team, turning over two acres of stubble each day. . . .

Finally the day came when the ground rang like iron under the feet of the horses, and a bitter wind, raw and gusty, swept out of the northwest, bearing gray veils of sleet. Winter had come! Work in the furrow had ended.

Yet, even at rest, the boys of the prairie played out a life farther west:

All the boys I knew talked on Colorado, never of New England. We dreamed of the plains, of the Black Hills, discussing cattle raising and mining and hunting. "We'll have our rifles ready, boys, ha, ha, ha-ha!" was still our favorite chorus, "Newbrasky" and Wyoming our far-off wonderlands, Buffalo Bill our hero.

Source: Hamlin Garland, A Son of the Middle Border, New York: Macmillan; London: The Bodley Head, 1962, pp. 68, 72, 73, 74, 75, 113. Copyright 1917 by Hamlin Garland, renewed 1945 by Mary I. Lord and Constance G. Williams. Reprinted courtesy of Macmillan Publishing Company and The Bodley Head.

In a week the news sped through California; in six months word spread to the East Coast; in December 1848, President Polk verified "the extraordinary character" of the California find in his farewell message to Congress. This precipitated an unprecedented rush to the gold fields. In 1849 alone 25,000 forty-niners booked ship's passage for California via Cape Horn, and an additional 55,000 simply walked and rode overland across the continent, following the Oregon and Sante Fe trails. In 1849, San Francisco, the major marketing center of the gold country, mushroomed into a city of nearly 25,000, with a harbor jammed by clipper ships abandoned by their crews in the rush for gold. Sutter's land was invaded and his buildings and livestock burned; he died in poverty thirty-two years after the discovery of gold on his property. In six years, gold production in the United States increased seventy-three times; 50 percent of the entire world's gold came from California. A new kind of society was arising on the frontier. By 1860, men outnumbered women six to one in the California census, and most of the latter were tact-

ROUGHING IT

In June 1861, Samuel Clemens traveled west with his brother Orion, who had just been appointed secretary of the Nevada Territory. After having worked as a printer and a riverboat pilot, Clemens, then twenty-six, became a writer for the Virginia City Territorial Enterprise using the name Mark Twain, and dug his pen into the society of the new mining country. Two years later, Clemens left his job as editor of the Enterprise to become a reporter in San Francisco, California. His reports from the field gained him fame back East, and he left San Francisco for New York in December 1866. These selections from Roughing It were written later in life:

It was in this Sacramento Valley, just referred to, that a deal of the most lucrative of the early gold mining was done, and you may still see, in places, its grassy slopes and levels torn and guttered and disfigured by the avaricious spoilers of fifteen and twenty years ago. . . . The men are gone, the houses have vanished, even the name of the place is forgotten. In no other land, in modern times, have towns so absolutely died and disappeared, as in the old mining regions of California.

It was a driving, vigorous, restless population in those days. It was a curious population. It was the only population of the kind that the world has ever seen gathered together, and it is not likely that the world will ever see its like again. For, observe, it was an assemblage of two hundred thousand young men—not simpering, dainty, kid-gloved weaklings, but stalwart, muscular, dauntless young braves, brimful of push and energy, and royally endowed with every attribute that goes to make up a peerless and magnificent manhood—the very pick and choice of the world's glorious ones. No women, no children, no gray and stooping veterans—none but erect, bright-eyed, quick-moving, strong-handed young giants —the strangest population, the finest population, the most gallant host that ever trooped down the startled solitudes of an unpeopled land. . . .

It was a splendid population—for all the slow, sleepy, sluggish-brained sloths stayed at home—you never find that sort of people among pioneers—you cannot build pioneers out of that sort of material. It was that population that gave to California a name for getting up astounding enterprises and rushing them through with a magnificent dash and daring and a recklessness of cost or consequence, which she bears unto this day—and when she projects a new surprise, the grave world smiles as usual, and says "Well, that is California all over."

Source: Samuel Clemens, Roughing It. New York: Harper & Row, 1900, Chapter 52.

fully classified as "neither maids, wives, nor widows." A restless, rootless society drawn from all over the world, many new Californians moved back eastward through the Rockies in search of new opportunities in Nevada, Colorado, Montana, Idaho, and Utah as the flow of gold dwindled in the 1860s. But others stayed on and sank roots in California, giving the state a distinctive regional tradition and culture.

Quite a different regional western culture was established in the valley of the Great Salt Lake in Utah. Two years before the gold rush to California, an astonishing body of fervently religious people, the Mormons, walked 1000 miles across the Great Plains and the Rocky Mountains into the western wilderness to create an ideal society beyond the frontier in a remote desert basin. The Mormons were a quiet, prosperous, polygamous people who, following divine precepts conceived in the visions of their prophet Joseph Smith, a farmer in western New York, believed themselves chosen of God. As much for envy of their prosperity as for their belief in plural marriage, they were hounded from New York State westward through Ohio, Missouri, and Illinois; their houses were burned, their banks looted, and the Mormon women raped. In 1844, the prophet Joseph Smith was shot to death in a cell in the Carthage, Illinois, jail; under the leadership of Brigham Young, the Mormons determined to build their holy city of Zion "up in the mountains where the Devil cannot dig us out . . . where we can live . . . as we have a mind to." After arriving in Utah in 1847, under the absolute rule of Young and his high council, the disciplined Mormons laid out the streets of their holy city, built irrigation ditches, and sowed the desert to convert the Salt Lake Basin into one of the most fertile regions of the American West. Two years later, California-bound miners "discovered" the prospering city of 8000 Mormons in the valley of the Great Salt Lake, and just before the Civil War, Mark Twain commented on the unusual character of "a city of 15,000 inhabitants with no loafers perceptible in it; and no visible drunkards or noisy people. . . ." Between 1847 and 1857, ninety-five cooperative (intentionally noncompetitive) Mormon communities were founded. In one generation the Mormon population swelled from 6000 to 200,000 as converts flocked to their well-ordered territory. Although the Mormons failed to establish an independent theocratic state in the American West, Brigham Young became the first governor of the fledgling state of Utah. Thus a new culture hearth based upon religious differences, in some ways mirroring the early history of New England, was implanted in the Great Basin country and has persisted to the present.

The last West to be conquered and settled was the Great Plains, a semiarid grassland *plateau*• that encompasses nearly a quarter of the continental

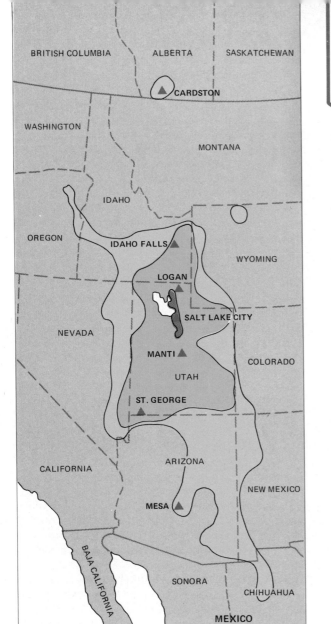

Figure 6. The Mormon Culture Region. The geographer Donald Meinig has delineated the scope and persistence of Mormon influence in the American West. The *core* of the Mormon culture region, focused on the valley of the Great Salt Lake, is the area of greatest density of occupance, intensity of organization, and homogeneity of belief and practice. The surrounding *domain* is still predominantly Mormon, but with markedly less cultural intensity and complexity of development. The *sphere*, areas where Mormons live in enclaves within Gentile (non-Mormon) populations, extends over much of the Rocky Mountains and Great Basin country from Alberta in Canada to Mexico. *Adapted from:* Donald W. Meinig, "The Mormon Culture Region: Strategies and Patterns in the Geography of the American West, 1847–1964," *Annals of the Association of American Geographers,* Vol. 55 (1965), p. 214, Fig. 7. Reproduced by permission.

United States, sloping eastward from the Rocky Mountains to the Mississippi Valley and extending northward from Texas into Manitoba, Saskatchewan, and Alberta. Generally level, treeless, and dry, the Great Plains was incorrectly perceived as "wholly unfit for cultivation," in the words of an 1820 government report, and a "Great American Desert" according to another. Prior to the California gold rush, many easterners considered the Great Plains to be an everlasting barrier to the westward migration of the American frontier; some even compared it to the desert wastes of Siberia. Indeed in the 1850s, at the urging of Secretary of War Jefferson Davis, Congress allocated $30,000 to import two boatloads of camels from the Middle East to Indianola, Texas, in an effort to duplicate Asian *pastoral nomadism*° in the arid southern plains. Uncertain rainfall, scanty fuel, winter blizzards, and summer grass fires made the Great Plains unattractive to trappers, miners, and pioneers; thus it remained the domain of mounted buffalo-hunting Indian tribes.

In 1860, some 250,000 Indians still inhabited the Great Plains. The strongest and most warlike tribes were the Sioux, Blackfoot, Crow, Cheyenne, and Arapaho in the north, and the Comanche, Apache, Ute, and Kiowa in the south. Trapped in a closing human vise of cattlemen and farmers advancing from the east and miners rebounding eastward from California, the Plains Indians still lived as nomadic hunters, migrating northward on horseback in summer and southward in winter feeding off enormous herds of buffalo. Some herds included as many as 12 million animals, on which the tribes relied for food, shelter, and clothing. As the railroads penetrated the plains, buffalo hunters, farmers, and cattlemen began to eliminate the herds, encroaching on hunting grounds granted by treaty to the Indians for "as long as water runs and grass grows." The very basis of Indian life was threatened. Record kills of 120 buffalo in forty minutes and 6000 in sixty days were logged by individual marksmen. In the late 1860s, 1 million animals were slaughtered every year, and buffalo all but disappeared from the northern plains. By 1873, only one large herd in the Texas Panhandle was still intact; by 1876, no more targets were left. In desperation, the Indians fought back in hundreds of pitched battles with army troops. One by one, the tribes were subdued and herded onto reservations, although outbreaks of war-

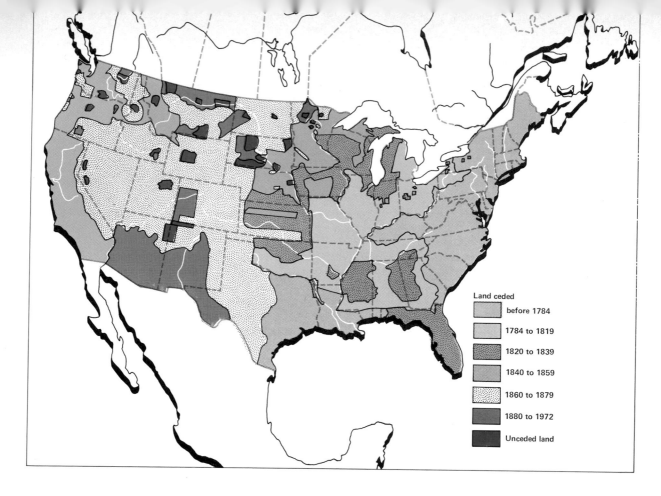

	Land ceded
	before 1784
	1784 to 1819
	1820 to 1839
	1840 to 1859
	1860 to 1879
	1880 to 1972
	Unceded land

Figure 7. Indian Land Cessions, 1784–1880. Land was alienated from the Indians of North America with extreme rapidity. By 1784, the lands of the eastern seaboard and the Gulf coast had already been seized by piecemeal expropriation. Indian lands in Canada remained larger, the Indians perhaps not as threatened by intensive white penetration. All the land of today's Indian reservations in the United States (50 million acres, or 2.2% of the nation's total) could fit in an area the size of Minnesota. *After:* **Sam B. Hilliard, "Indian Land Cessions," Map Supplement No. 16 to** *Annals of the Association of American Geographers,* **Vol. 62, No. 2 (June 1972). Cartographic design by Dan Irwin and the staff of the Southern Illinois University Cartographic Lab. Reproduced by permission.**

fare continued on the Great Plains frontier. The Indians' lands were taken by theft or purchase and their numbers drastically reduced by raids, disease, and hunger. But long before the pitiless massacre of the last of the Sioux at Wounded Knee, South Dakota, on New Year's Day 1891, the extinction of the buffalo had sealed the fate of the Plains Indians, and the Great Plains was open to settlement.

In the *ecological*• void left by the vanishing buffalo, several million semiwild longhorn cattle grazed on the central prairies from Texas to Canada in the 1860s. When railroads from the East reached the margins of these plains, *railhead*• cowtowns became the destinations to which well-fed longhorns gathered from the southern plains and northern prairies were driven for shipment to urban markets back

East. The idea was developed by a Chicago livestock trader, Joseph McCoy, who purchased the town of Abilene, Kansas, for $5 an acre in 1867 and sent riders to Texas offering as much as $40 a head, ten times the going local price, for cattle delivered to the railhead at Abilene. Recognizing that a fortune could be made by shipping cheap beef to eastern cities, McCoy boasted that he would ship 200,000 cattle out of his stockyards in ten years. In fact, he shipped over 2 million in only four years, and was, they said, "the real McCoy."

The first herd arrived in Abilene only 100 days after McCoy made his offer, driven from southern Texas up the Chisholm Trail. The typical drive took three months as cowboys moved 2500 longhorns at a rate of 15 miles a day along the 1200- to 1500-mile route. In the peak year of 1871, more than 600,000 cattle crossed the Red River heading north. Along the spreading rail lines, towns such as Abilene, Dodge City, and Ogallala sprang up—wild, disorderly boom towns with homicide rates ten to twenty times higher than that of modern New York City. Battles over cattle ownership, grazing rights, and water generated grim lawlessness and violence quite unlike the romantic legend that has been preserved. But the cattle trails and the Wild West lasted briefly. In only twenty years, the wide open spaces of the Great Plains, crisscrossed by rails and by the barbed-wire fences of homesteaders, were staked out in privately owned ranches and farms.

Between 1784 (when Congress first negotiated at Fort Stanwix) and 1880, Americans signed and broke 370 treaties with Indian tribes. As the frontier moved west, vaulted over the Rockies to Oregon and California, and then converged from both east and west on the Great Plains, millions of acres of land—two-thirds of a continent—were wrenched from the Indians. The tragedy of their fate was poignantly summarized by Chief Joseph of the Nez Percé, who, after a 1500-mile fighting retreat over mountain and plain, surrendered just short of asylum in Canada on October 5, 1877:

I am tired of fighting. Our chiefs are killed. Looking-Glass is dead. The old men are all dead. It is the young men who say yes and no. He who led on the young men is dead. It is cold and we have no blankets. The little children are freezing to death. My people, some of them, have run away to the hills and have no blankets, no food; no one knows where they are—perhaps freezing to death. I want to have time to look for my children and see how many I can find. Maybe I shall find them among the dead. Hear me, my chiefs. I am tired; my heart is sick and sad. From where the sun now stands I will fight no more forever.

As the settlement of the Great Plains got under way, Congress passed the Homestead Act of 1862, entitling every adult American, on payment of $10, to ownership to 160 acres of land simply by agreeing to work it and produce a crop within five years. An area as great as Great Britain and France combined was thrown open to homesteaders, most of it in the semiarid grasslands west of the one-hundredth **meridian.** Here, new settlers urged on by government and railroad persuasion, lured yet again by reports of fertile soil and almost free land, cut farms into the prairie turf, lived in underground sod dugouts, and suffered drought, blizzard, locust plagues, ceaseless wind, back-breaking work, and loneliness. It was a bleak, raw life that discouraged many. The isolation of the prairie home, according to *Atlantic Monthly* in 1893, resulted in "alarming amounts of insanity." One Nebraskan homesteader carved these words on a cabin wall and left: "Ten miles to water, twenty to wood; thirty miles to hell and I've gone there for good." But three inventions made life possible on the open plains: the steel plow, which turned the sod and opened the grassland soils to wheat farming; windmills, which supplied energy to pump underground water to the surface; and barbed wire, which fenced off the plains and separated crops from animals. Although only 1 acre in 8 of western land went to small settler-farmers (the rest went to land speculators and railroads), the population of the Great Plains increased rapidly. Nebraska's population tripled to nearly 500,000 in the 1870s, and Kansas achieved 1 million citizens early in the 1880s. Between 1870 and 1900, 430 million acres of new land were settled in America, more than the total amount of land that had been settled since the colonial period.

CENTENNIAL

In 1876, the 450-acre Centennial Exposition opened in Philadelphia with 30,000 exhibits from fifty nations to celebrate the first century of American independence. The nation was in the midst of a business depression and a scandalous election campaign, and was recovering from the political corruption that wracked the administration of President Ulysses S. Grant. In the East, hordes of European immigrants were filling growing cities and laboring in an expanding industrial base. The sensation of the exposition was the first public demonstration of Alexander Graham Bell's telephone. The South was beginning to regain economic momentum after the ravages of the Civil War and the excesses of the Reconstruction period. Its economy was improving, cotton was again the principal crop, and emancipation had not significantly altered the economic or social position of blacks. In the West, where seven years earlier the Union Pacific and Central Pacific had joined East and West by rail at Promontory Point, Utah, to create the first transcontinental railroad, people were stunned by news that one-third of the Seventh Cavalry under the command of General George Custer had been annihilated by the Sioux on the Little Bighorn River in Montana. Farther west, the rapacious carnival atmosphere of the gold rush had given way to organized industrial mining and agricultural development. To the north, Canada, with a population of around 4 million, had put down rebellion in the province of Manitoba, and the Canadian Pacific Railroad had been started under a cloud of scandal.

Overall, it had been a century of remarkable territorial expansion, population growth, and material progress. North Americans' faith in growth and progress, a constant impatience with the achievements of the present, had, as Tocqueville noted, won them a continent. A distinctive machine-run industrial economy was beginning to emerge. In a land rich in opportunity and resources and short of labor, North America would soon challenge Europe as the center of industrial power. The two nations had become the world's largest sources of cheap food, supplying the needs of their cities, providing purpose to the network of railroads that laced the continent together, and producing exports that would profoundly change their position in world affairs. In short, North America was rapidly moving toward economic independence, and although the environmental losses in ravaged land, destroyed forests, and discarded resources were enormous, the United States and Canada accomplished in a matter of years what Europe had been working toward for centuries.

NORTH AMERICA

REGIONAL PATTERNS

PHYSICAL FEATURES MAP
POPULATION DENSITY MAP

North America, considered here as the United States and Canada, is a striking example of an industrial society impressed on an ecologically diverse but socially unified environment. To explain the extraordinary growth of the North American economy, most scholars cite the continent's rich natural resources, its diverse and technically capable population of 236 million, its size, internal unity, and industrial capacity. But the key to the patterns of North America's geography lies in seeing that settlement of the continent and the Industrial Revolution were simultaneous events. After industrialization touched and sparked European society to exploration and conquest, the environmental transformation of North America took place in rapid succession. The region was formed and structured by the economic forces of industrialization.

Indian populations occupied North America for at least 40,000 years prior to the entry of the Europeans, but they were few in number and technologically limited. Only in favored locations—along the ocean coasts, on the shores of the Great Lakes, in the lower Mississippi Valley, and in parts of the Southwest— were Indian population densities higher than two people per square mile. Nothing like the dense preindustrial agrarian civilizations of India and China existed in North America to moderate and alter the amplitude and direction of European settlement. Weakened by newly introduced diseases and overwhelmed by European weaponry, Indians melted away before the European advance. They were only locally effective in hindering and redirecting the European penetration and exploitation of the continent. And because European settlement prior to the American Revolution was restricted to a narrow band of territory along the Atlantic coast, the full exploration and conquest of America were deferred until after the initial thrust of the industrial revolution. Colonial America, with its seigneurs, New England towns, and southern plantations, was dwarfed

and transformed by the rapid growth and geographical spread of a dynamic new type of economy and society.

The cultural geography of North America, therefore, is of recent origin, and compared with other world *regions,* relatively homogeneous. Large sections of the American West were occupied within living memory, and settlement in parts of Alaska and the Canadian North is a modern drama. For the most part, the political boundaries of North America—the provinces of Canada and the states of the United States—do not separate different peoples or beliefs. Rather, they represent expressions of the same culture set in different physical environments. There are exceptions—Mormon Utah, the Spanish Southwest, French-speaking Quebec—but by and large the regionality of North America is based on large-scale environmental features such as the Rockies, the Gulf Coast, and the *tundra* and *taiga* landscapes of the Canadian Shield rather than in differing languages, customs, and moral attitudes. Recognized American cultural subregions such as the South and the Midwest represent minor cultural variations compared with the differences between Spain and Germany, for example, or between Mongolia and the North China Plain. Compared with Europe, North America has no significant internal barriers to trade and communication. The United States and Canada form the largest uninterrupted platform of industrial economy, mobility, and communication in the world. Canada, with a national territory of 3.8 million square miles, and the United States with 3.6 million square miles, are the world's second and fourth largest nations.

Despite this apparent homogeneity, Canadians and Americans have clung staunchly to regional cultures, although most are clearly integrated into the national society and economy. New Englanders draw their cultural inspiration from different roots than do Southerners; French Canadians assert cultural independence in a nation built on English custom and law. At a more local level, Chinese immigrants, Germans, Poles, Czechs, and Amish frequently form small enclaves within specific cities and regions. Indians live on reservations implanted in a land they lost, and black Americans have become increasingly concentrated in the cores of metropolitan regions. The difficulty of describing both this cultural diversity and the essential unity of language, technology, and economy in North America is compounded by the variety of environments that slash across the continent and create vastly different settings for human activity. In an effort to compromise these differences, seven major regions are identified in this section: the Canadian Northlands, a virtually uninhabited land of tundra and taiga; French Canada, testimony to the persistence of the French colonial experiment in the New World; New England and the Atlantic Provinces, one of

The Canadian Arctic supports a population of less than 15,000 people, most of them Eskimos, whose stone-age culture is under severe strain as modern communications and education systems reach into this remote area. In the traditional way, these fish will be cleaned and cached under rock piles to provide food during the long winter; the men make the catch, and the women do the processing. *Photo:* Wide World.

colonial America's most influential culture hearths; the Industrial North, a belt of dense industrial and commercial activity stretching from the coastal *megalopolis* across the central Appalachians to the Upper Midwest; the South, an extension of northern landforms, but a psychologically powerful regional culture with its own literature, life style, and language; the Central Plains, the agricultural heartland of the continent; and the West, a vast sweep of mountains, plateaus, and deserts, densely urbanized on its Pacific periphery and thinly peopled elsewhere.

THE CANADIAN NORTHLANDS

The earth's ancient crust is exposed in the far north in the mostly uninhabited Canadian Shield. A taiga landscape of *coniferous forest* and a glacial waterscape of wide, shallow lakes and *braided streams,* the shield covers about half the territory of Canada (1.8 million square miles), projects south into Minnesota, Wisconsin, Michigan, and the Adirondack Mountains of New York, and is essentially devoid of human presence except for mines, air bases, and a unique society of traders, trappers, schoolteachers, priests, and Indians. In the farthest north,

beyond the shield, the Canadian *archipelago* forms a group of islands set in the Arctic Ocean stretching over 60 degrees of longitude from Banks to Ellesmere islands and reaching southeast over 1500 miles from north to south. Some 549,000 square miles of tundra, the Canadian Arctic supports a population of less than 15,000 people, mostly native Eskimos—stone-age peoples undergoing rapid change as modern communication systems, schools, and trading posts begin social transformations. A distinctive physical region of North America, the Arctic islands, like the Canadian Shield, are properly understood only in the reach of the continent as a whole.

FRENCH CANADA

Through social segregation and isolation, French Canada has remained the most distinctive culture region in North America. In many ways, French Canada served as a beginning for a separate Canadian identity in North America; French Canadians believe that Canada is their inspiration and that English Canada emerged independently only as a result of the northward flight of British loyalists away from the revolution in 1776. Although communities of French Canadians are diffused throughout Canada and the northeastern states, French Canada is essentially synonymous with the province of Quebec, the New France of colonial days. With an area of 594,861 square miles, nearly three times as large as France, Quebec has only 6 million people, more than nine-tenths of whom are descen-

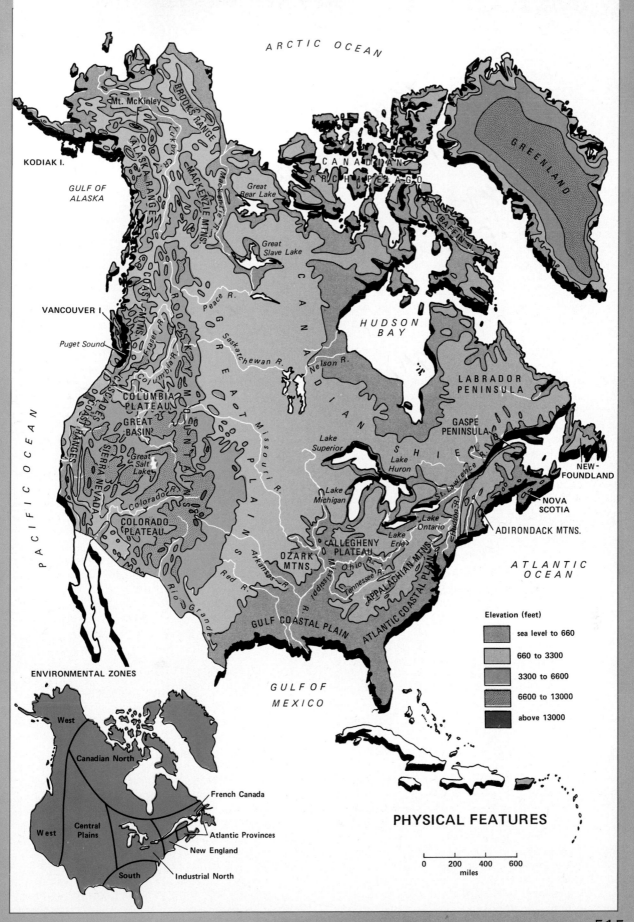

ARCTIC OCEAN

Mt. McKinley

BROOKS RANGE

Yukon R.

ALASKA RANGE

MACKENZIE MTNS.

(Mackenzie R.)

CANADIAN ARCHIPELAGO

GREENLAND

BAFFIN I.

KODIAK I.

GULF OF ALASKA

Great Bear Lake

Great Slave Lake

Peace R.

COAST MTNS.

VANCOUVER I.

Puget Sound

Fraser R.

Columbia R.

Saskatchewan R.

C A N A D I A N

HUDSON BAY

LABRADOR PENINSULA

PACIFIC OCEAN

CASCADES

COLUMBIA PLATEAU

GREAT BASIN

ROCKY MOUNTAINS

Nelson R.

G R E A T

S H I E L D

GASPÉ PENINSULA

COAST RANGES

SIERRA NEVADA

Great Salt Lake

Lake Superior

St. Lawrence R.

NEW-FOUNDLAND

NOVA SCOTIA

COLORADO PLATEAU

Colorado R.

P L A I N S

Missouri R.

Lake Huron

Lake Michigan

Lake Ontario

Lake Erie

Hudson R.

ADIRONDACK MTNS.

ATLANTIC OCEAN

Arkansas R.

OZARK MTNS.

Mississippi R.

Ohio R.

ALLEGHENY PLATEAU

Tennessee R.

APPALACHIAN MTNS.

ATLANTIC COASTAL PLAIN

Rio Grande

Red R.

GULF COASTAL PLAIN

Elevation (feet)

sea level to 660

660 to 3300

3300 to 6600

6600 to 13000

above 13000

GULF OF MEXICO

ENVIRONMENTAL ZONES

West

Canadian North

French Canada

West

Central Plains

Atlantic Provinces

New England

South

Industrial North

PHYSICAL FEATURES

0   200   400   600
miles

dants of the 65,000 French settlers in the New World in 1763—a remarkable *demographic*[*] persistence.

The French Canadians are concentrated in the lowlands of the Saint Lawrence River valley. Stretching 600 miles from the suburbs of Montreal to the tip of the Gaspé *Peninsula*,[*] the Saint Lawrence is framed on the north by the uplifted terrain of the Canadian Shield and on the south by the Sutton Mountains, a northern extension of the Appalachians into Canada. The Sutton *highlands*[*] of Quebec, known as the Eastern Townships, were settled by an English-speaking population of small farmers politically and culturally akin to New England and Toronto rather than to nearby Quebec or Montreal. The French Canadian population, on the other hand, extends well into eastern Ontario through the Ottawa River valley between Montreal and Ontario. The federal capital, Ottawa (population 450,000), is an enclave of English-speaking people amid a French Canadian population.

Well into this century, the Saint Lawrence River valley was a landscape of inherited family farms and small agricultural villages centered on parish churches. Agriculture remains an important source of income for the province, and the production of apples, wrapping tobacco, hay, oats, dairy products, and maple syrup is substantial in the Canadian context. Environmental conditions, however, limit the agricultural possibilities of French Canada. Even in the south, in Montreal, frosts occur late into May, and snow in October is not rare.

The expanding exploitation of timber, mineral, and energy resources in the province is altering the traditional agricultural economy of Quebec. The Saint Lawrence, itself tamed by the immense seaway project of the 1950s, provides access for seagoing vessels. The outlet for the entire *watershed*[*] of the Great Lakes, the Saint Lawrence has been dammed where it flows over the resistant rock of the Canadian Shield between Montreal and Lake Ontario to provide a channel for shipping and hydroelectricity. This project, funded by state, provincial, and both national governments, has deeply affected the economy of Quebec. Along the numerous rivers that thread swiftly southward off the Canadian Shield, the expansion of hydroelectric power resources has reinforced the importance of the timber, paper, and pulp industry that originally spurred settlement. Logging towns such as Shawinigan and La Tuque on the Saint Maurice River have been revitalized by cheap hydroelectric power. With energy demand rising in Montreal, Quebec City, Ottawa, and the northeastern United States, more remote reserves have been tapped by dams like that above Baie Comeau on the Manicouagan River—some 200 miles downstream from Quebec City. Quebec is the principal producer of Canada's most important export—pulp and paper—and is endowed with a hydroelectric energy surplus.

The mineral resources of the Canadian Shield have prompted a similar growth in the mining sector. Iron ore, aluminum, titanium, copper, gold, and other minerals are mined on the shield in such isolated centers as Rouyn-Noranda, Val d'Or, Gagnon, and Schefferville. Recently developed iron ore deposits in Labrador have benefited by being able to supply Great Lakes industry with metal at a time when high-grade Lake Superior ores are reaching exhaustion. But the natural resources of Quebec will not attract substantial new populations to the area. Efficient mining techniques now require only a minimum work force; hydroelectric development in the north could support a balanced economy of mineral treatment and metal production, but the more moderate environments of the Saint Lawrence are far more attractive. Population is so scattered on the Canadian Shield that less than 100,000 people live in the immense Quebec county of Saguenay, 315,176 square miles in area. The economy of French Canada, redirected from agriculture to the selective exploitation of natural resources, reflects a pattern of the human geography more common in the North American West: a dense core of intensive urbanization (Montreal) serves a vast and dispersed hinterland.

Montreal, the premier port of the Saint Lawrence, has a population of 2,700,000; it is Canada's largest city and a major industrial, financial, transportation, and educational center. Montreal is North America's sole *primate city*[*]—economically and culturally of overwhelming importance in French Canada. Compared with Quebec City (476,000) or Trois Rivières (85,000), the second and third cities of French Canada, Montreal is the residence of nearly half the French Canadian population. Marked by innovative urban planning, the city's central business district is connected by underground passages of shops, offices, and restaurants—a full complement of lower-level streets shielded from the harsh winter weather.

NEW ENGLAND AND THE ATLANTIC PROVINCES

New England and the nearby Canadian provinces of New Brunswick, Nova Scotia, Prince Edward Island, and Newfoundland are in the northern Appalachians, highlands that historically barred this subregion from easy access to the interior of the continent. Generally below 3000 feet in altitude and forested by second-growth hardwoods and conifers, the mountains of New England and the Atlantic Provinces are composed of three separate ranges. First, structurally related *folded mountains*[*]—the Taconics, which straddle New York, Vermont, Massachusetts, and Connecticut; the Berkshire Hills of Massachusetts; and the Green Mountains of Vermont—extend northward into the Shickshock

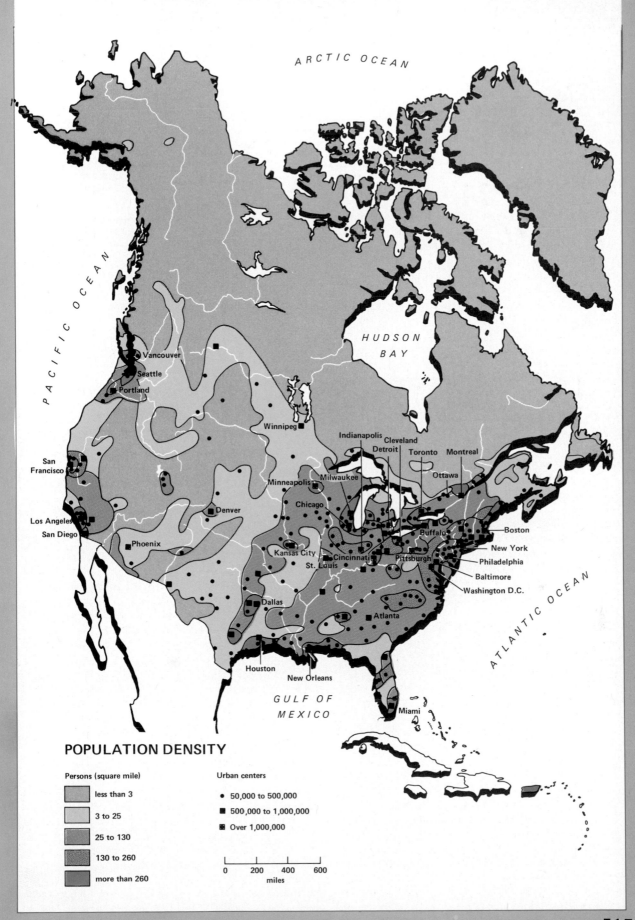

POPULATION DENSITY

Persons (square mile)

	less than 3
	3 to 25
	25 to 130
	130 to 260
	more than 260

Urban centers

● 50,000 to 500,000

■ 500,000 to 1,000,000

▣ Over 1,000,000

```
0    200   400   600
        miles
```

ARCTIC OCEAN

PACIFIC OCEAN

HUDSON BAY

ATLANTIC OCEAN

GULF OF MEXICO

Vancouver
Seattle
Portland
Winnipeg
San Francisco
Los Angeles
San Diego
Phoenix
Denver
Kansas City
St. Louis
Dallas
Houston
New Orleans
Minneapolis
Milwaukee
Chicago
Indianapolis
Cincinnati
Cleveland
Detroit
Toronto
Ottawa
Montreal
Buffalo
Pittsburgh
Boston
New York
Philadelphia
Baltimore
Washington D.C.
Atlanta
Miami

Port Clyde, Maine, a cluster of houses surrounded by lobster traps and sheltered in a small cove, is typical of the fishing towns of the northern coasts of New England. *Photo:* Wide World.

Mountains of the Gaspé Peninsula and the Long Range of northwestern Newfoundland. Second, a central mountain complex arches northeastward from the White Mountains of New Hampshire through Maine to the central uplands of New Brunswick and Newfoundland. A third band, noticeably lower in elevation, stretches from the coastal hills of Rhode Island and eastern Massachusetts, lies buried under the Gulf of Maine, and resurfaces in Nova Scotia and eastern Newfoundland. All three highland belts have undergone several cycles of *glaciation,* producing a beveled mountain landscape dotted by lowland lakes, *bogs,* brooks, and streams. Monadnocks, the scoured peaks of the White Mountains, and elongated glacial hills (drumlins) are distinctive landscape features of this area.

Although largely depopulated today, the New England highlands were intensively farmed and thoroughly logged over in the past. In the colonial period, these highlands supported subsistence farmers who grew hay, oats, rye, apples, and potatoes; raised poultry and dairy cows; and logged and made maple syrup on the side. As commercial agriculture spread into more fertile environments in the Central Plains of North America, these eastern highlands lost much of their population,

although local concentrations of activity remain. Dairy farming is profitable in southern Vermont and New Hampshire, where ready access to metropolitan markets is an important advantage. The flat, sandy soils, adequate water, and long summer days of Prince Edward Island and the Aroostook Valley of Maine favor commercial potato production. Apples, pears, and cherries are grown in the Annapolis Valley of Nova Scotia. Along the northern coasts, fishing fleets are sheltered in small coves from Maine to Newfoundland and ply the North Atlantic catching shellfish along the coast and cod in offshore fishing grounds. The Grand Banks, where cold waters of the Labrador Current flowing south from the Arctic Ocean collide with the warm waters of the *Gulf Stream,* are among the richest fisheries in the world. Increasingly, however, the economy of much of New England and the Atlantic Provinces depends on tourists from urban centers on the eastern seaboard, attracted to the rural vistas and rugged landscapes.

In the Atlantic Provinces, there are few cities of substantial size; the largest, Halifax in Nova Scotia (220,000 people) and Saint John's in Newfoundland (130,000), are oriented to the traditional economy of fishing and logging and a scattering of new mining interests. With incomes far below the average of the rest of Canada, the people of this area are poor. Planned government rejuvenation of the Atlantic Provinces, under way since the 1950s, has centered on attracting skilled industries to these picturesque but languishing urban centers and developing more efficient techniques of exploiting local timber and mineral resources. The Atlantic Provinces, however, have stronger historical ties to Boston than to French-speaking Montreal or the more distant Toronto: their location north of the international border hinders logical economic and cultural connections with the south.

The heartland of this region is the narrow coastal plain of southern New England, where dense agricultural and urban populations are concentrated in a band of rolling glaciated land set between the mountains and the sea. Both as the regional capital of New England and as the northeastern outlier of the Industrial North, Boston has steadily diminished in national importance as the shadow of New York has lengthened. But with a population of 2.9 million, Boston is still the eighth largest city in the United States and the northern terminus of a near continuous belt of urbanization extending from Washington, D.C., through Baltimore, Philadelphia, and New York—a megalopolis of contiguous *standard metropolitan statistical areas.* Boston's position at the head of an excellent natural harbor, its seagoing commerce based on nearness to Europe, and its role as a service center for southern New England's dense network of smaller cities and towns account for its continuing importance. Nearby, the early important textile centers of Lawrence, Lowell, and Fall River capitalized on cheap energy from the sudden drop in stream elevation where the coastal plain abuts the foothills along the fall line. South and west of Boston, the important industrial towns of Providence (906,000) and Hartford (721,000) dominate Rhode Island and Connecticut. The Connecticut River widens as it flows south to form the most valuable stretch of agricultural land in New England. Dairy, grain, tobacco, and truck farms compete with suburbs for space. Southern New England, a sprawling urban landscape, is thus a northern continuation of the intense concentrations of population and industry characteristic of the Industrial North.

THE INDUSTRIAL NORTH

The Industrial North is neither topographically nor culturally united; its people live in environments ranging from the bedroom suburbs of the eastern seaboard to the deep recesses of the central Appalachian Mountains. Yet the westward expansion of the United States in the nineteenth century bound the three subregions of the Industrial North—Megalopolis, the Central Appalachian Highlands, and the Great Lakes Interior—into an interdependent industrial economy, creating one of the world's richest, most diverse, and most productive manufacturing complexes. The initial east-west connection was made with the opening of the Erie Canal (1825) which joined Buffalo on Lake Erie with Albany on the Hudson River, bringing the agricultural wealth of the awakening continent into the economic orbit of New York City. Railroads soon intensified commerce and communication between coastal ports such as New York, Philadelphia, and Baltimore and the interior plains, augmenting the possibilities for industrial growth. Centers in the Old Northwest (Ohio, Indiana, Illinois, Michigan, and Wisconsin) sprouted as colonies of the East: Pittsburgh, Cleveland, Cincinnati, Chicago, and Milwaukee. With coal in Appalachia and iron in the Great Lakes, crop surpluses in the Middle West, and dense urban populations on the Atlantic coast, the Industrial North displays the single greatest concentration of human activity in North America.

The cities of the Atlantic coastal plain from Boston to Washington contain three-fifths of the industrial and commercial power of the United States in forty-two standard metropolitan statistical areas, ranging in size from New York (9,974,000 people) and four other cities of more than 1 million to smaller centers such as Wilmington, Delaware (500,000), and Trenton, New Jersey (304,000). The cities of Megalopolis form a continuous urban belt with endangered farmland interspersed among them. The intensity of urbanization in the 450-mile-long "Boswash" corridor is found elsewhere only in European manufacturing zones and the Tokaido corridor of Japan. New Jersey and Rhode Island, entirely within this urbanized region, have the highest population densities in North America. In 1970, New Jersey had 953 persons per square mile and Rhode Island 906—concentrations not appreciably different from those of southeastern England or the Low Countries. By contrast, California, the most densely urbanized state of the American West, has only 128 persons per square mile. Yet these statewide population figures convey neither the scope nor the intensity of the urban scene. New Jersey, despite its high population density, has relatively large open spaces in both the northwestern and southeastern parts of the state; the pine barrens of south Jersey have remained isolated from the main currents of American civilization despite their nearness to the urban core. Even today, their inhabitants are principally trappers and blueberry pickers, people who retain a remnant colonial accent and vocabulary much like isolated mountain folk in West Virginia and Kentucky. Areal statistics, therefore, do not reflect the true degree of urbanization: where the people live, densities are much higher.

With a metropolitan area population of 16,206,841 in three states, New York is the world's largest city. Urbanization spreads from two groves of ninety buildings over 500 feet high in Midtown and Lower Manhattan outward for more than 60 miles through suburban sprawl to Connecticut, the lower Hudson, Long Island, and New Jersey. As the nation's leading port, New York handles about half the nation's overseas air freight and passenger traffic and is the most important manufacturing and service center in the United States. The scale of human effort in New York City is difficult to grasp: the city employs more than 70,000 public school teachers, 24,000 police, and 10,000 fire fighters; Brooklyn, one of New York's five *boroughs*• and an independent city until 1898, would be the fourth largest city in the United States were it independent today. Forty-eight states, all with greater natural resource potential, have populations smaller than the New York metropolitan area. New York's black population is considerably larger than the entire population of Atlanta; New York's Puerto Rican population dwarfs that of San Juan. The long-term financial plight of the city is reflected in its citizens' needs, its size, and its cultural, social, and financial importance to the nation as a whole. Situated on the fine natural harbor of the Hudson River above Lower New York Bay, New York is the gateway to most of the eastern United States.

Two hours' driving time south of New York, the nation's fourth largest city, Philadelphia (population 4,818,000), is located at the head of the drowned *estuary*• of the Delaware River. The site was personally chosen by the Quaker William Penn in 1682. He designed the original geometrical street plan of the city straddling a narrow neck of land between the Schuylkill and Delaware rivers. Philadelphia's early industrial growth was based on the availability of waterpower for woolen mills, paper making, and printing. Today, Philadelphia has broadened its metal and textile manufacturing base to include oil refining and chemicals. Farther south, Baltimore (population 2,071,000), at the head of the Chesapeake Bay, is located in a transition zone between the Industrial North and the South. Although often perceived as a southern city, Baltimore is a center of heavy industry based on iron and other metal ore imports and coal transported overland from Appalachian fields. Baltimore is also, however, an important food-processing center for the agriculture of the Upper South. Nearby Washington (population 2,909,000), the nation's capital, was sited as a locational compromise between the North and the South. The French engineer Pierre L'Enfant, hired by George Washington, planned a spacious city with a radial street pattern to display its vistas of monuments and public buildings reached by wide, tree-lined avenues. L'Enfant's image of the city of democracy, however, was quickly and continuously jeopardized by urban growth. As the locus for disbursement of the federal budget, some $300 billion a year, Washington is an administrative center that increasingly governs the growth and direction of America as a whole.

From the deck of a Manhattan skyscraper, it is possible to look well into the Appalachian Highlands that form the western border of the urbanized Atlantic coastal plain. The ridges and valleys of the Appalachian Mountains form a corrugated band of sparsely inhabited land running northeast to southwest from the Catskill Mountains of New York south through the Alleghenies of Pennsylvania, western Maryland, and West Virginia, to the Blue Ridge Mountains of Maryland and Virginia. Still farther to the west, the coal-rich Allegheny Plateau, the largest topographical province in the Industrial North, is a highland zone bordering the main thrust of the Appalachians extending from western New York westward into Ohio and Indiana and running southward through Kentucky and into central Tennessee.

At first glance, the thinly populated Appalachian highlands appear to have little in common with the urban and industrial complexes in the interior and along the coast, but their intermediate location and strong resource base have welded their economy firmly to that of the Industrial North. Pittsburgh (population 2,400,000), the major metropolitan center of this subregion, is a classic example of the industrial geography of iron and steel. The city is located where the waters of the Allegheny River merge with those of the Monongahela to form the Ohio River. Coal lying close to the surface in uplifted Appalachian seams was exploited before the Civil War, fostering a wave of steel-based industrialization that rapidly brought labor and wealth to the area in the second half of the nineteenth century. Industrial towns set in hill-shadowed valleys grew up along the banks of the Allegheny, Susquehanna, and upper Ohio rivers; in their hinterlands, a population of small farmers and miners settled isolated mountain valleys. As local iron deposits were exhausted, ore from the Great Lakes was shipped by barge from Duluth at the western end of Lake Superior to growing ports on Lake Erie such as Cleveland and Erie and then inland by rail. Today, the metal-finishing factories of Pittsburgh (United States Steel, Kaiser) utilize the nearly inexhaustible coal resources of the Allegheny Plateau and import iron ore from more distant sources. Labrador iron is shipped down the Saint Lawrence Seaway, and Venezuelan ore is moved overland by rail from Baltimore to supply the industries of the cities that dot the Allegheny Plateau.

Farther west, where the Allegheny Plateau breaks onto the interior plains, the band of industrialization continues along the American and Canadian shores of the Great Lakes. The Great Lakes industrial centers are involved in the production of heavy metals, the transshipment of the agricultural products of the Great Lakes plain to world markets, and the pursuit of integrated specialized industries such as the manufacture of chemical, photographic, and pharmaceutical equipment, rubber, and automobiles. The ribbon of urbanization at the western end of Lake Ontario is virtually unbroken. Rochester, New York, sprang up as a milling town on the fall line of the Allegheny Plateau at the head of the rolling farmland of the Genesee Valley. Toronto and Buffalo are centers of heavy industry; Toronto fulfills its role as the second city of Canada by serving a broad hinterland that encompasses much of the nation. Lake Erie's largest center of population is Cleveland (2,064,000), whose long list of manufactures reflects the industrial diversity typical of the Great Lakes region. Detroit (4,431,000) is the capital of the automotive industry, situated at the narrowest point of the strait connecting Lake Erie with Lake Saint Clair and Lake Huron. Detroit has access to iron ore from Minnesota and Upper Michigan, and coal from Pennsylvania, West Virginia, and Ohio. Despite these locational advantages, the growth of Detroit as a base of American industry with the expansion of automobile transportation is the result of decisions by a few early capitalists—Olds, Dodge, and Ford.

Farther west, Chicago (6,980,000) grew as a railroad hub whose lines of steel tapped the agricultural potential of new lands to the north, west, and south of the city. In 1848, Lake Michigan was linked with the Mississippi River by canal; in 1852, Chicago was linked with New York by railroad, and a web of steel was drawn across the Middle West. Chicago evolved into a prairie metropolis, a heartland city of skyscrapers on the plain, stockyards, risk capital, organized crime, and ethnic politics. It has epitomized small-town America grown up, a town of go-getters and Babbitts whose dreams of progress and prosperity financed the development of a large portion of North America. Second only to New York in municipal population and the center of a substantial manufacturing zone and transport system, Chicago is the western focus of the Industrial North. North of Chicago on Lake Michigan, Milwaukee possesses a mixture of light and heavy industry characteristic of the Great Lakes cities. The twin cities, Minneapolis and Saint Paul, on the Mississippi, originally lumber towns, became the flour-milling centers for most of the northern plains as far west as Montana. Winnipeg, Chicago's alter ego to the north, is the center of the trans-Canadian transportation network. Marquette, Duluth, and Thunder Bay are port cities of Lake Superior which ship out the iron ore mined in the Mesabi, Vermilion, and other ranges on the southern projection of the Canadian Shield.

The cities of the Great Lakes Plain from Syracuse to Milwaukee are surrounded by important agricultural landscapes. Along Lake Ontario and Lake Erie in both Canada and the United States, production of fruit—apples, pears, peaches, cherries, and grapes—is substantial. Much of rural Michigan, under the warming influence of nearby Lake Michigan, is devoted to fruit cultivation, and the lower Lake Michigan shore is particularly well suited to the production of flowers and nursery stock—an important industry in a nation of suburban gardeners. Beyond the influence of the lakes, limited grain and hay farming is combined with dairying and poultry raising.

THE SOUTH

The American South covers a variety of terrain in the south-central and southeastern United States. It is an area distinguished by its warm climate and long growing season, occupied by a people bound to the fact and legend of the Civil War. Much of the region remains intensely rural and relatively isolated, a landscape of small towns and specialized farming. Rural poverty is great, and out-migration to southern industrial centers and to the cities of the Industrial North has been strong in this century. Foreign immigration largely bypassed the South in the nineteenth century, and only recently have fast-growing centers such as Houston, Atlanta, and Miami attracted migrants from the rest of the United States and abroad. Topographically a southern extension of the Atlantic coastal plain, the Appalachians, and the Mississippi Valley—all areas that farther north form core elements of the American industrial belt—the South has retained its cultural distance from the rest of the country and preserved elements of its colonial past, its plantation economy and society, racial segregation, and a coherent set of moral attitudes well into the present century. Today, the full brunt of the American industrial economy is impacting selected parts of the South, modifying and integrating this distinctive culture region into the broader framework of American society.

The lowland coast of the South is topographically similar from Virginia to Texas: wide, open bays and *inlets*° with *offshore bars*° set in a humid, swampy environment. In contrast to the Industrial Northeast, urbanization is quite limited. On the Atlantic coast, Norfolk, Virginia, has grown in response to important naval installations. Like Wilmington (North Carolina), Charleston, Savannah, and Jacksonville, Norfolk is an export center for the products of the coastal plain: cotton, tobacco, peanuts, lumber, and naval stores. Inland where the coastal plain abuts the piedmont in Virginia, the Carolinas, and Georgia, a string of cities grew up on the fall line poised between the plantations of the southern seaboard and the small farms of the Appalachian slopes. Richmond, Raleigh, Columbia, and Montgomery utilized the waterpower generated at this topographical break as the basis for a textile industry, and each today is an important manufacturing center.

521

A shuffleboard tournament at Bay Pines Trailer Park in St. Petersburg. Since World War II, much of Florida has become an age- and income-graded landscape of the elderly and winter tourists. *Photo:* Gunnell/Monkmeyer.

Farther south, the lowland South projects nearly 400 miles into the Atlantic in the form of the Florida Peninsula and grades westward on the wide coastal plain bordering the Gulf of Mexico as far as the Rio Grande of Texas. Until the early part of this century, the peninsula remained largely a wilderness, little influenced by the southern plantation past. Florida, set between the Atlantic Ocean and the Gulf of Mexico, is surrounded by warm water; the British Bahama Islands are but 90 miles offshore. A slightly differentiated, raised limestone platform, Florida has a near year-round growing season and rich soils ideal for citrus cultivation. The warm climate of the peninsula has attracted heavy migration from the North since World War II, and much of Florida has become a suburban landscape of age- and income-graded settlements for elderly citizens, refugees from megalopolis, and winter tourists. Tampa–Saint Petersburg (population 1,089,000) and Miami (1,268,000) are Florida's largest cities. Florida's distinctive culture and society are exclusively twentieth-century phenomena: in 1900 Miami was a trading post and yacht harbor with a winter population of only 1681.

To the west, the subtropical Gulf Coastal Plain is formed by a plain bordering the Gulf of Mexico

generally under 300 feet, succeeded inland by plains reaching elevations of up to 600 feet above sea level. The Mississippi River, below 300 feet elevation as far north as Cairo, Illinois, at the confluence of the Ohio River, divides the Gulf Plain into eastern and western sections. With the longest growing season in eastern North America, hot summers, mild winters, and rain throughout the year, the Gulf Plain proved ideal for the cultivation of cotton, which spread across this area in the first half of the nineteenth century. Much of the Gulf Plain, however, still remains in timber, and logging, especially in Louisiana and eastern Texas, is a large-scale industrial enterprise. Rice and sugarcane are important crops along the Louisiana and Upper Texas Gulf coast; the Texas cattle industry has bred animals uniquely suited to the hot, wet climate. In southern Texas, vegetable and citrus crops are grown on the *floodplain* of the Rio Grande Valley.

The major cities of the Gulf Coastal Plain are the ports of New Orleans (population 1,046,000) and Houston (2,000,000). New Orleans is the entrepôt of the Mississippi and the cotton capital of the southern coast. Built on forested lowland *bayou* country, Houston has grown from 285,000 in 1900 to become the fifth most populous city in the United States and one of the largest cities in the world in area (it covers parts of six Texas counties). Houston's diversified industrial base expanded when construction

Despite efforts to revitalize its economy, the valleys and plateaus of Appalachia form an isolated, poverty-stricken region caught in its history of hardship and human tragedy. *Photo:* Paul Conklin/Monkmeyer.

of a ship channel connected it to the gulf, diverting traffic away from the port of Galveston 50 miles away. The discovery of oil and natural gas in the region in the early 1900s made Houston the *petrochemical*• center of American industry. North and west of Houston, on the western frontier of the Gulf Coastal Plain, a 300-mile line of cities runs from Dallas–Fort Worth southward through Austin to San Antonio along the margin of the Central Plains. These cities serve both the Gulf South and the Central Plains, and their wide hinterlands encompass both environments.

The inland South, composed of the southern Appalachians and related highlands to the west, is distinctly southern in culture, but differs substantially in economy from the lowland South. Inland from the Atlantic coastal plain, on the Appalachian piedmont, a tradition of small, family-worked dairy farms and orchards contrasts strongly with the large-scale peanut and cotton plantation economy of the seaboard. Still farther inland beyond the Blue Ridge Mountains, settlement followed the long valleys of the major rivers—the Shenandoah, the Tennessee, and the Coosa. These narrow Appalachian valleys widen southward, with Knoxville,

Chattanooga, and Birmingham growing into industrial cities utilizing waterpower from the Tennessee Valley Authority and exploiting the coal and iron ore deposits of the terminal Appalachian folds. Atlanta (1,600,000), the largest city in the southern Appalachians, influences a large part of the eastern part of the South. It evolved from a marketing and railroad center to develop a large metal-refining capacity as well as textile mills, fertilizer, and agricultural machine industries.

The valleys and plateaus that spread north and west from the Blue Ridge Mountains form an isolated, poverty-stricken region with a history of hardship and human tragedy. Appalachia, as this region is generally called, remains a core area of unemployment because its mineral and lumber resources, thanks to technological advances, are now efficiently exploited by a dwindling labor force. Although federally sponsored programs have attempted to revitalize Appalachia's economy since the 1930s, the mountain and valley heartland of the southern Appalachians continues to be a zone of heavy out-migration and interior stagnation.

Farther west and north of Appalachia, settlement in the fertile blue grass basins of Kentucky and Nashville in Tennessee is more prosperous. Natural prairies in the hinterlands of Louisville and Lexington are rich farmlands noted for tobacco and finely manicured horse-breeding farms. Nashville, a center of country music and southern culture, is

Figure 8. Commodity Belts of the Central Plains.

also an insurance and clothing center. The bountiful farmland of central Tennessee was sufficiently attractive to make Nashville in 1784 the first city chartered west of the Appalachians.

Across the middle Mississippi River plain, dominated by the inland port of Memphis, lie additional southern highlands—the Ozarks in Missouri, the Boston Mountains in Arkansas, and the Ouachita Mountains of Oklahoma and Arkansas. Life there is similar to life in Appalachia, the origin of most of the settlers. Mining of coal, bauxite, and iron ore is locally important, and lowland farms specialize in apple orchards and dairies; upland farms are poor, and where the forest cover has been destroyed, erosion is severe. Little Rock (population 323,000), the largest city of the area, is on the western frontier of the South, and like Joplin and Springfield in Missouri, is a center for smelting the aluminum, lead, and zinc ores mined in the uplands.

THE CENTRAL PLAINS
[FIGURE 8]

The center of North America, a treeless prairie, was perceived as a vast wasteland until the middle of the last century. After 1850, the Central Plains were rapidly stripped of their thick sod and became the most productive grain field in the world. The extent of this natural prairie is defined by climate. To the north, the grasslands extend into central Alberta, beyond which the cold is too severe for abundant growth of grasses, and the taiga and *muskeg* begin. Eastward, prairie stretches into Indiana and Illinois; there, although rainfall is sufficient to support forests, the efficient nature of the grass plant (a single plant can put out 350 miles of roots in a year) choked off other vegetation, and fires, to which grasses are virtually immune, repelled trees. To the south, the grasslands fade far into Mexico. The Central Plains are clearly defined on the west by the Rocky Mountains.

In this agricultural environment, climate is of critical importance. Generally speaking, rainfall in the Central Plains declines from east to west as the *rain shadow* of the Rockies takes hold; average annual temperatures rise from north to south. Two contrasting air masses dominate the Central Plains. In winter, the flow of polar air from the Arctic sweeps southward unimpeded in "blue northers," and temperatures below 0 degrees Fahrenheit have been recorded as far south as Austin, Texas, on the edge of the Gulf Coastal Plain. Average winter temperatures in the north of the Great Plains are severely cold: Winnipeg, for example, has an average January temperature of −1 degree Fahrenheit. In summer, the land heats rapidly as Gulf air moves northward, pushing continental air back into the Arctic. Thunderstorms and tornadoes are common in spring; high daily temperatures occur far north into the Canadian prairie. The frost-free season varies in an orderly north-south progression starting with the 100-day limit for wheat cultivation reaching from Edmonton, Alberta, across central Saskatchewan to southern Manitoba; on the southern margins of the Central Plains, growing seasons up to 240 days occur in Texas.

The Central Plains are often pictured as undifferentiated, but from the Canadian prairie provinces of Saskatchewan and Alberta to the central United States there is considerable topographical and agricultural diversity. Broad belts of specialized commercial farming cover the Central Plains in a succession of agricultural regions graded according to climate and terrain. In the far north, a zone of spring-planted wheat extends from the northern limit of profitability (Edmonton–Saskatoon–Winnipeg) to the Dakotas and parts of Minnesota and Montana. Although called the spring wheat belt, more barley and rye grains are grown here than in any other section of America, and beef cattle, sold young for fattening to the corn belt farther south, are also important. Canada's cities in the spring wheat belt are much larger than those of the United States. The largest, Edmonton (population 491,000), has grown with the development of the Alberta oil fields after World War II. In Minnesota and Wisconsin, the dairy belt contrasts sharply with the wheatlands to the north and west. Rainfall is higher and winters less harsh; a wooded landscape of family dairy farms surrounded by hayfields predominates. Although not an environmental component of the grassland prairies, the dairy belt is a concentrated, contiguous market for grains from the prairies.

South of this area, in the heart of the Central Plains, the corn belt reaches from eastern Nebraska to the Allegheny Plateau of Ohio. The economy of the corn belt, like other farming regions in the Central Plains, is clearly related to local climate. Ideal conditions for corn are average July temperatures in the mid-70s and summer rainfall totals near 11 inches. In the corn belt, where these conditions are met, a cultivated carpet of dark green covers all of Iowa, Illinois, and Indiana, and significant portions of Missouri, Ohio, Michigan, Minnesota, South Dakota, Nebraska, and Kansas. Corn land is rotated with soybeans, winter wheat, and pasture; throughout the belt, cattle and hog feedlots fatten animals for market. The natural prairie sod of the corn belt, turned over and plowed at enormous effort, has disappeared; the entire area is now a

The Central Plains of North America have become the most productive grain field in the world. This combine near Regina in Canada is harvesting wheat that may likely find its way to some other country. *Photo:* Wide World.

landscape of large-scale commercial agriculture.

Elevation rises from 1500 to 5000 feet and rainfall declines westward in the Central Plains. This sparser grassland, often called the Great Plains, is a transitional zone between the humid East and the arid mountainous region of the West. The Great Plains are bounded by the Missouri River on the north, the Rocky Mountains on the west, and the Balcones *escarpment* of Texas on the south. To the east, a facade of east-running rivers drains across the Great Plains as the land dips toward the Mississippi River and the Gulf of Mexico. Water is the critical scarcity on the Great Plains, and periodic droughts have twice forced dramatic retreats of the agricultural frontier. Following initial homesteading after the Civil War, droughts struck in the 1880s and produced abandoned farms and human misery. But rising world market prices for wheat after World War I led to a renewal of speculative wheat farming on the dry margins of the Great Plains in the 1920s—a period of above-average rainfall. *Dust bowl* conditions resulted from below-average rainfall a decade later and again scarred the Great

525

Plains with ecological disaster. Since that time, rural population has declined considerably, and better farming methods—especially the no-till method of plowing and the utilization of former cropland for permanent sheep and cattle grazing—have stabilized the economy of the Great Plains. In the Llano Estacado of the Texas Panhandle, irrigation has converted former wheatlands to cotton production, but the *cap rock*• water being used is limited, and exhaustion of the water supply looms as a definite possibility.

Chicago, defined earlier as an important center in the Industrial North, is also the dominant urban center of most of the Central Plains because of its strong transportation network. The city's influence radiates outward to rule local manufacturing, food processing, agricultural service industries, and the commodity markets of the Central Plains. Within the heartland of the plains, smaller cities serve smaller hinterlands as processing and regional banking centers and as outposts of the U.S. Department of Agriculture, whose involvement in the organization of production and markets is considerable. Minneapolis–Saint Paul is the center of the dairy belt; Des Moines, Omaha, Kansas City, and Topeka are the major service centers for the corn belt. Farther south, wheat farms and cattle ranches on the Great Plains are served by Wichita in Kansas; Oklahoma City and Tulsa in Oklahoma; and Lubbock, Amarillo, and Fort Worth in Texas. Seemingly far to the east, but midwestern in industry and service is Indianapolis. Saint Louis, at the junction of the Mississippi and Missouri rivers, controls the commodities and river traffic passing southward to the Gulf of Mexico or north into the corn belt and the spring wheat belt.

THE WEST

The American West is a region of huge internal distances, great topographical variety, and a diversified history of settlement. Thinly populated except on the Pacific coast, the West is generally perceived in terms of its dominating physical geography—the Rocky Mountains, the *intermontane*• basins and plateaus, and the Cascade, Sierra, and Coast ranges and *fjords*• of the Pacific West. Settled within living memory, it was for thousands of years the domain of agricultural and hunting Indian tribes. But wagon trains crossing the Great Plains and the Rockies brought settlers to Oregon, the Mormons to Utah, and after the California Gold Rush of 1849, wave after wave of settlers seeking new lives and fortunes —a process that continues even today. Perhaps no other region has so captured the imagination of the North American people. Their restless movement has created a diversity of American wests side by side from Los Angeles to Las Vegas to the forbidding recesses of the Rockies, the barren *deserts*•

of the Southwest, and the *rain forests*• of Puget Sound.

The Rocky Mountains course southeast from the Brooks Range of Alaska through the Mackenzie and Franklin mountains of the Yukon and Northwest territories to the Canadian Rockies between British Columbia and Alberta. In the United States, the central Rockies are characterized by dome and park country—long, rounded, domed ridges rising above escarpments from wide valleys and frequently paralleled by equally high volcanic ranges such as the Absarokas of Montana and Wyoming. Volcanic activity was once extensive in portions of the American Rockies in northern New Mexico, Colorado, and Wyoming. The easternmost ranges of the Rockies are set dramatically above the Great Plains; they rise 10,000 feet above the prairies and are broken by only a few east-west passes. Farther north, the Canadian Rockies rise equally abruptly from a plain dotted by massive lakes and wide rivers that course across the taiga of the Canadian Shield into the Arctic Ocean and Hudson Bay.

There are few large towns in the Rockies; rural population, engaged in extensive sheep and cattle ranching, lumbering, and mining, is sparse. Mining of copper, lead, gold, and silver is the basis of most cities in the Rockies, but the limited population of their wide hinterlands has inhibited urban growth. In both Canada and the United States, the largest cities serve both the Rockies and the western Great Plains. Calgary (population 400,000) is the trading center for an extensive stock-raising and wheat-growing region in the Canadian plains; the lumber mills of the city are based on nearby mountain forests. Denver-Boulder (population 1,237,000) has a diversified industrial base and provides service functions for both the central Rockies and the neighboring Great Plains.

Between the Rockies and the Sierra ranges of the Pacific, three high plateaus—the Columbia Plateau in the northwest, the Great Basin centered on Nevada, and the Colorado Plateau—form a dry, rugged swath extending from the Canadian border to northern Mexico. In the north, the Columbia Plateau is a volcanized landscape of dry valleys and forested ridges. *Dry farming*• techniques make commercial grain agriculture feasible. In western Washington and British Columbia, irrigated valleys such as the Okanogan, Yakima, and Wenatchee are major national suppliers of apples and pears. In the more arid eastern and southern portions of the Columbia Plateau, thousands of unbroken acres of grain make this the wheat belt of the West. Water diverted from the Columbia River through the Columbia Basin Project is now transforming the agriculture of the Columbia Plateau; alfalfa and a wide variety of specialty crops, from mint to gladiolus, are being added to the agricultural economy of the region. Spokane (population 287,000), the largest city on the plateau, commands three passes through the northern Rockies and has a growing industrial base dependent upon the abundant hydroelectric power of the Columbia River.

The Great Basin, centered on upraised, highly *eroded** highlands in Nevada, has one of the driest climates in the United States. In the Sonora, Mojave, and Colorado deserts in the south, rain may not fall for a year or more, daytime temperature ranges are high, and life is restricted to irrigated *oases.** In general, the settled valleys of the Great Basin receive less than 10 inches of rain a year, with neighboring highland ranges receiving up to 20 inches. Agriculture is generally limited to cattle grazing over very large areas, dry farming of grain, and cultivation in isolated irrigated zones. The Salt Lake depression of Utah, the greatest population concentration in the Great Basin, is an oasis based on streams descending from the surrounding Wasatch Mountains. Originally settled by the Mormons, Salt Lake City is the chief distribution center for the Great Basin. Other cities (Las Vegas, Carson City, and Reno) serve specific extractive industries such as the gold, copper, lead, and zinc mining operations of Nevada. But attractive scenery, gambling, and the hot, dry climate have drawn people to this area. The spectacular growth of Phoenix and Tucson, Arizona, can be attributed directly to the search for a winter-free climate. Phoenix expanded from a small vegetable and fruit farming community of 5500 people in 1900 to become the twentieth largest city in the United States with a 1970 population of nearly 600,000; Tucson's 1950 population of 45,000 had grown to 300,000 by the mid-1970s.

The Colorado Plateau consists of the largely uninhabited highlands of central Utah, northern Arizona, New Mexico, and western Colorado. The deeply entrenched rivers of the area, best illustrated by the Colorado, are characterized by canyons incised into uplifted blocks of *sedimentary** rock. The area is rich in gold, silver, and copper, and its coal resources are increasingly attracting attention. Albuquerque, founded as a regional capital of New Spain in 1706, serves a broad section of this thinly populated land.

West of the intermontane region, the land rises sharply in the Sierra Nevada and the Cascade Mountains, falls abruptly in a succession of interior valleys, and rises again along the coast ranges in the United States. Over this varied terrain, a wide variety of agriculture and settlement patterns prevail: nowhere else in North America do such strong variations in climate prevail over short distances. In contrast with the rest of the West, urbanization is intense in California, and the urban centers of Portland, Seattle, and Vancouver punctuate the northern coast. The climate is dominated by polar Pacific air that reaches as far south as San Diego in winter; tropical air advances as far north as Vancouver Island in the summer. The seasonal shift of these Pacific air masses across rugged relief gives the Pacific West its special climates. The coasts from Alaska to San Francisco are characterized by humidity, high rainfall, and moderate temperatures; they contrast strongly with the winter *continentality** of the interior. Southern California, under dry air from spring until fall, exhibits characteristics of a *Mediterranean climate,** with little rainfall in summer and a maximum in winter, resulting from the southward march of maritime polar air. Throughout the region, the projected *relief** of the Coast Ranges and the interior Cascades and Sierra Nevada foster locally high rainfall totals.

The Sierra Nevada are young, folded inland mountains severely glaciated in their higher elevations and faulted on both eastern and western slopes. As in the Cascades, an uplifted platform studded by volcanic peaks, rainfall totals of up to 70 inches on the western slopes of the Sierras provide a reservoir of water important for the expansion of agriculture in the valleys below and for urban populations along the coast. The entrapment and channelization of the Sierra's runoff has been fundamental to the growth of modern California. Two centers of *irrigated** agriculture—the Central Valley and the Los Angeles Basin—draw water from the Sierra Nevada through hydrological engineering complexes whose maximum expansion has apparently been reached. To the north, the Sierra Nevada and the Cascades sweep westward merging with the Coast Mountains in British Columbia to culminate in the Alaska Range. In Alaska, recently uplifted mountains have created the highest peaks in North America; in the Alaska Range, Mount McKinley rises to 20,320 feet.

A line of topographical depressions—rich agricultural valleys—is located along the western face of the Sierra Nevada and the Cascades: Puget Sound in British Columbia and Washington, the Willamette Valley of Oregon, and the Central Valley of California. Filled with *alluvial** debris up to 2000 feet thick, they form the agricultural heart of the Far West. In the north, Vancouver, Seattle–Everett, and Tacoma line the fjord environment of Puget Sound. Portland has grown to serve the specialized dairyland of the Willamette Valley on the Columbia River. In California, a succession of urban centers, most notably Sacramento, dots an agricultural landscape of fruit and nut trees, vegetables, and cotton in the Central Valley.

The Coast Ranges rise out of the Pacific Ocean to border California, Oregon, and Washington before submerging in British Columbia and Alaska and appearing as a chain of islands of which Vancouver Island is the largest. Generally speaking, the Coast Ranges rise in elevation northward, from rolling hills 2000 to 6000 feet high north of Los Angeles to the 8000 foot Olympic Mountains of Washington. San Francisco–Oakland is an immense urban area encircling San Francisco Bay, a drowned estuary that provides direct access to the Central Valley. On this natural opening in the smooth coastline of California, San Francisco has developed as the premier Pacific port of North America. Devastated by earthquake in 1906, San Francisco lost its lead as the largest city of the West to Los Angeles in the decade that followed. A center for a wide variety of manufactures—heavy industry, shipbuilding, and light industries such as electronics—San Francisco is the home of two of the finest universities in North America, the University of California at Berkeley and Stanford University.

The growth of Los Angeles is often perceived as a symbol of the structural changes of North American life during the twentieth century. The city has evolved from a trade center based on fruit and vegetable agriculture in the Los Angeles Basin at the turn of the century into a multicored urban system more than 60 miles wide linked by automobiles. The work of Los Angeles is as varied as its population. Booming transport equipment industries—particularly aircraft—attracted thousands of Americans to southern California in the 1940s and 1950s. Earlier, in the 1930s, refugees from dust bowl conditions on the Great Plains migrated to California in search of employment. In 1900, southern California contained only a quarter of the state's population; by the early 1970s, the area from Santa Barbara to San Diego included two-thirds of California's people. At the same time, the population of Los Angeles jumped from 102,000 in 1900 to 2,810,000 in 1970. Today, the unstructured nature of growth in the Los Angeles Basin endangers those very features that attracted people to the region. Pollution is a critical problem; the scenic vistas of southern California appear only occasionally through the smog. Space and privacy have been jeopardized by suburban sprawl.

South of Los Angeles, the California scene is dominated by San Diego, an important naval base and retirement center. The Spanish sailed into San Diego's fine natural harbor as early as 1542, but the city was not founded until 1769. It was the first of a number of Spanish colonial efforts in California to convert the Indian population to Catholicism and redirect their hunting and gathering economy toward agriculture and herding. Inland, east of the low, brushy Coastal Range, the arid Imperial Valley around the Salton Sea is a center of intensive, irrigated agriculture conducted below sea level. Water diverted from the Colorado River by the All-American Canal allows the cultivation of cotton, alfalfa, date palms, and a wide variety of vegetables for both Californian and national markets.

From northern California along the Pacific coast to Alaska lies a wide expanse of land separated by

The smog that Los Angeles has made famous is now typical of many cities of the United States. This aerial view shows New Haven, Connecticut, in late October, just as a stagnant air warning was lifted. *Photo:* Wide World.

great distances from the rest of urban North America. The states of the Pacific Northwest (Oregon and Washington), British Columbia, and the twentieth-century frontier of Alaska are characterized by similar environments. Sea and the forest play important roles in the economy of this region; farming is restricted to favored locations set by the sea and carved out of the forest. The port cities of the Northwest have grown in proportion to the wealth of their fishing, forestry, and farming, and each serves a wide hinterland.

Although the salmon fisheries of the coast have steadily declined in output since the 1920s as the human imprint upon the environment has been more surely felt, the fishing industry has expanded to cover the entire northern Pacific. The amount of fish taken from the Pacific by the competitive fleets of all nations—especially the United States, Canada, Japan, Russia, Britain, and Denmark—is today some forty times greater than the catch from the Atlantic. Similarly, of all North American forests, those on the West Coast are by far the most valuable. The trees—dense stands of Douglas fir, western hemlock and cedar, ponderosa pine, Sitka spruce, and balsam fir—are used for construction, pulp, and furniture. The natural properties of these woods and the extent of the forests from Alaska to northern California have made lumbering the primary rural activity. Fully 70 percent of Washington and nearly 50 percent of Oregon is forest; some four-fifths is exploitable. In British Columbia, 15 percent of the total value of production comes from wood. Logging is facilitated by the numerous rivers of the region, which along with truck and rail transport, allow easy access to lumber mills.

Farming attracted the earliest pioneers to the Northwest, for they believed the thick forests were a sign of rich soils and potential agrarian prosperity. But the wooded, mountainous landscape rendered farming profitable only in a few wide valleys. The Willamette River Valley of Oregon and the lowlands of the Puget Sound area became notable dairy, cattle, and fruit centers. Farther north, in coastal British Columbia, farming is concentrated around the cities of Victoria and Vancouver, where vegetables and orchard crops can be produced during the long growing season (200 to 240 days) of the Fraser River delta and the plains of Vancouver Island. In Alaska, the Matanuska Valley, with good soils and shelter from harsh winds, was developed in the 1930s as a model for northern agriculture. Even though the growing season is barely over 100 days, the long, warm summer days provoke luxuriant growth of such crops as vegetables, oats, hay, and potatoes.

The settlements of the Northwest are typically clustered on inlets where interior valleys meet the sea. Each is a trade center for the fishing, logging, and farming products of its hinterland; specialized occupations have developed out of modern communications and the hydroelectric projects in the Columbia River Basin and along the fast-running streams of British Columbia. Industrial maturity and affluence have fostered diversification. Portland, at the juncture of the Willamette and Columbia rivers, boasts the most used harbor of any American port, although the value and tonnage of cargo is not exceptionally high. Seattle is the dominant urban center of Puget Sound, a drowned valley set between the Cascade and the Coast ranges. Seattle grew into an ocean port with trade based upon local raw materials; it is now the economic and social hub of the Northwest. Its contemporary fortunes rest on its relation to the aeronautics industry, its strategic location as the closest American link with the Orient, and its position as the financial and transportation service center for Alaskan development. At the head of Puget Sound, Vancouver Island lies between the Strait of Juan de Fuca facing the United States and the Strait of Georgia flanking the province. At Vancouver Island, the island and fjord environment of mountains, glaciers, rivers, and forests begins and extends northward to Alaska. Victoria is the capital of British Columbia, an oddly English urban landscape and society. Vancouver, the metropolis of the Canadian West at the mouth of the Fraser River,

was a trading post of the Hudson's Bay Company in the early 1800s and a lumber town in the early twentieth century; today it is an important industrial city and the export center for wheat from the prairie provinces.

Alaska, nearly 600,000 square miles in area, is connected to the south by both the Alaska Highway through the Yukon and northern British Columbia, and by the Inside Passage (Alaska Marine Highway) which threads through the coastal straits of the Pacific. Moderating oceanic influence is strongly felt in the Alaskan Panhandle: rainfall is heavy (up to 100 inches annually) and the climate remarkably free from severe cold. Settlements in the south-central portion of the state and the western chain of Aleutian Islands have capitalized on rich offshore fisheries and the dense forests of spruce, hemlock, and cedar inland. Anchorage, at the head of Cook Inlet on the south-central coast, has functions similar to those of the cities of the Pacific Northwest. High elevations are reached in the Alaska and Saint Elias ranges; peaks rising over 18,000 feet are common. Inland, beyond this great natural barrier, the Yukon Plateau is a basin landscape walled off from the far north by the Brooks Range. From the Yukon River Basin northward, rainfall declines to 15 inches or less in an Arctic desert. Extreme winter cold is interrupted by brief, yet surprisingly warm, summers. Beyond the Brooks Range, the vast tundra of the Arctic Coastal Plain stretches north to the Arctic Ocean. The Yukon Plateau, with little other natural wealth to offer, attracted a population of miners in search of gold in 1898. Towns such as Nome and Fairbanks grew so rapidly that Alaska was organized into a territory in 1912.

With statehood in 1959 and a rapidly increasing population, Alaska today is experiencing galloping industrial growth. With the discovery of substantial reserves of oil at Prudhoe Bay on the Arctic Ocean, the population of Alaska has reached 360,000; the state's budget has grown from $100 million in 1969 to $630 million in 1975–1976. The oil boom has launched Alaska toward a future fully integrated with that of the rest of the continent.

MODERN NORTH AMERICA
2

As the impact of the machine age and urbanization spread throughout the world, the twentieth century witnessed the full flowering of two capitalist societies on the North American landscape. The United States and Canada matured into dynamic technological societies with half the world's wealth and a total population of 236 million in 1975. In this drive to maturity, North Americans harnessed their diverse resource base to forge powerful national economies. The process drew North Americans, native and immigrant alike, into new urban centers that exploded in size. Diverse peoples created unexpected social adaptations in this urban world, responses to problems that reflected the increasing intensity and complexity of Canadian and American life. Perhaps most urgent was the question of the distribution of wealth. Technology manufactured prosperity. But in nations that prized utility and productivity, wealth tended to concentrate among the strongest and the most competitive. In the twentieth century, a recognition of persistent poverty among the less educated, the less mobile, and racial minorities began to dominate national debate. With the attainment of unprecedented affluence in the modern period, North Americans began to search for quality. Having conquered material problems, the principal concern of the rest of the world, they began to explore the inner frontiers of social geography—issues of quality of life, racial harmony, and environment. For the first time, Americans perceived limits imposed by reason on the material world, and they celebrated a "Bicentennial" debating questions of growth, freedom, and equity.

THE DRIVE TO MATURITY

In the last half of the nineteenth century, North American efforts to manipulate the environment gained momentum. An agricultural nation at the end of the Civil War, the United States had become an industrial giant whose production in 1900 dwarfed that of France, Germany, and Great Britain. During those thirty-five years, American manufactures increased seven times in value to a then-staggering $13 billion. Industrial horsepower increased five times, and nearly 5 million people were employed in factory labor.

There were several sources of this remarkable industrial growth. First, a storehouse of natural resources barely touched before was discovered and commercialized in these decades. Huge pools of oil were found; a substantial share of the world's coal was discovered; large deposits of iron, lead, zinc, copper, and silver came under exploitation. In an atmosphere of untrammeled competition, one mining strike followed another, and a frenzied rush to exploit the richest resource concentrations ensued. A few, heavily financed controlling interests quickly emerged to work resources to exhaustion, ravaging the land as they built empires of industry. Second, a flood of new inventions altered the life of the nation. Between 1865 and 1900, the Patent Office granted 500,000 patents; in the 1850s, fewer than 1000 patents per year were granted; in the 1890s, the annual figure was over 25,000. Thomas Edison, wedding scientific theory to practical convenience, single-handedly deluged the government with over 1000 requests for patents. The telephone, telegraph, sewing machine, camera, typewriter, and automobile were invented; new industrial processes, machines, and motors were developed. Industrialists zealously adapted these inventions to increase the productivity of the industrial worker, pioneering the system of mass production on which modern American society rests. Finally, as Tocqueville noted, a "thirst for riches" gripped North America's society. Success became a moral obligation in the United States; the Puritan gospel of hard work mandated accomplishment. As a Massachusetts bishop put it, "Godliness is in league with riches," and "wealth comes only to the man of morality." In the course of this saga of expansion, exploitation, greed, and material progress, the United States became the world's foremost example of economic development.

Railroad Empires

Perhaps the single most important element in North America's economic development was the expanding railroad network that linked the resources of the United States and southern Canada. In 1869, the first transcontinental railroad bridged the mountain walls of the Sierras and the Rockies when the Central Pacific, built by Chinese coolies, and the Union Pacific, constructed by gangs of Irishmen, met at Promontory Point, Utah, and a final golden spike was driven to complete the line. The next year railroad trackage in the United States passed the 50,000-mile mark: by 1880, 93,000 miles of track were in operation, and railroads were consuming nine-tenths of the rolled steel produced in the United States. The first Canadian transcontinental railroad was completed in 1885, and an ordinary spike, "just as good as any other used to build the railway" was driven at Eagle Pass, British Columbia. By 1890, 166,700 miles of railroad track spanned America, more than in all Europe combined. Five transcontinental trunk lines connected the East Coast with the West, and although railroading in the East and Middle West was less romantic and dramatic, the dozens of feeder lines that crisscrossed every state had great economic significance for local communities and industries. As one Indiana farmer remarked, "everybody and everything's going places." By 1900, state and federal governments had granted 180 million acres of land to the railroads, and private rail investors had tendered nearly $10 billion. The railroad debt was five times as large, and railroad revenues were twice as high, as those of the federal government.

The Central Pacific, built by Chinese laborers, and the Union Pacific, built by gangs of Irishmen, meet at Promontory Point, Utah, in 1869, to complete the first transcontinental railroad. *Photo:* **Union Pacific Railroad Museum Collection.**

Yet this enormous system of rapid and cheap transportation that hauled a flood of goods and people to all settled parts of the continent was in the hands of a few relentlessly ambitious, powerful individuals. Cornelius Vanderbilt, once captain of a ferryboat, operated a network of 4500 miles of track (the New York Central) between New York City and the largest cities in the Middle West in addition to owning a fleet of ocean freighters and a trans-Atlantic steamship line. The soft-spoken, cynical Jay Gould, archetype of the robber barons of the period and described by one competitor as "a perfect eel," rose from a position as grocery clerk in upstate New York to take control of a 9000-mile railroad system in the Southwest. Driven by fierce competition, uti-

In the late nineteenth century, the mines and mills of Pennsylvania supplied the coal and steel that made America a great industrial power. But the empires of magnates like Andrew Carnegie were built on exploitation of immigrant and child labor. These small boys separate slate from coal. *Photo:* Brown Brothers.

lizing ruthless maneuvers on the rim of the law, these railroad monarchs forged the network of steel that interlaced the nation. Nothing like it existed anywhere in the world.

Industrial Growth

Similar patterns of explosive growth and rapid consolidation of business empires occurred in steel, oil, and electricity—the most dynamic, fastest-growing segments of the American economy. After the invention of the Bessemer process of purifying iron into steel, that durable, once-rare commodity became widely available for bridges, buildings, railroads, and consumer goods. Steel production soared from 1 million tons in 1880 to 26 million in 1910, and a substantial share of the market belonged to one man, Andrew Carnegie (1835–1919), the immigrant son of a weaver from Dunfermline, Scotland. Recognizing that cheap steel was vital to the new industrial age, Carnegie began, by the time he was thirty, to buy up iron and steel mills, tributary iron and coal mines, limestone quarries, and the barges and railroads that connected ore fields to factories. The iron mines of Lake Superior were brought into production: the Menominee Range in Michigan, the Vermilion Range in Minnesota, and—largest of all—the Mesabi Range, also in Minnesota, where vast deposits of iron lay on the surface and were so soft they could be

strip-mined with steam shovels. Pittsburgh, in the heart of the Appalachian coalfields, burgeoned into the primary steel-producing center in America; additional multimillion-dollar steel complexes were developed in Alabama, Illinois, and Colorado. In the 1880s, the canal at Sault Sainte Marie linking western iron and eastern coal was carrying three times the tonnage of the Suez Canal. Exultant, Carnegie described the dynamics of his booming industry: "Two pounds of ironstone mined upon Lake Superior and transported 900 miles to Pittsburgh; one pound and one-half of coal mined and manufactured into coke and transported to Pittsburgh; one-half pound of lime mined and transported to Pittsburgh; a small amount of manganese ore mined in Virginia and brought to Pittsburgh—and these four pounds of materials manufactured into one pound of steel, for which the consumer pays one cent."

On this recipe for riches, Carnegie built an integrated industrial empire, the United States Steel Corporation, which owned 149 steel plants, 250,000 acres of coal land, 112 Great Lakes ore ships, and more than 1000 miles of railroad. Having devoted his life, as one biographer put it, to "a single-minded pursuit of the main chance that left behind a trail of ruined competitors," Carnegie sold the corporation to J. P. Morgan in 1901 for 250 million dollars, retired to a castle in Scotland, and spent the rest of his life donating his fortune to charity—30,000 public libraries, museums, foundations, peace endowments, and even pensions for the widows of former presidents.

John D. Rockefeller brought the same organizational genius to the oil industry. For nearly a cen-

Edwin Drake, at right, stands with a friend in front of the Oil Creek well at Titusville, Pennsylvania, on the day when oil was found at 70 feet. This first well produced about 20 barrels a day; by the 1880s, the Appalachian fields were producing 30 million barrels a year. *Photo: Wide World.*

tury, the petroleum that seeped to the surface in hollows in the western Appalachians fouled nearby farmland and was used only as a remedy for rheumatism, bronchitis, and a variety of other illnesses, marketed under spurious labels such as Snake Oil and Seneca Oil. In the 1850s, however, Edwin Drake, a former railroad express agent, drilled a well to tap this resource at Titusville, Pennsylvania. He struck oil at 70 feet, and the boom was on. Advances in technology made petroleum increasingly profitable, and wells were drilled throughout the Appalachian field. By the 1880s, it was producing over 30 million barrels of oil a year. Rockefeller, described by his friend Senator Mark Hanna as "mad about money, although sane in everything else," and by his enemies as "that bloodless Baptist bookkeeper," brought order to the chaotic oil fields by buying up oil refineries and monopolizing 95 percent of the nation's refining capacity through his firm, the Standard Oil Company. Like Carnegie, Rockefeller aimed at controlling an entire industry. He purchased producing wells in the Appalachians and the Southwest, barrel-making factories, pipelines and oil cars for transport, and even the retail stores where kerosene was sold for lighting. Eliminating or absorbing all competitors, Rockefeller arose as one of the most powerful men in America, the Mephistopheles of Cleveland, who, as more diverse uses for

petroleum became known, dominated a business empire whose products included asphalt, the raw materials for fertilizer, lubricating greases and oils, macadam binder, gasoline, and heating oil. Rockefeller was the first billionaire in history.

Other large-scale monopolies developed in public utilities—Western Union, American Telephone and Telegraph, and after a brutal seven-year business war, General Electric and Westinghouse. Swift, Cudahy, and Armour controlled meat packing; Pillsbury consolidated the flour-milling industry. The scale of these operations made new economies and efficiencies possible, and from a purely quantitative viewpoint, the accomplishments of American industry were astonishing. Total manufactures increased tenfold in the last half of the nineteenth century and doubled again before World War I. Living standards rose substantially. Technological advances, the driving energy of competitive businessmen, and an influx of willing immigrants from Europe were combining to make the United States the most formidable industrial nation in the world.

Problems of Growth

As early as the 1830s, Tocqueville had warned that "the manufacturing aristocracy which is growing up under our eyes is one of the harshest that ever existed"; uncontrolled industrial monopolies in the United States seemed to confirm this statement. The elimination of small independent businesses was generating a new sense of individual helplessness. It was no longer certain that enterprising individuals could achieve success and prosperity through hard work and strong character. Workers' slums were not breeding grounds for millionaires, and in a nation of wage earners, the dream of economic independence was, for many, fading fast. The rich viewed poverty as "the sternest of all schools" and unemployment as "an act of God." But by 1893, the richest 10 percent of Americans owned three-quarters of the national wealth. In desperation, workers formed unions to battle for reductions in the usual sixty- to eighty-hour work week, for minimum safety standards, and for some measure of job security. Corporations retaliated with private militias and federal troops; between 1881 and 1906, thousands of workers were killed in 38,000 strikes and lockouts involving 10 million workers. Immigrants from southern and eastern Europe and southern blacks were hired as strikebreakers to work on railroads, in

A view of Hester Street on New York's Lower East Side in 1898. Between 1880 and 1920, 24 million European immigrants arrived at East Coast ports. As many as 15,000 a day arrived at Ellis Island in New York harbor, where they were sorted and given cursory medical checks. *Photo: Byron/The Byron Collection, Museum of the City of New York.*

coal mines, and in urban sweatshops. Henry Frick, Carnegie's partner in steel, hired Hungarians to break a strike one year and Italians to break a similar strike by the Hungarians two years later. Ultimately the unions won better working conditions and a more secure living. But a chasm of distrust separated corporate business and the nation's workers, and bitter ethnic and racial tensions seethed in America's industrial cities.

THE URBAN WORLD

Urbanization and industrialization proceeded apace in the United States, with one process reinforcing the other. Between 1850 and 1900, the population of the country tripled from 23 million to 76 million and passed the 100 million mark by 1920. Although many Americans continued to move west in search of land and fortune, many more were lured to another frontier—the city. In 1860, four of every five Americans lived on the land, but by 1900, 30 million of the 76 million Americans were urbanites, and one-twelfth of the nation's population lived in New York, Philadelphia, or Chicago. By 1910, almost all America's great cities had established their regional dominance. The population of New York City soared to over 3 million, and the city dominated the ocean traffic of the Atlantic. San Francisco and to a lesser extent Los Angeles and Seattle played similar roles in the Pacific. Philadelphia was the nation's third largest city with 1.3 million people. Pittsburgh, the nation's greatest forge, and Saint Louis, the prairie entrepôt, were sited at important river junctions. At either end of the Mississippi, New Orleans and Minneapolis–Saint Paul were thriving cities. And Chicago, burned to the ground in 1871, had grown again to a population of 1.7 million by 1900. The nation's most active rail hub, Chicago was, in the words of author Carl Sandburg, "hog butcher, tool maker, stacker of wheat, player with railroads, and freight handler to the nation."

The rate and intensity of urbanization differed considerably from one part of the country to another. In 1910, the Industrial North included fourteen of the nineteen American cities with populations of more than 250,000, all three of the nation's cities with over 1 million (New York, Philadelphia, and Chicago), and the only Canadian cities with populations greater than 250,000 (Montreal and Toronto). Seven of every ten people in New England and the Middle Atlantic states lived in cities, as did half the Great Lakes population. On the West Coast, a comparable level of urbanization was reached; industrial growth based on exploitation of local resources, reliable railroad connections with the East, and ocean commerce had spurred the growth of several large urban centers. By contrast, the interior West, with its reliance on extensive grain farming and cattle raising, supported far fewer cities of substantial size. And the lowest rate of urbanization was in the South, where less than one of every five people lived in a city and only New Orleans had a population of more than 250,000. Overall, this urban movement in the United States and elsewhere in the technological world became the greatest of all migrations. The country seemed determined to go to town.

A Nation of Nations

Although many of America's new urbanites were drawn from native farming communities, millions were foreign immigrants who crossed the Atlantic in search of a better life. Between 1820 and 1880, more than 9 million foreigners entered the United States. Some 85 percent came from the British Isles, Germany, Scandinavia, and, lured by a greater range of opportunity, Canada. For most, out-migration was motivated by hard times in the old country. In the 1840s and 1850s, 1.7 million Irish sought refuge in the United States when life hit rock bottom in Ireland and hundreds of thousands died of "famine fever," dysentery, and scurvy in the wake of the five-year potato blight. Clustered in the Northeast, but gradually dispersing westward along the railroads they helped to build, one of every twenty-three Americans was Irish-born in 1850; one Boston priest suggested that "God had made America as an asylum for Ireland." In the 1850s, political repression and crop failures in Central Europe impelled 1 million Germans to cross the Atlantic; in the 1860s and 1870s, Germans formed the largest share of the incoming immigrants. Although some were professional people and artisans, most were farmers driven off the land by the cheap wheat flowing into Europe from the farmlands of North America and Russia. Along with Norwegians, Swedes, and a steady stream of English, Welsh, and Scottish immigrants, Germans settled on farms in the Middle West and the Canadian prairies, in the mining towns of Appalachia, and in the industrial towns of the Northeast.

Between 1880 and 1920, this immigrant stream swelled to flood as 24 million people, the vast majority of them from southern and eastern Europe, arrived at East Coast ports. Anti-Semitic massacres in Russia in the 1880s launched a wave of Jewish migration to America; cholera epidemics in the Italian Mezzogiorno had the same effect. Pressure of population growth and the inefficiency of peasant agriculture in eastern Europe left many Magyars, Czechs, Slavs, and Croatians with the choice of emigration or starvation. So they left for America by the hundreds of thousands. Emigrant trains starting deep in Russia picked up boxcars full of Austrians, Hungarians, and Lithuanians on the way to ports of embarkation. With North America's rapidly expanding industrial economy in need of cheap labor, thousands of commission agents for American and Canadian land interests, factories, and mines sought potential immigrants in Europe, making certain they had the three essentials for immigration—an exit paper, a $10 ticket, and $25 to spare. Between 1900 and 1914, 3.1 million Austro-Hungarians, 3 million Italians, 2.5 million Russians, and nearly 1 million people from the Balkans made the two- to eight-week passage across the Atlantic. As many as 15,000 a day arrived at Ellis Island in New York, where they were sorted and given cursory medical checks —chalked on their backs were H for heart disease, L for the limp of rickets (a bone disease), or a circle with a cross that indicated feeble-mindedness and mandated immediate deportation. Speaking many languages and of diverse faiths, these immigrants shared a vision of America as a land of opportunity. They were willing to do almost anything to seize their chance.

Urban Immigrants
[FIGURE 9]

With the open lands of the West filling up, the bulk of these new immigrants poured into cities in the North and were absorbed by the industrial sector. In 1910, 79 percent of them lived in urban centers, and a congressional report that same year indicated that in twenty-one major industries, 57.9 percent of all laborers were foreign-born, two-thirds of them from southern and eastern Europe. Russian Jews and Italians entered the garment trades of New York; Poles, Portuguese, Greeks, and Syrians joined the Irish in New England's textile mills; and Slovak, Polish, and Italian miners worked the coalfields of Pennsylvania. Almost unnoticed in this European tide, southern blacks also migrated northward, drawn by jobs in the expanding industrial belt. By 1910, 750,000 black Americans lived in the North and West, one-third of them in New York, Philadelphia, Chicago, and Saint Louis. The urban collision of black and ethnic Americans was beginning.

The scale of this migration transformed the American urban landscape. In 1910, four of every ten New Yorkers were foreign-born; the city had twice as many Irish as Dublin, more Italians than Naples, and probably the largest Jewish community in the world. Only Berlin and Hamburg had more Germans than Chicago. In industrial cities such as Milwaukee, Detroit, and Cleveland, more than 30 percent of the inhabitants were immigrants. The same was true in the entry ports of Boston and San Francisco. Poor, uneducated, and desperate for work, these people

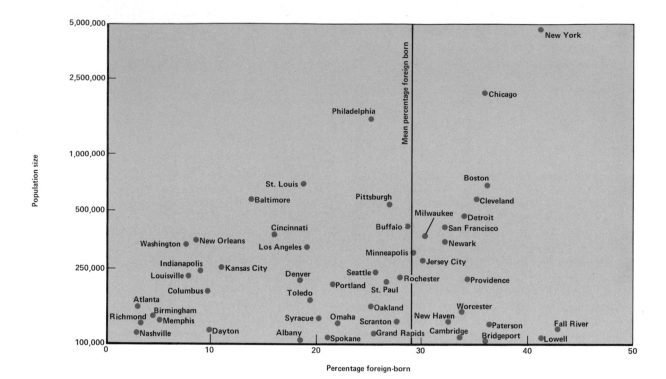

Figure 9. Percentage Foreign-Born, 1910. *Adapted from: David Ward, Cities and Immigrants: A Geography of Change in Nineteenth-Century America.* New York: Oxford University Press, 1971, p. 77, Fig. 2—6. Copyright © 1971 by Oxford University Press, Inc. Redrawn by permission.

were rapidly shunted into the nation's factories and airless tenement districts nearby. Large-scale immigration aggravated housing problems, insanitary conditions, street crime, and corruption in cities already strained by rapid growth. The newcomers clustered defensively in tightly knit neighborhoods to create a new ethnic urban geography in most industrial cities; each metropolis had its own Little Italy and Little Ireland.

Threatened by a babel of new voices, native movements composed of earlier northern European immigrants railed against "gross little foreigners" and "Europe's human garbage." Accepted into America themselves, they now protested that the open immigration policy of the United States would lead to "racial suicide," even though the proportion of foreign-born Americans had remained steady at 12 to 15 percent of the total population between 1850 and 1920. Nonetheless, in the 1920s the United States closed its door to large-scale immigration, but not before America had become not a melting pot, but a nation of nations.

Urban Conditions

Drawn from rural areas, most urban pioneers who crowded into New York, Chicago, Philadelphia, and other nineteenth-century cities faced problems of transport, health, and housing whose solutions lay beyond the reach of any single individual. Sewage facilities, primitive and in some cities nonexistent, lead to cholera and typhoid epidemics. Philadelphia's provisions for clean water were so inadequate as late as 1883 that the death rate from typhoid fever was double that of New York. In many cities, street cleaning was left to scavenger pigs which fed on refuse thrown into public thoroughfares. In Cincinnati, which relied on these animals for garbage disposal, the hogs were regularly rounded up and sold at auction when their number reached 6000. Somewhat earlier, a report of the day soberly castigated the pigs on Broadway in New York City as being too "weak in numbers and deficient in organization" to keep the city clean.

Public fire protection was but an emerging municipal concept; the nation's urban fire losses skyrocketed from $64 million to $150 million during the 1880s. And the crime rate soared with population growth, making daily life risky and public safety a central concern. The national homicide rate tripled during the 1880s, and the number of prison inmates increased by 50 percent. Everywhere urban growth outstripped road construction; in 1890, Chicago had 1400 miles of dirt streets. The "engineer" that laid out Boston's streets was, according to writer Ralph Waldo Emerson, a cow. Even before automobiles, urban traffic congestion was so intense that one 1867 New York paper claimed that the working population of the city—nineteenth-century commuters—was forced to spend as much as "a sixth-part of their working days on street cars or omnibuses.''

By the turn of the century, these urban problems had eased, and an *infrastructure*[•] of municipal services was available in most American cities. Police and fire departments were established; garbage removal was systematized; streets were paved. By 1898, 30 million square yards of asphalt were thrown down on city roads to replace cobblestones and wooden blocks. Cable cars were introduced in San Francisco in 1873; twenty years later, 850 trolley lines with 10,000 miles of track had been installed in American cities. One booster proudly discovered that a passenger could ride electric trolleys better than 1000 miles from Portland, Maine, via New York to Sheboygan, Wisconsin; it is not known whether anyone ever actually did. These facilities considerably extended the spatial reach of the city, spawning widening circles of suburbanization. They did little, however, to relieve traffic congestion; first New York and then Boston went underground to construct subways for moving people to and from work. Electric, gas, and telephone lines were installed in most cities, and aqueducts reaching far into urban hinterlands provided city dwellers with clean supplies of piped water, sharply reducing the incidence of epidemic. With urban real estate values soaring, architects built upward in steel. The words "skyline" and "skyscraper" were introduced into the vocabulary. The American city was beginning to take on its modern form.

The most serious urban problem, however, remained housing. Tenement slums, crowded warrens in which more people were crammed into less living space than ever before, spread out around the spacious avenues and skyscrapers of the central city. In parts of Lower Manhattan, population densities exceeded 900 people per acre, a staggering 500,000 people per square mile—and tenement buildings were rarely more than five stories high. Conditions of life in these airless blocks of low-cost housing were barely endurable—rates of infant mortality, tuberculosis, crime, vice, and delinquency were extremely high. In 1900, only two of five infants survived their first year in one Chicago slum. A Boston report noted that the average life span of the urban Irish was only fourteen years. In New York, one of every twenty people lived in a squalid cellar; in the poorest of these, boarders paid 37.5 cents a week for "first class" accommodations (straw pallets), 18 cents a week for second class (bare floor), and 9 cents a week for third class (space as available). Some groups survived better than others. Russian Jews, experienced urbanites, had a very low rate of tuberculosis; predominantly rural Italian immigrants usually had the highest death rate in the city. Unable and in some cases unwilling to flee crowded tenements for the expanding suburbs, the urban poor were manipulated by slum landlords, land devel-

opers, and corrupt city administrators who deferred to business interests. Denounced by Jacob Riis in his classic study, *How the Other Half Lives* (1890), the tenement slum remains a persistent blight on the American urban landscape. Seventy years old, having served generations of Irish, Italian, Polish, and German Americans, the same crumbling buildings house newer refugees today—black and Puerto Rican Americans, who have exchanged rural hovels for city slums and bitterly resent their impoverishment in a land of obvious plenty.

THE DISTRIBUTION OF WEALTH
In the 1920s, North Americans appeared to have discovered a method for maintaining permanent prosperity: the formula was scientific exploitation of resources and large-scale production and consumption of industrial goods. Unscathed and strengthened by World War I, the agricultural and industrial resources of North America had been mobilized to such a degree that the United States emerged more powerful than any nation in human experience. Creditor to the world, it owned some 40 percent of all the world's wealth and was as rich as all Europe combined. President Calvin Coolidge remarked that "the business of America is business." Indeed, no people pursued wealth with such enthusiasm and passion; few others had such faith in expansion and progress. Supported by a vast environment, the facts seemed to justify the faith. Industrial production in North America doubled in the decade after the war, and the real incomes of workers increased by half. With new energy sources more accessible and mobile, the average American consumed forty times more energy than a century earlier—almost half the world's total available power. The social significance of this achievement was not lost upon a nation suddenly able to afford a Model T automobile and move to the suburbs.

On the farms, large-scale mechanization and new fertilizers raised yields substantially; the nation was easily able to feed its population of 150 million and still remain the primary food exporter in the world. In agriculture, as in manufacturing, striking gains in productivity reflected new efficiencies, improved technology, and the electrification of manual work— all of which vastly increased the output of the individual laborer. Under these circumstances, most Americans were uncritical admirers of their system

THE IMMIGRANT

In The Rise of David Levinsky *(1917), Abraham Cahan follows the life of a Russian Jew from his native village and decision to leave for the New World to his rapid rise to power and wealth in the New York garment industry. Here, Levinsky discovers America in 1885 with his fellow immigrant Gitelson:*

When I say that my first view of New York Bay struck me as something not of this earth it is not a mere figure of speech. I vividly recall the feeling, for example, with which I greeted the first cat I saw on American soil. It was on the Hoboken pier, while the steerage passengers were being marched to the ferry. A large, black, well-fed feline stood in a corner, eying the crowd of newcomers. The sight of it gave me a thrill of joy. "Look! there is a cat!" I said to Gitelson. And in my heart I added, "Just like those at home!" For the moment the little animal made America real to me. . . .

We were ferried over to Castle Garden. . . .

The harsh manner of the immigration officers was a grievous surprise to me. As contrasted with the officials of my despotic country, those of a republic had been portrayed in my mind as paragons of refinement and cordiality. My anticipations were rudely belied. "They are not a bit better than Cossacks," I remarked to Gitelson. But they neither looked nor spoke like Cossacks, so their gruff voices were part of the uncanny scheme of things that surrounded me. These unfriendly voices flavored all America with a spirit of icy inhospitality that sent a chill through my very soul.

I lead the way out of the big Immigrant Station. As we reached the park outside we were pounced down upon by two evil-looking men, representatives of boarding-houses for immigrants. They pulled us so roughly and their general appearance and manner were so uninviting that we struggled and protested until they let us go— not without some parting curses. Then I led the way across Battery Park and under the Elevated railway to State Street. A train hurtling and panting along overhead produced a bewildering, a daunting effect on me. The active life of the great strange city made me feel like one abandoned in the midst of a jungle. Where were we to go? What were we to do? But the presence of Gitelson continued to act as a spur on me. I mustered courage to approach a policeman, something I should never have been bold enough to do at home. As a matter of fact, I scarcely had an idea what his function was. To me he looked like some uniformed nobleman—an impression that in itself was enough to intimidate me. With his coat of blue cloth, starched linen collar, and white gloves, he reminded me of anything but the policemen of my town. I addressed him in Yiddish, making it as near an approach to German as I knew how, but my efforts were lost on him. He shook his head. With a witheringly dignified grimace he then pointed his club in the direction of Broadway and strutted off majestically.

"He's not better than a Cossack, either," was my verdict.

At this moment a voice hailed us in Yiddish. Facing about, we beheld a middle-aged man with huge, round, perpendicular nostrils and a huge round, deep dimple in his chin that looked like a third nostril. Prosperity was written all over his smooth-shaven face and broad-shouldered, stocky figure. He was literally aglow with diamonds and self-satisfaction. But he was unmistakably one of our people. It was like coming across a human being in the jungle. Moreover, his very diamonds somehow told a tale of former want, of a time when he had landed, an impecunious immigrant like myself; and this made him a living source of encouragement to me.

"God Himself has sent you to us," I began, acting as the spokesman; but he gave no heed to me. His eyes were eagerly fixed on Gitelson and his tatters.

"You're a tailor, aren't you?" he questioned him.

My steerage companion nodded. "I'm a ladies' tailor, but I have worked on men's clothing, too," he said.

"A ladies' tailor?" the well-dressed stranger echoed, with ill-concealed delight. "Very well; come along. I have work for you."

As I learned subsequently, the man who accosted us on State Street was a cloak contractor, and his presence in the neighborhood of Castle Garden was anything but a matter of chance. He came there quite often, in fact, his purpose being to angle for cheap labor among the newly arrived immigrants. . . .

As we resumed our walk up Broadway the bejeweled man turned to me.

"And what was your occupation? You have no trade, have you?"

"I read Talmud," I said confusedly.

"I see, but that's no business in America," he declared. "Any relatives here?"

"No."

"Well, don't worry. You will be all right. If a fellow isn't lazy nor a fool he has no reason to be sorry he came to America. It'll be all right."

"All right" he said in English, and I conjectured what it meant from the context. In the course of the minute or two which he bestowed upon me he uttered it so many times that the phrase engraved itself upon my memory. It was the first bit of English I ever acquired.

The well-dressed, trim-looking crowds of lower Broadway impressed me as a multitude of counts, barons, princes. I was puzzled by their preoccupied faces and hurried step. It seemed to comport ill with their baronial dress and general high-born appearance.

In a vague way all this helped to confirm my conception of America as a unique country, unlike the rest of the world.

When we reached the General Post-Office, at the end of the Third Avenue surface line, our guide bade us stop. "Walk straight ahead," he said to me, waving his hand toward Park Row. "Just keep walking until you see a lot of Jewish people. It isn't far from here." With which he slipped a silver quarter into my hand and made Gitelson bid me good-by.

With twenty-nine cents in my pocket . . . I set forth in the direction of East Broadway.

Ten minutes' walk brought me to the heart of the Jewish East Side. The streets swarmed with Yiddish-speaking immigrants. The sign-boards were in English and Yiddish, some of them in Russian. The scurry and hustle of the people were not merely overwhelmingly greater, both in volume and intensity, than in my native town. It was of another sort. The swing and step of the pedestrians, the voices and manner of the street ped-dlers, and a hundred and one other things seemed to testify to far more self-confidence and energy, to larger ambitions and wider scopes, than did the appearance of the crowds in my birthplace.

The great thing was that these people were better dressed than the inhabitants of my town. The poorest-looking man wore a hat (instead of a cap), a stiff collar and a necktie, and the poorest woman wore a hat or a bonnet. . . .

"There goes a green one!" some of them exclaimed.

The sight of me obviously evoked reminiscences in them of the days when they had been "green ones" like myself. It was a second birth that they were witnessing, an experience which they had once gone through them-selves and which was one of the greatest events in their lives.

Source: Abraham Cahan, *The Rise of David Levinsky.* New York: Harper & Brothers, 1917, pp. 88–93. Copyright 1917 by Harper & Row Publishers, Inc.; renewed 1945 by Abraham Cahan. Reprinted by permission of the publisher.

In 1913, when this photograph was taken, it took 12.5 hours to build a Ford at the Ford Motor Company's first moving assembly line in Highland Park, Michigan. *Photo:* Ford Motor Company, Dearborn, Michigan.

of competitive enterprise and viewed industrial growth as an unmixed blessing. In 1928, Presidential candidate Hoover announced that the United States "was nearer to the final triumph over poverty than ever before in the history of any land." A year later, a director of General Motors, the chairman of the Democratic National Committee, noted that "anyone not only can be rich, but ought to be rich"; wealth was virtually a social obligation; it was also a national goal.

Perhaps the automobile best symbolized the mastery North Americans were gaining over material production. As early as 1908, advertising pro-claimed that the automobile was an American neces-sity, although there were only 650 miles of hard-surface road in the entire country. That year, Henry Ford produced his first Model T; in 1914 he controlled half the industry. By 1927, his corpora-tion had produced 15 million simple, sturdy cars that, according to Ford, a customer could buy "in any color you choose so long as it's black." Always ready to move, America became a nation on wheels as automobile registrations soared from 9 million vehicles in 1920 to 30 million in 1930. The auto-mobile industry redirected the focus of the American economy from farm to factory and transformed the

life and landscape of the nation much as the rail-roads had done two generations earlier.

This rapid expansion was made possible by Ford's use of efficient assembly line techniques aimed at mass production and mass consumption. In 1913, it took twelve and a half hours to build a Ford; a year later, Model Ts ran off the first electric conveyor belt in Highland Park, Michigan, at a rate of one every ninety-three minutes. By 1925, the production time was down to one car every ten seconds—and because of mass consumption the price of a Model T had fallen by half. As Ford saw it, if production increased 500 percent, production costs and market price could be cut in half, and the number of people able to buy an automobile would be multiplied by ten. Applied to other industries, these production methods led to store-bought shoes and clothing, de-partment stores, and, eventually, to supermarkets, shopping centers, drive-ins. The nation, woven to-gether by a network of paved highways, became a society of self-satisfying industrial producers and material consumers.

Persistent Poverty

But within this general prosperity, pockets of pov-erty, far broader and deeper than most people sus-pected, persisted. Some older industries, such as New England textile manufacturing, were in sharp

"Ladies, Men, Colored." A familiar sight in the American South, "separate but equal" facilities symbolized one of the deepest and most persistent divisions in the American social fabric. *Photo:* **Bruce Roberts/Rapho-Photo Researchers.**

decline, and hardship among Appalachian coal miners was acute despite high national rates of economic growth. Perhaps worst off were the farmers who had expanded their acreage and bought tractors (for the first time) to increase their production to meet the food needs of millions of Europeans during World War I. Promised that "food would win the war," American agriculture pushed wheat production up to the unprecedented total of 1 billion bushels in 1915. When this temporary demand for food waned, however, the farmers of Canada and the United States found themselves producing too much, particularly since they faced postwar competition on world markets from Russia, Argentina, and Australia. Grain prices plummeted, and small farmers were forced to abandon their land. Some 13 million acres were withdrawn from cultivation in the United States during the 1920s, but total American agricultural production continued to climb as new fertilizers, agricultural machines, and scientific cropping methods were developed. Between 1910 and 1930, the productivity of the average farm worker increased by 41 percent. Independent family-owned farms, such as those envisioned in the Homestead Act of 1862, could not compete with heavily capitalized large-scale farms—factories in the field—that did not grow wheat but manufactured it. As a result, total farm income fell by a third in the United States in the 1920s, and in thousands of farm towns, stores like future President Harry Truman's Kansas City haberdashery shop went out of business. By 1930, the farm population had dwindled to 21 percent of the total, one-quarter that of a century earlier; nearly half of those remaining on the land were tenant farmers.

Racial minorities also fared badly in the period of postwar prosperity. The antiforeigner sentiment that led to restrictions on immigration from southern and eastern Europe in the 1920s reinforced repression of black Americans, Mexican Americans, and the recently subdued Indians. A rigid segregation held sway in the South. "Equal but separate accommodations for the white and colored races" had been approved by the Supreme Court in 1890. Fewer than 10,000 black students were attending high school in the entire region in 1910—a purposeful barrier to full participation in an increasingly complex society. Between 1900 and 1914, an estimated 1100 black people were lynched in the South. By 1924, the Ku Klux Klan—an organization convinced that the native wealth of America was threatened by blacks, Jews, and Roman Catholics—reached a peak membership of nearly 5 million. It seemed that America, a nation once dedicated to a radical political experiment—democracy—was fast becoming a reactionary state.

When the 400,000 black Americans who enlisted in World War I returned to civilian life, many joined a growing northward migration rather than return to the South. The black population of the North rose from 1.4 million in 1920 to 2.3 million in 1930. Race riots, a focus of economic tension, broke out in northern cities such as New York, Chicago, Detroit, and Cleveland; in 1919, the year of the "red summer" in black folklore, racial conflict involved twenty-three cities and thousands of people. But even menial industrial jobs were better than **share-cropping,**[*] black children received some education in the North, and ghetto life in the brownstones and on the pavements of Harlem or Chicago's South Side seemed preferable to the lynch law of the agrarian South. Blacks were increasingly understanding what American educator Booker T. Washington meant in *Up from Slavery* by "Negro two-ness—an American, a Negro; two souls, two thoughts, two unreconciled strivings."

Despite prosperity and plans for a return to normalcy in the 1920s, signs of social unrest were widespread—labor strikes, race riots, a rising crime rate, more divorces, and an increasing taste for all kinds of luxury. The wilderness frontier had pitted pioneers against nature; its conquest exposed new social frontiers. Competition among individuals, business firms, and ethnic and racial groups claimed new casualties in an urban, industrial world that demanded cooperation and discipline for mutual economic advancement. But the American tradition of uninhibited individualism, unplanned growth, and competitive enterprise remained unchallenged despite the slums, the poverty in the countryside, and the neglected minorities. Be a Bull On America and Never Sell the United States Short were Wall Street slogans that reflected the optimism of the nation's past in a new setting of finance and fortune. However, North American productive power had raced far ahead of purchasing power. In 1929, 40 percent of all Americans earned less than $1500 a year, and the 24,000 richest families in the United States earned three times as much money as the 5.8 million poorest. For the first time in history, advertising stimulated the desire to buy, and credit provided the means; but neither increased the ability to pay. With too large a share of the nation's prosperity going into too few pockets, Henry Ford's system of mass production and mass consumption collapsed—an event that precipitated a major restructuring of the human geography of North America.

Depression

The Great Depression was one of the grimmest periods in the history of the nation. In the last week of October 1929, the bottom fell out of the New York stock market—the symbol of industrial society. The following year, 1300 banks closed; factories, business offices, and shops fell idle. Vastly reduced purchasing power and the subsequent underconsumption of factory-produced goods sped the downward economic spiral of the machine society, and by 1931 Henry Ford himself closed his Detroit plant, and 75,000 men lost their jobs. Nationwide, between 12 million and 13 million people were unemployed; one-third of Pennsylvanians were on some kind of relief, and 40 percent of the wage earners of Chicago had no jobs. In the South, plundering farming practices reaped a harvest of erosion. Dust bowl conditions buried wheat farms in sand, blocked railroad lines, and drove thousands of migrants to California: paradoxically, they were the first farmers in history to abandon their land in automobiles. In urban America, shantytowns (called, with grim humor, "Hoovervilles" after the president who had assumed the office in 1929) grew up overnight and filled with people who had lost their homes to banks. In the Northwest, unemployed timber workers set forest fires to earn a few dollars as fire fighters. In the midst of plenty, thousands of Americans actually faced starvation in 1932, while farmers burned crops they could not sell and threatened to cut off all

supplies to market until prices were raised. Unemployed war veterans sold apples on street corners; bread lines lengthened.

Under President Franklin D. Roosevelt, massive federal programs of construction were initiated to cope with these problems. In New England, idle master machinists, such as James English, my father, were put to work at quarries breaking rocks for federally sponsored buildings, roads, and dams. The Tennessee Valley Authority was created to revive the worn lands of seven states in the Southeast; huge dams—the Boulder (now Hoover) Dam on the Colorado River and the Grand Coulee on the Columbia River—were constructed in the West. Labor unions were given the right to bargain, and federal jobs were created by the thousands. Despite these efforts, there were still 10 million unemployed in 1938, and it was mobilization for World War II that ultimately brought economic recovery in both the United States and Canada.

But the Depression had forced a basic reexamination of American values. Under the New Deal, government took on the unprecedented roles not only of promoting but of underwriting the public welfare and curbing the individualism of private enterprise. For the first time, Americans acknowledged that unemployment could derive from forces other than laziness or improvidence and that even in the most affluent society, opportunities were not necessarily equal for all. Government intervention, previously perceived as destructive of individual freedom, was seen as the only means of restoring it. In Roosevelt's words, the nation must eliminate "entrenched greed" and pursue "social values more noble than mere monetary profit." Roosevelt was probably one of the most "conservative" presidents America ever had. These new attitudes impressed themselves on the American landscape and shaped the major issues of our day.

THE SEARCH FOR QUALITY

At the end of World War II, the United States stood unequaled in wealth and power. With unprecedented generosity, America helped rebuild France, Britain, West Germany, and Japan and initiated programs of military and economic aid throughout the developing world. Canada embarked upon a period of national prosperity; its postwar resource-oriented economy diversified to complement the increasing

On the night of February 13, 1932, this long line of men, oblivious to the lights of Times Square and the well-dressed theatergoers around them, waited for a sandwich and a cup of coffee. *Photo:* **Wide World.**

raw material needs of the United States and, indeed, its own strong industrial base. Canadian population grew as never before—from 12 million in 1945 to 21 million in 1970.

Although traditionally wary of entangling alliances, the United States signed treaties of protection with forty-three nations and became the leader of the free world: its mission, the international defense of liberty. Thomas Jefferson had written that "every man and body of men on earth possesses the right of self-government," and his successors now seemed determined to implement that principle. A costly arms race with the Soviet Union drained national resources to create a powerful and sophisticated nuclear arsenal. Stung by Russia's *Sputnik,* the finest minds and most sophisticated technologies in the country were directed to hurtle an American into outer space. To maintain peace, "limited" war and international intervention—"incursions"—seemed necessary. So American soldiers manned bases on every continent, fought skirmishes in Latin America, and endured bloody wars in Korea (1950–1953) and

Vietnam (1965–1975). To ensure the survival and success of liberty, President John F. Kennedy declared the United States prepared to "pay any price, bear any burden, meet any hardship." It was a lofty goal. As it turned out, the price was high, the burden heavy, and success elusive.

The Vietnam experience shattered the complacency of America's conspicuously affluent society and deeply divided the nation. The country was humiliated by the failure of its 500,000 soldiers to win a military victory, frustrated by the stamina of a simpler society fighting on its own soil (a lesson America taught Britain 200 years earlier), and embittered and saddened by the loss of 50,000 young men. At home, corruption in government, moral indifference, a rising crime rate, drugs, urban poverty, racial tensions, pollution, economic recession, and the demoralization of the young seemed to threaten the very fabric of American civilization. Remote from America, Vietnam was the catalyst that crystallized preexisting questions about national ideals and triggered the contemporary debate on future directions and priorities. Three major issues— the quality of life, race and the city, and the environment—emerged as central themes; their resolution will determine the future geography of the United States.

Kentucky-born Mary Owsley married an Oklahoma boy when he returned from World War I. From 1929 to 1936, they lived in Oklahoma.

There was thousands of people out of work in Oklahoma City. They set up a soup line, and the food was clean and it was delicious. Many, many people, colored and white, I didn't see any difference, 'cause there was just as many white people out of work than were colored. Lost everything they had accumulated from their young days. And these are facts. I remember several families had to leave in covered wagons. To Californy, I guess.

See, the oil boom come in '29. People come from every direction in there. A coupla years later, they was livin' in everything from pup tents, houses built out of cardboard boxes and old pieces of metal that they'd pick up—anything that they could find to put somethin' together to put a wall around 'em to protect 'em from the public. . . .

Oh, the dust storms, they were terrible. You could wash and hang clothes on a line, and if you happened to be away from the house and couldn't get those clothes in before that storm got there, you'd never wash that out. Oil was in that sand. It'd color them the most awful color you ever saw. It just ruined them. They was just never fit to use, actually. I had to use 'em, understand, but they wasn't very presentable. Before my husband was laid off, we lived in a good home. It wasn't a brick house, but it wouldn't have made any difference. These storms, when they would hit, you had to clean house from the attic to ground. Everything was covered in sand. Red sand, just full of oil.

The majority of people were hit and hit hard. They were mentally disturbed you're bound to know, 'cause they didn't know when the end of all this was comin'. There was a lot of suicides that I know of. From nothin' else but just they couldn't see any hope for a better tomorrow. I absolutely know some who did. Part of 'em were farmers and part of 'em were businessmen, even. They went flat broke and they committed suicide on the strength of it, nothing else.

A lot of times one family would have some food. They would divide. And everyone would share. Even the people that were quite well to do, they was ashamed. 'Cause they was eatin', and other people wasn't.

My husband was very bitter. That's just puttin' it mild. He was an intelligent man. He couldn't see why as wealthy a country as this is, that there was any sense in so many people starving to death. . . .

Source: Excerpts from Studs Terkel, *Hard Times: An Oral History of the Great Depression.* New York: Pantheon; London: Penguin, 1970, pp. 45–46. Copyright © 1970 by Studs Terkel. Reprinted by permission of Pantheon Books, a division of Random House, Inc., and Penguin Books, Ltd.

The Quality of Life
[FIGURES 10, 11]

In the postwar period, North Americans enjoyed a standard of living higher than any previously experienced. The gross national product of the United States doubled in the 1950s, and by the 1970s, North Americans were producing over $1 trillion worth of goods and services each year. Personal income quadrupled, and former luxuries became necessities without which people felt deprived. A remarkable one-third of American families earned $15,000 or more each year, and better than half more than $10,000 in the 1970s. Furthermore, the lives of most were protected by insurance, hospitalization, and retirement programs through a combination of government and private schemes. If freedom in colonial America meant political liberty, by the 1970s it had come to mean economic security and a diversified life. Unparalleled prosperity changed social styles and living patterns: people began to seek lives of higher quality rather than higher income, a direct challenge to the competitive work ethic that previously powered American society.

In fact, competition in the United States had already been circumscribed by the evolution of what Harvard economist John Kenneth Galbraith called "the corporate state." As early as 1956, 135 major corporations, most of them heavily reliant directly or indirectly on federal contracts, controlled 45 percent of the industrial assets of the country. Deploying billions of dollars of equipment in dozens of locations, employing hundreds of thousands of workers, these industrial giants applied increasingly complex technologies to the production and sale of material goods—a major reason why Americans were, compared with the rest of the world, well housed, well clad, and well fed. Important technological breakthroughs came in chemicals, computers, electronics, communications, and transportation—industries more mobile spatially than those that process raw materials such as iron and steel. Conversion from coal-based energy to petroleum and natural gas, and the increasing use of air travel for long-distance, short-term movement, enhanced locational flexibility. By 1960, four-fifths of all corporate research and development efforts were concentrated in these industries; virtually all of the 10 million new jobs created in the 1950s were for well-educated, technology-oriented, white-collar workers.

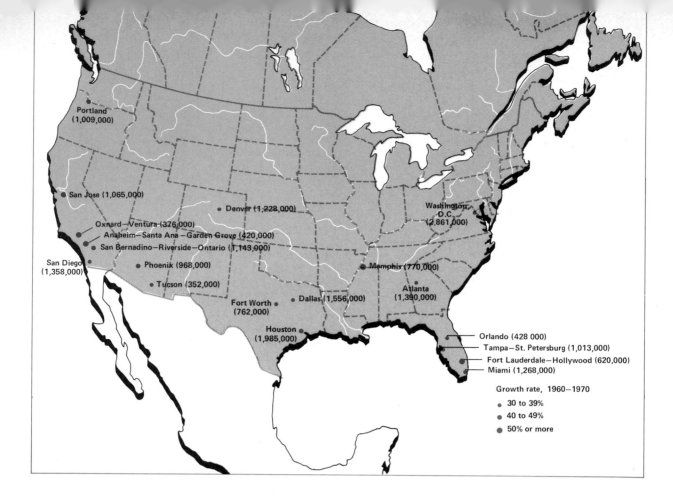

Portland (1,009,000)

San Jose (1,065,000)

Denver (1,228,000)

Washington D.C. (2,861,000)

Oxnard—Ventura (376,000)
Anaheim—Santa Ana—Garden Grove (420,000)
San Bernadino—Riverside—Ontario (1,143,000)

San Diego (1,358,000)

Phoenix (968,000)

Memphis (770,000)

Tucson (352,000)

Atlanta (1,390,000)

Fort Worth (762,000)

Dallas (1,556,000)

Houston (1,985,000)

Orlando (428 000)
Tampa—St. Petersburg (1,013,000)
Fort Lauderdale—Hollywood (620,000)
Miami (1,268,000)

Growth rate, 1960—1970

- 30 to 39%
- 40 to 49%
- 50% or more

Figure 10. America's Fastest-Growing Cities, 1960–1970. Of the 19 cities in the United States that grew 30 percent or more between 1960 and 1970, all but one were located in the South or West. The sole exception, Washington, D.C., was the seat of America's fastest-growing industry—the federal government.

The innovations that sprang from such corporations as IBM, Du Pont, General Electric, and Ford created products for which demands never before existed. The advertising industry usually managed to sell them: the failure of Ford's Edsel is remembered largely because it was so unexpected. With so many jobs and the welfare of so many at stake, the federal government attempted both to control and to support large corporations by using monetary policies to control inflation, to regulate markets, and to consolidate and subsidize bankrupt enterprises—notably aerospace and railroad companies. By 1970, government accounted for a quarter of all economic activity in the United States—a higher proportion than in some socialist countries. Free enterprise still existed in grocery stores, restaurants, and small shops, but the important decisions in North America were made by a complex web of institutions—corporations, unions, universities, and government agencies—not by individuals.

Changing technologies, institutions, and attitudes all contributed to a major spatial redistribution of wealth, power, and population in North America. A pronounced geographic shift occurred in population and income from the North and East to the Southern Rim, a broad arc of southern and western states extending from Florida through the South and Southwest to southern California. With America's mildest climates, most extensive coastline, well-developed inland waterways, and efficient rail and highway networks oriented to major ports, this region appealed to thousands of new and relocated industries. Defense and aerospace industries settled in southern California, Texas, Georgia, and Florida. **Agribusiness** made California, Texas, and Florida the three largest farm states. In Canada, too, population moved westward to capitalize on the development of oil fields in Alberta, and Canadians flocked to centers of capital and industry—the already predominant metropolises of Montreal, Toronto, and Vancouver. Resort and tourist businesses flourished and attracted hundreds of thousands of retired North Americans, whose numbers steadily increased as an extended life span and earlier retirement resulted in a larger proportion of citizens living beyond their economically productive years.

The traditional economic core in the Industrial North suffered accordingly; this region accounted for 70 percent of North America's manufactures and industrial employees in 1940; by 1970, these figures had dropped to 50 percent and 55 percent, respectively. Only 15 percent of the 10 million new people

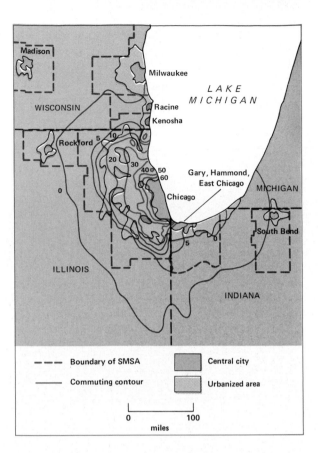

--- --- Boundary of SMSA   ▨ Central city

——— Commuting contour   ▨ Urbanized area

0   100
miles

Figure 11. The Urban Field of Chicago, 1960. Commuting contours document the suburban range of Chicago's influence and define the city's urban field. The percentage of the population commuting to the city decreases regularly from the metropolitan core. *Adapted from:* Brian J. L. Berry, "The Geography of the United States in the Year 2000," *Transactions,* The Institute of British Geographers, No. 51 (1970), p. 24, Fig. 1. Redrawn by permission.

added to the United States' population between 1970 and 1975 located in the North and Northeast; 85 percent of America's population growth occurred in the Southern Rim. The new rhythms of American life seemed to demand a new living environment, more leisure, a better quality of life; for many North Americans, these were to be found in the South and West. Between 1960 and 1970, all but one of the fastest growing cities in the United States were located in these regions. By 1970, this modern American migration had shifted the nation's center of population 27 miles westward to a soybean field just outside Saint Louis.

Far more North Americans, however, found their new opportunities not in the West, but in the suburbs. Between 1950 and 1960, suburban areas grew by 47 percent in population and in the next decade by an additional 27 percent. Fully two-thirds of the total population growth in the United States during these twenty years occurred on the developing peripheries of the largest cities. Although metropolitan centers continued to exert a gravitational pull on the rural poor and minorities, automobiles had extended to nearly 100 miles what English historian H. G. Wells called "the magic radius" of the city. Lured by open environments and greater recreational opportunities and repelled by crime, neglected schools, and congestion in the cities, Americans became willing to travel long distances between home and job. Suburbia spread in widening circles of decreasing density around each city, and the North American landscape was punctuated by urban fields or daily urban systems covering a substantial portion of the most desirable land of the two nations.

The term "daily urban system" indicates the profound structural changes that occurred in cities after World War II. ***Central business districts*** • became barren landscapes of high-rise office buildings inhabited by workers during the day only; formerly convenient and animated midcity neighborhoods became derelict districts owned by suburbanites and rented to those least able to purchase suburban privacy and most dependent upon the bankrupt services of central cities designed for the streetcar age. The middle and upper classes move over a vast urban field to sleep, eat, school their children, and pursue their careers. The urban field is the area habitually traversed by the modern urbanite; it is a geography of multiple suburbs focused upon shopping centers and schools, all economic and social offspring of the central city. Los Angeles, the archetype of the automobile-oriented metropolis, is a city of sixty-four separate municipalities spread over 455 miles of territory. Between a quarter and a third of the land area of Los Angeles is devoted to the needs of the automobile, and suburban growth stretches deep into its hinterland, making the urban field nearly four times larger than the area enclosed by the city's boundaries.

By 1975, the largest cities of the United States were losing population, and nonmetropolitan areas began to grow faster than metropolitan centers. A newfound preference for open spaces, and by implication a better quality of life, was actually beginning to reverse the century of migration that had brought North America to town. Despite this trend, three-quarters of the people of the United States and Canada live in cities; most urban geographers foresee the coalescence of North American metropolitan centers into gigantic multicored megalopolises that

Between 1950 and 1960, suburbia spread in widening circles around each city, and the North American landscape became punctuated by urban fields or daily urban systems. The photographs show Massapequa, on New York's Long Island, before and after. *Photo:* Skyviews.

will continue to be society's most vital and densely populated centers.

Poverty

With so many North Americans living in suburbia and connected to the city by private automobiles and high-speed freeways, and with youth preoccupied with new life styles, careers, and rising incomes, poverty in North America became less visible. During the Depression, Roosevelt had pledged to redeem "the forgotten man at the bottom of the economic pyramid," but by 1960, the poorest fifth of all American families had only 5 percent of the national wealth, a bare 1 percent gain over thirty years. While all Americans had gained in absolute wealth, the poor were no longer temporarily disadvantaged immigrants or disorganized labor groups as in the past; they formed a lower class frozen by racial discrimination, poor education, or inadequate skills into continuing economic deprivation. Segregated in the blighted ghettos of central cities, lodged in enclaves of rural poverty, the American poor remained outsiders to a technological society that yielded easy affluence to the well educated and the technically able. A permanent underclass, a ***culture of poverty,*** was "discovered" in the most prosperous nation in the world. John Kennedy made poverty

a national issue, claiming, "if a free society cannot help the many who are poor, it cannot save the few who are rich." The invisible poor had found a spokesman, and the total number of poor Americans declined from 38.8 million in 1960 to 25 million in 1972.

Poverty, however, remained closely identified with race. Although the white poor (16.2 million) outnumbered the black (7.2 million) by more than two to one, nearly a third of all black families lived below the poverty level; the same is true for Mexican Americans and Indians. A geographical shift of poverty to the cities occurred during the 1960s; 60 percent of the poor live in urban centers today, compared with 44 percent in 1960. At least partly for this reason, the total number of rural poor in the United States declined by half (to 10 million), but the spatial distribution of poverty in rural North America persisted. The 1000 poorest counties in the United States are densely clustered in the economically depressed farm areas of the rural South, in the strip-mined lands of the Appalachian coalfields, in the Ozarks, in the Spanish-speaking sections of south Texas, and on Indian reservations in the West. Rural poverty in these regions is slowly diminishing as interstate highways and programs of development achieve some economic balance; some urban migrants have even begun to return to the South. More intractable is the ghetto poverty of the large urban centers, where the twin issues of race and the physical structure of the city are closely entwined.

Turn on, tune in and drop out. . . . I urge any of you who are serious about life. . . . Find someone who knows more about consciousness than you and study . . . there's a tremendous amount of information which has been stored up for the last 3,000 or 4,000 years by men who have been making this voyage and who have left landmarks, guidebooks, footsteps in the sand, symbols and rituals which can be learned from and used.

. . . [Y]ou do not have to go on welfare or go around with a begging bowl. The odd thing about our society today is that in the mad lemminglike rush to the urban, antilove power centers and the mad rush toward mechanical conformity, our fellow citizens are leaving tremendous gaps and gulfs which make economic bartering very simple. For the first thing, consider moving out of the city. You'll find ghost towns empty and deserted 3 or 4 hours from San Francisco where people can live in harmony with nature, using their sense organs as 2 billion years of evolution had trained them to.

. . . Our countrymen are fed up with plastic and starved for direct, natural sensory stimulation. . . . [S]tart throwing things out of your house. And you won't need as much mechanical money to buy as many mechanical objects. . . . Trust your sense organs and your nervous system. Your divine body has been around a long, long time. Much longer than any of the social games you play. Trust the evolutionary process. It's all going to work out all right.

Source: Excerpts from Timothy Leary, *The Politics of Ecstasy.* New York: Putnam, 1965, pp. 358–361.

Race and the City
[FIGURES 12, 13, 14]

Beginning with an explosive demand for factory labor in World War II, the out-migration of black Americans from the South accelerated. Searching for jobs, better educational opportunities, and a less oppressive social existence, some 3 million blacks moved to the North and West between 1950 and 1970 in old family cars, Greyhound buses, and the Atlantic seaboard trains. Whereas two of every three blacks were southerners in 1950, only 53 percent of America's 23 million blacks still lived south of the Mason-Dixon line in 1970: the rest had moved to the largest cities of the North and West. This migration was more than a simple geographical shift: it was an economic move from field to factory, a social transition from small town to metropolis, a cultural leap from the segregated South to the city streets of black ghettos. Three of every four black Americans found themselves living in metropolitan areas and nearly 60 percent in the central cities. The old southern religious ideal of a black metropolis was coming to pass in a manner never before contemplated.

Clustered in metropolitan ghettos, the black population of America for the first time developed a philosophy of social action. For sixty years, the Supreme Court's separate but equal doctrine had stifled social mobility; this was successfully challenged when the literal promise of the Declaration of Independence that "all men are created equal" was reinterpreted. The Supreme Court ordered the integration of public schools in 1954 and, later, of all public facilities; voter registration procedures were simplified. As the civil rights movement gained momentum, disenfranchised blacks, Mexican Americans, and Indians made rapid legal gains. Although trouble was anticipated in the South in the early years and came at Little Rock, Arkansas, and Oxford, Mississippi, the tenacious northern resistance to the integration of black and white was unexpected.

Efforts at residential integration in New York City, Boston, and Chicago were frustrated by discriminatory real estate practices, the departure of whites from areas where blacks moved in, intransigent city councils, and newly formed resistance groups. The busing of black and white children to achieve racial balance in schools became an emotionally charged issue from New England to California. Treated by middle-class suburban whites as a moral issue, the clash of lower-income blacks and whites in the central cities was in fact a competition for housing, jobs, and education among the least advantaged in the most technological society.

As the black and Puerto Rican populations of northern and western cities grew by natural increase and continued immigration, the boundaries of the ghettos expanded, displacing the traditional Irish, Italian, Polish, and Jewish ethnic groups in the central city. Whites fled to the suburbs as the block-by-block encroachment of blacks into older urban areas induced panic selling. Only the old, the sick, and those too poor to move remained; integration, as one black leader cynically remarked, was the time it took for the last white to leave a neighborhood after the first black arrived. Barred from suburbs, blacks could not escape the ghetto; they could only extend it another fraction of an inch on the city map.

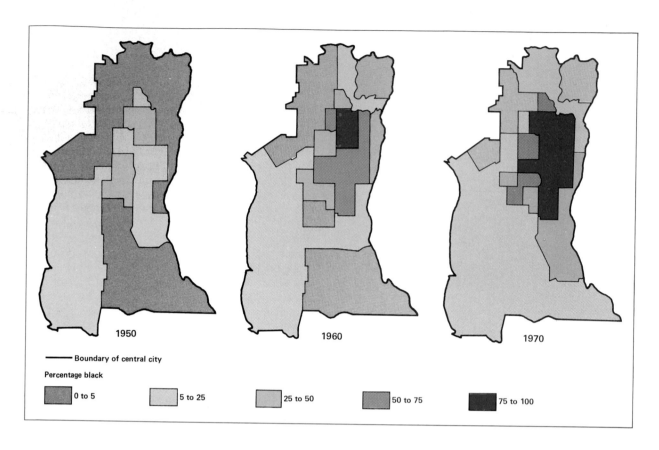

1950   1960   1970

—— Boundary of central city

Percentage black

[ ] 0 to 5   [ ] 5 to 25   [ ] 25 to 50   [ ] 50 to 75   [ ] 75 to 100

Figure 12. The Growth of a Ghetto: Seattle, 1950–1970. Between 1900 and 1950, the population of Seattle grew from 80,671 to 467,591—a remarkable increase based on the resources of a rich natural environment, the shift in population to the West, and the placement of the aeronautics industry in the area. But Seattle blacks, whose numbers grew from 15,666 in 1950 to 26,901 in 1960 and 37,868 in 1970, did not generally share in the residential expansion of the metropolis. As the central city population actually decreased between 1960 and 1970, the metropolitan (SMSA) population expanded. The relatively integrated center city of 1950 became an increasingly black and poor urban landscape of rented houses and suburban profits. *Adapted from:* Richard L. Morrill, "A Geographical Perspective of the Black Ghetto," originally published in Harold M. Rose and Harold McConnell, eds., *Perspectives in Geography 2: Geography of the Ghetto: Perceptions, Problems, and Alternatives.* DeKalb, Ill.: Northern Illinois University Press, 1972, p. 47, Fig. 2. Copyright © 1972 by Northern Illinois University Press. By permission of the publisher.

Spatial nearness had not produced a harmonious society in urban America; rather, the deepest, most persistent division was exposed and exacerbated.

The ghettos became blighted zones of high crime, low income, inadequate housing, and high unemployment. These conditions culminated in bloody race riots in metropolitan America, first in Los Angeles, then in Detroit, Newark, and most other large cities. The ghettos had become, as the English observer Kenneth Clark remarked, America's "social,

political, educational—and above all economic, colonies." Although blacks represent only 11 percent of the total American population, in 1970 they formed 71 percent of the population in Washington, D.C.; 50 percent in Atlanta; more than 40 percent in Baltimore, Detroit, and Cleveland; 30 percent in Chicago; and 20 percent in New York City. It is now clear that if integration and racial equality are realistic social goals, they will only be attained slowly as society redirects its values. Despite rising incomes and substantial educational gains within American society as a whole, the anger and frustration of ghetto communities remain strong. The discontent began, as Claude Brown noted in *Manchild in the Promised Land,* with an unfulfilled promise: the minorities migrated to the city for spiritual salvation; once there, deep-seated social prejudices reflected in spatial separation continue to blight their lives. Where, Brown asks, does one run to when you're already in the promised land?

By the 1970s, the central cities of older American metropolitan centers could hardly be thought of as promised lands. The white middle class had moved to the suburbs and had been replaced by the rural poor, racial minorities, and immigrants from countries new to the American experience such as Korea, Haiti, Ecuador, and Trinidad. Economic growth in the core area of the daily urban system declined.

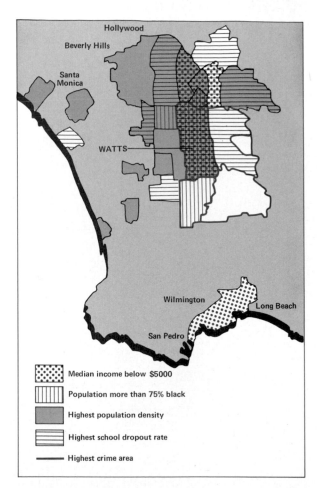

Figure 13. Anatomy of a Riot: Watts, 1965. In August 1965, a minor incident in which police attempted to arrest a black man for drunken driving triggered a bloody riot in the Watts district of Los Angeles. An estimated 10,000 rioters looted, burned stores and sniped at police and firefighters for an entire week. The toll was 34 people killed, 25 of them black; over a thousand wounded; and 977 buildings damaged or destroyed. The complex of social problems—low income, racial segregation, high population densities, high crime rates, and a high school dropout rate—that coincide in Watts and other inner-city ghettoes undoubtedly contributed to this explosion of anger. In 1967 racial disturbances took place in nearly 100 cities; 83 killed, 1,897 injured, and 16,389 arrested testified to the depth of black frustration. *After:* L. Lessing, "Systems Engineering Invades the City," *Fortune*, Vol. 77 (January 1968), p. 154. Map by Max Gschwind for Fortune Magazine. Copyright © 1968 by Time, Inc. Source: Space-General Corp.

Figure 14. The Economic Basis of Metropolitan Decline. This diagram of employment in five central cities and their suburbs between 1965 and 1972 illustrates the decline of urban manufacturing and the rapid growth of the suburban economy at the expense of the central city. The continuing decline of the commercial and industrial base that provides jobs, income, and tax revenues to municipalities is at the core of America's urban crisis. *From: The New York Times*, Sunday, October 19, 1975, "The Week in Review," p. 1. Copyright © 1975 by The New York Times Company. Reprinted by permission.

Businesses found it more profitable and pleasanter to move to the suburbs—a spatial dislocation that left the unemployed poor geographically and socially removed from new job opportunities in industrial parks and shopping centers throughout the urban field. With revenues declining, America's largest cities were saddled with salary demands by unionized teachers, firefighters, police, and garbage collectors; with high energy, rent, and land costs; with traffic congestion that drove up transportation costs; with high taxes, obsolete buildings, and a disproportionate share of society's disadvantaged. For the 31 percent of all Americans who lived in the 243 metropolitan areas of the United States in the 1970s, housing, crime, economic security, and pollution became compelling social issues. Bypassed by a technological society lured to new growth areas, the metropolitan centers, once the dynamic cores of America's surge to economic well-being, were economic and social disaster zones. New York, the largest and most complex of North America's great cities, seemed destined to celebrate the nation's bicentennial by going bankrupt.

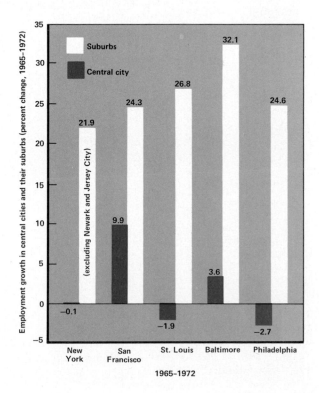

The black migration hit Brooklyn harder than any other part of the city. There were pockets of Puerto Ricans in Brooklyn, clustered around Smith Street in Boerum Hill, around the Williamsburg Bridge, and out in Sunset Park. But the really large numbers of Puerto Ricans had gone to East Harlem and the South Bronx. The Southern black man came to Brooklyn.

There were several reasons for this. It was far more difficult for a badly educated rural black man to get an apartment in Harlem than it was in Bedford-Stuyvesant. Harlem was a society, the black capital of America, with its already well-defined institutions: churches, numbers runners, landlords, restaurants, artists, after-hours places, con men, musicians, etc. Bed-Stuy was much looser, much less structured. . . .

Bed-Stuy was also easier to block-bust. A number of black real estate operators (in addition to whites) made fortunes busting Bed-Stuy. They often employed white salesmen, who would purchase a house in a white street, move in a black family, and then start calling up everyone else on the street. Since many of these areas had two-family houses or old elegant brownstones, this was much easier to do in Brooklyn than it was in Harlem. . . . Less money was involved, and more heartbreak, especially for the unfortunate hardworking black man who thought he had escaped the ghetto only to find that it was coming out behind him.

So Bedford-Stuyvesant exploded. Whites began leaving by the hundreds. In places like Brownsville, they left because Brownsville had almost always been a slum, and the second generation that was making it did not see any need for further loyalty. Others simply saw the whole thing as hopeless: Brooklyn, which in their youth had been the city of trees and free spaces and security, was being torn apart by drugs and gang wars. . . .

As Bedford-Stuyvesant expanded (any street that was occupied by blacks became Bedford-Stuyvesant, whether it was in Clinton Hill or Crown Heights), fear expanded. In Park Slope, across Flatbush Avenue from Bed-Stuy, real estate operators started breaking up the fine old brownstones into black boardinghouses. Most were occupied by transients, as boardinghouses have always been occupied, and they simply didn't care what neighbors thought about them. The streets became littered with broken bottles and discarded beer cans, the yards filled with garbage, drug arrests increased, hookers worked the avenues; there were knifings and shootings, and soon the merchants on Flatbush Avenue started folding up and moving away. No insurance could cover what they stood to lose.

Source: Adaptation from "Brooklyn: The Sane Alternative," in Pete Hamill, *Irrational Ravings.* New York: Putnam, 1971, pp. 63–64. Copyright © 1969 by Pete Hamill. By permission of Monica McCall, ICM.

Environment
[FIGURES 15, 16]

While the poor and the minorities strive for more jobs and higher incomes—goals most easily realized in an expanding economy—some Americans seek a lower rate of growth and less consumption. Pointing to the environmental damage the continent sustained during America's drive to affluence, environmentalists see North America as built on wastefulness; rapid and unplanned exploitation of resources, they note, has severely degraded its human and natural environments. In the South, the exhaustion of the soils of the southern Appalachians gave farmers a powerful incentive for migration. The first national soil conservation surveys of the 1930s revealed that 80,000 square miles of American soil—an area equal in size to England and Scotland combined—had been destroyed. In the North, the search for better timber completely stripped parts of southern Ontario and the Upper Midwest of forest. One study of southwestern Wisconsin showed that loggers and early settlers reduced the region's woodlands by 80 to 90 percent. In the Southwest and West, mineral resources were hurriedly removed. Some of the worst of these early environmental abuses were curbed by federal regulation in the first half of the twentieth century: programs of soil conservation, the national park system (established by President Theodore Roosevelt), the Tennessee Valley Authority, and the Prairie Farm Rehabilitation Act in Canada managed to preserve or renew substantial areas of North America. But today, new and more subtle environmental dangers have become apparent as scientists expose severe disruptions in natural **ecosystems** caused by what biologist Rachel Carson termed the "elixirs of death": the ecological side effects of the products and methods of a technological society.

As in other technological societies, air pollution has become a serious problem in North America. In 1973, 135 million automobiles in the United States and Canada—13.4 million in California alone—poured hydrocarbons and nitrogen oxide into the atmosphere; the gasoline combustion engine accounts for 60 percent of all airborne pollutants.

The playground in a New York slum. *Photo:* **Hugh Rogers/Monkmeyer.**

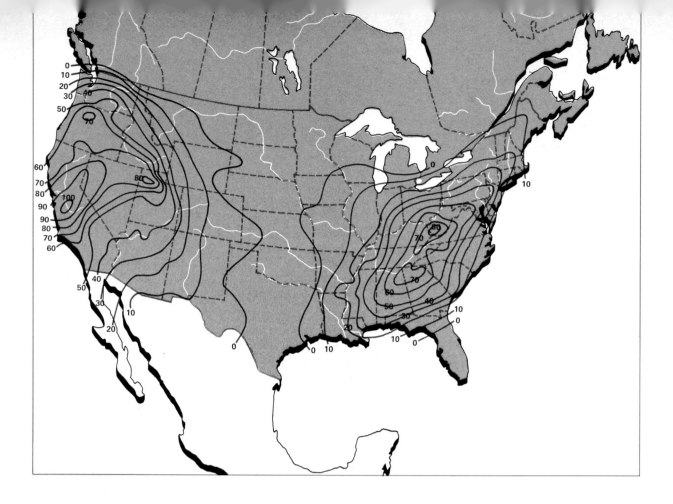

Figure 15. High Air Pollution Potential. The number of days on which high air pollution potential (defined as covering 75,000 square miles or more for at least 36 hours) was forecast in the eastern United States between 1960 and 1973 and between 1963 and 1970 in the western states is shown on this map. Topography, population density, industrial concentration, and weather conditions play an important role in determining this distribution. *After:* Virginia Brodine, "Episode 104," in *Air Pollution.* New York: Harcourt Brace Jovanovich, 1973, p. 23. Reproduced by permission of the publisher.

Metallurgical plants, iron and steel mills, petroleum refineries, fertilizer manufacture, and other industries contribute a further 25 percent. And with 90 percent of American electricity generated by burning coal and oil, power plants add their share. Overall, some 260 million tons of refuse are spewed into the atmosphere each year; despite the passage of a series of clean air acts, this figure remains stubbornly high. The intensity of air pollution is greatest in southern California owing to the interaction of the automobile culture and the physiography of the region, and in Appalachia, whose mountain folds trap the airborne pollutants from the Industrial North. In both areas, **temperature inversions** occur as pockets of cool air, trapped beneath stagnant warmer air, sit over populated areas and

accumulate pollutants. Regional death rates are measurably higher during inversions. In Donora, Pennsylvania, during a week in October 1948, half the population of 12,300 was made ill by trapped smoke from local wire, zinc, sulfuric acid, and steel factories; twenty people died. Yet virtually every large city, whatever its topographical setting, exhibits smog domes under certain weather conditions. In New York and Chicago, incoming sunlight during the smoggiest days is reduced by 25 to 40 percent. The capacity of urban industrial systems to concentrate natural energy and human activity in specific locations is producing a volume of waste that natural processes can no longer disperse.

A similar pollutant concentration is becoming apparent in the waterways of North America, although the danger is less acute than in Japan and parts of Europe, where space is far more limited and population densities greater. Sources of water pollution are manifold: sewage disposal from cities located on rivers and lakes; industrial wastes; pesticides, herbicides, and fertilizers from America's scientifically based agriculture; coastal oil refineries and offshore drilling rigs—in short, the elements that combined to produce the affluence of North American society. Perhaps the most dramatic incident of water pollution occurred in 1969 when the Cuyahoga River,

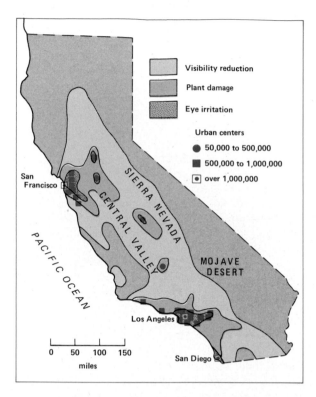

Figure 16. Ecological Geography of Air Pollution: California, 1961–1963. The artificial haze of polluted air is the least intense yet the most widespread characteristic of atmospheric degradation. Where the intensity of pollution is greater, plant growth is retarded, crop yields are reduced, and plants become more susceptible to insect attack. At the University of California at Riverside, researchers found that lemon trees in the polluted air of the Los Angeles Basin—the citrus bowl of the nation—yield 43 percent less fruit than trees in a controlled clean-air environment. Higher air pollution levels not only reduce visibility and damage plant life, but produce eye irritation in the healthy person. The long-term effects of air pollution—heart disease, bronchitis, emphysema—are less easily traced but surely as inevitable. *Adapted from:* "Extent of General Air Pollution in California, 1961–1963," *Geographical Review*, Vol. 56 (1966), p. 166. Copyrighted by the American Geographical Society of New York.

flowing through Cleveland laden with industrial chemicals, burst into flames and damaged two railroad bridges. Far more serious, however, is the gradual and general deterioration of water quality throughout the great watersheds of the continent— the Hudson, the Mississippi, the rivers of the Central Valley of California, the Columbia, and the greatest reservoir of fresh water on earth, the 31,820-square-mile Great Lakes.

Nitrogen and phosphorus from agricultural and suburban infiltration, industrial wastes from the heartlands of both the United States and Canada, and municipal sewage from shoreline urban centers have converted large areas of the Great Lakes into a carpet of algae: the water's oxygen content is reduced as fertilizing substances (such as the phosphates in detergents) are introduced, and the luxuriant growth of algae that ensues chokes out the normal, self-renewing biological processes of the water body. With less than 3.5 percent of the land area of the United States, the Great Lakes Basin today contains 14 percent of the American and an even higher proportion of the Canadian population. Chicago alone uses 4.25 billion gallons of water a day. The federal legislation enacted to regulate water pollution in North America utilizes different strategies from those in Europe and Japan, where polluters are forced to pay in proportion to the damage they create. Water quality has not significantly improved; industries and cities almost universally resist the high cost of water restoration. A striking exception, however, is the Willamette River in Oregon. A determined action group forced the paper industry and its unions to clean up the river; their success suggests that environmental issues are a matter of social commitment as much as of legislative competence.

At the heart of the environmental debate is the extremely high per capita energy consumption of North Americans, which is double that of other technological nations and six times greater than world averages. The affluence of North America was achieved by the sophisticated utilization of a natural abundance of energy sources—wood, water, coal, petroleum, natural gas—to continually increase the productivity of the industrial worker. Similarly, in agriculture, the lavish application of petroleum-derived pesticides and fertilizers enabled farmers to increase their productivity nearly 300 percent between 1947 and 1970. Environmentalists argue for a reduction of wasteful consumption and a decrease in the various forms of pollution that inevitably derive from the use of coal, oil, or nuclear power to generate energy. Lawsuits are filed to preserve wildlife, to prevent industry from constructing the trans-Alaskan pipeline, to eliminate offshore drilling for oil, to block the strip-mining of western coal. But in the 1970s, as domestic energy supplies dwindle and foreign oil becomes more expensive, as energy consumption increases at a rate of 4 percent a year, and as unemployment and inflation rise, the proponents of cleaner air and water appear to be losing ground to those who champion still greater industrialization as an answer to these more immediate economic problems. By 1975, however, when the National Cancer Institute identified environmental pollution as a prominent cause of the rapid increase in this disease, it had become clear that the introduction of largely untested chemical agents into the American environment has immediate bad consequences for all. Can the world's most powerful democratic societies, with their multiple pressure groups and competitive spirit, respond to a new vision that expects and demands less, and that seeks satisfaction more in quality than in quantity? The answer is far from certain.

BICENTENNIAL

There was no exposition in 1976, no central theme to celebrate two centuries of American independence. The country faced a business recession that confounded conventional economic theory, was recovering from the divisions of the Vietnam War, and had endured corruption at the highest levels of government that, for the first time in the nation's history, forced a president's resignation from office. In the 1960s innovative social programs in civil rights, medical care, environmental preservation, and poverty alleviation attempted to create opportunities for all Americans and to alter the shape of a society historically based on individual freedom, competition, and a minimum of social restraint in the pursuit of personal fulfillment. In fact, real progress had been achieved: Indians were skirmishing with bureaucrats rather than the cavalry; black Americans would never again endure official segregation or systematic disenfranchisement; some progress had been made toward improving the environment; and by any measure, America's poor were the richest poor people in the world.

Yet to be poor in the world's richest nation or to encounter racial prejudice in a land that promises social equality is to be truly poor and harshly oppressed. Further, the resistance and class resentments revealed by the enactment of the far-reaching social legislation of the last generation has illuminated the contradictions of life in a society beset by rapid change. Indeed, the rapidity of social change and the rise to material well-being is most often at the heart of America's disturbed social geography

and is most frequently forgotten. Viewed in a global framework of war and peace, famine and disease, poverty and suppression of liberty, North American society is at peace, rich, free, well fed, well housed, and healthy.

But the achievement of material abundance has solved only the most basic problems of human existence. North Americans have been able to defer vital social questions because the scale and variety of their resource base and the enormous size of their environment have provided places for dissidents, new lands for the landless, and opportunities for most. Yet North Americans are faced today with highly complex and technological issues that are double contradictions: they must be solved both within North America and in the rest of the world. The global view affects all national questions: freedom, racial harmony, social equality, and environmental well-being are issues discussed in terms of global solutions. Contemporary strategies involve the resources and promises of all nations, not just a favored few. North Americans debate the future in terms that still reflect their especially well-endowed past. But the value of maintaining economic growth through technological competence is contradicted by knowledge suggesting that an increase in the gross national product is not the sole measure of a society's substance and that a new social attitude must evolve that settles for fewer worldly goods and seeks personal fulfillment with a minimum of consumption. The global questions of the twentieth century—overpopulation, famine, social equity, and international harmony—are framed by this dialogue. New directions in North American society will have impact on both the technological and developing worlds. Paradoxically, while most other countries scorn American materialism, they strive in every way possible to match it. Although widely attacked as a conservative society, Americans, Swedish sociologist Gunner Myrdal points out, have traditionally attempted to preserve what are very radical principles indeed: personal freedom, political liberty, justice for all—seemingly diminishing commodities in the twentieth century. Despite turbulence and conflict, despite promises yet unfulfilled, the vitality and ingenuity of North Americans have been demonstrated too often to be disregarded.

NORTH AMERICA

THE INDUSTRIAL BASE

ENERGY AND MINERAL RESOURCES MAP

After a tour of North America in 1866, one British observer could not fail to be struck by the "extraordinary and wonderful character of American resources, surpassing by far anything of which we have the slightest experience in the Old World." These comments were made as the drive to American industrial maturity was just beginning; most of the resources of the continent lay undiscovered. Over the next century, the largest industrial machine in the world was created, and the abundant resources of North America fueled an unprecedented rise in industrial production and consumption. But today, continuously increasing energy demand, far outpacing population growth, has forced North Americans to reexamine reserves, to determine the feasibility of exploiting new energy fields remote from centers of consumption, and to increase output from existing sources. Although the total North American output of coal, oil, and natural gas declined slightly after 1970, demand for all forms of energy has increased and coal production, in particular, began to rise substantially. In September 1973, the Congressional Atomic Energy Committee predicted that by 1980, United States energy use would be triple that of 1950. Energy used in 1950 was equivalent to 16.1 million barrels of oil per day; in 1980, it will be 48.3. Underlying this dramatic increase is a tripling of the North American gross domestic product and a doubling of energy consumption between 1950 and 1970, while the population of the United States and Canada increased only 1.5 times over the same period. Never have so few consumed so much so quickly.

When Arab states placed an embargo on oil exports to nations supporting Israel in October 1973 and tripled the price per barrel of oil, the United States discovered it was a vulnerable consumer. Of the 14 million barrels of oil used each day in the United States in 1973, 5 million were imported. On November 7, 1973, President Nixon stated that the nation "had consumed beyond its resources and the price had to be paid." He called on citizens to dedicate themselves to the aim of attaining self-sufficiency in energy supplies by 1980. Project Independence emerged from this speech as a hitherto unforeseen and unplanned goal. Existing coal, hydroelectric, oil, and natural gas supplies came under greater scrutiny, and exploration for new supplies was sponsored. Costly technologies of energy exploitation and production became feasible as prices rose. Despite this, by 1976 the United States for the first time was importing more oil than it was producing.

An awareness of the finite nature of domestic supplies, of wasteful patterns of energy consumption, and of the social and environmental costs of exploitation and high use arose simultaneously. North Americans are now understanding with increasingly deeper perception the systematic nature of their own industrial culture.

With its 6.3 percent of the world's population consuming 35 percent of world energy, this continent occupies a privileged position among the world's peoples. Despite their agrarian history, the United States and Canada took on the characteristics of industrial society rapidly. The United States' population was more urban than rural by 1920; the Canadian population reached the same state by 1931. Agricultural workers as a percentage of the work force have steadily declined; fewer than 6 percent are actively engaged in farming today in either country. In contrast to Europe, however, the North American birth rate has remained relatively high, sustaining levels of natural population growth greater than in other technological nations. With a combined population of 236 million, the United States and Canada have, like the Soviet Union, large, sparsely populated areas and concentrations of densely populated land. Like all nations of the technological world, North Americans have a high level of personal income, a high level of literacy, a very high level of energy consumption, a low death rate, and a long life expectancy. The conditions that stimulated industrial growth in North America are not dissimilar from those in industrial regions elsewhere, but they are distinctive in terms of scale and abundance.

ENERGY SOURCES
[TABLE 1]

Statistics on industrial production and consumption reflect the scale and vitality of the North American resource base. In the United States and Canada, the productive potential, appetite for resources, and high per capita consumption of raw materials and finished goods exceed those of any other nation in the technological world. North Americans are pro-

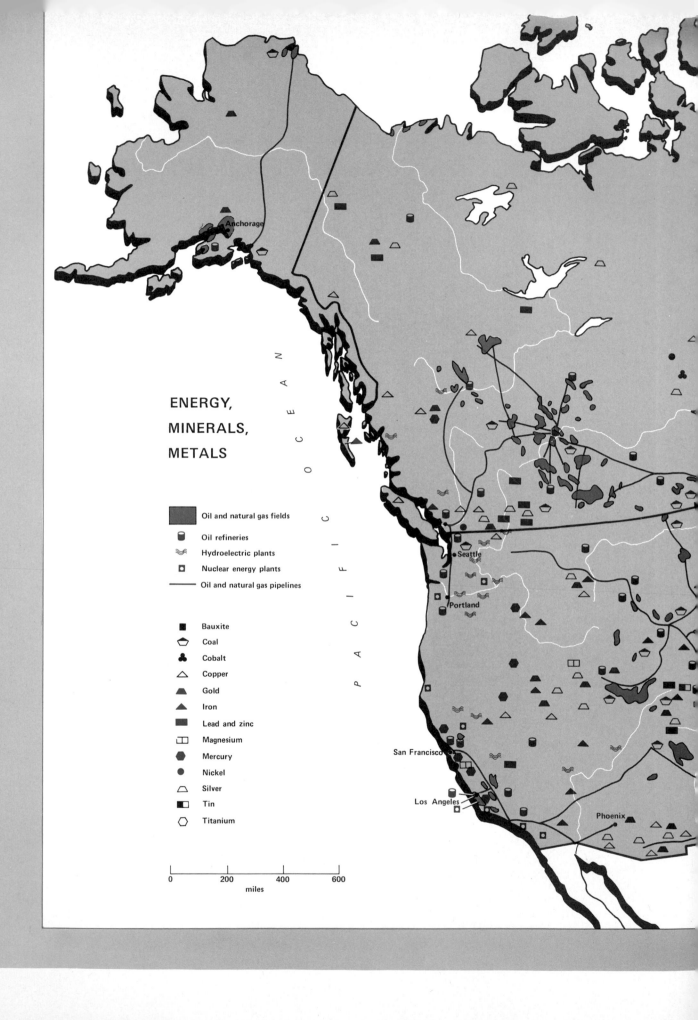

ENERGY,

MINERALS,

METALS

PACIFIC OCEAN

Anchorage

Seattle

Portland

San Francisco

Los Angeles

Phoenix

Oil and natural gas fields

Oil refineries

Hydroelectric plants

Nuclear energy plants

Oil and natural gas pipelines

Bauxite

Coal

Cobalt

Copper

Gold

Iron

Lead and zinc

Magnesium

Mercury

Nickel

Silver

Tin

Titanium

0   200   400   600

miles

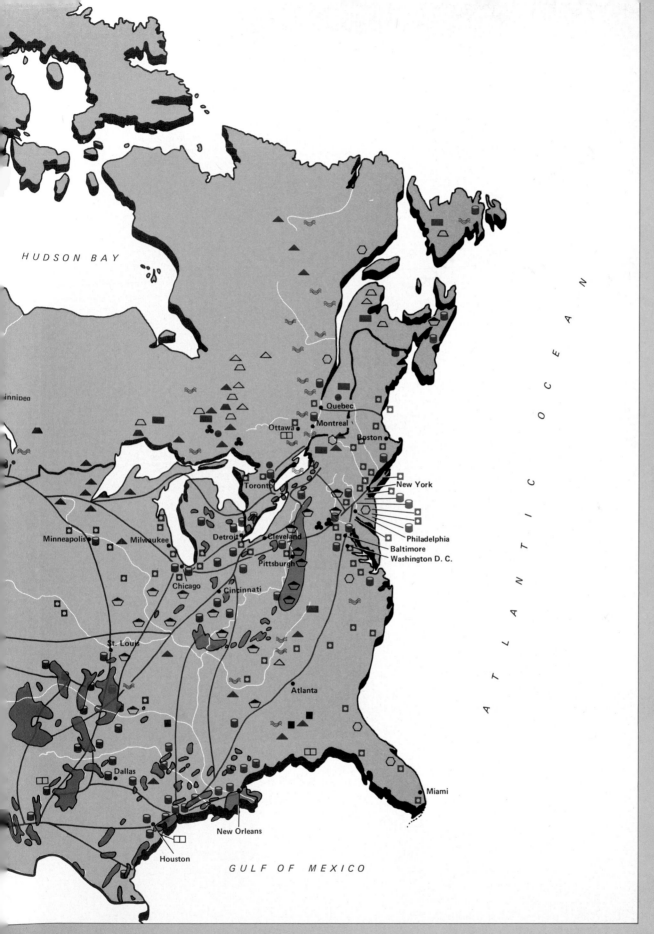

HUDSON BAY

ATLANTIC OCEAN

Quebec
Montreal
Ottawa
Boston

Toronto

New York

Detroit
Cleveland
Milwaukee
Minneapolis
Pittsburgh
Philadelphia
Baltimore
Washington D. C.
Chicago
Cincinnati

St. Louis

Atlanta

Dallas

Miami

New Orleans
Houston

GULF OF MEXICO

Winnipeg

Nation	Per capita GNP (dollars)	Per capita energy consumption (pounds)
United States	5,160	24,737
Canada	4,140	20,517
United Kingdom	2,430	12,115
Japan	2,130	7,187
Italy	1,860	5,900
Soviet Union	1,400	9,977

TABLE 1. Per Capita Gross National Product and Energy Consumption in Six Technological Nations, 1971
Source: Overseas Development Council, *The U.S. and the Developing World: Agenda for Action, 1974.* New York: Praeger, 1974.

ducers and consumers in a society of privileged affluence. A comparison of per capita gross national product and energy consumption in North America and in other technological nations (Table 1) shows the leading position of North Americans in resource consumption and purchasing power. The industrial complexes that mine, treat, and finish these resources are, as elsewhere in the technological world, fired by large supplies of coal, oil, natural gas, and hydroelectric power. Taken as a whole, the energy reserves of North America are notable for their total output (31 percent of world production in 1969), their geographical dispersion, and their relative accessibility, which allows petroleum and natural gas, especially, to be sold at rates far below world averages.

The United States contains nearly half the world's proved reserves of coal. Most underground mines are less than 1500 feet deep, and a large percentage of coal is mined by surface techniques. In 1974, 47 percent of soft, or *bituminous,*° coal was removed from beds lying at or near the surface by strip mining. Bituminous coal, which yields *coke*° for steel making, is widely used in industry. *Anthracite,*° or hard coal, once widely used for domestic heating, has declined to 1.2 percent of the coal market because petroleum and natural gas replaced coal for heating after World War II. In 1973, the five states of West Virginia, Kentucky, Pennsylvania, Illinois, and Ohio produced 77 percent of the coal mined in the United States. There are widespread and plentiful reserves; coal production is geared toward use in heavy industry, and most coal is mined near the greatest industrial concentrations, particularly the cities between the Ohio River and the Great Lakes.

The Appalachian coalfield, stretching from western Pennsylvania and eastern Ohio southward through valleys in the Appalachians to northern Alabama, and the eastern interior coalfield, cover-

ing much of Illinois, afford easy mining conditions. Strip mining, carried out with gigantic earth-moving equipment, is practicable and economic in both fields, although shaft mine production of both bituminous and anthracite seams in the Appalachian coalfield originally supported the steel industries of Pittsburgh, Cleveland, and Buffalo. Even today, one-fifth of the nation's steel-making capacity is concentrated in the Pittsburgh metropolitan area. Although strip mining is low in cost and high in production, it leaves a jumbled earth surface of subsoil materials. Some 2 million acres strip-mined in Kentucky, Illinois, and elsewhere in eastern coalfields lie in ecological flux where the earth, scarred by the mechanical upheaval of its crust, forms a landscape of man-made hills and gashed slopes. Restoration of these areas is generally possible, but only $9 million were spent on reclamation between 1969 and 1973. Today, increasing environmental awareness is forcing a recalculation of the long-term social and economic costs of inexpensive strip-mined coal.

The examination of this question is at an interesting juncture. In 1970 the United States Congress passed the Clean Air Act, recognizing that coal, the cheapest and most abundant American energy source, is also the dirtiest. The act sponsored industrial conversion to cleaner-burning fuel oil and natural gas by placing sanctions on industry-produced air pollutants. Five years later, however, growing national demand for petroleum and natural gas plus the political uncertainty of reliance upon Middle Eastern oil provoked a reinterpretation of the relative importance of coal energy and pollution control. In the Great Plains, Rocky Mountains, and Great Basin country, an estimated 86.1 billion tons of bituminous coal lie 50 to 100 feet beneath the surface. Some 90 percent of these western coal reserves cannot be mined under standards set by the Clean Air Act. As pressure mounts for increased coal production, the ecological integrity of remote areas of the West, until now largely unaffected by environmental deterioration, is in danger because virtually all western coal must be strip-mined. The coal reserves of the West—for use in eastern industries, regional electrical power production, and the extraction of oil from coal through the process of coal gasification—form a new energy frontier.

In contrast to the United States, Canada has a scant 1.4 percent of the proved global coal reserves. Moreover, economically productive Canadian coal reserves are located far from the centers of industry in Quebec and Ontario. Coal mined in New Brunswick and Nova Scotia has been useful in the development of limited industry in the Atlantic Provinces; the western coalfields of Alberta, however, are remote from industrial concentrations. Consequently, Canadian industry must import coal from closer sources in the eastern United States.

North American petroleum fields do not coincide with industrial concentrations—partly because of the historical precedence of coal as an industrial energy source and partly because oil and natural gas can be cheaply transported over long distances by pipeline and tanker. North America as a whole is self-sufficient in oil and natural gas, but strong differences exist between Canada and the United States.

Canada is a major world producer of oil; it has confirmed reserves of 9 billion barrels in central Alberta (one-fourth the United States total) and a potential reserve of more than 65 billion barrels (equal to that of Saudi Arabia) in the largely untapped oil-bearing *tar sands*• of northern Alberta. Except for the Soviet Union, Canada is the only oil-exporting nation in the technological world. Yet Canada's domestic oil situation is far from ideal. Canadian oil pipelines extend only as far east as Toronto, and the industrial Saint Lawrence Valley and Atlantic Provinces must depend on costly imported foreign oil. Recent exploration offshore from Nova Scotia has so far been disappointing, despite oil finds near Sable Island, 115 miles out in the Atlantic. Furthermore, oil derived from the Alberta tar sands is expensive to refine. And Canadian oil, largely an extension of the American industry, financed and developed by American capital for the benefit of the north-central states, has not been responsive to the Canadian domestic market. Until 1974, Canada supplied one-fifth of all United States oil imports; this percentage will diminish owing to limits placed on the export of Canadian oil, and by 1982, it is expected that Canada will no longer export oil.

The United States, until eclipsed by the Soviet Union in 1975, was the world's largest producer of both oil and natural gas; it remains the world's largest consumer and importer. The first (1859) oil field in the United States, at Titusville, Pennsylvania, produced 500,000 barrels annually; total American production rose slowly to 10 million barrels per year in the 1870s and 20 million in the 1880s. With the advent of the automobile, however, oil production and exploitation expanded into the major fields of the south-central states and California. In the 1920s, the present pattern of production began to emerge. By 1925, the United States produced about 20 percent of the world's oil; an average of 8,812,000 barrels was pumped each day. Today, 90 percent of all domestically produced oil and natural gas comes from three fields west of the Mississippi. Crude petroleum and natural gas production is concentrated in Texas and Louisiana, which together account for 60 percent of America's oil and 70 percent of America's natural gas. Only three nations—the Soviet Union, Saudi Arabia, and Iran—surpass Texas's output. These oil and natural gas deposits are found in a wide, nearly continuous belt along the Gulf Coast from the Mississippi Delta to the Mexican border. Offshore oil deposits, produced at operating costs two to ten times higher than those on land, were developed after World War II. Inland, the midcontinental oil field encompasses much of Kansas, Oklahoma, and Texas. It yields some 40 percent of the national total oil and natural gas production. The third largest concentration of production is in California, in and around Los Angeles, where large pools of oil are associated with folded rock structures. Natural gas is also produced for local consumption. Since there is little coal in this region, these energy resources of southern California have been vital in sustaining the growth of population on the West Coast in this century. Although California currently accounts for a tenth of the American oil yield, production is diminishing rapidly.

Elsewhere in the United States, oil and natural gas are produced in smaller quantities. Western Pennsylvania remains a significant producer of high-grade oil, but many wells of the Appalachians are near exhaustion. Substantial reserves exist in Wyoming, but the remoteness of the field has restricted production. In all, thirty-five of the fifty states and six of the ten Canadian provinces produce some oil or natural gas. But the area of greatest undeveloped potential lies 200 miles north of the Arctic Circle, near Prudhoe Bay, Alaska. There, on the North Slope of the Brooks Range, an estimated 10 billion barrels of oil—one of the largest fields in the world—lie 10,000 feet below the surface. In this frozen environment, the difficulties of drilling and transporting oil are complex and expensive. In early 1975, construction of a 799-mile, $6.37 billion pipeline from Prudhoe Bay to Valdez, on Prince William Sound, began in expectation of the production of 2 million barrels of North Slope oil a day by 1977. Although far removed from markets and consequently very expensive, and despite potential disruption of a vast wilderness, Alaskan oil fulfills current economic and political needs.

As new levels of energy demand are reached in the 1970s, new sources of oil and coal may be exploited for the first time. In the Gulf of Alaska and the Gulf of Mexico, offshore from southern California, New England, and New Jersey, oil and natural gas may exist in quantities far surpassing the potential of the North Slope. Some 16,500 square miles of public lands in Colorado, Utah, and Wyoming are believed to contain *oil-bearing shale*• capable of supplying 600 billion to 3 trillion barrels of oil—two to three times known world reserves. Pilot tests of Rocky Mountain oil shale are being made by private oil corporations. But the extraction process is so difficult and environmental damage so likely that exploitation of oil-bearing shale may prove an ecological nightmare: 99,000 cubic yards of shale must be moved to recover 40,000 barrels of oil; oil shale must undergo retortion (cooking) to remove the oil; the resulting landscape devastation far surpasses that of strip mining. The solution to America's growing demand for energy may result in heavy, long-term social and environmental costs.

The rivers of North America are a valuable potential source of renewable energy—hydroelectricity. Per capita use of hydroelectric power is far more important in Canada, where a relatively small population is well situated near economically feasible dam and power sites, than in the United States. The Saint Lawrence Valley is served by dams located on fast-running streams dropping southward off the southern rim of the Canadian Shield and by the Saint Lawrence Seaway project. In Quebec and Ontario, public power corporations have enough installed generating capacity to export electricity to Megalopolis. At Kitimat in British Columbia, 425 miles due north of Vancouver, new industry has been integrated with long-distance transmission of electricity produced on a tributary of the Fraser River. The economic difficulty of producing electricity in settings where no demand exists was overcome by the construction of an aluminum smelting plant at Kitimat, which is located on a coastal fjord. The Canadian North offers numerous locations where raw metals can be extracted with waterpower to achieve both the production of electricity and the initial processing of bulky mineral ores and metals.

In the United States, hydroelectric power is important in three areas. New York State is a beneficiary of the harnessed energy of Niagara Falls, a natural dam at the entry to Lake Erie, which was developed jointly by American and Canadian corporations to provide power for an area from Toronto to Buffalo. The power production of the Saint Lawrence Seaway also supplies New York State, as well as southeastern Ontario and Montreal. In the southern Appalachians, the Tennessee River watershed has been extensively developed by the Tennessee Valley Authority, a federal agency established by Congress as a rural-relief measure in 1933. The authority maintains twenty-seven major dams, sells hydroelectric power to 2 million customers in seven states, and regulates the flow of the Tennessee River, making its 650-mile length navigable from Knoxville to the Ohio River. A third region of large-scale hydroelectric development is the Pacific Northwest. The Columbia River was harnessed by the construction of Grand Coulee Dam, which produces more electricity than any other dam in North America. Nearly 1 million acres of agricultural land south of the Coulee have been irrigated, spurring a remarkable synthesis of agricultural development, power production, and industry in the Northwest. Despite these massive hydroelectric power projects and others on the Colorado, the Missouri, and streams in California, hydroelectric power in the United States accounted for a bare 1 percent of energy consumtion in 1970.

In 1975, there were nearly sixty nuclear power reactors operating in the United States and Canada, notably fewer per population than in Western Europe. In the United States, nuclear generating capacity represented less than 6 percent of the total electrical supply, although the Atomic Energy Commission has recommended that this proportion rise to 15 percent by 1980 and to 40 percent by 1990. Whether this recommendation will be realized depends on several factors, for nuclear power production may impose severe environmental penalties. The heat generated by nuclear power production is itself a pollutant, and large quantities of water must be used in cooling processes. In addition, not only must plant workers be shielded from nuclear radiation, but surrounding populations as much as several hundred miles distant must be safeguarded. The steadily rising prices of coal and oil have generated pressures for nuclear development, but the technological complexities of nuclear power production pose great danger. A leading nuclear safety expert at the Atomic Energy Commission, who resigned his post in 1974, stated that "unresolved questions about nuclear power safety are so grave that the United States should consider a complete halt to nuclear power plant construction while we see if . . . serious problems can . . . be resolved." In September 1974, the commission shut down twenty-one nuclear plants for safety inspections. While Project Independence envisions large-scale reliance upon nuclear power based on abundant domestic supplies of uranium, the fuel used for nuclear power generation, this kind of power production remains in an experimental state.

Energy from the earth's core, brought to the surface in fissures in the earth's crust, occasionally comes in contact with underground water, heating it to extremely high temperatures. Where this superheated water is pressured to the surface, tremendous energy is released, and *geothermal energy* can be efficiently exploited to generate electricity. In a single field in southern California stretching from the Salton Sea into northern Mexico, 20 million kilowatts of electricity per year will be generated continuously for 100 to 300 years. Project Independence estimates that geothermal power production in the United States will increase from 0.0001 percent of the 1970 energy budget to 0.004 percent in 1980 and that production will rise 250 times between 1974 and 1990. Largely because of the technological limitations, however, energy experts feel that large-scale geothermal power production is twenty years away.

Electrical power production from sunlight also lies in the future. Present use of solar energy in North America is restricted to test houses and water-heating devices. But technology inspired by space station research and solar power production for offshore oil rigs has led to increasing interest in harnessing solar energy for domestic use. In the United States, research and development spending on solar energy is expected to expand from $50 million in 1974 to $1 billion between 1975 and 1980; it is hoped that by 2000, solar energy may provide 15 to 30 percent of the total energy of the nation. A virtually unlimited resource with negligible environmental effects, solar energy looms as a desirable alternative for societies with high demand for energy, such as those of North America, and for other world regions, like Africa, which have limited conventional energy reserves.

MINERALS AND METALS

North America is remarkably well endowed with metal ores; both Canada and the United States are important producers of base metals such as iron ore, copper, lead, and zinc—the resources of heavy industry. Two great metal- and mineral-bearing structures exist in North America: the Canadian Shield and the Cordillera, a mountain system that arcs southward from Alaska through Canada to the Sierras and Rockies of the American West. The concentration of production in the United States is remarkable. Arizona, Minnesota, and Utah produce half the American total of metal ores, yet their population constitutes but 3 percent of the nation. As is true of energy sources, however, rising demand has outstripped finite supplies of metal ores, and the United States is now an importer of base metals. Domestic supplies are decreasing in output and quality; foreign sources are less costly owing to higher quality ores and lower labor costs.

Canada is an exporter of metals, as supplies exceed national needs. And Canadian production can be increased if the inaccessibility, rough terrain, and low population of the metal-bearing regions are overcome. Both Canada and the United States, it should be noted, are exporters or reexporters of virtually all minerals in the form of semifinished and finished manufactures.

Iron ore production is concentrated in two areas: the older mining districts at the western end of Lake Superior in Upper Michigan, northern Wisconsin, Minnesota, and Ontario; and newer finds in the Canadian Shield along the Quebec-Labrador border. Less important iron ore deposits are mined in eastern Newfoundland, the Adirondack Mountains of New York State, the southern folds of the Appalachians in Alabama, the Ozarks of Missouri, scattered sites in the Rockies and Sierra Nevada, and along the Pacific coast of British Columbia. Although iron ore imports provided only about 1 percent of America's needs in 1940, imports now constitute about half the national supply. Venezuela and Liberia are increasingly important exporters of iron to the United States, but Canada still supplies half of America's imports.

Expansion of Canadian production in the shield, in mining towns such as Gagnon and Schefferville, has been remarkable since World War II. Even so, the greatest concentration of production in North America is still in the Lake Superior uplands. Some 80 percent of the iron ore mined in the United States comes from this region, where, in the Mesabi field near Hibbing, Minnesota, half the total United States production is strip-mined to a depth of 350 feet. Iron ore is shipped south and east through the Great Lakes to cities from Chicago to Toronto, where coal from the Appalachian field provides the resource base for the North American steel industry. The steady decline in quality ore from the Lake Superior upland has created a ready market for iron ore shipped from Labrador and Quebec to the Great Lakes cities via the Saint Lawrence Seaway. With large reserves of low-quality iron ore and extensive unworked deposits far from centers of demand, the United States iron ore industry is in a period of flux pending technological advances in the use of less concentrated ores.

Like iron ore, nonferrous metal ore deposits are distant from existing markets. And mining does not attract increasing populations to centers of production; metal mining employment has declined steadily, dropping by over a third since 1940. Arizona produces half the nation's copper, and output is increasing; the declining copper content of the ore, however, has spurred research into the processing of less concentrated ores. Utah and Montana are also significant copper producers; in Canada, copper deposits north of Georgian Bay (Lake Huron) are the most important. The United States, first in copper production (23 percent of the world total), is also an importer. Canada, the fifth largest copper-producing country, is the third largest copper exporter.

Large-scale production by both countries, but export by Canada and import by the United States, is true for other metals also. Lead and zinc are mined in widely scattered areas in the Rockies and the Ozarks, in New Brunswick, and along the southern fringes of the Canadian Shield in Ontario, Quebec, and the Adirondacks. Canada is the primary world producer of nickel, and about half the world's supply is mined by the International Nickel Company in the Sudbury district. Cobalt, found in association with iron and nickel, is widely produced in North America. The continent's only significant source of bauxite in Arkansas produces but a fraction of demand; together, the United States and Canada import 70 percent of the bauxite sold on world markets. Tin is absent in North America. Gold and silver, historically a lure to the settlement of large areas of the West, are today of minor importance but are still mined in the American Rockies, in the Yukon, and on the southern Canadian Shield.

Of all mineral production—fuels, metals, and nonmetallic minerals—the last has experienced the greatest growth in demand in North America during the last generation. Between 1940 and 1970, there was a fourfold increase in the use of lime, salt, sulfur, phosphorus, phosphates, potassium, asbestos, boron, mica, magnesium, fluorspar, gypsum, and other nonmetallic minerals, including sand and gravel. This rise in demand, largely met by abundant resources, can be traced to the growth of the chemical, plastics, and construction industries. In addition, technical advances in older industries—such as steel—require many diverse nonmetallic materials.

BIBLIOGRAPHY

GENERAL

Boorstin, Daniel J. (ed.). *American Civilization: A Portrait from the Twentieth Century.* New York: McGraw-Hill, 1972. A beautifully illustrated collection of essays on the origins and intent of modern American society.

Boorstin, Daniel J. *The Americans: The Colonial Experience* (1958); *The Americans: The National Experience* (1965); *The Americans: The Democratic Experience* (1973). New York: Random House. A brilliant trilogy illuminating the diversity and direction of American intellectual and social development.

Gerlach, Arch C. (ed.). *The National Atlas of the United States of America.* Washington, D.C.: U.S. Department of the Interior, Geological Survey, 1970. In maps and text, a rich source on the geography and history of the United States.

Hart, John Fraser. *Regions of the United States.* New York: Harper & Row, 1972. A volume of essays on the regional geography of the United States.

Lerner, Max. *America as a Civilization.* New York: Simon & Schuster, 1965, 2 vols. An outstanding essay on the pattern and philosophical meaning of contemporary American civilization.

National Geographic Society. *We Americans.* Washington, D.C.: National Geographic Society, 1975. A brilliantly illustrated celebration of the American bicentennial.

Watson, J. Wreford. *North America: Its Countries and Regions.* London: Longmans, 1963. A fine regional text with emphasis on Canadian development.

White, C. Langdon, Edwin J. Foscue, and Tom L. McKnight. *Regional Geography of Anglo-America.* Englewood Cliffs, N.J.: Prentice-Hall, 1974. A detailed regional geography organized principally by physical areas.

Yeates, Maurice H., and Barry J. Garner. *The North American City.* New York: Harper & Row, 1971. A well-written geographical analysis of the American urban system, its processes and problems.

[1] THE FIRST NEW NATIONS

Brown, Ralph H. *Historical Geography of the United States.* New York: Harcourt, Brace, 1948. A comprehensive regional historical geography of the United States, the only study of this type extant.

Davidson, Marshall B. *Life in America.* Boston: Houghton Mifflin, 1974, 2 vols. A penetrating study of the American experience based on a wealth of original sources.

Fogel, Robert W., and Stanley L. Engerman. *Time on the Cross: The Economics of American Negro Slavery.* Boston: Little, Brown, 1974, 2 vols. A detailed statistical historical analysis of slavery in the South; highly controversial.

Garraty, John A. *The American Nation.* New York: Harper & Row, 1971. A well-written history of the growth of society and economy in America to 1877.

Jackson, John Brinckerhoff. *American Space: The Centennial Years, 1865–1876.* New York: Norton, 1972. The rural and urban landscapes of America a century ago, as described by a leading historical geographer.

Meinig, Donald W. "The Mormon Culture Region: Strategies and Patterns in the Geography of the American West, 1847–1964," *Annals, Association of American Geographers,* Vol. 55 (1965), pp. 191–220.

Meinig, Donald W. *Imperial Texas.* Austin: University of Texas Press, 1969. An important study of one of the American wests.

Meinig, Donald W. *Southwest: Three Peoples in Geographical Change, 1600–1970.* New York: Oxford University Press, 1970. A prominent geographer's detailed study of one area over four centuries.

Moir, John S., and Robert E. Saunders. *Northern Destiny: A History of Canada.* London: Dent, 1970. A modern survey of Canadian society from exploration to the present.

Rozwenc, Edwin C. *The Making of American Society.* Boston: Allyn & Bacon, 1972, 2 vols. A basic survey of the intellectual and institutional development of the United States.

Webb, Walter Prescott. *The Great Plains.* New York: Ginn, 1931. A controversial but brilliant exposition on the human occupance of the Great Plains mirroring both the nature of the region and the nature of man.

[2] MODERN NORTH AMERICA

Bach, Wilfrid. *Atmospheric Pollution.* New York: McGraw-Hill, 1972. A brief geographical introduction to the causes and costs of air pollution.

Berry, Brian J. L. "The Geography of the United States in the Year 2000." *Transactions, Institute of British Geographers,* No. 51 (1970), pp. 21–53. An interesting projection of America's future geography.

Davis, George A., and O. Fred Donaldson. *Blacks in the United States: A Geographical Perspective.* Boston: Houghton Mifflin, 1975. A perceptive and detailed historical and social geography of blacks in America.

Galbraith, John Kenneth. *The New Industrial State.* Boston: Houghton Mifflin, 1967. A noted economist's view of the dynamics of modern North America.

Manners, Ian R., and Marvin W. Mikesell (eds.). *Perspectives on Environment.* Washington, D.C.: Association of American Geographers, 1974. An excellent series of essays on geographical research into environmental problems.

Morrill, Richard L., and Ernest W. Wohlenberg. *The Geography of Poverty in the United States.* New York: McGraw-Hill, 1971. An outline of the spatial dimensions of poverty in the United States.

Rose, Harold M. *Geography of the Ghetto: Perceptions, Problems, and Alternatives.* De Kalb, Ill.: Northern Illinois Press, 1972. A penetrating series of geographical essays on the ghetto and the central city in modern American society.

Ward, David. *Cities and Immigrants: A Geography of Change in Nineteenth-Century America.* New York: Oxford University Press, 1971. An excellent study of urbanization and immigration at the turn of the century utilizing Boston as a case study.

Zelinsky, Wilbur. *The Cultural Geography of the United States.* Englewood Cliffs, N.J.: Prentice-Hall, 1973. A geographers appreciation of the origins and identity of American cultural patterns.

GLOSSARY

Note: Within a definition, terms defined elsewhere in the glossary are shown in boldface. Terms are shown in the text in boldface italic with a superscript bullet.

Acculturation: the process of cultural adjustment on either an individual or social level. In traditional social science literature, those changes inherent in the adjustment of a more "backward" group to a more "advanced" society, such as acceptance of new styles of dress, language, and customs.

Agglomerated settlement: a relatively compact **settlement** formed around closely spaced nuclei—clustered farmsteads, hamlets grown together, or adjoining villages; found throughout much of Europe, Asia, Africa, and Latin America.

Agrarian: the characteristics of a preindustrial, dominantly rural, agriculturally based society.

Agribusiness: a huge farm under corporate management, dependent upon reserves of capital and sale to a large geographic market; developed in agriculturally dependable environments throughout the United States and Canada.

Al Maghrib al aqsa: see **Maghrib.**

Alloy mineral: a mineral such as chromium, nickel, magnesite, manganese, molybdenum, tungsten, silica, and vanadium, which contains elements that when added to iron yield a desirable property—strength, durability, or flexibility.

Alluvial fan: cone- or fan-shaped deposits of **alluvium** in a plain or open valley; in arid regions, alluvial fans are often valuable agricultural environments, endowed with renewable soils and retrievable water.

Alluvial plain: a level stretch of land near a river upon which **alluvium** has been deposited in time of flood; often characterized by thick beds of sub-surface alluvial material and good drainage, this is fertile agricultural land.

Alluvial soil: fertile deposit of topsoil adjacent to sources of water.

Alluvium: rock fragments, soil, and other fragmented materials deposited by water in low-lying areas such as stream beds, **deltas,** and **estuaries.**

Anthracite: a long-burning hard coal that has the highest carbon content of all types of coal and burns with almost no smoke. In the United States, anthracite mines in northeastern Pennsylvania originally supplied coal for the steel industry until **coking** processes allowed the use of lower-grade **bituminous** coal.

Apartheid: a spatial solution to the problems posed by the multiracial nature of society in the Republic of South Africa. In theory, apartheid envisions the creation of a loose federation of **bantustans.** In practice, it is a political device to preserve the power of the white population in a society where they form only 17 percent of the total population.

Arable: the agricultural space of a society; the land suitable for cultivation.

Archipelago: a group of geologically related islands located in close proximity to one another; originally restricted to the islands of the Aegean Sea, the term now embodies the idea of a chain of islands such as the Aleutians or the Florida Keys.

Arroyo: dry rock- and silt-laden stream bed found in **desert** environments that channels runoff during brief periods of rainfall; in the Middle East, the term wadi is used.

Autocracy: government by a single ruler with unlimited power; see also **despotism.**

Balkanization: the breaking of a region into many small and often hostile units. The term comes from the political evolution of the Balkan peninsula of southeastern Europe, which was governed, with minor exceptions, by either the Ottoman or the Austrian empires from the 1400s until national movements in the nineteenth century created a profusion of small independent states.

Bantustan: separate, self-governing reserve for the African population of South Africa.

Barrage: an earthen or concrete obstruction built across a river to control the flow of water for **irrigation** and flood control.

Basin irrigation: a system of irrigation in which the floodwaters of a river are trapped in a series of basins; seasonal in nature, it supplements inadequate rainfall for a relatively short period of time.

Bayou: a local term for the slow-moving marshy creeks, **tributaries,** and minor rivers of the Gulf coastal plain of the southern United States, particularly in Louisiana and Texas.

Benelux: an acronym for the three European nations of Belgium, the Netherlands, and Luxembourg, which formed an economic union in 1958.

Bituminous: soft coal, generally containing less than a third volatile matter; refined into **coke,** it provides the energy for most iron and steel production.

Black country: descriptive term for the landscapes of early industrialized, congested regions of Europe, derived from the dense concentration of smoke and soot generated by the burning of coal in the production of iron and steel, often so great as to blacken the surrounding countryside.

Bog: a low-lying area of water-logged ground composed of decaying plantlife, especially moss, and characteristic of the **taiga** and of the shallow standing water of **glacial** lakes and ponds; known as muskeg in Canada.

Bolshevik: the radical wing of the Russian Social Democratic Party in prerevolutionary Russia. Under the leadership of V. I. Lenin, the Bolsheviks displaced the moderates and seized power in 1917.

Borough: a political subdivision: New York City is divided into five boroughs—Brooklyn, Queens, the Bronx, Staten Island, and Manhattan.

Bourgeoisie: the urban middle class whose members conducted the business affairs of the town, owned property, and were concerned with correct social behavior; in modern political terms, a self-serving propertied class whose interests are based on the investment and expansion of capital for personal gain.

Braided streams: a complex pattern of interweaving shallow channels of a river system, each stream with insufficient volume or velocity to carry its load of **alluvium.**

Break in bulk point: a transfer point on a transportation route where the mode of transport of a specific good changes. Timbuktu, for example, became the premier trade center of the western Sahara by virtue of its location at the farthest navigable inland point on the Niger River. Goods traveling upstream were transferred from river boats to camels; goods traveling downstream were transferred from camels to boats.

Cap rock: a layer of resistant rock set above a less resistant layer of water, oil, or ore; in Texas, cap rock overlies a layer of sandy water-laden soil, and extensive drilling for this water has transformed cap rock plains into an **irrigated** agricultural environment.

Caravel: a sailing ship developed by the Portuguese and instrumental in furthering European voyages of discovery to Africa, India, the East Indies, and the New World in the fifteenth and sixteenth centuries.

Cartel: a combination of individual enterprises designed to limit competition by setting common market conditions, particularly with respect to the production and pricing of products; see also **OPEC.**

Cartography: the science of map-making; the representation of two common measures of geography—distance and scale—in map form.

Cataract: a series of rapids or waterfalls in a river caused by a sudden steepening of slope or outcrops of resistant rock in the riverbed; in Africa, river cataracts formed a major obstacle to European penetration of the interior.

Central business district (CBD): the "downtown" or main commercial district of a North American city, characterized by a high concentration of business, usually lodged in a vertical core of office buildings, in a small area.

Central place: a location that functions as a service center for a surrounding area by providing various goods, employment, and services. Central places, usually towns, may be ranked in a hierarchy of importance by population, the number and range of goods and services provided, and the area over which their influence is felt.

Chernozem: a Russian name for the fertile black soils that cover much of the Ukraine in Russia and the Great Plains of North America; these soils, high in organic content, develop in **midlatitude** grasslands.

City-state: an autonomous state consisting of a city and its surrounding territory; well-known examples are the Greek city-states of ancient times and the Italian city-states of the Middle Ages and the Renaissance.

Civilizational hearth: a center of innovation, stable social institutions, and regional culture such as the Yellow River valley in China, the Ganges and Indus river valleys in India, and the Tigris-Euphrates Valley in Mesopotamia; the earliest sites of the environmental transformation.

Coke: bituminous coal that has been burned at high temperatures and transformed into a residue which burns at higher temperatures than coal; used to fire steel blast furnaces.

Collectivization: an administrative restructuring of rural society in which all land holdings are grouped together into a single unit and operated under the cooperative control of those who live and work on the land. Collectives have existed throughout history, but the term is now most often used in connection with Russian and Chinese systems for rationalizing agricultural production.

Commune: a settlement based on collective ownership and use of property, goods, and the means of production.

Concessions: the grants of commercial privileges, property, and immunity from civil law obtained by European commercial interests from the traditional societies of China, India, and Africa that produced enclaves of foreign influence in these areas and allowed Europeans to dominate the economy and often the politics of the host area.

Conifer: a conically shaped tree with straight trunk, short branches, and needlelike leaves. Most conifers, such as the spruce, fir, and pine, are **evergreen**; a coniferous forest is characterized by little undergrowth (due to the continuous and deep shade) and poor soils.

Conquistador: name given to the sixteenth-century Spanish conquerors of Mexico and Peru.

Continentality: measure of indexes of a continental climate, which is characterized by seasonal extremes of temperature and marked differences in precipitation, due mainly to great distance from the sea.

Conurbation: an extensive urban area formed of two or more cities, originally separate, which have coalesced to form a single continuous metropolitan region with multiple nodes.

Copra: the dried meat of the coconut, which yields coconut oil and is also used as animal feed; grown on commercial **plantations** in the southwestern Pacific and in parts of tropical Africa.

Cordillera: a continental mountain system consisting of numerous ranges set in parallel ridges. The Andes cordillera forms the mountainous spine of South America; in North America, the western cordillera includes the Rockies, Sierra Nevada, Sierra Madre, and Coast ranges.

Cosmography: historically, the description and mapping of the physical universe; limitation of the scope of geography to the study of the earth's surface occurred in the nineteenth century.

Crevasse: a deep crack in a **glacier**, not unlike a fault line. Crevasses frequently occur either at the top of a valley glacier where the ice is brittle and fractures easily, or downslope where a glacier moves more rapidly over a steeper grade or is bent around a curve.

Crop rotation: a farming technique designed to protect and even increase soil fertility and yields. In its simplest form, as in **shifting agriculture**, crop rotation involves the successive use of different planting sites. More generally today, the same field is used to produce different crops during each growing season, utilizing the knowledge that each crop has different nutritive demands and yields different by-products in its cycle of growth and decay.

Cross plowing: tilling a field with a wooden plow first in one direction and then across the furrows, reworking the entire field to break up the soil. With the appearance of the heavier iron plow in Europe in the early medieval period, cross plowing was no longer necessary.

Cultural landscape: the impress of a society on its physical environment. In early twentieth-century geography, the study of the cultural landscape was seen as a fundamental area of inquiry.

Culture hearth: a region in which a distinctive cultural complex either originated or exists. In North America, modern American civilization can be traced to four culture hearths in French Canada, New England, the Middle Colonies, and the South—each with different economic foci, social organization, and patterns of intellectual development.

Culture of poverty: according to the anthropologist Oscar Lewis, a set of behavior, a culture, derived from relative deprivation. A vague term, this concept depends upon the identification of social traits of poverty that can be shown to be independent of cultural characteristics such as race, language, religion, and nationality.

Deciduous: shedding leaves seasonally—at the onset of winter or a dry season—and renewing them in spring or with the arrival of wet-season rains.

Delta: a flat, fertile lowland plain formed by a river as it deposits its burden of **alluvium** near its mouth.

Demographic transition: a four-stage model of the impact of the scientific revolution on population growth. In the early phases of industrialization, a population is characterized by high birth rates and, before the general introduction of modern health practices, high death rates. Population remains static. In the second stage, fertility remains high but mortality rates decrease as sanitary conditions dramatically improve: a sharp increase in population ensues. In the third stage, the birth rate declines to a level comparable with the death rate, slowing population growth. In the final stage, the total population is much larger that at the beginning of the cycle of growth, but is again stabilized with both birth and death rates at low levels.

Demography: the study and description of population by nationality, race, age, sex, religion, health, education, and other vital characteristics.

Desert: tract of land in which precipitation is so scanty and undependable that vegetation is noticeably absent; **sedentary** human activity is restricted to the extraction of specific minerals and metals, or to irrigated **oasis** agriculture.

Despotism: oppressive and abusive individual rule; absolutism.

Dhow: boat with a single triangular sail attached to a low mast, commonly found in the coastal waters of the West Indian Ocean. These boats remain important commercial carriers of agricultural products and traditional manufactures along the Arabian and East African coasts.

Diffusion: geographical spread of cultural elements from a given point over a progressively wider area. Geographers identify the study of cultural diffusion—its causes and effects, propagation, amplitude, and direction—as an important means of understanding the relationships between different societies and the course of culture through time and space.

Dike: an earthen bank constructed alongside low-lying ground to prevent it from being flooded by the sea, a lake, or a river. In the Netherlands, dikes form protective rings around vast areas of agricultural land reclaimed from the sea.

Dispersed settlement: widely spaced, scattered rural farmsteads, often distributed along roads, streams, and canals. Dispersed settlement is characteristic of rural North America.

Distributary: an individual channel formed by the splitting of a river which does not rejoin the main stream but reaches the sea independently.

Double-cropping: the practice of planting two crops in succession in the same field in the same year.

Drip irrigation: an agricultural technique whereby crops receive measured quantities of water in a rhythmic, driplike fashion from underground sprinkler systems. Drip irrigation, particularly useful for tree crops, is an effective way of reducing water loss from evaporation, seepage, and runoff while providing crops with as much moisture as the soil is capable of absorbing and retaining.

Dry farming: techniques used in arid and dry-season environments to retain as much moisture as possible in the soil. Year-long plowing and mulching of **fallow** land were among the dry farming practices of medieval Europe; in modern agriculture, dry land is left unplowed and seeded by no-till planters to conserve moisture.

Dust bowl: a semi-arid area from which exposed topsoil is being or has been removed by the wind after a period of low rainfall.

Ecology: the science of the mutual relationship of organisms to their **environment**.

Economic take-off: as advanced by the economic historian W. W. Rostow, that stage in the development of an industrial society when the conditions for an internal industrial revolution are met and sudden change—"the great watershed in the life of modern societies"—begins to take hold. Thereafter, increasing production, consumption, wealth, and the notion of continual progress become the normal and expected course of events. Economic take-off, measured by growth in vital industries such as metal production and transport, occurred in Britain during the last twenty years of the eighteenth century, in Japan one hundred years later, and is now occurring in China.

Ecosystem: an organic community of plants and animals within its **environment**—for example, a **bog**, an **oasis**, or a **lagoon**.

Elite: a privileged social class, small in number, whose members control political, administrative, intellectual, artistic, religious, and economic affairs. In traditional nonindustrial societies, the elite form the single center of power.

Entrepôt: a center to which goods in transit are brought for temporary storage and transshipment; often a port city. The economy of an entrepôt is based on commerce and trade rather than manufacturing.

Environment: the sum of the surrounding conditions within which organisms or communities exist; in modern terms, environments tend to be centered on the role of the human community as the modifier and organizer of nearly all other kinds of life.

Erosion: the wearing away of the earth's surface by the action of water or wind; a natural process, erosion is accelerated when the vegetative cover is removed or disturbed by human populations.

Erosional silt: particles of **alluvium** coarser than clay but finer than sand, loosened and carried away by water or wind erosion.

Escarpment: a sharply defined inland cliff produced by **faulting** or **erosion**, rimming a **plateau**.

Estuary: the tidal mouth of a river where fresh water mixes with sea water, an estuary is a delicately balanced aquatic **ecosystem** noted for shellfish production and a rich variety of marine life.

European Common Market (EEC): a trading union of nine nations founded in 1958 to foster economic cooperation through a geographic consolidation of markets and resources, and common tariffs on imported goods. Although the Treaty of Rome which established the European Economic Community envisioned political integration, its member states have not relinquished their sovereignty.

Evergreen: a descriptive term for plants that remain green throughout the year—plants with such persistent leaves or needles include **conifers**, many grasses, and succulents.

Extended family: a family in which grandparents, any number of their children, and the offspring of the second generation live under one roof and function as an economic unit.

Fall line: a line joining points where parallel-flowing rivers drop suddenly from a **piedmont** to a coastal plain in falls or rapids; the upstream limit of river navigation. Because of the availability of waterpower at these locations, a string of industrial cities frequently grew up along fall lines.

Fallow: cultivated acreage that lies idle for one crop year, or is plowed but not planted to crops in an attempt to maintain soil fertility. In medieval European agriculture, a third of the cultivated land was in fallow each year; in arid zones, land is often fallowed by plowing so that precipitation may more easily penetrate the soil.

Faulting: the fracturing of the earth's crust into blocks of land along lines of pressure. Along with **folding**, it is one of the principle mountain-building processes.

Favela: slum ringing Rio de Janiero, Sao Paulo, and other fast-growing cities of Brazil.

Fen: low-lying land often covered by a thin sheet of water, and characterized by plants and animals adapted to a water environment. A fen is often fertile land susceptible to draining and subsequent settlement: in eastern England, there is a region of fenlands; in Boston, Fenway Park is an example of a fen reclaimed from the sea.

Ferroalloy: any of the many minerals such as tungsten, vanadium, or molybdenum that are alloyed with **pig iron** to yield steel of a desired quality.

Fertile Crescent: a well-watered, semicircular band of land arcing northward from the southeastern coast of the Mediterranean, through the Lebanon Mountains, east to the **alluvial plains** of Mesopotamia, and south again along the foothills of the Taurus and Zagros mountains.

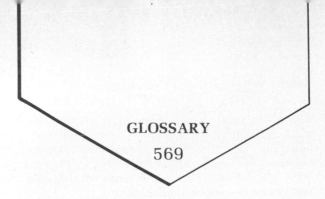

Feudalism: the most prevalent system of political organization in Europe during the Middle Ages, based on bonds of loyalty between peasant and lord. The political map of Europe was a patchwork of lordly domains worked by **peasants** or **serfs** who comprised 90 percent of the population and were bound to their lord in land, labor, arms, and other services; feudal systems were also characteristic at various periods in China, Japan, India, and the Middle East.

Fief: an expanse of land controlled by a feudal lord and worked by his **serfs**.

Fjord: long, narrow **inlet** of the ocean found in Norway, Greenland, and Chile, on the North American Pacific coast from Vancouver to Alaska, and in Labrador. Scoured and deepened as valley **glaciers** made their way to the sea, fjords were filled with seawater after the retreat of the glaciers.

Floodplain: level, low-lying valley floor bordering a river, subject to flooding when the river rises and overflows its banks. **Alluvium** deposited during floods creates a rise of higher land along the river, a natural levee, with lower marshes farther away. Thick concentrations of population frequently exist on floodplains, whose fertile soils support dense networks of human settlement.

Fog desert: desert on the west coast of a continent between 15° and 30° latitude. When cool air overlying cold ocean currents paralleling the shore moves inland, these deserts are blanketed by fog. Dew forms a substantial portion of the total moisture budget and modifies vegetation, hence the descriptive term fog desert.

Folded block mountains: mountains initially produced by **faulting** and later folded (compressed into ridges and valleys) to create a highly irregular landscape that is difficult to traverse.

Folded mountains: mountains constructed by the compression of the earth's crust into alternating ridges (mountain ranges) and valleys, much like a washboard.

Fragmentation: successive subdivision of inherited land into ever-smaller and less economic parcels. Inheritance systems encourage fragmentation when law or custom dictates that land be divided among children.

Gallery forest: a corridor of tropical **rain forest** along a stream.

Gentry: a rural social class of high standing, characterized by ownership of large properties, economic privilege, and conspicuous wealth. Gentries are usually found in societies with rigid class distinctions, where the mass of the rural population is composed of **peasants**.

Geohydrology: the science of managing and utilizing the earth's water resources as a complex system of precipitation, infiltration, and renewal.

Geothermal: of or relating to the heat of the earth's interior. Geothermal electricity is produced by capturing this heat in locations where instability in the earth's crust has brought it near the surface in the form of **geysers**, whose hot water is capped or drawn off to generate power.

Geyser: a deep hot spring which at intervals shoots a jet of steam and hot water as high as 200 feet into the air; commonly found along **fault** lines.

Glacier: a river of ice, of one of two types: valley (or alpine), are found where thick accumulations of ice in **highland** zones begin to move downslope; and continental (or sheet), which occur when cold climates cause a higher proportion of the earth's water to be stored in ice, as in the polar latitudes.

Greenbelt: encircling swath of forest and farmland on the periphery of a built-up urban area, usually purchased by a municipality and designed to maintain some balance within the metropolitan region between urban and rural landscapes.

Gross national product (GNP): the total value of all goods and services produced within a country (or smaller administrative unit) in any given year. The GNP of a country reflects population size, level of industrialization, material well-being, and economic power. When divided by the total population, GNP is a relative measure of the purchasing power of each individual.

Growth pole: a service center that serves as a base for economic development and **diffusion** into a region chosen for growth. In planned and centrally organized modern societies, growth poles increase in population and economic functions very rapidly. In the Soviet Union, for example, the progression of settlement in the developing East has been organized around growth poles selected as strategic economic nodes.

Guano: hardened deposit of bird or bat excrement, rich in nitrates and used in the manufacture of fertilizers and explosives. Bat guano is mined in caverns; bird guano collects in arid habitats with large bird populations.

Guild: organizations of artisans whose hereditary membership maintained standards of quality and scale of production as well as methods of merchandising specific products in preindustrial urban societies.

Gulf Stream: a warm-water ocean current that flows out of the Gulf of Mexico, passes through the Florida Straits, parallels the east coast of the United States, and turns eastward across the North Atlantic toward northwestern Europe, where it is known as the North Atlantic Drift. The Gulf Stream is responsible for higher than average temperatures in adjacent coastal zones.

Headman: the recognized leader and symbol of authority in a hamlet, village, or small town in traditional preindustrial societies.

Headwaters: the source of a stream or river.

Heartland: the center of action, a vital and strategic place. In geography, the heartland indicates the area most characterized by the cultural or physical phenomenon under study.

Heath: a tract of wasteland where heather, a shrubby **evergreen**, berry plants, mosses, and sorrel have replaced woodlands as the dominant vegetation.

Highland: a general term referring to any kind of elevated land—mountains, **plateaus**, hills.

Hijaz: the western Red Sea coast and mountain region of Saudi Arabia, differentiated from the central **plateau** by a low north-south trending mountain range of the same name. This **region** includes three of Saudi Arabia's principal cities—Mecca, Medina, and Jidda.

Hinterland: the surrounding area over which a city or any **central place** exerts influence, and on which it draws to sustain services, industry, and population.

Hoe cultivation: small-scale, labor-intensive agriculture, often **terraced** and **irrigated**, which produces high yields due to the skillful application of human energy. In China in particular, this type of cultivation was primarily done with the hoe, a hand tool allowing great sensitivity in cultivating, weeding, and loosening the earth around plants.

Homesteading: a movement in North America rooted in the belief that the public domain belonged to the people and that every family was entitled to a debt-free home or farm. It culminated in the Homestead Act of 1862 under which all heads of family in the United States were entitled to 160 acres of land in the public domain after occupancy and cultivation for five years. Similar legislation was passed in Canada.

Humus: a black, nutrient-rich layer of decomposed and decomposing organic matter derived from dead plants and animals; the top layer of **midlatitude** soils.

Hydroponics: a modern form of agriculture in which the root systems of plants grow in a liquid solution of vital nutrients with their leaf systems suspended above the surface. Although still largely experimental, hydroponics has long been practiced in the production of sprouts for Oriental cuisine and is commercially important in some technologically advanced countries where water, space, or temperature are limiting factors.

Iberia: a 230,000-square-mile peninsula composed of Spain and Portugal. **Mediterranean climate** predominates throughout Iberia, named by the ancient Greeks after the population near the river Iberus (the modern Ebro) in Spain.

Indentured servitude: a system by which an individual was bound by contract to work for another for a given length of time; a common feature of rural society in medieval Europe and colonial America.

Indigo: a plant whose leaves yield a dark blue dye. Indigo was cultivated as early as 2500 BC in India and later along the fringes of the Mediterranean, in Britain, and Peru. It was an important item of colonial trade in the Americas, but was replaced by chemical dyes after 1880.

Industrial node: a **central place** with an overwhelming number of services, distributive functions, and material goods produced and consumed; a large concentration of industry and population supported by transport and supply networks.

Infrastructure: the physical underpinnings of industrial society, permanent installations that facilitate the input and output of goods, services, and people, and communication. An urban infrastructure includes as well those installations that maintain the well-being of the urban population —sewage lines, water treatment plants, electrical generating plants, hospitals, schools, police stations, post offices.

Inlet: a small opening in the shoreline of an ocean, lake, or river.

Intermontane: descriptive of land lying between mountain ranges, or facets of life in such regions: intermontane society; intermontane agriculture.

Iron smelting: the process of extracting purer iron from iron ore by burning the ore at high temperatures, usually with **coke**.

Irrigation: artificial distribution of water where rainfall is irregular or insufficient by the construction of channels from the water source or storage place to a point of need. More complex forms of irrigation involve the construction of dams or

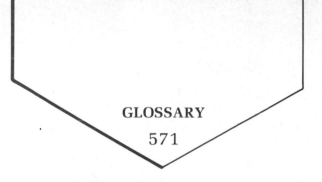

barrages to create reservoirs for agricultural, residential, and industrial use. See also **basin irrigation**; **drip irrigation**; **perennial irrigation**.

Isthmus: a narrow, connective neck of land bordered on both sides by water and set between two larger bodies of land.

Jungle: a dense, impenetrable tangle of low trees, climbing vines, and thick undergrowth that occurs where streams and highways in the **tropics** open **rain forests** to sunlight. Commonly called a jungle, such an area is more properly referred to as a **gallery forest**.

Lagoon: shallow stretch of coastal water separated from the open sea by a narrow strip of land—a coral reef, atoll, island, **offshore bar**, or spit. Lagoons sometimes become filled with **alluvial** deposits from rivers or with sediment carried in by tides or waves during storms.

Land reform: the giving of farmland to landless **peasants** to achieve a more equitable distribution of agricultural land among the rural population and to end absentee landlordism and **tenancy**. If poorly planned, land reform programs may adversely affect productivity, replacing large, efficient estates with a patchwork of small, uneconomic farmsteads.

Laterite: a soil commonly found in the humid **tropics**, rich in iron and aluminum but poor in **humus**, and **leached** of other soil nutrients. Exposed to the atmosphere, laterite hardens into a rocklike material and supports agriculture only when intensively fertilized.

Leaching: a process by which minerals and organic matter percolate downward through successive layers of soil, or are entirely removed from the soil structure by intense and prolonged rainfall. Leached soils such as **laterites** are rich in heavy minerals (particularly iron and aluminum) but deficient in nutrients and poor for agriculture.

Legume: a plant family consisting of forage grasses and vegetables that produce seed pods and return nitrogen to the soil. Peas, beans, clover, and alfalfa are legumes.

Levant: a name given to the shores of the eastern Mediterranean Sea. Historically, the economy of the Levant has been based on international commerce; it is a cosmopolitan region with urban populations composed of many nationalities and many religious and ethnic groups.

Lignite (brown coal): a low-grade coal, intermediate in hardness, burning qualities, and moisture content between **peat** and **bituminous** coal. Like peat, lignite is economically unimportant except in regions where bituminous coal or some alternate fuel is economically unavailable.

Littoral: a seacoast that is directly affected by its neighboring water body; a seashore. Low-lying littoral **environments** are often rich in vegetation and animal life, and are especially sensitive to disruptions caused by industrialization.

Llanos: a tropical grassland located in the Orinoco Basin of Venezuela and the Guiana Highlands on the northern margins of the Amazon Basin; see also **pampas**; **savannah**.

Loess: airborne dust which is carried on prevailing air currents and falls to create a deposit of fine soil that in some places may cover large areas with a thick mantle. Loess soil is highly porous and generally very fertile; it is the basis of rich agricultural environments in north China, the Ukraine, central Europe, and parts of the American Midwest and Argentina.

Maghrib: an area set between the Atlas Mountains, the Atlantic, the Mediterranean, and the Sahara in northwest Africa. Meaning in Arabic the land lying farthest west, the Maghrib is one of the primary regional divisions of the Middle East and is composed of the nations of Morocco, Algeria, and Tunisia.

Magnetic anomaly: area where large concentrations of iron, nickel, or other magnetic materials exist, causing compass bearings to deviate. Everywhere else on the earth's surface, compass needles align to magnetic north in the Canadian Arctic or magnetic south in Antarctica.

Malthusian: name given to the doctrines of Thomas R. Malthus (1766–1834), who held that when unchecked by war, famine, or disease, population would increase at a rate faster than its means of subsistence. This contradiction between the geometrical growth of population and the arithmetic increase of subsistence, in his view, set a natural control, a "strong and constantly operating check," which prevented a population from outstripping its resource base. Unfortunately, Malthus has been continually misconstrued, so that a Malthusian doctrine or policy has come to mean a pessimistic view of population growth that suggests dire consequences for societies whose numbers increase rapidly.

Mandate: a commission given by the League of Nations after World War I to a member nation for the establishment of a responsible government in a former German colony or conquered territory. With the exception of South West Africa (Namibia), mandated territories became United Nations Trust Territories after World War II.

Marchland: a frontier or border region whose boundaries are vaguely defined and subject to conflicting national claims, invasion, and repeated transfers of power.

Market area, market town: trading center where the produce of the surrounding countryside (the **hinterland** or market area) is sold, exchanged, or bartered for a limited number of urban services and nonagricultural goods. In traditional China, basic-level market towns were small, lower-order settlements woven into a network throughout the countryside; higher-level market towns offered a greater range of services, had larger populations, and drew upon this network.

Market economy: an economy in which monetary transactions are universal. Production is geared for cash sale; consumption stems from money paid for goods and services, in contrast to systems such as barter.

Mason-Dixon Line: the cultural boundary between the North and the South in the United States. In the 1760s, Charles Mason and Jeremiah Dixon surveyed the disputed boundary between Pennsylvania and Maryland and fixed Pennsylvania's border (except for the westernmost 36 miles). With the Missouri Compromise (1820) setting limitations on the practice of slavery in the West, the Mason-Dixon Line came to mean the dividing line between southern slave states and northern free states.

Massif: a mountainous block of land whose peaks do not form lines as in a mountain range. The Massif Central of France has given this word to geography; the Adirondack Mountains of New York State are an American example.

Mediterranean climate: transition climate between the **subtropical deserts** nearer the equator and the cool, moist climates farther poleward. Best displayed in the Mediterranean Basin, this climate is characterized by summer drought and a winter rainfall maximum; it is unique among climactic types. The distinctive vegetation of low **evergreen** trees and **scrubland** commonly found in Mediterranean climates is able to withstand both a summer drought of two to four months and frequent heavy winter rains.

Megalopolis: a great urban **region** including many cities that have expanded and coalesced to form an extensive, continuous zone of urbanization. A megalopolis encompasses all other urban levels—town, city, suburb, and **conurbation.** In the technological world, the Boston–Washington megalopolis of the eastern seaboard of the United States is a prime example. In the developing world, rapidly expanding populations are increasingly urban; in Brazil, Rio de Janeiro–São Paulo is a megalopolis in the making.

Meltwater: run-off derived from melting snow or a **glacier;** in unusually warm weather, meltwater may cause flooding.

Mercantilism: an economic system developed in Europe in late medieval times by which nations attempted to increase the power and wealth of the state by securing a large supply of precious metals, a favorable balance of trade through **protectionism,** and the establishment of trade monopolies in international commerce—policies that gave impetus to colonial ventures.

Meridian: a line of longitude stretching 180° from pole to pole and serving as a measurement of distance east or west of the standard meridian (0°), which passes through Greenwich, England. One degree of longitude (one meridian) progressively decreases in distance poleward.

Meteorology: a science that deals with the earth's atmosphere in order to predict weather and understand climate. Meteorologists study the interrelated physical processes of the air and the land in terms of atmospheric pressure, temperature, winds, precipitation, insolation, humidity, and other variables.

Midlatitude: the zone between 35° and 55° north and south latitude on either side of the equator. Here, contrasts between seasons are strong, but neither winter nor summer is harsh enough to seriously limit human activity.

Miscegenation: marriage or cohabitation between persons of different races.

Modernization surface: concept used to analyze the spread of modernization in a country by comparing the spatial **diffusion** of components of the economic **infrastructure**—hard-surface roads, railroads, hospitals, and central government administrative offices—over time.

Moraine: masses of boulders, rocks, and soil carried and ultimately deposited by a **glacier** and the resulting landform. Moraines left behind during a period of glacial retreat often appear on the landscape as parallel ranges of low hills, their surfaces pockmarked by depressions holding ponds or small lakes, with an irregular drainage pattern.

Mulatto: a person of mixed white and black descent. Mulattos form an important proportion of the population in Latin America, in the former

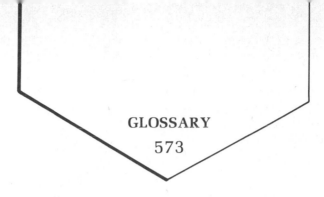

Portuguese African colonies, and in South Africa, where they are known as Cape Coloured.

Muskeg: see **bog.**

Nation-state: a country inhabited by people who in large part share the same religion, language, and ethnic heritage. In Europe, nations of people such as the Germans and the Italians joined together to form nation-states. In Africa, by contrast, many newly independent states defined by boundaries drawn during the colonial period are in search of a national identity.

New town: an urban center constructed in a nonurban landscape, designed and financed by a central government to plan and regulate urban growth. Developed in Britain, new towns are now found in most European countries, the Soviet Union, and to a lesser degree in many countries of the developing world.

Nonferrous metal: any metal not containing iron. Nonferrous metals fall into two general categories: those used alone or in combination with other nonferrous metals to yield materials known for specific properties, such as copper, aluminum, or brass; and those alloyed with iron to yield special irons and steels—the **ferroalloys.**

North Atlantic Treaty Organization (NATO): defense alliance formed in 1949 in response to the Soviet military threat to Western Europe after World War II, by the United States, Canada, and ten Western European nations, who agreed that "an armed attack against one or more of them . . . shall be considered at attack against all."

Oasis: a fertile, watered area in the midst of a **desert.** It may consist of a clump of palm trees dependent upon an isolated spring, or encompass several hundred square miles where a stream or reservoir provides water for extensive **irrigation.** Large oases such as the Nile Delta support dense agricultural and urban populations dependent upon complex systems of irrigation management.

Offshore bar: ridge of sand deposited a short distance offshore by the action of waves, winds, and currents.

Oil-bearing shale: a kind of rock containing oil in dispersed form; supports the theory that petroleum originates when microscopic marine plants are transformed into oil droplets on the ocean floor. Although much less concentrated than in pools set between **sedimentary** rock strata, the vast amounts of petroleum held in suspension in oil-bearing shale can be commercially exploited through mining and retorting in high-technology societies like those of North America.

Oligarchy: rule by an **elite** that frequently exercises political control for corrupt and selfish purposes.

OPEC: a thirteen-member **cartel** of oil-producing nations, the Organization of Petroleum Exporting Countries, formed in 1960.

Organization of American States (OAS): grouping formed at the Ninth International Conference of American States in Bogotá, Colombia, in April 1948, that now joins twenty-four nations of the western hemisphere in a common effort to promote political, social, and economic cooperation in the Americas. Canada and Cuba are noticeably not members.

Outback: a local term for Australia's nearly 3 million square miles of **desert**, a vast expanse with one of the lowest population densities on earth.

Pampas: the **midlatitude** grasslands of Argentina. Like the Russian **steppe** and the North American prairie, the pampas are highly productive grain and grazing lands. See also **llanos; savannah**.

Parallel: a line drawn parallel to the equator (0°) in ever smaller concentric circles to the north or south. One degree of latitude (one parallel) is equal to approximately 69 miles everywhere on the earth's surface.

Pastoralist: herder of animals found in a wide variety of cultural and natural settings. The pastoralists of the Middle East, tropical Africa, Scandinavia, and Asia range from short-distance semi-nomadic sheep, cattle, and goat herders and seasonal **transhumants** to long-distance camel and reindeer herders. In North America, the cowboy, the sheepherder, and the goatroper most closely resemble pastoralists, although they are generally tied to the central focus of a ranch.

Peasantry: an agricultural class of low status in a society of rigid class structure; often landless agricultural laborers.

Peat: a black or brown fibrous low-grade fuel of decomposed organic matter that accumulates in a **bog.**

Peneplain: a near totally eroded mountain range; almost a plain.

Peninsula: a stretch of land projecting into a sea or lake. Peninsulas vary considerably in size;

Iberia (Spain and Portugal) and Florida are both very large peninsulas.

Peon: a member of the rural landless class in Latin America, frequently in debt servitude to a landlord.

Perennial irrigation: a system in which one or more **barrages** or dams are constructed to create a permanent reservoir of water for year-round use. In many river valleys of the developing world, facilities for perennial irrigation have been constructed to replace simpler systems of water entrapment such as **basin irrigation**. This shift from basin to perennial irrigation has led to dramatic changes in the agricultural environment, particularly in the Nile Valley.

Periodic market: a temporary market that rotates in time through a network of specific locations, servicing consumers one or two days a week. The periodic market system is common in preindustrial societies where manufactured goods enter rural areas in limited quantities, where non-agricultural services are restricted in variety, and where the product of the countryside is uniform. Levels of economic demand and consumption of manufactured goods are low in the **hinterlands** of periodic markets.

Petrochemicals: the wide variety of industrial chemicals derived from petroleum or natural gas, from benzene for insecticides to polyvinylchloride for plastics.

Piedmont: hilly, rolling land, lying at the foot of a mountain range and forming a transition between mountain and plain. Piedmonts are crossed by swiftly flowing rivers that drop rapidly in elevation at the point of contact between the piedmont and plain (the **fall line**).

Pig iron: iron ore that has been partially refined by burning with **coke**. Cast into molds called "pigs," this crude iron may be further refined into cast iron, wrought iron, or steel.

Placer deposit: naturally occurring concentration of metals carried down a stream or washed ashore with sand, soil, and other particles. Gold, platinum, diamonds, and other heavy minerals are found in placer deposits.

Plantation: large agricultural estate, usually devoted to the cultivation of a single export crop such as rubber, bananas, cotton, sugar cane, sisal, or coffee. Often owned and directed by foreign capital and located in nonindustrial societies, plantations employ large numbers of unskilled workers (in the past slaves) in the production of commercial agricultural exports.

Plateau: an extensive level stretch of land raised above the surrounding landscape, often exhibiting sharply defined edges in the form of cliffs or

escarpments. Intermontane plateaus, however, are level highlands partly or totally enclosed by mountains, and are higher only in reference to land beyond the mountainous region.

Podzol: acid, infertile soil that underlies **evergreen** forests (**taiga**) in cool, moist climates and covers large areas of Canada and Russia.

Polder: land reclaimed from the sea or an inland lake by the construction of protective *dikes*; the enclosed area is pumped dry and the resulting polderland is carefully brought under cultivation. Polderlands have enlarged the **arable** of the Netherlands by nearly 25 percent.

Population implosion: a change in the distribution of population from a pattern of thinly dispersed groups dependent upon a variety of **environments** to relatively densely settled communities in agricultural environments. Urbanization is the principal modern population implosion.

Primacy, primate city: a measure of the relative dominance of a given city over the total urban system of an area, usually a **nation-state**, as expressed in terms of population size vis à vis other national cities. A primate city dominates the social, political, and economic functions of a nation. In France, for example, Paris, with a population of 2.6 million, overshadows all other French cities in size and influence.

Primary manufacturing district: an urban region with ready access to iron ore, coal, or water-power that became the dominant manufacturing area of a European nation early in the Industrial Revolution. Tyneside, Yorkshire, and Liverpool-Manchester were primary manufacturing districts in Britain; in Belgium and northern France, they were the valleys of the Sambre and Meuse rivers.

Proletariat: the lowest class in an industrial society, composed of people completely lacking in capital assets who live by selling their labor for wages.

Protectionism: a national trade policy of protecting domestic products from cheaper foreign imports by levying high tariffs and duties on foreign goods so that domestic goods are relatively cheaper in the home market. Protectionism may prolong inefficient domestic production or, alternatively, safeguard national production from underpriced foreign competition.

Railhead: a railway terminus; also used to describe a city that has numerous terminuses and is thus a strategic node in the transportation network of a country.

Rain forest: forest located in a belt straddling the equator where rainfall is heavy and there is no dry season. Due to high temperatures and sustained precipitation, forest growth is luxuriant,

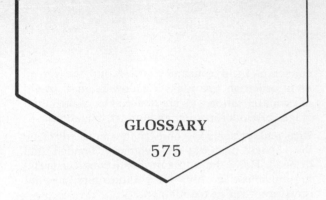

and a leafy canopy of evergreen trees forms a roof over the forest floor. The number of different species of flora and fauna in the tropical rain forest is greater than in any other natural **environment**. Its **laterite** soils are poor, low in **humus** content, and when cleared of vegetation swiftly harden and become useless for agriculture.

Rain shadow: an area with relatively lower precipitation on the lee side of a mountain range. When moisture-laden air crosses a mountain range, it is forced to rise and drop its moisture on the windward slopes as the air mass cools; when it descends, this air is warmed and dried, so that the lee area receives less rain than surrounding areas. A notable example of a rain shadow is found on the eastern slopes of the Sierra Nevada in California and Nevada; the Western Ghats of India also produce a distinct rain shadow.

Refractory: heat-resistant ceramic material often used to line oven, forges, and blast furnaces.

Region: in geography, the name for a distinctive set of physical and/or cultural features that lend special character to a place and set it off from other places. An elastic term, region may refer to large-scale areas such as the world regions discussed in this text or to smaller scale, more local areas. Japan, for example, is a *world* region by virtue of the fact that it is the homeland of the Japanese state and society. But each Japanese island can be considered a separate *physical* region. At a still more local scale, the trade area of the city of Tokyo forms an *economic* region and Tokyo itself forms an *urban* region within the hierarchy of Japanese cities. Within Tokyo, regions could be delimited by land use, occupation, religious affiliation, language, architecture, or other criteria. Important in a discussion of region are questions of scale, the criteria under study, and one's purpose in conceptualizing and measuring this mental construct.

Relief: the difference in elevation between the highest and lowest points in any given area of the earth's surface; the physical shape of the surface of the earth.

Revolution of rising expectations: the quantum leap in aspirations common to societies undergoing rapid change as a result of modernization; closely tied to increasing wealth, availability and consumption of consumer goods, and the spread of information and ideas via new modern media of communications, all characteristics of the initial stages of modernization and industrialization.

Rice paddy: specially constructed field edged by low banks that can be regularly flooded and drained. Here, the optimum conditions for growing lowland rice—high temperature and constant moisture—can be maintained.

Riverine: descriptive of an environment that includes a river and its **floodplain**, a transitional **ecological** system fixed between water and high ground that contains a wide variety of flora and fauna.

Sahel: the transitional **savannah** country located between the southern border of the Sahara Desert and the **rain forests** of tropical Africa.

Savannah: a grassland with scattered trees and bushes usually found on the margins of equatorial **rain forests**. Where precipitation declines, the rain forests thin out and grasslands dominate. With distinct wet and dry seasons, savannahs are used for both agriculture and herding. In southern Africa, the savannah is called the **veld**; in South America, the **llanos** of Venezuela and the campo serrado of Brazil are savannah environments.

Scarped plateau: plateau set sharply above adjoining lowlands by a cliff or steep slope. Much of South Africa consists of a massive scarped plateau set above a narrow coastal plain.

Scrubland: area covered with vegetation consisting of low trees, bushes, and drought-resistant plants, often found on the margins of forests where rainfall is insufficient or soils too poor for the growth of denser plant life. When scrub is removed, the landscape resembles a prairie or **steppe** and may be used for grazing.

Sedentary, sedentarization: permanently settled, fixed to fields and towns; the process of anchoring nomads and **shifting cultivators** to a permanently settled existence. Sedentarization has been official government policy in some Middle Eastern states.

Sedimentary: descriptive of rocks formed by the deposition of **alluvial** materials in distinct layers called strata. These strata, generally laid down in horizontal beds, may be subsequently faulted or folded, or undergo transformation into a different kind of rock.

Sedimentary basin: a trough underlain by warped sedimentary rock or filled by sedimentary strata over time. Sedimentary basins are often likely locations for oil and natural gas, which are caught in pockets between strata. Coal may also be exposed to the surface by **folding** in a sedimentary basin, and become easily accessible for mining.

serf: a worker bound in servitude to a lord or master by personal and hereditary ties. The serf's residence, occupation, and movement beyond the lord's manor or estate were strictly circumscribed, although unlike slaves, serfs owned their own cottages and plots of land. Serfs were common in medieval Europe and in Russia until the mid-nineteenth century.

Sericulture: the raising of mulberry trees and silkworms to produce commercial silk cloth. The silkworm (a moth larva) thrives on the leaves of the white mulberry tree; it weaves a web of raw silk that is subsequently harvested and spun into cloth.

Settlement pattern: the way a population is distributed over the landscape and organizes its spatial network of homes, roads, and fields. **Cultural landscapes** can be categorized according to types of settlement pattern. Two of the most common are **agglomerated** and **dispersed**, as defined by the degree of concentration or dispersion of dwellings in a given area.

Shantytown: unplanned residential zone constructed of cast-off materials on vacant land in or near the city; generated by population growth and urban migration and usually inhabited by people new to urban life and unable to find housing and jobs. The shantytown is known by different names in different societies: **favela** in Brazil, bidonville in French-speaking Africa, barrio in Mexico, bustee in India.

Sharecropping: a system of farming in which the cultivator raises crops and pays for the use of the land by giving a fixed share of the harvest to the landlord as rent. Sharecropping is especially common in the Middle East and Latin America; see also **tenancy**.

Shield: a continental platform of extremely ancient rocks exposed above sea level; soils are poor and human population densities low. Examples are North America's Canadian Shield and Europe's Fennoscandian Shield.

Shifting agriculture: cultivation by the periodic, piecemeal removal of forest or scrub cover by burning or slashing; also known as slash and burn agriculture. Crops are planted in the newly cleared ground as long as soil fertility remains high; when fertility decreases, the land is abandoned and a successive site is cleared. Rejuvenation of the vegetative cover and soils takes place through cyclical agricultural abandonment. Shifting agriculture, found in a wide variety of settings and societies from the **tropical** forests of West Africa to the **scrublands** of Central America today and in much of southern China and central Europe in the past, requires sufficient time and territory to allow for continued productivity.

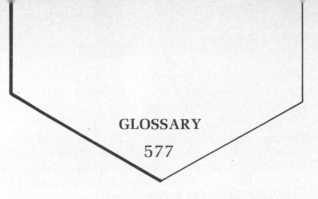

Shogunate: the feudal government of Japan, under which a shogun (generalissimo) and his clan ruled in the name of the emperor, who was kept cloistered and powerless. The Tokugawa shogunate, which lasted for 250 years, was the government with which Perry dealt when he went to Japan in 1853.

Slash and burn agriculture: see **shifting cultivation**.

Spanish Main: originally, the coast of Latin America from the shoulder of Brazil to Central America and the east coast of Mexico. Later, when Spanish colonial trading patterns focused on the Caribbean, the Spanish Main came to include the islands of the Caribbean.

Standard Metropolitan Statistical Area (SMSA): United States Bureau of the Census measure of urbanization; a county that contains a central city of 50,000 population or more, or a group of contiguous counties, each with a central city of 50,000 or more. In 1974, 265 metropolitan areas in the United States were considered SMSAs.

Steppe: **midlatitude** grassland, generally treeless and level plain, the covers a vast area in the interior of the Eurasian landmass; often suitable for grain cultivation, with thick, fertile soils known as **chernozem**. In North America, the steppe-like environments of the Great Plains are called prairies; in Latin America, the term **pampas** is used to refer to the **midlatitude** grasslands of Argentina, Paraguay, and Uruguay.

Strip farming: a pattern of cropping in medieval Europe whereby fields were laid out in long, narrow strips. Strip farming came to dominate field paterns when oxen were used to plow the land; the difficulties involved in turning the ox and plow are usually cited as a reason for this field shape.

Strip mining: the removal of the earth's soil mantle to expose a vein or lode of minerals near the surface; advantageous because a greater percentage of the deposit can be extracted, lower-grade deposits can be worked, there is less danger to miners, and the productivity of each miner is higher because of the use of giant earth-moving machinery. But strip mining disrupts large areas of the earth's surface and if no restoration takes place, leaves behind a landscape useless for agriculture, **ecologically** disturbed, and susceptible to **erosion**.

Subtropical: descriptive of latitudes from the tropics to approximately 35° both north and south of the equator characterized by distinct seasonal changes in climate. In the dry subtropics, a **Mediterranean climate** is characterized by winter rainfall maximums and summer drought; in the humid subtropics, there is a summer rainfall maximum and no clearly defined dry season.

tableland: a broad, level elevated mass set off from the sea or adjoining lowlands by steep, cliff-like edges; see also **plateau**.

Taiga: the **coniferous** forests that cover much of sub-Arctic Russia, Scandinavia, and North America. Trees are well spaced and the ground is covered by lichens and mosses; **podzol** soils, covered by a surface layer of **humus**, are typical.

Tailing hills: mounds of crushed rock debris from which ore has been extracted located near mines and ore processing plants. Tailing hills are a prominent feature of mining landscapes, are notoriously unstable, and often pose a direct threat to nearby settlements.

Take-off stage: see **economic take-off**.

Tar sand: sand holding vast quantities of petroleum in a suspended, dispersed state. Commercial exploitation through mining and retorting is feasible in high-technology societies like those of North America. See also **oil-bearing shale**.

Tax farming: the practice of assigning the right to collect taxes to individuals, often military men, who are allowed wide liberty in methods of tax collection. In traditional India, China, and the Middle East, central governments were often represented in rural areas solely by tax farmers.

Temperature inversion: an increase of warm air with altitude, so that warm air overlies colder, contrary to the normal state. Temperature inversions are common over snow-covered surfaces, but can also be induced by concentrations of pollutants and heat production within a stable air mass. In these cases, air carrying a load of pollutants rises and reaches an upper level of stability at night. This upper-level air settles over areas enclosed by mountains, entrapping and increasing pollution levels until new air moves it away.

Tenancy: a system of farming whereby a farmer pays the landowner a cash rental for the right to farm the land. Tenancy flourishes where land prices are high and where farmers utilize land on a seasonal basis; see also **sharecropping**.

Terrace: in agriculture, a raised and embanked plot of hillside land made level and planted to crops; found where level land is scarce—for example, Japan.

Tertiary: descriptive of the service sector of an economy. The primary sector is involved in the production of goods—agriculture, mining, fishing; the secondary sector is involved in the processing of raw materials into finished goods.

Theocracy: a government directed by religious officials or a single leader regarded as divinely guided.

Tideland: see **tidewater.**

Tidewater: the coastal plain of eastern Virginia, a lowland cut by the Potomac, Rappahannock, York, and James rivers, and indented by **estuaries** and bays. In the colonial period, the first tobacco and rice **plantations** were established here.

Time zone: measure used in the system of reckoning time throughout the world, standardized at an international congress held in Washington, D.C., in 1884. Each time zone extends 7½° west and 7½° east across standard 15° lines of longitude (**meridians**). Greenwich Observatory near London is the standard point of origin, so that all time zones are described in terms of the number of hours they differ from Greenwich Mean Time (GMT). There are 24 time zones in all, 12 east of and 12 west of Greenwich.

Tithe: a tenth part of income, paid in kind or in money as a tax or contribution, usually for the upkeep of a church. During the twelfth and thirteenth centuries in Europe, tithing of the agricultural product was generally law and the basis for sustaining churches, abbeys, and religious orders.

Township and range: system by which most of the United States west of the Appalachians was laid out and mapped. The basic unit of land division was the township, 6 miles square in area, laid out along an east-west base line—a line of latitude also called the township line. Every 6 miles along it, a line of longitude called a range line divided the townships into equal units. In this way, a geometrical grid of latitude and longitude (here called township and range) was imposed on the landscape in advance of settlement.

Transhumance: the seasonal movement of people and animals from lowland to highland environments in search of pasture. In Mediterranean lands, winter is spent in snow-free lowlands and summer in the cooler highlands.

Transmontane: descriptive of an area lying beyond, or across, a mountain system.

Tributary: a stream or river that joins a larger one.

Troglodyte: person who lives underground in a natural cave or earthen dugout; usually applied to primitive peoples.

Tropics: the area between the Tropic of Cancer (23½° north latitude) and the Tropic of Capricorn (23½° south latitude), characterized by the relative absence of a cold season, high daily temperatures, and strong sun. Although the term tropics is often used to refer to those parts of the tropical latitudes with hot and wet climates, hot and dry climates are also found there.

Tundra: a zone between the northern limit of trees and the polar region in North America, Europe, and Asia. Tundra areas have only one summer month with an average temperature above freezing; their vegetation is composed of grasses, sedges, lichens, and shrubs that grow rapidly during the long days of brief summer. Tundra soils are generally poor, the product of mechanical weathering of rocks by freezing and thawing, and in some areas are permanently frozen (permafrost) except in summer.

Veld: the open grassland that covers the **tableland** of South Africa. Three divisions of the veld are generally identified: the high veld, between 5000 and 6000 feet, is typified by treeless grassland; the middle and low veld, located between 1000 and 3000 feet, are mixed **scrubland** interrupted by low hill ranges locally known as rands.

Volcanic soils: soils formed of volcanic dust, ash, rock fragments, and weathered lava (solidified molten rock); if well watered, they are very fertile and excellent agricultural environments.

Wadi: see **arroyo.**

Watershed: a "river basin" or "drainage basin" —all the territory drained by a given stream. As streams join, their watersheds merge into a single system.

Wattle and daub: a preindustrial building technique using abundant local building resources— branches, reeds, straw, small stones, and mud— to erect walls, houses, and other structures cheaply and quickly. Daub (a plaster of soil materials) is added to wattle (a skeleton of sticks or straw) to yield a structure dried and hardened by the sun and varying in complexity from a hunting shelter to an adobe house.

Zero population growth (ZPG): a contemporary term indicating a population in equilibrium (births and deaths per 1000 population approximately equal). Advocates of ZPG stress the importance of achieving population stability so that environmental and social needs can be met and improvements in the quality of life sustained over time.

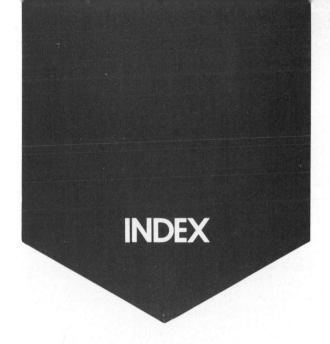

INDEX

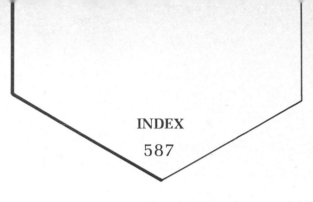

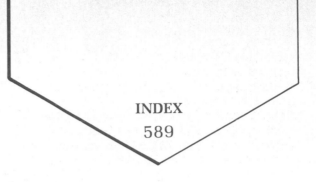